Managerial Finance in a Canadian Setting

Second Edition

Peter Lusztig/ Bernhard Schwab

BUTTERWORTHS
Toronto

CANADA: BUTTERWORTH & CO. (CANADA) LTD.
TORONTO: 2265 MIDLAND AVE., SCARBOROUGH, M1P 4S1

ENGLAND: BUTTERWORTH & CO. (PUBLISHERS) LTD.
LONDON: 88 KINGSWAY, WC2B 6AB

AUSTRALIA: BUTTERWORTH PTY. LTD.
SYDNEY: 586 PACIFIC HIGHWAY, CHATSWOOD, NSW 2067
MELBOURNE: 343 LITTLE COLLINS STREET, 3000
BRISBANE: 240 QUEEN STREET, 4000

NEW ZEALAND: BUTTERWORTHS OF NEW ZEALAND LTD.
WELLINGTON: 26/28 WARING TAYLOR STREET, 1

SOUTH AFRICA: BUTTERWORTH & CO. (SOUTH AFRICA) (PTY.) LTD.
DURBAN: 152/154 GALE STREET

Canadian Cataloguing in Publication Data

Lusztig, Peter A., 1930—
Managerial finance

First ed. published in 1973 under title: Managerial finance in a Canadian setting.

Bibliography: p.
Includes index.
ISBN 0-409-84700-3

1. Corporations — Canada — Finance. 2. Finance — Canada. 3. Business enterprises — Canada — Finance. I. Schwab, Bernhard, 1942— II. Title.

HG4090.L88 1977 658.1'5'0971 C77-001410-0

To
Elisabeth Schwab
and to the memory of
Suzanne Lusztig
Alfred Peter Lusztig
and
Martin Schwab

PREFACE

In the teaching of basic finance it has been necessary to rely on texts written for students in the United States. This has proven frustrating for all concerned, not simply because examples and illustrations related exclusively to the U.S. scene but, more importantly, because of the significant differences in the relevant institutional environments of Canada and the United States. This book was written in answer to this problem. Standard topics in financial management are treated in a Canadian setting, with due consideration given to the Canadian environment with regard to taxation, forms of business organization, the banking system, and the financial markets.

As is now quite generally appreciated, financial theory has developed rapidly during the last two decades and today involves new approaches and perspectives along with a changed emphasis in teaching. Given the increased reliance on economic theory and quantitative analysis, the emergence of a widening gap between academics and practitioners has come to be anticipated. It is our belief that any such rift is undesirable, and throughout this second edition we have worked to avoid this dichotomy. Thus, while the standard body of modern finance is introduced and developed, our emphasis in presenting the material is away from mathematical analysis and formalism *per se*, and centered instead on relating the theory, its assumptions, and conclusions to the world of the practitioner. It is hoped that, as a consequence, this text will be of use not only to students at academic institutions and to those entering the professions, but to the interested executive as well.

A number of important changes are to be found in this second edition, prompted by our own experience in teaching business executives and students at both the undergraduate and graduate level while using this text. After careful review, major sections of the book have been essentially rewritten with a view to improving the clarity of presentation, and providing the beginning student with additional support. Numerous examples and exercises have been added to clarify the material presented. A section of problems with detailed solutions is provided at the end of most chapters, while problem and question sections throughout the book were reworked and updated. In attempting to review both the existing theory and the necessary institutional detail, the level of difficulty of the material covered in most finance texts becomes, by necessity, somewhat uneven. In order to alleviate this problem, and to allow instructors to cover the material at different levels of sophistication, more advanced topics have been placed in clearly identified, starred sections at the end of chapters. These starred sections can be omitted without loss of continuity. A glossary of terms has been added at the end of the book for students who may lack familiarity with the technical terms and jargon commonly used in finance.

Institutional material has been updated throughout the text. To reflect recent important conceptual developments in finance, we have added a chapter introducing portfolio theory, risk-return trade-offs, and the capital asset pricing model. We feel that development in this area has reached a stage where it can no longer be ignored even in a basic finance course. The presentation seeks to highlight those concepts which are of relevance in a practical setting, without attempting to provide a complete review of the theory, as this more properly belongs in more advanced and specialized courses on the subject.

In recent years, the environment within which financial decisions have had to be made has been characterized by persistently high rates of inflation, and by important changes in the international financial system. Both have important implications for financial decision-making, particularly in an open economy such as our own. Finance texts have tended to either ignore the issues which these developments have posed, or have mentioned them in passing, perhaps by dedicating one chapter to issues in international finance. It is our belief that the issues of inflation, and of financial decision-making in an international environment, if they are to be treated in a meaningful way, must be fully integrated into the standard topics of finance as treated in this text. We have attempted this integration throughout, and we believe that a more relevant and up-to-date treatment of financial topics has resulted.

In summary, we are confident that this second edition represents a significant improvement over the earlier version, a view which has been confirmed by a variety of students, executives, colleagues, and reviewers who have assisted us with our drafting.

Instructors teaching basic finance will have different preferences regarding the order in which the standard major topics are to be covered in an introductory course. While the order of topics in the book reflects our preference, many alternatives are possible and viable. To accommodate such varying preferences, the book is divided into ten parts. Each of these parts is relatively self-contained, which not only makes it possible to teach these parts in various sequences, but also enables an instructor to omit certain parts altogether to better fit his particular course objectives. Thus, for example, Part 5 (The Canadian Monetary System), Part 9 (Expansion), and Part 10 (Some Conceptual Developments in Risk-Return Relationships) are likely candidates for omission, where either the length of the course or the preparation and objectives of the students do not warrant a full coverage of the text. Similarly, an instructor may want to omit Chapter 6 (Capital Expenditure Decisions Under Uncertainty) and Chapter 20 (Dividend Policy and the Valuation of Common Shares) in a more elementary treatment of the subject.

We are obviously indebted to many people for their assistance in making both the first and the second editions of this book possible. We are particularly grateful to Philip White and Noel Hall, former deans of the Faculty of Commerce and Business Administration and to Acting Dean Stan Hamilton. We also acknowledge financial support from the Committee on Research of the Faculty of Graduate Studies at UBC and from the Certified General Accountants' Association of Canada. In this context, we appreciate the encouragement received from Chris Trunkfield, formerly of the CGA Association of Canada.

We are indebted to a number of our colleagues who assisted us more directly, including Professors Michael Brennan, Dan Gardiner, David Lam, Maurice Levi, Ralph Loffmark, John Murray, Eduardo Schwartz, and Bob White. Significant help was also received from many of our students and former students, most particularly Messrs. Trinh Binh, Jack Byeman, Bevan Clarke, Ross Dafoe, Bob Ford, Lawrence Kryzanowski, Doug Schram, Gordon Sick,

Jim Wort and Derek Yee for which we express appreciation. Special thanks are due to Miss L. Dureau, Mrs. L. Wey, and Ms. Jane Wood for typing the manuscripts a number of times. Lastly, we thank our wives, Penny and Beatrix, for their encouragement, patience, and understanding during this book's two rather lengthy gestation periods.

P. Lusztig
B. Schwab
Vancouver, 1976.

CONTENTS

INTRODUCTION

The major functions of financial management may be viewed as the procurement of funds for the business, and control over the disbursement of these funds into various investments and activities. Both the procurement and the disbursement of funds are broken down into several subheadings, and for purposes of exposition one of the major categorizations will be into long-term and short-term financial decisions. Two other important, although somewhat ancillary areas of financial management are financial analysis and control, and the institutional environment within which financial decisions take place. A summary of the main areas of financial management is given below:

An overview of the major areas of financial management

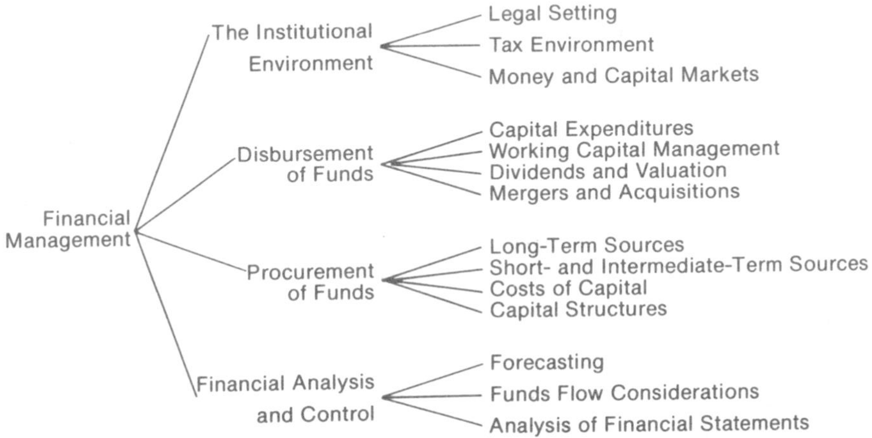

This book is divided into ten parts as follows:

Part 1 starts with an introductory chapter which describes the scope and function of managerial finance and discusses the objectives of financial management. Two chapters on the institutional environment follow, which assist in providing the framework within which financial decisions take place: Chapter 2 introduces the legal setting, and Chapter 3 provides a description of the Canadian tax environment.

Part 2 covers long-term investment decisions. Chapter 4 introduces the mathematics of finance which is relevant for long-term financial decisions. Chapter 5 discusses the basic concepts involved in evaluating long-term investments, while Chapter 6 introduces the measurement and evaluation of risk in the context of capital budgeting.

Part 3 is concerned with the procurement of long-term funds. After an introductory chapter dealing with the role and functioning of capital markets, several chapters provide detailed discussions of the various alternative instruments on which a firm can rely when raising long-term funds externally. Thus, Chapter 8 deals with long-term debt, Chapters 9 and 10 with preferred and common shares respectively, and Chapter 11 with convertible securities, warrants, and units. Chapter 12 outlines how a firm goes about selling securities in the capital markets and describes the functions of investment dealers and the underwriting process. Having reviewed the various individual sources of long-term funds, Chapters 13 and 14 are concerned with the firm's overall long-term financing policies. Chapter 13 details the computation of the firm's overall cost of capital, which is to be used as a yardstick in evaluating returns on investments, while Chapter 14 discusses policies regarding capital structure and outlines how the best mix of funds is to be found.

Intermediate- and short-term sources of funds are discussed separately in Part 4, as financial decision-making in this area tends to be dominated by considerations which are different from those prevailing with regard to long-term financing. The banking system and the money markets, trade credit, various intermediate-term sources of funds, and leasing are each dealt with separately in Chapters 15 through 18.

Part 5 provides a brief overview of the Canadian monetary system, which is an important aspect of the institutional environment. Its treatment is deferred until this point as we thought it desirable for the reader to have a good grasp of financing and the role of interest rates, as introduced in Parts 3 and 4 before dealing with this material.

Dividends and valuation are the topics treated in Part 6. Again, one can argue that the reader is better equipped to deal with these topics after he has had exposure to earlier sections, particularly Parts 2 and 3. Chapter 20 covers the more conceptual issues which are relevant in this context and sets out a general framework within which alternative dividend policies can be evaluated, while Chapter 21 is concerned with a description of actual dividend policies as pursued by Canadian corporations, and provides relevant institutional details.

Part 7 introduces financial analysis and control, including techniques for the analysis of financial statements in Chapter 22, and the analysis of sources and uses of funds as well as financial forecasting in Chapter 23.

Working capital management and investments in current assets are taken up in Part 8. Again, the techniques and considerations for assessing such short-term investments are quite different from the ones which were introduced in the context of long-term investments in Part 3, and exposure to financial analysis and control as it was developed in the preceding section provides a useful background for many of the issues which are raised here. Chapters 24 to 26 review major categories of current assets: cash and marketable securities, accounts receivable, and inventories. Chapter 27 is concerned with introducing some general principles which are relevant in managing working capital.

The topic of external expansion—mergers and acquisitions—is left to Part 9 as it is a subject which may be viewed as somewhat ancillary in a finance course, and hence, may be omitted. The techniques of analysis are similar to those which are used to evaluate internal expansion through capital budgeting and which were reviewed in Part 2. However, some of the procedural aspects differ sufficiently to warrant separate treatment.

Finally, Part 10 reviews, at a conceptual level, a major aspect of financial decision-making, namely the trade-off between risk and return. Placing this discussion at the end is useful for two reasons. For one, it may serve to pull together the conceptual foundations of financial management as discussed throughout this book. Secondly, for a more basic or elementary level course, or for the reader who lacks exposure to elementary probability and statistics, this part can again be omitted.

PART 1

The Institutional Environment

Chapter 1
The Scope and Objectives of Financial Management

1-1. INTRODUCTION

In this chapter, we start by outlining the role of the financial executive within the overall firm, his typical duties and responsibilities and his place within the organizational structure. We then move on to discuss the objectives of financial decision-making. It is important to have some understanding of the motivating goals of financial decision-making, as the quality of financial decisions can only be judged if one has some clear objective in mind.

Two major issues arise when one attempts to specify the objectives of financial decision-making. To begin with, one needs to discuss the role of financial versus broader, non-financial objectives such as social responsibility and the likes. Secondly, after one has narrowed the discussion to strictly financial objectives, one needs to formulate goals which are both valid and operational. Our discussion will center mainly around the latter issue, as the topic of financial versus non-financial goals in business is better taken up in a business policy course.

1-2. THE ROLE OF THE FINANCIAL EXECUTIVE

The importance of effective financial management and the advantages of having first-rate fianancial people as senior executives is increasingly being recognized in the larger corporations. Meanwhile, in smaller businesses, the frequent lack of financial expertise is being recognized as a serious deficiency.

The financial executive was formerly regarded as part of a staff function and generally unsuited for promotion to the presidency. Today, however, financial executives are frequently being chosen to head firms because of their involvement in broad policy areas.

A recent survey, based on the largest one-hundred industrial concerns ranked by *Fortune*, shows that the proportion of chief executives with backgrounds in finance moved from 13 percent in the period 1953 to 1957 to 24 percent during 1963 to 1967. The proportion of marketing and production people holding the post of chief executive fell from 29 percent to 18 percent and from 16 percent to 12 percent respectively.[1]

One of the basic reasons for this trend is made clear by Weston and Brigham.[2] They note that a variety of policy decisions, most of them financial, affect the

[1]From a study by management consultant H. Golightly as reported in the *Wall Street Journal*, June 6, 1968, p. 1.
[2]J. Weston and E. Brigham, *Managerial Finance* (5th ed.), Hinsdale: Drydon Press, 1975, pp. 13-14.

risk and profitability of a firm, and that, in turn, it is risk and profitability which determine not only whether the firm is to survive but also at what price its shares will trade.

Other reasons have been cited for this growth in the importance and scope of finance.[3] To begin with, the scale of operations of business firms has greatly increased. The growing concentration of assets into large corporations results in added responsibilities for financial executives, for example, the evaluation of large expenditures for new plants and equipment; the analysis of mergers and acquisitions; the sorting out of tax and foreign exchange problems; and combines and antitrust matters. Secondly, the merger movement and widespread diversification of products have magnified the complexity of operating a business. Instead of firms with one division and a few products, we now have multiproduct, multidivisional, and even multinational corporations. This change has required a substantial increase in both the amount and quality of financial information as well as the speed with which it must be collected and interpreted, in order to facilitate control of such diverse operations. Lastly, rapid technological developments together with the large investments made by firms call for more long-range planning than was characteristic of earlier years.

The trend has not developed without problems. The need to include at least one able financial officer as part of the corporate management team has resulted in a shortage of capable and experienced financial personnel. One noteworthy situation precipitated by this shortage, occurred during 1970. At this time, Air Canada experienced considerable difficulty in filling the position of vice-president of finance, and the inevitable delays were widely reported, prompting Mr. Pratte, its president, to observe that:

> This man doesn't have to be an expert on public financing, we can get that outside when we need it. But he has to be a man of ideas. It is very urgent that we find him soon.[4]

Organizational structure in which the financial executive functions

The previous discussion should not be taken to mean that a company's operations are always centered around and dependent upon the financial executive. The finance function is handled in a great variety of ways depending upon the firm's organizational structure and the financial executive's role will vary according to the activities involved, the size of the firm, his own ability, and the abilities of other officers and directors. Thus, in a large corporation the financial executive will likely be the only insider to give advice to the president and the board of directors on important financial decisions, such as a new issue of common shares. In a small company, on the other hand, the financial executive as an entity may not even exist, with the president in all probability performing the duties of the chief financial officer. Unfortunately, it is also quite possible that the president's competence in financial matters will be limited.

[3]R. Johnson, *Financial Management* (4th ed.), Boston: Allyn & Bacon, Inc., 1971, p. 17.
[4]"Pratte Continues Extensive Search for Finance Man", *The Financial Post*, May 23, 1970, p. 37.

Most presidents of small companies are one of the original promoters of the company, often individuals who have developed either a new product idea or have a marketable technical competence. Computer companies, for example, are often formed by engineers, programmers, or salesmen; mining and oil companies by geologists and security salesmen; while manufacturing firms are often established by engineers and inventors.

Since financial decisions affect the destiny of the entire business, in larger firms at least, financial management is now more properly viewed as part of the overall management of the enterprise. After all, financial decisions cannot be made independently of decisions in other functional areas such as production or marketing. As a consequence, even in the most decentralized operations with independent management, perhaps in various parts of the world, financial management tends to remain quite centralized. A report on a sampling of 289 giant corporations (members of *Fortune Magazine's* list of the 500 largest corporations) notes that in 91 percent of the cases the senior financial officer had the rank of vice-president and reported directly to either the president or the chairman of the board. It was the opinion of the author of this report that: "Finance is emerging as the business function that holds the corporation together at the top management level."[5]

Duties of the financial executive

Today's financial officer is oriented toward the *future* goals of the enterprise. In contrast to the traditional accountant who is more concerned with keeping an up-to-date score on past operations, the financial executive is more likely to be participating in forecasting operations and forward planning.[6] This has created tremendous direct and indirect pressures on the financial executive. He must be thoroughly familiar with accounting and financial theory and practice; continually become involved in the development of information systems by which data are made available both in a timely fashion and in a form which facilitates decision-making; learn the strengths and limitations of computers since computers play such an important role in gathering and processing information; and have an increased knowledge of the newer analytical techniques and related tools such as management science and statistics, in order to participate effectively in decision-making.[7] Finally, he must be versed in macro-economics so that he is capable of providing information on monetary and fiscal policy, flexible or floating exchange rates, the behavior of national income, general price levels, interest rates, and the money and capital markets from an international perspective.

The financial executive typically is involved in all areas of finance as outlined

[5]J. Krum, "Who Controls Finance in the Industrial Giants?", *Financial Executive*, March 1970, pp. 20-28. This fact, has, of course, been recognized by most, if not all, conglomerates.

[6]For a complete expression of this, see R. MacDonald, "The Financial Executive and Senior Management", *Financial Executive*, March 1969, pp. 15-19.

[7]See, for example, *Development of Financial Managers*, a research study prepared for the Financial Executives Research Foundation, New York, 1970, pp. 131-132.

in the introduction which precedes this chapter. An actual job description of the chief financial officer for a major Canadian corporation is provided as an appendix of this chapter. It illustrates that, in terms of time spent rather than importance of function, the financial officer is still most deeply concerned with working capital management. This is particularly true when the economic scene is best described as a combination of inflation and recession. Working capital management would include activities such as credit and collections, accounting systems and operations, contacts with chartered banks, and preparation of budgets. Other time-consuming duties include advising on dividend policy; the purchase of raw materials (likely to be in short supply); the handling of pensions; and public and shareholder relations. The fact is that the financial executive, like all other executives, is required to spend a great deal of his time on the more routine and possibly less exciting aspects of corporate management.

1-3. OBJECTIVES IN FINANCIAL MANAGEMENT[8]

Finance is primarily concerned with how "better" financial decisions can be made. But, before exploring methods that result in "better" decisions, we must decide on the goal or goals for which financial decision-making should strive.

Whose goals? More traditional economic writing accepts without question the hypothesis that firms are operated on behalf of their shareholders, even when ownership is diffused. Such economic literature argues that the stockholders in effect are the real entrepreneurs of the firm since they have the final say. For instance, should they become dissatisfied with the operations of the firm they can sell their holdings and invest elsewhere. The price of the firm's shares will probably fall as a consequence, indicating to management that "something is wrong". If the situation persists, the unsatisfactory management will eventually be replaced by the shareholders.

Other economic literature[9] suggests that in reality there is some degree of separation between shareholders and management and that their objectives are not likely to be identical. Specifically, it is argued that management tends to "play it safe"—brilliant decisions that result in great success may go unrewarded, while bold decisions that result in failure will surely come to the attention of stockholders and the financial community, and result in penalties.[10] If, for example, a particular investment decision turns sour and results in substantial losses, a manager has more than a drop in earnings per share at stake, for both

[8]Much of the following discussion is drawn from E. Solomon, *The Theory of Financial Management*, New York: Columbia University Press, 1963, pp. 1-25; and J. Weston, *The Scope and Methodology of Finance*, Englewood Cliffs, N.J., Prentice-Hall, Inc., 1966, pp. 1-30.

[9]R. Gordon, "Stockholdings of Officers and Directors in American Industrial Corporations", *Quarterly Journal of Economics*, August 1936, pp. 622-657; R. Gordon, "Ownership by Management and Control Groups in the Large Corporation", *idem*, May 1938, pp. 367-400; R. Gordon, "Ownership and compensation as incentives to corporation executives", *idem*, May 1940, pp. 455-473; A. Berle Jr. and G. Means, *The Modern Corporation and Private Property*, New York: Macmillan Co., 1944, pp. 119-125. Also J. Elliott, "Control, Size Growth, and Financial Performance in the Firm", *Journal of Financial and Quantitative Analysis*, January 1972, pp. 1309-1320.

[10]This argument derived support from psychological theories that corporate management seeks to "satisfice" rather than maximize. See, for example, H. Simon, "Theories of Decision-Making in Economics and Behavioral Science", *American Economic Review*, June 1959, pp. 253-283.

his job and his career may terminate at that point. This despite the fact that the original decision may be the best which could have been made under the circumstances. It is not surprising then, that a manager whose career and personal future are tied to his performance may be more risk-averse than a shareholder who holds a diversified portfolio of securities and whose investment in the firm may be purely temporary.

Some writers have suggested that, quite apart from the issue of management *versus* shareholder objectives, the traditional view is too narrowly centered. They question whether the criterion of maximizing benefits from the standpoint of shareholders of a firm is appropriate in a world comprising many participating agents, each with a limited role. The agents usually mentioned are management, interested in growth and continuity of operations; customers, interested in quality and lower prices; unions, interested in higher wages, greater fringe benefits, and job security; and stockholders, interested in larger dividends and/or price appreciation. This position has been clearly set out by Professor Donaldson:

> The concept of relative parity may be employed by professional management in relating the conflicting interests of stockholders, employees, customers, the general public, government, and so on, to each other. Having abandoned the idea of absolute priority of the stockholder's interest, which existed only when management and ownership were one (and perhaps not even then), management continues to attach more weight to its responsibility to owners than to any other vested interest. This means, of course, that where a conflict of interest develops, management must determine how much of the stockholder's interest will be sacrificed in order to behave "more responsibly" toward other interests such as the labor union or the customer.[11]

He concludes that, as a result, the shareholder's point of view will be subordinate to management's point of view, with management arbitrating between various groups which have an interest in the operations of the firm. Therefore, the objectives and criteria of decision-making are altered.

We would concur with Donaldson that, despite the legitimate and possibly conflicting interests of various groups, management continues to attach more weight to its responsibilities to owners than to any other vested interest. In recent years, the significant concentration of shareholder power has contributed to this. Thus, we have witnessed a tremendous increase in the percentage ownership of outstanding corporate shares by financial institutions such as mutual funds, trusteed pension plans, and the likes. This has resulted in a stronger, more active, and unified shareholder front. In face of this, management may be seen as becoming more responsive to shareholders, rather than less, and the split

[11]G. Donaldson, "Financial Goals: Management vs. Stockholders", *Harvard Business Review*, May-June 1963, p. 119. It might be noted that the growing phenomenon of "co-determination" or the legally imposed representation of unions on corporate boards, as found in Germany, for example, gives Donaldson's arguments particular relevance.

between ownership (shareholders) and control (management) which was prevalent when shareholdings were widely dispersed may become less important. The recent proxy fight relating to the Supertest Petroleum Corporation and BP Canada merger illustrates how major institutional shareholders and fiduciaries are rejecting more passive roles. In this instance, Central Fund of Canada, a closed-end investment fund, Alfred Bunting & Co., a Toronto-based brokerage house, and Jarislowsky, Fraser and Co., a Montreal investment counselling firm, sought to improve terms of the merger agreement which were labelled "neither fair nor equitable".

The emphasis on the interests of shareholders warrants one further comment. While the principle of maximization of shareholder wealth as a global objective for the firm is subject to question, it is nevertheless one of several possible criteria to guide management's thinking. Clearly, even if a firm has a broad set of objectives, at least one important dimension of these objectives will be financial performance, as without adequate financial performance the firm may not survive in a competitive market economy. This is of particular relevance in the area of financial decision-making. Where trade-offs need to be made, the financial officer should be aware of their likely implications for share prices both because of concern for existing shareholders and because of a need to maintain ready access to capital markets at reasonable terms.

Hence, the principle of maximization of shareholder wealth will form the basis for much of the conceptual analysis in financial decision-making throughout this book. The reader should keep this initial discussion in mind so to be able to interpret the derived results in a broader context.

In the next section, the difficulties inherent in devising an operational form of maximizing shareholder wealth will be explored together with how shareholder wealth can best be measured.

Difficulties inherent in the financial objective of maximizing shareholder wealth

Maximization of profit has long been accepted in standard price theory as the best operational form of maximizing shareholder wealth.[12] To quote from the work of one respected economist:

> That the entrepreneur aims at maximizing his profits is one of the most fundamental assumptions of economic theory. So much so that it has almost come to be regarded as the equivalent of rational behavior . . . we have a vested interest in maintaining this assumption—it makes economic analysis so much simpler.[13]

Justification for this objective is to be found in classical economic theory. Thus, given certain assumptions about perfect competition, perfect information, a pricing system which fully reflects costs or benefits external to the firm, and rational behavior, we can show that maximization of profits by firms will lead to

[12]See, for example, R. Leftwich, *The Price System and Resource Allocation* (rev. ed.), New York: Holt Rinehart and Winston, 1964, pp. 174, 205, 270, and 308 under a variety of market structures.

[13]P. Scitovsky, "A Note on Profit Maximization and Its Implications", *Review of Economic Studies, 1943-1944*, p. 57.

an efficient allocation of resources in the economy.

The appropriateness of this operational form has been under increasing criticism during the past quarter-century. Some earlier criticisms were essentially an indictment of private enterprise. More rationally, the validity of the assumptions which underly the above economic analysis has been questioned, and governments have increasingly intervened where it became clear that "laissez-faire" policies by government coupled with profit maximization by firms would lead to suboptimal decisions for society. For example, legislation on the disclosure of true interest rates on loans aims at removing imperfections in the flow of information; pollution controls attempt to reduce social costs external to the firm; and anticombines legislation seeks to ensure workable competition. However, government intervention of this type, while imposing constraints on business, leaves the role of profits intact in the basic framework of allocating resources.

The more recent dissent comes from those who accept the private enterprise framework but believe that the objective of profit maximization is inherently ambiguous, and hence is neither the goal of business nor the objective businessmen say they pursue.[14]

In reviewing possible objections to profit as the item to be maximized, we should start by noting some clear inconsistencies which may arise if one is concerned about shareholder wealth. Thus, a firm can increase its total profits by selling additional common shares, and by investing the funds thus raised in projects yielding positive rates of return. If, however, such returns are below the average returns which the firm earns on its existing projects, a reduction in earnings per share would follow. Such a dilution in earnings per share would clearly suggest an inappropriate interpretation of profit maximization, as the original shareholders are now worse off.

Example

> Consider a firm with 1,000 common shares outstanding and after-tax profits of $1,000 per year, implying earnings per share of $1.00. A further 1,000 shares are sold and are assumed to net the company $7,000. These monies are then invested to generate an additional after-tax profit of, for example, only $500 per year. Thus, despite total profits having been increased significantly to a total of $1,500 per year, the position of the original shareholders has been diluted. Earnings per share have dipped from $1.00 to $0.75.

Allowing for the interpretation of profits as per-share earnings, further failings can be noted. An annual earnings stream of one dollar per share over twenty years and known with *certainty* may well be preferred by those who are risk-averse over a stream with *an expected value* of $1.20 per share over a like time horizon, if the expectation reflects equal probabilities of either an annual loss of $1.20 per share or earnings of $3.60 per share. In effect, then, preferences

[14]Various alternative proposals such as the revenue maximization hypothesis have been proposed. Under this approach, sales should be maximized subject to a minimum profit level being maintained. See W. Baumol, *Business Behavior, Value and Growth* (rev. ed.), New York: Harcourt, Brace and World, 1967, pp. 45-52.

of decision-makers and investors between risk and return cannot be ignored.

Even ruling out uncertainty, there are other shortcomings to contend with. Given that money has a time value, and like amounts received in different periods are not the same, the timing of earnings to be maximized needs to be recognized. It is necessary, therefore, to think of maximizing the present value of earnings per share in order to evaluate different time patterns of earnings. For example, earnings per share of one dollar per year for the next five years on the one hand must be differentiated from zero, zero, one, two, and two dollars over the next five years on the other. The concept of present values will be discussed in detail in subsequent chapters.

A further shortcoming is the problem of dividend policy. It is evident that if the net return on dollars retained is positive, then earnings per share can only be maximized with complete retention of all earnings. Is it then valid to deduce that all earnings should be retained, or is it not useful to recognize the preferences of shareholders who might favor dividend payments, perhaps because they have significantly more attractive reinvestment opportunities? Obviously, some consideration of investor preference is necessary. It would be unreasonable, for example, to have a firm pay no dividends, while increasing its earnings per share through earning interest on cash balances at six percent, if shareholders have the opportunity of reinvesting dividends which are paid out at rates of returns which are significantly higher.

It is evident from the above that the goal of profit maximization is too vague to be a satisfactory objective in financial management. A more meaningful and operational alternative which gets around many of the objections raised is the goal of *wealth maximization*—that is, maximizing the market price of the firm's common shares.[15]

Maximizing the market price of shares over the longer run[16] would take into account present and future expected earnings; the timing and uncertainty of these earnings; as well as dividend policies. Basically, investors active in the capital markets become the judge on such issues, and the firm should behave in a way which is consistent with preferences as expressed by the market. Such corporate conduct will attract investors to buy the firm's shares, with share prices increasing as a consequence. Even if a particular shareholder becomes distressed by the policies being pursued, perhaps because he has preferences which differ from those which prevail in the market, he can now sell his shares for a good price if he so desires, and pursue other activities which are more consonant with his preferences. On the other hand, if a firm makes decisions which are not in line with market preferences, share prices would decline. Thus, for example, if a firm assumed undue risks for the returns generated, investors would find the firm's shares to be a relatively unattractive investment. The firm's share prices would fall as a consequence, declining until they reached a level at which investors could once again expect to receive a return which was

[15]The goal of wealth maximization also applies to other organizational forms such as partnerships and single proprietorships. In such cases, the goal could be the maximization of the residual interest of the owner-participants in the organization.

[16]The terminology "maximization over the longer run" serves to isolate actions leading to quick but short-lived price appreciation.

commensurate with the risks to be borne.

For the objective of maximizing long-run share prices to become operational, we need to know what the preferences of the market are with regard to alternate financial policies and with regard to the major trade-offs as outlined above. We need to deal with the issue of valuation, or how investors ascribe a value to common shares. In recent years, much of the research in finance has been addressed to this issue and in later discussions throughout the text we will make reference to the various findings reported to date.

Where the shares of a firm are not publicly traded, the specific objectives of the owners will form the basis for decision-making. However, even in those cases the timing of profits, and tradeoffs between risks and returns more generally, are likely to be important aspects of financial decision-making. Thus, comparisons may usefully be made with other similar enterprises whose shares are publicly traded to obtain at least rough indications of performance and value in a market setting.

Difficulties through time

Maximizing the market price of shares, while conceptually sound, is not without some operational problems. Thus, the financial officer may need a criterion for choosing between alternative patterns of market prices over time.[17] With rational and well-informed investors who correctly anticipate future developments, this issue does not arise since share prices at any time will fully reflect future developments. Actions which maximize share prices and are therefore "best" at some point in the future are also best now.

Under conditions of uncertainty, and in real life situations involving investors who may not always be rational and well-informed, however, the market prices of shares can fluctuate more widely, and the price which prevails at some point in the future will not necessarily correspond to the prices which were observed during preceding time periods. Thus, two alternative financial strategies could easily result in share price time patterns with crossings as exhibited in Figure 1-1.

Thus, a firm which severely curtails discretionary expenditures such as research and development, advertising and maintenance may be able to increase short-term earnings figures at the expense of long-term earnings potential. If the market does not fully recognize this, its share prices may move as shown in Figure 1-1, curve *B*, posting initial gains at the expense of long-term growth; whereas *A* may have resulted if more conventional policies had been pursued. In such a case, the objective of maximizing share price has little operational meaning unless a basis for choosing between the criss-crossing price patterns can be developed. While formal approaches for resolving this issue are easily formulated, they draw on concepts which are not developed until later chapters.[18] At this point, we remind ourselves that shareholder wealth should be

[17]The discussion below is adapted from J. Mao, "Survey of Capital Budgeting: Theory and Practice", *The Journal of Finance*, May 1970, pp. 349-360.

[18]It involves taking, over the relevant time horizon, the present value of price differences by subtracting say, the share price depicted by curve A for each period from the price indicated by curve B. Then, if the result is a positive present value, time pattern B is selected, and if negative, the choice is pattern A.

viewed in terms of *long run* share prices which a firm should strive to maximize. This implies that short-run fluctuations caused, for example, by investor ignorance or irrationality, should not dominate considerations in chosing between alternative financial policies.

FIGURE 1-1

Share Price Patterns Over Time

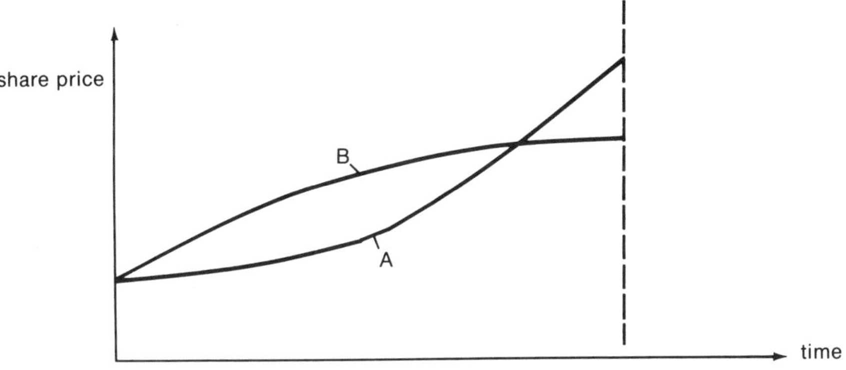

The financial objective as perceived by the financial executive

It is of interest to analyse what a sample of interviewed financial executives regarded as "the objective of financial management".

> Our objective is to finance the high growth rate of this company. Since we do not use debt, we have to make sure that we earn enough profit to finance the growth. It may be that share value is maximized as well, but we don't think about that.
>
> We have a goal of earnings per share which we manage astutely every quarter. Because this is a young, growing company, it is important in terms of future financing that we do not disappoint the investing public. The thing that means the most to the stockholder is the value of their stock. In determining the value of stock, the most critical factor is probably the earnings per share, but it also involves the fact that you are not static but moving forward and increasing your earnings per share.
>
> To increase earnings, you have to have sales growth which is the lifeblood of any business.
>
> The goal of the financial manager is to have his company produce a record that will enable it to raise capital at the lowest possible cost. To accomplish this goal, he needs a proper concept of stability and a proper concept of growth. In this company, we try to achieve a growth rate of 15 to 18 percent, compounded annually, in both sales and earnings.[19]

[19]Mao, *op. cit.*, p. 352.

These responses have been interpreted as evidence that although management may not have specifically identified maximization of the firm's share value as their objective, such reasoning was implicit in the responses. Given management's operational orientation, the goal of maximizing share prices was more naturally expressed in terms of combining both operating targets for growth with stability in earnings.[20]

1-4. SUMMARY

In this chapter we first considered the growing importance of the financial executive and his role within the firm. Considerable attention was directed at explaining the need for carefully formulated financial objectives and setting out the theoretical and operational problems. The potential for conflict between management and the shareholders was touched on while ambiguities in simply defining the firm's goals as the maximizing of profits or even profits per share were noted. It was concluded that, for purposes of this text, one reasonable objective for making financial decisions is the maximization of shareholders' wealth. It was also determined that, operationally, a shareholder's wealth is best measured by the price at which his shares are trading. However, some of the difficulties and limitations which were pointed out in the discussion should be kept in mind in order to view properly any results which will be derived in subsequent chapters.

Questions for discussion

1. It has been said that the risk attitudes of management often diverge from those required for maximizing shareholder wealth. How would you explain the discrepancy and what can be done to minimize its effect?
2. What operational difficulties are involved in using the maximization of shareholder wealth as a financial objective?
3. "The sole corporate objective should be the maximization of shareholder wealth as this would lead to the most efficient allocation of resources in our economy." Discuss this statement.
4. In several countries, unions have gained official representation on boards of directors. What do you see as the potential advantages and/or disadvantages of such a development, and how might this affect the objectives of financial management?
5. With regard to pollution, should firms simply abide by the minimal legal requirements or go beyond the statutes in order to be good corporate citizens? Should management lobby against anti-pollution legislation where such lobbying might increase shareholder wealth?
6. Research project: Using data supplied in annual reports, plot EPS and market price over a ten-year period for any company listed on the Toronto Stock Exchange. Do you see any similarity between these series?

[20]For a discussion of how this essential similarity is often missed, see E. Fama and M. Miller, *The Theory of Finance*, New York: Holt, Rinehart and Winston, 1972, pp 74-75.

7. Should a financial institution like a bank voluntarily disclose the effective interest rate on consumer loans? Should lenders as a group lobby against legislation forcing the disclosure of effective interest rates on loans? Discuss.
8. Review the published Annual Reports of several different corporations to see whether corporate objectives are set out in any way. Discuss your findings.
9. Prepare numerical examples to illustrate the potential weaknesses of using the following criteria as objectives to be maximized by a firm:
   (a) profits after taxes
   (b) total sales (or total revenues)
   (c) earnings per share

Selected references

R. Anthony, "The Trouble With Profit Maximization", *Harvard Business Review*, November-December, 1960, pp. 126-134.

A. Booth, "Frivolous? Not This Power Play", *Financial Post*, April 5, 1975, pp. 15-16.

B. Branch, "Corporate Objectives and Market Performance", *Financial Management*, Summer 1973, pp. 24-29.

G. Brioschi, "How Olivetti's Treasury Department Functions", *Euromoney*, December 1974, pp. 53-55.

M. Friedman, *Essays in Positive Economics*, Chicago: University of Chicago Press, 1953, pp. 3-43.

E. Lerner, *Managerial Finance*, New York: Harcourt Brace Jovanovich, Inc., 1971, Ch. 1.

C. Phillips, Jr., "What is Wrong With Profit Maximization?", *Business Horizons*, Winter 1963, pp. 73-80.

J. Van Horne, *Financial Management and Policy* (4th. ed.), Englewood Cliffs; Prentice-Hall, Inc., 1977, Ch. 1.

J. Weston, "New Themes in Finance", *Journal of Finance*, March 1974, pp. 237-243.

CHAPTER 1: APPENDIX

POSITION DESCRIPTION OF THE CHIEF FINANCIAL OFFICER FOR A MAJOR CANADIAN CORPORATION

NUMBER	E.	TITLE	VICE-PRESIDENT—FINANCE
DEPARTMENT	FINANCE	DIVISION	HEAD OFFICE
ACCOUNTABLE TO	PRESIDENT	DATE	JANUARY 1 1971

SUMMARY

Under the general administrative direction of the PRESIDENT, the VICE-PRESIDENT—FINANCE is responsible for formulating financial policies, planning and executing financial programs, supplying financial services, appraising and reporting on the financial results of the operation, and recommending action to be taken. The VICE-PRESIDENT—FINANCE is responsible for the supervision of all financial functions of the company including accounting, auditing, banking, budgetary control, cash receipts and disbursements, credit and collections, accounting methods and statistics, financing, insurance, and payrolls.

DUTIES & RESPONSIBILITIES

Organization Planning

Develops and directs his supporting organization; establishes the duties and responsibilities for positions reporting to him.

Initiates, develops, and establishes changes in the Financial Division organization when necessary due to changing conditions or new objectives.

Financial Planning

Develops, recommends, and supervises operation of an adequate system of forecasting the company requirements for working capital.

Investigates, develops, and formulates financial plans to ensure provision of adequate funds to meet the long- and short-term requirements of the company on the most economical and practical basis consistent with sound financial practices.

Assesses alternatives and recommends the most profitable utilization of company funds.

Policies

Formulates or causes to be formulated all company policies, practices, and procedures covering accounting, auditing, banking, budgetary control, cash receipts and disbursements, credit and collections, accounting methods and statistics, financing, payroll procedures, and insurance; makes provision for the rendering of assistance and guidance to the operating divisions in these matters when needed.

Management Reports

Issues appropriate reports on the financial affairs of the company; interprets financial results, developments, and conditions of the company for the PRESIDENT and the BOARD OF DIRECTORS.

Establishes the management report structure that best meets the planning and control needs of the company.

Appraisal of Financial Results

Consults with the PRESIDENT as required on general policy matters; keeps him informed of the overall performance and results of the company's financial activities and matters of particular interest and importance.

Assists other executives in appraising their activities in terms of financial results, pointing out significant trends in operations as indicated by analysis of reports; assists other executives in determining future policies based on applying sound business judgment to the conclusions deduced from such facts.

Co-ordination

Co-ordinates Financial Division activities for effective, efficient internal operation; co-operates with other executives of the company in co-ordinating Financial Division activities with other operations as required to provide effective service to them and to facilitate reaching overall company objectives.

Administration and Control

Directs, co-ordinates, and controls the work, delegates responsibilities and commensurate authority to the following personnel:

COMPTROLLER
INSURANCE MANAGER
SECRETARY
PROPERTY MANAGER
ANALYST
INTERNAL AUDITOR

Prepares and recommends a program of expense for the Financial Division; manages its operations efficiently within cost limitations; selects and assigns subordinates; guides and assists them in their work; reviews performance and keeps them fully informed of company policies affecting their responsibilities.

Personnel Administration

Selects, trains, transfers and promotes, adjusts compensation, measures effectiveness of effort, maintains discipline and control, takes appropriate corrective action according to established company policies and procedures; co-operates with the VICE-PRESIDENT & SECRETARY in securing all assistance in administering these personnel responsibilities.

Keeping Informed

Keeps informed on overall policies and procedures of the company to the extent that is necessary to administer the Finance Division activities; interprets such policies and procedures to subordinates and associates to help them to determine proper courses of action.

Keeps currently informed of business and economic conditions in all areas affecting the company; appraises the financial implications of such conditions upon the company.

Keeps informed on current practices in financial, accounting, and operating control fields through professional and related association activities, technical and business publications, etc.

Accounting

Sees that accounting methods and procedures adequate to control and appraise the financial needs of the enterprise are established and maintained.

Capital Expenditures

Establishes procedures and criteria for assessment of capital expenditure proposals; directs the review and appraisal of requests and the preparation of a consolidated capital expenditure request for consideration and approval of the PRESIDENT and BOARD OF DIRECTORS.

Credit and Collection

Directs the establishment of criteria and their application in the authorization of credit and collections of money due.

Insurance

Directs the establishment and control of an adequate program of insurance for the company.

Security of Assets

Establishes and administers such control standards as may be required to ensure the conservation, effective utilization, and control of the company's assets and capital structure.

Inventory Control

Consults with and advises divisional VICE-PRESIDENTS and other company personnel on inventory policy; assists in making most effective use of funds invested in inventories.

Tax Management

Directs the determination of tax liabilities and filing of proper tax returns.

Employee Welfare Plans

Directs the financial operation of the company's employee welfare programs.

Internal Audit

Directs a program of internal audit designed to strengthen and improve security and control over assets, adherence to standard policies and procedures, and staff training.

Investment of Surplus Funds

Invests surplus cash funds in accordance with general policies established by the PRESIDENT.

Chapter 2
The Legal Setting and Financial Management

2-1. INTRODUCTION

The financial manager or student of finance needs to be aware of certain basic concepts of business law, since the environment within which financial decisions are made is molded by such regulation. In this chapter, we first provide a brief introduction to Canada's legal system. We then discuss various legal forms of business organization, such as the sole proprietorship, the partnership, and the corporation. Finally, we briefly review legislation which is relevant in the case of bankruptcies and compositions. Many of the topics presented in this chapter are introduced in a fairly brief and general way, since the main purpose is to provide a general understanding of basic concepts. For a more detailed and technical treatment of these subjects, the reader should refer to the extensive literature in this field.

2-2. CANADA'S LEGAL SYSTEM

By simple definition a law is a binding rule prescribed by a supreme controlling authority. A rule is a law, however, only if the authority has the means and intention of enforcing it. In the interest of convenience, laws have been categorized as being either *substantive* or *procedural.*

Subtantive law prescribes rights and duties.

Procedural law sets out the machinery by which the rights and duties are realized and enforced.

A substantive law, for example, requires directors of widely held corporations to report their shareholdings to a Securities Commission. The related procedural law details the method by which the Securities Commission can impose sanctions on a director for failing to file such a report. Substantive laws are further divided into *public* and *private* law.

Public law deals with relations between the government and private persons. "The government" includes agencies such as the Securities Commission, while "private persons" includes such entities as individuals, clubs, and corporations.

Private law is concerned with the relationship between private persons. A contract dispute between an employee and the company he worked for is an example in which private law would be invoked.

Two main systems of law have evolved, namely *civil* law and *common* law. Civil law in this context[1] means a system that uses as its authority a *civil code*

[1]Civil law is also used to mean law between individuals such as contract or tort law.

with courts settling disputes after reference to such a code to find the applicable law. Where the code does not contain a rule which pertains exactly to the facts disputed, the court is free to reason by analogy a solution to the problem or to refer to previous cases. Only the code is binding on the court's decision.

The second main system is common law. Unlike civil law systems, common law jurisdictions recognized the need for consistency and predictability. They, therefore, adopted the doctrine of *Stare Decisis*, a Latin phrase meaning *to let it stand decided*. Thus, there is under the system no code on which to base decisions, but rather a history of case law precedent. If a factual situation arises involving a dispute, the court will look to previous cases to determine how the dispute should be settled. A previous case with no distinguishing features from the present case will bind the court.[2] Like civil law, however, if there are no previous cases on point, a court may reason by analogy a solution to the dispute. Perhaps because of its desirable features of predictability and consistency, the common law system is predominant in the English-speaking world. It is used in Great Britain, Canada, and the United States of America with the exception of French-speaking areas such as the Province of Quebec.

In addition to the precedent case law just described, there is within the common law system a second major source of law comprised of statutes—laws enacted by various jurisdictions. By authority derived from the *British North America Act*, the federal and provincial governments are empowered to pass legislation. The validity of any piece of legislation is dependent on where the authority granted by the BNA Act resides.[3] Statutes may be attacked as *ultra vires*, or outside the power granted, if it is thought that the enacting government lacked the required jurisdiction. If, for example, a province passed legislation concerned with bankruptcy, anyone affected by it could apply to the courts to have the legislation quashed since authority to legislate in that field is explicitly given to the federal government.

The courts of Canada which provide the machinery required to put our system of law into effect can be divided into tiers at both the provincial and federal levels. The lowest level of court in the province is a trial court having jurisdiction over less serious criminal cases, juvenile and domestic relations problems, and small claims cases. These courts are often termed Magistrate's or Provincial Courts depending on the province. County or District Courts are of a higher level and usually hear cases involving medium-size claims and more serious criminal cases. This level of court may also hear appeals from the lower courts. Each province also has one higher court of first instance called the High Court of

[2]Our rapidly changing society has, in fact, prevented blind adherence to *stare decisis*. See, for example, J. Smyth and D. Soberman, *The Law and Business Administration in Canada*, (3rd ed.), Toronto: Prentice-Hall, 1976, pp. 47-48.

[3]It is primarily section 91 which gives the federal government powers in certain areas. Sections 92 and 93 give the provinces jurisdiction over other areas, while municipalities only acquire rights delegated to them by the provinces. If a particular field is not explicitly referred to in the BNA Act, it is usually assumed that, under a general clause in section 91, the federal government has the authority.

Justice or the Supreme Court.[4] It has jurisdiction to hear all criminal and civil cases as well as appeals from lower courts. The highest provincial court is the Court of Appeal. Cases reach this level only on appeal after being tried in lower courts.

At the federal level, the Federal Court of Canada has a division of original jurisdiction to try cases in such limited areas as federal taxation, patents, copyrights, trademarks, and disputes relating to shipping. Furthermore, an appeal division of this same court provides for appeals to be heard. The Supreme Court of Canada is the land's highest appeal court with appeal to it coming from decisions of both the Federal Court and the highest provincial courts. It also rules on constitutional issues referred to it by the federal cabinet.

2-3. LEGAL FORMS OF BUSINESS ORGANIZATION

Business activity in Canada is conducted largely by organizations which take one of three legal forms. These three most widely used legal forms of business organization are the *sole proprietorship*, the *partnership*, and the *corporation*. Their relative importance in particular areas of endeavor is reflected in Tables 2-1, 2-2, and 2-3. In manufacturing, for example, where larger amounts of capital are required to establish viable operations, the corporate form of organization dominates; while in retailing, which includes the corner store, the role of the sole proprietorship is significant. Generally speaking, however, the dominant form is the limited company or corporation. Much of its appeal stems from income tax, legal liability and fund-raising considerations, and the attribute of permanency. The implications of each of these considerations will be explored in greater detail below.

TABLE 2-1

The Percentage Distribution of Establishments in the Manufacturing Industries by Type of Organization

Selected Years only

	Sole Proprietorships	Partnerships	Corporations	Co-operatives
1964	31.1	8.1	58.7	2.1
1969	24.2	6.1	68.1	1.6
1970	23.2	5.7	69.5	1.6
1971	22.1	5.5	70.9	1.5
1972	21.4	5.3	72.0	1.3
1973	20.3	5.3	73.0	1.4

Source: Statistics Canada, *Manufacturing Industries of Canada, 1973.*

[4]The terminology "a court of first instance" or "trial court" is used so as to distinguish it from a court of appeal. A court of appeal can never hear a case for the first time. By definition, a appeal is from a case which has already been tried.

TABLE 2-2

Percentage Distribution of Value of Shipments of Goods of Own Manufacture by Type of Organization and Value of Shipments Per Establishment, 1972.

	Under $ 25,000	$ 25,000- $ 99,999	$ 100,000- $ 499,999	$ 500,000 and over
Sole Proprietorships	70.9	36.6	5.3	0.1
Partnerships	9.6	11.5	3.0	0.2
Corporations	19.2	51.5	89.6	98.2
Co-operatives	0.2	0.3	2.1	1.6

Source: Correspondence with Statistics Canada, February, 1975.

TABLE 2-3

Retail Trade by Form of Organization, 1966

	Number of Establishments	Percentage	Sales ($ 000)	Percentage
Total, All Stores	153,620	100.00	22,686,418.2	100.00
Sole Proprietorships	103,341	67.27	5,703,137.3	25.14
Partnerships	11,744	7.64	1,197,881.8	5.28
Corporations	35,956	23.41	14,738,380.3	64.96
Co-operatives	893	0.58	251,148.9	1.11
Others	1,686	1.10	795,869.9	3.51

Source: Dominion Bureau of Statistics, *Retail Trade, Miscellaneous Data, 1966 Census.*

Many consequences flow from the type of business organization selected. Whether reevaluating an earlier choice or choosing a form for the first time, awareness of the different aspects of each form of organization is essential.[5] What is perceived to be an advantage by one entrepreneur may well appear disadvantageous to another. In evaluating alternatives, the specific situation has to be kept in mind.

The sole proprietorship

There is no legislation pertaining to the sole proprietor as such, and a discussion of the legal consequences of this form of business is really little more than a discussion of the rights and duties of an individual in society.

The sole proprietorship certainly is the oldest form of business organization, the simplest one to establish, and the one most often used by small businesses which comprise much of the service industries. The individual need only acquire

[5]Choice is not always possible since particular forms of organization may be mandatory or prohibited by statute. Thus, the practice of law may not be carried on through corporations.

the necessary licences and he can legally begin to operate. The owner, if aware of his responsibility to creditors, can avoid collective decision-making and lay claim to all profits after taxes. Also, he can readily maintain a personal relationship with most of his customers.

Looking beyond these considerations, however, there are very few advantages to be gained from setting up a business as a proprietorship. In many regards the sole proprietorship is characterized by significant weaknesses and disadvantages. The most serious of these is likely to be the risk posed for the owner through the feature of *unlimited liability* as this prevents an owner from shielding whatever assets he may hold outside of the business from the claims of the proprietorship's creditors. Expressed another way, creditors may look to the owner's business, to his personal assets, or to both for satisfaction of their claims. A second negative consequence of this type of organization is its *lack of permanence*, with life of the business limited to that of its owner. Only the net assets remain to be passed on to heirs and, in fact, valuable leases and other contracts may not be transferable.

One of the other consequences of organizing as a sole proprietorship relates to taxes to be paid. This may prove to be favorable or unfavorable depending on the particular circumstances. Profits of a sole proprietorship are fully taxed at the owner's marginal tax rate, which may be higher than the corporate tax rate which would be applicable. On the other hand, there are no further levies to be faced should funds subsequently be transferred from the business to its owner. This is in contrast to a corporate setting where corporate levies are paid on business profits, but the owners face additional personal taxes if they withdraw funds from the business through dividends.

As the sole proprietorship is typically built around one individual, most managerial chores tend to fall entirely on the sole proprietor. When he finds such functions and/or the effort of maintaining adequate finances too great a burden, he may consider a joint undertaking. Recognition of the obvious benefits to be gained by such a pooling of resources may result in the formation of a partnership.

The partnership

The partnership is identical to the sole proprietorship in many fundamental ways. Thus, for example, the partners, or at least one of them in the case of a limited partnership, face unlimited liability; the partnership's lifetime is limited to the life of any partner, or by agreement; and earnings are taxed at the personal rate in the hands of the partners. But the formation of a partnership has serious consequences differing from those of a proprietorship. These differences are best illustrated by first defining a partnership and by identifying the legal implications of entering into one.

Unlike the sole proprietorship, the partnership is given statutory recognition in all provinces. Many of the statutes define a partnership as the relation which subsists between persons carrying on business in common with a view of profit.[6]

[6] *Partnershp Act*, R.S.B.C., 1960, C.277, s 3.

The partnership is entered into in one of two ways. First, a partnership may be established under statute, and persons associated in partnership are required to make a written declaration to that effect. Such a declaration automatically gives legal status to the partnership.

Secondly, a partnership may be held by law to exist if two or more persons act in such a way as to cause other people to believe they are partners. This "implied" partnership results in all the legal consequences that flow from a "declared" partnership. Whether or not an implied partnership is found to exist depends on a number of factors. While joint ownership or the sharing of profits or returns from jointly owned property does not necessarily create a partnership, it may serve as a strong indication that a partnership, in fact, exists.

The relationship of partners *inter se* (among, or between themselves) adds significantly to the legal consequences which may emerge from this form of business organization. To begin with, it must be appreciated that a partner is the agent of all other partners and that his acts, while within the scope of the partnership's business, bind his partners personally.[7] This agency relationship may be restricted by agreement between the partners, but only if a third party knows or can reasonably be expected to know of such restraints are the other co-owners protected. For most acts of one partner, such as incurring debts for instance, the other partners are *jointly* liable. This means that if the partnership is sued for the debt each member must contribute towards its repayment, and, if some are unable to do so, the other partners end up having to pay larger amounts.

For more serious acts by one of the partners, the others are held both *jointly* and *severally* liable. If, for example, a partner misappropriates the funds of one of the partnership's customers, the customer may sue that individual. Were the partners only jointly liable, the customer could not later sue the other owners to recover what the first partner did not repay. However, when the partners are jointly and severally liable the client can sue one partner, and if not satisfied, can bring an action against any of the other partners for his claim. The liability of a partner, like that of the sole proprietor, extends beyond partnership property to his personal assets. To face unlimited liability under the circumstances just described quite obviously requires that the partners have a great deal of confidence in and respect for one another.

Liability does not necessarily end on death or retirement from the partnership. Contracts entered into by the partnership before either death or retirement will remain the liability of a former partner or his estate unless there is a discharge by both the other party to the contract and the other owners. A retiring partner may, furthermore, be liable for arrangements entered into by the partnership after his retirement if he has failed to give public notice about having left the organization. It is possible to protect oneself against such liability by advertising retirement and disclaiming any liability for future contracts in the official gazette of the province. Death of a partner will always obviate his estate's liability for

[7]Whatever is necessary for the usual conduct of the firm's business is held to be in the scope of the partnership's business. It would, for example, include buying the usual or necessary goods, selling the goods or chattels of the firm, receiving payments and giving receipts, and hiring servants.

partnership debts contracted after his death.

Apart from liability for partnership acts, there are other legal consequences flowing from the relationship of partners *inter se*. Unless agreement is reached to the contrary between the partners, their relationships will be determined by the legislation in the partnership's jurisdiction. Statutory provisions will usually provide the following:

(a) Property acquired for the partnership shall be used exclusively for the partnership and not for the private purposes of individual partners. Property purchased with partnership money is deemed to be partnership property.
(b) All partners are to share equally in the capital and profits of the business, and must contribute equally toward the firm's losses.
(c) A partner shall be indemnified by the other partners for any liability incurred on behalf of the partnership.
(d) A payment made by a partner for the purposes of the partnership in excess of his agreed subscription shall earn interest.
(e) Each partner may take part in the management of the business.
(f) No remuneration shall be given for partnership activity in the business.
(g) No new member may be admitted to the partnership without the consent of all partners.
(h) Disputes regarding the partnership business may be decided by a majority, but the nature of the partnership may not be changed without the consent of all members.
(i) Partnership books shall be kept at the partnership's place of business and all partners shall have access to them.
(j) No majority may expel any partner.

Subject to agreements between the partners, legislation will also provide for termination of the partnership under certain circumstances. Thus, a partnership will terminate

(a) if entered into for a fixed term, by the expiration of that term;
(b) if entered into for a single venture or undertaking, by the termination of that venture or undertaking;
(c) by any partner giving notice to the others of his intention to dissolve the partnership; and
(d) following death, insanity, or bankruptcy of a partner.

The above statutory enactments only apply when the partners have failed to cover the points in an appropriate agreement. Provincial legislators do recognize that many people would prefer not to be bound by such externally imposed restrictions and have allowed partners to agree on their relationships including the termination of the partnership. An agreement between partners, to be sufficiently comprehensive, should cover at least the following points:

(a) The firm's name.
(b) Contributions to be made by each partner.
(c) The nature, location, and scope of the partnership business, including its duration.
(d) A buy-sell agreement, including a basis for valuation of the business and provision for arbitration.

(e) The ratio or basis for the payment of salaries, interest, and distribution of profits and losses.
(f) The treatment of partnership loans, salaries, and drawings.
(g) Provisions to delegate and assign the authority, duties, and responsibilities of the partners.
(h) The general criteria for the admission or expulsion of partners.
(i) The treatment of any outside ventures of the partners.
(j) Factors terminating the partnership (*e.g.*, death).

Unlike the corporation, a partnership is for most purposes not a separate legal entity. This is evident from our earlier comments about the personal liability of partners for acts of the partnership. In some ways, however, a partnership holds a separate identity. It can, for example, sue and be sued in its own name without each partner being named as a plaintiff or defendant, and, for accounting purposes, it issues its own financial statements.

The many legal consequences of forming a partnership as detailed above may make this form of business organization quite risky for the individuals involved. A way of curtailing some of the risk by avoiding unlimited personal liability while staying with a business carried on as a partnership is to become a special partner in a *limited partnership*. The limited partnership, is generally restricted to the transacting of particular businesses. It requires two classes of partners. In addition to the *special* or *limited* partners with limited liability, there must be at least one *general* partner personally liable for an unlimited amount. The liability of the special partners is held to amounts contributed by them as capital. Certain conduct by special partners, including an active role in management of the firm, results in their being deemed general partners. The loss of limited liability also occurs when operations extend beyond the period provided for in the certificate setting out the limited partnership.

Partnerships are particularly prevalent in certain lines of business which have often been precluded by law from incorporating, and where the pooling of resources from various individuals enhances the ability of the business to compete. Thus, through various legislations, professionals such as lawyers, doctors, and accountants have been refused the right to incorporate. The reasoning behind such legislation is complex, but includes the fact that we may not want to grant limited liability to such professionals.

The corporation

Today, the corporation or limited company is the most important form of business organization as judged by its contributions to the economy. As we know it in Canada, the corporate form of business organization is not a new institution, having evolved quite slowly from the English joint-stock companies of the sixteenth century. While economic historians point to visible expressions of corporate character in the Anglo-Saxon and Anglo-Norman gilds,[8] it is generally agreed that the Russia Company (1553), chartered directly by the

[8] W. Scott, *The General Development of the Joint-Stock System to 1720*, Cambridge: University Press, 1912, p. 3.

Crown, is one of the earliest examples of business application of the corporation.

Incorporation was, and continued to be, a matter of special grant by King or Parliament until passage of the *Joint Stock Companies Registration and Regulation Act* of 1844. By this statute, certain privileges of incorporation were made generally available, and registration requirements were set out for protection of the general public. However, English law continued to preclude limited liability as a matter of general right until 1855.[9] It was the right to establish limited liability companies that provided the means by which much needed aggregations of capital could be gathered and efficiently administered. Developing from the English pattern, the corporation became an important if not the dominant form of business organization in the more vital fields of Canadian business endeavor.

The corporation is a unique business form. Unlike a partnership in which the partners are the "business", and a sole proprietorship where the proprietor is the "business", *a corporation is a distinct legal entity*, separate from the people who set it up, own it, and manage it. Its feature of limited liability stems from this fact. The landmark case in company law illustrating these considerations is *Salomon vs. Salomon & Co. Ltd.* In this instance, Salomon formed a company and sold all his assets to it, taking both shares and secured debt instruments in exchange. His wife and other members of his family each held one share because seven shareholders were required under the *Companies Act* applicable in 1892. Since these shares were held in trust for Salomon, he was the beneficial owner of all shares of the company and it subsequently went into insolvency. When Salomon tried to enforce his rights as a secured creditor, the general creditors sued him for recovery of what was owed them by the firm. They essentially argued that as he owned all the shares, managed the company, and was its sole employee, he was, in fact, the company. The House of Lords deciding in favor of Salomon rejected the creditors' arguments and held that there was a company distinct from the shareholders and management and the money was owed by the company. This fact of separate legal personality has many important consequences which will be more fully apparent as we consider how the corporation comes into being.

2-4. THE FORMATION OF A CORPORATION

A company may be incorporated either *provincially* or *federally* to carry on a trading, manufacturing, or service type of business. The choice actually made is influenced by the scope of the proposed activity. If the initial plan is to carry on business across Canada, the firm should in all probability incorporate federally. On the other hand, because of costs, time, and effort to be saved, a company intending to function in just one or two provinces might find it advantageous to incorporate provincially. A provincial corporation may trade throughout Canada by registering as an *extra-provincial* company in other provinces.

There are three basic approaches to incorporation in Canada, the method to be used depending on the jurisdiction. The *letters patent* system is the method of incorporation resorted to in Manitoba, Quebec, Prince Edward Island, and New

[9] B. Hunt, *The Development of the Business Corporation in England, 1800-1867*, Cambridge, Mass.: Harvard University Press, 1936, p. 89.

Brunswick. The remaining provinces except for Ontario use a *registration system*, while the federal government and Ontario use the *certificate of incorporation system.*

In letters patent jurisdictions, the persons desiring incorporation must file an application for a charter or letters patent. The application will include the corporate name, the objectives of the company, details on the authorized share capital desired, and the names of the initial subscribers for shares. The registrar of companies or like authority has complete discretion over whether or not to register the letters patent applied for. A letters patent company may also apply to have its bylaws, which are the rules by which the internal management is to proceed, registered. On acceptance of the application and granting of letters patent, the separate corporate entity is born.

A registration jurisdiction involves two basic procedural differences respecting incorporation. Firstly, the persons desiring incorporation file a *memorandum of association* instead of an application for letters patent. The memorandum includes similar information. If, however, the memorandum complies with the statute, the registrar of companies may not refuse registration. Secondly, the registration jurisdiction requires a company to have its internal management procedures made public. A memorandum company must therefore file its articles, which are similar to the bylaws of a letters patent company, with the registrar. Should a company fail to file articles, it is deemed to have adopted the set prescribed by the jurisdiction's *Companies Act*. When the memorandum is accepted, the corporation's life commences.

A third system of incorporation, the certificate of incorporation approach, was designed in Ontario and subsequently adopted for federal incorporations under the *Canada Business Corporations Act*.[10] This approach is not substantially different from the registration system with potential incorporations submitting their articles of incorporation to the appropriate offices. If the statutory requirements for incorporation are met, the registrar of companies has no discretion and must issue a charter or certificate of incorporation. As with the other systems, once the certificate is issued, a new entity is created and from that moment the consequences of a separate existence emerge.

The consequences of this separate legal existence can be most clearly demonstrated by contrasting the corporation with the partnership or sole proprietorship. One upshot is that the shareholders or owners of the business have limited personal liability. With the company a legal entity able to act in its own name, any debts incurred or wrongful acts committed remain those of the corporation, and creditors or other persons who in some way have a claim against the company must sue it and not its owners. A shareholder's total liability is, therefore, limited to the amounts paid out for the purchase of company stock.[11] If the corporation loses more money than its assets are worth, the shareholder's total investment has obviously been dissipated but his assets outside the business remain untouched. If, on the other hand, a partnership or

[10]Statistics of Canada, 1974-75, c. 33.

[11]Provided the shares are fully paid for and nonassessable. This will be detailed in a separate chapter dealing with common shares.

sole proprietorship has the same experience, the creditors will be free to go after the personal assets of the proprietor or partners. It should be noted that in a small business setting, lenders who are obviously aware of the limited liability implied in the corporate form of business organization may be reluctant to provide funds for the business unless one or more of the major shareholders provide a personal guarantee to cover the loan. Thus, such shareholders may lose the benefits of limited liability which are otherwise derived from incorporation.

Secondly, the fact of incorporation allows for easy transfer of ownership, and a shareholder wishing to take his money out of a business may simply sell his shares. He is also free to bequeath shares in his will, and neither act will affect the life of the corporation directly. A partner trying to take his investment out of a partnership, however, will probably end up having to dissolve the partnership to achieve this, or sell his interest to someone the other partners are willing to accept. Even if a partner can retire from the firm and take his money out without serious problems, he may still be liable for debts of the firm. Furthermore, a partner cannot freely pass his partnership interest to an heir. Death or bankruptcy of a shareholder has no direct effect on the life of the corporation; but in the event of a partner's death or bankruptcy, a partnership will often be ended.

Thirdly, a shareholder is not necessarily the agent of the company or of its other shareholders. This means that neither the corporation nor its other shareholders are liable for acts by individual owners, and investors may feel quite safe buying shares in a company without knowing a thing about the other minority shareholders. On the other hand, a person wanting to enter into a partnership must be infinitely more cautious and should know a great deal about each of his prospective partners.

A fourth consequence of the separate corporate identity is that the corporation pays its own taxes. Since 1917, the income of the corporation has been subject to taxation quite apart from the taxation of its owners. Such double taxation of income, first in the hands of the corporation, and then in the hands of the shareholders if corporate earnings are distributed, has been subject to debate. While tax considerations will be more fully explored in the next chapter, the following quotation from the 1966 *Report of the Royal Commission on Taxation* is opportune:

> Although we can see no grounds in principle for taxing corporations and other organizations, we have reluctantly reached the conclusion that there are good and sufficient reasons for continuing to collect a tax from them. The main reason is the practical difficulty of taxing accrued share gains as required under the ideal approach just described. Another is the loss of economic benefit to Canada that would result if non-residents holding shares in Canadian corporations were not taxed by Canada on their share of corporate income at approximately the rates that now prevail.[12]

[12]Canada, *Report of the Royal Commission on Taxation*, Vol. IV, Ottawa: Queen's Printer, 1967, pp. 4-5.

A shareholder of a corporation will be taxed if he earns a salary from the company, receives a dividend from it, or realizes a capital gain from the sale of his shares. Advantages, in the form of reduced or deferred taxes, may sometimes be gained by the appropriate splitting of distributions to shareholders between dividend and salary payments. The ultimate effect hinges on a variety of factors including the corporate tax rate; the marginal tax rate of the relevant group of shareholders; their general financial position; and like variables which will differ from one corporate situation to another. It is significant that the partnership and sole proprietorship enjoy no such options, with all income from the business taxed at personal rates.

There are additional legal considerations relating to differences between corporations and other forms of business organization besides the separation of the corporation from its shareholders. Thus, a corporation is not as free to function as is an individual, and must, in fact, act through human agents. It is also limited by objectives stated in its letters patent, memorandum of association, or certificate of incorporation. Although the granting of a charter or letters patent effectively gives a letters patent corporation all the powers of a natural person, a shareholder may sue it for any detriment if the corporation acts in deviation from its objects. The capacity of a memorandum company is even more strictly constrained by its stated objectives. If a company acts outside its defined scope, the act is said to be *ultra vires* and is subject to attack by any party to the act as well as by shareholders.[13]

An example will show the possible consequences of deviating from stated objectives.

Example

> Consider Constructs Limited, a letters patent company incorporated with the stated object of building and selling houses. It subsequently begins to carry on the business of giving advice to land developers, which is clearly not an object of the firm. A shareholder, engaged in similar endeavors, could therefore sue the company to restrain it from engaging in such competitive consulting. Next, consider the same circumstance but substitute a typical memorandum company for the letters patent firm. The corporation in this case only has legal capacity to act within its objectives, and if the land developer defaulted on an agreement to pay consultant's fees, the company could not win its case because it lacked the legal capacity to enter into such contracts in the first place.[14]

2-5. THE DUTIES OF DIRECTORS

The fact that a corporation is a legal entity distinct from its shareholders requires that the latter elect individuals as directors to manage the firm on their behalf.

[13]British Columbia, though a memorandum jurisdiction, has used a section of its *Companies Act* to set aside the *ultra vires* doctrine as has Ontario, while the Federal Act does not require the charter to set out a corporation's objectives.

[14]For purposes of the illustration, an Ontario or B.C. company would fall into the former category.

Those elected by the shareholders make up the company's board of directors. For federally incorporated firms, a majority of the board must be comprised of resident Canadians.[15] When the board is quite large it is usual to find a management committee of the board dealing with many of the more routine matters to be faced.

When a potentially large number of shareholders vest the management of the corporation in the hands of a few directors, there must be safeguards to protect the owners from fraudulent or unscrupulous acts by the directors. Such safeguards have developed in the form of directors' duties. By case law precedent and, to a lesser degree, by statute it has been established that directors have two broad categories of obligations to meet. The first is that the director has a duty to exercise care and skill in carrying out his functions. Unfortunately for the shareholders, however, the degree of care and skill required is generally quite modest though some statutory enactments are adding to the obligations. In Ontario, for example, directors are called on to exercise the degree of care, diligence, and skill that a reasonably prudent person would exercise in comparable circumstances. Under the *Canada Business Corporations Act*, directors who do not attend meetings or delegate their authority, can not thereby avoid liability if the persons who did act failed to exercise care and skill.

The second category of obligations is termed *fiduciary duties*.[16] It is more extensive and imposes a higher standard of performance on the director. There are a number of such fiduciary duties. The first is to act honestly and in the best interests of the firm. Secondly, all acts of directors must be for the furtherance of the objects of the company, not their own. Thirdly, a director must act on his own initiative in making decisions, and lastly, he must not place himself in a position where there is a possibility that his duty will conflict with his personal interests. This latter point is based on the equitable doctrine that a trustee must not profit from a position of trust, and bars directors from gains through contracts with the company or profits generated because of relationships with the company and knowledge gained as a result.

2-6. THE RIGHTS AND DUTIES OF SHAREHOLDERS

In addition to the protection afforded owners by the responsibilities imposed on directors, the shareholders are aided to some degree by statutory requirements relating to financial disclosure. Thus, all corporations must file annual income statements and balance sheets and make documents, such as the minutes of meetings, available to their shareholders. Widely held companies must release additional information including, for example, reports on share transactions taking place on behalf of insiders.[17] Furthermore, all provinces except Prince Edward Island provide for an investigator to look into the affairs of a company if

[15]A resident Canadian is defined as either a Canadian citizen or a landed immigrant who has been resident in Canada for less than six years.

[16]Fiduciary duties refer to relationships between persons where one acting as a trustee for the other incurs particular obligations.

[17]Insiders generally include directors, senior officers of the company, and individuals holding controlling blocks of shares.

a sufficient number of shareholders approach the court to have one appointed. Under the federal and some provincial acts, when a corporation has been wronged and neither management nor the board can be moved to act, minority shareholders may obtain court permission to take legal action on behalf of their company and all other shareholders. This right is particularly useful if a firm has suffered at the hands of one or more of its directors or officers.

Statutes also provide that shareholders be given notice of and be allowed to attend shareholders' meetings at least one of which must be held every year. Under certain circumstances, the shareholders may also require management to call a special meeting. At any of the meetings questions may be asked and criticisms voiced of the company's officers. Additionally, nearly all common shares issued today allow the holder to vote on issues raised at shareholders' meetings and to vote in the election of directors. It is through such voting that a shareholder can express approval or disappointment over the way in which management is performing.

A shareholder has a right to dividends if and when declared by the board of directors. He also has the right to share in the assets of the corporation if it is wound up or liquidated. Any other rights which may attach to shares can be established by contract between the shareholder and the issuing company.

While all shareholders enjoy certain rights, some, because they are in a position of controlling the corporation, are governed by particular rules and have certain obligations. Majority shareholders, for example, must not vote so as to intentionally discriminate against a minority shareholder. Statutory court orders may afford some protection to minority owners in situations where a controlling block of shares is voted in such an oppressive way. The order could require an involuntary winding-up of the company to allow the minority shareholders to get their money out; or prescribe some other action which the court holds to be just and equitable. Unlike directors, however, shareholders may, in all other circumstances, vote any way they wish even if they vote for their own best interests and against what is best for the corporation.

2-7. THE NATURE OF CORPORATE SECURITIES

A further feature of incorporation is the broad choice of ways in which the firm can raise monies externally. Whereas partnerships and sole proprietorships are limited to borrowing, and usually only in quite a constrained fashion, a corporation can resort to debt or equity financing in different forms and combinations.

As will be detailed in later chapters covering long-term external sources of funds, the distinction between debt and equity financing is fundamental. Debt involves a loan to the company taking the form of bank loans, bond or debenture issues, leases, or mortgages, with the lender becoming a creditor of the corporation. Such creditors under normal circumstances have no voice in company affairs. On the other hand, equity financing through the sale of new shares implies the sale of fractional ownership of the company.

From the investor's standpoint, the consequences flowing out of holding different financial instruments are significant. If the investor is, in fact, a creditor, he has a right to agreed upon interest payments and to repayment of principal when the obligation comes due. A shareholder enjoys no such claim against the corporation and is only entitled to a share of the assets if the company is wound up. Furthermore, creditors have a prior claim to assets if the company fails while the shareholder's position is residual. The several types of securities used to finance the corporation will be looked at individually in subsequent chapters to ascertain in more detail the rights and features attaching to each of them.

In discussing financing, it must be made clear that, for the protection of investors, there are restrictions on the ways in which a corporation may seek financing from the general public. Securities legislation establishes who may solicit public financing and what procedures must be followed. The two methods of control relied upon by provincial securities commissions are

(1) the licensing of those in the securities business and
(2) the requirement that public offerings of securities only be made after extensive and complete information regarding the offering and the issuing firm is made available to the general public. The document containing this information which also has to be filed with the relevant Securities Commission is called a *prospectus*. An abridged example of a prospectus is set out in Appendix A at the end of this book.

2-8. TERMINATION OF CORPORATE EXISTENCE

Just as a partnership may be dissolved or a sole proprietor may die, a corporation, although a more permanent form of business organization, may also cease to exist. Thus, it may be wound up voluntarily by agreement of the required number of shareholders, or wound up involuntarily by court order because of bankruptcy or abuse of minority shareholders. Since very few areas of corporation law are as complex as those touching upon corporate reorganization and the winding up of companies, no review of the subject matter will be undertaken in this text.

2-9. THE VOTING TRUST

One outgrowth of the corporate form of business organization is the voting trust, a device used periodically to exercise control over a corporation. It effectively secures the continuity of management for a designated period but without the need for holding a significant block of common shares to attain this end. The setting up of a voting trust entails depositing a block of the controlling stock with trustees and receiving *voting trust certificates* in exchange. The controlling group then sells such voting trust certificates to the public, recovering in the process an amount which would approach what must be tied up in common shares to ensure control.[18] In the meantime, the trustees become the legal owners of the shares and exercise the inherent right of voting the shares and collecting the dividends due. The shares are voted in accordance with the trust agreement entered into when the shares were deposited, while dividends are

[18]The monies released may, of course, be used to gain control of another firm, and the process repeated.

redistributed to holders of the voting trust certificates.

The certificates are freely transferable in the market, but such transfers in no way affect the voting rights of the shares held by the trustees. Upon termination of the trust, the voting trust certificates are taken up and the deposited shares distributed to certificate holders.

The voting trust is not just a device for extending control. It may also be used when a company is undergoing reorganization and there is a need to continue with a particular management group until the firm is revitalized. The voting trust involving the shares of Westcoast Transmission Company between 1959 and 1963 is an example of the former category of usage, while the 1958 to 1963 voting trust relating to the Greater Winnipeg Gas Company exemplifies the latter.

2-10. THE HOLDING COMPANY

The holding company is another outgrowth of the corporate form of organization and is the term used to describe a parent corporation which owns a substantial number of the outstanding voting shares of subsidiary corporations.[19] Though the holding company vehicle may be used for a variety of purposes, one of its important applications is in extending control over other corporations with only minimal commitments of funds. To illustrate how the holding company may evolve and achieve such ends, consider investors Smith, Jones, and Brown owning twenty-six, fifteen, and ten percent respectively of the voting shares of Alpha Company. They form a new corporation, Beta, transferring to it their shares in Alpha to comprise the new firm's only assets. With shares of Beta distributed to the three investors in proportion to assets contributed, Smith, having just over fifty percent of these shares (26/51), ends up with control of Beta and hence of Alpha. If Beta were next to raise additional funds through issuance of debt and use the proceeds to buy a block of shares in a third corporation, while Alpha also acquired such shares with its surplus cash, the entire expansionary process could be extended further. Excessive pyramiding of both control and profits may naturally result, which, in the utility field in particular, can give rise to difficulties in rate regulation.

The British Columbia Telephone Company as part of a much larger complex of utilities and an operating subsidiary of two "layers" of holding companies is an interesting and useful example of the functioning of such devices. Figure 2-1 sets out the relationships in somewhat simplified fashion.

The particular complex illustrated was, in fact, of some concern to the Attorney General for British Columbia who made submissions before the 1971 rate-revision hearings of the Canadian Transport Commission. One specific submission was that, since the Company's costs are inflated by imprudent purchasing policies designed to enhance the profits of its ultimate parent, no increases in telephone tolls are warranted.

[19]A parent company need not own fifty percent plus one share of a second firm to qualify, because the ability to control the board of directors may be achieved with far fewer voting shares, provided all others are widely distributed.

FIGURE 2-4
A Utility Holding Company Complex

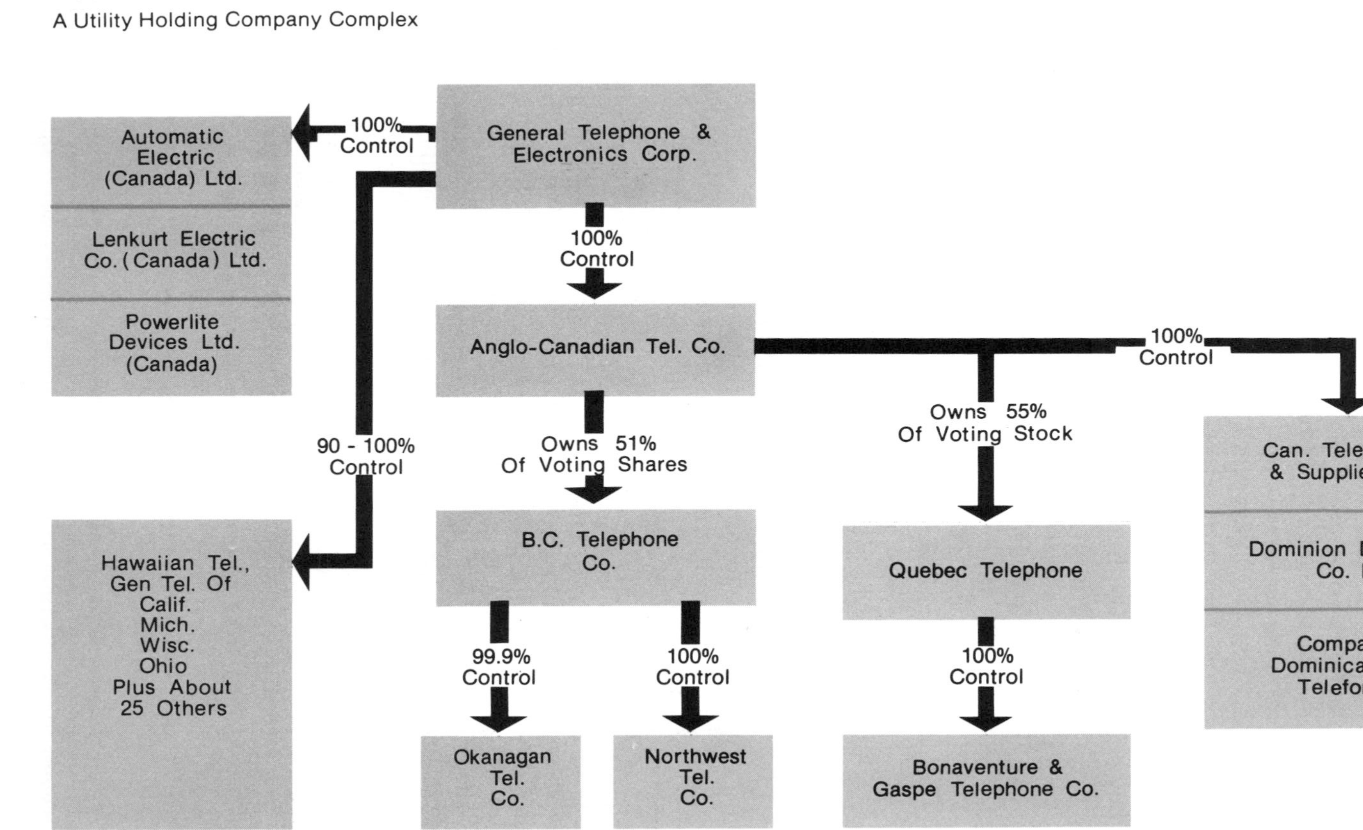

Commissioner G. F. Lafferty, in awarding far more modest increases than were requested, noted in his decision that:

> Officers of Dominion Directory Company Limited and Canadian Telephones and Supplies Ltd., filed financial statements of both companies for 1969 and 1970, as witnesses subpoenaed by Counsel for the British Columbia Federation of Labour. Counsel for the Applicant objected to that evidence on the ground that it was irrelevant. We permitted the filing of the statements reserving our decision on the objection. Having examined the documents, I do indeed find them to be relevant. The evidence shows that some 80% of the income of Dominion Directory Company Limited is derived from British Columbia Telephone Company and that 90% of the work of Canadian Telephones and Supplies Ltd. is performed for British Columbia Telephone Company.
>
> The shareholders' equity of Dominion Directory Company Limited amounted to $631,428 and $697,075 at December 31, 1969 and 1970 respectively. The earnings after taxes were $514,952 in 1969 and $613,647 in 1970. The shareholders' equity of Canadian Telephones and Supplies Ltd. amounted to $778,779 and $820,486 at December 31, 1969 and 1970 respectively. The earnings after taxes were $230,707 in 1969 and $298,957 in 1970. Both companies paid substantial dividends in both years to Anglo-Canadian Telephone Co. which holds a controlling interest in the ordinary shares of the Applicant.
>
> I am not satisfied that the Applicant has taken all reasonable and proper steps to negotiate more favourable terms under these two contracts. No satisfactory explanation was given as to whether it would not be feasible and more profitable for the Applicant either to provide the service directly or to establish a wholly owned directory subsidiary. In the case of Canadian Telephones and Supplies Ltd., I am not satisfied that the services contracted for could not be performed more economically by the Applicant for its own account.
>
> These considerations have not been without influence on my finding as to the amount of rate increases that I believe it would be appropriate to authorize at this time.[20]

A 1975 enquiry into the intercorporate relations, including procurement practices of the British Columbia Telephone Company was somewhat more encouraging. Thus, it was stated that:

> The return on the owner's equity in the unregulated affiliates has been significantly greater than that yielded on either the overall investment in the Canadian communications equipment manufacturing industry or on the average of all industries in Canada. There is no evidence to indicate that this situation results from excessive pricing of goods or services provided to B.C. Tel by affiliates.[21]

[20]Canada, Canadian Transport Commission, Decision of July 30, 1971, pp. 6-7.

[21]G. Pelletier, Minister of Communications, "Review of the Procurement Practices and Policies and the Intercorporate Financial Relationships of the British Columbia Telephone Company", Ottawa, July, 1975, p. 5.

The holding company is also a commonly used device for firms operating in a multinational setting. It allows the parent company to establish separate legal entities in the various national jurisdications in which operations are maintained. Thus, a multinational corporation may consist of a parent company which essentially functions as a holding company, and a variety of wholly owned or partly owned subsidiaries which are incorporated in different host countries. The issue of dealings between various subsidiaries belonging to the same overall corporate structure gains particular significance in this context. As illustrated above where one subsidiary purchases goods and/or services from another subsidiary, profits can be shifted from one subsidiary into another through an appropriate setting of prices for such transactions. Thus, a subsidiary operating in a country with relatively modest tax rates could purchase goods from another subsidiary operating in another country characterized by much higher tax rates. By setting a low price for such goods, profits of the buying subsidiary can be increased at the expense of profits of the selling subsidiary, and an overall reduction of taxes to be paid may be achieved. Also, where a host country has imposed restrictions on the payment of dividends to nonresidents, similar techniques may be used in an attempt to transfer earnings out of that particular country. Naturally, governments of the host country are quite concerned about these possibilities of shifting profits as such practices could severely reduce national tax revenues. Hence, dealings between related companies and the transfer prices charged on such transactions are typically subject to close surveillance by the relevant tax authorities. Prices which cannot be justified in terms of fair market value may be challenged, and appropriate adjustments to reported profits and consequent tax liabilities may be imposed.

2-11. BANKRUPTCY AND COMPOSITION

A person who cannot meet his debts when they come due is said to be insolvent and, in such circumstances, remedies are needed for both the debtor and his creditors. The debtor will likely find it very difficult to satisfy any obligations while under pressure from various sources, and may need to be released from his predicament so as to attempt a fresh start. The creditors of an insolvent debtor may also seek a solution, being in most cases more interested in quickly salvaging what they can from their position, rather than hanging on to the remote possibility of full payment at some distant future date. It is for the benefit of both interests that bankruptcy legislation exists in Canada. Such legislation is extensive and complicated and no effort will be made in this section to review all the aspects in detail. We will discuss briefly to whom the *Bankruptcy Act* applies, the procedures involved, and how it benefits the parties.

Either creditors who are owed at least $1,000 by the insolvent, or the debtor himself, may petition for a bankruptcy order. The *Act* does not apply where the debtor is a bank, insurance company, trust or loan company, or railway company, nor does it apply to farmers, fishermen, or employees earning less than $2,500 a year. To instigate bankruptcy proceedings, a creditor or group of creditors may petition a court for an order holding that a particular debtor is bankrupt and the insolvent debtor may voluntarily submit to such a court order.

The order may be granted if it is shown that the debtor has committed an act of bankruptcy within the last six months. Such acts include:

(a) a fraudulent conveyance, gift, delivery, or transfer of property;
(b) a departure from Canada with intent to defraud creditors;
(c) removal, secretion, or disposal of property with intent to defraud creditors; and
(d) failure to meet liabilities when they become due.

Once a court order is issued, a licensed trustee is appointed to take possession of all the assets of the bankrupt debtor including any relevant books and documents, and generally to handle affairs in the best interests of the creditors. Inspectors will be appointed by the creditors to help ensure that their interests are adequately protected.

When all the assets and liabilities of the debtor have been ascertained, the trustee will then attempt to settle the claims against the debtor. First, the creditors whose loans were secured through some collateral may have their securities realized. Once secured claims have been settled, the remaining assets become available to preferred creditors whose claims would include trustee's fees, legal fees, taxes, wages payable, rent, and claims of the Crown. Any residual is then released to the unsecured creditors. It is important that creditors file their claims with the trustee, providing details and substantiating evidence of their claim. As it is unlikely that the liquidation of assets will yield enough cash to satisfy all claimants, detailing of both the amounts owed and the collateral involved is vital.

An insolvent debtor who is not forced into bankruptcy by his creditors and who does not voluntarily assign his assets to a trustee in bankruptcy may seek relief under the *Bankruptcy Act* in another way. He can make a proposal to his creditors, through a trustee, whereby he agrees to pay a certain number of cents on each dollar owed. If creditors representing over three-quarters of the sum owing agree to the scheme, the trustee may then submit the proposal to the Court for approval. Such a settlement is called a *composition.*

Whether through involuntary bankruptcy, voluntary assignment, or proposal to creditors, the debtor may apply for discharge after the trustee's work is completed. Such a discharge can only be granted by court order, and its effect is to cancel any remaining debts. If the bankrupt is a company, it will then be dissolved. If it is an individual, he will be free to start afresh without being subject to claims and harrassment from old creditors. A discharge is not always given, however. Thus, if the assets have not yielded at least fifty cents on each dollar's worth of debt, discharge may be denied. Other reasons for refusal include misconduct of the debtor ranging from extravagant living to intentionally committing acts of bankruptcy.

2-12. SUMMARY

This chapter provides a brief introduction to the legal setting within which business must function, with emphasis on those features of the law which are relevant to financial management.

We started by providing a brief discussion of our legal system, including the court system required to put such law into effect. With the exception of Quebec, Canada's legal system is based on common law or case precedent. The British North America Act apportions authority to pass legislation between the provinces and the federal government. Accordingly, separate court systems exist at the provincial and federal levels.

The legal form of organization which a business selects has important implications which include the area of financial management. The main forms of business organization are the sole proprietorship, the partnership, and the corporation. Certainly in terms of dollar volume, the corporation has become the dominant form of organization in the western industrialized countries. It can be viewed as a prerequisite for being able to raise the significant sums of money from the general investing public which are required to finance large scale projects characterizing a developed economy. The salient features of the various forms of business organizations are as follows:

Sole proprietorship

easy to establish; little in terms of reporting requirements; all profits taxed at owner's personal tax rates;
proprietor faces unlimited liability, meaning creditors can lay claim against any of his personal assets;
lack of permanency;
the proprietor faces a lack of liquidity in that his business interests are not easy to dispose of.

Partnership

allows pooling of resources, both managerial and financial;
established under law ("declared partnership") or implied by business conduct ("implied partnership");
limited reporting requirements;
profits taxed at partners' personal tax rates;
partners face unlimited liability, not only for their own actions, but also for those of other partners, with the exception of special partners in a limited partnership;
lack of permanency and difficulties in disposing of business interests.

Corporation

separate legal entity;
limited liability with shareholders only liable for their equity investment;
permanency which transcends the life of individual shareholders;
shareholders have liquidity since shares are freely transferable and easily disposable;
extensive reporting requirements;

the corporation as a separate entity is taxed on its business income and further taxes may be levied if such income is distributed to shareholders in the form of dividends.

Incorporation in Canada is governed by legislation which differs by jurisdiction. Three basic approaches to incorporation exist and are called the letters patent system, the registration system, and the certificate of incorporation system.

The shareholders of a corporation are its legal owners. They elect directors to manage the firm on their behalf. Directors are required to exercise due care and skill in carrying out their functions and to act in the best interests of the firm. Apart from the election of directors, shareholders have the right to attend and vote at shareholders' meetings, to receive dividends if and when declared by the board of directors, and to be supplied with relevant information such as the firm's annual financial statements. In addition, minority shareholders enjoy certain protection from oppressive acts of a controlling majority.

One of the major strengths of the corporate form of business organization is its ability to raise funds in the capital markets. The two major categories of funds are debt (such as bonds and debentures) and equity (common shares). Issuance of debt involves contractual obligations by the firm to pay interest and to repay principal in accordance with the provisions of the particular debt issue. Failure to comply can result in legal action by creditors and potential bankruptcy. Equity owners, on the other hand, have no such legal rights. To protect the investing public, extensive disclosure of information regarding the firm and the securities to be issued has to precede any public offering of securities.

Two outgrowths of the corporate form of business organization are the voting trust and the holding company. A voting trust is generally set up to exercise periodic control over a corporation. A holding company is a corporation which owns substantial parts of other firms. It can be used for a variety of purposes such as extending control over other corporations, and is also found where firms engage in multinational operations. Given various corporations related through such shareholdings, the transfer prices charged for goods and services between subsidiaries can become contentious. Both in a regulatory setting and in a multinational environment, it affords the potential for a shifting of profits.

A corporation can terminate its existence either voluntarily, or by court order as, for example, in the case of bankruptcy. Bankruptcy legislation is intended to afford protection to both creditors and the debtor, and establishes orderly procedures to be followed where a firm faces insolvency.

Questions for discussion

1. What are the most popular forms of business organization? Why is the sole proprietorship more popular in retailing than in manufacturing?
2. What are the distinct characteristics which make the corporation different from the partnership or sole proprietorship?
3. What are the fiduciary duties of directors of a corporation? What are the purposes of these requirements?
4. What are some of the benefits a major shareholder can receive when he deposits his shares in a voting trust?
5. Define a holding company. What is its main purpose?
6. Why is the partnership the predominant form of business organization in such areas as law and accounting?

Additional problem

1. Using the Financial Post's *Survey of Industrials,* identify a major holding company, trace through the recent history of takeover bids made by the company and explain possible reasons behind each attempted move.

Selected references

L. Gower, *Principles of Modern Company Law*, (3rd ed.) London: Stevens and Sons, 1969.

J. Smyth and D. Soberman, *The Law and Business Administration in Canada*, (3rd ed.), Scarborough: Prentice-Hall of Canada, 1976.

M. Taylor *Partnership Law*, (10th ed.), London: MacDonald and Evans, 1966.

Chapter 3

After this book was typeset, another federal budget was introduced (March 31, 1977), proposing a set of changes which, if passed by Parliament, would affect a few of the numerical illustrations set out in **Chapter 3**.

The basic concept we have seen fit to illustrate will not be violated, however.

We urge readers to recognize that from 1978 on, the following key changes may become law:

- a more generous dividend tax credit
- a right to apply some realized capital gains against the $1,000 tax-free amount of interest or dividends received
- a right to treat stock dividends as capital gains.

Subsequent budgets should also be watched since continuing change must be expected as governments adapt to political and economic realities.

Chapter 3
The Tax Environment

3-1. INTRODUCTION

Selection of the appropriate form of business organization involves taxation considerations and this has already been alluded to. Corporate taxes also play a very significant role in a variety of other managerial decisions, financial ones in particular. To provide specific examples: corporate taxes affect the economic desirability of investments; returns realized by investors holding securities are influenced by taxes levied on interest or dividend income; and after-tax earnings reflect allowable expenses deducted in arriving at taxable income. The tax environment will also affect corporate financing, negotiations relating to the fusion or acquisition of separate businesses, and the evaluation of leasing. Generally, the results of financial decisions on an after-tax basis differ significantly from measures obtained without a full consideration of the particular tax environment involved. Thus, detailing of some of the more pertinent tax provisions will not only provide a grasp of the environment within which Canadian firms must operate, it will also clarify a major variable influencing financial decisions.

The areas of tax legislation and regulation which are particularly pertinent to financial decision-making include:

- the taxation of corporate income,
- the taxation of individual income including dividends and interest received,
- the taxation of capital gains, and
- expenses and other deductions allowed in determining taxable income.

Each area will be looked at in turn.

In Canada, both the federal and provincial governments levy taxes on individuals and corporations, with provincial tax rates varying from province to province. Both levies will have to be considered for it is the combined tax bill which is relevant in deriving the after-tax cash flows.

The subject of taxation is far too complex to be treated here in any great detail, but some general understanding of the tax structure is obviously required in order to undertake any studies in the area of financial management. What follows is a concise overview of the tax environment which has existed since January 1, 1972 as a result of the extensive amendments to the *Income Tax Act*. It is worth noting that while one of the major areas of amendment relates to the tax treatment of corporations and their shareholders, the tax changes were so far-reaching and have subsequently been altered so frequently that their total impact remains almost indeterminant at this stage.

3-2. TAXATION OF CORPORATE INCOME

Because the *Act* stipulates quite different treatments of public, private, and

Canadian-controlled private corporations, the basic distinctions between such categories need to be clarified. For purposes of this brief survey, a public corporation is one resident[1] in Canada with at least one class of its shares publicly traded in Canada. The Minister of National Revenue may himself, however, designate a company to be a public corporation. A private corporation is simply a corporation resident in Canada which is neither a public corporation nor controlled by one. Lastly, a Canadian-controlled private corporation is a private corporation which meets the following requirements:

(a) it was at one time a resident corporation and was either incorporated in Canada or resident here after June 18, 1971, and

(b) it is not controlled directly or indirectly by nonresident persons (corporate or natural) or by one or more public corporations or by any combination of nonresidents and public corporations.

The need for such distinctions will become clearer in subsequent sections. It essentially relates to a range of tax incentives which are available to various categories of Canadian-controlled corporations.

Rates

In most industrialized countries of the Western world, the tax rate on corporate income is close to 50 percent. This uniformity is explained, in part, by the international mobility of capital, which could be attracted to countries with lower tax rates if significant discrepancies appeared.[2]

In Canada, the combined federal and provincial tax levied on corporate income follows this pattern and may be taken as just under 50 percent. Many exceptions can be noted, however, and any generalization applied indiscriminantly can prove to be misleading. In practice we must not only recognize that provincial tax rates on corporate income, which are built into the total rate, do vary significantly, but that various abatements or deductions exist. These deductions are important with respect to small business income; income derived from manufacturing and processing operations in Canada; and income from the production of minerals, oil and gas. Since deductions seem to be varied in some way by almost every budget introduced by the Minister of Finance, no attempt is made here to provide much more than an overview.

The rate which the federal government has set as a basis for the computation of corporate tax in Canada is 46 percent.[3] The federal government then grants a reduction of 10 percentage points to accommodate taxes imposed by the provinces. Thus, the combined federal and provincial tax is computed as follows:

[1]By general rule of law, a corporation is resident in the country where its central management and control is located. Additionally, however, the *Act* provides that a company incorporated in Canada after April 26, 1965, is deemed to be resident in Canada as a simple consequence of such incorporation and regardless of any other factors. In the case of earlier incorporations, Canadian residence is established either through the general rule of law or by carrying on business here.

[2]Developing countries, for example, often design special tax incentives with a view to attracting foreign industry.

[3]The 46 percent figure is the consequence of predetermined rate reductions of one percentage point annually, starting from 50 percent in 1972 and ending in 1976. It does not reflect any surtax on corporate profits which may be introduced from time to time.

Total tax payable = general tax rate of 46% on taxable income

MINUS 10% of the corporation's taxable income earned in each province

PLUS provincial taxes, with various rates applied against taxable income earned in particular provinces.

Since provincial tax rates on corporate income vary, ranging upward from 10 percent, the actual tax rate paid is generally somewhat above 46 percent, and will depend on the particular province in which income is earned.

Example

Consider two corporations, one with all of its activities conducted in a maritime province where the provincial tax rate is assumed to be 10 percent, and another operating in a western province where the rate is taken as 12 percent. Assuming identical taxable incomes of $10,000,000, taxes to be paid and effective rates of taxation are computed as follows:

	Maritime Province	Western Province
Taxable Income	$10,000,000	$10,000,000
Tax (46%)	4,600,000	4,600,000
Deduction for Provincial Tax (10%)	1,000,000	1,000,000
Net Federal Tax	3,600,000	3,600,000
Provincial Tax	1,000,000	1,200,000
Total Corporate Tax	4,600,000	4,800,000
Total Tax as % of Taxable Income	46%	48%

The consequences of such rate differentials should not be overlooked, as they may affect decisions on where to locate a business, and decisions regarding transfer prices for goods and/or services of various operating units which are located in provinces with varying tax rates.

As an incentive to *smaller* Canadian-controlled private corporations, there is provision for a reduced rate of taxation as long as income doesn't exceed some specified limit. Specifically, the first $150,000 (as of 1976) of such firms' income from an active business in Canada may be eligible for small business deduction, with the general rate applicable only on any excess.[4] Thus, considering an operation in a western province with a 12 percent provincial tax rate qualifying for the small business reduction, the actual rate to be paid on the first $150,000 would be 27 percent determined as follows:

General Tax Rate (1)	Small Business Deduction (2)	Net Federal Tax (3)=(1)−(2)	Deduction for Provincial Tax (4)	Provincial Tax Rate (5)	Total Tax Rate (6)=(3)+(4)+(5)
46%	21%	25%	10%	12%	27%

[4]The actual amount of the reduction in taxes is constrained in a number of fairly complex ways. The limitation of the deduction to the lesser of four different amounts is not described since only the more basic concepts are being highlighted here.

It should be stressed that the resultant tax saving is neither available to a foreign-controlled corporation nor to a public one.

To confine the tax concession to smaller corporations, the deduction is available only so long as the company's taxable income accumulated over the years is under some specified limit, which in 1976 was set at $750,000. The accumulation, termed the *cumulative deduction account*, is very approximately determined by summing each year's taxable income from 1972 on and deducting 4 dollars for every 3 dollars of taxable dividends distributed to the shareholders.[5]

Example

A corporation with annual business income of $150,000 and paying no dividends would lose the benefits of the small business deduction after 5 years. However, by paying $21,000 a year in dividends, for example, deductions on a $4-for-each-$3 paid basis ($21,000 × 4/3 = $28,000) mean that after 5 years a further 5 × $28,000 = $140,000 of business income can be received before eligibility for the reduced tax rate is lost.

Tax legislation is one important way in which the government can provide incentives to industry, and varied provisions are frequently introduced to reflect particular economic situations and priorities. Without going into any of the intricate details here, and recognizing the frequency with which the legislation is changed, it should be mentioned that manufacturing and processing profits from an active business carried on in Canada currently qualify for tax deductions. Further the profits of resource industries, as a consequence of certain abatements, may also be subject to reduced tax rates.

3-3. TAXATION OF INDIVIDUAL INCOMES

Personal taxes are payable on individual income. Depending on the source of income, different income tax provisions may apply. There is, however, no statutory definition of income, and no general criterion by which "income" as such may be defined. Examples of the many items which individuals must generally treat as income for taxation purposes include wages, salaries, interest, dividends, rental income, and the net income of proprietorships and partnerships.

Various deductions from income are available to individual taxpayers in arriving at their taxable income. Personal exemptions, medical expenses and charitable donations are some examples. It is particularly significant that to cushion the effect of inflation, personal exemptions increase in line with earlier rises in the Consumer Price Index. To illustrate one consequence of such indexing, the personal exemption of single status taxpayers has risen from $1706 in 1974 to $1878 in 1975, reflecting an index factor for inflation of 10.08 percent ($1706 × (1 + 0.1008) = $1878).

[5]The gap between $750,000 termed the *total business limit* and the cumulative deduction account also has a bearing on the actual reduction in annual taxes. (See previous footnote.) The reduction in tax actually allowed is generally the *lesser* of 21 percent of business income or 21 percent of the difference between the total business limit and the cumulative deduction account of the preceding years.

For a variety of social and political reasons, the tax bite faced by individuals in Canada is *progressive* rather than proportional. In other words, successive increments to incomes are taxed at increasingly higher rates. Once again, however, to offset the impact of inflation, an indexing plan is provided which has the effect of raising each tax bracket over time in accordance with earlier price-level changes. If such indexing were not provided for, most individuals whose incomes increase with inflation would be pushed automatically into higher tax brackets and would face an increasing tax burden, even if their *real* incomes had remained unaltered.

Table 3-1 illustrates both the progressive nature of our income tax system with its sharply increasing rates on marginal income, and the relief provided through indexing across a two-year timespan. It shows, for example, that an individual with annual taxable income which remained constant at $45,786 would have paid federal taxes of $15,673 ($12,755 on the first $39,000, plus 43 percent on the remaining $6,786) in 1973, and $14,939, or $734 less, in 1975.

TABLE 3-1

Sample Federal Income Tax Rates 1973 and 1975

1973		1975	
Taxable Income	Tax	Taxable Income	Tax
in excess of		in excess of	
$7,000	$ 1,435 + 25% on next $ 2,000	$ 8,218	$ 1,649 + 25% on next $ 2,348
9,000	1,935 + 27% on next 2,000	10,566	2,236 + 27% on next 2,348
11,000	2,475 + 31% on next 3,000	12,914	2,870 + 31% on next 3,522
14,000	3,405 + 35% on next 10,000	16,436	3,962 + 35% on next 11,740
24.000	6,905 + 39% on next 15,000	28,176	8,071 + 39% on next 17,610
39,000	12,755 + 43% on next 21,000	45,786	14,939 + 43% on next 24,654
60,000	21,785 + 47% on remainder	70,440	25,540 + 47% on remainder

In addition to the federal tax, each province imposes its own levy on individual income earned within the province. In all cases except Quebec, the provincial tax rate is expressed as a percentage of the basic federal tax, with this percentage ranging between 26 percent and 42.5 percent. In the case of Quebec, tax rates of between zero and 28 percent are imposed on taxable income. Application of the two levels of tax rates to income are demonstrated in subsequent sections of this chapter.

Taxation of dividends received

Where some portion of after-tax corporate income is distributed to shareholders in the form of dividends, these distributions may once again be taxed in the hands of individual recipients. This clearly indicates double taxation of the same income; once at the corporate level, and then again when it is distributed and received by the individual investor in the form of dividends.

Some relief from double taxation is afforded by what is labelled the 20 percent federal *dividend tax credit*. This credit is based on the taxable or grossed-up dividends received from taxable Canadian corporations, and its workings and impact are best appreciated by reviewing a set of numerical illustrations.

Example

Consider an investor residing in a province where the *provincial* income tax rate respecting individuals is 30.5 percent of the basic federal tax. He faces a *marginal federal* rate of 39 percent and receives $1000 in dividends from shares of a widely held Canadian corporation, all of which is deemed fully taxable in his hands. In the absence of any relief through the dividend tax credit, the investor's receipt of $1000 would be reduced by:

(i) the federal tax of 39 percent of $1000 or $390.00 and

(ii) the provincial tax of 30.5 percent of $390, or $118.95, providing a net after-tax dividend of $491.05. Thus, his overall tax rate on such dividends would have been almost 51 percent.

Given a dividend tax credit, the investor computes his tax bill and net retention as follows:

Dividend		$1000.00
Add 33⅓% gross-up[6]		333.33
Taxable dividends		$1333.33
Federal tax before credit (39% of $1333.33)	$520.00	
Less 20% dividend tax credit on taxable dividends (20% of $1333.33)	266.67	
Federal tax		253.33
Provincial tax (30.5% of federal tax)		77.27
Combined tax		330.60
Before-tax dividends received		1000.00
Net amount retained		$ 669.40

Hence, through the tax credit device, the investor's taxes are reduced by $178.35 (from $508.95 without the tax credit to $330.60 with it) taking the effective net tax rate on the dividends to 33 percent.

The net effect of the dividend tax credit depends on the marginal federal tax rate applicable to an investor, and it tends to have most favorable results for those investors in the lower marginal tax brackets. In extreme cases, where the dividend tax credit exceeds the federal tax on the dividends, the excess may reduce the shareholder's tax payable on other income.

More recently, it has been provided that up to $1000 received from Canadian sources either as interest, or as "grossed-up" amounts of taxable dividends, or some combination of both, may essentially be exempted from taxation. The reasoning for the deduction offered by the Minister of Finance

[6]This "gross-up" relates to the requirement that an individual receiving a taxable dividend must take into his or her income 100 percent *plus* an additional 33⅓ percent of such dividends.

was set out in the 1974 Fall Budget. In conjunction with other measures, he was seeking to protect individual savings against the eroding effects of inflation, while both encouraging the purchase of Canadian shares and shoring-up the stock markets.

In most instances, dividends received by a public corporation from another Canadian corporation are exempt from tax altogether, and the dividend tax credit does not apply.

In terms of minimizing the impact of double taxation, the special 15 percent tax on "1971 undistributed income" is also worthy of consideration. The *Income Tax Act* allows a corporation resident in Canada to pay a 15 percent tax on its undistributed income (roughly its retained earnings) accumulated between the years 1950 to 1971 inclusive. The remaining 85 percent, a so-called "tax-paid undistributed surplus on hand" may then be distributed as a tax-free dividend to shareholders. The corporation has the option of paying the 15 percent tax on less than the full amount of its 1971 undistributed income. In addition, what has been defined as the *1971 capital surplus* may subsequently be available for tax-free distribution as well.[7] However, since this provision entails fairly complex definitions, it will not be pursued here. The reasoning behind these concessions has to do with removal of certain inequities introduced with the imposition of capital gains taxation after 1971.

It must be appreciated that where dividends are distributed on a tax-free basis, the recipient may not take advantage of the dividend tax credit. Furthermore, shareholders receiving the tax-free distribution, which may be viewed as a return of capital to the owners, must adjust the cost base of their shares accordingly, thereby altering ultimate capital gains or losses realized in the disposition of the shares as the case may be. Hence, what we have termed tax-free distributions in this section may strictly speaking be viewed as a deferral of taxes to the time at which the shares were disposed of.

Example

> To illustrate this adjustment of the cost base, consider the investor who purchased a share for $60 in 1972. Over the years, he has received $25 in the form of such tax-free distributions. He now sells his share for $100. In computing his capital gain, he has to reduce his original purchase price by the amount of tax-free dividends received. Thus, the cost of his share is assessed as $60 – $25 = $35, implying a capital gain on disposition of $100 – $35 = $65.

More detailed consideration of such distributions and subsequent adjustments to the cost base will be found in subsequent chapters dealing with preferred shares, common shares and dividend policy.

3-4. TAXATIONS OF CAPITAL GAINS

As of 1972, the taxation of capital gains became part of the Canadian tax system. A capital gain may arise when an asset is sold for a price which exceeds the

[7]Amounts approximated by the sum of capital gains and other tax-free amounts on hand or accrued as at the end of 1971 are identified as the *1971 capital surplus*. Once a corporation has paid the special tax on all its 1971 undistributed income, then without additional taxes, the 1971 capital surplus is generally available for tax-free distribution as well. Adjustment to the cost base of the shares is again required.

original purchase price. One-half of realized capital gains is now to be included in the taxpayer's income to be taxed at personal or at corporate rates, as the case may be.

Example

> An investor purchased 100 shares at $15 a share and subsequently sold the investment to net $20 a share. A realized capital gain of $5 a share, or $5 × 100 = $500 would be involved. One-half of this amount, or $250, must be added to the individual's taxable income in the year of disposal.

The fact that only one-half of capital gains are included in income provides some incentive to investors considering more risky ventures. Furthermore, given our experiences with inflation, it is useful to have a built-in cushion since in many cases it is the effect of price-level changes rather than real gains which are being taxed.

One-half of any capital losses can be applied against taxable capital gains. Corporations may not apply a capital loss against other income but can carry losses back one year and then forward until absorbed by taxable capital gains. Individuals, on the other hand, may apply up to $1,000 of deductible capital losses against ordinary income and, if the losses are not absorbed, they may be applied against the previous year's annual limit of $1,000 and then against the $1,000 limits of the requisite number of future years.

Example

> An individual has ordinary income of $20,000, capital gains of $1,000, and capital losses of $3,000. One-half of his capital loss ($1,500) is first applied against taxable capital gains ($500), with the remaining deductible capital loss ($1,000) applied against ordinary income. His total taxable income thus becomes $19,000.

The rationale for the capital gains tax in Canada may be summarized by the statement:

> Taxation at progressive rates of increments in economic power represents the fairest measure of ability to pay, and is the only means of achieving an equitable and neutral tax system. Gains realized on dispositions of property come within this concept naturally and logically. Such gains increase the taxpayer's economic power and thus enhance his ability to pay.[8]

3-5. EXPENSES AND DEDUCTIONS

Taxes are computed by applying tax rates to taxable income. In this section, we are concerned with factors influencing the calculation of taxable income, and in particular with some of the more important expenses and deductions which can be claimed against gross income, thereby reducing the firm's taxable income. Interest on debt instruments is considered to be a business expense, and hence, is generally deductible in arriving at taxable business income. Similarly, rent and lease payments are treated as deductible business expenses. On the other hand, dividends on both common and preferred shares must be paid out of after-tax

[8] Canada, *Report of the Royal Commission on Taxation*, Volume 3, Ottawa: Queen's Printer, 1966, p. 337.

earnings.

There are provisions in the Act under which ordinary business losses incurred in a particular year may be carried back and applied against income of the preceding year (through filing of an amended return) or carried forward and deducted from income of the next five years starting with the earliest possible year. Thus, a loss in 1973 may be deducted from the income of 1972, 1974, 1975, 1976, 1977, and 1978, in that order. As might be expected, there is set out a detailed definition of a loss.

Under the *Act*, taxpayers, including corporations, in arriving at taxable income may deduct capital cost allowances (CCA) up to particular limits, the idea being that all capitalized outlays on depreciable assets should eventually be deducted from income, in most cases not all at once. Put another way, provision is made for an investor to recover, over some time frame, the original amount he has invested without having to pay tax on that portion of his proceeds. In this context it should be borne in mind that the amount of capital cost allowances deducted from income for tax purposes in a particular year may be something very different from the depreciation a corporation shows on its own books of account. To reduce taxes, maximum capital cost allowances may be claimed while the depreciation deducted in computing income reported to shareholders may be based on accounting concepts of income measurement.[9] We note that in subsequent chapters of this book the distinction between the terms, "capital cost allowances" and "depreciation" will be dropped.

Ideally, the cost of an asset with an economic life of 20 years should be charged against income over that same span of time. In practice, however, not only is the useful life of most assets difficult to predict, but taxpayers and tax collectors are hardly likely to reach anything approaching a common prediction. Understandably, our tax regulations leave little room for debate. As a general rule, depreciable assets fall into one of over 30 classes with each class treated separately.[10] Capital cost allowances and asset values are not computed for individual assets but for the aggregate of all assets comprising an asset class. Maximum capital cost allowance rates, ranging from 1-100 percent are prescribed for each class and these rates generally are applied against declining asset balances in each class. Purchase prices of new assets are added to the total asset class value while sales up to an asset's original cost are deducted. If assets in an asset class are disposed of and the selling price exceeds the original cost, capital gains for individual assets are realized. More commonly, if the selling price is lower than the asset's original cost, the sale just reduces the aggregate asset value of the class, and as a consequence future capital cost allowances for the class are reduced accordingly.

Exceptions to this treatment of sales arise only if all assets in a class are sold and a balance still remains in the asset class; or if sales of assets and the consequent adjustment to the book value of the class result in a negative value for the asset class:

[9]With capital cost allowances the larger, a deferred tax liability will appear on the balance sheet.

[10]Some election of transfer of assets between classes is possible, but will not be pursued here.

In fairly general terms, the legislation states that:

(i) if all assets in a class are sold and a positive balance remains in the class, or in other words, if on disposal of such assets the amount realized is less than the undepreciated capital cost of the particular class, the difference may be viewed as a terminal loss and deducted from income; and

(ii) if the sale of any part or all of the assets would render the balance remaining in the class negative, that is, if proceeds on a disposition exceed the undepreciated capital cost in the class, the excess to the extent of capital cost already taken is treated as income. Any part of the sale price not absorbed by past and undepreciated capital costs is held to be a capital gain.

Examples of such possibilities are presented as a problem with solution at the end of this chapter.

Selected examples of assets, the classes to which they are normally assigned, and the maximum annual capital cost allowance rates prescribed are set out below:

Asset	Class	Maximum Rate
Chinaware, cutlery and tableware	12	100%
Mining equipment	10	30%
General machinery	8	20%
Frame buildings	6	10%
Brick buildings	3	5%
Catalysts	26	1%

Application of the specified maximum rate against declining balances can be illustrated by considering general machinery included in class 8. Where $100,000 of assets belonging to this class are held, the maximum capital cost allowance to be claimed in each of the next several years is the undepreciated capital costs multiplied by the specified rate of 20 percent. This is reflected in Table 3-2.

The actual allowances claimed (column 4 above) give rise to a *tax shield* or reduction in taxes in the sense that tax deductible expenses of $20,000, $16,000, and $12,800 are available in each of the next 3 years respectively. Taking a corporate tax rate of $t = 46\%$, actual taxes to be paid would be reduced by $9,200, $7,360, and $5,888 in the respective periods, or generally by $Cdt(1-d)^{n-1}$ in year n. Thus, capital cost allowances give rise to a reduction in cash outflows for taxes.

This tax shield over the next several years may be expressed in notation as: sum of tax shield for n years $= Cdt + Cdt(1-d) + Cdt(1-d)^2 + \ldots + Cdt(1-d)^{n-1}$ which can be simplified and rewritten[11] as $Ct[1-(1-d)^n]$. Taking our earlier example, the total tax shield for the first 3 years ($9200 + $7,360 + $5,888 = $22,448) could also have been computed using $Ct[1-(1-d)^n] = 100{,}000 \times 0.46\,(1-0.8^3) = \$22{,}448$.

We must keep in mind that when an asset is sold, the value of the asset class is

[11]This is easily derived by using the well known formula for geometric series which specifies $1 + x + x^2 + \ldots + x^{n-1} = (1-x^n)/(1-x)$. Setting $x = (1-d)$, the above result is obtained.

reduced by the price realized. Thus, reductions in the subsequently available capital cost allowances and tax shields will occur. Clearly then, the tax shield implications extend both to the acquisition and the disposition of depreciable assets.

TABLE 3-2

Illustration of Maximum Capital Cost Allowances

Taxation Year (1)	Undepreciated Capital at Start of Taxation Year (2)	Maximum Rate (20%) (3)	Maximum Capital Cost Allowance (4) = (2) × (3)	Undepreciated Capital at End of Taxation Year (5) = (2) −(4)
1	$100,000	20	$20,000	$80,000
2	80,000	20	16,000	64,000
3	64,000	20	12,800	51,200

With starting asset values taken as C and the maximum rate for capital cost allowances set at d, each year's maximum claim may be written in notation as follows:

Taxation Year (1)	Undepreciated Capital at Start of Taxation Year (2)	Maximum Rate (3)	Maximum Capital Cost Allowance (4) = (2) × (3)	Undepreciated Capital at End of Taxation Year (5) = (2) − (4)
1	C	d	Cd	$C-Cd = C(1-d)$
2	$C(1-d)$	d	$C(1-d)d$	$C(1-d)^2$
3	$Cd(1-d)^2$	d	$C(1-d)^2d$	$C(1-d)^3$
⋮				
n	$C(1-d)^{n-1}$	d	$C(1-d)^{n-1}d$	$C(1-d)^n$

Though the significance of tax shields created in applying capital cost allowances is taken up more fully in the chapters to follow, it is useful to recognize that accelerated depreciation, which increases the size of earlier tax shields, is an important element of government policy designed to stimulate the economy.[12] Such periodic tax incentives which permit a faster write-off of assets are frequently set out in federal budgets.[13]

The effects of providing for accelerated capital cost allowances are readily illustrated. Assume a 50 percent corporate tax rate, a piece of general equipment just acquired for $100,000, and tax incentives providing for the equivalent of two-year straight-line depreciation on new machinery. Differences in the tax shields appear as follows:

[12]Establishing the totals and mix of government receipts and disbursements is termed fiscal policy. As explained in introductory economics, both monetary and fiscal policy play vital roles in regulating economic activity.

[13]It has, for example, been provided that machinery and equipment purchased for use by a Canadian manufacturing or processing business may be depreciated up to 50 percent in the year of acquisition and completely written off in the second year.

	Class 8 Rate of 20%		Accelerated Depreciation	
Year	Capital Cost Allowance	Tax Shield	Capital Cost Allowance	Tax Shield
1	$20,000	$10,000	$50,000	$25,000
2	16,000	8,000	50,000	25,000
3	12,800	6,400	0	0
4	10,240	5,120	0	0

It should be noted that under existing approaches to accounting, which are based on historical costs, taxable income may be significantly overstated in periods of high inflation. An unfair tax bill is one immediate consequence. The difficulty can frequently be traced to inadequate allowances for depreciation since original costs of items pooled in the various asset classes in no way reflect replacement costs. For example, a capital cost allowance of $10,000 may be taken in the current year on an asset which was acquired 5 years ago for $100,000. This amounts to 10 percent of the original purchase price. Because of inflation, the current replacement costs of that asset may have increased to $200,000. Thus, $10,000 or 10 percent of the original purchase price would prove inadequate if 10 percent of the asset actually needed replacing. In such circumstances, the firm would be forced to draw on its earnings to maintain its asset base. The problem is most acute in capital intensive industries, where, in periods of rising price-levels, tax as well as dividend payments are based on overstated earnings, which could lead to a gradual liquidation of the business.

3-6. GENERAL

The business income of a proprietorship and each partner's share of partnership

TABLE 3-3

Tax Revenues by Level of Government in Selected Years (millions of dollars)

	1967	1970	1974
Direct Taxes — Persons	7,011	11,406	20,739
Federal	4,291	7,398	13,368
Provincial	1,871	3,003	5,762
Pension Plans	849	1,005	1,609
Direct Taxes — Corporations*	2,397	2,854	6,464
Federal	1,786	2,142	4,699
Provincial	611	712	1,765
Indirect Taxes**	9,442	11,975	20,292
Federal	3,705	4,033	8,495
Provincial	2,982	4,150	7,095
Local	2,755	3,792	4,702
Withholding Taxes on Nonresidents:			
Federal	218	267	433

*Excludes refundable tax on corporate profits

**Indirect taxes include excise and other taxes, such as federal sales tax, tariffs, and the likes.

Source: Statistics Canada, *National Income and Expenditure Accounts:* Various Issues

income is treated as personal income. Such income is subject to taxation at the proprietor's or partners' individual rates regardless of whether it is drawn out or retained for use in the business. Clearly, at some levels of income a business might achieve immediate tax savings through incorporation, but each individual situation should be studied carefully as tax considerations are but one factor in the selection of an appropriate organizational form.

Table 3-3 provides some appreciation of the relative importance of the several forms of taxes levied by governments. It is evident from the data that direct corporate taxes do not provide nearly as significant a portion of total revenues as the political attention it receives would suggest, but that their relative contribution may be increasing.

3-7. SUMMARY

This chapter provides some basic appreciation of the Canadian tax environment. A number of the tax provisions most relevant to financial decision-making were reviewed including the tax rates on corporate income, the taxation of dividends, and the treatment of expenses which are applicable in deriving taxable income, including capital cost allowance.

Corporate income taxes in Canada, composed of both a federal and a provincial tax, amount to about 50 percent of taxable income. A variety of special deductions are available, for example to smaller Canadian-controlled private corporations and to firms engaged in manufacturing and processing. Individual income tax rates are progressive and also represent a combination of federal and provincial taxes. Dividends, which are paid out of after-tax corporate earnings, are generally taxed again as income in the hands of the recipient. A dividend tax credit provides at least partial relief from double taxation. The taxation of capital gains, at both corporate and individual levels, was introduced in Canada in 1972. One-half of any gains realized from the sale of assets is to be included into taxable income in the year of disposition, with provisions for similar inclusion of capital losses.

In arriving at taxable income, various expenses and deductions are permitted, the more important ones being the deduction of interest on most debt as an expense and capital cost allowance on depreciable assets. In Canada, assets are grouped into asset classes, with capital cost allowance computed on the aggregate values in each class. The capital cost allowance is taken mostly on a declining balance basis, with applicable rates specified for each asset class. Capital cost allowances serve to reduce taxable income and, hence, provide an important tax shield or saving in tax payments.

Attention was also focused on more recent legislative innovations designed to cope with inflationary distortions. One important illustration used was indexing tied to personal exemptions and tax brackets. In this same context, unresolved issues were also identified including understated capital cost allowances and overstated capital gains.

Quite significant differences in provincial tax rates applicable to corporate income were identified and the implications for location and transfer-pricing decisions by business noted.

Questions for discussion

1. Why do you think the corporate income tax rate is quite similar in most industrial countries while the personal rate tends to vary significantly?
2. The owner of a sole proprietorship is considering incorporation. From a tax point of view what are the main considerations? Discuss.
3. Discuss some of the potential inequities and distortions which may be introduced into a tax system through inflation. How might legislation relating to corporate and individual taxation be amended to take account of inflation?
4. Provide a rationale for including just one-half of realized capital gains in a taxpayer's income.
5. How, if at all, would a rise in the provincial rate on an individual's taxable income alter the dividend yield required? Assume the investor wants as much current income as would be provided by a 10 percent bond.

Problems with solutions

1. The income tax rate imposed by a province on corporate taxable income was 13 percent in 1976. What is the total corporate tax bill of a public corporation which had taxable income of $17,000,000?

Solution

Taxable Income	$17,000,000
Federal Tax (46% × $17,000,000)	7,820,000
Minus Deduction for Provincial Tax (10% × $17,000,000)	1,700,000
Net Federal Tax	6,120,000
Plus Provincial Tax (13% × $17,000,000)	2,210,000
Total Corporate Tax	$ 8,330,000

2. (a) An individual faces a federal tax rate of 47 percent at the margin, and a provincial tax of 30.5 percent of basic federal tax. On an investment of $50,000, he receives $3,300 of dividends, all of which is eligible for the dividend tax credit. Considering after-tax returns only, would he be better off to invest in a debt instrument paying 9¼ percent interest? Ignore the $1,000 deduction on investment income which is assumed to have been exhausted already.
   (b) What if his provincial rate were 42.5 percent?

Solution

(a)

		Interest Alternative
Interest		$4,625
Federal tax (47% × $4,625)	$2,174	
Provincial tax (30.5% × $2,174)	$ 663	
Total tax		$2,837
Amount retained		$1,788

		Dividend Alternative
Dividend		$3,300
Gross-up		$1,100
Taxable dividend		$4,400
Federal tax before credit (47% × $4,400)	$2,068	
Less tax credit (20% × $4,400)	$ 880	
Federal tax		$1,188
Provincial tax (30.5% × $1,188)		$ 362
Combined tax		$1,550
Amount retained		$1,750

Based on the above figures, the investor would better off with the debt instrument.

(b)

	Interest Alternative
Provincial tax (42.5% × $2,174)	$ 924
Total tax	$3,098
Amount retained	$1,527

	Dividend Alternative
Provincial tax (42.5% × $1,188)	$ 505
Combined tax	$1,693
Amount retained	$1,607

Hence, the answer is reversed and the dividend income becomes preferable.

3. Consider an individual who is subject to the 1975 tax rates as set out in Table 3-1, with the provincial tax rate being 42.5 percent of the federal tax. Assume the individual to be the majority shareholder of a firm which allows him to determine the firm's dividend policy. Dividends amounting to $100,000 are contemplated for the current year. Given "1971 undistributed income" on hand, how should this dividend be paid to minimize the particular shareholder's tax payable? Assume that the shareholder intends to hold the shares indefinitely, so that potential capital gains taxes on disposition of the shares can be ignored. Also assume that this dividend income is the only income the investor receives.

Solution

The corporation, by paying $15,000 in taxes on $100,000 of 1971 undistributed income, would then have $85,000 of tax-paid undistributed surplus on hand, available for distribution as a tax-free dividend.

If, \$100,000 are simply paid out as regular dividends, we compute taxes as follows:

Dividend			\$100,000
Gross-up			\$ 33,333
Taxable dividends			\$133,333
Less: \$1,000 exemption			\$ 1,000
Net taxable dividends			\$132,333
Federal tax before credit:	on first \$70,440	\$25,540	
	plus 47% of \$61,893	\$29,090	
		\$54,630	
Less tax credit* (20% of \$133,333)		\$26,667	
Federal tax			\$ 27,963
Provincial tax (42.5% × \$27,963)			\$ 11,884
Combined tax			\$ 39,847
Amount retained			\$ 60,153

*At the time the solutions are being prepared, the 20 percent dividend tax credit is computed based on taxable dividends *before* the \$1,000 exemption.

Thus, the former approach should be selected. Note that under this approach the shareholders would have to reduce the cost base for the shares. This may have tax consequences if disposition of the shares is contemplated.

4. A firm is faced with a total corporate tax rate of 48 percent. It acquires certain equipment (class 10, maximum rate 30 percent) for \$1,000,000.
   (a) If the equipment was only to be paid for when the first year's tax shield became available, what would the net cash outflow be for that year?
   (b) What tax shield would be available in the fourth year?

Solution

(a) Net cash outflow = purchase price − tax shield from CCA in first year
$= 1{,}000{,}000 - Cdt$
$= 1{,}000{,}000 - (1{,}000{,}000)(.30)(.48)$
$= 1{,}000{,}000 - 144{,}000$
$= \$856{,}000$

(b) Tax shield in year 4 $= Cdt(1-d)^3$
$= 144{,}000(0.70)^3$
$= 144{,}000(0.3430) = \$49{,}392$

5. For the situation described in problem 4 above, assume the Minister of Finance, in his budget speech, had just introduced tax incentives including an accelerated depreciation provision. Specifically, the equipment may now be written off over two years on a straight-line basis. What is the incremental tax shield from such legislation over the first two years?

Solution

Year 1 New tax shield – previous tax shield = 500,000 × 0.48 – Cdt = 240,000 – 144,000 = 96,000

Year 2 500,000(.48) – $Cdt(1-d)$ = 240,000 – 100,800 = 139,200

Total Incremental Tax Shield = \$96,000 + \$139,200 = \$235,200

6. Given: C = \$100,000
   d = 20%
   t = 40%

   Find: a) Capital cost allowance in year 5:
   b) Tax shield in year 5:
   c) Sum of capital cost allowances years 1-5:
   d) Book value at end of year 5:

Solution

(a) \$100,000 × 0.2 $(0.8)^4$ = \$8,192

(b) \$8,192 × 0.4 = \$3,277

(c) \$100,000 $[1 - (0.8)^5]$ = \$67,232

(d) BV_5 = original book value – sum of capital cost allowances years 1-5
= \$100,000 – \$67,232
= \$32,768

7. John Babashoff is looking to dispose of either his tractor (placed in class 10 which provides for a 30 percent capital cost allowance rate) or a spreader (class 8 and a 20 percent capital cost allowance rate). He now has a total of \$330,000 of undepreciated capital cost in class 8, while the tractor is the only class 10 asset he has ever owned. He can obtain \$30,000 by selling either the spreader or the tractor. Both were purchased 30 months ago for \$29,000 and \$21,00 respectively, and maximum capital cost allowances have been claimed for two years. Babashoff's tax rate at the margin is 52 percent.
   (a) How much total tax might he have to pay on each of the possible dispositions?
   (b) What would the situation be if the assets only realized \$10,000 in a sale?

Solution

(a) Sale of the spreader will see class 8 assets reduced from \$330,000 to \$301,000. Since the sale realized \$1,000 more than the original purchase price, 52 percent tax or \$260 will have to be paid on taxable capital gains of ½(30,000 – \$29,000). The other tax effect will result from lower CCA to be claimed in subsequent years.

Sale of the tractor, however, does create an immediate tax liability totalling \$7,909.20. Specifically, if the tractor is sold, we have:

original purchase price		\$21,000
CCA in year 1 (\$21,000 × 30%)	\$6,300	
CCA in year 2	\$4,410	
total CCA years 1 and 2		\$10,710
undepreciated capital cost in the asset class at time of sale		\$10,290

The selling price of $30,000 exceeds the original purchase price, and when the original price is subtracted from the undepreciated capital cost of the asset class, a negative balance is left. To compute the tax liability arising from the sale, the selling price of $30,000 is thought of being composed of the following amounts:

undepreciated capital cost	$10,290
capital cost allowance taken in past periods ($21,000 – $10,290)	$10,710
capital gain ($30,000 – $21,000)	$ 9,000
	$30,000

The tax liability is then computed as follows:

recapture of capital cost allowance taken in past, taxed as ordinary income (0.52 × $10,710)	$5,569.20
capital gains of $9,000, with half of such gains taxed (0.5 × $9,000 × 0.52)	$2,340.00
total tax liability arising from sale	$7,909.20

(b) Sale of the spreader for $10,000 will see class 8 assets reduced to $320,000, without other tax effects.

Sale of the tractor leaves asset class 10 without assets, but with a remaining book value of $10,290 – $10,000 = $290. This $290 is considered a terminal loss, as the proceeds from the sale are less than the undepreciated capital cost. Taking this loss into income will save Babashoff 0.52 × $290 or $150.80 in taxes.

Additional problems

1. A shareholder's total investment income consists of $1,900 in annual dividends from Calgary Power. Assuming his marginal federal tax rate to be 40 percent and the provincial rate to be 26 percent, calculate his dividend net of taxes.
2. At the end of 1972, a taxpayer has a $1,000 capital gain, a $2,000 capital loss and income of $60,000 from all other sources. Assuming the average tax rate of the taxpayer to total 40 percent, compute his total tax payable and his total income (including capital gains and losses) after tax.
3. M.T. Corporation has a business loss of $1,200,000 during 1973. Assuming the company has a taxable income of $1,000,000 in 1972, and paid taxes at 50 percent,
   (a) respecting 1972, calculate the refundable tax if any.
   (b) How is any remaining loss to be absorbed?
4. General machinery worth $80,000 is purchased by a firm with a 27 percent tax rate. Capital cost allowance is taken on a declining balance at a rate of 20 percent. Compute the total *tax shield* over the first 4 years.
5. A partnership is comprised of two partners, *A* and *B*, who have marginal tax rates of 45 and 50 percent respectively. The income received from the partnership will be distributed equally to each partner. At the end of 1976, the

partnership has income before taxes of $100,000. *A* withdraws $30,000 from the partnership for his own use while *B* leaves the whole $50,000 for use within the partnership.

(a) What is the amount of tax payable by *A*?

(b) What is payable by *B*?

6. John Smith, age 45, owns and operates a pizza parlor which is now a sole proprietorship. The net income from operations last year was $50,000 before taxes. In the past, Smith has been taking a salary of $30,000 per year and leaving $20,000 in the business so as to accumulate sufficient funds for a proposed expansion in the next year or so. Smith is married and has two children, aged 12 and 18 attending school. His wife maintains the household and has no income of her own.

Calculate Smith's present tax liability and advise him whether or not he should incorporate. If he were to do so, he would draw a salary of $24,000 and pay himself $6,000 in dividends to maintain his previous income.

Assume: (a) No fees for incorporation;

(b) Taxes are calculated by applying actual 1975 rates (see Table 3-1);

(c) Provincial *Individual* Tax Rate of 30.5%;

(d) Smith's business is not a Manufacturing and/or Processing operation;

(e) Exemptions of the following items:

i) Basic	$1878
ii) Married	1644
iii) Child under 16	352
iv) Child over 16	646
v) Standard Medical/Charitable	100

Required: Calculate, in addition to Smith's present tax liability, his *total* tax liability including *both* personal and corporate income taxes if he were to incorporate. Determine any amounts saved/spent over and above his present tax payments.

Selected references

Canada, National Revenue, *Taxation, Corporate Tax Guide, Tax Reform and You*, Ottawa: 1972.

Canada, *Report of the Royal Commission on Taxation, Volumes 1-6*, Ottawa: Queen's Printer, 1966.

Canadian Tax Foundation, *Corporate Management Tax Conference 1974*, Toronto: Canadian Tax Foundation, 1974.

D. Smith, *Effects of Taxation: Corporate Financial Policy*, Boston: Harvard Graduate School of Business Administration, 1952.

PART 2

Long-Term Investment Decisions

Chapter 4
Compounding, Discounting, and Bond Yields

4-1. INTRODUCTION

Financial decisions will, in almost all cases, involve consideration of cash flows across different time periods. With the existence of interest, money has a time value, and like amounts received in different periods are not equivalent.[1] Even in a world of certainty, for example, an investor whose objective is to maximize his ultimate wealth, would not be indifferent to choosing between the alternatives of receiving $100 now or $100 a year hence. On the $100 received now, interest or some other return can be earned over the year, leaving the investor in a better financial position at year-end than would be the case under the second alternative. Hence, a dollar received today is generally worth more than a dollar received sometime in the future. Similarly, most investors prefer to defer costs so as to earn interest on their funds in the interim. Economically speaking, money has an opportunity cost which is determined by the opportunities which exist for its investment and the returns which these opportunities promise. Thus, in striving to maximize shareholders' wealth, financial analysis must recognize the time value of money. Consequently, the fundamentals of compounding and discounting are of critical importance.

This chapter deals mainly with the mathematical foundations and the mechanics of compounding and discounting. The economic rationale behind the time value of money, its usage, and its relationship to the maximization of shareholder wealth, will be taken up in subsequent chapters, in particular in Chapter 5.

4-2. INTEREST AND COMPOUNDING

Interest may be termed the price paid for the use of borrowed money. When interest is paid on the sum originally borrowed but not on any subsequently accrued interest, one is involved with *simple interest*. The rate of interest is usually expressed as a percentage per year. A common application of simple interest is to be found in bond issues. If interest coupons are not clipped, there is no compensation to the investor.[2]

[1] For an expansion of the concept of "time value of money", see H. Bierman and S. Smidt, *The Capital Budgeting Decision*, (3rd ed.) New York: Macmillan, 1971, Ch. 4.

[2] A bond is a document acknowledging corporate debt and entitling the bearer or the registered owner (depending on the particular form of the bond) to receive interest as specified. Some bonds have coupons attached to them, each coupon with a due date indicated. Coupons are "clipped" and exchanged for the periodic interest payments.

For subsequent use in formulations, the following variables, most of which are discussed in more detail further on, are defined:

P = the principal amount
i = the stated or nominal annual interest rate
r = the effective annual interest rate or yield
n = the number of years
I = the dollar amount of interest earned over the total period
V = the ending value or principal plus interest earned
F = the amount of a future receipt
PV = the present value of future cash flows
A = the amount on an annuity, where the amount A is invested or paid every year for a given number of years
AR = the annual repayment required on a loan

In the case of simple interest, annual interest payments are given as iP. If interest is paid over n periods, we have $I = niP$ and

$$V = P + I = P + niP$$

(1)
$$= P(1 + ni)$$

Example

A firm borrows $1,000 at 8 percent simple interest, with all payments due at the end of 3 years. What amount must be repaid?

$$\begin{aligned} V &= P(1 + ni) \\ &= 1{,}000[1 + (.08)(3)] \\ &= 1{,}000(1.24) \\ &= 1{,}240 \end{aligned}$$

Thus, $1,240 must be paid.

Where interest earned during a particular period is added to principal and in subsequent periods earns interest itself, one is involved with *compound interest*. A common application of compound interest is to be found in the proffered return on personal savings accounts of chartered banks. The appropriate formulation for this case is derived as follows. At the end of the first year, interest on principal will be iP, and the value of principal plus interest becomes

$$V_1 = P + iP = P(1 + i)$$

During the second year, interest is paid on this amount (principal plus interest earned in the first year) and the ending value after two years becomes

$$V_2 = V_1(1 + i) = [P(1 + i)]\,(1 + i) = P(1 + i)^2.$$

Similarly, we obtain

$$V_3 = V_2\,(1 + i) = P(1 + i)^3$$

and, generally, for the ending value after n years

(2)
$$V_n = P(1 + i)^n$$

Example

A person invests \$1,000 at 8 percent interest compounded annually. How does this amount grow over time, and what is the total amount received at the end of 4 years?

Year	Amount at beginning of year		Amount at end of year		
1	1000 =	P	1000(1 + 0.08) = 1080	=	$P(1+i)^1$
2	1080 =	$P(1+i)$	1080(1 + 0.08) = 1166	=	$P(1+i)^2$
3	1166 =	$P(1+i)^2$	1166(1 + 0.08) = 1259	=	$P(1+i)^3$
4	1259 =	$P(1+i)^3$	1259(1 + 0.08) = 1360	=	$P(1+i)^4$

The total amount due at the end of the fourth year is $P(1 + i)^4 = 1000(1 + 0.08)^4 = 1360$. Note that Table 1, reproduced in Appendix B, gives the values for the compound interest factor $(1+i)^n$. Thus, for $n = 4$ and $i = 8\%$, we find this factor to be 1.360, obviating the need for computation.

Compounding often takes place more frequently than once a year, for example, quarterly. In such cases, the stated annual interest rate must be divided by the frequency of compounding, called k, to obtain the rate per period, while n must be multiplied by this frequency. The compound interest formula becomes

(3) $$V_n = P(1 + \frac{i}{k})^{nk}$$

Note that formula (3) is equivalent to formula (2), with i/k now being the interest rate *per compound period*, and the exponent nk being the *number of compound periods.*

Example

A firm borrows \$1,000 at 8 percent interest, compounded quarterly, with all payment due at the end of 3 years. What amount must be repaid?

$$\begin{aligned} V_3 &= P(1 + \frac{i}{k})^{nk} \\ &= 1{,}000(1 + \frac{.08}{4})^{3 \times 4} \\ &= 1{,}000(1 + .02)^{12} \\ &\simeq 1{,}000(1.2682) \\ &= 1{,}268.20 \end{aligned}$$

Thus, \$1,268.20 must be paid. Note that 8 percent annual interest compounded 4 times per year over 3 years is identical to 8/4 = 2 percent interest per quarter, compounded over 3 × 4 = 12 quarters. This is reflected in $V_3 = 1000(1 + 0.02)^{12}$ above.

Where a stated annual interest rate may be compounded more than once per year, it becomes necessary to distinguish between the stated annual rate of interest, that is, the *nominal* rate, and the *effective* rate. The effective rate of interest may be defined as:

> That rate which, when compounded once a year, gives the same amount of interest as a nominal rate compounded k times per year.[3]

Example

If a bank states that on its savings accounts it will pay 8 percent interest per year (the nominal rate as stated), compounded quarterly, a $1 deposit would grow to $1(1 + \frac{0.08}{4})^4 = 1.0824$ within one year, implying an effective yield to the investor of 8.24%. Note from equation (3) that $V_n = P(1 + i/k)^{nk}$. If r is defined as the effective annual rate, then $V_n = P(1 + r)^n$. Hence

$$(1 + r) = (1 + \frac{i}{k})^k \quad (4)$$

and

$$P(1 + r)^n = P(1 + \frac{i}{k})^{nk}$$

Example

A bank offers an annual interest rate of 12 percent, compounded monthly, on its savings accounts. What is the effective rate being paid?

$$\begin{aligned}(1 + r) &= (1 + \frac{i}{k})^k \\ &= (1 + \frac{0.12}{12})^{12} \\ &= (1 + 0.01)^{12}\end{aligned}$$

From Table 1 we find $(1 + 0.01)^{12} = 1.127$ implying that $r = 12.7\%$.

It should be recognized that, as the interest is compounded more frequently per year, the effective rate of interest is increased. To illustrate, Figure 4-1 shows r as a function of k for $i = 10\%$.

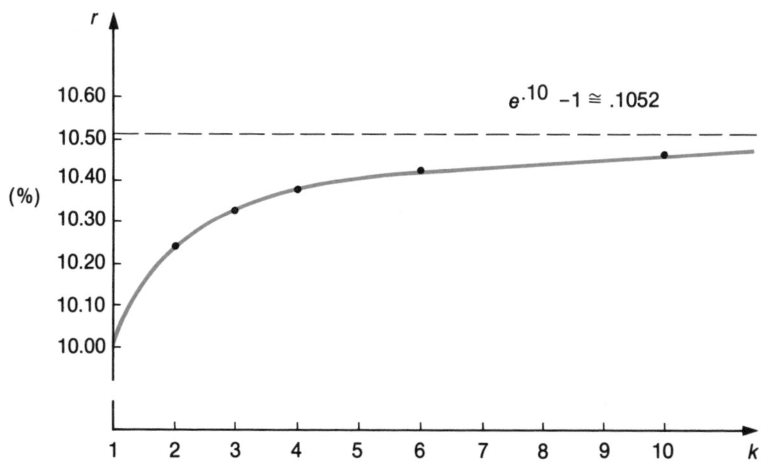

[3] J. Howell and D. Teichroew, *Mathematical Analysis for Business Decisions*, Homewood, Ill.: Irwin, 1963.

When interest is *compounded continuously*, that is when k increases indefinitely, equation (3) becomes

(5) $$V = \lim_{k \to \infty} P\left(1 + \frac{i}{k}\right)^{kn}$$

By drawing on basic mathematics, it is possible to show that

(6) $$\lim_{k \to \infty} \left(1 + \frac{i}{k}\right)^{k} = e^{i}$$

where $e \simeq 2.718$ is the base of natural or Napierian logarithms. Equation (5) can now be rewritten as

(7) $$V = Pe^{in}$$

A graph of the function e^x is given in Figure 4-2.

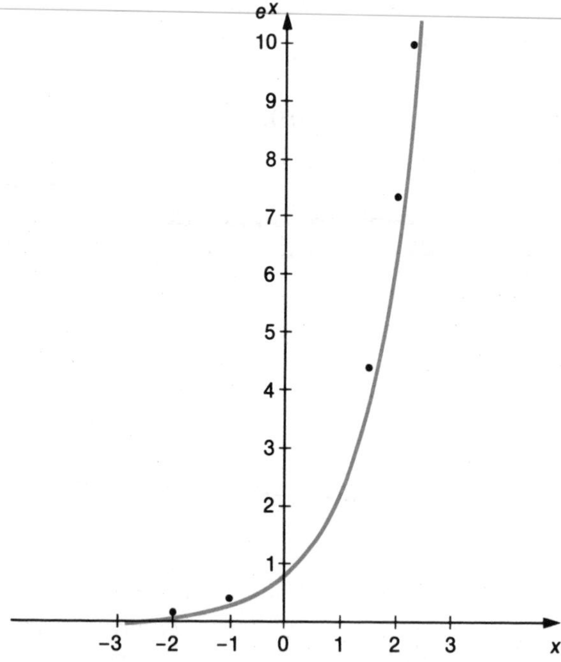

Example

A firm borrows $1,000 at 8 percent interest compounded continuously, with all payments due at the end of 3 years. What amount must be paid?

$$
\begin{aligned}
V &= Pe^{in} \\
&= 1{,}000e^{(.08)(3)} \\
&\simeq 1{,}000 \times 2.718^{.24} \\
&\simeq 1{,}000(1.271249) \\
&= 1{,}271.25
\end{aligned}
$$

Thus, \$1,271.25 must be paid.[4]

Continuous compounding assumes that interest is calculated and added to the principal at every instant in time. Although continuous compounding is unlikely to be used in loan transactions, the use of continuous functions is of great importance in the development of financial theory and financial models. As can be seen from the previous examples at normal rates of interest, results obtained through continuous compounding do not differ significantly from results obtained by monthly or even quarterly compounding. Use of continuous functions, however, allows application of calculus, thereby often facilitating analysis which otherwise would be difficult to carry out. For our purposes, however, the mathematics of continuous compounding is of limited significance.

For an additional understanding of the long-run effects of compounding, Table 4-1 illustrates the amount to which \$1 deposited at a compound interest rate of 3 percent per year would grow after selected numbers of years.

TABLE 4-1

Growth of \$1 compounded at 3 percent per annum

\$1 deposited at 3 percent compound interest grows		
in 10 years	to \$	1.34
in 100 years	to \$	19.22
in 250 years	to \$	1,620.—
in 500 years	to \$	2,621,877.—
in 1000 years	to \$	6,870,000,000,000.—
in 2000 years	to \$	4.7×10^{25}

The above numbers, which are also reflected in Figure 4-2, illustrate that in spite of an initial growth which appears modest, continuous compounding at even low rates, if applied over a longer period of time, will lead to explosive growth exceeding all bounds (note that the figure to which \$1 compounded at the modest rate of 3 percent grows over 1000 years exceeds the current gross national product of all of North America). While over the last few decades, due to rapid technological improvements, we have become accustomed to rates of compound growth of several percentage points per year, the basic mathematical properties of compound growth raise serious doubts as to the longer

[4]Where no calculator or table is available, computations such as the above are carried out by resorting to logarithms. Taking the natural logarithm of both sides of the equation, one obtains $ln(V/P) = in$. Thus, V/P simply becomes the antilog of *in*.

term viability of such a system, as reflected in current concerns over population growth, growth in demand for natural resources, and interest and inflation rates.

4-3. PRESENT VALUES AND DISCOUNTING

The preceding material has been concerned with determining value at some period in the future. In financial management, it is often necessary to calculate the current equivalent of a sum to be received at some future point of time. This current value is known as the discounted or *present value* and denoted by *PV*.

The formula for the present value of an amount, F, due in n years, given i as the time value of money, is given by

$$PV = \frac{F}{(1+i)^n} = F(1+i)^{-n} \tag{8}$$

By comparing equations (8) and (2), it is apparent that present value is simply the reciprocal of compounding.

Example

In the previous example on compound interest, we saw that an amount of \$1000 invested at 8 percent interest per year would grow at the end of 4 years to $P(1+i)^n = \$1360$. If an investor wants to maximize his wealth at the end of the 4 years, and if he can invest monies at 8 percent, we conclude that he would be indifferent between receiving \$1000 now or \$1360 4 years hence, as \$1000 received now would just grow to \$1360 in 4 years. While \$1360 is called the future value at the end of 4 years of \$1000, \$1000 is called the present value of \$1360, indicating an indifference between \$1000 at present and \$1360 4 years hence. The future value of \$1000 was computed by compounding, namely

$$F = P(1+i)^n = 1000(1+0.08)^4 = 1360$$

whereas the present value of \$1360 is given by

$$PV = \frac{F}{(1+i)^n} = \frac{1360}{(1+0.08)^4} = 1000$$

Table 3 in Appendix B gives the values for the present value factors $\frac{1}{(1+i)^n}$, *e.g.* for $n = 4$ and $i = 8$ percent we find $\frac{1}{(1+0.08)^4}$ to be 0.735, and $1360 \times 0.735 = 1000$.

Note that the above formula has 4 variables, PV, F, i, and n. Thus, if we know any three of these variables, we can derive the fourth.

Example

If \$2000 grew in a savings account to \$3222 in 5 years with annual compounding, what was the interest rate being paid?

We have

$$PV = \frac{F}{(1+i)^n}$$

or $$2000 = \frac{3222}{(1+i)^5}$$

or $$\frac{2000}{3222} = 0.621 = \frac{1}{(1+i)^5}$$

Looking in Table 3 in the row for $n = 5$ years, we try to find an interest rate which will give an entry as close as possible to 0.621, obtaining $i = 10$ percent.

Note that we could also have used Table 1 as follows:

$$2000 = \frac{3222}{(1+i)^5}$$

or $$(1+i)^5 = \frac{3222}{2000} = 1.611$$

and again, for 5 years we obtain $i = 10$ percent.

If interest is compounded more than once a year, the annual rate must again be adjusted. The adjustment alters equation (8) to the following form:

(9) $$PV = F(1 + \tfrac{i}{k})^{-nk}$$

Example

What is the present value of $1,000 to be received 4 years from now, with $i = .08$ compounded quarterly?

$$\begin{aligned} PV &= F(1 + \tfrac{i}{k})^{-nk} \\ &= 1{,}000(1.02)^{-16} \\ &\simeq 1{,}000(.728) \\ &= 728 \end{aligned}$$

The present value is $728.

The concept of present values is extremely important in making financial decisions, particularly where the situation entails cash flows occurring at different points in time. It is, for example, used by financial executives when evaluating longer term investment of financing decisions; hence the reader should acquire a full understanding of the concept.

4-4. ANNUITIES

Attention has thus far focused on the value of a single future sum. The problems discussed to this point can, of course, be extended to cover a series of equal payments for a specified number of years termed *annuities.*

Example

Suppose a sum A of $1000 is invested at the end of each of $n = 4$ years to earn an interest rate of $i = 10$ percent. We are interested in the total amount having accrued at the end of the fourth year.

If we analyze each of these payments separately, we calculate the future values at the end of year 4 and just add up for the total. The first payment of \$1000 will have 3 years compound interest accrued at the end of the fourth year for a total of $A(1+i)^3 = 1000(1+0.1)^3 = \$1331$. Similarly, the payment at year 2 will have grown to $A(1+i)^2 = 1000(1+0.1)^2 = 1210$, the payment in the third year will be at $1000(1+0.1) = \$1100$ with the fourth payment being just at \$1000. The total future value of this 4-year annuity is \$4641, as shown below, or

$$V = A(1+i)^3 + A(1+i)^2 + A(1+i) + A$$

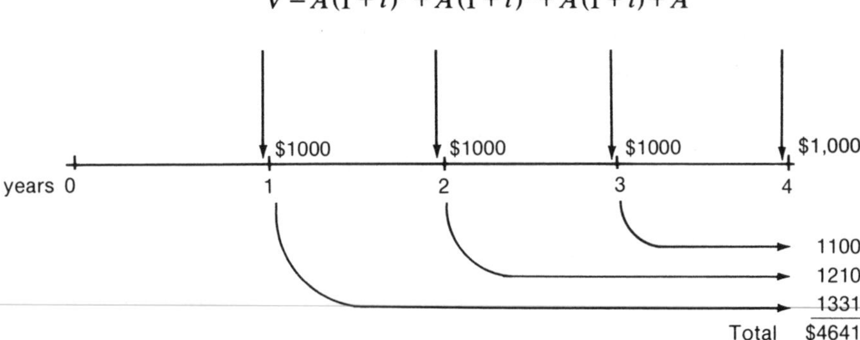

More generally, for an annuity involving equal payments at the end of each of n years, we have

(10) $$V = A(1+i)^{n-1} + A(1+i)^{n-2} + \ldots + A(1+i) + A$$

Sums of this type occur frequently in finance, for example in periodic interest payments on bonds, or where bank loans are to be repaid in equal instalments. If n is large, they could involve many terms which would be inconvenient computationally. They can easily be transformed, however, into an equivalent but shorter and more convenient form as follows. Multiplying both sides of equation (10) above by $(1+i)$ results in

(11) $$(1+i)V = A(1+i)^n + A(1+i)^{n-1} + \ldots + A(1+i)$$

Then subtracting equation (10) from (11) yields (12) as follows

(11) $$(1+i)V = A(1+i)^n + A(1+i)^{n-1} + \ldots + A(1+i)$$

minus (10) $$V = \qquad\qquad + A(1+i)^{n-1} + \ldots + A(1+i) + A$$

(12) $$iV = A(1+i)^n \qquad\qquad - A$$

and by simplifying, one obtains

(12a) $$V = A\left[\frac{(1+i)^n - 1}{i}\right]$$

Equation (12a) is the *future value of an annuity of A* dollars per period for n periods at an interest rate of i per period.

Example

How much will $1,000 deposited in a bank at the end of each of 10 years amount to immediately after the last deposit, assuming 8 percent interest compounded annually?

$$V = 1{,}000\left[\frac{(1+.08)^{10}-1}{.08}\right]$$
$$\simeq 1{,}000\,[14.487]$$
$$= 14{,}487$$

The amount will be $14,487.

Note that Table 2 in Appendix B gives the values for the annuity factor $\left[\frac{(1+i)^n-1}{i}\right]$, which for i = 8 percent and n = 10 years we find to be 14.487.

Finally, consider the present value of a series of payments to be received at the end of each of the next n years. It should be clear that the discounted or present value of the first payment to be received a year hence is $A(1+i)^{-1}$. The present value of the second payment is $A(1+i)^{-2}$, and that of the final payment to be received n years from now is $A(1+i)^{-n}$.

For this series

$$PV = A(1+i)^{-1} + A(1+i)^{-2} + \ldots + A(1+i)^{-n}$$

It is left as an exercise for the reader to show that by applying the technique discussed above, this reduces to

(13) $$PV = A\left[\frac{1-(1+i)^{-n}}{i}\right]$$

Equation (13) represents the *present* value of an annuity of A dollars per period. To simplify, we write $(a_n i\%) = [1-(1+i)^{-n}]/i$, where $(a_n i\%)$ is simply the present value factor for an annuity of n years at i percent. We have

(13a) $$PV = (a_n i\%)A$$

Example

What is the present value of $1,000 received at the end of each year for 10 years, assuming 8 percent as the time value of money and annual compounding?

$$PV = 1{,}000\left[\frac{1-(1+.08)^{-10}}{.08}\right]$$
$$\simeq 1{,}000\,[6.710]$$
$$= 6{,}710$$

The present value is $6,710.

Table 4 in Appendix B gives the values of the present value factors for annuities ($a_n i\%$), once again obviating the need for tedious computations. For $i = 8$ percent and $n = 10$ years, we find the entry of (a_{10} 8%) = 6.710 in the Table.

If payments are due at *the beginning* of each year, the above formulas are easily modified and the tables may still be used. Consider the present value of $1000 received at the beginning of each year for 10 years, assuming again 8 percent as the time value of money and annual compounding. This is equivalent to $1000 at the beginning of year one, plus an annuity of $1000 for 9 years with payments received at *the end* of each year. Thus, we obtain

$$PV = 1000 + 1000\left[\frac{1-(1+.08)^{-9}}{.08}\right]$$

$$\simeq 1000 + 1000[6.247]$$

$$= 7{,}247$$

Situations exist where, at least theoretically, an annuity is to be paid in perpetuity. We see that as n in formula (13) becomes very large, the expression $(1+i)^{-n}$ approaches zero, so that for a perpetual annuity, equation (13) simply reduces to $PV = A/i$.

Example

For $1,000 received at the end of each year in perpetuity, with the time value of money at 8 percent, the present value becomes $PV =$ $1,000/0.08 = $12,500.

4-5. BOND YIELDS

An important application of annuity tables is found in computing bond yields. Bonds are debt instruments originally issued by a borrower with interest payments which were competitive in the capital markets at the time of issue. The face value of the bond acknowledges the amount of the debt while the maturity specifies the date by which the corporation has to repay the debt. Owners of bonds may subsequently resell them at the going market price to other investors; in other words, there is a secondary market for most bonds where regular trading takes place. The market price of a bond will be a function not only of its face value, maturity and interest payments, but also of prevailing market conditions including interest rates on alternative investments available to investors at that time. Thus, a bond may have a face value of $1000, a remaining maturity of 20 years, and an interest rate originally specified (also called the coupon rate or the nominal yield) of 8 percent. If since issue, general interest rate levels have increased, and investors can find comparable investments yielding 10 percent, the bond can only be sold if its *effective yield* to a purchaser also becomes 10 percent, implying that its market price will have to be reduced to a point where the effective interest rate becomes competitive. The face value of a bond, its maturity and its coupon or nominal yield are generally known. If in addition, the effective yield is known, then the market value can be computed, and *vice versa.* This section is concerned with such computation of market value and effective yield.

The determination of bond yields is related to the concept of discounting. More precisely, the effective bond yield is determined by finding the rate of discount, r, which equates the present value of all future interest and principal payments to the market price of the particular bond. Future payments consist of an annuity of I for n years (annual interest payments) and a lump sum payment of the face value at the end of year n (repayment of principal at maturity). The equation for calculating bond yields becomes

$$P = \frac{I}{(1+r)} + \frac{I}{(1+r)^2} + \ldots + \frac{I}{(1+r)^n} + \frac{FV}{(1+r)^n} \tag{14}$$

where P is the current market price, FV the face value, I the annual dollar interest payment, and n the number of years to maturity. The above formula assumes annual interest payments; recognition to the usual pattern of semi-annual interest payments is given below.

The rationale for formula (14) is as follows: The purchase of a bond entitles the investor to annual interest payments $I = iFV$, and to a repayment of FV at the maturity date of the bond. If the investor demands an effective yield of r percent, the present value of those future receipts are found simply by discounting at that rate. For reasons set out earlier, an investor should then be indifferent between this present value and the future cash flows as indicated; hence, the maximum amount he should be willing to pay for the bond is given by this present value, which becomes the market value of the bond *i.e.* P in equation (14).

Example

What is the market price P of a bond with a face value of \$1000, a nominal interest rate of 5 percent, and a maturity of 10 years if the effective yield demanded by investors is 7 percent?

By purchasing the bond, an investor would be entitled to annual interest payments of $I = 1000 \times 0.05 = \$50$, payable at the end of years 1 through 10 (*i.e.* an annuity of \$50 for 10 years), as well as a payment of \$1000 at the end of the tenth year to retire the debt. Discounting these cash flows at 7 percent, we obtain a present value of

$$P = 50\,(7.024) + 1000\,(0.508)$$
$$= \$859.20$$

where 7.024 is the present value factor for an annuity with $n = 10$, $i = 7$ percent from Table 4 and 0.508 is the present value factor from Table 3. The present value of future cash flows works out to be \$859.20, which is at the same time the amount an investor should be willing to pay for the bond and, consequently, its market value.

Similarly, we can use formula (14) to compute the effective yield of a bond if we know the current market value.

Example

What is the yield to maturity of a 5 percent, \$1000 bond with 10 years to final maturity and a current market price of \$926?

We have

$$926 = \frac{50}{(1+r)} + \frac{50}{(1+r)^2} + \ldots + \frac{50}{(1+r)^{10}} + \frac{1,000}{(1+r)^{10}}$$

which has to be solved for r. The equation is complex because of the powers of r which appear in it. An algebraic solution which would leave r on one side and would allow us to find its value by simple computation is generally not available. We have to use trial and error to arrive at a value for r which satisfies the equation, meaning that we must simply try various values of r to see how close we can come to making the right side of the equation equal to \$926. Since the market value of \$926 is below the face value of \$1000, we know that the effective yield r will have to exceed the nominal yield of 5 percent. It follows that we could start by trying a value of r = 7 percent. For the right hand side, we obtain

$$\$50 \times 7.024 + \$1000 \times 0.508 = \$859.20$$

If the effective yield were 7 percent, the market value would only be \$859.20. The actual market value of \$926 suggests an effective yield which is somewhat lower, *i.e.* between 5 and 7 percent. Trying r = 6 percent next we obtain

$$\$50 \times 7.360 + \$1000 \times 0.558 = \$926$$

which satisfies the equation. Hence, the bond's effective yield is 6 percent.[5]

Extensive bond yield tables do exist in fact, obviating the need for tedious computations; and more generally standard computer programs are available (even on some pocket-size electronic calculators) which follow similar procedures to find effective yields.

Equation (14) can be used in a variety of ways. If any three of the variables *I, P, FV,* and r are given, we can use this equation to compute the values of the unknown fourth variable.

As outlined above, the effective yield of a bond and, hence, its market price reflects prevailing market interest rates. If the prevailing market rate is higher than the bond's coupon rate, the instrument will have to trade at a discount to be attractive to investors (*i.e.*, the market price will be below the face value) and *vice versa*. Everything else being equal, this discount or premium will increase with increasing time to maturity for the bond; the longer the time to maturity, the more sensitive is the market price of a bond to changes in prevailing interest rates.

Example

What are the current market prices of each of three 5 percent, \$1,000 bonds if the prevailing market rate of interest is 6 percent and the years

[5]In using the tables, one may want to interpolate to obtain more accurate results. Problem 1 with solution at the end of this chapter illustrates the process of interpolation.

to maturity are (a) 5 years, (b) 10 years, and (c) 20 years? Assume interest to be paid annually.[6]

(a) $$P = \sum_{n=1}^{5} \frac{50}{(1.06)^n} + \frac{1000}{(1.06)^5} \simeq 210.60 + 747 \quad = 957.60$$

(b) $$P = \sum_{n=1}^{10} \frac{50}{(1.06)^n} + \frac{1000}{(1.06)^{10}} \simeq 368.00 + 558 \quad = 926.00$$

(c) $$P = \sum_{n=1}^{20} \frac{50}{(1.06)^n} + \frac{1000}{(1.06)^{20}} \simeq 573.50 + 312 \quad = 885.50$$

If, as is usually the case, interest on a bond is paid more than once a year, equation (14) is easily altered using the same approach as in equation (4) above, yielding

(15) $$P = \frac{I/m}{\left(1 + \frac{r}{m}\right)} + \frac{I/m}{\left(1 + \frac{r}{m}\right)^2} + \ldots + \frac{I/m}{\left(1 + \frac{r}{m}\right)^{mn}} + \frac{FV}{\left(1 + \frac{r}{m}\right)^{mn}}$$

where m is the number of times interest is paid per year.

Example

What is the current market price of a 5 percent 10-year bond with a face value of $1,000 and paying interest semiannually if the prevailing market rate is 6 percent?

$$P = \frac{50/2}{\left(1 + \frac{.06}{2}\right)} + \frac{50/2}{\left(1 + \frac{.06}{2}\right)^2} + \ldots + \frac{50/2}{\left(1 + \frac{.06}{2}\right)^{20}} + \frac{1{,}000}{\left(1 + \frac{.06}{2}\right)^{20}}$$

$$= \sum_{n=1}^{20} \frac{25}{(1.03)^n} + \frac{1{,}000}{(1.03)^{20}}$$

$$\simeq 371.93 + 554$$

$$= \sum_{n=1}^{20} 925.93.$$

The current market price is $925.93.

Note that half the annual interest is paid in each period, but the number of semiannual periods over which discounting takes place becomes twice the number of years to maturity, with discounting taking place at half the annual interest rate.

Some bonds (and other fixed income securities) which have no maturities do exist. They are called *perpetuals* or *consols* and, at least theoretically, generate interest payments forever. Drawing on the formula for perpetual an-

[6]The Greek symbol Σ is standard mathematical notation and stands for "sum". Thus, $\sum_{n=1}^{5} \frac{50}{(1.06)^n}$ stands for "sum of $\frac{50}{(1.06)^n}$ from $n = 1$ to $n = 5$", or $\frac{50}{(1.06)} + \frac{50}{(1.06)^2} + \ldots + \frac{50}{(1.06)^5}$.

nuities, the yield on such a perpetual is simply given as

(16) $$r = \frac{I}{P}$$

This result, which may be intuitively obvious, could also have been derived more formally by inserting $FV = 0$ in equation (14), transforming this series along the lines presented in the development of equation (12) above, and then inserting ∞ for n. It is left as an exercise for the reader to verify this procedure.

Example

If in the above example of a 5 percent, \$1000 bond and a prevailing market interest rate of 6 percent, the bond was a perpetual with no maturity, what would its market price be?

We have

$$r = \frac{I}{P} \text{ or } P = \frac{I}{r} = \frac{50}{0.06} = \$833.33$$

4-6. EFFECTIVE INTEREST AND REPAYMENT SCHEDULES ON LOANS

Many loans such as bank loans and mortgages entail periodic repayments of equal amounts which cover interest and repayment of principal until the loan is amortized. Thus, a \$10,000 loan may call for repayments of \$3500 per year for 4 years, with payments due at the end of each year. The techniques discussed above can readily be extended to compute the effective interest charged on such a loan, or where the effective interest rate is known, to compute the size of periodic payments to be made. If P is the amount of the loan, AR the annual repayment and n the number of years over which payments are to be made, the effective interest rate of the loan is again given by solving for r the equation

(17) $$P = \frac{AR}{(1+r)} + \frac{AR}{(1+r)^2} + \ldots + \frac{AR}{(1+r)^n}$$

Note that trial and error procedures are not necessary here, however, as we have a standard annuity of AR for n years. Using formula (13), we can write the equation (17) as

$$P = AR\left[\frac{1-(1+r)^{-n}}{r}\right]$$

To simplify, we again write

$$(a_n r\%) = \left[\frac{1-(1+r)^{-n}}{r}\right]$$

where $a_n r\%$ is the present value factor for an annuity of n years at r percent, the values of which are listed in Table 4.

We have

(18) $$P = (a_n r\%) AR$$

or $$(a_n r\%) = \frac{P}{AR}$$

For a given n, we can find the correct r from the tables. In the above example, we would find

$$(a_4 r\%) = \frac{10{,}000}{3{,}500} = 2.86$$

Looking at Table 4 in the row for $n = 4$ years, we try to find an entry which comes as close as possible to 2.86, which in this instance implies an effective interest rate of between 14% ($a_4 14\% = 2.914$) and 16% ($a_4 16\% = 2.798$).[7]

Example

A mortgage of $30,000 calls for equal annual repayments of $3,825 over 25 years. What is the effective interest rate being charged?

$$(a_{25} r\%) = \frac{30{,}000}{3{,}825} = 7.843$$

and from Table 4 with $n = 25$ years, we find $r = 12$ percent.

Similarly, equation (18) can clearly be used to establish the amount of the annual repayments if the amount and life of the loan and the effective interest rate being charged are known.

Example

A $10,000 loan carries an effective interest rate of 12 percent and calls for equal annual repayments over 3 years. What is the amount of each repayment?

$$AR = \frac{P}{(a_n r\%)} = \frac{\$10{,}000}{2.402} = \$4163.20$$

Finally, it is often necessary for tax purposes to break the annual repayments up into the portion which constitutes interest and that portion which constitutes repayment of principal, as only the interest portion is considered an expense and hence is deductible for tax purposes. Pursuing the above example, we have

Year	(1) Principal Outstanding at Beginning of Year	(2) Annual Repayment	(3) Interest on Principal Outstanding $r\% \times (1)$	(4) Repayment of Principal $(4) = (2) - (3)$	(5) Principal Outstanding at End of Year $(1) - (4)$
1	10,000.00	4,163.20	1,200.00	2,963.20	7,036.80
2	7,036.80	4,163.20	844.42	3,318.78	3,718.02
3	3,718.02	4,163.20	445.18	3,718.02	0

[7]Interpolating, we obtain $\left[\begin{array}{ll} 16\% & 2.798 \\ \left[\begin{array}{l} r\% \\ 14\% \end{array}\right. & \left.\begin{array}{l} 2.86 \\ 2.914 \end{array}\right] \end{array}\right]$

or $\frac{r - 14}{16 - 14} = \frac{2.86 - 2.914}{2.798 - 2.914}$, yielding $r = 14.93\%$

The interest portion is calculated by applying the interest rate to the principal outstanding at the beginning of the year. The remaining portion of the annual repayment is then used to reduce the amount of principal outstanding.

We see that the annual repayments of $4,163.20 indeed incorporate interest of 12 percent on the amount of principal outstanding and a total amortization of the principal at the end of 3 years.

It is left for the exercises at the end of the chapter to deal with situations calling for repayments on a quarterly or monthly basis.

4-7. SUMMARY

The time value of money is a fundamental concept in finance. Interest computations enable one to determine the value to which a sum of money grows over a period of time given certain rules governing interest payments, such as simple or compound interest (compounded once or several times per year). Discounting is computationally the opposite of compounding; it is used to derive the present value of future cash flows, a prerequisite for being able to compare and evaluate cash flows which occur in different time periods. Computation of investment yields is closely related to discounting, which was applied to bonds. Thus, the effective yield of a bond is arrived at by finding the discount rate which equates future interest and principal payments with the current market price. This relationship may also be used to compute the market values of such securities for given effective yields. Computation of effective interest rates on loans and loan repayment schedules are a further application of the same techniques.

Naturally tables exist to alleviate computations for most of the problems surveyed and some appear in Appendix B.

Questions for discussion

1. (a) If the general level of interest rates rises, what do you think will be the effect on market prices of outstanding bonds? Give reasons.
   (b) Further to your answer in (a) above, would you expect bonds with a longer term to maturity or with a shorter term to maturity to be more significantly effected?
2. (a) If a person can invest monies for one year at 10 percent, and we say that therefore he should be indifferent between receiving $100 today or $110 a year from now, what assumptions are we making?
   (b) How reasonable are these assumptions in the context of a business firm?
3. What is the relationship between the entries in Table 1 (Compound Sum of $1) and Table 3 (Present Value of $1) as reproduced in Appendix B? For example, how could one derive the entry of 0.650 for 5 years and an interest rate of 9 percent as given in Table 3 if one only had access to Table 1?
4. What impact do service charges and commissions have on the effective interest cost of a bank loan? Explain.
5. (a) Explain the difference between a nominal and an effective interest rate. Give a practical example of where these two rates may differ. Which is more relevant for financial decision-making?

(b) Why have some financial institutions which lend money frequently quoted a nominal rate rather than the effective rate of interest?

6. An older version of the *Bank Act* provided for a maximum rate of interest which chartered banks could impose. To what extent would such a statutory limitation be difficult to administer? Why?

Problems with solutions

1. (a) A bond with a 4-year maturity, face value of $1000 and coupon rate of 5 percent is selling on the market at $950. Calculate the effective yield.

Solution

The market value of the bond is equivalent to the present value of all expected receipts from the bond discounted at the effective yield rate (r%)

$$\text{Market Value} = \sum_{n=1}^{4} \frac{\text{Coupon}}{(1+r)^n} + \frac{\text{Face Value}}{(1+r)^4}$$

$$950 = \frac{50}{(1+r)} + \frac{50}{(1+r)^2} + \frac{50}{(1+r)^3} + \frac{50}{(1+r)^4} + \frac{1000}{(1+r)^4}$$

This can be written as:

$$950 = (50)(a_n r\%) + \frac{1000}{(1+r)^4}$$

(where notation $a_n\ i\%$ is the present value of an annuity of $1 for n years at i%)

By trial and error, we find r% to be between 6% and 7%.

i.e. If $r = 6\%$, then the right side of the equation is

$$(50)(3.465) + (1000)(.792) = 965.25$$

If $r = 7\%$,

$$(50)(3.387) + (1000)(.763) = 932.35$$

The value which we are seeking must lie between these two since $932 < \underline{950} < 965$.

We can use interpolation to find r, the effective yield on the bond.

Interpolation:

$$\begin{bmatrix} 7\% & 932 \\ \begin{bmatrix} r\% \\ 6\% \end{bmatrix} & \begin{bmatrix} 950 \\ 965 \end{bmatrix} \end{bmatrix}$$

$$\frac{r\% - 6\%}{7\% - 6\%} = \frac{950 - 965}{932 - 965} = \frac{-15}{-33} = .45.$$ Hence, $r = (7-6)(.45) + 6 = 6.45\%$

(b) If instead of an annual coupon payment of $50, the bond in part (a) pays $25 semiannually, compute the effective yield.

Solution:

We can now expect eight semiannual receipts of $25, and a receipt of $1,000 at maturity.

The unit period is now a half-year, and we first determine the effective interest rate per half-year period called r'.

$$\text{Market value} = \frac{25}{(1+r')} + \frac{25}{(1+r')^2} + \ldots + \frac{25}{(1+r')^8} + \frac{1000}{(1+r')^8}$$

or

$$950 = \sum_{n=1}^{8} \frac{25}{(1+r')^n} + \frac{1000}{(1+r')^8}$$

By trial and error and interpolation as in 3(a), we find that r' is equal to 3.22%

(at $r' = 3\%$, market value equals 964.50,
at $r' = 4\%$, market value equals 899.33,
interpolated figure for market value of 950 is $r' = 3.22\%$).

Thus, we have an effective yield of 3.22% per half-year. An approximation of the annual effective yield can be derived by simply multiplying r' by 2, *i.e.* $r = 2r' = 6.44\%$. However, more exactly we have to consider the compounding effect, *i.e.*

$$(1+r) = (1+r')^2 = (1+0.0322)^2 = 1.0654$$

yielding $r = 6.54\%$.

2. (a) A \$1000 par value bond with a maturity of 3 years has a coupon rate of 10 percent. Calculate the market price of the bond if the effective yield is 8 percent.

Solution

$$\text{Market value} = \sum_{n=1}^{3} \frac{100}{(1+r)^n} + \frac{1000}{(1+r)^3}$$

$$= (100)(a_{3}8\%) + \frac{1000}{(1+.08)^3}$$

$$= (100)(2.577) + (1000)(.794)$$

$$\text{Market value} = \underline{\$1051.70}$$

(b) If the bond in part (a) had a maturity of 10 years instead of 3 years, calculate the market price.

Solution

$$\text{Market value} = \sum_{n=1}^{10} \frac{100}{(1+.08)^n} + \frac{1000}{(1+.08)^{10}}$$

$$= 100\,(a_{10}8\%) + \frac{1000}{(1+.08)^{10}}$$

$$= (100)(6.71) + (1000)(.463)$$

$$= \underline{\$1134}$$

(c) If the bond in part (a) had no maturity date, but was rather a claim to the receipt of \$100 annual interest in perpetuity, calculate its market value.

Solution

$$\text{Market value} = \sum_{n=1}^{\infty} \frac{100}{(1+.08)^n}$$

$$= \frac{100}{.08}$$

$$= \underline{\$1250}$$

3. (a) A firm borrows \$10,000 from the bank at an effective interest rate of 10 percent. This loan is to be paid off by the end of 3 years through 3 equal annual repayments. What should be the amount of these equal payments?

Solution

$$\text{Loan Amount} = \frac{\text{Annual Repayment}}{(1+r)} + \frac{\text{A.R.}}{(1+r)^2} + \frac{\text{A.R.}}{(1+r)^3}$$

$$= \sum_{n=1}^{3} \frac{\text{A.R.}}{(1+r)^n} = (\text{A.R.})\,(a_3 r\%)$$

$$\$10{,}000 = (\text{A.R.})\,(a_3\,10\%)$$

$$\text{A.R.} = \frac{10{,}000}{a_3\,10\%} = \frac{10{,}000}{2.487}$$

$$= \underline{\$4{,}020.91}$$

(b) Break down the annual payments of part (a) into principal and interest.

Solution

	(1) Unamortized Principal	(2) Annual Repayment	(3) Interest on unamortized Principal (10%) × (1)	(4) Amortization Payment (2) − (3)	(5) New Unamortized Principal Amount (1) − (4)
Yr. 1	10,000	4,021	1,000	3,021	6,979
Yr. 2	6,979	4,021	698	3,323	3,656
Yr. 3	3,656	4,021	366	3,656	⊖

Note: figures above are rounded to the nearest dollars.

4. (a) Suppose you obtain a personal bank loan of \$3,200 which you are to repay by making three annual payments of \$1,200, with the first payment to be made on the first anniversary of the loan date. What is the effective interest cost on your loan?

Solution

$$\text{Loan Amount} = (\text{Annual Repayment})\,(a_n r\%)$$

$$a_n r\% = \frac{\text{Loan}}{\text{A.R.}}$$

$$a_3 r\% = \frac{3200}{1200} = 2.67$$

From "*P.V.* of annuity" table for 3 years, we see that $a_3 6\% = 2.673$, so the effective interest rate (r) equals 6%.

(b) If for the loan in part (a), you must make quarterly payments of $300 instead of annual payments of $1,200, would you expect the effective interest cost to be higher or lower? Calculate the new effective interest rate.

Solution

As in problem 1(b) we will let r' stand for the quarterly interest rate.

$$3200 = \frac{300}{(1+r')} + \frac{300}{(1+r')^2} + \ldots + \frac{300}{(1+r')^{12}}$$

This can be written as

$$3200 = (300)\,(a_{12}r')$$

$$a_{12}r' = \frac{3200}{300}$$

$$= 10.67$$

Interpolation from the tables gives us

$$r' = 1.86\%$$

An approximation to the effective annual rate would again be

$$r = 4r' = 7.44\%$$

More exactly, considering compounding effects, we have,

$$(1+r) = (1+.0186)^4$$

$$1+r = 1.0765$$

$$r = 7.65\%$$

(c) Assume the situation given in part (a). If at the time of the loan, the bank charges you a service fee of $51, what is the effective interest cost of the loan?

Solution

The service fee in effect decreases the amount of the loan, while the amount of the repayment remains the same. Thus, one would now expect the effective interest cost to be higher.

$$a_n r\% = \frac{\text{Net Loan Amount}}{\text{Annual Repayment}}$$

$$a_3 r\% = \frac{3200 - 51}{1200}$$

$$= \frac{3149}{1200}$$

$$= 2.624$$

From the tables we can see that r is now 7%.

Additional Problems

1. (a) A $1,000 5-year bond with a coupon rate of 6 percent is selling at $1,075. Compute the effective yield.
   (b) What is the effective yield if the coupon rate is 3 percent to be paid semiannually instead of the 6 percent annual payment?
2. (a) Calculate the market price of a bond having the following characteristics: par value of $1,000, maturity 3 years, coupon rate 4 percent, and effective yield of 6 percent.
   (b) Compute the market price of the bond in part (a) assuming that it matures in 10 years.
   (c) What would be the market value of the bond if it had no maturity date?
3. (a) What annual payment would be required to pay off a 4-year $20,000 loan, if the effective interest being charged is 7 percent?
   (b) Break down these payments into principal and interest.
4. (a) A 5-year loan of $50,000 is to be repaid in 5 annual payments of $12,000. What is the effective interest cost of this loan?
   (b) If, instead, this loan were to be repaid through payments of $4,000 every 4 months for 5 years, what would be the effective interest cost?
   (c) Assume that the borrower had made a deal with an intermediary to pay him a 0.5 percent commission (of the loan amount) if he could locate a lender who would agree to certain terms. A lender was located and the arrangement in part (a) was consummated. What was the effective interest cost to the borrower?
5. If a $5,000 loan requires repayment of principal and 5 percent simple interest in 4 years time, how much will be repaid?
6. (a) If a bank pays 6 percent interest compounded annually on a $1,000 savings deposit, what will be the value of this deposit at the end of 5 years?
   (b) If another bank pays 6 percent interest on the same $1,000 deposit but compounds interest quarterly, what will be the value of this deposit at the end of 5 years? What is the effective rate being paid?
   Note: Interpolate in using tables.
   (c) If interest were paid continuously at 6 percent on this $1,000 deposit, what would it be worth in 5 years?
7. What is the present value of a lump sum payment of $500 to be received 10 years from now if interest is compounded annually at 6 percent? What is the present value if interest is compounded semiannually?
8. If $3,000 is placed in a savings account at the end of every year for 5 years, what is the value of this account at the end of the fifth year given that interest is 7 percent and is compounded annually?
9. What is the present value of $3,000 to be received at the end of each year for 5 years if interest is 7 percent and is compounded annually?
10. Suppose an 8 percent $1,000 bond with 8 years left to maturity is selling for $1,124.19. What is the effective yield, assuming interest is paid annually?

11. If, in question 10, interest were paid semiannually, what would the bond sell for given that the effective yield remained unchanged?
12. (a) If a $1,000 note is sold to a bank one year before maturity at a *simple* discount of 4 percent for each 6 months, how much will the bank pay for the note?
    (b) What is the rate of interest that the bank will earn on this investment?

Selected References

R. Cissell and H. Cissell, *Mathematics of Finance.* Boston: Houghton Mifflin, 4th ed., 1973.

H. Ferns, *Mathematics of Canadian Finance,* Toronto: McGraw-Hill, 1963.

J. Howell, and D. Teichroew, *Mathematical Analysis for Business Decisions,* Homewood: Irwin, 1963, Chapter 10.

Chapter 5
Capital Budgeting

5-1. INTRODUCTION

This chapter and the next are concerned with the firm's capital-expenditure decisions, that is, with the commitment of funds to projects which are expected to generate returns extending at least one year into the future. Attention is therefore directed to such longer-term projects as investments in plant or equipment, certain types of promotional campaigns, and research and development. Shorter-term investment, such as seasonal allocations to inventories and accounts receivable, are considered as part of working-capital management. The one-year cutoff on returns to distinguish long-term investments (capital budgeting) from short-term investments (working-capital management) is admittedly somewhat arbitrary[1] and certain projects may not lend themselves readily to such simple categorization.

There is justification, however, for treating longer-term commitments of funds under a separate heading because the managerial problems which must be faced often differ significantly from those encountered in working-capital management. For example, since benefits accrue over an extended period, the time value of money will play an important role in establishing the economic desirability of the investment. Special emphasis may also have to be placed on risk analysis, not only because of uncertainties inherent in any long-term forecast of cash flows, but also because a significant percentage of the firm's resources may be committed by a single capital-expenditure decision. Furthermore, while the abandonment of a project is always a possibility, some expenditures are sunk costs and, once the decision to invest in a long-term project is taken, funds are generally tied up for fairly lengthy periods. Lastly, while working-capital decisions largely determine the liquidity and hence the short-run viability of a firm, capital-budgeting decisions are crucial to establishing longer-term profitability and hence the value of the firm.

The importance of an efficient allocation of these longer-term resources to the Canadian economy can be surmised from Table 5-1 which shows gross business investment in absolute figures and as a proportion of gross national expenditure for selected years.

As you might expect, the relative magnitude of capital assets to total assets varies significantly between industries: for instance, being more modest in forestry or retailing where large sums are tied up in inventories and accounts receivable; and quite significant in the communications and utilities fields which are characterized by massive investments in plant and equipment. Data for selected industries are shown in Table 5-2.

[1]It is however, relevant for accounting and tax purposes since expenditures which are expected to be recovered within one year will be expensed, while investments with a longer economic life may have to be capitalized and subsequently depreciated.

TABLE 5-1

Gross Business Investment (Construction, Machinery and Equipment) and Gross National Expenditure at Market Prices (in millions of dollars)

Year	Business Investment	Gross National Expenditure	Business Investment as a Proportion of G.N.E.
1974	26,826	139,493	0.1923
1973	22,107	118,902	0.1859
1972	18,540	103,493	0.1791
1971	16,640	93,307	0.1783
1970	14,842	85,685	0.1732

Source: Statistics Canada, *National Income and Expenditure Accounts*, various issues.

TABLE 5-2

The ratio of Capital Assets to Total Assets for Selected Industries, 1971

Industry	Net Depreciable Assets as a Proportion of Total Assets
Communications	0.8051
Public Utilities	0.7748
Transportation	0.7047
Fishing	0.6148
Paper and Allied Industries	0.4685
Metal Mining	0.4095
Chemicals	0.3943
Textile Mills	0.3474
Rubber Products	0.3417
Food	0.3150
Forestry	0.3065
Agriculture	0.3036
Furniture	0.2211
Retail Trade	0.1956
Tobacco Products	0.1093
Clothing	0.1008
Finance, Insurance	0.0845

Source: Statistics Canada, *Corporation Financial Statistics, 1971*, October, 1974.

Regardless of industry, substantial amounts are involved nevertheless for most individual firms, and Table 5-3 sets out the absolute amounts as well as the proportions of total assets represented by capital assets for a sample of companies. The additional amounts invested in capital assets during 1974 are also indicated.

TABLE 5-3

Capital Assets of Selected Canadian Companies
(in thousands of dollars)

	Capital Assets	Total Assets	Capital Assets as a Proportion of Total Assets	Gross Capital Investments During Fiscal 1974
	As at End of Fiscal Year 1974			
Alcan Aluminum Limited	1,329,460	2,957,646	0.4495	201,870
British Columbia Forest Products Ltd.	240,250	358,345	0.6704	44,563
British Columbia Telephone Co. Ltd.	1,002,500	1,076,697	0.9311	201,484
Calgary Power Limited	578,134	601,564	0.9610	119,156
The Molson Company Limited	131,874	345,316	0.3819	15,580
Canadian Pacific Limited	3,774,790	5,434,527	0.6946	1,207,699
Cominco Limited	370,329	765,717	0.4836	35,243
Woodward Stores Limited	82,526	205,086	0.4024	23,270
Home Oil Limited	284,389	381,819	0.7448	44,283
Northern Electric Company Limited	119,986	567,795	0.2113	33,728
Sherrit Gordon Mines Limited	107,243	189,843	0.5649	8,903
Steel Company of Canada Limited	812,093	1,340,336	0.6059	135,500

Source: 1974 Annual Reports

It is useful to recognize several distinct steps or phases in the capital-budgeting process since each of these entails its own management problems.[2] Thus, one can identify

- The generation of project ideas
- The estimation of cash flows
- Project selection (which is based on the application of selection criteria to determine investment worth)
- Implementation of investment decisions including controls and periodic reevaluations

Each of these topics will be looked at in turn.

5-2. THE GENERATING OF PROJECTS

While for most firms it is not difficult to come up with notions about possible investment projects, good ideas are quite scarce. The generation of worthwhile ideas is of critical importance and contributes to the success of any program of capital expenditures. Successful companies have been built around one good idea as illustrated, for example, by the Xerox Corporation whose success was based largely on the invention of a new copying mechanism; or by Digital Equipment Corporation which set out to build small, modestly priced computers for which there was a ready market.

Timing may be a critical factor. Thus, during the late sixties a number of entrepreneurs made large gains on entry into such fields as computer services and leasing, largely because the market was ready. One year later others went bankrupt while trying to exploit the same opportunities because the general environment had changed.

[2]See for example J. Bower, *Managing the Resource Allocation Process*, Boston, Harvard University Press, 1970, especially Part I of the book.

While new ideas are often generated in a somewhat random manner, systematic search efforts such as those undertaken in research and development departments, play a major role in certain industries.[3] Sources for ideas are bound to vary according to the type of investment considered.[4] For instance, suggestions relating to product lines are most likely to emerge from either the marketing or the research and development departments; approaches aimed at a reduction in production costs may come from plant or engineering personnel; while suggestions for external acquisitions may originate from outside contacts including banks and investment dealers. The key is to systematically establish channels of communication which facilitate the transmission of ideas and, further, to provide people with an incentive to contribute. This may be implemented in a variety of ways ranging from suggestion boxes on the production floor coupled with financial rewards for ideas acted upon, to sophisticated research management as encountered, for example, in the chemical and aerospace industries. Senior management will generally impose constraints and give policy directives on the areas in which the search for new projects is to be centered, specifying, perhaps, that new products are to remain within the same general industry, or that internal growth rather than external acquisitions is to be relied on. Such policies should be reevaluated periodically in light of a changing environment.Thus, a firm which views itself as being in the railroad business may, at some stage, find it advantageous to reconsider its position and, like the Canadian Pacific, expand into other areas of transportation or even into quite unrelated fields.

In most cases, the financial officer's responsibility will not encompass the generation of new investment proposals, but will generally be limited to their evaluation. Nevertheless, as part of the top management team, he can make contributions to the formulation of overall policies as well as to improving the flow of ideas throughout the organization.

5-3. ESTIMATING THE CASH FLOWS

Next to the generation of project ideas, the estimation of future cash flows, occasioned by commitment to an investment project, is probably the most important step in the capital-budgeting process. The problem of forecasting cash flows can be divided into two parts: one is concerned with the basic method to be used in isolating the relevant cash flows; and the other deals with the problem of quantifying and analysing the uncertainties which are inherent in any projection. We shall concentrate first of all on the former aspect, leaving the discussion and analysis of uncertainty until the following chapter.

Forecasting cash flows is quite a complex task. Thus, if the investment involved the launching of a new product, forecasts several years into the future would have to be made of the following: expenditures on new production

[3]It is worth noting that under some circumstances it is possible to obtain government support for research and development efforts. Possible sources of funds include the Program for Advancement of Industrial Technology sponsored by the Department of Industry, Trade and Commerce, and programs under the *Industrial Research Development Incentives Act*.

[4]See, for example, D. Quirin, *The Capital Expenditure Decision*, Homewood: Richard D. Irwin, 1967, pp. 16-19.

facilities; sales quantities and product prices; possible effects of the new product on sales of existing lines; additional investments required in working capital; and operating expenditures. Many of these forecasts would have to include estimates of future inflation rates. Where sales involve foreign markets, foreign exchange considerations and costs of protecting against foreign exchange risks may also have to be projected. All of these forecasts then have to be translated into cash flows relating to the proposed investment since it is these flows which determine the attractiveness of the investment to the firm.

The choice of an appropriate time horizon to be considered when evaluating investments which potentially have a long life may become a problem. Consider the case where a firm acquires another company which then becomes one of its divisions.[5] The initial outlay will result in subsequent cash inflows, and these cash inflows may continue indefinitely. Therefore, we have to decide for what period of time forecasted cash flows are to be included in the analysis, recognizing that predictions are likely to become more and more uncertain the further we move into the future.

One approach is to specify a particular cutoff date and to ignore all cash flows beyond that time. While admittedly arbitrary, this approach is frequently implemented in practice because of its operational simplicity. Where future cash flows are discounted across reasonably long timespans (say over 25 years) any errors due to a neglect of cash flows beyond then are likely to be minor, since cash flows discounted over many years have low present values (as will be more fully discussed in the next section).

Alternatively, we could just assume constant annual cash flows beyond a certain point in time, or cash flows growing at some constant rate, conceptually *ad infinitum*, and then deal with the present value of such forecasts.

As can be seen, forecasting cash flows to be generated by an investment project can be a difficult task, requiring sound judgment which potentially hinges on many unproven assumptions. However, even the most sophisticated analytical techniques are dependent upon the quality of the inputs and, regardless of the evaluation criteria used, poor forecasts of cash flows will simply increase the probability that a project's economic worth will be misevaluated. It is not difficult to cite illustrations of companies with very sophisticated managements—for example, various firms in the aerospace industry—which found themselves in severe difficulties either because they were unable to generate new ideas or because their forecasts proved to be quite inaccurate.

In estimating cash flows, we are interested in the *incremental* or marginal effect which the undertaking of a new investment will have on the *total* operations of the firm. If, for example, the installation of a new machine makes the sale of an older model possible, the outflow to be recognized for the investment is a net figure reflecting receipts for the sale. Where a company brings out a new product the sales of which will cut into the market of an existing item, the resultant decrease in existing revenues needs to be recognized in the

[5]Note that acquisitions of other ongoing businesses can be viewed as just another investment which is subject to normal capital-budgeting procedures. Mergers and acquisitions and their institutional settings will be discussed more fully in a separate chapter.

appraisal. Further, when the new product can be produced in part on existing equipment which is idle because of excess capacity, there is then the question of whether the new investment should be charged for using this equipment. The answer hinges on what other opportunities the firm has for making use of the machines, and the concept of *opportunity cost* becomes relevant. Thus, if the firm expected to be back at full production again within two years, the new product should be charged with such future expenditures as might be required to replace "borrowed" capacity. Even if we never expected the machines to be used again, recognition should be given to any residual market value at which they might be sold.

Many of the points discussed in this section are best illustrated through numerical examples. While the problems with solutions at the end of this chapter provide detailed illustrations, the following simplified example will introduce some of the basic concepts.

Example

A firm currently operates a machine which was purchased five years ago. If currently sold, its market value would be $100,000. The machine is expected to last a further five years by which time it will have no salvage value. A new and improved version of the equipment is now on the market at a cost of $130,000, and could replace the old machine. Its expected economic life is five years with an estimated salvage value of zero at the end of that time. Operating costs for the old machine are $15,000 per year, while the new machine would only require operating costs of $9,000 per year. Both machines belong to the same asset class, and capital cost allowance can be taken at a rate of 30 percent on the declining balance. The corporate tax rate is 40 percent. The problem posed is to isolate the net cash flows resulting over the next five years from the new investment, and ultimately to decide whether the anticipated operating savings warrant the initial investment.

Pursuing the above points, we start by establishing the net or marginal investment in the new machine to be $130,000 (cost of new machine) – $100,000 (current market value or trade-in of old machine) = $30,000 (net new investment). If the new machine is acquired, the old one can then be disposed of, reducing the amount of the net new investment).[6]

All costs and benefits over the entire estimated life of the project should be considered on a period-by-period basis including any salvage values or costs at the end of the project's life. In using *discounted cash flow* techniques such as the *net present value* or the *internal rate of return*, both to be discussed below, it is permissible to net the costs and benefits for each period, leaving net cash flows to be worked with. Because of the time value of money, however, netting across time periods must *not* be undertaken. In other words, a $6,000 saving in

[6] The first problem with solution at the end of the chapter provides a more detailed illustration of the determination and use of marginal cash flows.

operating costs three years hence cannot be directly applied against a current cash outflow.

Continuing with the above example, incremental, before-tax operating savings from investment in the new machine are found to be $15,000 – $9,000 = $6,000 per year for years one to five. As will become apparent from our discussion below, it is the net cash flows generated by an investment project which are of primary importance for any economic evaluation. These are not equivalent to incremental net profits or after-tax operating savings, the major difference being noncash charges such as capital cost allowances (CCA) which also have to be considered. Thus, in order to determine the investment's total cash flows, we need to derive the amounts of capital cost allowance to be taken and the resulting tax savings from capital cost allowance claimed in each period.

If the new machine is acquired and the old machine is sold, the resulting changes in the total book value of the *asset class* are as follows

	beginning book value of asset class	BV_{before}
minus:	proceeds from sale of old machine	$100,000
plus:	purchase price of new machine	$130,000
equals:	book value of asset class after transactions	BV_{after}
that is	$BV_{after} = BV_{before} + \$30,000$	

In the *asset-class system* of capital cost allowances, whenever an asset is sold/purchased, its selling/purchase price is generally subtracted/added from the total book value of the asset class, and future capital cost allowances are taken on the new book value for the class.[7] In our example, we add a net $30,000 to the asset class, resulting in additional CCA on this amount. The incremental capital cost allowances resulting from the new investment are detailed below for the first five years.

	Incremental Book Value at Beginning of Year (1)	Capital Cost Allowance* (2) = (1) × 30%	Incremental Book Value at Year End (3) = (1) – (2)
Year 1	30,000	9,000	21,000
2	21,000	6,300	14,700
3	14,700	4,410	10,290
4	10,290	3,087	7,203
5	7,203	2,160	5,042

*As set out in Chapter 3, the maximum claim for *CCA* in year n is $Cd(1-d)^{n-1}$ while the book value at the end of the nth year is $C(1-d)^n$, with C the original value of the asset and d the maximum rate at which *CCA* may be taken.

From this, we can now compute the net cash flows for each year. Given an increase in operating revenue (operating revenue = all revenue – all current

[7]We assume here that there are always enough assets in the class so that a particular sale will not empty the asset class, as otherwise more complicated tax adjustments such as recapture of capital cost allowance may be called for.

operating expenses, excluding taxes and CCA), net after-tax cash flows for each year can be computed in two equivalent ways as follows:

Alternative (1) for computing net cash flows

	Net Operating Revenue
minus	Capital Cost Allowance
	Taxable Income
minus	Tax Payable
	Net Income or Profit
plus	Capital Cost Allowance
	Net Cash Flow

Thus, net cash flows are given by adding noncash charges (CCA) back to net profits.

Alternative (2) for computing net cash flows

	Net Operating Revenue
minus	Tax on Operating Revenue
	After-Tax Operating Revenue
plus	Tax Savings from CCA
	Net Cash Flows

After computing tax on the full amount of operating revenue, we then add back the tax savings available from being able to claim CCA as a tax-deductible expense. This would reduce the firm's tax bill and, consequently, increase its cash flows. The above two methods for computing cash flows are exactly equivalent[8], so that the choice is merely one of computational convenience.

Computing the cash flows for our numerical example using alternative (1), we obtain

	Years				
	1	2	3	4	5
Operating savings or increase in net operating revenue	6,000	6,000	6,000	6,000	6,000
less CCA	9,000	6,300	4,410	3,087	2,160
Taxable income	(3,000)	(300)	1,590	2,913	3,840
less tax payable* (40%)	(1,200)	(120)	636	1,165	1,536
Net income	(1,800)	(180)	954	1,748	2,304
add CCA	9,000	6,300	4,410	3,087	2,160
Net incremental cash flow	7,200	6,120	5,364	4,835	4,464

*A negative taxable income results in tax savings when applied against income from other sources.

[8]Mathematically, this equivalence is easy to show. Let OR be operating revenue NI net income and CF net cash flows. We have $CF = (OR - CCA)(1 - T) + CCA = OR(1 - T) + T \times CCA$.

By resorting to alternative (2), we obtain the same results as follows

	Years				
	1	2	3	4	5
Operating savings or increase in net operating revenue	6,000	6,000	6,000	6,000	6,000
less tax on operating revenue (40%)	2,400	2,400	2,400	2,400	2,400
After-tax operating revenue	3,600	3,600	3,600	3,600	3,600
Add reduction in taxes or tax shield from CCA = 0.4 × CCA	3,600	2,520	1,764	1,235	864
Total net cash flows	7,200	6,120	5,364	4,835	4,464

Note at the end of year 5 we still have a book value of $5,042 which will continue to be written off at 30 percent per annum on a declining balance, conceptually *ad infinitum*. We will deal with this issue below. Thus, our investment project is now characterized as follows

	Years					
	0	1	2	3	4	5
Incremental net cash flows	–$30,000	$7,200	$6,120	$5,364	$4,835	$4,464

Figure 5-1 will further clarify the relationship between profits and cash flows (where profits, net income and earnings are held to be synonymous). It is apparent from the diagram that capital cost allowances are a part of the cash flow available to the firm. In arriving at taxable income, capital cost allowances appear as a deductible expense, hence contributing to a reduction in taxes. It is, however, an expense which is simply an accounting entry with no corresponding cash outflow and needs to be recognized as part of the cash flows generated by the firm through operations. Thus, total cash flows accruing to the firm from an investment are comprised of after-tax operating revenues plus the *tax-shield effects* of capital cost allowances attributable to the investment.

FIGURE 5-1

Relationship Between Cash Flows and Earnings

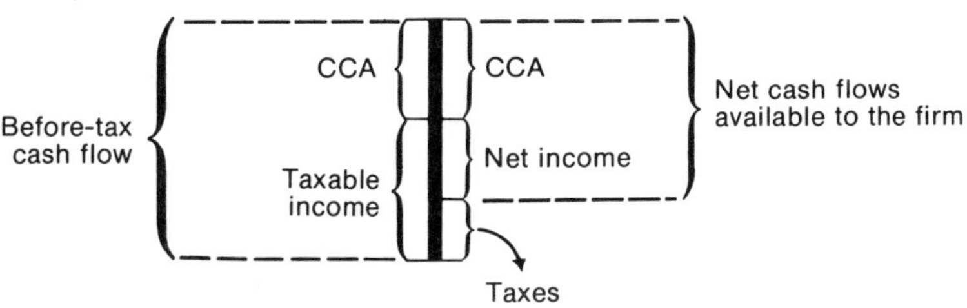

5-4. TAX SHIELDS FROM DECLINING BALANCE CAPITAL COST ALLOWANCE

As noted in Chapter 3, capital cost allowances in Canada are almost always taken as a percentage of the declining balance in an asset class, making the computation of annual cash flows quite cumbersome, particularly since the process may go on to infinity. In our example, capital cost allowances would continue to be taken at a rate of 30 percent per annum on the book value of $5,042 remaining at the end of year 5, resulting in tax savings in subsequent years which cannot be ignored. Fortunately, it is easy to derive a formula for the *total present value* of the tax savings (or tax shield) due to claiming capital cost allowance, which can then be used in the overall evaluation of investment projects. Using the notation and concepts introduced in Chapter 3, recall that we derived the following formulas for declining balance capital cost allowance:

Contributions to *CCA* in year n: $Cd(1-d)^{n-1}$

Tax shield from *CCA* in year n: $Cdt(1-d)^{n-1}$

where C is the starting value of the asset, d is the rate at which *CCA* is taken and t is the corporate tax rate. Given a discount rate k, the present value of the total tax shield from *CCA* claimed over time on an asset is equal to the discounted sum of the individual tax shields for each year, or

$$\frac{Cdt}{(1+k)}+\frac{Cdt(1-d)}{(1+k)^2}+\frac{Cdt(1-d)^2}{(1+k)^3}+\ldots+\frac{Cdt(1-d)^{n-1}}{(1+k)^n}+\ldots$$

$$=Cdt\left[\frac{1}{1+k}+\frac{(1-d)}{(1+k)^2}+\frac{(1-d)^2}{(1+k)^3}+\ldots+\frac{(1-d)^{n-1}}{(1+k)^n}+\ldots\right]$$

Because theoretically, the declining balance approach to depreciation leads to an infinite number of years, the above is a sum of an infinite series. Using the well-known formula for an infinite geometric series[9], it is easy to show that the above sum simplifies to

$$\begin{matrix}\text{Present value of total}\\ \text{tax shield from } CCA\end{matrix} = C\left(\frac{dt}{d+k}\right)$$

Hence, the present value of the tax shield associated with depreciating a capital investment can be found by using the above formulation in the analysis of capital-expenditure decisions, obviating the need for computing separate tax shields for each year throughout the life of a project.

Applying this formula to our example and assuming a discount rate or time value of money of 10 percent, the present value of the total tax shield from taking *CCA*, theoretically *ad infinitum*, becomes

$$\$30{,}000\left(\frac{0.3\times 0.4}{0.3+0.1}\right)=\$9{,}000$$

[9]The formula for the infinite geometric series is $1+x+x^2+\ldots=1/(1-x)$. Setting $x=(1-d)/(1+k)$, we have $\frac{Cdt}{(1+k)}(1+x+x^2+\ldots)=\frac{Cdt}{1+k}\times\frac{1}{1-(1-d)/(1+k)}$ which simplifies to $Cdt/(d+k)$.

To conclude the example, and in anticipation of our subsequent discussion on discounted cash flow analysis, we are now in a position to compute the total present value of all relevant cash flows associated with the investment. In order to integrate use of the formula with the computation, we derive cash flows by taking the present value of after-tax operating revenues and adding the present value of the tax shield from *CCA*, along lines discussed above in Alternative (2) for computing cash flows. The total present value for all cash flows generated by the investment becomes

Total present value = – initial investment
+ present value of all after-tax operating savings
+ present value of total tax shield from *CCA*
= – \$30,000 + \$3,600 × $a_5 10\%$ + \$9,000
= – \$30,000 + \$3,600 × 3.791 + \$9,000
= – \$7,352.40

If in our example we had assumed a salvage value of S_n = \$20,000 for the new machine at the end of year 5, this could easily have been incorporated in the above formulation. Generally, we saw that if an asset is sold at the end of *n* years for a salvage value of S_n, this salvage value is deducted from the aggregate book value of the asset class at the time of disposition, reducing the capital cost allowances for subsequent years.[10] Thus, at the time of salvage a total tax shield with a present value, computed at the end of year *n*, of $S_n\left(\frac{dt}{d+k}\right)$ is lost, which, if brought back to the present, amounts to

$$\text{present value of tax shield lost from salvage} = \frac{S_n}{(1+k)^n}\left(\frac{dt}{d+k}\right)$$

Applying this to our example, the effect of a salvage value would be as follows:

Total present value = previous total present value
+ present value of inflow from salvage
– present value of tax shield lost from salvage

$$= -\$7{,}352.40 + \frac{\$20{,}000}{(1+0.1)^5} - \frac{\$20{,}000}{(1+0.1)^5}\left(\frac{0.3\times 0.4}{0.3+0.1}\right)$$

= – \$7,352.40 + \$12,420 – \$3,726
= \$1,341.60

Table 5-4 summarizes the formulas used to derive the above results. Problems with solutions at the end of this chapter provide further illustrations pertaining to the derivation of cash flows; tax shields from capital cost allowance; and present values for evaluating investment projects.

[10]As noted earlier, this assumes that other assets are in the asset class with an aggregate book value exceeding S_n. If no other assets are in the class, or if the salvage value exceeds the aggregate book value of the asset class, the tax treatment is more complicated as recapture of capital cost allowance and capital gains or capital losses may have to be recognized, as outlined in Chapter 3.

TABLE 5-4

Summary of Formulas for Present Value of Total Cash Flows from an Investment where Capital Cost Allowance is taken on a Declining Balance by Asset Class

Notation:

C = net initial investment
R_j = contributions to operating revenue (before tax) in year j
S_n = salvage value of asset realized at end of year n
t = corporate tax rate
k = discount rate or time value of money
d = maximum rate for capital cost allowance
n = total life of the investment

Present value of all cash flows with no salvage value

$$PV = -C + \sum_{j=1}^{n} \frac{R_j(1-t)}{(1+k)^j} + C\left(\frac{dt}{d+k}\right)$$

Present value of all cash flows, with salvage value S_n.

$$PV = -C + \sum_{j=1}^{n} \frac{R_j(1-t)}{(1+k)^j} + C\left(\frac{dt}{d+k}\right) + \frac{S_n}{(1+k)^n}\left[1 - \frac{dt}{d+k}\right]$$

5-5. CASH FLOWS vs. EARNINGS AS A BASIS FOR INVESTMENT EVALUATION

Because the approach of working with cash flows is often misunderstood, it may be helpful to discuss more fully the reasons for its use in evaluating investments. As we have seen, a period's net cash inflows generated by an investment can be split into two components: one being depreciation and reflecting the somewhat discretionary recovery over time of the original amounts invested; and the remainder representing cash flows in excess of depreciation termed net income or profit after taxes. It would clearly be inappropriate to accept a project only if the present value of profits were in excess of the original investment since depreciation has already been taken to recover the original investment, and profits are really amounts in excess of what is needed to recoup the funds invested. On the other hand, it would also be unreasonable to equate the initial investment with subsequent depreciation charges and to conclude that a project yielding a positive present value of profits alone will automatically be acceptable. Depreciation charges accumulate throughout the life of the project and, because of the time value of money, their present value cannot equal the original amount invested. Some portion of profits must, therefore, make up for this deficiency, ruling out the simple division of cash flows along lines suitable for accounting purposes.

The best alternative is to include original investment, depreciation charges, and profits in the evaluation, and to consider net cash flows as the relevant input on which to base an economic analysis.

Example

Consider an investment of $100,000, depreciated for illustrative purposes on a straight-line basis over 5 years. The expectation is that operating revenues of $30,000 per year will be generated in years 1 through 5. With taxes at 40 percent, we have:

Operating revenues	$30,000
less depreciation	(20,000)
Taxable income	$10,000
less taxes payable	(4,000)
Net profit	$ 6,000
add depreciation	20,000
Net Cash Flow	$26,000

It would be inappropriate to contrast the initial investment of $100,000 with subsequent annual profits of $6,000 over the next 5 years, concluding that profits of $30,000 do not make up for an initial investment of $100,000. These profits are cash flows *in excess* of depreciation, with $20,000 of additional cash flows per year actually being taken in by the firm and contributing to the recovery of the original investment.

On the other hand, it would also be inappropriate to conclude that the investment is acceptable simply because profits in excess of depreciation are projected. The initial investment of $100,000 has to take place immediately while cash inflows represented by depreciation accrue over the next several years. Thus, while the aggregate amount of depreciation (5 × $20,000 = $100,000) equals the initial outlay, given the time value of money, its present value will not. If, for example, the appropriate discount rate is 12 percent, the present value of $20,000 a year for 5 years is 20,000 × 3.605 = $72,100, and falls short by $27,900 in making up for the initial investment.

It must be concluded that net incremental cash flows, in this instance $26,000 a year for five years viewed against the initial $100,000 investment, form the only valid basis for sound evaluation of investment projects.

One last point to be raised in the context of estimating future cash flows for investments concerns provision for price-level changes over time. In an environment characterized by inflation, it is important to decide whether future cash flows should be estimated in constant current dollars (*i.e.*, ignoring inflationary increases), or in dollar figures which are likely to prevail in the future in full consideration of anticipated inflation. In order not to unduly complicate our discussion, we will ignore for the time being price level changes and assume constant costs and prices over the life of investment projects. The issue of inflation and how to adjust cash flows for price level changes will be discussed separately in section 5-9 after some of the basic concepts of investment evaluation have been covered.

5-6. INTANGIBLES AND EXTERNAL EFFECTS

Those benefits expected from an investment which are difficult to quantify in dollars are often referred to as *intangibles*. Rather than trying to provide for them in the cash flow computations, they are frequently just noted at the end of an investment proposal.[11] Examples of intangible benefits would include more timely and accurate reporting based on a new computer application; improvement in employee morale stemming from new office surroundings; or increased customer goodwill as a consequence of shorter delivery times following additional investments in the distribution system. It can be very difficult to express some of these items numerically and any figures are likely to be very rough estimates indeed.

However, to decide between competing alternatives, a tradeoff involving such benefits and straight dollar items will have to be made—either explicitly or implicitly. The real issue is not whether or not the tradeoff should be made, as it cannot really be avoided, but rather who should make it. It could be the analyst drawing up the proposal or, at the other extreme, the final granting authority within the firm. No standard answers can be offered as it will depend on the importance of the decision as well as on how knowledgeable various levels of management might be, and on their willingness to delegate. When, however, investment recommendations involve significant consideration of intangibles, this should generally be interpreted as signalling the need for careful investigation, because even the crudest approximation of how the intangibles may translate themselves into dollars is frequently better than no estimate at all.[12] For instance, a good number of firms have acquired sophisticated computers largely on the basis of vaguely defined intangibles and have subsequently failed to attain anything approaching the economic benefits projected.[13]

External effects are the costs, benefits, or both, which accrue to units outside the firm and which will not therefore be reflected in the firm's financial statements.[14] Such externalities include recreational benefits of mining or logging roads which accrue to the general public; the costs of pollution which are generally not fully borne by the polluters; and the likes. As far as external benefits go, there is little debate; they will generally be excluded from the firm's project evaluation process as the investment has to be justified based on benefits accruing to the investor.

A more difficult issue is how, for example, the costs of pollution, which are largely shifted to the community at large, should be accounted for in evaluating construction of a new smelter or pulp mill. It can be argued that in a competitive industry with limited profit margins, a firm cannot afford to go beyond such basic requirements as are imposed on all competitors, for to do so could seriously jeopardize its own ability to compete. This then suggests that it is the role of government to impose regulations which are binding on all concerned. Carrying the argument one step further, in markets which are competitive internationally, multinational cooperation may be called for to ensure both adequate and reasonably uniform regulation.

[11]See, for example, The Conference Board, *Managing Capital Expenditures*. New York: National Industrial Conference Board, 1963, p. 17.

[12]See, for example, E. Joslin, *Computer Selection*, Reading, Mass.: Addison Wesley, 1968, Ch 2.

[13]D. Sanders, *Computers in Business*, New York: McGraw-Hill, 1965, pp. 253-254 and also McKinsey & Company, *Unlocking the Computer's Profit Potential*, New York, 1968.

[14]See, for example, D. Quirin, *op. cit.*, pp. 71-79, on which the following discussion draws, as well as W. Baumol, *Business Behavior, Value and Growth*, New York: Macmillan, 1959, Ch. 6-8.

The situation may be quite different when one focuses upon corporations with significant market powers or, more particularly, on monopolies. It can be argued that public utilities and certain domestic air carriers, for instance, should include some consideration of external costs into their analyses of investment projects in order to ensure that such projects are in the best interests of society at large.

5-7. EVALUATION CRITERIA

With forecasts of an investment's incremental cash flows given,[15] the next step in the capital-budgeting process involves their input into selection criteria in order to reach an accept-or-reject decision. Several different measures of investment worth are used in industry and have been discussed in financial literature, the most important ones being the *payback period*, the *average rate of return*, the *net present value*, and the *internal rate of return*. Each of these will be looked at in turn.

Payback

A useful point of departure for any discussion of investment criteria is the *payback* concept, a technique particularly popular with business executives,[16] but dismissed as misleading by most academic writers.

Payback simply measures the time required for the expected after-tax cash inflows to equal the original cash outlay.

Basic project rankings and accept-or-reject decisions are made on the basis of the quicker paybacks being preferred. In some cases, a maximum allowable payback period is set, beyond which projects are deemed unacceptable.

As a measure of investment worth, payback has at least two major weaknesses. First, it ignores the timing of proceeds prior to the payback period and, secondly, it ignores inflows projected to follow the payback period.

Example

Assume two mutually exclusive projects *A* and *B*, a three-year payback requirement, and the following expected after-tax cash flows:

Project A

Time period (years)	t_0	t_1	t_2	t_3	t_4
Initial after-tax cash outlay	\$400				
After-tax cash inflows		\$100	\$100	\$200	\$200

Project B

Time period (years)	t_0	t_1	t_2	t_3	t_4
Initial after-tax cash outlay	\$400				
After-tax cash inflows		\$200	\$100	\$100	\$500

Both opportunites afford a three-year payback and hence appear equivalent. The extreme nature of the example makes it obvious, however, that *B* is superior to *A*, not only because it generates larger inflows in the year following the

[15]For ease of exposition we continue for the moment to exclude direct consideration of uncertainty.

[16]See *e.g.*, C.G. Hoskins and M.J. Dunn, "The Economic Evaluation of Capital Expenditure Proposals under Uncertainty: The Practice of Large Corporations in Canada", *Journal of Business Administration*, Fall 1974, pp. 44-55.

payback limit ($500 vs. $200 in t_4), but also because during the payback period the larger $200 flow is generated earlier.

It should also be pointed out that the choice of what payback period is deemed to be acceptable is arbitrary, as there is no rational basis of deciding which cutoff period is appropriate.

Before dismissing payback as a meaningless computation which owes its popularity largely to its simplicity in application, it is well to consider the thrust of a paper by Weingartner.[17] He contends that the payback criterion should not be viewed solely as a measure of return, but rather as a tool for evaluating risk. It provides the manager with an indication of the time period during which he is exposed to the risk of not recovering his original investment and, in trying to limit his risk of exposure, the manager may set a payback constraint. He may specify, for example, that no project with a payback period extending beyond five years will be accepted. If used as a constraint, however, additional criteria will have to be relied on for choosing between those competing projects which satisfy the constraint.

Suppose two mutually exclusive projects each have a payback period of four years based on estimated cash flows. Additional measures of economic desirability will have to be applied before a valid choice can be made. Furthermore, based on best estimates of cash flows, both projects may have an expected payback period of four years yet the projected cash flows which were used in deriving these payback estimates could be subject to different degrees of uncertainty.

In summary, the payback criterion is widely used in practice as a quick and readily applicable rule of thumb. In identifying the time it should take to recoup the original investment, it may provide a rough indication about the economic desirability of a project. Like most rules of thumb, however, it has failings which can result in faulty conclusions and, therefore, it must be used with caution.

Average rate of return

The *average* or *simple accounting rate of return* technique is a straightforward criterion. During the late fifties it was used as a primary measure of investment worth by about one-half of the larger corporations in the United States. Since then, however, its use has declined significantly both in the United States and Canada.[18] It is discussed here not because we recommend its usage, but because it may still be encountered in business practice.

The average rate of return (ARR), measured in percent, is computed as follows:

$$\text{ARR} = \frac{\text{average annual profits after tax}}{\text{average book value of investment over life of project}} \times 100\%$$

[17]M. Weingartner, "Some New Views on the Payback Period and Capital Budgeting Decisions", *Management Science*, August 1969, pp. B-594 to B-607.

[18]T. Klammer, "Empirical Evidence of the Adoption of Sophisticated Capital Budgeting Techniques", *Journal of Business*, July 1972, pp. 387-397, and also C.G. Hoskins and M.J. Dunn, *op. cit.*, pp. 48-49. Hoskins and Dunn found that the use of simple, nondiscounted techniques has remained fairly constant, but that most large firms now use more sophisticated techniques based on discounted cash flows as well and collaterally, so that the importance of techniques such as the ARR for decision-making has declined.

Straight-line depreciation is generally assumed in arriving at the denominator but variations are possible. Projects can be ranked according to their average rates of return with higher rates preferred while, to qualify as an acceptable investment, the project's ARR must exceed some figure set by management as the hurdle rate.

Example

An investment of $3,000 generates profits after taxes of $1,500, $1,000, and $500 in each of the next three years, after which it has no residual value. The original investment of $3,000 is assumed to be depreciated on a straight-line basis over the project's three-year life as follows:

Year	1	2	3	4
Book value at beginning of year	$3,000	$2,000	$1,000	$0

With straight-line depreciation, the average book value over the life of the investment becomes

$$\text{Average book value} = \frac{\text{Beginning book value} - \text{Ending book value}}{2}$$

$$= \frac{\$3{,}000 - \$0}{2} = \$1500$$

and it is this $1,500 base against which the accounting rate of return is computed. The rationale for this approach stems from looking at an investment strictly from the accounting point of view, and equating book values with amounts invested.

Average annual profits are computed next and, with a useful project life of n years we derive

$$\text{Average annual profits} = \frac{\text{sum of all profits over project's life}}{n}$$

$$= \frac{\$1500 + \$1000 + \$500}{3} = \$1000$$

We then compute the accounting rate of return as

$$\text{ARR} = \frac{\$1000}{\$1500} \times 100\% = 66^2/_3\%$$

This percentage supposedly measures the average annual profit made on the average book value of the investment.

Apart from the fact that the method can be grasped very quickly and uses standard accounting concepts, there is little to be said in its favor. As with the payback period, there is no rational way to decide what an appropriate cutoff rate for the firm would be. Furthermore, the average rate of return ignores timing of the proceeds and is unable to distinguish between average annual profits of $1,000 made up of individual profits of $500, $1,000, and $1,500, or $1,500, $1,000, and $500 in each of three succeeding years. It is based on accounting income and book values rather than on cash flows, the direct consequences of which have already been reviewed. The fallacy is readily apparent, however, from the following brief illustration.

Example

Consider an initial investment of $1,000 generating net cash inflows of $0 and $1,200 in years 1 and 2; in other words, the initial cash outflow of $1,000 results in a cash inflow of $1,200 at the end of two years. By assuming no salvage value and using straight-line depreciation, we have

Year	0	1	2
Net cash flow	–$1000	$0	+$1200
Depreciation of original investment	0	$500	$500
Net profits (cash flows – depreciation)	0	–$500	$700

with net profits simply being cash flows minus depreciation. The accounting rate of return is then computed as

$$\text{ARR} = \frac{(-500 + 700)/2}{(1000 + 0)/2} \times 100\% = \frac{100}{500} \times 100\% = 20\%$$

It is misleading to construe the $200 gain over a *two-year* period as a 20 percent average annual rate of return on investment. It can, in fact, be shown that the accounting rate of return overstates the true return on a project as measured, for example, by the *internal rate of return* discussed below.[19]

Discounted cash flow criteria

This comprises the next two criteria to be discussed — the *net present value* and the *internal rate of return* — which give explicit consideration to the *time value of money*, incorporated through the discounting of cash flows generating from investment projects. Thus, it is recognized that with the existence of interest, money has a time value, and identical sums received in various time periods are not equivalent. Cash received today can be reinvested to earn a return and, hence, is more valuable than the same amount received sometime in the future. If the value of the firm as reflected in its share prices is to be maximized, this time value needs to be recognized. Investors can earn interest on funds invested otherwise, and a firm which does not recognize this opportunity cost of funds provided to the firm by its shareholders does not act in their best economic interest. While differences can be shown to exist between the various discounted cash-flow criteria presented in this section it is probably fair to say that these differences are seldom significant. A consistent application of any of the discounted cash-flow techniques will, in most practical situations, suggest identical decisions. It is well to note that the use of discounted cash-flow criteria has increased significantly over the last decade. Hoskins and Dunn report in their study covering large Canadian corporations that by 1972, 79 percent of the firms surveyed used evaluation criteria based on discounted cash flows, as compared to only 35 percent in 1962.[20]

[19]See M. Gordon, "The Payoff Period in the Rate of Profit, reprinted in E. Solomon (ed.), *The Management of Corporate Capital*, New York, The Free Press, 1959, pp. 48-55.
[20]See C.G. Hoskins and M.J. Dunn, *op. cit.*, p. 48.

Net present value

The net present value is defined as the sum of all future cash flows generated by a project, but with each cash flow discounted back to the present. The discount rate used reflects the value of money to the firm and is generally given by the firm's cost of capital.

The concept of the firm's overall or *weighted average cost of capital* is developed in Chapter 13, and at this stage will be taken as given.[21] Briefly, it represents the annual percentage cost at which the firm can raise new monies. A firm raises these monies from various sources, either internally through retained earnings and depreciation, or externally by issuing additional common shares or debt obligations. The overall cost of capital is simply the average cost from these various sources.

The rationale for the net present value approach stems from the view that an investment has to earn at least the equivalent of costs incurred by the firm, including costs of funds provided to finance the investment. The net present value itself indicates the excess or shortfall of cash flows in present value terms, once financing charges are met. Hence, a positive net present value indicates that a project is acceptable, contributing cash flows to the firm in excess of the cost required to finance it. In equation form, the net present value is expressed as

$$NPV = \sum_{t=0}^{n} \frac{C_t}{(1+k)^t}$$

where C_t is the net after-tax cash flow (inflows minus outflows) in period t, and is positive for net inflows and negative for net outflows,

k is the discount rate applied per period, representing the time value of money to the firm after taxes, and

n is the number of periods comprising the expected life of the investment.

Example

Consider a project requiring an initial investment of \$10,000 and generating net cash inflows of \$4,000, \$5,000, and \$6,000 assumed to occur at the end of the first, second, and third years respectively.[22] Given a cost of capital of $k = 0.1$ or 10 percent, we obtain

Year	Cash Flows (1)	Present Value Factors (2)	Present Value of Cash Flows (3) = (1) × (2)
0	-\$10,000	1.000	-\$10,000
1	4,000	0.909	3,636
2	5,000	0.826	4,130
3	6,000	0.751	4,506
		Net Present Value	\$ 2,272

[21]Although in the interest of simplicity we generally assume the discount rate to be constant over time, it has been recognized that the rate may be a function of time, varying from one period to another. See, A. Robichek and S. Myers, *Optimal Financing Decisions*, Englewood Cliffs: Prentice-Hall, 1965, p. 10.

[22]In the previous chapter covering the mathematics of finance, the possibility of discounting on a quarterly, monthly, or even continuous basis was noted. Annual discounting is, however, generally applied in capital budgeting and will in most instances yield sufficiently accurate results.

Expressed more formally,

$$NPV = -10{,}000 + \frac{4{,}000}{(1+0.1)} + \frac{5{,}000}{(1+0.1)^2} + \frac{6{,}000}{(1+0.1)^3}$$

$$= 2{,}272.$$

Note that Table 5-4 already introduced the formulas for the net present values of cash flows generated by investments where capital cost allowances are taken on a declining balance by asset class.

The economic interpretation of this net present value is that the project is expected to generate a gain of $2,272 over and above financing charges of 10 percent on the unrecovered portion of the investment. Specifically, if the initial $10,000 along with a return of 10 percent on any outstanding balance, was to be repaid from cash flows subsequently generated, we would have

Year (1)	Principal Outstanding at Beginning of Year (2)	Interest on Principal Outstanding (3)=10%×(2)	Amount of Inflow (4)	Repay-ment of Principal (5)=(4)−(3)	Principal Outstanding at Year End (6)=(2)−(5)
1	$10,000	$1,000	$4,000	$3,000	$7,000
2	7,000	700	5,000	4,300	2,700
3	2,700	270	6,000	2,700*	0

*This leaves an additional amount of $3,030 in year 3.

Thus, one can recover the initial investment plus 10 percent on unrecovered principal and in the third year, given the $6,000 inflow, be left with a gain of $6,000 − ($2,700 + $270) = $3,030. The present value of this gain is $3,030/(1 + 0.1)^3 = $3,030 × 0.751 = $2,275, which is the net present value of the project as computed earlier. (The small difference between the two figures is due to rounding.)

Computation of the net present value and the internal rate of return for the numerical example used in the earlier section 5-3 on cash flows is provided as a problem with solution at the end of this chapter. Other problems with solutions provide further illustrations of applying discounted cash flow criteria.

The internal rate of return

The *internal rate of return* is, by definition, the rate of discount which, when applied to the cash flows of an investment, will yield a net present value of zero. Arithmetically, it is the discount rate i which satisfies the equation

$$\sum_{t=0}^{n} \frac{C_t}{(1+i)^t} = 0$$

with the notation as defined earlier for use with the net present value.

To illustrate derivation of the internal rate of return, we first consider what is termed the *net present value profile* of an investment. It shows net present value as a function of the discount rate.

Example

Consider once again our earlier example which called for an initial investment of $10,000, and was expected to generate net cash inflows of $4,000, $5,000 and $6,000 in years one to three respectively. It is possible to compute the net present value for various levels of discount rate as follows:

		Present Value Factors at Discount Rate			
Year	Cash Flow	0%	10%	20%	28%
0	-10,000	1	1	1	1
1	4,000	1	0.909	0.833	0.781
2	5,000	1	0.826	0.694	0.610
3	6,000	1	0.751	0.579	0.477
Net Present Values		$5,000	$2,272	$ 276	-$ 964

This net present value profile is pictured graphically in Figure 5-2.

FIGURE 5-2

Net Present Value Profile Showing
Net Present Value as a Function of the Discount Rate

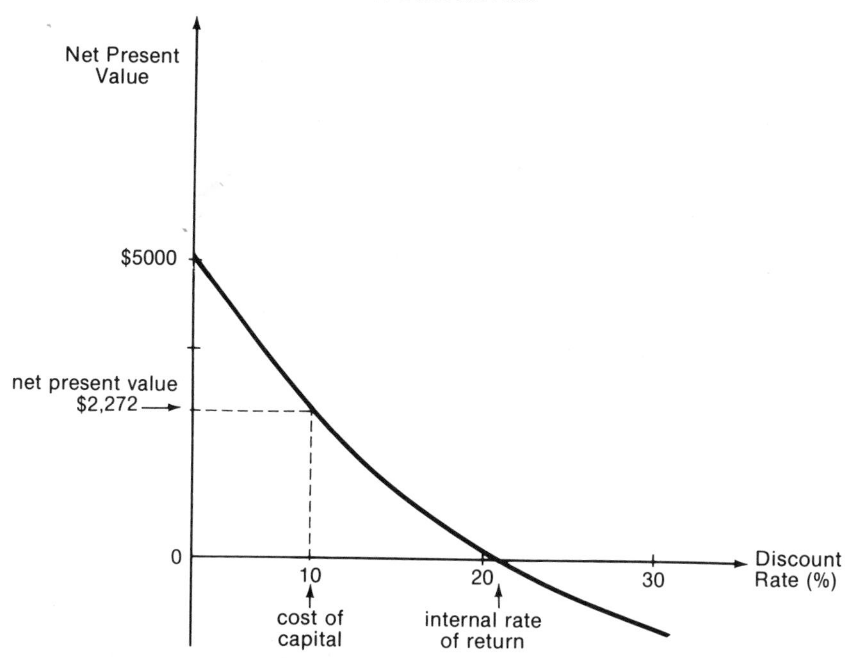

It is easy to see that the shape of the profile is similar for all investments which involve an initial outlay and subsequent inflows. The initial outlay at time zero is unaffected by discounting, while the present value of future cash inflows decreases as the discount rate rises. It follows, therefore, that the present value of a project decreases as one increases the discount rate. Assuming that the cash flows are such that we start with a positive net present value at a discount rate of zero (in other words that the total undiscounted cash inflows exceed the initial outflows) then by increasing the discount rate we decrease the net present value until, at some stage, the net present value passes through zero and becomes negative. In our example, we find the internal rate of return to be roughly 22 percent (the point at which the net present value profile crosses the horizontal axis in Figure 5-2).[23]

Computationally, the exact derivation of i would require solution of the above equation setting the present value of cash flows equal to zero, which is a polynomial of nth degree. Since, as shown in Figure 5-2, the net present value is generally a steadily decreasing function of the discount rate, that is, the larger the discount rate the smaller the net present value derived, it is in most instances relatively easy to arrive at least at an approximate solution. It can be found either by trial and error and interpolation, as outlined above, or through the use of one of the many standard computer packages available. If the former approach is used, we start by simply choosing any reasonable discount rate and compute the net present value. If the net present value is positive, the discount rate for the next calculation should be increased as the flows must be further reduced, or *vice versa*. The process is repeated until we find a discount rate for which the net present value is close to zero. With some experience at straddling the actual internal rate of return and then working toward it by interpolating, its identification is generally possible after only a few trials.

The reader may have noticed a similarity between the internal rate of return and the effective yield (for example on bonds) as discussed in Chapter 4. The internal rate of return is, in fact, the effective yield of the investment given by the subsequent cash flows.

In evaluating investment projects, a *hurdle rate* is usually established to identify the minimum return which projects must generate to be acceptable, and larger internal rates of return are favored. Generally, the hurdle rate is deemed to be the firm's weighted average cost of capital.

A project yielding more than the costs incurred to finance it will make a positive contribution to the firm and hence should be accepted. In interpreting the economic meaning of the internal rate of return, it must be appreciated that this rate is the effective yield to be earned over time on the *unrecovered* portion of the investment, that is, on any portion of the initial investment still tied up in the project.

[23] Interpolating between a discount rate of 20% and 28%, from the above we obtain

$$\left[\begin{array}{ll} \left[\begin{array}{l} 20\% \\ x\% \end{array}\right. & \left.\begin{array}{r} \$276 \\ \$0 \end{array}\right] \\ 28\% & -\$964 \end{array}\right] \quad \text{giving} \quad \frac{276-0}{276-(-964)} = \frac{20-x}{20-28}$$

from which we compute $x = 21.8$ percent.

Example

This can be illustrated by once again using the above numerical example.

Year (1)	Investment outstanding at beginning of year (2)	Cash inflow (3)	22% return on outstanding investment (4)=22%×(2)	Reduction in outstanding investment (5)=(3)–(4)	Investment outstanding at year end (6)=(2)–(5)
1	10,000	4,000	2,200	1,800	8,200
2	8,200	5,000	1,804	3,196	5,004
3	5,004	6,000	1,101	4,899	105*

*The figure of $105 remaining at the end of the third year is due to rounding of both the internal rate of return and the individual cash flows.

The total net cash inflows in each period (column 3) can be thought of as being made up of (i) a 22 percent return on the outstanding investment (column 4), and (ii) some recovery of the original investment (column 5). Thus, of the $4,000 flowing in during the first year, $2,200 can be viewed as a 22 percent return on the original $10,000 investment and the balance of $1,800 as a reduction in the outstanding investment, leaving it at $8,200. Following the procedure through, it is shown that future cash inflows over the life of the project provide for the full recovery of the amount originally invested, plus a return of 22 percent on any funds tied up in the project.

Referring back to Figure 5-2, it is easy to appreciate that generally the net present value and the internal rate of return will yield equivalent results. If for a desirable project the net present value is positive, using as a discount rate the cost of capital, this normally implies that at the same time the internal rate of return has to be larger than the cost of capital. The two techniques may be viewed as two equivalent ways of looking at the same problem.

In one case (net present value), we discount at the cost of capital, and look for the total benefit to be achieved after meeting the cost of funds invested.

In the other case (internal rate of return), we insure that the effective yield of the project exceeds the cost of capital.

Conflicts between these two criteria can only occur in special cases. In order to keep the basic concepts as clear and as simple as possible, cases where such conflicts may arise will not be pursued here, but dealt with in a separate section at the end of this chapter.

5-8. LIMITATIONS OF DISCOUNTED CASH FLOW METHODS IN INVESTMENT EVALUATION

In spite of the apparent strengths of discounted cash flow approaches to investment evaluation, we should not lose sight of several limitations. Discounted cash flow criteria provide measures of economic worth, but inasmuch as a firm has objectives of a nonmonetary nature, these will not be reflected in the methods described above. The issue of economic versus other objectives is particularly important in the public sector. In the context of corporate finance, it has been discussed in Chapter 1 and need not be repeated here.

While it may be more difficult for a widely held public corporation to justify extensive *nonmonetary objectives*, it is certainly the prerogative of the owner-manager to have almost any goals he chooses. Thus, he may well build a new warehouse using the very best materials if the resultant attractive appearance gives him satisfaction and pride of ownership, and he may do so even if it is evident that a shack of corrugated sheet-iron would yield a higher net present value. In such circumstances, however, discounted cash flow techniques might still prove useful in that they would indicate what costs are being incurred in pursuing nonmonetary goals.

Another objection which is frequently raised rests on the possible discrepancy between cash flows as used in the techniques described, and earnings reported in the firm's financial statements.[24] Thus, it is perfectly possible for a project which is favorable according to a discounted cash flow analysis to have negative effects on reportable earnings in the initial periods, either because of heavy startup expenses, or significant depreciation charges, or both. In a world of perfect information and rational investors, this would not be disturbing because investors would accept the early decline in earnings recognizing that they would be adequately compensated through favorable cash flows and earnings in later periods. In a realistic environment of imperfect information and sometimes irrational investors, however, where any decline in reported earnings per share is often interpreted as a sign of weakness, management's concern about the immediate effect of their decisions on the firm's published financial statements is understandable.

While this does not deny the importance of discounted cash flow analysis in capital budgeting, it does suggest that management may need additional information for a complete evaluation. The effect of capital budgeting decisions on cash budgets, projected future balance sheets and income statements may be of particular importance.

In the past, this information was often difficult to obtain. The drafting of financial statement forecasts was time-consuming and expensive and, hence, when used at all, only a limited number of new investment alternatives were evaluated. With the advent and increasing usage of computers the situation has changed.[25] *Computer-based financial models* can readily provide future financial statements based on management's forecasts of business operations such as sales, production costs, new investments and the likes. For example, by feeding the computer with the operational changes introduced following acceptance of certain investment proposals, we can easily obtain projected financial statements for several periods into the future which both reflect these changes and

[24]See, for example, S. Henrici, "Eyeing the ROI", *Harvard Business Review*, May-June, 1968, pp. 83-97, and also E. Lerner, and A. Rappaport, "Limit DCF in Capital Budgeting", *Harvard Business Review*, September-October, 1968, pp. 133-139.

[25]A detailed description of a corporate financial model is given in G. Gershefski, "Building a Corporate Financial Model", *Harvard Business Review*, July-August, 1969, pp. 61-72. See also G. Dickson, J. Mauriel, and C. Anderson, "Computer Assisted Planning Models, A Functional Analysis", in A. Schrieber (ed.) *Corporate Simulation Models*, Seattle, University of Washington, 1970, pp. 26-42.

show the effect of the investment decision on the balance sheets and income statements. Furthermore, once a model has been built, each computer run is relatively inexpensive, making possible a detailed evaluation of many alternative forecasts and assumptions at little cost or delay. Corporate models of this type are gaining rapid acceptance by industry, both in the United States and Canada,[26] and provide management with much additional insight and information, thereby complementing the traditional methods of discounted cash-flow analysis.

In recognizing the time value of money, we have seen that discounted cash-flow methods place relatively heavier emphasis on early results and, at normal discount rates, the impact of long-term costs or benefits which accrue, for example, fifty years hence will become almost negligible. While the approach has its justification in corporate finance, care should be taken to recognize possible limitations when dealing with decisions made by governments, including Crown corporations. It is beyond the scope of this text to review the extensive discussion in the literature as to what discount rate, if any, would be appropriate for decisions in the public sector.[27] It should be pointed out, however, that discounted cash-flow analysis has limitations in this context. It may be difficult, for example, to justify conservation of natural resources, replanting of trees, strong antipollution legislation, investments in education, or even basic research, with discounted cash-flow type evaluations and discount rates as they may be appropriate in a competitive industrial setting. The consequences evolving from such investments will rest with future generations many years hence. On the other hand, some of the negative side effects of our advancing technology now being experienced were perhaps viewed as very distant when various developments were initiated and were, therefore, ignored. Since we know that the future lies around the corner, it is essential to appreciate that many costs of short-sighted decisions will become very real and have to be faced by others. The growing public concern about such issues including specific consideration of nonmonetary objectives is, therefore, understandable. Where longer-term decisions and policies are involved, limitations of techniques which by their nature heavily favor the short run should be understood.

5-9. DISCOUNTED CASH FLOW ANALYSIS AND INFLATION

Given the current inflationary environment it becomes important to establish whether projected cash flows for new investments should reflect fully the anticipated price-level changes, or whether such forecasts should be made in constant current dollars. We noted earlier that both the discount rate applied to future cash flows to derive their present value, and the hurdle rate used in internal rate of return evaluations, typically reflect the costs at which a firm can raise new funds in the capital markets. New investments are expected to yield

[26]For a survey of the use of corporate models by industry, see G. Gershefski, "Corporate Models—The State of the Art", in A. Schrieber, *op. cit.*, pp. 43-70.

[27]For a general introduction to the issue of the cost of capital in the public sector see, for example, D. Quirin, *op. cit.*, Ch. 7. A more rigorous discourse is to be found in P. Dasgupta, A. Sen, and S. Marglin, *Guidelines for Project Evaluation*, New York: United Nations, 1972, Ch. 13.

returns which will cover the costs of funds used in their financing.

The cost of raising funds in capital markets (which will be discussed in detail in subsequent chapters) does reflect the inflation expectations held by investors. If, for example, inflation is expected to run at 10 percent per annum, it would be difficult to find investors willing to make funds available at an interest rate of, say, 5 percent per annum, as even on a before-tax basis the real return to the supplier of funds would be negative. Thus, the cost of raising funds tends to parallel the inflation rate, as investors strive for a real return over and above the rate of general price level changes.

In order to be consistent, and given that the discount rate to be applied fully reflects inflationary expectations, projected cash flows should reflect anticipated price-level changes as well.

Example

> Assume that the inflation rate has gone to 50 percent per year (as in some Latin American countries, for example) with the result that the cost of new capital to the firm is above that figure, say at 55 percent. If a discount rate of 55 percent is applied to future cash flows which are based on constant costs and prices, very few feasible investments would remain as they would have to provide *real* returns of at least 55 percent per year.

Many firms still fail to incorporate specific forecasts of price-level changes into their capital-budgeting procedures and, while this may have been defensible when inflation rates were low, the double-digit figures experienced recently may result in significant distortions. Consider, for example, an investment in reforestation, with a harvest cycle of 80 years. If a 10 percent average inflation rate for the cost of lumber is applied over this time period, every \$1,000 in current prices would become $\$1,000(1 + 0.1)^{80} = \$2,048,400$ in prices 80 years hence—hardly a negligible effect to be ignored for reasons of convenience or ease of computation.

It should also be noted that price-level changes for different goods and services in the economy may be subject to quite different rates, which may not coincide with any average inflation rate as measured, for example, by the consumer price index. Different rates may have to be applied to such different components of cash flows as labor costs, raw material costs, or prices of goods sold. As a matter of fact, one of the thrusts for automation has been that labor costs were viewed as subject to more rapid increases than other cost items. While not suggesting that the forecasting of price-level changes over extended periods is easy, it can no longer be ignored. A crude forecast, even if subject to uncertainty, may be better than a forecast which ignores inflation.

5-10. INTERDEPENDENCIES BETWEEN PROJECTS

Even ignoring uncertainty as assumed thus far, it may not be possible to view each project in isolation, and attention to the overall "basket" of investments may be required. Specifically, we need to be concerned with interdependencies among projects.[28] Extreme cases are projects which are *mutually exclusive* and projects which are *contingent* upon each other.

Location problems are typical examples of mutually exclusive projects. If a firm is considering any one of three different locations for a new warehouse, the alternatives are mutually exclusive as the choice of one site will preclude a warehouse in any other location even if a separate analysis of each alternative reveals that a positive net present value may have been attainable in more than one location. Another example would be the purchase of machinery, where a choice of several different machines may be available for the one particular task. To deal with this type of situation, all mutually exclusive alternatives are analyzed as a group, and only the best one is chosen.

Contingent investments imply that the viability of one project is dependent on the prior acceptance of another. Acquisition of a trailer may hinge, for instance, on the purchase of a truck to go with it, and *vice versa.* Again the contingent projects have to be considered in a group and evaluated together. The possibility that a project upon which other projects are contingent may be accepted even if it, by itself, proves economically undesirable should be noted. This may be the case where an offset is provided by returns received from other projects in the contingent group.

More generally, the interdependence of projects may be either *complementary* or *negative.* For example, two new products may have some market overlap and, hence, some negative interdependence, while two other products may complement each other thus increasing total sales. Under conditions of dependence among projects, all possible subgroups of investments making up a capital budget should ideally be evaluated in order to find the best possible combination of investment projects. However, though this approach may be theoretically appealing, the operational consequences may prove prohibitive given the large numbers of combinations which would generally have to be considered. Thus, it may only be possible to recognize the more important dependencies, perhaps making some intuitive initial selections or later adjustments as required.

5-11. CAPITAL RATIONING

Our rule thus far has been that a firm should accept all projects which, after taking account of the time value of money, yield benefits in excess of costs. At a given point in time, however, a firm may have limited resources at its disposal and be constrained as to the activities which it may be able to pursue. While the following discussion focuses on financial constraints, we should recognize that other constraints such as scarcity of manpower or managerial talent may be limiting as well. Where financial constraints are operating, we term this *capital rationing*—monies have to be rationed to projects competing for the scarce funds. We could argue that a firm which creates enough attractive investment opportunities to face financial constraints should simply raise additional capital, to the point where marginal costs equal marginal benefits, thereby taking advantage of such opportunities. So long as investments undertaken yield more

[28]For a quantitative treatment of this subject, see M. Weingartner, "Capital Budgeting of Interrelated Projects: Survey and Synthesis", *Management Science*, March, 1966, pp. 485-516.

than the cost of raising the necessary capital, they will make an economic contribution to the firm and increase the wealth of its owners.

While this may be a reasonable longer-term policy guideline for a publicly held corporation, it may not always be applicable. For one thing, raising new capital often involves significant time lags, so that in the short run, at least, it may not be possible to remove all constraints. Furthermore, and more importantly, in many closely held firms where either control or the use of debt are of concern, resort to external financing is simply limited by policy. Hence, in many practical situations, capital rationing becomes a very real source of concern.

In the light of capital rationing, a firm can no longer accept all investment proposals yielding returns in excess of its cost of capital. The hurdle rate has to be raised, with *opportunity costs* becoming the relevant yardstick against which new investments are to be measured. This opportunity cost is given by the internal rate of return or effective yield of the most attractive project foregone.

Example

> Consider a corporation with an overall cost of capital of 12 percent. The firm has more investment opportunities than can be handled with the limited capital currently available to it, and several investment projects promising returns of around 16 percent have to be passed up. It is clear then that the opportunity cost of 16 percent becomes the standard against which new investment proposals must be measured, for this is the amount which could be earned on any uncommitted funds.

5-12. PROJECT IMPLEMENTATION AND ABANDONMENT

Once the decision to invest has been taken, the project-implementation phase begins. The involvement of the financial officer does not end with approval of the project and its assignment to operating divisions for implementation, because important control and follow-up activities remain to be performed. Continuous budgetary control and progress reports, including revisions of forecasts at periodically scheduled intervals, are required both in order to spot difficulties in implementation and to facilitate prompt remedial action. We must bear in mind that proposals are approved on the basis of best estimates and that variations will be common once the project is initiated. Difficulties may initially have been underestimated and tight controls are indicated to guarantee the continued success of a project which, in a competitive environment, may only have promised a fairly narrow profit margin to begin with. It has been reported, for example, that 90 percent of all new computer installations exceed the initial implementation schedule, and that 40 percent of all computers installed have not proven themselves in an economic sense.[29] Failure to exercise proper control after the initial approval may well account for a large percentage of these cases.

Related to the above is the need for a continued reappraisal of each project as to whether it should be continued or abandoned. If unforeseen difficulties are experienced or, quite generally, if at any point the present value of forecasted

[29]Sanders, *op. cit.*, p. 254.

cash flows becomes negative, a project should be abandoned no matter how much money has already been sunk into it.[30] The concept of *sunk costs* may sometimes be psychologically difficult to accept and the temptation may be there to keep a project alive based on efforts already expended. This is analogous to the gambler who, having already lost one-thousand dollars and not wanting to face that fact, is determined to play just until he breaks even. Chances are he would be better off to take his "lumps" and quit immediately rather than risk further losses. Generally it is difficult to abandon an existing project which has gathered some momentum and to which people with their expectations and interests are attached. Nevertheless, a realistic assessment of ongoing projects, including the willingness to abandon where necessary, can make an important contribution to the success of a firm. Corporate annual reports provide repeated examples of situations where losses could have been avoided through more rapid withdrawal from projects.

Finally, a post-audit of an investment project may provide feedback which can be useful in reappraising the soundness of established procedures and which hopefully will improve the performance of participating management at all levels.

***ADDITIONAL SELECTED TOPICS*

**5-13. THE RELATIONSHIP OF CAPITAL BUDGETING TO OTHER AREAS OF FINANCIAL DECISION-MAKING

The capital-budgeting decision does not stand in isolation but is intertwined with two other major areas of corporate financial decisions, namely, *capital structure* and *dividend policy*.

Capital budgeting decisions, for instance, will affect the stability and magnitude of future cash flows; these, in turn, will be important in determining how much debt the firm can afford to carry in its capital structure, and what amount is available to be paid out in dividends. On the other hand, the particular capital structure determines the overall cost of capital to be used as a discount rate in capital budgeting, and earnings which are not paid out as dividends become available for reinvestment.

When we are concerned with maximizing the market value of the company's shares, we should recognize the interdependencies of the several variables identified in share-valuation models. Ideally we should express the value of the shares as a function of such factors and set out to maximize the function by choice of a proper value for each of the influencing variables simultaneously. Thus, if the market value of shares (V) is determined by the firm's investment portfolio (I), its capital structure (C), and dividend policy (D), we should try to estimate the function.

$$V = f(I, C, D)$$

[30]See, for example, A. Robichek and J. Van Horne, "Abandonment Value and Capital Budgeting". *Journal of Finance*, December, 1967, pp. 570-590. E. Dyl and H. Long, "Abandonment Value and Capital Budgeting, Comment", *Journal of Finance*, March, 1969, pp. 88-95.

and to maximize it by proper simultaneous choice of I, C, and D.

Such models may be theoretically appealing since they recognize that a decision to invest in a particular asset can have a broad impact on the firm in influencing earnings, both in size and stability. The decision may also alter dividend payout and debt equity ratios, especially if internal sources of financing are to be relied upon. Furthermore, while each of these variables affects share values, any one of them may, under certain conditions, offset another. Thus, a lowering of the dividend payout could contribute to the firm's investment activities, but may itself be viewed as a negative indicator by the investors.

The operational difficulties of such an integrated approach are, however, apparent. Even if it were agreed that maximization of share prices should be the sole objective of the firm (see Chapter 1 for a detailed discussion), it would be very difficult to estimate and update an overall function of share values like the one described above, particularly in an environment characterized by change and uncertainty.

For operational convenience, therefore, we choose to analyze the capital expenditure decision in isolation—in other words, we hold constant the other variables such as capital structure and dividend policy. In our previous discussions we took the capital structure and hence the cost of capital for the firm as given and proceeded to analyze the capital-budgeting decision in the light of constant financing policies. This approach is reasonable where an established firm is dealing with incremental decisions, none of which will substantially alter the predetermined complexion of the firm. If, however, the magnitude of an individual decision is such that it may alter the way the firm is perceived by investors, or if a significant shifting in overall policy occurs, the approach taken becomes questionable. Suppose a firm which was exclusively in the forest-products industry makes the decision to diversify and to enter the plastics and chemicals business in a significant way. Such an investment decision could well affect both the way investors would look at the firm, and the terms under which the firm would be able to raise capital in the future. Thus, this capital-budgeting decision could alter the cost of capital, which would in turn alter the basis of capital-budgeting decisions. In such circumstances, the firm would do well to weigh the interdependencies of the various decision areas.

**5-14. THE BENEFIT-COST RATIO

A further criterion based on discounted cash flow analysis which is sometimes encoutered in practice is the *benefit-cost ratio*, or *profitability index*. It is simply given as the ratio of discounted benefits over discounted costs. As with the net present value criterion, the discount rate applied represents the time value of money to the firm. Projects with ratios greater than one are held to be acceptable and larger ratios are favored. Two variations, namely, the aggregate and the netted ratio have been proposed.[31] With the *aggregate ratio*, operating revenues

[31]See B. Schwab and P. Lusztig, "A Comparative Analysis of the Net Present Value and the Benefit-Cost Ratio as Measures of the Economic Desirability of Investments", *Journal of Finance*, June, 1969, pp. 507-516, on which the following discussion draws.

generated by a project are placed in the numerator, while all cash outflows, including the initial investment and operating expenses over the life of the project, are assigned to the denominator.

Under the *netted ratio*, a distinction is made between initial cash outlays required to get the project going and subsequent operating expenses which can be met from inflows generated by the project. While the former have to be provided out of the firm's capital budget, the latter are in a sense financed by the investment. Only the initial costs are placed in the denominator of the ratio, with operating expenses being subtracted from the cash inflows accruing in each period. The net inflows are then left to be discounted and aggregated into the numerator.

Example

Consider a project characterized by the following figures, where the cost of capital is given to be 12 percent.

Year	Initial investment (1)	Operating cash inflows (2)	Operating cash outflows (3)	Net operating cash flows (4) = (2) − (3)
0	−$12,000			
1		$10,000	$4000	$6000
2		10,000	4000	6000
3		10,000	4000	6000

$$\text{Aggregate benefit-cost ratio} = \frac{(a_3 12\%)10{,}000}{12{,}000 + (a_3 12\%)4{,}000}$$

$$= \frac{2.402 \times 10{,}000}{12{,}000 + 2.402 \times 4000} = 1.112$$

$$\text{Netted benefit-cost ratio} = \frac{(a_3 12\%)\,6{,}000}{12{,}000}$$

$$= \frac{2.402 \times 6{,}000}{12{,}000} = 1.201$$

It has been shown that the aggregate ratio is misleading as a criterion for the economic evaluation of investments and that operating cash flows should be netted and related to just the initial investment as described above. It is the relationship of net benefits to initial investment which is relevant in judging the soundness of an investment rather than total cash inflows over total cash outflows.

In comparing the netted benefit-cost ratio with the net present value, both methods will generally yield equivalent results. It is obvious that only if the present value of net benefits is larger than the initial investment, that is, only if the netted benefit-cost ratio is greater than one, can the net present value be positive. Thus, both measures actually establish the same cutoff criterion. When, however, *mutually exclusive* projects are involved (projects such that only one of a set can be undertaken) it can be shown that application of the netted ratio and the net present value techniques might suggest conflicting decisions, particularly when the investments differ in terms of size. Consider, for example, the following alternatives:

	Project A	Project B
Initial investment required	$50,000	$15,000
Present value of expected net cash inflows	70,000	30,000
Net present value of project	20,000	15,000
Netted benefit-cost ratio	1.4	2

According to the net present value technique project *A* should be preferred, whereas the benefit-cost ratio holds out project *B* as superior. In such circumstances, the net present value is the better criterion, since it measures the economic contribution of the project to the firm in absolute terms. The benefit-cost ratio suffers from the usual limitations of percentages and index numbers in that it conceals absolute magnitudes. A project may have a high benefit-cost ratio but be small in terms of the absolute dollar amounts and hence less desirable than another opportunity characterized by a more modest ratio but a larger contribution.[32] In our illustration above, if project *B* were selected, and the remaining $35,000 could only be invested to produce a net present value of under $5,000, then the wrong decision would have been made because the resultant contribution to the firm would be less than that available from *A*.

A decision-maker can easily compute both measures simultaneously and then compare projects both in terms of relative profitability and absolute contributions. Given the basis for the conflicting decisions which might be suggested by the two criteria, the net present value is generally preferred.

**5-15. COMPARING THE NET PRESENT VALUE AND THE INTERNAL RATE OF RETURN

The net present value and the internal rate of return are probably the most widely advocated criteria for sound capital-budgeting decisions. In actual practice the two approaches will usually provide equivalent results and consistent application of either should prove satisfactory. Conflicting rankings by the two methods may occur, however, making a brief analysis of such situations useful.

Example

Consider two mutually exclusive projects *A* and *B*, both entailing an initial investment of $10,000 and subsequent after-tax cash inflows given as follows:

	Project A	Project B
Year 1	$ 2,000	$10,000
2	4,000	3,000
3	12,000	3,000

The internal rates of return can be computed as $i_A = 27$ percent and $i_B =$ 38 percent, while using 6 percent as the assumed appropriate discount

[32]Thus, a farmer evaluating the opportunity of investing in a hand shovel would come up with a high benefit-cost ratio but low net present value. The alternative of investing in a large tractor would probably offer a much lower ratio but a more significant net present value.

rate, the net present values become $5,500 and $4,600 for projects *A* and *B* respectively.

According to the internal rate of return, project *B* should be selected, while the reverse decision is indicated by the net present value approach. The problem arises because the cash flows generated by the projects have different time patterns,[33] and each of the techniques implies a different reinvestment rate for these flows.

The nature of the difficulty may be illustrated by using the notion of terminal values and applying it to a simplified example.

Example

Consider two mutually exclusive projects, each requiring the initial investment of $1,000 and with subsequent after-tax cash inflows as indicated:

Year	Project A	Project B
1	+ 1200	0
2	0	0
3	0	+$1520

The internal rates of return are 20 percent and 15 percent in the case of projects *A* and *B* respectively. Choice of the investment with the highest internal rate could prove unwise if the $1,200 cash throwoff of project *A* in the first year can only be reinvested at a rate below 20 percent. Assuming the best reinvestment opportunity available yields only 10 percent after taxes, the terminal position at the end of the third year would be $1,520 from investment in *B* but only $1200(1+0.1)^2 = \$1,452$ from the selection of *A* with its higher internal rate of return.

Reliance on internal rates of return assumes that funds released from any project can be reinvested at a particular project's internal rate of return. If in the above example early cash inflows from project *A* can be reinvested at 20 percent (the internal rate of return) project *A* is indeed superior. However, an assumption that throwoffs from one particular project are reinvested at 20 percent, while those of a second earn 15 percent, is basically inconsistent. The net present value method, on the other hand, implies that reinvestment opportunities provide a return which is equal to the discount rate being used. Because highly productive opportunities are unlikely to be readily available for cash released early from high return investments, the more conservative and stable reinvestment rate assumption of the net present value technique is appealing.[34]

[33]Projects with different lives or of different sizes pose the same problem.

[34]J. Hirshleifer, "On the Theory of Optimal Investment Decisions", *Journal of Political Economy*, August 1958, pp. 95-103. The existence, however, of special situations and a more general variability of reinvestment rates may have to be recognized. See C. Doenges, "The Reinvestment Problem in a Practical Perspective", *Financial Management*, Spring 1972, pp. 85-91.

Net present value profiles (which we discussed earlier) can be used to provide a more generalized view of the problem and this is done in Figure 5-3 which relates to our earlier example of the two $10,000 investments. The internal rates of return are given by the intersections of the curves with the horizontal axis at which points the net present values are zero. Contradictory rankings between the NPV and IRR criteria occur whenever the present value profiles of two proposals cross over at some rate beyond (or to the right of) the cost of capital, the crossover being caused by a difference in the time patterns of the cash inflows. This is illustrated in a more general way in Figure 5-4. The net present value of project *A* with its more distant cash inflows will be more sensitive to changes in the discount rate. In applying a discount factor $1/(1+k)^n$, any increase in k gets magnified by the exponent n. On the other hand, the relatively immediate cash returns of project *B* will be much less sensitive to such changes, implying a "flatter" net present value profile with a more modest slope. If for a discount rate of zero the present value of cash flows from project *A* exceed those of project *B*, it is easy to see that a crossover may occur given the steeper slope of the profile for project *A*.

The desirability of project *B* will depend on the rate at which its early cash returns can be reinvested: if this reinvestment rate is low, the larger but more distant cash returns of project *A* will be preferred; if on the other hand the reinvestment rate can be raised, project *B* becomes progressively more attractive.

FIGURE 5-3

Net Present Value Profiles

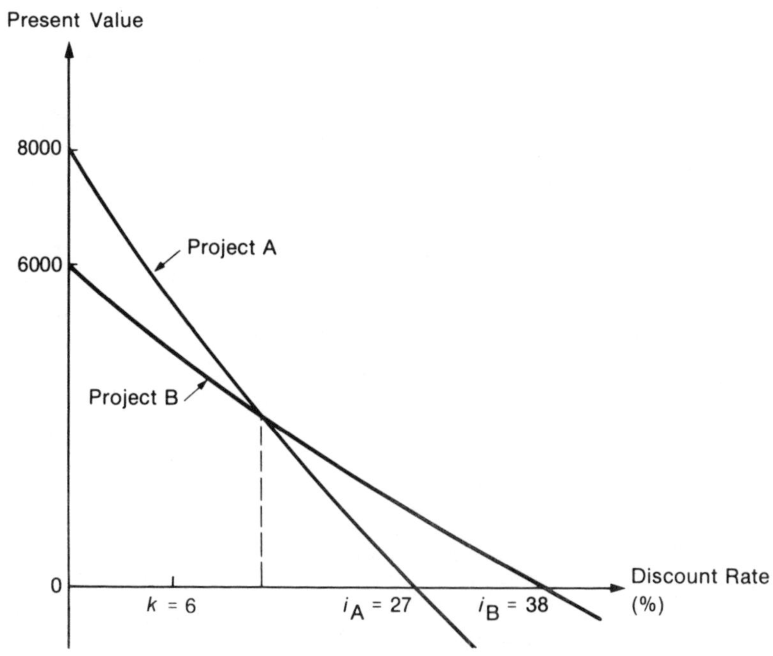

FIGURE 5-4

Two Investments with Net Present Value Profiles Which May Cross Over

Project *A*. Initial investment creates relatively large returns in more distant future

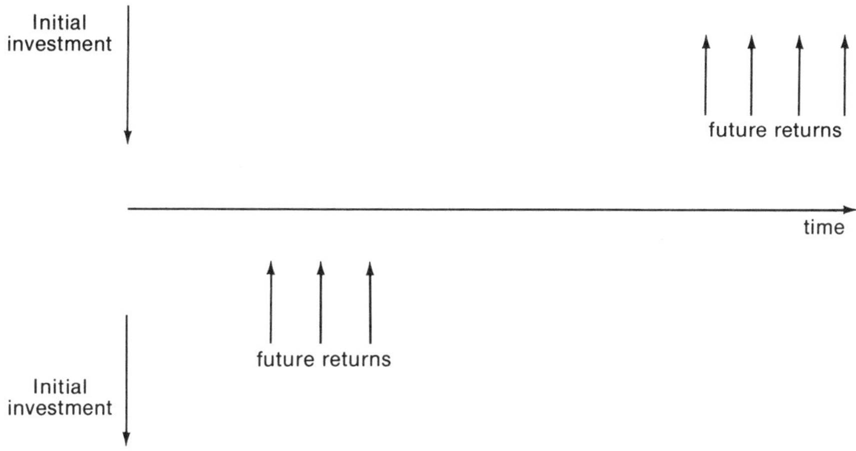

Project *B*: Initial investment creates more modest returns in near future

The internal rate of return technique does have redeeming features. An advantage is that no discount rate needs to be specified in advance of any project evaluation. This point gains significance when we recognize that there are often practical difficulties in estimating the firm's cost of capital. While a hurdle rate still needs to be specified, projects can at least be ranked by their internal rates of return.

In any case, management need not feel constrained to use just one criterion— in fact it may increase the decision-maker's understanding of a specific situation to have both the net present value and the internal rate of return on hand.

**5-16. MULTIPLE INTERNAL RATES OF RETURN

Where an investment is characterized by an initial cash outflow followed by cash inflows (there is but one reversal of signs with cash flows going from negative to positive) the shape of its net present value profile will conform to the curve in Figure 5-2 on p. 105 and only one value for the internal rate of return is possible.

With some projects, however, there could be more than one reversal of direction in the cash flows. We could start with an initial investment, followed by cash inflows, and at the end of the project's life face cash outflows once again. In strip-mining, for example, costs may be associated with meeting legal requirements for restoring the environment after the ore body has been mined out. In such circumstances there could be two different values for the discount rate, each of which satisfies the criterion of an internal rate of return by providing a net present value of zero.

Example

Examine the often cited example[35] expenditure of $1,600 for a new and larger pump than currently in use to result in larger oil production but earlier exhaustion of the supply. The subsequent net incremental cash flows are assumed to be + $10,000 in period t_1, and – $10,000 in t_2 yielding an internal rate of return of both 25 percent and 400 percent. The reason for the multiple rate stems from the two reversals in sign of the net cash flows during the project's life. The initial cash outflow is followed by a sign reversal and net inflow in year one, and then by a second reversal in sign or net outflow in year two. Using a zero discount rate, total outflows exceed total inflows leaving a net balance of – $1,600. With positive rates, cash flows in the more distant period will be most heavily reduced and, at some point, discounted benefits start to exceed discounted costs. As the discount rate continues to increase, the cash inflow in year one is drawn down to the point where the present value of all flows again produces a negative total. This is illustrated in Figure 5-5 which shows the profile for the above case.

FIGURE 5-5

Net Present Value Profile of Pump Illustration

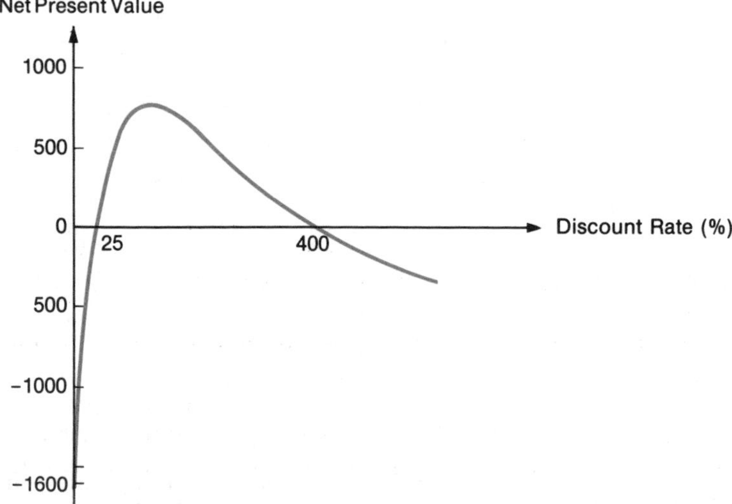

It can be shown that two or more reversals in the flows of cash are needed to give multiple rates of return; although a project with more than one reversal in cash flows need not necessarily have multiple rates of return.[36]

The interpretation of multiple rates is difficult and it has been shown that

[35]See J. Lorie and L. Savage, "Three Problems in Capital Rationing", *Journal of Business*, October, 1966, pp. 236-237, for the idea, and E. Solomon, *The Theory of Financial Management*, New York, Columbia University Press, pp. 129-130, for the numerical example.

[36]Mathematically speaking, more than one reversal of signs is a necessary but not sufficient condition. For a more complete discussion, see D. Quirin, *op. cit.*, pp. 56-57.

mechanically derived results may actually be incorrect.[37] Using our pump example, a full pattern of cash flows would appear as follows:

Year	With Continued Use of Old Pump	With New Pump	Incremental Cash Flow on Replacement
0	$ 0	$ -1,600	$ -1,600
1	10,000	20,000	10,000
2	10,000	0	-10,000

Given these figures, it is clear that the arithmetic solution has failed to provide a meaningful rate of return for the decision-maker. We see that, by investing $1,600 in the new pump, the investor receives $10,000 one year ahead of time. The true economic desirability of the project will depend on the rate at which this $10,000 can be reinvested.

Assuming, for example, that the investor can earn 23 percent on the extra $10,000 received in year one, he ends up with an additional $2,300 in year two. In such circumstances, the true internal rate of return—the discount factor which equates $1,600 spent with $2,300 received two years hence—is 20 percent.

**5-17. CAPITAL RATIONING AND MATHEMATICAL PROGRAMMING

If separate constraints exist for several time periods (budgetary limits, for example), the selection of an optimal investment portfolio which takes full account of all the constraints may prove a difficult problem. It has been suggested that mathematical programming can play a useful role in this context by selecting a portfolio of investments which, subject to all of the constraints imposed, will maximize net present value.[38] In the simplest case, this could take the form of a linear programming model, with the possibility of introducing integer constraints and/or nonlinearities as required. The interested reader is referred to the Appendix in this chapter for a basic review of mathematical programming.

While potentially useful, there are several practical difficulties in applying mathematical programming techniques to problems of this type. They include the difficulty of selecting an appropriate time horizon; inadequate knowledge of future constraints; and inadequate knowledge of future investment opportunities. Problems also arise in that the opportunity cost (or discount rate to be used in the objective function) cannot be specified until the optimal solution is found and it is known which opportunities have to be foregone and *vice versa*.[39]

[37]E. Solomon, *op. cit.*, pp. 130-131, is the source for what follows.

[38]For a complete treatment of the subject, see M. Weingartner, *Mathematical Programming and the Analysis of Capital Budgeting Problems*, Englewood Cliffs: Prentice-Hall, 1963, and also R. Bernhard, "Mathematical Programming Models for Capital Budgeting—A Survey, Generalization, and Critique", *Journal of Financial and Quantitative Analysis*, June, 1969, pp. 111-158.

[39]See, for example, W. Baumol and R. Quandt, "Investment and Discount Rates Under Capital Rationing—A Programming Approach", *Economic Journal*, June, 1955, pp. 317-319; P. Lusztig and B. Schwab, "A Note on the Application of the Linear Programming to Capital Budgeting", *Journal of Financial and Quantitative Analysis*, December, 1968, pp. 427-431; S. Myers, "A Note on Linear Programming and Capital Budgeting," *Journal of Finance*, March, 1972, pp. 89-92; and G. Whitmore and L. Amey, "Capital Budgeting under Rationing: Comments on the Lusztig and Schwab Procedure," *Journal of Financial and Quantitative Analysis*, January 1973, pp. 127-135.

It appears likely, therefore, that the greatest benefit of linear programming to capital budgeting is to be found in the information which may be extracted from operating models which optimize the current physical operations of the firm rather than in the direct applications as detailed above. Such models are, for instance, widely reported in the oil industry for the scheduling of refinery operations; in the forest products industry for the allocation of logs to mills, and the scheduling of various activities within the plants.[40] The models, while primarily geared to current operations, can also be of considerable benefit in deciding on capital expenditures. To the extent that various capacity constraints are binding and, therefore, limit operations, the *dual variables*[41] for these constraints (obtained from the optimal solution to the model) give a good indication of incremental benefits which may be obtained by relaxing each particular constraint. Thus, the comparative benefits of various capital expenditures made to increase operating capacities can readily be evaluated. For complex production systems, the absence of such models would make evaluations of this type a difficult undertaking.

5-18. SUMMARY

Capital budgeting is concerned with the long-term investment decision of the firm. In this chapter we have been concerned with establishing the framework for evaluating such investment decisions under the idealized case of ignoring uncertainty. The capital budgeting process can be viewed as comprising the (i) generating of project ideas, (ii) estimation of cash flows for proposed investments, (iii) evaluation of these cash flows by application of appropriate selection criteria, and (iv) implementation of investment decisions including controls and periodic reevaluations. The generation of good project ideas and the proper estimation of cash flows are crucial to the success of any capital-budgeting program.

Cash flows should be estimated on an incremental, after-tax basis. Evaluation criteria include the payback period, the average rate of return, and discounted cash flow criteria, with only the latter giving explicit consideration to the time value of money.

The net present value method, benefit-cost ratios, and the internal rate of return are the better known discounted cash flow criteria. While the consistent application of any of these techniques is likely to yield satisfactory decisions, some potential contradictions warrant attention. Furthermore, some general limitations inherent in discounted cash flow approaches need to be recognized. Corporate financial models may provide management with useful additional information, such as the impact of new projects on future financial statements.

Investment proposals cannot be viewed in isolation and interdependencies such as mutual exclusion and contingency have to be recognized.

[40]For the discussion of a refinery application see, for example, L. Rappaport and W. Drews, "Mathematical Approach to Long Range Planning", *Harvard Business Review*, May-June, 1962, pp. 75-87. An application in the forest products industry is given by J. Dickens, "Linear Programming in Corporate Simulation" in Schreiber, *op. cit.*, pp. 292-314.

[41]See Appendix 1 of this chapter for an elaboration.

Capital rationing may preclude investments which might otherwise be attractive and the opportunity cost of funds, therefore, becomes important. If various constraints over several periods are imposed, the problem of choosing the best investment portfolio which would satisfy these constraints may be viewed in a mathematical programming context.

After an investment decision has been made, proper controls should be exercised. Ongoing projects should periodically be reevaluated and abandonment should be considered where projects are no longer expected to generate adequate returns.

Questions for discussion

1. (a) Why are incremental cash flows the appropriate basis for evaluating investment projects rather than contributions to reported earnings?
   (b) Should management consider earnings at all?
   (c) Might a project with a positive NPV make negative contributions to earnings in the short run? Why?
2. How can the government influence (stimulate or reduce) the level of business investments?
3. The payback technique is considered misleading by many writers.
   (a) What are its major weaknesses?
   (b) Why is it nevertheless so popular with practitioners?
4. Discuss some of the limitations of discounted cash flow criteria.
5. If the government liberalizes depreciation and depletion allowances, what impact will this have on capital investments by industry?
6. As the general manager of a firm, you are presented with an investment proposal by one of your divisions. Its net present value if discounted at the cost of capital for your firm (which is 15 percent) is \$100,000, and its internal rate of return is 20 percent.
   (a) What is the economic interpretation of the NPV and IRR figures—*i.e.*, what do they mean?
   (b) What, if any, additional information would you like to have before approving the project?
7. Briefly explain why the net present value and the internal rate of return may occasionally produce contradictory rankings for two investment projects, *i.e.* for two projects A and B we may have

$$\text{NPV}_A > \text{NPV}_B$$

$$\text{IRR}_A < \text{IRR}_B$$

   If the two projects are mutually exclusive, how should a decision-maker resolve this conflict?

Problems with solutions

1. A firm is contemplating construction of a new production facility and its management wishes to determine the effective size of the investment involved. The building would go on a piece of vacant land which the firm has owned for 10 years. When first acquired, the land cost \$200,000 but its current market

value is estimated to be $1,000,000. The building itself can be erected for $350,000. Machinery worth $100,000 needs to be purchased although, in addition, certain essential equipment would be produced by one of the firm's own divisions. Production costs for the equipment are expected to total $50,000 and to have a ready market price of $60,000. Corporate taxes are 40 percent. Lastly, additional investments of $30,000 in working capital (mainly inventories) are required initially.

Solution

In working towards a solution it must be recognized that there are really two alternatives under consideration. Management may either build the facility or decide to pass up this particular investment opportunity. We therefore focus on the incremental cash flows attributable to building the facility as opposed to not doing so. If the new building were not put up the land could be sold for $1,000,000 and the production equipment for $60,000. It follows that in not building the new facility we have:

Receipts from sale of production equipment	$60,000	
Less tax on profits from sale (60,000 – 50,000)0.4	4,000	
Net cash inflow from sale of production equipment		$56,000
Receipts from sale of land	$1,000,000	
Less capital gains tax on profits from sale ½(1,000,000 – 200,000)0.4	160,000	
Net cash inflow from sale of land		840,000
Total potential cash inflows from sale of assets to be used in project		$896,000

It should be noted that whether or not the land is actually sold, if the new facility is not constructed, is immaterial. The fact remains that the land could be sold and if the project goes forward the firm foregoes the opportunity of realizing cash inflows either from a sale or from an alternative use. Hence, the new project should be charged with such cash flows.

In building the new facility we have the following cash outflows:

Building	$350,000
Purchase of machinery	$100,000
Investment in working capital	$ 30,000
Total potential cash outflows relating to the new investment	$480,000

Thus the effective size of the investment involved is given by the sum of actual cash outflows of $480,000 and the cash inflows foregone by committing assets which could otherwise have been sold for $896,000, or a total of $1,376,000.

2. Investment in a new machine which can be bought for $100,000 is under consideration. The machine would produce before-tax operating savings of $20,000 per year. Maximum annual capital cost allowances (20 percent on the declining balance) would be taken and the firm's tax rate is 40 percent. Management wishes to know what cash flows can be looked for over the next 3 years.

Solution

Amounts to be claimed as capital cost allowances over the next 3 years must first be set out.

	Book Value of Asset at Beginning of Year (1)	Capital Cost Allowance* (2)=(1)×20%	Book Value of Asset at Year End* (3)=(1)minus(2)
Year 1	$100,000	$20,000	$80,000
2	80,000	16,000	64,000
3	64,000	12,800	51,200

*As set out in Chapter 3, the maximum claim is $Cd(1-d)^{n-1}$ while book value at year end is $C(1-d)^n$

The cash flows are then computed as follows:

	Years 1	2	3
Operating savings	$20,000	$20,000	$20,000
Less capital cost allowances	(20,000)	(16,000)	(12,800)
Taxable income	0	$ 4,000	$ 7,200
Less tax payable	0	(1,600)	(2,880)
Net income	0	$ 2,400	$ 4,320
Add non-cash expense items, *i.e.* capital cost allowances	$20,000	$16,000	$12,800
Net incremental cash flow	$20,000	$18,400	$17,120

An alternative line of reasoning could also be used. Thus, with operating savings taxed at 40 percent, the firm would net $20,000 × 0.6 = $12,000 annually. Actually, however, tax savings are available through being able to deduct capital cost allowances in arriving at taxable income. This would reduce the firm's tax bill and consequently increase its cash flow. Computation of cash flows would involve the following format:

	Years		
	1	2	3
(1) Capital cost allowance (*CCA*) = reduction in taxable income	$20,000	$16,000	$12,800
(2) Reduction in taxes 0.4 × *CCA*	8,000	6,400	5,120
(3) Net operating savings	12,000	12,000	12,000
(4) Total net cash flows, row (2) plus row (3)	$20,000	$18,400	$17,120

3. (a) A firm is contemplating the purchase of a $10,000 machine. If it is purchased, the firm expects that it can save labor costs of $5000 in each of years 1 and 2, and $6000 in each of years 3 and 4. The machine is not expected to have a salvage value at the end of the 4th year; and capital cost allowance may be claimed at the rate of 30 percent. If the company's tax rate is 40 percent and its cost of capital is 8 percent, calculate:

   (i) the net present value of this proposal.
   (ii) the internal rate of return.
   (iii) the payback period.

Solution

(i) The cost of this investment is the initial outlay of $10,000. The benefits are the after-tax inflows in years 1 through 4, and the tax savings the company realizes by claiming maximum capital cost allowance (CCA).

NPV = –initial investment + present value of after-tax inflows + present value of tax shield from CCA.

	Years			
	1	2	3	4
Before-tax benefits (inflows)	5000	5000	6000	6000
After-tax benefits (t = 40%)	3000	3000	3600	3600

$$\text{PV of tax shield} = \text{Capital cost}\left(\frac{\text{CCA rate} \times \text{tax rate}}{\text{discount rate} + \text{CCA rate}}\right)$$

$$= 10{,}000\left(\frac{.30 \times .4}{.08 + .30}\right)$$

$$= \$3{,}158$$

The present value of the tax shield is equivalent to the sum of all future discounted tax savings which result from claiming the maximum allowable capital cost allowance each year, as shown below:

	Undepreciated Capital Cost (1)	Capital Cost Allowance (2)=30%×(1)	Tax Saving (3)= 40%×(2)	PV factor at 8% (4)	PV of Tax Savings (3)×(4)
Year 1	10000	3000	1200	.926	1111.2
2	7000	2100	840	.857	719.9
3	4900	1470	588	.794	466.9
4	3430	1029	411.60	.735	302.5
5	2401	720.3	288.12	.681	196.2
6	1680.7	504.2	201.68	.630	127.1
7	1176.5	352.9	141.16	.583	82.3
8	823.5	247.1	98.84	.540	53.4
9	576.5	172.9	69.16	.500	34.6
10	403.5	121.1	48.44	.463	22.4
11 and subsequent					41.0
			Present Value of Tax Shield =		$3158

Having determined the initial outlay, the after-tax benefits and the present values of the tax shield, we can calculate the net present value as follows:

$$\text{NPV} = -10{,}000 + \frac{3000}{(1+.08)} + \frac{3000}{(1+.08)^2} + \frac{3600}{(1+.08)^3} + \frac{3600}{(1+.08)^4} + 3158$$

$$= -10{,}000 + 3000(.926) + 3000(.857) + 3600(.794) + 3600(.735) + 3158$$

$$= \$4{,}011$$

Instead of using the four present value factors to discount the inflows, we can visualize them as a 2-year annuity of $3,000 (in years 1-2) and another 2-year annuity of $3,600 (in years 3-4). In more complex problems, it may be advantageous to use this idea to express the above equation as follows (although either method may be used):

$$\text{NPV} = -10{,}000 + (3000)(a_2 8\%) + (3600)(a_4 8\% - a_2 8\%) + 3158$$

(where: $a_n i\%$ is the present value of an annuity of $1 for n periods at i%).

$$= -10{,}000 + 3000(1.783) + 3600(3.312 - 1.783) + 3158$$

$$= -10{,}000 + 5{,}349 + 5{,}504 + 3{,}158$$

$$= \$4{,}011$$

(ii) The internal rate of return is the discount rate which would give the project a net present value equal to zero.

$$0 = -10{,}000 + (3000)(a_2 i\%) + (3600)(a_4 i\% - a_2 i\%) + 10{,}000\left(\frac{0.3 * 0.4}{0.3 + i}\right)$$

Present value at various discount rates:

Year	Cash Flow	0%	10%	20%	28%	24%
			Present Value Factors at			
0	−10,000	1	1	1	1	1
1-2	3,000 per yr.	2	1.736	1.528	1.392	1.457
3-4	3,600 per yr.	2	3.170−1.736 = 1.434	2.589−1.528 = 1.197	2.241−1.392 = .849	2.404−1.457 = .947
tax shield	10,000	.12/.3	.12/.4	.12/.5	.12/.58	.12/.54
Total net present value		7200	3370.40	803.60	−698.63	2.42

By trial and error, *IRR* (i%) works out to 24%.

$0 \simeq -10{,}000 + 3000(1.457) + 3600\,(2.404 - 1.457) + 2222$

(iii) To calculate the payback period, we must find out when the project has returned (on a cumulative basis) the amount of the initial investment, $10,000. To do this, we must show the annual cash flows:

Time period	1	2	3	4
		Years		
Initial Outlay 10,000				
After-tax cash inflows	3000	3000	3600	3600
CCA tax savings $[Cdt(1-d)^{n-1}]$	1200	840	588	412
Cumulative "paid-back" amount	4200	8040	12228	16240

The payback period (to the nearest year) is therefore 3 years.

(b) Calculate the net present value of the proposal in part (a) if a salvage value of $1,000 is expected after the 4-year life of the machine.

Solution

If the company receives $1,000 for the machine after 4 years, this inflow will have to be discounted and included in NPV, thereby increasing it. However, the disposal of the machine will mean that the undepreciated capital cost of the asset class will be reduced by $1,000. This means that at the *end of year 4* the present value of the tax shield lost equals

$$1000\left[\frac{dt}{d+k}\right]$$

The present value (discounted to the present) of this loss is therefore:

$$\frac{1000\left[\frac{dt}{d+k}\right]}{(1+k)^4}$$

Therefore, net present value with the salvage value is now:

$$NPV = -10000 + 5349 + 5504 + 3158 + \frac{1000}{(1+.08)^4} - \frac{1000\left[\dfrac{.30 \times .4}{.30 + .08}\right]}{(1+.08)^4}$$

(first fraction: PV of salvage inflow; second fraction: PV of loss of tax shield)

$$= -10{,}000 + 5349 + 5504 + 3158 + \frac{1000\left[1 - \dfrac{.12}{.38}\right]}{(1+.08)^4}$$

$$= \$4514$$

(c) Assume that the company is operating under a tax system which allows only linear depreciation for tax purposes (over the expected useful life of the asset).

(i) What is the net present value of the investment if the machine is expected to have no salvage value?

(ii) Compute also the average rate of return.

Solution

(i) The amount of annual depreciation will now be \$10,000/4 = \$2,500. The present value of the tax shield will be:

$$\frac{(\text{tax rate})(2500)}{(1+.08)} + \frac{(t)(2500)}{(1+.08)^2} + \frac{(t)(2500)}{(1+.08)^3} + \frac{(t)(2500)}{(1+.08)^4}$$

$$= \sum_{n=1}^{4} \frac{(.4)(2500)}{(1+.08)^n}$$

$$= (a_4 8\%)(1000)$$

$$= (3.312)(1000)$$

$$= \$3312$$

Now $NPV = -10{,}000 + 5{,}349 + 5{,}504 + 3{,}312$

$$= \$4{,}165$$

It might seem curious that NPV should now be higher with linear depreciation than it was under declining balance CCA (part a), since declining balance or acceleration of depreciation is generally viewed by business as an advantage over the linear method.

The reason for this is the short duration of the investment. In effect, the company is claiming 25% for 4 years under the straight-line method. Using declining balance CCA, the annual depreciation figures are:

	Years					
	1	2	3	4	5	6
CCA at $d = 30\%$	3000	2100	1470	1029	720	504
% of original capital cost	30%	21%	14.7%	10.3%	7.2%	5%

In 4 years, the company has claimed 100% of the asset's value as depreciation expense with linear depreciation. However, with declining balance, the 4-year proportion claimed is only about 76%.
A capital asset (where $d = 30\%$) will usually be expected to have a life longer than 4 years, so that a greater proportion of the tax benefits will be anticipated in the earlier years under declining balance than under linear depreciation.
For example where the useful life is expected to be ten years;

Capital Cost $10,000
$d = 30\%$

	Years					
	1	2	3	4	5	...
Straight line depreciation	1000	1000	1000	1000	1000	...
Declining Balance depreciation	3000	2100	1470	1029	720	...

In this case (as in additional problem 1(a)(i) vs. 1(c)(i)) the faster write-off afforded by using the declining balance depreciation method for tax purposes is beneficial.

(ii) $\text{Average rate of return} = \dfrac{\text{Average annual after-tax profits}}{\text{Average Investment}}$.

Year	Gross savings	Depreciation	Taxable Income	After Tax Profits
1	5000	2500	2500	1500
2	5000	2500	2500	1500
3	6000	2500	3500	2100
4	6000	2500	3500	2100

Average profits $= (1500 + 1500 + 2100 + 2100)/4 = 1800$

The book value of the investment at the beginning of years 1 to 5 is $10,000, 7500, 5000, 2500 and 0 respectively for an average of $5000.

$$\text{Average rate of return} = \frac{\$1800}{\$5000} = 36\%$$

(d) If the company uses linear depreciation (as in part c) but there is once again a $1,000 expected salvage value, compute the net present value.

Solution

The expected residual value results in a lower annual straight line depreciation expense, and a $1,000 inflow in year 4.

$$\text{Annual depreciation} = \frac{\$10{,}000 - \$1{,}000}{4\text{ yrs.}} = \$2250$$

The new net present value is therefore:

$$NPV = -\text{initial investment} + \text{discounted inflow} + \text{p.v. of tax shield} + \text{p.v. of \$1000 in yr. 4.}$$

$$= (-10{,}000) + (5349 + 5504) + \sum_{n=1}^{4} \frac{(.4)(2250)}{(1+.08)^n} + \frac{1000}{(1+.08)^4}$$

$$= -10{,}000 + 10{,}853 + (3.312)(900) + (1000)(.735)$$

$$= \$4{,}569$$

4. We pursue, with slight modifications, the now familiar example which was used to derive cash flows in sections 5-3 and 5-4 of the chapter. A firm currently operates a machine which was purchased 5 years ago at a cost of $150,000. If currently sold, its market value would be $100,000. The machine is expected to last a further 5 years by which time it will have no salvage value. A new and improved version of the equipment is now on the market which could replace the old machine, at a cost of $130,000. Its expected economic life is 5 years. Operating costs for the old machine which is more labor intensive are $15,000 per year, while the new machine would only require operating costs of $9,000 per year. Both machines belong to the same asset class, and capital cost allowance can be taken at a rate of 30 percent on a declining balance. The corporate tax rate is 40 percent, and the cost of capital is 10 percent.
   (a) In the chapter, we computed a net present value of NPV = −$7,352.40 assuming no salvage value for the new machine, and NPV = $1,341.60 assuming a salvage value $20,000 for the new machine. How high would the salvage value of the new machine have to be in order for the new machine to become attractive, *i.e.*, at which point do we have NPV = 0?

Solution

Given we want NPV = 0, we must set the equation derived in section 5-4 to 0 as follows:

Total present value = 0 = previous total present value (see chapter) + present value of inflow from salvage − present value of tax shield lost from salvage

$$NPV = -\$7{,}352.40 + \frac{\$x}{(1+0.1)^5} - \frac{\$x}{(1+0.1)^5}\left(\frac{0.3 \times 0.4}{0.3+0.1}\right) = 0$$

or

$$\$7{,}352.40 = \frac{\$x}{(1+0.1)^5} - \frac{\$.3x}{(1+0.1)^5}$$

from which we compute

$$11{,}841 = .7x$$

and

$$x = \text{salvage value} = \$16{,}916$$

   (b) For a salvage value of $20,000, derive and draw the net present value profile for the investment, and determine the internal rate of return.

Solution

In order to devise the net present value profile of any investment it is useful to have at least three values. We need the NPV at a 0% discount rate (*i.e.*, without regard to the time value of money), we need the IRR value (where NPV becomes 0), and we need at least one value in between which will give a rough idea of the shape of the NPV profile.

In section 5-4 of the chapter we computed the NPV of this project at 10%. The NPV with a salvage value of $20,000 was found to be $1,341.60.

We determined this value by solving the following equation, substituting 10% for i:

$$NPV = -30{,}000 + 3600a_5 i\% + 30{,}000\left(\frac{.3 \times .4}{.3+i}\right) + \frac{20{,}000}{(1+i)^5} - \frac{20{,}000}{(1+i)^5}\left(\frac{.3 \times .4}{.3+i}\right)$$

For an explanation of any of these terms refer to section 5-4.

We have our intermediate term for the profile, we now need a value for 0% and the IRR.

To determine the NPV at 0% we simply substitute 0 for i in the above equation.

$$NPV = -30{,}000 + 3600a_5 0\% + 30{,}000\left(\frac{.3 \times .4}{.3+0}\right) + \frac{20{,}000}{(1+0)^5} - \frac{20{,}000}{(1+0)^5}\left(\frac{.3 \times .4}{.3+0}\right)$$

$$= -30{,}000 + 3600(5) + 30{,}000\left(\frac{.12}{.3}\right) + \frac{20{,}000}{1} - \frac{20{,}000}{1}\left(\frac{.12}{.3}\right)$$

$$= \$12{,}000$$

To arrive at the IRR, we must set the above equation equal to zero, and derive the corresponding value of i by trial and error. We know the NPV of the project is still positive at 10%, so the IRR must be greater than this.

Substituting $i = 14\%$ we get:

$$NPV$$

$$= -30{,}000 + 3600a_5 14\% + 30{,}000\left(\frac{.3 \times .4}{.3 + .14}\right) + \frac{20{,}000}{(1 + .14)^5} - \frac{20{,}000}{(1 + 1.4)^5}\left(\frac{.3 \times .4}{.3 + .14}\right)$$

$$= -30{,}000 + 3600\,(3.433) + 30{,}000\left(\frac{.12}{.44}\right) + 20{,}000\,(.519) - 20{,}000\,(.519)\left(\frac{.12}{.44}\right)$$

$$= -1910.29$$

The IRR is therefore somewhere between 10% and 14%. By substituting $i = 12\%$ in the equation the value may be determined to be (–350.57). Thus the IRR is between 10% and 12%.

Interpolating we find:

value at 10%	+ 1341.60
value at x%	0
value at 12%	– 350.57

$$\frac{x - 10\%}{12\% - 10\%} = \frac{-1341.60}{-1341.60 - 350.57}$$

$$x = 10\% + \left[\frac{1341.60}{1692.17} \times 2\%\right] = 10\% + 1.59\% = 11.59\% = \text{IRR}$$

We now may plot the net present value profile with our values of

$12,000 at a discount rate of 0%
$1,341.60 at a discount rate of 10%
IRR of 11.59%

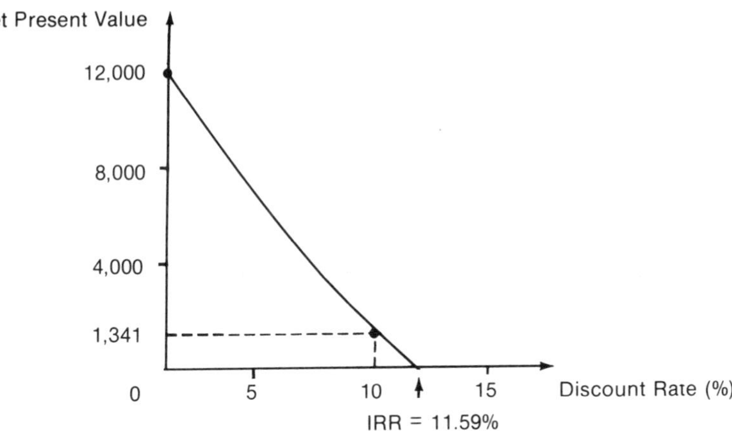

Note that substituting other discount rates, for example 5%, would have given additional points on the curve and, hence, a more accurate profile.

(c) Due to inflation, labor costs are expected to increase at an average rate of 15 percent per annum, and this increase will be reflected in the operating costs of both machines, which are also expected to grow at a rate of 15 percent per annum. Assuming no salvage value for the new machine, recompute the net present value of the investment.

Solution

It should first be noted that the initial $30,000 investment and the present value of the total tax shield from CCA will not be affected by inflation.

The new NPV may be computed as follows. Operating costs of $15,000 for the old machine and $9,000 for the new will increase by 15% per year. Thus we must increase both of these costs by 15% per year, find the after-tax increment and compute the present value of the savings. This is done in the following table.

Operating Costs for the Two Machines Given a 15% Inflation Rate

Year	Old Machine Operating Costs (1)	New Machine Operating Costs (2)	Difference (3)=(1)-(2)	After-Tax Difference (4) = (1-40%)×(3)	Present Value Factor at 10% (5)	Present Value of Saving (6)=(4)×(5)
1	15,000.00	9,000.00	6,000.00	3,600.00	.909	3,272.40
2	17,250.00	10,350.00	6,900.00	4,140.00	.826	3,419.64
3	19,837.50	11,902.50	7,935.00	4,761.00	.751	3,575.51
4	22,813.13	13,687.88	9,125.25	5,475.15	.683	3,739.53
5	26,235.09	15,741.06	10,494.03	6,296.42	.621	3,910.08
				Total Present Value of Savings		$17,917.16

From here it is an easy matter to substitute the new present value of all after-tax operating savings for the old value of \$13,647.60 derived in the chapter, giving:

Total Present Value = – initial investment
+ present value of all after-tax operating savings
+ present value of total tax shield from CCA
= – 30,000 + 17,917.16 + 9,000
= – \$3082.84

The net present value of the investment is now – \$3082.84.

5. A firm operates a computer on which it has a 5-year lease. The computer is not operating at capacity, and it is expected that this situation will prevail in the future. It is company policy *not* to rent out spare computer capacity to outside clients. Management is currently investigating whether to develop a new program to automate certain aspects of production-scheduling in the plant. Costs (before tax) of developing the program are estimated at \$20,000. These costs would be capitalized, with capital cost allowance taken at a rate of 30 percent. In addition, a consultant would have to be hired who would demand a fee of \$3,000 with this amount being expensed in the current accounting period. The firm's computing center, to recover its leasing costs, normally charges departments for use of computer time at a rate of \$200 per hour, and it would take 50 hours of computer time per year to run the above program. Savings (before-tax) in production costs in the plant are expected to be \$8,000 per year for 5 years if the new production-scheduling system is implemented. In addition, one of the machines which is currently required would no longer be needed and could be sold for \$10,000. This machine belongs to an asset class on which capital cost allowance is taken at a rate of 30 percent. At the end of 5 years, it is expected that the entire production process will be obsolete thus requiring a major overhaul. The firm's after-tax cost of capital is 15 percent, and the marginal corporate tax rate is 40 percent. Should the program be developed if an assessment is to be based on its net present value? (Assume there are other assets in each CCA class.) What is the program's internal rate of return?

Solution

To derive the NPV the first step must be to isolate all relevant cash flows in order to establish the time of their impact.

Relevant figures are as follows: where t_n is the period of their occurrence:

t_0	Initial cost of development	– \$20,000
	After-tax cost of consultant (\$3000 × 60%)	– \$ 1,800
	Sale of old machine	+ \$10,000
	Total initial outlays	– \$11,800
$t_1 - t_5$	Savings per year, after tax (\$8000 × 60%)	+ \$ 4,800

The present value of these savings is

$$\$4,800\ a_5 15\%, \text{ or } \$4,800 \times 3.352 = \$16,090.$$

In addition, the present value of the tax shield from depreciation will be:

$$\$10{,}000 \left[\frac{dt}{d+k}\right] = 10{,}000 \left[\frac{.12}{.45}\right] = \$2667$$

$20,000 is added to the asset class, with $10,000 lost from the sale of the old machine, for a net gain in depreciable assets of $20,000 – $10,000 = $10,000. Note that leasing costs are not included in the analysis. As it is company policy not to rent out spare capacity, all leasing costs would have to be paid anyway. Thus, there are no *incremental* cash flows with respect to leasing, and no opportunity costs.

We may now compute the NPV of the program.

NPV = –initial cost + sale of old machine – consultant's fee (after tax) + NPV of production savings (after tax) + NPV of the tax shield from additional depreciation

= –$20,000 + $10,000 – $1,800 + $16,090 + $2,667

= $6,957

Additional Problems

1. (a) A firm is purchasing a $10,000 machine and expects to realize annual operating savings of $3000 per year for the first 4 years and $4000 per year from the 5th to the 8th year inclusive. The company's tax rate is 40 percent and its discount rate is 8 percent. Depreciation expense is recorded using the declining balance method and a rate of 30 percent with no salvage value anticipated. For this investment, what is:

   i) the net present value
   ii) the internal rate of return
   iii) the payback period

   (b) If the machine in part (a) can be salvaged at the end of its useful life for $750, recalculate the NPV of the investment.

   (c) If the company decided to use straight-line depreciation, and if this method were allowable for tax purposes,

   (i) what would the net present value of the project be, assuming no salvage value?

   (ii) Also compute the average rate of return.

   (d) Calculate the NPV assuming the case as in part (c), but with the $750 salvage value at the end of the useful life.

2. Consider an investment project with the following facts:

Initial investment	$10,000
Net cash benefits before depreciation and taxes	
year 1 and year 2	$ 4,000 each year
year 3 and year 4	$ 4,500 each year

Given that the discount rate to be used is 6 percent, that the maximum rate for capital cost allowances on the declining balance basis appropriate for the class of assets is 20 percent, and that the firm's tax rate is 40 percent, calculate:

(a) The net cash flows generated by the project during the first 4 years.
(b) The present value of the total tax shield.
(c) The net present value and internal rate of return for this project.
(d) The payback period to the nearest year (round up).
(e) The net present value of the project, assuming a salvage value of $2,000 can be realized at the end of the 4th year.

3. Consider two Projects, *A* and *B*, given the following facts:

	Project *A*	Project *B*
Initial investment	$10,000	$20,000
Net benefits before taxes and depreciation		
Year 1	$ 8,000	$12,000
Year 2	$ 8,000	$12,000
Year 3	$ 8,000	$16,000
Year 4	$ 8,000	$16,000
Year 5	$ 8,000	$20,000

Assuming that the weighted average cost of capital to be used as the discount rate is 8 percent, a corporate tax rate of 40 percent, and the maximum rate for capital cost allowances on the declining basis appropriate for the class of assets to be 20 percent, calculate:
(a) NPV of Project *A*.
(b) NPV of Project *B*.
(c) Which project do you prefer? Discuss.

4. Consider a machine in use which can be sold for $3000 or which could be used for another 3 years with no salvage value at the end. A new machine can be bought at a total cost of $15,000 (including freight and installation cost). It also has an estimated life of 3 years and has no salvage value. If the new machine is purchased, direct cash savings could be expected to be $10,000 the first year and $5,000 in each of the next two years. Assuming that the corporate tax rate is 40 percent, the maximum rate for capital cost allowances is 30 percent, and the discount rate is 8 percent, calculate:
(a) The internal rate of return and net present value of the cash flows for the new machine.
(b) If the salvage value of the new machine at the end of the third year is estimated at $1000, what would be the internal rate of return and the net present value?

5. A restaurant chain considers opening a new restaurant. A suitable lot could be acquired for $400,000. It would cost $200,000 to erect the building, with capital cost allowance on the building taken at 30 percent. Kitchen facilities and furniture have already been bought for another restaurant which at the last moment could not be put in operation. They were acquired a year ago at a cost of $80,000 and have a current market value of $60,000, with capital cost allowance taken at a rate of 20 percent. Landscaping can be done at a cost of $10,000 and would be expensed in the current accounting period. The firm's

tax rate is 40 percent, and its cost of capital is 12 percent. Including the present values of tax shields from capital cost allowance into your considerations, what is the total net investment if the chain decides to go ahead with the new restaurant?

6. A firm currently operates a machine which was purchased at a cost of \$150,000 two years ago. It has a current market value of \$100,000. A new improved version of the equipment is now on the market at a cost of \$130,000. The machines are part of a general asset class, and capital cost allowance is taken at a rate of 30 percent. Special foundations for the new machine would need to be laid requiring 200 man hours. The work can be done by the firm's own employees with \$20 per man hour generally being charged. As there is currently some slack and excess capacity due to a sales slump, the foundations could be laid and the 200 man hours could be provided without disrupting other operations in any way. The firm does not contemplate laying off employees at this time as the current sales slump is expected to be short-lived and the firm wants to retain its employees. Costs for laying the foundations would simply be expensed in the current accounting period. The firm's tax rate is 40 percent and its cost of capital is 12 percent. Including the present values of tax shields from capital cost allowance into your considerations, what is the total net investment if the firm disposed of the old machine and bought the new machine.

7. A firm is considering building a new and improved production facility for one of its existing products. It would be built on a piece of land which the firm has owned for many years and which is vacant. This land was acquired four years ago at a cost of \$200,000; it has a current estimated market value of \$1,000,000. The building can be erected for \$350,000. Machinery worth \$100,000 needs to be bought. Certain other necessary production equipment will be produced by one of the firm's own divisions, with production costs estimated at \$50,000, and a market price of \$60,000. Capital cost allowance on a declining balance will be taken on all depreciable assets at a rate of 20 percent. Operating savings from the new production facility are expected to be \$300,000 per year for the next 10 years. The salvage value at the end of the 10 years is expected to be \$1,500,000, which is solely the value of the land. The firm's tax rate is 40 percent, with capital gains taxed at half their value. The firm's weighted average cost of capital is estimated at 15 percent. Based on a discounted cash flow analysis, should the investment be undertaken?

8. A financial manager is looking at a report which contains the following information:

	Project *A*	Project *B*
Initial outlays	\$100,000	\$100,000
Net present value of expected net cash flows	\$ 30,000	\$ 50,000
Internal rate of return of expected net cash flows	15%	10%

(a) You are asked to explain why Project *B* has a higher NPV but a lower IRR.

(b) If you are in a position to make the decision, which project would you choose? Why? (Assume that the weighted average cost of capital of the firm is 6 percent.)

9. You are presented with two proposals, *A* and *B*, with equal risks, requiring initial investments of \$10,000 and \$8,000 respectively. Subsequent net cash inflows are given as follows:

Year	Project *A*	Project *B*
1	\$ 3,250	\$2,500
2	\$ 3,250	\$2,500
3	\$ 3,500	\$3,000
4	\$ 3,500	\$3,000

(a) Assuming the weighted average cost of capital to be used as the discount rate to be 6 percent, rank the two projects in terms of:
  (i) payback period,
  (ii) internal rate of return, and
  (iii) net present value.

(b) How do you account for the differences in ranking? Which project do you prefer? Why?

10. Consider two projects, *A* and *B*, with the following facts:

	Project *A*	Project *B*
Initial cash outlays	\$20,000	\$10,000
Present value of expected net cash inflows	\$50,000	\$30,000

(a) Compute the net present value and netted benefit-cost ratio for each project.

(b) Which project is preferred if they are mutually exclusive? Why?

Case

The Consolidated Logging Company Ltd.

Early in 1975, the financial manager of Consolidated Logging Company (C.L.C.) was investigating the possibility of either replacing one of the company's 7 log-loaders with a new model or substantially refitting the existing machine. The company is engaged in supplying timber-loading services to a large lumber concern in British Columbia. C.L.C. has been in business for approximately 12 years and has built up a reputation for dependability and quality service throughout its life. Although not yet the leader in the industry, it was expected that given another 3 to 4 years, C.L.C. would likely attain this position.

Initially, the financial manager decided to look at replacing or refitting just one machine. Based on the outcome of that analysis, he felt he would be in a better position to decide on the other loaders. The following information, on a per-annum before-tax basis, indicated the approximate costs of operating each loader:

Maintenance and Repair	$10,000
Wages of Operators (2)	31,900
Gasoline	8,200
Storage	4,800
Miscellaneous Servicing	5,000
Total Operating Costs	$60,500

Although the "average" loader appears in the asset class at approximately $40,000, if it were to be sold today, a market price of only $20,000 could be obtained. If refitting were undertaken, the financial manager estimated that the machine could conceivably be run for another 10 years. The cost of each refitting was estimated at $85,000.

Alternatively, Consolidated Logging could purchase a new, more powerful loader at a cost of $150,000 from a local manufacturer. In addition, special tires and parts would have to be purchased at at price of $15,000 and would last the useful life of the basic machine. The new machine was essentially the same as the older one since it could perform the same basic functions. This model had not been previously produced, however, and in a sense it was "first off the production line". This fact seemed to trouble the financial manager, for the manufacturer of these loaders had unsuccessfully attempted to introduce a similar model some years earlier. On the other hand, the new model promised lower operating costs primarily in the form of reduced labor expense (only one highly trained "engineer" was needed to operate the machine) and lower maintenance and repair costs. A detailed breakdown of the pre-tax, annual operating costs follows:

Maintenance and Repair	$ 6,500
Wages of Operator	19,500
Diesel Fuel	8,900
Garage Facilities	6,000
Miscellaneous Servicing	4,000
Total Operating Costs	$44,900

The financial manager estimated that the new machine would last at least 10 years without any major refitting or overhaul. Beyond this point, no one could estimate with reasonable accuracy what was going to happen. Given the rapid technological advances within this industry, salvage value was estimated to be only $2,400 or approximately one-half of the loader's book value at that time.

Other considerations that would affect the decision on whether to replace or refit included the current general decline in the lumber industry; labor unrest; and the opportunity costs associated with tying-up funds in either project. Concerning the general decline in the lumber industry, just how long the downturn could last remained to be seen, but at that time, the effects of it were starting to be felt in industries associated with lumber production. Consolidated Logging's revenues were slightly lower than they were for a similar period last year. Furthermore, labor strife was not at all uncommon. The manufacturer of the new machines had experienced considerable labor unrest at his plant over the past two or three months. As a result, customers were not getting delivery of much-needed equipment on time and one large purchaser even cancelled his order at the very last moment. Another factor that the financial manager had to consider was the implicit opportunity cost associated with tying up scarce funds in either the purchase of the new loaders or the refitting of the older ones. It was estimated that in order to invest in any project of this nature, after-tax annual returns of 12 percent or greater had to be met for the project to be attractive. Although this was a rather high figure, the financial manager believed it to be reasonable given the risks associated with this particular category of investment. All of these loaders belonged to the Class 10 pool of assets and were depreciable at the maximum rate of 30 percent per annum. It was C.L.C.'s policy to always have something in that asset class so as to avoid the possible recapture, or terminal loss implications of current tax laws. Consolidated Logging's overall tax rate at this time was 40 percent.

Required: Assume you are the financial manager. You are required to submit to the Board of Directors a written analysis concerning the advisability of either refitting the existing loader or acquiring a new one. Your report should separate the qualitative and quantitative considerations.

Selected References

W. Baumol, and R. Quandt, "Investment and Discount Rates under Capital Rationing—A Programming Approach," *The Economic Journal*, June, 1965, pp. 317-329.

R. Bernhard, "Mathematical Programming Models for Capital Budgeting—A Survey, Generalization, and Critique," *Journal of Financial and Quantitative Analysis*, June, 1969, pp. 111-158.

H. Bierman, and S. Smidt, *The Capital Budgeting Decision*, (3rd ed.). New York: Macmillan, 1971.

The Conference Board, *Managing The Resource Allocation Process*, New York: National Industrial Conference Board, 1963.

P. Dasgupta, A. Sen, and S. Marglin, *Guidelines for Project Evaluation*, New York: United Nations, 1972.

C. Doenges, "The Reinvestment Problem in A Practical Perspective," *Financial Management*, Spring 1972, pp. 85-91.

C. Dudley, "A Note on Reinvestment Assumptions in Choosing Between Net Present Value and Internal Rate of Return," *Journal of Finance*, September, 1972, pp. 907-915.

C. Edge, *A Practical Manual on the Appraisal of Capital Expenditure* (rev. ed.), Hamilton: The Society of Industrial Accountants of Canada, 1971.

R. Fogler, "Ranking Techniques and Capital Rationing", *Accounting Review*, January, 1972, pp. 134-143.

S. Henrici, "Eyeing the ROI," *Harvard Business Review*, May-June, 1968, pp. 88-97.

J. Hirshleifer, "On the Theory of Optimal Investment Decisions," *Journal of Political Economy*, August, 1958, pp. 95-103.

C. G. Hoskins, "Benefit-Cost Ratios Versus Net Present Value: Revisited", *Journal of Business Finance and Accounting*, Summer, 1974, pp. 249-265.

C. G. Hoskins and M. J. Dunn, "The Economic Evaluation of Capital Expenditure Proposals under Uncertainty: The Practice of Large Corporations in Canada", *Journal of Business Administration*, Fall 1974, pp. 44-55.

I. Kilpatrick, *Capital Expenditures, Key to Profits*, Toronto: Sir Isaac Pitman (Canada) Ltd., 1971.

T. Klammer, "Empirical Evidence of the Adoption of Sophisticated Capital Budgeting Techniques", *Journal of Business*, July, 1972, pp. 387-397.

E. Lerner, and A. Rappaport, "Limit DCF in Capital Budgeting", *Harvard Business Review*, September-October, 1968, pp. 133-139.

J. Lorie, and L. Savage, "Three Problems in Capital Rationing", *Journal of Business*, October, 1955, pp. 229-239.

P. Lusztig, and B. Schwab, "A Note on the Application of Linear Programming to Capital Budgeting", *Journal of Financial and Quantitative Analysis*, December, 1968, pp. 427-431.

J. Mao, "Internal Rate of Return as a Ranking Criterion", *Engineering Economist*, Winter, 1966, pp. 1-13.

S. Myers, "A Note on Linear Programming and Capital Budgeting," *Journal of Finance*, March, 1972, pp. 89-92.

S. Myers, "Interactions of Corporate Financing and Investment Decisions—Implications for Capital Budgeting", *Journal of Finance*, March, 1974, pp. 1-25.

D. Quirin, *The Capital Expenditure Decision*, Homewood: Irwin, 1967.

A. Robichek and J. Van Horne, "Abandonment Value and Capital Budgeting", *Journal of Finance*, December, 1967, pp. 577-590.

B. Schwab and P. Lusztig, "A Comparative Analysis of the Net Present Value and the Benefit-Cost Ratios as Measures of the Economic Desirability of Investments", *Journal of Finance*, June, 1969, pp. 507-516.

E. Solomon, "The Arithmetic of Capital-Budgeting Decisions", *Journal of Business*, April, 1956, pp. 124-129.

E. Solomon, *The Theory of Financial Management*, New York: Columbia University Press, 1963.

J. Van Horne, "A Note on Biases in Capital Budgeting Introduced by Inflation", *Journal of Financial and Quantitative Analysis*, January 1971, pp. 653-658.

J. Weaver, "Organizing and Maintaining a Capital Expenditure Program," *Engineering Economist*, Fall, 1974, pp. 1-36.

M. Weingartner, "Capital Budgeting of Interrelated Projects: Survey and Synthesis", *Management Science*, March, 1966, pp. 485-516.

M. Weingartner, "Some New Views on the Payback Period and Capital Budgeting Decisions", *Management Science*, August, 1969, pp. B-594 to B-607.

M. Weingartner, *Mathematical Programming and the Analysis of Capital Budgeting Problems*, Englewood Cliffs: Prentice-Hall, 1963.

G. Whitmore and L. Amey, "Capital Budgeting under Rationing: Comments on the Lusztig and Schwab Procedure", *Journal of Financial and Quantitative Analysis*, January, 1973, pp. 127-135.

CHAPTER 5: APPENDIX

Mathematical Programming

1. Introduction

A number of practical problems, some of which are encountered in finance, take the following form: a decision-maker wants to maximize (or minimize) some quantity which is a function of a number of variables but is subject to some constraints on these variables. In capital budgeting, for example, the total net present value of a portfolio of projects is a function of the individual investments chosen and the amounts invested in each case. We may wish to maximize this net present value subject to budgetary constraints in various periods; constraints on other resources such as manpower; or legal constraints in the case of financial institutions. For reasonably well-structured situations, we can formulate such a problem in terms of mathematical equations, thereby constructing a *mathematical model* of the decision situation. Quite generally, such a model may take the form,

$$\text{(1)} \quad \begin{aligned} &\text{maximize} \quad f(x_1, x_2, \ldots, x_n) \\ &\text{subject to} \quad g_i(x_1, x_2, \ldots, x_n) \leq b_i, \text{ for } i = 1, 2, \ldots, m, \end{aligned}$$

where $f(x_1, \ldots, x_n)$ is the *objective function* which we want to maximize, there being m constraint equations $g_i(x_1, \ldots, x_n) \leq b_i$ expressing restrictions imposed on the values which we may choose for the *decision variables* $x_1, x_2, \ldots, x_n$. It should be noted that problems of maximization and minimization (we may, for instance, wish to minimize costs rather than maximize revenue) are completely equivalent mathematically, maximization of $f(x)$ being the same as minimization of $-f(x)$. While simple problems with only a few equations and variables may often be solved by inspection or intuition, larger-scale problems involving several dozen equations and/or variables require more systematic solution procedures. Mathematical programming provides us with computational techniques for finding solutions to problems of this type. In the following sections several branches of mathematical programming are identified depending on the types of equations found in the objective function and in the constraints which, in turn, determine the mathematical techniques required to derive the optimal solution.

2. Linear Programming

The easiest case, mathematically speaking, arises when all equations in the model are linear (a linear function of one variable would be represented by a straight line). The most common form of linear program is

$$
(2)\quad
\begin{aligned}
\text{maximize}\quad & c_1x_1 + c_2x_2 + \ldots + c_nx_n \\
\text{subject to}\quad & a_{11}x_1 + a_{12}x_2 + \ldots + a_{1n}x_n \le b_1 \\
& a_{21}x_1 + a_{22}x_2 + \ldots + a_{2n}x_n \le b_2 \\
& \quad\vdots \qquad\qquad\qquad\qquad\qquad\qquad \vdots \\
& a_{m1}x_1 + a_{m2}x_2 + \ldots + a_{mn}x_n \le b_m \\
& x_1, x_2, \ldots, x_n \ge 0
\end{aligned}
$$

where $x_1, \ldots, x_n$ are the decision variables, and all the a's, b's, and c's are constants which may be positive or negative. Staying with our capital budgeting example and assuming that we have n different projects in which to consider investing, $x_1, x_2, \ldots, x_n$ represent the amounts of project $1, 2, \ldots, n$ respectively to be included in the portfolio. The decision variables are to be chosen in such a way as to maximize the objective function while at the same time satisfying all the constraints. The coefficients in the objective function are $c_1, \ldots, c_n$ which specify the unit contributions of projects $1, \ldots, n$ respectively. The total net present value contribution of project 1, for instance, is given by c_1x_1, namely, the unit contribution of project 1 multiplied by the number of units undertaken. The total amount of a particular resource available may be represented by b_1 for example, the budget ceiling in period 1; and the first constraint simply states that we cannot use more of this resource than is available. For example, a_{11} would be the amount of capital needed to finance one unit of project 1 during the first period, a_{12} the amount needed to finance one unit of project 2, and so on, while the amount of capital used is again obtained by multiplying these unit figures with the number of units to be undertaken, given by $x_1, \ldots, x_n$. Generally it is required that all activities undertaken be positive.

Example

Consider only two investment proposals, labelling the amounts to be invested x_1 and x_2 respectively. Each dollar invested in project 1 yields a net present value of 1.2, and each dollar invested in project 2 yields 1.0. The total amount of capital available is \$100,000 and, for reasons of diversification, it has been decided that not more than \$80,000 is to be invested in project 1 and not more than \$60,000 in project 2. While this example is oversimplified, and the optimal values for x_1 and x_2 could clearly be found without the use of mathematical techniques, it can serve to show the basic principles employed in finding solutions to more complex linear programming problems which defy intuitive analysis.

Mathematically, we have,

$$(3)\quad \begin{array}{lrl} \text{maximize} & 1.2\,x_1 + x_2 & \\ \text{subject to} & x_1 + x_2 & \leq 100{,}000 \\ & x_1 & \leq \;\; 80{,}000 \\ & x_2 & \leq \;\; 60{,}000 \\ & x_1, x_2 & \geq \;\; 0 \end{array}$$

and, relating (3) to (2), $c_1 = 1.2$, $c_2 = 1.0$, $a_{11} = 1$, $a_{12} = 1$, $a_{21} = 1$, $a_{22} = 0$, $a_{31} = 0$, $a_{32} = 1$, $b_1 = 100{,}000$, $b_2 = 80{,}000$, $b_3 = 60{,}000$, $n = 2$, and $m = 3$. Since the example involves only two variables, x_1 and x_2, we may portray the above relationships graphically, as shown in Figure 1. The shaded area in Figure 1 represents the *feasible region* for this problem, that is, all points (x_1, x_2) such that all the constraints of the problem are satisfied. It is necessary to find the point in this feasible region for which the objective function $1.2x_1 + 1.0x_2$ assumes the largest possible value.

FIGURE 1

Geometrical Solution of a Linear Programming Problem with Two Decision Variables. (Shaded area shows feasible values of x_1 and x_2.)

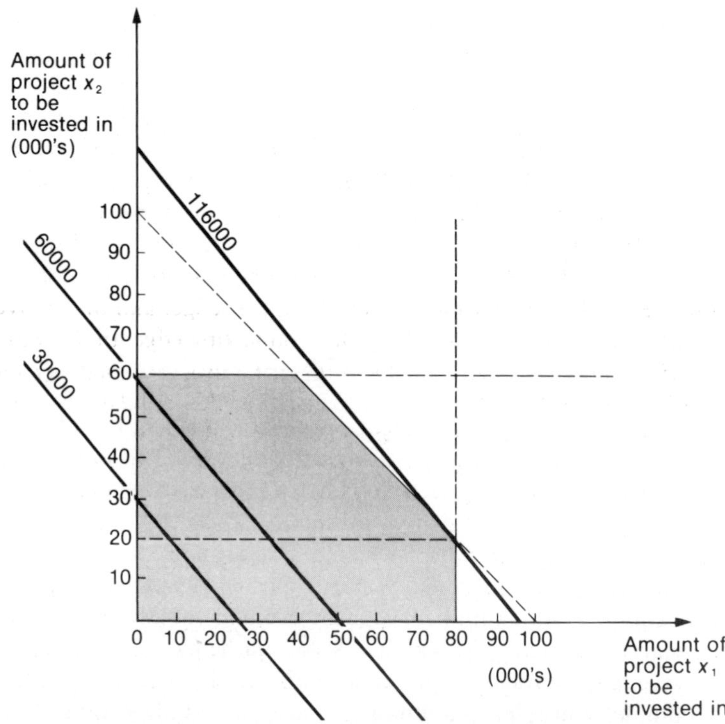

We may start by seeing if a net present value of \$30,000 can be achieved, finding all the points for which this is possible. The line marked 30,000 is derived, which is given by the equation $1.2x_1 + 1.0x_2 = 30{,}000$. Next, an attempt is made to increase the net present value to \$60,000, obtaining a line $1.2x_1 + 1.0x_2 = 60{,}000$ which is parallel to the first line but further removed from the origin. We can try to further increase the net present value, obtaining parallel lines which are successively further away from the origin, as long as these lines have at least one point which falls within the feasible region. It is easy to see that the highest net present value which can be achieved in this way is \$116,000 and is determined by the line which just touches the feasible region at one of its cornerpoints where $x_1 = 80{,}000$ and $x_2 = 20{,}000$, this being the optimal solution for our problem.

The concepts used in this graphical solution form the basis for the *simplex algorithm* which is used to solve general linear programming problems. In linear programming, the feasible region is always bounded by straight lines or planes, having a number of cornerpoints where these boundary lines or planes meet (where there are more than three variables, these planes and cornerpoints cannot be represented graphically, but they can be adequately characterized and described mathematically). The objective function is again a line or a plane which we want to push as far in one direction as possible. This implies that the optimal solution will generally be at a cornerpoint of the feasible region. Since there are only a limited number of cornerpoints (five in the above example), in principle we could find the optimal solution by just computing the value of the objective function for all possible cornerpoints, and then picking the best one. The difficulty is that for problems with many variables the number of possible cornerpoints can become extremely large, and trying to solve a linear-programming problem in this fashion would be inefficient at best. We require an efficient search procedure for searching through cornerpoints, and this is in essence what the simplex method provides. It starts at any one cornerpoint, looks at the various edges connecting this cornerpoint with other cornerpoints, chooses an edge in such a way that the improvement in the value of the objective function is greatest per unit movement along this edge, and then moves to an adjacent and better cornerpoint along this connecting edge. In this way, we are able to find the optimal cornerpoint by looking at only a very small percentage of all possible cornerpoints. The simplex method is clearly amenable to computerization, and standard computer programs are widely available. Its efficiency permits solution of linear-programming problems with several thousand variables and constraint equations in only a few hours of computer time.

In order to obtain an appreciation for the potentials and limitations of linear programming, we should have a proper understanding of the underlying assumptions, some of which may be removed by techniques which shall be described subsequently. Linear relationships as discussed above imply *proportionality, divisibility,* and *additivity*. Thus, in our portfolio example, the net present value derived from an individual investment was assumed to be directly proportional to the amounts of the investments undertaken; and twice the amount of a particular investment activity implies twice the contribution of this activity to the objective function. In a straight-line relationship there is no room for economies or diseconomies of scale and, while underlying assumptions of linearity are illustrated by focusing on the objective function, the constraint equations are similarly restricted. The contributions of each type of investment were assumed to be independent of the levels of activity chosen for other investments, and no interactions such as synergistic or substitution effects are possible, the joint contribution of two activities being given just by the sum of each individual contribution. It was also assumed in the preceding analysis that individual activities can be undertaken in any amount, fractional or integer, that is, the *x*'s are continuous variables. Many investment projects, the purchase of a new machine for example, can only be undertaken in integer amounts and we must look to extensions of linear programming to accommodate such cases. Finally, linear programming assumes that all the coefficients (the *a*'s, *b*'s, and *c*'s in (2)) are constants whose values are known with certainty. While these assumptions may appear restrictive to the extent of limiting the usefulness of linear programming, they are sufficiently well-met in enough situations to make linear programming probably the most widely applied technique of operations research in industry. A number of extensions allow us to deal with situations in which the above assumptions cannot be fully accepted.

3. Sensitivity Analysis

Some of the coefficients in (2) above may not be known with certainty but may simply represent best estimates such as the amount of capital available one or two periods hence. Such budgetary constraints may even be subject to alteration through, for example, additional borrowing. Referring to the graphic solution of Figure 1, we see that a change in the constant of a constraint simply means a parallel shift of the boundary line for that constraint. Thus, if b_1 is increased in (3) from \$100,000 to \$110,000, the corresponding constraint boundary line in Figure 1 would be moved away from the origin as indicated in Figure 2a, entailing a shift in the optimal solution from A to B, with an increase in the total net present value by \$10,000 from \$116,000 to \$126,000.

One of the very useful items of additional information provided by the simplex algorithm is the increase in the objective function occasioned through an increase in any constraint coefficient by one unit. These figures are often called *shadow prices* or optimal solutions for the *dual variables*. For the three constraints in (3) above we would obtain values of 1, 0.2, and 0 respectively. Thus an increase in b_2 by one unit from \$80,000 to \$80,001 would imply an increase in the objective function by \$0.20 from \$116,000 to \$116,000.20.

If we are in a position to alter a constraint, perhaps because it is merely a policy constraint, this information allows for ready assessment of the implicit cost of a particular policy, and it may be very useful in evaluating alternatives.

Variations of coefficients in the objective function may be similarly dealt with. Referring again to the graphic solution, a change in one of the unit net present value contributions, for example in project 1 a change from \$1.2 to \$1.1, would merely be reflected in a change of the slope of the objective function from line *a* to line *b*, as indicated in Figure 2b.

FIGURE 2a

Geometrical Representation of the Impact of a Shift in a Constraint

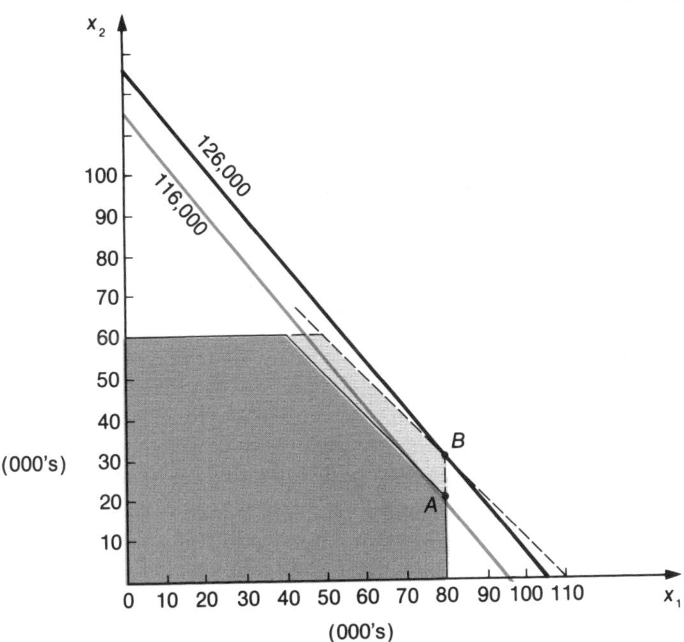

FIGURE 2b

Geometrical Representation of the Impact of Varying Coefficients in the Objective Function

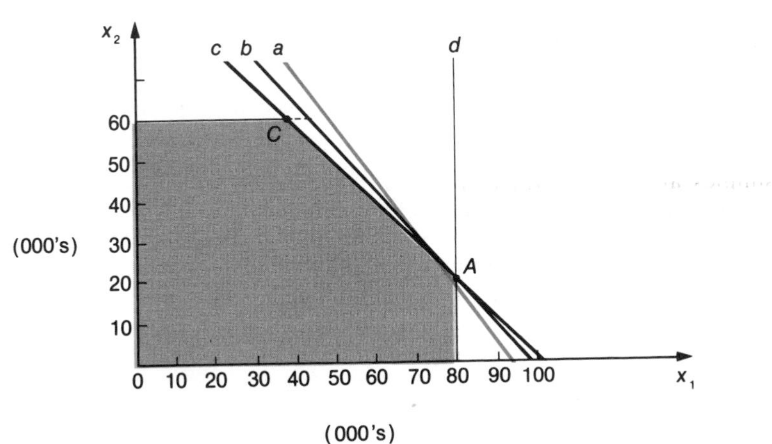

Given uncertainty about the true value of a particular coefficient in the objective function, we may be interested in knowing how sensitive the optimal solution is to changes in the value of this coefficient, in other words, what deviation from the estimated value can be tolerated without jeopardizing the optimality of the solution. Graphically, it is easy to see from Figure 2b that as long as the slope of the objective function falls between lines c and d, A will remain the optimal solution. In our example, this implies that as long as the unit contribution of project 1 is greater than one, it will be optimal to invest \$80,000 in project 1 and \$20,000 in project 2, as originally derived. However, should the unit contribution, c, fall below one, the optimal solution would shift from A to C implying investments of \$40,000 and \$60,000 in projects 1 and 2 respectively. Again, this information is readily obtained from the simplex method, and it allows us, to some extent at least, to incorporate uncertainty into an otherwise deterministic approach such as linear programming. Changes in the other coefficients (the a_{ij} in (1)) may be analysed in similar fashion. *Parametric linear programming* permits limited analysis of simultaneous variations in several coefficients.

4. *Nonlinear Programming*

If the above assumptions of linearity do not hold, in particular if the equations entail terms with powers of the decision variables (such as x^2, x^3, etc.) or interaction terms (such as x_1x_2 or x_1/x_2) possibly signifying economies of scale or substitution effects, we are faced with a nonlinear model, and generally we have to resort to nonlinear-programming techniques. For example, the linear programming problem in (3) above would become nonlinear if we changed the objective function slightly to maximize $1.2x_1 + 1.0x_2 + 0.1x_1x_2$, the last term implying some interaction between the two variables such that the net present value derived from project 1 depends in some way on the amount of project 2 undertaken. It is beyond the scope of this brief introduction to elaborate in even an elementary fashion on the techniques of nonlinear programming. The problem is considerably complicated by the fact that we no longer need have a nicely bounded feasible region with cornerpoints and that the optimal solution need not be on the boundary of the feasible region. Nevertheless, various techniques are available for solving nonlinear problems, although computationally they are not nearly as efficient as the simplex method. We are restricted in the size of problems which can be solved both in terms of the number of variables and the number of constraints. An alternative is to approximate a nonlinear relationship by a linear one, that is, by fitting a line to a curve, which transforms the problem back into a linear programming format. Clearly, the solution will not correspond exactly to the solution which we would ideally have sought; nevertheless, in practice we often have to be content with less than the ideal, and the real issue becomes whether the solution derived by some approximation is useful in the sense of being an improvement over previous practice.

5. *Integer Programming*

Techniques of integer programming apply when some or all of the variables are restricted to integer values. Certain investment projects, such as installation of a new machine for example, cannot be undertaken in fractional amounts, thereby necessitating integer constraints. In finance, the case where a variable may only assume two values, zero or one (such a variable is called a *binary variable*), is of particular importance; the values of one and zero may signify that a particular indivisible investment project will or will not be undertaken respectively. Again, the solutions of integer programming problems pose additional difficulties necessitating special solution techniques which are limited in their efficiency and scope if compared with standard techniques of linear programming. This restricts the size of problems which we may solve. Computer codes do exist, however, for the solution of moderate-size problems (for example, several dozen variables and/or constraints) and many of the potential applications in finance fall within this category.

6. *Stochastic and Chance-Constrained Programming*

As demonstrated in the preceding discussion, it is generally assumed in formulating and solving linear programming problems that the coefficients in (2) above are known. Sensitivity analysis provides a powerful tool for analysing possible variations in the values which these coefficients may assume. A further step in relaxing the above assumption is an explicit incorporation of uncertainty into the model by interpreting each coefficient as a random variable with an associated probability distribution. Stochastic and chance-constrained programming offer solution techniques at least for certain models of this type. Several complications arise: if the coefficients of the objective function are random variables, then the objective function which is just a sum of random variables becomes itself a random variable with its own probability distribution, and the concept of maximizing the objective function needs some redefinition. We may, for instance, just maximize the expected value of the objective function. Random variables in the constraint equations give rise to two different interpretations of these constraints: in stochastic programming, the constraints have to be met for any values which the coefficients may assume, whereas in chance-constrained programming, a small probability of a constraint being violated is allowed for, with the decision-maker being able to specify the risk he is willing to assume in this regard. Since many problems in finance deal with inherently uncertain situations, an increasing number of applications of stochastic and chance-constrained programming have been suggested in recent literature.

7. *Summary*

Mathematical-programming techniques offer efficient solution procedures to the problems for which they were designed: to find the optimal course of action from a given set of alternatives in a generally well-structured situation with reasonably complete and accurate information available. While proving useful in the formulation and solution of a wide variety of problems in industry, it is probably fair to say that most applications in finance are somewhat peripheral. The reason may well be that in financial decisions the main difficulties are often faced in structuring the problem and in obtaining the necessary information, for example, formulating an appropriate objective function (with which some of the literature in capital budgeting is concerned); finding the set of feasible alternative actions; and determining values or probability distributions for parameters. These steps generally have to be solved before an application of mathematical programming can be initiated.

Problems (Appendix)

1. Consider a firm manufacturing two products *X* and *Y*. Each unit of product *X* requires 10 hours of foundry time, 6 hours machining, and 4.5 hours for finishing. Each unit of product *Y* requires 5 hours of foundry time, 6 hours machining, and 18 hours finishing. Each week the firm has available 50 hours of foundry time, 36 hours of machine time, and 81 hours of finishing. It is assumed that the firm can sell all it produces and makes a profit of $9 on each unit of *X* and $7 on each unit of *Y*. Given these circumstances, what combination of products *X* and *Y* should be manufactured to maximize profits?
2. A firm wishes to invest in two projects requiring cash outlays in each of the next three periods. The firm is subject to budget constraints in these periods and must decide how to allocate optimally its available funds to the projects in order to maximize the overall net present value. Assume here that the projects are divisible, that is, it is possible to carry out a fraction of a project but it is not possible to carry out more than one unit of each project. The following table shows the cash outlays that would be made in each period per unit of each project undertaken, the unit net present values of the projects, and the budgetary constraints.

Project	Cash Outlay per Unit			Net Present Value
	in period 1	in period 2	in period 3	of Investment
1	20	15	6	2
2	20	5	18	1
Budget Constraint	12	6	9	

(a) What combination of projects 1 and 2 maximizes the net present value?
(b) What is the change in the net present value given that the period 2 budget is increased from 6 to 7?
(c) If the objective function were to maximize $2.9x_1 + x_2$, what would the optimal solution be?

Selected References (Appendix)

F. Hillier, and G. Lieberman, *Introduction to Operations Research*, San Francisco: Holden Day, 1968, Chapters 5 and 15-17.

H. Wagner, *Principles of Operations Research*, Engelwood Cliffs: Prentice-Hall, 1969, Chapters 2-5, 13, 14.

M. Weingartner, *Mathematical Programming and the Analysis of Capital Budgeting Problems*, Chicago: Markham Publishing Co., 1967.

Chapter 6
Capital Expenditure Decisions Under Uncertainty

6-1. INTRODUCTION

In the previous chapter, we assumed that the cash flow forecasts characterizing a particular investment were given. We concentrated our discussion on the proper application of evaluation criteria to such forecasted cash flows. In this chapter, we will explore the effects of uncertainty and risk on the evaluation of investment projects.[1]

Any business forecast, including the estimation of future cash flows, is subject to uncertainty. Thus, when a staff analyst forecasts $100,000 as the cash flow to be generated by a new investment three years hence, he does not imply a belief that a cash flow of *exactly* $100,000 will be realized. As a matter of fact, he would probably be amazed if his forecast proved completely accurate. The single-value estimate of $100,000 has to be interpreted as some sort of "best estimate", which either may not be reached or may be exceeded. More precisely, the actual outcome may cover a range of dollar figures, and some probability may be associated with each possible range of values. The estimate of $100,000 which was put forward may merely represent an average or expected value of such a probability distribution.

Managers and investors generally are fully aware of risk and rely not only on the use of average figures to evaluate the economic desirability of investments but also consider the associated uncertainties.

Such uncertainties can have wide implications for the financial decisions of a firm. Risks associated with a firm's investments affect returns to both creditors and shareholders. More specifically, the greater the perceived riskiness of ventures entered into by the corporation, the greater will be the reluctance of investors to advance funds. Investor reluctance will quite obviously be reflected in the terms, including costs, at which the firm is able to raise funds; also, the proportions of various funds (in particular equity and debt) on which the firm typically relies for its financing may be influenced by the riskiness of the firm's investments.[2] Thus, as the uncertainty regarding future cash flows increases, a firm may become increasingly reluctant to borrow funds and become committed to fixed debt charges.

As we can see, the firm's cost of capital is directly related to the risk of the firm's investments.

[1]Formal distinctions which are sometimes made between risk and uncertainty will be dropped here, and we will use both terms interchangeably. See A. Robichek and S. Myers, *Optimal Financing Decisions*, Englewood Cliffs: Prentice-Hall, 1965, pp. 67-69, on the matter of definitions in the context of finance.

[2]For a formal exposition, see D. Tuttle and R. Litzenberger, "Leverage, Diversification and Capital Market Effects on a Risk-Adjusted Capital Budgeting Framework", *Journal of Finance*, June, 1968, pp. 427-443.

Two main problems must be faced in the analysis of investments subject to uncertainty. First of all, the uncertainties have to be measured. This is generally accomplished through the use of probability distributions. Then the uncertainties have to be evaluated, taking into consideration the objectives of the firm and its management. This latter step will involve identifying tradeoffs between expected profitability and risk.

6-2. PROBABILISTIC ESTIMATION CASH FLOWS[3]

As noted above, a single-value estimate typically represents someone's best approximation of a whole range of possible values, each with a particular probability of occurring. It is typically the first step in any explicit consideration of uncertainty to obtain additional information from the forecaster, asking him to express his predictions in terms of probabilities. Ideally, this will result in a complete probability distribution.

FIGURE 6-1

Probability and Cumulative Probability Distributions

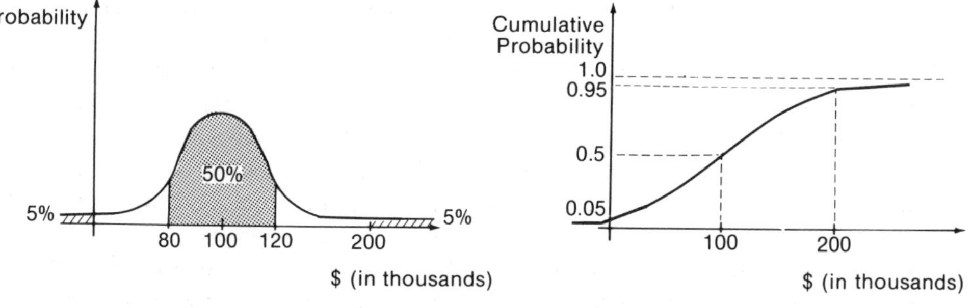

(a) Regular Probability Distribution

(b) Cumulative Probability Distribution

Probabilities can be represented either in the form of a regular probability distribution, or in the form of a cumulative probability distribution, as shown in Figure 6-1. With a regular probability distribution, the proportion of the area under the curve falling within any given range indicates the probability of the forecasted variable falling between the two specified values.

Example

> If 50 percent of the total area under the curve in Figure 6-1(a) falls between the values of $80,000 and $120,000, this implies a 50 percent probability that forecasted cash flows will fall within this range. Similarly, the probability of negative cash flows would be 5 percent according to Figure 6-1(a).

A cumulative probability distribution is just another way of portraying the same

[3]For a review of some of the basic concepts of probability on which the following sections draw, the reader is referred to any standard introductory text in the field.

information. It allows us to read off on the vertical axis (cumulative probabilities) the probability of forecasted cash flows being below any corresponding value on the horizontal axis.

Example

Probabilities of anticipated cash flows being below $0 are read off Figure 6-1(b) as 5 percent, and there is a 50 percent probability of cash flows falling short of the "best estimate" or expected value of $100,000.

Distributions such as the ones presented in Figure 6-1 provide a manager who is assessing an investment project with more relevant information than a statement such as: "cash flows from this project three years hence are anticipated to be $100,000".

One should recognize that probability distributions thus derived are merely an explicit presentation of the forecaster's subjective beliefs about a particular situation. Depending on the quality of the forecaster's judgment, a probability distribution may or may not be a good representation of reality. However, there are several advantages to be gained in making one's judgment explicit.[4]

First of all, having to be explicit about an opinion forces us to think through a particular situation, which in turn may help to improve the forecasting. It is one thing to be able to say "I think chances are good that we will make a profit on this one", but quite another thing to have to be more precise and to make explicit the reasoning behind such a statement. This is not to say that intuitive judgments are unimportant in deriving business forecasts, but rather to suggest that such judgments are best made within some systematic framework of analysis.

Secondly, and related to the above, probability distributions can improve the quality of communication and advance the exchange of information within the organization. Statements such as "there is a good chance of breaking even" or "we have to be lucky to get a fair return on this project" are difficult to interpret. A probability distribution is a much more precise way of presenting and interpreting beliefs regarding uncertainty, and its use can serve to reduce distortions and misunderstandings.

Finally, probabilistic information is a prerequisite if a variety of projects are to be compared and consistently evaluated.

Although these points may appear to be obvious, obtaining data from key personnel in the form of probability distributions could prove difficult. Managers, frequently unfamiliar with statistical terminology and techniques, may have trouble pulling the information together and may even distrust an explicit quantitative approach to the point of turning their backs on it. Compromises can be made, however, to adapt to the particular situation. Rather than forcing a manager to provide a complete probability distribution for a particular forcasted figure, one may simply ask for three point estimates along

[4]See, for example, D. Woods, "Improving Estimates that Involve Uncertainty", *Harvard Business Review*, July-August, 1966, pp. 91-98.

the lines of standard PERT[5] forecasts. Thus, it may be possible to elicit one most likely forecast, a pessimistic one, and an optimistic one, where the pessimistic and the optimistic estimates may be defined as levels or values such that there is only a 5 percent chance of the outcome being either below or above.

Example

> Referring to the example presented in Figure 6-1, a forecaster would supplement the most likely value of $100,000 with optimistic and pessimistic values of $200,000 and $0 respectively, thus providing some measure of the uncertainty inherent in the forecast.

One could then fit a probability distribution to these points. As suggested by the wide acceptance of PERT techniques, no significant difficulties need exist with such an approach. Even more sophisticated methods requiring considerably more input from personnel who have no special training have been found to work satisfactorily.[6]

Another approach, which reduces some of the operational difficulties encountered when working with probability distributions, considers only selected measures of the distribution, the most common ones being the expected value and the variance or standard deviation.

Example

> Assume the standard deviation for the distribution portrayed in Figure 6-1 to be $30,000. The forecaster would simply specify the expected value of $100,000 and this measure of variation for the forecast.

The variance or standard deviation is commonly viewed as a reasonable measure of risk, corresponding with the intuitive notion that risk is somehow related to the variability of returns around an expected value.[7] Such an approach has the advantage of simplifying comparisons between various investment proposals, as it is much easier to base a comparison on just two numbers than it is to work with entire probability distributions. On the other hand, by compressing a probability distribution into only two measures, some information is lost.

A further weakness is that managers may find it difficult to work with the

[5]PERT (which stands for Program Evaluation and Review Technique) was originally developed by a leading firm of consultants for the U.S. Navy to control progress on the Polaris Ballistic Missile Program. A complex project is broken down into the individual tasks which have to be performed, and any precedence relationship which may exist between these tasks is specified in terms of a network. Completion times for each individual task are estimated, generally in the form of three-point estimates (pessimistic, most likely, optimistic) and based on these, the total completion time for the project and the "critical path" are derived. The network with the corresponding probabilistic time estimates (which is often stored on a computer) can then be used to control and monitor the progress of the actual project implementation. PERT techniques are widely used in certain industries, as they became a requirement on many U.S. government contracts, particularly in the defence and aerospace industries. They are also widely used in Canada in industries such as construction. For further detail, the interested reader is referred to F. Hillier and G. Lieberman, *Introduction to Operations Research*, San Francisco: Holden Day, 1968, pp. 225-234.

[6]See L. Kryzanowski, P. Lusztig, and B. Schwab, "Monte Carlo Simulation and Capital Expenditure Decisions. A Case Study", *The Engineering Economist*, Fall, 1972, pp. 31-48.

[7]This approach was originally set out by H. Markowitz. See, "Portfolio Selection", *Journal of Finance*, March, 1952, pp. 77-91. Since that time, other measures such as the semi-variance, which was also noted by Markowitz, have been proposed as more appropriate. See, for instance, J. Mao and J. Brewster, "An E-S_h Model of Capital Budgeting", *Engineering Economist*, Winter 1970, pp. 103-121.

variance or standard deviation and may resist or be unable to express uncertainties in such terms. Nevertheless, because of their computational convenience these measures have taken hold and are widely used in the literature of finance.

Instead of the variance or standard deviation, sometimes *the coefficient of variation* is used to express the dispersion of a particular probability distribution. The coefficient of variation is simply a probability distribution's standard deviation divided by its expected value.

Example

With a standard deviation of \$30,000 and an expected value of \$100,000 the coefficient of variation becomes \$30,000/\$100,000 = 0.3.

Setting the dispersion in relation to a distribution's expected value is reasonable. Certainly, a variation of ±\$10,000 has to be viewed differently on a project with expected returns of \$500,000 than on a project with expected returns of \$20,000. However, the standard deviation or variance, being *absolute* measures of dispersion, would be the same in either case. The coefficient of variation, by setting a project's standard deviation in relation to its expected value, provides a *relative* measure of risk which is often more meaningful.

6-3. EVALUATION CRITERIA

Once risk has been assessed, criteria must be established for evaluating and ranking investment proposals which may differ both in terms of risk and expected returns. This is illustrated by the two projects set out in Figure 6-2.

FIGURE 6-2

Risk and Return on Two Projects

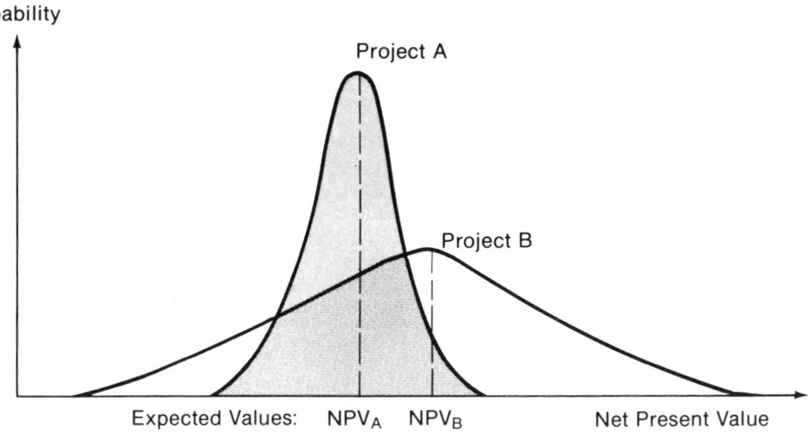

We can no longer say that project B will be preferred to project A just because it yields a higher expected net present value, since any ranking of the two projects will also have to reflect the decision-maker's attitudes towards risk. Given some degree of risk aversion, it may well be that project A with its much lower variability is preferred, even if this implies sacrificing some potential profitability. For example, a mining company may limit its exploration budget in a particular area even though the potential payoffs are perceived to be high, simply because the risks may appear excessive. The company may prefer to see funds used for investment in additional production equipment to reduce unit production costs: in which case, the potential payoffs may be more modest but more highly predictable.

Over the last two decades, a variety of approaches have been proposed to evaluate risk in investment decisions. We cannot undertake a comprehensive coverage of the extensive literature in this area. Rather, we will concentrate on some of the basic concepts and techniques, placing particular emphasis on methods which over the years have proven to be useful in practice.

Some of the more conceptual aspects of risk analysis, such as utility theory, will be discussed at the end of this chapter, while general theoretical considerations for trading off risks *versus* returns in financial decisions are deferred until Chapter 29.

In devising criteria for evaluating risk, we face a trade off between operational simplicity and theoretical validity. That is, some evaluation techniques, while being crude rules of thumb, are easily understood and implemented. Others, while attempting to encompass more of the complexities of the real-life situation, become more cumbersome and are operationally less convenient. Accordingly, we have classified various evaluation techniques as set out in Table 6-1. We will discuss each of these in turn.

The review of certainty equivalents will be found at the end of the chapter—this technique does not appear to be widely used in practice, and is most easily illustrated in the context of utility theory.

TABLE 6-1

Summary of Techniques for Evaluating Risk in Capital Budgeting

- Simple rules of thumb
  - Ignoring risk
  - Conservative estimates
  - Payback period
- More sophisticated rules of thumb
  - Risk-adjusted discount rates
  - Certainty equivalents
- Other decision-making aids
  - Sensitivity analysis
  - Monte Carlo simulation
  - Decision trees

Simple rules of thumb

Ignoring risk

Quite commonly, risk is not explicitly considered when investment projects are evaluated in practice. Instead, evaluations are just based on best estimates or forecasted average values. It should be evident from the above discussion that results obtained in this way may not reflect the true preferences of the firm and its management, most particularly where there are marked differences in risk between various projects under consideration.

Example

To illustrate how misleading decisions based on expected returns can be we present the classic example which was formulated over a hundred years ago by the famous mathematician Bernoulli. It has since been known as the *St. Petersburg paradox*. While originally formulated in a gambling context in the casinos of St. Petersburg, the conclusions derived can readily be transposed to a business setting. The rules of the gamble as proposed by Bernoulli are set out in Table 6-2. If asked how much we would be willing to pay for the privilege of being allowed to play this game, few of us would offer more than fifty dollars, even though the expected returns of the game are easily shown to be infinitely large. Because of risk aversion, people shy away from the relatively high probability of losing some money, even if the potential but risky compensation may be very high.

TABLE 6-2

The St. Petersburg Paradox

Assume a coin is tossed repeatedly, until heads (H) appears for the first time, after which the game is terminated. The various events which can occur, their probabilities which are easily computed, and the payoffs to be received for each possible sequence of tosses which can occur are given below:

Event (sequence of tosses)	probability	payoff
H (heads on first toss)	½	\$3
TH (heads on 2nd toss)	¼	\$3 × \$3 = \$9
TTH (heads on 3rd toss)	⅛	\$3 × \$3 × \$3 = \$27
heads on n^{th}	$(½)^n$	$(\$3)^n$

That is, if H appears for the first time after the nth toss, the payoff is $(\$3)^n$.

The expected value (EV) of this game is easily computed as

$$EV = ½ \times 3 + ¼ \times 9 + ⅛ \times 27 + \ldots + (3/2)^n + \ldots = \text{infinity}$$

Since the payoffs increase faster than the decrease in the associated probabilities, the expected value of this game becomes infinitely large.

The only setting where it may be quite reasonable to ignore risk analysis in investment evaluations is where projects are relatively small in relation to the firm's total resources. In such cases risk aversion is generally not very pronounced, and the operational convenience of straightforward evaluation procedures is likely to outweigh any benefits to be derived from more sophisticated analysis. Given that there are likely to be a fair number of such smaller projects which are reasonably independent of each other, any deviations from anticipated returns tend to balance out to some extent, with some projects exceeding expectations and others falling short.[8] Therefore, it may be reasonable for a firm to establish a limit based on project size, with investments below this limit being judged simply on expected values.

Conservative estimates

Another widespread approach for dealing with uncertainty simply seeks to limit downside risk by scaling down estimates. Thus a manager, presented by a subordinate with a forecast of $100,000 which is subject to uncertainty, may in fact use a scaled down figure of $80,000 in his own evaluations. As we shall see below when discussing certainty equivalents, this technique has merit and can be quite useful if properly devised and implemented. In most practical settings, however, such subjective adjustments tend to be made in an *ad hoc* manner, without much information about the underlying probability distributions. Consequently, the decisions resulting may be less than optimal. To illustrate, the subordinate who provided the $100,000 figure may have already toned down the forecast in order to protect himself in case things failed to work out as anticipated. If successive layers of management each make their own subjective adjustments, each without knowledge of what the other has done and without a full appreciation of the actual uncertainties underlying the original forecasts, the figures on which the final evaluation is based may bear little resemblance to the actual project under consideration. As already mentioned, we shall pursue this approach further when discussing certainty equivalents and utilities and will develop a conceptual framework within which such adjustments can be made properly.

Payback period

The payback period and some of its limitations were discussed in Chapter 5. In spite of its shortcomings, however, it does provide management with at least a rough indication of exposure to risk. In particular, where management is concerned with the possibility of having to abandon an investment prematurely, information about a project's payback period may be useful.

Example

> If a new product is launched, its useful life may be difficult to forecast accurately as it will depend on such uncertain events as competitor reaction, technological obsolescence, and the likes. If the project has an expected payback period of three years, management knows that at least the original investment should be recovered by that time. The estimated useful life of the product can be viewed in relation to this figure, and if it is expected to exceed the payback period significantly, this may be perceived as providing adequate protection against risk.

The payback period can be made more useful by adding the following refinements. For one, the time value of money should be incorporated, with the

[8]This concept, which is related to the idea of diversification, will be explored more fully in Chapter 29 dealing with the capital asset pricing model.

payback period redefined as the point in time where the *net present value of cash inflows* equals the original investment. With discount rates of 15 percent and above becoming common in industry, the bias introduced by not incorporating the time value of money will be significant.

Example

Consider an investment of $100,000, generating net cash inflows of $20,000 per year for 7 years, and undertaken by a firm with a cost of capital of 15 percent. Without discounting, the payback period would normally be computed as 5 years, as after 5 years the undiscounted cash inflows have "repaid" the original investment. Recognizing, however, that money has a time value, we should discount future cash flows to compare their present value with the current investment. In so doing, we find that this project will never pay back. As illustrated in Table 6-3, the present value of $20,000 for seven years discounted at 15 percent equals only $83,220.

Thus, it can be seen that the payback period as commonly computed without discounting, will understate the true time until "breakeven" has been reached.

More generally, a firm may not only be interested in the breakeven point as represented by the payback period, but also in the magnitude of its exposure to loss if abandonment occurs prior to the payback period.[9]

Example

Given a payback period of 4 years, it may also be relevant to know how much would be lost if, due to unforeseen circumstances, the project had to be abandoned after only 1 or 2 years. We can plot, as shown in Figure 6-3, the net present value of a project as a function of time, *assuming abandonment of the project at time t.* Thus, the project shown in Figure 6-3 has an expected life of 7 years, with an ultimate net present value of $150,000. Its payback period is 4 years and, if it is abandoned at this time, the total net present value of all cash flows is just zero with the firm breaking even. If, however, unforeseen events should force a liquidation of the project after only 1½ years, the firm stands to lose $100,000 in present value terms, for initial investment and startup expenses would have been incurred by this time without the project having started to generate net cash inflows.

As illustrated in Figure 6-3 a curve showing not only the project's ultimate net present value and its payback period based on discounted cash flows, but also the firm's exposure throughout the project's life, provides much more complete information regarding exposure to risk than any single number.

[9]See B. Schwab and P. Lusztig, "A Note on Abandonment Value and Capital Budgeting", *Journal of Financial and Quantitative Analysis*, September, 1970, pp. 377-379, and B. Schwab and P. Lusztig, "A Note on Investment Evaluation in Light of Uncertain Future Opportunities", *Journal of Finance*, December, 1972, pp. 1093-1100, on which papers this section draws. For a more mathematical treatment, see also S. Brumelle and B. Schwab, "Capital Budgeting With Uncertain Future Opportunities: A Markovian Approach", *Journal of Financial and Quantitative Analysis*, January, 1973, pp. 111-122.

TABLE 6-3

Payback Period Based on Undiscounted and Discounted Cash Flows

				YEARS			
	1	2	3	4	5	6	7
Cash flows (undiscounted)	$20,000	$20,000	$20,000	$20,000	$20,000	$20,000	$20,000
Cumulative cash flows	20,000	40,000	60,000	80,000	100,000	120,000	140,000
Discount factor (at 15%)	0.870	0.756	0.658	0.572	0.497	0.432	0.376
Discounted cash flows	17,400	15,120	13,160	11,440	9,940	8,640	7,520
Cumulative discounted cash flows	17,400	32,520	45,680	57,120	67,060	75,700	83,220

FIGURE 6-3

Net Present Value as a Function of Time, Assuming Abandonment at Time t

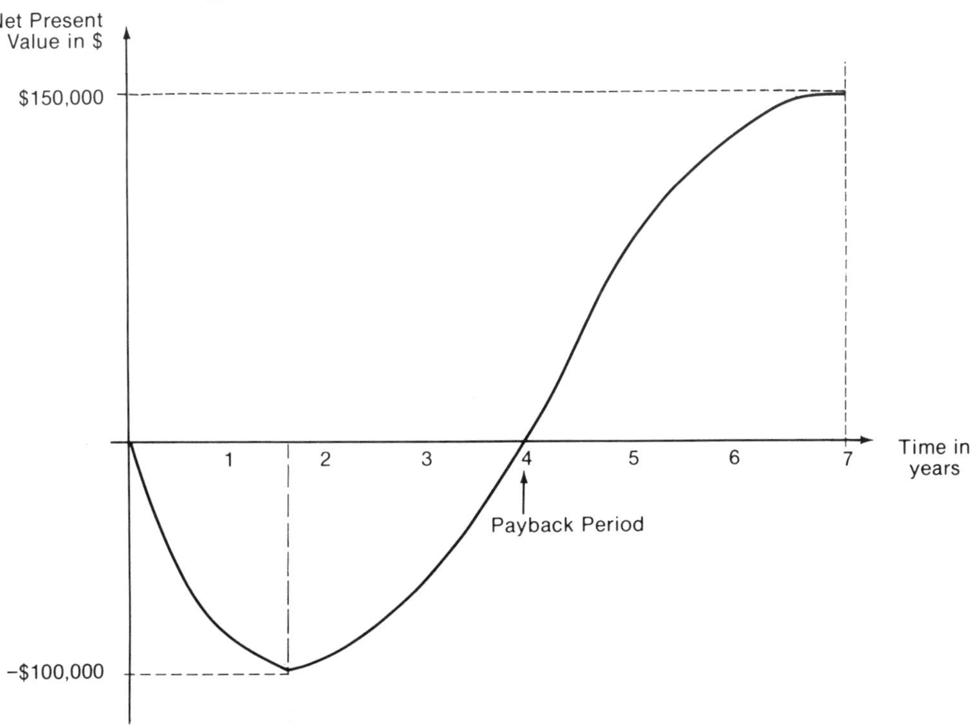

More sophisticated rules of thumb

Risk-adjusted discount rates

As the term suggests, an approach relying on risk-adjusted discount rates implies varying the discount rate applied to a project's expected cash flows on the basis of perceived risk. Typically, investment projects are grouped into several risk classes, and the rate employed in discounting expected cash flows is made to vary for each class of expenditures, with higher rates used for more risky investments.

Example

A firm may use the following classifications:

Project class	Discount rate applied
I Low-risk, cash flows highly predictable	12%
II Normal business risk	15%
III Speculative	18%

Consider a project requiring an initial investment of $100,000 and promising cash inflows of $30,000 per year for 5 years. Applying the various discount rates as set out above, the project's net present values become:

Discount rate applied	Net present value of investment
12%	$8,150
15%	$ 605
18%	–$6,190

While the project would be acceptable in the low-risk category and marginally acceptable given normal business risk, it would be rejected if it entailed higher than usual risks.

Generally, an increase in the discount rate to reflect increased risk will reduce the project's net present value and, hence, its economic desirability. In effect, we are relying on a rule of thumb related to the notion of a risk premium: a higher risk must be compensated for by a higher expected return if the project is to be attractive.

This approach to dealing with risk is appealing because it is easily understood and operationally convenient to implement. This may account at least in part for its popularity with practicing managers. Also, as we saw, a firm's cost of capital tends to increase with increasing risk of its operations, since investors become more reluctant to advance funds. Therefore, there is some economic rationale for applying higher discount rates to riskier projects.

There are also weaknesses, however. For one, the question of what adjustments to the discount rate are appropriate is often left unanswered. If such adjustments are to be representative of investor attitudes towards risk, and not merely a reflection of subjective assessments by management, an answer may not easily be derived. While noting the difficulty, we will postpone discussion of this point until further on in this chapter.

Secondly by tying together the time value of money (discounting) and an evaluation of risk, blanket adjustments to discount rates imply questionable assumptions about the risk of a project's cash flows over time. For instance, because of the mathematics of the discounting process, a short-term opportunity with a large element of risk is relatively unaffected by adjustments to the discount rate, whereas the adjustment effect on a moderately risky project with longer-term benefits is likely to prove significant.

Example

Consider the drilling of an oil well costing $500,000 which may result in either a dry well with a probability of 85 percent, or in a find with a probability of 15 percent. In the latter case, a gain of $5,000,000 is anticipated from the sale of the well. The expected cash inflow at the end of the year becomes 0.15 × $5,000,000 = $750,000. The results of the drilling will be realized within a period of one year. Even if, because of the high risk, the discount rate to be applied is raised to say 25 percent per annum, the effect of such an increased discount rate is not very dramatic. Discounting only takes place across one year and the expected benefits are only reduced by a factor of $1/(1 + 0.25) = 0.8$. The project's net present value remains positive at

$$\text{NPV} = -\$500{,}000 + \frac{\$750{,}000}{(1 + 0.25)} = \$100{,}000$$

On the other hand, if another project's benefits accrued 10 years hence, a discount rate of 25 percent would reduce every dollar of future benefits by a factor of $(1/1.25)^{10} = 0.11$, or to just 11 cents.

Even if it is felt that risk increases over time (since the more distant future becomes more difficult to forecast), it would be an unlikely coincidence if the increase in perceived risk just paralleled the decreases in present values brought about by the risk-adjusted discount rate.

To overcome this deficiency, we could vary the risk-adjusted discount rate over time, with the discount factor applied in each time period corresponding to the particular risks perceived. Such explicit specification of the added risk premiums required in each period is not unlike the use of *certainty equivalents* (discussed on p. 174) where the cash flows for each period are individually adjusted for risk.[10] However, while conceptually more appealing, such complex approaches become unwieldy and do not appear to be used very frequently in practice.

We conclude that risk-adjusted discount rates are a useful and practical approach to handling the problem of risk, often representing a good compromise between what is operationally workable and what may be conceptually desirable. Nevertheless, we should be aware of its limitations in order to be able to make modifications which may become necessary—for example where the perceived risk of a project's cash flows clearly does not match the adjustments effected through use of a higher discount rate.

Other decision-making aids

Various techniques have proven to be useful in attempting to evaluate risk in capital budgeting. Their purpose is generally to provide the manager with more precise information regarding potential outcomes of an investment and the attached probabilities. It is felt that such information enhances management's ability to make good investment decisions. In this section, we briefly describe three of the techniques which have found relatively widespread application in practice: sensitivity analysis, Monte Carlo simulation, and decision trees.

Sensitivity analysis

Sensitivity analysis determines how vulnerable a project's economic desirability is with regard to changes in the values being forecast. This is best illustrated through an example.

Example

Consider an investment in a machine costing $100,000. Net cash inflows of $30,000 per year are anticipated over the next 5 years. The applicable

[10]For a discussion of the potential superiority of the certainty-equivalent approach over risk-adjusted discount rates, see P. Lusztig, "The Application of Certainty Equivalents in Capital Expenditure Decisions", *Cost and Management*, January-February, 1971, pp. 53-55.

discount rate is 12 percent. Thus the investment's net present value is given as

$$\text{NPV} = -\$100{,}000 + \$30{,}000 \times 3.605 = \$8{,}150$$

suggesting the project is acceptable. However, since the forecasted cash inflows are subject to uncertainty, a manager may be interested to find out by what amount the figure of $30,000 per year could be reduced before the project's net present value becomes negative. This is easily computed, setting

$$\text{NPV} = -\$100{,}000 + 3.605 \times \text{annual cash flows} = 0$$

from which we derive

$$\text{annual cash flows} = \frac{100{,}000}{3.605} = \$27{,}739$$

With annual cash inflows of $27,739, the project just breaks even, implying that a drop of less than 10 percent from the original forecast will mean an unattractive investment. Hence, the acceptability of the project is fairly sensitive to forecasting errors associated with the anticipated annual cash inflows.

Such sensitivity analysis and consequent determination of breakeven values can be carried out for a variety of variables influencing a project's cash flows. For instance, where the launching of a new product is under consideration, we may determine how sensitive its net present value is with regard to future sales, selling price, useful life, production costs, and other forecasted variables. Not only does this information provide a manager with insights into the main determinants of risk in a particular situation, but it also allows him to concentrate on those variables which are most critical for the project's ultimate success.

Sensitivity analysis can be used alongside corporate financial models which were discussed in the previous chapter. As we saw, such models can generate forecasted income statements and balance sheets. Thus, the impact of an investment proposal on the projected operations of the firm can be tested, indicating how sensitive the firm's projected financial performance is with regard to changes in forecasts. As most financial models are computer-based, it is relatively easy to assess a variety of alternatives quickly and inexpensively. The manager, by being able to test the effects of various forecasts, can better cope with the problem of risk.

Monte Carlo simulation

Sensitivity analysis is most appropriate where the impact of variations in variables is to be assessed one at a time. In a typical investment project, however, many variables may interact in a complex way to determine the overall risk of the project. For example, a project's net present value is determined by net cash flow figures for several periods. The net cash flows themselves are made up of several cost and revenue figures, and each of these cost and revenue figures may again depend on several operating variables, including production schedules and quantities, market variables, and the likes. With uncertainties inherent in each of these interrelated variables, the overall impact on the final net present value of the investment is, in most instances, far from obvious.

In mathematical terms, we are confronted by the following problem. A measure such as the net present value (NPV) is a function of a number of variables which may be labelled $x_1, x_2, \ldots, x_n$, or in other words, NPV $= f(x_1, x_2, \ldots, x_n)$. Each of the x's is subject to uncertainty and has a probability distribution associated with it.[11] The problem is to find the probability distribution for the net present value, given that we know the function f and have received from operating personnel probability distributions for all the variables identified.

Direct mathematical solutions deriving probability distributions of net present values are possible only under very special circumstances.[12] More generally, however, such direct solutions are not available, and we must resort to Monte Carlo simulation. Monte Carlo simulation is a computer-based technique offering solutions, based on sampling, for problems of practically any degree of complexity.[13] This technique calls for (i) the identification of key variables which are expected to affect the investment project's cash flows and (ii) the assignment of probability distributions to each factor. Then, giving due recognition to the likelihood of particular outcomes, the computer is programmed to randomly select values for each variable and to combine them to generate estimated cash flows and net present values or internal rates of return. Interdependencies between variables as they may exist, for example, between anticipated sales and selling price are recognized.

Through a sufficient number of trials, a graphic distribution of these returns is provided for the decision-maker, allowing for a more complete and precise appreciation of the overall risk inherent in a project.[14]

This is illustrated graphically in Figure 6-4, where a Monte Carlo simulation model is used to derive the probability distribution for the project's net present value (or for some other evaluation criterion identified in Chapter 5), given that the uncertainties associated with the project's forecasted variables and their interrelations have already been quantified.

[11]It should be noted that these variables need not be independent. For example, the sales forecast for a particular year may be strongly influenced by the predicted selling price which, in turn, reflects expectations about labor costs.

[12]For a good introductory discussion, see C. Springer, R. Herlihy, R. Mall, and R. Beggs, *Probabilistic Models*, Homewood, Ill.: Richard D. Irwin, 1963, Ch. 4. Where, for example, the function simply consists of a sum of variables which are normally distributed with known means, variances, and covariances, the resulting probability distribution is readily computed.

[13]See, for example, D. Hertz, "Investment Policies That Pay Off", *Harvard Business Review*, January-February, 1968, pp. 96-108; D. Hertz, "Risk Analysis in Capital Investment", *Harvard Business Review*, January-February, 1964, pp. 95-106; and L. Kryzanowski, P. Lusztig, and B. Schwab, *op. cit.* .

[14]Results obtained must be interpreted with care. Thus, distributions of the simulated IRR's and NPV's would not generally be identically distributed nor would an expected IRR be equal to the mean of the distribution of IRR's obtained through simulation. For greater detailing, see A. Robichek, "Interpreting the Results of Risk Analysis", *Journal of Finance*, December, 1975, pp. 1384-1386.

Figure 6-4

Monte Carlo Simulation Model to Derive the Probability Distribution for a Project's Net Present Value from Various Input Variables

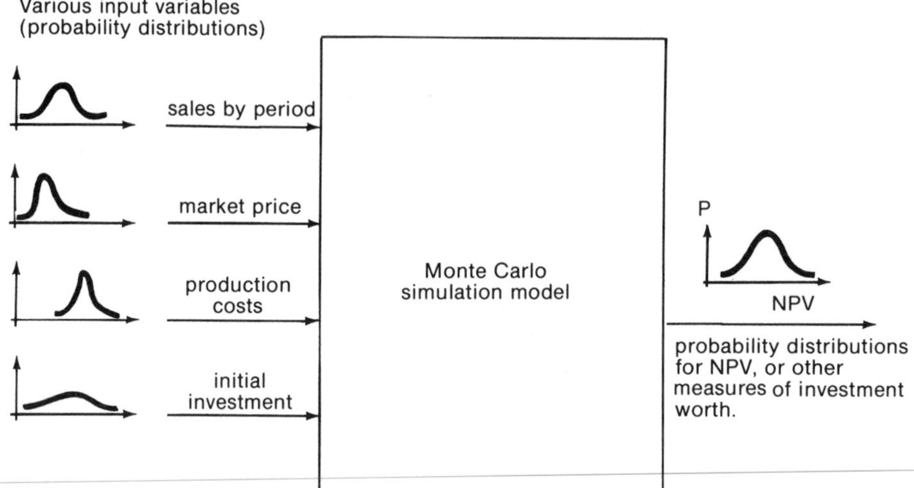

With the widespread availability of computers at decreasing costs and of programming languages especially designed for simulation applications, Monte Carlo simulation is becoming an increasingly useful tool in the analysis of investment decisions.

Decision trees

Decision trees have been advocated as another operational tool for assessing project risk.[15] While decision trees are limited in the degree of complexity and the number of variables which can reasonably be incorporated, this technique can be useful in analyzing dependencies between a lesser number of key variables. It may also provide a useful framework for analyzing certain types of sequential decisions. A simplified illustration is provided in Figure 6-5.

The optimal decision is reached by moving back toward the decision point from the right-hand extremities of the branches.

Example

> The expected present value of cash flows for the larger store is found to be .3(22,000,000) + .5(9,800,000) + .2(8,000,000) = \$13,100,000, yielding an expected net present value of \$13,100,000–\$10,000,000=\$3,100,000. For the investment in the smaller store, the expected present value of cash flows is .3(8,000,000) + .5(7,000,000) + .2(6,000,000) = \$7,100,000, yielding an expected net present value of \$7,100,000 – \$6,000,000 = \$1,100,000. The desirability of the large versus the small store will in part depend on how profitably the \$4,000,000 saved if the small store is

[15] J. Magee, "How to Use Decision Trees in Capital Investment", *Harvard Business Review*, September-October, 1964, pp. 79-96; also R. Hespos and P. Strassmann, "Stochastic Decision Trees for the Analysis of Investment Decisions," *Management Science*, August, 1965, pp. B244-259.

built can be invested elsewhere. If the $4,000,000 can only be invested in marginal projects yielding returns close to the firm's cost of capital and, hence, a net present value which is close to zero, the larger investment with its higher expected net present value is indicated. A more careful scrutiny of Figure 6-5 would show, however, that despite the apparent attractiveness of the larger project, there is in fact a 70 percent chance of it having a negative net present value. It is also evident from the decision tree that, for those who are risk-averse, the smaller store offers a more attractive range of outcomes—there being no possibility of a loss.

FIGURE 6-5
Simplified Decision Tree Showing Limited Number of Branches

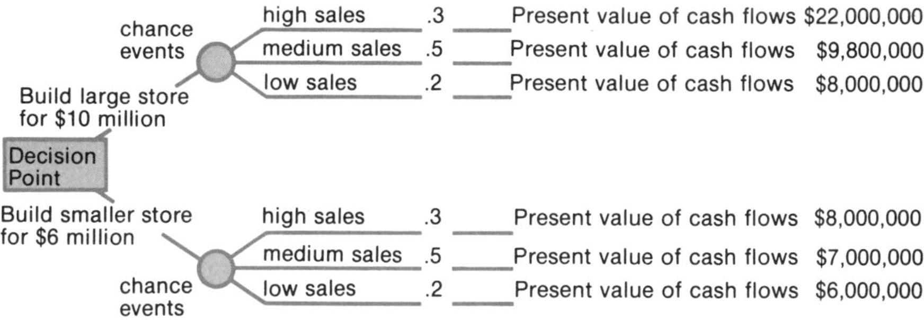

Decision trees are most useful, however, in analyzing projects involving sequential decisions and dependent variables such as cash flows over several time periods. Figure 6-6 provides a simple illustration of projects with a two-period life.

Example

In the case of the small store, if low sales prevail during the first period, another decision point is reached where the decision-maker can choose between abandoning the project (that is, selling the store for $3 million) or continuing with it. Probabilistic results of the latter course of action are shown in the subsequent branches of the tree. The probabilities indicated for period 2 are conditional probabilities, that is, 0.1 is the conditional probability of observing high sales in period 2 given that sales were low in period 1. The joint probability of low sales in period 1 and high sales in period 2 is shown as 0.1 × 0.5 = 0.05 at the end of the particular branch. In analyzing the abandonment decision, we obtain an expected present value of only 0.9(1,500,000) + 0.1(4,000,000) = $1,750,000 for continuing the operation of the store, indicating the $3,000,000 abandonment as the appropriate decision if low sales are in fact experienced in period 1. The overall expected net present value if the optimal course of action or strategy is followed through is found to be

$$\begin{aligned} PV &= 0.5\ [\ (4{,}000{,}000) + 0.8\ (5{,}000{,}000) + 0.2\ (3{,}000{,}000)\ ] \\ &\quad + 0.5\ [\ (3{,}000{,}000) + (3{,}000{,}000)\ ] - 6{,}000{,}000 \\ &= 0.5\ (8{,}600{,}000) + 0.5\ (6{,}000{,}000) - 6{,}000{,}000 \\ &= \$1{,}300{,}000. \end{aligned}$$

FIGURE 6-6

Two-period Decision Tree

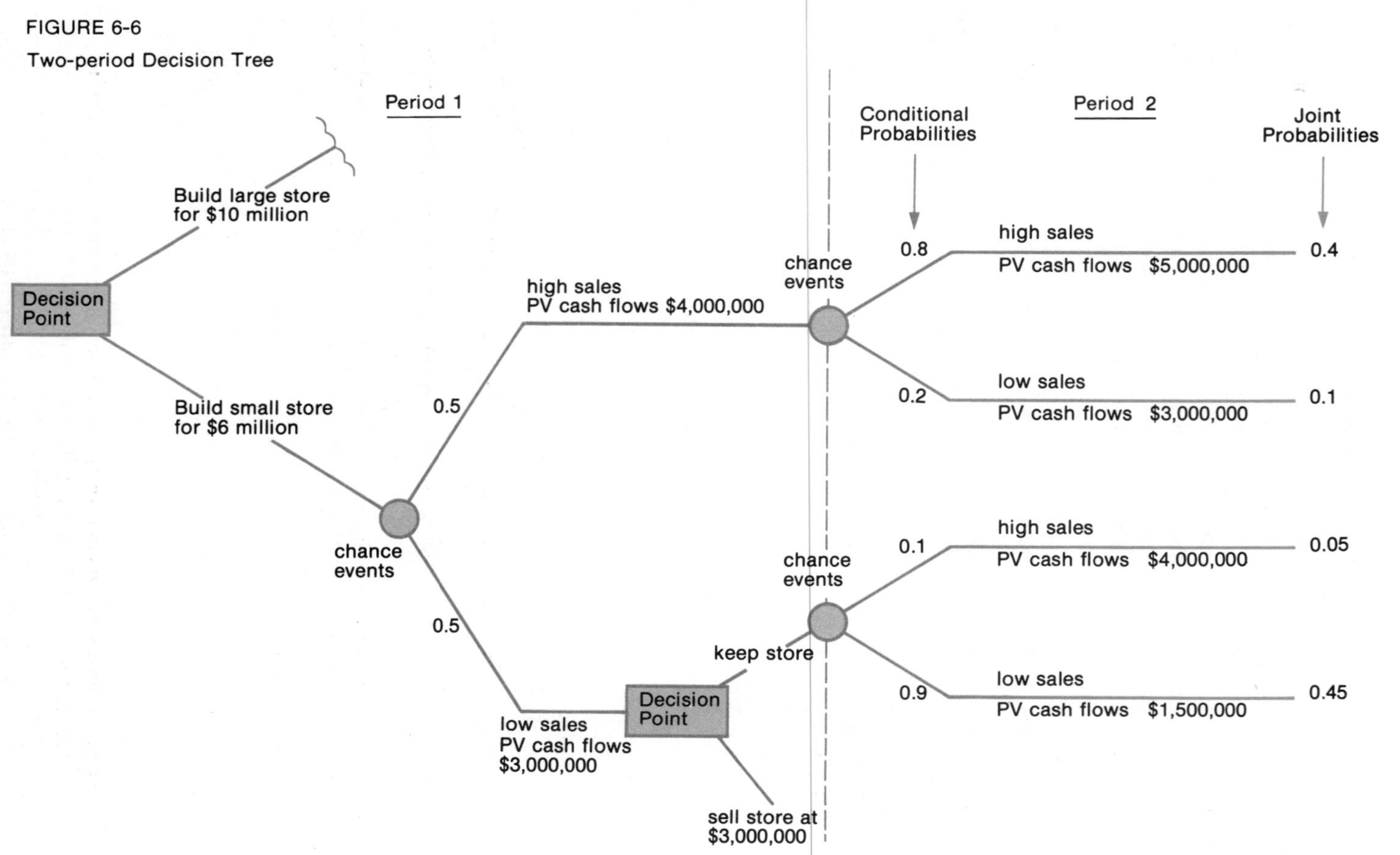

6-4. PORTFOLIO CONSIDERATIONS

Discussions to this point have focused on the assessment and evaluation of risk of individual investment proposals treated in isolation. However, the uncertainties inherent in a variety of projects interact to determine the overall risk of the firm. Therefore, we should assess how new projects under consideration "fit" with the firm's current portfolio of investments as well as with other opportunities currently being looked at, or those already underway. In this section, we restrict ourselves to a simplified introduction of some basic concepts of portfolio management. A more complete treatment will be provided in Chapter 29.

Consider a business contemplating two risky investments A and B. Individual risk analysis as described above has been carried out yielding the two probability distributions for the net present values NPV_A and NPV_B. It is, however, the probability distribution of NPV_{A+B}, reflecting the sum of both projects' net present values, which is of concern in evaluating the overall risk of the capital budget. The risk or dispersion of NPV_{A+B} depends not only on the risk of the individual projects, but also on the interrelation between the two.

Consider the individual probability distributions of net present values for projects *A* and *B* as shown in Figure 6-7:

FIGURE 6-7

Probability Distributions of Net Present Values for Project A, Project B and Projects A + B

Probability

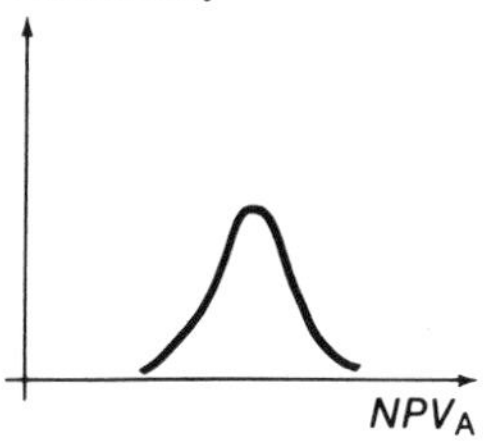

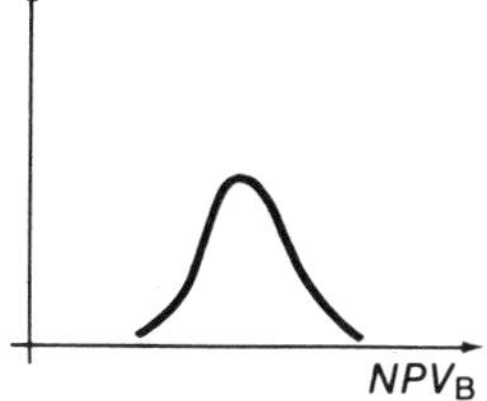

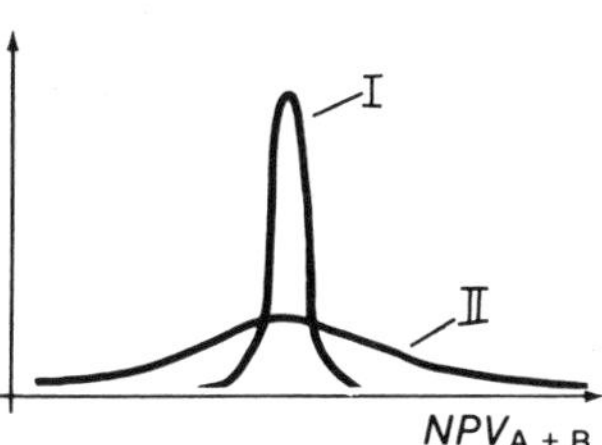

If, for example, high values in project *A* tend to go together with low values in project *B* and *vice versa*, so that the two projects are *negatively correlated*, the two individual risks cancel out to some degree. The resulting distribution of NPV_{A+B} may have a lower dispersion than each individual project taken by itself (curve I for NPV_{A+B}).

If on the other hand, projects *A* and *B*, being *positively correlated*, tend to move together, with high or low values appearing simultaneously in both projects, the overall risk becomes magnified as illustrated by curve II for NPV_{A+B}.

Where projects *A* and *B* are independent of each other, an intermediate curve would result.

These concepts are related to the common sense notion of "not putting all your eggs in one basket", and account for the efforts of many firms to diversify their operations. The attempts of several tobacco companies to diversify into other lines of endeavor are indicative in this context. A broadening of the market base would reduce the firm's vulnerability to direct or government-sponsored action against smoking. Other examples reflecting portfolio diversification are to be found in the management of investment funds and in the fairly recent trend to conglomerate mergers.[16] It should be noted, however, that in general it is difficult to find projects with negative correlation, largely because most business ventures are linked to the state of the economy and fluctuate with it.

The ideas introduced above can be expressed more formally. In order to simplify our exposition, we assume that the variance of a project's probability distribution is a good measure of its risk. Given the variances σ_A^2 and σ_B^2 associated with the individual projects, the concern is to determine σ_{A+B}^2. It is evident from elementary probability theory that σ_{A+B}^2 is not just dependent on the values of σ_A^2 and σ_B^2, but on the statistical relationships which may exist between the risks of the individual projects as well. Expressed more formally,

$$\sigma_{A+B}^2 = \sigma_A^2 + \sigma_B^2 + 2Cov_{AB}$$

where Cov_{AB} is the covariance between projects *A* and *B*. The covariance can also be expressed as $Cov_{AB} = \rho_{AB}\sigma_A\sigma_B$, with ρ_{AB} the correlation coefficient between *A* and *B*.[17] As we can see from the above formula, where projects are negatively correlated (so that their covariance or correlation coefficient is negative), σ_{A+B} is reduced accordingly and *vice versa*. The numerical example given below underlines this point.

Example

A firm with a portfolio of investments *A* is assessing two mutually exclusive new investment projects *B* and *C*. The relevant data may be summarized as follows:

Project	Expected NPV	σ^2
A	$100	400
B	20	25
C	20	36

It is also given that $\rho_{AB} = 0.90$ and $\rho_{AC} = -0.80$, indicating that project *B* is highly correlated with the firm's current investments, while for project *C* this correlation is negative. The expected net present value of either *A* + *B* or *A* + *C* is $100 + $20 = $120. If projects are considered in isolation, then the less risky *B* would be selected. Considering the projects as additions to a portfolio, however, we find

$$\sigma_{A+B}^2 = 400 + 25 + 2\,(.9)\,(20)\,(5) = 605$$

and

$$\sigma_{A+C}^2 = 400 + 36 + 2\,(-.8)\,(20)\,(6) = 244$$

[16] It has been questioned whether conglomerate mergers do, in fact, create opportunities for diversification beyond those available to investors thereby increasing the combined market values of the fused firms. See, for example, W. Alberts, "The Profitability of Growth by Merger", in W. Alberts and J. Segall (eds.), *The Corporate Merger*, Chicago: University of Chicago Press, 1966, pp. 235-287. Also, H. Levy and M. Sarnat, "Diversification, Portfolio Analysis and the Uneasy Case for Conglomerate Mergers", *Journal of Finance*, September, 1970, pp. 795-802.

[17] For a look at such application of statistics to capital budgeting, see N. Paine, "Uncertainty and Capital Budgeting", *Accounting Review*, April, 1964, pp. 330-332.

Thus, the impact of the negative correlation coefficient, ρ_{AC}, is quite apparent and project C becomes a more attractive addition to the firm's investment portfolio.

In practice, explicit analysis incorporating the effect of new investments on portfolio variances based on correlations may not be feasible, mainly because of the difficulty of estimating quantitatively correlations between projects. Nevertheless, when evaluating major investment projects, it is important for the manager to be aware of possible portfolio effects, bearing in mind that diversification to reduce risk depends on the interrelationships of various projects.

6-5. PRESCRIPTIVE COMMENTS ON ATTITUDES TOWARD RISK

Thus far our concern has been with the evaluation of risky investments, given some set of attitudes toward risk held by the decision-maker. What should these attitudes be? Since it is once again impossible to prescribe risk attitudes for the owner-manager or even for the closely held firm, our discussion is focused on the publicly held corporation. Assuming the objective of maximizing shareholder wealth, the disposition of investors in the capital markets toward risk becomes the determinant factor, as a firm will only be able to maximize the price of its shares if it acts in a manner which is consistent with the prevailing preferences of the general investing public.

Several attempts have been made to identify market tradeoffs between risk and expected returns. We defer a more complete discussion of this important issue to Chapter 29, and merely provide here a brief outline of the techniques which may be used. For example, one study measured the expected returns and variability of returns for 59 industries (each represented by a sample of individual companies) over a period of 16 years, and derived a linear regression equation as illustrated in Figure 6-8.[18] The findings confirmed the common notion of risk-averse investors who would require compensation through higher expected returns for bearing increased risk. Some support for these results is also to be found in the bond markets, where realized yields on corporate debt is found to increase as the quality of the firm issuing the debt decreases. While limitations

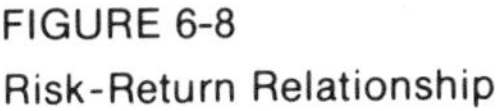
FIGURE 6-8
Risk-Return Relationship

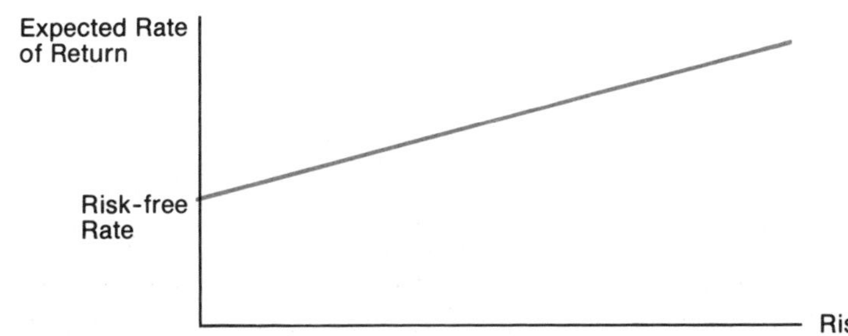

[18] G. Conrad and I. Plotkin, "Risk Return: U.S. Industry Pattern", *Harvard Business Review*, March-April, 1968, pp. 90-99.

of statistical analyses using historical data have to be recognized, a statistically derived relationship of market tradeoffs can serve as a useful guideline to management in determining suitable criteria for risk-return appraisals. If, for instance, a particular investment has expected returns which fall short of what might be expected from situations with comparable risks, then caution or at least further analysis may be indicated.

It has been pointed out that the attitudes of managers toward risk may differ from what is perceived as being most appropriate for the organization, and that these attitudes may, in fact, differ between levels of management, thus leading to inconsistencies in decision-making.[19] If a manager is penalized for failing to attain forecasts, while results which exceed projections are largely attributed to good fortune, then conservatism in forecasts and behavior are almost inevitable. Excessive caution will also be exercised if earnings growth is merely noted while losses precipitate intensive investigations. Thus, the control and reward system of an organization, as sensed by management, is an important instrument for promoting reasonable and consistent attitudes toward risk.

6-6. CAPITAL BUDGETING: THEORY VERSUS PRACTICE

Several studies and surveys can be looked at for information about current business practices in the areas of capital budgeting touched upon in this and the previous chapter.[20] For example, a staff study by Helliwell for the Royal Commission on Taxation surveys the practices of larger Canadian corporations. The evidence suggests that only a fairly low percentage of the companies responding resorted to discounting cash flows and that only one-half of total expenditures (by value) were subject to any form of rate of return calculation.[21] Helliwell goes on to note that:

> The data presented suggest quite strongly that the rate of return calculations made in many firms neither represent very accurate estimates of the probable outcome of investment projects . . . nor matter very much to the officials responsible for making investment decisions.[22]

A more current work by Ronald Williams was based on 100 respondents drawn largely from *Fortune*'s top 500 corporations.[23] Again, the study reflects a relatively large gap between the theory on capital budgeting and industry practice: 39 percent of the companies responding failed to recognize the time

[19]See, for example, R. Swalm, "Utility Theory—Insights Into Risk Taking", *Harvard Business Review*, November-December, 1966, pp. 123-136.

[20]See, for example: Canada, Studies of the Royal Commission on Taxation, *Taxation and Investments: A Study of Capital Expenditure Decisions in Large Corporations*, Ottawa: Queen's Printer, 1967; R. Williams, "Industry Practice in Allocating Capital Resources", *Managerial Planning*, May-June, 1970, pp. 15-22; J. Mao, "Survey of Capital Budgeting: Theory and Practice", *Journal of Finance*, May 1970, pp. 349-360; J. Mao, and J. Helliwell, "Investment Decisions Under Uncertainty: Theory and Practice", *Journal of Finance*, May, 1969, pp. 323-338; T. Klammer, "Empirical Evidence of the Adoption of Sophisticated Capital Budgeting Techniques", *Journal of Business*, July, 1972, pp. 387-397; and C.G. Hoskins and M.J. Dunn, "The Economic Evaluation of Capital Expenditure Proposals under Uncertainty: The Practice of Large Corporations in Canada", *Journal of Business Administration*, Fall 1974, pp. 45-55.

[21]Canada, Studies of the Royal Commission on Taxation, *op. cit.*, pp. 18-20.

[22]*Ibid.*, p. 24.

[23]R. Williams, *op. cit.* .

value of money. Reasons given for failing to use discounted cash flows included preference for payback bench marks, failure of the techniques to consider earnings per share, and the view that projecting future cash flows often is, at best, a futile exercise. Limited understanding or a total lack of familiarity with discounting techniques at various management levels may also be important in explaining this discrepancy.

At the same time, however, the study indicated that sophistication in the area of capital budgeting had improved significantly since 1955, to a point where a number of firms even used subjective probabilities as inputs. Such improvements in management practice are confirmed by other reports in the literature. Thus, Hoskins and Dunn's survey of the largest 100 non-government, non-financial corporations in Canada found that the use of discounted cash flow criteria increased significantly during the last decade, with 79 percent of the firms responding now making use of such techniques.[24]

In the area of risk analysis, their study indicates that conservative estimates of revenues and/or costs remains the single most popular technique in use. However, more sophisticated approaches such as risk-adjusted discount rates, sensitivity analysis and simulation have gained much ground during the same period.

We also note that corporate financial models which were unheard of in the early 1960's are now used to a point where a number of consulting firms have developed expertise and even standard packages in the area because growing demand warranted the effort.

Successful applications of mathematical programming and Monte Carlo simulation in financial decision-making, although not as widespread, are no longer a curiosity.

With growing managerial awareness and appreciation of quantitative tools, and with wider availability of computers at relatively low cost, the trend is expected to continue, particularly in larger organizations where problems of coordination and communication often make explicit analysis imperative.

On the other hand, some limitations of the techniques considered should be noted. For one thing, some executives find they are able to make reasonable decisions based largely on intuitive judgments. It is hard to convince a successful businessman whose managerial style takes this pattern (particularly one who finds it difficult to state explicitly how he arrived at decisions which ultimately prove sensible) that his approach is faulty and that modern management techniques should be substituted. Secondly, while we may often find that analytical techniques are useful in structuring problems and in guiding intuitive judgments, we must recognize that even the most sophisticated methods leave some of the fundamental problems in capital budgeting unresolved—the generation of accurate forecasts being but one. The inputs to capital-budgeting models are, in the final analysis, provided by people and based on subjective assessments of a particular situation.

[24]C.G. Hoskins and M.J. Dunn, *op. cit.* .

Therefore, while increasing thoroughness of analysis is desirable and can often improve the decision-making process, good intuitive judgment will remain a crucial ingredient of good capital expenditure decisions.

***ADDITIONAL TOPICS*

**6-7. CERTAINTY EQUIVALENTS

This is a relatively sophisticated technique for evaluating risk which overcomes some of the limitations of risk-adjusted discount rates, already discussed. As mentioned earlier, however, it is cumbersome to implement and, consequently, is seldom used in practice. Nevertheless, its discussion coupled with an introduction to utility theory, may serve to clarify some of the conceptual issues inherent in evaluating risk.

Assume a financial officer is faced with the choice (i) of receiving, in some period, an uncertain cash flow characterized by a particular probability distribution, or (ii) of receiving an amount X dollars with certainty. If the amount X dollars is such that the financial officer is indifferent to choosing between the two alternatives then X is termed the *certainty equivalent* of the uncertain cash flow.

Example

> Suppose, net cash flows for the next period may have an expected value of $10,000 and be characterized by a particular probability distribution as shown in Table 6-4. If the decision-maker is indifferent to either the prospect of such cash flows or the receipt of $8,000 without fail in the same period, then the $8,000 becomes the certainty equivalent of the uncertain cash flow forecasted. The discrepancy between the expected value of $10,000 and the certainty equivalent of $8,000 is an expression of his risk aversion.

TABLE 6-4

Hypothetical Probability Distribution of Cash Flows and its Certainty Equivalent

cash flow	probability of occurrence
$17,000	0.3
$10,000	0.4
$ 3,000	0.3

Expected value: $10,000

Certainty equivalent assumed to be $8,000

As can be seen, certainty equivalents are related to the approach of using conservative estimates to scale down uncertain forecasts.

In using the method of certainty equivalents to evaluate an investment project which is to yield uncertain cash flows, we first assign a certainty equivalent to the cash flow distribution specified for each period.

For the above example which covers only one period, the certainty-equivalent coefficient would have been 0.8, as

$$\text{certainty equivalent} = \text{certainty equivalent coefficient} \times \text{expected value of uncertain cash flows}$$

or, 8,000 = 0.8 × \$10,000.

In a multi-period case this would be accomplished by multiplying each period's expected cash flow by a certainty-equivalent coefficient which reflects the decision-maker's particular risk preferences. The resultant certainty equivalents are then discounted to reflect the time value of money.

Since the discount rate is being applied to certainty equivalents with risk fully accounted for, care should be taken to ensure that the rate reflects only the time value of money without in any way including a premium for risk.

We denote α_t as the certainty-equivalent coefficient for period t, with $0 < \alpha_t \leqslant 1$ for risk averse decision-makers, and values for α_t decreasing with increasing risk.

Example

Consider an investment of \$1,000 to yield uncertain cash flows with expected values of \$500 at the end of each of the next three years. Assume that risk increases over time so that management views the certainty-equivalent coefficients as $\alpha_0 = 1.0$, $\alpha_1 = 0.9$, $\alpha_2 = 0.8$, and $\alpha_3 = 0.7$. The time value of money for a riskless investment is given by $k = 4$ percent. Thus we have

Year	Uncertain cash flows (expected values)	Certainty Equivalent Coefficients α_t	Certainty Equivalent
0	-\$1000	1.0	-\$1000
1	\$ 500	0.9	\$ 450
2	\$ 500	0.8	\$ 400
3	\$ 500	0.7	\$ 350

and the net present value for the investment becomes

$$\begin{aligned}\text{NPV} &= \sum_{t=0}^{n} \frac{\alpha_t C_t}{(1+k)^t} \\ &= 1(-1000) + \frac{0.9\,(500)}{(1+0.04)} + \frac{0.8\,(500)}{(1+0.04)^2} + \frac{0.7\,(500)}{(1+0.04)^3} \\ &= \$113.70.\end{aligned}$$

Since after full consideration of the risks involved, the project does yield a positive net present value, it should be accepted.

Practical problems in implementation stem from the decision-maker's need to specify a certainty-equivalent coefficient for every distribution of uncertain cash flows, and having to repeat the process for each new investment opportunity proposed. The difficulty could be overcome to some extent if it were possible to measure comprehensively a decision-maker's attitudes toward risk. The findings could then be applied more mechanically in adjusting cash flows for uncertainty. *Utility theory* provides insights for this more general measurement of attitudes towards risk.

**6-8. THE APPLICATION OF UTILITIES

Economists have been concerned for some time with the development of acceptable yardsticks for measuring the satisfaction which people derive from the ownership or use of goods or services. In the late forties, the concepts were extended to include analysis under conditions of uncertainty. Von Neumann and Morgenstern in some pathfinding work[25] introduced a method which now bears their name for measuring relative values under conditions of risk and uncertainty. Their work has laid a solid foundation for analyzing decision problems involving uncertainty, and the superiority of their approach has led to its widespread use particularly in economic and financial theory.[26]

While the concept of utilities is quite generally applicable, our review will focus on its role in decision-making where the outcomes are monetary.

Utilities measure the *relative* value which a decision-maker places on the gain or loss of various sums of money.

Before discussing how such utility values may be derived, it is useful to summarize their application very briefly. By working not with dollar amounts, but rather with utility values which a decision-maker associates with the gain or loss of each dollar amount, it becomes possible for decision-makers' attitudes towards risk to be accounted for. Alternatives are then ranked according to their expected utility, with equal expected utilities implying indifference between the choice of alternatives.

It is often convenient to portray utility functions of monetary gains and losses graphically, and an example is set out in Figure 6-9. In interpreting the graph we should note, for instance, that the positive utility value of 6.5 placed on the gain of the first \$500,000 is greater than the 3.5 value placed on the gain of an additional \$500,000 or, in other words, the utility of 10 placed on a gain of \$1,000,000 is less than twice the value placed on a gain of \$500,000. This reflects the typically observed phenomenon of diminishing marginal utilities. Furthermore, since monetary gains and losses are not equally weighted, the negative 4.5 utility value placed on a loss of \$100,000 is as large as the positive value placed on a gain of \$250,000. Thus, a 50 percent chance of making a profit of \$250,000 would be just offset by a 50 percent chance of incurring a \$100,000 loss, since the expected utility, E(U), of such a proposition would be

$$E(U) = 0.5\ (-4.5) + 0.5\ (+4.5) = 0.$$

Similarly, a 50 percent chance of making a profit of \$1,000,000 is offset by a 50 percent chance of losing \$200,000 as the respective utility values are plus and

[25] J. Von Neumann and O. Morgenstern, *Theory of Games and Economic Behavior*, (2nd ed.), Princeton: Princeton University Press, 1947.

[26] For an introductory treatment, see J. Hammond, "Better Decisions With Preference Theory", *Harvard Business Review*, November-December, 1967, pp. 123-141.

minus 10, reflecting risk aversion as it is prevalent with investors.

FIGURE 6-9

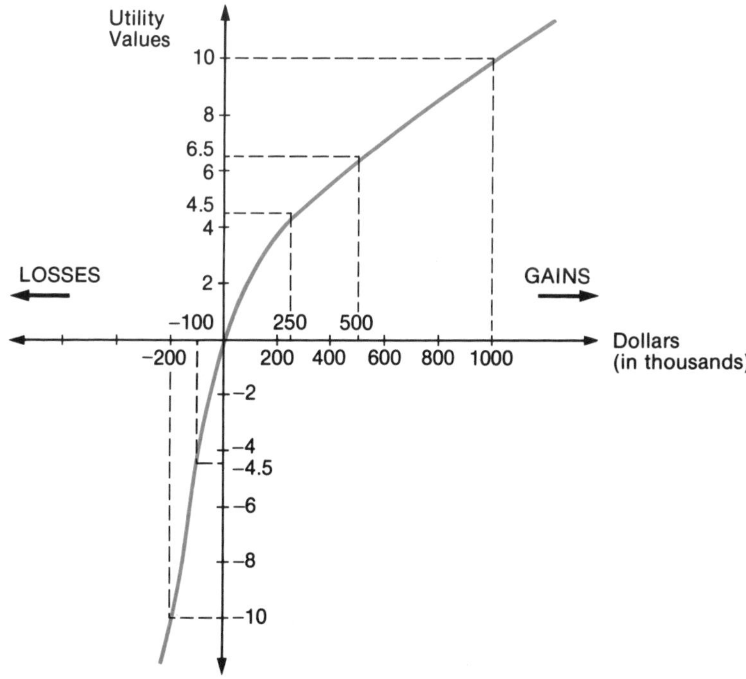

If, on the other hand, the odds were 70 to 30 for making $1,000,000 or losing $200,000, the expected utility becomes

$$E(U) = 0.7\ (+10) + 0.3\ (-10) = 4$$

Given a decision-maker is indifferent to choosing between any two alternatives yielding the same expected utility, we can readily determine the certainty equivalent for the above gamble. By noting from the graph that the dollar amount corresponding to a utility of +4 is a gain of about $230,000 the receipt of $230,000 with certainty affords the same satisfaction as, and is equated with, a 70 to 30 chance of either making $1,000,000 or losing $200,000.

The derivation of utility functions

The question which remains to be answered is how a decision-maker's utility function is to be derived. This is most readily achieved through the use of a step-by-step process in which the manager is repeatedly asked to identify his preferences or indifferences in decision situations of the simplest kind. We start by defining the scale against which we want to measure utilities. Since we are interested in expressing *relative* values, choice of the unit of measurement is arbitrary. Numerical utility values can be assigned to any two dollar amounts and this will define the scale.[27]

Example

Assume that a utility of zero is assigned to an amount of \$0 and a value of 10 to a gain of \$1,000,000. Utilities for other dollar amounts are obtained by presenting the decision-maker with choices between alternatives. If there is indifference in choosing between any pair of alternatives, the expected utilities of these alternatives have to be equal. Suppose we offer the decision-maker the choice between a 50-to-50 chance of receiving \$1,000,000 or nothing, and of receiving X dollars with certainty. Assuming he specifies \$270,000 for the value of X to be indifferent, it is then implied that the utility of this certain receipt is equal to the expected utility of the first alternative and we obtain

$$\begin{aligned} U\,(270{,}000) &= 0.5\ U(1{,}000{,}000) + 0.5\ U(0) \\ &= 0.5\ (10) + 0 \\ &= 5 \end{aligned}$$

Having identified the utility value of a certain gain of \$270,000, the procedure moves to offer other choices: the next, for example, between a 25 to 75 chance of \$1,000,000 or nothing, and receiving Y dollars with certainty. Should Y dollars at indifference turn out to be \$100,000, its utility would be $0.25 \times 10 + 0.75 \times 0 = 2.5$. Further possibilities are then considered including the chance of losses which is handled in the same way. A curve along the lines of the one shown in Figure 6-9 can next be plotted to provide a full description of the attitudes toward risk held by a particular executive at some point in time. If his behavior is consistent, he should evaluate risky investments and their respective probability distributions of monetary gains and losses according to the attitudes depicted by the curve, choosing those opportunities which maximize his expected utility.

Example

To illustrate the process of selection among alternatives, consider two cash flow distributions for projects A and B, with possible monetary results and probabilities as shown below. The corresponding utility values are read from Figure 6-9.

Proposal A

(1) Monetary Result	(2) Utility	(3) Probability	(2) × (3)
+ \$1,000,000	+ 10.0	0.3	+3.0
+ 400,000	+ 6.0	0.4	+2.4
− 200,000	− 10.0	0.3	−3.0
	Expected Utility		+2.4
	Certainty Equivalent		+\$120,000

[27]This is analogous to the assignment of 0 and 100 degrees to the freezing and boiling points of water, respectively, which then defines the centigrade scale.

(Certainty Equivalent = monetary gain having a utility of 2.4, read off Figure 6-9 as approximately +$120,000).

Proposal B

(1) Monetary Result	(2) Utility	(3) Probability	(2) x (3)
+ $600,000	+7.3	0.2	+1.46
+ 400,000	+6.0	0.6	+3.60
+ 200,000	+3.5	0.2	+0.70
		Expected Utility	+5.76
		Certainty Equivalent	$380,000

(Certainty Equivalent = monetary gain having a utility of 5.76, read off Figure 6-9 as approximately +$380,000)

While proposal *A* yields the same expected monetary value of $400,000 as project *B*, on the basis of risk-aversion the decision-maker clearly prefers *B* with its lower dispersion of results over *A*, as reflected by the expected utility figures and the corresponding certainty equivalents.[28]

FIGURE 6-10

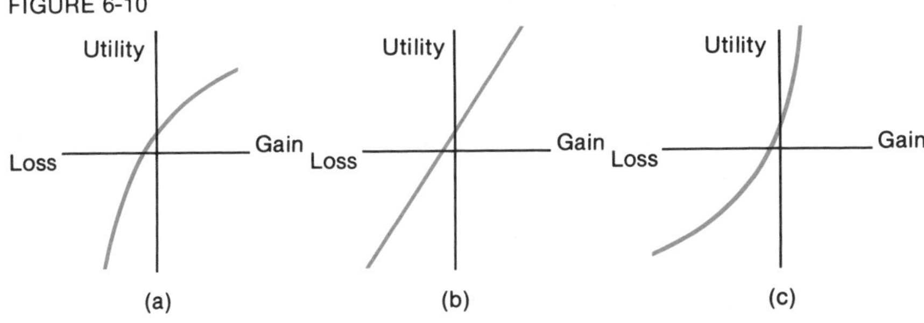

Once the decision-maker's utility function is established, it can be used repeatedly to derive certainty equivalents. Attitudes toward risk obviously may change over time. They are affected by the affluence of the decision-making entity and, therefore, it is important that the derived utility function be reviewed periodically.

Figure 6-10 depicts various utility functions.[29] Persons having a utility function of the type labelled (a) are risk-averse. It can easily be shown that they will require some positive premium in expected values before undertaking a risky venture. At the other extreme, there are those individuals with utility functions of the general form labelled (c). Such individuals are risk-seekers who accept gambles even when the expected value is known to be negative. Their contributions to Monte Carlo and Nevada are evident from the splendor of the casinos. The linear utility function (b) reflects indifference towards risk. Here,

[28]Such analysis can readily be extended to continuous probability distributions. The expected utility of a proposition simply becomes $E(u) = \int xu(x)f(x)dx$, where x represents the various monetary results and $f(x)$ is the continuous probability density function.

[29]For an example of utility functions which were derived by interviewing managers, see R. Swalm, *op. cit.*.

the value experienced by monetary losses or gains is strictly proportional to the amounts involved. It can be shown that ignoring uncertainty by just maximizing expected monetary receipts is only appropriate where the utility function is linear. When this is the case, the maximization of expected monetary value and expected utility are equivalent. Quite understandably, the criterion of maximizing expected monetary value is adequate where relatively small amounts are involved, as the relevant utility function may then be approximated by a straight line. As the sums involved become larger, however, to a point where losses come to represent a significant strain on the firm's resources, nonlinearities in the utility function will generally become increasingly important and cannot be neglected if realistic decisions are to be reached.

In situations where more than one person is involved in the decision process, a serious limitation of utility analysis as described must be underlined. Namely, the approach does not allow for interpersonal comparisons. The difficulty arises because we measure utilities on arbitrarily assigned interval scales rather than on an absolute scale. This precludes the conclusion that a particular action, involving two individuals and resulting in utility values of +2 and −1 respectively, is less attractive than another proffering values of +1.6 and +0.5. Constraints on interpersonal comparisons severely limit the application of utility analysis in finance. It cannot, for example, be used to determine the financial risk of a corporation which is most congruent with the risk preferences of *all* shareholders, even if their individual utility functions were known.

The preferences of a majority shareholder should pose no problems, however, and those investors with similar attitudes might subsequently be attracted to the firm.

6-9. SUMMARY

Considering that investors and management are generally not indifferent toward risk, an explicit evaluation of the uncertainties inherent in capital-budgeting decisions becomes important. It is useful to quantify the uncertainties surrounding cash-flow forecasts in terms of probabilities, as this provides a concise way of communicating information regarding uncertainty.

Several evaluation criteria can be relied on to assess risky investments. We distinguished between crude rules of thumb, more sophisticated rules of thumb, and other decision-making aids. Crude rules of thumb which are widely used in practice include ignoring risk, conservative estimates, and the payback period. Ignoring risk and simply working with expected forecasts is only reasonable where the projects being considered are relatively small in relation to the size of the financial resources of the firm. Conservative estimates are mostly applied in practice in a very informal and intuitive way. In particular in larger organizations, where several people are typically involved in the decision-making process, this can lead to severe distortions and inconsistent decision-making. The payback period, in spite of its weaknesses, has a useful role to play in the evaluation of risk, particularly if several refinements are considered. These include specific consideration of the time value of money, and the use of graphs portraying the net present value of a project under the assumption of abandonment at various points in time.

Under more sophisticated rules of thumb, we discussed risk-adjusted discount rates and certainty equivalents. Risk-adjusted discount rates, because of their operational convenience, are more widely used in practice. They have limitations where the uncertainties in a project's cash flows over time do not match the effects of discounting cash flows at an increased rate. However, this approach probably represents the most useful compromise between operational simplicity and theoretical validity. Certainty equivalents, while conceptually more appealing and providing greater flexibility, suffer from being cumbersome and difficult to implement in an operational setting.

Several other aids to decision-making under uncertainty were reviewed. Their main purpose is to provide the manager with information which will enhance decision-making. Specifically, we discussed sensitivity analysis, Monte Carlo simulation and decision trees. Sensitivity analysis is a powerful and easy-to-use tool requiring no great sophistication, yet providing exceedingly useful information. It assesses the sensitivity of a decision to changes in various input variables and determines break-even points. It can be used in conjunction with corporate financial models.

Monte Carlo simulation is a more sophisticated, computer-based technique. It allows us to assess how the uncertainties of several variables interact and work together to determine the overall risk of a project. Such risk may be measured, for example, by a probability distribution over the project's net present value. It requires some effort to set up a Monte Carlo simulation model, and, hence, its use is probably restricted to larger and more important projects. Decision trees are a useful way of structuring problems, in particular if they are of a sequential nature involving a series of decision points over time, with later ones being dependent on earlier decisions and events.

Major investment proposals should not be viewed in isolation, as the incremental risk which they contribute to the total investment portfolio of the firm has to be taken into account. This incremental risk depends largely on the correlation of cash flows between the various projects comprising the portfolio. Diversification to reduce such correlations is a well-known tactic often pursued in practice.

The risk attitudes of management should reflect those exhibited by investors, at least for widely held public corporations. Discrepancies may develop, however, given the system of rewards and penalties as perceived by executives.

Utility theory provides a conceptual framework within which decisions under uncertainty can be analyzed. Investors and managers alike ascribe different values to various amounts of monetary gains and losses. These values can be made explicit by deriving a decision-maker's utility function. Uncertain alternatives are then ranked according to their expected utilities. While this approach has seldom been used operationally, it provides very useful insights into the main issues of evaluating uncertain alternatives.

When comparing current industrial practices in capital budgeting with theory, a relatively wide gap is to be noted. Given increasing managerial sophistication, however, a significant narrowing of differences has been and will continue to be observed.

Questions for Discussion

1. Any business forecast is subject to uncertainty. Discuss the benefits of making such uncertainty explicit by asking forecasters to provide probability distributions. Why are probability distributions seldom used in practice to quantify uncertainty?
2. Why is an explicit evaluation of risk important in capital budgeting? How does risk affect a firm and its management? Under what circumstances may it be reasonable to ignore risk and to evaluate investment projects merely on their expected values?
3. Discuss the potentials and limitations of the payback period, including various refinements which were discussed in the chapter.
4. Discuss the strengths and limitations of using risk-adjusted discount rates to evaluate investment projects. Under what circumstances may their application lead to distorted results? How should the risk adjustments which are made to the discount rates be determined?
5. Discuss the relation which may exist between the accuracy of forecasts obtained from an individual, and the reward structure for performance as perceived by the individual?
6. Several researchers have found that many managers are exceedingly conservative in their forecasts, and are overly risk-averse in their evaluations of new projects, especially in larger corporations. What may be some of the reasons for this? If such behavior is not in the best interests of the corporation, how could it be overcome?
7. Discuss the concept of portfolio diversification. Why is this idea important in evaluating new investment projects? What are practical difficulties in its implementation?
8. It has been argued that firms should not be concerned about diversification. After all, if a shareholder wants diversification, he can achieve it himself by simply diversifying his holdings and investing, for example, in shares of a variety of corporations. Thus, it is argued that diversification at the corporate level is of no benefit to the shareholder. Discuss your reactions to this argument. Why do you think many firms are nevertheless concerned about diversifying their operations?
9. Derive your own utility function for money gains and losses for the range between minus \$3,000 and plus \$3,000. Would you use this utility function to make investment decisions? Discuss.

Problems with Solutions

1. Derive your own subjective probability distribution for the annual inflation rate 5 years hence. Note that such a forecast would be important not only to assess future cash flows from investment projects, but also to forecast long-term developments in interest rates, etc.

Solution

The specific distribution derived will obviously vary from individual to individual according to subjective beliefs. However, we will explore the procedure by which such a distribution may be derived.

Consider a roulette wheel with 100 numbers from 1 to 100. On the turn of the wheel, each number has the same probability of occurring. Assume you are confronted with having to choose between the following two alternatives:

Alternative 1: You receive $10 if the annual inflation rate 5 years hence is below or equal to zero percent, and you receive nothing if it is above zero percent.

Alternative 2: You receive $10 if the number which turns up in spinning the roulette wheel is smaller than or equal to x, and you receive nothing if it is larger than x.

The question is: how large does x have to be for you to be just indifferent between these two alternatives. For example, you may feel that at $x = 15$, you prefer alternative 2, as you have a 15 in 100 chance of winning, which you think is higher than under alternative 1. On the other hand, you may feel that for $x = 2$, you prefer alternative 1. Let us assume that at $x = 4$, you are just indifferent between the two alternatives. The implication is that you assign a probability of 4 percent or 0.04 to the event of an inflation rate of zero or below.

Next, we change alternative 1, with you receiving $10 if the inflation rate is below or equal to 3 percent. Again, you ask yourself for which value of x you would be indifferent between alternatives 2 and 1. The value of x should now be larger, as clearly under alternative 1 you stand a better chance of winning if the inflation rate can be anywhere below 3 percent than if it can only be below zero. Assume your indifference value for x now becomes 7. Thus, you assign a probability of 7 percent or 0.07 to the event of an inflation rate not exceeding 3 percent.

We continue in the same way, successively altering the limit for the inflation rate under alternative 1 and determining values for x which make us indifferent between the two alternatives. Assume we derive the following additional values:

Alternative 1	Alternative 2 (values of x which make both alternatives equally desirable)	Probability of Event
Inflation $\leqslant$ 6%	$x = 15$	0.15
9%	$x = 30$	0.30
12%	$x = 50$	0.50
15%	$x = 70$	0.70
18%	$x = 85$	0.85
21%	$x = 95$	0.95

From this, we can easily plot the cumulative probability distribution representing this particular set of beliefs regarding the future inflation rate, as follows:

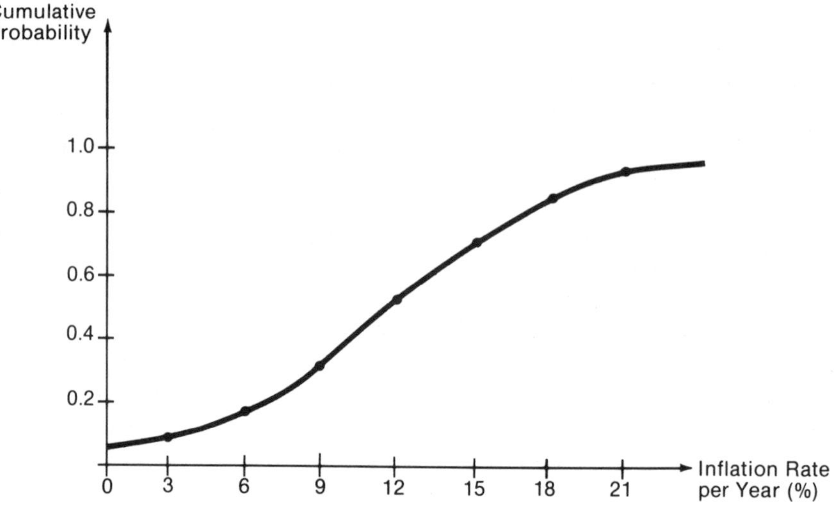

We can also derive the regular probability distribution. Note that, for example, the probability of an inflation rate between say, 9 and 12 percent, is simply given by the difference in cumulative probabilities. If there is a probability of 50 percent for inflation to be smaller than or equal to 12 percent, and a probability of 30 percent for inflation to be smaller than or equal to 9 percent, then the probability of inflation being between 9 and 12 percent must just be 20 percent. Thus, we derive:

Range for Inflation	Probability
⩽ 0%	0.04
0% – 3%	0.07 – 0.04 = 0.03
3% – 6%	0.15 – 0.07 = 0.08
6% – 9%	0.30 – 0.15 = 0.15
9% – 12%	0.50 – 0.30 = 0.20
12% – 15%	0.70 – 0.50 = 0.20
15% – 18%	0.85 – 0.70 = 0.15
18% – 21%	0.95 – 0.85 = 0.10
>21%	1.00 – 0.95 = 0.05

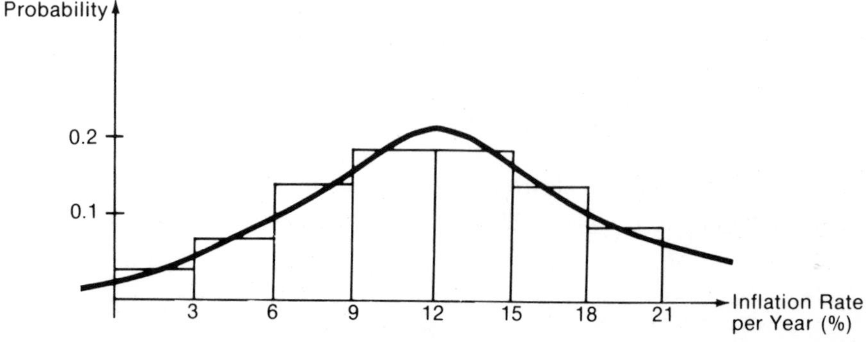

By confronting a person with simple choices between alternatives as illustrated above, you can derive subjective probability distributions in a systematic way. The process may have to be repeated several times: if after the first round, the resulting probability distribution is not really credible, you may want to change some of the indifference points derived earlier, until you feel that the distribution derived is more realistic.

2. Based on what was derived in problem 1 above, assume the following simplified probability distribution:

Inflation Rate Five Years Hence	Probability
−2 %	0.04
1.5%	0.03
4.5%	0.08
7.5%	0.15
11.5%	0.20
13.5%	0.20
16.5%	0.15
19.5%	0.10
23 %	0.05

Derive the expected value, the variance, and the standard deviation for this distribution.

Solution

EXPECTED VALUE: this may be derived by obtaining the sum of all the products of the probability and the inflation rate forecast.

Thus,

$$\text{E.V.} = (-2\%\times 0.04) + (1.5\%+0.03) + (4.5\%\times 0.08) + \ldots + (23\%\times 0.05)$$
$$= 12.03\%$$

VARIANCE: the variance is the average of the squares of the deviations about the expected value (mean).

Thus,

$$\text{VARIANCE} = .04(12.03-(-2))^2 + .03(12.03-1.5)^2 + \ldots + .05(12.03-23)^2$$
$$= 33.90$$

STANDARD DEVIATION:

$$\text{STANDARD DEVIATION} = \sqrt{\text{VARIANCE}}$$
$$= \sqrt{33.90}$$
$$= 5.82\%$$

3. An investment project is characterized by the following net cash flows over time.

Year	Net Cash Flows
0	–$100,000
1	–$ 20,000
2	+$ 20,000
3	+$ 40,000
4	+$ 60,000
5	+$ 60,000
6	+$ 40,000
7	+$ 20,000

The firm's cost of capital is 14 percent.

(a) Compute the project's payback period to the nearest year without discounting cash flows.

(b) Compute the project's payback period to the nearest year using discounted cash flows.

(c) Derive the project's net present value as a function of time t, assuming abandonment at time t.

(d) Given that the project might have to be abandoned early, what is the maximum amount the firm stands to lose (in present value terms) if early abandonment comes at the worst possible time?

Solution

(a) Without discounting future cash flows, the payback period may be ascertained as follows:

Year	Cumulative Amount Invested to Date	Cumulative Amount Returned to Date	Difference
0	$100,000	$ 0	$100,000
1	$120,000	$ 0	$120,000
2	$120,000	$ 20,000	$100,000
3	$120,000	$ 60,000	$ 60,000
4	$120,000	$120,000	$ 0

The payback period is *4 years.*

(b) The payback period now involves discounted cash flows. These may be computed as follows:

Year	Net Cash Flows	P.V. Factor (14%)	Discounted Cash Flow
0	–$100,000	1	–$100,000
1	–$ 20,000	.877	–$ 17,540
2	$ 20,000	.769	$ 15,380
3	$ 40,000	.675	$ 27,000
4	$ 60,000	.592	$ 35,520
5	$ 60,000	.519	$ 31,140
6	$ 40,000	.456	$ 18,240
7	$ 20,000	.400	$ 8,000

The payback period may now be obtained in the same fashion as under (a) above.

Year	Cumulative Amount Invested to Date (Discounted)	Cumulative Amount Returned to Date (Discounted)	Net Present Value to Date (– Investments + Returns)
0	$100,000	$ 0	–$100,000
1	$117,540	$ 0	–$117,540
2	$117,540	$ 15,380	–$102,160
3	$117,540	$ 42,380	–$ 75,160
4	$117,540	$ 77,900	–$ 39,640
5	$117,540	$109,040	–$ 8,500
6	$117,540	$127,280	+$ 9,740

The discounted payback period is about *5½ years.*

(c) This may be derived from the first column and the last column in the above table. For year 7, the value for the last column may be calculated as +$17,740.

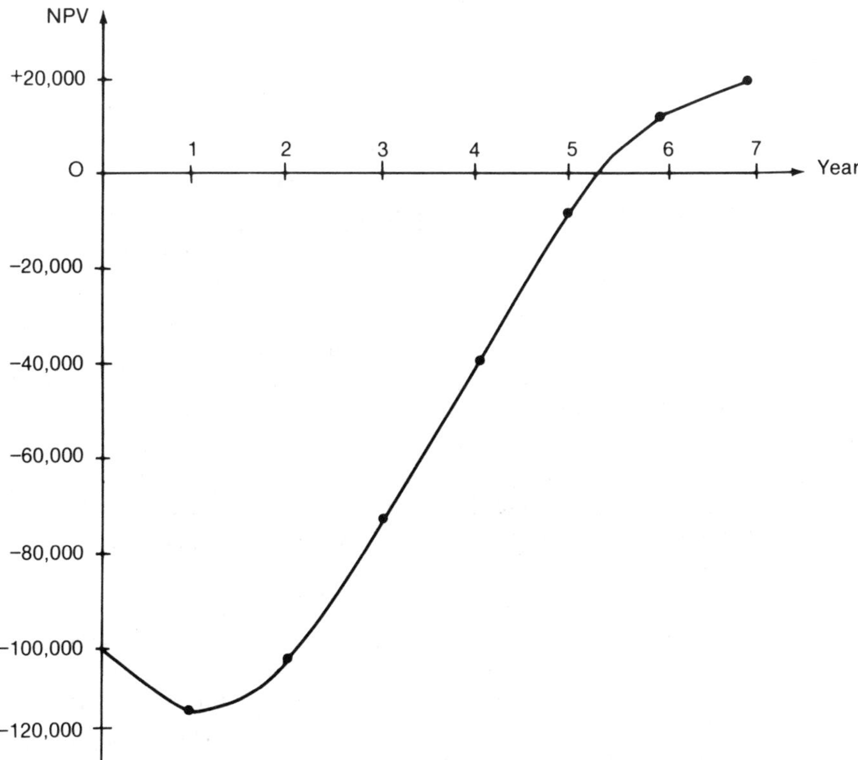

(d) From the graph, it is apparent that the worst that could happen is for the company to be forced to abandon the project at the end of year 1, thus losing $117,540 (in present value terms).

4. Assume expected after-tax cash inflows of $100 a year for 20 years from two projects, where project *B* is viewed to be somewhat riskier than project *A*, with project *A* corresponding to the firm's usual investments. The risk-adjusted discount rate deemed appropriate for project *B* is 15 percent, raised from the usual 10 percent which is otherwise applied.
   (a) Derive the ratio of present values for the annual net cash flows of projects *A* and *B* for years 5, 10, 15, and 20; that is *PV*(cash flows from *A*)/ *PV*(cash flows from *B*).
   (b) Based on your findings under 4 (a) above, what is inferred about the riskiness of cash flows from project *B* relative to the cash flows of project *A* over time?
   (c) Graph the present value of annual cash flows from each project as a function of time.

Solution

(a)

Period	Present Value of Annual Cash Flows Normal Project A Cash Flows Discounted at 10%	Present Value of Annual Cash Flows Risky Project B Cash Flows Discounted at 15%	Ratio A/B
t = 5	62	50	1.24
10	39	25	1.56
15	24	12	2.00
20	15	6	2.50

Note: The above figures are rounded to the nearest dollar.

(b) The above figures illustrate the risk adjustment which is implied when using risk-adjusted discount rates. Through the discounting process, later cash flows are affected more severely by an increase in the discount rate. Thus, from the figures derived under (a) above, it is inferred that, for example, the riskiness of the 20th period's cash flows of project *B* relative to the flows of the more typical project *A* is double the relative riskiness of the fifth period's projection. Even if the relative risk of project *B* as compared with project *A* does increase over time, it would be an unlikely coincidence for the relationships implied by the ratios to parallel such increases.

(c) *PV* of the cash flows for each 5-year mark were derived under (a) as follows:

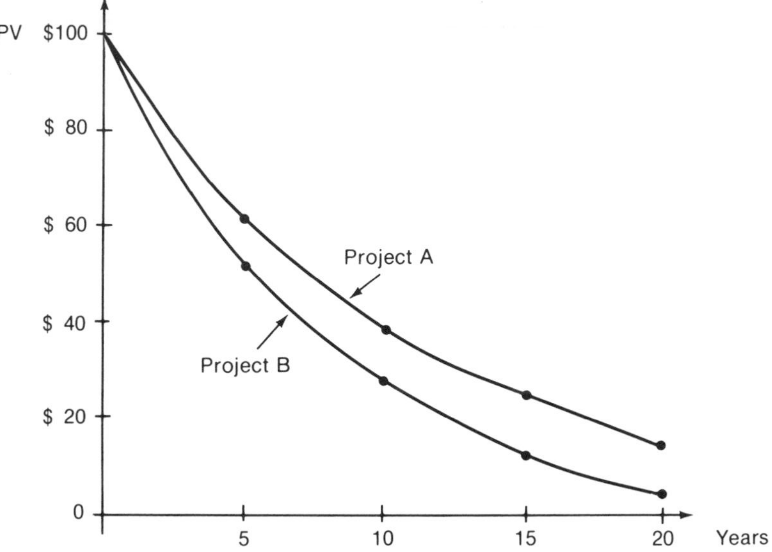

5. Excellent Enterprises considers investing in a new machine which would produce operating savings on the manufacture of one of the firm's major products. The new machine would cost $100,000 and is expected to produce before-tax savings of $33,333 per year for 10 years, at which point the machine could be sold for $4,500. CCA may be used on a declining balance method at a rate of 30%. Cost of capital for the company is 12% and the tax rate is 40%.
   (a) Derive the net present value of the project. Based on this figure, should the firm proceed?
   (b) A more careful forecast is prepared by the divisional manager, including possible variations in anticipated cash inflows. Savings from use of the new machine are a direct result of use of the machine, and it is possible sales could vary from expected values. This in turn could vary the before-tax saving achieved by the new machine by up to $15,000 per year. However, once sales patterns are established in the new year, sales are expected to remain at this level over the 10-year life of the machine.

   As well, the new machine may last up to 12 years, allowing savings to continue for another 2 years. Finally, the divisional manager feels that the expected salvage value of the machine at the end of the tenth year is largely a conjecture, and the actual value realized may vary between zero and $6,000.

   Conduct a sensitivity analysis showing the effects on the desirability of the project of the worst possible result occurring for savings, length of life, and salvage value, one at a time.
   (c) Where applicable, plot the net present value as a function of these three key variables (one at a time), also showing the break-even values, where the NPV just becomes equal to zero.

Solution

5. (a) Initial outlay on project = \$100,000

Expected after-tax annual cash inflows = \$ 20,000 for ten years

PV at 12% = \$ 20,000 × 5.650 = \$113,000

Salvage value of machine = \$ 4,500 in year 10

PV at 12% = \$ 4,500 × .322 = \$1,449

PV of tax shield from depreciation (formula derived in Chapter 5) $= C\left(\frac{dt}{d+k}\right) = \$100{,}000\left(\frac{.30 \times .40}{.30 + .12}\right)$

= \$ 28,571

PV of tax shield lost on sale of machine in year 10 $= \$4{,}500\left(\frac{.30 \times .40}{.30 + .12}\right) \times .322 = \$414$

NPV = – initial outlay + PV of annual cash inflows + tax shield from depreciation + salvage value of machine – tax shield lost on sale of machine.

= – \$100,000 + \$113,000 + \$28,571 + \$1,449 – \$414

= \$42,606

Based on this figure, Excellent Enterprises should proceed with the project.

(b) After-tax savings of only (33,000 – 15,000)0.6 = \$11,000 per year (worst possible case) would mean a NPV of annual cash inflows of \$11,000 × 5.650 = \$62,150.

NPV = – \$100,000 + \$62,150 + \$28,571 + \$1,449 – \$414

= –\$8,244

Length of life of the machine is not expected to be less than 10 years.

Assuming the worst with respect to salvage value (\$0), the NPV of the project would change by only \$1,449 – \$414 = \$1,035

NPV = \$42,606 – \$1,035 = \$41,571

(c) To plot these functions, we compute three points for each

(i) After-tax cash inflows:

We know if after-tax cash inflows are \$20,000, NPV = \$42,606

\$11,000, NPV = –\$ 8,244

At \$0 cash inflow, NPV = –\$100,000 + \$28,571 + \$1,449 – \$414

= –\$70,394

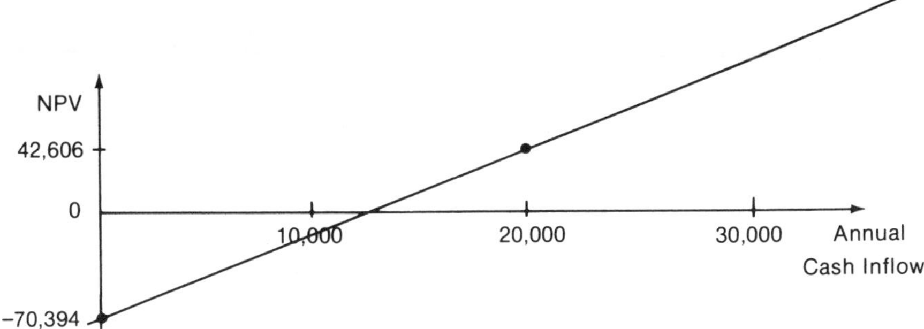

The equation for the net present value as a function of annual cash inflows can be derived as

NPV = –70,394 + 5.650 × annual inflows

From the above it is easy to see that in order to break even, the present value of all annual after-tax savings has to equal \$70,394. Given an annuity discount factor of 5.650, the break-even value is derived as: break-even value $= \dfrac{\$70{,}394}{5.650} = \$12{,}459$.

(ii) Length of life:

Varying the length of life of the project varies the annuity factors. We already know the NPV of a 10-year project is \$42,606. Given 8 years of operating life, the NPV becomes:

$$
\begin{aligned}
NPV &= -\$100{,}000 + \$20{,}000a_8 12\% + \$28{,}571 + \$4{,}500(.404) \\
&\quad - \$1{,}286(.404) \\
&= -\$100{,}000 + \$99{,}360 + \$28{,}571 + \$1{,}818 - \$520 \\
&= \$29{,}229
\end{aligned}
$$

A life of only 2 years would result in a NPV of:

$$
\begin{aligned}
NPV &= -\$100{,}000 + \$20{,}000a_2 12\% + \$28{,}571 + \$4{,}500(.797) \\
&\quad - \$1{,}286(.797) \\
&= -\$35{,}067.44
\end{aligned}
$$

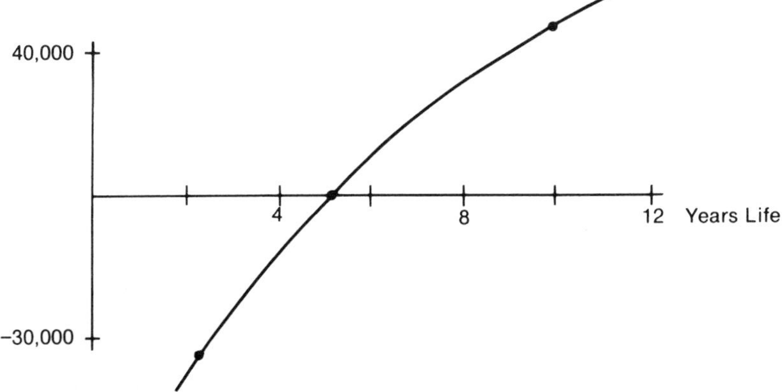

Break-even is about 5 years.

(iii) Salvage value affects only the last two terms in the NPV equation. At a salvage value of \$4,500, we have NPV + \$42,606, and at a salvage value \$0 (worst possible case), NPV = \$41,571. Given the insignificance of the change, it would not be worthwhile to analyze the NPV function. Naturally, there would be no break-even value.

6. The financial manager of B.T. Company with an existing portfolio of investments, z, is assessing two mutually exclusive projects, x and y. The relevant data may be summarized as follows:

Project x		Project y		Portfolio z	
Possible NPV	Probability	Possible NPV	Probability	Possible NPV	Probability
\$100	0.2	\$80	0.3	\$100	0.2
80	0.3	60	0.5	80	0.4
40	0.5	50	0.2	70	0.4

(a) Calculate the variance (σ^2) of x, y, and z.

(b) Assuming that the correlation coefficient between x and z is −.8 and between y and z is +.8, compute the variance of the combination of x and z and of y and z.

(c) Which project would you recommend to the financial manager?

Solution

6. (a)

	Project x	Project y	Portfolio z
Expected NPV	\$64	\$64	\$80
Variance (σ^2)	624	124	120

(b)

$$\begin{aligned}\sigma^2_{x+z} &= \sigma^2_x + \sigma^2_z + 2\rho_{xz}\,\sigma_x\,\sigma_z \\ &= 624 + 120 + 2(-.8)(\sqrt{624})(\sqrt{120}) \\ &= 744 - 437.83 \\ &= 306\end{aligned}$$

$$\begin{aligned}\sigma^2_{y+z} &= \sigma^2_y + \sigma^2_z + 2\rho_{yz}\,\sigma_y\,\sigma_z \\ &= 124 + 120 + 2(.8)(\sqrt{124})(\sqrt{120}) \\ &= 244 + 195.17 \\ &= 439.17\end{aligned}$$

(c) Project x has a higher σ^2 than does project y when considered in isolation, but if the covariance between each project and the existing portfolio z is taken into account, project x should be selected because it results in a lower overall variance (306 vs. 439).

7. The P.L. Company is considering an investment project with the following characteristics:

Initial outlay	—\$500,000
Net benefits before taxes and depreciation—	
year 1	\$400,000
year 2	\$300,000
year 3	\$180,000
Salvage value at the end of year 3	\$ 35,000

The corporate tax rate is assumed to be 50%, capital cost allowances for the class are taken at a rate of 20% on a declining balance, and the risk-free discount rate is 6 percent. Assume that risk increases over time, so that management views the certainty-equivalent coefficients for the cash flows anticipated in years 0 to 3 as $\alpha_0 = 1.0$, $\alpha_1 = 0.8$, $\alpha_2 = 0.7$, and $\alpha_3 = 0.6$.

(a) Using certainty equivalents, calculate the internal rate of return of the project. Would you accept the project?

(b) If risk-adjusted discount rates were used to evaluate this project instead of certainty equivalents as under 7(a) above, how high would the risk premium on the discount rate be (over and above the 6% risk free rate) in order for the project to just remain acceptable?

Solution

(a) Internal rate of return calculation:

$$500{,}000 - 500{,}000\left(\frac{.20 \times .50}{.20 + i}\right) = \frac{200{,}000(.8)}{1 + i} + \frac{150{,}000(.7)}{(1 + i)^2} + \frac{90{,}000(.6)}{(1 + i)^3}$$

$$+ \frac{35{,}000(.6)}{(1 + i)^3} - \frac{35{,}000(.6)}{(1 + i)^3}\left(\frac{.20 \times .50}{.20 + i}\right)$$

By trial and error, $IRR \simeq 5.5\%$.
Since $5.5\% < 6\%$, we would reject the project.

(b) Computing the internal rate of return for the original cash flows as given above, we obtain:

$$0 = -\$500{,}000 + \$500{,}000\left(\frac{0.2 \times 0.5}{0.2 + i}\right) + \frac{\$200{,}000}{(1 + i)} + \frac{\$150{,}000}{(1 + i)^2}$$

$$+ \frac{\$90{,}000}{(1 + i)^3} + \frac{\$35{,}000}{(1 + i)^3} - \frac{\$35{,}000}{(1 + i)^3}\left(\frac{0.2 \times 0.5}{0.2 + i}\right)$$

By trial and error, we obtain:
for $i = 16\%$ NPV $= -\$3{,}368.05$
for $i = 15\%$ NPV $= \$5{,}927.14$
Interpolating, we obtain:
IRR $\simeq$ 15.6%

Thus, any risk premium of less than $15.6\% - 6\% = 9.6\%$ would imply that the project remains acceptable, whereas if the risk adjusted discount rate is raised to above 15.6%, the project should be rejected.

Additional Problems

1. Derive your subjective probability distribution for the value which you think the Dow Jones average will assume (a) one year hence, and (b) 3 years hence.
2. Assume the following discrete probability distribution:

Possible Value for the Dow Jones Average	Probability
1150	0.02
1075	0.10
1025	0.25
1000	0.25
950	0.20
900	0.10
875	0.06
800	0.02

Derive the expected value, the variance, and the standard deviation for this distribution.

3. Given a cost of capital of 12 percent, the following investment is being considered. The project would require $50,000 to be invested initially, another $50,000 in the first year, and $10,000 in the second year. These investments will result in net after-tax returns of $30,000 per year for years 1 to 3, and $40,000 per year for years 4 to 7.

   (a) Compute the project's payback period to the nearest year using both discounted and non-discounted cash flows.
   (b) Derive the project's net present value as a function of time t assuming abandonment at time t.

4. (a) A one-period decision tree is given as follows:

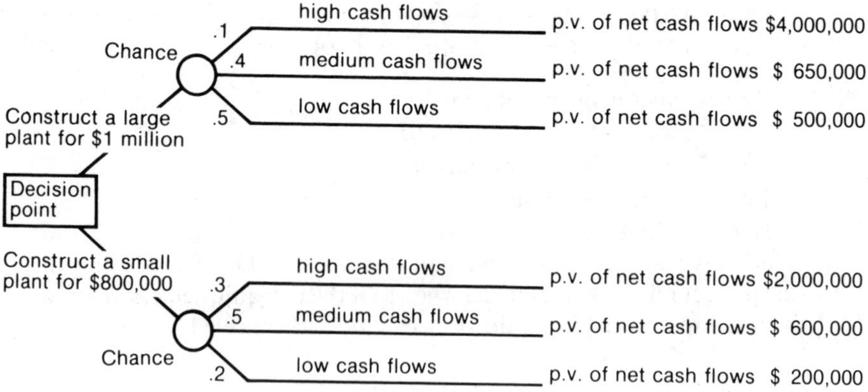

   Which alternative should be selected? Why?

   (b) Suppose you make the decision to build a small plant and market conditions have changed such that you now face the following decision tree:

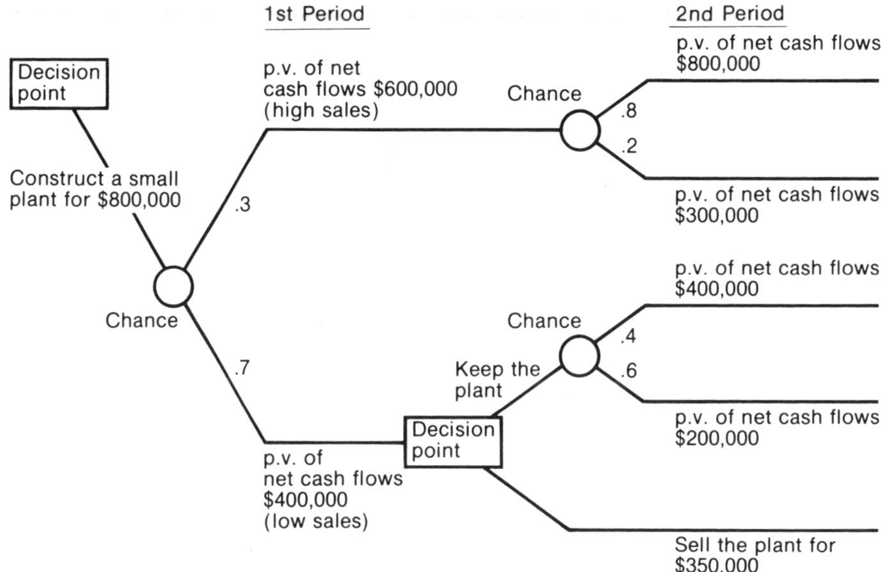

If low sales are indicated, would you keep the plant or sell it? What is the expected net present value of cash flows if a small plant is built?

5. The financial manager of P.B. Company is considering two projects, *x* and *y*, with the following information:

Project *x*

possible monetary result	utility	probability
$500,000	+10.0	0.4
300,000	+ 7.0	0.3
–100,000	–10.0	0.3

Project *y*

possible monetary result	utility	probability
$800,000	+12.0	0.2
200,000	+ 5.0	0.3
80,000	+ 2.0	0.5

(a) Assume that the certainty-equivalent coefficient for project *x* is .5. Calculate the expected monetary value, the expected utility, and the certainty equivalent (dollar amount) of *x*.
(b) Do the same calculations as in (a) for project *y* assuming that the certainty-equivalent coefficient for *y* is .65.
(c) Which project do you think the financial manager would accept? Why?

6. Assume that a utility of zero is assigned to an amount of \$0 (zero) and a utility of 100 to a gain of \$100 million. A financial manager is indifferent to a 50–50 chance of winning \$100 million or nothing, and a certain amount of \$30 million.
   (a) What is his utility for the \$30 million?
   (b) What is the appropriate certainty-equivalent coefficient, α, for the uncertain gain of \$100 million?
7. An investment is available to a company which would require an initial outlay of \$250,000. Returns over the next 6 years would be somewhat uncertain, but it is felt that \$75,000 per year would be a reasonable estimate. The cost of capital for the company is 14%.
   (a) Derive the net present value of the investment.
   (b) Do a sensitivity analysis on the effect of changes in:
      (i) the amount of anticipated annual cash inflows, and
      (ii) the number of years the inflows will last (one at a time).
      This includes plotting the NPV as a function of these variables, and identifying break-even values.
8. An airline is considering the purchase of a large plane to add to its fleet. The board of directors has asked you for a recommendation as to whether the plane should be purchased, and what the expected net present value of the investment would be. The following data and conditional probabilities were produced by the company's staff:

Purchase price of aircraft	\$15,000,000
First period	
good sales	\$ 7,000,000 probability .6
bad sales	\$ 4,000,000 probability .4
Second period	
good sales/first period good	\$ 8,000,000 probability .8
bad sales/first period good	\$ 6,000,000 probability .2
good sales/first period bad	\$ 6,000,000 probability .4
bad sales/first period bad	\$ 3,000,000 probability .6
Third period	
good sales/first period good/second period good	\$ 8,000,000 probability .8
bad sales/first period good/second period good	\$ 6,000,000 probability .2
good sales/first period good/second period bad	\$ 7,000,000 probability .4
bad sales/first period good/second period bad	\$ 3,000,000 probability .6
good sales/first period bad/second period good	\$ 7,000,000 probability .5
bad sales/first period bad/second period good	\$ 4,000,000 probability .5
good sales/first period bad/second period bad	\$ 5,000,000 probability .2
bad sales/first period bad/second period bad	\$ 2,000,000 probability .8

   Resale value of aircraft
      Aircraft could be sold after the first period only.
      If first period sales good — price \$12,000,000
      If first period sales bad — price \$10,000,000
   Note: All the above figures are present values of net cash inflows per period.
   (a) Draw the decision tree for this purchase.
   (b) What is the expected value of the purchase assuming the optimal course of action is followed?

SELECTED REFERENCES

M. Adler, "On Risk-Adjusted Capitalization Rates and Valuation by Individuals," *Journal of Finance*, September, 1970, pp. 816-836.

R. Bower and D. Lessard, "An Operational Approach to Risk-Screening", *Journal of Finance*, May, 1973, pp. 321-337.

S. Brumelle and B. Schwab, "Capital Budgeting With Uncertain Future Opportunities, A Markovian Approach", *Journal of Financial and Quantitative Analysis*, January, 1973, pp. 111-122.

Canada, Studies of the Royal Commission on Taxation, *Taxation and Investments: A study of Capital Expenditure Decisions in Large Corporations*, Ottawa, Queen's Printer, 1967.

J. Grayson, *Decisions Under Uncertainty: Drilling Decisions by Oil and Gas Operators*, Boston: Harvard Graduate School of Business Administration, 1960.

D. Hertz, "Investment Policies that Pay Off", *Harvard Business Review*, January-February, 1968, pp. 96-108.

D. Hertz, "Risk Analysis in Capital Investment," *Harvard Business Review*, January-February, 1964, pp. 95-106.

R. Hespos and P. Strassmann, "Stochastic Decision Trees for the Analysis of Investment Decisions", *Management Science*, August, 1965, pp. B244-B259.

C. Hoskins and M. Dunn, "The Economic Evaluation of Capital Expenditure Proposals Under Uncertainty: The Practice of Large Corporations in Canada", *Journal of Business Administration*, Fall, 1964, pp. 45-55.

M. Joy and J. Bradley, "A Note on Sensitivity Analysis of Rates of Return", *Journal of Finance*, December, 1973, pp. 1255-1261.

R. Keeley and R. Westerfield, "A Problem in Probability Distribution Techniques for Capital Budgeting", *Journal of Finance*, June, 1972, pp. 703-709.

L. Kryzanowski, P. Lusztig, and B. Schwab, "Monte Carlo Simulation and Capital Expenditure Decisions: A Case Study", *The Engineering Economist*, Fall, 1972, pp. 31-48.

R. Litzenberger and M. Joy, "Decentralized Capital Budgeting Decisions and Shareholder Wealth Maximization", *Journal of Finance*, September, 1975, pp. 993-1002.

P. Lusztig, "The Application of Certainty Equivalents in Capital Expenditure Decisions", *Cost and Management*, January-February, 1971, pp. 53-55.

J. Mao, "Survey of Capital Budgeting: Theory and Practice", *Journal of Finance*, May, 1970, pp. 349-360.

J. Mao and J. Brewster, "An E—S_n Model of Capital Budgeting", *Engineering Economist*, Winter, 1970, pp. 103-121.

J. Mao and J. Helliwell, "Investment Decisions Under Uncertainty: Theory and Practice", *Journal of Finance*, May, 1969, pp. 323-338.

N. Paine, "Uncertainty and Capital Budgeting", *Accounting Review*, April, 1964, pp. 330-332.

A. Robichek, "Interpreting the Results of Risk Analysis", *Journal of Finance*, December, 1975, pp. 1384-1386.

A. Robichek and S. Myers, "Risk Adjusted Discount Rates", *Journal of Finance*, December, 1966, pp. 727-730.

B. Schwab and P. Lusztig, "A Note on Investment Evaluation in Light of Uncertain Future Opportunities", *Journal of Finance*, December, 1972, pp. 1093-1100.

B. Schwab and P. Lusztig, "A Note on Abandonment Value and Capital Budgeting", *Journal of Financial and Quantitative Analysis*, September, 1970, pp. 377-379.

B. Schwab and H. Schwab, "A Method of Investment Evaluation for Smaller Companies", *Management Services*, July-August, 1969, pp. 43-53.

R. Swalm, "Utility Theory—Insights into Risk Taking", *Harvard Business Review*, November-December, 1966, pp. 123-136.

D. Tuttle and R. Litzenberger, "Leverage, Diversification and Capital Market Effects on a Risk-Adjusted Capital Budgeting Framework", *Journal of Finance*, June, 1968, pp. 427-444.

W. Whisler, "Sensitivity Analysis of Rates of Return", *Journal of Finance*, March, 1976, pp. 63-69.

D. Woods, "Improving Estimates That Involve Uncertainty", *Harvard Business Review*, July-August, 1966, pp. 91-98.

PART 3

Long-Term Sources of Funds

Chapter 7
Long-Term Sources of Funds

7-1. INTRODUCTION

In this chapter, we are concerned with providing a brief overview of the role of financial markets, and the processes by which they function. Given that a large proportion of the funds obtained by business are raised in the financial markets, it is essential for business executives to have some understanding of the workings of such markets. We start by reviewing the role which financial securities play in facilitating the flow of funds from savers and investors to ultimate users, and examine the functions which financial intermediaries perform in this context. Next we discuss the basic purposes and workings of financial markets in facilitating the trading of securities. Finally, we review the various sources of funds which businesses typically rely on, and identify their relative importance. The final section of the chapter provides an introduction to the financial flow accounts (which summarize the flows of funds between various sectors of the economy) as prepared by Statistics Canada.

7-2. THE ROLE OF FINANCIAL ASSETS[1]

An appreciation of the concept of *assets* and *liabilities* has undoubtedly been gained from work taken in introductory accounting or economics. For our purposes it is useful to note the distinction between *real* and *financial* assets. Such physical properties as land, buildings, inventories, or more generally durable goods, are examples of real assets. Financial assets, on the other hand, are created by borrowing and lending activities and are represented by a paper claim against an economic unit, entitling the holder to some payments of funds. The creation of financial assets necessarily involves at least two parties—an issuer to whom the instrument represents a liability, and the purchaser to whom it is an asset. It follows that every financial instrument is simultaneously an asset in the hands of an investor and a liability of the issuer. Corporate shares, while not representing a liability in the legal sense, are also included under financial assets in this context, as they are issued by corporations to raise funds, providing the holders with some claim on corporate income and assets. Examples of financial assets are bonds and debentures, common and preferred shares, bank or trust company deposits and money.[2]

In a barter economy lacking money and other financial assets, each economic unit has, by definition, a balanced budget in every time period, with current consumption and expenditures on real assets self-financed out of current

[1]Much of this section is drawn from J. Gurley and E. Shaw, "Financial Aspects of Economic Development", *American Economic Review*, September, 1955, pp. 515-538; and J. Van Horne, *Functions and Analysis of Capital Market Rates*, Englewood Cliffs, N.J.: Prentice-Hall, Inc., 1970, pp. 3-8.

[2]Money represents a claim against the issuing central bank.

productivity.[3] There being no financial assets, units can neither purchase or invest more than they earn, nor can they save more than is committed to real assets. To illustrate, consider the farmer requiring a plow to improve his output. He must either make the plow himself or trade part of his current crop to obtain a plow made by someone else. In all probability, however, the farmer will not only be ill-equipped and quite inefficient in plow construction but will also find it difficult to locate a person willing to make the trade. It is obvious, therefore, that given such a setting we are unlikely to find resources in the economy allocated to their most productive use.

With the introduction of money, economic units are provided with somewhat more flexibility since money balances can now be accumulated. Nevertheless, in the absence of other financial assets a unit's investment behavior is still constrained, and resource allocation in the economy remains less than satisfactory. Many worthwhile investments in real assets may be deferred or even rejected altogether because of the inadequate savings of economic units.

The introduction of other financial assets and some limited form of financial markets improves the situation considerably. In such circumstances there are three means by which individual economic units can finance levels of investment in real assets in excess of current savings:

- a unit may reduce its accumulated money balances,
- it can sell financial assets from its investment portfolio which it may have accumulated in the past,
- it can increase its own financial liabilities through borrowing.

Financing under the first two approaches essentially involves a shift in the composition of the economic unit's asset portfolio from money or other financial assets to real assets. The third method of financing simply entails the addition of real assets to the portfolio. Acquisition is made possible by the direct borrowing of the *deficit-spending unit* (which issues primary or newly created securities and claims against itself) from a *surplus-spending unit*. Deficit-spending units are those which disburse on goods and services more than their current income and surplus-spending units are the converse.

Such an economic setting avoids many of the problems cited earlier. Individual deficit-spending units no longer need to postpone promising investment opportunities for lack of accumulated savings; while surplus-spending units benefit because they can hold their savings in the form of financial securities yielding a positive return.

Nevertheless, problems still remain. A deficit-spending unit must seek out surplus-spending units and, if there is a sizeable project to be invested in, surplus-spending units may have to be found in larger numbers. The requisite searching involves expenditures of both time and effort and, as a consequence, may produce relatively expensive funds. Surplus units may similarly experience difficulty in placing their funds effectively. Therefore, the allocation of resources in the economy is still less than optimal. For instance, those located in one part of the country may be advancing monies to entrepreneurs at eight percent

[3] This is not strictly correct, for some saving is still possible. Unconsumed nonperishable consumption goods provide an example.

interest while borrowers of comparable standing in another region may be eager to pay up to twelve percent for funds.

To rectify these inefficiencies, better distribution techniques are inevitably developed. A communication system emerges to provide more information to both surplus- and deficit-spending units. In time, *non-monetary financial intermediaries* are formed both to simplify and reduce the cost of contact between borrowers and lenders and to broaden the range and characteristics of financial assets to better suit participants in the financial markets.

7-3. THE ROLE OF FINANCIAL INTERMEDIARIES

Financial intermediaries create a system of *indirect* financing. Rather than surplus-spending units providing funds directly to deficit-spending units, funds are channeled from surplus-spending units to such intermediaries, who in turn make the monies available to deficit-spending units. Figures 7-1a and 7-1b portray both direct and indirect financial channels. By issuing claims against themselves, and in this way raising funds from ultimate lenders or investors, financial intermediaries introduce a new set of financial instruments and services, the so-called *indirect claims:* such indirect claims, for example life insurance contracts and certificates of deposit, are issued by the intermediaries, and added to the portfolios of the surplus-spending units. The intermediaries meanwhile commit their newly raised funds to the purchase of securities issued by the deficit-spending units. Such *direct claims* are then held as assets. Figure 7-2 illustrates a greatly simplified version of the process.

FIGURE 7-1a

Direct Financing Channels

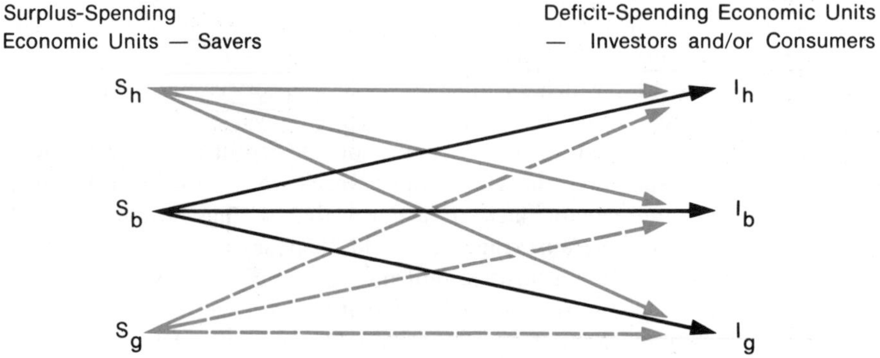

where S_h: Households — Savings

S_b: Business — Retained earnings, depreciation, depletion

S_g: Government — Budgetary surplus

I_h: Household — New housing, durables, education

I_b: Business — New plant and equipment

I_g: Government — Social capital, roads, schools, dams.

It must be recognized that financial intermediation will not alter the fact that the direct and indirect financial assets held by surplus-spending units must equal the securities and obligations of deficit-spending units. The sum of financial assets is greater, however, than would be the case if only direct financing were possible.

FIGURE 7-1b

Indirect Financing Channels

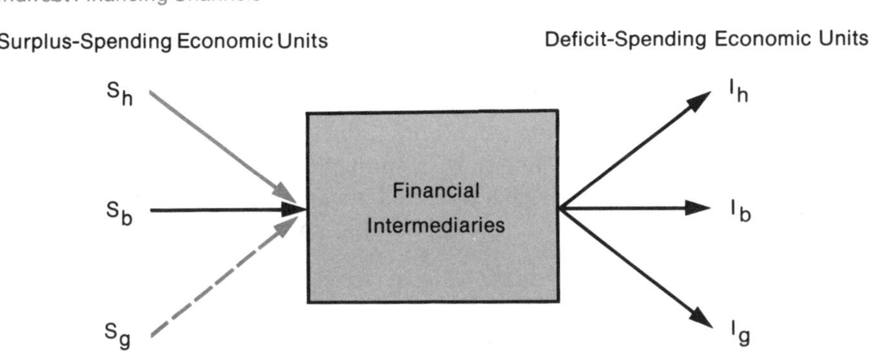

FIGURE 7-2

A Simplified Illustration of the Relationship of Balance Sheet Claims Given Financial Intermediation

Business Sector

Financial Assets	Liabilities
Real Assets	Net Worth

Household Sector

Financial Assets	Liabilities
Real Assets	Net Worth

Financial Institutions

Financial Assets [DIRECT DEBT OF VARIOUS SECTORS]	Liabilities [INDIRECT DEBT]
Real Assets	Net Worth

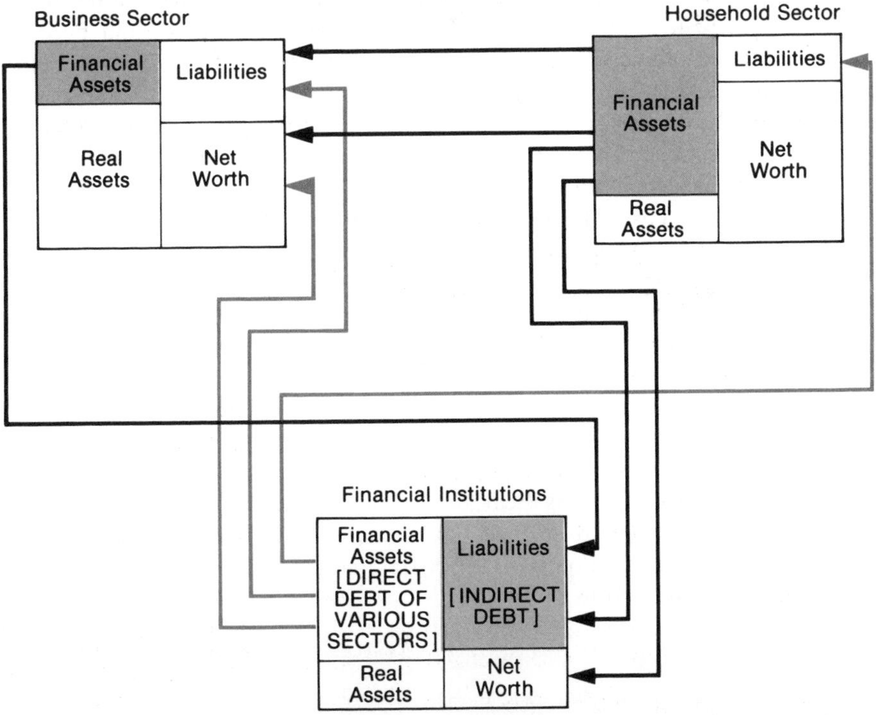

The growth of financial intermediaries and indirect finance is a most important innovation, because investors no longer need to expend major efforts to locate the right borrowers and *vice versa*. Also, services provided by intermediaries and the range of indirect securities which they make available improve opportunities and available alternatives for both investors and businesses seeking funds. The following statement from the *1964 Report of the Royal Commission on Banking and Finance* provides a good summary:

> . . . no matter how efficient the markets and how much liquidity or saleability they add to such instruments as bonds, stocks, and mortgages, they cannot meet all the needs of final lenders and borrowers. If financial institutions did not exist to take these claims into their balance sheets and to issue their own claims to final lenders in their place, much of the credit which now flows from lenders to borrowers in this way would only move at higher rates and under more restrictive conditions, while a good deal of it would probably not flow at all.
>
> The financial institutions, being relatively well known to both those with funds to invest and those requiring them, are able to do business on a large scale, to acquire diversified portfolios of assets, and to develop specialized skills and efficient procedures for processing credit applications. This greatly reduces their own risks of loss and enables them to offer liabilities to savers in a variety of forms meeting their demand for diversification, safety, yield, liquidity, or prospect of capital gain. Savers will hold these claims for a lower yield than they would require on the underlying debt because these liabilities can be tailored more closely to their requirements, because risk is reduced, and because related financial services are provided to them. At the same time, the skill and size of the institutions enable them to provide better service and lend at lower rates than the borrowers could get from direct lenders, while still earning a margin of profit for the institutions. In short, their activities facilitate the flow of funds from lenders to borrowers by reducing costs and improving liquidity, by increasing the number of routes over which credit may pass, and by enhancing the flexibility of the financial system.[4]

Neufeld, in a recent comprehensive work, reviews the emergence and growth of financial intermediaries in Canada over the past 170 years.[5] A few of the more important institutions identified in his study include the chartered banks, life insurance companies, mortgage loan companies,trust companies, credit unions and caisses populaires, trusteed pension funds and mutual funds. Whether we think of deposit accounts created, policies and shares issued, or retirement benefits contracted for, it is clear that each institution offers some form of indirect financial asset to be included in the portfolios of savers. Table 7-1 provides some indication of the relative sizes and patterns of growth of a few of these financial institutions.

[4]Canada, *1964 Report of the Royal Commission on Banking and Finance*, Ottawa: Queen's Printer, 1964, pp. 91-92.

[5]E. Neufeld, *The Financial System of Canada*, Toronto: Macmillan, 1972.

TABLE 7-1

Assets of Selected Financial Intermediaries
(in millions of dollars)

	1965	1970	1975
Chartered banks	26,233	47,307	108,378
Life insurance companies	11,856	15,673	21,656 (1974)
Local credit unions and caisse populaires	2,542	4,570	10,315
Mortgage loan companies	2,438	3,778	8,017
Mutual funds	1,574	2,704	2,801
Quebec savings banks	430	568	971
Trust companies	3,488	6,564	14,559

Sources: *Bank of Canada Review*, May, 1976 and *Canadian Life Insurance Facts*, various issues.

7-4. FINANCIAL MARKETS

Financial markets essentially encompass the institutions and procedures involved in the purchase and sale of financial assets. By facilitating the channeling of savings into the more attractive investment opportunities available, financial markets foster capital formation and economic growth. The main purpose of these markets is to match buyers and sellers in an efficient way. Prices at which various financial assets are traded will be determined by supply and demand. At the equilibrium price, the total offerings of all sellers at that price will equal the total amount that buyers in aggregate are prepared to purchase. This price is essentially determined by *investors at the margin*, or those investors who are marginally willing to buy or to sell at the market price. For example, a particular security may sell for $100. To some investors, the security may appear undervalued at this price, and they would not be willing to sell unless the price were to increase by an amount which was felt to be excessive. Other investors might view the same security as overvalued, and they would sell even if the market price were to slide somewhat lower. Neither of these two groups of investors are influenced by moderate changes in the market price, which implies that the supply or demand which they generate may be viewed as constant. On the other hand, for investors at the margin, the security just represents a marginal investment at the given price and any changes in that price will modify their behavior. Thus, supply and demand is adjusted and made equal through the effect of the market price on the behavior of such marginal investors. This whole concept is significant to the financial executive since the price of a firm's shares is determined by marginal investors, making it important to assess the impact of various financial policies on such investors.

In any review of financial markets, two general types of trading are to be observed.

There is trading in the *primary securities market*, which involves the sale of new security issues to investors. By facilitating primary distributions, financial markets provide for the efficient allocation of savings. Previously issued securities will be the subject of resale, or trading in the *secondary market*, simply changing hands from one investor to another. The facilitating of such secondary trading is of importance since it provides liquidity to investors, thereby increasing their willingness to enter the market in the first place. Consider an investor who purchased corporate bonds with a maturity of 20 years. Without a developed secondary market, the investor would have no meaningful choice but to hold such securities until maturity, and few investors would be able to enter into such long-term commitments. Given secondary markets, however, which provide opportunities for resale, the investor knows he can quite readily convert his holdings to cash by selling the bonds to other investors. Thus, it is reasonable to conclude that the existence of a reasonably efficient secondary market is almost a prerequisite for the issuance of securities with longer maturities.

To indicate the size of Canadian financial markets, we note for example, that during 1975 various levels of government issued or guaranteed a total of almost $15 billion of new securities, while primary distribution by industry amounted to just over $5.4 billion. The maximum size of a single new issue of corporate securities in Canada is probably around $150 million. Where larger amounts need to be raised, the issuer may have to go to the market in New York, as the American financial markets are much larger in size than their Canadian counterparts. In fact, one of the main reasons given by Canadian financial institutions for their large investment in securities listed on the New York Stock Exchange is that the size of the New York market makes it much easier to buy and sell large blocks of securities in secondary trading, thereby improving their flexibility and liquidity. The total quoted 1975 market value of all outstanding shares of industrial, mining, and oil companies listed on the Toronto Stock Exchange was $195 billion, with $4.1 billion worth of shares traded on that exchange during the same year. The total 1975 market value of all shares on the New York Stock Exchange was $685 billion with $126.7 billion worth of shares traded that year.

Classification of financial markets

Depending on the types of financial assets traded, we can subdivide financial markets into the *money markets* and *capital markets.* The money market involves the trading of short-term debt with maturities under three years, but in actual fact, securities with maturities under one year dominate. Typical instruments issued and traded in this market include treasury bills (short-term debt issued by the federal government) and commercial paper (short-term debt issued by corporations).

Securities with longer maturities or without maturity (such as shares) are traded in the capital markets. The capital markets can be subdivided further, with the most important segments for our purposes being the *bond market*, which involves the trading of long-term debt, and the *equity market* in which corporate shares are traded.

The functions of financial markets

The Canadian money market is basically a telephone market, with a number of major authorized dealers, who are in constant contact with each other, active in maintaining the market. The money market is heavily used by the government and money market dealers are expected to maintain an orderly market in short-term government securities such as treasury bills. To this end, these dealers may either act as agents in bringing buyers and sellers of money market instruments together, or they may act as principals, trading on their own account. They enjoy special arrangements with the Bank of Canada, which will act as a "lender of last resort" in supplying such dealers with temporary credit when necessary—a facility which adds to the stability of this market. The business sector is increasingly availing itself of opportunities available in this market as well and the greater sophistication of corporate financial officers has facilitated their participation. The role which the money market plays for business financing will be discussed in more detail in the chapter dealing with short-term sources of funds.

Shares are typically traded on organized security exchanges, or through the less formalized "over-the-counter market". Organized stock exchanges are competitive market places where brokers, acting on behalf of their investor clients, arrange to match buy and sell orders through an auction system. Trading takes place on the floor of the exchange between representatives of brokers who are members of the exchange. In order to become members they first had to purchase the necessary "seat".[6] In exchange for their services, brokers charge a commission which typically is some percentage of the value of the transaction.

Generally, only "listed" securities are bought and sold on the exchange. In order to qualify for a listing, the corporation concerned must both meet and comply with the various requirements of the particular stock exchange. Requirements typically include a fairly wide distribution of outstanding shares, assets of at least a certain magnitude, and willingness to disclose financial information. Trading in listed shares may be suspended and the shares may even be delisted by order of the exchange. It must be appreciated that listing as such is neither a guarantee nor a recommendation of the security by the exchange.

The relative positions of the six major Canadian stock exchanges, and the dominant position of the New York Stock Exchange, are reflected in Table 7-2.

TABLE 7-2
Trading Records, 1971

Exchange	Value (000,000 of dollars)	Number of Shares (000,000 of shares)
New York Stock Exchange	147,372	4,404
Toronto Stock Exchange	4,716	546
Montreal and Canadian Stock Exchanges	1,598	305
Vancouver Stock Exchange	488	607
Calgary Stock Exchange	12	21
Winnipeg Stock Exchange	1	1

Source: Toronto Stock Exchange, *Canadian Equity Market and Economy*, 1971.

[6] During 1971, two seats on The Toronto Stock Exchange were sold at prices of $80,000 and $95,000. These prices represent a sharp drop from the four sales of 1970 whose prices ranged from $115,000 to $132,500.

Shares of a corporation may be traded on more than one exchange. Thus, many Canadian issues are listed not only on various Canadian stock exchanges, but on the New York Stock Exchange or the American Stock Exchange as well. Where securities are traded on more than one exchange, investors will see to it that their prices remain closely aligned; otherwise the possibility of making immediate profits through *arbitrage* exists. The term arbitrage refers to the simultaneous buying and selling of the same good at two different locations in order to make a profit.

Example

> Consider a company whose shares trade for $100 on the Toronto Stock Exchange, while at the same time being quoted at $105 on the Montreal Stock Exchange. Barring transaction costs such as brokerage commissions, an investor could make an immediate profit of $5 per share by purchasing shares in Toronto and offering them for sale in Montreal. Such action would increase the demand for shares in Toronto, pushing up their price, and would result in an increased supply of shares in Montreal, decreasing the price there. The process would continue until the prices of both exchanges were aligned.

More generally, such arbitrage results in the economic *law of one price*, which states that, at any point in time, the price differential for the same good traded in two different locations cannot exceed transaction and transportation costs. Given world-wide markets, not only for financial assets, but also for commodities and foreign exchange, the importance of this concept and its role in maintaining a uniform equilibrium price needs to be stressed.

A large number of Canadian companies are either unable to qualify for listing on an exchange, or have elected to remain unlisted. Shares of these corporations are traded *over-the-counter* and the issuers are not bound by any of the restrictions which usually go with listing on an organized exchange. The so-called over-the-counter market is made up of some three hundred broker-dealers located in Canada's major financial centers. Information on bid and ask prices as well as on actual trades is available from investment firms active in the market and partial lists appear on the financial pages of various newspapers.

In this context, it is useful to distinguish between the function of a broker and a dealer, while noting that both functions may be performed side by side by the same investment firms. A *broker* acts as an agent for his client, buying and selling securities for the client's account, without taking title to the securities himself. As we saw, he derives his compensation from commissions. A *dealer*, on the other hand, purchases the securities from the seller and then attempts to resell them to a buyer. His remuneration comes from the spread between his buying price (also called *bid price*) and his selling price (*asking price*). The majority of trades in the over-the-counter market take place in this latter fashion. As an alternative to immediately reselling previously purchased securities, investment firms may buy and sell for their own account, thus maintaining inventories of securities.

In addition to common shares, most debt instruments such as bonds and debentures are traded in the over-the-counter market, thus adding to its importance. While this market serves a most useful function, it lacks the efficiency of our major stock exchanges, implying higher transaction costs and possibly reduced liquidity for investors.

7-5. SOURCES OF FUNDS—BUSINESS UNITS

The business sector, on a netted aggregate basis, is a deficit-spending sector of the economy. Thus, the representative firm can be depicted as supplementing its internally generated funds by drawing on outside sources. The ultimate providers of the financing are surplus-spending units in the economy and they can be businesses, households, governments, or foreign investors. The requisite funds may become available directly through the sale of various types of securities to investors, or they may be channeled indirectly through financial intermediaries.

Over any particular period, a firm's main sources of internally generated long-term funds are retained earnings, capital cost allowances, and possibly depletion. Depletion write-offs are an important source for the mining and petroleum sectors of the economy. Debt and equity are the principal sources of externally generated long-term funds. As will be detailed in the next chapter, debt can take a variety of forms. Most usually, however, it is classified as either a bond or debenture issue, depending on whether the debt is secured by specific collateral (bonds) or not (debentures).

FIGURE 7-3

Forms of Long-Term Business Sources of Funds

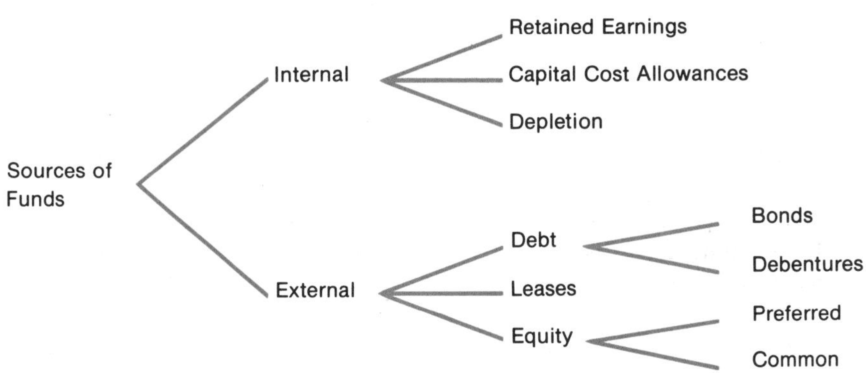

The relative importance of the several external sources of funds and the impact of shifting patterns is pictured in Table 7-3. Unfortunately, historic data on Canadian corporate financing leaves much to be desired as information must be derived from several sources, that are, strictly speaking, not always comparable. Consequently, Table 7-3 should be used or interpreted with some caution.

With the recent publication of financial flow accounts by Statistics Canada, both the magnitude and the relative importance of each source of funds to nonfinancial corporations became readily ascertainable on a period-by-period basis. Table 7-3 portrays the relevant information for the period 1968 to 1974. Several trends and patterns are worth noting. Thus, we see that the period under consideration was characterized by a rapid growth in the absolute amounts of funds generated, more particularly for the period from 1971 to 1974. The resultant stress in the capital markets, reflected in significantly higher costs required to service these funds, is quite understandable. Undoubtedly, the increased volume was related largely to inflation. With the inflationary growth in sales, firms had to maintain proportionately higher investments in assets such as inventories and accounts receivable. Furthermore, capital cost allowances, which are based on the assets' historical acquisition costs, may no longer be sufficient to provide for adequate replacement of plant and equipment.

Example

> Consider assets which were purchased 10 years ago at a cost of $10,000,000, but which have a current replacement value of $20,000,000. It is clear that capital cost allowance of 10 percent on the original purchase price is wholly inadequate to replace 10 percent of such assets, and the shortfall of $1,000,000 may have to be met from other sources.

In this context, it is worth noting that for some industries, the rate of price level changes has exceeded considerably the growth rate of such indicators as the widely publicized consumer price index.

Internally generated funds have always been of major importance to the financing of business, typically providing over 60 percent of all available funds. The decreasing proportion of these amounts in recent years can be attributed to the inadequacy of capital cost allowance during periods of inflation as just discussed, and disappointing earnings performances in an environment which has often been characterized by simultaneous inflation and stagnation. The almost inevitable consequence has been a relatively larger reliance on outside funds, notably debt. The dramatic increase in trade payables (credit granted by suppliers) reflects the increased dollar volume of purchases, largely caused by price level changes. The high level of bank loans over the period 1972 to 1974 may in part reflect borrowing by small- and medium-sized businesses which, because of their limited size, do not have ready access to the capital markets. The high level may also reflect that, with long-term interest rates having been at historical highs, many firms attempted to postpone long-term debt financing by drawing temporarily on shorter-term sources such as bank loans.

Relatively wide fluctuations in the volume of new equity issues are worth noting. To a large extent, this volatility reflects varying receptiveness in the equity market to new issues. When prices are low, a firm has to issue a relatively larger number of shares in order to raise a given amount of capital than would be the case when share prices reach higher levels. The larger the number of outstanding shares, the more difficult it becomes for the firm to maintain earnings and dividends per share, and existing shareholders may suffer some dilution. Therefore, given the volatility of the stock markets, timing is critical when planning for new issues of common shares, with such offerings drying up almost completely when adverse capital market conditions like those of 1974 prevail.

TABLE 7-3

Sources of Funds, Nonfinancial Corporations
1968-1974 inclusive

Sources of Funds	1968		1969		1970		1971		1972		1973		1974	
	millions of $	%	millions of $	%	millions of $	%	millions of $	%	millions of $	%	millions of $	%	millions of $	%
Total funds generated	8,289	100.0	9,102	100.0	9,982	100.0	12,389	100.0	14,814	100.0	19,919	100.0	26,618	100.0
Internally generated funds	4,796	57.9	4,993	54.9	6,670	66.8	7,271	58.7	8,716	58.8	10,717	53.8	11,448	43.0
Capital consumption allowances	3,922	47.3	4,103	45.1	4,683	46.9	4,958	40.0	5,886	39.7	6,739	33.8	7,536	28.3
Net domestic saving	874	10.5	890	9.8	1,987	19.9	2,313	18.7	2,830	19.1	3,978	20.0	3,912	14.7
Externally generated funds	3,493	42.1	4,109	45.1	3,312	33.2	5,118	41.3	6,098	41.2	9,202	46.2	15,170	57.0
Trade payables	438	5.3	578	6.4	293	2.9	1,153	9.3	1,660	11.2	2,334	11.7	4,857	18.2
Bank and other loans	123	1.5	1,078	11.8	161	1.6	209	1.7	2,451	16.5	2,896	14.5	3,549	13.3
Mortgages	59	0.7	192	2.1	199	2.0	271	2.2	336	2.3	518	2.6	507	1.9
Bonds	553	6.7	780	8.6	1,329	13.3	1,910	15.4	863	5.8	825	4.1	1,435	5.4
Equity capital	842	10.2	1,266	13.9	705	7.1	586	4.7	376	2.5	1,032	5.2	788	3.0
Finance company and other short term commercial paper	186	2.2	302	3.3	40	0.4	326	2.6	—238	—1.6	—65	—0.3	783	2.9
Claims on associated enterprises: corporations	719	8.7	84	0.9	492	4.9	73	0.6	302	2.0	497	2.5	789	3.0
Other	573	6.9	—71	—0.8	93	0.9	508	4.1	348	2.3	1,165	5.8	2,462	9.2

Source: Statistics Canada, *System of National Accounts, Financial Flow Accounts*, various issues.

As we can see, sources of financing relied on by business may change over time, both in absolute amounts and in relative terms. Changed conditions in the economy in general, and in the financial markets in particular, require adaptations in financing policies. Financial decisions can only be assessed as good or bad in a given context and proper timing is an essential ingredient for success. In order to anticipate developments and thereby to efficiently plan the financing of the firm, the executive needs to have a broad understanding of the economy and financial markets.

TABLE 7-4

Corporate Liabilities and Net Worth 1935, 1951, and 1967-1971.
(Shown in percentage)

	1935	1951	1967	1968	1969	1970	1971
Total Current Liabilities	8.0	18.9	37.9	38.6	39.3	37.6	38.1
Net Long-Term Debt	24.9	18.7	16.5	16.5	16.6	20.1	20.6
Other Noncurrent Liabilities	n.a.	n.a.	9.0	9.3	9.2	8.9	8.5
Preferred Shares	50.1	29.3	4.8	4.6	4.5	4.1	3.8
Common Shares			9.7	9.3	9.3	8.6	8.3
Surplus and Retained Earnings	17.0	33.1	22.1	21.7	21.1	20.7	20.6

Sources: 1935 and 1951 data based on 603 companies is drawn from Montreal Stock Exchange, *Brief to the Royal Commission on Banking and Finance*, 1962, p. 101. Subsequent data from Statistics Canada, *Corporation Financial Statistics*, various issues.

Small business

The growth of our economy has been accompanied by a continued growth and institutionalization of financial intermediaries, with such intermediaries becoming a dominant force in Canada's financial markets. These intermediaries naturally find it easier and more efficient to deal with a more limited number of larger, better-known companies whose stocks and bonds are publicly held and traded. As a result, smaller businesses have experienced some difficulty in obtaining long-term funds through existing channels. Unfortunately, such businesses are of necessity more dependent on external sources of funds than are the larger corporations. Despite favorable tax treatment, their earning streams are more modest relative to requirements for new capital which have recently been inflated by price level changes. Also, because of their limited size, and because small public issues of corporate securities tend to become prohibitively expensive, such firms have difficulties in finding direct access to investors and, as a consequence, have become more dependent on the services provided by financial intermediaries.

Any attempt at detailing small business financing in Canada is hampered by an almost complete absence of current factual information.[7] Looking specifically at the availability of longer-term financing from external sources, the Canadian Manufacturers Association brief to the 1961 Royal Commission on

[7]For one reasonable piece of research in the area, see F. Wildgen, *Financing Small Business*, a mimeographed research staff working paper prepared for the 1961 Royal Commission on Banking and Finance.

Banking and Finance provides some limited insights for manufacturing concerns. Results of a CMA survey on the adequacy of long-term financing revealed a marked discrepancy between the responses received from small private companies controlled in Canada and those from public companies and larger or foreign-controlled businesses. A more complete picture is provided in Table 7-5. The evidence does suggest inadequate access to long-term financing in the case of smaller Canadian-controlled private companies engaged in manufacturing. It is important to record, however, that the survey also revealed some considerable aversion toward the sale of common shares or convertible debt by this category of respondent. Of 114 replies from those with sales under $1 million, 59 indicated a lack of interest in such long-term external financing.

TABLE 7-5

Summary of Survey on the Adequacy of Long-Term Financing
Categorized by Number, Nature, and Source of Responses

	Sales Class of Respondent (millions of $)			
	All Classes	Under $0.25	$0.25- $0.99	$1.0 and over
Private Companies — Cdn. Controlled				
No. answering "adequate"	130	19	46	65
No. answering "inadequate"	91	26	42	23
Private Companies — Foreign Contr.				
No. answering "adequate"	88	1	15	72
No. answering "inadequate"	2	0	1	1
Public Companies — Cdn. Controlled				
No. answering "adequate"	48	1	3	44
No. answering "inadequate"	4	0	1	3
Public Companies — Foreign Contr.				
No. answering "adequate"	35	0	0	35
No. answering "inadequate"	0	0	0	0

Researchers have also noted the impact of geographic location on the availability of financing. According to one study,

> Interviews with a broad cross-section of small business operators leave the writer with the impression that small businesses in outlying communities may not find financial facilities as adequate as those businesses located in larger cities.[8]

It would appear that the urban concentration of the general financial community and of individual financiers is to the disadvantage of those smaller firms in need of external funds but located outside metropolitan centers. Several programs designed by various levels of government to remedy this situation will be discussed in a subsequent chapter on intermediate-term sources of funds.

[8] *Ibid.*, p. 82.

7-6. YIELDS OF FINANCIAL SECURITIES

One of the major issues at the heart of most financial decisions is the trade-off between risk and return. For the firm seeking financing, this may take the form of a trade-off between the cost of funds, and the risk of using such funds. While individual attitudes towards risk do vary, in aggregate investors active in the financial markets have proven to be risk averse. With the existence of financial assets whose returns are subject to different degrees of risk, the riskier securities must provide higher expected returns to be attractive to investors. Similarly, in many instances firms will be able to reduce their direct costs of financing only at the expense of assuming additional risk themselves. Thus, both the investor and the financial manager are continually faced with having to trade-off expected profitability against the increased risk which inevitably follows. In practice, this is often one of the more difficult elements of decision-making which faces the financial executive. The topic of risk-return trade-offs will be discussed in more detail in subsequent chapters, with our final chapter which introduces the capital asset pricing model providing the conceptual framework within which such trade-offs should take place. The purpose of this section is simply to provide a brief introduction to this issue as it applies to corporate long-term financing.

TABLE 7-6

Summary of Characteristics and Trade-offs of Debt, Preferred Shares, and Common Shares (yield/cost figures as of October, 1975)

		For Investor			For Corporation		
Bonds	Risk		Low			High	
	Yield/Cost	11%	Low	(6.60)	11%	Low	(5.5)
Preferred	Risk		Medium			Medium	
	Yield/Cost	9.36	Medium	(7.8)	9.36	Medium	(9.36)
Common	Risk		High			Low	
	Yield/Cost		High			High	
		Div. Yld.	6.31	(5.2)	Div. Yld.	6.31	(6.31)
		E/P*	12.58	(10.4)	E/P*	12.58	(12.58)

Note: Figures in brackets are after-tax data based on the assumption of a 50% corporate tax rate and a 40% individual tax rate (combined federal and provincial, with provincial tax at 30% of federal). The above yields are based on average figures as published in the *Financial Post*.
*E/P = current annual earnings/current market price per share = current earnings yield.

Table 7-6 presents a brief overview of the costs and yields of the main external sources of long-term financing, namely debt, preferred shares, and common shares. Each of these securities, and their characteristic features, will be reviewed in detail in the chapters which follow. We note that, from an investor's point of view, bonds may be taken as the least risky investment, followed by preferred shares and finally by common shares. Interest on debt represents a fixed contractual obligation of the issuing corporation, while dividends on preferred shares are normally a set amount, but need not be paid if, for example, the firm were to encounter financial difficulties. Dividends on common shares are fully discretionary with the firm's board of directors, but can only be paid after dividends on preferred shares have been met. Similarly, in the case of bankruptcy and liquidation, claims of bondholders and preferred shareholders rank ahead of claims held by common shareholders. For all these reasons, bonds and preferred shares are often termed *senior securities.*

Quite obviously, it is the after-tax yields which are of primary relevance to an investor. For purposes of illustration, the figures shown in brackets in Table 7-6 assume a 40 percent overall tax rate for the investor, with provincial tax being 30 percent of the federal tax. Interest income on bonds is assumed to be fully taxable, while dividends on either preferred shares or common shares are held to qualify for the dividend tax credit as outlined in Chapter 3.

The yield on common shares, while discussed in detail in subsequent chapters, warrants a brief introductory comment. Shown in the table are both the current dividend yield (current dividends/current market price), and the current earnings yield, or current earnings over current market price (E/P). If the firm paid out all its earnings in dividends, the dividend yield would equal the earnings yield. However, a given proportion of earnings are typically retained in the business to finance new investments and future growth. Clearly, shareholders should only pass up current dividends if such reinvestments are expected to provide an adequate compensation in the form of increased future dividend payments and/or capital gains. Thus, the value of reinvested earnings to investors in the form of capital gains and/or increased future dividends should at least equal, if not exceed, the value which investors would derive if these same earnings were paid out in current dividends. It follows that for introductory purposes, the current earnings yield can be used as a rough approximation and perhaps as a conservative minimum estimate of the true yield which investors expect to realize when holding common shares. With the discussion of the cost of capital in a subsequent chapter, a more complete and accurate measure will be developed.

Given these observations, we see from Table 7-6 that after-tax yields do indeed increase with increasing risk, with bonds on the low end, both in terms of risk and returns, and common shares providing high expected returns as compensation for a high degree of risk. Obviously, we can further differentiate between different types of bonds, preferred and common shares, with the figures in Table 7-6 merely representing aggregate averages. A look at the financial pages of the newspaper will reveal the broad spectrum of securities available, and the pervasiveness of the trade-off between risks and returns.

From the corporation's point of view, debt represents the riskiest form of financing, given that any default on payments can lead to bankruptcy. Ranking next in terms of risk are preferred shares, with common share financing providing the greatest degree of flexibility and the lowest degree of risk. At the same time, we see that debt entails by far the lowest direct cost of financing, implying increased potential profitability for the firm. Therefore, in planning the procurement of funds, the financial officer has to weight low costs (or high expected profitability) against higher risks.

Summarizing the above discussion, we may observe that in relatively efficient and sophisticated financial markets, there are no bargains to be found. If a particular financial asset promises a high expected yield, it is normally because such potential yield is subject to greater risk. Otherwise, it is likely that many other investors would also have found the particular security to be an attractive investment, and have bid up its price until its expected return was once again in line with that of other securities which are available in the market.

***ADDITIONAL SELECTED TOPICS*

**7-7. THE FINANCIAL FLOW ACCOUNTS

As part of its *National Accounts*, Statistics Canada publishes *Financial Flow Accounts* which provides relatively detailed statistics on the flow of funds between various sectors of the economy. It shows by period which sectors of the economy have been surplus spenders or net providers of funds, and which sectors have used such funds to finance their deficit spending. Information about the types of financial assets issued as part of such flows from net savers to net users, and on the role played by financial intermediaries in the process, is also included. Analysis of the financial flow accounts not only enables the financial officer to gain a better understanding of the workings and magnitudes of financial markets, but also helps in assessing trends which are likely to be reflected in future capital market conditions. An early detection of such developments is of major importance in planning and scheduling the firm's external financing. In this section, we briefly review the types of information contained in the financial flow accounts, and some basic issues which have to be kept in mind when interpreting such information.

The concepts of *flows* and *stocks* are fundamental to the understanding of financial flow accounts. A *stock* represents the total amount of a certain asset outstanding at some particular point in time. In contrast, a *flow* variable measures the volume of transactions per unit of time. Hence we could think of the stock of wealth, of real or financial assets at some instant in time, and of the flow of income, savings, or investment in a given year. Stock and flow variables, however, are intimately related. A stock variable may be considered as the summation of previous net flows, while a flow variable is the difference in the level of a stock, measured at the beginning and end of the time period under consideration. With respect to financial assets, we speak of the stock or holdings of assets, and of the flow or transactions occasioned by the purchase and sale of new or existing assets.

A logical way to explain the role and operation of the flow accounts is to view them in the context of typical financial statements of business corporations. The corporate balance sheet represents the stocks of assets, liabilities, and net worth as at a particular point in time. Changes in the items on balance sheets drawn up at two different time periods may be categorized and presented as a standard source-and-use-of-funds statement. By taking source-and-use statements for all units in the economy, and grouping these into sectors, we can prepare a *financial flows matrix* for the entire economy. Each sector represents a column in such a matrix, and each type of financial transaction is portrayed in a row. Statistics Canada, in its *Financial Flow Accounts*, prepares just such matrices as well as summaries of these accounts, as shown in Table 7-7.[9]

In interpreting the information provided in Table 7-7, we identify, for example, the main surplus spending and deficit spending sectors of the economy. By looking at category number 1900, we see that during 1975 the main net lenders of funds were persons and unincorporated business ($8,703 million), social security funds ($1,991 million), and "rest of the world" ($5,074 million), where rest of the world essentially means foreign monies which were invested in Canada. We note that Canada has typically been a net importer of capital, and has traditionally drawn on foreign sources to balance its sources and uses of funds. It is clear that if the inflow of foreign capital was curtailed, such curtailment would have to be matched by a reduction in spending by deficit-spending units, or by increased domestic savings. We also see that the main deficit-spending sectors of the economy (net borrowers) were non-financial private corporations ($4,339 million), non-financial government enterprises ($4,591 million), the federal government ($4,611 million), and provincial and local governments and hospitals ($2,538 million).

We can further analyze how the various sectors of the economy invested their funds, and what liabilities they took on. For example, foreign investors providing funds to the Canadian economy did so mainly through the purchase of bonds ($4,454 million), of which by far the largest category were provincial government bonds ($3,165 million). Households (persons and unincorporated business), on the other hand, invested mainly in deposits with banks and other institutions ($12,559 million), again in bonds ($3,446 million) and in life insurance contracts and pension funds ($4,553 million). It is interesting to note that the latter represents what might be termed "forced savings" by individuals having to meet their life insurance or pension fund commitments. Combining this figure with deposits at financial institutions, we can appreciate the importance of financial intermediaries in channeling funds from surplus to deficit spending units. The main uses of funds by non-financial private corporations were for fixed capital formation ($17,311 million) and accounts receivable ($4,117 million), with funds provided internally through capital cost allowances ($8,388 million), and net domestic saving or retained earnings ($3,571 million), and externally through accounts payable or trade credit ($2,543 million), loans ($2,314 million), and the sale of bonds ($2,116 million) and stocks ($1,009 million).

Clearly, analysis of such detailed statistics will not only provide a good grasp of the major forces shaping the activities taking place in the financial markets but, if compared with statistics from other periods, will also enable the manager to detect trends and to assess future developments. Such analysis is obviously critical in financial planning, since the type of funds to be drawn on and the

[9]See, for example, Statistics Canada, *System of National Accounts, Financial Flow Accounts, Fourth Quarter 1971*, Ottawa: Queen's Printer, March, 1972. It should be noted that the Canadian system of national accounts is in line with standards outlined in the United Nations publication, *A System of National Accounts*, New York: Department of Economic and Social Affairs, 1968.

TABLE 7-7

Financial Flow Matrix for 1975

Category No.	Transaction Category	I. and II. Persons and Unincorporated business	III. Non-financial private corporations	IV. Non-financial government enterprises	V. The monetary authorities	VI I. Chartered banks
		Sector				
		millions of dollars				
1100	**Gross domestic saving**	**15,042**	**11,959**	**1,287**	**1**	**532**
1101	Residual error of estimate, income and expenditure accounts	—	—	—	—	—
1200	Capital consumption allowances and miscellaneous valuation adjustments	5,683	8,388	1,088	1	60
1400	Net domestic saving	9,359	3,571	199	—	472
1500	**Non-financial capital acquisition**	**6,339**	**16,298**	**5,878**	**11**	**200**
1501	Residual error of estimate, income and expenditure accounts	—	—	—	—	—
1600	Gross fixed capital formation	7,508	17,311	5,879	11	200
1700	Value of physical change in inventories	62	—1,098	167	—	—
1800	Net purchases of existing and intangible assets	—1,231	85	—168	—	—
1900	**Net lending or borrowing (1100-1500)**	**8,703**	**—4,339**	**—4,591**	**—10**	**332**
2000	**Net financial investment (2100-3100)**	**6,470**	**—2,974**	**—4,076**	**—9**	**387**
2100	**Net increase in financial assets**	**21,428**	**6,631**	**645**	**377**	**8,479**
2210	Official international reserves:	—	—	—	—404	—
2211	Official holdings of gold and foreign exchange	—	—	—	—565	—
2212	International Monetary Fund, general account	—	—	—	154	—
2213	Special Drawing Rights	—	—	—	7	—
2310	Currency and deposits:	12,559	335	393	—	—172
2311	Currency and bank deposits	7,777	678	300	—	529
2312	Deposits in other institutions	5,149	—92	39	—	—
2313	Foreign currency and deposits	—367	—251	54	—	—701
2320	Receivables:	71	4,117	—187	—	2,337
2321	Consumer credit	71	63	—	—	2,337
2322	Trade	—	4,054	—187	—	—
2330	Loans:	—	160	32	12	4,849
2331	Bank loans	—	—	—	—	4,849
2332	Other loans	—	160	32	12	—
2340	Government of Canada Treasury Bills	120	16	—12	492	—269
2350	Finance and other short-term paper	—765	208	5	—96	—
2410	Mortgages	—	6	1	—	1,695
2420	Bonds:	3,446	150	46	339	275
2421	Government of Canada Bonds	2,888	—6	10	339	—61
2422	Provincial government bonds	—538	182	35	—	175
2423	Municipal government bonds	193	67	3	—	23
2424	Other Canadian bonds	903	—93	—2	—	138
2430	Life insurance and pensions	4,553	—	—	—	—
2510	Claims on associated enterprises:	—	1,189	15	45	—159
2512	Corporate (1)	—	1,189	21	—	—159
2513	Government	—	—	—6	45	—
2520	Stocks (1)	—22	—29	176	—	—
2530	Foreign investments	—53	—69	—1	—	13
2610	Other financial assets	1,519	548	177	—11	—90
2700	Official monetary reserve offsets	—	—	—	—	—
3100	**Net increase in liabilities**	**14,958**	**9,605**	**4,721**	**386**	**8,092**
3210	Official international reserves:	—	—	—	—	—
3211	Official holdings of gold and foreign exchange	—	—	—	—	—
3212	International Monetary Fund, general account	—	—	—	—	—
3213	Special Drawing Rights	—	—	—	—	—
3310	Currency and deposits:	—	—	—	1,346	7,713
3311	Currency and bank deposits	—	—	—	1,346	7,775
3312	Deposits in other institutions	—	—	—	—	—
3313	Foreign currency and deposits	—	—	—	—	—62
3320	Payables:	5,047	2,543	—496	—	—
3321	Consumer Credit	3,206	—	—	—	—
3322	Trade	1,841	2,543	—496	—	—
3330	Loans:	1,860	2,314	596	—	—8
3331	Bank loans	1,855	1,421	359	—	—
3332	Other loans	5	893	237	—	—8
3340	Government of Canada treasury bills	—	—	—	—	—
3350	Finance and other short-term paper	—	102	—32	—	—
3410	Mortgages	7,986	345	122	—	—
3420	Bonds:	65	2,116	3,005	—	173
3421	Government of Canada Bonds	—	—	—18	—	—
3422	Provincial government bonds	—	—	3,024	—	—
3423	Municipal government bonds	—	—	—	—	—
3424	Other Canadian bonds	65	2,116	—1	—	173
3430	Life insurance and pensions	—	—	—	—	—
3510	Claims on associated enterprises:	—	707	1,342	—898	—
3512	Corporate (1)	—	707	—	—	—
3513	Government	—	—	1,342	—898	—
3520	Stocks (1)	—	1,009	50	—	173
3530	Foreign investments	—	—	—	—	—
3610	Other liabilities	—	469	134	—62	41
3700	Official monetary reserve offsets	—	—	—	—	—
4000	**Discrepancy (1900-2000)**	**2,233**	**—1,365**	**—515**	**—1**	**—55**

Sector										
VI 2. Near-banks	VII. Insurance companies and pension funds	VIII. Other private financial institutions	IX. Public financial institutions	X. Federal government	XI. Provincial and local governments & hospitals	XII. Social security funds	XIII. Rest of the world	XIV. Residual error of estimate	Total	Category No.
millions of dollars										
222	**274**	**401**	**—102**	**—3,425**	**3,071**	**1,991**	**5,580**	**—171**	**36,662**	1100
—	—	—	—	—	—	—	—	—171	—171	1101
13	24	17	4	395	1,794	—	—	—	17,467	1200
209	250	384	—106	—3,820	1,277	1,991	5,580	—	19,366	1400
54	**142**	**50**	**218**	**1,186**	**5,609**	**—**	**506**	**171**	**36,662**	1500
—	—	—	—	—	—	—	—	171	171	1501
59	56	42	87	1,048	5,128	—	—	—	37,329	1600
—	—	—	—	31	—	—	—	—	—838	1700
—5	86	8	131	107	481	—	506	—	—	1800
168	**132**	**351**	**—320**	**—4,611**	**—2,538**	**1,991**	**5,074**	**—342**	**—**	1900
167	**132**	**351**	**—377**	**—4,145**	**—2,991**	**1,991**	**5,074**	**—**	**—**	2000
5,908	**5,234**	**1,928**	**2,640**	**441**	**3,099**	**1,991**	**6,009**	**—**	**64,810**	2100
—	—	—	—	—	—	—	—	—	—404	2210
—	—	—	—	—	—	—	—	—	—565	2211
—	—	—	—	—	—	—	—	—	154	2212
—	—	—	—	—	—	—	—	—	7	2213
314	108	210	120	—752	152	—	813	—	14,080	2310
—230	57	181	92	—752	140	—	416	—	9,188	2311
331	53	—2	28	—	3	—	1	—	5,510	2312
213	—2	31	—	—	9	—	396	—	—618	2313
579	213	65	7	22	23	—	—	—	7,247	2320
579	91	65	—	—	—	—	—	—	3,206	2321
—	122	—	7	22	23	—	—	—	4,041	2322
295	—10	424	669	582	183	—	62	—	7,258	2330
—	—	—	—	—	—	—	—	—	4,849	2331
295	—10	424	669	582	183	—	62	—	2,409	2332
8	7	164	11	—	—	—	34	—	571	2340
335	246	205	40	6	14	—	408	—	606	2350
3,782	1,245	360	1,012	—15	360	—	—	—	8,446	2410
268	2,555	—12	535	4	1,022	1,399	4,454	—	14,481	2420
—12	36	—93	72	1	24	10	190	—	3,398	2421
160	1,029	91	332	—1	642	1,389	3,165	—	6,661	2422
94	98	—4	52	—	348	—	356	—	1,230	2423
26	1,392	—6	79	4	8	—	743	—	3,192	2424
—	—	—	—	—	—	—	—	—	4,553	2430
99	10	656	27	1,084	1,268	591	391	—	5,216	2510
99	10	656	—	—	—	—	391	—	2,207	2512
—	—	—	27	1,084	1,268	591	—	—	3,009	2513
83	676	—135	133	53	—151	—	87	—	871	2520
11	145	47	—	—7	—	—	—	—	86	2530
134	39	—56	86	—536	228	1	—240	—	1,799	2610
—	—	—	—	—	—	—	—	—	—	2700
5,741	**5,102**	**1,577**	**3,017**	**4,586**	**6,090**	**—**	**935**	**—**	**64,810**	3100
—	—	—	—	—	—	—	—404	—	—404	3210
—	—	—	—	—	—	—	—565	—	—565	3211
—	—	—	—	—	—	—	154	—	154	3212
—	—	—	—	—	—	—	7	—	7	3213
5,276	—	—	232	69	—	—	—556	—	14,080	3310
—	—	—	—	67	—	—	—	—	9,188	3311
5,276	—	—	232	2	—	—	—	—	5,510	3312
—	—	—	—	—	—	—	—556	—	—618	3313
—	29	—	12	11	101	—	—	—	7,247	3320
—	—	—	—	—	—	—	—	—	3,206	3321
—	29	—	12	11	101	—	—	—	4,041	3322
40	—	424	79	56	529	—	1,368	—	7,258	3330
5	—	161	4	—	405	—	639	—	4,849	3331
35	—	263	75	56	124	—	729	—	2,409	3332
—	—	—	—	571	—	—	—	—	571	3340
—85	—	197	—18	—	442	—	—	—	606	3350
—	—	7	5	—	—19	—	—	—	8,446	3410
134	—	676	6	3,416	4,890	—	—	—	14,481	3420
—	—	—	—	3,416	—	—	—	—	3,398	3421
—	—	—	6	—	3,631	—	—	—	6,661	3422
—	—	—	—	—	1,230	—	—	—	1,230	3423
134	—	676	—	—	29	—	—	—	3,192	3424
—	4,575	—	—	—22	—	—	—	—	4,553	3430
48	—92	170	2,461	69	35	—	441	—	4,283	3510
48	—92	170	—	—	—	—	441	—	1,274	3512
—	—	—	2,461	69	35	—	—	—	3,009	3513
128	66	235	143	—	—	—	—	—	1,804	3520
—	—	—	—	—	—	—	86	—	86	3530
200	524	—132	97	416	112	—	—	—	1,799	3610
—	—	—	—	—	—	—	—	—	—	3700
1	**—**	**—**	**57**	**—466**	**453**	**—**	**—**	**—342**	**—**	4000

Source: Statistics Canada, *System of National Accounts, Financial Flow Accounts*, Fourth Quarter, 1975.

timing of any external financing will hinge on prevailing conditions in the financial markets.

Detailed treatment of the limitations and problems associated with the preparation of financial-flow accounts are beyond the scope of this book.[10] A few basic points, however, should be noted. Firstly, when data on economic units comprising a particular sector are aggregated, transactions between units belonging to the same sector are netted out. In other words, the residual information is concerned only with activity between sectors, and information about any activity within sectors is lost. As a consequence, a great deal of insight into procedures employed by economic units is lost.

A second and related problem concerns the strategy for grouping the many types of economic units into a meaningful yet small enough number of sectors to be conducive to analysis. Categorization should depend primarily on the economic unit's importance in the overall flow-of-funds picture, and on the economic unit's degree of homogeneity with respect to its sector classification. Reference to the Financial Flows Matrix shows that Statistics Canada, mindful of the trade-offs involved, has essentially classified economic units into thirteen sectors.

Finally, we must recognize that difficulties in valuation do occur because market values of various assets at particular points in time are normally used in deriving the flows. Such values, unfortunately, combine incremental new flows as well as capital gains or losses on outstanding securities. In addition, when market values are unavailable, estimates are based on book values. The possibility that holders of financial assets record values differing from those noted by the issuers of claims is apparent and leads to the "discrepancy" entries as noted in the accounts.

7-8. SUMMARY

One of the prerequisites for a modern industrialized economy is the development of efficient financial markets to channel funds from surplus-spending units (savers) to deficit-spending units. Financial assets acknowledge such transfers of funds. They represent a paper claim in the hands of savers or investors, and a liability on the part of deficit-spending units (the units which issued the paper in the process of raising external funds). While some of the funds flow directly from savers to users, financial intermediation plays an increasingly important role in our economy. Funds are channeled from a variety of surplus-spending units to financial intermediaries, with the latter issuing indirect claims against themselves. Such funds are then committed to the purchase of securities issued by the ultimate users of funds. Financial intermediaries relieve surplus-spending units of the burden of seeking out deficit-spending units on their own, and in addition allow greater portfolio diversifications by investors. By pooling funds from many individual savers, economies of scale are realized, and users of funds are able to deal with only one or a few large financial institutions, rather than with a multitude of small individual investors.

[10]A concise introduction to this topic is found in B. Moore, *An Introduction to the Theory of Finance*, New York Free Press, 1968, pp. 21-28.

Financial markets encompass the institutions and procedures involved in the selling and trading of financial assets. Their primary purposes are to provide for the efficient distribution of new issues (primary trading), and for the trading of previously issued securities among investors (secondary trading). The existence of such secondary trading provides liquidity to investors, who can readily dispose of their financial assets at fair value when the need arises. We can categorize financial markets by distinguishing between the money market (trading of short-term debt instruments with a maturity of under three years) and the capital market. The capital market can be subdivided further into the bond market, where long-term debt is traded, and the equity market, where trading in preferred and common shares takes place.

The money market is basically a telephone market with a number of authorized dealers in constant telephone contact to actively maintain the market. Shares are traded either on organized security exchanges, or on the over-the-counter market. Stock exchanges typically have a variety of listing requirements, and many corporations either do not qualify for listing or choose to remain unlisted. The over-the-counter market is again a telephone market in which a variety of dealer-brokers are active. Most long-term debt trades in this market along with unlisted shares. Where the shares of a corporation are listed on more than one exchange, arbitrage will ensure that prices on various exchanges remain in line with each other. The process of arbitrage is important wherever the same good is traded in geographically dispersed markets.

Long-term sources of funds for Canadian business can be divided into internally generated funds (retained earnings, capital cost allowances, and depletion allowances), and externally generated funds (bonds and debentures, and preferred and common shares). Reliance on various sources of funds changes over time in accordance with changes in economic conditions and with altering conditions in the financial markets. Therefore, it is important for the financial officer to project trends and developments in the financial markets in order to properly plan for new financing. Questions have been raised about the adequacy of the Canadian financial markets in providing financing to small businesses, particularly those which are located outside major metropolitan centers.

The trade-off between risk and return is critical for many financial decisions, including long-term financing. In selling financial assets, higher risks have to be compensated through higher expected returns, since on aggregate investors have proven to be risk averse. This is easily illustrated by referring to current yields of various types of securities traded in the capital markets. Instruments providing low risk to investors, through strong guarantees and high priority claims, will place a higher risk on the issuer who has to honor such stringent commitments.

As part of its national accounts, Statistics Canada publishes financial flow accounts which provide relatively detailed statistics on the flow of funds between various sectors in the economy. Such information is useful to managers attempting to gain a better understanding of both the relative magnitudes of the flows which have a bearing on capital market conditions, and of patterns and trends which may be developing.

QUESTIONS FOR DISCUSSION

1. Briefly explain the term "financial asset", giving several examples of such assets. Why are financial assets a prerequisite for modern industralized economies?
2. What are some of the useful functions performed by financial intermediaries? Illustrate with a specific example.
3. Why is it important to have financial markets which provide for efficient secondary trading of financial securities? How do you define efficiency in this context?
4. When we say that a particular financial asset has a greater degree of liquidity than some other financial asset, what do we mean?
5. One of the key issues in financial decision-making is the trade-off between risk and return. Provide several specific examples of decisions where this trade-off is important.
6. By resorting to the financial pages of the newspaper, find the current average yield for long-term corporate bonds, for preferred shares, and for common shares (use current earnings yield). Using a marginal tax rate of 40 percent for an investor (combined federal and provincial tax, where provincial tax is 30 percent of federal tax), and of 45 percent for a corporation, compute the after-tax yields to the investor (assuming he pays taxes on both interest and dividend income), and the after-tax costs to the corporation. Explain your findings.
7. By referring to the relevant Statistics Canada publication, find the financial flow accounts for the most recent period. Briefly summarize and interpret any salient features.

SELECTED REFERENCES

Canada, *1964 Report of the Royal Commission on Banking and Finance*, Ottawa: Queen's Printer, 1964.

G. Conway, *The Supply of, and Demand for Canadian Equities*, Toronto: Toronto Stock Exchange, 1970.

Dominion Bureau of Statistics, *Financial Flow Accounts 1962-67, A Preliminary Report*, Ottawa: Queen's Printer, 1969.

R. Goldsmith, *Financial Institutions*, New York: Random House, 1968.

R. Goldsmith, *Flow of Funds in the Postwar Economy*, New York: National Bureau of Economic Research, 1965.

J. Gurley and E. Shaw, "Financial Aspects of Economic Development", *American Economic Review*, September, 1955, pp. 515-538.

J. Gurley and E. Shaw, *Money in a Theory of Finance*, Washington: Brookings Institution, 1960.

W. Hood, *Financing of Economic Activity in Canada*, Ottawa: Queen's Printer, 1958.

B. Moore, *An Introduction to the Theory of Finance*, New York: Free Press, 1968.

E. Neufeld, *The Financial System of Canada*, Toronto: Macmillan, 1972.

R. Robinson, *Money and Capital Markets*, New York: McGraw-Hill, 1964.

J. Van Horne, *Functions and Analysis of Capital Market Rates,* Englewood Cliffs: Prentice-Hall, 1970.

CHAPTER 7: APPENDIX

The Stock Market[1]

It is useful for students of finance to have an appreciation of a few of the more common types of transactions which take place in our stock markets. While straight purchases and sales account for the bulk of trading which is carried on, important departures from the usual market contracts are to be noted.

Regardless of the contract involved, trading will be in *board lots* or *odd lots.* A board lot is simply the unit of trading specifying, for a particular share, the minimum number of shares normally traded, and it varies according to the security's value. Odd lots involve transactions with volumes below this specified unit of trading. It is a reasonable generalization to state that odd lots must normally be purchased at a slight premium, or sold below the going market price for board lots. Table 1 provides an indication of the size of board lots, but it should be noted that there may be special cases and exceptions from time to time. For example, where a firm's shares trade at $5 per share, usual purchase orders would be placed in multiples of 100 shares. Where an investor wishes to purchase an odd lot of less than 100 shares, higher transaction costs per share will typically be involved. The effect is to discourage small transactions.

TABLE 1

Board Lots, Toronto Stock Exchange

Effective January 2, 1974

On securities selling under	$ 0.10	:	1000 shares
On securities selling at	$ 0.10 and under $ 1.00	:	500 shares
On securities selling at	$ 1.00 and under $100.00	:	100 shares
On securities selling at	$100.00 and over	:	10 shares

Apart from straight purchases or sales of shares, three less frequently used, but nonetheless important transactions to be aware of include *buying on margin, selling short*, and *stop-loss orders.* While it has been suggested that the first two are probably of greater interest to speculators than to normal investors, we feel that such trades, if properly understood and used in a way which is consonant with the investor's objectives, can afford opportunities for all market participants. Buying on margin involves borrowing part of the purchase price from the broker, the expectation being that market prices will rise. As a consequence of financing the investment partly with borrowed money, the investor can purchase an increased number of securities with a given investment of his own. The return (positive or negative) which the investor will derive from any subsequent

[1]For a very interesting review of the market see, for example, B. Malkiel, *A Random Walk Down Wall Street*, New York: Norton, 1973, or A. Smith, *The Money Game*, New York: Dell Publishing Co., 1969. A good introductory treatment of the stock market, its functioning, and terminology is provided in L. Engel, *How to Buy Stocks*, Boston, Bantam, 1967.

fluctuations in the market price of the securities purchased will be magnified through such a transaction, an effect which is commonly termed as *leverage.* Margin requirements limit the amount which may be borrowed and are usually set by stock exchange regulations, typically at 50 percent of the value of the shares. The margin requirements, expressed as a percentage rate, indicate the proportion the purchaser must provide from his own funds, with the balance to be borrowed. Thus, a 60 percent margin requirement would allow 40 percent of the market price to be borrowed. Should market price subsequently fall, the purchaser will be expected to put up additional monies to keep margin requirements from being violated. Naturally, interest is charged by the broker on the sum borrowed, and the securities purchased are pledged as a collateral against the loan. Margin requirements vary depending on the type of security purchased, typically being lower for bonds than for stocks.

Where investors anticipate a decline in share prices, they may elect to sell short. This entails selling securities they do not own, with the whole transaction made possible by borrowing the necessary shares through a broker. The seller's intention is to buy back and replace the securities some time in the future, presumably at a lower price than that at which the sale was transacted. The short-seller must maintain cash with the broker at least equal to the value of securities borrowed and subsequently sold. It has been argued that the facility to sell short tends to support declining markets on the down-side, with short-sellers buying shares back to take their profits. Short sales, it is held, may also curtail unrealistic and unjustified upswings. Since, contrary to expectations, share prices may subsequently rise, the risks to the short-seller are obvious.

Example

> An investor may feel that at the current price of $10 per share, the shares of a particular firm are overpriced, and that a drop in prices is imminent. He can borrow 1,000 shares which he immediately sells at the prevailing market price. If three weeks later the share price has indeed dropped to $7 per share, the investor repurchases the shares in the market at the new price and replaces the previously borrowed shares. He has made a gross profit of 1,000($10 − $7) = $3,000.

An order to sell when the shares touch a particular price level is termed a stop-loss order. It is useful where an investor feels he or she may be out of touch with the market and wishes to protect a profit made in a previous upswing, or to minimize a potential loss. A stop-loss order at $40, placed when the market is $45 is an instruction to sell once the market price drops to $40. In a rapidly falling market, the order may only be completed well below $40 and this risk should be recognized. The possibility of momentary market swings touching off a sale must also be considered.

Following the success of the Chicago Board Options Exchange, which in 1973 became the first exchange in the world to deal in stock options, the Toronto and Montreal Exchanges introduced option trading, but in a selected number of issues only. During 1976, only *call options* were being traded in Canada although the possibility of introducing *put options* was being explored. A call option is the right to acquire a share within a predetermined period of time and at a specified price called the *exercise price.* Resort to such options enables the investor to control a larger number of shares than would be possible through outright purchase. It is, of course, the option purchaser's belief that before expiry of the option, the value of the underlying stock will rise sufficiently above the exercise price to cover the cost of the option, the commission charged, and afford some profit as well.

Example

Consider a share selling at \$23, with a 6-month call option on the same share with an exercise price of \$23 selling for \$2.09. Ignoring transaction costs, for \$2,300 an investor could pick up either 100 shares or buy calls on a total of 1,100 shares,[2] which provide the right anytime over the next six months to buy shares at \$23. If the share price jumps to \$35 within that period, the options per share could be sold at around \$35 – \$23 = \$12, for a total of 1,100 × \$12 = \$13,200, affording a far greater profit than the \$1,200 to be realized from a straight share purchase. Clearly, however, should the shares fail to rise above \$23, the purchaser of the call option loses his entire investment, though a purchaser of shares would incur no loss.

A put option is just the reverse of a call, giving the purchaser the right to sell a share at an established price and over a specific period of time.

An important cost associated with market orders is the broker's commission. Canadian stock exchanges limit members to a basic commission for buying and selling shares, but during 1976, the notion of negotiated charges was being debated. Rather than reproducing the complete schedule, which will change periodically, the following basic rates on orders up to and including \$20,000 are given for illustrative purposes:

(a) shares selling under \$14
    2.5% of the value of an order

(b) shares selling at \$14 and up to, and including, \$30
    22.575¢ per share plus 0.8875% of the order value

(c) shares selling at over \$30
    1.64% of the value of the order

It should also be noted that on orders of \$5,000 or over, a 10 percent surcharge on the regular commissions applies.

Students of finance will frequently find reference being made to *stock price indices* or *market averages* which purport to provide an indication of the condition of the stock market and the directions in which it is moving. Reliance on various averages is based partly on a view that the movements of certain common share prices are strongly correlated. The major indices available, which include the Dow-Jones, the Standard and Poor's, the Montreal Stock Exchange, and the Toronto Stock Exchange averages are calculated in various ways. Some are almost straightforward additions of prices adjusted for stock splits and substitutions while others are also weighted by the amount of stock

[2]In actual practice, each call involves an option on 100 shares.

outstanding. Quotations are available several times daily.

The Toronto Stock Exchange had four major indices, namely the *Industrial* Index made up of 151 different stocks in 16 categories, the *Gold* Index of 12 stocks, the *Base Metal* Index of 28 stocks, and the *Western Oil* Index of 19 stocks. Figures 1 and 2 illustrate the movement of the TSE and Dow-Jones Industrial Averages over the past several years. As of January 1977, the TSE replaced its index system with a more sophisticated approach called the "TSE 300" index. It represents 14 groupings of firms, each with their own index as well. The arbitrary starting level of the "TSE 300" was 1000.

A casual look at the stock price quotations to be found on the financial pages of any daily newspaper could leave you quite perplexed. More careful scrutiny will show that fairly complete and meaningful data are being provided. For instance, the actual number of shares traded, the opening, highest, lowest, and last or closing prices of the day's transactions, as well as the net change from the previous day's closing price are often reported. To what extent such information is useful in assessing future stock price movements is debatable. While stock price movements can be a fascinating topic, its complexity makes it impossible to deal with in a text on managerial finance. The interested reader can refer to specialized courses or books in securities analysis.[3]

[3]See, for example, D. Hayes, Investments: Analysis and Management, (3rd ed.) Riverside: Macmillan, 1976.

FIGURE 7-1—APPENDIX

Toronto Stock Exchange 1934-1973

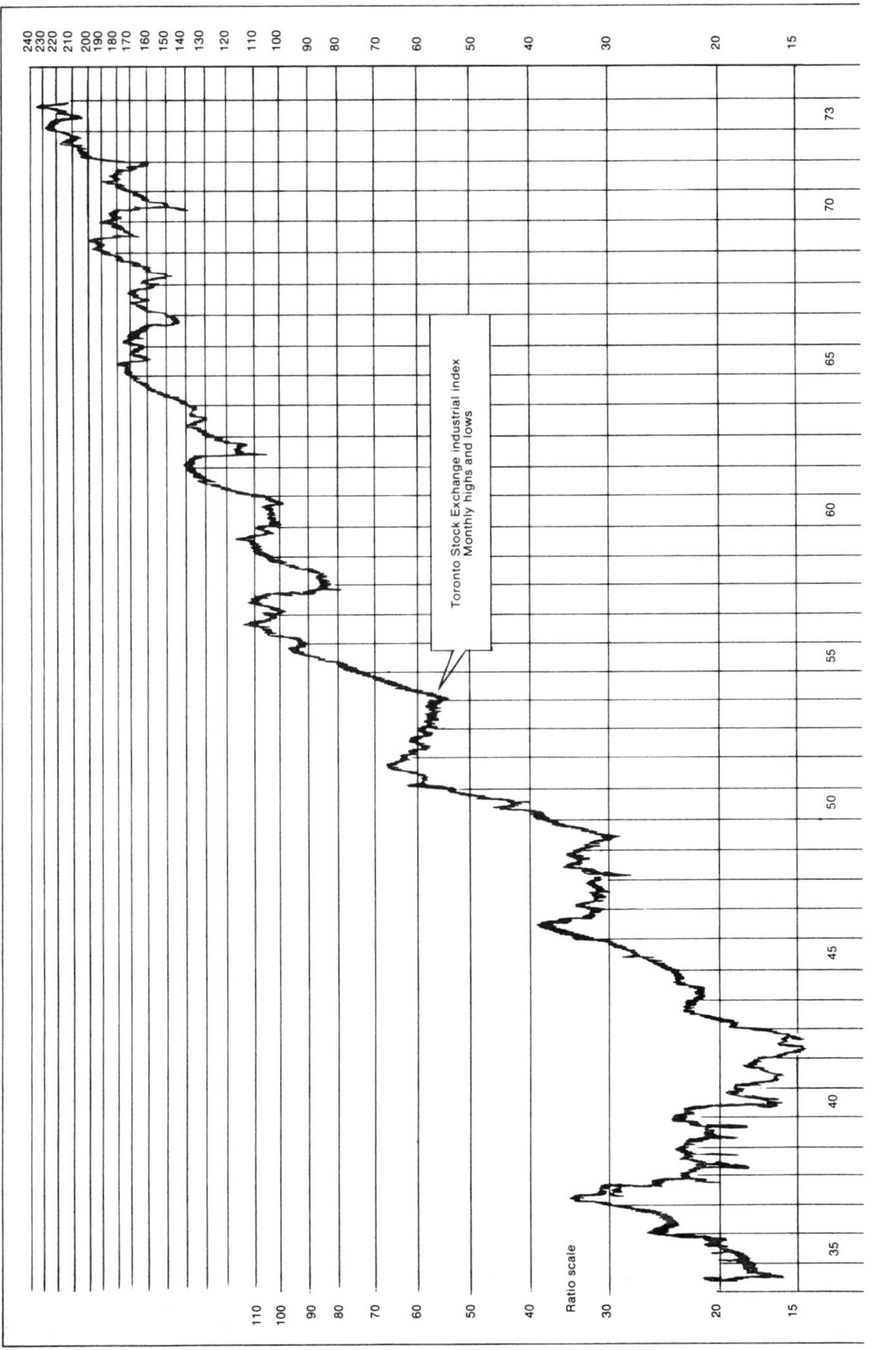

Source: F. H. Deacon & Company Limited, Toronto, Ontario.

FIGURE 7-2—APPENDIX Dow-Jones Industrial Average 1929-1977

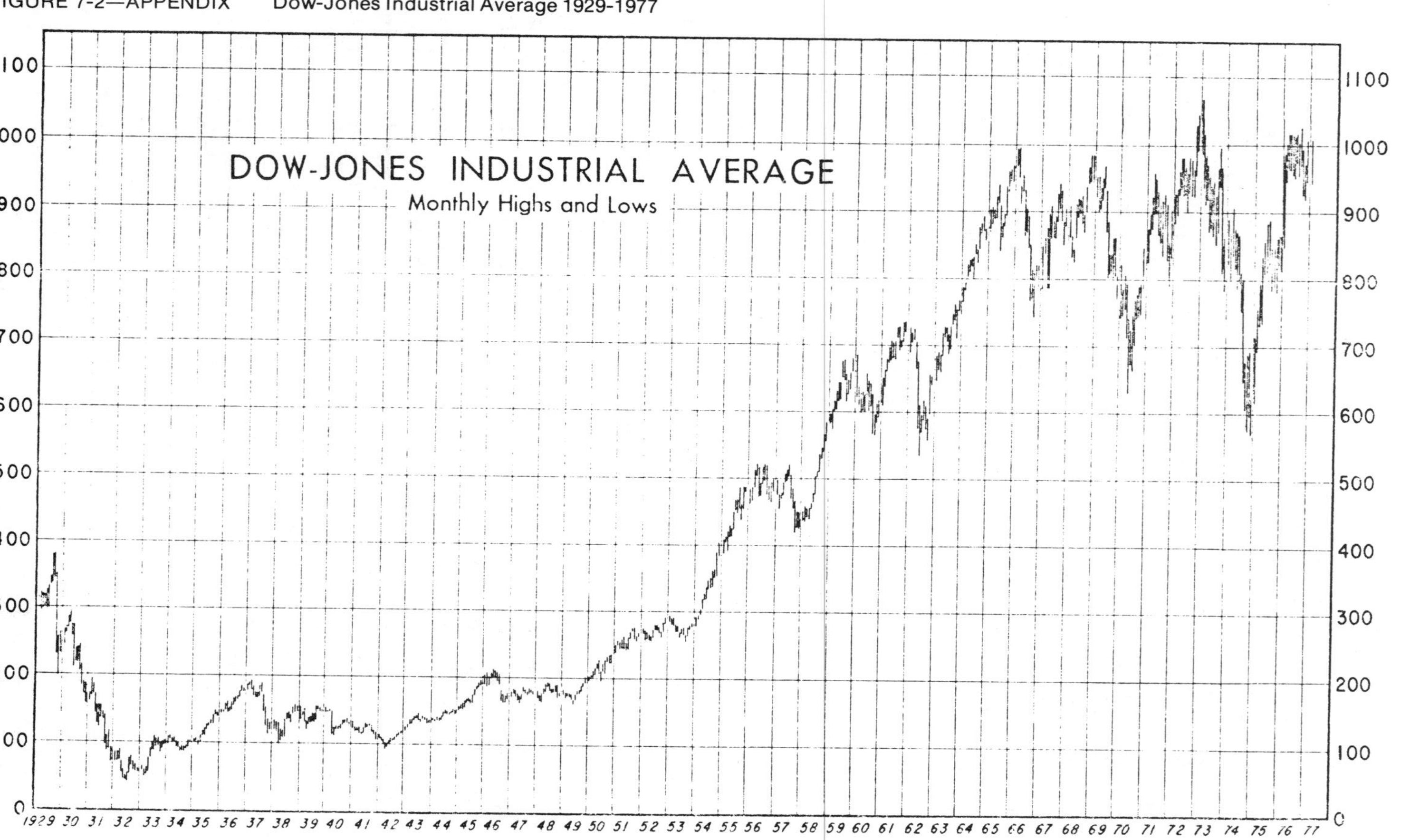

Source: *Moody's Handbook of Common Stocks*, Winter 1976-77, Moody's Investor Services Inc., N.Y.

Chapter 8
Long-term Debt

8-1. INTRODUCTION

Long-term debt is a contractual liability. By using debt certificates, the firm acquires funds under conditions which usually provide for both a definite final repayment date and periodic interest payments.[1] In corporate-debt financing, "long-term" is usually taken to be an issue maturing ten or more years after the date of sale; in Canada, the average maturity of new long-term offerings is somewhere between fifteen and twenty years.[2]

Before proceeding, it is useful to review the terminology most frequently encountered in any discussion of long-term debt. The fixed interest return provided by a long-term debt instrument is denoted by the *coupon rate.*

Example

> The Westcoast Transmission Company's 7½'s of 1991 indicate a 7½ percent coupon rate and a final maturity in 1991. Debt is commonly issued in multiples of $1,000, and accordingly, Westcoast will pay $75 of interest per annum for every $1,000 face value bond held.

As detailed in Chapter 4, the *yield* or effective rate of return on a debt instrument is the discount rate which equates the present value of expected cash inflows to the investor with the current market price of the debt instrument. The actual composition of these cash inflows depends upon the holding period. Where the instrument is held to maturity, cash inflows would consist of the return of principal, that is the face value of the debt, and interest payments. If the instrument is disposed of before that date, the selling price of the security and interest payments until the date of sale would comprise the inflows. The yield to maturity may, therefore, differ from the holding-period yield if the debt instrument is sold prior to maturity.

Holders of debt instruments are creditors of the firm. Though entitled to a fixed return and ultimate repayment of principal, they have neither a voice in corporate management nor the right to participate in any residual earnings available to the borrowing firm. To the issuer, such indebtedness (with the exception of income bonds) represents a constant, but limited cash drain regardless of earnings. Failure to meet interest charges or to comply with any of the provisions in the loan agreement represents default to creditors and may lead to acceleration of debt repayment, seizure of any assets pledged to secure the loan, and possibly to bankruptcy proceedings. As noted in Chapter 2, in the event of liquidation, the claims of debt holders and other creditors rank ahead of those of preferred and common shareholders. There is also a priority of ranking

[1]Some perpetual debt is in existence. Canadian Pacific Limited, for example, has almost $560,000,000 of four percent perpetual consolidated debenture stock issued. A feature of this rarely used debt instrument borrowed from English practice is its right to vote in event of default on interest. Some of it is pledged as collateral for the corporation's Collateral Trust Bonds.

[2]D. Fullerton, *The Bond Market in Canada*, Toronto, Carswell, 1962, p. 10.

claims between the various creditors of a company with the ordering dependent upon the nature of the debt instrument held.

The debt instrument is itself a secondary contract. The primary contract is a *trust deed* or indenture drawn between the issuing corporation on the one hand and a trust company acting as trustee for the creditors on the other. Such a trust deed covers a variety of items including:

(a) size of the issue, maturity or maturities, sinking fund provisions, and redemption or call features if any,
(b) frequency and size of interest payments,
(c) the character and extent of assets against which creditors have claims, the nature of the claims, and arrangements to be made for the protection of assets pledged, and
(d) restrictions placed on the borrowing corporation respecting further issues of debt, the pledging of assets, and dividend payments. These restrictions, known as *protective covenants*, are similar to those contained in term-loan agreements and serve to protect creditors.

Should the issuer default on any of the provisions of the trust deed, the trustee, on behalf of the bondholders, can take action to correct the situation. If unsuccessful, he is generally required to report the situation to the bondholders and with their consent take action to force the corporation to comply with the provisions. Assuming this move also fails, he must then seek to satisfy the bondholder's demands in some other way, perhaps by calling for the immediate repayment of the entire outstanding issue or by initiating bankruptcy proceedings.

A corporation may issue either *bearer bonds*, which are payable to the bearer, or *registered bonds*, which are promises to pay to those whose names are registered in the books of the corporation. Ownership of a registered bond may be transferred on written assignment by the registered owner when it is presented at the office of the corporation or the designated transfer agent. In order for the transfer of ownership to be completed, however, the corporation's bond register must be amended to reflect the change.

Unlike registered bonds, bearer bonds are payable to any person having possession of them. Since ownership passes simply with delivery and no endorsement is required, the purchase and sale of such bonds is greatly facilitated. Obviously, however, the hazards of ownership also increase because of possible theft. Fully registered bonds appeal to institutional investors and others expecting to hold the securities for an extended period of time, while those in bearer form appeal to those investors more prone to trade.

In the case of bearer bonds, or with bonds which are registered as to principal only, interest payments take the form of dated coupons attached to the bonds and payable to the bearer. On or after each interest payment date, bondholders may clip their coupons and present them to a financial intermediary such as a chartered bank to receive their cash. When a bond is fully registered, that is, registered both as to principal and interest, interest is paid by cheque to the owner of record as at a predetermined date, and the nuisance of handling and accounting for bond coupons is avoided.

8-2. INTEREST RATES

Interest rates represent the pricing mechanism in the financial markets and, as such, play a key role in the allocation of savings in the economy. Interest rates are dynamic and change significantly over even relatively short periods of time. This is illustrated in Table 8-1. Furthermore, as will be discussed below, the relationships between long- and short-term interest rates vary over time as well. While both the determination of interest rates and their movement over time entail complex phenomena, it is nevertheless important that the financial manager has at least a basic understanding of such movements, and of the determination of equilibrium rates. Financial officers have some discretion in the timing and maturities of their firm's borrowings, and astute management, including proper timing of new debt issues to take advantage of favorable interest rate movements, can save the firm significant sums of money.

In an introductory text such as this, we have to restrict ourselves to a basic outline of some key factors which affect interest rates. Economists have been debating interest rate theories for some time, and more than a few issues still remain to be resolved.[3] Difficulties in attempting to focus on interest rates in a simplified fashion stem not only from the fact that debt markets are linked in a complex way to other internal and international capital markets, but that interest rates are also influenced by changes in the level of economic activity, by liquidity considerations of investors, and by savings and investment generally.

TABLE 8-1

Selected Canadian Bond Yield Averages and Other Interest Rates

	Canada Bank Rate	Canada Treasury Bill Yields		Government of Canada Bonds			McLeod, Young, Weir, Index of 10 Industrial Bonds [a]	90-Day Finance Company Paper
		3 Mo.	6 Mo.	3-5 Yr.	5-10 Yr.	10 Yr. and over		
April 26/72	4.75	3.64	3.93	6.43	6.86	7.27	8.28	5.88
April 9/73	5.25	4.90	5.37	6.67	6.90	7.39	8.30	6.00
April 15/74	8.25	7.64	7.96	8.56	8.57	8.81	9.91	11.04
April 30/75	8.25	6.85	7.31	7.52	7.99	9.04	10.75	7.64
April 28/76	9.50	8.99	9.02	8.46	8.93	9.34	10.64	8.73

[a]Average term about 20 years.

The Canada Bank Rate is the rate at which the Bank of Canada lends to chartered banks.

Treasury Bills are promissory notes of the federal government with a maturity of under one year.

Finance Company Paper represent short-term borrowing by finance companies.

Source: *Bank of Canada Review*, May, 1976.

[3]See, for example, B. Moore, *An Introduction to the Theory of Finance*, New York: Free Press, 1968, Ch. 5.

With these qualifications in mind, three major sets of factors can be identified as having a major influence on interest rate movements and, therefore, on the pricing of long-term debt.[4] Firstly, interest rate levels will be influenced by the supply of newly issued debt and the availability of loanable funds in a given period of time. Therefore, everything else being the same, if monies made available by investors for the purchase of new debt instruments are limited while the volume of new offerings increases, then interest rates would tend to rise and *vice versa*. In economics literature, this explanation is referred to as the *loanable funds theory*.

Secondly, at any point in time, in addition to new offerings of debt, a stock of previously issued debt is held in the portfolios of investors. Clearly, the supply and demand for debt instruments will also be influenced by investors wanting to sell part of this previously issued stock of debt, or seeking to buy such debt to adjust their portfolio balances. If investors on aggregate are inclined to switch out of long-term debt into more liquid assets such as cash, the increased supply of debt instruments in the market would cause their price to fall. As a consequence, the effective yield on debt and hence interest rates would tend to rise, as only higher interest rates would induce investors to buy additional debt. This explanation of interest rate movements which extends beyond the loanable funds theory, and incorporates consideration of investor preferences with respect to portfolio liquidity is commonly referred to as the *liquidity preference theory*. Since at any point in time the existing stock of debt instruments held in investor portfolios will be much larger than the flow of current new offerings, adjustments by investors to the stocks of securities held in their existing portfolios may be of far greater consequence than flows of new financing. In this regard, the particular actions of investors and their demand for money and similar liquid balances will be influenced by their expectations regarding general economic activity.

Of particular importance in this context are investor expectations about inflation. Typically, in order to loan funds, we would expect investors to demand a positive *real return*. The term "real" in this context refers to a return being measured in constant dollars, or a return net of price level changes. Assume that the inflation rate is currently measured at 10 percent per year. It follows that a lender loses 10 percent of the purchasing power of his outstanding principal each year due to inflation. Hence, debt will only provide a real return (before tax) if it carries a nominal or coupon rate which exceeds 10 percent. It comes as no surprise, then, that the level of interest rates tends to move with inflation, increasing when the inflation rate moves up and *vice versa*.

In spite of this apparent compensation for inflation through higher interest rates, however, the tax treatment of interest both at the investor and at the corporate level can cause important distortions.

Example

Consider an investor who faces a marginal tax rate on interest income of 40 percent, and who purchases a $1,000 bond from a corporation facing

[4]Fullerton, *op. cit.*, pp. 188-190.

a corporate tax rate of 50 percent. Inflation currently runs at 10 percent per year, and the bond provides for coupon payments of 12 percent. In the absence of taxes, such a bond would provide a modest real return of 12% – 10% = 2% to the investor, and this would also be the real cost to the corporation. However, interest is taxed as income in the hands of the investor, and is treated as a tax deductible expense at the corporate level. Thus, the after-tax nominal return to the investor is reduced to (1 – 40%) × 12% = 7.2% (or in real terms *minus* 2.8%), while the after-tax cost to the corporation is only 6% (in real terms *minus* 4%).

It follows that taxes have the effect of reducing both returns to investors and the costs to the borrower quite drastically, and the probability of both negative real returns and costs in periods of substantial inflation must be recognized. Pursuing the above example, it becomes a simple arithmetic exercise to show that if coupon rates remain just marginally higher than the inflation rate, the distortion increases with increasing rates of inflation. Given the above, the drastically increased indebtedness of Canadian corporations during the last few years (which was discussed in the previous chapter) becomes understandable. Provided a corporation pays taxes, and can generate the necessary cash to service its debt, debt appears to have been one of the few available bargains in the market.

Finally, the willingness of foreign investors to add to their holdings of Canadian longer-term debt will clearly affect domestic interest rates. A following section of this chapter supports the suggestion that, in fact, foreign holdings of Canadian debt have been increasing.

The term structure of interest rates

Interest rates vary with maturity of the debt, among other things. In this section, holding all other aspects of a debt issue constant, we discuss the relationship which exists between interest rates and debt maturity. This relationship is commonly called the *term structure of interest rates* and when plotted depicts a *yield curve*.[5] Several factors influence the particular shape which the yield curve may assume at a given point in time. The most important ones are the risk differential between long-term and short-term debt, and expectations regarding future interest rate movements. We will discuss both of these factors in turn. Excellent basic surveys of the different hypotheses on yield-maturity relationships are available to interested readers.[6]

Everything else being equal, from the point of view of the investor, the risk of a particular debt issue increases with its maturity. Two reasons may be given for this. First, the financial position of the borrower is more difficult to forecast as one moves out into the more distant future, thus increasing the potential risk of default on payments of both principal and interest. Even where the risk of

[5]The depictions are, in fact, only an approximation of the true relationship because even Government of Canada securities are not identical in every respect.

[6]For example, J. Van Horne, *Function and Analysis of Capital Market Rates*, Englewood Cliffs, Prentice-Hall, 1970, Ch. 4.

default is negligible, however, such as on debt issued by the federal government, an investor faces greater risks in holding debt with long maturities. The risk in question is termed *interest-rate risk*, and is introduced by potential fluctuations in general interest rate levels over time. We saw in Chapter 4 that changes in interest rate levels will affect the market price of previously issued bonds, with increases implying a drop in bond prices and *vice versa*. We also saw that the sensitivity of the market price of a bond to changes in prevailing interest rates increases with the length of its maturity, making the market prices of long-term debt more volatile than those of shorter-term issues.[7] Consider, for example, a bond issued some time ago and carrying a 6 percent coupon. Current interest rates on comparable debt have moved to 8 percent. In order for anyone to purchase this bond, it will have to provide an effective yield which is competitive under prevailing market conditions. This would be possible only if the bond sold at a discount, with the discount having to make up for the difference between the coupon rate and the prevailing market rate. At an intuitive level, it would be clear that the opportunity cost of investing in a bond paying a low coupon increases with the number of years over which a person is tied to such low interest payments. Thus, to make the bond attractive, the discount at which it has to be sold will have to increase with increasing maturities. Table 8-2 shows the market price of a $100 bond as a function of its maturity, given that interest rate levels have changed. In light of such increased risk with increasing maturity, we would expect interest rates on long-term debt to be higher than interest rates on shorter-term issues, since investors will have to be compensated for such additional risk. This is reflected in Figure 8-2, which shows an upward-sloping yield curve. In order to hold other aspects such as the risk of default constant, this curve is based solely on debt issued by the federal government.

TABLE 8-2

Selected Price Data for a $100 Debt Instrument with a 6% Nominal Interest Rate

Years to Maturity	Price to Yield 8% to Maturity	Price to Yield 5% to Maturity
1	$98.11	$100.96
2	96.37	101.88
5	91.89	104.38
10	86.41	107.79
20	80.21	112.55
25	78.52	114.18

From our discussion, it follows that the only debt which is riskless is debt which has both a short enough maturity to eliminate interest-rate risk and on which there is no possibility of default. In financial theory, it is often useful to refer to the riskless or pure rate of interest. This risk-free rate is usefully approximated by the yield on short-term borrowing by the federal government, which commonly takes the form of treasury bills.

Part of the additional interest rate which has to be paid by a borrower on debt

[7]B. Malkiel, *The Term Structure of Interest Rates*, Princeton, Princeton University Press, 1966, p. 54.

of longer maturities is called a *liquidity premium*. In this context, the term liquidity refers to ready conversion of a security into cash on short notice while achieving a fair price at least equal to the amount originally invested. Given the risk of loss in principal inherent in longer-term debt, such securities are deemed less liquid than those with short maturities, and must offer investors a liquidity premium in the form of higher interest rates. The magnitude of this premium need not be constant over time, however, and will likely fluctuate as the level of interest rates varies from perceived historical norms. Thus, when interest rates are high and are felt to have peaked, interest rate risk will obviously be perceived as low, with the potential for capital gains from falling interest rates outweighing any concern about potential losses. The liquidity premium can be expected to adjust accordingly.

The second major factor affecting the yield curve is the expectation of investors regarding future interest rate movements. Consider the following example.

Example

> Current short-term interest rates are at 8 percent, and are expected to fall to 7 percent within a year, and to 6 percent two years hence, stabilizing at that level for the indefinite future. For an investor who wants to invest his money for several years, a long-term bond offering an interest rate of 7 percent may be quite attractive, in spite of the 8 percent which he could currently obtain on short-term loans. If interest rate expectations as given above are borne out, such short-term loans would have to be reinvested at lower yields in the future, producing a return of only 6 percent at any time after the first two years.

Thus, if short-term interest rates are expected to fall from currently high levels, we may observe an inverted term structure of interest rates, and over some ranges at least, the slope of the yield curve may be negative, implying short-term rates above long-term ones. An example of such a situation is portrayed in Figure 8-1. The often advanced *expectations hypothesis* states that long-term interest rates reflect the expectations about future short-term rates, as discussed above; and more particularly that the longer-term interest rates are merely an average of present short-term rates and expectations about future short-term rates.

Some recent empirical studies lend support to the expectations theory adjusted by the notion of liquidity premiums. Nevertheless, much more work is required to test conclusively the often conflicting hypotheses which are being advanced in the academic literature regarding interest rates.[8]

[8]An alternate explanation for the term structure of interest rates is found in the so-called *market segmentation theory*. This theory rejects the expectations hypothesis which holds long- and short-term securities to be substitutes for one another. It contends instead that both borrowers and lenders maintain preferences for particular maturities despite differences in yields. As a consequence, it would be appropriate to recognize distinctly separate markets with interest rates in each independently determined.

FIGURE 8-1
Yield Curve as at April 24, 1968
Government of Canada Securities

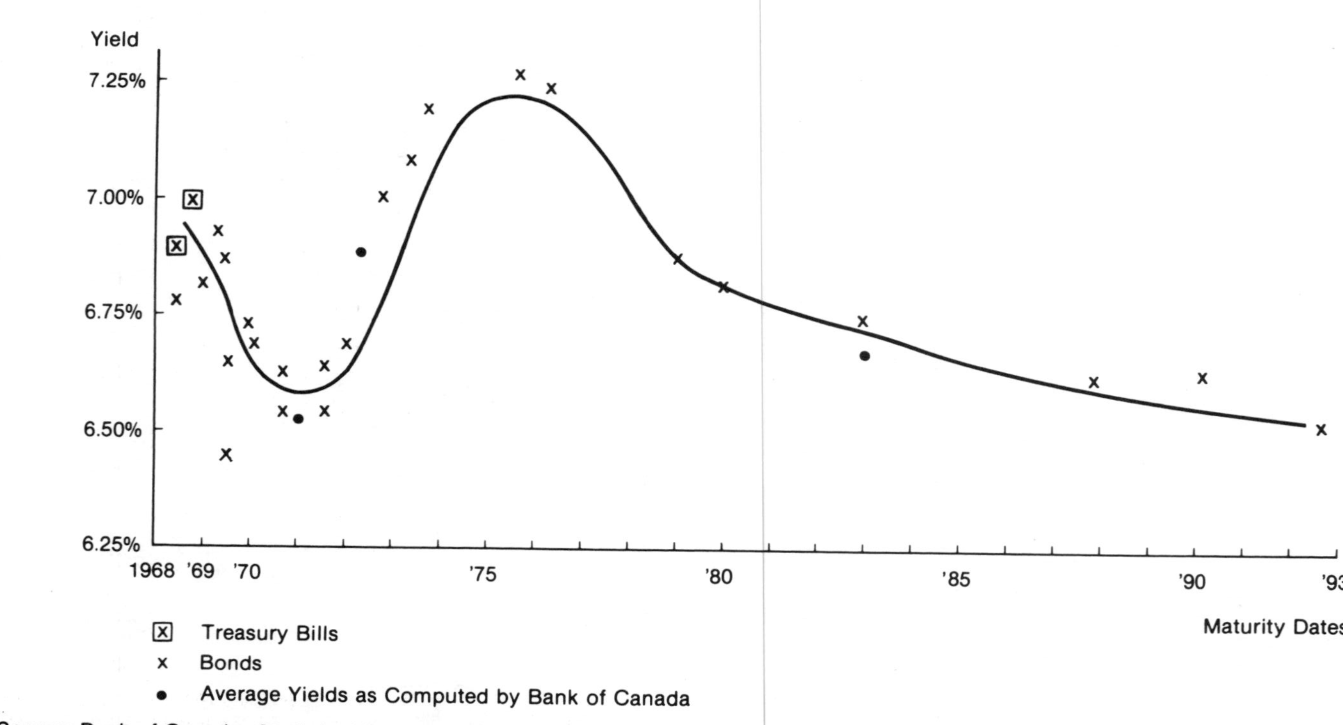

Source: Bank of Canada, *Statistical Summary*, May, 1968.

FIGURE 8-2

Yield Curve as at April 29, 1970
Government of Canada Securities

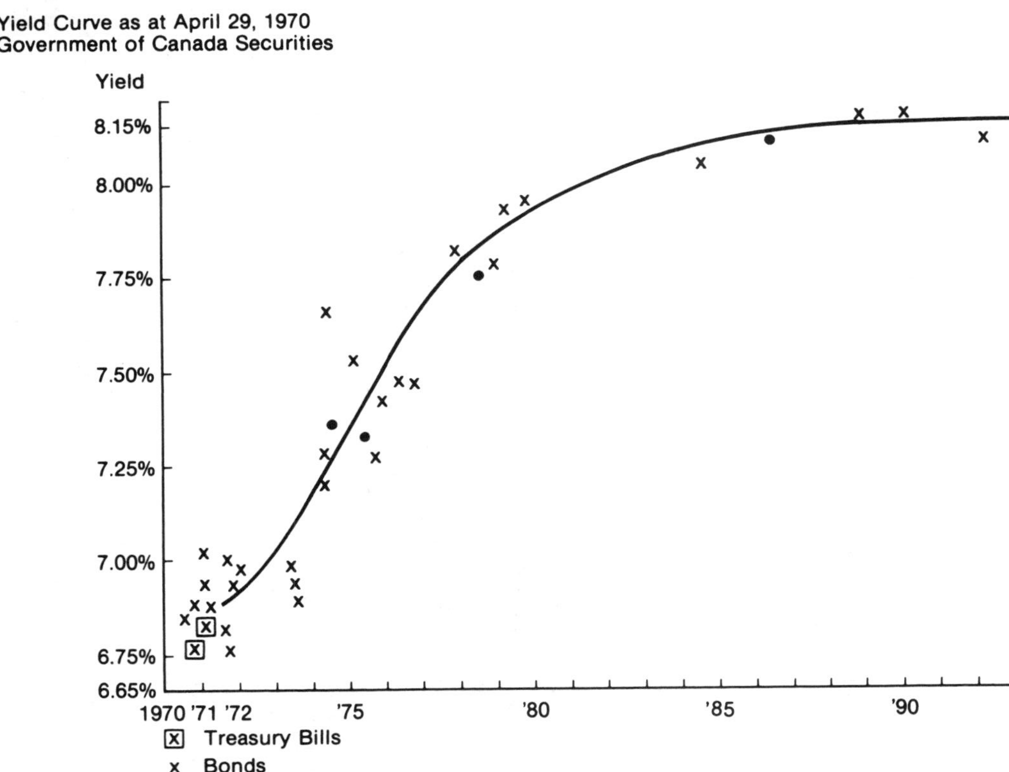

Source: Bank of Canada, *Statistical Summary*, May, 1970.

Interest rates and the risk of default

Having seen that the investors will generally demand increased returns as a compensation for bearing increased risk, it is not surprising to find that the yield provided by otherwise similar debt issues depends on the financial strength of the borrower as perceived by investors. As the perceived risk of default increases, so does the interest rate which borrowers have to offer in order to make their debt issues attractive. Typically, debt issues by the federal government are considered to be the safest, with the risk of default being negligible. It is interesting to note, and easy to verify by scanning the financial pages of any newspaper, that even among various provincial issues, interest rate differentials do exist, suggesting varying degrees of investor confidence. For instance, debt issued by some of the Atlantic provinces and by Quebec typically tends to carry a higher yield than similar debt issued by Ontario. Similarly, the yield provided on corporate debt issues varies depending on the perceived credit worthiness of the issuing firm. Some independent agencies, notably Moody's Investor Service and Standard and Poor's Corporation, supply rating information on the quality of a wide range of bonds, debentures, and corporate short-term debt, making it somewhat easier for investors to evaluate various offerings. Standard and Poor's has more than 10,000 bond and preferred share ratings outstanding.[9] Various keys and abbreviations are typically used to summarize such information, with Moody's letter ratings being widely used. Table 8-3 provides a brief overview of this rating system.

TABLE 8-3

Summary of Moody's Corporate Ratings

Aaa	Best quality; carrying the smallest degree of investment risk.
Aa	High quality; margins of protection may not be up to those of Aaa group.
A	Higer medium grade; present position adequate, but future impairment a possibility.
Baa	Lower medium grade; certain protective elements lacking.
Ba	Possess speculative elements; protection of interest and principal payments may be very moderate.
B	Generally lack characteristics of a desirable investment.
Caa	Poor standing; may be in default or in danger of default.
Ca	Speculative in a high degree; often in default.
C	Lowest grade; have extremely poor prospects of attaining any real investment standing.

Ratings are useful for categorizing issues into broad ranges of investment quality. The basis used reflects (i) the availability of financial resources, (ii) past earnings and future earnings potential, (iii) collateral protection afforded in terms of the firm's assets, (iv) management's demonstrated ability and sense of responsibility, and (v) protective provisions provided for in the trust deed. Bond ratings cannot be classed as an exact science, however, and to some extent have

[9]B. Harris, "How Corporate Bonds and Commercial Paper are Rated", *Financial Executive*, September, 1971, pp. 30-36.

to be based on subjective judgment. Therefore, bond ratings, while providing useful information, should not be the sole basis for investment decisions.

8-3. CLASSIFICATION OF DEBT INSTRUMENTS BY COLLATERAL REQUIREMENTS

While the continued earning power of the issuing organization is of primary importance to investors in assessing a particular issue of debt, other factors also contribute to the risks as perceived by lenders. The collateral being offered and the retirement schedule provided are of particular significance. Several differing collateral and retirement arrangements are possible and debt instruments are classified accordingly.

Corporate debt may (a) be secured by the pledge of specific assets, (b) be completely unsecured, backed largely by the earning power of the borrower and a claim against residual assets, or (c) provide a *floating charge* against assets. The floating charge gives lenders an all-embracing claim against any corporate assets not otherwise pledged and effectively ranks them ahead of unsecured or general creditors in the event of liquidation. When specific assets are pledged, the debt instrument is called a *bond*, whereas the term *debenture* is applied in the other two cases.

Bonds

When, under a trust deed, specific assets are pledged, the market value of such collateral will usually exceed the amount of the bond issue by a reasonable margin. Most frequently, the assets pledged are land, plant, and equipment. These debt instruments are labelled *mortgage bonds*.

It often becomes necessary for a company to float debt after an issue of mortgage bonds is already outstanding. Whether such a subsequent offering is possible will depend on particular provisions of the original trust deed including possible constraints placed on the right to issue additional debt under the same mortgage. Thus, the trust deed can provide for an *open-end, closed-end, or limited open-end mortgage*. With an open-end arrangement, subsequent debt can be issued freely under the same trust deed. Obviously, this is appealing to the borrower in that it provides flexibility for future financing and minimizes subsequent issuing expenses.

To protect the original bondholders against excessive new offerings which would erode the security provided originally, it is customary for trust deeds containing an open-end mortgage to include some protective provisions. They may, for example, limit new bonds to some fraction of the value of properties or improvements to be acquired or specify that bond interest be covered a certain number of times by reported earnings before interest and taxes. An *after-acquired property clause* usually is included as well. It provides that all subsequently acquired properties will fall under the mortgage agreement and be pledged as further security.

The limited open-ended mortgage places a ceiling on the amount of bonds issuable under the trust deed, but unlike the closed-end variety, this maximum is not immediately binding. When the mortgage is closed-end, further offerings of bonds respecting the property pledged under the mortgage would have to be issued under another trust deed and a secondary mortgage.

Example

A $5,000,000 bond issue pledging real property with a current market value of $10,000,000 was placed in 1969. By 1974, about half of the debt had been repaid while, with inflation and pressures on land, the market value of the property increased to $20,000,000, implying a much more generous safety factor. The margin of $17,500,000 between the debt outstanding and the market value of the collateral would justify the issuance of additional debt, but with the closed-end mortgage new bonds could be issued only under another trust deed and mortgage and would rank strictly behind the original debt in terms of claims against assets.

Such secondary bonds are termed *second* or *general mortgage bonds.*

As long as investors are satisfied that collateral will continue to have a realizable value, assets other than real property may be used to secure debt. One example of this is the *collateral trust bond,* secured by the pledging of securities such as common shares of other corporations which the issuer may hold and which are deposited with a trustee.

Debentures

As noted, debentures are not secured by claims against specific assets. In practice, their use has been limited to corporations which have exhausted the ability to issue bonds, or which have credit standing high enough to make the pledging of specific assets unnecessary. From the issuer's point of view there are advantages to using debentures, with or without a floating charge, rather than pledging particular assets. Debentures afford increased flexibility, not just for future financing but also in the management of corporate assets. The sale of assets, for example, may not be constrained by mortgage provisions in the trust deed. When the earning power and general credit standing of a corporation are perceived as high by investors, debentures may find almost the same acceptance as bonds. As a general rule, however, debentures must provide slightly higher yields than are available on comparable bonds.

As with bonds, trust deeds covering debentures typically contain a variety of protective clauses which strengthen the investor's position. The *negative pledge clause* is a fairly critical one in that it prevents the company's pledging of any of its assets to other creditors under subsequent borrowings. Such a provision may, of course, severely restrict management's ability to obtain additional financing.

Obligations with claims which rank behind those of ordinary debenture holders are termed *subordinated debentures.* Since such debentures are subordinated to other existing and future funded debt, they are often regarded by creditors as being equivalent to equity. It is quite possible to have more than one subordinated debenture issue and, in such cases, one offering may be subordinate to another and labelled a junior subordinated issue.

As the least secure form of debt, subordinated debentures must provide a higher risk premium or yield to be marketable. Some borrowers, however, may rely on subordinate debentures, using either conversion features or warrants to "sweeten" the offering, thereby making it attractive to investors even at a reasonable rate of interest. Such special features will be discussed in more detail in a subsequent chapter.

Equipment trust certificates

Although they are a form of long-term external debt financing, *equipment trust certificates* are quite different from the debt instruments already reviewed. Not only are they derived from a direct leasing arrangement, but they are almost always placed with financial institutions rather than individual investors. Resorted to by railroads and other transport companies where obsolescence is not a factor, their use entails the following procedures:

(i) An order for rolling stock is placed by the railroad with a manufacturer. A down payment of 20 to 25 percent is made with the balances raised through the sale of equipment trust certificates.

(ii) All payments to the manufacturer are made through a trustee. The equipment is placed in the trustee's name and is the collateral behind the certificates.

(iii) The equipment trust obligations are sold with varying maturities of up to 15 years, and are to be retired more rapidly than the assets depreciate, thus improving the collateral security of the outstanding certificates over time. By way of illustration, the Canadian Pacific's $25,000,000 (U.S.) 5 percent equipment trust certificates series P, were dated January 6, 1966, and $1,668,000 of the issue was to mature each January 6 from 1967 to 1981 inclusive.

(iv) A detailed lease is drawn up between the trustee and the railroad. Rental payments sufficient to meet interest charges and redemptions are provided for. Provision is also made for the protection of assets, their assembly in event of default, and the transfer of ownership once all certificates are retired.

In terms of attractiveness, equipment trust certificates rank with the most senior secured debt. Their strength is attributable to a combination of factors including the essential nature of the equipment pledged, the ease with which it can be transferred to another lessee, the increasing margin between the value of collateral and the certificates outstanding, and finally the fact that with equipment owned by the trustee, in the event of the lessee's insolvency, legal tangles are avoided.

Income bonds

Income bonds are a potentially weak form of debt instrument, which may appear as either bonds or debentures. Under provisions of such issues, interest becomes payable only when earnings are reported by the borrower, and generally the amount of interest unpaid does not accumulate. Unlike the U.S. pattern, for purposes of Canadian income tax, interest on such securities is to be treated as a preferred dividend by both the firm and recipients.

Given the weak position of such bondholders, for a successful offering of income bonds, the issuer must incorporate some fairly attractive features, including liberal arrangements for orderly retirement of the debt.[10] In practice, income bonds are mainly issued in unusual circumstances, including cases of corporate reorganization where there is a readjustment of the capital structure because of actual or imminent default on payments to creditors. Given the choice between liquidating the company and receiving perhaps 25 cents on the dollar, or of accepting income bonds in exchange for their present holdings, creditors generally make the best of a bad situation and accept income bonds.

Convertible bonds or debentures

Convertible debt is a financial instrument which can be converted into a certain number of the firm's common shares at the holder's option. The number of shares to be received upon conversion is specified in the trust deed. Quite clearly, upon conversion, the bondholder relinquishes his position as a creditor and takes an equity position in the firm. A thorough analysis of convertible securities and their use is provided in Chapter 11.

Form of debt chosen

The form of debt chosen in any given situation will not only depend on a corporation's particular circumstances, but on conditions prevailing in the capital markets as well. Though offerings proposed by the firm have to be attractive enough to find acceptance in the market, there typically will be room for trade-offs, which must be considered by corporate management. Therefore, management may have to weigh the value of flexibility resulting from liberal provisions in the trust deed against higher interest costs, with the ultimate decision likely to be made on the basis of informed judgment.

8-4. CURRENCY CONSIDERATIONS

When it comes to the form, collateral and maturity of long-term debt, an issuing corporation's management must give careful consideration to attitudes prevailing in the bond markets and, on the basis of their findings, choose from among the many alternatives available. In actual fact, matters become even more complicated since, for many Canadian borrowers, the relevant bond market is an international one.[11] Should the issue be offered abroad, management must determine the currency or currencies in which the debt is to be denominated. Furthermore, a decision to move into the international bond market also raises the question of whether to deal through the larger and more active *Euro-bond market* or through the *foreign bond market.*

As the name suggests, the Euro-bond market is centered in Europe and covers "bonds . . . sold principally in countries other than the country of the currency in which the issue is denominated."[12] The sale of U.S. dollar debentures by a Canadian corporation to investors in Paris is an example of a Euro-bond issue.

[10]S. Robbins, "A Bigger Role for Income Bonds," *Harvard Business Review*, November-December, 1955, pp. 100-114.

[11]Many Canadian corporations as well as provincial governments, Crown corporations, and municipalities are active in the international bond market.

[12]R. Rodriguez and E. Carter, *International Financial Management*, Englewood Cliffs: Prentice-Hall, 1976, p. 501.

It is the availability of a number of different currencies, including dollars, outside of their country of origin which makes such activity possible.[13]

An offering in the foreign bond market, on the other hand, would involve sales being made primarily in the country of the currency denominating the debt. For instance, an issue by the same Canadian corporation denominated in Swiss francs and sold to investors in Zurich and Geneva, or U.S. dollar borrowings taking place in New York, would be considered offerings in foreign bond markets.

In cases where longer-term international borrowing is involved, foreign exchange risks generally become an important consideration. With flexible rather than fixed exchange rates prevailing, these risks have increased dramatically. Furthermore, as many provincial and corporate borrowers are learning to their great sorrow, exchange risks are absorbed by the debtor corporation if bonds and debentures are denominated in other than the borrower's currency.[14] To clarify the nature and extent of such foreign exchange risks, it is useful to draw on a simplified numerical example.

Example

> Consider a firm which required $15,000,000 back in 1970. Rather than paying 9 percent on a 15-year issue to be sold in Canada, the financial officer approached the European capital markets where an issue denominated in German marks could be placed at 8 percent. With the then prevailing *spot rate*[15] on German marks at $0.2830 per mark, the decision was made to sell a DM 53,000,000 issue to gross about $15,000,000. No sinking fund feature was incorporated.
>
> In January 1976, with the spot rate at $0.3895 to the mark, the liability of the Canadian borrower in terms of Canadian dollars stood at 0.3895 × 53,000,000 or $20,643,500. In addition, to meet the year's interest payment, which is also payable in German marks, the corporation had to find 8 percent of $20,643,500, or $1,651,480. Had $15,000,000 been borrowed in Canada at the higher 9 percent figure, the interest charge would have come to only $1,350,000.

Therefore, a corporation issuing debt in a foreign currency has to weigh anticipated interest rate savings against the risk of foreign exchange. It should be clear that fluctuations in exchange rates can work both ways. Pursuing our example above, the indicated shifts in exchange rates would clearly have been

[13]Such external currency balances are known as Euro-dollars, Euro-sterling, and the likes. Threats of political interference, foreign currency restrictions, and tax considerations all help to perpetuate these balances. For example, U.S. banks have been restricted by law as to the maximum amount of interest which they can pay on deposits. No such restrictions existed for dollar deposits held in branches abroad, prompting the holding of dollar balances in various other countries. Such balances found ready users when, to solve U.S. balance of payments problems, restrictions were imposed on U.S. firms moving funds abroad for investment. From time to time, other countries were moved to impose similar restrictions, thus contributing to the establishment of Euro-markets for various other currencies.

[14]When it comes to debt involving more than one currency, this may not always be true. Such securities are commented on later in this section.

[15]The spot rate may be defined as the going rate of exchange for immediate delivery of one currency against another.

very favorable to a German borrower who issued debt in Canadian dollars.

It should be appreciated that borrowers do not turn to the New York, Frankfurt, and Zurich markets just to save on coupon rates, as other considerations may be important. To begin with, very large issues of bonds or debentures cannot easily be handled in Canada because of the limited size of Canadian capital markets. Secondly, studies have shown that firms which obtain a relatively large and stable proportion of their total revenues in foreign currencies often try to arrange for a portion of their longer-term liabilities to be denominated in those same currencies. To protect their positions, they will do so even when the interest costs may be higher. Lastly, it has been suggested that borrowers wanting to sell their obligations directly to institutional lenders without going through a general public offering of their securities often have little choice but to enter the New York market to arrange such private placements, usually because Canadian institutional investors are not large enough to take up an issue.[16]

During late 1975 and early 1976, with comparatively high interest rate levels prevailing in Canada, Canadian borrowers relied more heavily than ever on the international bond markets, where new issues during the first quarter of 1976 totalled $10.2 billions.[17] Such foreign borrowings undoubtedly contributed to the strength of the Canadian dollar and to the improved liquidity of many corporations, municipalities, and governments. What must not be lost sight of, however, is that the new debt will require servicing and, as discussed above, will increase the borrower's foreign exchange exposure accordingly. Table 8-4 identifies the sharp increase in international borrowings by Canadian corporations.

TABLE 8-4
Net New Issues of Debt (in millons of dollars)
Placed in Domestic Markets and Abroad

Years and Quarters		Corporations				Provinces & Municipalities	
		Placed Domestically	Placed Abroad	Total Placed	% of Total Placed Abroad	Total Placed	% of Total Placed Abroad
1974	I	269	42	311	13.5	937	52.3
	II	532	31	563	5.8	1,144	29.2
	III	309	86	395	21.8	811	39.6
	IV	476	78	554	14.1	1,510	39.5
1975	I	845	56	901	6.2	1,515	40.9
	II	991	36	1,027	3.5	2,070	39.4
	III	415	129	544	23.7	1,307	46.7
	IV	159	454	613	74.1	2,385	61.2
1976	I	460	829	1,289	64.3	3,056	69.2

Source: Derived from *Bank of Canada Review*, May, 1976.

[16]For some elaboration of these considerations, see K. Stroetmann, *The Theory of Long-Term International Capital Flows and Canadian Corporate Debt Issues in the United States*, unpublished Ph.D. dissertation, Faculty of Commerce and Business Administration, The University of British Columbia, May, 1974.

[17]During the first quarter of 1976, over 22 percent of the $4.7 billions issued in the Euro-bond market was by Canadian borrowers. See, for example, Federal Reserve Bank of Chicago, *International Letter*, July 2, 1976.

In attempts to shift, spread, or generally reduce the foreign exchange risk, a variety of mixed-currency debt instruments have been introduced and now appear alongside simple currency offerings which have long dominated the Euro-bond markets. Multiple currency bonds have been used since 1957 and provide the lender with options from among a group of currencies for all future payments of interest and principal. Set parities between the various currencies are specified at the time of issue, and periodic payments will obviously be requested by lenders in currencies which have improved the most from those pre-established parities. While being attractive to investors because of the options provided, such multiple currency bonds have proved quite unattractive to borrowers. As an alternative, since 1961 a variety of issues have been designed which are denominated in weighted mixes of currencies termed "currency baskets".

The objective behind the several currency baskets which have been implemented in this context was to either spread the exchange risk between borrowers and lenders, or to minimize fluctuations in values. Examples of such currency baskets, which have grown in popularity in recent years, include debt denominated in *Special Drawing Rights*,[18] the *European Composite Unit* or EURCO, and the *European Unit of Account* or EUA. While descriptions of such increasingly complex securities is beyond the scope of this text, any financial officer looking to the Euro-bond market for funds will need to become familiar with such alternatives.[19]

8-5. RETIREMENT FEATURES

One of the characteristic features of any debt is that it comes due.[20] While the specified maturity is of great significance to both the debtor and his creditors, attention must also center on provisions for repayments prior to maturity. The retirement of bonds and debentures can come about in any one of several ways. Debt can be retired by payment of face value at maturity, by periodic repayments of principal over the life of the debt, by conversion if the securities are convertible, or by calling the debt before maturity if there is a call feature. Gradual retirement of obligations may be provided for either through a sinking fund or the use of serial bonds; each of which is considered in turn. Call features on debt are examined next, while conversion is reviewed in a later chapter.

Sinking fund provisions and serial bonds

Though examples of perpetual debt are to be found, practically all debt issues do have a specified maturity. To avoid possible problems at the time of maturity, borrowers inevitably provide for a sinking fund feature. This feature not only relieves the borrower of the pressures associated with attempting a single critical repayment but also may be attractive to investors concerned about the liquidity

[18]A creation of the International Monetary Fund, Special Drawing Rights or SDR's are an asset created to augment the level of international reserves. Its value since June 1974 has been based on a weighted value of 16 currencies. Hence, while its composition remains set, its value changes as exchange rates fluctuate.

[19]For a description of these instruments, see P. Lusztig and B. Schwab, "Units of Account and the International Bond Market", *Columbia Journal of World Business*, Spring, 1975, pp. 74-79.

[20]Exceptions exist as noted in footnote 1, page 229.

of their holdings. Marketability is improved by periodic demand for the debt to meet sinking fund obligations.

Under a sinking fund provision, the corporation issuing the debt makes periodic payments toward the retirement of the outstanding debt. These payments may involve equal instalments paid to the trustee over the life of the debt, although less rigid repayment schedules designed to meet the borrower's particular circumstances can be negotiated.

Example

A 10-year $10,000,000 bond issue could provide for equal payments of $1,000,000 for each of the 10 years, or it could provide for payments of $500,000 for each of the 10 years with a final "balloon" payment of $5,000,000 at maturity.

Even less rigid sinking fund features may link the amounts to be paid to corporate earnings in some fashion. The date of the first payment or the period over which payments are made may be flexible also with all such clauses subject to negotiation prior to floating the issue.

Example

The $20,000,000 5¾ percent Subordinated Debentures of Quebec Natural Gas Corporation issued in 1957 and due in 1978 incorporated a balanced approach in providing the feature. In this instance, annual sinking fund payments did not commence until March 31, 1966 and then amounted to the lesser of $500,000 or 50 percent of the net income of the previous fiscal year.

Use of very rigid conditions is unlikely to be in anyone's interest as it may, over the term of the issue, impair managerial performance by requiring the debtor corporation during periods of poor earnings to meet heavy fixed sinking fund commitments.

The procedure generally followed in making sinking fund payments is for the issuer to transfer monies to the trustee who will then use the funds to retire the debt. Redemption may be accomplished either through a purchase on the open market, or by calling some proportion of the issue. When bonds or debentures are to be called, a random drawing is used based on serial numbers of the securities. This call provision is normally provided for to avoid having to purchase the debt at a premium in the event that interest rates declined. To illustrate, if the going interest rate for comparable bonds has fallen to 8 percent, then a 10 percent $1,000 bond with 10 years to mature will trade at a market price of about $1,134. A $1,000,000 sinking fund payment, therefore, would be sufficient to retire debt with a face value amounting to only $1,000,000/1.134 = $881,834 because of the market premium over face value caused by lower rates of interest. To protect the issuer against having to bid significantly above face value when trying to meet the sinking fund obligations provided for, a trust deed usually allows the trustee to call the required amount of debt at face value or at a very modest premium.

With serial bonds, too, a specified proportion of the debt is retired periodically over the life of the issue. Unlike the workings of a sinking fund issue, however, the serial bonds, when originally offered, provide for staggered maturities for different serial numbers in the issue. The effect is very similar to that of a sinking fund provision although, by the specification of different maturities from the outset, investors can be attracted to bonds meeting their specific needs. The bond issue, consequently, has wider market appeal.

In Canada, the largest issuers of serial bonds have been the municipalities and, in these situations, the interest coupons have varied with the maturities to reflect the term structure of interest rates. A poor resale market for municipal bonds has tarnished serial bonds to some extent and restricted their use by corporate borrowers.

Extendibles and retractables

Some borrowers have catered to investor uncertainty about future interest-rate movements and concern about interest-rate risk by issuing long-term *retractable debt*. In effect, such bonds give investors the right to cash in the debt instrument at full face value at a particular date well before maturity. Thus, the 7¼ percent Bank of Montreal issue, maturing in 1987, allows investors to cash in on August 1, 1979 at face value. As illustrated by the nonredeemable 8 percent bonds of Bell Telephone, *extendibles* are simply a variation of retractables. Issued in 1969 and maturing in 1977, the securities were exchangeable at the holder's option between November 1, 1970 and November 1, 1975, into 8¼ percent bonds due in 1990. The onus to move such debt out of the short- or intermediate-term into the long-term category rests entirely with the investor. Given the passive stance of many individual investors, this may well increase the probability of the borrower having to enter the capital market more frequently as such debt is not extended, and it explains the greater reliance by corporations on retractables.

It is difficult to accurately comment upon the attractiveness of retractables and extendibles. Figure 8-3 shows the development of interest rates and bond prices over the period 1963 to 1975. Given the pattern of increasing interest rates and eroding bond prices, the widespread use of retractable or extendible features on debt in order to protect investors becomes understandable, and it has been suggested that coupon rates on new issues might be reduced by perhaps one-half of one percent through the inclusion of the retractable feature during periods of rising interest rates and investor uncertainty, with even greater savings available in the case of extendibles.

Call features

Call features are commonly associated with fixed income securities such as debt or preferred shares. The call feature gives a corporation the option to repurchase its debt at a stated price before maturity. Such call provisions give the company flexibility in its financing. If interest rates should decline significantly, the firm can refund before maturity at a lower interest cost. In addition, the call feature may be advantageous to the company if it finds that the protective provisions in the trust deed are unduly restrictive. By calling the bonds before maturity, the

FIGURE 8-3

Relationship Between Market Price of Debt and the Movement of Interest Rates

Government of Canada 5% Bonds Due June 1, 1988

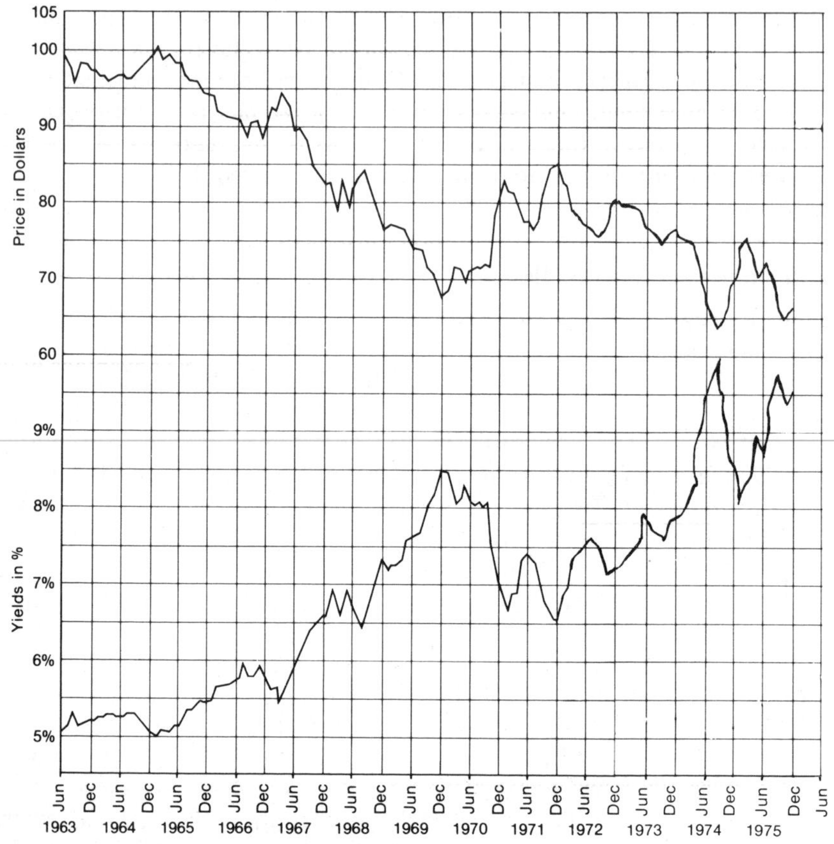

Source: *Bank of Canada Review*, June 1963 to January 1976.

company can eliminate such provisions providing, of course, that a new refunding issue can be floated without similar restrictions.

Security holders know that if bonds or debentures are to be called, it will likely be when interest rates have declined. Following the call the debt holder has no other choice than to reinvest the funds at a lower rate of interest for at least some portion of the remaining years.[21] Hence, the call privilege represents a potential

[21]We should appreciate that the bond holder is also confronted with costs involved in reinvesting, for example, the cost of search and transaction costs.

loss of yield, and it is in the investor's interest to minimize this type of risk or at least to seek compensation for any early redemption of the issue. The usual practice is to spell out a call price which exceeds the debt's face value when redemption is for other than sinking fund purposes. This premium required by potential bond or debenture holders hinges on expectations about future interest rates. In practice, the premium for the earlier years is established at about one year's interest. For example, if the coupon rate is 7½ percent, the initial call price may be $1,075 per bond with a $1,000 face value. Subsequently, the premium decreases over time. This takes cognizance of the fact that as time passes the investor loses less through the calling of an issue, and therefore requires less by way of compensation.

There are two types of call provisions. Some issues provide a call privilege which is immediately operative; in other instances, the privilege is deferred for a time and the debt cannot be called for example during the first five years of its life. All other things being equal, the former would be more risky for investors. The most widely used deferrals are for five- and ten-year periods.

If a debt issue is called by the issuing corporation to take advantage of lower interest rates through a refunding operation, it is clear that this gain to the corporation is a loss to the investor. To compensate the investor for the increased risk which he bears if he invests in a bond which provides for liberal call features, not only does the call price generally have to be set above the face value of the debt, but such callable debt will generally have to pay somewhat higher interest rates than comparable debt without such call features.[22]

The question of whether the increased interest rate to be paid on callable debt is worth the potential flexibility gained by the corporation depends, partly at least, on the interest-rate movements anticipated by the issuing corporation and by investors respectively. We might expect that where the corporation and the investing public have similar expectations about future interest rates, the market will demand a risk premium in the form of higher interest which should just about offset the issuer's expected gain from a potential refunding. Empirical evidence does not support this conclusion[23], and there is some suggestion based on U.S. data that the market may undervalue the call privilege.[24] If this is really the case, the firm's optimal strategy would be to take advantage of this market imperfection by paying the higher interest in obtaining a full call privilege. Consistent with this observation is the fact that traditionally most debt has been issued with a call feature. During recent periods of unusually high interest rates, however, many issuers of long-term debt increased the attractiveness of their offerings by curtailing the right of early redemption. Such curtailment guaranteed investors attractive returns over an extended period despite the possibility of subsequent declines in levels of interest rates.

[22]See W. Winn and A. Hess, Jr., "The Value of the Call Privilege," *Journal of Finance*, May, 1959, pp. 183-195.

[23]Considerations other than expectations about interest rates may play a role here and some factors such as the concern about restrictive provisions in the trust deed already have been cited.

[24]F. Jen and J. Wert, "The Effect of Call Risk on Corporate Bond Yields," *Journal of Finance*, December, 1967, pp. 637-651.

8-6. REFUNDING OF DEBT[25]

Refunding refers to the transaction by which a firm replaces an issue of outstanding bonds or debentures at or before maturity by a new issue of debt. Major reasons for refunding include the following:

(a) A debt issue matures, implying repayment of principal, but the firm wishes to extend the term of the borrowing. New debt is issued, with proceeds used to repay the old creditors.

(b) The firm has debt outstanding at interest rates which exceed those currently prevailing in the capital market. The old debt may be called and new debt issued at lower interest rates. Proceeds from the new debt issue are again used to repay the old debt.

(c) The firm may have debt outstanding under terms which impose certain restrictions on the firm, such as limitations on additional borrowing or on dividend payments. Management may find such restrictions, likely negotiated many years earlier, overly constraining. Again, by issuing new debt to retire an outstanding issue, such restrictive provisions may be removed.

We will discuss each of these reasons for refunding in turn.

Many firms rely on longer-term debt as a permanent part of their capital structure. Therefore, if debt is to be retained, refunding needs to take place as the maturity date of an outstanding issue approaches. For larger firms which may have a variety of debt issues outstanding, such refundings may take place with some frequency. Given that almost all debt issues have a sinking fund provision alongside a final maturity date, regular sinking fund payments may initially be met from short-term debt sources. Eventually, however, built-up balances of short-term debt need to be refunded, along with balloon payments at maturity, through new issues of long-term debt.

When the objective in refunding is a reduction in interest charges, a decision is reached after analysis which draws on evaluation techniques developed in our discussion of capital budgeting. Calling an issue of outstanding debt for redemption and arranging the refunding through issuance of new debt will entail a variety of costs. These costs are incurred in order to achieve interest savings in years to come. In deciding whether such an operation is profitable, we draw on net present value analysis, comparing the present value of future interest savings with the current outlays required for refunding. A positive net present value indicates that refunding is profitable.

In order to carry out the actual analysis, we first need to isolate all the relevant after-tax cash flows. The main outlays involved in a refunding operation are:

(a) the costs associated with the issuance of the new debt, which include legal and professional fees, and commissions paid or discounts offered for the selling of such securities to the public. Such costs are termed *issuing and underwriting expenses*. Detailed tax treatment of such expenses can become quite complex. To simplify the exposition we will assume that all such

[25]For an excellent detailed treatment, see O. Bowlin, "The Refunding Decision", *Journal of Finance*, March, 1966, pp. 55-68.

expenses are fully deductible for tax purposes in the period in which they are incurred.[26]

(b) the costs of calling the old debt issue. This outlay which equals the call premium stipulated in the debt contract, cannot be treated as an expense for tax purposes, and has to be met out of after-tax income.

The following example will clarify the decision process further.

Example

A corporation has a $20,000,000 issue of 10 percent debentures outstanding, with 10 years left to maturity. Interest rates have dropped somewhat, and the corporation could now refund the outstanding debt with an otherwise identical issue, but at an interest rate of only 8 percent. The maturity of this new issue would also be 10 years. The call premium on the old debentures is 5 percent of face value, while issuing and underwriting expenses for the new issue would amount to $600,000. The corporate tax rate is 45 percent, and no sinking fund features are called for under either debenture issue. Initial cash outflows associated with the refunding may therefore be given as:

	Before Tax	After Tax
Issuing and underwriting expenses	$ 600,000	$ 330,000
Call premium on old issue (5% × $20,000,000)	$1,000,000	$1,000,000
Total after-tax cash outflows		$1,330,000

Subsequent interest savings on a before-tax basis will amount to the 2 percent reduction in the coupon rate on $20,000,000, or $400,000 annually for 10 years. With interest charges a tax deductible expense, these savings will result in a reduced tax shield bringing after-tax annual interest savings to (1−0.45) × $400,000 or $220,000.

Before computing the net present value of the refunding proposition, one additional and frequently incurred cost needs to be recognized. If the old debentures are called, for example, effective January 1, a corporation would usually issue the new debt several weeks earlier. This caution makes good sense, protecting against unexpected delays in the issuance of the new debt. It would obviously be embarassing to have January 1 approach without having the needed funds available. Thus, an overlap period is provided for during which both the old and the new debt are outstanding, with interest having to be paid on both issues. Given the large sums normally involved, these duplicate interest charges cannot be ignored.

Assume that in our example the firm plans for a 2-month overlap. Rather than realizing the projected interest savings from the date of the

[26]It should be noted that the actual tax treatment of issue and underwriting expenses is quite complex and is varied from time to time, with the *Income Tax Act* providing for numerous special conditions and exceptions. For a brief overview see, for example, Canadian Tax Foundation, *Corporate Management Tax Conference 1974*, Toronto: Canadian Tax Foundation, 1974, pp. 78-81, in particular.

new issue, additional interest will have to be paid on the old debt for a further 2 months. On the other hand, excess funds which are available during the overlap period can be invested in short-term securities such as treasury bills to earn some return, which for purposes of our example we assume to be 7 percent. The additional expenses attributable to the overlap are then computed as follows:

	Before Tax	After Tax
Additional interest paid on old debt (2/12 × 10% × \$20,000,000)	\$333,333	\$183,333
Yield on short-term investments	\$233,333	\$128,333
Additional after-tax expenses during overlap period		\$ 55,000

Thus, given an overlap period, we have to contrast total immediate after-tax cash outflows of \$1,330,000 + \$55,000 = \$1,385,000 with after-tax cash savings of \$220,000 per year for 10 years.

The choice of the proper discount rate to be applied to future interest savings warrants some discussion. In the chapters on capital budgeting, we showed that the firm's cost of capital should be used in computing net present values of investments. Computation of a firm's cost of capital, and consideration of the various factors which influence it, will be the subject of extensive discussion in subsequent chapters on cost of capital, capital structure, and the capital asset pricing model. Nevertheless, in order to appreciate the issues involved in bond refunding, some brief commentary is appropriate at this point.

As was discussed earlier, the cost at which funds can be raised is in part a function of risk. More particularly, the overall business risk of a firm as reflected by its typical investment projects determines, in part, how and at what cost the firm can raise funds. This cost of capital is appropriate where a firm evaluates typical investment projects which have risk characteristics similar to the overall risk of the firm. Consider, however, an investment in debt refunding: the future cash savings are essentially known with certainty as they are specified in the debt contracts, and very little risk is associated with such projections. Hence, it is not consistent to apply a discount rate which contains a risk premium—such as the firm's overall or average cost of capital—to a project which is clearly much less risky than the firm's overall activities. In essence, a riskless project could be financed entirely through debt, and in floating new debt, the firm could easily have chosen to issue an additional amount to cover expenses of refunding.[27]

[27]This can be shown more rigorously in the following highly simplified context. Assume \$20,000,000 of 10 percent *perpetual* debt to be outstanding. Refunding can be undertaken with a new perpetual issue at 8 percent. The firm intends to finance any refunding expenses by simply issuing additional debt. Interest of 10% × \$20,000,000 or \$2,000,000 per year is being paid on the old debt. In order for refunding to be attractive, annual interest payments on the new debt can amount to at most \$2,000,000. At 8 percent interest, this implies that the maximum amount of new debt which can be issued is \$2,000,000/0.08 = \$25,000,000, and that refunding expenses must not exceed \$5,000,000. Such refunding expenses have to yield a return equal to the after-tax cost of the new debt. Given a tax rate of 45 percent, this works out to (1 − 0.45) × 8% or 4.4 percent, and this becomes the discount rate to be applied to future interest savings of (1 − 0.45) × (10% − 8%) × \$20,000,000 = \$220,000. When these are discounted at 4.4 percent, the present value of such savings becomes \$220,000/0.044 = \$5,000,000, confirming that this is the maximum amount which the firm can afford to spend on refunding. The argument as outlined can be shown to carry over into more general situations involving fixed maturities and sinking fund payments.

Thus, the appropriate time value of money to be applied in this case becomes the firm's cost of issuing new debt, on an after-tax basis, which for our example is given as $(1-0.45) \times 8\% = 4.4\%$.

Given the discount rate, computation of the net present value is purely mechanical. The annuity factor for 10 years and 4.4 percent can be found by interpolation from the tables as being approximately $a_{10}4.4\% = 7.9554$, resulting in a net present value for refunding of:

$$\begin{aligned} NPV &= -\$1{,}385{,}000 + 7.9554 \times \$220{,}000 \\ &= \$365{,}188 \end{aligned}$$

Thus, based on a net present value analysis, refunding is indicated.

Whether refunding is actually undertaken may depend on some additional considerations, the most important one being timing, which will be discussed in further detail below. For example, if interest rates are declining and this decline is expected to continue, management may prefer to delay the refunding. At a later date, new debt could presumably be sold at even lower rates of interest, thus making the refunding operation even more attractive. Also, because call premiums on outstanding debt usually decline in a stepwise manner as such debt approaches its maturity, the refunding may be postponed in order to refund at a reduced future call price.

Finally, as already noted, refunding may be considered attractive in order to remove restrictive provisions imposed on the firm through terms of an old debt issue. Such a provision may, for example, restrict the firm from undertaking additional borrowings and may have been included in order to provide added security to the holders of the original debt. Because of continued price level changes, both the firm's dollar volume of business and the collateral value of its assets may have increased beyond original expectations, placing the firm in a position where it could comfortably service additional debt. Under such circumstances, refunding may be indicated to restore management's flexibility in pursuing financing policies which are in the best interests of the firm. Clearly, management must weigh the costs of refunding against the benefits to be obtained, where the assessment of such benefits may become largely a matter of subjective managerial judgment.

Despite everything said thus far, possible loss of investor goodwill may force the debtor corporation's management to rule out refunding. Institutional investors may resent having their portfolio balances upset by a redemption, more particularly if they lose debt instruments with exceptional protective provisions or an attractive coupon rate. A natural reaction would be to avoid further investments in securities of the firm undertaking the refunding.[28]

Timing

In the issuing of new debt, as well as in considering a refunding operation, timing becomes critical and the eventual decision must be based on forecasts of

[28]Implicit agreements barring calls except in very exceptional circumstances may also block obviously attractive refunding opportunities.

future interest-rate movements. Ideally, a company would want to hold off on new long-term debt issues in times of sliding interest rates so as to take advantage of the more favorable conditions being anticipated, perhaps arranging for some short-term financing in the interim. On the other hand, with postponement, significant losses might be incurred if forecasts of declining interest rates did not materialize, and it should be recognized that the lead time to prepare for and negotiate a new debt issue is in the order of several months.

The critical nature of a timing decision is evident if we think, for example, of a $40,000,000 issue and a one percent change in interest rates. The annual "loss" through financing at an interest rate which has increased by one percent, even after tax at a rate of 50 percent, would amount to $200,000. While models have been developed which view future interest rates as a random variable with particular probability distributions, they are primarily theoretical and are more appropriate in an advanced treatment of financial theories.[29] In a practical context, we might more usefully call for forecasts and actions based on an informed interpretation of activities in the international capital markets, the economy, actions by the Bank of Canada, and general political considerations. This illustrates how important it is for the financial executive to have a firm grasp of the workings of capital markets, and to be able to spot developments and shifts as they take place—for a wrong assessment of trends in interest rate movements could clearly be quite costly. We conclude that timing can be viewed as something of an art, with decisions dominated more by informed judgment than by scientific techniques.

8-7. SUMMARY

Long-term debt may be viewed as an interest-bearing promissory note with a life of ten or more years. The holders of such financial instruments are creditors of the corporation, and are entitled to periodic interest payments and to repayment of principal. Failure by the corporation to meet such contractual payments can result in bankruptcy proceedings. In the event of liquidation, the claims of debt holders rank ahead of those of preferred or common shareholders. Because of their prior claims, debt, and sometimes preferred shares, are often termed senior securities.

Interest rates play a key role in the allocation of savings in the economy. Interest rate levels vary over time, and are also a function of the maturity of the debt, and of the risk of default as perceived by investors. The general level of interest rates is influenced by the supply and demand for newly issued securities. It is also influenced by the propensity of investors to retain various types of previously issued securities in their portfolios. Finally, the willingness of foreign investors to add to their holdings of Canadian long-term debt will further affect domestic interest rates.

[29]Weingartner has drawn attention to a dynamic programming model for handling the timing of refunding decisions. See M. Weingartner, "Optimal Timing of Bond Refunding", *Management Science*, March, 1967, pp. 511-514. Interested readers are also referred to J. Mao, *Quantitative Analysis and Financing Decisions*, New York: Macmillan Co., 1969, pp. 357-362.

Expectations regarding inflation will have a bearing on investor attitudes and will influence interest rates, since holdings of debt instruments are normally expected to provide positive real returns. Even where interest rates are marginally higher than the inflation rate, however, real returns may not materialize because of the distortions introduced by taxes. With interest income taxable, and interest expense tax deductible, the after-tax returns and the after-tax real costs of debt have tended to be negative in recent periods of inflation.

The term structure of interest rates, or the yield curve, relates interest rates to the maturity of debt. Long-term debt typically is riskier than short-term debt, both in terms of default risk and in terms of interest-rate risk. Interest-rate risk refers to fluctuations in the market price of debt as a consequence of shifts in interest rate levels. Thus, we would expect higher interest rates, reflecting a liquidity premium, for longer maturities, and an upward-sloping yield curve. However, expectations about future movements in short-term interest rates will also be relevant. Where expectations are for short-term rates to fall, this may result in an inverted term structure which may have a negative slope, at least over some range.

Debt may be classified by collateral requirements. Where debt is secured by a claim against specific assets it is called a bond, as distinct from a debenture which may have a general floating charge against all assets or be unsecured. Bonds or debentures may take various forms, and may incorporate a variety of features and provisions. Equipment trust certificates and income bonds were briefly reviewed.

For many borrowers, the relevant bond market is an international one. The main trade-off in moving abroad is between lower interest rates and the risk of future loss from unfavorable changes in the exchange rate. Recently, Canadian firms appear to have been less worried about foreign exchange risks, approaching the Euro-bond and foreign bond markets with increasing frequency. Where a firm regularly receives income in foreign currencies, it may hedge against foreign exchange risks. Foreign exchange risk may also be shifted or spread through the use of mixed-currency debt.

Periodic retirement of debt before its final maturity may take place either through sinking fund payments or by resorting to serial bonds. Purchases for sinking fund purposes create a demand for the bonds, thus improving investor liquidity. Extendible and retractable debt provide investors with some options for choosing the maturity of their debt. An issuing corporation may call debt prior to its maturity and may do so for several reasons, including refunding if interest rates have declined.

Refunding should be viewed as an investment, with the corporation committing funds in order to achieve future interest savings. Therefore, net present value analysis is appropriate. As refunding is essentially riskless and could conceptually be financed with debt, the discount rate to be applied is the after-tax cost on the new debt. Timing is critical in both refunding decisions and original issues of debt, making it important for the financial officer to exercise good judgment in assessing future movements of interest rates.

Questions for Discussion

1. What do you see as the effect of inflation on long-term debt issues? In your discussion recognize the problems faced both by investors and by the issuing corporation.
2. Briefly describe the general relationship between the market price, the maturity of a bond, and the prevailing interest rates. Verify your findings by providing examples using published financial data.
3. If bonds were floated with variable interest rates tied to prevailing market rates, what implications do you see for:
   (a) the investor?
   (b) the issuing corporation?
4. (a) Under what circumstances would you encourage a corporation to borrow in the international bond market?
   (b) How, if at all, would your answer change if the borrower were a municipality?
5. As a corporate financial officer contemplating debt financing, what would your reaction be if you noted that the yield curve had a negative slope?
6. It has been suggested that as the average maturity of a firm's borrowings is reduced, risk is being increased. Comment on this view.
7. Is the foreign-exchange risk greater for a Canadian firm borrowing in U.S. dollars in New York with or without a sinking fund provision? Assume that with the sinking fund debt is to be retired periodically.
8. Based on quotations of Government of Canada bonds as published in the financial pages, derive the current term structure of interest rates and prepare a graph along the lines of those given in Figure 8-1 and Figure 8-2. Briefly interpret the yield curve which you derive.
9. Canada Savings Bonds generally provide for redemption by the investor at any time at full face value. If prevailing interest rates should rise, what do you see as a consequence? What can the Government do to minimize such consequences?
10. By consulting the financial pages, and looking at bonds with a similar maturity, compare the current effective yields on debt issued by the Government of Canada, by various provincial governments, by various municipalities, and by corporations. Give a brief explanation of the yield differentials which you observe.

Problems with Solutions

1. A corporation has a $10 million, 25-year bond issue outstanding, carrying an 8% interest rate. This issue was sold 5 years ago (it has 20 years left to maturity), and can be called by the company at a premium of 7% on face value. A new $10 million, 20-year bond issue, carrying a 6% interest rate can be floated to replace the old issue. Issuing expenses for the new debt would be $100,000. The new bonds would be sold one month before the old issue is called, and excess funds could temporarily be invested to yield interest at 5%. The corporation has a 40% tax rate. Based on net present value analysis, should the old issue be retired and replaced with the proposed new issue?

Solution

The costs of proceeding with the refunding are: the issue costs, the call premium, and the interest expense on the old issue during the overlap period less the interest revenue earned during that period. The annual benefits are given by the decreased interest expenses on the new issue for the next 20 years.

(a) Initial costs of refunding (outflows)

	Before Tax	After Tax
Total issuing expenses	\$100,000	\$ 60,000
Call premium	\$700,000	\$700,000
Interest expense during overlap period (1/12 × .08 × \$10 million)	\$ 66,666	\$ 40,000
less: Interest received during overlap period (1/12 × .05 × \$10 million)	(\$41,666)	(\$ 25,000)
Total after-tax cash outflows		\$775,000

(b) Annual cash benefits (inflows)

	Before Tax	After Tax
Current annual interest payment	\$800,000	\$480,000
New annual interest payment	\$600,000	\$360,000
After tax annual savings		\$120,000

The discount rate to be applied is the after-tax cost on the *new* debt, or $(1 - 0.4) \times 6\% = 3.6\%$. The annuity factor is derived by interpolating between 3% and 4% as follows:

$$\left[\begin{array}{ll} \left[\begin{array}{ll} a_{20}3\% & 14.877 \\ a_{20}3.6\% & x \end{array}\right] & \\ a_{20}4\% & 13.590 \end{array}\right]$$

$$\frac{3.6\% - 3\%}{4\% - 3\%} = \frac{x - 14.877}{13.590 - 14.877}$$

From which we compute:

$x = a_{20}3.6\% = 14.10$

P.V. of annual savings $= \$120{,}000 \times a_{20}3.6\%$
$= \$120{,}000 \times 14.10$
$= \$1{,}692{,}000$

As the P.V. of the annual benefits exceeds the costs incurred, the issue should be refunded.

2. QT Ltd. has a \$25,000,000 bond issue with an original maturity of 20 years outstanding which pays a coupon rate of 9%. The issue, sold 10 years ago, has a call feature specifying varying premiums for early retirement. The premium applicable if the issue is retired during the current year is 5% of face value. Bond interest rates have fallen recently to 7.5% and QT is considering refunding with a new 10-year issue at the lower rates. Before-tax issuing expenses would amount to 1½% of the face value of the new issue. The corporate tax rate is 40%. Funds invested during the two-month overlap period between issuing the new bonds and calling the old ones would provide

a before-tax interest return of 6%. The after-tax average cost of capital for QT Ltd. is given as 12%.

(a) Based on a net present value analysis, should refinancing proceed?

(b) Assume further research indicates that all of the following will occur:

(i) Interest rates are expected to fall a further ½% in the next year.

(ii) During the year, underwriting and issuing expenses are expected to rise to 2% of face value, up from the current 1½%.

(iii) The call premium will drop to 4% of face value within the next year. If everything else remains as under item (a) above, should refinancing be undertaken now or be postponed the extra year?

Solution

(a) Costs and benefits relating to this refunding may be computed in the same manner as in question (1) above.

Initial costs of refunding (outflows)

	Before Tax	After Tax
Total issuing expenses	$ 375,000	$ 225,000
Call premium	$1,250,000	$1,250,000
Interest expense during overlap period (2/12 × .09 × $25 million)	$ 375,000	$ 225,000
less: Interest received during overlap period (2/12 × .06 × $25 million)	($ 250,000)	($ 150,000)
Total after-tax cash outflow		$1,550,000

Annual cash benefits (inflows)

	Before Tax	After Tax
Current annual interest payment	$2,250,000	$1,350,000
New annual interest payment	$1,875,000	$1,125,000
After-tax annual savings		$ 225,000

Present value of annual savings $= \$225,000 \times a_{10}4.5\%$

$= \$225,000 \times 7.917$*

$= \$1,781,325$

Benefits of refinancing exceeds costs by ($1,781,325 – $1,550,000) = $231,325, thus refinancing should proceed.

*4.5% is the after-tax cost of the new debt, here (1–.4)7.5%. $a_{10}4.5\% = 7.917$ is derived by interpolation of the appropriate figures in Table 4.

(b) Again, we must find the net advantage of refinancing. It should be kept in mind, however, that this advantage will accrue a year from now. Thus, this figure must be discounted back to the present when comparing net present values of part (a) and part (b).

Initial costs of refunding (outflows)

	Before Tax	After Tax
Total issuing expenses	$ 500,000	$ 300,000
Call premium	$1,000,000	$1,000,000
Interest expenses during overlap	as in part (a)	$ 225,000
Interest received during overlap*	as in part (a)	($ 150,000)
Total after-tax cash outflow		$1,375,000

*Note: This assumes that short-term interest rates have remained at 6% as under part (a) of this question.

Annual cash benefits (inflows)

	Before Tax	After Tax
Current annual interest payment	$2,250,000	$1,350,000
New annual interest payment	$1,750,000	$1,050,000
After-tax annual savings		$ 300,000

Present value of annual savings (as of the time of refunding, which is one year from now)

= $300,000 × $a_{9}4.2\%$
= $300,000 × 7.370
= $2,211,000

Benefits of refinancing exceed costs by
($2,211,000 – $1,375,000) = $836,000.

Thus, in itself this project should be undertaken. However, to compare the two alternatives available to QT Ltd., which are to refinance now at 7½% or to wait a year and refinance at 7%, we must discount to the present the benefit computed above for the second alternative. The question of what discount rate to use in arriving at this present value is no small question. While the after-tax cost of debt has been used for discounting future interest savings to this point, it is not applicable in this case. The after-tax cost of debt is only used because the savings generated are essentially riskless. However, in evaluating the second alternative and discounting to the present, there is some question whether the interest rate will fall to the anticipated 7% within one year. Hence, we should revert back to using a discount rate which reflects risk, such as the after-tax cost of capital, here 12%. Alternatively, some of the other techniques for risk analysis as discussed in Chapter 6 could be applied.

Discounting the total benefit of $836,000 at 12% for one year to bring it back to the present, we obtain the present value of this benefit as $836,000 × .893 = $746,548. This is still above the total benefit of refinancing immediately at 7½%, and indicates that refinancing should be postponed for a year.

The framework of analysis is further illustrated in the following graph:

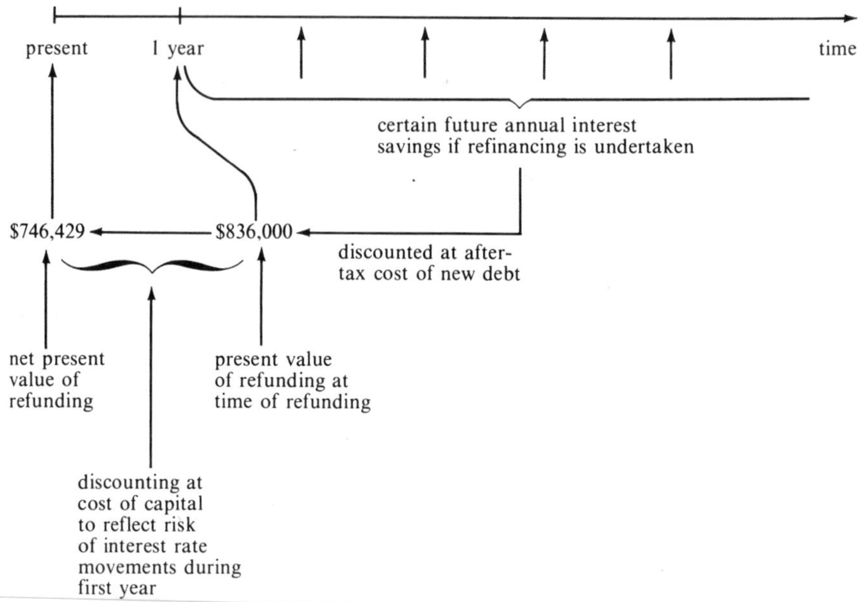

3. A Canadian company, Merlin Ltd., wishes to borrow enough money to finance a major plant expansion planned for next year. The money could be borrowed in Canada with a 10% interest rate, or in New York with only an 8% interest rate.
   (a) Given that the present spot rate is now $1 Cdn = $1.0275 US, to what value could the Canadian dollar fall in terms of the US dollar before annual interest charges of a loan negotiated in New York would exceed those of a loan arranged in Canada?
   (b) If Merlin wishes to borrow $20,000,000 Canadian dollars for a period of three years, and the expectations are that the exchange rate will adjust once over the next twelve months and then hold steady, how much can the Canadian dollar fall before it would make borrowing in New York unattractive? Ignore the time value of money.

Solution

(a) Given the present exchange rate, the total amount of US dollar borrowings would have to be 1.0275 times the Canadian funds required. For example, suppose Merlin needs to borrow Cdn $10,000,000. If it borrows in New York, it will be necessary to raise US $10,275,000. Thus, annual interest payments will be either 10% of Cdn $10,000,000 = Cdn $1,000,000, or 8% of US $10,275,000 = US $822,000. To eliminate the differential on annual interest payments, the exchange rate would have to adjust such that paying $1,000,000 interest in Canadian funds just equalled paying $822,000 in US funds. This would occur where the Canadian dollar was worth:

$$\frac{\$\ 822{,}000}{\$1{,}000{,}000} = \$0.822 \text{ US}$$

(b) If Merlin borrowed in Canada, the schedule would be as follows:

		Payments
Year 0	Borrow $20,000,000	
Year 1	Interest	$ 2,000,000
Year 2	Interest	$ 2,000,000
Year 3	Interest + Principal	$22,000,000

If Merlin borrowed in New York, the schedule would be as follows:

		Payments
Year 0	Borrow $20,000,000 Cdn = $20,550,000 US	
Year 1	Interest (.08 × Principal)	$ 1,644,000 US
Year 2	Interest	$ 1,644,000 US
Year 3	Interest + Principal	$22,194,000 US

Merlin must determine which of these cash flows is more favorable, given that the exchange rate may change during the next year. Note that the amount of American dollars to be paid if the loan is arranged in New York is certain, but because of the uncertainty of future exchange rates, the amount of Canadian dollars needed in this case is uncertain.

Merlin, if borrowing in Canada, would pay a total of $2 million + $2 million + $22 million = Cdn $26,000,000 until the debt is retired in Year 3. If borrowing in New York, total payments in US dollars would be $1,644,000 + $1,644,000 + $22,194,000 = $25,482,000.

Thus, in order to make borrowing in Canada attractive, the exchange rate would have to adjust so that paying $26,000,000 in Canadian funds was just equivalent to paying $25,482,000 in American funds. This would occur when the exchange rate went to:

$$\$1.00 \text{ Cdn} = \frac{\$25{,}482{,}000}{\$26{,}000{,}000} = \$0.980 \text{ US}$$

Note that the exchange rate determined above is not a function of the amount borrowed, but it does depend on the length of time for which the money is borrowed. For example, if the money was borrowed for four years instead of three, the exchange rate at which borrowing in New York would become unattractive would be:

$$\frac{\$25{,}482{,}000 + \$1{,}644{,}000}{\$26{,}000{,}000 + \$2{,}000{,}000} = \$0.969 \text{ US}$$

Additional Problems

1. Assume that on February 1, 1967, an investor purchased a 4 percent $1,000 Government of Canada bond which matures on February 1, 1981. The bond was priced to yield 5.75 percent to maturity.
   (a) Calculate the purchase price of the bond assuming that no brokerage charges were levied.
   (b) On February 1, 1970, this same bond was trading at $659.70. Calculate the yield to maturity from this later date.

2. Assume that on February 1, 1967, the 4 percent Government of Canada bonds due on February 1, 1973, were priced to yield 5.50 percent.
   (a) Calculate the price at which the bonds were trading.
   (b) On February 1,1970, this same bond issue was trading at $905.70. Calculate the yield to maturity from this later date.
3. Refer to problems 1 and 2 above. What is the difference in the yields and the market values of the bonds on February 1, 1967? On February 1, 1970? Is there any significant difference between the yields of the bonds on the two dates? Is there any significant difference in the market values on the two dates? Explain.
4. The ABC Company presently has $20,000,000 of 10½ percent long-term debentures outstanding. These debentures are due in 20 years and have a call premium of 5 percent. At present, the company can float a new issue of similar debentures with a 9 percent coupon. The issuing expenses will be $450,000. There will be a two-month overlap and any surplus funds can be reinvested at 4 percent in Treasury Bills. The corporate tax rate is 45 percent. No sinking fund feature is called for. Should the refunding be undertaken?
5. Company A has to decide whether or not to refund an outstanding bond issue. The old bonds are a $5 million issue which matures in 10 years. They carry a 10% coupon rate. The new bonds which can be issued are 10-year bonds of the same principal amount, but with an 8% coupon rate. Before-tax issuing expenses would be $20,000, while underwriting costs would be $100,000. There will be a two-month overlap period, during which 8% before-tax interest can be earned on the newly acquired funds. If Company A is taxed at 40% and the existing bond indenture requires an 8% call premium, decide whether Company A should take advantage of this bond-refunding opportunity.
6. Hardnose Corporation is faced with deciding whether or not to replace an existing 12% debenture issue with 20 years to maturity, callable at a 6% premium, with a similar 20-year issue at a nominal rate of interest of 10%. The new $30 million issue would be floated at par which corresponds to the amount still outstanding on the old issue. Legal and other issuance fees are estimated to be $110,000 if refinancing should occur. The corporate tax rate is 40 percent.
   (a) Based on a net present value analysis, should the refunding be undertaken? Assume there is no overlap period.
   (b) Assuming now that there is an overlap period of two months during which both issues will be outstanding, recompute the net present value of refunding. Note that excess funds (all new proceeds) can be invested in Treasury Bills (short-term government paper) to yield a before-tax interest return of 6 percent.
   (c) Given the problem as stated under item (a) above (without an overlap period), what is the maximum amount the firm could afford to pay in legal and issuing expenses in order for refunding to remain economically feasible? This information may be useful in negotiating the new issue, and in assessing whether the refunding decision is sensitive to changes in issuing costs.

(d) Assume that refunding is indicated based on a net present value analysis. Does that imply that the firm should automatically proceed, or are there any other considerations? Briefly discuss.

7. Assume a province's municipal financing authority borrowed 30 million Euro-Swiss francs in 1970 when the spot rate was 1 franc = $0.242. Repayment of principal was to be made 6 years later. Three percent in coupon rate was saved annually by having borrowed in the Euro-bond market at 6 percent rather than domestically. With interest paid annually at the end of each year, and the relevant spot rates as shown, analyze the wisdom of the decision using hindsight. Assume a discount rate of 12% for the financing authority in computing present values.

1971	1 franc = $0.246
1972	$0.259
1973	$0.318
1974	$0.330
1975	$0.394
1976	$0.385

Selected References

H. Bierman, "The Bond Refunding Decision", *Financial Management*, Summer, 1972, pp. 27-29.

O. Bowlin, "The Refunding Decision", *Journal of Finance*, March, 1966, pp. 55-68.

R. Dobell, and T. Sargent, "The Term Structure of Interest Rates in Canada", *Canadian Journal of Economics,* February, 1969, pp. 65-77.

L. Fisher, "Determinants of Risk Premiums on Corporate Bonds", *Journal of Political Economy*, June, 1959, pp. 217-237.

D. Fullerton, *The Bond Market in Canada,* Toronto: Carswell, 1962.

F. Jen, and J. Wert, "The Effect of Call Risk on Corporate Bond Yields", *Journal of Finance*, December 1967, pp. 637-651.

A. Kraus, "The Bond Refunding Decision in an Efficient Market" *Journal of Financial and Quantitative Analysis*, December, 1973, pp. 793-806.

R. Litzenberger and D. Rutenberg, "Size and Timing of Corporate Bond Fluctuations", *Journal of Financial and Quantitative Analysis*, January, 1972, pp. 1343-1359.

P. Lusztig and B. Schwab, "Units of Account and the International Bond Market", *Columbia Journal of World Business*, Spring, 1975, pp. 74-79.

B. Malkiel, *The Term Structure of Interest Rates,* Princeton: Princeton University Press, 1966.

R. Peters, *Economics of the Canadian Corporate Bond Market,* Montreal: McGill-Queens University Press, 1971.

G. Pinches and K. Minge, "A Multivariate Analysis of Industrial Bond Ratings", *Journal of Finance*, March, 1973, pp. 1-18.

T. Pogue and R. Soldofsky, "What's in a Bond Rating?", *Journal of Financial and Quantitative Analysis,* June, 1969, pp. 201-228.

G. Pye, "Value of a Call Option on a Bond", *Journal of Political Economy,* April, 1966, pp. 200-205.

G. Pye, "The Value of Call Deferment on a Bond: Some Empirical Results", *Journal of Finance,* December, 1967, pp. 623-636.

S. Robbins, "A Bigger Role for Income Bonds", *Harvard Business Review,* November-December 1955, pp. 100-114.

J. Scanlon, "Bell System Financial Policies", *Financial Management,* Summer, 1972, pp. 16-26.

J. Van Horne, *Function and Analysis of Capital Market Rates,* Englewood Cliffs: Prentice-Hall, Inc., 1970.

J. Van Horne, "Implied Fixed Costs in Long-Term Debt Issues", *Journal of Financial and Quantitative Analysis*, December, 1973, pp. 821-833.

M. Weingartner, "Optimal Timing of Bond Refunding", *Management Science*, March, 1967, pp. 511-524.

W. Winn, and A. Hess, Jr., "The Value of the Call Privilege", *Journal of Finance*, May, 1959, pp. 182-195.

Chapter 9
Preferred Shares

9-1. INTRODUCTION

As the name would suggest, the holder of preferred shares enjoys certain priorities and privileges as compared to the common shareholder. Actually, in terms of safety, the preferred shareholder finds himself somewhere between the investor in common shares and creditors including bond and debenture holders. Thus, in most but not all cases, in the event of liquidation the preferred shares rank ahead of the common stock in claims on corporate assets.[1] Furthermore, no dividends are payable to common shareholders until the dividend claims of preferred shareholders are satisfied. It is important to appreciate, however, that in most cases the preferred shareholders are entitled only to a fixed dividend and then only when declared by the corporation's board of directors. As will be seen, failure to declare a dividend on the preferred shares can cause management considerable inconvenience but will in no way place the company in default of its legal obligations.

9-2. THE USE OF PREFERRED SHARES

Table 9-1 summarizes the net new issues of longer-term corporate securities in Canada for selected years to 1975. A pattern of modest reliance on preferred shares is suggested. Further probing would show that privately owned public utilities account for a significant proportion of the preferred stock issues.

This is readily explained. Privately owned public utilities, like government-owned ones, have large capital requirements which can only be met by massive external financing. Unlike the Crown corporations, however, which can issue debt backed by government guarantees, privately owned public utilities have no such advantage and must maintain a credit rating for their debt instruments. Such ratings are very sensitive to the relative size of the equity base which underlies corporate borrowing. To maintain this equity base, that is, the level of contributions made by investors as distinct from creditors, without unduly diluting the position of common stockholders, utilities often turn to preferred stock issues.

[1]By way of illustration, the following wording is taken from the prospectus covering the Hudson's Bay Oil and Gas Company Limited five percent Cumulative Redeemable Convertible Preferred Shares Series A:

> In the event of liquidation, dissolution or winding up of the Company or other distribution of assets to shareholders, the holders of Preferred Shares Series A shall be entitled to receive the par value thereof together with all accrued and unpaid preferential dividends and, if such distribution shall result from voluntary action on the part of the Company, a premium of $3.50 per share if the date of distribution is before October 15, 1977 or $1.00 per share if such date is on or after that day, *all in priority to the holder of Common Shares* and any other shares ranking junior to the Preferred Shares Series A.

TABLE 9-1

Net New Issues of Longer-Term Corporate Securities and the Relative Position of Preferred Shares.

(in millions of dollars)

Years	Bonds	Preferred Shares	Common Shares	Total Long-Term External Sources	Preferred Shares as % of Long-Term External Sources
1966	972	177	388	1,537	11.5
1971	1,839	111	230	2,180	5.1
1972	1,670	199	417	2,286	8.7
1973	1,604	89	518	2,211	4.0
1974	1,844	452	280	2,576	17.5
1975	3,172	628	408	4,208	14.9

Source: Bank of Canada, *Bank of Canada Review.*

Apart from broadening the firm's equity base and thereby increasing its borrowing power, the issuance of preferred stock offers other advantages. In particular, it may appeal to a different class of investor—perhaps to an investor who wants more regular and certain income than would be provided by common shares, and a higher after-tax yield than would be offered by debt instruments.

During recent periods of inflation combined with high costs for money, investors have tended to view preferred shares with some suspicion. They have demanded and received relatively more attractive dividend rates along with added protective provisions. If we think back to our discussion of interest-rate risk in the previous chapter and recognize that preferred shares are almost always issued without maturity, the caution of investors is not difficult to appreciate. Thus, given increases in market yields of securities including dividends on preferred shares, caused perhaps by accelerating inflation, the market price of outstanding preferred shares would drop severely, mainly because preferred shares have no maturity and are, in essence, perpetual securities.

Example

The problem is dramatically illustrated by the 5½ percent $100 par value issue of Gaz Metropolitan which had a 1975-76 trading range of between $49 and $53. With no maturity date involved, and barring a future decline in the cost of money, an investor having to sell his shares would have lost about 50 percent of the original investment.

Example

The issue of convertible preferred shares by the Canada Development Corporation in 1975 serves to illustrate tailoring by an issuer to overcome market resistance. In terms of protective provisions, there was included a retractable feature providing for redemption at full face value between October 2 and December 31, 1980, at the holder's option. Therefore, the interest-rate risk as referred to above was mininized. Despite further inducements like a convertible feature allowing for conversion into common shares, and a bonus of two common shares to be received at specified future dates, the original dividend rate of 7 percent had to be adjusted to 8 percent to move the 125 million dollar offering which verged on collapse.[2]

9-3. RIGHTS OF PREFERRED SHAREHOLDERS

Though preferred shareholders have voting rights, the normal practice is to limit such voting privileges to special circumstances. A company will usually grant preferred stockholders the right to vote or perhaps to elect a specified number of directors if the corporation has been unable to pay preferred dividends for a specified period of time. Page 17 of the Trans-Canada Pipe Lines Prospectus (set out in Appendix A) typifies such provisions respecting voting rights. An unrestricted right to vote may prove quite meaningless in any case as the number of preferred shares outstanding is generally but a fraction of the number of common shares issued.

As mentioned, the preferred stockholders' right to income lies somewhere between the claim of common shareholders and those of creditors. The same is typically true in the event of liquidation, although in some instances their claim against company assets may not have priority over those of the common shareholders. To strengthen their position, preferred shareholders often insist on certain protective provisions not unlike those to be found in the trust deed of a debt issue. Provisions used may relate, for example, to limits *on further issues* of debt or preferred shares or to the maintenance of working capital and liquidity above a particular level. An investor should seek out the details as they do vary quite widely between issues.

9-4. FEATURES OF PREFERRED SHARES

Apart from the protective provisions cited, preferred shares have several vital features critical to both the issuing corporation and to the investors. Because their inclusion or exclusion may drastically change the nature of the financial instrument under discussion, the features warrant careful scrutiny.

Cumulative and noncumulative shares

Most issues of Canadian preferred shares have a *cumulative* feature which provides that any unpaid dividends mount up. Such previous defaults in dividend payments are called arrears which must be removed before any dividends can be paid on common shares or before the preferred shares can be redeemed. While the cumulative feature offers protection in the case of well established firms which in normal times would pay some dividends on their common shares, in extreme cases of financial difficulty even a cumulative feature may be of limited value. Clearly, until directors contemplate paying dividends to their common shareholders, investors holding cumulative preferred shares with dividends in arrears have almost no exercisable leverage

[2]For a more complete review see R. Jamieson, "By Gosh But (Second Time Around) the Price was Right", *Financial Post*, September 6, 1975, p. 13.

and may have to watch the market value of their holdings decline.[3] Only when earnings improvements suggest that the corporation may wish to make payments to common shareholders or may require additional external financing for expansion will the situation improve. In such circumstances, there may be anticipation of either cash dividends large enough to clear up the arrears on the preferred or, where the arrears are too great, of a recapitalization. An example of such a recapitalization might involve an offer to preferred shareholders to accept a combination of cash and other securities, such as common shares, in exchange for their preferred shares. Given resort to recapitalization, the relatively weak position of preferred shareholders may result in acceptance of quite a bit less than the equivalent of the arrears.

Example

> Perhaps the most striking recent illustration of this is to be found in a United States situation. By October of 1961, the Virginia-Carolina Chemical Company had arrears of over $90 on its $100 par value preferred shares. Despite good earnings over more recent periods, quarterly dividends were still withheld on the preferred, and arrears were allowed to increase. With voting power only 40 percent of that available to common shareholders, the preferred shareholders were unable to gain representation on the board of directors and accepted recapitalization. The plan entailed acceptance of a mix of one common share (market price around $37), 1.3 of a $50 par value 5 percent senior preferred share, and one $50 par value 5 percent convertible preferred share (convertible into 1.1 common shares), or roughly $145-worth of new securities for each share of the old preferred including arrears.

Where a share is noncumulative, dividends not declared in any period do not accrue and are lost to the shareholder. The investor's only protection stems from the fact that where dividends are passed up in a particular period, nothing can be distributed in that same period to common shareholders either. From earlier comments on cumulative shares, the very weak position of noncumulative preferred is obvious and tends to explain their infrequent usage.[4] The issuance of such securities is usually limited to situations involving reorganization to avoid bankruptcy or trade-offs where certain other benefits are substituted for the cumulative feature. The Class C *participating* preferred shares of Argus Corporation Limited exemplify such substitution for the cumulative feature.

Participating and nonparticipating shares

Nonparticipating preferred shares are more usual, and here the preferred shareholders receive nothing more than the specified dividend regardless of amounts distributed in dividends to the common shareholders. On the other

[3]It is becoming more common for preferred shareholders to gain token representation on boards of directors when there is nonpayment of dividends. To illustrate the type of provision that makes such representation possible, the preferred shares of George Weston Ltd. are nonvoting unless for two consecutive years the company fails to pay certain dividends; then, as a class, such shareholders may elect two directors.

[4]From the investor's standpoint, noncumulative preferred are even less attractive than income bonds.

hand, given a participating feature, investors in the preferred shares might be entitled to share in the good fortunes of the corporation over and above the regular dividends prescribed. Both the method and extent of participation can vary greatly, and, in some instances, the privilege is so limiting as to be essentially worthless.

Example

Cimco Limited Class A shares illustrate a constraint on the extent of participation. The Class A shares are preferred shares calling for annual cumulative dividends of $0.80. After paying dividends of $0.60 in any one year on the common shares, the Class A are entitled to additional noncumulative dividends of $0.10. Should $0.80 be paid on the common shares in any one year, the Class A are entitled to a further noncumulative $0.10 for a total of $1. There is no participation beyond this amount. The following dividend record shows the impact of both this noncumulative participation and the limit on participation. Note that in 1967 the company consciously paid a divided of $0.95 which fell short of the $1.00 normally called for. However, since dividends are noncumulative, this shortfall has no effect on subsequent dividend payments.

	1969	1968	1967	1966
Dividend Paid on Common	1.00	1.00	0.90	0.60
Dividend Paid on Class A	1.00	1.00	0.95	0.80

Example

A much more liberal participating feature is found with the Class A shares of Canadian Tire Corporation Limited. Here, the preferred shares carry a regular cumulative dividend of $0.08 per annum. When, in a fiscal year, dividends of $0.08 have been paid on common shares, all further dividends must be shared equally.

Corporate issuers must be cautious in their use of participating preferred shares, for such shares can restrict management's flexibility. If a firm has participating preferred shares outstanding, it may no longer be justifiable, for example, to recommend temporarily reduced dividend payments on common shares. The potential longer-term benefits from such sacrifices—namely the increased future profits attributable to the reinvestment of a larger proportion of earnings—must be subsequently apportioned to investors holding preferred shares.

Redemption features

Unlike debt instruments, preferred shares have no maturity date. Along with common shares, they are generally viewed as a permanent source of funds. Nevertheless, provision is often made for periodic retirement of preferred shares through a sinking fund feature and call provisions. Occasionally, preferred shares may also be redeemed at the investor's option, a feature which is designed to reduce the interest-rate risk. We saw an example of this in the 1975 offering of the Canada Development Corporation which was discussed above.

The Sinking Fund Feature

Sinking fund provisions are to be found in many issues of preferred shares, thereby allowing for gradual redemption of the securities. However, since no critical maturity dates are faced, the amounts involved are generally smaller than called for in the case of debt issues. The feature typically provides for a specified sum, which may vary over time, to be committed each year. Monies are then used either for the purchase of shares on the open market if they trade below a particular price or, failing that, for redemption of the necessary number of shares called by lot or tender. Other things being equal, issues with a sinking fund feature are more attractive to investors. With the issuing company, through a trustee, active in the open market to meet its sinking fund commitments, demand for the shares is enhanced. A secondary benefit of such redemptions is that the coverage of preferred dividends is increased as the number of outstanding shares declines.

Though the firm may benefit from inclusion of the sinking fund provision by getting away with a lower preferred dividend rate than would otherwise be the case, there are also disadvantages. A sinking fund commitment may, for example, represent a significant drain on corporate cash resulting in an increase in perceived financial risk. This would cause embarrassment when cash is scarce. For the protection of investors in preferred shares, dividend payments to common shareholders may be conditional upon sinking fund requirements being met.

Example

National Hees Industries Limited's 6 percent $10 par value cumulative convertible first preferred shares serve to illustrate possible weaknesses in the provisions just discussed.[5] Here, it was required that on or before March 1 of each year commencing with 1966, the company credit to a purchase fund an amount equalling *the lesser* of either (i) 3 percent of the par value of the greatest number of these preferred shares already issued or (ii) the previous fiscal year's consolidated net earnings after deducting dividends on the first preferred shares. Since the firm showed losses for a number of years, this provision proved to be rather ineffective as far as preferred shareholders were concerned.

The Call Feature

Most issues today include a call feature. This provision enables corporations to redeem an issue without having to rely on such potentially inexpedient procedures as the purchase of shares in the open market. Downward drifts in interest and dividend rates often invite refinancing of an outstanding issue with a new issue in order to obtain a more attractive dividend rate. Restrictive conditions connected with the issue might also prompt refinancing. In either circumstance, the advantage of a call feature is apparent. In practice, various types of call features are to be found, almost all calling for a premium to be paid to the investor as a compensation for the early retirement of the preferred shares. In

[5]Sometime after this issue, the firm was reorganized and renamed National Hees Enterprises Limited.

some cases, the premium changes over time, and the usual change is downward.

Example

The 6 percent $100 par value redeemable preferred shares of Canadian Utilities Limited, issued in February 1967, are redeemable at $105 on or before February 1, 1972. They are redeemable thereafter at $104 on or before February 1, 1977, at $103 on or before February 1, 1987, and after that date at a $1 premium.

9-5. THE REFINANCING DECISION

The motives for and the principles involved in refinancing an issue of preferred stock are similar to those involved in refunding bonds and were detailed in the previous chapter. The most common objective is to reduce the burden of dividend payments. Refinancing may be entered into when current dividend yields on preferred shares decline from previous levels. A firm then could float a new issue of preferred shares to replace an outstanding one, doing so at a lower dividend rate. On occasion, refinancing may also be considered in order to eliminate undesirable restrictions or provisions which are part of an outstanding issue.

Where refinancing takes place to reduce dividend costs, the analysis closely parallels that developed in the previous chapter for debt refunding. The present value of future dividend savings is compared with the initial after-tax outlays required to carry out the refinancing and, where a positive net present value results, a new issue is indicated. Differences between the analyses stem from the following factors:

(i) dividend payments on preferred shares are not tax deductible, hence no adjustments for taxes need to be made respecting savings in such outlays;
(ii) savings on future dividends, conceptually at least, accrue in perpetuity since preferred shares typically have no maturity.

Example

Consider a firm which has a $10,000,000, 9 percent issue of preferred shares outstanding. Because of declining yields in the capital markets, this issue could currently be refinanced with an otherwise identical offering, but at an 8 percent dividend rate. Issuing and underwriting expenses would be $250,000. The outstanding issue would have to be called for redemption at a premium of 7 percent. The firm would allow for an overlap period of 3 months during which time both issues would be outstanding. Excess funds which are available as a consequence of the overlap can be invested in treasury bills yielding interest of 8 percent before taxes. The firm's tax rate is given as 40 percent.

The initial after-tax outflows associated with refinancing are then computed as follows:

	Before Tax	After Tax
Issuing and underwriting expenses	$250,000	$150,000
Call premium on outstanding shares (7% × $10,000,000)	700,000	700,000
Dividend payments on old issue during overlap period (3/12 × 9% × $10,000,000)	225,000	225,000
Less: Interest on treasury bills during overlap period (3/12 × 8% × $10,000,000)	($200,000)	($120,000)
Total after-tax cash outflows on refinancing		$955,000

As a consequence of refinancing, annual savings in dividend payments would amount to $10,000,000 (9% – 8%) = $100,000. This is an after-tax figure as dividend payments are not tax deductible. Theoretically, at least, these savings are available in perpetuity. To compute their present value, we again discount using the firm's after-tax cost on long-term debt, for the same reasons as outlined in the previous chapter.[6] Assuming the firm's before-tax interest rate on long-term debt to be 10 percent, the present value of future dividend savings is found to be $100,000/.06 = $1,666,667. The net present value of refinancing is, therefore, $1,666,667 – $955,000 = $711,667, indicating that refinancing is appropriate.

Whether refinancing is actually undertaken at that time will depend on anticipated movements of dividend yields. If yields were expected to fall further, refinancing might be postponed to take advantage of even lower future rates. Similarly, if a drop in the call premium is provided for the near future, the firm may consider a postponement in order to save on redemption costs.

9-6. YIELDS

The set dividend on preferred shares combined with the lack of maturity date gives rise to significant price swings as monetary conditions and interest and dividend rates change. During periods of tight monetary posture and increasing interest rates, for reasons already noted, the outstanding issues of preference shares can be expected to fall away from their par values. During 1975, at a time when yields on long-term industrial bonds exceeded 10½ percent, the $100 par value 4⅜ percent B.C. Telephone preferred share reached a low price of $40.

[6]For this case we offer the following intuitive explanation for using the firm's after-tax cost of debt as the discount rate. From management's point of view, preferred dividends should always be met. Hence, any savings in dividend payments may, for the practical purposes of an internal decision, be considered certain. The financing necessary, therefore, for undertaking such a "sure investment" may be entirely through the less expensive source of long-term debt, with added leverage in the capital structure allowed for in recognition of the safe investment opportunity. Clearly, then, for the refinancing to be viewed as attractive, it must produce after-tax benefits which cover or exceed the after-tax cost of debt used to fund initial outlays.

Since interest rates tend to move with inflation, uncertainty about future inflation rates contributes to the risk of holding preferred shares.

Bondholders are creditors in receipt of protective provisions and remedies unavailable to preferred shareholders and, unlike preferred shareholders, have a legal right to periodic interest payments. Hence, in order to compensate for the increased risk, one would expect *a priori* a higher yield on a corporation's preferred issue than on its debt offering. A look at Canadian data, however, shows this not to be the case, and the greater before-tax yield on debt requires comment.

The irregularity is, in fact, the direct result of the dividend tax credit. With dividends from preferred shares qualifying for the dividend tax credit, while interest is fully taxed as income, many investors for tax reasons have a preference for dividend income. Therefore, while gross yields (that is, before personal income taxes) on preferred shares are below those of comparable bonds, on an after-tax basis their yield is generally greater.

Quite commonly, preferred shares are convertible, at the option of the holder, into another class of securities which are typically common shares. The terms of the conversion vary and, in most cases, expire with the passage of time. Such conversion features are provided as "sweeteners" designed to increase the attractiveness of the preferred shares. Consequently, preferred shares which are characterized by liberal conversion features may be issued at a lower dividend yield than would otherwise be possible. Analysis of convertible securities including convertible preferred shares can become quite involved and is of sufficient importance to warrant further treatment in a separate subsequent chapter.

9-7. ADVANTAGES AND DISADVANTAGES OF FINANCING WITH PREFERRED SHARES

Use of preferred shares, on a after-tax basis, costs the issuing corporation about twice as much as debt. The reason is that interest payments on debt are an allowable tax deductible expense, whereas dividends on preferred shares have to be paid out of after-tax earnings. Thus, a firm's reliance on preferred shares is frequently criticized. Their issuance might, however, be warranted on several grounds, particularly where the corporation is faced with large long-term requirements for funds. From the point of view of a creditor, preferred shares are viewed as equity capital, as any claims of preferred shareholders always rank junior to those of creditors. Thus, issuance of preferred shares will broaden the firm's equity base and increase its borrowing power without diluting the position of common shareholders. Furthermore, while the *cost* of preferred shares is higher than that of debt, the sinking fund provisions on most bonds will require after-tax cash outflows which may well overshadow both dividend and sinking fund requirements on the preferred shares.[7]

[7]A $10,000,000 twenty-year bond issue at eight percent could, in addition to interest of $400,000 in the first year, require a sinking fund payment of $500,000—both after tax. A comparable seven percent preferred issue might go with a one percent sinking fund feature and would, in the first year, entail $700,000 in dividends and a $100,000 sinking fund payment, all after tax.

Example

Compare a $10,000,000 bond issue carrying 10 percent interest with the same amount of preferred shares at a 9 percent dividend rate. Given a corporate tax rate of 45 percent, the after-tax cost of debt and of preferred shares becomes 5.5 percent and 9 percent respectively. However, the debt may call for sinking fund payments of $1,000,000 per year for 10 years, whereas the preferred shares require no such payments to be made. During the first year, the effective after-tax cash outflows become:

Debt: after-tax interest payment + sinking fund

= (1 − 0.45)$1,000,000 + $1,000,000

= $1,550,000

Preferred Shares: dividend payments = $900,000

This increasing drain on cash which frequently characterizes debt financing, combined with the contractual nature of debt obligations, will often curtail debt financing in cyclical industries. Additional debt may also be ruled out because of constraining provisions already in effect, or because of unacceptable conditions being proposed for the issue. Should the financial markets be unreceptive to new offerings of common shares, preferred shares could remain the only alternative.[8]

In a frequently cited paper, Donaldson has defended the use of preferred shares while making the following observations:

1. The similarities between preferred stock and debt should not lead to a disregard of important distinctions between the relative risks of financing by these two securities. When the chips are down—when cash inadequacy threatens—these differences can be all-important. The major difference is that the legal obligation of meeting interest payments on debt creates a risk of insolvency, while the discretionary obligation of meeting dividends does not.
2. Comparisons between the merits of debt and preferred stock tend to mislead and confuse the issue, for the real contest is not between debt and preferred shares. Debt is a cheaper source than preferred and should be used up to an acceptable limit.
3. Preferred stock should be used as a complement, and not as a substitute, for debt whenever the debt capacity of the company is fully utilized.
4. The real contest is between preferred stock and retained earnings. A policy which automatically gives priority to retained earnings as a source of funds by curtailing dividend payments on common shares

[8]Preferred shares may also play a useful role in financing the take-over of other firms, particularly in situations where shareholders of the corporation to be acquired seek not only an immediately identifiable price for their shares, but attractive dividends and some opportunity for future capital gains as well. By using convertible preferred shares when making their offer, the acquiring firm may not only meet the seller's desires, but can postpone the dilution which would result when its own common shares are used to finance the acquisition. Quite complex tax implications may also encourage resort to convertible preferred shares, but such considerations are beyond the scope of this text.

may be favoring the high-tax-bracket shareholder at the low-tax-bracket shareholder's expense.[9]

This last issue will be explored more fully in Chapter 20. Briefly, retention of earnings tends to make the firm's shares more valuable, implying a trade-off between current dividend income and capital gains.

**ADDITIONAL SELECTED TOPICS*

**9-8. TAX-DEFERRED PREFERRED SHARES

As noted in our earlier discussion of the tax environment, it is possible under existing legislation for a corporation to declare dividends payable out of the firm's tax paid undistributed surplus and subsequently out of its 1971 capital surplus on hand. In such instances, the dividends would not constitute taxable income in the hands of investors, though in computing capital gains the adjusted cost base of each holder's shares would have to be reduced by the amount of the dividends received. Expressed another way, dividends in this form may be viewed as a nontaxable return of capital, with taxes deferred until capital gains are realized.

Corporations very quickly recognized the benefits this provision could confer on certain investors. With such opportunities in mind, securities including preferred shares were especially designed and offered to take full advantage of these legislative provisions.

Example

Such an offering is provided by the 1976 issue of 8 percent tax deferred preference shares by the Algoma Steel Corporation. It provides an excellent illustration of such financial instruments tailored to meet the needs of particular groups of investors with funds raised at a lower dividend rate than would otherwise have been possible.

The interesting wrinkle to this issue was an exchange privilege any time after September 1, 1988 extended to investors. Under the option, each $25, 8 percent preferred share could be exchanged for one 9¾ percent cumulative redeemable preferred share, with the exchange *not* regarded as a disposition for income tax purposes. To illustrate the full significance of this option, consider that if tax-deferred dividends were paid without interruption until September 1, 1988, they would have totalled $24.76 per share, reducing the cost base of an initial purchaser from $25 to $0.24. If the initial purchaser were to sell his shares in the market, at say $25, one half of the excess over the $0.24 adjusted cost base, or $12.38, would have to be included in his 1988 income as a taxable capital gain.

If the shares were retained, one-half of any subsequent tax-deferred dividend would have to be viewed as a taxable capital gain in the year of receipt.[10] Through exercise of the exchange privilege, however, taxes

[9] G. Donaldson, "In Defense of Preferred Stock", *Harvard Business Review*, July-August, 1962, pp. 123-136.

[10] When an adjustment to the cost base brings the base to a negative amount, that amount is immediately considered a capital gain.

would again be deferred, with the new preferred shares assuming the adjusted cost base of the old tax-deferred issue. Thus, in effect, no taxable capital gains need be recognized, although dividends on the new preferred shares must, of course, be normal taxable dividends. Since preferred shares do not have a maturity date, the attractiveness of such an issue to investors faced with high marginal tax rates is understandable.

We note that the 1977 Budget proposals of the Minister of Finance, if approved, may eliminate both tax-deferred preferred and common shares by 1979.

9-9. SUMMARY

In terms of claims on income and assets, preferred shares fall somewhere in between debt and common shares. Preferred shareholders are entitled to a dividend which is normally fixed and expressed as a percentage of the shares' par value. However, such dividends do not represent a contractual obligation on the part of the issuing corporation. While failure to meet dividend payments on preferred shares may result in inconveninece to the firm's management, and preclude it from paying dividends on common shares, it does not have any legal consequences and cannot lead to bankruptcy. Dividend payments on preferred shares have to be met out of after-tax income, making preferred shares a more expensive source of financing than debt. In the hands of investors, such dividends qualify for the dividend tax credit. In case of liquidation, claims of preferred shareholders on assets rank ahead of those of common shareholders, but are junior to the claims of creditors.

Features attached to preferred shares vary significantly between issues. The main distinguishing features include whether dividends are cumulative or noncumulative, whether shareholders participate in additional earnings, whether and under what circumstances shareholders have voting rights, whether and under what conditions the preferred shares can be redeemed, whether a sinking fund is provided for, and whether conversion privileges are attached. A special feature sometimes encountered provides for dividends which are paid out of the firm's tax paid undistributed surplus and which are tax deferred in the hands of investors. Most preferred shares outstanding are cumulative, nonparticipating, nonvoting, redeemable, nonconvertible, and have a sinking fund feature.

Refinancing may be undertaken to remove restrictive provisions or, more commonly, to reduce dividend charges. Analysis of refinancing closely follows the approach discussed for the refunding of debt. Important distinctions to be recognized are that there is no tax shield on dividend savings, and that preferred shares do not have a maturity date, so that savings in dividends conceptually accrue in perpetuity.

Questions for Discussion

1. Discuss the comparative advantages and disadvantages of preferred shares versus bonds from both the investor's point of view and the corporation's point of view. Would you expect preferred shares or bonds to provide a higher before-tax yield? Briefly discuss.
2. Would you generally expect the interest-rate risk to be higher for bonds or for

preferred shares? That is, would you expect the market prices of bonds or of preferred shares to be more sensitive to changes in prevailing interest rates?
3. With debt being cheaper for a corporation than preferred shares, why would any corporation issue preferred shares and not debt?
4. How would you evaluate a sinking fund feature both from the corporation's and from an investor's point of view? In deciding whether or not to provide for a sinking fund, what are the tradeoffs facing the corporation?
5. Everything else being equal, would you expect a preferred share with a call feature to have a higher or a lower dividend rate than a preferred share without a call feature? Discuss.

Problems with Solutions

1. Preferred shares with a face value of $50 and entitling the holder to dividends of $4.50 a year are outstanding. Compute the market price of the shares, given that:
   (a) current dividend rates on comparable preferred shares are 10%,
   (b) current dividend rates on comparable preferred shares are 7%.
   (c) Given the shares are currently trading at $57, compute their effective yield.

Solution

(a) The formula for the present value of an annuity was derived in Chapter 4 as:

$$PV = A \left[\frac{1-(1+i)^{-n}}{i}\right]$$

Where, as in dividends on preferred shares, we have conceptually a perpetual annuity, the number of periods n becomes infinite. The above formula simply reduces to:

$$PV = \frac{A}{i}$$

Thus, we have $A = \$4.50$ and $i = .10$:

$$PV = \frac{\$4.50}{.10} = \$45.00$$

The preferred shares should trade at the present value of the future dividends, here $45.00. The result is intuitively obvious, in that a perpetual annuity of $4.50 will provide a 10 percent return each year on a $45.00 investment.

(b) In exactly the same fashion as in (a), we find:

$$PV = \frac{\$4.50}{.07} = \$64.29$$

(c) Simply rearrange the formula in (a):

$$\frac{A}{PV} = i$$

$$\frac{\$\ 4.50}{\$57.00} = 7.9\%$$

2. In 1971, Blazer Ltd. issued 50,000 cumulative preferred shares each with a par value of $100 and with an 8 percent annual dividend, payable quarterly. At the same time the company issued 500,000 common shares to bring the total number of common shares outstanding to 1,000,000.

   In 1974, Blazer started having financial difficulties and from the third quarter of 1974 on, the dividends on the preferred shares were missed.

   By late 1975, the financial difficulties seemed to be clearing up, and by early 1976 Blazer's management wished to pay off the arrears on the preferred so as to be able to pay dividends on the common stock. The current depressed price of Blazer's common stock was of some concern as it was hoped that a new common issue may be floated in early 1977.

   The tax rate for Blazer Ltd. was 40%.

   (a) Calculate the amount in arrears on each preferred share as of the end of the fourth quarter of 1975.
   (b) Assume before-tax earnings for 1976 turned out to be $3,000,000. Given that shares traded at 7 times earnings which were available to common shareholders, what was the market price of the common shares in early 1977?

Solution

(a) Dividends on preferred shares due each quarter may be calculated as:

$$50{,}000 \times \$100 \times 8 \text{ percent} \times \tfrac{1}{4} = \$100{,}000$$

Blazer Ltd. missed dividend payments for the two last quarters of 1974 and the full year of 1975. Thus, they were six quarters, or $600,000, in arrears.

There were 50,000 preferred shares ($5,000,000/$100 face value per share) outstanding, so arrears per share as of the end of 1975 were:

$$\frac{\$600{,}000}{50{,}000} = \$12 \text{ per share}$$

(b) Earnings per share could be calculated as follows:

Earnings before taxes	\$3,000,000
Tax (40%)	1,200,000
Net income	\$1,800,000
Payment of arrears on preferred stock	600,000
Payment of preferred stock dividends for 1976	400,000
Net earnings available for common shares	\$ 800,000

Earnings per share: $\frac{800{,}000}{1{,}000{,}000 \text{ shares}} = \$0.80$ per share

Market price of the common shares was \$0.80 × 7 = \$5.60.

3. Cracker Corp. has 50,000 preferred shares outstanding. The dividend on each \$100 par value share is \$10 per annum. Mr. Lester, the president, is considering refinancing the issue as the now prevailing dividend rate is only 9%. A call premium of 5% would have to be paid if the old preferred issue was retired. Cracker Corp.'s tax rate is 40%. Issuing expenses for the new issue would be \$200,000. To be safe, Mr. Lester is allowing for an overlap of six months, during which time the money could be placed with a bank to yield 7%. The rate at which new debt could currently be floated is 10%.

   (a) Determine if it is currently worthwhile refinancing the preferred shares on a net present value basis.
   (b) If the financing proceeds, how many years will pass before the present value of dividend savings equals the refinancing costs, that is, until the company breaks even on the refinancing?
   (c) Assume there is a possibility that in the near future dividend rates may fall further to 8%. Assume all other factors remain the same. Given a .5 chance of rates going to 8%, .1 of them staying at 9%, and .4 of them going back to 10%, should Cracker refinance now or later if the decision is to be based on expected net present value?

Solution

(a)

	Before Tax Cost	After Tax Cost
Issuing and underwriting expenses	\$200,000	\$120,000
Call premium	250,000	250,000
Dividend payments on the old issue during overlap period	250,000	250,000
Interest received during overlap period	(175,000)	(105,000)
Total cost of refinancing		\$515,000

Annual savings by refinancing: \$5,000,000 (10% − 9%) = \$50,000

Debt could be floated at 10 percent, or at an after-tax cost of $(1-0.4) \times 10\% = 6\%$. Taking 6% as the discount rate, the present value of perpetual future dividend savings becomes:

$$\frac{\$50{,}000}{.06} = \$833{,}333$$

$$\begin{aligned} \text{Present value of refinancing} &= \text{present value of savings} - \text{refinancing costs} \\ &= \$833{,}333 - \$515{,}000 \\ &= \$318{,}333 \end{aligned}$$

Based on a net present value analysis, it would be worthwhile to refinance.

(b) Dividend savings are \$50,000 per year. Total costs were \$515,000, and the present value of future dividend savings over n years just has to equal this amount. We have \$50,000 $a_n 6\%$ = \$515,000.

$$a_n 6\% = \frac{\$515{,}000}{\$\ 50{,}000} = 10.3$$

Consulting an annuity table, we find for 6% and 16 years, $a_{16}6\% = 10.106$, and for 17 years, $a_{17}6\% = 10.477$. By interpolating we find that it would take about 16.5 years of dividend savings to recover the initial refinancing costs.

(c) To arrive at a decision, it is first necessary to compute the advantages or penalties for various possible changes in dividend rates. In item (a) above, we calculated the net advantage of refinancing to be \$318,333. As rates are already 9%, there is no further advantage to be gained if rates later are still 9%. However, should rates move back to 10%, we would lose the \$318,333 advantage presently available. Should rates move down to 8%, the dividend saving would be an additional \$50,000 per year over the 9% rate. Computing the present value as in item (a) above, this would result in a further present value of future dividend savings of \$833,333. The expected present value of waiting can be computed as follows:

	Additional Gain/(Loss)	Probability	Gain/(Loss) × Probability
10% dividend	(\$318,333)	.4	(\$127,333)
9% dividend	0	.1	0
8% dividend	\$833,333	.5	\$416,667

Based on expected net present value (E(NPV) = \$289,334), we should wait and refinance later. We note that such action would entail some risk, with a 40 percent probability of losing even the gains which are currently available. Therefore, this trade-off between expected gains and risk needs to be considered before arriving at a final decision.

Additional Problems

1. Coronet Sales Ltd. has $1,500,000 in 9% preferred shares outstanding. Current dividend rates have fallen so that a similar issue today would carry an 8% dividend rate. Mr. Grey, the vice-president, is considering the possibility of refinancing.

   If the issue were refinanced, new issuing and underwriting expenses would be $250,000. There is an overlap period during which the extra costs of dividend payments on the old issue exceeds after-tax revenue from short-term investments by $10,000. Also, a call premium of 8% would have to be paid on the old preferred issue. The tax rate for Coronet is 40% and bonds could currently be issued bearing 11% interest.
   (a) Should refinancing be undertaken?
   (b) How far would dividend rates have to drop so that refinancing just became marginally attractive?
2. The Super Hot Pizza Parlor undertook an extensive expansion program 10 years ago. The funds needed for this purpose were obtained by issuing $5,000,000 of 7 percent cumulative preferred shares. Dividend rates have declined since, and the company is now considering refinancing its preferred shares. The old shares have a call premium of 6 percent if called within 20 years from the date of the original issue. Issuing and underwriting expenses for a new issue are expected to be 4 percent of the gross dollar amount issued. There would be a one-month overlap if the refinancing were undertaken. Excess funds could be invested and would generate $12,332 in interest revenue (before tax). The corporation's tax rate is 40 percent. The corporation could currently issue debt at an interest rate of 10 percent. The company feels that any refinancing should pay for itself in at most 30 years; thus, dividend savings will only be considered for the first 30 years in the analysis. What would be the maximum rate of dividend on its new issue, expressed in percent, that the company could afford to pay if refinancing is to be undertaken?
3. Preferred shares with a dividend rate of 8 percent and a face value of $30 are held by an investor. What is the market price of such a share if currently prevailing dividend yields in the market are:
   (a) 9%
   (b) 6%

   Calculate the effective yield of the share if it is trading at:
   (c) $36
   (d) $19
4. FGH Co. in a given year has total earnings after tax of $2,400,000. Outstanding are 200,000 common shares and 200,000 $50 par value 10% preferred shares. Dividends on the preferred shares are paid quarterly, and the dividend for the first quarter of the year was not paid. Calculate earnings per common share for the year and dividend payments per preferred share assuming the preferred shares are:
   (a) cumulative, nonparticipating; arrears have been cleaned up.
   (b) noncumulative, nonparticipating.

5. Canbye Limited is a corporation engaged in general wholesaling. In order to finance an expansion 7 years ago, Canbye issued $1,000,000 in 8%, $50 par value preferred stock, which is callable at a 7% premium. The expansion turned out to be ill-timed with the result that starting 5 years ago, the dividends were missed.

This year earnings are finally back to a reasonable level (after 40% tax, earnings are $600,000) and Canbye would like to pay off the arrears so as to bolster the sagging market price of the common shares, which currently trade at $6. 500,000 common shares are currently outstanding.

Canbye is considering the following two alternatives:

(a) Pay off the arrears and call the preferred issue. The retirement of the preferred could be financed 50% by a short-term bank loan with an interest rate of 11%, and 50% by long-term debt at an interest rate of 8%.

(b) Exchange each preferred share for 8 common shares. In this case, arrears would not be paid. It is expected that preferred shareholders would accept such an offer.

Which alternative would leave the present common shareholders with higher current earnings per share?

Selected References

J. Bildersee, "Some Aspects of the Performance of Non-Convertible Preferred Shares", *Journal of Finance*, December, 1973, pp. 1187-1201.

G. Donaldson, "In Defense of Preferred Stock", *Harvard Business Review*, July-August, 1962, pp. 123-136.

H. Elsaid, "The Function of Preferred Stock in the Corporate Financial Plan", *Financial Analysts Journal*, July-August, 1969, pp. 112-117.

D. Fischer and G. Wilt, Jr., "Non-Convertible Preferred Stock as a Financing Instrument, 1950-1965", *Journal of Finance*, September, 1968, pp. 611-624.

G. Pinches, "Financing With Convertible Preferred Stock, 1960-1967", *Journal of Finance*, March 1970, pp. 53-63.

R. Sprecher, "A Note on Financing Mergers with Convertible Preferred Stock", *Journal of Finance*, June, 1971, pp. 683-686.

R. Stevenson, "Retirement of Non-Callable Preferred Stock", *Journal of Finance*, December, 1970, pp. 1143-1152.

Chapter 10
Common Shares

10-1. INTRODUCTION

Common shares[1] are certificates of residual ownership. Collectively, therefore, common stockholders own the company and assume the ultimate risk associated with ownership. Their liability, however, is usually restricted to the amount of their investment. Shareholders are entitled to corporate earnings and assets only after all prior and senior claims such as bond interest and sinking fund payments, preferred share dividends and provisions for income taxes have been satisfied. For this reason, shareholders are also called residual owners.

Common shares have no maturity. The purchase or sale of outstanding shares usually involves no legal formalities, and usually has no direct impact on corporate operations. If the firm is publicly owned, the shares are traded either on a stock exchange, or on the over-the-counter market. Some purchase and sale of securities approved or listed for trading on a stock exchange may take place in the *"third market"*. This term refers to transactions in listed securities which are not put through the stock exchange but are effected elsewhere. For instance, financial institutions may arrange for the purchase or sale of a large block of securities without going through the stock exchange, partly in order to reduce transaction costs.

Common shares have been described as *risk capital.* The basis for this appellation is not simply their weak residual position in the event of reorganization or liquidation following insolvency. Some other factors can quite readily be illustrated.

Example

Consider a corporation with debt preferred and common shares as follows:

Long-term debt at	8 percent	$10,000,000
Preferred shares at	7 percent	$5,000,000
Common shares	1,000,000 authorized and issued.	

With corporate taxes taken at 50 percent, assume that annual operating revenue before financing charges and taxes (commonly called earnings before interest and taxes or EBIT is normally $2,600,000. Case A below reflects resultant earnings per share. Cases B and C, on the other hand, illustrate the impact of a 50 percent shift in EBIT in either direction.

As can be seen, the assumed variations in EBIT only affect common shareholders, as interest payments on debt and dividend payments on preferred shares are maintained at a constant level. Furthermore, a given percentage change in EBIT can cause a magnified percentage change in earnings per share. Therefore, a ±50 percent change in EBIT causes earnings per share to fluctuate by ±118 percent ($1.20/$0.55).

[1]The terms share and stock are used interchangeably and refer to the certificate evidencing ownership interest.

	Case A (Norm)	Case B (50 percent decline in EBIT)	Case C (50 percent increase in EBIT)
EBIT	$2,600,000	$1,300,000	$3,900,000
Interest charges	800,000	800,000	800,000
Taxable income	$1,800,000	$ 500,000	$3,100,000
Income after tax	$ 900,000	$ 250,000	$1,550,000
Dividends on preferred	350,000	350,000	350,000
Earnings available to common shareholders	$ 550,000	($ 100,000)	$1,200,000
Earnings per share	$0.55	($0.10)	$1.20

The residual position of the common shareholder who receives earnings only after all other financing charges have been met gives rise to this more pronounced variability in earnings per share and the "risk capital" designation.

10-2. FEATURES OF COMMON STOCK

Share certificates are usually issued as an engraved or printed form with space on the front for the owner's name and the number of shares owned. Like most financial assets, the stock certificate is generally engraved on quality paper so as to minimize the possibility of forgery. A *street certificate* is a share certificate generally made out in the name of an investment dealer or a stockbroker. Like a bond in bearer form, the share certificate in street form is more conveniently bought and sold as the name of the owner does not need to be changed every time the share changes hands. All dividend cheques, financial reports, and other communications between the corporation and its owners are sent to the party named on the certificate. Where the shares are in street form, such communications will reach the ultimate owner via the broker or dealer named on the certificate. It follows that if an investor held dividend-paying shares in street form, dividend cheques might have to be tracked down, making it more sensible to have such shares registered in the owner's name.

Authorized, issued, and outstanding shares

A firm's corporate charter specifies the number of shares *authorized*, and this authorization represents the maximum number of shares the company can issue. A company is able to amend its charter, however, to alter the number of authorized shares. Although amending the charter is not a difficult procedure, it does require the approval of existing stockholders, and will take time. For this reason corporate management typically prefers the position of having a significant number of shares authorized but as yet unissued. These unissued shares introduce flexibility in that it remains possible, for example, to grant stock options, to issue additional shares to pursue mergers, or to raise additional capital on short notice.

Outstanding shares represent the portion of authorized stock which has been sold or otherwise issued by the corporation and is presently held outside the company. If the firm has not repurchased any of its issued shares, then the amounts issued can be equated with outstanding stock.

Subject to various constraints, several provincial statutes and the *Canada Business Corporations Act* allow companies to repurchase their outstanding common shares. The federal legislation, for example, authorizes such actions provided the firm is solvent before any repurchases and will not be pushed into insolvency through the transactions. There is the further requirement that the realizable value of the corporation's assets after any repurchase of shares be at least equal to the sum of its liabilities and stated capital of all classes.[2] Any purchase can either be made by simply buying shares in the open market, or it may be initiated by invitation addressed to all shareholders for tenders of shares, and purchases have to be made *pro rata* from the shares tendered. The repurchase of shares and its motivations and effects will be discussed in more detail in the section of this book dealing with dividends.

Par and no par value

The shares of Canadian companies either have a *par value* or are without par value.[3] The par value of a share is its stated monetary face value. A stock may have a par value of one cent, or $100,000, or any other value. The more usual par value for mining stocks is one dollar, while par values of five, ten, and twenty-five dollars are common for shares of industrial corporations. At one time all shares issued had a stated par value. In 1912, when the issuance of no par value shares was first authorized by New York, this changed. Today, shares being issued are predominantly without par value, and firms incorporated federally under the *Canada Business Corporations Act* may no longer issue shares having a par value.[4]

The advantage of shares without par value is that such shares are always fully paid and nonassessable, regardless of the price at which they are sold to the public. The terms fully paid and nonassessable imply that investors who purchased these shares have paid the full price for these shares, and cannot be required to make any additional payments. Mining stock excepted, shares with a par value cannot be issued as fully paid and nonassessable unless cash, or a fair equivalent in property or past services at least equal to par value, is received by the company as consideration. Present shareholders are potentially liable for the difference between par and original issue price if the shares held were initially sold at a discount from par value and are still not fully paid. The company, if the need arises, can call on present shareholders for all or part of this difference. This reflects, for example, the position of shareholders in certain Canadian insurance companies.

Once shares are fully paid and nonassessable, the significance of par value

[2]1974-75 (Can.), c.33, s.32.

[3]See, for example, *Bank Act*, R.S.C. 1970, c. B-1, s.9 which calls for bank shares to have a par value of one dollar or any multiple thereof but not to exceed ten dollars.

[4]1974-75 (Can.), c. 33, s.24(1).

becomes quite limited. A par value figure simply provides information identifying the lowest possible investment behind the company's historical offerings of shares. Unfortunately, common shares having a par value can confuse uninformed investors in that a particular value for the security may be incorrectly assumed. Thus, when a stock with a par value of, say, ten dollars is selling at five dollars, an uninformed investor may deem it to be worth ten dollars and therefore underpriced and a good buy. Such an investor may not realize that there is usually little relationship between the market price which reflects current operating conditions and future prospects, and the par value of common shares which merely provides some historical information. Hence, the mandatory use of no par value common shares is an understandable development.

The accounting treatment differs somewhat depending on whether or not the shares have a par value.

Example

Suppose a newly formed provincially incorporated company sold 100,000 common shares priced to net the company 20 dollars a share, and that the par value was 5 dollars per share. The equity portion of the balance sheets would appear as:

Common stock ($5 par value)	$ 500,000
Paid-in capital	1,500,000
Net worth	$2,000,000

The paid-in capital indicates the amount by which proceeds from the issue exceeded the par value. If the same shares were without par value, the balance sheet would generally read:[5]

Common stock	$2,000,000
Net worth	$2,000,000

Book, market, and other values of common stock

The value of a share of common stock can be measured in a variety of ways. The more commonly used gauges are *book value, market value*, and *intrinsic value.* Each measure will be considered in turn.

The book value of a common share is the net worth of a firm as shown on the balance sheet less the par value of preferred stock outstanding, divided by the number of common shares outstanding. Thus, book value is determined by a firm's balance sheet, and is influenced by accounting practice.

Example

The aggregate book value of the common stock of British Columbia Forest Products Limited as at December 31, 1971 may be determined from the firm's equity position as set out in Table 10-1. It is found to be ($94,433,000 − $10,138,000)/3,718,569 = $22.67.

[5]Shares without par value may be carried on the books either at the market price at which they are issued or at some stated value. In the latter case, the difference between issuing price and stated value would be reflected on the books as paid-in capital.

TABLE 10-1

British Columbia Forest Products Limited
Shareholders' Equity Section
of Consolidated Balance Sheet
as at December 31, 1971

Shareholders' Equity	
Share Capital	
6% cumulative preferred shares of $50 par value, 1966 issue, redeemable at $53	
Authorized — 240,000 shares	
Issued — 202,760 (1970 — 209,960 shares)	$10,138,000
Common shares of no par value	
Authorized — 5,000,000 shares	
Issued — 3,718,569 shares	32,052,000
	$42,190,000
Retained Earnings	52,243,000
	$94,433,000

Source: *1971 Annual Report.*

In general, the market value of an object or asset is the price at which it can be sold. In the case of common shares we may distinguish between two market values—a liquidating value and a value as a going-concern. The *liquidating value* of a common share is its proportionate interest in the residual amount to be realized when a firm's assets are sold off. The share's going-concern value, on the other hand, can be viewed as its proportionate interest in the net amount to be realized when the firm is sold as a complete operating concern.

Conceptually, the total book value of common shares could correspond to the liquidating value of the company. In practice, however, the two values seldom coincide. Even if we disregard the costs of liquidating assets, we would find liquidation value to be the lesser amount for many firms because many assets are saleable only at distress prices. For example, a smelter somewhere in the north may have a considerable book value based on its original costs, yet be almost unsaleable if it had to be liquidated. On the other hand, when companies show certain assets such as land and mineral rights at conservative values on their books the liquidating value may be significantly higher than the book value.

An inflationary setting such as the one recently experienced contributes to a relative increase in liquidation values as compared to book values, as market prices increase continually whereas book values continue to be based on historical acquisition costs. Occasionally, the estimated liquidating value may exceed market value of the firm's common shares.

A firm may have shown poor operating performance with several years of losses which caused a depressed market price for its shares. Yet, such a firm may have substantial land holdings which could be quite valuable, causing the firm's estimated liquidation value to exceed the market price of its common stock. Under these circumstances the company becomes a candidate for raiding and take-over. A raider buys company stock either in the open market or by a tender offer to existing shareholders so as to obtain a controlling interest. Once control is attained, at least partial liquidation may follow. A profit per share is realized which equals the net liquidating value per share less the price paid per share. The managements of firms susceptible to such raids are naturally wary of major transactions in the company's stock and watch for signs of accumulation.

The going-concern value of a common share is reflected by the current price at which the stock is traded. For shares of listed companies and actively traded over-the-counter stocks, price quotations on actual trades are readily available. However, for the shares with thin or inactive markets, or shares of closely held corporations, price quotations may not be readily available or, if available, they may reflect only the sale of a few shares and not the market value of the shares as a whole. In such cases, quoted prices may become a poor approximation for the overall going-concern value of the firm.

The going-concern market value of common shares will almost always differ considerably from its book and liquidating values. It is a function of the supply and demand for the firm's common shares in the market place, which in turn depends on the current and future returns which investors can expect, and the perceived risk of holding the stock. As these factors bear only a partial relationship to the book and liquidating values of the company, we would not expect to find the going-concern value closely aligned. The valuation of common shares by investors will be discussed in considerable detail in subsequent chapters.

In assessing whether the current market price of a firm's common shares appears to be unduly inflated or depressed, reference is often made to the *intrinsic value* of common shares. This intrinsic value is the price which appears justified based on the firm's current operations and its future prospects, including anticipated returns and perceived risks. Where, for example, the market price of a share has been bid up by what may appear to be excessive speculation, the intrinsic or fundamental value of the firm's shares could be considerably lower than the current market price. The term intrinsic value basically refers to the price which a rational and fully informed investor ought to pay for the common shares, and if the stock market was dominated by such rational and fully informed investors, the market price of common shares would probably equal their intrinsic value.

Resale of shares

The purchase or sale of shares in broadly held corporations[6] is usually not constrained and involves no legal formalities. There are, however, a few instances where this is not so and such cases are worth noting.

Letter Stock

Letter stock essentially involves a block of shares sold by an issuer to an individual, corporate, or institutional investor, but without the normal disclosure and information requirements or other documentation which have to be

[6]Broadly held corporations are to be distinguished from closely held ones which are referred to as private companies in some jurisdictions and non-reporting corporations in others. The right to sell or transfer shares of closely held corporations is restricted.

provided if shares are to be sold to the general public. Such sales are sometimes considered, mainly by smaller companies with an immediate need for capital, in order to avoid the immediate expenses and time delays which a public offering of shares would entail. The resale of such letter stock is generally restricted. It can be resold as a block only with the blessing of the appropriate stock exchange, and to the general public only when the term of the letter expires and the requisite documents have been prepared and filed. Given this lack of marketability, letter stock of six to twelve months' duration may initially sell at a discount of around twenty-five percent from the market price of the identical but publicly traded shares.[7] During periods of economic growth and rising share prices, this provides potential for gain on letter stock, which may make such issues attractive in spite of the initial restrictions on trading.

Escrow Shares

Shares are said to be escrowed when they are turned over to a trustee, usually at the request of someone like a securities commission or stock exchange. Once escrowed, such shares are not transferable until the escrow agreement expires unless consent is obtained from the appropriate securities commission or exchange following a formal request. Escrow agreements are used largely in connection with new offerings of common shares. Their purpose in most cases is to prevent the selling of shares by the original or founding shareholders who may have obtained significant blocks of shares in exchange for properties or services rendered. Such selling could disrupt the public offering or depress the share price after the issuing has taken place as additional numbers of shares would be released for sale.

Listing

In Canada, the shares of most new public corporations trade on the over-the-counter or unlisted market—a market which is made up of security dealers. Bonds are also traded in the over-the-counter market, adding to its importance. The market's dollar volume, including bonds is, in fact, much greater than that of all securities listed on stock exchanges. When *sponsorship* exists for the securities of a corporation, one or more dealers "make the market" by buying and selling at bid and ask prices respectively which they quote. A supporting dealer will maintain an inventory of securities, and when necessary trade on his own account, thereby speeding up the trading process and helping to maintain price stability. When sponsorship does not exist, dealers execute orders only when buyers and sellers can be matched. Sponsorship may exist either because a dealer was involved in the original offering of the shares and feels an obligation to assure a smooth market for some time after such offering, or simply because a dealer finds it profitable to continue trading in a particular stock. As a company grows and its number of stockholders increases, it may qualify for listing on one or more stock exchanges. By listing, a security qualifies for trading on the exchange which is simply an organized and competitive market place where buy

[7]Examples of letter stock used in Canada include, for example, Dylex Diversified Ltd., J. Harris and Sons Ltd., and Seaway Multi-Corp. Ltd.

and sell orders are matched efficiently.[8]

Listing requirements of Canadian exchanges vary quite significantly with the more stringent qualifications being those of the Toronto Stock Exchange (TSE) and the Montreal Stock Exchange.[9] To qualify for listing, the TSE recently required net tangible assets of at least $1,000,000 and earnings of at least $100,000 in the previous year as well as in three of the last five years. At the same time, the Vancouver Stock Exchange, being much less stringent, called for net tangible assets and earnings to be "adequate". Once a company meets the requirements of a stock exchange, it should consider the benefits of listing in its own particular case. Listing generally increases the marketability of the shares and, as a consequence, shareholders stand to gain in liquidity. Listing may also improve the value of shares as collateral, the prestige and perhaps even the market price of the stock. It has also been suggested that the more prestigious and well-known the exchange, the greater such effects.[10] Not surprisingly, the shares of a number of important Canadian firms are listed on Canadian as well as foreign exchanges. Massey Ferguson, Inco and Canadian Pacific are examples, with listings on the New York Stock Exchange as well as on Canadian exchanges.

However, not all companies which are eligible decide to have their shares listed. In fact, stocks of many major corporations continue to trade in the over-the-counter market. Clearly, certain firms see no tangible advantage to listing while others, perhaps those more closely held, may wish to avoid greater financial disclosure requirements associated with listing.

10-3. RIGHTS OF SHAREHOLDERS

In order of theoretical authority, the principal parties concerned with corporate affairs are the shareholders, directors, officers, and employees of the company.

The shareholders elect the members of the board of directors, who are to set general policies for the corporation on behalf of the shareholders. The board of directors, in turn, hires and controls the senior officers of the corporation and delegates to such officers the day-to-day management of the firm. In this section, we review the actual rights of shareholders who, as we have seen, are the ultimate owners of the business. Shareholders of broadly held corporations have the right

- to do as they wish with their stock holdings,
- to share in the earnings of the company if and when cash dividends are declared by the board of directors,

[8]The matter of efficiency has been challenged. See, for example, W. Baumol, *The Stock Market and Economic Efficiency*, Fordham University Press, New York, 1965.

[9]P. McQuillan, *Going Public in Canada*, Toronto: Canadian Institute of Chartered Accountants, 1971, pp.220-221.

[10]An empirical study by Van Horne for the United States does not support this belief. His findings suggest that listing of a stock from the over-the-counter market to either New York or American Stock Exchange does not in itself create value. Moreover, stock prices do not appear to rise upon the announcement to list in any systematic manner that could be exploited profitably by market participants buying the stock upon the announcement to list and selling it upon actual listing. See J. Van Horne, "New Listings and Their Price Behavior", *Journal of Finance*, September, 1970, pp. 783-794.

- to benefit from retained earnings once all claims of senior securities such as bonds and preferred shares are satisfied,
- to elect directors,
- to vote on general questions relating to company affairs such as the selection of auditors and the amendment of the corporate charter, and
- to examine the company's books and records.

These rights should now be considered more specifically and in greater detail than was possible in Chapter 2.

Disposal of share holdings

The common stockholder, by owning shares, is the owner of a negotiable financial asset. He may decide at any time to withdraw as an owner, sell his shares, and use the funds to advantage elsewhere.

When a corporation offers its shares for sale to investors, the net proceeds received from such a sale belong to the firm. After this original sale of shares, however, the buying and selling of outstanding stock neither increases nor decreases the capital of the company. Shares, therefore, may be transferred from one owner to another without directly affecting the operation or financial resources of the firm. When previously issued shares are sold by a shareholder, the selling price is paid not to the corporation but to the seller of the shares, and the effect of such a sale is simply that a new name will appear on the company's register of shareholders. The sale of shares is attended by no legal formalities, beyond the witnessed signing of a registered security or the delivery of the certificate when in street-form.

Following patterns set in the United States some forty years ago, Canadian jurisdictions have enacted legislation over the past several years requiring detailed disclosure of trading in company securities by the firm's officers and directors.[11] Reports on such insider trading are generally published monthly by Securities Commissions of the provinces involved and have probably curtailed transactions by insiders. The purpose of such legislation is to prevent insiders from taking advantage of inside information which they may possess. For example, a director having access to important information regarding his firm's mineral exploration activities, which has not yet been publicly released, could take advantage of his position by trading on his own account, to the detriment of the general shareholder. Full disclosure of insider trading is intended to inhibit such abuses. In any case, the more flagrant abuses of insider information can generally be prosecuted as a criminal offence.

Maturity

An important benefit enjoyed by common shareholders is that shares cannot be taken away by call for sinking fund purposes or redemption.

For all practical purposes, an issue of common stock is not tagged with a maturity date. Common shareholders cannot be required to sacrifice their

[11]See, for example, *Business Corporations Act*, R.S.O. 1970, c.53, ss.148 (am. 1971, Vol. 2, c.26, s.23), 149.

claims to net assets and future income, except perhaps in cases involving reorganization or bankruptcy.

Claim on income

Common stockholders have no right to dividends or any other fixed return. They share in the earnings of the company only when dividends are declared. Stockholders can, however, prosper from appreciation of the market value of their shares. Dividend payments are set by the board of directors with respect to amount, type, timing, and frequency, thereby placing the common shareholder in a quite different position from that of a creditor. Shareholders have no legal recourse against a company for not distributing profits; their only recourse is to attempt to change the board of directors.

Claim on assets

All earnings after taxes, interest charges, and preferred dividends accrue to the benefit of common shareholders. Even if such earnings are not paid out in current dividends, this is a significant consideration as retained earnings may be used to finance new investments which, in turn, will enhance the future earning power of the firm. Such shareholders also enjoy a residual claim against the corporation's assets in case of liquidation. Unfortunately, in a forced liquidation, the amount at which assets may be shown on the books bear little relation to the sums actually realized. In the case of voluntary liquidation, though common stockholders are quite likely to do better, the amount netted may still fall short of book value.

Voice in management

Under the *Canada Business Corporations Act*, in the absence of other provisions every shareholder is entitled to as many votes at all general meetings of the company as shares he owns in the company. This voting power may be exercised in person or by *proxy*. As illustrated in Figure 10-1, a proxy is a revocable power of attorney given to somebody else entitling that person to vote the shares at stockholder's meetings. Proxies are generally solicited by company management from shareholders who do not attend the general meeting and are given for one meeting though, on occasion, the request is made for an assignment of the right to vote for one full year. Solicitation of proxies is subject to regulations, and management is required to disseminate information to shareholders along with the proxy mailings.

In evaluating the significance of the right to vote, it should be recognized that, when exercised, the vote must be cast either by the stockholder or by the individual holding his proxy.

Because of the costs involved and because stockholders are often apathetic, they do not attend the company's meetings. If they vote at all, it is by proxy. Consequently, management will actively solicit proxies from stockholders prior to the annual meeting. If the shareholder is satisfied with company management, he will return the signed proxy to management. If dissatisfied but unwilling to

FIGURE 10-1

An Example of a Proxy Solicitation

CANADIAN OCCIDENTAL PETROLEUM LTD.

PROXY SOLICITED BY MANAGEMENT
FOR ANNUAL AND SPECIAL GENERAL MEETING OF SHAREHOLDERS

May 1, 1972

I hereby appoint ROBERT A. TEITSWORTH or failing him J. HOWARD HAWKE, or failing him DAVID B. CHALMERS, or in their stead ______________ as proxy, with power of substitution, to attend the Annual and Special General Meeting of Shareholders of Canadian Occidental Petroleum Ltd. to be held on May 1, 1972, and at any and all adjournments thereof, and to vote on my behalf:

	For	Against
(1) To approve the Company's financial statements for 1971	☐	☐
(2) To approve a by-law conferring borrowing powers upon the Board of Directors	☐	☐
(3) To approve a by-law increasing the quorum to 25% for shareholders' meetings	☐	☐
(4) To approve a by-law decreasing the number of directors from twelve to eleven	☐	☐

	For	Abstain
(5) To elect eleven directors to serve for the ensuing year	☐	☐

	For	Against
(6) To appoint Arthur Andersen & Co., as the Company's independent auditors for 1972	☐	☐

(7) To consider and act on any other business which may properly come before the meeting.

The shares represented hereby will be voted for the election of the directors named in the accompanying proxy statement (or for a substitute if any of those named is unable to serve), unless abstention is specified. The shares will be voted in accordance with the choices specified hereon in connection with Proposals Nos. 1, 2, 3, 4, and 6; if no choice is specified with respect to a proposal, the shares will be voted in favor thereof. If the shareholder's address appears on the Company's records to be in the United States, the proxy will not be used in connection with Proposal No. 1.

(PLEASE DATE AND SIGN BELOW)

Except as otherwise expressly provided herein said attorneys shall have discretionary authority with respect to all matters which may properly come before the meeting or any adjournments thereof, and I hereby ratify and confirm all that my said attorneys may do by virtue hereof.

I hereby acknowledge receipt of the notice of the meeting and accompanying proxy statement dated April 3, 1972.

Dated this ______________ day of April, 1972.

____
Shareholder's Signature

Shareholder's signature should be exactly as the name appears at the left. Corporations should affix their seals. When signing as attorney, executor, administrator, trustee or guardian, please give your full title as such.

YOU MAY APPOINT SOMEONE OTHER THAN THE PERSONS DESIGNATED ABOVE TO ATTEND AND ACT ON YOUR BEHALF AT THE MEETING BY FILLING IN THE NAME OF SUCH PERSON IN THE SPACE PROVIDED. Please date, sign and return the proxy promptly. You may revoke this proxy at any time before it is exercised.

PRINTED IN CANADA

sell his holdings, he may elect one of several possible courses of action. He may solicit proxies himself, or he may assign his vote to some outside group desiring to replace the present directors. He may follow either course despite the knowledge that current management has a distinct advantage in any *proxy fight* mainly because management is able to solicit proxies and mail information to stockholders at the company's expense.

Alternatively, he may decide not to vote. Many common stockholders follow this course of action because they feel that their vote is in any case unimportant. Finally, the stockholder may choose to attend the meeting and express his dissatisfaction in person. The following item from the *Financial Post* is illuminating with regard to this alternative course of action.

> To get to the annual meetings of Steep Rock Iron Mines Ltd., you have to fight your way through the crowds at Toronto Airport, fly to Thunder Bay, then rent a car and drive through 130 miles of scrubby brush and frozen lakes until you come to Atikokan, a northern company town like all the others, except that here the dust that covers everything is a bright, boxcar red.
>
> You drive up a rust-colored hill, past a sign warning that the public isn't welcome past this point, and keep driving. The landscape is a series of immense holes. . . .
>
> Finally, after your 1,000-mile journey from Toronto, you come to a sort of boxcar-red bunkhouse. You climb its stairs, walk down the hall past various offices and enter a small room, a cubicle almost.
>
> With its hard chairs, its blackboards, its wooden desk at the front, it looks like a classroom for retarded children, circa 1936. This is the scene of Steep Rock's annual meeting, a truly inspiring exercise in shareholder democracy.
>
> Considering that Steep Rock reported a 1969 "paper" loss of $33.5 million, you'd be entitled to suppose that one or two shareholders might have braved the journey from the south to find out what's happening to their money. But no, Steep Rock's body count is spot on. The company has provided exactly 30 hard-backed chairs for the meeting, and that turns out to be plenty.[12]

Given the weakness of the voting mechanism, it has been suggsted that management is self-perpetuating, especially as shares become widely distributed. Thus, in the early 1930's, Berle and Means[13] presented evidence to suggest that economic and financial power was slipping into the hands of professional managers, with the shareholders assuming, for the most part, quite passive roles. In other words, there had emerged a clear split between ownership and effective control. Currently, this trend appears to be reversing again, given increasing concentration of shareholdings in the hands of institutional investors such as pension funds, mutual funds, insurance companies and the likes. For example, such institutions already account for close to one-half of all the trading taking

[12]Alexander Ross, "The Sad Story of How Steep Rock Divorced Its Auditors", *The Financial Post*, April 11, 1970, p. 7.

[13]A. Berle and C. Means, *The Modern Corporation and Private Property*, New York: Harcourt Brace and Co., 1959, p. 124 *et. seq.*

place on the Toronto Stock Exchange. While such financial institutions often have a policy of not becoming active in exercising their voice in management, they sometimes cannot escape some involvement. This is particularly true in Canada, as large blocks of shares are not easily disposed of and, hence, a financial institution holding a significant number of shares may have an active interest in the firm for longer periods of time. An interesting aside is whether we can today, in Canada at least, identify a transition of power, that is, whether stockholders—this time institutional investors—are in the position of re-acquiring control.[14]

Under the normal voting system, each shareholder receives one vote for each share held. In electing directors, a vote can then be cast for each vacant position. For instance, a stockholder with ten shares can cast ten votes respecting each contested position. Each contestant requires a majority of the votes cast for that position. Thus a minority group of shareholders may be precluded from winning any representation, and somebody controlling over 50 percent of the shares can elect the full board of directors.

In an attempt to strengthen the hand of minority shareholders, an increasing number of jurisdictions in the United States are requiring the use of *cumulative voting* in place of normal or statutory voting. This device can provide some minority representation on boards of directors. In Canada, it is provided for federally, as well as in a few provincial statutes, and will likely gain greater acceptance.

Unlike normal voting procedures where shareholders cast one vote per share for their choice on each vacant position, in cumulative voting the available votes need not be spread. They may be accumulated and cast for just one or two aspirants. Slates of candidates are not involved and individuals garnering the largest number of votes are elected. Given an investor who holds ten shares, and nine vacancies to be filled on the board of directors, ninety votes are available which can be cast in favor of a single candidate. Under normal procedures, only ten votes could be cast for each of the nine candidates, and control of one vote more than 50 percent of those cast would guarantee election of the entire board.

Example

A firm has 1,000 shares outstanding, and we assume that all shares are to be voted at the upcoming annual meeting. Seven new directors are to be elected, and two opposing shareholder groups each have their set of competing candidates. One group of shareholders holds 252 shares, with the other group holding 748 shares. Given normal voting where each of the seven positions is voted on separately, the minority group would be outvoted on the separate ballot for each position by 748 to 252 and, hence, the majority group would control the entire board of directors. Under cumulative voting, the minority group has a total number of 252 × 7 = 1764 votes versus 748 × 7 = 5236 votes for the majority group. Only the seven candidates with the largest number of

[14]This point was touched upon in a provincial and federal study of mutual funds. See, *Report of the Canadian Committee on Mutual Funds and Investment Contracts*, Ottawa: Queen's Printer, 1969, p. 7.

total votes win a position on the board. If the minority group concentrates its votes on just two candidates, each of these candidates would obtain 1764/2 = 882 votes. In order for candidates of the majority group to rank ahead in the election, each such candidate will have to exceed this figure of 882 votes. Given its 5236 votes, the majority group can only vote in a maximum of five directors (with 5236 votes spread evenly over five candidates, each candidate receives 5236/5 = 1047 votes; with 5236 votes spread evenly over six candidates, each candidate only receives 5236/6 = 872 votes which falls short of the 882 votes which the candidates of the minority group have accumulated). If in our example a group controls 252 shares, cumulative voting would ensure that such a group could obtain representation on the board with at least two directors, even if all other 748 shares were voted for competing candidates.[15]

As is evident, cumulative voting gives minority interests a better opportunity to be represented on the board of directors. Even with cumulative voting, however, management might preclude minority interests from obtaining a seat on the board of directors by either reducing the number of directors or by staggering their terms so that only a portion are elected each year. If in the above example the new positions to be filled were reduced to two members, it is easy to verify that even with cumulative voting the minority group would be shut out.

Right to examine books

A stockholder is legally entitled to examine certain of the corporation's books and records including the stockholder register. Corporate management may not want to encourage the practice, and in most cases access to audited financial statements as presented, for example, in the corporation's annual report, is deemed to be quite adequate.

10-4. TYPES OF COMMON SHARES

For most companies, the common stock authorized is of a *non-classified* nature. This means that one share of common stock of the company gives its holder the same rights as would any other common share of that same company. A company may, however, have more than one class of common stock, with its common stock *classified* on the basis of its voting power, the type of dividend to be paid, or any of the other rights commented on earlier.

[15]A formula exists to determine the minimum number of shares required under a cumulative voting system to ensure the election of a specific number of directors. Let n = total number of shares to be voted, n_1 = minimum number of shares required, k = number of vacant positions, x = number of directors desired. One obtains $n_1 = (nx/(k+1)) + 1$. Pursuing our above example, for $n = 1000$, $k = 7$, and $x = 2$, one obtains $n_1 = 2000/8 + 1 = 251$, with 251 shares ensuring the election of 2 directors. The formula is easily derived. n_1 shares entitle kn_1 votes. Spreading these evenly over x candidates gives kn_1/x votes per candidate. For the remaining $(n - n_1)$ shares not to be able to elect more than $(k - x)$ candidates, we have to have

$$\frac{n_1 k}{x} \geq \frac{(n - n_1)k}{k - x + 1}$$

This ensures that any opposing group can at most have $(k - x)$ candidates with votes exceeding kn_1/x. From the above formula, one simply derives by algebraic manipulation $n_1 \geq (nx/(k+1))$, which implies that if $n_1 = (nx/(k+1)) + 1$ election of x directors is guaranteed.

Example

R. L. Crain Ltd. affords a useful illustration. The company's capital stock consists of both common and special shares. The former carries one vote per share while the special shares are equal in all respects except that the *original* holders of such special shares are entitled to ten votes per share. Once transferred, the special shares lose their multiple voting rights. The St. Lawrence Cement Company provides a similar pattern. It has Class A and B shares outstanding. Class A carries one vote per share and Class B carries three, but they rank equally in every other respect.[16]

Classified shares are primarily used by the firm's original founders or promoters and corporate management to ensure that control of the company is retained within a select group in spite of subsequent sales of additional shares to the general public.

To confuse matters slightly, two classes of common shares are also used by many Canadian companies in order to give investors the option of either receiving the usual taxable dividends, or of receiving dividends which are not immediately taxable in the hand of shareholders but on which the corporation itself pays a special fifteen percent tax, with the investor merely adjusting the cost base of his shares for purposes of computing capital gains upon disposition. This possibility was reviewed in Chapter 3.

Example

Using John Labatt Limited as an illustration, Class A and Class B common shares have been issued by that firm with the securities interchangeable one for the other at the investor's discretion. Both classes of shares are subject to identical rights and conditions except when it comes to dividends. Distributions on Class B shares are equivalent to those paid on the Class A except that the special fifteen percent tax has been paid by the corporation on behalf of the former class of shareholders. Further elaboration on these particular classified shares is to be found in the chapter dealing with dividend policy.

10-5. USE OF COMMON SHARES

To the issuing corporation, there are both advantages and disadvantages in the use of common shares to raise funds as opposed to other types of securities. On the positive side the following merit attention:

- There is no critical maturity date to worry about—the funds received are made available permanently.
- There are no fixed charges to be met by the issuer. In case of financial difficulties, no contractual obligations for any payments to shareholders exist, and any dividend payments are strictly at the discretion of the board of directors.

[16]Note that the concept of Class A and Class B divulges nothing. Thus, in the case of Traders Group Ltd., it is the Class B which enjoys normal voting rights; Class A elects two directors only, and otherwise is nonvoting.

- During particular time spans characterized by buoyant stock markets, investors may be more receptive to common share issues than to other types of securities.
- The credit standing of the business is enhanced by the increase in shareholders' equity. Since creditors have a claim on the corporation's cash flows and assets which ranks prior to that of common shareholders, their position is enhanced if a large proportion of the firm's financing comes from equity sources.
- Related to the previous point, the corporation's reserve borrowing power and flexibility for future financing is preserved if not increased.

There are, on the other hand, disadvantages to be considered. The disadvantages need not apply in every situation, but the following points bear watching:

- A controlling group of shareholders may suffer dilution of voting control if additional shares are issued.
- Various costs and issuing expenses associated with the sale of common shares may be comparatively high.

With an increasing number of common shares outstanding, there may be a reduction in earnings per share. Whether the market price of the firm's common shares will drop as a consequence, to the detriment of existing shareholders, will depend on the use which the firm can make of the new funds which were raised through the sale of the additional common shares. Thus, if these funds can be invested to yield high rates of return, any drop in earnings per share may be short lived, and a reduction in the market price of the firm's shares through such dilution may be avoided.

The mood of the capital markets will play an important role in the timing of new issues. Thus, in face of the 1970 stock market decline, several proposed issues were temporarily or perhaps permanently shelved including the Bagel King, Bear Foods, and Sanco Steel Tube offerings. To quote from one very comprehensive recent work, which stressed the importance of timing,

> If the new issue is in a fad industry, late entrants in offering shares . . . will . . . encounter public saturation.
>
> . . . If the company is growing rapidly it may be advisable to defer the public offering until a later date when total earnings may have doubled.
>
> . . . On occasion the public will be unwilling to buy the company's dream. By waiting until the dream has partially passed into the realm of reality, the public may become enthusiastic subscribers.[17]

The receptiveness of the stock market to the issuance of the firm's shares will determine the market price which the firm can expect to realize for its shares. Thus, in times of buoyancy in the stock market the prices to be realized on the sale of shares will greatly exceed those which would prevail in a depressed market. Consider a firm which needs to raise a given amount of new funds. Clearly, the higher the market price per share, the lower the number of new shares to be issued, and consequently the lower the dilution suffered by current

[17]McQuillan, *op. cit.*, p. 37.

shareholders in terms of earnings per share or voting control.

Example

Assume a firm needs to raise $30,000,000 of new capital through an offering of common shares. Shares currently could be sold to net the company $15 per share, which implies that $30,000,000/$15 = 2,000,000 new shares would have to be issued. Assume that the current state of the stock market is considered to be unduly depressed, and that management expects a recovery of share prices, with the firm's share price climbing to at least $20 per share within the next 18 months. If shares could be sold to net the company $20 per share, only $30,000,000/$20 = 1,500,000 new shares would have to be issued. Hence, there would be a strong incentive for the company to consider postponement of the new financing until general conditions in the stock market improve.

Considerations such as these are reflected in the fact that new offerings of shares abound in times when shares trade at historically high prices, whereas they dry up almost completely at times of depressed market conditions. It leaves the financial manager with the difficult task of forecasting movements in the stock market, as proper timing may be the most critical ingredient in a successful new offering. Clearly, no simple recipes or formula-type answers exist to assist the manager in this task, and experienced judgment will probably have to play the dominant role in reaching decisions.

10-6. SUMMARY

Common shares are certificates of ownership in a corporation. They have no maturity, and can be freely transferred from one owner to another. The purchase or sale of outstanding shares involves no legal formalities and generally has no impact on corporate operations.

Shareholders are entitled to corporate earnings and assets only after the claims of all creditors and preferred shareholders have been satisfied. Given the firm has fixed obligations, such as interest payments to creditors, a given percentage variation in the firm's operating revenue will generally result in an increased percentage variation in earnings per share. For these two reasons, common shares are often referred to as risk capital.

We may distinguish between authorized, issued, and outstanding shares. Authorized shares are those which the firm's management is entitled to issue and are specified in the corporate charter or approved by shareholders. Issued shares are those which have actually been sold. If the corporation has not repurchased any of its own shares, the number of shares outstanding will equal the number of shares issued.

Shares may have a par value, or be without par value. Shares having a par value cannot be issued as fully paid unless cash or a fair equivalent at least equal to the par value is received for consideration. It follows that the significance of a par value is quite limited. It merely provides information identifying the lowest possible investment behind the company's historical offerings of shares. Many shares are issued without a par value, and for federally incorporated companies the notion of a par value was entirely abolished in 1975.

In valuing common shares, various measures may be used. These include the share's book value, its market value, and its intrinsic value. The market value may further be subdivided into a liquidating value and a going-concern value. The book value is determined by the equity section of the balance sheet, and is strongly influenced by accounting practice. It often bears little resemblance to market value and is of limited significance. Clearly, investors are mainly concerned with market value. Under normal circumstances, the going-concern value is of primary significance, with the liquidating value becoming important when the firm faces financial difficulties with the threat of bankruptcy, or when in unusual circumstances the firm's liquidating value exceeds its current market value as a going concern. The intrinsic value attempts to specify a market price which would be justified based on the firm's operations and prospects, and also attempts to eliminate any unjustified moods of the market which may have distorted the actual current market price.

Generally, there are no restrictions to the purchase or resale of common shares. Exceptions are letter stock and escrow shares. Letter stock is sold to a large investor, but without the normal legal requirements associated with a public sale. Escrow shares are those deposited with a trustee, and are not transferable until the escrow agreement expires. Shares may be listed and sold on a stock exchange, or they may be sold on the over-the-counter market.

The rights of a shareholder include the right to dispose freely of his shares, the claim on dividends if and when declared by the board of directors, a residual claim on assets in the case of liquidation, the right to examine the corporation's books and records, and his right to vote at shareholder meetings, which includes the election of directors.

Questions for Discussion

1. You represent a minority group of shareholders with two representatives on the corporation's 9-man board of directors. Cumulative voting has enabled you to obtain such representation. It is being proposed that elections to the board be staggered with 3 positions to be filled each year (3-year term). What is your reaction and why?
2. Explain why the residual position of common shares makes such securities particularly attractive to individuals electing to invest in more risky ventures.
3. With Royal Assent given to the *Canadian Business Corporations Act* in March of 1975, the issuing of par value shares by federally incorporated firms was expressly ruled out. What arguments can you advance to support the abolition of par value common shares?
4. Tax considerations aside, as the company's chief financial officer what advantages and disadvantages would you cite for a policy of holding dividends constant and using any excess cash for the redemption of some of the corporation's common shares?
5. Some common shares have recently been trading below their book values. Comment on the statement that "given double-digit inflation, the earnings of public utilities and hence their retained earnings have been overstated,

making reported book values per share considerably higher than is actually warranted."

6. Why is it very difficult to replace the existing board of directors of a corporation?
7. Is it useful to have the statutory requirement that "insiders" disclose any share transactions? Why or why not?
8. In November, 1970, Molson Industries Ltd. offered to exchange 4 Molson class *A* common shares plus $20 cash for every 5 common or class *A* shares of Beaver Lumber Company Limited. At the time the offer was made, it represented a premium of 28 percent over the market price for Beaver. What are some of the factors that a shareholder in Beaver should consider in determining whether the offer should be accepted or rejected?

Problem with Solution

1. Premier Industries Ltd. has a 15-man board of directors. After resisting pressure for some years, a decision has been made by the board to introduce cumulative voting to accommodate an organized group of shareholders able to command proxies for 32 percent of the 1,000,000 outstanding shares. For practical purposes it can be assumed that all outstanding shares are voted. If the entire board is to be re-elected at one time, show that the minority group will be able to elect at least 5 directors.

Solution

The minority group has 15 × 320,000 = 4,800,000 votes, with other shareholders having 15 × 680,000 = 10,200,000 votes. If the minority group spread its votes evenly over five candidates, each candidate would receive 4,800,000/5 = 960,000 votes. If the other shareholders spread their votes evenly over 10 candidates, each candidate would receive 10,200,000/10 = 1,020,000 votes, implying that these 10 candidates and the 5 candidates of the minority group would be elected. If these votes were spread over 11 candidates, each candidate would receive 10,200,000/11 = 927,272 votes, implying that the five candidates of the minority group now have the largest number of votes and are elected, plus 10 of the remaining 11 candidates (the tie in votes would have to be broken in some way). Thus, regardless of how all other shareholders vote, the minority group is guaranteed a representation of 5 men on the board of directors.

This result could have been obtained more directly by resort to the formula which was derived in footnote 15. We have

$$\text{minimum number of shares required} = \frac{(\text{Total number of shares to be voted}) \times (\text{number of directors desired})}{\text{Total number of positions} + 1} + 1$$

or

$$320{,}000 = \frac{1{,}000{,}000\, x}{15 + 1} + 1$$

where x is the number of directors desired. We can compute

$$x = \frac{319{,}999 \times 16}{1{,}000{,}000} = 5.12$$

In using this formula, all fractions should be dropped. Thus, we confirm our above result that a holding of 320,000 shares will ensure election of at least 5 of the 15 directors.

Additional Problem

Use the information provided in the preceding problem with solution. Assume that the existing board of directors is interested in keeping minority representation as small as possible, while having the term of office limited to 3 years. The current board proposes that terms should be staggered, with 5 positions filled each year. What effect would this proposal have on minority representation, and how many representatives would the minority group have on the board of directors at any one time?

Selected References

R. Bear and A. Curley, "Unseasoned Equity Financing," *Journal of Financial and Quantitative Analysis*, June, 1975, pp. 311-325.

R. Duvall, and D. Austin, "Predicting the Results of Proxy Contests", *Journal of Finance*, September, 1965, pp. 467-471.

R. Furst, "Does Listing Increase the Market Price of Common Stocks?" *Journal of Business*, April, 1970, pp. 174-180.

D. Logue, "On the Pricing of Unseasoned Equity Issues: 1965-1969," *Journal of Financial and Quantitative Analysis*, January, 1973, pp. 91-104.

H. Lowe, "The Classification of Corporate Stock Equities", *Accounting Review*, July 1961, pp. 425-433.

P. McQuillan, *Going Public in Canada*, Toronto: Canadian Institute of Chartered Accountants, 1971.

D. Shaw, "The Allocation Efficiency of Canada's Market for New Equity Issues", *Canadian Journal of Economics*, November, 1969, pp. 546-556.

R. Soldofsky, "Classified Common Stock", *The Business Lawyer*, April, 1968, pp. 899-902.

H. Stevenson, *Common Stock Financing*, Ann Arbor: University of Michigan, 1957.

H. Stoll and A. Curley, "Small Business and the New Issues Market for Equities", *Journal of Financial and Quantitative Analysis*, September, 1970, pp. 309-322.

J. Van Horne, "New Listings and Their Price Behavior", *Journal of Finance*, September, 1970, pp. 783-794.

C. Walsh, "Does Listing Increase the Market Price of Common Stocks?—Comment", *Journal of Business*, October, 1975, pp. 616-620.

C. Williams, *Cumulative Voting for Directors*, Boston: Graduate School of Business Administration, Harvard University, 1951.

Chapter 11
Warrants, Convertibles, and Units

11-1. INTRODUCTION

When contemplating new offerings of senior securities such as debt or preferred shares, a corporation's financial officer may see benefits in the use of "sweeteners" including warrants and conversion features. The expectation is that by such supplementing of straight preferred or debt issues, or through the use of packages of securities termed units, the issuing firm will be able to reduce the costs associated with a particular offering. Even quite superficial consideration of the use of sweeteners would reveal that the issuing firm is engaged in a tradeoff—while being able to finance at a lower interest or dividend rate than would otherwise be the case, the corporation is in fact granting potentially valuable *options* to new investors.

In a more general sense, options may be defined as a right to buy or sell particular assets, including securities and commodities, at a predetermined price and over a specified period of time prior to a maturity or expiry date.[1] Some of the more impressive recent developments in the theory of finance have been concerned with the pricing or valuation of various options. These advances were stimulated by the work of Black and Scholes[2] and furthered, no doubt, by development of new options markets in both Canada and the United States.[3] As has been suggested, option-trading appears as the "new game in town" with the option market where the action is.[4]

11-2. WARRANTS

Warrants represent a transferable option to buy, within a given period of time, a certain number of a corporation's shares. Purchases of the shares are to be made at a predetermined price termed the *exercise* or *striking price.* Through their issue, warrants become in a sense a liability of the issuing corporation which must provide the requisite number of shares in return for cash when the options are exercised.

In almost all cases, the option associated with a warrant is granted for a prescribed period of time, with use of perpetual warrants a great rarity in Canada.[5] Warrants are generally not issued by a corporation as a separate offering,

[1]This defines what has been called the American option. In contrast, a European type option may be exercised only at the expiry date.

[2]F. Black and M. Scholes, "The Pricing of Options and Corporate Liabilities", *Journal of Political Economy*, May-June, 1973, pp. 637-659. A review detailing subsequent modifications and extensions is to be found in C. Smith, "Options Pricing: A Review", *Journal of Financial Economics*, January-March, 1976, pp 3-51.

[3]The Chicago Board Options Exchange (CBOE) opened trading on April 26, 1973, as the world's first exchange established expressly for trading in stock options.

[4]J. Laing, "New Game in Town", *Wall Street Journal*, April 22, 1974, p. 1.

[5]The Alleghany Corporation's perpetual warrants are a U.S. example.

but are sold in conjunction with an issue of debt or preferred shares for the purpose of making the issue more attractive to investors. Once made available to the purchasers of senior securities, warrants can be detached and are traded in their own right. Many of the industrial warrants which have been issued in Canada are listed on the Toronto or the Montreal Stock Exchanges, and trading in warrants can be very active. While warrants represent options of a particular type, the term option in the context of common shares has recently come to have a different meaning. Options traded under that name on securities exchanges or on specialized options exchanges are the creation of individual investors who elect to sell (write) such options. For example, an investor may offer for sale the option to purchase a specified number of shares (which the investor may hold anyway) at a specified price for a given period of time with the investor having to provide such shares if the option is exercised by the purchaser. From the point of view of a person purchasing such an option, its features are very similar to those of a warrant. Unlike warrants, however, such options are not issued by a corporation, but merely represent contracts between individual investors. Hence, warrants should not be confused with general options just described.[6]

Example

> The outstanding warrants of Husky Oil Ltd., serve to illustrate the use of such sweeteners. In August 1971, the company issued $15,000,000 of 8½ percent sinking fund debentures and 20 warrants were attached to each $1,000 principal amount of debentures being offered. Each warrant, labelled Series E for purposes of identification, entitled its holder to purchase one unissued common share of Husky Oil at $18 on or before August 15, 1976 and at $21 thereafter until August 15, 1981 when the warrants were to expire. The corporation reserved 300,000 common shares for exercise of the warrants and, as is usually the case, the initial exercise price of $18 was set somewhat above the prevailing market price of the common shares at the time of issue. It is well to recognize, however, that inclusion of a jump in the exercise price by Husky Oil is not the usual practice.

In determining the value of a warrant, we can distinguish between its *floor value* which is readily computed and its actual *market value*, with the latter likely exceeding the warrant's floor value for reasons to be explored below. A warrant's floor value is simply determined by the gain which can be realized should the warrant be exercised immediately. If we define the symbols:

W_F = the floor value of a warrant
n = the number of shares each warrant entitles the holder to purchase
P = the current market price of one share, and
S = the exercise price on one share, as specified on the warrant

The formula for computing the floor value of a warrant simply becomes:

$$W_F = n(P - S)$$

[6]Interested students are referred to G. Gastineau, *The Stock Options Manual*, New York: McGraw-Hill Book Co., 1975.

Where the current market price of the shares is lower than the exercise price, the floor value of the warrant is zero.

Example

To illustrate, we refer to our previous example of the warrants issued by Husky Oil Ltd. Thus, on April 2, 1976, the market price of Husky Oil's common shares was at \$21.50. With each warrant entitling the holder to purchase one share at an exercise price of \$18, an immediate gain of \$21.50 – \$18 = \$3.50 could be realized on exercise of the warrant, and the floor price of the warrant according to the above formula becomes:

$$W_F = 1(\$21.50 - \$18) = \$3.50$$

As the term floor price indicates, a warrant cannot trade below this value. If it did, investors could make an immediate profit by buying warrants and exercising them. Suppose Husky Oil warrants were to trade at \$2. An investor who bought a warrant, exercised it and sold the purchased share for \$21.50 could realize a net gain of \$3.50 – \$2 = \$1.50. In such circumstances a strong demand for the warrants would develop, until their market price is bid up to approximate their floor value. In actual fact, warrants may trade at prices which significantly exceed their computed floor value. Thus, the warrants of Husky Oil were trading at \$6.75 on April 2, 1976. This raises interesting questions as to how the actual market price of warrants is determined. The concepts explored in the Black and Scholes model and in subsequent works can be particularly useful in suggesting some answers.

The floor value of a warrant, as computed by the above formula, is shown diagrammatically in Figure 11-1. Several basic factors influence the actual market price of warrants, and can be drawn on to explain why warrants generally trade at prices which exceed their floor value. The most important factors are:

- The current price of the firm's shares, the exercise price, and the anticipated variability of share prices. The current market price of the shares and the exercise price not only determine the warrant's floor price, but they also influence the degree of leverage which speculators are afforded in buying the warrants, as will be detailed below. Since warrants are typically viewed as speculative investments, a greater variability in the price of the underlying shares will enhance the desirability of the warrants, implying a higher market price.
- The time to expiry of the warrant. The longer the time to expiry, the greater is the potential for capital gains through subsequent appreciation in the market price of the shares and, hence, the higher the market price of the warrant. Close to their expiry dates, however, warrants will trade at their floor value, since they can only be exercised, or the options will be forfeited.
- The dividends paid on the common shares, and the level of interest rates. Warrants can be transformed into shares at any time. If generous dividends are paid on the shares, holding of shares becomes comparatively more attractive, and the market price of warrants should be lower as a consequence. Similarly the level of interest rates may affect the market price of warrants along lines detailed below.

Each of the above points are discussed in turn, and illustrated through a series of numerical examples.

FIGURE 11-1
Hypothetical Relationships Between Floor and Market Values of a Warrant and Share Prices. (Exercise Price = $18)

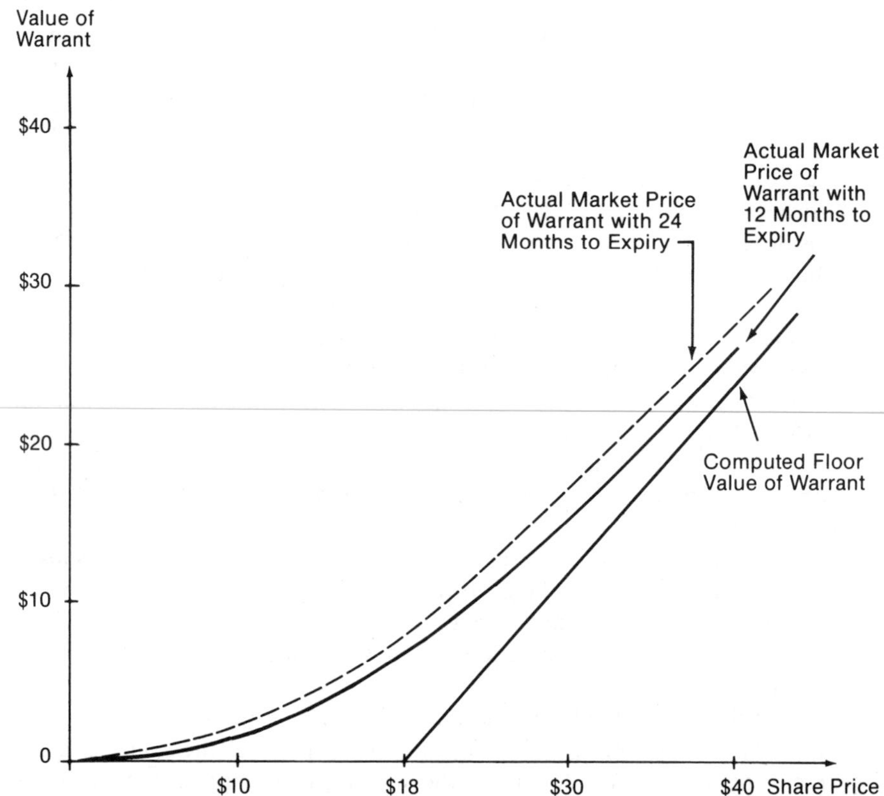

One of the main attractions of buying warrants rather than the underlying common shares lies in the fact that warrants provide investors with leverage. That is, a given percentage change in the market price of the common shares will result in a magnified percentage change in the value of the warrants, and it is for this reason that warrants are generally considered to be a more speculative type of instrument.

Example

Consider a 50 percent increase in the market price of Husky Oil shares from $21.50 to $32.75. As a consequence, the floor price of the warrant would move from $3.50 to 1($32.25 – $18.00) = $14.25, for an increase of 307 percent. Even if the warrant's earlier market price of $6.75 is taken as a basis, this would still represent a 111 percent increase from that level. With the expiry date of the warrants some years off, their market price would certainly be above the $14.25 floor value, implying a still greater gain. Pursuing the example, consider an investor having

$215 to commit. He could purchase 10 shares, at $21.50 a share, or alternatively 31 warrants (31 × $6.75 = $209.25). Given the above increase in share prices and ignoring taxes and brokerage costs, his gain from holding shares would be 10($32.25 – $21.50) = $107.50. On the other hand, his minimum gain from holding warrants would amount to 31($14.25 – $6.75) = $232.50. However, to fully understand the implications of leverage as afforded by holding warrants, we should appreciate that results would be similarly magnified if share prices were to drop. For instance, with the price of Husky Oil shares falling below $18, the floor value of the warrants becomes zero. Furthermore, if share prices appear to stabilize at a level which is significantly below $18, the market price of the warrants may become minimal as well, with the investor losing most of his invested capital.

The implication of dividend payments and interest rates for the valuation of warrants are readily illustrated by extending our above example. For instance, the same investor, aware of the increased risk inherent in warrants, may decide to purchase only 20 warrants for 20 × $6.75 = $135.00, and to invest the remaining $215 – $135 = $80 in short-term interest-bearing securities. Such investment of a portion of funds in more stable short-term debt instruments may be viewed as an attempt to balance the risks inherent in the overall investments. In addition, shareholders may have received dividends of $1 per share during the period under consideration. Both of these facts would alter the returns to be realized from investing in shares or in warrants. Based on the 50 percent increase in share price as assumed above, and again ignoring taxes and transaction costs, returns from holding 10 shares would now be given as:

capital gains on 10 shares + dividend payments during holding period
= 10 × ($32.25 – $21.50) + 10 × $1
= $117.50

whereas the returns from investing in a combination of warrants and short-term debt would include capital gains on 20 warrants and some interest on debt during the holding period.

Some other important considerations are reflected in Figure 11-1. To begin with, the longer the time to expiry of the warrant, the greater are the opportunities for investors to realize capital gains, since there is more time for share price movements to take place. Hence, the spread between the computed floor value and the actual market price of the warrant will increase with increasing time to expiry. Consider two warrants identical in every respect except for their maturities. One warrant has a year until expiry while the other expires two years hence. Clearly, the longer lived instrument must be more valuable. Not only does an investor holding it enjoy everything available to the holder of the one-year warrant but he has, in addition, an option which survives for an extra twelve months. It should be clear that as the expiration date of a warrant approaches, its market price will move towards the computed floor price. The day before expiration, a warrant can only be exercised or the option forfeited, but it no longer offers an opportunity for additional capital gains.

Figure 11-1 also shows that as the share price rises, so will the warrant price.

High warrant prices, in turn, reduce leverage opportunities since the possibilities for large percentage gains decrease if the starting price is already high. This will narrow the spread between the actual market and computed floor values.

Lastly, it is evident from Figure 11-1 that even when the market price of the underlying shares is at or below the exercise price, and the floor value of the warrant is computed to be zero, such warrants may have a positive market value. The explanation for this is to be found in the variability of the share's prices and in investors' expectations about share price movements over the life of the warrants.

Example

Consider a case where there is a year until expiry of the warrant which entails the option to buy one share at an exercise price of $18. With a current market price for the underlying shares assumed at $17, the computed floor value of the warrant is found to be zero. Assume investors have the following expectations for the market price of the shares at year end:

a probability of 0.20 that the share price will increase 30 percent to $22.10

a probability of 0.25 that the share price will increase 20 percent to $20.40

a probability of 0.30 that the share price will increase 10 percent to $18.70

a probability of 0.10 that the share price will hold at $17

a probability of 0.10 that the share price will decrease 5 percent to $16.15

a probability of 0.05 that the share price will decrease 10 percent to $15.30

Given a probability of 0.75 or three chances out of four that share prices will exceed the exercise price before the warrants expire, investors may well bid a positive price for the warrant. They may do so even after allowing for the time value of money and making present value adjustments to their expectations. Only when there is complete certainty that the share price would never exceed $18.00 would the warrant be worthless.

Quite obviously, the extent to which investors in senior securities are willing to accept reduced yields and less attractive provisions in exchange for warrants which are attached to their debt instruments or preferred shares depends on the attractiveness of the option offered. Its duration and the exercise price in relation to the share price are, as we have seen, of particular significance.

A corporation resorting to such sweeteners can expect to receive additional monies when warrants are finally exercised since new shares will be sold at the exercise price. As we saw, the exercise price is generally set above the market value of the underlying common shares when the warrants are first issued. Hence, the corporation ends up realizing a price per share which exceeds the price which could have been obtained if common shares had been sold as part of the original offering. Because of the potential for capital gains and the leverage afforded, and given that warrants generally trade at prices which are above their exercise or floor value, warrants typically are held and traded, and are not exercised until they approach their expiry date.

It is interesting to note that studies which have analyzed the experience of warrant holders suggest that warrants have performed more poorly than the general equity market, and show that shortdated warrants offered very little compensation for the high risks involved.[7]

11-3. CONVERTIBLES

Conversion features associated with issues of senior securities such as bonds or preferred shares are another form of "sweetener" relied on by corporations when attempting to minimize the costs of their external financing. To facilitate exposition, the focus of this section is largely on debt instruments which incorporate such features. Most of the discussion, however, also applies directly to issues of convertible preferred shares.

Convertible instruments, whether preferred shares, bonds, or debentures, are securities which, at the option of the holder, may typically be converted into the common shares of the issuing firm. The basis for switching a convertible security into common shares is spelled out either in terms of a *conversion price* or a *conversion ratio.* In the case of a convertible debenture, for example, the conversion price is the face value of debt to be surrendered for each common share when the option to convert is exercised. Given a debenture with a face value of \$1,000, a conversion price of \$25 indicates that the security is convertible into \$1,000/\$25 = 40 common shares. The conversion ratio is the number of common shares received when a debt-holder converts—40 in this case. Thus, we have the following relation between conversion price, conversion ratio and face value of the debt:

$$\text{face value of debt} = \text{conversion price} \times \text{conversion ratio}.$$

The conversion price is generally set above the prevailing market price of the common shares at the time of the convertible offering and may be varied over time.

Example

> The \$1,000 face value, 7½ percent convertible debentures of Westcoast Transmission Company Limited with a maturity of 20 years were issued in December 1970. They provided for a conversion price of \$22 if converted prior to January 1, 1976 and \$25 thereafter but prior to January 1, 1981. It is also significant that the conversion feature expires 10 years before the maturity date of this issue. Such limitations on conversion rights are frequently found.

In connection with convertible securities, reference is often made to their *conversion value*, which is simply defined as:

$$\text{conversion value} = \text{conversion ratio} \times \text{current market price per common share}$$

[7]R. Brealey, *Security Prices in a Competitive Market*, Cambridge: The M.I.T. Press, 1971, pp. 188-189.

Example

The 7 percent subordinate convertible debentures of Industrial Acceptance Corporation due in 1985 provide for conversion of each $1,000 debenture into 80 common shares prior to October 31, 1972; and then into 70 shares to October 31, 1977. With the market price of the common shares on April 28, 1976 at $18, the conversion value at that time is computed as $18 × 70 = $1,260.

The conversion value indicates the value of the conversion feature alone to the investor, or the value which could be realized if the investor converted immediately and then sold all the common shares. The market price of a convertible security will generally exceed its conversion value for two reasons.

- First, a convertible security, apart from the possibility of immediate conversion, provides the option to convert for an extended period of time, with the consequent potential for future capital gains.
- Secondly, investors are entitled to periodic interest payments on the underlying debt while holding such securities.

The spread between the market price of the convertible security and its conversion value is called the *conversion value premium*, which is generally measured as a percentage of the conversion value.

Example

The convertible debentures of IAC traded at $1,270 on April 28, 1976. The conversion value premium on that date is computed as $1,270 – $1,260 = $10, or ($10/$1,260) × 100% = 0.79 percent.

Another concept which is important in evaluating a convertible bond or debenture is its *straight debt value*, which represents the value of the debt alone.[8] If no conversion feature was attached to the debentures the securities would trade as straight debt, with their market price determined by the standard bond value formulas as outlined in Chapter 4. Using notation, we have:

$$DV_m = \sum_{t=1}^{T-m} \frac{I}{(1+i)^t} + \frac{F}{(1+i)^{T-m}}$$

where

DV_m = the convertible's straight debt value at time m,
T = the original term to maturity,
i = market rate of interest on a straight debt issue of equivalent risk,
F = face value of the debt paid at maturity, and
I = dollars of interest paid each year.

We see that the straight debt value of a convertible debenture is determined by the interest paid on the convertible debt in relation to the then prevailing market interest rates on straight debt, and by the remaining maturity of the convertible security. Generally, one of the attractions of a conversion feature to the issuing corporation is that, by increasing the appeal of the security to investors, the corporation can reduce the interest rate below prevailing market

[8]The following concepts are drawn from E. Brigham, "An Analysis of Convertible Debentures", in E. Brigham, ed., *Readings in Financial Management*, New York: Holt, Rinehart and Winston, 1971, pp. 305-329.

rates for comparable straight debt issues. Given $I < iF$, the straight debt value of convertibles is generally well below their face value.

Example

To illustrate the computation of straight debt value, consider the IAC convertible debentures introduced earlier, which are assumed to mature nine years hence. If an ordinary but otherwise comparable debenture issue of the company had to yield nine percent in order to attract investors, the convertible's straight debt value would be:

$$DV = \sum_{t=1}^{9} \frac{70}{(1.09)^t} + \frac{1000}{(1.09)^9} = \$878.95$$

The spread between the straight debt value of a convertible security and its market price is termed the *bond-value premium*, which may also be measured as a percentage of the current market price of the convertible security. It provides the investor with an indication of how much he would stand to lose if the conversion feature became of little or no value, for example because of continually depressed share prices.

Example

For the above illustration, the bond value premium is computed as \$1,270 − \$878.95 = \$391.05, or (\$391.05/\$1,270) × 100% = 30.79 percent.

A convertible debt instrument has a market value no less than the greater of either its conversion value or, where the common share prices are depressed, its straight debt value. In other words, conversion value and straight debt value combine to provide a price floor for the convertible bond or debenture. Convertible securities such as the IAC debentures sell above this price floor and give rise to a conversion and bond value premium for three reasons. Firstly, not only is there a capital gains potential, but it is combined with protection against downside risk through their straight debt value. Such limiting of loss is unavailable when investment is made in the corporation's common shares rather than in its convertibles. Secondly, financial intermediaries may be legally constrained from purchasing or holding corporate common shares, but not convertible senior securities, again making the convertibles attractive. Thirdly, investors face lower margin requirements on bonds and debentures than on common shares. This greater borrowing capability serves to attract speculators to convertible debt.

Before proceeding with our discussion, we will review the new terminology and key features of convertible securities which were introduced in the preceding pages in the context of the following hypothetical example.

Example

A firm needs to raise \$10,000,000. Its shares are currently trading at \$40 per share, but the firm's management believes that they are undervalued and expects the share price to increase to at least \$50 per share over the next few years.

The firm plans to sell 20-year convertible debentures at their face value of \$1,000 each with an interest rate of 9 percent, where each debenture can be converted at the option of the holder into 20 common shares. If the firm were to issue otherwise comparable straight debt, an interest rate of 10 percent would have to be paid to make such debt competitive in the market. From this information, we derive the following values for various variables at the time of issue:

$$\text{Conversion ratio} = 20$$

$$\text{Conversion price} = \frac{\text{face value}}{\text{conversion ratio}} = \$50$$

$$\text{Conversion value} = 20 \times \$40 = \$800$$

$$\text{Conversion premium} = \$1{,}000 - \$800 = \$200$$

$$\text{or } \frac{\$1000 - \$800}{\$800} \times 100\% = 25\%$$

$$\text{Straight debt value} = \sum_{t=1}^{20} \frac{\$90}{(1+0.1)^t} + \frac{\$1000}{(1+0.1)^{20}}$$

$$= \$766 + \$149 = \$915$$

$$\text{Bond value premium} = \$1000 - \$915 = \$85$$

$$\text{or } \frac{\$1000 - \$915}{\$1000} \times 100\% = 8.5\%$$

Let us now look at the same issue three years hence. Assuming that the general level of interest rates has not changed and remains at 10 percent for straight long-term debt, the straight debt value of the convertible security at that time becomes

$$\sum_{t=1}^{17} \frac{\$90}{(1+0.1)^t} + \frac{\$1000}{(1+0.1)^{17}} = \$722 + \$198 = \$920$$

The security's conversion value will depend on the prevailing market price of the common shares at that time and be given by

$$\text{conversion value} = 20 \times \text{market price}$$

Figure 11-2 portrays the straight debt value and the conversion value as a function of the market price of the underlying common shares for the above example, with the heavy lines providing a floor below which the market price of the convertible cannot fall. We have seen that the market price of the convertible is likely to be above this floor, as shown in Figure 11-2. If the market price of the common shares is very depressed so as to render the conversion feature almost worthless, the convertible's market price will be close to the straight debt value. On the other hand, with a very high market price for the common shares, investors will buy the convertibles mainly for their conversion feature, and the market price of the convertible securities will approach their conversion value.

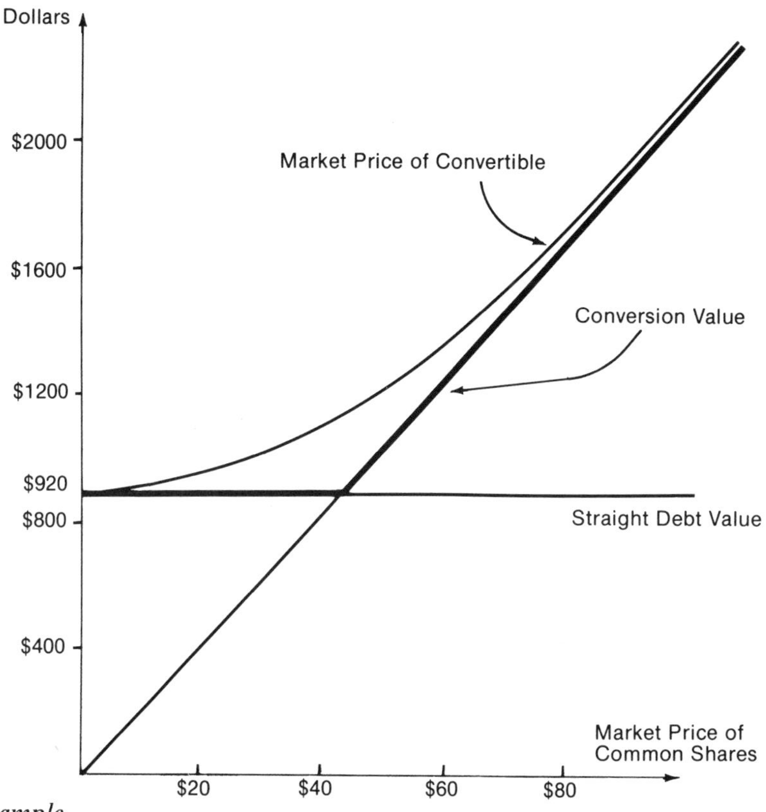

FIGURE 11-2

Price of a Convertible Debenture as a Function of the Market Price of the Firm's Common Shares (assumes risk of default unaffected by Share Price)

Example

Assume that in our previous example the market price of the common shares three years after the date of the original issue was actually $55, and the convertible securities traded at $1,200.We can then compute:

conversion value	$1100	conversion value premium =	$1200 − $1100 = $100; $\frac{\$1200 - \$1100}{\$1100} = 9\%$
market price	$1200		
straight debt value	$ 920	bond value premium =	$1200 − $ 920 = $280; $\frac{\$1200 - \$\ 920}{\$1200} = 23\%$

To the investor, the bond value premium indicates the potential loss due to a slide in the stock market which would render the conversion feature worthless. The conversion value premium indicates the percentage by which the firm's common shares have to appreciate in order for the conversion value to exceed the current market price of the convertible securities. In our example, a collapse in the stock market would expose an investor to a potential loss of 23 percent of the

> investment, while the market price of the common shares would have to go up by an additional 9 percent if an investor who pays $1,200 for the convertible securities is to break even on exercising the conversion privileges.

It should be recognized that the lines as shown in Figure 11-2 will change over time. For example, the straight debt value of the convertible security may not only be altered by shifts in prevailing interest rates or by changes in the risk of the borrowing corporation as perceived by investors, but also by the remaining time to maturity. Thus, as the maturity of the convertible debt issue approaches, the straight debt value will move towards the face value of the security. Also, if there is a time limit on exercising the conversion option, any conversion premium will disappear. As such a deadline approaches the investor has no choice but to convert or to forfeit the option, and no opportunity exists for additional future gains. A similar effect occurs if the security can be called by the issuing corporation, a possibility which will be discussed below.

From the issuing corporation's point of view, issues of convertible securities are typically viewed as deferred common equity financing. In most cases, convertible securities are issued with the full intention and expectation that conversion will become attractive and will take place. As we saw, the conversion price generally is set above the prevailing market price of the common shares at the time of the convertible offering. Thus, convertible securities are designed to net the corporation more for each share which is ultimately issued than could have been obtained under current market conditions, with the minimizing of dilution of ownership as one consequence.

Example

> Pursuing the above numerical example, Figure 11-3 contrasts the effects of immediate financing through issuance of new common shares at $40 per share with the issuing of convertible debentures as outlined. We note that under the latter alternative, and given the conversion price of $50, $10,000,000/$50 = 200,000 new common shares would have to be issued upon conversion. On the other hand, if the $10,000,000 had been raised through a straight issue of common shares at $40 per share, an additional $10,000,000/$40 = 250,000 common shares would be outstanding.

To enable the issuing corporation to force conversion once the price of its common shares has made conversion viable, convertible securities are generally issued with a call feature.

Example

> Assume again that three years after the original issue the firm's common shares trade at $55 per share, and that the market price of the convertible security is $1,200. If the convertible debenture was subject to a call feature allowing the corporation to redeem the debentures with a call premium of 5 percent, or for $1,050, clearly investors could be forced to convert. Given a few weeks' notice with a deadline at which time they would receive the call price of $1,050 for each debenture they

hold, rational investors would choose to convert before the call date as the securities' conversion value of 20 × \$55 = \$1,100 exceeds the call price.

It is easy to appreciate from the above why the market price of convertible securities which are subject to being called will not substantially exceed their conversion value.

FIGURE 11-3

Consequences of Immediate Equity Financing Versus Issuance of Convertible Debt which is Converted after Three Years

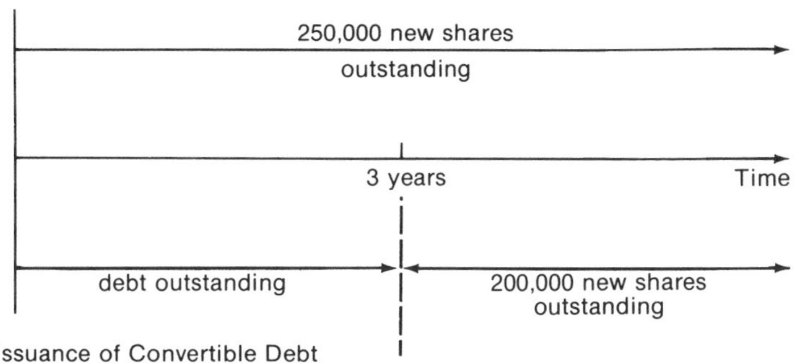

By now the reasons for using convertibles might be quite obvious but they are nevertheless worth pulling together. The more important advantages include the following:

- Permits cheaper financing or perhaps financing with fewer restrictive covenants. The conversion privilege is a "sweetener" with broad appeal to investors. Combines the safety of a senior security with the capital gains potential of common shares.
- Provides a vehicle for common share financing at prices above those prevailing at the time the convertibles are first issued. This minimizes dilution. Underwriting costs are likely to be lower as well.
- Enables the issuer to enlarge the market for its securities by attracting investors, such as financial institutions, faced with legal constraints on direct investment in common shares.

The issuer must also recognize potential disadvantages in the use of convertibles. The plan to resort to deferred rather than immediate equity financing may backfire. If corporate performance is below expectations, leaving the price of common shares depressed, forced conversion through a call for redemption is not feasible. For instance, if in our previous example the firm's share price had remained at \$40 per share, the resulting conversion value of 20 × \$40 = \$800 would have ruled out any possibility of forcing conversion. The resultant "overhanging" issue of convertible debt may impair future flexibility in financing and serve to remind prospective investors of the company's past failings.

The dilution potential inherent in a convertible is recognized by the market. When an issue is first announced, a drop in the market price of the issuing corporation's common shares may take place.[9] This potential for dilution will be of concern to management and the reason for it should be well noted.

Example

Assume that in our previous example, the firm had originally 750,000 common shares outstanding, with no debt or preferred shares in its capital structure. Earnings before interest and taxes (EBIT) are $16,000,000, and this figure is expected to increase to $18,000,000 once the monies received from the new issue have been invested. The corporate tax rate is 40 percent. The partial impact of dilution is illustrated by the indicated per share earnings in the calculations below.

	Presently	With Convertibles Outstanding	With Debentures Converted
EBIT	$16,000,000	$18,000,000	$18,000,000
9% debenture interest	—	900,000	—
Taxable income	$16,000,000	$17,100,000	$18,000,000
Tax at 40%	$ 6,400,000	$ 6,840,000	$ 7,200,000
Profit after taxes	$ 9,600,000	$10,260,000	$10,800,000
Number of common shares outstanding	750,000	750,000	950,000
Earnings per common share	$12.80	$13.68	$11.37

Note that dilution would have been even larger if the additional $10,000,000 had been raised through an issue of straight common shares at $40 per share. With 250,000 new shares issued, earnings per share would drop to $10,800,000/(750,000+250,000) = $10.80.

11-4. UNITS

On occasion, Canadian corporations package together two or more different types of securities and options in order to increase the attractiveness of an offering, or in an attempt to appeal to a wider range of investors.[10]

The use of packaging has, of course, varied and we can point to no standard unit or approach.

Example

The one-hundred-million-dollar Bell Canada arrangement offered in 1974 provides an interesting illustration. In this instance, 2,000,000

[9]When attempting to ascertain the full impact of dilution on market price of the issuer's common shares an analyst must, in addition, subjectively estimate shifts in the price earnings ratio brought about by changes in financial risk or leverage. This is discussed in detail in the chapter on capital structure.

[10]We could question whether such packaging really serves a useful purpose. Setting potential savings in issuing and underwriting expenses aside, we could argue that investors would have a wider choice if various securities were issued separately without being tied into prepackaged units.

> units were issued, each comprising one $4.23 cumulative redeemable convertible voting preferred share with a par value of $47.00 and one warrant to purchase from Bell Canada one common share of Northern Electric Company Limited. Northern Electric is a 90 percent owned subsidiary of Bell Canada and, on exercise of all 2,000,000 warrants, 82 percent of its shares would still be owned by Bell Canada. The preferred shares have a conversion ratio of one and are convertible into common shares of Bell Canada at any time before December 2, 1986. The warrants have an exercise price of $21.50 and expire after November 30, 1979. This "double option" package was priced at $50 and was well received by investors in the market.

Units of greater complexity and comprising even more of a mix of securities are sometimes used by smaller or less established firms in periods of high interest rates. If the senior securities being offered were not made more attractive through appropriate packaging, the yield on the debt or preferred shares would have to be increased, its features and protective covenants tightened, and the underwriter's compensation raised. The combination of these considerations has frequently prompted resort to units.

The components of a unit may be tied together for some specified period of time after issue in an attempt to curb, or at least defer excessive speculation which otherwise may develop around certain component securities of the unit, such as warrants. Practice in this regard will vary and hinges on the particular circumstances and the attitudes of the underwriters involved.

11-5. SUMMARY

In an attempt to lower the cost of raising funds, firms will often use warrants, convertibles and units as "sweeteners".

A warrant is a transferable option to buy a number of common shares for a given exercise price. The option is generally made available for a specified time period of several years. A floor value for warrants is easily computed from the difference between the current market price of the firm's common shares and the exercise price. The market price of warrants is generally higher than this computed floor value since warrants offer investors potential for future capital gains if the market price of the underlying shares should increase. The market price of warrants is more volatile than that of the underlying shares, thus offering investors leverage to speculate. Other things being constant, the value of a warrant increases with increasing time to expiration, and at the expiry date, warrants will trade at their computed floor values.

Convertible instruments, whether preferred shares, bonds or debentures, give the holder an option of converting the security into common shares on some prescribed basis. From the issuing firm's point of view, convertible securities are generally viewed as delayed equity financing, and are issued with the full expectation that in the future conversion will take place. They are generally issued with call features which enable the corporation to force conversion once conversion is economically attractive for investors. From an investor's point of view, a convertible security may combine the attractions of relatively low-risk fixed-income securities with the speculative appeal and potential for capital gains associated with equity investments.

From the issuer's point of view, certain differences between warrants and convertibles are to be noted. Warrants will provide the firm with additional funds when exercised as new shares are purchased at the subscription price. Exercising of conversion privileges, on the other hand, will not provide the firm with additional funds as investors simply exchange their convertible debt for share certificates. Exercising of both warrants and convertible options can lead to some improvement in the corporation's debt-equity ratio, though exercise of warrants will leave unchanged the actual amount of debt outstanding.

Units are combinations of securities or options packaged to appeal to investors. The components of a unit may be tied together for some specified period of time after the issue, after which each security making up the package can be traded separately and in its own right.

Questions for Discussion

1. Contrast rights with warrants from an issuer's point of view with particular reference to (i) how they come into being
   (ii) what the issuer expects to receive and
   (iii) the balance sheet implications.
2. Why are warrants usually traded at prices which are higher than their computed floor values? Give some examples to illustrate your argument.
3. What are the main factors to be considered in the evaluation of warrants? Is it correct to say that the higher the price of common shares the closer the market value of warrants to their floor price (other things being equal)? Why?
4. What are convertibles? Can you cite some potential benefits in their use?
5. What is the floor value of a convertible debenture? Why does a convertible trade at a premium above its floor value? When might it not?
6. Which of warrants or convertibles are generally riskier for the investor? Why?
7. Why may an outstanding warrant be viewed as a corporate liability?
8. Why is the market price of a warrant influenced by the variability of the underlying share's price, the warrant's maturity date, and whether dividends are paid on the underlying shares?
9. Why would a deferred call privilege on an issue of convertible bonds be attractive to investors, particularly if the conversion feature has a long life?

Problems with Solutions

1. A firm's common shares currently trade at \$10 per share. The firm has warrants outstanding which entitle the holder to purchase two shares at an exercise price of \$9 per share, with an expiry date which is three years hence.
   (a) Compute the floor value for the warrants.
   (b) Show why the warrants could not trade at a market price which is below the computed floor value.
   (c) Show the percentage change in the computed floor value for a ±25 percent change in the market price of the shares.

(d) Assume that a year later the firm's shares trade at \$20 per share. Recompute the floor value of the warrants, and again derive the percentage change in the computed floor value for a ±25 percent change in the market price of the shares.

Solution

(a) Here the formula $W_F = n(P-S)$ is used, as developed in the chapter, section 11-2, where:

$$P = \$10 \qquad S = \$9 \qquad n = 2$$

Thus, the warrant floor value = 2(10 − 9) = \$2

(b) Suppose the warrants were trading at \$1 (that is, below their computed floor value). Then an investor could buy a warrant for \$1 and thereby purchase 2 shares for a total of \$18. Immediately this investor could sell these shares for \$20, realizing a net profit from his transactions of \$20 − \$18 − \$1 = \$1. There would be a profit made by this process until the warrants traded at \$2—just the floor value.

(c) Again, we use the formula $W_F = n(P - S)$, where:

$$n = 2 \qquad S = \$9 \qquad P = \$10 \pm 25\%$$

Thus, as P assumes values of \$7.50, \$10, \$12.50

$$W_{F_1} = 2(7.50 - 9) = -\$3.00$$

$$W_{F_2} = 2(10 - 9) = \$2.00$$

$$W_{F_3} = 2(12.50 - 9) = \$7.00$$

Note the value of W_{F_1} is negative. Obviously, this is not possible and the value of the warrant would simply be \$0.

Thus, the percentage changes are:

$$+25\%: \quad \frac{W_{F_3}}{W_{F_2}} = \frac{2(12.50 - 9)}{2(10 - 9)} = \frac{\$7}{\$2} = 350\%$$

−25%: W_F becomes 0, thus change must be −100%.

(d) Use $W_F = n(P - S)$. This formula is not affected by the passage of time.

$$W_{F_1} = 2(20 - 9) = \$22$$

With a share price of \$20 a ±25% change would yield \$15 or \$25. The new floor values may then be computed:

$$W_{F_2} = 2(25 - 9) = \$32$$

$$W_{F_3} = 2(15 - 9) = \$12$$

This price change of ±25% yields a warrant floor price change of:

$$\left.\begin{array}{l} \dfrac{32 - 22}{22} = 45.5\% \\ \text{and} \\ \dfrac{12 - 22}{22} = -45.5\% \end{array}\right\} \pm 45.5\%$$

Comparing this solution to the solution under 1(c) above, we see that as the market price of the underlying shares increases, the leverage potential of the warrants decreases.

2. The S.D. Company is planning a major expansion program requiring new capital of \$20,000,000. The firm currently has 8,000,000 shares outstanding and \$20,000,000 in long-term debt at an interest rate of 10 percent. Earnings before interest and taxes for the year just ended were \$15,333,333. With the new financing, they are expected to increase to \$17,000,000 by the end of the current year, and to increase at a rate of 12 percent per annum for the indefinite future. The firm's shares have typically traded at a price-earning ratio of 10 and it is expected that they will continue to do so. The corporate tax rate is 40 percent.
   (a) Compute the current market price of the firm's shares.
   (b) Assume new shares could be issued to net the company 10 percent less than the current market price. If the new capital were raised through an issue of common shares, how many shares would be outstanding? Compute earnings per share and the market price per share at the end of the current year and at the end of year 3.
   (c) Alternatively, the new capital could be raised through issuing 20-year convertible debentures, \$1,000 each, at an interest rate of 8 percent. The conversion price would be set 20 percent above the current market price of the shares. A call feature would be provided allowing the corporation to call the issue at any time after year 3 at a premium of 5 percent. Current interest rates on a comparable straight debt issue would be 11 percent.
      (i) Assuming that projections materialize as anticipated, compute the straight debt value and the conversion value at the end of year 3. Can the corporation force conversion at the end of year 3?
      (ii) Assuming conversion has taken place, compute earnings per share and market price per share at the end of year 3.
   (d) Based on the information given, which alternative method for raising the funds appears preferable? What are the risks or tradeoffs?

Solution

(a) The market price of the shares is simply 10 times the earnings per share. Earnings per share may be calculated as follows:

Earnings before interest and taxes	\$15,333,333
Interest (10% × \$20,000,000)	2,000,000
Taxable earnings	\$13,333,333
Tax (40%)	5,333,333
Net earnings	\$ 8,000,000

$$\text{Earnings per share} = \frac{\$8,000,000}{8,000,000} = \$1/\text{share}$$

The market price per share is ten times this amount, or \$10.

(b) New shares at 10% less than current market price would net the company \$9/share.
Thus, to raise the necessary \$20,000,000, the S.D. Company would need

to issue $\dfrac{\$20{,}000{,}000}{\$9/\text{share}} = 2{,}222{,}222$ shares

Earnings per share for the current year, given that the new shares were issued, would be:

Earnings before interest and taxes	\$17,000,000
Interest (10% × \$20,000,000)	2,000,000
Taxable earnings	\$15,000,000
Tax (40%)	6,000,000
Net Earnings	\$ 9,000,000

There are now 8,000,000 + 2,222,222 = 10,222,222 shares outstanding, so earnings per share are

$$\frac{\$9{,}000{,}000}{10{,}222{,}222 \text{ shares}} = \$0.88/\text{share}.$$

This would translate into a share price of \$8.80.
Three years hence earnings before interest and taxes, growing at 12% per annum, would become:
17,000,000 × 1.405 = \$23,885,000
Earnings per share are calculated in the usual manner:

Earnings before interest and taxes	\$23,885,000
Interest (10% × \$20,000,000)	2,000,000
Taxable earnings	\$21,885,000
Tax (40%)	8,754,000
Net earnings	\$13,131,000

$$\text{Earnings per share} = \frac{\$13{,}131{,}000}{10{,}222{,}222 \text{ shares}} = \$1.285$$

Share price is ten times this, or \$12.85

(c) (i) The straight debt value is calculated through use of the formula:

$$DV_m = \sum_{t=1}^{T-m} \frac{I}{(1+i)^t} + \frac{F}{(1+i)^{T-m}}$$

Where, from the problem we know:

$T = 20$ $\quad I = \$80$ $\quad F = \$1{,}000$

$m = 3$ $\quad i = 11\%$

$$DV_3 = \sum_{t=1}^{17} \frac{\$80}{(1+.11)^t} + \frac{\$1000}{(1+.11)^{17}}$$

$$= 80(7.571) + 1000(.1696)$$

$$= 605.68 + 169.60 = \$775.28$$

$$\text{Conversion Ratio} = \frac{\text{Face Value}}{\text{Conversion Price}}$$

We know that:

Face Value = \$1,000

Conversion Price = 20% above current market price of \$10 = \$12

Thus,

$$\text{Conversion Ratio} = \frac{\$1000}{\$12} = 83.33$$

Thus, the *current* conversion value is 83.33 × \$10 = \$833.33

To determine the conversion value at the end of year 3 requires computation of the market price and earnings per share at the end of year 3.

We compute the earnings per share as before, remembering an additional \$1,600,000 interest charge (\$20,000,000 × 8%) will have to be included.

Earnings before interest and taxes	\$23,885,000
Interest (10% × \$20,000,000 + 8% × \$20,000,000)	3,600,000
Taxable earnings	\$20,285,000
Tax (40%)	8,114,000
Net earnings	\$12,171,000

$$\text{Earnings per share} = \frac{\$12,171,000}{8,000,000} = \$1.521$$

Market price = \$1.521 × 10 = \$15.21

Conversion value is thus: \$15.21 × 83.33 = \$1,267.45 and the corporation *could* force conversion.

(ii) Assuming conversion had taken place, we would find that interest payments had decreased to \$2,000,000 (10% × \$20,000,000), and that the number of shares outstanding had increased by

$$\frac{\$20,000,000}{\$12} = 1,666,667.$$

Earnings before interest and taxes	\$23,885,000
Interest (10% × \$20,000,000)	2,000,000
Taxable earnings	\$21,885,000
Tax (40%)	8,754,000
Net Earnings	\$13,131,000

Earnings per share are thus $\dfrac{\$13{,}131{,}000}{8{,}000{,}000 + 1{,}666{,}667} = \$1.358$

and the market price is $13.58 per share.

We note that with a convertible issue outstanding, investors realize the potential dilution which would come about if the issue is converted, with additional common shares outstanding. Thus, in our example, the common shares may have traded at a market price which is less than 10 times earnings or $15.21, as computed under (c)(i) above, in anticipation of such dilution.

(d) From an earnings-per-share viewpoint, the preferable decision is clearly to issue convertible debt. Both initially and in three years, earnings per share, and hence, market price per share are considerably higher. The main reason for this is that under a convertible issue, new shares are effectively sold for $12 per share, as compared to $9 per share under the immediate common share issue. The main risk is that projections may not materialize as anticipated—either if earnings are off, or if the price earnings ratio of the firm's shares drop, the firm may not be able to force conversion with the issue overhanging. Thus, the tradeoff is between higher earnings per share and higher share prices, given anticipated future developments, and the risk of such forecasts not materializing. In the latter case, an immediate common share issue might have been preferable.

3. The S.P. Company is considering a plan to expand its operations, and $500,000 is needed for the expansion. There are two possible alternatives open to the firm:

Alternative 1: Sell convertible debentures with a coupon rate of 8 percent, convertible into shares at $16.

Alternative 2: Issue 8 percent debentures with each $1,000 debenture carrying 100 warrants, each warrant entitling the holder to purchase one common share at an exercise price of $16.

The financial statements for the current year are given below:

S.P. Company
Balance Sheet
As at December 31, 197X

Total current assets	$ 800,000	Total current liabilities	$ 600,000
Total fixed assets	200,000	Shares ($1.00 par)	300,000
		Retained earnings	100,000
Total assets	$1,000,000	Total liabilities	$1,000,000

S.P. Company
Income Statement
For the year ended December 31, 197X

Sales	$1,900,000
Total costs (except interest charges)	1,325,000
Gross profit	$ 575,000
Interest charges	75,000
Income before tax	$ 500,000
Tax (40%)	200,000
Income after tax	$ 300,000
Number of shares outstanding	300,000
Earnings per share	$1.00

Assume that one-half of the funds secured through the new issue will be used to pay off bank loans, with the other half used for investment in fixed assets. When warrants are exercised, the proceeds will be invested in current assets.

(a) Show the balance sheets after conversion of the convertibles or exercise of warrants under alternatives 1 and 2 as outlined above.

(b) What will be the debt/total assets ratio under each alternative?

(c) What will the earnings per share be under each of the alternatives, assuming conversion has taken place and the warrants have been exercised, if net income after tax is assumed to be 25 percent of total assets?

Solution

(a) Alternative 1: The \$500,000 will increase fixed assets by \$250,000 and decrease current liabilities by \$250,000. The \$500,000 long-term debt issued would be converted into $\frac{\$500,000}{\$16} = 31,250$ shares, increasing the share account by 31,250 × \$1 = \$31,250 and creating a paid-in capital account of (31,250 × \$15) = \$468,750.

S.P. Company
Balance Sheet
Alternative 1

Total current assets	$ 800,000	Total current liabilities	$ 350,000
Total fixed assets	450,000	Long-term debt	—
		Shares ($1.00 par)	331,250
		Paid-in capital	468,750
		Retained earnings	100,000
Total assets	$1,250,000	Total liabilities	$1,250,000

Alternative 2: Again fixed assets increase and liabilities decrease. However, in this case the long-term debt remains

outstanding. A total of 50,000 warrants will be issued (500 debentures each carrying 100 warrants). The exercise of all warrants will result in the issuance of 50,000 shares for a total of 50,000 × \$16, or \$800,000. Hence, current assets increase to \$1,600,000, the share account increases by \$50,000, and a paid-in capital account of 50,000 × \$15 = \$750,000 arises.

S.P. Company
Balance Sheet
Alternative 2

Total current assets	\$1,600,000	Total current liabilities	\$ 350,000
Total fixed assets	450,000	Long-term debt	500,000
		Shares (\$1.00 par)	350,000
		Paid-in capital	750,000
		Retained earnings	100,000
Total assets	\$2,050,000	Total liabilities	\$2,050,000

(b)

	Alternative 1	Alternative 2
Total debt	\$ 350,000	\$ 850,000
Total assets	\$1,250,000	\$2,050,000
Debt/total assets	28%	41%

(c)

	Alternative 1	Alternative 2
Total assets	\$1,250,000	\$2,050,000
Net income after tax (25% of assets)	\$ 312,500	\$ 512,500
Number of shares outstanding	331,250	350,000
Earnings per share	\$0.94	\$1.46

4. The floor value of a warrant is computed as $W_F = n(P - S)$. Assume the market price of the shares changes by x% from P to P^1. That is:

$$x = \frac{P^1 - P}{P} \times 100\%$$

This will cause a change in the computed floor price of the warrant from W_F to W_F^1, or a percentage change of:

$$y = \frac{W_F^1 - W_F}{W_F} \times 100\%$$

To illustrate the leverage afforded by warrants, compute the percentage change in the computed floor price of the warrant as a function of the percentage change in the market price of the shares, or y as a function of x.

Solution

Given $P^1 = (1 + x)P$, we have:

$$W_F^1 = n(P^1 - S) = n[(1 + x)P - S]$$
$$= n(P - S) + xnP$$
$$= W_F + xnP$$

We obtain:

$$W_F^1 - W_F = xnP$$

and

$$\frac{W_F^1 - W_F}{W_F} = y = x\frac{nP}{W_F}$$

For example, assume:

$n = 1 \qquad P = \$10 \qquad S = \$6$

We have $W_F = 1(\$10 - \$6) = \$4$

A 20 percent increase in P to $P^1 = \$12$ would cause $W_F^1 = 1(\$12 - \$6) = \$6$, which is equivalent to a 50 percent increase from W_F. According to the above formula, we would have obtained:

$$y = x\frac{nP}{W_F}$$
$$= 20\%\frac{1 \times \$10}{\$4} = 20\% \times 2.5 = 50\%$$

From the formula $W_F = n(P - S)$, we see that the value of W_F can range between zero (for $P \leq S$) and nP (for $S = 0$). From the formula $y = x\frac{nP}{W_F}$, it is clear that the leverage potential of a warrant increases with decreasing values of W_F. The formula can be portrayed diagramatically as follows:

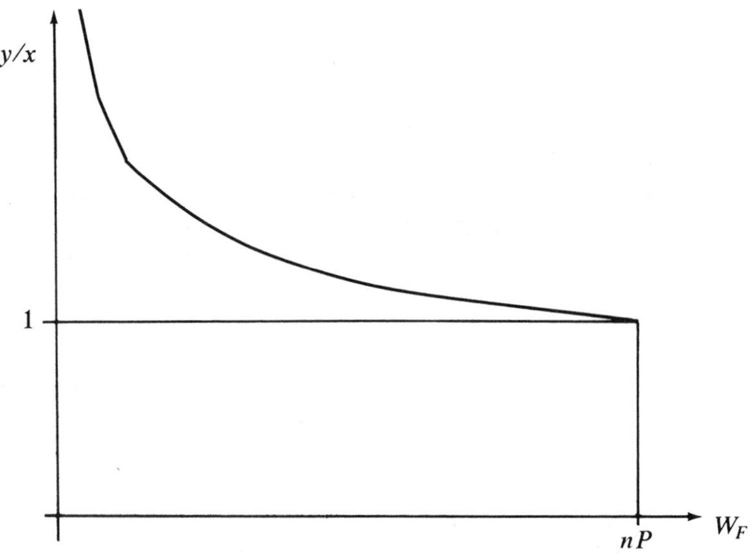

We conclude that the smaller S is in relation to P, the closer W_F will be to nP, and the lower the leverage potential of the warrants.

Additional Problems

1. Shares of Child Corp. presently trade at $37.50. The firm has warrants outstanding entitling the holder to purchase one share for $40. These warrants are currently trading at $2.
   (a) Compute the floor value of the warrants.
   (b) Why might the warrant trade above the floor value?
   (c) A year later the shares of Child Corp. trade at $52.50. Compute the floor value of the warrants now.
2. Warrants for the purchase of shares of Q Co. Ltd. are outstanding. The warrants entitle the holder to purchase 5 shares per warrant at $16.50 a share. The warrants have a computed floor value of $17.50.
   (a) Compute the current market price per share.
   (b) Show the percentage change in the floor value for a 10% change in the market price of the shares.
   (c) Share price moves to $16. Compute the new floor value of the warrant and the effect of a 10% change in the new share price on the warrant's floor price.
3. Sixtue Corp. has outstanding an issue of 25-year 7% convertible bonds with a total face value of $15,000,000, which was issued two years ago. Each $100 face value of bonds is convertible into 7 shares of Sixtue common stock. Had Sixtue issued debt without the convertible feature, it would have faced an interest rate payable of 9%. Interest rate levels have remained constant during the last two years. Shares of Sixtue are currently trading at $18.
   (a) Compute the current straight debt value.
   (b) Find the conversion price and the current conversion value.

   Two years later, the outlook for Sixtue is quite dismal. Accordingly, the share price has dropped to $10. The convertibles have a market price of $90. Interest rates on long-term debt are still 9 percent.
   (c) Compute the new straight debt value and the bond value premium percentage.
   (d) What is the conversion value and the conversion value premium now?
4. Sunrise Ltd. wishes to issue $1,000,000 of $1,000 face value convertible bonds. These bonds would be convertible into 40 shares of Sunrise common stock, which currently trades around $21 per share. This bond issue would be a 20-year issue and could be floated at an interest rate of 9%. Similar issues without conversion privileges generally bear interest of 10%.
   (a) Compute the conversion premium.
   (b) Compute the bond value premium.

   Four years later, Sunrise Ltd.'s stock trades at $24, with interest rates having remained constant.
   (c) Compute the new straight debt value and the current conversion value.
5. The following financial statements of Depliant Industries were released for the year just ended:

Balance Sheet

Current assest	$2,400,000	Current liabilities	$1,200,000
Investments	200,000	Long-term debt(8%)	5,000,000
Plant & equipment	6,000,000	Common shares—	
Land	4,100,000	$2 par value	
		authorized 2,000,000	
		issued 1,000,000	2,000,000
		Paid-in capital	3,500,000
		Retained Earnings	1,000,000
	$12,700,000		$12,700,000

Income Statement

Sales	$4,000,000
Cost of goods sold	2,600,000
Earnings before interest and taxes	$1,400,000
Interest expense	400,000
Taxable income	$1,000,000
Tax (40%)	400,000
Net income	$ 600,000

Shares have generally traded at 7 times earnings.

Depliant's vice-president, Mr. Smith, would like to take advantage of a new investment possibility, but this would require additional capital of $4,000,000.

Before reporting at an upcoming board meeting, Mr. Smith would like to have more information in order to make a recommendation as to whether the new investments should be pursued.

Preliminary indications are that a straight debt issue could be floated at 11% interest, a debt issue with warrants attached at 9% interest, a convertible debt issue at 8% interest, or common shares to net Depliant $4 per share.

If the debt with warrants alternative were taken, each $1,000 face value of debt would carry 100 warrants, with each warrant entitling the holders to purchase one share at an exercise price of $4.75. The warrants would have a life of four years. If the convertible debt was decided upon, the conversion price would be set at $4.75.

Mr. Smith believes that if the new investments are undertaken, earnings before interest and taxes will grow at a rate of 8% per year for five years and also that the price/earnings ratio will immediately adjust upward to 10.

(a) Compute the present market price of Depliant's shares.

(b) Given the above projections, show the effect of issuing the $4,000,000 in straight debt on share price at the end of the coming year and also at the end of the fourth year.

(c) as in item (b), but issuing only common shares.

(d) as in item (b), but issuing debt with warrants attached. Assume that all warrants would be exercised during the fourth year.

(e) as in item (b), but issuing convertible debt. Assume that investors base their valuation of Depliant's shares on fully diluted earnings per share, that is, on earnings per share given all the new shares outstanding once conversion has taken place. Could Depliant force conversion at the end of year 4?

(f) Show the balance sheet as it would appear under the following conditions at the end of year 4. Assume that all earnings for the four years were paid out in dividends. Also assume any increase in capital will go 60% to plant and equipment and 40% to land.
   (i) issuance of straight debt.
   (ii) issuance of common shares.
   (iii) issuance of debt with warrants, all warrants converted prior to expiry.
   (iv) issuance of convertible debt, not yet converted.

Selected References

P. Bacon and E. Winn Jr., "The Impact of Forced Conversion on Stock Prices", *Journal of Finance*, December, 1969, pp. 871-874.

W. Baumol, B. Malkiel and R. Quandt, "The Valuation of Convertible Securities", *Quarterly Journal of Economics*, February, 1966, pp. 48-59.

F. Black and M. Scholes, "The Pricing of Options and Corporate Liabilities", *Journal of Political Economy*, May-June, 1973, pp. 637-659.

A. Bladen, *Techniques for Investing in Convertible Bonds*, New York: Salomon Brothers and Hutzler, 1966.

R. Brealey, *Security Prices in a Competitve Market*, Cambridge: The M.I.T. Press, 1971, Ch. 16 and 17.

E. Brigham, "An Analysis of Convertible Debentures" in E. Brigham, ed., *Readings in Financial Management*, New York: Holt, Rinehart and Winston, 1971, pp. 305-329.

P. Cretien, Jr., "Premiums on Convertible Bonds: Comment", *Journal of Finance*, September, 1970, pp. 917-922.

D. Duvel, "Premiums on Convertible Bonds: Comment", *Journal of Finance*, September, 1970, pp. 923-927.

S. Hayes and H. Reiling, "Sophisticated Financing Tool: The Warrant", *Harvard Business Review*, January-February, 1969, pp. 137-150.

E. Jennings, "An Estimate of Convertible Bond Premiums", *Journal of Financial and Quantitative Analysis*, January, 1974, pp. 33-56.

Midland-Osler Securities Ltd., *Share Purchase Warrants*, 1966.

G. Mumey, "Premiums on Convertible Bonds: Comment", *Journal of Finance*, September, 1970, pp. 928-930.

G. Pinches, "Financing with Convertible Preferred Stocks, 1960-1967", *Journal of Finance*, March, 1970, pp. 53-64.

O. Poensgen, "The Valuation of Convertible Bonds: Parts I and II", *Industrial Management Review*, Fall, 1965, and Spring, 1966, pp. 77-92 and pp. 83-98.

D. Rush and R. Melicher, "An Empirical Examination of Factors Which Influence Warrant Prices", *Journal of Finance*, December, 1974, pp. 1449-1466.

P. Samuelson, "Rational Theory of Warrant Pricing", *Industrial Management Review*, Spring, 1965, pp. 13-31.

J. Shelton, "The Relation of the Price of a Warrant to the Price of its Associated Stock: Parts I and II", *Financial Analysis Journal*, May-June, and July-August, 1967, pp. 143-151 and pp. 88-89.

L. Skerratt, "The Price Determination of Convertible Loan Stock: A UK Model", *Journal of Business Finance and Accounting*, Autumn, 1974, pp. 429-443.

C. Smith, "Options Pricing: A Review", *Journal of Financial Economics*, January-March, 1976, p. 3-51.

J. Van Horne, "Warrant Valuation in Relation to Volatility and Opportunity Costs", *Industrial Management Review*, Spring, 1969, pp. 19-32.

R. Weil Jr., J. Segall, and D. Green Jr., "Premiums on Convertible Bonds", *Journal of Finance*, June, 1968, pp. 445-464.

R. Weil Jr., J. Segall, and D. Green Jr., "A Reply to Premiums on Convertible Bonds: Comment", *Journal of Finance*, September, 1970, pp. 931-933.

Chapter 12
Investment Dealers, the Underwriting Function and Rights Offerings

12-1. INTRODUCTION

In the preceding chapters we reviewed the available sources of long-term external financing along with the peculiarities and characteristics of the various types of securities involved. This chapter is concerned with the institutional arrangements for issuing new securities. The major alternatives open to a firm intent on selling new securities are reviewed in this chapter and include public offerings, private placements and rights offerings.

In the case of public offering, new securities are made available for sale to the general public. While a few corporations may undertake to retail their own securities, they generally lack the expertise and required facilities for floating large public issues. Hence, the services of an investment dealer are generally engaged to *underwrite* the issue. Underwriting as applied to the investment field is a term borrowed from insurance and refers to the purchase of a new offering of securities by the investment dealer. Purchase takes place at a set price and on a particular date. In effect then, once the underwriting is contracted, the success of the offering from the issuer's standpoint is assured. The dealer meanwhile arranges to retail the securities to investors at a somewhat higher price than was paid the issuer, with the spread providing dealer compensation. We can see from this that an investment dealer not only provides marketing services and advice on timing, type and terms of the issue, but also assumes all risks associated with the offering which would otherwise have to be borne by the issuer. In public offerings of securities, the issuing corporation has to publish a *prospectus* which is a document spelling out details of the offering and providing financial and other material information about the firm.

In private placements of securities, the issuing corporation sells the entire offering to one or a very limited number of investors, typically financial institutions like insurance companies or, in the case of issues by smaller concerns, venture capitalists.[1] Private placements eliminate the need for a concerted marketing effort on behalf of the issues as well as the need for a prospectus including the public disclosure therein. The services of an investment dealer may nevertheless be engaged to provide advice on the issue and to bring the interested parties together.

[1]Venture capital refers to equity investments often packaged with some debt and invested in private companies. It is a useful source of funds until such time as a public offering can be made. Venture capitalists include the federal and provincial governments as well as wealthy individuals, banks, and public and private corporations. Their roles will be explored in subsequent chapters.

In a rights offering, the firm's current shareholders are given the right to subscribe to a new issue of securities at a specified subscription price. Because the firm deals with its own shareholders, the marketing effort called for is quite limited and the arrangements relatively straightforward.

Given the importance of public offerings in corporate finance, we start this chapter with a discussion of the underwriting process, followed by comments on private placements, and we conclude with a section on rights offerings.

12-2. APPROACHES TO UNDERWRITING AND THE UNDERWRITING AGREEMENT[2]

The most common approach to underwriting involves a *firm commitment* under which the investment dealer purchases the entire issue. In exchange for the risk assumed through the purchase, as well as the management and subsequent selling effort required, the dealer is compensated by the spread between the price at which the security is to be sold to the public and the amount actually paid to the issuing corporation. Table 12-1 taken from the prospectus of Kaiser Resources Ltd. provides an illustration of just such a spread. Expenses of issue incurred by the corporation include audit and legal fees as well as other costs of preparing the prospectus.

TABLE 12-1

Estimated Net Proceeds
from Sale of 2,500,000 New Common Shares

	Price to Public	Underwriting Discount	Proceeds to Company (1)
Per Share	$12	$0.80	$11.20
Total	$30,000,000	$2,000,000	$28,000,000

(1) Before deducting expenses of issue estimated not to exceed $100,000.

Option underwriting is a method used chiefly in connection with mining issues where risks of underwriting tend to be greater, as new capital is often raised to perform further exploratory work on a property which does not yet have proven economic viability. Here, over time, the underwriter receives a series of options on blocks of unissued shares in exchange for *firm commitment underwriting* of a set amount with the usual form of compensation. The options, exercisable at identified future dates, give the underwriter the right to buy set numbers of shares at predetermined prices generally above the original issue price and rising over time. If the mine prospers and share prices rise above the option price, the

[2]Excellent descriptions of the underwriting process in Canada are to be found in a variety of sources including: Investment Dealers' Association of Canada, *Brief to the Royal Commission on Banking and Finance (Volume II)* mimeographed, 1962, pp. E-7 to 17; Canada, *1964 Report of the Royal Commission on Banking and Finance*, Ottawa: Queen's Printer, 1964, pp. 307-314; P. McQuillan, *Going Public in Canada*, Toronto: The Canadian Institute of Chartered Accountants, 1971; and R. Peters, *Economics of the Canadian Corporate Bond Market*, Montreal: McGill-Queen's University Press, 1971. These sources are relied upon for most of the detail which follows.

dealer stands to make gains in addition to his original compensation. Unexercised options do not carry forward.

In cases involving firm commitment underwriting, the corporation may either contact a dealer with whom it has an established relationship, or just shop around to choose an underwriter.[3] Once contact is made, an informal agreement is drawn, usually in the form of a *letter of intent* from underwriter to issuer. The letter broadly describes the security involved including the size of the offering, and it constitutes an offer by the dealer to purchase the issue under certain conditions. Should any pricing be discussed, it will be given in a range and not defined until just before the securities are offered to the public. The conditions set out in the letter include some standard ones. Thus, the issuing corporation is expected to meet statutory requirements pertaining to the issuance of securities and their offer to the public, including compliance with the applicable companies act and provincial securities acts. The necessary prospectus, trust deed, financial statements, and other documents are to be prepared and registration procedures initiated.

Once the prospectus has been cleared by the appropriate securities commission, a formal *underwriting agreement* is entered into. Provision is made in this agreement for a so-called *market out clause* giving the underwriter the option of termininating the agreement without penalty. Though use of the clause is generally contingent on some extraordinary occurrence or governmental action, it does provide for the agreement to be terminated on the basis of the underwriter's "assessment of the state of the financial markets", and thus limits the risk which the underwriter assumes.

While still negotiating the formal underwriting agreement, the underwriter often selects other dealers to form a *banking group* or underwriting syndicate. The group is likely to be assembled on the basis of past relationships with the principal underwriter. Once a particular banking group has become associated in financing an issuer, individual dealers will expect to be invited to participate in future offerings of the same issuer and the principal underwriter will expect them to take up their standard proportion of new offerings. According to the Porter Commission, these practices introduce ridigity into the industry and place great power into the hands of a few managers.

> Syndicates once formed tend to ossify; the new firm finds it almost impossible to obtain participations, while the aggressive and growing members of the syndicate experience equal difficulty in expanding theirs. Participants in syndicates, particularly of corporation issues also complain that they are seldom seriously consulted often being given less than 24 hours to decide whether or not they will participate. Given the lack of flexibility in syndicates, they usually must go along whether or

[3]Established relationships often exist because the investment dealer is represented on the borrower's board of directors. The potential conflict of interest is apparent and discussed in a recent paper. See D. Shaw, "The Cost of Going Public in Canada," *Financial Executive*, July, 1969, pp. 27-28.

not they believe the issue is attractive, since rejection means they will not be invited to distribute subsequent issues.[4]

The principal underwriter will be both a member of the banking group and its syndicate manager. The managing firm's name will head the list of underwriters in a prospectus—a mark of prestige about which investment dealers are quite conscious. The front page of the March 1972 prospectus of Trans-Canada Pipe Lines convertible preferred issue shown in Appendix A of this text illustrates the point quite vividly, as only the name of the principal underwriter appears.

There is no formal banking agreement among the members—only individual letters from the syndicate manager to each of the groups. The letter provides tentative details on the securities involved and is an offer of specific participation to prospective members of the banking group. Acceptance of the offer constitutes a committment to purchase the allocated participation from the managing firm. A special percentage of each member's participation is reserved for sales to financial intermediaries such as insurance companies which make up the so-called *"exempt list"*. The exempted institutions are only approached by the syndicate manager. In this way, large buyers are both shielded from a flood of selling offers and blocked from attempting to break the minimum issue price specified.

The offering prices will depend on the type of securities offered and will differ among buyers. There may be prices to the public, exempted institutions, various dealers, and banking group members. Expenses of the issue are borne by the members in proportion to participation, and profits on sales to dealers and institutions are similarly split.

Larger issues may also involve a *selling group* formed by the syndicate manager. The manager may invite orders from selected dealers to assist with sale of the securities. Unlike banking group members, however, these dealers do not take title to the securities but simply offer marketing services for a fee, while acting as brokers.[5]

To illustrate compensation procedures, consider the following hypothetical prices on a bond purchased from the issuing corportion at $970 by the syndicate manager:

Cost to banking group members	$ 977.50
Draw-down price to banking group members and selling group members	985.00
Price to casual dealers	992.50
Price to exempted institutions	1000.00
Retail price	1000.00

[4] *1964 Report of the Royal Commission on Banking and Finance, op. cit.*, p. 309. The *Report* expresses the hope (p. 310) that greater flexibility will develop in Canada as the industry is now large enough to allow competitive forces to work without impairing the services provided borrowers. There is evidence to suggest that the system still lacks flexibility; see J. McMahon, "Undercurrents of Criticism in the Underwriting World", *Financial Times of Canada*, March 30, 1970, p. 5.

[5] Both brokers and dealers assist in the selling of goods. The distinguishing feature is that a dealer becomes party to the transaction and in the process actually takes title to the goods. A broker on the other hand just offers a service in bringing the buyers and sellers together without becoming a party to the transaction.

The syndicate manager is compensated by the spread of $7.50 between the price at which the issue is bought from the corporation and the cost to banking group members. The difference between the $977.50 cost to banking group members and the $985.00 draw-down price is a withholding by the syndicate manager to cover the expenses of the issue with any unused portion being returned to the members. Banking group members and dealers again derive their compensation from the spread which exists between the price they have to pay for the securities and the price at which they retail them to the investing public. Usually, the price to exempted institutions equals the retail price at which the issue is sold to the public.

The banking group will work toward providing downside price support for an issue *during* and perhaps immediately *after* distribution. Should the market price of the securities fall below the issuing price during this period, banking group members will take an active role in the market, temporarily buying up excess supply in order to support the price.

A significant break in price during the offering period could obviously involve the syndicate in serious losses, while a weak after-market for the security would very quickly produce a list of disgruntled ex-clients. Stabilization efforts might include overselling an offering (selling more securities than are available), and subsequently buying up sales of short-term speculators who are willing to sell immediately after this offering, thereby being able to fill all the outstanding orders.

In contrast to firm commitment underwriting, and most often with smaller speculative issues, the entire arrangement will be on a *best efforts distribution* basis. In such instances, the dealer undertakes to do little more than attempt to retail the securities for the issuer and he receives a commission on sales made. Where the firm seeking funds has a doubtful future, certain dealers may be willing to handle its issues but not guarantee their sale. As the fees are likely to be less, best efforts distribution may also be favored by an issuer when it is felt that the quality of offerings is such that they will require no underwriting.

12-3. THE PROSPECTUS

Securities legislation is a provincial responsibility and statutes in the several jurisdictions have the protection of investors as a major objective. Protection is, in part at least, achieved by requiring the use of a prospectus.[6] It is expected that the document will contain full, true, and plain disclosure of all material facts relating to the proposed public offering.

Using the B.C. *Securities Act* by way of illustration, Part VII of the statute—concerned with new public distributions—is introduced by the following:

> No person or company shall trade in any security issued by a person or company either on his own account or on behalf of any other person or company where the trade would be in the course of primary distribution to the public of the security until there has been filed with and accepted

[6]Federally incorporated companies are also regulated by the prospectus provisions of the *Canada Corporations Act*.

> by the Superintendent a prospectus in respect of the offering of the security and a receipt therefor in writing has been obtained from the Superintendent.[7]

In several jurisdictions, including B.C., various related requirements are set out in the companies acts and must also be complied with.

The prospectus will contain several essential parts:

- a set of financial statements including the auditor's statements;
- additional information likely to be of interest to investors, such as full details on securities to be issued, disclosures of interests in the corporation received or to be received by any experts or directors referred to in the prospectus, and the remuneration of directors and senior executives—stock options included;
- the estimated amount to be raised and how the proceeds are to be used by the issuer;
- a letter over the company president's signature giving salient but broad facts about the company; and
- approval of the contents by the corporation's directors and appropriate certification by other experts where their statements or reports appear in the prospectus.

After the prospectus has been prepared it is filed with the appropriate Securities Commissions, and in the case of federally incorporated companies with the Department of Consumer and Corporate Affairs, to await so-called "blue-skying" or approval. When all requirements are met and approval is obtained the public offering is made. It is worth noting that, within a time constraint, a purchaser may have an agreement to buy securities rescinded if he did not receive a prospectus before placing the order. Rescission may also occur where false statements appear in the prospectus. Shareholders may, in addition, have a right of action against directors and promoters for damages in case of deliberate misrepresentation. For illustrative purposes an abridged copy of a prospectus pertaining to the March 1972 issue of convertible preferred shares by Trans Canada Pipelines is reproduced in Appendix A of this text.

12-4. EFFICIENCY OF UNDERWRITING IN CANADA

Critiques of underwriting procedures in Canada focus on three issues in addition to the lack of flexibility already noted.[8] To begin with, it is suggested that larger well-established underwriters avoid the more speculative issues. Concern about image and reputation has apparently led to this posture and has resulted in operational issues of smaller corporations having to face underwriting costs as high as 10 percent, while in cases of promotional or more speculative issues, 20 percent can be exceeded.[9]

Secondly, underwriters, by avoiding any final agreement on price until the last hour and by having the escape clause in the agreement as well, are hardly

[7] *Securities Act*, 1967 (B.C.) ch. 45, s. 37, as am. 1973, ch. 78, s. 6 and 1974, ch. 82, s. 25.

[8] See *1964 Report of the Royal Commission on Banking and Finance*, *op. cit.*, p. 313.

[9] Best efforts distributions have involved fees approaching ten percent.

assuming very meaningful risks. The fact that institutional and other purchase commitments are often nailed down by the underwriters before the underwriting agreement is signed is supportive of the criticism levelled.

Finally, the continued absence of competitive tendering for corporate issues is often a matter of concern. Given competitive tendering, competing dealers are invited to bid for the underwriting agreement, with the contract going to the dealer offering the most attractive price for the issue under consideration. In the United States, competitive tendering is mandatory for issues of most public utility holding companies, of railroads, and of securities that fall under the jurisdiction of the Federal Power Commission, presumably to ensure efficient pricing. In Canada, arguments against competitive bidding which stress the benefits of receiving continued advice from the dealer with whom there is an ongoing relationship appear to hold sway. As one recent writing suggests, however, the price for such advisory services may be too high. A sampling of United States and Canadian bond issues in the $10 to $49.9 million range shows underwriting spreads in Canada averaging 2.75 times those in the United States.[10]

Total costs of issuing securities should vary according to size of the issue and the degree of risk. There are certain expenses which are more or less fixed regardless of the size of issue. Such expenses include, for example, legal fees and preparation of the prospectus. With respect to the balance, or underwriting costs, there is greater risk assumed with the less well-known or smaller issues and with junior securities, particularly common shares. Table 12-2, drawn from the brief to the Porter Commission submitted by the Investment Dealer's Association, sets out the underwriters' compensation. It is based on a survey of members.

TABLE 12-2

Underwriters' Compensation
(Average Gross Mark Up as a Percentage Cost)

	Percentage		
	Arithmetic Average	Median	Range
Common stock issues —			
(a) under $3 million	8.43	9.09	2.00 - 14.00
(b) over $3 million	6.98	6.38	5.00 - 10.00
Preferred stock —			
(a) under $3 million	6.05	4.77	3.50 - 11.00
(b) over $3 million	4.75	4.00	3.50 - 6.50
Bonds and Debentures —			
(a) under $3 million	4.62	4.90	1.00 - 10.00
(b) over $3 million	2.82	2.85	.50 - 5.00

Source: I.D.A. Brief, Volume II, p. E-14.

[10] R. Peters, *Economics of the Canadian Corporate Bond Market*, *op. cit.*, p. 69.

A more recent study of underwriting costs by Shaw covers the period 1966-1968. Figure 12-1 taken from his work establishes a linear relationship between underwriting costs and issue size. The following comments made in his paper about Figure 12-1 are quite revealing:

> This is a surprising result in view of the expected decreasing relationship between underwriting cost and size of issue. . . . The . . . almost perfectly linear relationship . . . observed . . . taken in conjunction with the assumption that much of the underwriter's costs are substantially fixed, suggests that either underwriters make greater relative profits on larger issues than smaller ones, that they recoup losses on small issues through their larger ones, or that the riskiness of these issues is directly related to size of issue—an unlikely possibility. The relationship . . . is surprising for another reason. These issues do not appear to be equivalent in risk. . . . If underwriting costs do vary with risk within the operational class of issues, then the underwriting cost of higher risk issues should lie above the regression line . . . and underwriting costs of lower risk issues below it. . . . While . . . underwriting costs do vary across operational and promotional classes, . . . tests do not indicate any risk distinction reflected in the underwriting costs for recent operational issues. Since a major function of the underwriter's role is to absorb the risk of the offering for the issuing firm, it is surprising to find the actual underwriting costs so insensitive to these tests of risk.[11]

FIGURE 12-1

Relationship Between Underwriting Cost and Size of Issue For Operational Issues in Canada 1966-1968

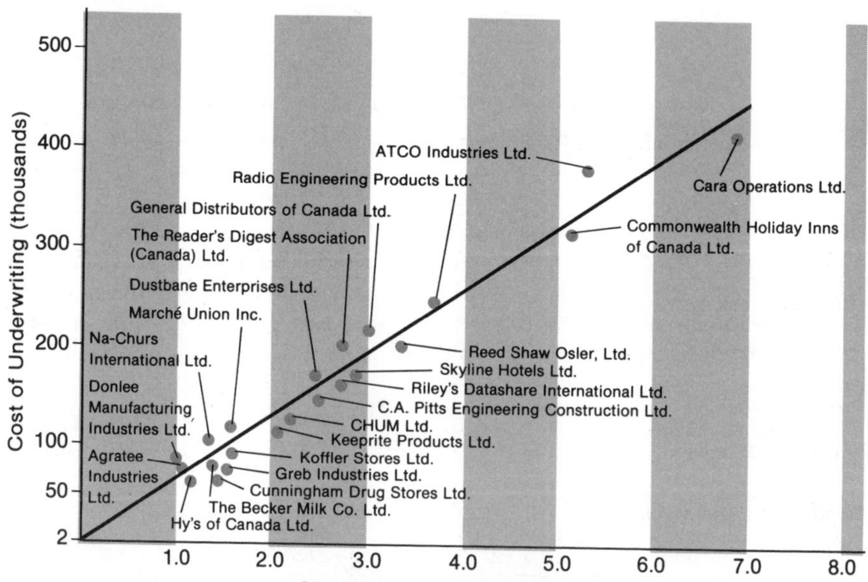

Source: D. Shaw, "The Cost of Going Public in Canada", *Financial Executive*, July, 1969.

[11]D. Shaw, "The Cost of Going Public in Canada", *op. cit.*, pp. 21-22.

12-5. PRIVATE PLACEMENTS

In addition to underwritten public offerings, securities may be privately placed with one or a few large institutional investors such as life insurance companies and pension funds. In the issuing of corporate dept, private placements are quite common; as shown in Table 12-3, about a quarter of recent debt offerings fall into this category. Furthermore, smaller firms will frequently rely on direct sales to insiders or to those intimately acquainted with its operations, including venture capitalists.

TABLE 12-3

Gross New Corporate Debt Issues
(in Millions of Dollars, Par Value)

Year	Public Offerings Amount	Public Offerings Percentage	Private Offerings Amount	Private Offerings Percentage
1960	$ 482.1	71.1	$195.2	28.9
1962	303.5	32.1	641.1	67.9
1964	382.5	34.4	728.2	65.6
1966	607.9	53.3	529.5	46.7
1968	1,190.4	75.9	378.5	24.1
1970	1,507.7	91.5	140.9	8.5
1972	1,571.2	85.0	276.2	15.0
1974	1,801.0	71.0	735.9	29.0

Source: Adapted from the Financial Post Corporation, *Record of New Issues*, for 1970 to 1974, and J. Ross Peters, *Economics of the Canadian Corporate Bond Market*, Montreal: McGill-Queen's University Press, 1971, p. 16.

The issuing corporation may have direct contacts with interested financial institutions, obviating the need to use the services of an investment dealer. In other cases a dealer may be engaged to act as an agent for the issuer or simply to bring the parties together. For such services the dealer receives a commission of between ¼ and 1½ percent of the offering depending on the work involved and the size of the issue. With legal requirements minimized for private institutional placements, other issuing expenses are also lower than for a public offering. Furthermore, a borrower has the opportunity of arranging to draw funds at predetermined future dates and at agreed-to interest rates. Such provisions are referred to as deferred or delayed take-downs and may be particularly useful where funds are raised to finance large capital investment projects, since monies for construction are usually required in installments spread over several years. On the other hand, the lender may strive to tailor the issue to his own needs, for example by seeking a slightly better yield, better security and more protective covenants than would be given with a public offering. Careful tailoring is understandable since lenders cannot readily divest themselves of the securities acquired through private placement. Negotiations are therefore clearly indicated.

Given the size and efficiency of the capital markets and financial institutions in the United States relative to those of Canada, Canadian borrowers including corporations often find private placements, particularly for larger issues, easier to arrange through New York.

12-6. RIGHTS OFFERINGS

In certain instances, neither the general public nor selected financial institutions are approached with an additional or new offering of securities. The firm's common shareholders may have first right by corporate policy or by law to buy any further new offerings of common shares or securities convertible into common shares. Such right by law is termed the *pre-emptive right.* It is, for example, to be found in Canada under the *Bank Act* which states:

> Any of the original unsubscribed capital stock or of the increased capital stock shall be offered to the persons who are shareholders according to the books of the bank, pro rata, at such price not less than par, at such time and on such terms as the directors determine except that . . . no share need be offered to a shareholder whose recorded address is . . . outside Canada. . . .[12]

The reasoning behind such statutory provisions includes the fact that it helps assure Canadian shareholders of equitable treatment and precludes stock options to management.[13]

The right to maintain proportionate shareholdings by investors is recognized by corporations. Even where not required by law, the equivalent of pre-emptive rights is often granted existing shareholders by having the securities sold through an offering to them rather than to the public at large. This approach is termed selling by *privileged subscription,* and entails granting each shareholder one right for each share held. A certain number of rights will enable the holder to purchase one share of the new offering. Such rights are issued in the form of a negotiable instrument termed a "subscription warrant." Fractional shares are not normally available, but a market for rights evolves almost immediately, thus permitting their purchase or sale as required.

The usual procedure followed in a rights offering is for directors to set a *date of record.* Investors registered as shareholders on that date receive the rights, one for each share held. Shares will trade ex-rights (meaning that ownership of a share no longer entitles the shareholder to the receipt of a right) two days prior to the date of record to allow for lags in registering changes on the company's list of shareholders. Obviously, following announcement of the rights offering but before the shares trade ex-rights, the market price of shares will adjust to reflect both the proposed increase in the number of shares outstanding and more particularly, the assurance that to each share traded there is one right attached.

The time span within which rights can be exercised is quite short and, at the end of the period, the rights expire thereby losing any former value.

By offering new securities to existing common shareholders who are presumably satisfied with the way their firm is performing, the probability of a successful sale is enhanced. Worthy of note, however, are additional direct advantages to both shareholders and the corporation. For example, issuing expenses and costs of underwriting are reduced below what might be incurred through a public flotation. Furthermore, rights offerings make it possible for

[12] *Bank Act,* R.S.C. 1970, ch. B-1, s. 33(1).

[13] *1964 Report of the Royal Commission on Banking and Finance, op. cit.,* p. 144.

existing shareholders to preserve their pro rata share of the business including its future prospects, and to maintain their own voting position. Where this is of no concern to a shareholder, the rights may simply be sold.

Disadvantages associated with a rights offering include the time it takes to complete the sale of the issue, and the perpetuation of an existing base of ownership which may be narrower than desirable or perhaps fall too heavily outside of Canada. The disadvantage of having corporate financing heavily dependent on the stability of the stock market during a critical four- or five-week period while the rights are exercisable is very real as will be detailed below.

The numerical relationships in a rights offering are best illustrated through an example. We are concerned with relationships between the market price of a firm's shares during both the *rights-on* and *ex-rights* periods,[14] the subscription price for the new securities, the amount of money to be raised, and the theoretical value which a right should have. Our illustration will involve use of the following notation:

P_O = the market price per share during the rights-on period
P_X = the market price per share ex-rights
R = the theoretical value of a right
S = the subscription price for new shares
N = the number of rights required to subscribe to one new share.

Initially we will develop the conceptual relationships which you would expect to find, and later on we will discuss how these relationships may be modified in practice.

Example

Consider a firm with one-million shares outstanding, the shares trading at a price of $25.00 rights-on, $2.2 million to be raised through a rights-offering at a subscription price of S = $22 per share.[15] Assuming no issue expenses, net proceeds to the corporation would also be $22 a share, implying $2,200,000/$22 or 100,000 new shares having to be issued. With one right issued for each share outstanding, an investor will require N = 1,000,000/100,000 or 10 rights to subscribe to one new share.

If the firm has no other securities such as debt or preferred shares outstanding, the total value which investors placed on the firm just prior to the issuing of new shares was $25 × 1,000,000 = $25,000,000. Immediately after issuance of the new shares the firm remains basically unchanged except that it now has 1,100,000 shares outstanding and an additional $2,200,000 in cash from the new share subscriptions. Hence, it is reasonable to expect, *ceteris paribus*, that the firm's total value after the offering should be $25,000,000 + $2,200,000 = $27,200,000, implying a market price per share of $27,200,000/1,100,000 or $24.73. These

[14]Shares are said to trade rights-on from the time the rights offering is announced almost until the date of record because during this period the purchaser of a share also acquires a right. This is no longer the case during the ex-rights period which, as already noted, starts two days prior to the date of record.

[15]It should be noted that the subscription price has to be set below the current market price of the shares or it would be cheaper for investors to buy additional shares on the open market and there would be no incentive to subscribe.

relationships are summarized below:

	Before Offering	After Offering
Total value of firm	$25,000,000	27,200,000
Number of shares outstanding	1,000,000	1,100,000
Market price per share	$25.00	$24.73

We see that as a consequence of the offering, the market price of the shares should decline from P_O = $25.00 to P_X = $24.73. This is so because after the offering more shares are outstanding and the new shares issued brought in less money per share than the earlier market price.

To derive the theoretical value of a right, we recall that 10 rights allowed the purchase of one new share at a subscription price S = $22.00. Since the shares have an anticipated market price of $24.73 after the rights offering, for every 10 rights you stand to make a gain of $24.73 – $22.00 = $2.73. Thus, the theoretical value of one right becomes

$$R = \frac{P_X - S}{N}$$

which for our example becomes R = ($24.73 – $22.00)/ 10 = $0.27.

Following through on the wealth position of a shareholder who owned 10 shares before the rights offering and who exercised those rights, we have

	Before Offering	After Offering
Shares held	10	11
Market price per share	$25.00	$24.73
Total value of holdings	$250.00	$272.03

Considering that $22 was spent in subscribing to the new shares, it is clear that the shareholder's total wealth position stands unchanged by the offering. Similarly, if those rights had not been exercised they could have been sold for 10 × $0.27 or $2.70, again leaving the shareholder's total wealth after the offering unchanged at 10 × $24.73 + $2.70 = $250. We see that the expected drop in the market price of the shares from P_O = $25.00 to P_X = $24.73 just equals the theoretical value of the right, so that sale of the right exactly compensates for the drop in market price experienced by the shareholder. We now have

$$R = P_O - P_X$$

from which it is quite simple to derive that[16]

$$R = \frac{P_O - S}{N + 1}$$

[16]This equation is easily derived by substituting $P_X = P_0 - R$ into the equation $R = \frac{P_X - S}{N}$ introduced above. It may then be rewritten as $R = \frac{P_0 - R - S}{N}$ or $NR + R = P_0 - S$, giving $R = \frac{P_0 - S}{N + 1}$. Intuitively, the $(N + 1)$ in the denominator reflects the fact that P_0 comprises the value of the share and the value of one right which attaches to the share.

To summarize our main results, we found that *ceteris paribus*, the following three consequences should be observed following a rights offering:

- The market price of the firm's shares should drop as a consequence of the increasing number of shares outstanding. This number of shares and the drop in price will increase as the subscription price for new shares decreases.
- The theoretical value of a right is such that it will just compensate for the drop in share prices, with $R = P_O - P_X$.
- The total wealth position of any shareholder should be unaffected by a rights offering, regardless of whether the rights are exercised or sold. The subscription price of the new offering is immaterial in this regard.

The above points are sometimes not intuitively obvious for on a casual inspection it may appear that shareholders are getting a "deal" by being able to subscribe to new shares at a subscription price which is below the current market price. An extreme example may offer further clarification of this matter. Assume that the firm had set the subscription price at zero, in effect giving away one new share fore every ten shares held.[17] It is clear that the firm immediately before and immediately after the offering is itself unchanged except that after the offering ten percent more shares are outstanding. Each share is worth less, however, since shareholders have received nothing of value by just holding additional pieces of paper, with their proportionate ownership of the firm and the firm itself standing unchanged.

While the considerations as outlined are conceptually straightforward, there are several reasons why we may not find the above relationship exactly replicated in practice. Rights often do trade at more than their theoretical value because of opportunities afforded speculators. With a fixed amount of money to invest, potential gains can be realized in an upward-moving stock market through the purchase of a company's rights rather than its common shares. Reasons for this are best illustrated through an actual example.

Example

Consider an investor having \$1300 to invest as at January 3. 1969. Assume that his interest focused on Inland Natural Gas which had just issued rights, with terms of the offering and other pertinent information as follows:

Expiry date of rights, February 3, 1969
Number of rights required for one new share $N = 10$
Subscription price $S = \$10$
Market price of shares ex-rights as at January 3, 1969 $P_X = \$13$.

While the theoretical value of a right was $R = (\$13 - \$10)/10 = \$0.30$, rights were actually trading at \$0.333. At this price, the investor could have purchased \$1300/\$13 = 100 shares, or alternatively, \$1300/\$0.333 or 3900 rights. With an expectation that the market price of shares would climb to \$15 by February 3, 1969, the expected gain (neglecting

[17] This could actually be termed a stock split, or if retained earnings are capitalized, a stock dividend. These actions are discussed in more detail in Chapter 21.

transactions costs) would have been 100($15 – $13) or $200 with the purchase of shares. On the other hand, just before expiry, rights would be expected to trade at no less than R = ($15 – $10)/10 or $0.50 suggesting a potential gain of 3900 ($0.50 – $0.333) or $650.

Clearly, should share prices in fact move downward, relatively greater loss would occur where rights were purchased. It should also be noted that the longer the time until the rights expire the more likely it is that speculative activity and a market price above theoretical value for the rights will develop. Just prior to the expiry date, opportunities no longer exist for speculators as the rights can only be exercised, and by implication the market price of the rights will equal their theoretical value.

By reference to a recent offering, the entire process can be more fully detailed. Common shareholders of the Bank of Montreal on record on February 14, 1969 were offered rights to subscribe to 3,796,875 additional shares on the basis of one new share at twelve dollars for each eight shares held. The market price at the time was just over sixteen dollars. Subscription rights were transferable and expired on April 8, 1969. The market price for shares, rights, and the theoretical value of rights are set out in Table 12-4. It is apparent from the table that, with the approach of the expiry date, the market price of the rights approximates their theoretical value.

TABLE 12-4

Market Prices of Shares and Rights and the Theoretical Value of Rights of the Bank of Montreal

Date	Market Price of Shares	Market Price of Rights	Theoretical Value of Rights
Feb. 10, 1969	$16⅛	$0.46	$0.458
Feb. 14, 1969	15⅝	0.44	0.422
Feb. 17, 1969	15⅝	0.43	0.422
Feb. 19, 1969	15	0.41	0.375
Feb. 21, 1969	14⅞	0.38	0.359
Apr. 1, 1969	14⅜	0.30	0.297

While it was noted above that, from the shareholder's viewpoint, the level at which the subscription price was set really should not matter, practical considerations will often dictate the level. The subscription price in Canada generally appears to be set fifteen to twenty percent below market price of the outstanding shares and choice of this discount does have some practical significance. Clearly, should the market value of the shares fall below the subscription price before expiry date of the rights, shareholders will not subscribe as they would not be willing to buy new shares from the corporation for a price which exceeds the price at which shares can currently be bought in the market. Thus, the offering would fail. This possibility has been termed the primary risk in rights offerings.[18] To avoid such risk and consequently to reduce

[18]For a more detailed discussion, see P. Bacon, "The Subscription Price in Rights Offerings", *Financial Management*, Summer 1972, pp. 59-64.

underwriting costs, an issuer will be tempted to offer a large discount, as protection against fluctuations in the shares' market price during the several weeks which may elapse between the announcement and expiry of a typical rights offering. A significant spread between subscription price and current market price also enhances the value of a right. This should encourage shareholders who elect not to exercise their rights to sell them, rather than just letting them lapse.

On the other hand, the lower the subscription price the more shares must be sold to raise a fixed amount of new capital, and the greater the drop in the market price which can be expected on outstanding shares. Furthermore, adjustments to historical financial data of a firm are seldom made to reflect the effects of a rights-offering. Given the increased number of new shares outstanding, the growth rate in reported earnings per share may well be slowed while the cash needed to maintain previous dividends per share will increase.

Example

Pursuing our previous example, Table 12-5 summarizes the short-run theoretical impact on key financial variables of varying the subscription price. Again, a million shares with a market price of $25 (rights-on) are currently outstanding with $2.2 millions to be raised. The tabulation is based on the assumption that before the offering, reported earnings for the firm are $2.50 per share and dividends are $1.00 per share. No additional earnings are expected from investment of new monies raised for at least two years and are therefore ignored in analyzing the short-run impact of the offering.

TABLE 12-5

The Theoretical Impact of Various Subscription Prices on Key Variables.

	Subscription Price ($)			
	22.00	19.80	11.00	4.40
Percentage Discount of Subscription Price over Previous Market Price: $(P_O\text{-}S)/P_O$	12.0	20.8	56.0	32.4
Number of Additional Shares to be Issued $2,200,000/*S*	100,000	111,111	200,000	500,000
Number of Rights Required for 1 New Share	10	9	5	2
Value of a Right: *R*	$0.27	$0.52	$2.33	$6.87
Market Value of Share Ex-rights: P_X	$24.73	$24.48	$22.67	$18.13
Earnings per Share	$2.27	$2.25	$2.08	$1.67
Annual Cash Requirements to Sustain Dividends per Share	$1,100,000	$1,111,111	$1,200,000	$1,500,000

It is apparent from the above tabulations that if investors expect past dividend levels to be maintained, and if short-run earnings per share are important, then financial executives face some real tradeoffs when selecting the spread between market and subscription price. There is on the one hand an incentive to set a low subscription price in order to minimize the risks of the offering and on the other hand there is the conflicting objective of minimizing the number of new shares issued. The typical discount of fifteen to twenty percent reflects this tradeoff. We have shown that theoretically, a shareholder's wealth position should not be affected by a rights offering regardless of the subscription price selected, with the market price of shares from rights-on to ex-rights dropping by just the value of the right. The ex-rights market price of the shares will also be influenced, however, by shareholder expectations as to how the new funds raised by the firm are to be invested. If particularly good returns are foreseen for such new investments, the market price of shares may well remain higher than we would otherwise expect. Perhaps because the offering of new shares is often seen to be a positive action signalling the availability of good investment opportunities, a positive impact on the firm's share prices is frequently to be observed.

Additional issues regarding the choice of subscription prices and potential effects on shareholder wealth have been raised in the recent financial literature.[19] A reasonable review of it, however, would go beyond our survey treatment of the subject. Unfortunately, it is difficult to obtain conclusive evidence regarding some of these issues through empirical testing, for example by observing share price behavior during actual rights offerings. A firm's share prices are influenced by many different factors and it is difficult to isolate the effects of a rights offering in observing actual share price behavior.

In practice, the success of a rights offering hinges on a variety of factors. The more pertinent ones include:

- the relationship between the market price and the subscription price. Given five weeks or so between announcement and expiry of typical rights offerings, a healthy price spread is required to cushion against the market price dipping below subscription price;
- the size of the issue relative to what is already outstanding. The size and dispersion of present holdings must also be recognized. If most existing shareholders each held just a few shares, there may be greater difficulties than would be the case with a significant number of different institutional investors in dominance. As many small shareholders may lack the sophistication or interest to either exercise or sell their rights, new shares will remain unsubscribed;
- the mood and stability of the financial markets—it always being more difficult to sell new shares in a depressed or declining market;
- cash flow requirements to cover dividend payments on the larger number of shares outstanding. This point certainly relates to the use to which funds raised will be put and the additional earnings which are expected as a consequence of new investments. It is possible to shift the risk of under-

[19]See, for example, G. Wakoff. "On Shareholders' Indifference to the Proceeds Price in Preemptive Rights Offerings", *Journal of Finance and Quantitative Analysis*, December 1973, pp. 835-836; M. Jones-Lee, "Underwriting of Rights Issues—A Theoretical Justification", *Journal of Business Finance*, Spring 1971, pp. 20-25; S. Keane, "The Significance of the Issue Price in Rights Issues", *Journal of Business Finance*, Autumn 1972, pp. 40-45; and H. Levy and M. Sarnat, "Risk, Dividend Policy, and the Optimal Pricing of a Rights Offering", *Journal of Money, Credit, and Banking*, November 1971, pp. 840-849.

subscription in a rights offering by entering into a *standby* underwriting agreement with an investment dealer. Under such an arrangement, which would of course involve additional costs, the underwriter stands ready to pick up any unsold securities.

12-7. RIGHTS AND WARRANTS

It is important not to confuse rights with warrants which were reviewed in the previous chapter. Though both are options to purchase common shares they are quite different in several respects. While rights evolve from a decision to raise additional capital through common equity and essentially from existing shareholders, warrants are the by-product of raising funds from the public at large through the sale of senior securities, most typically bonds or debentures. Furthermore, duration of the two options differ significantly with rights expiring after several weeks while the maturity of warrants is measured in years. Finally, it should be noted that while an issue of rights is expected to produce significant new monies for the issuer, exercising of the warrants is not. Warrants, typically exercised only years after issue, are essentially used to improve the marketability of the securities to which they initially attach, and give rise to the issuance of very much fewer shares than is the case in rights offerings.

12-8. SUMMARY

A firm can sell new securities through a public offering, a private placement, or a rights offering. In a public offering, the services of an investment dealer will generally be engaged to underwrite the issue. The investment dealer purchases the securities from the issuing firm and then retails them to the general public. Here, the principal underwriter may cooperate with other investment dealers, forming a syndicate or banking group. Comparing Canada with the U.S., criticisms have been levied against underwriting in Canada as it appears to be less competitive and less efficient.

In a public offering, the issuing firm must file and publish a prospectus, which is a document containing all the material facts regarding the offering and which is to provide investors with the necessary information for evaluation of the new securities.

A private placement entails direct selling of the securities to one or a few large investors, mainly financial institutions. It is subject to less legal requirements, and the deal can be more closely tailored to the specific needs of the contracting parties. Because of reduced liquidity, the yield which investors demand may be marginally higher than in a comparable public offering. Private placements are common in corporate debt, and for small businesses where public offerings are impractical.

In a rights offering, new securities are offered on a pro-rata basis to existing shareholders. Rights are issued which are options to purchase new securities at a specified subscription price. Such rights are negotiable, and have a life which is generally limited to between four and six weeks. Conceptually, the wealth position of existing shareholders should be unaffected by a rights offering, regardless of the subscription price—we expect the market price of shares to decline from the rights-on to the ex-rights period by just the theoretical value of the right. In practice, some of these conceptual relationships may be modified somewhat as rights may have speculative appeal. Furthermore, the subscription price influences the number of new shares to be issued and, hence, future dividend payments and reported earnings per share figures. Expectations as to the returns to be achieved from investment of the new funds is also of importance in this context.

Questions for Discussion

1. Define the terms underwriting, firm commitment underwriting, and option underwriting.
2. What are letters of intent and the market-out clause? Why does an underwriter need the market-out clause in its agreement with the issuing company?
3. It is said that with present practices, the underwriting syndicates are rigid with a few syndicate managers enjoying great power. Do you think this is true? Discuss.
4. What is a best-efforts distribution of securities by a dealer? Is it correct that only those companies issuing high risk securities make use of this method because underwriters are unwilling to assume the necessary risks?
5. Discuss the similarities and the differences between warrants and rights.
6. As the financial executive of a firm which plans a major new issue of common shares, you are contemplating the alternatives of a public offering, a private placement and a rights offering. What would be some of the main considerations and tradeoffs in evaluating these alternatives?
7. If you, as the financial executive of your firm, had decided on a public offering of new securities, how would you evaluate various investment dealers who are interested in underwriting the issue, and what would be major topics of negotiation before signing an agreement?
8. In the chapter, we derived several theoretical relationships which ought to exist between the subscription price, the market price of shares, and the value of rights. How might you test empirically the extent to which these relationships prevail in practice? What are some of the likely difficulties you will encounter? Be as specific as possible.
9. Discuss the results portrayed in Figure 12-1. How would you interpret the information presented? How could you gather additional evidence to substantiate the points which the author tries to make regarding the efficiency of underwriting in Canada?

Problem with Solutions

1. Consider a firm which currently has 5,000,000 shares outstanding at a market price of $20 per share. New equity capital in the amount of $16,000,000 is to raised through an issue of common shares which are to be sold through a rights offering.
   (a) Assuming the subscription price is set at 20 percent below the current market price, how many new shares need to be issued? If one right is

associated with each outstanding share, how many rights will be required to subscribe to one new share?

(b) Compute the total market value which the firm's outstanding common shares should have just before and just after the new offering, as well as the market price per share.

(c) Compute the theoretical value of a right, using both the formulas based on the market price per share during the rights-on period and on the market price per share ex-rights.

(d) Show that the total wealth of an investor who held 5 shares before the offering remains unchanged through the offering, regardless of whether he exercises or sells his rights.

(e) Assume that an investor had $1,000 to invest and either purchases shares ex-rights at $19.33 per share, or rights at $0.67 each. Compute the absolute and the percentage gain or loss if just prior to the expiry of the rights the market price of the shares had increased/decreased by $1. Ignore the transaction costs.

Solution

(a) Subscription price per share:

$$S = 0.8 \times \text{current market price} = \$16$$

Number of new shares to be issued:

$$n = \$16{,}000{,}000/\$16 = 1{,}000{,}000$$

Number of rights required to purchase one new share:

N = current shares outstanding/new shares to be issued

= 5,000,000/1,000,000 = 5

(b) Before offering:

Market price per share = $20

Total market value of firm's common shares = 5,000,000 × $20 = $100,000,000

After offering:

Total market value of firm's common shares = Market value before new offering + Amount raised through offering

= $100,000,000 + $16,000,000

= $116,000,000

$$\text{Market price per share} = \frac{\text{total market value}}{\text{number of shares outstanding}}$$

= $116,000,000/6,000,000

= $19.33

(c) Formula based on rights-on market price:

$$R = \frac{P_O - S}{N + 1} = \frac{\$20 - \$16}{6} = \$0.67$$

Formula based on ex-rights market price:

$$R = \frac{P_X - S}{N} = \frac{\$19.33 - \$16.00}{5} = \$0.67$$

(d) Investor exercises rights:

Wealth before offering	5 × \$20.00 = \$100.00
Wealth after offering	
shareholdings	6 × \$19.33 = \$116.00
minus: subscription price paid for one new share (.8 × \$20)	\$ 16.00
Net wealth	\$100.00

Investor sells rights:

shareholdings	5 × \$19.33 = \$ 96.65
Proceeds from sale of 5 rights	5 × \$ 0.67 = \$ 3.35
Total wealth	\$100.00

(e) Increase in share price to \$19.33 + \$1.00 = \$20.33. Given a \$1,000 investment, the investor could have purchased 51 common shares (51 × \$19.33 = \$985.83, spare cash = \$14.17) or 1,492 rights (1,492 × \$0.67 = \$999.64, spare cash = \$0.36). Given the increase in the market price of the shares, the theoretical value of a right would have increased to:

$$R = \frac{P_X - S}{N} = \frac{\$20.33 - \$16.00}{5} = 0.87$$

Investor's ending wealth under share purchase alternative:

51 × \$20.33 + \$14.17 (shares) (spare cash)	= \$1,051.00
absolute gain	= \$51.00 (= \$1.00 per share purchased)
relative gain	= 5.1%

Investor's ending wealth under purchase of rights alternative:

1,492 × \$0.87 + \$0.36 (rights) (spare cash)	= \$1,298.40
absolute gain	= \$298.40
relative gain	= 29.8%

Note: We have neglected any interest which may be earned on the spare cash during the holding period.

Decrease in share price to \$19.33 – \$1.00 = \$18.33

Investor's ending wealth under share purchase alternative:

51 × \$18.33 + \$14.17 = \$ 949.00
(shares) (spare cash)

absolute loss = – \$51.00

relative loss = – 5.1%

Investor's ending wealth under purchase of rights alternative:

$$R = \frac{\$18.33 - \$16.00}{5} = \$0.47$$

1,492 × \$0.47 + \$0.36 = \$701.60
(rights) (spare cash)

absolute loss = – \$298.40

relative loss = – 29.8%

Additional Problems

1. The shares of P.X. Company are trading on the stock market at \$60 per share during the ex-rights period. The shareholders are offered one new share for every 5 shares held at a subscription price of \$50.
   (a) What is the theoretical value of one right?
   (b) If a speculator, who has \$3000 to place in the stock market, believes that the price of P.X. shares would advance from \$60 to \$80 a month from now, should he gamble on stocks or on rights assuming that he can buy P.X. rights on the market at \$2.50 each?
2. The S.T. Company is listed on the Toronto Stock Exchange and its shares are trading at \$20 per share. The company offers the existing shareholders one new share for every 5 shares held at a subscription price of \$14.
   (a) Determine the theoretical value of each right during the rights-on period.
   (b) Leslie owns 100 shares of S.T. Company. Assuming that the market value for each S.T. right is equal to its theoretical value, prepare a statement showing the changes in her position if she decides to sell all her rights.
   (c) What do you think Leslie's position would be in a real-world situation?
3. X Ltd. is a company whose shares are traded actively on the Vancouver Stock Exchange at \$80 per share. Because of the need for additional funds, the company is offering its shareholders one new share for every 10 shares held at a subscription price of \$69.
   (a) Calculate the theoretical value of X Ltd.'s rights using two different methods.
   (b) Would the actual market price of rights be identical with the theoretical value? Discuss.
   (c) What do you think will happen to the price of X's common shares on the stock exchange? Why?

4. Successful Enterprises currently has 10,000,000 common shares outstanding which trade at a market price of $10 per share. Ten-million dollars of new equity capital is to be raised through a rights offering. The company has been debating whether to set the subscription price for the new shares at $9, $8, or $7 per share.
   (a) For each alternative, compute the number of additional shares to be issued, the number of rights required for subscription to one new share, the theoretical value of a right and the market price per share ex-rights.
   (b) If, regardless of the offering, total after-tax earnings for the coming year are expected to be $12,000,000 and dividends are to be maintained at $0.60 per share, compute the impact of various subscriptions prices as given above on earnings per share and on total cash needed to pay dividends.
   (c) What are the practical tradeoffs in setting the subscription price?

Selected References

P. Bacon, "The Subscription Price in Rights Offerings" *Financial Management*, Summer, 1972, pp. 59-64.

R. Briston, "A Note on the Underwriting of Rights Issues", *Journal of Business Finance*, Vol. 4, No. 2, 1972, pp. 68-70.

R. Briston and P. Herbert, "The Measurement of Underwriting Performance in a Depressed Market", *Journal of Business Finance*, Vol. 4, No. 2, 1972, pp. 88-95.

J. Brown, "Post-offering Experience of Companies Going Public," *Journal of Business*, January, 1970, pp. 10-18.

E. Dyl and M. Joehnk, "Competitive versus Negotiated Underwriting of Public Utility Debt", *The Bell Journal of Economics*, Autumn, 1976, pp. 680-689.

G. Evans, "The Theoretical Value of a Stock Right," *Journal of Finance*, March, 1955, pp. 55-61.

S. Hayes, III, "Investment Banking: Power Structure in Flux", *Harvard Business Review*, March-April, 1971, pp. 136-152.

Investment Dealers' Association of Canada, *Brief to the Royal Commission on Banking and Finance* (Volume II) mimeographed, 1962.

M. Jones-Lee, "Underwriting of Rights Issues—A Theoretical Justification", *Journal of Business Finance*, Vol. 3, No. 1, 1971, pp. 20-25.

M. Jones-Lee, "Underwriting of Rights Issues: A Rejoinder", *Journal of Business Finance*, Vol. 4, No. 4, 1972, pp. 71-73.

S. Keane, "The Significance of the Issue Price in Rights Issues," *Journal of Business Finance*, Vol. 4, No. 3, 1972, pp. 40-45.

H. Levy and M. Sarnat, "Risk, Dividend Policy, and the Optimal Pricing of a Rights Offering", *Journal of Money, Credit and Banking*, November, 1971, pp. 840-849.

P. McQuillan, *Going Public In Canada*, Toronto: The Canadian Institute of Chartered Accountants, 1971.

R. Nelson, "Price Effects in Rights Offerings," *Journal of Finance*, December, 1965, pp. 647-650.

G. Newbould and P. Wells, "Underwriting of Rights Issues—A Theoretical Justification: A Reply", *Journal of Business Finance*, Vol. 3, No. 1, 1971, pp. 53.

R. Peters, *Economics of the Canadian Corporate Bond Market*, Montreal: McGill-Queen's University Press, 1971.

G. Sears, "Public Offerings for Smaller Companies", *Harvard Business Review*, September-October, 1968, pp. 112-120.

D. Shaw, "The Cost of Going Public in Canada," *Financial Executive,* July, 1969, pp. 20-28.

D. Shaw, "The Performance of Primary Common Stock Offerings: A Canadian Comparison," *Journal of Finance*, December, 1971, pp. 1101-1113.

R. Soldofsky and C. Johnson, "Rights Timing," *Financial Analysts Journal*, July-August, 1967, pp. 101-104.

H. Thompson, "A Note on the Value of Rights in Estimating the Investor Capitalization Rate", *Journal of Finance*, March, 1973, pp. 157-160.

Chapter 13
The Cost of Capital

13-1. INTRODUCTION

Several very important questions on corporate financial policy will be pursued in this chapter. First, we will deal with the calculation of costs to a firm of funds acquired from the various sources dealt with in previous chapters. Specifically, we will develop formulas for computing the cost to a firm of debt, preferred shares and common equity. We will then discuss how to combine these individual cost figures into a weighted average cost of capital figure for the firm. This weighted average cost of capital represents the overall cost at which the corporation can raise new funds.

It should be appreciated that in order to simplify the exposition we are again holding other financial policies which affect the firm constant. For example, capital budgeting policies affect both the profitability and the risk faced by a firm, as perceived by investors. This in turn will influence how investors value the various securities which a firm may issue and, hence, the terms under which new financing may be available. In this chapter, we will concentrate on determining a firm's cost of capital given that its financial policies in other areas such as capital budgeting have been determined and remain unaltered. This is a reasonable assumption for most ongoing businesses which do not contemplate drastic changes in financial policy. Where major departures from past financial policies are contemplated, interrelationships between various areas of financial decision-making need to be recognized; consequently, the analysis becomes more complex.

A clear appreciation of the costs at which a firm raises its funds is not only of general importance to senior management, but also it has direct applicability when determining the discount rate or hurdle rate to be applied in capital-budgeting decisions. In most cases, we have seen that the appropriate rate is the firm's weighted average cost of capital.

In the absence of capital rationing, the internal rate of return criterion suggests acceptance of projects only where the internal rate of return exceeds the corporation's cost of capital; while the net present value technique requires a positive net present value when cash flows associated with the projects are discounted at the cost of capital. In the application of either criterion, it is important to have a good estimate of the firm's cost of capital. Furthermore, regulatory authorities such as the Canadian Transport Commission, in trying to establish fair rates of return for privately owned utilities, air carriers and other regulated industries, use the cost of capital as a basis for their deliberations regarding fair rates of return. Their task is to ensure that such regulated firms are able to attract necessary new funds to finance expansion and improve services, but without reaping excessive profits.

We start by computing the cost of capital for a given capital structure. That is, we assume that the corporation has decided on the proportions of debt, preferred, the common equity financing it will undertake, and that funds will continue to be raised in proportions which prevailed in the past. Alterations in a firm's capital structure and their effect on the operations of the firm and on the cost of capital will be dealt with in the following chapter.

13-2. MARKET YIELD AND COST OF CAPITAL

Any financial security issued by a corporation for purposes of raising additional funds typically involves an immediate cash inflow to the firm (equivalent to a cash outflow for the investors) to be followed by periodic outflows (equivalent to receipts for the investors). These flows are illustrated in Figure 13-1.

FIGURE 13-1

Typical Cash Flows From Sale of a Financial Security.

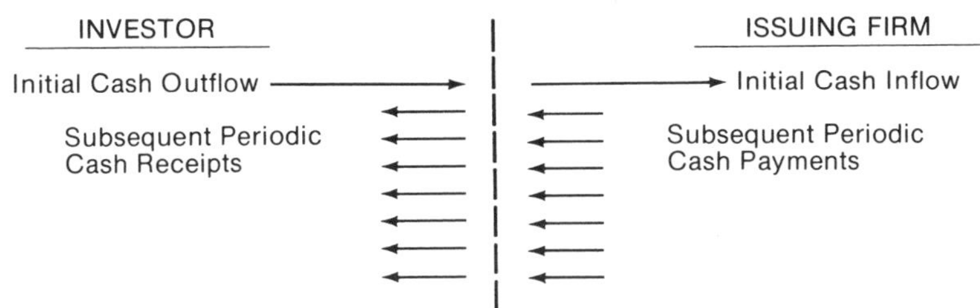

The initial cash inflow for the firm arises from the sale of financial securities such as bonds or shares. The subsequent cash outflows take the form of interest and repayment of principal in the case of debt, and of dividends in the case of common shares. Preferred shares may involve a sinking fund as well as dividends.

In the absence of corporate taxes, underwriting costs, and issuing expenses, cash flows from the firm's point of view and from that of the investor would just be mirror images of each other, with every outflow to the issuer representing an inflow of equal magnitude to the investor and *vice versa.* Drawing on material presented in the chapter on discounting, the yield of the security to the investor *(before individual income taxes),* also termed the *market capitalization rate,*[1] would be given by the internal rate of return which equates anticipated future returns with the current outflow or price. Similarly, to the firm, the cost of funds provided by the sale is equivalent to the internal rate of return which equates the

[1]The term "market capitalization rate" derives from the fact that it is the rate of return which investors find appropriate in establishing a market value for a security which is expected to produce a stream of cash flows. In the above context, it is therefore the rate at which investors in the market discount or capitalize anticipated cash flows to determine current market or capital value. For instance, if a 10-year bond of \$1000 with an annual 10 percent coupon sells for \$887, it provides an effective yield of 12 percent, which is the equivalent of saying that investors capitalize future interest payments at 12 percent, thus deriving a market price of \$887.

present value of future cash outflows with the funds originally received. It is clear that, with all the cash flows identical, these two internal rates will be the same, implying that for a given financial security issued, the cost of capital to the firm would be identical to the investors' yield.

The presence of corporate taxes and costs of issuing new securities, however, does drive a wedge between market capitalization rates and costs of funds to the firm. With issuing expenses on new securities paid from the gross proceeds of an issue, the firm's initial cash inflow no longer matches the monies provided by investors. To illustrate, new preferred shares may be sold to the public at a price of $100 per share, but with a price to the underwriter of $97 and issue expenses as well, the firm may only receive $96 per share. The tax deductibility of interest payments made by the firm further serves to separate the cost of debt from the corresponding market yield. With interest payments being a tax deductible expense, the firm's taxes are reduced as a consequence of such payments, and this results in reduced after-tax interest costs to the firm.

Example

> Assume a corporation pays $1,000 in interest and faces a tax rate of 40%. As a consequence of the interest payment, corporate taxes would be reduced by 40% × $1,000 = $400, resulting in after-tax interest expenses of $1,000 – $400 = $1,000 (1 – 0.4) = $600.

Therefore, in subsequent discussions, it will be necessary to distinguish between market capitalization rates which will be denoted by $\hat{k}_b$, $\hat{k}_p$ and $\hat{k}_e$ for debt, preferred, and common shares respectively, and costs of capital to the corporation which will be represented by k_b, k_p and k_e. While the costs of capital to the firm will include full consideration of corporate taxes, it should be noted that personal investor taxes (*e.g.* on interest or dividend payments) are not considered when computing market capitalization rates. The reason for this is that investors face widely varying tax rates so that the effective after-tax yields of securities would have to be computed individually for each investor to reflect the investor's particular tax situation. Hence, it is more convenient and common to derive market capitalization rates without consideration of investor taxes, recognizing that tax adjustments will have to be made by individual investors to determine their after-tax effective yields.

13-3. COSTS OF INDIVIDUAL SOURCES OF FUNDS

The cost of debt capital

We start by looking at the cost of long-term debt which is generally issued in the form of bonds or debentures. Consider a bond which is sold at its face value of F dollars and pays interest of I dollars until maturity at which time the face value is repaid. Given a corporate tax rate of T, and neglecting underwriting and issue expenses, the relevant cash flows would be as given in Figure 13-2A, with the firm's outflows for interest payments shown on an after-tax basis.

FIGURE 13-2A

Typical Cash Flows Associated with an Issue of Debt

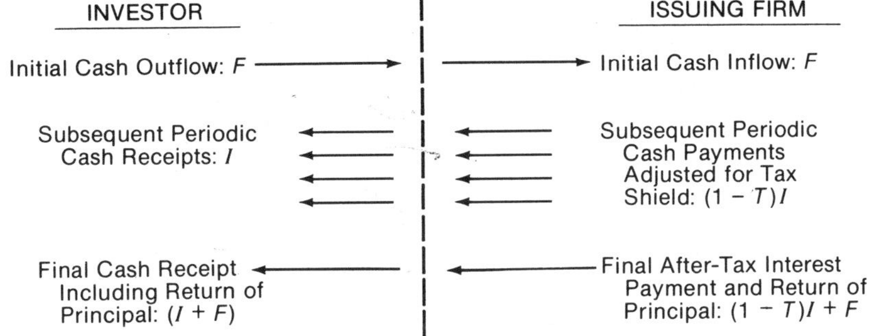

FIGURE 13-2B

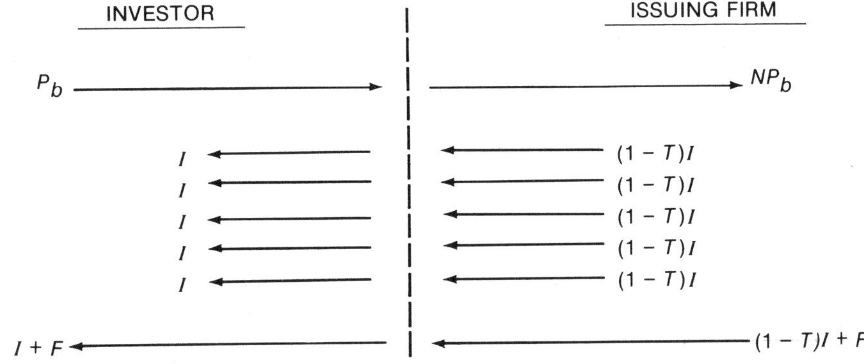

Solving for the internal rate of return, we simply find

(1) $\hat{k}_b = \dfrac{I}{F}$

(2) $k_b = \dfrac{(1 - T)I}{F}$

Example

Suppose a firm with a 40 percent marginal tax rate issued $1000 bonds at par to pay a coupon rate of 8 percent, and underwriting and issuing expenses were neglected. We would have $\hat{k}_b = \dfrac{\$80}{\$1000} = 8$ percent and $k_b = \dfrac{(1 - 0.4)\$80}{\$1000} = 4.8$ percent.

Note that formulas (1) and (2) above remain unchanged, even if principal is repaid through periodic sinking fund payments.[2]

[2]The following simplified example will illustrate this fact. Assume an 8 percent bond of $1000 and a corporate tax rate of 40 percent. Half the principal is to be repaid at the end of the first year with the balance due at the end of year 2. Interest payments in year 1 would be $1000 × 8% = $80, and $500 × 8% = $40 in year 2, resulting in after-tax cash outflows for the firm of $548 in the first year and $524 in the second, comprised of $500 in sinking fund payments and the after-tax interest expense. It is readily verified that the internal rate of return which equates

In actual situations, several additional variables need to be considered. Specifically, in the above example we have ignored underwriting and issue expenses as well as the possibility of selling to the public at a premium or discount from face value.[3] Drawing on our earlier review of investment dealers and the underwriting function, we recognize underwriting costs borne by the issuer to be a payment for both the retailing services provided by the dealers and their bearing of risks associated with the offering. Issuing expenses, on the other hand, include audit costs, legal fees, and other charges associated with preparation of the prospectus. With large debt issues, these expenses can amount to several hundred thousand dollars. Underwriting costs, issue expenses and sales to the public at prices below par value decrease the net proceeds available to the issuer to below the security's face value.

In order to establish the actual cost of debt we must determine the relevant cash flows after considering the tax implications for the issuer of underwriting and issue expenses, and of selling the debt at a premium or discount. Following common practice, we will simplify the subsequent discussion by assuming that expenses and discounts on new issues of securities are fully expensed, giving rise to a corresponding tax shield at time of issue. It should be noted, however, that the tax treatment of issue expenses and underwriting and other discounts is varied from time to time and that the tax aspects are complex, with the *Income Tax Act* providing for numerous special conditions and exceptions.[4] The following section is intended, therefore, as a typical illustration of the basic framework for analysis which can be extended to include any such tax effects as may be applicable, rather than as a set of rules on how such matters should specifically be dealt with for tax purposes.

Net proceeds to an issuer will be given by the par value *minus* underwriting and other discounts and issue expenses, *plus* the related tax shields. Following on our earlier discussion, we use this notation:

F = the face value of the debt instrument;
I = the annual interest or coupon payment on the debt;
n = the number of years to maturity;
P_b = the market price at which the bond is sold to the public, which may be higher or lower than F;
NP_b = the net proceeds from the bond to the issuer, including tax shields from expenses and discounts;
T = the issuing corporation's tax rate.

Relevant cash flows are set out in Figure 13-2B.

$\$1000 = \frac{\$548}{(1 + k_b)} + \frac{\$524}{(1 + k_b)^2}$ is again 4.8 percent.

[3]Capital market conditions, including interest rates may change during the final days of preparation preceding a new issue. If interest rates rise, for example, rather than increasing the coupon rate and revising documents including the prospectus, the bond may simply be offered at a discount, to improve the yield.

[4]For a brief overview, see for example, Canadian Tax Foundation, *Corporate Management Tax Conference 1974*, Toronto, Canadian Tax Foundation, 1974, pp. 78-81 in particular.

The market capitalization rate $\hat{k}_b$ and the cost of debt k_b are derived by finding the values which equate present values of current and future cash flows as follows:

Market capitalization rate

$$(3) \qquad P_b = \frac{I}{(1+\hat{k}_b)} + \frac{I}{(1+\hat{k}_b)^2} + \cdots + \frac{I}{(1+\hat{k}_b)^n} + \frac{F}{(1+\hat{k}_b)^n}$$

$$= \sum_{t=1}^{n} \frac{I}{(1+\hat{k}_b)^t} + \frac{F}{(1+\hat{k}_b)^n}$$

Cost of debt

$$(4) \qquad NP_b = \frac{(1-T)I}{(1+k_b)} + \frac{(1-T)I}{(1+k_b)^2} + \cdots + \frac{(1-T)I}{(1+k_b)^n} + \frac{F}{(1+k_b)^n}$$

$$= \sum_{t=1}^{n} \frac{(1-T)I}{(1+k_b)^t} + \frac{F}{(1+k_b)^n}$$

Example

A 20-year \$1000 par value bond with an 8 percent coupon is sold at a discount of 3 percent. The underwriting discount is a further 3 percent of the par value, additional issue expenses are \$20 per bond and the corporate tax rate is 40 percent. Following our earlier simplifying assumption regarding the tax treatment, we assume these underwriting and issuing expenses to be fully deductible for tax purposes. Accordingly, annual cash flows are computed as follows:

	For Investor	For Corporation
Year 0	\$970 outflow	\$952 inflow
Year 1-19	\$80 inflow	\$48 net outflow
Year 20	\$1,080 inflow	\$1,048 outflow

with the initial cash inflow for the corporation derived as the par value of \$1000 minus the discount to the public (\$30) minus underwriting discount (\$30) minus issue expenses (\$20) plus tax shields of these discounts and expenses [0.4 × (\$30 + \$30 + \$20)], or \$1000 – \$80 (1 – 0.4) = \$952. Substituting into equations (3) and (4) we obtain

$$\$970 = \sum_{t=1}^{20} \frac{\$80}{(1+\hat{k}_b)^t} + \frac{1000}{(1+\hat{k}_b)^{20}}$$

and

$$\$952 = \sum_{t=1}^{20} \frac{48}{(1+k_b)^t} + \frac{1000}{(1+k_b)^{20}}$$

Unless, as discussed in Chapter 4, a computer terminal with corresponding programs is available, values for $\hat{k}_b$ and k_b have to be determined by trial and error. In this case, we would find that $\hat{k}_b$ = 8.3 percent and k_b = 5.2 percent.

For maturities of over 10 years, good approximations for $\hat{k}_b$ and k_b can generally be found by slightly modifying formulas (1) and (2) above to

$$\hat{k}_b = \frac{I}{P_b} \quad \text{and} \quad k_b = \frac{(1-T)I}{NP_b}$$

For our previous example this would result in $\hat{k}_b = 80/970 = 8.25$ percent and $k_b = 48/952 = 5.04$ percent. As can be seen, the above approximations come quite close and will suffice in many practical situations. We note, however, that failure to consider discounts and underwriting and issue expenses altogether (using formulas (1) and (2)) would have yielded less acceptable estimates of $\hat{k}_b = 80/1000 = 8$ percent and $k_b = (1 - 0.4)80/1000 = 4.8$ percent.

It should be recognized that a firm's debt may entail various maturities and a variety of forms other than bonds and debentures. For example, part of a firm's financial needs are generally met by short-term debt which may consist of credits granted by suppliers (trade credit), of loans advanced by banks and other financial institutions, or of short-term promissory notes which the firm may issue. As we shall see later, leasing is also properly viewed as a source of debt financing. These various short and intermediate sources of borrowed funds and their costs are reviewed in detail in subsequent chapters. Conceptually, the same techniques of discounted cash flow analysis as presented in this section apply in assessing the relevant costs and yields. For simplicity, in the following examples in this chapter we will refer to a single cost of debt, k_b, computed from bonds or debentures to be issued. However, it should be recognized that in reality a firm's cost of debt may be an average of the individual costs of various maturities and forms of debt which make up the firm's capital structure.

The cost of preferred shares

Computation of the yield, $\hat{k}_p$, and the cost of preferred shares, k_p, follow the same general approach as outlined above, but since preferred shares generally have no maturity date, more straightforward formulations are involved. Specifically, only the stated dividends D_p, the market price of shares to the investors at time of issue P_p, and net proceeds to the issuing firm NP_p need to be considered, with the cash flows as shown in Figure 13-3. Because dividends are not deductible by the corporation for tax purposes, future cash flows from the investor's and firm's point of view are identical. Net proceeds NP_p are derived again by subtracting from the market price P_p any after-tax issuing and underwriting expenses.

FIGURE 13-3

Cash Flows on an Issue of Preferred Shares

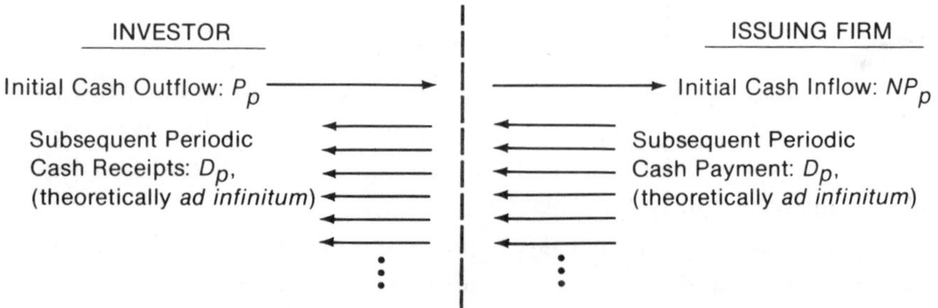

To solve for the internal rate of return from an investor's point of view we have[5]

$$(5) \quad P_p = \sum_{t=1}^{\infty} \frac{D_p}{(1+\hat{k}_p)^t} = D_p \sum_{t=1}^{\infty} \frac{1}{(1+\hat{k}_p)^t} = \frac{D_p}{\hat{k}_p}$$

with the market capitalization rate simply reduced to dividends over market price, or

$$(6) \quad \hat{k}_p = \frac{D_p}{P_p}$$

Similarly, the cost of preferred shares to the firm is given by

$$(7) \quad k_p = \frac{D_p}{NP_p}$$

Example

Consider a corporation issuing 8 percent preferred shares with a market price of $100. Issuing and underwriting expenses are 5 percent of the issue price, are assumed to be tax deductible, and the firm's tax rate is 40 percent. Thus net proceeds would be $100 – (1 – 0.4) $5 = $97. The market yield is simply 8 percent, while the cost to the firm is k_p = 8/97 or 8.25 percent. With dividends on preference shares providing no tax shield to the issuing firm, the cost of preferred shares is generally much higher than the cost of debt.[6]

The rationale for the treatment of preferred dividends as fixed costs in deriving the above formulas needs explaining. While dividends on preferred shares do not represent legal obligations to the same extent as debt charges, few firms would issue preferred shares without intending to pay regular dividends. Failure to do so can have serious consequences in terms of future financing, general credit standing, control of the corporation and paying dividends on the common shares.[7]

The cost of common equity capital

There are two potential sources of common equity capital open to the firm. First, the firm can increase its equity base by retaining part of its earnings rather than paying them out to shareholders in dividends. Secondly, the firm can raise equity by a further offering of its common shares. The costs of these two approaches to raising equity will usually differ. We will first derive the cost of common equity from new issues, and then discuss retained earnings as a source of equity capital.

[5] Note that in the formula below, it can be shown that $\sum_{t=1}^{\infty} \frac{1}{(1+\hat{k}_p)^t} = \frac{1}{\hat{k}_p}$ by applying the well-known formula for the infinite geometric series $1 + x + x^2 + \ldots + x^n + \ldots = \sum_{n=0}^{\infty} x^n = \frac{1}{1-x}$ and setting $x = \frac{1}{1+\hat{k}_p}$.

[6] In Canada, dividends which an investor received from preferred shares qualify for the dividend tax credit, whereas income is fully taxed. Hence, given an equal interest rate on debt and dividend rate on preferred shares, the effective yield after personal investors' taxes would generally be higher for preferred shares. Consequently, firms find that they can sell preferred shares at a dividend rate which is lower than the before-tax interest on long-term debt in spite of the higher investor risk typically associated with preferred shares. This narrows the gap between k_b and k_p.

[7] See also D. Quirin, *The Capital Expenditure Decision*, Homewood: Richard D. Irwin, 1967, p. 102.

New Issues

When a firm raises funds from investors through the sale of new shares, the investors again provide these funds in expectation of future cash returns.[8] These future cash flows which the firm provides take the form of dividends as shown below.

FIGURE 13-4

Cash Flows on an Issue of Common Shares

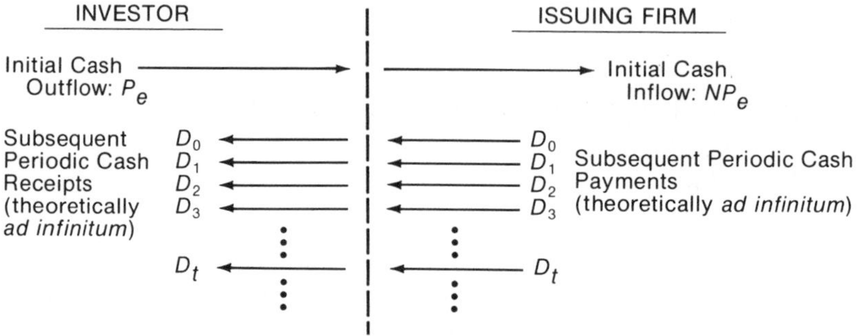

Following much of the standard financial literature, we term P_e as the price of the shares to the investor, NP_e the net proceeds to the firm, and D_t the dividend expected at the end of period t.

It is clear that the market capitalization rate and the cost of new equity funds to the firm can be found by solving for the internal rate of return of the following equations:

Market Capitalization Rate

$$(8)\quad P_e = \frac{D_0}{(1+\hat{k}_e)} + \frac{D_1}{(1+\hat{k}_e)^2} + \ldots + \frac{D_t}{(1+\hat{k}_e)^{t+1}} + \ldots.$$

$$= \sum_{t=0}^{\infty} \frac{D_t}{(1+\hat{k}_e)^{t+1}}$$

Cost of New Issue

$$(9)\quad NP_e = \frac{D_0}{(1+k_e)} + \frac{D_1}{(1+k_e)^2} + \ldots + \frac{D_t}{(1+k_e)^{t+1}} + \ldots.$$

$$= \sum_{t=0}^{\infty} \frac{D_t}{(1+k_e)^{t+1}}$$

Note that D_0 is the dividend at the end of the current period which is assumed to have just started; hence it is discounted for one period.

The difficulty in applying these formulations lies in the fact that future dividend payments, being at the discretion of the firm's board of directors, are unknown and uncertain. Some simplifying assumptions generally need to be made to obtain at least a first approximation of the cost of new common equity.

[8]While an investor may purchase shares (or other securities) essentially in the hope of making a capital gain, the selling price of the shares should ultimately reflect dividend expectations, with a higher selling price simply reflecting improved earnings and dividend prospects for the firm. This point will be developed more fully in the chapter on dividend theory.

If we assume dividend payments to remain constant at current levels, the above formulas have the simple solution of $\hat{k}_e = \frac{D_0}{P_e}$ and $k_e = \frac{D_0}{NP_e}$. However, generally some fraction of earnings is reinvested and consequently we would expect corporate earnings and dividends to grow. Inflation may also contribute to this expectation. Under such circumstances, the most straightforward assumption would be to apply a constant annual growth rate g to dividend payments. Conceptually, the assumption of a constant growth rate can be justified if, for example, a firm reinvests a constant proportion of its earnings and such reinvestments, on average, produce a given constant return. The assumption of a costant growth rate of dividends implies

$$(10) \qquad P_e = \frac{D_0}{(1+\hat{k}_e)} + \frac{D_0(1+g)}{(1+\hat{k}_e)^2} + \frac{D_0(1+g)^2}{(1+\hat{k}_e)^3} + \ldots + \frac{D_0(1+g)^t}{(1+\hat{k}_e)^{t+1}} + \ldots .$$

or

$$(11) \qquad P_e = \frac{D_0}{(1+\hat{k}_e)} \left[1 + \frac{(1+g)}{(1+\hat{k}_e)} + \left(\frac{1+g}{1+\hat{k}_e} \right)^2 + \ldots . \right]$$

The sum in the bracket is an infinite geometric series, which can be simplified arithmetically and rewritten as

$$1 + \left(\frac{1+g}{1+\hat{k}_e} \right) + \left(\frac{1+g}{1+\hat{k}_e} \right)^2 + \ldots . = \frac{1}{1 - (1+g)/(1+\hat{k}_e)} = \frac{1+\hat{k}_e}{\hat{k}_e - g}$$

Inserting in (11), we obtain

$$(12) \qquad P_e = \frac{D_0}{\hat{k}_e - g}$$

from which the market capitalization rate is derived as[9]

$$(13) \qquad \hat{k}_e = \frac{D_0}{P_e} + g$$

Similarly, we would have obtained for the cost of capital to the firm

$$(14) \qquad k_e = \frac{D_0}{NP_e} + g$$

with k_e being greater than $\hat{k}_e$ because of the underwriting and issuing expenses which the firm has to bear ($NP_e < P_e$).

[9]For those comfortable with calculus, equation (13) is readily derived if you assume dividends to be paid at a continuous rate and continuous compounding. Thus, in the constant growth case with

$$D_t = D_0 e^{gt}, \text{ and } NP_e = \int_0^\infty D_t e^{-k_e t} dt, \; NP_e \text{ can be written as:}$$

$$\int_0^\infty D_0 e^{-t(k_e - g)} dt,$$

and integrating (if $k_e > g$)

$$NP_e = \frac{D_0}{k_e - g} \quad \text{or} \quad k_e = \frac{D_0}{NP_e} + g.$$

While for purposes of investor expectations the assumption of a constant growth rate may not be completely accurate, it is an approximation which can provide a fairly reasonable indication of the cost of new common equity, and as such is widely used.[10] The growth rate g may be derived from historic data, or it may be a figure estimated from current and expected industry and corporate performance, inflation rates and the likes. Growth rates which are not constant over time can be handled in a similar way, although the mathematics become more complex. An example of this is provided in the problems with solutions at the end of this chapter.

Note that basing a firm's cost of equity on dividend payments does not imply that, because a firm currently pays little or no dividends, its cost of equity is automatically low. To illustrate, a firm characterized by rapid growth may be retaining all of its earnings to finance attractive new investment opportunities and paying no dividends. While the reinvestments are expected to yield increased earnings in the future, no firm can expect to grow forever at a rate which is above that of the economy. At some future time, the increased level of earnings and declining reinvestment opportunities will logically dictate that increased amounts be paid out in dividends.[11]

And as we saw, k_e is not only determined by the current dividend cost $\frac{D_0}{NP_e}$, but also by growth expectations g. For example, if shares can be sold to net the company \$100 per share, with current annual dividends at \$5 per share and an annual growth rate projected for the foreseeable future at 10 percent, the cost of new equity is determined as

$$k_e = \frac{5}{100} + 0.1 = 0.15 = 15\%$$

The use of dividends (which are not explicitly promised but declared at the discretion of the firm's board of directors) as the basis for computing the cost of capital requires further comment. If the required rate of return on equity is $\hat{k}_e$ as determined by current dividend expectations of investors, and the firm raises new equity on which it can earn only a return less than $\hat{k}_e$, the result will be that investors will revise their valuation of the corporation's shares downward, with share prices declining so that at the new price the shares will once more offer a prospective return equal to $\hat{k}_e$.

Pursuing the above example, if investors require a return of 15 percent but the firm, in reinvesting its funds, can only sustain a growth rate of 7 percent instead

[10]In this case, D_0 is the current dividend rate. For a detailed discussion see M. Gordon, *The Investment, Financing and Valuation of the Corporation*, Homewood: Richard D. Irwin, 1962 pp. 46-47.

[11] As mentioned earlier, an investor may buy a share because of expected capital gains without regard to current dividend payments. His expected return may be given by

$$P_0 = \frac{D_0}{(1+\hat{k}_e)} + \ldots + \frac{D_t - 1}{(1+\hat{k}_e)^t} + \frac{P_t}{(1+\hat{k}_e)^t}$$

where P_t is the expected selling price after t periods. With a high expected terminal value P_t, the return $\hat{k}_e$ can be high even if current dividend payments are low. The high expected stock value at time t, however, has to have some justification. It is likely to be found in the increased earnings per share, for as reinvestment opportunities stabilize, the earnings are expected ultimately to find their way into dividends.

of 10 percent as expected, then by formula (12) the shares will trade at the reduced market price of

$$P_e = \frac{D_0}{\hat{k}_e - g} = \frac{\$5}{0.15 - 0.07} = \$62.50$$

and once again provide the required yield of

$$\hat{k}_e = \frac{D_0}{P_e} + g = \frac{\$5}{\$62.50} + 0.07 = 15 \text{ percent}$$

If the corporation is to avoid this decline in its share prices resulting from inadequate returns on its investments it must undertake to offer a return on its equity capital at least equal to $\hat{k}_e$.[12] Hence, in raising new equity, the corporation must expect to be able to invest it and earn a return on it at least equal to the market capitalization rate $\hat{k}_e$. This rate forms the basis for determining the required rate of return or specific marginal cost of equity capital.

Example

Assume a firm which can sell new shares to the public at \$93 per share. Issuing and underwriting expenses (which are assumed to be tax deductible) amount to \$5 per share, with the corporate tax rate at 40 percent. Hence, net proceeds become \$93 – (1 – 0.4) \$5 = \$90. The firm's shares now trade at \$100 with current annual dividends of \$4.50 per share. The history of dividend payments for the last 10 years is as follows:

Year	1965	'66	'67	'68	'69	'70	'71	'72	'73	'74
Dividends	\$3	\$3	\$3	\$3.50	\$3.50	\$4	\$4	\$4	\$4.25	\$4.50

The increase from \$3 to \$4.50 over a 9-year period implies an approximate average annual growth of 5 percent ($\$3 \times 1.05^9 \simeq \$4.50$), a figure slightly above the average inflation rate for the period. In light of comparatively high current inflation rates of around 9-10 percent, management feels it reasonable to assume that investors expect earnings to continue to grow at a rate slightly above that of price level changes, and that a growth rate of about 11 percent would be reasonable. Thus, the cost of new common equity is estimated as

$$k_e = \frac{\$4.50}{\$90} + 0.11 = 0.16 = 16 \text{ percent}$$

[12]This point can be made more rigorously. Let r be the perpetual yield on a new investment, n the number of common shares initially outstanding, m the additional shares sold at price P to finance the project, and $\bar{E}_t$ the expected earnings per share in period t. Then, for a non-growth situation with no senior securities and no change in business risk through acceptance of the project,

$$\bar{E}_{t+1} = \frac{n\bar{E}_t + mPr}{n + m}.$$

For the price of shares to hold up, $\bar{E}_{t+1}$ must match the current expectation $\bar{E}_t$. In notation, therefore,

$$\frac{n\bar{E}_t + mPr^*}{n + m} = \frac{n\bar{E}_t}{n}$$

with r^* the particular yield on the new investment which will keep the shareholder's position unchanged. It follows that r^* equals the earnings-price ratio or cost of equity capital $\bar{E}_t/P$. If, in fact, r, the actual rate of return achieved, is below k_e, then as suggested above P will decline.

As previously discussed, determination of the approximate cost of new equity capital requires judgment and is subject to uncertainties which limit the accuracy of any figure derived. The above techniques, however, do provide a useful starting point for the derivation of first approximations. While the basic problem of assessing future expectations always remains, more sophisticated tools which go beyond the scope of this text are available for the derivation of more refined results.[13]

Retained Earnings

As was shown in Chapter 7, corporations frequently generate significant funds through earnings which are then retained for reinvestment. While a firm would have no direct commitments in the form of future cash outflows associated with these funds, the opportunity cost related to alternative uses of such monies must not be overlooked. Specifically, earnings are benefits accruing to shareholders, which if not retained in the firm would be paid out as dividends. Since shareholders can reinvest dividends and if management wants to act in the best interests of its shareholders, earnings should only be retained within the firm provided they can be reinvested at yields which match or exceed returns which shareholders could achieve on reinvesting additional dividends themselves. shareholders could always invest by purchasing additional shares in this or similar companies to yield $\hat{k}_e$ as computed above, it follows that earnings would have to yield at least that amount if they are retained by the firm. For the cost of retained earnings, therefore, we would have $k_{re} = \hat{k}_e$, which is generally smaller than the cost of raising new common equity capital k_e, because underwriting and issue expenses do not arise.

The above argument needs to be modified because of taxes which investors generally have to pay on dividends received. If the investor's marginal tax rate on dividend income, net of the dividend tax credit, is t and the corporation distributes one dollar in dividends, the net amount received by the investor is only $1(1 - t)$ dollars after tax has been paid. The investor then has the opportunity to invest this amount in the shares of this corporation (or of another corporation with similar risk characteristics) to produce an annual expected return of $\hat{k}_e (1 - t)$. Therefore, if the corporation is to provide the investor with an equivalent expected return by retaining and reinvesting the dividend, it must earn a return of only $\hat{k}_e (1 - t)$ on the common equity portion of its investment.[14] Hence the specific marginal cost of equity from retained earnings would be given by:

(15) $$k_{re} = \hat{k}_e (1 - t)$$

In practice, it may be difficult to use the above formula. While in a closely held firm the marginal tax rates which the owners pay on dividends may be accurately determined, this becomes very intricate in a situation where the shares are widely

[13]See, for example, S. Myers, "Finance Theory in Rate Cases," *The Bell Journal of Economics and Management Science*, Spring 1972, pp. 58-97.

[14]To simplify exposition, the capital gains tax is ignored. Where the investor purchases securities to hold them indefinitely, this assumption is realistic since no capital gains are realized. More generally, provided that the impact of the capital gains tax is smaller than that of the tax on dividends, the position that retained earnings provide a cheaper source than floating a new common share issue holds. For a development of this point, see W. Lewellen, *The Cost of Capital*, Belmont: Wadsworth Publishing Co. Inc., 1969, pp. 67-68.

held and where the tax rate faced by investors may exhibit wide variations. Accordingly, we can either use a rough subjective assessment and estimate a tax rate for the "typical" investor, or we can ignore the tax effect altogether. The latter stance leads to a conservative estimate[15] for the cost of retained earnings, namely having it equal to the current market yield on the corporation's shares. Again, perfect answers in this difficult area are generally not available and we have to make do with the limited information available.

Example

To illustrate, we pursue the example used in the previous section to compute the cost of new equity. Ignoring the tax effect on dividends, we would have derived

$$k_{re} = \hat{k}_e = \frac{\$4.50}{\$100} + 0.11 = 15.5 \text{ percent}$$

which is lower than the 16 percent computed for k_e because underwriting and issue expenses are avoided. If we consider a situation involving a closely held firm, with the shareholders' marginal rate on dividends net of all credits estimated to be t = 20 percent, we obtain

$$k_{re} = (1 - t)\hat{k}_e = 0.8 \times 15.5 = 12.4 \text{ percent}$$

As we can appreciate from these figures, the difference due to the tax effect is significant, further highlighting the need for reasoned judgment before any computations are made.

Depreciation

As noted in earlier chapters, depreciation charges along with retained earnings provide a significant source of funds for business investment. Again, while no direct cash outlays are associated with the use of funds available through depreciation, there is an opportunity cost reflecting alternative uses for such monies which needs to be considered. We can show, however, that the appropriate opportunity cost is really the firm's overall cost of funds, a fact which will enable us to ignore depreciation when computing the firm's cost of capital.

Example

Let us consider an oversimplified situation. A business endeavor comprises a single investment of \$100,000 which is financed by issuing \$30,000 of debt at a cost k_b = 4 percent and \$70,000 worth of equity at a cost k_e = 8 percent, for a weighted average cost of $0.3 \times 4 + 0.7 \times 8 = 6.8$ percent. During the first year, depreciation of \$20,000 is charged. The firm can either reinvest these monies or commit to retire a portion of the capital originally contributed, as depreciation charges represent a recovery of the capital which was originally invested. If the firm wishes to maintain its original capital structure it would use the \$20,000 to repay \$20,000 × 0.3 = \$6,000 worth of debt and retire \$20,000 × 0.7 = \$14,000 worth of equity (for example by declaring a liquidating

[15]Ignoring the tax may really be quite reasonable. Given the \$1,000 exemption for tax purposes on certain investment income plus the dividend tax credit, some individuals' dividend income will not be fully taxed while some may escape tax altogether.

dividend). This would save future financing charges of \$6,000 × 0.04 + \$14,000 × 0.08 = \$1,360, which as a percentage works out to \$1,360/\$20,000 = 6.8 percent, a figure just equal to the firm's weighted average cost of capital.

13-4. THE WEIGHTED AVERAGE COST OF CAPITAL

Before dealing with issues which arise when computing the weighted average cost of capital, the rationale for its use as the discount rate on which capital budgeting decisions are to be based needs explaining. Put another way, if a new long-term loan is negotiable at an after-tax cost of k_b = 5 percent to finance a new expansion, we must stand ready to answer the question of why this figure cannot serve as the yardstick against which investment performance is measured.

Within reasonable limits, most corporations have a policy of maintaining, over the longer-term, a particular capital structure with given proportions of debt, preferred shares and common equity. The structure is usually one which management feels is reasonable given the firm's business risk. When actually raising funds, however, financing is generally "lumpy" with one form of security used at a time so as to minimize underwriting and issue costs as well as the expenditure of management time. This means that the mix reflected in the capital structure is only adhered to over the longer-term. Thus, a firm may float a new issue of long-term debt this year at an after-tax cost of 5 percent and finance its investments essentially out of retained earnings over the next three years in order to rebuild its equity base and return the capital structure to the desired debt-to-equity mix. It would clearly lead to inconsistent decision-making if in one year the firm accepted all investment projects yielding above 5 percent simply because debt financing was used, while in succeeding years investments yielding 10 and 11 percent were rejected because the cost of retained earnings was 12 percent. It is more sensible not to match an investment with its specific source of financing, but rather to take the long-term view and consider the total corporate pool of funds, raised at various times from different sources at varying costs. The average cost of such funds should then be applied against investment projects being financed from the pool.

It should also be clear that the relevant costs to consider when evaluating new investments projects are not the historical costs at which monies were raised in the past, but current marginal costs of raising the required funds. It is irrelevant for purposes of evaluating new capital expenditures that past interest rates were much lower and that significant amounts of such inexpensive debt may currently be carried on the company's books. What matters are the various costs of today's capital requirements and it is these costs against which the projected returns of new investments should be measured.

An example illustrating the appropriate weighting to be given retained earnings and new common equity issues when computing the overall cost of capital will further clarify the marginal principle—that of using the marginal costs occasioned by incremental investments.

Example

Assume a firm to have a total capital budget of \$10,000,000 for the coming year. Appropriations of \$9,000,000 have already been decided on and management is evaluating the final \$1,000,000 project, a new machine to automate certain aspects of the production process. In the past the firm has had a capital structure consisting of 50 percent debt and 50 percent equity which it wishes to maintain. Equity financing consists of retained earnings and the issuance of new common shares. Retained earnings are cheaper and will generally be drawn on first, and only if there is a shortfall in equity funds from this source will additional common shares be issued. Given \$3,000,000 in retained earnings, the capital budget for the year is to be financed as follows:

\$5,000,000 debt at k_b = 5 percent
\$5,000,000 common equity, comprising
  \$3,000,000 from retained earnings at
    k_{re} = 10 percent
  \$2,000,000 from a new issue of common shares at
    k_e = 15 percent

If the new machine is not acquired only \$9,000,000 need be raised, \$4,500,000 in debt and \$4,500,000 in equity of which \$3,000,000 is internally available in any case. Therefore the firm would reduce its outside offering of new shares by \$500,000 raising:

\$4,500,000 from debt at k_b = 5 percent;
\$3,000,000 from retained earnings at k_{re} = 10 percent; and,
\$1,500,000 from a new issue of common at k_e = 15 percent.

Hence savings in financing charges of \$500,000 × 0.05 + \$500,000 × 0.15 = \$100,000 per year are involved if the final \$1,000,000 project is not undertaken. Expressed in percentages, the \$1,000,000 investment in machinery would, therefore, have to yield at least

$$k = \frac{\$\ 500{,}000}{\$1{,}000{,}000} \times 5\% + \frac{\$\ 500{,}000}{\$1{,}000{,}000} \times 15\% = 10\%$$

which becomes the appropriate weighted average cost of capital to be used in discounting.

Generalizing from this illustration, we can state that where the common equity portion of a capital budget is financed partly through retained earnings and partly through an offering of new shares, generally only the higher cost of issuing new shares is relevant for computation of the overall cost of capital. This follows from the fact that if an incremental investment is not undertaken, the cutback on the equity side will be of the more costly new share issue. While firms generally do have policies regarding the proportion of equity to be maintained in their capital structure, there is no reason to maintain constant proportions of retained earnings and new common shares within the equity category and, as already mentioned, the cheapest source of equity funds will be drawn on first.

The actual computation of the weighted average cost of capital is quite straightforward.

Example

Assume that \$100,000,000 will be required by a firm to finance a major new expansion program and that in keeping with the existing capital structure, funds are to be raised from the following sources:

debt:	\$25,000,000
preferred shares:	\$15,000,000
new common shares:	\$30,000,000
retained earnings:	\$10,000,000
depreciation:	\$20,000,000

debt:	8% coupon \$1,000 par value 20-year bonds. Issuing and underwriting expenses are 3% of par value.
preferred shares:	each 7% \$100 par value share to net the company \$97 (this includes the tax shields from issuing and underwriting expenses).
common shares:	shares are currently trading at \$45; a new issue would net the company \$40 per share (again, including tax shields of expenses and commissions). The company wants to maintain the current annual dividend at \$2 per share while sustaining a long-term average growth of dividends of 10% per year.
retained earnings:	assume all shareholders to pay roughly 30% net tax on dividends received.

The corporate tax rate is 45%.

Using the approximation formula discussed earlier in this chapter for the cost of debt, we compute:

$$k_b \simeq \frac{(1-T)I}{NP_b} = \frac{0.55(80)}{1000 - 0.55 \times 30} = 4.47\%$$

$$k_p = \frac{D_p}{NP_p} = \frac{7}{97} = 7.2\%$$

$$k_e = \frac{D_0}{NP_e} + g = \frac{2}{40} + 0.1 = 15\%$$

$$k_{re} = (1-t)\left(\frac{D_0}{P_e} + g\right) = (0.7) \times \left(\frac{2}{45} + 0.1\right) = 10\%$$

The cost of depreciation will equal the weighted average cost of capital. Hence, computation of the weighted average cost of capital is unaffected by depreciation, and this source will be dropped from further consideration. The remaining \$80,000,000 is raised in the following proportions:

Source	Amount (1)	Proportion (2)	Cost In % (3)	Weighted Cost (4) = (2) × (3)
debt	$25,000,000	$\frac{25}{80} = 0.31$	4.47	1.40
preferred	$15,000,000	$\frac{15}{80} = 0.19$	7.2	1.35
equity[16]	$40,000,000	$\frac{40}{80} = 0.5$	15	7.5

Weighted Average Cost of Capital k = 10.25%

The discount rate to be used in evaluating new investments becomes slightly over 10%.[17]

Alternative choices of weights

While the weights to be used in computing the weighted average cost of capital should reflect the proportions in which the firm intends to finance future investment projects, convenience sometimes makes it tempting to compute the weighted average cost of capital using existing financial data. Regulatory bodies, for example, in establishing prices which will provide a fair rate of return for the regulated firm, generally appear interested in approximating the firm's weighted average cost of capital from published financial statements. In drawing on public financial information, the two main approaches for approximating the weights of various sources of funds to be used in computing the weighted average cost of capital are: (1) to use the book value proportions of debt, preferred shares and common equity as weights, or (2) the use of proportions based on current market values of the various securities outstanding.

Example

Assume a firm with the following balance sheet figures:

Source	Book Value Amount	Proportion
Debt	$50,000,000	50%
Equity		
5,000,000 common shares at $5 each	$25,000,000	25%
Retained Earnings	$25,000,000	25%

While the firm's debt is assumed to have a market price roughly equal to its book value, the shares, reflecting the growth potential perceived by investors, are currently trading at $20 per share, giving rise to the following market values:

[16] Based on the above discussion of the marginal principle, the cost of new equity is used for the entire equity financed portion.

[17] Note that adding back depreciation at a cost of 10.25 percent does not alter the result, as we obtain $k = 0.8 \times 10.25 + 0.2 \times 10.25 = 10.25$.

Source	Market Value Amount	Proportion
Debt	$50,000,000	33⅓%
Equity		
5,000,000 shares at $20 each	$100,000,000	66⅔%

Note that retained earnings do not appear explicitly in this computation since such retentions are already reflected in the market values at which the shares trade. That is, investors take the firm's retained earnings into consideration when valuing the firm's shares, and the same would hold true for funds provided through depreciation.

If in the above example we find that $k_b = 5\%$, $k_{re} = 10\%$ and $k_e = 15\%$, then using book value weights we obtain:

$$k = 0.5 \times 5\% + 0.5 \times 15\% = 10\%$$

On the other hand, using market weights:

$$k = 0.333 \times 5\% + 0.667 \times 15\% = 11.67\%$$

Thus, whenever the market price of common shares is higher than the book value of equity, which is often the case, the use of market values implies that equity will weigh more heavily in the weighted average cost of calculation, pushing up k.

Which set of weights to use has been a controversial issue. Market value weights do have strong appeal on theoretical grounds.

Book value proportions merely reflect financial history. If the market currently values a firm's common equity at $100,000,000, it seems more reasonable to use that figure rather than one of $50,000,000 which in terms of retained earnings reflects past reinvestment policies, and the fact that perhaps 20 years ago shares were first sold at $5 each. Looked at another way, if historical weightings were to suggest a cost of capital *higher* than market weightings, say 14 percent rather than 10 percent, it would clearly not be in the shareholders' interests to use 14 percent as a hurdle and to reject a 12 percent project when new financing under current market conditions could in fact be provided for at 10 percent.

The use of market values, however, may raise a different set of problems. Market values, those of equities in particular, can fluctuate rapidly and over relatively wide ranges, making it necessary to average over time so as to obtain reasonably stable weights. Furthermore, it takes more effort to determine market values while book values are readily available from the firm's financial statements.

Obviously if market value proportions govern the firm's future financing policies, its book value proportions will change over time.

Example

Pursuing our earlier example, assume that the firm raised an additional $5,000,000 in market value proportions, that is $33,333,333 = 0.667 ×

$50,000,000) in new common shares and the balance of $16,666,667 = 0.333 × $50,000,000 in new debt. This new financing would give rise to the following book value figures:

Source	Book Value Amount	Proportion
Debt	$66,666,667	44%
Equity		
Common Shares	$58,333,333	39%
Retained Earnings	$25,000,000	17%

With continued new financing based on market values, the book value proportion will gradually shift to approach market value proportions, and in this example, would increase the equity weighting on the balance sheet.

The question also arises as to whether investors judge the financial risk of a firm from balance sheet data, market value proportions or some other basis such as cash flow considerations. If the balance sheet plays a major role in guiding investors' thinking, then the new financing as outlined in the above example will alter the risk characteristics of the firm as perceived by investors and this must be taken into account when setting financing policies.

From the above discussion it is easy to appreciate why the choice of weights remains a controversial issue which is not easily resolved. It is our view, however, that the firm's policies regarding its future financing mix should provide the basis for the choice of appropriate weights. How a firm should evaluate various alternatives in this regard is discussed in the following chapter which deals with the evaluation of alternative capital structures.

By way of summary and to reinforce the earlier discussions it may be useful to formalize the concept of the weighted average cost of capital using market value weights. Assume that a corporation makes new investments in an amount J to yield an annual rate of return k and finances these investments by increasing the amount of outstanding debt, preferred shares, and common equity by amounts ΔB, ΔP and ΔE respectively. Then,

$$J = \Delta B + \Delta P + \Delta E$$

since the amount of financing must equal the amount invested. If the investment is to be worthwhile, it must earn a rate of return sufficient to cover its financing costs. This minimum rate of return a project must earn if it is to be worthwhile is referred to as the corporation's cost of capital, k, and is given by:

$$kJ = k_b \Delta B + k_p \Delta P + k_e \Delta E$$

where k_b, k_p and k_e are the required rates of return or *specific marginal costs* of debt, preferred and common equity funds—that is, the returns from the project, kJ must be large enough to cover the overall costs of financing it. We next obtain:

$$k = k_b \frac{\Delta B}{J} + k_p \frac{\Delta P}{J} + k_e \frac{\Delta E}{J}.$$

where $\frac{\Delta B}{J}$, $\frac{\Delta P}{J}$ or $\frac{\Delta E}{J}$ are the proportions of debt, preferred shares and equity to be used in financing the contemplated investments.

With the new investment financed in the same proportions of debt, preferred and common equity as given by the current market values of the firm's outstanding securities, we have

$$\frac{\Delta B}{J} = \frac{B}{V}, \quad \frac{\Delta P}{J} = \frac{P}{V}, \text{ and } \frac{\Delta E}{J} = \frac{E}{V}$$

where B, P and E are the existing amounts of debt, preferred shares, and equity already outstanding and V is the total market value of the corporation ($V = B + P + E$).

Hence, the corporation's cost of capital may be written as:

$$k = k_b \frac{B}{V} + k_p \frac{P}{V} + k_e \frac{E}{V} \qquad (16)$$

k, which is the appropriate cost of capital for capital expenditure decisions, is referred to as the corporation's *weighted average cost of capital,* for it is a weighted average of the specific marginal costs of each of the individual sources of funds where the weights are the proportions of the total value of the corporation contributed by each source of funds.

***ADDITIONAL SELECTED TOPICS*

**13-5. THE COST OF COMMON EQUITY CAPITAL WITH FINANCING THROUGH RIGHTS

Where new common shares are issued through a rights offering, underwriting commissions may not be incurred. Except for certain minor expenses, the corporation receives the full subscription price which investors pay for the new shares. As noted in Chapter 12, the market price of the corporation's share is usually affected by a rights offering, with a drop in share price brought about by the initial dilution. Consequently, we saw that after a rights offering investors typically hold more shares at the lower per share price and their total wealth should remain unaffected.

In assessing a firm's cost of new equity which is issued through rights, much will depend on how a firm adapts its dividend policy to deal with the increased number of lower priced shares outstanding. Generally, it appears that following rights offerings corporations do strive to maintain existing policies regarding per share dividends. It follows, therefore, that to compute the cost of new common shares sold through rights, the formulas derived in this chapter for the cost of common equity remain valid, with the net proceeds NP_e being given by the subscription price S. If, due to the rights offering, a firm should contemplate a change in per share dividends this clearly would have to be considered in computation of k_e.

**13-6. THE COST OF CONVERTIBLE SECURITIES

An assessment of the costs of a convertible security is difficult because forecasts of fairly uncertain future events are called for. As discussed in Chapter 11, a convertible security is generally viewed as delayed equity financing, and is issued with the expectation that at some future time conversion into new common shares will take place. Hence a convertible debenture has to be treated as debt for a number of years until conversion takes place, and as common equity thereafter. The relevant cash flows are shown in Figure 13-5. As a consequence, not only are estimates regarding future dividend payments beyond the conversion date called for, but the time of conversion, which may not be the same for all investors, needs to be assessed as well. Any figure derived can only be viewed as a rough estimate, highlighting once more the need for judgment and the difficulty and lack of precision in this important area of finance.

FIGURE 13-5

Cash Flows of an Issue of Convertible Debt

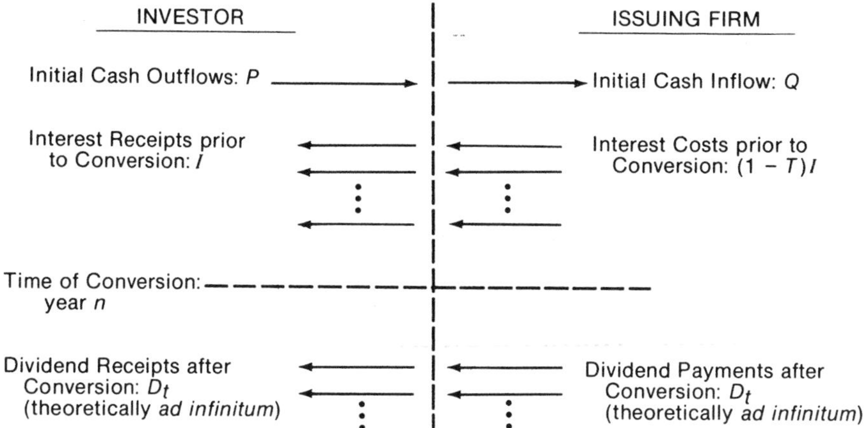

13-7. SUMMARY

The weighted average or overall cost of capital is an important concept in corporate finance. It reflects the overall cost at which the firm can raise new monies to finance new investments and, in the absence of capital rationing, it becomes the yardstick against which investment returns are to be measured.

A firm typically finances its operations from several sources, the most important external ones being debt, preferred shares and new common shares; while the major internal sources are retained earnings and depreciation. Respecting securities which a corporation sells to investors, we can distinguish between the security yield to the investors, called the market capitalization rate, and the cost of the security or cost of capital to the firm. The two are not identical because of various expenses in issuing new securities, and because of tax effects, the most notable one being the tax deductibility of interest at the corporate level. Both the market capitalization rates and the costs of capital for various securities are computed by deriving internal rates of return for the relevant net cash flows available respectively to investors and the corporation. Particular difficulties arise in the case of common shares because the analysis has to be based on investor expectations about future dividend payments which are not governed by any contractual commitments.

With internally generated funds, the notion of an opportunity cost needs to be recognized. Thus, the cost of retained earnings is established as the opportunity cost to the shareholders of having dividends withheld. The opportunity cost of depreciation is simply the weighted average cost of capital, as funds from depreciation could be used to repay or retire capital which was initially invested.

The weights to be used in computing the average cost of capital should primarily reflect current financing policies of the firm, just as the costs should be marginal costs reflecting current capital market conditions.

A compendium of formulas for market yields and the specific marginal costs of capital to the corporation, as introduced in this chapter, appears below. Notation used includes:

$\hat{k}$ = market capitalization rate or market yield
k = overall cost of capital
b, p, e, re = subscripts for debt;, preferred shares, common shares and retained earnings respectively
F = par value of debt
I = annual interest payments
n = number of years to maturity
P = market price of security
NP = net proceeds of security to the firm
D = annual dividend payments
g = average long-term growth rate in dividends
T = corporate tax rate
t = net tax rate on dividends for "typical investor"

Debt:

with underwriting and issue expense as well as discounts ignored

$$\hat{k}_b = \frac{I}{F} \qquad k_b = \frac{(1-T)I}{F}$$

Approximations, recognizing the presence of underwriting and issue expenses as well as discounts:

$$\hat{k}_b = \frac{I}{P_b} \qquad k_b = \frac{(1-T)I}{NP_b}$$

Preferred Shares:

$$\hat{k}_p = \frac{D_p}{P_p} \qquad k_p = \frac{D_p}{NP_p}$$

Common Shares, assuming constant growth rates in dividends:

$$\hat{k}_e = \frac{D_0}{P_e} + g \qquad k_e = \frac{D_0}{NP_e} + g$$

Retained Earnings:

$$k_{re} = (1 - t)\hat{k}_e$$

Depreciation:

cost equals the weighted average cost of capital k.

Questions for Discussion

1. In computing the cost of equity capital, should we use the cost of retained earnings or the cost of new issues? Discuss.
2. In computing the weighted average cost of capital, should we use weights based on market value? What arguments can be put forward against using book value weights?
3. Keeping the opportunity cost concept in mind, discuss some approaches to specifying the appropriate hurdle rate for a Crown corporation. Assume an absence of capital rationing.
4. Discuss connections between the notion of a "required rate of return" as established during public utility type rate hearings, and the cost of capital.
5. Under what circumstances could it be argued that dilution will not take place following an issue of common equity?
6. What are some of the main difficulties in trying to assess a firm's weighted average cost of capital in practice?
7. How does the tax environment influence a firm's financing decision and its cost of capital?

Problems with Solutions:

1. The Vice President Finance of XYZ Corporation has asked you to estimate the weighted average cost of capital to the firm. The firm plans on financing major new expansion programs by drawing on funds in the following proportions which roughly correspond with its current capital structure:

long-term debt	30%
preferred shares	10%
new common shares	20%
retained earnings	20%
depreciation	20%

Issuing and underwriting expenses can be neglected throughout. Debt can be issued at a coupon of 12 percent; dividends on preferred shares would be 9 percent. Common shares currently trade at $50 per share, and new shares would be sold at a 10 percent discount. The current dividend is $2.25 per share. Management feels that on average over the long run, growth in dividends should at least match inflation which is anticipated to run at about 10 percent per annum. The corporate tax rate is 40 percent and you may assume an investor tax rate on dividends of 30 percent.

Solution

Given that issuing and underwriting expenses can be neglected, the computations are greatly simplified, and we obtain

$$k_b = (1 - T)\hat{k}_b = 0.6 \times 12\% = 7.2\%$$

$$k_p = \hat{k}_p = 9\%$$

$$k_e = \frac{D_0}{NP_0} + g = \frac{2.25}{45} + 0.1 = 0.15 = 15\%$$

$$k_{re} = (1 - t)\hat{k}_e = 0.7\left(\frac{2.25}{50} + 0.1\right) = 10.15\%$$

Note that if retained earnings are used, the discount at which new shares would have to be sold is avoided; hence the denominator in the above equation becomes \$50 (current market price) and not \$45 (discount price for new shares).

Because of the marginal principle as outlined in the chapter, k_{re} will not appear in the weighted average cost of capital calculation as only the more expensive source of equity capital (new common shares) will be used for the equity portion of new financing. Depreciation can be ignored, and the weights of the various sources of funds should be adjusted accordingly. We obtain:

$$k = 3/8 \times 7.2\% + 1/8 \times 9\% + 4/8 \times 15\% = 11.33\%$$

The cost of depreciation is simply $k_d = k = 11.33\%$

2. Assume a firm with the following balance sheet figures

Source	Book Value Amount	Proportion
Debt	\$48,000,000	40%
Equity		
5,000,000 shares at \$4 each	\$20,000,000	16.7%
Retained earnings	\$52,000,000	43.3%

Given the substantial rise in interest rates in recent years, the firm's debt currently has a market price of only \$30,000,000.

The common shares are trading at \$25 each. New debt can currently be issued at an after-tax cost of k_b = 7%, while the cost of new equity is estimated at k_e = 15%. Issuing and underwriting expenses can be neglected.

(a) Compute the firm's weighted average cost of capital using both book and market value proportions.

Solution

k_b = 7%

k_e = 15%

k_{re}: we can assume k_{re} is less than k_e, and therefore we do not need it, as only the more expensive source of equity is relevant in computing the weighted average cost of capital.

Using book value weights:

$$k = 0.4 \times 7\% + 0.6 \times 15\% = 11.80\%.$$
Debt Equity

Using market value proportions the following values are computed:

Source	Market Value	Proportion
Debt	$ 30,000,000	19.35%
Equity: 5,000,000 shares at $25 each.	$ 125,000,000	80.65%

The cost of capital using market value weights becomes:

$$k = 0.1935 \times 7\% + 0.8065 \times 15\% = 13.45\%.$$

(b) Assume that the firm raised an additional $30,000,000 using market value proportions. What would its book value proportions be after completion of such new financing?

Solution:

Market value proportions:	Debt	19.35%
	Equity	80.65%
Amounts raised:	Debt	.1935 × $30,000,000 = $5,805,000
	Equity	.8065 × $30,000,000 = $24,195,000

The new book value proportions are computed as follows:

Source	Book Value Amount	Proportion
Debt:	$48,000,000 + $ 5,805,000 = $53,805,000	35.87%
Equity:		
Shares	$20,000,000 + $24,195,000 = $44,195,000	29.46%
Retained Earnings	$52,000,000 + 0 = $52,000,000	34.67%

The new proportions are 35.87% debt, 29.46% shares, and 34.67% retained earnings.

(c) Assume that the firm raised the additional $30,000,000 using book value proportions, what would its market value proportions be after such financing?

Solution

Book Value Proportions:	Debt	40%
	Equity	60%
Amounts raised:	Debt	.40 × $30,000,000 = $12,000,000
	Equity	.60 × $30,000,000 = $18,000,000

The new market value proportions are:

Debt	$30,000,000 + 12,000,000 = $42,000,000	22.7%
Equity (shares)	$125,000,000 + 18,000,000 = $143,000,000	77.3%

The new proportions are 22.7% debt and 77.3% equity.

3. Given current capital market conditions and the characteristics of XYZ corporation, investors demand a market capitalization rate of $\hat{k}_e = 15$ percent on the common shares which are currently trading at $30 per share. Dividend payments for the current year are expected to be $1.50 per share.

   (a) What is the implied long-term average growth rate in dividends which shareholders expect?
   (b) If because of changed business conditions investors adjust their growth expectations down to a zero growth rate but still demand a 15 percent market return on the shares, what do you expect will happen to the market price of the shares?
   (c) Conversely, if because of a buoyant economy, investors reassess their growth expectations to 15 percent per annum but still demand a 15 percent market rate of return, at what price should the common shares trade?

Solution

(a) Using the formula

$\hat{k}_e = \frac{D_0}{P_e} + g$ where, from the problem,

$\hat{k}_e = 15\%$, $D_0 = \$1.50$, and $P_e = \$30$, we solve for g

$$
\begin{aligned}
g &= \hat{k}_e - \frac{D_0}{P_e} \\
&= .15 - \frac{1.50}{30} \\
&= .15 - .05 \\
&= .10
\end{aligned}
$$

The implied growth rate is 10%

(b) Using the formula $P_e = \frac{D_0}{\hat{k}_e - g}$, and setting $g = 0$, with $\hat{k}_e$ staying constant at .15, the price of the shares, P_e, must fall.

$$P_e = \frac{\$1.50}{0.15 - 0} = \$10$$

Note the fairly dramatic change in share prices from $30 to $10 as investors adjust their growth expectations from $g = 10\%$ to $g = 0\%$.

(c) Again use $P_e = \frac{D_0}{\hat{k}_e - g}$

Here it is obvious that the formula cannot be solved, as the denominator $(\hat{k}_e - g)$ becomes zero for $g = \hat{k}_e$ implying $P_e = \infty$ for $g = 15$ percent.

If the dividends which the firm pays are expected to grow at a rate of g, and the equity capitalization rate which investors apply is $\hat{k}_e = g$, the growth in future dividends just cancels the effect of discounting. We have

$$P_e = \frac{D_0}{(1 + \hat{k}_e)} + \frac{D_0(1+g)}{(1+\hat{k}_e)^2} + \ldots + \frac{D_0(1+g)^t}{(1+\hat{k}_e)^{t+1}} + \ldots .$$

For $g = k_e$, this reduces to

$$P_e = \frac{D_0}{(1+\hat{k}_e)} + \frac{D_0}{(1+\hat{k}_e)} + \ldots + \frac{D_0}{(1+\hat{k}_e)} + \cdots$$

With an infinite stream of dividends, $P_e = \infty$.

The implication of this mathematical derivation is that such a situation is unstable and cannot prevail. A firm cannot grow at a rate which exceeds that of the general economy or of competing, similar firms forever, as before long it would have taken over the entire economy. Conversely, if general growth expectations for the economy were to increase, so would the yield investors would demand on their investments and, hence, $\hat{k}_e$. While a firm's projected growth rate may exceed $\hat{k}_e$ temporarily, this situation cannot prevail indefinitely.

4. A company can currently issue new shares to net \$20 per share. Dividends to be paid at the end of the current period are \$1 per share. Dividends are expected to grow at an average rate of 15 percent for the 5 years following the current year, after which growth is expected to normalize and settle down to 10 percent per year for the indefinite future. Compute the cost of equity for the firm.

Solution

We have

$$NP_0 = \frac{1}{(1+k_e)} + \frac{1(1+0.15)}{(1+k_e)^2} + \ldots + \frac{1(1+0.15)^5}{(1+k_e)^6}$$

$$+ \frac{1(1+0.15)^5\,(1+0.1)}{(1+k_e)^7} + \ldots.$$

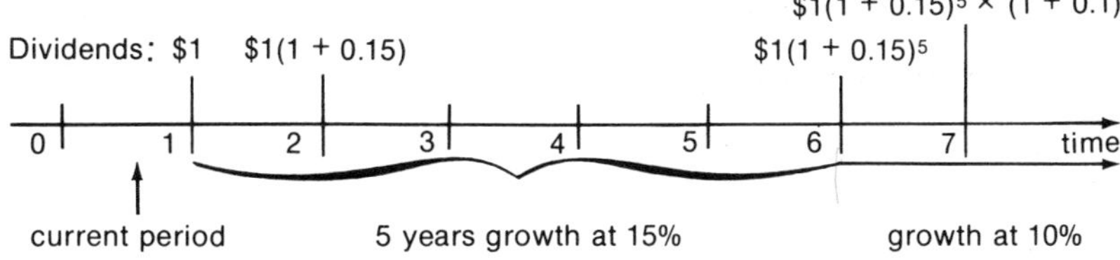

Calling $g_1 = 0.15$, $g_2 = 0.10$ the growth rates for the initial 5 years and the subsequent years respectively, we obtain the following formulas:

$$NP_0 = \sum_{t=0}^{5} \frac{D_0(1+g_1)^t}{(1+k_e)^{t+1}} + \sum_{t=6}^{\infty} \frac{D_0(1+g_1)^5\,(1+g_2)^{t-5}}{(1+k_e)^{t+1}}$$

Imagine we place ourselves at the beginning of the 5th year and look at the present value (computed in relation to the beginning of the 5th year) of future dividend payments. With dividends at the end of the 5th year at

$$1(1+0.15)^5 = \$2.01$$

we have

$$PV\text{ (future dividends)} = \frac{2.01}{(1+k_e)} + \frac{2.01(1+0.1)}{(1+k_e)^2} + \ldots + \frac{2.01(1+0.1)^t}{(1+k_e)^{t+1}} + \ldots$$

which is identical to formula (11) of the chapter. Thus, using formula (12), we can write

$$PV\text{ (future dividends)} = \frac{\$2.01}{k_e - 0.1}$$

Bringing this present value back from the beginning of the 5th year to the present (beginning of year 0), we have to discount by 5 additional years, obtaining

$$PV_{\text{today}}\text{ (dividends after year 5)} = \frac{\$2.01}{(1 + k_e)^5\,(k_e - 0.1)}$$

For the dividends paid in the first 4 years, we have

$$PV_{\text{today}}\text{ (dividends years 0-4)} = \sum_{t=0}^{4} \frac{D_0(1+g)^t}{(1+k_e)^{t+1}}$$

Thus, considering all future dividends, we have

$$NP_e = \sum_{t=0}^{4} \frac{\$1(1+0.15)^t}{(1+k_e)^{t+1}} + \frac{\$2.01}{(1+k_e)^5\,(k_e - 0.1)}$$

for which k_e could be derived by trial and error. The first term in the above equation could be further simplified by using the following formula for geometric series

$$1 + x + x^2 + \ldots + x^{n-1} = (1 - x^n)/(1 - x)$$

giving

$$\sum_{t=0}^{4} \frac{(1+0.15)^t}{(1+k_e)^{t+1}} = \frac{1}{(1+k_e)} \sum_{t=0}^{4} \left(\frac{1+0.15}{1+k_e}\right)^t$$

and for $(1 + 0.15)/(1 + k_e) = x$ and $n = 5$, the first term can be simplified to

$$\frac{(1+k_e)^5 - \$2.01}{(1+k_e)^5\,(k_e - 0.15)}$$

giving

$$NP_e = \$20 = \frac{(1+k_e)^5 - \$2.01}{(1+k_e)^5\,(k_e - 0.15)} + \frac{\$2.01}{(1+k_e)^5\,(k_e - 0.1)}$$

Trying various values of k_e and computing the above expression, we find that for $k_e \simeq 16\%$ the equation is satisfied. Hence, the cost of equity for the firm is approximately 16 percent. Note that for $k_e < 0.1$ the second term on the right-hand side becomes ∞, as the long-term growth rate in dividends exceeds the discount rate. Also, for $k_e = 0.15$, the first term on the right-hand side in this form becomes undefined (0/0), and in order to compute its value at this point it is best to resort back to its long form $\sum_{t=0}^{4} \frac{(1+0.15)^t}{(1+k_e)^{t+1}}$.

Additional Problems

1. XYZ Company Limited sold a \$1,000, 8 percent bond having a 10-year maturity. If before-tax issue costs were \$40 and the corporate tax rate is 40 percent, what is the company's after-tax cost of debt?
2. The XYZ Co. issues a 10 percent preferred share at its par value of \$100 with after-tax issue costs of \$1/share. What is the cost to the firm?
3. The XYZ Co. issues 100,000 common shares at \$10 par. After-tax issue costs amount to \$100,000. Growth in earnings has been steady at 5 percent and it is assumed that this will continue. It is expected that current dividends of \$1/share will grow at the same rate. What is the firm's cost of equity capital for new issues?
4. If, in the above problem, the investor's marginal tax rate on dividends is a net 20 percent (after dividend tax credit) and shares are selling at par, what is the cost of equity capital if all new equity is from retained earnings?
5. Assume that the XYZ Company Ltd. has a capital mix of ½ debt, ¼ preferred stock, and ¼ equity. What is its weighted average cost of capital (based on data obtained in problems 1 to 4)? Do your computations (a) assuming that some common shares are issued to raise new equity and (b) assuming that new equity is solely financed through retained earnings.
6. The total assets of P.L. Company were \$50 million at the beginning of the year. It is estimated that assets will have to be \$75 million at the end of the year and new financing needs to be arranged to fund this growth. The capital structure of the firm is considered to be optimal and can be shown as follows:

Debt	\$20,000,000
Preferred stock	\$ 5,000,000
Common stock and retained earnings	\$25,000,000
Total	\$50,000,000

Common shares which are selling on the market at \$60 a share, would be floated to net the company \$54. Stockholders expect to earn a 12 percent rate of return on their investment, with current dividends at \$3 per share. Retained earnings are expected to be \$2.5 million. New bonds and new preferred shares can be issued at par with 9 and 10 percent rates respectively.

Assume that the corporate tax rate is 50 percent, and investors' average net marginal tax rate on dividends 40 percent.

(a) How much of the \$25 million growth should be financed by equity to keep the financial structure unchanged?
(b) Compute the cost of each of the equity components (namely, retained earnings and common stock).
(c) What is the weighted average cost of capital of the P.L. Company?

7. A firm could issue common shares to net the company \$10 per share. Dividends at the end of the current period will be \$0.50 per share. Dividends are expected to grow at a rate of 20 percent per year for 3 years following

the current year, after which time no further growth will take place. Compute the cost to the firm of issuing new equity .

8. Investors currently require a market capitalization rate of 12% on the shares of Dime Corporation, whose dividend payments for this year are expected to be 60 cents. The current market price per share is $12.50.
   (a) What is the implied long-term average growth rate of dividends?
   (b) Should growth expectations for Dime grow to 9.5%, at what price should the shares trade?
   (c) If instead growth expectations fall to only 3%, what share price would be anticipated?

9. Gumball Corporation currently has the following capital structure which it wishes to maintain in the future:

Debt	30 percent
Preferred Shares	10 percent
Common Stock	40 percent
Retained Earnings	20 percent

New debt financing is available in the form of 20-year, 8 percent bonds which can be sold at face value (issuing and underwriting expenses can be neglected). New preferred shares would net the company $6 per share, with a 50 cent dividend per share. Common shares could be sold to the public at $30 per share, with 5 percent issuing costs (after taxes). Shareholders expect a dividend of $1 this year, with an average long-term annual growth of 10%. The company's tax is 40% while the net tax which investors pay on dividends is 30%.
   (a) Compute Gumball's weighted average cost of capital to be used in evaluating new investment projects.
   (b) If the firm has 10 million dollars of depreciation (CCA) charges this year, what is the appropriate cost to use for such funds? Briefly discuss.

10. The ABC Manufacturing Company has the following capital structure as of April 15, 1976; the board of directors has decided that these same proportions of debt, preferred, and equity capital are to be maintained.

Short-term Debt	minimal
Long-term Debt (9½%)	$60,000,000
Preferred Stock (7½%)	$30,000,000
Net Worth	$90,000,000

Earnings per share have grown steadily from $1.25 in 1969 to $2.50 estimated for 1976. The investment community, expecting this growth to continue, capitalizes current earnings per share at about 5 percent, giving a current market price of $50. ABC is paying a current annual dividend of $.80, and it expects the dividends to grow at the same rate as earnings.

New securities can be sold as follows: bonds to yield 9½ percent; preferred to yield 7½ percent; and common stock at the current market price less $2 a share selling commission, which is to be treated as a tax deductible expense.

Ignore issuing and underwriting expenses on bonds and preferred shares. The corporate tax rate is 40 percent. These figures all assume that the capital relationships set out above are maintained.

The firm has desirable investment opportunities at hand which require it to raise $20,000,000 additional capital.

Compute ABC's cost of capital for these additional funds.

Case

John Labatt Limited[1]

John Labatt Limited is a management holding company active (through its subsidiaries) in the Canadian brewing industry (the "brewing group"), and engaged in the distribution and production of wines, frozen foods, confectionary products (the "consumer products group"), and in the manufacture and distribution of milk products, organic chemicals and grain and flour products (the "industrial products group"). Although the company enjoyed a 20% increase in consolidated sales in 1975 over the previous year, with high rates of inflation plus "widespread recession", overall net income decreased approximately 2% from the 1974 level. (See *Exhibit 1*). Higher costs of production (raw materials, labor etc.) were the main factors accounting for this decline.

The outlook for the 1976 fiscal year looked more favorable, however, with respect to improving earnings, especially in the brewing industry. Production costs were expected to stabilize relative to the 1975 level and, coupled with increased beer consumption, it looked like a good year for Canadian brewers.[2] Given this more "optimistic" position, the company wanted to develop and expand its businesses and planned to undertake a $200 million capital expenditure program over the next five years. In the past, the necessary funds for capital expenditures were derived primarily from five sources: debt (sinking fund debentures), equity (preferred and Class A and B common), retained earnings, depreciation and deferred income taxes.[3] Over the long run, it was thought that the proportion of each of the above sources in the total capital structure would be roughly the same as in the past.

Given that on a per annum basis, this expenditure program represented a significant increase over investments in previous years, and given growing concern over the deterioration of Canadian competitive ability both externally and internally, it was extremely important to accurately evaluate the attractiveness of the proposed capital outlays. The President asked the Vice-President of Finance (you) to assume overall responsibility for the capital expenditure program. This would entail evaluating each proposal on a net present value

[1]This case is based on the actual 1975 financial statement data of John Labatt Limited, London, Ontario. The authors would like to thank this firm for their kind permission to reproduce in whole or in part their 1975 Annual Report (Exhibit 1 through 3).

[2]See Richardson Securities of Canada Information Reports, dated January and July 1975, entitled "Brewing Industry".

[3]Because of differences between capital cost allowances claimed and depreciation as reported to the shareholders, deferred income taxes result. The income taxes shown on the income statement are based on depreciation and are allocated between the actual tax liability payable each year and a deferred income tax account.

basis and recommending the most "desirable" one(s). You recall your days at university and remember that in order to use net present value (NPV) analysis, an appropriate "discount" rate—*i.e.* weighted average cost of capital—is required. In order to calculate this rate, you need some "guidelines". After emphasizing the importance of this concept to the President, both of you decide that the most appropriate framework to work within includes that:

(a) market capitalization rates as well as the specific marginal costs to the firm should be calculated;

(b) all component costs of debt and equity are to be computed solely on a *per bond* ($1,000 face value, 20-year maturity) and a *per share* basis;

(c) for debt, allow for a 1% discount to the public, a further 3% of face value for underwriting costs and $15 per debenture for additional issuance expenses (all of which are fully tax deductible and expensed immediately);

(d) for preferred equity, assume underwriting costs to be 4% of market value (par at time of issuance) and issuance costs to be $0.15 per share with tax deductibility as per (c) above;

(e) for common equity, 6% of the per share market price would represent underwriting expenses and $0.12 per share for issuance costs would appear reasonable (tax deductibility as per (c) above);

(f) bond market quotations around the end of April, 1975 for comparable industrial corporations issuing new debt indicated an average yield in the range of 9¾%-10¾%;

(g) stock market quotations and dividend rates on new preferred indicate yields of 8-10% to be reasonable, while dividend yields for common were in the neighborhood of 5%;[4]; and

(h) expectations for interest rates were such that a slight decline was expected in the 1976 fiscal year, with the rate of inflation being closer to 10%, down from the previous year's 12% rate.

Unfortunately however, both of you are unable to decide on whether the weighted average cost of capital should be computed using book value weightings or market value weightings. Given this fact, the President asks you to calculate it *both* ways and recommend the most "appropriate" one.

[4]Note that an expected long-term dividend growth rate of 11% was forecasted (in light of current inflationary trends) for John Labatt Limited, as published in the McLeod, Young, Weir and Company publication, "Value In the Breweries," *Monthly Market Review*, November 12, 1974, p. 5.

EXHIBIT 1

John Labatt Limited

Consolidated Statement of Earnings
For the year ended April 30, 1975
(with comparative amounts for the year ended April 30, 1974)

	1975	1974
INCOME		
Gross Sales	$727,457,000	$603,014,000
Less excise and sales taxes	133,266,000	123,414,000
	594,191,000	479,600,000
OPERATING COSTS		
Cost of products sold	368,533,000	280,233,000
Selling and administrative expenses	164,051,000	139,473,000
Depreciation	13,377,000	11,394,000
Interest (long-term portion 1975—$10,113,000; 1974—$7,806,000)	14,290,000	10,860,000
	560,251,000	441,960,000
OPERATING INCOME	33,940,000	37,640,000
OTHER INCOME		
Investment income	3,008,000	2,625,000
Gain on sale of investments and other assets	602,000	681,000
	3,610,000	3,306,000
EARNINGS BEFORE INCOME TAXES	37,550,000	40,946,000
Income taxes—current	11,731,000	11,367,000
—deferred	3,391,000	7,434,000
	15,122,000	18,801,000
EARNINGS BEFORE MINORITY INTEREST	22,428,000	22,145,000
Minority interest	252,000	(419,000)
NET EARNINGS	$ 22,176,000	$ 22,564,000
NET EARNINGS PER COMMON SHARE	$ 2.09	$ 2.15
FULLY DILUTED NET EARNINGS PER COMMON SHARE	$ 1.84	$ 1.87

EXHIBIT 2

John Labatt Limited

Consolidated Balance Sheet
April 30, 1975
(with comparative amounts at April 30, 1974)

Assets	1975	1974
CURRENT		
Cash	$ 1,713,000	$ 1,393,000
Marketable securities at cost (market value $3,516,000—1975; $9,287,000—1974)	3,522,000	8,778,000
Accounts receivable	62,048,000	58,629,000
Inventories	98,711,000	75,760,000
Prepaid expenses	7,350,000	4,627,000
	173,344,000	149,187,000
INVESTMENTS AND OTHER ASSETS		
Investment in corporate joint ventures	12,520,000	8,589,000
Investment in other companies	2,843,000	3,209,000
Mortgages, loans and advances	7,900,000	7,390,000
Due from trustees and employees under share purchase and option plans	839,000	937,000
	24,102,000	20,125,000
FIXED AT COST		
Land	10,491,000	10,591,000
Buildings and equipment	284,177,000	252,256,000
	294,668,000	262,847,000
Less accumulated depreciation	125,457,000	112,124,000
	169,211,000	150,723,000
UNAMORTIZED DEBT FINANCING EXPENSE	1,598,000	1,694,000
GOODWILL, STORE LICENCES AND TRADEMARKS	57,895,000	54,956,000
	$426,150,000	$376,685,000

Liabilities	1975	1974
CURRENT		
Bank advances and short-term notes	$ 61,355,000	$ 35,285,000
Accounts payable	41,941,000	38,537,000
Taxes payable	14,198,000	6,688,000
Dividends payable	727,000	754,000
Long-term debt due within one year	1,073,000	861,000
	119,294,000	82,125,000
DEFERRED INCOME TAXES	22,876,000	18,916,000
LONG TERM DEBT[1]	116,185,000	118,632,000
MINORITY INTEREST IN SUBSIDIARY COMPANIES		
Preferred shares	1,554,000	1,637,000
Common shares and retained earnings	1,337,000	1,205,000
	2,891,000	2,842,000
Shareholders' equity		
SHARE CAPITAL		
Authorized		
4,000,000 preferred shares of $18 par value each[2]		
14,000,000 Class A convertible common shares of no par value[3]		
14,000,000 Class B convertible common shares of no par value[3]		
Issued and outstanding		
2,762,918 preferred shares (2,869,209—1974)	49,732,000	51,646,000
9,092,440 Class A common shares (8,964,933—1974)		
251,391 Class B common shares (239,933—1974)	23,222,000	20,729,000
	72,954,000	72,375,000
RETAINED EARNINGS	91,950,000	81,795,000
	164,904,000	154,170,000
	$426,150,000	$376,685,000

EXHIBIT 3

John Labatt Limited

Five Year Review

	1975	1974	1973	1972	1971
OPERATIONS DATA (thousands of dollars)					
Gross sales	$727,457	$603,014	$517,685	$466,973	$426,757
Earnings before income taxes and minority interest	37,550	40,946	37,148	33,368	33,038
Income taxes	15,122	18,801	16,750	15,996	16,753
Earnings before extraordinary items	22,176	22,564	20,435	16,991	15,997
Net earnings	22,176	22,564	17,836	13,676	15,997
Cash income before extraordinary items	38,121	39,609	32,447	27,809	24,402
Dividends paid—preferred	2,802	2,916	2,991	3,026	3,027
—common	9,219	8,153	7,783	6,482	6,452
Capital expenditures	28,328	27,415	23,086	27,456	22,760
FINANCIAL DATA (thousands of dollars)					
Working capital	54,050	67,062	43,470	39,946	38,697
Land, buildings and equipment—net	169,211	150,723	135,740	121,945	97,913
Long term debt	116,185	118,632	91,093	61,878	57,579
Shareholders' equity	$164,904	$154,170	$142,671	$134,732	$130,164
RATIOS AND PERCENTAGES					
Earnings before extraordinary items as a percent of gross sales	3.05%	3.74%	3.95%	3.64%	3.75%
Ratio of current assets to current liabilities	1.45	1.82	1.65	1.56	1.69
Long term debt as a percent of assets employed	37.86%	40.27%	36.61%	29.11%	27.92%

EXHIBIT 3

(Continued)

	1975	1974	1973	1972	1971
PER COMMON SHARE DATA					
Earnings before extraordinary items	$ 2.09	$ 2.15	$ 1.93	$ 1.55	$ 1.45
Fully diluted earnings before extraordinary items	1.84	1.87	1.70	1.41	1.34
Dividends paid	.98	.89	.86	.72	.72
Cash income before extraordinary items	3.81	4.01	3.26	2.75	2.39
Shareholders' equity	12.33	11.14	9.79	8.91	8.42
Price range—high	25⅞	27⅞	31¾	25½	25¾
Price range—low	12⅝	20¼	23⅞	20⅜	18¾
STATISTICAL DATA AT YEAR END					
Number of shares outstanding					
preferred	2,762,918	2,869,209	2,975,564	3,026,026	3,026,581
—Class A common	9,092,440	8,964,933	9,098,325	9,006,528	8,988,938
—Class B common	251,391	239,933			
Number of shareholders—preferred	5,293	5,540	5,970	6,150	6,710
—common	9,205	9,110	9,300	9,250	9,805
Number of employees	11,600	11,500	10,100	10,000	10,500

Notes to the Financial Statements

1. Particulars of sinking fund debentures are as follows:

Series	Coupon	Maturity	Book Value	Bid Price*	Yield*
B	6%	January 2/79	$ 862,000	88¾	9.72%
C	6¼%	May 15/81	1,921,000	84	9.83%
D	6¼%	June 15/87	5,711,000	74	10.00%
E	6¼%	October 1/89	3,770,000	70⅛	10.25%
F	7⅛%	April 15/92	5,475,000	73½	10.50%
G	9¼%	September 1/90	28,951,000	89⅝	10.73%
H	8¼%	March 1/93	30,000,000	82	10.50%
I	9%	March 15/94	30,000,000	86	10.75%

*For April 30, 1975 as kindly supplied by Wood Gundy Limited, Vancouver, B.C. Bid price based on $100 worth of debt. Note that the difference between the total of the book values and the actual balance sheet figure represents long-term liabilities of subsidiaries ($10,568,000) less current portion of long-term debt due within one year and included in current liabilities ($1,073,000).

2. Market value per $1.00 preferred share was $16.50 as at close of trading on the Toronto Stock Exchange, May 2, 1975, as quoted in The Financial Times of Canada, May 5, 1975, p. 30. Dividends of $1.00 per share were paid from the years 1969-1975 inclusive. The low dividend yield is explained by the fact that these preferred shares are convertible into common shares. For purposes of analysis, assume that any new preferred shares to be issued will be straight preferred shares without conversion features.
3. Class A market value on May 2, 1975 was $16⅝ per share as quoted in The Financial Times, May 5, 1975. Class B common shares did not trade in 1975 but could reasonably be assumed to have the same market price as the Class A shares.

Selected References

As the material covered in chapters 13 and 14 is intimately related, the bibliography which is given at the end of chapter 14 covers both of these chapters.

Chapter 14
The Evaluation of Capital Structures

14-1. INTRODUCTION

In this chapter we will analyze the effects of using alternative capital structures, with special attention given to the consequences of firms varying the proportions of debt and equity used to finance their operations. We will first be concerned with the consequences of increasing leverage through the use of debt in the capital structure. In particular, we will consider how common shareholders are affected by leverage, including its influence on earnings per share. With simple tools such as breakeven analysis we can illustrate, and to some extent quantify, the risk-return tradeoff implied by leverage, with higher leverage promising greater expected returns at the expense of increased volatility and risk. To determine optimal corporate financing policies we have to assess how investors in the capital markets approach such risk-return tradeoffs. After presenting the more important issues, we will look at the practical considerations facing firms when formulating policies on capital structure. Finally, we will introduce some current theories on how various degrees of leverage should be valued including the optimal policy regarding capital structure which is implied.

14-2. LEVERAGE AND FINANCIAL RISK

Broadly speaking, the concept of leverage is encountered whenever use is made of funds entailing fixed costs (*e.g.* debt with fixed interest charges) and these funds are then employed in operations generating variable amounts of revenue. Thus, financial leverage is primarily concerned with use by business firms of securities such as bonds, debentures and preferred shares. Just as forces are magnified by the use of physical levers, through the use of fixed income securities the financial results accruing to an equity investor will be magnified. The concept is best introduced with a numerical example, and while we use debt financing to illustrate the workings and effects of financial leverage, it should be noted that analysis using preferred shares would be analogous.

Example

> Let us consider the possibility of launching a new business venture requiring an initial investment of $100,000. With taxes at 50 percent, the investment can either be financed entirely through common equity contributed by the prospective owners, or it can be financed by drawing on a $50,000 loan at 10 percent interest and having an equity investment of just $50,000. In analyzing the effects of such alternative capital structures, the starting point is generally net operating revenues or earnings before interest and taxes (EBIT) as these figures only reflect business results without any distortions cropping up because of the actual capital structure employed. The figure is taken on a before-tax basis because the tax paid will be influenced by the tax shield from

interest expense and hence will be dependent on the capital structure. Assuming expected earnings before interest and taxes for the first year of operations to be $20,000, we obtain the following financial results for the two alternative capital structures proposed:

	All Equity	50% Debt ($50,000 at 10% interest)
EBIT	$ 20,000	$20,000
Interest	—	5,000
Taxable Earnings	$ 20,000	$15,000
Tax Payable	10,000	7,500
Earnings Available to Common Shareholders	$ 10,000	$ 7,500
Percentage Return on Equity Investment	$\frac{\$10,000}{\$100,000} = 10\%$	$\frac{\$7,500}{\$50,000} = 15\%$

We see that the use of debt financing has increased the expected return on equity from 10 percent to 15 percent. Intuitively, it is clear that equity investors stand to make an extra gain. If they can raise funds through debt at an after-tax interest cost of say 5 percent, as in the above example, and are able to invest these funds to yield a return which is above that cost, any difference accrues to them as residual claimants.

The increased expected gain comes at the expense of increased risk, however, for just as equity gains are magnified if operating results are favorable, potential losses to equity investors are enlarged if performance falls short of expectations.

Example

Pursuing the above example, assume that the estimated EBIT of $20,000 could, in fact, turn out to be as high as $35,000 or, if the results fall short of expectations, could be as low as $5,000.

The consequences of such fluctuations work out as follows:

	All Equity		50% Debt	
EBIT	$ 35,000	$ 5,000	$ 35,000	$ 5,000
Interest	—	—	5,000	5,000
Taxable Earnings	$ 35,000	$ 5,000	$ 30,000	0
Tax Payable	$ 17,500	$ 2,500	$ 15,000	0
Earnings Available to Common Shareholders	$ 17,500	$ 2,500	$ 15,000	0
Percentage Return on Equity Investment	$\frac{\$17,500}{\$100,000} = 17.5\%$	$\frac{\$2,500}{\$100,000} = 2.5\%$	$\frac{\$15,000}{\$50,000} = 30\%$	0%

Summarizing the percentage return on equity figures we have

EBIT	All Equity	50% Debt
$35,000	17.5%	30.0%
20,000	10.0%	15.0%
5,000	2.5%	0%

As we can readily see, variations in EBIT will cause variations in equity returns which are magnified through the use of leverage.

Variations in net operating revenues or EBIT are inherent in any business and are simply the result of business cycles, uncertainty about the economy, well-being of the particular industry and the likes. Such potential variations are termed the *business risk* of an enterprise, which in the above examples is reflected in the variations of return on equity for the all equity firm. As we have seen, this risk can be magnified through the use of leverage by the firm. The additional variability introduced through the use of fixed cost senior securities is labelled the *financial risk* of a firm.[1]

Management exerts control over business risk through its decisions on capital expenditures including the types of investment projects it chooses. Management also exerts control over financial risk by establishing the degree of leverage to be incorporated into the firm's capital structure when financing such investments. If no senior securities are employed, equity investors have a claim against a cash flow characterized by a particular business risk. If, however, debt were to form part of the capital structure, creditors lay a prior claim which has to be met, making that portion of the cash flow committed with certainty. It is obvious that cash flows remaining after debt charges have been met, must be subject to greater *relative* variations, a point illustrated in a simplified fashion below.

FIGURE 14-1

The Effect of Fixed Charges on the Relative Uncertainty of Cash Flows

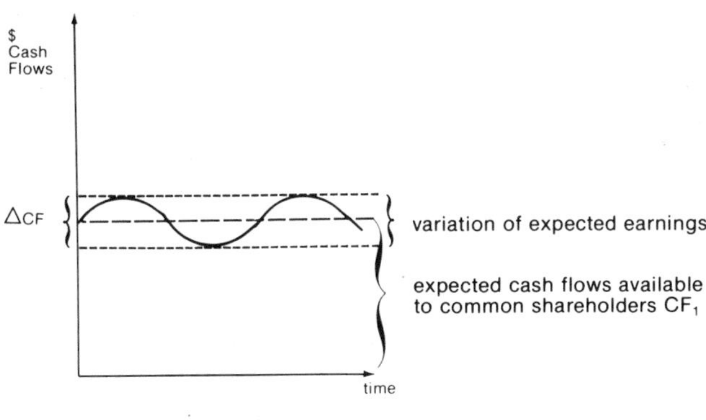

No fixed charges

$$\text{Relative variation} = \frac{\Delta CF}{CF_1}$$

[1]A narrower definition of financial risk which is sometimes used just considers additional variations in shareholder returns caused by the use of leverage. However inclusion of debt in a corporation's capital structure may also create liquidity problems for the firm if cash flows generated by operations turn out to be inadequate given sinking fund provisions as well as interest charges. This aspect is considered in more detail further on in the chapter.

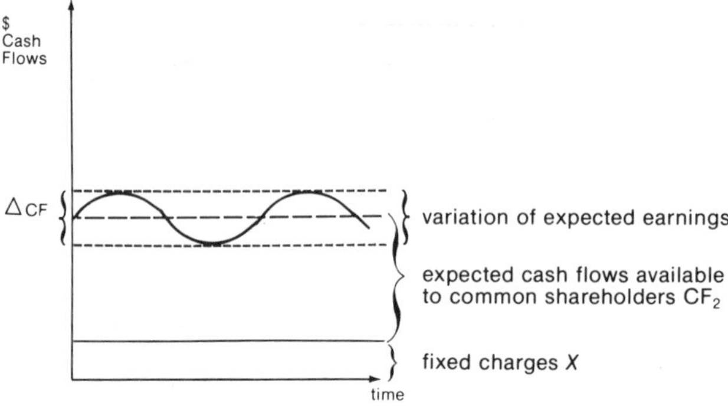

Given fixed charges X

$$\text{Relative variation} = \frac{\Delta CF}{CF_2} = \frac{\Delta CF}{CF_1 - X}$$

Considering our earlier example, it was shown that in the absence of leverage, a plus or minus 75 percentage change in EBIT caused an identical change in reported earnings. Where 50 percent debt financing was introduced, however, a 100 percent change in earnings resulted. Looking at matters in a narrower but more exact way, the percentage change in return on equity or earnings per share flowing from a given percentage change in EBIT can be defined as the "degree of financial leverage". In our example, in the case of no leverage, a 75% change in EBIT ($20,000 ± $15,000) resulted in a 75% change in return on equity (10% ± 7.5%), giving a value of 1.0 for the degree of financial leverage. With $50,000 debt introduced into the capital structure, the resulting change in return on equity was magnified to 100% (15% ±15%) and hence the degree of financial leverage increased to 100%/75% = 1.33.[2] We see that if only equity is employed,

[2]Results in the above example can be generalized by deriving the appropriate formulas. We measure return on equity through earnings per share, and we use the following notation:

- *EBIT:* earnings before interest and taxes
- *EPS:* earnings per share (after taxes)
- *I:* annual interest expense
- *T:* corporate tax rate
- *n:* number of shares outstanding

We measure return on equity through earnings per share, and we have

$$\text{EPS} = \frac{(\text{EBIT} - I)(1 - T)}{n}$$

From this identity, a percentage change in EPS is easy to derive arithmetically

$$\text{Degree of financial leverage} = \frac{\text{Percentage change in EPS}}{\text{Percentage change in EBIT}} = \frac{\text{EBIT}}{\text{EBIT} - I}$$

As previously derived, for the above illustration with 50 percent debt,

$$\frac{\text{EBIT}}{\text{EBIT} - \text{I}} = \frac{20{,}000}{20{,}000 - 5{,}000} = 1.33$$

It is clear from the formula, that for a given level of interest charges I, the degree or magnitude of financial leverage becomes a function of the particular level of EBIT at which the firm operates.

Where interest charges are small relative to the level of EBIT, little leverage exists and changes in EBIT cause quite similar percentage changes in EPS, yielding a ratio close to one. Where EBIT are close to I with EPS very small, a minor change in EBIT can cause a significant percentage change in EPS, simply because whatever change is caused is viewed in relation to the current EPS level which is close to zero.

changes in returns on equity reflect only business risk and the degree of financial leverage, according to the above definition, equals one. A degree of financial leverage which exceeds one signals the use of debt in the capital structure with consequently magnified relative variations in returns on equity.

14-3. INDIFFERENCE ANALYSIS

We have seen that earnings per share (EPS) depend on the level of earnings before interest and taxes (EBIT) which the company achieves from its operations, as well as on the particular capital structure which the firm employs. The purpose of indifference analysis is to determine the effects of alternative capital structures and specifically of alternative new financing schemes, on EPS for various levels of EBIT.

Example

Consider a corporation with 10,000 common shares outstanding (n_1) and subject to a tax rate of T = 50 percent. The firm needs to raise an additional $100,000 to finance an expansion program and is weighing the alternatives of issuing 10,000 additional common shares (n_2) or of issuing 6% debt which would involve annual interest payments of I = $6,000. After financing has taken place, earnings per share under the alternatives are readily computed. With all equity financing,

$$\text{EPS} = \frac{(1-T)(\text{EBIT})}{n_1 + n_2} = \frac{0.5\,\text{EBIT}}{20{,}000} = \frac{\text{EBIT}}{40{,}000} \tag{1}$$

With the introduction of debt financing,

$$\text{EPS} = \frac{(1-T)(\text{EBIT} - I)}{n_1} = \frac{0.5\,(\text{EBIT} - 6000)}{10{,}000} = \frac{\text{EBIT}}{20{,}000} - 0.3 \tag{2}$$

TABLE 14-1

Impact of Capital Structure on Earnings per Share

Common Share Financing

EBIT	$10,000	$12,000	$15,000	$20,000
Income tax	5,000	6,000	7,500	10,000
After-tax earnings	$ 5,000	$ 6,000	$ 7,500	$10,000
Earnings per share (20,000 shares)	$ .25	$ .30	$ .375	$ .50

Bond Financing

EBIT	$10,000	$12,000	$15,000	$20,000
Bond interest	6,000	6,000	6,000	6,000
Before-tax earnings	4,000	6,000	9,000	14,000
Income tax	2,000	3,000	4,500	7,000
After-tax earnings	$ 2,000	$ 3,000	$ 4,500	$ 7,000
Earnings per share (10,000 shares)	$ .20	$ .30	$ .45	$ .70

Table 14-1 gives the earnings per share for various levels of EBIT under both financing alternatives while Figure 14-2 illustrates graphically the relationships between EPS and EBIT, and reflects that both equations (1) and (2) above represent straight lines. The intercept on the horizontal axis to the right of the ordinate reflects the before-tax interest cost. With debt financing used, an EBIT level of $6000 must be reached before any earnings accrue to the common shareholders. The higher slope of the line representing new financing through debt is due to the fact that fewer common shares are outstanding, and indicates that for a given change in EBIT, the change to earnings per share is greater under the debt alternative, confirming our previous conclusion that debt financing results in increased risk to equity investors.

FIGURE 14-2

Indifference Chart

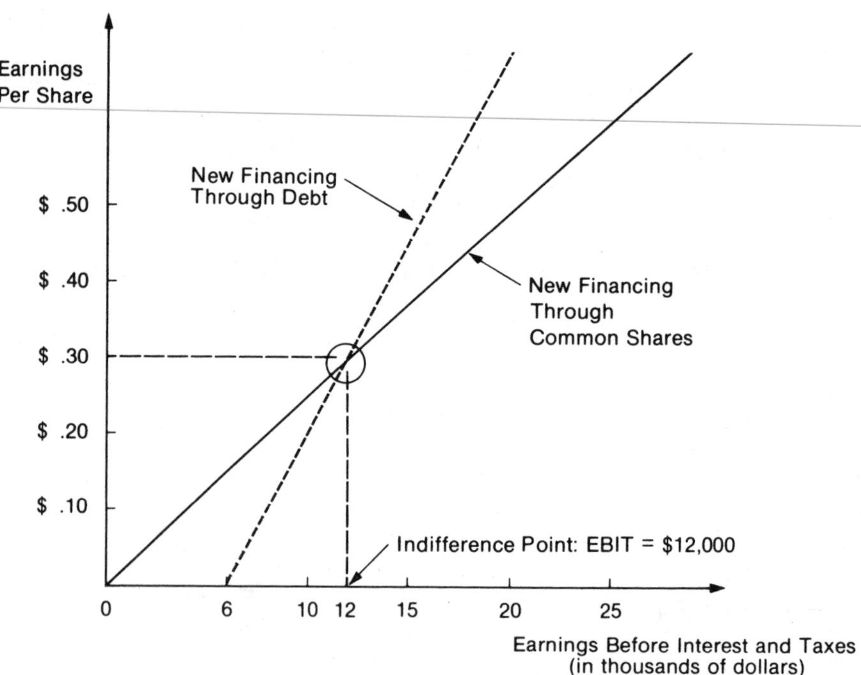

The indifference point may also be computed. Letting EBIT* equal the level of EBIT at the indifference point, an equation can be set up such that EPS are equal at that point. We then have

$$(3) \qquad EPS_{\text{new common}} = \frac{EBIT^*(1-T)}{n_1+n_2} = \frac{(EBIT^*-I)(1-T)}{n_1} = EPS_{\text{new debt}}$$

which is easily solved for EBIT*, giving

$$(4) \qquad EBIT^* = \left(\frac{n_1+n_2}{n_2}\right) I = \frac{20{,}000}{10{,}000} \times \$6000 = \$12{,}000$$

Hence, for EBIT levels greater than $12,000, debt financing will result in larger amounts of EPS, while for EBIT below $12,000, common share financing will yield higher values of EPS.

A further numerical example will illustrate how the above concepts are easily extended to cover more complex situations involving other financing alternatives.

Example

Assume a firm with 500,000 common shares outstanding (n_1) alongside $10,000,000 of debt with a 10 percent coupon requiring annual before-tax interest payments of I_1 = $1,000,000. The corporate tax rate is 40 percent. An additional sum of $3,000,000 is to be raised and the following financing alternatives are being considered:

1) *New common:* the company can sell additional shares, to net $30 a share. This approach would therefore require a further 100,000 shares (n_2) to be issued.
2) *New Debt:* the company can issue debt at 10%, to net face value. Additional annual interest payments would amount to I_2 = $300,000 on a before-tax basis.
3) *Preferred Shares:* an issue with a 7 percent dividend to net par value, requiring annual dividends of D = 0.07 × $3,000,000 = $210,000.

Earnings per share for each alternative may then be computed as follows:

1) Common shares

$$\text{EPS} = \frac{(1-T)(\text{EBIT}-I_1)}{n_1+n_2} = \frac{0.6(\text{EBIT}-\$1{,}000{,}000)}{600{,}000}$$

2) Debt

$$\text{EPS} = \frac{(1-T)(\text{EBIT}-I_1-I_2)}{n_1} = \frac{0.6(\text{EBIT}-\$1{,}300{,}000)}{500{,}000}$$

3) Preferred

$$\text{EPS} = \frac{(1-T)(\text{EBIT}-I_1)-D}{n_1} = \frac{0.6(\text{EBIT}-\$1{,}000{,}000)-\$210{,}000}{500{,}000}$$

It should be noted that the second parentheses in the numerators always represent taxable income which, when multiplied by $(1-T)$ yields after-tax earnings. Preferred dividends (D) are paid out of such after-tax earnings. The denominator simply gives the total number of common shares outstanding to derive earnings per share figures.

The above equations are portrayed graphically in Figure 14-3, resulting in indifference points of

$EBIT_1^* = \$2,800,000$ between new debt and new common, and

$EBIT_2^* = \$3,100,000$ between preferred and new common[3]

FIGURE 14-3

Indifference Chart

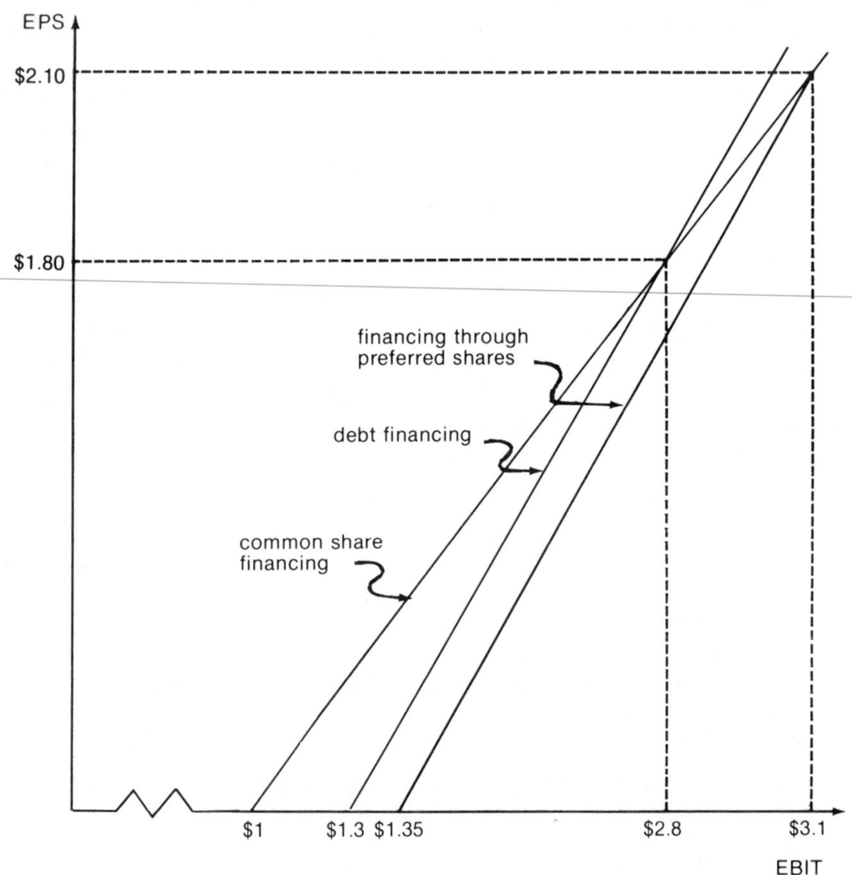

[3]The intercepts of the various lines with the EBIT axis are found by simply setting EPS = 0 in the above equations. Thus, for the common share alternative, we obtain $EPS = 0 = \frac{0.6(EBIT - \$1,000,000)}{600,000}$, giving EBIT = \$1 million. The slope of the line is given by the coefficient of EBIT, or $0.6/600,000 = 10^{-6}$ signifying a \$1 increase in EPS for every \$1 million increase in EBIT. The breakeven points are derived by equating EPS for the various alternatives as in the previous example.

Notice that the lines for the new debt and new preferred share financing in Figure 14-3 have identical slopes[4] with debt providing higher EPS values at any EBIT level. Why then would a firm ever issue preferred shares rather than debt under such conditions? Two answers are possible. First, the issuance of preferred shares broadens the equity base and should therefore be compared to common equity financing. An alternative answer would be that dividends on the preferred, in contrast to the interest on debt, do not represent a contractual obligation which can force a firm into bankruptcy. Hence, if EBIT levels should fall significantly short of expectations, causing liquidity problems for the firm, dividend payments on the preferred shares can be withheld without posing any threat of bankruptcy. The lower returns in the form of earnings per share inherent in the preferred share alternative are compensated through the reduced risk of financial insolvency should operating performance prove to be inadequate.

Limitations of indifference analysis

Indifference analysis demonstrates the impact of various capital structures on earnings per share as a function of earnings before inteιest and taxes. It is a useful approach to analysis and planning for analysts and financial executives. There are, however, certain limitations associated with indifference analysis which must be recognized. For instance, earnings per share considerations need to be supplemented by cash-flow analysis including cash budgeting as outlined in Chapter 24. Thus, where senior securities are issued, sinking fund provisions for the periodic retirement of either the debt or preferred shares usually exist, and such commitments are generally not allowed for in the indifference analysis as they come out of after-tax earnings. Such sinking fund payments can, however, represent a very significant cash drain. Consider our earlier example involving $3,000,000 of 10 percent debt and assume the issue is to be retired through annual sinking fund payments of $300,000 over ten years. It is easy to see that sinking fund payments will exceed after-tax interest charges every year, and by an increasing proportion of the total amount as the debt outstanding declines over the issue's life. Hence, while at a particular level of EBIT earnings per share may be higher in the levered case, where new financing is through debt, cash flows available to the corporation may actually be reduced.

Also, indifference analysis does not include considerations of how equity investors may react to the increased risk imposed by leverage in the light of uncertain future EBIT figures. With EBIT levels well above the indifference point, preliminary indications may point to positive effects on earnings per share from leverage. Nevertheless future EBIT levels are inherently uncertain and, as we have seen, any deviations from expected EBIT values will result in magnified EPS fluctuations once leverage is introduced. If investors are risk averse, they may demand higher expected returns on their shares to compensate for the increased risk and this higher required rate is in effect an increase in the firm's

[4]In both instances 500,000 common shares are outstanding and it is this figure which determines the slope.

cost of equity capital. For example, the use of cheaper debt financing may result either in an increase in the firm's cost of common equity or equivalently in a drop in current common share prices should investors perceive the firm to be more risky. This *indirect or implicit cost of debt financing* is not taken account of in simple breakeven analysis and will receive attention in the sections which follow. Clearly, such implicit costs must be recognized in considering the question of optimal capital structures.

14-4. EVALUATION OF ALTERNATIVE CAPITAL STRUCTURES

It is useful right at the outset to define specifically what is meant by an optimal capital structure and how the "goodness" of a particular capital structure can be evaluated. Based on our discussion of financial objectives in Chapter 1, the desirability of a capital structure is measured by its likely impact on the market price of a firm's common shares, with the optimal capital structure being the one which maximizes share values, other factors being held constant. The optimal capital structure also minimizes the firm's overall or weighted average cost of capital which includes as one of its components the cost of common equity.

Given that the points made are important and relate to the ensuing discussion, we will formalize the argument somewhat, starting with a simplified hypothetical example.

Throughout this section we neglect underwriting and issue expenses so that the cost of equity to the firm k_e equals the yield to the investor $\hat{k}_e$ which is also called the market capitalization rate. This simplification will greatly simplify the subsequent exposition without compromising the derived results in any way.

Example

Consider a newly established corporation requiring an initial investment of $1,000,000. Two alternative capital structures are under consideration. One would involve no leverage with 10,000 common shares to be issued at $100 each, while the other would comprise $500,000 of debt and an issue of only 5000 common shares, also at $100 each. Debt can be issued at 10 percent interest and the corporate tax rate is 50 percent.

Earnings before interest and taxes are expected to be $200,000 per year and to remain at the level, with all earnings to be paid out in dividends. If no leverage is employed, in light of the anticipated business risk shareholders require a return of $\hat{k}_e = k_e = 10$ percent to make the purchase of the shares attractive. Considering the financial risk of leverage, however, assume that this return would have to increase to 12 percent if half the funds are raised through debt. To establish which of the two alternatives represents the better capital structure we perform the following computations:

	No Debt Alternative 10,000 Common Shares	50% Debt Alternative 5,000 Common Shares and \$500,000 Debt at 10%
EBIT	\$200,000	\$200,000
Interest	—	50,000
Taxable Earnings	\$200,000	\$150,000
Tax Payable	100,000	75,000
Earnings to Shareholders	\$100,000	\$ 75,000
Earnings per Share	\$10	\$15
Required Return on Equity: $\hat{k}_e = k_e$	.10	.12
Market Price/Share: $\frac{EPS}{k_e}$	$\frac{\$10}{.10} = \$100$	$\frac{\$15}{.12} = \$125$
Total Value of all Securities	10,000×\$100 = \$1,000,000	5000×\$125+\$500,000 = \$1,125,000

Although shares are originally to be sold for \$100 each, in the levered case earnings of \$15 per share (all to be paid out as dividends) exceed the required return of 12 percent. Investors seeking to acquire such shares for their high yield will push up the market price until it reaches \$125, implying an effective return of 12 percent. The total market value of the firm is computed by adding the market values of all the different types of securities it has outstanding. Thus, for the levered case we have \$500,000 in debt plus 5,000 shares with a market price of \$125 each, for a total of \$1,125,000.

The weighted average cost of capital in the case of all common equity financing is simply $k = k_e = 10\%$. The after-tax cost of debt is $k_b = (1 - T)10\% = 5$ percent. Hence, with leverage introduced and using weights appropriate for the initial financing[5] we obtain

$$k = (0.5 \times .05) + (0.5 \times .12) = 8.5\%.$$

Summarizing the results of the criteria which are relevant for any evaluation of capital structures, we have

	No Debt 10,000 Shares	\$500,000 Debt and 5,000 Shares
Market price per share	\$100	\$125
Total value of the firm, V	\$1,000,000	\$1,125,000
Weighted average cost of capital, k	10%	8.5%

[5]To facilitate our exposition we use weights from the initial financing. Had we used subsequent market weights, then drawing on the notation introduced in the previous chapter, we would have had $k = \frac{B}{V}k_b + \frac{E}{V}k_e = \frac{\$500,000}{\$1,125,000} \times .05 + \frac{\$625,000}{\$1,125,000} \times .12 = 8.88\%$. We could also have computed an average yield (before investor taxes) provided by the firm on all its securities, also called the firm's overall market capitalization rate. For all common equity financing we again have $\hat{k} = \hat{k}_e = 10\%$. With leverage introduced we obtain $\hat{k} = 0.5 \times .10 + 0.5 \times .12 = 11\%$ or using market value weights $\hat{k} = \frac{\$500,000}{\$1,125,000} \times .10 + \frac{\$625,000}{\$1,125,000} \times .12 = 11.11\%$.

It is evident that the levered capital structure produces the better results in terms of all three criteria listed and should be selected. The important general result to be learned from this example, however, is that all three criteria are really synonymous. In other words, if a particular capital structure results in higher market prices per share it will always entail a lower weighted average cost of capital and a higher total value of the firm. Hence, any one of these three criteria can be used to evaluate alternative capital structures and the choice is merely one of computational convenience.

In the above example it comes as no surprise that the levered capital structure emerged as the appropriate choice. By raising funds through debt at an after-tax cost of $k_b = 5\%$ and investing these monies to generate EBIT of 20 cents on every dollar invested, gains in excess of after-tax interest payments accrued to the common shareholders thereby increasing earnings per share from \$10 to \$15. With investors only requiring an increase in returns from 10% to 12% to compensate for the additional financial risk, share prices went up from \$10/.10 = \$100 to \$15/.12 = \$125.

It is interesting to consider what would have transpired had investors been more risk averse and required a return of 17% on any common equity investment in the levered situation. Specifically, the market price per share, instead of increasing to \$125, would have dropped to \$15/.17 = \$88.24 since the increase in earnings per share would not have been enough to compensate for the added financial risk perceived by investors. Similarly, the total value of the firm would have decreased to V = \$500,000 + 5,000 × \$88.25 = \$941,200 while the weighted average cost of capital would have risen to $k = 0.5 \times .05 + 0.5 \times .17 = 11\%$, all of which implies that complete common equity financing should have been implemented. Summarizing the situation where risk averse common shareholders demand a return of 17% to compensate for increased financial risk, we now have

	No Debt 10,000 Shares	\$500,000 Debt and 5,000 Shares
Market value per share	\$100	\$88.24
Total value of the firm, V	\$1,000,000	\$941,200
Weighted average cost of capital, k	10%	11%

Clearly, then, the merit of alternative capital structures hinges on how investors view and evaluate the increased risk produced by leverage.

Conceptually, it is useful to distinguish three possibilities. First, the case where investors appear to be reasonably risk neutral, implying that increasing leverage will result in lower costs of capital. Next there is the situation where investors are risk averse to the point of just neutralizing any advantage gained by the use of cheaper debt funds, and thirdly the case where investors are risk averse to such a degree that use of leverage becomes undesirable. These three circumstances are illustrated diagrammatically in Figure 14-4.[6]

FIGURE 14-4

Consequences of Investor Attitudes Towards Risk

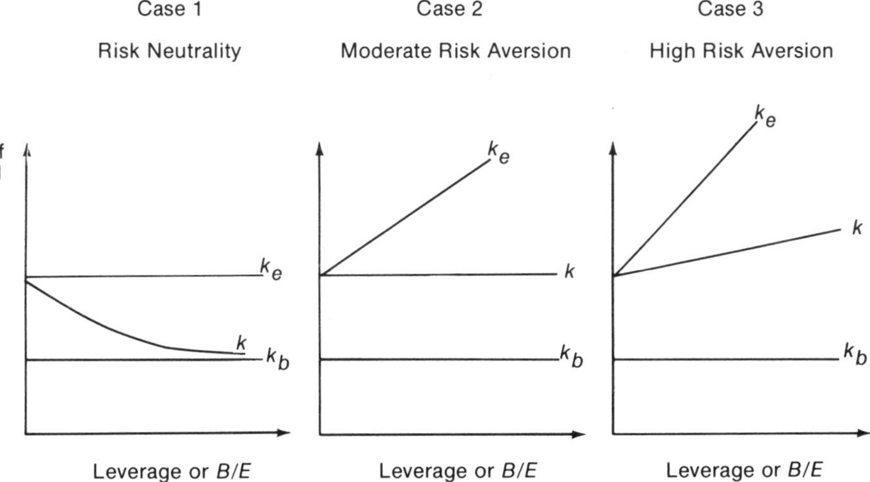

In this conceptual discussion we are obviously assuming that the cost of debt remains unaffected by the degree of financial leverage employed by the firm. Further on, we in fact recognize that where there is significant reliance on debt, creditors will not only introduce restrictive provisions but may be unwilling to advance additional funds except at higher interest rates. It is to be noted, however, that the cost of debt k_b is always below the cost of equity k_e, reflecting the relatively lower risk borne by creditors and the tax deductibility of interest at the corporate level.

In case 1, with risk neutral investors who ignore the additional risks introduced by leverage and are concerned solely with the maximizing of expected gains, the cost of common equity remains constant. Thus, with k_e and k_b unaffected by leverage, it is clear that the weighted average cost of capital $k = k_b \frac{B}{V} + k_e \frac{E}{V}$ decreases as cheaper debt is substituted for more costly equity, and resort to high degrees of leverage is indicated.

In case 2 investors are risk averse. k_e therefore rises with increasing leverage reflecting the higher returns demanded by shareholders as compensation for assuming increased financial risk. Thus, debt not only has a direct cost k_b, but an indirect cost as well in the form of a rising k_e. The increases in k_e are such that

[6]If *all* investors in the capital markets were risk neutral, we would observe $k_e = k_b$ in case one of Figure 14-4, as investors would not demand a premium in the form of $k_e > k_b$ for investing in common shares. However, the diagram as shown need not be inconsistent with the assumption of risk neutrality as stated above if we view the bond and the equity markets as separate markets, with risk neutrality only applying to equity investors. It should also be noted that various functions of k_e for varying degrees of leverage need not be caused solely by investors' risk attitudes but may be derived from risk-return tradeoffs available to equity investors through use of personal leverage, as will be detailed in Section 14-7.

they just compensate for the lower direct cost of additional debt financing, leaving the overall cost of capital $k = k_b \frac{B}{V} + k_e \frac{E}{V}$ constant regardless of capital structure.[7] This implies that there exists no optimal capital structure and that one degree of leverage is as good as any other. It is left as an exercise for the reader to show that this circumstance would have arisen in our earlier numerical example, if in the levered case the rate of return required by shareholders had risen to 15 percent. We shall see later on that case 2 has strong theoretical justification.

In the third case, the cost of equity increases with leverage at an even faster rate implying very conservative or risk averse investors. The use of cheaper debt financing becomes unattractive as it fails to offset the high premiums demanded by investors for assuming additional risk. In this case the weighted average cost of capital is lowest if leverage is avoided altogether. This was reflected in our earlier numerical example where equity investors demanded a 17 percent return for bearing the financial risk and the unlevered capital structure turned out to be superior.

The question naturally arises as to which of the above cases is observable in practice and how investors actually do trade off risks and returns. As it turns out, this is an easy question to pose but an extremely difficult one to answer for evidence, when available, is controversial and inconclusive. For a widely held corporation with a constantly changing shareholder group it is clearly not feasible to poll shareholders directly and such specific policy issues as capital structures are normally not brought before general meetings of shareholders. An alternative and more promising approach would be to gather statistical data about a variety of otherwise similar publicly traded firms and to see, for example, how leverage is related to the earnings-price ratios at which the firm's shares typically trade, where said ratio may be used as a readily measurable, albeit rough, substitute for the more elusive cost of equity capital k_e. Unfortunately, this approach is also fraught with difficulties.

First, similar firms also tend to use similar proportions of debt in their capital structures, allowing little insight to be gained about the effects of alternative capital structures. Second, several other factors such as growth expectations may also influence a firm's earnings-price ratio and share price, clouding whatever impact leverage may have. These and other statistical problems are discussed in greater detail in a theoretical section at the end of this chapter. The consequence, however, is that we lack clear and precise answers to the important question of actual investor tradeoffs between risk and return; and also that the specification of optimal capital structures for firms in practice involves rough approximations where subjective judgment has a major role to play.

[7]With $k = k_b \frac{B}{V} + k_e \frac{E}{V}$ = constant, it follows that $k_e = \frac{kV - k_b B}{E} = \frac{k(B+E)}{E} - \frac{k_b B}{E} = k + (k - k_b)\frac{B}{E}$, implying that k_e increases in proportion to a firm's debt-equity ratio $\frac{B}{E}$.

14-5. THE TRADITIONAL POSITION

Before turning to the controversial and more rigorous issue of developing normative theories about investor behavior and share valuation we will address some more practical matters concerned with corporate choice of capital structures and debt-equity ratios. It would appear that most firms react to what has been termed the traditional position on capital structure and the use of leverage. This traditional position is actually a mix of the three conceptual cases presented above, and is diagrammatically reflected in Figure 14-5.

FIGURE 14-5

The Traditional Position on Capital Structure and the Cost of Capital

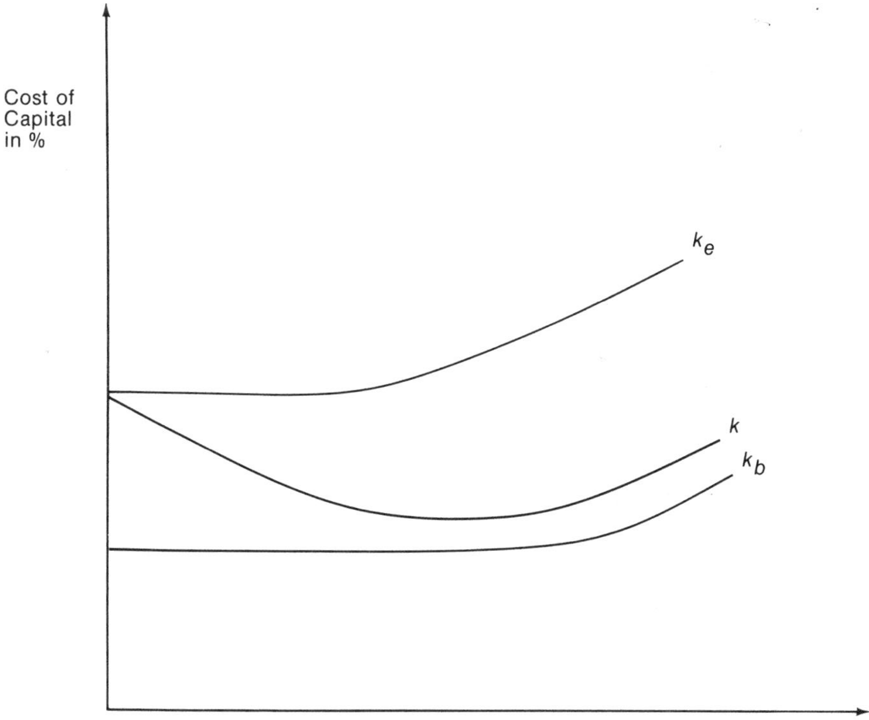

The traditional view has been that a corporation is able to issue a reasonable amount of debt without appreciably affecting the risk and therefore the cost of equity capital, k_e. Therefore, since the cost of debt, k_b, is less than k_e, the addition of moderate amounts of debt to the capital structure will reduce the average cost of capital. The cost of capital schedule falls over its initial range, but as the amount of debt in the capital structure rises beyond a certain level, shareholders begin to require a higher rate of return to compensate for the additional financial risk they must bear. Furthermore, as the firm's use of debt financing increases, lenders will become increasingly reluctant to provide the corporation with additional funds. This attitude is reflected initially through higher interest charges demanded by creditors, and in extreme cases it could take the form of a flat refusal to lend. After a certain point, k_b will also show an increasing slope. Hence, after flattening out, the weighted average cost of capital will start to increase again, indicating that leverage beyond this point becomes undesirable.

Most corporations do make use of debt funds to take advantage of the positive aspects of leverage. At the same time, however, firms limit the amount of debt they carry, in most cases to amounts which are below any constraints imposed by lenders. Thus, their actions appear to be consistent with the traditional position outlined above and imply a belief that an optimal capital structure exists and is achieved by using moderate proportions of debt in the overall financing mix. The likely existence of an optimal capital structure implying a saucer-shaped cost of capital curve as portrayed in Figure 14-5 can also be justified through more rigorous theoretical arguments as outlined in the final section of this chapter.

14-6. CONSIDERATION OF CASH FLOWS

A natural question which arises is how this optimal point or range of leverage is to be found. In most practical situations, where the answer prescribed is not just one of intuitive judgment, analysis is based on cash flows and a firm's ability to generate large enough flows to service any contractual commitments related to debt financing.[8] The specific charges alluded to comprise both interest and sinking fund payments. As a firm increases the amount of debt in its capital structure, these charges, which are generally fixed contractual obligations, increase.[9] A failure to meet such payments results in considerable financial embarrassment at the very least, with a strong possibility that the maturity of the debt is moved to the date of default and, hence, the debt becomes immediately redeemable. Naturally, a firm will only plan to issue additional obligations if its expectations are such that the monies raised can be invested well enough to generate sufficient cash to service the securities. Unanticipated economic downturns do occur, however, and given sales below expectations with no concurrent net reduction of investment in current assets, liquidity problems can arise.

Example

> Assume a firm operating with annual fixed cash obligations of \$12,000,000. Of this amount, \$7,000,000 are fixed costs incurred in operations, and \$5,000,000 relate to outstanding debt, with \$2,000,000 of interest payments (tax deductible) and \$3,000,000 for sinking fund purposes (the latter to be met on an after-tax basis). Annual sales are expected to total \$44,000,000 while variable cost should run at 50

[8] For an excellent paper on the subject, see G. Donaldson, "New Framework for Corporate Debt Capacity", *Harvard Business Review*, (March-April 1962), pp. 117-131 and also G. Donaldson, *Strategy for Financial Mobility*, Homewood, Ill.: R.D. Irwin, 1971, especially Part II.

[9] The charges referred to here are not always fixed. Corporate debt is on occasion issued with flexible sinking fund provisions. For instance, the Canadian Pacific Hotels Limited 8⅝% First Mortgage Bonds Series A, dated April 13, 1972 and due April 15, 1992, provide for a sinking fund to retire \$500,000 of debt per annum between April 1978 and 1991 inclusive. In addition, however, an optional sinking fund of a like amount and duration is provided for.

percent of sales, and depreciation amounts to $5,000,000. With the corporate tax rate at 40 percent we obtain:

Sales		$44,000,000
Variable costs	$22,000,000	
Fixed costs	7,000,000	
Depreciation	5,000,000	
Total expenses		34,000,000
Earnings before interest and taxes		$10,000,000
Interest		2,000,000
Taxable earnings		$ 8,000,000
Taxes		3,200,000
Net earnings		$ 4,800,000

Clearly, the firm should experience no difficulty in meeting all of its obligations since the expected net after-tax cash flow is positive. Specifically, net cash flows amount to $4,800,000 plus depreciation of $5,000,000 less the $3,000,000 sinking fund payment for a net of $6,800,000. Assume, however, that sales unexpectedly drop to half their forecasted level, perhaps because of a severe recession. We then have

Sales	$22,000,000
Total expenses ($11,000,000 + $7,000,000 + $5,000,000)	23,000,000
Earnings before interest and taxes	$(1,000,000)
Interest	2,000,000
Net earnings	$(3,000,000)

Expected net after-tax cash flows are now $5,000,000 – $3,000,000 – $3,000,000 = –$1,000,000 (depreciation – losses – sinking fund payments) and unless the previous year's taxes paid are recaptured the corporation may well face a liquidity problem.

It is clear that when entering a debt commitment, a firm needs to assess the likelihood of sales being below expectations and to balance the risk of insolvency against the favorable leverage which low-cost debt financing may provide. Most corporations want to keep such risk at low levels, only incurring fixed charges to a point where the probability of meeting the obligations, given normal operating conditions, is very high. In this context, we see that the cash budget becomes the starting point for establishing policy on capital structure, with cash budgets being prepared not simply with future expectations in mind but under an assumption of adversity as well, in order to obtain data on the "worst possible" outcome. While considerable judgment is obviously called for when assessing future business conditions, past operating experience often provides a good starting point for estimating the variability of cash flows.

It follows that in practice, the stability of revenues becomes a key criterion for determining a firm's debt capacity, with many corporate decisions respecting capital structure being based on such considerations. Quite obviously, the stability of revenues and cash flows is strongly dependent on the particular type of business and it is not surprising, therefore, that different degrees of leverage are viewed as typical for different industries. Table 14-2 provides some evidence in this regard.

TABLE 14-2

Corporate Long-Term Financing
Aggregated to 1970 by Industry
in Proportions of Total Capital Employed

Industry	Long-Term Debt (%)	Preferred (%)	Common Equity (%)
All Corporations	41	8	51
Mining	23	6	71
Manufacturing	29	5	66
Retailing	30	9	61
Utilities including Transport	52	11	37
Wholesaling	31	9	60

Source: Adapted from Statistics Canada, *1970 Corporation Financial Statistics*, Ottawa, 1974.

We see that regulated industries such as utilities, which enjoy stable revenues, typically employ high leverage, while cyclical industries like mining, which are significantly affected by changes in the economy, can only afford quite modest reliance on senior securities.

We are left with the question of whether emphasis on cash-flow considerations as found in practice is consistent with the previously specified objective of maximizing shareholder wealth. The two are not unrelated for inasmuch as shareholders suffer real losses in the event of bankruptcy, it is in their interest that careful attention be given to anticipated cash flows. Corporate management, however, may on occasion tend to be even more conservative than shareholders' interests would warrant and understandably so. There are other parties who incur real losses when a firm goes bankrupt and their losses may be much more severe than those of shareholders who hold the company's shares as part of a diversified investment portfolio. These other parties include the community at large, employees, creditors and management itself. Consequently, where risks of complete financial failure have to be reckoned with, an approach focussing solely on the more immediate interests of shareholders appears too narrow; and conservatism on the part of management, reflected in their primary concern for liquidity, becomes understandable.

*****ADDITIONAL SELECTED TOPICS***

**14-7. THE THEORY OF OPTIMAL CAPITAL STRUCTURES

A normative theory on capital structure, which doesn't simply describe how things are or might be, but which attempts to derive how things should be was developed by Modigliani and Miller,[10] henceforth identified as M-M.

[10]See F. Modigliani and M. Miller, "The Cost of Capital, Corporation Finance and the Theory of Investment," *American Economic Review*, June 1958, pp. 261-297 and also F. Modigliani and M. Miller, "Corporate Income Taxes and the Cost of Capital: A Correction," *American Economic Review*, June 1963, pp. 433-442.

The first notion we need to discuss in reviewing their theory is that of personal vs. corporate leverage. We have seen in the preceding sections how corporations can use debt in their capital structures to achieve financial leverage. An individual investor can also create personal financial leverage and risk by, for example, purchasing common shares and financing the investment in part with borrowed funds while paying the necessary interest charges.[11] Consequently, in seeking a particular level of leverage an investor can either buy the shares of a firm which employs enough debt in its capital structure to provide the desired leverage, or buy the shares of corporations which use less than the desired amount of debt in their capital structure while using personal debt to finance the share purchases. In either case, the ultimate result from the investor's viewpoint is quite similar and, in effect, given certain assumptions which we will detail further on, corporate leverage and personal leverage are substitutable, leaving the investor indifferent between the two. This being the case, M-M have gone on to show that, taxes aside, a firm's capital structure is irrelevant. Expressed another way, their view is that apart from a tax effect, there is no optimal capital structure and any amount of debt in the capital structure is as good as any other, and the conditions portrayed in Figure 14-4, case 2, should prevail. Before discussing the implications and limitations of their position, we will formalize some of the arguments they have advanced.

Arguments about the interchangeability of corporate and personal leverage are heavily dependent on the tax structure and rates. To facilitate an explanation it is useful first to develop the M-M case in the absence of taxes. The conclusions derived will then be modified to take into account the realities of taxation. Further assumptions made by M-M in developing their basic argument include:

- Securities markets are perfect, in that besides an absence of taxes, there are no transaction costs for buying or selling securities, and the interest rates at which the borrowing and lending of money takes place is the same for all corporations and investors. Note that in the absence of taxes and transaction costs, the cost of capital for debt and common equity, k_b and k_e, are identical to the market capitalization rates $\hat{k}_b$ and $\hat{k}_e$.
- Firms can be grouped according to business risk, with the EBIT stream of firms in the same risk class being subject to the same degree of uncertainty. Investors have common perceptions about firms and common expectations regarding the mean value and the risk or variability of future operating income levels.

While these assumptions may appear to be overly restrictive, the reader is cautioned against rejecting the M-M theory out of hand because of the lack of realism in the assumptions; what is important is not how realistic the assumptions are, but the extent to which the M-M conclusions carry over to a more realistic world.

With these assumptions, M-M are able to show that if two firms in the same risk class do not have the same total market value and hence weighted average

[11]In other words, buying shares on margin is one example of the use of financial leverage by the individual.

cost of capital, then, regardless of the leverage of the two firms, it will pay investors to sell their shares in the higher-priced firm and invest the proceeds in the lower-priced one. This arbitrage process [12] will continue until both firms trade at the same overall market value, and end up with the same cost of capital.

Rather than reproducing the M-M argument in full, only the nature of their proof will be illustrated by numerical example.

Example

Firms U (unlevered) and L (levered), for which data are presented in Table 14-3, are two corporations in the same risk class, so that their operating income or EBIT streams, X, are perfectly correlated and have the same mean value, $\overline{X}$ = \$100, which remains constant with all earnings paid out as dividends. Firm U has no debt outstanding, whereas firm L has \$200 of debt outstanding at an interest rate of 5 percent.

TABLE 14-3

Data on Firms U and L in same Risk Class

	Firm U	Firm L
Expected level of EBIT*, $\overline{X}$	\$ 100	\$ 100
Interest charges, k_bB	—	\$ 10
Earnings to common shareholders, $\overline{X} - k_bB$	\$ 100	\$ 90
Equity capitalization rate, $\hat{k}_e = k_e$	.10	.10
Market price of equity, $E = \frac{1}{\hat{k}_e}(\overline{X} - k_bB)$	\$1,000	\$ 900
Total market value of firm, $V = E + B$	\$1,000	\$1,100

* An assumption of no taxes was made.

Assume initially that the costs of equity capital, k_e, are the same for the two firms—implying that equity investors are risk neutral along lines outlined earlier in Figure 14-4, case 1. We see from Table 14-3 that firm L's value is \$1,100 or \$100 more than firm U's. The reason for the higher total value of L comes from the fact that the part of EBIT which services debt (\$10) is capitalized at a rate of only 5 percent, supporting debt with a market value of \$10/0.05 = \$200 on which interest is paid at a rate of only 5 percent (typically, because of its lower risk, $k_b < k_e$).

It is now possible to show that it will pay an investor in the levered firm L to sell his shares, substitute personal borrowing for corporate borrowing, and

[12]The term arbitrage refers to the process of buying and selling the same or similar goods at the same time for a profit. It is related to the economic law of one price which holds that at any point in time prices for the same goods in different locations cannot differ by more than transportation and transactions costs because otherwise the opportunity for profit will attract groups or individuals to act in ways which would quickly drive prices together. The concept is clearly important in finance, particularly in the securities and foreign exchange markets. Take, for example, a firm whose shares are traded on several stock exchanges including New York and Toronto. The possibility of arbitrage will ensure that shares trade at quite similar prices in both locations, for if the price in New York was lower than that in Toronto, investors would buy shares in New York and simultaneously sell them in Toronto. They would continue to do so as long as profit margins greater than transaction costs were available. In other words, the process would end where, for all practical purposes, the price spread disappeared.

to invest the proceeds in firm U with its lower market value.

In evaluating these alternatives, we will have to consider both the investor's *expected return* and the *variability of returns.* Where a tilde is placed over a symbol, this indicates that the cash flow associated with this symbol is uncertain.

Example

In Table 14-3, operating income is uncertain ($\tilde{X}$), whereas interest payments are not ($I = k_b B$). Assume the investor initially owns 10 percent of the equity of firm L with a market value of \$90. Then, his income from this holding, $\tilde{Y}_L$, is given by $\tilde{Y}_L = .10\,(\tilde{X} - I) = 0.10(\widetilde{100} - 10) = \widetilde{10} - 1$. Suppose next that the investor sells his investment in L at its market value of \$90, borrows \$10 and uses the resulting \$100 to purchase 10 percent of the equity of U. Now his gross income from the new investment is $0.10\tilde{X} = 0.10(\widetilde{100})$ and, after paying interest on his personal borrowing at the same rate as corporate borrowing (\$10 × 0.05), his net income becomes:

$$\tilde{Y}_U = .10(\widetilde{100}) - .05(10) = \widetilde{10} - 0.5.$$

Comparing $\tilde{Y}_U$ to $\tilde{Y}_L$, we see that the investor's uncertain income stream is the same in both cases, but that $\tilde{Y}_U$ is greater than $\tilde{Y}_L$ by \$0.5 which is certain.

The above transaction enables the investor to increase income without any increase in risk, and M-M are able to argue that the hypothesized difference in value between the two firms cannot persist. As set out in Table 14-4, rational investors will continue the arbitrage process until the total market values of U and L are identical.

TABLE 14-4

Equilibrium Values for Firms U and L

	Firm U	Firm L
Expected level of EBIT, $\bar{X}$	\$ 100	\$ 100
Interest charges, $k_b B$		10
Earnings to common shareholders $\bar{X} - k_b B$	\$ 100	\$ 90
Equity capitalization rate, $\hat{k}_e = k_e$	.10	0.1125
Market price of equity $E = \frac{1}{\hat{k}_e}(\bar{X} - k_b B)$	\$1,000	\$ 800
Total market value of firm, $V = E + B$	\$1,000	\$1,000
Weighted average cost of capital $k = k_b \frac{B}{V} + k_e \frac{E}{V}$	.10	.10

At this point, the total market values and the weighted average costs of capital are identical for firms U and L. No opportunity for further arbitrage exists as an investor owning 10 percent of the equity in L achieves exactly the same returns (\$10 – \$1) which he would obtain if he sold his holdings for \$80, borrowed \$20 and bought 10 percent of the equity in firm U (returns: \$10 – \$1).[13]

To summarize this part of the M-M argument, given constant risk, a firm's total market value should only be determined by the level of its operating income and in equilibrium a firm cannot command a higher total market value simply because of the leverage it employs. Investors can create their own leverage by borrowing and purchasing shares on margin, and hence would not pay any premium for corporate leverage which they can duplicate themselves. Since the value of the two firms must be the same, so must be their overall cost of capital, and M-M conclude with their basic proposition, specifically, that the average cost of capital to a firm is independent of its capital structure and is therefore equal to the cost of equity for an unlevered firm of the same risk class.

The implication is that, regardless of degree, use of debt increases the risk assumed by owners of the firm. Consequently, any seemingly desirable reliance on proportionately more debt financing should be exactly offset by a rise in the cost of equity.

With the overall cost of capital $k = k_e \frac{E}{V} + k_b \frac{B}{V} =$ constant, it is easy to show how the cost of equity capital must vary with leverage. We have:

$$(5) \qquad k_e = \frac{kV - k_b B}{E} = \frac{k(B+E)}{E} - \frac{k_b B}{E}$$

or

$$(6) \qquad k_e = k + (k - k_b)\frac{B}{E}$$

The relationship between the cost of equity, k_e, and the debt equity ratio as set out in equation (6) is shown in Figure 14-6 which corresponds to the case discussed earlier and portrayed in Figure 14-4, case 2.

FIGURE 14-6

Relationship Between the Cost of Capital, Cost of Equity Capital and Leverage

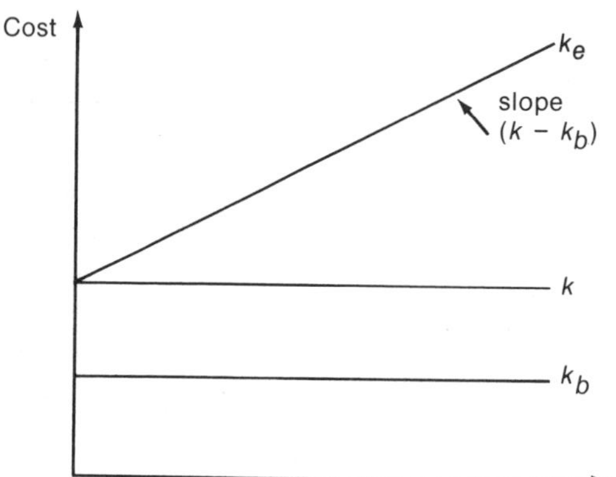

[13]A similar argument could have been presented for the case where an unlevered firm U commands a higher total market value than a levered but otherwise identical firm L. We assume throughout that the firm which is overvalued is an isolated case with a small equity value relative to other firms in that same risk class, so that the arbitrage process only affects the market price of that firm's shares.

Note that unlike the traditional position which holds that k_e will not rise noticeably for moderate amounts of leverage, the M-M hypothesis asserts that the cost of equity is an increasing function of leverage at all levels of leverage.

Before proceeding further, it is useful to detail and discuss some of the more common criticisms of the M-M assumptions.

- The existence of transaction costs prevents the arbitrage mechanisms from functioning smoothly; we should therefore expect to find some differences in valuation which could not be profitably eliminated by arbitrage.

First, it should be noted that while the M-M argument runs in terms of an arbitrage process, this is not necessarily the way in which equilibrium is achieved. There is a constant turnover of the shares of most publicly held companies, and choices by potential buyers between firms *U* and *L*, unaffected by transaction costs, will serve to keep their values equal. Secondly, even if transaction costs did impede the equilibrating process significantly, there is no reason to believe that this would have a systematic tendency to keep the value of the levered firm above that of the unlevered. We should, in fact, expect to find that the higher value would sometimes be found with the levered firm and at other times with the unlevered.

- It is not reasonable to believe either that investors can assign firms to risk classes, or that investors agree about expected operating income streams.

Again, it does not seem probable that the failure of this assumption leads to any systematic bias. In any case, it has recently been shown that under certain conditions the M-M position can be proven without reference to risk classes.[14]

- The argument implicitly assumes that personal borrowing is a perfect substitute for corporate borrowing. This is, in fact, not the case. Personal borrowing leads to the risk of personal bankruptcy, whereas there is no such risk associated with corporate borrowing because of limited liability. M-M moreover assume that investors are able to borrow at the same rate as corporations whereas, in reality, because of their superior credit standing, corporations are often able to borrow at rates considerably below those at which private investors can borrow. For both these reasons it is maintained that investors prefer corporate leverage to personal leverage, and are therefore prepared to pay a premium for the levered firm over the unlevered one.

M-M admit that personal and corporate leverage may not be perfect substitutes for the reasons cited, but question whether the magnitude of the bias due to treating them as equivalent is significant. The following reasons may be advanced for believing that this bias is unimportant:

Many investors hold mixed portfolios of bonds and shares. By selling bonds out of the portfolio the investor can create personal leverage at an effective cost equal to the corporate bond rate and without any increase in the risk of personal bankruptcy. In this case, therefore, personal and corporate leverage are perfect substitutes.

The relevant borrowing rate is, at worst, the rate on brokers' loans which is not

[14]See J. Stiglitz, "A Re-examination of the Modigliani-Miller Theorem," *American Economic Review*, December 1969, pp. 784-793.

significantly above the corporate borrowing rate. Furthermore, for most corporations the leverage ratio does not exceed thirty to forty percent; the risks of personal bankruptcy in borrowing to this extent against a large and well diversified share portfolio are small.

If investors did have a preference for corporate leverage over personal leverage, investment companies would be set up to provide such leverage by buying unlevered shares and issuing debt against them on behalf of investors. These investment firms would bid up the prices of unlevered corporations until they were equal to those of levered ones in the same risk class.

The above arguments were developed under the assumption of no taxes, or more generally similar tax rates at the corporate and personal levels. The logical extension is to consider the effects of the corporate income tax on the Modigliani-Miller theory. In addition, some explicit attention should be given to the possibility of firms going bankrupt through the use of excessive leverage.

**14-8. TAXES, BANKRUPTCY COSTS AND OPTIMAL CAPITAL STRUCTURES

We saw that in the absence of taxes, corporate and personal leverage are substitutable. The choice of capital structure should then be irrelevant with the weighted average cost of capital remaining constant regardless of the degree of financial leverage employed. The question now arises as to how the above conclusion is altered if different tax rates are applicable to both corporations and investors, and in particular if the corporate tax rate exceeds investor tax rates. With corporate tax rates generally around 50 percent this situation is usual, as the marginal tax rates of most investors are likely to be lower. Again, to simplify presentation of the basic argument, we consider the extreme case where only the corporation pays taxes and does so at rate T. Where tax-exempt institutional investors like pension funds are involved this would not be unrealistic. We keep in mind that the gist of the conclusions reached carries over to any situation in which investors face lower marginal rates than do corporations and this is certainly the case for most widely held corporations.

Under circumstances where investors pay no taxes, personal leverage is no longer a perfect substitute for corporate leverage. It then becomes advantageous for shareholders if the corporation incurs tax-deductible interest expenses which will minimize the total tax burden and hence maximize the amount of funds available to security holders. If a firm becomes too highly levered for the particular risk preferences of an investor, the investor can always invest part of his holdings in fixed income securities (perhaps in the same corporation's debt issues) to "undo" the leverage and to reduce his personal risk.

To illustrate the point, we pursue our earlier examples, as depicted in Table 14-4 but include consideration of a corporate tax rate $T = 50$ percent. Calculations and the resultant equilibrium values for firms U and L are shown in Table 14-5, and it is useful to compare both tables to fully appreciate the effect of corporate taxes. Because of the tax induced reduction in earnings available to the common shareholders, the market prices of equity are proportionately reduced, from \$1,000 to \$500 and from \$800 to \$400 respectively. However interest payments and hence the value of debt B for the levered firm is unaffected by taxes, maintaining a value of \$200. The net effect is that as a consequence of corporate taxes the levered firm has a higher total market value than the unlevered firm and hence a lower weighted average cost of capital, with $k_u = 10$ percent whereas $k_L = \frac{200}{600} \times .025 + \frac{400}{600} \times .1125 = 8.33$ per cent). The explanation is apparent: in the no-tax situation detailed in Table 14-4, the total amount paid out to shareholders and bondholders was the net operating income or \$100 regardless of financial leverage. The only effect leverage had was to apportion these total payments and their inherent risk among the various types of security holders. Thus, while values of E and B varied depending on capital structure, the total value of the firm $V = E + B$ remained constant. However, with corporate taxes introduced, and because of the tax deductibility of interest, the total amounts available to be paid to security holders (shareholders and bondholders) are no longer constant, but increase with the amount of debt in the firm's capital structure (\$50 in the case of U and \$45 + \$10 = \$55 in the case of L).[15] It is the "bonus of the tax shield" which causes the total value of a levered firm to be higher. In fact, we can show arithmetically[16] that the value of levered firm V_L

TABLE 14-5

Equilibrium Values for Firms U and L Given Corporate Taxes

	Firm U	Firm L
Expected level of EBIT, $\bar{X}$	\$ 100	\$ 100
Interest charges, k_bB		10
Taxable income, $\bar{X} - k_bB$	\$ 100	\$ 90
Tax payable, $T(\bar{X} - k_bB)$	50	45
Earnings to common shareholders $(1 - T)(\bar{X} - k_bB)$	\$ 50	\$ 45
Equity capitalization rate, $\hat{k}_e$	0.10	0.1125
Market price of equity, $E = \frac{1}{\hat{k}_e}(1 - T)(\bar{X} - k_bB)$	\$ 500	\$ 400
Total market value of firm, $V = E + B$	\$ 500	\$ 600

[15] To show this more clearly, consider the total after-tax amounts $\bar{X}_t$ expected to be available to a corporation's security holders

$\bar{X}_t = (\bar{X} - k_bB)(1 - T) + k_bB$

= after-tax earnings plus interest on debt

Rearranging the terms, we have

$X_t = \bar{X}(1 - T) + Tk_bB$ showing $\bar{X}_t$ to be an increasing function of the amount of debt outstanding.

[16] The value of an unlevered firm V_U is given by $V_U = \frac{\bar{X}(1 - T)}{k_U}$ with k_U the market capitalization rate for the unlevered firm. As shown in footnote 15, for a levered firm, $\bar{X}_t$ is equal to the income of an unlevered firm $\bar{X}(1 - T)$ plus tax savings due to debt of Tk_bB. If the debt is taken to be perpetual, then the present value of these future tax savings is $Tk_bB/k_b = TB$.

We can conclude that $V_L = V_U + TB$. Note that while the proper capitalization for $\bar{X}(1 - T)$ is k_U, which is an equity capitalization rate reflecting the business risk of the firm, the tax savings due to debt are subject to considerably less uncertainty and hence are capitalized at the lower rate k_b. For further detailing on this point, see e.g., also the discussion on the discount rate to be chosen in bond refunding in Chapter 8.

increases with increasing amounts of debt, or that

$$V_L = V_U + TB$$

This is confirmed by the example set out in Table 14-5, where $V_L = \$500 + 0.50\ (\$200) = \$600$.

It follows from the above that the firm's weighted average cost of capital declines with leverage and by implication that debt financing is always superior to the use of equity. The actions of financial managers belie this, however, raising the question of why firms do not in fact exploit the tax advantage of leverage to the full by issuing large amounts of debt. Three possible reasons may be advanced for this:

- Lenders may be reluctant to lend once the capital structure becomes too highly levered because of the increasing risks of cash-flow shortages leading to default on loans provided. In addition to high interest rates or even outright refusal to lend, this reluctance may take the form of highly restrictive debt contracts which curtail management's freedom to assume additional debt and take advantage of attractive new investment opportunities.[17]
- As the leverage rises, the probability of the firm being forced into financial difficulties and possible bankruptcy also rises. Bankruptcy is likely to entail direct costs to equity investors since the value of the firm would no longer be determined by its earnings potential as a going concern, but by the liquidation value of its assets, some of which may have to be sold at distress prices. Therefore, if we consider both the probability of bankruptcy which increases with leverage and its costs, the cost of equity capital should increase more rapidly. This in turn causes the overall cost of capital curve to flatten out, or even to turn up, once the reasonable use of leverage is exceeded.[18] More importantly, however, bankruptcy will generally entail significant costs for most other parties having an interest in the corporation and, as was suggested earlier, it appears unrealistic not to take these costs into account.
- Lastly, the phenomenon of managerial risk aversion has been offered as an explanation for the use of quite conservative capital structures. While large corporations are rarely forced into bankruptcy, temporary financial difficulties may well make them targets for a takeover which would result in replacement of the existing management team. Hence, concern by management about job security may cause firms to select a leverage ratio such that the cost of capital schedule is still downward-sloping.

Contrary to the traditional position which is purely based on judgment, the theory on capital structure as set out by Modigliani and Miller has provided us with a systematic framework within which to analyze the issue. In their argument M-M have noted that, for more highly levered firms, restrictions in borrowings and other considerations will raise the real cost of debt. Clearly, once such costs are recognized we return very quickly to the conclusion that for most corporations an optimal capital structure does exist and that some

[17]See J. Van Horne, "A Linear Programming Approach to Evaluating Restrictions Under a Bond Indenture or Loan Agreement," *Journal of Financial and Quantitative Analysis*, June 1966, pp. 68-83.

[18]For a discussion of bankruptcy costs, see N. Baxter, "Leverage, Risk of Ruin, and the Cost of Capital," *Journal of Finance*, September 1967, pp. 395-403; and A. Robichek and S. Myers, *Optimal Financing Decisions*, Englewood Cliffs: Prentice-Hall, 1965, pp. 40-44.

reconciliation of the M-M and traditional positions is possible.[19] Our own conclusion is that the optimal capital structure for many firms may be at higher levels of leverage than has traditionally been assumed and that the minimum in the weighted average cost of capital curve as previously shown in Figure 14-5 may well be flat, suggesting that within a particular range the cost of capital is relatively insensitive to changes in capital structure.

**14-9. EMPIRICAL TESTS OF COST OF CAPITAL THEORIES

As a consequence of the controversy surrounding the cost of capital question, considerable research has been directed towards establishing what actually happens in practice and towards testing alternative theories to see which provides the most adequate explanation of the real world. Unfortunately, there are severe difficulties impeding the construction of adequate empirical tests, some of which were alluded to earlier, so that it is difficult to reach unequivocal conclusions from the evidence thus far produced.

Statistical tests can involve either longitudinal or cross-sectional data. Longitudinal or time series data imply that information is gathered on one firm through time. Using the data we might then try to determine how, for example, a change in capital structure through an issue of debt which took place at some time in the past has affected the firm's share price or the earnings-price ratio. In such circumstances, the earnings-price ratio may serve as a convenient and readily measurable surrogate for k_e. Two difficulties arise however. To begin with we know that a variety of factors can influence the price of a corporation's stock including the general level of stock prices, prospects for the industry of which it is a member, and so on. These and similar factors cannot be held constant over time and their effect may well overshadow any changes caused by an alteration of the capital structure. Thus, in looking at time series data it is very difficult to isolate and measure with any degree of confidence changes brought about by one of many factors influencing share prices. Secondly, even if we succeed in providing a rough analysis for one particular case, it is difficult to generalize the findings and lend support to or refute a general theory. It is for these reasons that studies involving cross-sectional data are more prevalent.

In a cross-sectional study, we would consider a single point in time but look at data for a variety of firms, trying to establish statistical relationships which may exist between capital structure and various indicators for the cost of capital. Generally, the statistical tool employed is regression analysis. Once again, however, we face the difficulty of being unable to hold constant those other factors which may influence the dependent variable, as well as the difficulty of being able to suitably measure all potentially relevant variables. In addition, all of the common limitations of regression analysis prevail. For example, the dangers of extrapolating observed relationships beyond the range of observed data points to extreme degrees of leverage must be recognized. Considering that debt proportions observed in practice for firms of similar business risk tend to

[19]For an attempt to do so see A. Robichek and S. Myers, *Optimal Financing Decisions*, Englewood Cliffs: Prentice-Hall, 1965, pp. 42-44.

cluster around industry norms, the usefulness of statistical results obtained is limited. Stability over time also becomes an issue as it is not clear that a relationship which was observed for data representing a particular point in time need prevail at other times. Finally, it is dangerous to infer causality simply because a relationship is identified. Spurious relationships are not uncommon in analyses involving many difficult-to-measure variables which potentially could have a link.

To illustrate, for a sample of 43 electric utilities for the period 1947-1948, M-M regressed the ratio of total funds available to all security holders after tax to total market value of the firm, $\frac{\overline{X}_t}{V}$, on the leverage ratio $\frac{B}{V}$. $\frac{\overline{X}_t}{V}$ is used as a surrogate for the firm's weighted average cost of capital. In the traditional view there would be a negative relationship between the average cost of capital and leverage, whereas the unrevised[20] M-M hypothesis predicts their independence. The result obtained was $\frac{\overline{X}_t}{V} = 5.3 + .006\frac{B}{V}$, where the standard error of the coefficient is .008 and the correlation coefficient $r = 0.12$. By any of the standard statistical tests these results are consistent with the null hypothesis that there is no relationship between the variables, and M-M took them as confirming their theory. Furthermore, neither in this case nor in cross-sectional samples of 42 oil companies was there any suggestion of the saucer-shaped curve traditionalists would expect to find. However, these early results which M-M put forward as being only preliminary, and which were in any case inconsistent with their revised hypothesis that due to taxes the cost of capital declines with leverage, were submitted to critical analysis. Weston[21] argued that M-M had omitted the all-important growth term from their estimated equation. $\overline{X}_t$ measures only the current stream of after-tax income plus interest on debt for the firm; however, the value investors are willing to place on the corporation and, hence, the ratio $\frac{\overline{X}_t}{V}$ will depend on the rate at which earnings are expected to grow in the future. There is a high negative correlation between g and $\frac{B}{V}$, as many growth firms rely heavily on equity financing, while more stable firms use larger proportions of debt. Hence, Weston argued that M-M's results were biased by the omission of g. Replicating M-M's tests for a larger sample of electric utility firms for 1959, Weston obtained:

$$\frac{\overline{X}_t}{V} = 4.27 + \underset{(.007)}{.027}\frac{B}{V}, \text{ with } r = .46$$

where the standard error of the coefficient is written in parentheses below the coefficient. With the cost of capital shown to rise with leverage, this result contradicts both M-M and the traditional view; however, as Weston argues, it is biased by omission of the expected growth term g. Weston then estimated g from the rate of growth of earnings per share for the period 1949-1959. Adding in

[20]Corrections were made in their 1963 paper.

[21]F. Weston, "A Test of Cost of Capital Propositions," *Southern Economic Journal*, October 1963, pp. 105-112.

this growth estimate, he obtained:

$$\frac{\overline{X}_t}{V} = 5.91 - \underset{(.008)}{.0265}\frac{B}{V} - \underset{(.002)}{.082}\,g, \text{ with } r = .53$$

The negative coefficient of the leverage variable implies that, holding growth constant, the cost of capital decreases as the debt ratio grows. Hence, he concluded that the cost of capital schedule does slope down. Before taking the Weston results at face value, some caution should be exercised.

As can be seen from the above, growth expectation of investors forms a critical variable yet it cannot be directly measured. To simply insert past growth as a proxy for anticipated future growth may result in biases which could affect significantly the results of a regression analysis. In the Weston study, for example, the sluggish state of the economy in 1959 may well have led investors to expect lower future growth rates than had been experienced over the past decade. Furthermore, the analysis should be conducted among firms subjected to equal business risk and again we face a problem. Business risk as perceived by investors is difficult to measure[22] and the grouping of companies into equivalent risk classes is subject to errors and inaccuracies. Biased regression coefficients can easily result. Thus firms with low business risk tend to have a higher proportion of debt in their capital structure than firms with high business risk. If there are significant differences between the risks of the various companies in the sample this may cause the coefficient for the leverage ratio in the regression equation to be strongly distorted. Since all empirical cost of capital studies require both that the companies in the sample be drawn from the same risk class and that expected growth rates be estimated, they are all subject to potential biases of unknown magnitude which must reduce the credibility which can be placed in the results and in the conclusions drawn from them.[23] It should be mentioned, nevertheless, that a second empirical study by M-M made significant progress even if the issue remains unresolved.[24]

Clearly, we are not in a position to state authoritatively how equity investors react to various degrees of leverage and hence how the firm's cost of capital behaves as a function of its capital structure. Decisions in this area have to be based on informed judgment and while progress has been made to at least pinpoint and conceptualize the major factors which have a bearing on the issue, the conclusions to be drawn remain controversial and no universally valid formula-type solutions are available.

[22]See the final chapter where portfolio theory and the capital asset pricing model are reviewed.

[23]Additional biases have been flagged by researchers. Wippern notes that the measure of leverage incorporates the market value of equity. Such value is a function of several variables including financial structure. For example, if shares are highly valued for reasons in addition to financial structure, the leverage ratio will be lowered, underlining the fact that the variable is not a pure measure of financial risk. Other conceptual problems are commented on by Wippern but no complete review is possible in these notes. See R. Wippern, "Financial Structure and the Value of the Firm," *Journal of Finance*, December 1966, pp. 615-633.

[24]See F. Modigliani and M. Miller, "Some Estimates of the Cost of Capital to the Electric Industry, 1954-57," *American Economic Review*, June 1966, pp. 333-391. A full discourse on the statistical and measurement techniques used is beyond the scope of this text. It is sufficient to note that the debate continued in the December 1967 issue of the *American Economic Review* with comments by J. Crockett and I. Friend, M. Gordon and others.

14-10. SUMMARY

The use of fixed-cost financing such as debt or preferred shares in a firm's capital structure gives rise to the phenomenon of leverage. If funds thus raised can be invested to generate expected returns which exceed their costs, the benefits reaped from such transactions accrue to common shareholders in the form of higher expected returns. Financial leverage, however, magnifies any variations in earnings per share brought about by changes in operating income, thereby creating financial risk, and it follows that the use of debt or other senior securities in a firm's capital structure basically becomes an issue of trading off increased expected returns for increased risk.

Financial breakeven analysis is a common tool used to show the relationship between earnings before interest and taxes and earnings per share as a function of alternative capital structures. Breakeven or indifference points respecting EPS can be established to provide a rough indication of the desirability of alternative capital structures, given certain expectations about EBIT levels.

A firm's capital structure is optimal if it maximizes the market price of the firm's shares. This is synonymous with minimizing the weighted average cost of capital or maximizing the total market value of the firm. The desirability of financial leverage depends on equity investors' tradeoffs between risk and returns. Conceptually, we can distinguish between risk-neutral investors, implying that leverage is desirable, risk-averse investors, implying that leverage does not matter, and strongly risk-averse investors, implying that leverage should be avoided. The traditional position, which appears to have a widespread following in practice, is basically a combination of these three cases and postulates a saucer-shaped cost of capital curve which has a minimum for moderate degrees of leverage.

In practice, a firm's debt capacity is often derived through cash-flow analysis, whereby one establishes levels of fixed obligations which can be sustained even in the face of adverse developments affecting revenues and cash inflows. Thus, debt capacity is influenced by the perceived stability of cash flows and, as a consequence, norms regarding capital structures tend to vary from industry to industry.

Normative theories on how investors should trade off risks and returns were first advanced by Modigliani and Miller (M-M). In the absence of taxes M-M show that rational investors would behave in a way that makes the firm's capital structure irrelevant with the weighted average cost of capital remaining constant regardless of leverage. A cornerstone of this argument is that personal leverage is a perfect substitute for corporate leverage. Where corporate taxes are allowed for, financial leverage becomes desirable because of the tax deductibility of interest; and the extent to which a firm might employ leverage is only limited by the increasing threat of bankruptcy costs.

Empirical tests to determine how investors actually behave in trading off risk against return are characterized by difficulties and have not produced conclusive findings. A multitude of factors have the potential to affect the market price of securities, and some of the variables which are of concern are difficult if not impossible to measure. Consequently, the evaluation of alternative capital structures remains a controversial issue in finance. While significant progress has been made in gaining at least a conceptual understanding of the issues involved, for practical decision-making in this area, informed judgment remains an important ingredient.

Questions for Discussion

1. Define and discuss the concept of financial leverage. What are the potential advantages and disadvantages of using financial leverage? Provide a numerical example to illustrate.
2. The choice of an optimal capital structure is based on a risk-return tradeoff. Discuss.
3. Why does one observe different typical capital structures in different industries? What do you think are some of the main factors determining a firm's debt capacity?
4. Why is it difficult in practice to assess the optimal capital structure for a firm?
5. If a firm is able to reduce its cost of capital by accepting a greater leverage ratio, why do firms not utilize this advantage to the full by issuing large amounts of debt?
6. Discuss the potentials and limitations of breakeven analysis in evaluating alternative capital structures. What additional analyses would you draw on before making decisions in this area?
7. Explain the concept of corporate leverage and personal leverage. Under what circumstances can they be viewed as substitutes?
8. Critically evaluate the theory regarding capital structure as advanced by Miller and Modigliani. From the point of view of a practicing manager, what can you learn from their arguments? Where are their arguments and conclusions weakest?

Problems with Solutions

1. A firm has 1,000,000 common shares outstanding with a current market value of $12 per share. An additional $10,000,000 needs to be raised. The firm's tax rate is 40 percent.
   (a) The alternatives are to issue an additional 1,000,000 common shares which would net the company $10 per share, or to place a 20-year debenture calling for annual interest payments of 12 percent. Carry out a financial breakeven or indifference analysis, illustrating for what ranges of EBIT each of the above alternatives appears superior. Provide a diagram, and compute the breakeven point.

Solution

Using formulas (1) and (2) from this chapter we may compute the breakeven point:

Earnings per share issuing new common.

$$\frac{\text{EBIT}(1-T)}{n_1 + n_2} = \frac{\text{EBIT}(0.6)}{2{,}000{,}000} = 0.3 \times 10^{-6}\ \text{EBIT}$$

Earnings per share issuing debt:

$$\frac{(\text{EBIT}-I)(1-T)}{n_1} = \frac{(\text{EBIT} - 1{,}200{,}000)0.6}{1{,}000{,}000} = 0.6 \times 10^{-6}\ \text{EBIT} - 0.72$$

Equating these two expressions we may find the breakeven point where earnings per share (EPS) are equal for both alternatives.
Breakeven point:

$$0.3 \times 10^{-6}\ \text{EBIT} = 0.6 \times 10^{-6}\ \text{EBIT} - 0.72$$
$$0.3\ \text{EBIT} = 720{,}000$$
$$\text{EBIT} = 2{,}400{,}000$$

Substituting back into our original equations it is apparent that EPS at this level are 72¢ per share.
Diagramatically, this can be shown as follows. Note that by issuing only equity, EPS = 0 occurs for EBIT = 0. However, issuing debt requires a fixed charge of $1,200,000 to be covered before EPS may become positive, so that EPS = 0 for EBIT = $1,200,000.

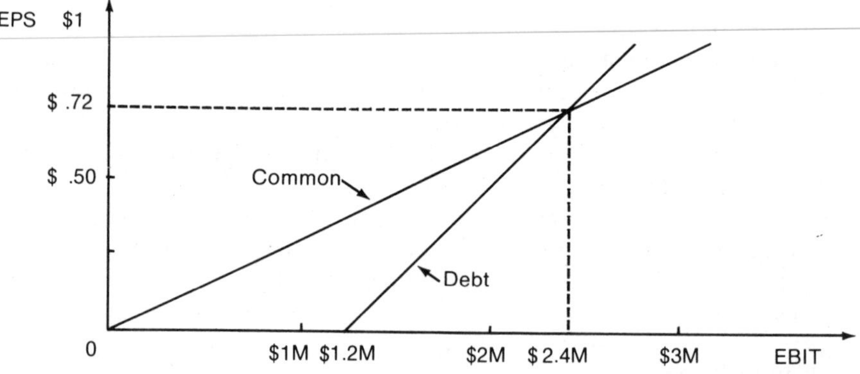

From the above it is apparent that issuing new shares is the more favorable decision for EBIT less than $2.4 million, and debt is superior for EBIT above $2.4 million.

(b) Why is the above analysis based on EBIT?

Solution

The above analysis is based on EBIT because EBIT are not influenced by the capital structure of the firm. Only the operations of the firm influence this figure. In evaluating alternative capital structures, we need as a starting point a measure of the operations of the firm which is independent of the particular capital structure employed. We then assess how the particular capital structure transforms this independent measure of a firm's operations (EBIT) into earnings per share.

(c) The additional $10,000,000 could also be raised through a preferred share issue of 100,000 shares to net the company $100 per share at a dividend rate of 10 percent. Redraw your diagram from part (a) and include the proper line for the preferred share alternative.

Solution

For preferred shares,

$$\text{EPS} = \frac{(\text{EBIT})(1 - T) - D}{n_1} = \frac{\text{EBIT}(0.6) - 1{,}000{,}000}{1{,}000{,}000}$$

$$= 0.6 \times 10^{-6}\ \text{EBIT} - 1$$

Breakeven between issuing common shares and issuing preferred shares:

$$0.6 \times 10^{-6}\ \text{EBIT} - 1 = 0.3 \times 10^{-6}\ \text{EBIT}$$
$$0.3 \times 10^{-6}\ \text{EBIT} = 1$$
$$\text{EBIT} = \$3{,}333{,}333$$

$$\text{EPS at breakeven} = \frac{3{,}333{,}333(.6) - 1{,}000{,}000}{1{,}000{,}000} = \$1 \text{ per share}$$

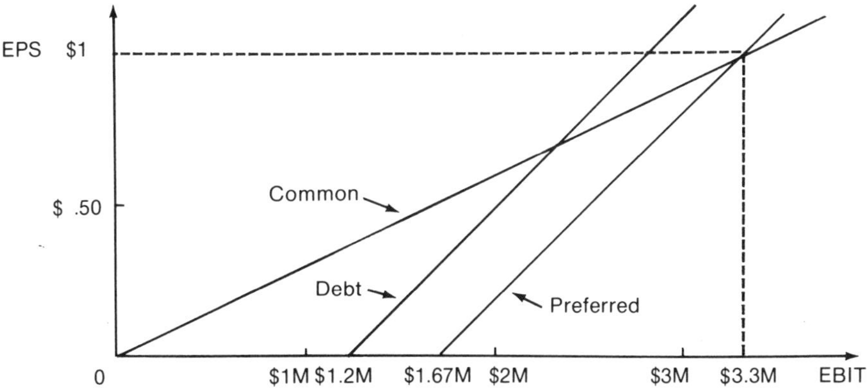

(d) Based on your analysis in (c) above, should a firm consider the preferred share alternative at all—if so under what circumstances might the preferred share alternative offer potential advantages?

Solution

Preferred shares should be considered only where EBIT may be expected to be above $3,333,333. Even so, the generated EPS will be below that which could be achieved with debt. Thus preferred should be issued only where EBIT could potentially fall below the breakeven point between common and debt. If operating performance is uncertain and EBIT could potentially be very low or even negative, issuance of preferred shares is less risky than issuance of debt. Dividends on preferred shares need not be paid if the firm faces a liquidity squeeze, and generally no sinking fund payments are called for. Therefore, given disappointing levels of EBIT, the issuance of preferred shares would help minimize the embarrassing potential cash-flow problems and eliminate consequent trouble in servicing the debt.

(e) EBIT are expected to be \$4,000,000 but they could be 10 percent higher or lower than this figure. What would be the resulting percentage change in earnings per share under each of the above financing alternatives? What would be the "degree of financial leverage" under each of the above financing alternatives?

Solution

To determine the percentage change in EPS given a 10% change in EBIT we must determine the values of EPS given EBIT of \$4 million, \$4.4 million, and \$3.6 million.

EBIT \$4 million:

Common shares:	$EPS = (0.3 \times 10^{-6})\ EBIT$	= \$1.20
Debt:	$EPS = (0.6 \times 10^{-6})\ EBIT - .72$	= \$1.68
Preferred:	$EPS = (0.6 \times 10^{-6})\ EBIT - 1$	= \$1.40

Similarily for EBIT \$4.4 million:

		% change*
Common shares:	EPS = \$1.32	+ 10.0%
Debt:	EPS = \$1.92	+ 14.3%
Preferred:	EPS = \$1.64	+ 17.1%

*e.g. for common shares $\frac{1.32 - 1.20}{1.20} = +10.0\%$

And for EBIT \$3.6 million:

Common shares:	EPS = \$1.08	− 10.0%
Debt:	EPS = \$1.44	− 14.3%
Preferred:	EPS = \$1.16	− 17.1%

The degree of financial leverage under the three alternatives is determined by

$$\frac{\text{percentage change in EPS}}{\text{percentage change in EBIT}}$$

Common shares: $\frac{\%\Delta EPS}{\%\Delta EBIT} = \frac{10}{10} = 1.00$

Debt: $\frac{14.3}{10} = 1.43$

Preferred: $\frac{17.1}{10} = 1.71$

(f) Do your answers in (e) above depend on the expected value of EBIT?

Solution

Yes, the answer does depend on the expected value of EBIT. The degree of financial leverage relates the percentage change in EPS to the *percentage* change in EBIT. It should be clear that these *percentage* changes depend on the absolute levels of EBIT and EPS. For example, given EBIT = \$1,200,000 we have EPS = 0 for the debt alternative. At this point, any increase in EBIT will create an infinite *percentage* increase in EPS.

2. Kulich Corporation is a large firm engaged in light manufacturing. Mr. Kulich has asked Mr. Bullen, controller and treasurer, to prepare figures useful in determining whether there are any risks regarding cash flows for the company in the upcoming year. The firm's tax rate is 40 percent.

   Mr. Bullen presents the following budgetary forecast of items affecting cash flows for the coming year.

   Kulich Corp.

Expected sales	$2,400,000
Cost of direct materials used	400,000
Direct labor cost	325,000
General supplies	10,000
Misc. labor	70,000
Overtime and idle time	40,000
Rent	100,000
Depreciation	95,000
Interest on outstanding debt	300,000
Insurance	8,000
Sales commissions	100,000
Sales salaries	140,000
Shipping expense	105,000
Administrative expense	180,000
Sinking fund requirements on outstanding debt for upcoming year	257,000

   If there are no cash flow problems, Mr. Kulich would like to borrow an additional $500,000 at 10% interest (before tax) for expansion. This would entail additional interest and sinking fund payments of $50,000 and $60,000 respectively next year.

   (a) Compute the net cash flow for the upcoming year. What would you recommend to Mr. Kulich concerning the loan if the above forecasts prove to be accurate?
   (b) Mr. Kulich feels feels there might be a chance that sales could in fact drop to a value as low as $1,700,000. Determine the firm's cash flows in this case. Would you change your recommendation concerning the loan?

Solution

(a) and (b) are solved in the same way with different figures.

Firstly, the various expenses should be broken into fixed and variable over the upcoming year.

Assumed to be fixed: Rent, depreciation, insurance, sales salaries, and administrative expense.

Assumed to be variable: Direct materials, direct labor, general supplies, misc. labor, overtime and idle time, sales commissions, and shipping expense.

We may then determine net earnings:

	(a)		(b)	
Expected sales		$2,400,000		$1,700,000
Total variable costs	$1,050,000		$743,750*	
Total fixed costs	428,000		428,000	
Depreciation	95,000		95,000	
Total expenses		1,573,000		1,266,750
Earnings before interest and taxes		$827,000		$433,250
Interest		300,000		300,000
Taxable earnings		$527,000		$133,250
Tax (40%)		210,800		53,300
Net earnings		$316,200		$ 79,950

*From (a) we determine that variable costs are 43.75% of sales (1,050,000/2,400,000). Thus, if sales drop to $1,700,000, variable costs should drop to 43.75% × $1,700,000 = $743,750.

Net cash flow (NCF) = net earnings + depreciation – sinking fund requirements. Note: sinking fund payments come out of after-tax earnings and are not tax deductible. Without the additional loan, we have

for (a) NCF = $316,200 + $95,000 – $257,000 = $154,200
for (b) NCF = $ 79,950 + $95,000 – $257,000 = –$82,050

The additional loan would increase interest by $50,000, reducing taxable earnings by that amount and reducing net earnings by (1–.4)50,000 = $30,000. As well, sinking fund requirements would increase by $60,000. Hence net cash flow would be reduced by $90,000. This could easily be met in the case of earnings of $2,400,000 (a), but could lead to severe cash-flow problems should sales actually amount to only $1,700,000 (b).

(c) Given the additional $500,000 are borrowed, what is the lowest value which sales could assume in order for cash flows not to be negative?

Solution

Cash flows as a function of sales are given as

$$\text{cash flows} = (\text{sales} - \text{variable costs} - \text{fixed costs} - \text{depreciation} - \text{interest}) \times (1 - T) + \text{depreciation} - \text{sinking fund payments}$$

$$= (\text{sales} - 43.75\% \times \text{sales} - 428{,}000 - 95{,}000 - 350{,}000) \times 0.6 + 95{,}000 - 317{,}000$$

We want to find the sales level at which cash flows just equal zero. By setting cash flows equal to zero in the above equation, we have

$$0 = (\text{sales}\ (1 - 0.4375) - 873{,}000) \times 0.6 - 222{,}000$$

or

$$\text{sales} = \left(\frac{222{,}000}{0.6} + 873{,}000\right) \times \frac{1}{1 - 0.4375}$$

$$= \$2{,}209{,}777$$

3. Companies A and B are identical in all respects, except that A is financed entirely by equity while B has $20,000 of 5 percent debt in its capital structure.
   (a) Company A achieves net operating earnings of $10,000 per annum which the market capitalizes at a rate $\hat{k}_e = 10\%$. What is its market value, or the total value of its stock?
   (b) If the market value of company B is $120,000, which is higher than that of company A, what would happen according to the M-M theory? What are some of the crucial assumptions behind the arbitrage process?
   (c) Suppose you own one-tenth of company B stock, and you carry out the arbitrage process as assumed by the M-M theory. What is your net gain after the switch?

Solution

(a) Market value of stock $= \dfrac{\$10{,}000}{.10}$

$= \$100{,}000.$

Since company A has no debt in its capital structure, the market value of the firm is also $100,000.

(b) If $V_B > V_A$, according to the M-M theory company B is overvalued relative to company A. Hence, investors holding shares of company B will sell their shares, borrow on their personal accounts and buy shares of company A. By so doing, they will drive company B's share price down. The arbitrage process will stop when $V_A = V_B$.
The crucial assumptions behind this arbitrage process are:
(i) no tax considerations
(ii) no difference between corporate debt and personal debt.

(c)

	Company A	Company B
Net operating income	$10,000	$10,000
Interest on debt	—	1,000
Earnings available to shareholders	$10,000	$ 9,000
Equity-capitalization rate	.10	.09*
Market value of stock	$100,000	$100,000
Market value of debt	—	20,000
Total value of firm	$100,000	$120,000

*The equity capitalization rate of 9% for company B is derived from the problem statement which specifies a total market value for company B of $120,000, with $20,000 debt (market value of stock = $120,000 – $20,000 = $100,000) at 5 percent interest. Interest payments are $20,000 × 0.05 = $1,000, implying earnings to common shareholders of $10,000 – $1,000 = $9,000. It follows that $\hat{k}e$ = $9,000/$100,000 = 9 percent.

Expected current income from B = .10($9,000) = $900.

Sell shares of B for $10,000 (1/10 × $100,000).
Borrow an amount equivalent to 10% of B's debt ($2,000) at the same interest rate (5%).

(i) Invest in A $8,000 of the proceeds from the sale of B's stock plus the $2,000 borrowed on personal account at 5% interest. You now own 10% of A.

Gross earnings	$1,000
Less interest on personal account	100
Net income	$ 900

Results: same net income
same financial risk
reduced investment (by $2,000).

(ii) Invest the entire $10,000 received from the sale of B's stock plus $2,000 borrowed on personal account at 5% interest. You now own 12% of A.

Gross earnings	$1,200
Less interest on personal account	100
Net income	$1,100

Results: increased net income
same financial risk
same investment.

Additional Problems

1. A firm has 1,000,000 common shares outstanding with a current market value of $11 per share. An additional $10,000,000 needs to be raised. The firm's tax rate is 45 percent.
   (a) The alternatives are to issue an additional 1,000,000 common shares which would net the company $10 per share, or to place a 25-year debenture calling for annual interest payments of 14 percent. Carry out a financial breakeven or indifference analysis, illustrating for what ranges of EBIT each of the above alternatives appears superior. Provide a diagram, and compute the breakeven point.
   (b) The additional $10,000,000 could also be raised through a preferred share issue of 200,000 shares to net the company $50 per share at a dividend rate of 9 percent. Redraw your diagram from part (a) and include the proper line for the preferred share alternative.
   (c) EBIT are predicted to be $5,000,000 but they could be 15 percent lower or higher than this figure. What would be the resulting percentage change in earnings per share under each of the preceding financing alternatives? What would be the "degree of financial leverage" under each of the above financing alternatives?
2. A firm has 500,000 common shares outstanding with a current market value of $11 per share and a $1,000,000 debenture at 10 percent interest. An additional $1 million needs to be raised. The alternatives are to issue an additional 100,000 shares which would net the firm $10 per share, or to place

an additional 20-year debenture calling for interest payments of 12 percent. The firm's tax rate is 40 percent. Carry out a financial breakeven or indifference analysis, illustrating for what ranges of earnings before interest and taxes each of the above alternatives appears superior.

3. The Snapper Corporation is considering a new product and has a need for $10 million. It has reviewed a number of financing alternatives and has narrowed the choice down to 2 methods of financing: either 7½% debt due in 20 years and sold at a discount of 2% or an additional 400,000 shares of common to be sold at $25 per share. Already outstanding were 5 million common shares and $20 million 6% preferred shares. Recent experience indicated that Snapper's earnings before interest and taxes might range from $5 million to $12 million. The corporate tax rate is 40%.
   (a) Calculate the range in earnings per share which can be expected under each financing alternative.
   (b) If debt is chosen, how much must the firm's earnings be before interest and taxes in order not to sustain an operating loss?
   (c) At what level of earnings before interest and taxes would the two methods yield identical earnings per share? Which method is preferred in the range set by management?

4. Wining Corporation has reached the point where it feels that to grow any further its product lines should be expanded. The vice-president of finance for the company has been looking for suitable projects and has come up with two projects of apparently equal potential. The first of these projects would require additional outside financing of approximately $400,000. The second would be a much larger undertaking which would require $1,300,000 from outside sources. In either case, the new project could be financed entirely through debt, and because of the tax deductibility of interest this appeals to management. The first project could be financed by a 9% debt issue and a sinking fund requirement of $60,000 per year, but the second, due to different financial backing could be financed with debt bearing only 8% interest. Sinking fund requirements here would be $160,000 per year.

   In either case it would take a couple of years before the new projects would start to generate inflows of their own. Forecasts for the upcoming year suggest probable sales of $3,000,000 which could fluctuate within a range of ±10%. Variable costs have traditionally been 60% of sales, and fixed costs (excluding depreciation and interest on current debt) are $600,000 per year. Depreciation for the coming year will be $100,000, interest charges on debt currently outstanding are $150,000, with sinking fund requirements of $200,000. The tax rate for Wining Corporation is 40%.
   (a) Compute the expected net cash flow for the coming year, excluding the effects of any new project.
   (b) Suggest to the vice-president whether either of these projects appear acceptable from a cash-flow point of view. Would 100% debt financing of either project be safe even if sales were at the low end of the anticipated range?

5. Consider two firms, U and L, which are identical in every respect except for the fact that while the former is not levered, the latter firm has $3,000,000 in

5% debentures outstanding. Ignore any tax considerations. Valuation of the two firms is shown as follows:

	Firm U	Firm L
Net Operating Income	$ 1,000,000	$ 1,000,000
Interest on Debt	—	150,000
Earnings Available	$ 1,000,000	$ 850,000
Equity-Capitalization Rate	.08	.10
Market Value of Stock	$12,500,000	$ 8,500,000
Market Value of Debt	—	3,000,000
Total Market Value of Firm	$12,500,000	$11,500,000

An investor initially owns 1% of the unlevered firm.

(a) According to the Modigliani-Miller (M-M) hypothesis, can this valuation occur? Why or why not?

(b) Assuming the investor wants to maintain his *same* proportionate ownership, outline the arbitrage process as put forth by M-M and calculate the amount of increased return available to this investor.

(c) When will this process cease, according to M-M? In reality, will this always be the case? Why or why not?

Case

National Bridge

Mr. Charles Hull, chief financial officer of National Bridge, a well regarded firm of steel producers, was reviewing a list of capital expenditures planned over the next two years. The projects had been tentatively approved by the firm's board of directors subject to satisfactory financing arrangements being worked out. In Hull's opinion, the capital investments which represent the final phase of National Bridge's modernization program, underway since 1972, would in no way alter the firm's business risk.

The board has requested Mr. Hull to develop plans for raising $15,000,000 externally so as to provide for additional net investments during 1976 and 1977. Internally generated funds were expected to provide for the basic replacement of fixed assets, some additions to such assets, and increases in working capital when required. Issues to be addressed specifically in his report included:

(a) the sequencing of the different securities to be issued,

(b) the question of injecting more leverage into the capital structure, and

(c) the use of convertible debt.

Hull knew that while some members of the board were very concerned with the impact of any new financing on earnings per share, others, including the chairman, were more interested in the coverage of fixed charges and limitations to management flexibility which borrowing could introduce. In addition, he appreciated that the board recently appeared to favor a balance sheet showing long-term debt below 60 percent of net worth. As far as he knew, however, there was no policy on the use of senior securities, and determination of the optimal capital structure for National Bridge had never been explored.

Following a long series of meetings with underwriters, Hull learned that:

(a) a private placement of 15 million dollars of 15-year debentures was possible at a coupon rate of 12 percent. Sinking fund requirements of $1,000,000 per year would be specified, issues of additional senior debt beyond amounts now outstanding would be ruled out, and no call for other than sinking fund purposes would be permitted for the first 10 years of the issue.

(b) the market would probably be receptive to a $10,000,000 mortgage bond issue with an 11 percent coupon, or $15,000,000 at 11½ percent. Regardless of the issue's size, a 20-year maturity would be possible with the sinking fund provision specified on a straight-line basis. The issue would be callable after 5 years.

(c) a 20-year $10,000,000 convertible bond issue could be moved out at 10 percent provided the conversion feature remained in effect for 8 years. The conversion price would have to be set at the last possible moment and at no more than 20 percent above the going market price of the common shares. No sinking fund feature would be expected and the issue would be callable after 5 years.

(d) up to $5,000,000 of 10 percent cumulative, redeemable, preferred shares could also be sold, with the sinking fund requirement held to no more than $200,000 per year.

(e) an issue of up to 1,000,000 additional common shares could be expected to net $15 per share at this time.

In looking to the future, Hull believed that the additional net investments during 1976 would increase earnings before interest and taxes by $2,500,000 in fiscal 1977, while sums invested in 1977 would raise the following year's EBIT by an additional $600,000. Corporate taxes during this period were expected to work out to about 52 percent.

The exhibits which follow provide relevant financial data to be used by Mr. Hull in preparing his report for submission to the board of directors. An increase in quarterly dividends to 15 cents per common share should be noted from Exhibit 2. It was the chairman's view that dividends should not be jeopardized under any circumstances.

EXHIBIT 1

National Bridge
Capital Market Statistics

		TSE Industrial Index Closing Quotation at Month-End	McLeod, Young, Wier Long-Term Industrial Bond Yield	TSE Industrial P/E Ratio
1974	Jan	215.0	8.98	12.43
	Feb	222.9	8.98	11.96
	Mar	215.3	9.26	11.40
	Apr	198.2	9.91	9.98
	May	187.5	10.12	9.21
	Jun	183.4	10.45	8.98
	Jul	184.9	10.81	8.70
	Aug	167.0	11.02	7.60
	Sep	151.4	10.99	6.90
	Oct	165.6	10.40	7.31
	Nov	156.2	10.34	6.67
	Dec	156.8	10.72	6.64
1975	Jan	179.9	10.44	7.66
	Feb	183.9	9.99	7.85
	Mar	180.3	10.15	7.83
	Apr	182.9	10.75	8.19
	May	186.3	10.62	8.36
	Jun	189.4	10.57	8.44
	Jul	189.8	10.93	8.73
	Aug	188.5	10.94	8.82
	Sep	177.2	11.40	8.22
	Oct	168.0	11.15	7.59
	Nov	177.4	11.15	8.51
	Dec	172.3	11.06	8.20
1976	Jan	187.5	10.60	8.97

EXHIBIT 2

National Bridge
1975 Share Price, EPS and Dividends

	1975 Jan	Feb	Mar	Apr	May	Jun	Jul	Aug	Sep	Oct	Nov	Dec	1976 Jan
Market Price	15.20	15.60	15.50	16.00	16.50	16.50	16.60	16.50	16.10	16.00	16.10	16.00	16.50
Quarterly EPS	0.38			0.39			0.41			0.41			0.50
Quarterly Dividends	0.12			0.12			0.12			0.12			0.15

EXHIBIT 3

National Bridge
Data from Earnings Statements
for the Years Ended January 31, 1973-1976
(in millions of dollars)

	1973	1974	1975	1976
Net sales	135.5	141.3	140.7	160.1
Manufacturing expenses	94.0	98.1	98.0	110.5
Depreciation	1.7	3.1	4.0	5.7
Sales and administrative costs	6.1	6.3	6.4	7.0
Earnings before interest and taxes	33.7	33.8	32.3	36.9
Interest charges	2.5	2.4	3.3	3.1
Taxable income	31.2	31.4	29.0	33.8
Taxes	16.2	16.3	15.1	17.6
Earnings after taxes	15.0	15.1	13.9	16.2
Preferred dividends	0	0	0	0
Common dividends	3.6 (0.40/sh)	3.8 (0.40/sh)	4.6 (0.48/sh)	4.8 (0.51/sh)
Sinking fund payments	1.5	1.5	1.5	2.0
Common shares outstanding	8,900,000	9,500,000	9,500,000	9,500,000

EXHIBIT 4

National Bridge
Balance Sheets as at January 31, 1973 to 1976
(in millions of dollars)

	1973	1974	1975	1976
Cash	1.4	9.6	3.2	1.5
Accounts receivable	10.1	10.8	11.2	12.3
Inventories	29.0	33.2	36.0	39.3
Other	0.3	0.4	0.5	0.2
Total current assets	40.8	54.0	50.9	53.3
Plant and equipment	61.0	73.5	89.7	107.2
Less accumulated depreciation	18.7	21.8	25.8	31.5
Net fixed assets	42.3	51.7	63.9	75.7
Total assets	83.1	105.7	118.0	129.0
Accounts payable	4.7	4.8	4.9	5.1
Bank loan	1.1	—	—	0.9
Current portion, long-term debt	1.5	1.5	2.0	2.0
Accruals and other	4.1	3.5	4.2	7.9
Total current liabilities	11.4	9.8	11.1	15.9
Long-term debt	35.0	42.5	41.0	39.0
Common stock	8.9	9.5	9.5	9.5
Capital surplus	10.2	15.0	15.0	15.0
Retained earnings	17.6	28.9	38.2	49.6
Net worth	36.7	53.4	62.7	74.1
Total liabilities and net worth	83.1	105.7	114.8	129.0

Selected References

W. Alberts and S. Archer, "Some Evidence on the Effect of Company Size on the Cost of Equity Capital," *Journal of Financial and Quantitative Analysis*, March 1973, pp. 229-245.

E. Altman, "Corporate Bankruptcy Potential, Stockholder Returns, and Share Valuation," *Journal of Finance*, December 1969, pp. 887-900.

J. Ang, "Weighted Average Versus True Cost of Capital," *Financial Management*, Autumn 1973, pp. 56-60.

F. Arditti, "Risk and the Required Return on Equity," *Journal of Finance*, March 1967, pp. 19-36.

F. Arditti and M. Tysseland, "Three Ways to Present the Marginal Cost of Capital," *Financial Management*, Summer 1973, pp. 63-67.

A. Barges, *The Effect of Capital Structure on the Cost of Capital,* Englewood Cliffs: Prentice-Hall, 1963.

D. Baron, "Default Risk and the Modigliani-Miller Theorem: A Synthesis," *American Economic Review*, March, 1976, pp. 204-212.

N. Baxter, "Leverage, Risk of Ruin and the Cost of Capital," *Journal of Finance*, September 1967, pp. 395-403.

M. Brennan, "A New Look at the Weighted Average Cost of Capital," *Journal of Business Finance*, Spring, 1973, pp. 24-30.

J. Coates and P. Woolley, "Corporate Gearing in the EEC", *Journal of Business Finance and Accounting*, Spring 1975, pp. 1-18.

J. Crockett and I. Friend, "Some Estimates of the Cost of Capital to the Electric Utility Industry, 1954-57: Comment," *American Economic Review*, December 1967, pp. 1258-1267.

G. Donaldson, "New Framework for Corporate Debt Capacity," *Harvard Business Review*, (March-April 1962), pp. 117-131.

G. Donaldson, *Strategy for Financial Mobility*, Homewood, Ill.: Richard D. Irwin, 1971.

D. Durand, "The Cost of Debt and Equity Funds for Business: Trends, Problems of Measurement," in *Conference on Research in Business Finance*, New York: National Bureau of Economic Research, 1952.

D. Durand, "The Cost of Capital, Corporation Finance, and the Theory of Investment: Comment," *American Economic Review*, September 1959, pp. 639-654.

M. Gordon, "Some Estimates of the Cost of Capital to the Electric Utility Industry, 1954-57: Comment," *American Economic Review*, December 1967, pp. 1267-1278.

A. Kraus and R. Litzenberger, "A State-Preference Model of Optimal Financial Leverage," *Journal of Finance*, September 1973, pp. 911-922.

P. Kumas, "Growth Stocks and Corporate Capital Structure Theory," *Journal of Finance*, May 1975, pp. 533-547.

B. Lev and D. Pekelman, "A Multiperiod Adjustment Model for the Firm's Capital Structure," *Journal of Finance*, March 1975, pp. 75-91.

W. Lewellen, *The Cost of Capital*, Belmont: Wadsworth Publishing, 1969.

B. Malkiel, *The Debt-Equity Combination of the Firm and the Cost of Capital: An Introductory Analysis*, New York: General Learning Press, 1971.

J. Mao, "The Valuation of Growth Stocks: The Investments Opportunities Approach," *Journal of Finance,* March 1966, pp. 95-102.

M. Miller and F. Modigliani, "Some Estimates of the Cost of Capital to the Electric Utility Industry, 1954-57: Reply," *American Economic Review,* December 1967, pp. 1288-1300.

F. Modigliani and M. Miller, "Corporate Income Taxes and the Cost of Capital: A Correction", *American Economic Review*, June 1963, pp. 433-442.

F. Modigliani and M. Miller, "Some Estimates of the Cost of Capital to the Electric Industry, 1954-57", *American Economic Review*, June 1966, pp. 333-391.

F. Modigliani and M. Miller, "The Cost of Capital, Corporation Finance and the Theory of Investment," *American Economic Review,* June 1958, pp. 261-297.

G. Mumey, *Theory of Financial Structure*, New York: Holt, Rinehart and Winston, 1969.

S. Myers, "The Application of Finance Theory to Public Utility Rate Cases," *Bell Journal of Economics and Management Science*, Spring 1972, pp. 58-97.

J. Porterfield, *Investment Decisions and Capital Costs*, Englewood Cliffs: Prentice-Hall, 1965.

D. Quirin, *The Capital Expenditure Decision*, Homewood, Ill.: Richard D. Irwin, 1967.

A. Robichek and S. Myers, *Optimal Financing Decisions*, Englewood Cliffs: Prentice-Hall, 1965.

A. Robichek, J. McDonald, and R. Higgins, "Some Estimates of the Cost of Capital to the Electric Utility Industry, 1954-57: Comment", *American Economic Review*, December 1967, pp. 1278-1288.

D. Scott, "Evidence on the Importance of Financial Structure," *Financial Management,* Summer 1972, pp. 45-50.

J. Scott, "A Theory of Optimal Capital Structure," *Bell Journal of Economics,* Spring, 1976, pp. 33-54.

E. Solomon, "Measuring a Company's Cost of Capital", *Journal of Business*, October 1955, pp. 240-252.

E. Solomon, *The Theory of Financial Management*, New York: Columbia University Press, 1963.

E. Solomon, "Leverage and the Cost of Capital," *Journal of Finance*, May 1963, pp. 273-279.

J. Stiglitz, "A Re-examination of the Modigliani-Miller Theorem", *American Economic Review*, December 1969, pp. 784-793.

I. Tepper, "Revealed Preference Methods and the Pure Theory of the Cost of Capital", *Journal of Finance*, March, 1973, pp. 35-48.

F. Weston, "A Test of Cost of Capital Propositions", *Southern Economic Journal*, October 1963, pp. 105-112.

R. Wippern, "Financial Structure and the Value of the Firm", *Journal of Finance*, December 1966, pp. 615-634.

PART 4

Short- and Intermediate-Term Sources of Funds

Chapter 15
Major Short-Term Sources of Funds

15-1. INTRODUCTION

As discussed earlier, the external sources of funds available to the firm can be classified in several ways, with by far the most practical approach involving consideration of the time period between the raising of the monies and their final repayment. Thus, short-term financing generally encompasses loans or advances with maturities of one year or less; intermediate-term financing implies maturities from one to ten years; while long-term financing refers to financing that extends beyond ten years or is permanent. Such breakdowns are admittedly somewhat arbitrary, although the sources of funds and the arrangements which are typically involved vary with the terms of financing, making such classification by maturities convenient. In considering long-term sources, the importance of having corporate financial officers who are fully aware of the several alternatives available was noted. A similar grasp of short- and intermediate-term sources, including some feel for their advantages and disadvantages, is also necessary, not simply to permit rational choice within such categories but across the complete range of alternatives as well.

The major sources of short-term credit include the chartered banks and other financial institutions such as credit unions and finance companies of various types, trade creditors, factors, and corporations willing to place their surplus funds into money-market instruments. More sophisticated borrowers may also look to the international money market as a source. The purpose of this chapter is to examine the short-term lending activity of the chartered banks, reviewing certain key sections of the *Bank Act* which regulates banking in Canada, and to consider a few of the other important sources as well. Trade credit, a quite unique source of short-term funds in that it is spontaneously generated through ordinary business activity, is important enough to warrant discussion in a separate chapter.

15-2. THE BANKING SYSTEM

The Canadian banking system has been termed a system of *branch-banking*. It is a system characterized by banks operating on a national basis, with business being conducted through branches scattered right across the country. This is in contrast to the United States situation, where banks are often restricted in the geographical range of their activities, and commonly have to confine themselves to operations in a particular state. Such restricted activity is known as *unit-banking*. The system of branch-banking has some implications for the lending activities of banks. Operating on a national scale, banks typically can maintain a broader and more balanced portfolio of loans, hence are less susceptible to changes in economic conditions in one particular geographic area or in one particular industry. As a consequence, individual branches need not be overly concerned about concentrating their lending in, for example, one particular industry, as on a national scale even such a local concentration of lending activities is likely to have only a minor effect on the overall loan portfolio of the bank. Given the size of the asset base of the five major Canadian banks, it would be virtually impossible for any single industry to account for a significant share of any of these banks' lending. In this context, it is worth noting that the so-called "big five", The Royal Bank of Canada, the Canadian Imperial Bank of Commerce, the Bank of Montreal, the Bank of Nova Scotia, and the Toronto Dominion Bank not only rank among the 50 largest banks in the world, but as of January 31, 1976, controlled about 90 percent of the assets of our chartered banks which totalled almost $110 billions.[1]

The traditional view of banks is that they should be sources of short-term credit, which is a reflection of the fact that over 90 percent of their own liabilities are current and have short maturities. Although a tradeoff must be made between profitability and risk as far as the distribution of bank assets is concerned, it follows that their managements lean toward the granting of short-term loans rather than ones with intermediate or longer maturities because of the increased liquidity afforded by the first category.

Efficiency demands that loan requests be acted upon with reasonable promptness and, to achieve such performance, each branch is granted a discretionary lending limit. Officers of the branch may make loans up to that limit without prior reference to higher authority. The 1964 *Report of the Porter Commission* stated that 90 percent of all acceptable loan requests were approved at the branch level.[2] Should the credit application be beyond a branch's lending limit, a detailed report must then be prepared and forwarded to the divisional office and, if it falls within that level's lending limit, it will be dealt with there. Should the sum requested fall outside divisional authority, the latter's comments will be appended and the application forwarded to the credit department at head office. For very major requests the board of directors may have the final say. The Porter Commission noted that under one percent of credit applications had to be referred back to head office.[3]

Lending by banks, whether over the short or intermediate term, is usually arranged at a rate of interest expressed as some percentage over the *prime business loan rate*. The prime rate in this context is the interest rate charged by the bank to its most credit worthy borrowers. The prime rate is published by the banks, and is adjusted from time to time to reflect changes in economic conditions. It follows that most bank loans are characterized by a variable interest rate which is adjusted periodically to reflect shifts which have taken place in the prime rate.

[1]For greater historical detail, see D. Peters, "Competition and Canada's Banking Structure", *The Banker*, October, 1971, p. 23.

[2]Canada, *1964 Report of the Royal Commission on Banking and Finance*, Ottawa, Queen's Printer, 1964, p. 132.

[3]*Loc. cit.*

Loans secured under sections 82, 86, and 88 of the Bank Act

A large percentage of business loans made by banks are *secured loans*, meaning that the borrower has to pledge some assets as collateral to provide security to the lender in event of default. The types of assets which are acceptable as collateral vary, with regulations as set out in the *Bank Act* having some relevance in this context. One of the important provisions enables the Canadian banks to extend credit to producers on the strength of articles to be produced. This feature, which is now formulated under Section 88, was originally introduced into the *Bank Act* in 1861 to enable banks to take certain inventories as security against business loans. Since the chartered banks occupied a very dominant position in the nineteenth century financial scene, the introduction of such pledge-sections became the means by which the government facilitated access to reasonably priced short-term funds for primary producers. Introduced in 1954, Section 82 of the *Bank Act* has facilitated the development of oil and natural gas production in Canada. This section permits banks to take as security for loans both hydrocarbons in storage and under the ground. Under Section 86, banks are permitted to lend on the security of warehouse receipts or bills of lading covering any goods, wares, or merchandise stored in independent warehouses or under the control of a shipper.

In taking security under any of these statutory sections, a bank must ensure that the requirements of the act are closely followed. For example, to enable a bank under Section 88 to exercise its legal rights over the assets in question, a notice of intention to provide the security must be registered with the Bank of Canada's provincial office. Before time of the first advance, the borrower would be required to complete an application and promise to give security under Section 88. Further, an agreement as to loans and advances would also be signed, with promissory notes provided by the borrower as funds are actually drawn. After the loan is granted, the borrower may be required to complete a statement of security and forward it to the bank. This statement should assist in determining whether or not the firm's business is proceeding satisfactorily. Figure 15-1 is an example of a statement of security under Section 88 of the *Bank Act*.

The ability of the chartered banks to grant loans secured in these ways has developed and advanced efficiency in manufacturing, fishing, farming, and the extractive industries. Though the actual impact of the lending activity of banks is difficult to determine, there is little doubt that various sectors of the economy benefitted significantly from these pledge-sections of the statute. While the more successful firms may in any case have obtained credit without these provisions, the cost even for them would likely have been higher.[4]

[4]The Canadian Bankers' Association, *Submissions to the Royal Commission on Banking and Finance*, Supplement to the *Canadian Banker*, Spring 1963, p. 25.

FIGURE 15-1

L.F. 151 Rev. July 1967.
CAN.
Statement of Security under Section 88 of the Bank Act.
53380 Printed in Canada

To the Manager,
BANK OF MONTREAL ....19..........

....

The undersigned submits the following true statement of products, stock, goods, wares and merchandise and/or grain and the values and locations thereof as at..19..........., assigned by the undersigned to the Bank of Montreal to secure advances made to the undersigned under Section 88 of the Bank Act. The said products, stock, goods, wares and merchandise and/or grain are free from any mortgage, lien or charge thereon (except previous assignments to the Bank, if any, or as stated below).

The wages, salaries or other remuneration owing by the undersigned to persons employed do not now exceed $..............................., of which not exceeding $............................ are in arrears.

Moneys owing to growers of perishable products of agriculture and/or producers of dairy products for such products do not now exceed $................................ (List on reverse side accounts over $7,500.)
(Information in this paragraph required from manufacturers only.)

The undersigned hereby agrees with the Bank of Montreal that should this statement be found to be incorrect in any material particular, then the person for the time being acting as manager of the above-mentioned branch of the Bank, may declare to be due and payable all moneys owing by the undersigned to the Bank and not then due and payable and all bills and notes held by the Bank in respect thereof and not then due and payable, and on such declaration being made, the said moneys and bills and notes shall thereupon become and be due and payable.

N.B.—Description of Products, etc., may be continued on reverse side or on sheets to be attached. LOCATION	QUANTITY AND DESCRIPTION OF PRODUCTS, Etc. (Indicate Grade or Quality)	MARKET PRICE PER BUSHEL, 1,000 FT. OR AS CASE MAY BE	TOTAL MARKET VALUE (OMIT CENTS)
		TOTAL $	

THE FOLLOWING SUMS ARE NOW OWING:—

To the Provincial Government, for:

	TOTAL	DELINQUENT
(a) Personal Property and Income Tax	$......................	$......................
(b) Royalty and/or Stumpage	$......................	$......................
(c) Workmen's Compensation	$......................	$......................

To the Government of Canada, for:

	TOTAL	DELINQUENT
(a) Income Tax	$......................	$......................
(b) Sales Tax	$......................	$......................
(c) Royalty and/or Stumpage	$......................	$......................

Overdue Rental of Premises in which Products, etc., are located..$......................

Overdue Taxes on Property on which Products, etc., are located..$......................
(If customer is tenant, this information is required only if he is assessed for such taxes)

NOTE:—If a customer is a Corporation the Corporate Seal is to be affixed.

....
Customer to sign here

AFFIX SEAL

Lines of credit

Quite simply expressed, a *line of credit* is a stated maximum which a bank may be willing to lend to a customer for a set period of time. Once a line is approved, the borrower may draw on the funds as he needs them, up to the specified limit. Almost all operating loans granted to business are part of a line of credit arrangement. Virtues of the line include that it lets a firm's financial officer know how much bank credit he can expect, that borrowings are limited to amounts actually needed, and that it permits the bank's branch manager to make instant advances up to the maximum amount prescribed without having to process further loan applications. To continue using the line of credit, the business must maintain its credit standing and have fulfilled conditions which have been agreed upon in negotiating the loan. For instance, most lines are granted on the understanding that they will be subject to annual review; in addition, the bank often reserves the right to reduce the negotiated maximum. General credit conditions may precipitate such reductions.

With the 1967 revision of the *Bank Act*, banks are required to disclose the full effective cost of borrowing, which includes interest payments, discounts, and any other charges. Furthermore, *compensating balances*—a requirement which has the borrower maintaining a fixed percentage of a loan as an interest-free deposit—can only be required when expressly agreed to by the borrower. In some circumstances the banks do charge standby fees and require compensating balances, both of which effectively increase the cost of borrowing. Standby fees, tied to the maximum amount authorized, have been introduced to discourage requests by borrowers for lines of credit they are unlikely to require. Such fees may take different forms including a levy against the difference between the line granted and the maximum actually borrowed. One consequence of the charge is that banks find it easier to project their total loans and thereby to effectively manage their resources. In the absence of any standby fee the borrowing firm enjoys the advantage of paying interest on just those funds actually borrowed. Avoiding a standby fee may also have advantages for the bank, since by the absence of such charges, a contractual arrangement is avoided, leaving the bank with increased flexibility in its operations. Table 15-1 shows the amounts outstanding under various lines of credit. It is interesting to note that only about forty percent of authorizations greater than five million dollars appeared drawn down, while in the case of smaller authorizations usage was considerably higher. Also worth noting is the rapid growth of the absolute dollar amounts in the various categories over time, illustrating the increased importance of this source of funds.

TABLE 15-1

Business Loans Authorized and Outstanding Categorized by Size of Authorization (in millions of dollars) as at December 31, 1961, 1966, 1971, and 1975.

Authorized Limit	1961 Auth.	1961 Out.	1966 Auth.	1966 Out.	1971 Auth.	1971 Out.	1975 Auth.	1975 Out.
5 million or more	1480	474	3066	1328	9793	3858	22900	9085
1.0 to 5.0 million	1674	737	2787	1543	4716	2374	9545	5071
Less than 1.0 million	2086	2311	2933	3300	4623	4836	n/a	9054

Source: *Bank of Canada Review*, various issues.

15-3. THE MONEY MARKET

The *money market* comprises the places and institutions where debt instruments with short maturities—sometimes referred to as "near-money"—are traded. Though the definition often relates to securities with maturities under three years, the bulk of activity centers around debt instruments coming due within one year.[5] A limited number of shorter-term instruments which are important for business financing will be reviewed in this section.

The Canadian money market has expanded significantly since its inception in 1954 and, apart from governments, its facilities are used in one way or another by most large financial and nonfinancial corporations.[6] Since 1957, a reasonable market has been provided for the promissory notes of better corporate borrowers. The use of such commercial and finance company paper (discussed below) for many firms has proven to be an increasingly important source of short-term external financing. This fact is reflected in Table 15-2. Since many firms experience seasonality in their cash flows, money-market activity will continue to increase as appreciation of its functions continues to spread.

TABLE 15-2

Estimates of Commercial and Finance Company Paper Outstanding; Selected Years (in millions of dollars)

End of	Commercial Paper Issued in Canadian $	Commercial Paper Issued in Other Currencies	Finance Co. Paper Issued in Canadian $	Finance Co. Paper Issued in Other Currencies
1965	95	2	757	157
1969	633	26	1451	116
1973	1156	75	2356	121
1974	2919	59	2761	189
1975	2938	184	2668	340
March 1976	2745	342	2807	311

Source: *Bank of Canada Review*, May, 1976.

[5] Wood Gundy Securities Limited, *The Canadian Money Market*, 1969, p. 9.

[6] See, for example, J. Wilson, "The Canadian Money Market Experiment," *Banca Nazionale del Lavoro Quarterly Review*, March 1958, pp. 3-38.

Rather than providing for periodic interest payments, money-market instruments commonly sell at a discount from face value. The investor realizes his return at maturity when the borrower redeems the paper at face value. Given the relatively short maturities, it is more convenient to provide for returns in this way rather than by the mailing out of interest cheques or the likes. When such instruments are traded, the discount at which they sell will gradually decrease as the maturity date approaches. The effective yield is simply the discount rate which equates the current market price with future receipt of the face value. However, because of the short maturities, the yield is commonly approximated by prorating the discount on an annual basis.

Example

To illustrate, consider a security with a face value of \$100 which currently trades at \$98 and has 91 days to maturity. By purchasing this paper and holding it to maturity, an investor receives \$2 on an investment of \$98 for three months. The effective annual yield is simply approximated as:

$$\text{effective annual yield} = \frac{\text{discount}}{\text{market price}} \times \frac{365}{\text{days to maturity}}$$

$$= \frac{\$\,2}{\$98} \times \frac{365}{91}$$

$$= 0.0819 \text{ or } 8.19\%$$

More exactly, the effects of compounding will have to be taken into consideration. The interest rate for 91 days is computed as 2/98 = 2.04 percent. Referring back to our discussion in Chapter 4, and compounding over four quarters, the effective annual interest rate r is found from the equation:

$$(1+r) = (1+0.0204)^4 = 1.0841$$

yielding r = 8.41 percent per year.

Commercial and finance company paper

Commercial paper consists of short-term unsecured promissory notes issued mostly by major corporations which are well-known to investors and which enjoy excellent credit reputations.[7] Such debt is sometimes also referred to as *corporate paper*, and excludes the issues of finance companies. The paper may be either interest-bearing, or sold at a discount from face value to provide a particular yield to maturity when it is redeemed at face value. Issued in large denominations, often of not less than \$100,000, the maturities vary from *demand notes* which can be cashed on 24-hour notice, to 365-day paper. By far the most common, however, are 30-, 60-, and 90-day notes.

[7]The following sample of regular borrowers illustrates the point: Bell Canada, DuPont of Canada, Imperial Oil, MacMillan Bloedel, Simpson's Ltd., Steinbergs, and United Grain Growers.

Finance company paper is basically quite similar except that it is usually secured by a pledge of receivables in amounts providing a reasonable margin. The value of receivables pledged typically amounts to anywhere from 112½ percent to 125 percent of the value of paper outstanding. Unsecured finance paper would almost certainly have to be guaranteed unconditionally as to principal and interest by a parent corporation.

To an issuer, corporate paper provides the vehicle for tapping funds in the money market, most often at lower costs than would be faced in borrowing from financial institutions such as the chartered banks. Data on comparative costs are provided in Figure 15-2. However, the borrower's relations with those providing the funds (through the purchase of such paper) are much more impersonal than would be the case in dealing with a bank. This factor should not be overlooked by firms likely to face a credit squeeze. Unfortunately, the value of such bank support in periods of temporary difficulties is hard to assess, making meaningful comparisons between the alternatives of issuing commercial paper or drawing bank loans difficult.

The market generally expects issuers of paper to have bank lines of credit available to cover the dollar value of issues outstanding. Actual access to the market is provided by investment dealers who act as intermediaries in some transactions and as principals in others. Where the dealer does not take title to the paper, commissions of between ⅛ to ¼ of one percent per annum of the face value are charged to the issuer. If a dealer is unable to locate an investor willing to purchase the paper, he may buy such a paper himself and hold it in his own inventory. At a later date, it may be sold to an investor at a price which represents a sufficient return to justify the hold in inventory.

While finance companies use commercial paper as a fairly permanent part of their borrowings, the issuance of commercial paper is most appropriate for the financing of seasonal peaks in receivables and inventories. Commercial paper may also be used to provide flexibility in the timing of longer-term external financing. For instance, a firm in need of longer-term funds may temporarily use short-term paper in anticipation of a drop in long-term interest rates. If such a drop materializes, long-term debt would then be issued, and the short-term liabilities liquidated with the proceeds. As a consequence of recent high interest rates, commercial paper has been built into the debt financing of some utilities and other corporations almost permanently. The risks of such policies are apparent. Not only may longer-term interest rates fail to decline as anticipated, but if money generally becomes tight, or if the issuing corporation should experience business difficulties, the firm may find that access to such short-term funds could dry up, leaving the firm in a most difficult financial position.[8] It follows that short-term borrowers should view commercial paper not as a substitute for longer-term funds, but as an alternative or complement to other

[8]The risks and widespread repercussions of this practice were vividly displayed by the collapse of the Penn Central Transportation Company, the largest railroad in the United States. It immediately started a rush for liquidity and search for quality on the part of investors in money-market instruments, and firms dependent on the market for funds found reluctant lenders. See P. Nadler, "Banking After the Penn Central Collapse", *The Canadian Banker* March/April, 1971, pp. 15-17. Also, R. Murray, "The Penn Central Debacle: Lessons for Financial Analysis", *Journal of Finance*, May 1971, pp. 327-332.

FIGURE 15-2

Key Money Market Rates 1970, 1971, and 1972

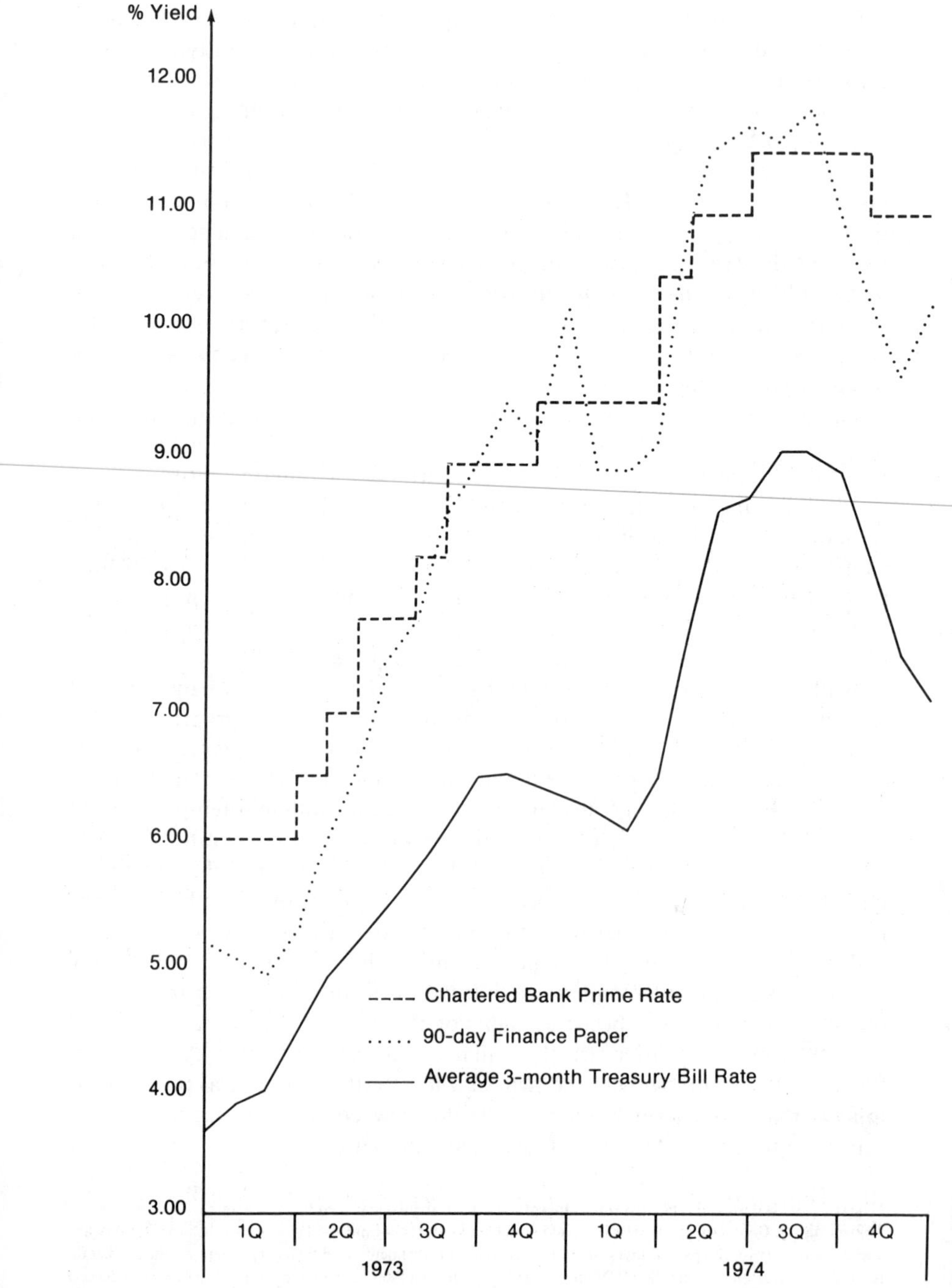

Source: *Bank of Canada Review*, January, 1975.

such sources of short-term funds as bank loans. Choice of the particular source of short-term financing to be relied on will be influenced largely by the relative costs, and to some extent by the more subjective considerations outlined above. Even if commercial paper is not used as a major source of short-term funds, the mere fact that a firm could issue such paper may prove useful in negotiating the terms of a loan; and it may also temper a banker's inclination to resort to compensating balances and other similar devices in periods when money is tight.

It is clear that in order to issue commercial paper, a firm has to be well-known and have a high credit standing. This typically implies that the firm has adequate working capital, effective management, a sound capital structure, and unused bank lines equal to the expected issues of paper. Smaller firms, even if all of the requirements could be met, generally find that they are not well enough known by the investment community for their paper to be accepted, restricting use of such instruments to the larger and better known firms. Once a firm decides to go to the market, and in order to build market acceptance, an *offering memorandum* is prepared with the help of legal counsel and an investment dealer. This memorandum typically consists of:

- the authority to borrow as set out in the corporation's by-laws;
- an indication of the maximum amount of notes authorized to be issued;
- a certificate of incumbency supplying signatures of the signing officers; and
- legal opinion on a variety of points relating to the issue including its suitability for insurance and trust company investment.

While buyers may peruse such offering memoranda carefully, they may also consider various ratings which are published on the quality of commercial paper.[9] Such ratings are largely concerned with the ability of the borrower to meet cash obligations on time. On the Standard and Poor's measure, a rating of A would indicate reasonable liquidity ratios; long-term senior debt which generally enjoys an A rating or better; ready access to alternative sources for borrowings; favorable trends in earnings and cash flows; and the issuing corporation enjoying a sound position in a strong industry. A rating of C, on the other hand, would suggest that the issuer's long-term senior debt is not of investment quality, and further, that there are wide swings in the firm's liquidity ratios.

Increased availability of assistance and advice to investors, and the greater breadth of understanding and sophistication of corporate financial officers should encourage even further growth in the use of commercial and finance company paper. An increasing desire to avoid holding temporary cash surpluses idle should certainly provide added stimulus on the demand side.

Bankers' acceptances

In addition to using corporate paper, a larger corporation may undertake some of its short-term financing through *bankers' acceptances*. Such an instrument is nothing more than a draft, drawn by the firm seeking funds for a specified

[9]B. Harries, "How Corporate Bonds and Commercial Paper are Rated", *Financial Executive*, September 1971, pp. 30-36.

transaction, and providing for payments as at particular dates. The payments are, however, guaranteed by the chartered bank which accepts the draft. Once these securities are countersigned by the bank they are usually purchased by investment dealers and traded in the money market. Table 15-3 provides some estimates on the increased use of bankers' acceptances since their introduction to Canada in 1962.

Bankers' acceptances are issued for periods of between 30 and 90 days and in multiples of $100,000, which is their minimum size. Their eligibility for purchase by the Bank of Canada makes it possible for money-market dealers, who are temporarily short of cash yet holding acceptances in inventory, to either use the instruments as security for day-to-day loans from the chartered banks[10], or to rediscount them at the central bank. The resultant combination of being virtually default free and extremely liquid makes them saleable at quite modest yields or discounts from face value. An issuer must, however, add to such interest costs the charge levied by the chartered banks for the guarantees provided. This acceptance fee ranges between the annual equivalent of one-half of one percent and one percent of face value. Table 15-4 provides some measure of the comparative yield on 30-day bankers' acceptances.

TABLE 15-3

Estimates of Canadian Dollar Bankers' Acceptances
Outstanding: Selected Years
(in millions of dollars)

End of Year	Amount
1962	7
1966	170
1970	395
1973	342
1974	903
1975	1047

Source: *Bank of Canada Review*, May, 1976.

TABLE 15-4

Selected Interest Rates and Yields
as at Dates Indicated, 1972-76

Dates	30-day Bankers' Acceptances	3-month Canada Treasury Bills	90-day Finance Co. Paper	Average Rate on New Demand Loans of Chartered Banks
May 31, 1972	5.50	3.73	5.50	6.28
May 30, 1973	6.05	5.18	6.48	6.95
May 29, 1974	10.75	8.63	11.57	11.32
May 28, 1975	6.88	6.87	7.12	9.45
Mar. 31, 1976	9.93	9.07	9.99	10.27

Source: *Bank of Canada Review*, May, 1976.

[10]To the chartered banks, day loans are a useful vehicle for investing temporarily surplus cash. They are granted to investment dealers in multiples of $100,000 and can be called by either party before noon for settlement that same day. Day loans form part of the banks' secondary reserves.

Securities issued by banks and trust companies

The instruments used by the chartered banks to obtain shorter-term funds from savers include *certificates of deposit, deposit receipts* and *bearer deposit term notes.* Certificates of deposit, or CD's, are nonredeemable, fully registered, transferable, interest-bearing notes with maturities of between 1 and 6 years. Denominations may vary between banks, but will range upward from $5,000. Deposit receipts are transferable term deposits with maturities of between 30 and 364 days. As shown in Figure 15-3, the interest rates on deposit receipts are quite competitive with other money-market instruments, such as finance company paper. The attractiveness of deposit receipts to the lender is further enhanced by their being cashable at any time, subject only to an interest penalty. Bearer deposit term notes are issued in amounts exceeding $100,000 and for fixed maturities of up to 7 years. These securities are also transferable and will sell at discounts from face value to provide the necessary yields.

Competing securities have been issued by trust companies, credit unions, and other financial institutions and labelled deposit receipts, guaranteed investment certificates, and the likes. The instruments of trust companies may have terms as short as 24-hour demand.

Bank *swapped deposits* are a somewhat more complex money-market instrument involving the chartered banks. They comprise a foreign currency short-term deposit purchased by an investor with Canadian dollars. To eliminate foreign exchange risks, a swap or hedge is arranged whereby the purchase of foreign currency necessary for the deposit is combined with a *forward sale*[11] of a like amount of the currency to coincide with the term of the deposit. The use of forward contracts is discussed in more detail in the following section. Yields on such swaps are quoted by banks to include both the deposit rate and effects of the spot purchase and forward sale of foreign exchange. The propensity of investors to purchase swapped deposits hinges on both international short-term interest rate differentials and forward exchange premiums or discounts.

15-4. INTERNATIONAL BORROWING

The international money markets located in such major financial centers as New York, London, Zurich, and Frankfurt, are often frequented by larger corporate borrowers. Short-term loans may be sought in these markets for a variety of reasons. For example, borrowings may be part of a covering or hedging operation involving foreign exchange exposure in accounts receivable.[12] Consider a Canadian exporter with U.K. sales and receivables, part of which are

[11]Movements of short-term funds to take advantage of international interest-rate differentials require a means of protecting against adverse shifts in foreign exchange rates. Purchasing U.S. dollar deposits for a half percentage point above what is available in Canada would make little sense to a corporate financial officer if the U.S. dollar were to depreciate by one percent against the Canadian dollar. In fact, however, this exchange rate risk can be taken care of through a forward exchange contract to sell the foreign currency at some future agreed-to date and at a prearranged price.

[12]We shall use the terms "covering" and "hedging" interchangeably.

FIGURE 15-3

MONEY MARKET RATES

Morning March 14, 1975.

BANK RATE—8¼%

PRIME RATE—9%

TREASURY BILLS

Average Tender Rates

	91 Days	182 Days
Mar. 13/75	6.28%	6.22%
Mar. 6/75	6.28	6.21
Feb. 6/75	6.37	6.39

SELECTED CANADA BONDS DUE WITHIN 3 YEARS

Coupon	Maturity	Market	Yield
5½	Oct. 1, 1975	99.53-.58	6.25
5½	Apr. 1, 1976	99.30-.40	6.08
7	Sept. 1, 1977	101.60-.70	6.25

SHORT TERM NOTES AND DEPOSITS

	30-59 Days %	60-89 Days %	90-179 Days %	180-269 Days %	270-365 Days %
PROVINCIAL BILLS & NOTES	6.40	6.40	6.40-6.25	6.25	6.25
CHARTERED BANK CERTIFICATES OF DEPOSIT	6.25-6.75	6.25-6.75	6.25-6.75	6.25-6.75	6.75-7.00
BANKERS' ACCEPTANCES	6.45	6.45	—	—	—
TRUST COMPANY DEPOSIT RECEIPTS	6.00	6.25	6.50	6.75	6.75
FINANCE COMPANY NOTES (True Yield)					
Associates Acceptance Company	6.78-6.82	6.69-6.73	6.73-6.77	—	—
Builders Financial Co. Limited	6.25	6.37	6.50	6.75	7.00
Chrysler Credit Canada Ltd.	7.16-7.20	7.20-7.25	7.25-7.38	7.38-7.52	7.52-7.67
T. Eaton Acceptance Co. Ltd.	6.64-6.66	—	—	—	—
Ford Motor Credit Company of Canada Limited	6.53-6.57	6.57-6.60	6.47-6.58	6.71-6.82	6.82-7.09
General Motors Acceptance Corporation	6.40-6.44	6.44-6.47	6.60-6.71	6.71-6.82	6.82-6.95
IAC Limited	6.40-6.44	6.44-6.47	6.60-6.71	6.71-6.82	6.82-6.95
International Harvester Credit Corp.	6.78-6.82	6.82-6.86	6.86-6.98	6.98-7.10	7.10-7.23
Laurentide Financial Corporation Limited	6.53-6.57	6.69-6.73	6.73-7.25	7.25-7.38	7.38-7.52
Niagara Finance Company Limited	6.53-6.57	6.57-6.60	6.60-6.84	6.84-6.96	6.96-7.09
Traders Group Limited	6.53-6.57	6.69-6.73	6.73-7.25	7.25-7.38	7.38-7.52
United Dominions Corporation (Canada) Limited	6.75	6.75	6.75	—	—
CORPORATE NOTES					
Bell Canada	6.37	—	—	—	—
Firestone Canada Limited	6.50	6.62	6.62	—	—
Honeywell Holdings Limited	6.50	6.62	6.62	—	—
John Labatt Limited	6.50	—	—	—	—
Lombard Natwest Canada Limited	6.62	6.75	6.75	7.00	7.00
NCR Canada Ltd.	6.75	—	—	—	—
The Royal Trust Company Mortgage Corporation	6.25	6.25	6.50	6.50	6.50
Simpsons-Sears Limited	6.50	6.50	6.50	—	—
TohCan Limited	6.62	6.62	6.75	—	—

A. E. AMES & CO. LIMITED

320 BAY STREET, TORONTO
TELEPHONE 867-4000

denominated in pounds sterling and payable 60 days hence. In the absence of any hedging operation, the sterling receivables represent a foreign exchange risk in that their value in terms of the exporter's domestic currency will be affected by the exchange rate prevailing between the Canadian dollar and pound sterling in two months' time. Actually, however, the Canadian firm could borrow an equivalent amount in sterling with a maturity of 60 days, and immediately convert proceeds of the loan into dollars at the current rate of exchange. Foreign exchange risk is clearly eliminated in the process, with subsequent sterling receipts from the collection of the receivables available to repay the sterling loan. These and other procedures relating to the management of cash and accounts receivable will be detailed in subsequent chapters.

Short-term borrowing may also be undertaken abroad to take advantage of lower interest rates. If, for example, U.S. funds for 3 months were available in New York at the equivalent of 7 percent per annum, while a loan of the same maturity denominated in Canadian dollars and arranged in Toronto would require 12 percent interest, this differential would make foreign borrowing seem more attractive. When, however, a borrower arranges for a loan in a foreign currency, he faces additional risks, namely the possibility of changes in the exchange rate between Canadian and U.S. dollars over the term of the loan. Thus, if during a loan period, the Canadian dollar relative to U.S. currency dropped in value, a Canadian borrower having to repay a loan denominated in U.S. funds would incur added costs in terms of Canadian dollars.

Example

> Consider a Canadian borrower, requiring Cdn. $1,000,000 for a 3-month period, making arrangements for a loan in New York. Assume the above interest-rate differential and a current exchange rate between the two currencies of U.S. $1.00 = Cdn. $0.9706. The amount of the New York loan would, therefore, be $1,000,000/0.9706 = U.S. $1,030,290, while interest charges on that amount at a rate of 7 percent per annum, to be paid at maturity, would total U.S. $1,030,290 × 0.07 × 3/12 = $18,030. If, at the end of the 3-month period, the exchange rate had shifted, with the Canadian and U.S. dollars now trading at par, the borrower would repay the equivalent of $1,048,320 in Canadian funds. This amount on an original loan of Cdn. $1,000,000 implies an effective cost of 4.83 percent over 3 months or 4 × 4.83 = 19.32 percent per annum. Obviously, the unfavorable shift in the exchange rate would more than offset the initial interest differential.

The existence of *forward* currency markets and forward currency contracts permit borrowers to eliminate the foreign exchange risks associated with such transactions. Contracts in forward markets involve the purchase or sale of one currency against another, with delivery and payment to be made at some specified future date. The exchange rate which governs the transaction is set, however, when the contract is first entered into. Thus, a forward contract specifying the purchase of U.S. dollars with Canadian funds, for delivery three months hence, may be quoted at an exchange rate of U.S. $1 = Cdn. $0.9798. Forward market activity is usually confined to dealings in more important currencies and while contracts allowing for various settlement dates can be written, quotations are more readily available for 1-, 2-, 3-, 6- and 12-month contracts. Quotes on rates are available from banks and are frequently given in terms of a premium or discount from the current or spot exchange rate. Table 15-5 provides an illustration of spot and forward rates,[13] and of the notion of premiums or discounts.

TABLE 15-5

Illustrative Foreign Currency Exchange Rates
(Canadian dollars per foreign currency unit)

Spot Rate (S)	1 U.S. $ = Can. $ 0.9706
Forward rate (F)	
1 month forward (*n*)	0.9739
Discount (-) or premium (+) in % per annum*	+4.08
3 month forward	0.9798
Discount or premium in % per annum*	+3.79
6 month forward	0.9857
Discount or premium in % per annum*	+3.11
12 month forward	0.9967
Discount or premium in % per annum*	+2.69

*The formula for converting the forward rate into an annual percentage premium or discount figure is $\frac{F-S}{S} \times \frac{12}{n} \times 100$ with notation as set out in the tabulation, and *n* the number of months of the forward contract.

Example

> Pursuing our earlier example, it is easy to illustrate the role of forward exchange markets in the hedging transaction to eliminate exchange risk from foreign borrowing. At the time the original loan was contracted, and based on rates quoted in Table 15-5, the Canadian borrower could have purchased U.S. dollars for forward delivery 3 months hence at a rate of U.S. $1.00 = Cdn. $0.9798. Then at maturity of the loan, regardless of any changes in the spot rate which may have taken place during the 3-month term of the loan, the borrower would pay Cdn. $1,048,320 × 0.9798 = Cdn. $1,027,144 to liquidate his liabilities. In this way, the loan is free of exchange risk for the borrower, with an effective cost of 2.71 percent over the 3-month period, or 2.71 × 4 = 10.8 percent per annum.

In this context, the premium on the forward rate, which increases foreign borrowing costs, may be viewed as an insurance premium paid to cover against the risk of currency fluctuations during the term of the loan. It should be noted that a relationship generally exists between prevailing interest rates in two currencies and their forward exchange rates. Thus, the currency of a country where lower interest rates prevail will normally sell at a forward premium relative to a currency with a higher interest rate, so that hedging through a forward contract will eliminate at least part of the interest differential. With

[13]Bid and offer prices are available from a bank, but to simplify the discussion no distinction is made here.

higher interest rates in Canada than in the United States, the data in Table 15-5, showing forward premiums on the U.S. dollar illustrates the point.[14]

15-5. FACTORING

Many businesses, particularly smaller firms, may obtain financing from factors who purchase the firm's available accounts receivable outright. In effect, all problems associated with the receivables, such as collecting any balances owed, pass over to the factor. The factor derives his compensation by paying less than the book value on the receivables outstanding. Firms engaged in factoring are generally finance companies or their subsidiaries. Thus, Aetna Factors Corporation Ltd. is part of the Traders Group and the following excerpt from the latter's *1971 Annual Report* is revealing:

> Factoring and accounts receivable financing showed a continued strong growth trend in 1971 as volume reached a record high of $219.9 million, compared with $165.5 million in 1970. . . . The division also benefitted from lower borrowing costs through 1971 which, combined with reduced credit losses, make this portfolio an excellent profit performer and left no question of its preeminent role in factoring in Canada.[15]

Almost all factoring is done on a notification basis, that is, the seller's customers are notified and instructed to remit directly to the factor. This reduces the factor's risk of having the seller make collections on the receivables. The potential loss of customer goodwill as a consequence of the sale of receivables, which forces customers into dealings with a third party, should be kept in mind.

Because the risk of bad debt losses is shifted to the purchaser, the factor takes on the task of making credit checks as well as collections. The savings to a smaller business through curtailment of its own credit and collections function may be significant. It is, in fact, probable that a highly seasonal business may find it relatively uneconomical to maintain its own credit and collections unit and would be attracted by the prospect of dispensing with these functions. Such savings need to be considered when assessing the costs of factoring.

Though factoring is generally not all that much more costly than many other short-term sources, it is not resorted to by some businesses because it may be viewed as evidence of financial weakness. When money is scarce, however, many firms tend to assume more realistic postures and find factoring quite a satisfactory means of financing.

[14]Reasons for this pattern are clear. Because of arbitrage opportunities in free markets, the differential in interest rates on the one hand and the spread between forward and spot rates on the other, would exactly offset each other leaving no room for gain by borrowing abroad on a fully covered basis. If, for example, one-year interest rates in Canada were 12 percent while those in the United States were 10, the forward exchange rate of the Canadian dollar would be driven down by arbitragers who, on investing in Canadian dollars for one year, would sell the same amount forward 12 months at which time their investment would mature. Transactions costs aside, the Canadian dollar's forward discount relative to the U.S. dollar would increase until returns free of exchange risk would be equal in both currencies. In actual fact, however, given such imperfections as exchange controls, capital flow restrictions, differing perceptions of political risk and tax considerations, it may be possible to borrow abroad and save.

[15]Traders Group Limited, *Annual Report 1971*, p. 24.

15-6. SUMMARY

Short-term credit is defined to cover loans or advances with maturities of one year or less. Important sources for such funds are the banking system, money markets, both domestic and international, factoring, and trade credit.

The ability of the chartered banks to take secured loans under various sections of the *Bank Act* has facilitated lending to manufacturing concerns, wholesalers, retailers, farmers, fishermen, and the oil and gas industry at quite reasonable rates of interest. Unsecured loans granted under lines of credit represent another important approach by the banks to providing short-term financing and such lines are of significance to a very wide range of businesses.

The use of money-market instruments such as commercial and finance company paper is quite impersonal when contrasted with borrowing at a bank. Nevertheless, it is being used increasingly by major corporations able to take advantage of this comparatively cheap source of debt financing. The increased sophistication of corporate financial officers and their reluctance to hold temporary cash surpluses idle has stimulated additions to the available range of money-market instruments. Some of the more interesting ones include bankers' acceptances, certificates of deposit, chartered bank and trust company deposit receipts, guaranteed investment certificates, and bank swapped deposits.

Short-term borrowing may be undertaken abroad and, given forward exchange markets with the opportunity for hedging, loans may be arranged which are free of exchange-risks. Typically, the currency of a country where lower interest rates prevail will sell at a forward premium relative to a currency with a higher interest rate, eliminating, at least in part, existing interest-rate differentials on a fully hedged basis.

Factoring or the outright sale of accounts receivable not only provides short-term financing, but also makes possible the shifting of both the risk of bad debts and the credit and collections functions. Factoring may, therefore, prove quite useful to smaller businesses as well as to firms with very seasonal sales.

Questions for Discussion

1. Outline the comparative advantages and disadvantages of using:
   (a) a bank loan,
   (b) commercial paper.
   Why is the use of commercial paper restricted to large, well-known firms?
2. What is factoring? Why might it be advantageous to a firm engaged in a highly seasonal business? Do you see any problem for the user?
3. What is a line of credit? What are some possible costs when a line of credit is granted by a chartered bank? Why might the bank require a standby fee?
4. Why are interest rates on commercial paper usually lower than the rates on bank loans? Why might firms still use bank credit even though interest rates are lower on the commercial paper?
5. What is a forward market? Why is this market important when considering foreign borrowings?

6. From recent issues of the Financial Post, obtain the yields for finance company paper, commercial paper, bankers' acceptances, and Canada treasury bills. Are there differences in the yields? Why?
7. Why and in what ways does a well developed and efficient money market contribute to greater efficiency in the economy?
8. Why are interest rates on bank loans typically variable?

Problems with Solutions

1. A short-term note with a face value of $10,000 and a maturity of 15 days sells for $9,971. What is its effective yield? Compute using the approximation and the exact formula as discussed in the chapter.

Solution

Approximation:

$$\frac{\$29}{\$9971} \times \frac{365}{15} = 0.0708 \simeq 7.1\%$$

Exact Solution:

interest per 15-day period $= \frac{\$29}{\$9971} \times 100\% = 0.2908\%$

number of compounding periods $= \frac{365}{15} = 24.33$

$(1 + r) = (1 + 0.002908)^{24.33}$ $= 1.0732$

effective annual interest rate r $= 7.32\%$

2. On a one-year loan of $1,000, a bank charges an interest rate of 10 percent. In addition, the bank charges an application fee of $30 to cover processing expenses. What is the effective cost (computed as an annual rate) being paid by the borrower?

Solution

The borrower only receives a net amount of $970, and pays interest of 10% on $1,000, or $100 per year. Therefore, the effective cost on the $970 received becomes:

$$\frac{\$100}{\$970} \times 100\% = 10.31 \text{ percent}$$

3. A Canadian borrower in need of short-term funds is asked to quote on the maximum interest rate he would be willing to pay on a loan of 10 million German marks (DM) available for 3 months. The following data are relevant:

3-month forward rate on the German mark	Cdn. $0.4040
Spot rate on the German mark	Cdn. $0.3990
3-month borrowing rate in Canada	12% per annum

Assuming he wishes to quote realistically while avoiding foreign exchange exposure, what interest rate could the potential borrower bid?

Solution

DM 10,000,000 is the equivalent of Cdn. $3,990,000 which could be borrowed in Canada at interest of $3,990,000 × 12/100 × 3/12 = Cdn. $119,700. It follows that on DM 10,000,000, he could pay *I*% interest for 3 months, buy the necessary DM 3 months forward at $0.4040, while holding total outflows to $119,700 plus the principal repayment of $3,990,000.

Thus $[10{,}000{,}000 + 10{,}000{,}000 \times I/100 \times 3/12]0.4040 = 119{,}700 + 3{,}990{,}000$

$$10{,}100I = 69{,}700$$
$$I = 6.90\%$$

Transactions costs aside, 6.90% would be the maximum bid *i.e.* the point of indifference. If borrowing in German marks is available at an interest rate of less than 6.90%, this alternative is preferred to domestic borrowing in Canada.

Additional Problems

1. A short-term note with a face value of $25,000 and a maturity of 30 days sells for $24,865. What is its effective yield? Compute using the approximation and the exact formula as discussed in the chapter.
2. A firm with $600,000 of receivables outstanding on average, is considering the factoring of its receivables. The factor would charge interest of 6 percent per annum on the receivables outstanding net of commission charges, and would also charge a commission of 3 percent. These commission charges are deducted from each advance. If receivables turn over 6 times a year, find:
   (a) The amount received by factoring receivables during the year.
   (b) the effective cost (computed as an annual rate) being charged by the factor.
3. The financial vice-president of Poker Ltd., Ms. Gose, is exploring the possibility of borrowing English pounds to finance short-term needs for the next 6 months. A lender has been found who would lend 2,000,000 pounds sterling. If the 6-month forward rate for English pounds is $1.9294 and the current spot rate is $1.9032, what is the maximum interest rate Ms. Gose would be willing to pay? The 6-month borrowing rate in Canada for Poker is 11 percent.

Selected References

E. Addison, "Factoring: A Case History", *Financial Executive*, November 1963, pp. 32-33.

R. Anstie, "The Historical Development of Pledge Lending in Canada", *The Canadian Banker*, Summer 1967, pp. 81-90.

N. Baxter and H. Shapiro, "Compensating Balance Requirements: The Results of a Survey", *Journal of Finance*, September 1964, pp. 483-496.

Canada, *1964 Report of the Royal Commission on Banking and Finance*, Ottawa: Queen's Printer, 1964.

Canadian Bankers' Association, "Banking in the Sixties—A Statistical Review", *CBA Bulletin*, June 1969.

Canadian Bankers' Association, "Bank Profits: The Changing Mix", *CBA Bulletin*, May 1971.

Canadian Bankers' Association, "Current Banking Statistics: Midsummer 1971", *CBA Bulletin*, August 1971.

Canadian Bankers' Association, "Government Guaranteed Loans: Supplement to Normal Bank Credit", *CBA Bulletin*, November 1970.

Canadian Bankers' Association, "The Growth of Banking—Some Statistical Highlights", *CBA Bulletin*, August 1968.

Canadian Bankers' Association, *Submissions to the Royal Commission on Banking and Finance*, Supplement to the *Canadian Banker*, Spring 1963.

First National City Bank, *Corporate Foreign Exposure Management*, New York, 1975.

W. Fulton, "Farm Credit Under the Microscope", *The Canadian Banker*, May-June 1969, pp. 15-20.

B. Harries, "How Corporate Bonds and Commercial Paper are Rated," *Financial Executive*, September 1971, pp. 30-36.

F. Johnson, "Financing Small Business", *The Canadian Banker*, February 1971, pp. 13-15.

J. Little, *Euro-Dollars: The Money Market Gypsies*, New York: Harper and Row, 1975.

R. Murray, "The Penn Central Debacle: Lessons for Financial Analysis", *Journal of Finance*, May 1971, pp. 327-332.

P. Nadler, "Banking After the Penn Central Collapse", *The Canadian Banker*, March-April, 1971, pp. 15-17.

P. Nadler, "Compensating Balances and the Prime at Twilight", *Harvard Business Review*, January-February, 1972, pp. 112-130.

E. Neufeld, "Canadian Financial Intermediaries", *The Canadian Banker*, Spring 1967, pp. 143-150.

D. Peters, "Competition and Canada's Banking Structure", *The Banker*, October 1971, p. 23.

F. Shadrack, "Demand and Supply in the Commercial Paper Market", *Journal of Finance*, September 1970, pp. 837-852.

B. Stone, "The Cost of Bank Loans", *Journal of Financial and Quantitative Analysis*, December, 1972, pp. 2077-2086.

R. Styles, "Export Development Corporation", *The Canadian Banker*, September-October 1969, pp. 16-20.

J. Wilson, "The Canadian Money Market Experiment", *Banca Nazionale del Lavoro Quarterly Review*, March 1958, pp. 3-38.

Wood Gundy Securities Ltd., *The Canadian Money Market*, 1969.

Chapter 16
Trade Credit

16-1. INTRODUCTION

An examination of the various types of short-term financing which Canadian business relies on would identify trade credit as the most significant single source in terms of volume. Trade credit is the financing extended by a supplier to his customers when allowing payment for goods or services to be made some time after delivery. Such credit will show on the buyer's books as accounts payable. This chapter focuses on various aspects of the management of such accounts payable including the use of trade credit, the several forms in which it is available, the terms offered, and the costs entailed by its use.

16-2. THE USE OF TRADE CREDIT

One of the more significant characteristics of trade credit from the buyer's point of view is that, when required, it arises *spontaneously*. For example, standard payment procedures in an industry may call for payment of the invoiced amount 30 days after receipt of the goods. A purchaser receiving $15,000 worth of merchandise would, in fact, automatically receive a credit of $15,000 for 30 days from his supplier. Where repeated purchases are made, such credit may essentially become a permanent source of financing.

As the volume of business and therefore the purchase of supplies increases or decreases, so too does the amount of trade credit generated. To illustrate, where a firm buys $15,000 into inventory every 15 days with payment due 30 days after receipt of the goods, it will at any given time have approximately $30,000 in accounts payable. This is shown in Figure 16-1. Should business expand and require a 20 percent increase in inventory purchases, it is easy to see that trade credit will increase spontaneously, thus adding another $6,000 to the accounts payable. This becomes particularly important in an inflationary setting like the one recently experienced, which implies just such increases in the dollar volumes of purchases made by business. In the presence of price level changes, even constant physical operations will require increasing dollar values of inventories and purchases. Such increases have been financed, at least in part, through corresponding increases in trade credit and accounts payable.

From balance sheet information for 1971, trade credit in use by all Canadian corporations totalled some 16.1 billion dollars. By way of comparison, bank loans amounted to only 10.1 billion dollars.[1] As shown in Table 16-1, the use of trade credit as a source of new funds has grown significantly in recent years. In part, this growth has been caused by inflation. Given general price level in-

[1]Statistics Canada, *Corporation Financial Statistics, 1971*, Ottawa: Queen's Printer, October 1974, p. 53.

creases, the dollar amounts of purchases made by businesses must increase, even if physical volumes were to remain constant. Such increases in the dollar volume of purchases are reflected in corresponding increases in trade credit.

FIGURE 16-1

Example Illustrating the Financing of Inventories through Trade Credit

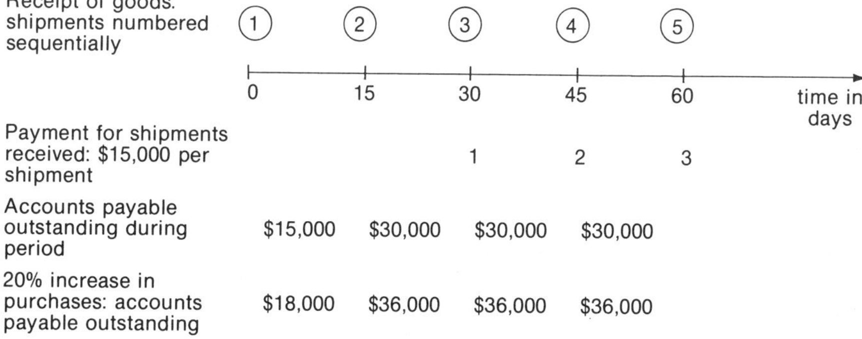

TABLE 16-1

Trade Credit as a Source of New Funds, Canadian Nonfinancial Corporations, 1972-74.

	Increase in Millions of $	% of All Short-Term Sources of Funds
1972	1,680	49.6
1973	2,322	50.0
1974	4,857	55.7

Source: Statistics Canada, *System of National Accounts, Financial Flow Accounts*, various issues.

One of the chief reasons for the wide use of trade credit is its convenience to both suppliers and purchasers, with a minimum of red tape involved. Once the account has been accepted by the seller, where the buyer maintains his credit standing, trade credit becomes a continuing source of financing. There are no negotiations to be entered into or detailed forms to be filled out as subsequent orders are placed. Furthermore, trade credit, in contrast to many alternative sources, is generally unsecured. Consequently, assets suitable for collateral purposes remain unattached, thereby adding to the flexibility afforded the debtor corporation's management.

Trade credit generally remains available when, in periods of monetary constraint, funds from other sources, including financial institutions, become scarce. Suppliers usually operate with reasonable markups and, in addition, may be anxious to cultivate and maintain reliable outlets for their products. Underutilization of plant and equipment can be costly, and it follows that suppliers may have to assume greater risks than do the financial institutions. Also, competition may well determine the credit terms to be offered.

One relevant aspect of trade credit is its wider use by the smaller concern. This reliance is quite understandable since such firms have more limited access to financial markets even under most favorable economic conditions[2] and then only at higher cost. The effects of tight-money policies which tend to place a particularly heavy burden on small business simply compound the problem.[3]

16-3. TYPES OF TRADE CREDIT

Open account

Today's most frequently used type of trade credit is the *open account*. It is also the most informal arrangement, with no precise evidencing of the amount owed. Once the seller accepts the account, he merely fills the buyer's order and sends out a dated invoice indicating the items forwarded under the order, their price, and the credit terms. The supplier's evidence of the credit extended essentially consists of his book entries and the purchase and shipping orders. The wide use of open account trade credit is an indication of the degree of confidence and trust which prevails between firms doing business in a developed economy.

Promissory note

In certain lines of business, especially those like jewelry wholesaling which involve higher cost items, suppliers frequently request formal evidence of indebtedness from the buyer. Formal evidence may also be asked for when a customer's credit worthiness no longer warrants selling on an open account basis and amounts are still outstanding. One satisfactory vehicle for formalizing the credit arrangement is the *promissory note* which provides a written commitment to pay a stated obligation no later than a specified date. In situtations where an open account becomes past due and the customer requests an extension, the seller may insist on a promissory note so as to formalize the claim.

Trade acceptance

Formal acknowledgment of the debt can also take the form of a *trade acceptance*. Under this form of trade credit, the supplier prepares a draft drawn on the buyer requiring payment of the invoiced amount by a particular date. The draft is then signed as accepted by the buyer and only then are the goods turned over. The signed draft, now a trade acceptance, may be held by the seller until the due date, appearing on the balance sheet as a note receivable. It could also be sold at a discount to a finance company, for example. The actual marketability of the trade acceptance will be determined largely by the signer's credit-standing.

Since at maturity the acceptance is presented for payment at the debtor's bank, an inability to meet the obligation would very quickly and significantly impair the debtor's credit-standing. It follows, therefore, that this form of trade credit can be most attractive to suppliers facing difficulties in credit dealings with certain of their customers.

[2]The authors' views differ with those of the Porter Commission which held that "there has not been a wide gap in Canadian financing facilities for small business... short-term lending facilities appear to have been adequate." Canada, *1964 Report of the Royal Commission on Banking and Finance*, Ottawa: Queen's Printer, 1964, p. 45.
[3]Interestingly enough, the Porter Commission shared this view despite its previously cited judgment. *Ibid.*, p. 474.

16-4. SELLING TERMS

The relative importance of the open account type of trade credit has already been noted, leaving the various terms of sale used in conjunction with this type of credit to be looked at.

Selling terms can be classified by the timing of called-for payments and the discount provisions afforded. *Cash discounts* are often offered by suppliers to induce customers to make prompt payments. When offered, the actual size of the cash discount is expressed as a percentage of the invoice price. A discount period is also set out designating the brief time span within which the invoice must be paid so as to qualify for the reduction. Such cash discounts offered in this context of trade credit must not, however, be confused with either quantity or trade discounts.

Cash before delivery

Terms of *cash before delivery*, or C.B.D.[4], involve no credit or discount whatsoever. While such terms may reflect uncertainty about the buyer's credit-standing, poor credit worthiness need not be implied. The sale may not have warranted the expense of credit analysis or perhaps there were serious time constraints involved. In any case, the arrangement virtually relieves the seller of any risk.

Cash on delivery

Under terms of *cash on delivery*, or C.O.D., the seller requires payment before the buyer takes possession of the goods. Since under this arrangement shipment precedes payment, the supplier faces the risk of a possible refusal of the goods by the purchaser, and perhaps having to absorb transportation and handling charges.

Credit periods with and without cash discounts

The extension of credit for a particular period with no cash discount can be set out in several ways. Terms of *net 45*, for example, indicate a credit period of forty-five days from the date of invoice, while terms of *net/10 EOM* call for payment ten days following the end of the month.

In some industries, the more usual terms of trade credit comprise a percentage cash discount, a discount period, and a credit period. Thus, terms of *2/10, net 30*, are quite common. Such terms provide for a two percent discount where payment is made within ten days but call for payment of the full invoiced amount within thirty days in any case. Terms of *2/10 EOM, net/30*, may exist in situations where a buyer places frequent orders. The discount period extends to ten days following the end of the month in which the purchase is made, with full payment due 30 days after the end of the month. Such terms allow the buyer to make one payment for all orders placed within a single month without foregoing any discounts. Under such an arrangement, the actual length of both discount and credit periods depends upon the exact timing of purchases, with both periods being larger for purchases made toward the first part of the month.

[4]Not to be confused with progress payments required in certain lines of manufacturing.

Datings

Manufacturers of products for which there is a seasonal demand, snow skis for example, often encounter problems in forecasting sales and therefore in establishing production schedules. To minimize the difficulty, attempts may be made to stimulate orders during the off-season by means of seasonal datings. Thus, during the summer months, the ski manufacturer may offer terms of net/30 November 1, indicating that payment on the goods will not be required until 30 days after November 1, or November 30th. While the supplier has to finance the cost of the skis during this period, sales may become more predictable, with production problems and storage costs minimized, and shipping bottlenecks reduced. Hence, seasonal datings can be advantageous to all parties concerned.

16-5. THE COST OF TRADE CREDIT

Trade credit is often thought of as a "free" source of funds, with no costs being incurred. This is generally an oversimplification. Even setting aside the effects of cash discounts, some indirect costs may have to be considered. For instance, the granting of credit terms represents a cost to the supplier. Where competitive forces permit, the supplier may attempt to pass on the cost of extending credit to the purchaser in the form of higher selling prices.

When cash discounts being offered are not taken, additional explicit costs are incurred and these may be substantial.

Example

Assume that selling terms specify 2/10, net 30, thus offering a cash discount if payment is made within ten days from receipt of the invoice. Consider an invoice amount of $100. The choice for the purchaser is to either pay $98 by the tenth day, or to pay the full $100 at the end of 30 days. The cost of not taking the discount is payment of an additional $2, and the benefit is to have the use of $98 for an additional 20 days. This is illustrated in Figure 16-2. In comparing the cost of foregoing the discount with the costs of alternative sources of funds, such as a bank loan, it is useful to derive the effective annual interest rate implied in foregoing the cash discount. In paying $2 to obtain the use of $98 for 20 days, it is easy to see that the interest paid during this 20 day period is $2/$98, or 2.04 percent. On an annual basis, such cost would be incurred 365/20 = 18.25 times a year. Hence, the implied annual interest rate of foregoing the cash discount becomes

$$\frac{2}{98} \times \frac{365}{20} = 37.2 \text{ percent}$$

Note that this interest rate represents a before-tax figure. By foregoing the discount, the firm increases its expenses and, hence, reduces its taxable income and its tax liability. If the firm's tax rate was $T = 40$ percent, the after-tax annual interest rate of foregoing the cash discount would become $(1 - T)\ 37.2\% = 0.6 \times 37.2\% = 22.32$ percent.

As can been seen, the costs of foregoing cash discounts can be significant, and the rates implied when not taking discounts are generally so high that borrowing from other sources, where available, is indicated. Nevertheless, when a business experiences an acute cash shortage and has exploited its other sources of financing to the limit, increasing its accounts payable by not taking discounts may prove to be the only alternative available to generate badly needed additional funds.

FIGURE 16-2

Costs of Foregoing Cash Discounts

Assumed terms: 2/10, net 30

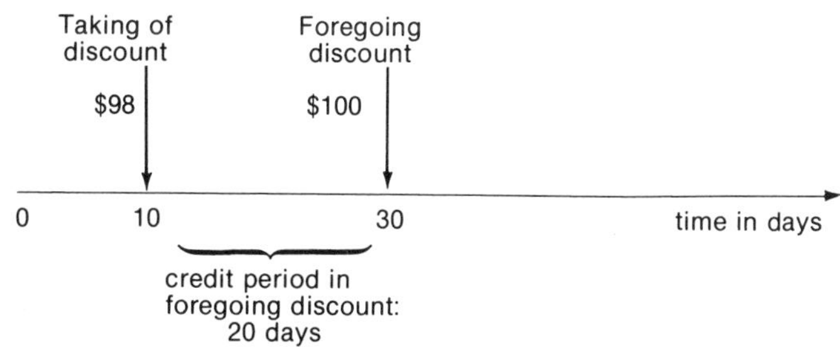

Costs of Foregoing discount: $\frac{2}{98} \times \frac{365}{20} = 37.2\%$

16-6. THE MANAGEMENT OF ACCOUNTS PAYABLE

Besides simply recognizing the convenience of drawing on trade credit, the financial officer should give consideration to the efficient management of accounts payable. For instance, the time value of money would suggest payment at the latest time specified. Once a discount has been missed, payment should then be made at the end of the credit period. The basis for this position can quite readily be illustrated by once again considering terms of 2/10, net 30. Foregoing the discount and making payment on the 15th day gives the firm the use of funds ($98) for just an additional 5 days. This indicates a significant increase in the annual percentage cost to

$$\frac{2}{98} \times \frac{365}{5} = 149.0 \text{ percent.}$$

It should be clear from this example that the cost of not taking discounts decreases the longer payments are delayed. This raises questions about stretching payables beyond the credit period. To pursue our example, if payment were made 60 days after receipt of the invoice, the implied annual cost of foregoing the discount would be reduced to $(2/98)(365/50) = 14.9$ percent. While suppliers may be reluctant to force payment by the end of the period, the long-run costs of such stretching should not be overlooked. A history of late payments is viewed as a weakness by credit analysts and the buyer's credit-standing could become impaired. Given temporary financial difficulties, however, it may be possible to negotiate with the supplier about stretching the credit period. In such circumstances, a straightforward approach with full disclosure of the situation involved will generally provide the best results.

Where international transactions are involved, the currency in which an invoice is denominated may become of concern. Consider a Canadian purchaser who receives goods from an American supplier and draws on trade credit, implying delayed payments. If the invoice is denominated in U.S. dollars, such a purchase would entail foreign exchange risk, as any shift in the value of the Canadian dollar in relation to the U.S. dollar during the credit period would affect the amount of the payment ultimately to be made. In order to determine the impact of such foreign exchange risk on the overall operations of the firm, it has to be viewed in relation to the firm's other assets and liabilities which are denominated in foreign currencies. Such foreign exchange exposure, which can be particularly significant given flexible exchange rates, will be discussed in more detail in a later section of this book which deals with the management of working capital.

16-7. SUMMARY

By volume, trade credit is the most important source of short-term funds for Canadian business. It arises spontaneously with the purchase of goods if payment is called for sometime after delivery. Given the same credit terms, the volume of trade credit increases automatically with the dollar volume of purchases. This is important in an inflationary setting, as trade credit is used to finance, at least in part, increases in the dollar volumes of purchases brought about by price level changes.

Trade credit can take on several forms, the most common one being the open account. More formal acknowledgments of debt are provided if promissory notes or trade acceptances are resorted to.

Credit terms also vary, and can be classified by the timing of called-for payments and the discount provisions afforded. Terms specifying cash before delivery (C.B.D.) or cash on delivery (C.O.D.) do not involve the granting of credit by the supplier. Datings are commonly used in highly seasonal industries and provide for delayed payments to stimulate sales during off-season periods.

Granting of trade credit represents a cost to the supplier. This cost is likely to be reflected in his prices, implying that trade credit may not be a "free good". Where cash discounts are foregone, the cost of doing so can be computed and is most conveniently expressed as an equivalent annual interest rate. Foregoing cash discounts is generally expensive, and where other sources of funds such as a bank loan are available, these are typically less costly.

In managing accounts payable, care should be taken that payments are made towards the end of either the discount or the credit period in order to take full advantage of the availability of such funds. Where invoices are denominated in foreign currencies, the purchaser may be subject to foreign exchange risk. Such risk should be dealt with as part of the firm's overall management of its foreign exchange exposure.

Questions for Discussion

1. The availability of trade credit is said to be more important for a small firm than for a large firm. Discuss.
2. A large supplier is contemplating changing the terms offered to its customers. At present, the terms are net 30 days. The new proposal is to offer a 2 percent discount for payment within 10 days, or the balance due within 60 days. What effects might such a proposal have on both the supplier's and the purchaser's cash flows?
3. Some firms attempt to stretch their payables in order to reduce the cost of financing their short-term credit needs. Discuss some of the adverse effects such a practice could have on the firm.
4. Some firms offer a greater percentage cash discount than do other firms. Discuss what factors may affect the level of discount to be offered.
5. The comptroller of a local company stated that while he realized it was expensive to forego the trade discount, he did so because of a lack of funds. The firm's main cash inflow from receivables occurred about one week after the end of the payables' discount period. The comptroller disbursed the funds for the payables as soon as the cash position of the firm allowed. The firm generally paid all its invoices within 20 days of receipt despite the fact that terms of 2/10, n/30 were allowed. What recommendations would you make with regard to this area of the company's operations?

Problems with Solutions

1. Assume the terms of payment are given as 2/10, net 30. Demonstrate that the annual interest rate implied in not taking the cash discount is independent of the amount of the invoice.

Solution

Call the amount of the invoice X. The choice is between paying $X - 0.02X = 0.98X$ after 10 days, or X after 30 days. According to the chapter, the effective annual interest rate is computed as

$$\frac{0.02X}{0.98X} \times \frac{365}{20} = \frac{0.02}{0.98} \times \frac{365}{20} = 37.2\%$$

with the amount of the invoice cancelling out of the equation.

2. Given terms of 2/10, net 30, compute the cost of not taking the discount as a function of the time of payment. Provide a graph illustrating the nature of this relationship. Assume no penalties are associated with late payments.

Solution

Call the number of days after receipt of the invoice until payment is made t. The cost of not taking the discount becomes

$$\frac{2}{98} \times \frac{365}{(t - 10)}$$

For selected values of t, we obtain:

t (in days)	annual cost of not taking discount (in percent)
10	∞
15	148.98
20	74.49
30	37.24
60	14.90
90	9.31
120	6.77
360	2.13
∞	0

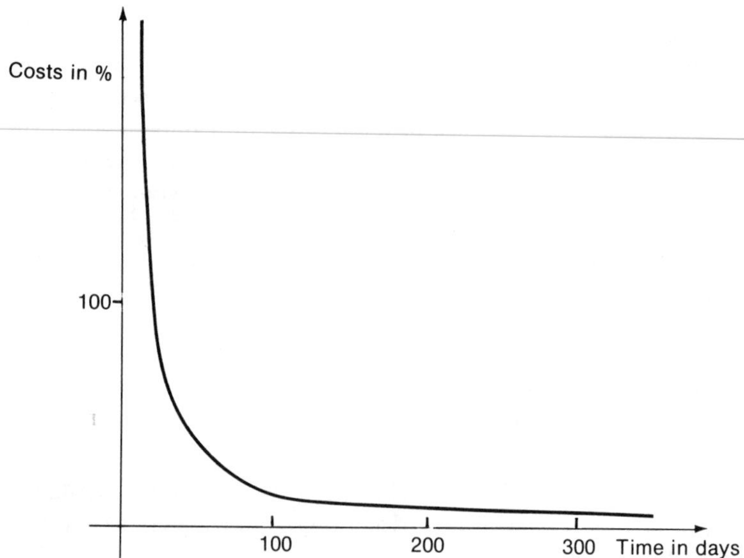

3. Compute the effective annual cost of not taking the discount if the terms of payment are 1/15 EOM, net 60.

Solution

A one percent discount is available if payment is made within 15 days after the end of the month. Otherwise, full payment is called for within 60 days from the end of the month. Thus, if the discount is not taken, funds are available for an additional (60 – 15) = 45 days. The effective annual cost becomes

$$\frac{1}{99} \times \frac{365}{45} = 8.19 \text{ percent}$$

4. Terms of trade credit are 2/10, net 90. You have a partially unused line of credit with the bank on which you can draw money at an interest rate of 10 percent (before-tax). Rank the following 3 alternative actions regarding payment in order of their desirability.

payment on 10th day
payment after 60 days
payment after 90 days

Also show the relevant implied annual interest rates for monies used in each of the cases indicated.

Solution

Costs of not taking discount and paying after 60 days:

$$\frac{2}{98} \times \frac{365}{50} = 14.90\%$$

Costs of not taking discount and paying after 90 days:

$$\frac{2}{98} \times \frac{365}{80} = 9.31\%$$

Where the cash discount is taken and payment is made on the 10th day, financing for such payment can be viewed as coming from the line of credit at 10 percent. Since payment after 90 days implies an interest rate which is lower than what is currently being paid for funds drawn from a line of credit (10 percent interest), it does not pay to take the discount. Funds which can be obtained through drawing on trade credit (at 9.31 percent) can be used to reduce the balance owing to the bank, saving 10 percent in interest. On the other hand, payment after 60 days is clearly not attractive. Thus, the ranking becomes:

most desirable:	payment after 90 days
second choice:	payment on 10th day
least desirable:	payment after 60 days

Note that all the above calculations were made on a before-tax basis. The effect of taxes would be to reduce the costs under each alternative by a factor $(1 - T)$, where T is the corporate tax rate. Clearly, the relative rankings of the three alternatives are left unaltered if each of them is multiplied by the same factor $(1 - T)$.

Additional Problems

1. Calculate the implied annual interest cost of not taking the discount, where the selling terms are:
(a) 1/10, n/20 (b) 2/10EOM, n/60 (c) 2/10, n/20
(d) 2/10, n/40 (e) 1/10, n/40

2. The Nufit Shoe Company is experiencing a temporary shortage of funds. The treasurer has suggested two ways by which funds can be raised. Firstly, the company could forego the trade discounts it has been taking and pay the invoices at the end of the period. At present, terms of 2/20, n/60 are received from the firm's suppliers. Secondly, the company could borrow funds from the local bank at an interest rate of 10 percent. Which alternative should be chosen?
3. Terms of trade credit are 3/10, net 120. You have a partially unused line of credit with the bank on which you can draw money at an interest rate of 12 percent. Rank the following 3 alternative actions regarding payment in order of their desirability. Also show the relevant implied annual interest rates for monies used in each of the cases indicated.

   payment on 10th day

   payment after 60 days

   payment after 120 days
4. a) Two different suppliers offer the same product. Supplier A's price is \$1000 with terms of payment 1/10, net 30. Supplier B offers the same product at a price of \$1005 with terms of net 60. You have a partially used line of credit with the local bank at 13 percent annual interest. From which suplier would you purchase?

   b) A third supplier offers the same product C.O.D. What would his price have to be for you to consider purchasing from him?

Selected References

J. Brosky, *The Implicit Cost of Trade Credit and Theory of Optimal Terms of Sale*, New York: Credit Research Foundation, 1969.

J. Coates, "Trade Credit: A Case-Study", *Journal of Industrial Economics*, June, 1965, pp. 205-213.

J. Mao, *Quantitative Analysis of Financial Decisions*. New York: The Macmillan Company, 1969, chapter 13.

T. Mayer, "Trade Credit and the Discriminatory Effects of Monetary Policy", *National Banking Review*, June, 1966, pp. 543-545.

A. Meltzer, "Mercantile Credit, Monetary Policy and the Size of Firms", *Review of Economics and Statistics*, November, 1966, pp. 429-437.

A. Reinhardt, "Economics of Mercantile Credit: A Study in Methodology", *Review of Economics and Statistics*, November, 1957, pp. 463-467.

A. Robichek, D. Teichroew, and J. Jones, "Optimal Short Term Financing Decisions," *Management Science*, September, 1965, pp. 1-36.

R. Schwartz, "An Economic Analysis of Trade Credit," *Journal of Financial and Quantitative Analysis*, September, 1974, pp. 643-658.

W. White, "Trade Credit and Monetary Policy: A Reconciliation", *Economic Journal*, December, 1964, pp. 935-946.

Chapter 17
Intermediate-Term Sources of Funds

17-1. INTRODUCTION

An intermediate-term loan is held to be one which is repayable anywhere between one and ten years' time, but such a classification is admittedly arbitrary. Resort to these somewhat longer maturities makes sense in situations in which the need for funds is more permanent than is the case, for example, with cash shortages occasioned by seasonal fluctuations or similar phenomena. Also, small- and medium-sized businesses may find it difficult, if not impossible, to secure long-term debt financing in the capital markets. Investors may be unreceptive to issues of firms which are not well-known, with the consequence that both interest costs and underwriting expenses could become prohibitively high. Consequently, for such firms, term loans may be the only sensible alternative to including debt into their capital structure.

Sources of intermediate-term financing may be divided into two broad categories, namely private financial institutions including banks, and agencies set up and sponsored by various levels of government. We will review each of these groupings in turn.

You may well ask why governments have assumed such active roles in setting up various programs and agencies to provide intermediate-term sources of funds to business, rather than simply leaving it for the forces in the marketplace to determine the allocation of funds to various lenders. Two reasons may be given. For one, governments may view such agencies as a vehicle for the achieving of social objectives which may not be strictly economical. For instance, such agencies may be used to subsidize certain endeavors which are deemed to be socially desirable, even if they do not result in the greatest economic efficiency. Incentives to locate industries in depressed areas characterized by high unemployment, or direct and indirect subsidies to small business are examples of such thinking. Under certain circumstances, government agencies and programs may be viewed as complementing offerings available from private institutions, and many government agencies in fact do stipulate that borrowers will only qualify as clients if comparable loans could not be obtained elsewhere under reasonable terms. In other words, they play the role of "lenders of last resort". Secondly, government agencies, on occasion, have also taken it upon themselves to compete directly with private institutions. The rationale for such action typically is to be found in charges of monopoly power and/or excessive profits by private institutions, with the government claiming that it can provide better service at more reasonable rates. Sometimes it is also claimed that private financial institutions neglect certain geographical areas, with local governments stepping in to protect the interests of their constituents. Needless to say, arguments such as these are subject to considerable discussion, with different parties taking quite different positions in the debate, depending on the interests and political philosophies involved.

Without discussing details in this chapter, we also note that at the international level many countries, developing countries in particular, have set up incentive programs and/or special agencies for the purpose of attracting industries. A wide variety of programs and services are offered, ranging from financing arrangements to special tax concessions. In many instances, host country governments will offer to become partners in industrial ventures. Competition between countries vying for foreign investment capital has led, on occasion, to undercutting and hence to offering terms which are so favorable to the investor that benefits to the host country are questionable. Interestingly enough, in some geographical areas, countries have started to cooperate in drafting uniform terms for incentives in order to reduce damaging competition.

17-2. PRIVATE FINANCIAL INSTITUTIONS

A variety of private financial institutions are active in providing intermediate-term financing to Canadian businesses. Some of them may also take equity positions in their clients' companies alongside the loans they have granted. The chartered banks have recently emerged as one of the most important sources for term funds, both to the business and personal sectors of our economy. Credit unions and caisses populaires also play a vital role, more particularly for small- and medium-sized business at the local level.

In addition, a growing number of companies exist which view term-lending as one of their major activities. In a number of instances, such firms are either wholly or partially owned subsidiaries of major financial institutions such as banks, who find it convenient or necessary to provide certain financial services or activities through the vehicle of a subsidiary corporation. For example, the *Bank Act* has restricted the activities of the chartered banks in a variety of areas which are not viewed as an integral part of banking. As a consequence, banks have only been able to participate in such areas indirectly, mainly through equity participation in other investment and financing companies.

While the particular forms which term loans may take are too numerous to review, often being tailored to meet specific circumstances, a few provisions appear to be quite prevalent and are worth discussing. Most term loans are secured loans, with the lender demanding some type of collateral. The most common collateral is probably real property, although chattel mortgages (on movable assets) are also prevalent. In mining, term loans for mine development have also been granted on the strength of long-term ore delivery contracts. Typically, the market value of the collateral will exceed the amount of the loan by some margin, thus providing additional protection to the lender. This margin will understandably depend on the saleability of the asset in case of default. Where the borrowing firm is a small- or medium-sized incorporated business, lenders will often require additional collateral in the form of a personal guarantee from management or the principal owners. In addition, life insurance may have to be taken out on key personnel. Borrowers are frequently required to supply the lender with periodic information about their operations in the form of up-to-date financial statements. The debt contract may also impose various restrictions on the borrowing firm's operations, which serve to protect or strengthen the position of the creditor. The provisions which were discussed in Chapter 8 on long-term debt and which are commonly found in trust indentures are also typical in this context. Finally, and in contrast to long-term debt raised through a public offering, interest rates on term loans are almost inevitably variable and are tied to fluctuations in the prime rate in some fashion. Given the uncertainty about future interest-rate movements, and the fact that institutions such as banks continually have to pay competitive rates on the money which they raise through deposits, this provision becomes understandable. It is well to remember that almost all provisions in a term loan will be negotiable, with the results of such negotiations depending on the competitive strength of both the borrower and the lender.

The banks

As noted in Chapter 15, the traditional view of banks has been that they should provide temporary financing of a self-liquidating type, the expectation being that longer-term requirements of business were to be sought elsewhere in the capital markets. In the past, however, some few borrowers did obtain intermediate-term credit from chartered banks. Such loans were usually granted to smaller firms whose requests were moderate and for whom the cost of a market issue of debt would have been disproportionately high, both in terms of the coupon rate and the underwriting costs.[1]

With the rapid growth in their assets, banks have been able to diversify their loan portfolios to a larger degree and to place greater emphasis on term loans. In 1966, term loans outstanding with limits of under one-million dollars accounted for 4.3 percent of total business loans; by December 31, 1970, this same ratio had risen to 13.3 percent.[2] It has been suggested more recently that banks have become a major source of term loans for business expansion—approximately one-third of all commercial loans over $200,000 granted by banks fall into this category.[3] From time to time, the *Bank Act* contained provisions which have affected the banks' ability to be active in this area. For example, until March 1967, bank lending was subject to an interest-rate ceiling of 6 percent. Though this particular restriction was readily circumvented by banks through service charges and other devices, increased activity in term-lending was certainly fostered with the abandonment of this constraint.

A significant move into personal loans with maturities of up to 5 years is also to be noted. Since entering the consumer loan field, the chartered banks have become the largest single source of personal loans. The total of such loans outstanding as at December 31, 1975 exceeded 14 billion dollars, providing a striking 11.5 billion dollar increase over the December 31, 1966 level.

[1]Canadian Bankers' Association, "Bank Profits: The Changing Mix", *CBA Bulletin*, May, 1971.

[2]*Loc. cit.*

[3]Canadian Bankers' Association, *As Others See Us* (a booklet in a sense dealing with 1977 revisions to the *Bank Act*), May, 1976, p. 10.

Banks are apparently working to increase their share of the consumer loan market with the introduction of vacation, cottage, mobile-home, and even investment loan plans. Under this latter scheme, one bank will lend between $1,500 and $10,000 for the purchase of shares in listed Canadian corporations.[4] The loan is repayable over a period not to exceed 10 years with a pledge of the shares being purchased as security. The prime criterion on which the loan is judged is the individual debtor's ability to service the obligation.

In addition to granting more term loans, banks may well be contemplating the purchase of equity. Thus, in reference to a recently negotiated bank loan, the *1970 Annual Report* of British Columbia Forest Products Limited noted the following:

> . . . in connection with certain banking arrangements made during the year, the company granted an option to the bank to purchase 45,000 shares at the price of $23.71 per share exercisable at any time up to and including June 30, 1975.[5]

It is not unreasonable to suppose that arrangements along similar lines will become fairly common in the not too distant future as banks develop the concept of servicing the total financial requirements of a firm to compete with other intermediaries. Sections of the Canadian Bankers' Association brief to the Minister of Finance, for example, suggest amendments to the *Bank Act* which would extend the ability of banks to take equity positions.[6]

Caisses populaires and credit unions

These financial institutions are really savings and credit cooperatives. The first caisse populaire was founded in Quebec in 1900, modelled largely on Europe's nineteenth century movement which established Peoples' Banks. The caisses encouraged savings and provided for loans to members in emergencies or for productive purposes. Canadian credit unions first evolved in Nova Scotia in the early 1930's, tracing their origins to Europe's eighteenth century mutual savings banks. Concentrated first of all in farm and fishing communities they attracted savings from, and quite readily granted credit to, both individuals and small local business. Growth of both movements has been impressive as reflected in Table 17-1.

TABLE 17-1

Selected Assets of Caisses Populaires and Credit Unions
(in millions of dollars)

Year	Total Assets	Municipal Securities	Mortgages	Loans	
				Personal	Other
1955	653	n.a.	211	n.a.	n.a.
1967	3,382	281	975	1094	167
1970	4,570	355	1327	1493	180
1974	10,315	432	4035	2762	213

Source: *Bank of Canada Review*, May, 1976.

[4]Certain restrictions on the types of shares and their number are naturally imposed.

[5]British Columbia Forest Products Limited, *Annual Report 1970*, p. 25.

[6]Canadian Bankers' Association, *The Industry Brief* (a booklet in a sense dealing with 1977 revisions to the *Bank Act*), October, 1975, p. 22.

The divergent attitudes held by the caisses populaires and credit unions toward borrowing by members is reflected in their very different patterns of asset investment. Credit unions are very heavily committed to lending to their members though there has been a marked move by some of them toward actively seeking unrelated business accounts. The caisse populaires, on the other hand, have held consumer loans to a modest total while appearing to take an active role in the financing of local municipalities and school boards.

It is reasonable to expect continued growth by both institutions, particularly at local levels. Their contributions to the total financial system should become more significant, with local governments or their agencies and smaller enterprises as the principal beneficiaries.

Investment and development companies

Rather than attempting to detail the many types of other firms engaged in providing intermediate-term financing to business, we will illustrate the available range by reviewing RoyNat Limited, one rather typical and well-known firm with a major emphasis on small- and medium-sized business financing.[7] The reader, however, must keep in mind that, because of rapid changes in the activities of such financial institutions, complete and up-to-date information will have to be researched when required for any particular situation.

RoyNat Limited

RoyNat Limited was founded in 1962 to provide a source of intermediate- and longer-term financing for medium-sized Canadian businesses. It was formed and is owned by 5 major financial institutions, namely the Royal Bank of Canada, Banque Canadienne Nationale, Canada Trust, Montreal Trust, and General Trust of Canada. For its operations, the company maintains 11 district offices across Canada and, in addition, it can serve its clients through the roughly 1,700 branch offices of its shareholders.

Through the purchase of mortgage bonds, debentures, income bonds, or some combination of such instruments, RoyNat provides 3- to 15-year debt financing in amounts of between $25,000 and $2.5 million. In some instances, the company will also purchase equity. The funds advanced are normally used for one or more of the following:

- expenditures on plant and equipment,
- additions to working capital,
- refinancing, and
- the acquisition of other companies.

RoyNat, in combination with other institutions, will provide credit in excess of $2.5 million to corporations whose shares are widely held. Given the difficulties and expenses of placing smaller debt issues in the capital markets, this aspect of operations may well increase in importance.

[7]Other well-known firms include Charterhouse Canada Ltd., United North Atlantic Securities Ltd., and Canadian Enterprise Development Corporation Ltd.

Credit is provided to most types of enterprise including manufacturing, the wholesale and retail trades, transportation, communication, and personal services. Firms whose principal business is land development or real estate investment for rental purposes are specifically excluded, however. In 1968, a wholly owned subsidiary, TanYor Limited, was formed to provide combined mortgages of up to ninety percent of appraised value to private homeowners. RoyNat Leasing Limited, another wholly owned subsidiary, was set up in 1969 as a natural adjunct to the term-financing field. This recently established service provides RoyNat's clients with the useful option of either borrowing funds to purchase any required assets or of obtaining use of the same assets through a leasing arrangement.

17-3. PROGRAMS AND AGENCIES OF THE FEDERAL GOVERNMENT

Federally guaranteed loan plans[8]

The first guaranteed loan plan was a joint effort of the federal and provincial governments introduced during the great depression. The scheme provided guarantees on loans granted by the banks to farmers for the purchase of seed grain. Since that time varied federal legislation has extended the guarantees, thereby enabling householders, small businessmen, fishermen, and students to have easier access to the credit facilities of chartered banks and certain other institutions. No government monies are involved directly and, therefore, the total availability of funds from lending institutions has not been expanded. Under most of the plans, the federal government guarantees reimbursement on defaults up to an annual maximum, where this limit is generally set as a percentage of total advances made under a particular lending program. Table 17-2 shows the amounts outstanding under various guaranteed loan plans.

TABLE 17-2

Amounts Outstanding Under Various Federally Guaranteed Lending Programs (in millions of dollars)

	As At December 31			
	1967	1972	1974	1975
Canada Student Loans	120	381	473	543
Farm Improvement Loans	433	373	457	478
Small Business Loans	76	82	117	160
Home Improvement Loans	77	44	43	44

Source: *Bank of Canada Review*, May, 1976.

Of particular significance to those interested in business finance is credit extended under the *Small Businesses Loans Act*, which was brought into force in early 1961. Its purpose is to increase the availability of low-cost intermediate-

[8]This section draws on Canadian Bankers' Association, "Government Guaranteed Loans: Supplements to Normal Bank Credit", *CBA Bulletin*, November, 1970.

term loans to a variety of small businesses which are in need of funds for purposes of capital expansion. Loans of up to $50,000 may be made to firms engaged in manufacturing, the wholesale or retail trade, transportation, construction, communications, and to companies which provide services. Repayment must take place within 10 years, and a borrower is generally required to provide between 10-20 percent of the cost of a project from his own resources. To qualify as a small business, gross revenues of a firm during the year in which the loan application is made must not exceed $1,000,000. The government guarantee provides that valid claims of loss filed by a chartered bank are paid in full to a limit of 10 percent of business improvement loans made by it during any lending period. The guarantees to all banks, however, apply only to a maximum of $300,000,000 of loans. An important condition of the guarantee, is, of course, the constraint placed on a rate of interest to be charged. This rate is established at 6-month intervals.

From its inception until December 31, 1974, over 33,000 loans totalling over $300,000,000 were made under this program, while payments to the chartered banks under the guarantee provision amounted to over $1,000,000 on 264 claims. During 1974, over 2,800 loans were made to small businesses, with the service industry accounting for 34 percent, retailing 24 percent, and construction 15 percent of the loans granted. A total of $32.3 million was advanced, or an average of $11,000 per loan.[9] Interestingly enough, over one-half of the loans were with the Royal Bank of Canada.

The Federal Business Development Bank

Prior to 1944, no financial institution in Canada provided regular sources of medium- or long-term financing for smaller-sized businesses which were unable to raise funds in the capital markets. Short-term credit was available from the banking system but, in general, longer-term funds were difficult to obtain. Recognition of this situation led to the establishment of the Industrial Development Bank (IDB) by an act of parliament in 1944, as a wholly owned subsidiary of the Bank of Canada. In 1975, it was succeeded by a new Crown corporation, the Federal Business Development Bank (FBDB).

Section 20 of the *Federal Business Development Bank Act* empowers the Bank to extend credit to any industrial enterprise in Canada provided that such credit would not otherwise be available on reasonable terms and conditions, and provided also that the character of the investment and the amount invested by others are such as to afford the Bank reasonable protection. The legislation also indicates that the FBDB was to be particularly concerned with the financing problems of smaller business enterprises investing in Canada. Beyond this, it is reasonable to expect that the FBDB will undertake more equity financing than had previously been engaged in by the IDB, and that it will also be very active in providing management-counselling services to business.

[9] Canada, Department of Finance, *Small Business Loans Act, Annual Report, 1974*, Ottawa: Information Canada, 1976, p. 6.

The purposes for which the FBDB lends may be classified as follows:

- to increase the purchase of fixed assets,
- to increase working capital,
- to finance a change of ownership, and
- to repay term obligations.

Costs of such loans, which typically have to be fully secured, are normally at least one percent above the chartered bank prime rate.

While the form of security varies between loans, the principal forms of collateral are mortgages on real property and chattel mortgages. In cases involving incorporated businesses, the personal guarantee of one or more of the owners for a portion of the loan may be required. Insurance on the life of the principals of the business is occasionally required. Where a subsidiary company is involved, it may be necessary for the parent concern to provide a guarantee. It is a normal condition of all loans that the borrower maintain and assign to the Bank adequate insurance on the mortgaged assets.

Subject to requirements regarding eligibility, unavailability of funds from other sources on reasonable terms, and credit worthiness, the FBDB is permitted to enter into underwriting agreements respecting stock, bond, or debenture issues. Such securities can be purchased or otherwise acquired for resale. In actual fact, the bank, though willing, may have little opportunity to participate in equity financing due to the typical unwillingness of shareholders of small businesses to dilute their own holdings.

Tables 17-3, 17-4, and 17-5 provide an overview of the activities of the old IDB and its successor, the FBDB. The very prominent role which the former Industrial Development Bank has played in the area of intermediate financing must be emphasized. In the 31-year period ended September 30, 1975, it authorized 65,000 loans totalling $3 billion and thereby has assisted 48,000 businesses. In fiscal 1975, the IDB approved 9,461 loans totalling $401,000,000 and it had nearly 28,000 customers on the books at the fiscal year end. To make its activities known and to provide service, the bank has 80 branches and 5 regional offices spread across the country.

On occasions, the IDB has come under criticism for employing too conservative a lending policy and for taking too long to process an application for credit.[10] The problem of reducing the turnaround time on loan applications has received constant attention and, the time taken to reach a decision has now been reduced to less than 20 days. However, the very deliberate caution exercised in lending and the desire for tangible security still appear to be prevalent with the ratio of losses to loans granted persisting at under one percent. It can be hoped that a somewhat less cautious lending policy will be resorted to by the FBDB, which need not be profit-motivated, but which is charged with stimulating development, and acting as a lender of last resort.

[10]See, for example, Canada, *1964 Report of the Royal Commission on Banking and Finance*, Ottawa: Queen's Printer, 1964, p. 228.

TABLE 17-3

IDB Loan Approvals (by number) Classified by Industry

	Fiscal			
	1968	1971	1974	1975
Manufacturing	29%	22%	17%	17%
Transportation and Storage	4	4	3	3
Construction	6	5	5	6
Agriculture	8	8	9	7
Wholesale and Retail Trade	23	24	30	32
Tourism	14	20	19	18
Other	16	17	17	17
	100%	100%	100%	100%

Source: *Annual Reports*, Industrial Development Bank.

TABLE 17-4

1975 Loan Approvals Classified by Size

	Number	Amount ($,000,000)
$5,000 or less	461	1.9
Over 5,000 — 25,000	4127	64.5
Over 25,000 — 50,000	2802	106.1
Over 50,000 — 100,000	1453	110.0
Over 100,000 — 200,000	501	73.2
Over 200,000	117	45.8
Total	9461	401.4
Average Size	—	42

Source: *1975 Annual Report*, Industrial Development Bank.

TABLE 17-5

Provincial Distribution of Loans on Books as at September 30, 1975

	No. of Businesses	Amounts Outstanding or Committed ($,000,000)
Newfoundland	699	25.1
Prince Edward Island	232	7.3
Nova Scotia	888	27.5
New Brunswick	758	30.3
Quebec	4,899	259.4
Ontario	7,255	309.1
Manitoba	784	38.4
Saskatchewan	780	29.8
Alberta	2,866	119.0
British Columbia	8,094	440.8
Yukon	129	10.2
N.W. Territories	124	7.3
Total	27,508	1304.1

Source: *1975 Annual Report*, Industrial Development Bank.

The Export Development Corporation

With passage of the *Export Development Act*, the Export Development Corporation (EDC) was established, and on October 1, 1969, it succeeded the Export Credits Insurance Corporation. The main functions of the EDC are to insure overseas investments and transactions, to guarantee loans, and to finance exports for terms of between 7 and 20 years. Though its activities extend well beyond intermediate financing, the EDC can be most usefully treated in this section.

Federal government sponsorship of EDC is, in part, a direct recognition that export trade involves particular risks and particular problems. As far as the corporation's insurance activities are concerned, they relate to (a) commodities sold on short-term credit, or shipped on consignment or for exhibition purposes, (b) capital goods sold on terms of up to five years, and (c) engineering, construction, or similar services. Described quite generally, the perils insured against include insolvency of a foreign buyer or failure to pay after 6 months of accepting goods, blockage of funds, war in the buyer's country, and unexpected restrictions against importation. To discourage indiscriminate extensions of credit, an exporter, through coinsurance, will be expected to assume 10 percent of any loss. Since the insurance coverage may be assigned to a bank, considerable aid in financing is provided indirectly because the collateral value of foreign receivables is significantly enhanced.

Through a program of EDC guarantees, banks and other financial institutions are encouraged to participate more actively in lending where exports are involved. Guarantees may be given to such institutions when financing is provided for foreign importers of Canadian capital goods or services. In instances where commercial financing is not available, the corporation may itself make intermediate- and long-term loans to foreign importers of Canadian capital equipment and engineering services, and it may even finance certain local costs involved in capital projects. All this, no doubt, assists Canadian exporters in matching credit terms offered by their foreign competitors and the amounts involved are fairly impressive. Thus, the maximum which may be outstanding in loans and guarantees at any one time is $4.25 billion, though a further $850,000,000 may be used to finance export sales which, in the government's view, are in the national interest. Single transactions engaged in during 1975 ranged between $1,000,000 and $155,000,000, with operations authorized totalling almost one-half the maximum specified.[11]

The Canada Development Corporation

Incorporated in 1971, the Canada Development Corporation (CDC) is not a Crown corporation and the *CDC Act* does specify that up to 90 percent of the voting shares will ultimately be held by Canadian citizens and residents, with the federal government owning the balance. In early 1976, however, the Government of Canada was the only holder of CDC common shares.

[11]Export Development Corporation, *1975 Annual Report*.

At this stage, the CDC may be viewed as a potential equity investor in firms able to undertake large, longer-range development projects, particularly those involving an upgrading of resources, a high technological base, or prospects for building up a Canadian-controlled presence in international markets. The achieving of profits commensurate with risks involved is an essential policy criterion, though some wait through years of earnings buildup is quite acceptable. The corporation is also prepared to help mobilize the capital of other investors, both domestic and foreign, in joint ventures which are under Canadian control.

CDC not only expects to invest in selected fields as described, but through significant common equity interests in three closely held venture-capital companies,[12] is active in providing more modest amounts of capital to those business ventures in their conceptual or early development stages which have substantial potential for earnings growth over the longer-term.

17-4. PROVINCIAL CROWN CORPORATIONS AND PROVINCIALLY GUARANTEED LENDING PROGRAMS

With the 1973 establishment of the British Columbia Development Corporation, all provinces now have public agencies to further economic development by lending funds and providing other services to particular types of business enterprises. The purpose of these agencies is to stimulate economic development in their respective provinces. They are generally designed to complement the lending of private financial institutions and confine their support to firms which are otherwise unable to obtain financing on reasonable terms. In certain provinces, however, they are quite prepared to compete directly with private institutions. For example, the Manitoba Development Corporation, has clearly affirmed that it is not a lender of the last resort.

Examples of provincial development corporations include the Ontario Development Corporation, the General Investment Corporation of Quebec, The British Columbia Development Corporation, the Alberta Commercial Corporation, the Saskatchewan Economic Development Corporation, the Manitoba Development Corporation, the Industrial Development Board of New Brunswick, Industrial Estates Limited of Nova Scotia and the Nova Scotia Industrial Loan Fund, the Prince Edward Island Industrial Enterprises, and the Industrial Development Board of Newfoundland. This brief listing is hardly complete, however, and details of the functioning of these and similar organizations may be obtained from promotional materials and annual reports published by the various agencies. To illustrate the range of programs and services available, we offer a review of the major activities of the Ontario Development Corporation.

[12]The three are Venturetek International Limited, Innocan Investments Ltd., and Ventures West Capital Ltd.

The Ontario Development Corporation

The Ontario Development Corporation (ODC), a parent corporation of the Northern Ontario Development Corporation and the Eastern Ontario Development Corporation is designed to offer a comprehensive program of financial services to qualified companies wishing to locate new manufacturing plants or expanded existing operations in Ontario. The three corporations offer loans, term loans, leaseback and rental arrangements, and guarantees for loans from private lenders. Incentive loans are also offered and are largely related to attempts at spreading the benefits of industrial development to various parts of the province.

For instance, in northern Ontario, the Ontario Business Incentives Program offers repayable loans of up to 90 percent of the cost of eligible assets with a maximum of $500,000; while in eastern Ontario, the plan provides up to 75 percent of eligible assets with the same maximum. Repayments may be deferred until the borrower becomes established and interest charges waived for up to 5 years. Loans are granted essentially for the construction or expansion of manufacturing plants and, where economically justifiable, to service organizations closely allied to manufacturing. During a 10-month period ended January 31, 1975, over 80 loans totalling $29 million were approved under the Business Incentives Program.

Under their term-loan program, the ODC will lend money to those secondary manufacturing companies and firms in the service industry able to show that increased employment will follow from their new or expanded activities. Particular attention is directed to those businesses operating in slow growth areas. Many different loan programs fall under the term-loans categorization including Small Business Loans, Venture Capital for Canadians, Tourist Industry Loans, Pollution Control Equipment Loans, and Export Support Loans. The service to exporters does not infringe on the activities of the chartered banks, the Export Development Corporation, or any other financial institutions. To obtain a loan under the export support program, which must be repaid within a 5-year period, an applicant must show that reasonable arrangements could not be obtained elsewhere.

The significant majority of businesses approaching the ODC for financial assistance expect a loan to solve their most serious problems. In a number of instances, possibly because of ineffective management this has simply not been the case. In an attempt to strengthen the management of small companies, the ODC has introduced an advisory service plan whereby consultants will visit a firm and offer assistance or advice. This service is generally withheld from those who could afford to hire private consultants.

By way of summary it is reasonable to suggest that the total program presented by the Ontario Development Corporation is one of the most comprehensive and imaginative efforts to be found among provincial agencies. It is also a very active program. During the 10-month period ended January 31, 1975, a total of 526 loans and guarantees totalling over $90 million were authorized.

This represents a 51 percent increase in amounts authorized during the previous 12-month fiscal year.[13]

17-5. SUMMARY

Intermediate-term loans are held to be those which are repayable anywhere between 1 and 10 years' time. Such loans form an important source of funds for business, in particular for smaller firms which, because of their limited size, find it difficult to raise long-term debt in the capital markets.

Sources of intermediate-term debt may be divided into two broad categories: private financial institutions including banks, and agencies set up and sponsored by various levels of government. The chartered banks, through their term-lending programs as well as the credit they extend under government-guaranteed lending plans, constitute a major source of intermediate-term credit in our economy. Credit unions and caisses populaires play an important role, in particular for small- and medium-sized business at the local level. There exists a variety of other financial institutions which are active in this area and discussions in this chapter were limited to providing no more than a sampling of firms active in serving the needs of business. While term loans are characterized by a variety of provisions, the following features are commonly found:

- most term loans are secured.
- lenders will often require personal guarantees where the borrowing firm is incorporated.
- the borrower will have to provide the lender with periodic information about the operations of the firm.
- various restrictive provisions may be imposed on the borrowing firm in order to strengthen the position of the lender.
- interest rates charged are typically variable, often being tied to fluctuations in the prime rate.

It should be noted that there is no such thing as a standard contract, and almost all provisions in a term loan agreement are negotiable.

Federal programs and agencies discussed included the Federal Business Development Bank, the Export Development Corporation, the Canada Development Corporation, and federally guaranteed loan plans like those extended under the *Small Businesses Loans Act*.

All provinces have set up public agencies which seek to stimulate economic development by making funds available to particular types of business enterprises. These agencies may either act as lenders of last resort, restricting the availability of funds to firms which could not obtain financing elsewhere under reasonable terms, or they may play a more aggressive role by competing with private institutions. A wide range of services may be offered, and, by way of example, we briefly reviewed the activities of the Ontario Development Corporation.

[13]Ontario, Ministry of Industry and Tourism, *Ontario Industry, Trade and Tourism Review*, July, 1975, p. 43.

Questions for Discussion

1. Discuss the desirability of governments' becoming active as lenders in the financial markets. What arguments can be made for and against such action? What restrictions, if any, should be placed on government activities in this area?
2. The *Small Businesses Loans Act* may be viewed as one way in which the government subsidizes small businesses. Discuss the desirability of government subsidies to small business.
3. Why is the interest rate variable on most term loans granted by private financial institutions, and in some way tied to movements in the prime rate? Why was it more common ten years ago to grant term loans with a fixed interest rate?
4. What are some of the provisions typically included in a contract for a term loan?
5. The Manitoba Development Corporation has been involved in financing a pulp and paper complex known as Churchill Forest Industries. Search out the details and evaluate the situation which developed.
6. It has been charged that the former Industrial Development Bank, now the Federal Business Development Bank, has been overly conservative in its lending policies, sustaining only very small losses from defaults on loans. Discuss the merits of such an institution liberalizing its credit policies.
7. Do you see any dangers in the fact that, in their efforts to attract industry, various Canadian provinces may be competing against each other? What possible remedies can you suggest?

Selected References

Canada, *1964 Report of the Royal Commission on Banking and Finance*, Ottawa: Queen's Printer, 1964.

Canada, Department of Finance, *Small Businesses Loans Act Annual Report 1974*, Ottawa: Information Canada, 1976.

Canadian Bankers' Association, "Bank Profits: The Changing Mix", *CBA Bulletin*, May 1971.

Canadian Bankers' Association, "Government Guaranteed Loans: Supplements to Normal Bank Credit", *CBA Bulletin*, November 1970.

Canadian Bankers' Association, *The Industry Brief*, October, 1975, p. 22.

D. Hayes, *Bank Lending Policies: Issues and Practices*, Ann Arbor, Michigan: Bureau of Business Research, University of Michigan, 1964, Chapter 6.

J. Middleton, "Term Lending—Practical and Profitable", *Journal of Commercial Lending*, August 1968, pp. 31-43.

Nova Scotia, Industrial Estates Limited, *Annual Report 1971.*

Ontario, Ontario Development Corporation, *Annual Report 1968.*

Ontario, Ontario Development Corporation, *Programs For Prosperity.*

D. Rogers, "An Approach to Analyzing Cash Flow For Term Loan Purposes", *Bulletin of Robert Morris Associates*, October 1965, pp. 79-85.

Wells Fargo Bank, *Commercial Lending*, San Francisco: Wells Fargo Bank, 1975.

Chapter 18
Lease Financing

18-1. INTRODUCTION

We have defined intermediate-term financing as debt involving final maturities of between one and ten years. Given this somewhat arbitrary designation, most forms of leases fall into the category of intermediate-term financing and are reviewed here. Under a leasing arrangement, the lessor, who retains title to the asset, makes this asset available to the lessee in return for periodic lease payments. Hence, a lease may be viewed as akin to a longer-term rental agreement. The following, taken from a brochure prepared for RoyNat Leasing Ltd., provides a useful foreword to this chapter:

> Profits are earned through the use of equipment, not through its ownership. The extent to which this concept has been recognized is reflected in the wide range of assets being leased for business purposes. To name only a few: manufacturing equipment, production lines, office and professional equipment, aircraft, warehouse and handling equipment, boats and barges, equipment for oilfields and mining operations, radio and T.V. equipment, printing presses, store fixtures, tractors, trucks, trailers, etc. There is virtually no end to the list.
>
> Equipment leasing is becoming increasingly popular because it fills a definite need in the Canadian economy.[1]

The fact that leasing has developed wide popularity in recent years can be documented. The Conference Board of Canada estimated in 1975 that between 12.4 to 13.9 percent of all capital goods in Canada were acquired through leases, while the Equipment Lessors Association of Canada estimated 2.5 billion dollars of gross lease receivables as at December 31, 1975.[2] In a subsequent section of this chapter, attention will be directed to those sections of the 1976 Federal Budget which will likely curtail further growth of leasing activity.

Before evaluating the alternatives of leasing an asset on the one hand and owning it on the other, a distinction should be drawn between two very different types of leasing arrangements, namely *operating leases* and *financial leases.* Operating leases are very similar to straight rentals in that the contractual commitment covers a time span which is short relative to the life of the asset. However, compared to straight rentals the commitment on operating leases is somewhat longer, typically running beyond one year. Given terms which are fairly short relative to the life of the asset, a leasing firm is likely to recoup the asset's cost through lease payments only if the original lease is repeatedly renewed, or if it can enter into a second or third leasing arrangement with other lessees. From the lessee's standpoint, under an operating lease there is a commitment to a set of lease payments, but only for a fairly brief period of time, and the fixed charges entailed are unlikely to total the value of the asset involved.

[1]RoyNat Ltd., *Equipment Leasing for Canadian Business*, p. 5.

[2]Roy Marine Leasing; *Roy Marine: What We Are and What We Do*, 1976, p. 3.

Therefore, the leasing firm assumes any risk of obsolescence, and this fact is most likely reflected in comparatively high leasing charges. This point can be quite important, for example, where equipment such as computers, which have been subject to rapid rates of technological obsolescence, are involved.[3]

Operating leases may be advantageous in a variety of circumstances. For one, financial managers can be expected to turn to operating leases when their reading of the risk of obsolescence inherent in a particular asset is higher than that of the lessor. Secondly, operating leases provide the lessee with considerable flexibility for altering his operations when required, since under such leases assets can be exchanged on relatively short notice and without penalties. Such flexibility may be of particular value to firms whose operations are subject to rapid changes which are difficult to anticipate. Finally, under an operating lease, maintenance for the asset is typically provided by the lessor. This may appeal to lessees as there is no risk of equipment deterioration or of having to face unknown maintenance and repair costs.

Financial leases have also been called "full payment" leases in that the contractual arrangement covers a longer time period which allows the lessor to recover the full cost of the asset plus a return during the period of the lease. For all practical purposes, the contractual commitment is noncancellable prior to its expiration. Costs of insurance, repairs, and maintenance typically rest with the lessee. Consequently, the lessor only provides a financing service, which makes acquisition and subsequent use of the asset by the lessee possible. The lessor then recovers his outlays plus an implied return through lease payments made over the life of the contract.[4]

Financial leases can either take the form of a *direct lease*, where use is obtained of an asset not previously owned, or involve a *sale and leaseback* arrangement. In the latter case, the corporation sells an asset to a financial institution such as an insurance company, and that intermediary, as lessor, then leases the asset back to the corporation. For the sale, the lessee receives cash which is then available for employment elsewhere in the business.

From the point of view of a lessee, reliance on a financial lease is very similar to the raising of funds through debt. While there are important differences which will be explored below, fixed contractual charges have to be met in either case, with both arrangements having similar impacts on considerations regarding capital structure and on the financial risk of the firm. It follows, therefore, that financial leases are best evaluated against the alternative of purchasing the asset with funds raised through a term loan.

In this context, we are primarily interested in the financing arrangements implied by leasing. Hence, in the remainder of this chapter, attention is focused on financial rather than operating leases. We note that, in spite of the increasing popularity of leasing, approaches to the analysis of leasing have tended to be

[3]A. Pantages, "An Introduction to Leasing", *Datamation*, August, 1968, pp. 26-32.

[4]Leases should not be confused with *conditional sale agreements* by which transfer of the ownership of the asset sold is postponed until the purchaser has met certain obligations, such as full payments on any financing provided. To be construed as a lease for tax purposes, the arrangement must not involve a subsequent transfer of the asset involved at a nominal price.

somewhat crude, and in the literature the topic of leasing has only recently begun to receive the attention it deserves.[5]

18-2. EVALUATION OF FINANCIAL LEASES

Quantitative evaluation of leasing versus borrowing

Consider a situation where, on the basis of earlier capital budgeting evaluations, a decision has been taken to acquire a particular asset. What remains to be decided is how the acquisition of the asset is to be financed. With financial leasing considered a viable alternative, the firm must next assess whether terms available through leasing are more or less favorable than other financing arrangements which could be made. For reasons already referred to, the most reasonable comparison to make is between leasing on the one hand and borrowing-to-purchase the asset on the other.

To arrive at a rational choice between these two financing alternatives, we must focus on the cash flows which are expected as a consequence of each course of action. However, only flows which are unique to one or the other of the alternatives need be considered, as it is only these flows which can affect the relative desirability.

The relevant cash flows for leasing and borrowing-to-purchase are summarized in Table 18-1. Lease payments are fully deductible as an expense for tax purposes and hence, give rise to a tax shield. In the case of periodic loan payments, only the interest component is deductible for tax purposes, while repayment of principal is not. Other major differences between the two alternatives arise out of asset ownership, which only in the case of borrowing-to-purchase resides with the firm. Ownership affects cash flows in two important ways. First of all, only if the firm owns the asset can it claim capital cost allowances and reap the benefits of corresponding tax shields. Secondly, where the asset is expected to have a residual value at the end of the lease period, any future benefit of this residual value is lost if the asset is leased, as such benefits then rest with the lessor.

Once the relevant cash flows have been determined, present value analysis can be used to establish the relative attractiveness of the two financing alternatives. We can either compare the present value of all cash flows under leasing with those of the borrowing-to-purchase alternative, or we can just compute the present value of the incremental cash outflows of the one alternative over the other.

To complete our framework for the quantitative analysis of leasing against borrowing, we must specify the discount rate to be used in computing the present value of future cash flows. Considerable controversy surrounds the choice of the proper discount rate, and we will discuss this topic further in the section at the

[5]Some recent and more impressive works include: R. Bower, "Issues in Lease Financing", *Financial Management*, Winter, 1973, pp. 25-33; M. Gordon, "A General Solution to the Buy or Lease Decision: A Pedagogical Note", *Journal of Finance*, March, 1974, pp. 245-250; and L. Schall, "The Lease or Buy and Asset Acquisition Decisions", *Journal of Finance*, September, 1974, pp. 1203-1214.

TABLE 18-1

Relevant Cash Flows for Leasing and Borrowing

Leasing	Borrowing-to-Purchase
– lease payments	– loan repayments
+ tax shield from lease payments	+ tax shield from interest portion of repayments
	+ tax shield from CCA
	+ residual value
	– tax shield lost from CCA due to disposition of asset*

Note: Positive signs indicate cash inflows or cash savings. Negative signs indicate cash outflows.

*More complex tax adjustments may be necessary when an asset is disposed of; see our discussion in Chapter 3 for details.

end of this chapter dealing with the cost of leasing.[6] At an introductory level, we may view the comparison of the two financing alternatives as being quite similar to decisions regarding debt refunding or preferred share refinancing which were analyzed in earlier chapters. In these instances, we argued that the after-tax interest cost of debt was the proper rate to be used in discounting future cash flows. Given that the cash flows associated with the various financing alternatives were known with a fair degree of certainty, application of the firm's cost of capital with its built-in risk premium became inappropriate. For similar reasons, we will use the *after-tax interest cost of debt* as the discount rate applicable in evaluating the leasing versus borrowing-to-purchase decision.

Example

Assume a firm has decided to acquire a piece of equipment costing $10,000. The asset is part of an asset class with the maximum rate for capital cost allowances given at 30 percent on a declining balance. The estimated life of the equipment is 10 years, and after this time the asset is expected to have no residual value. The asset can be purchased for cash using a 10 percent bank loan, or leased for 10 years at $1,478 per year. For simplicity, we assume lease payments to be made at the end of each year, with the tax shield available at the same time.[7] The corporate tax rate is 40 percent.

The relevant cash flows for this example are set out in Tables 18-2 and 18-3A. In analyzing the borrowing-to-purchase alternative, we typically look at a term loan which is to be repaid in equal annual installments over a period which is equivalent to the life of the lease. As outlined in Chapter 4, equal annual installments to repay a 10-year, $10,000 loan at

[6]See, for example, R. Bower, *op. cit.*

[7]Lease payments are, in fact, made at the beginning of a period and the tax shield would be available sometime afterwards. Recognition of this in our example would have suggested an unreal advantage for borrowing, whereas a more accurate analysis incorporating monthly payments would show the advantage to be largely illusory. Simplifying assumptions were therefore made in this illustration.

an interest rate of 10 percent are computed as follows:

$$\$10{,}000 = a_{10}10\% \times \text{annual repayments}$$

from which we have:

$$\text{annual repayments} = \frac{\$10{,}000}{a_{10}10\%} = \frac{\$10{,}000}{6.145} = \$1{,}627$$

These installments must now be broken down into interest at 10 percent on the principal outstanding at the beginning of each year, and repayment of principal.[8] Interest payments are shown in column 2 of Table 18-3A, with annual amounts of depreciation shown in column 3. To simplify the illustration, capital cost allowances in Table 18-3A are not carried beyond the 10th year. The annual after-tax cash outflows for owning are simply computed as the loan repayment minus the tax shields available on interest payments and on capital cost allowances. It should be noted that, for two reasons, tax shields are largest in the early years. First, using capital cost allowances based on a percentage of declining balances is a method of accelerated depreciation providing for larger amounts to be claimed against income in early years. Secondly, initial loan repayments contain a larger component of interest charges, since larger balances are still owing. The combination of these two effects decreases initial net outflows for the borrowing-to-purchase alternative, with the annual outflows gradually increasing over time. In contrast, net outflows under leasing remain constant throughout the term of the lease.

TABLE 18-2

After-tax Cash Outflows: Leasing

Year	Lease Payments (1)	Tax Shield (2) = 0.4(1)	After-tax Cash outflows (3) = (1) − (2)
1-10	$1,478	$591	$887

[8] This can be accomplished by using the approach which was detailed in Chapter 4. Alternatively, formulas are available for determining the proportion of a periodic installment which represents interest and the proportion which represents repayment of principal. We use the following notation.

A = annual repayment

I_t = interest payment on instalment in period t

P_t = repayment of principal on instalment in period t

P = total amount originally borrowed

One can show that:

$P_t = (A - iP)(1 + i)^{t-1}$

$I_t = A - P_t = A - (A - iP)(1 + i)^{t-1}$

Pursuing our above example, with $A = \$1{,}627$, $i = 0.1$, and $P = \$10{,}000$, interest payments in year $t = 6$ would be computed as:

$I_6 = \$1{,}627 - (\$1{,}627 - 0.1 \times \$10{,}000)(1 + 0.1)^5 = \$617.$

TABLE 18-3A

After-tax Cash Outflows: Owning

Year	Loan Payment (1)	Interest (2)	Depreciation (3)	Tax Shield (4)=0.4[(2)+(3)]	After-Tax Cash Outflows (5)=(1)−(4)
1	$1,627	$1,000	$3,000	$1,600	$ 27
2	1,627	937	2,100	1,215	412
3	1,627	868	1,470	935	692
4	1,627	792	1,029	728	899
5	1,627	709	720	572	1,055
6	1,627	617	504	448	1,179
7	1,627	516	353	348	1,279
8	1,627	405	247	261	1,366
9	1,627	283	173	182	1,445
10	1,627	148	121	108	1,519

Note: the numbers in this table are rounded to the last digit.

To make the presentation more explicit and easier to understand, the cash flows for "owning" are shown in Table 18-3A in considerable detail, including the annual amounts of depreciation and the resulting tax shields. Also, these detailed tabulations are important as a basis for cash budgeting and financial planning, to be discussed in subsequent chapters. As we saw in Chapter 5, it is computationally more convenient to derive the total present value of the tax shield from capital cost allowance by the formula:

$$\text{present value of tax shield from CCA} = \frac{Cdt}{d+k}$$

where:

C = original purchase price of the asset
d = rate at which CCA is taken
t = corporate tax rate
k = applicable discount rate

For our example, given $C = \$10{,}000$, $d = 0.3$, $t = 0.4$, and k = after-tax interest cost of the loan = $(1 - 0.4)10\% = 0.06$, we compute the present value of the tax shield from capital cost allowances to be:

$$\frac{\$10{,}000 \times 0.3 \times 0.4}{0.3 + 0.06} = \$3{,}333$$

In practical computations, we could omit column 3 in Table 18-3A. Only the tax shield from interest payments is then taken into account as shown in columns 3 and 4 of Table 18-3B.

It should come as no surprise to find that the present value of after-tax loan repayments just equals \$10,000, or the original amount of the loan (the minor difference being due to rounding in the computations of Table 18-3B). The after-tax loan repayments, which imply an after-tax interest rate of $(1 - 0.4)10\% = 6\%$ on principal outstanding, just yield the original amount of the loan when discounted at this same rate of 6%.

TABLE 18-3B

After-Tax Cash Outflows: Owning, Excluding Tax Shields from CCA

Year	Loan Payment (1)	Interest (2)	Tax Shield From Interest (3)=0.4(2)	After-Tax Cash Outflow (4)=(1)−(3)	Present Value Factor at 6% (5)	Present Value of Cash Flows (6)=(4)×(5)
1	$1,627	$1,000	$400	$1,227	0.943	$1,157
2	1,627	937	375	1,252	0.890	1,114
3	1,627	868	347	1,280	0.840	1,075
4	1,627	792	317	1,310	0.792	1,038
5	1,627	709	284	1,343	0.747	1,003
6	1,627	617	247	1,380	0.705	973
7	1,627	516	206	1,421	0.665	945
8	1,627	405	162	1,465	0.627	919
9	1,627	283	113	1,514	0.592	896
10	1,627	148	59	1,568	0.558	875
					Total	$9,995

Note: The numbers in this table are rounded to the last digit.

We can now compute the present value of the total cash outflows for both alternatives. For leasing, we simply have:

$$\text{present value of cash outflows: leasing} = a_{10}6\% \times \$887 = 7.360 \times \$887 = \$6{,}528$$

For borrowing-to-purchase, using the present value computations shown in Table 18-3B, we obtain:

$$\text{present value of cash outflows: owning} = \text{amount of loan to purchase} - \text{present value of tax shield from CCA}$$
$$= \$10{,}000 - \$3{,}333$$
$$= \$\ 6{,}667$$

We see that the present value of cash outflows is slightly lower for leasing than for owning, with the margin which favors leasing being $6,667 – $6,528 = $139. In fact, in this example the difference between the two alternatives is so small that the decision would probably be based on other considerations which were not included in the quantitative analysis and which will be discussed below.

Where an asset is expected to have some residual or salvage value at the end of the lease period, an estimate of this contribution should be treated as an after-tax inflow available under the borrowing-to-purchase alternative. In contrast with other cash flow projections involved in the analysis, the asset's residual value some years hence understandably represents a very uncertain estimate. To reflect this increased risk, the cash flows anticipated from the residual value should be discounted at a rate higher than the after-tax cost of debt, and the firm's cost of capital might be more appropriate.

Example

Pursuing our numerical illustration, assume that the asset under consideration could be sold for $1,000 at the end of the 10th year, and that the appropriate discount rate (given the risk inherent in this estimate) is the firm's weighted average cost of capital which is given at

12 percent.[9] For year 10, the cash flows under the alternative of owning must be adjusted in two ways. First, there will be an expected cash inflow of \$1,000 from the sale of the asset. Secondly, as was discussed in Chapter 5, the book value of the asset class is reduced by the amount of the sale, with a consequent loss in future capital cost allowance beyond year 10. Assuming that there is other equipment in the asset class, the cash flow effects due to the residual value in year 10 become:

$$\text{effective cash inflow in year 10} = \text{selling price} - \begin{array}{c}\text{loss of tax shield}\\ \text{from subsequent CCA}\end{array}$$

$$= \$1{,}000 - \frac{\$1{,}000 \times 0.3 \times 0.4}{0.3 + 0.12}$$

$$= \$714$$

It should be noted that the lost tax shield from subsequent capital cost allowances is as uncertain as the estimated residual value and, accordingly, the discount rate used to compute the present value of the lost tax shield is also 12 percent. In bringing this amount of \$714 back from year 10 to the present at a discount rate of 12 percent, the benefit of the anticipated residual value is further reduced to a present value of \$714 × 0.322 = \$230, and the total present value of all cash outflows under the borrowing-to-purchase alternative drops down to \$6,667 − \$230 = \$6,437.

The loss of the residual value under leasing may gain particular significance in periods of substantial inflation. This is especially true with assets which are not subject to rapid technological obsolescence, such as land and buildings. If, for example, a firm contemplates leasing a piece of land for a period of 10 years and, during the lease period, land appreciates in value at an average rate of 10 percent per year, the residual value of the land at the end of the contract would be over two-and-a-half times its original purchase price. Such considerations could clearly tip the balance against leasing.

Qualitative considerations

When evaluating leases, several qualitative factors which were not included in the numerical analysis just outlined need to be recognized. Some of the more important items include the following:

- Leases generally do not appear as debt in the firm's balance sheet, and are only disclosed in footnotes to the financial statements. Therefore, under leasing as opposed to borrowing, a firm's capital structure may appear less levered and various financial ratios may appear to be more attractive.

  While sophisticated analysts and investors will certainly recognize that such

[9]If the asset had originally been purchased and has an economic value beyond the lease period, the firm may simply continue using it, rather than selling it at the end of year 10. In such an event, in order to make the two alternatives comparable, we would simply assume that under the lease alternative, the firm could purchase the asset at its fair market value at the end of the lease period. In that case, leasing would entail an additional outflow at the end of year 10, which is equivalent to the asset's residual value minus tax shields from future capital cost allowances, and the relative desirability of the two alternatives would be as outlined above.

"off-balance-sheet" lease financing will burden the corporation as much as would other debt obligations, to the casual observer the financial position of the firm may appear to be stronger than it actually is.

- It may not be practical to raise external debt every time an asset is acquired. Where external debt financing is "lumpy", excess balances of cash may have to be held temporarily, or short-term funds may have to be drawn on until needs have built up to a level where an offering of longer-term debt is warranted. Under leasing, the arrangement is specifically tailored to the particular assets being acquired, and no such problems arise.
- With current uncertainty regarding future rates of inflation and interest-rate movements, many term loans provide for variable interest rates which are tied in some way to the prime rate. Given that lessors often finance a large proportion of their investments through debt of their own, lease agreements in some instances also provide for variable lease payments which are tied to the general level of interest rates. Variable payments of this type represent additional uncertainty to the lessee or borrower. Where only one of the two alternatives (leasing or borrowing) provides for variable payments, this may affect its relative desirability and needs to be recognized. If, for example, payments on a loan are variable, whereas lease payments are fixed, the borrowing alternative contains an additional element of uncertainty which may detract from its desirability.
- Under a lease, restrictive provisions and protective convenants which are usually associated with debt may be avoided. Given that the lessor retains title to the asset, he is in a stronger position than creditors in case of default as he can simply repossess the asset, without having to become involved in lengthy bankruptcy proceedings or similar litigation. Thus, there may be no need for him to secure additional protective provisions in the lease agreement.[10]
- Leases generally provide for 100 percent financing and involve no down-payments. In contrast, where a loan is to be obtained and secured with the asset as collateral, a lender may only be willing to advance a certain proportion of the asset's value, while requiring the purchaser to provide some funds on his own. Hence, when borrowing, the purchaser may be left to raise additional funds from secondary sources for the downpayment.

Where less than 100 percent financing is available on a term loan to purchase the asset, the numerical analysis as presented earlier has to be modified to take this into account. If an additional source of debt can be found at a higher interest rate, to cover the shortfall, the extension of the analysis is quite straight-forward.[11] In this case, two loans might be outstanding under the purchase alternative, each covering a portion of the purchase price and each carrying its own interest rate. The total cash flows for owning are computed by simply adding the individual cash flows from the two loans, and the analysis proceeds in

[10]In this context, it should be mentioned that in the event of the lessee's insolvency or bankruptcy, the lessor can simply repossess the asset. He is not, however, entitled to recover subsequent lease payments beyond some specified amount which is typically set at one year's obligations.

[11]If no debt arrangement can be found and the shortfall has to be made up with equity funds, the proper framework for the analysis would become quite complex. The two alternatives now imply different amounts of debt financing and, hence, different degrees of financial risk. As such, they are no longer strictly comparable.

the same fashion as previously outlined.[12] A numerical example of this alteration is provided in the problem section at the end of the chapter.

18-3. TAXATION AND LEASING

Given that the lessor is the legal owner of a leased asset, he is entitled to claim the appropriate capital cost allowances on the asset and to receive the benefit of any consequent tax shelter. Leasing used to be particularly attractive where a firm required the use of an asset, but was unable to take advantage of the tax shields from capital cost allowances. This situation can arise either because the firm is not subject to taxation, as is the case for Crown corporations and the likes, or because it lacks sufficient profits against which capital cost allowances can be applied. By arranging for a lease, the benefits of capital cost allowances could be shifted to a lessor who is able to take full advantage of the tax shelter which such allowances afford. In return, the lessor would pass back part of this benefit to the lessee in the form of reduced lease payments. In essence, tax benefits from capital cost allowance could be shifted to the taxpaying unit which had the greatest use for them, with resultant savings accruing to both parties in the transaction.

The 1976 Federal Budget dealt a severe blow to the leasing industry in Canada by placing restrictions on the amount of capital cost allowances which may be claimed by lessors on leased equipment. Specifically, after May 26, 1976, capital cost allowances on the leasing of moveable property is limited to the lessor's "net rental income". Net rental income is defined as income from lease payments received minus overhead expenses and interest charges on debt which the lessor entered into in financing acquisition of the assets. Basically, this provision precludes the lessor from applying the capital cost allowance on a leased asset against any other income not directly associated with the lease. Given that many lessors previously used the substantial capital cost allowances arising out of their leasing business to shelter unrelated income from taxes, this move by the government has made leasing much less attractive for many lessors. As a consequence, lessors will have to demand higher lease payments to make up for the lost tax shelter, and it is reasonable to expect that leasing will become a comparatively less attractive and more expensive form of financing.

In light of the above, an understandable question to pose is whether lessees will now look abroad to jurisdictions where the tax treatment of lessors is still attractive and tax benefits are available to be shared. Because of other fairly recent fiscal policy, a negative answer is indicated. Specifically, the 25 percent Canadian withholding tax on lease payments to non-residents which is now in effect will serve as a barrier to foreign-source leases.

18-4. FINANCIAL LEASES AND THE COST OF CAPITAL

With a sizable number of firms (such as airlines and other transportation companies) financing a significant portion of their assets through lease

[12]Note that the proper discount rate now becomes the after-tax interest cost on the most expensive loan used, as this is the firm's marginal cost of debt.

arrangements, such leases need to be recognized and included in the firm's weighted average cost of capital calculations. To do this, both the costs of leasing and the relevant weighting must be determined.

Where a firm intends to finance a certain proportion of its assets through leasing, with this proportion remaining roughly constant over time, the proper weighting to be applied to leasing is simply given by the value of the assets to be leased in relation to the total value of assets to be financed. For instance, where a firm plans new investments totalling $100 million over the next several years, with $20 million financed through financial leases, the appropriate weight for leasing in weighted average cost of capital calculations simply becomes $20/100 = 0.20$.

To determine the proper costs of leasing in this context, we stay within the same framework which was developed in Chapter 13 to derive specific costs for various sources of funds. Accordingly, the cost of leasing is given as the internal rate of return which equates the funds originally provided with the present value of after-tax cash outflows resulting from leasing the asset. Leasing can be viewed as providing immediate funds equivalent to the market value of the assets being leased. In return, the firm is committed to future lease payments. Furthermore, in choosing this form of financing, the firm loses the tax shields from capital cost allowances and any benefits associated with a residual value. It follows that the proper cost for leasing is given as the internal rate of return which satisfies the equation:

$$\begin{aligned} \text{original asset value} = {} & \text{discounted future lease payments} \\ & + \text{present value of tax shield from CCA lost due to leasing} \\ & + \text{present value of benefits from residual value lost due to leasing} \end{aligned}$$

Pursuing our numerical example which was previously introduced and assuming no residual value for the asset, we obtain:

$$\text{original asset value} = a_{10}i\% \times \$887 + \$10{,}000 \frac{0.3 \times 0.4}{0.3 + i}$$

The internal rate of return which represents the cost of leasing is found by trial and error to be $i \simeq 5.7$ percent. We note that this is an after-tax cost as it is computed based on after-tax cash flows.

An alternative way of comparing the desirability of leasing against that of borrowing is to compare the cost of leasing as just computed with the after-tax interest cost on the loan. We see again that leasing with its after-tax cost of 5.7 percent is slightly more attractive than borrowing which carries an after-tax interest cost of $(1 - 0.4) \times 10\% = 6$ percent. For reasons detailed in Chapter 5, both our approaches to evaluate leasing should generally yield equivalent results: the approach introduced earlier in this chapter was based on a net present value analysis, while the procedure just outlined relies on a comparison of internal rates of return.

We noted earlier that the discount rates to be applied to various cash flows in a net present value analysis of leasing versus owning have been the subject of considerable controversy, with a variety of approaches having been proposed.[13] To some extent, reliance on internal rates of return allows us to sidestep this issue. We note, however, that some of the cash flows, such as the residual value of the asset, which are used to derive the internal rate of return for leasing may be subject to considerable uncertainty. This uncertainty then carries over into the computed cost of leasing. Thus, cost of capital calculations and comparisons of internal rates of return should not be viewed as a purely mechanical exercise, and may require considerable judgment.

Where net present value analysis is relied on, sensitivity analysis which tests how sensitive the conclusion reached is with regard to changes in the discount rate may be quite useful. Given the large initial tax shields available from CCA and interest payments, increases in the discount rate typically favor borrowing, since under this alternative the larger cash outflows occur in the more distant future. If borrowing is favored using a low discount rate such as the after-tax cost of debt, the decision will only be strengthened by applying higher discount rates, and the choice of the proper rate may for practical purposes become an irrelevant issue.

18-5. SUMMARY

Under a leasing arrangement, the lessor, who retains title to the asset, makes this asset available to a lessee in return for periodic lease payments. In other words, a lease may be viewed as akin to a longer-term rental agreement. By retaining title, the lessor takes capital cost allowance on the asset and reaps the benefits arising out of any residual value which the asset may have upon termination of the lease agreement.

We distinguished between operating leases and financial leases, and essentially limited ourselves to discussing financial leases in this chapter. Operating leases, being very similar to straight rentals, provide for a contractual commitment which is short relative to the life of the asset. The risk of obsolescence thus rests with the lessor. On the other hand, financial leases, also called full payment leases, call for a contractual arrangement which covers a time period which is long enough to allow the lessor to recover the full costs of the asset plus a return. The lessor assumes no risks of obsolescence and basically provides a financing service. From the point of view of a lessee, reliance on a financial lease is very similar to the raising of funds through debt. In either case, fixed contractual charges have to be met, and the impact on the financial risk of the firm is similar. It follows that financial leases are properly evaluated by comparing them against the alternative of purchasing the asset with funds raised through a term loan.

[13]We argued earlier that the after-tax cash outflows associated with leasing and borrowing are known with relative certainty, and should therefore be discounted at the after-tax cost of debt. Some authors have suggested that future tax shields hinge on future tax rates and on the future availability of taxable income, both of which involve some uncertainty, thus calling for a higher discount rate. Further, the rate at which the estimated residual value should be discounted depends on the uncertainty inherent in the estimate, and the cost of capital or some other rate may be appropriate depending on the specific circumstances. For a good review, see R. Bower, "Issues in Lease Financing", *op. cit.*

The quantitative analysis of leasing versus borrowing is best carried out within the framework of discounted cash flow analysis. Relevant cash outflows for leasing are given as the lease payments minus the tax shield derived by claiming such payments as an expense. Under borrowing, the relevant cash outflows are given as the payments on the loan, minus tax shields from interest payments and capital cost allowance, and minus benefits resulting from any residual value of the asset. Present values of cash outflows are derived by applying as a discount rate the firm's after-tax cost of debt. The asset's residual value may be discounted at a higher rate, such as the cost of capital, to reflect the uncertainty inherent in this estimate. The financing alternative resulting in the lower present value of cash outflows is favored. Alternatively, we can also compute the cost of leasing as an internal rate of return, and contrast this cost with the after-tax cost of borrowing-to-purchase. The internal rate of return thus computed can be used as the cost of leasing in the firm's weighted average cost of capital calculations.

Several qualitative factors which are not included in such formal evaluation procedures need to be recognized and may have a bearing on the final decision. These include the accounting treatment of leases in the firm's financial statements, the lack of restrictive provisions which are typical for lease agreements, and the fact that leasing normally provides for 100 percent financing which may not be readily available elsewhere.

Recent tax legislation in Canada has made leasing less attractive by preventing lessors from claiming capital cost allowance on leased equipment against other income which is unrelated to leasing. As a consequence, leasing is likely to become less competitive as a financing alternative. Withholding tax on lease payments to nonresidents serves as a barrier to foreign-source leasing.

Questions for Discussion

1. What are the differences between operating leases and financial leases? Under what conditions do firms find operating leases attractive?
2. Is it correct to say that leasing is the best way to hedge against obsolescence without paying any cost? Why?
3. Why might a leasing firm be willing to lease an asset to a company whose financial position is such that banks would be unwilling to lend money to finance the purchase?
4. Comment on the statement that "if double-digit inflation continues and taxation authorities do not permit capital costs to be revised upward through some form of indexing, assets will be leased rather than purchased".
5. Under what circumstances, if any, is a firm's total debt capacity increased through leasing? Discuss.
6. Why are leasing firms quite willing to undertake what amounts to 100% financing under a financial lease when various financial institutions frown on 100% borrowing?
7. Lessors lost part of their competitive advantage when restrictions were placed on the amount of capital cost allowances such firms could claim on leased equipment. Explain why this is so.

Problems with Solutions

1. A steel distributor must acquire a piece of land for open-air storage. The distributor is weighing the alternatives of leasing the land for a 10-year period or of borrowing-to-purchase. The current market value of the land is \$1,000,000. Lease payments would be \$180,000 per year, payable at the beginning of the year. Assume that the tax shields from the lease payments are available at the time of payment. A loan of \$1,000,000 can be obtained as follows: no payments to be made until the end of the 10th year, at which time \$2,600,000 must be repaid. The value of the land at the end of year 10 (when it would be sold) is estimated to be \$1,300,000. The firm's tax rate is 40%, with capital gains included for taxation at half the amount realized. The firm's after-tax weighted average cost of capital is 15%, but it can generally borrow at a before-tax cost of 10%. Which alternative is more attractive?

Solution

Outflows: lease alternative (payments to lessor start immediately)
\$180,000 × 0.60 = \$108,000/year after-tax in periods t_0 to t_9

$$PV \text{ at } 6\% = \$108,000 + \$108,000 \times a_9 6\%$$
$$= \$108,000 + \$108,000 \times 6.802$$
$$= \$842,616$$

Outflows: borrowing alternative

$$PV = .558\,[\$2,600,000 - 0.40(\$1,600,000)] - .247\,[\$1,300,000 - (.40)(\$150,000)]$$
$$= \$1,093,680 - \$306,280$$
$$= \$787,400$$

Note that the lease payments and the loan repayment are relatively certain and should be discounted at the after-tax cost of borrowing (10%(1 − 0.4) = 6%), but the proceeds from the sale of the land are uncertain and hence are discounted at the weighted average cost of capital (15%). Note also that land is not depreciable, so no capital cost allowances are involved in the comparison.

Conclusion: borrowing is more attractive.

2. Using problem 1 above, compute the cost of leasing to be used in weighted average cost of capital calculations. Compare this with the cost of borrowing.

Solution

We need to find the internal rate of return i which solves the equation:

$$\text{original purchase price} = \begin{array}{l}\text{present value}\\ \text{of lease payments}\end{array} + \begin{array}{l}\text{present value of benefits}\\ \text{lost from residual value}\end{array}$$

$$\$1,000,000 = [\$108,000 + a_9 i\%\ \$108,000]$$
$$+ \left[\frac{1}{(1+i)^{10}}\ (\$1,300,000 - 0.4 \times \$150,000)\right]$$

By trial and error, the internal rate of return is found to be $i \simeq 13.7\%$. This cost is again higher than the 6% after-tax interest cost on borrowing.

3. An asset can be purchased for $25,000. It has an estimated economic life of 4 years, and no residual value is anticipated after that time. Capital cost allowance can be taken at a rate of 40% on a declining balance. The asset can be leased, with annual lease payments amounting to $10,000. Lease payments are due at the end of the year. Alternatively, a loan of $20,000 could be obtained from the bank at 10%, with the asset pledged as collateral. An additional unsecured loan of $5,000 could be obtained at 15%. Both loans are to be repaid in equal annual installments over the 4 years. The corporate tax rate is 40%. Conduct a net present value analysis evaluating the alternatives of leasing and borrowing-to-purchase.

Solution

As the discount rate, we use the marginal cost of borrowing, which is (1 − 0.4)15% = 9%.

Leasing: cash outflows

years 1 to 4—after-tax lease payments = (1 − 0.4) × $10,000 = $6,000

present value of cash outflows for leasing = $a_4 9\%$ × $6,000 = 3.240 × $6,000 = $19,440

Borrowing-to-purchase: cash outflows

$20,000 loan at 10%

$$\text{annual payments} = \frac{\$20{,}000}{a_4 10\%} = \frac{\$20{,}000}{3.170} = \$6{,}309$$

Year	Principal at Beginning of Year (1)	Annual Repayment (2)	Interest (3)=10%×(1)	Repayment of Principal (4)=(2)−(3)	Principal at Year End (5)=(1)−(4)
1	$20,000	$6,309	$2,000	$4,309	$15,691
2	15,691	6,309	1,569	4,740	10,951
3	10,951	6,309	1,095	5,214	5,737
4	5,737	6,309	573	5,737	—

$5,000 loan at 15%

$$\text{annual payments} = \frac{\$5{,}000}{a_4 15\%} = \frac{\$5{,}000}{2.855} = \$1{,}751$$

To illustrate their use, we draw on the formulas provided in footnote 8 in the chapter to compute annual interest and principal payments. For year t, we have:

$$I_t = \$1{,}751 - (\$1{,}751 - 0.15 \times \$5{,}000)\,(1 + 0.15)^{t-1}$$

$$= \$1{,}751 - \$1{,}001\,(1 + 0.15)^{t-1}$$

$$P_t = (\$1{,}751 - 0.15 \times \$5{,}000)\,(1 + 0.15)^{t-1}$$

$$= \$1{,}001\,(1 + 0.15)^{t-1}$$

Inserting, we obtain:

Year	Interest (I_t)	Repayment of Principal (P_t)
1	$750	$1,001
2	600	1,151
3	427	1,324
4	229	1,522

Combining both loans, we derive the following cash outflows for borrowing:

Year	Total Loan Payments (1)	Total Interest Payments (2)	Tax Shield From Interest Payments (3)=0.4×(2)	After-Tax Cash Outflows (4)=(1)–(3)	PV Factors at (1–0.4)15%=9% (5)	Present Value of Cash Outflows (6)=(4)×(5)
1	$8,060	$2,750	$1,100	$6,960	0.917	$6,382
2	8,060	2,169	868	7,192	0.842	6,056
3	8,060	1,522	609	7,451	0.772	5,752
4	8.060	802	321	7,739	0.708	5,479
			Present value of cash flows:			$23,669

Note: Entries in the above table are rounded to the nearest dollar.

$$\text{Present value of tax shield from CCA} = \$25{,}000 \times \frac{0.4 \times 0.4}{0.4 + 0.09} = \$8{,}163$$

$$\text{Total present value of cash outflows for borrowing and owning} = \$23{,}669 - \$8{,}163 = \$15{,}506$$

Thus the present value of cash outflows is lower for owning and borrowing ($15,506) than for leasing ($19,440) and the asset should be purchased.

Alternatively, the solution could have been derived as follows:

Cost of leasing:

Find the discount rate (IRR) which solves

$$\$25{,}000 = a_4 i\%\ \$6{,}000 + \$25{,}000 \times \left(\frac{0.4 \times 0.4}{0.4 + i}\right)$$

Through trial and error, we find for the after-tax cost of leasing $i \simeq 13.8\%$.

The after-tax average cost of borrowing is computed as

$$\frac{20}{25}(1 - 0.4)10\% + \frac{5}{25}(1 - 0.4)15\% = 6.60\%$$

which again indicates that borrowing is the cheaper source of financing.

Additional Problems

1. Alpex Company has a need for working capital, but its bank has refused to give any additional loans to the company unless the current ratio is improved. The company is considering a sale-and-leaseback of one of its major machines and to use half of the proceeds to repay bank loans and the other half to reduce accounts payable. The profit figure and balance sheet for the current year are shown below:

Alpex Company
Balance Sheet
As at December 31, 1976

Cash	$ 300,000	Accounts payable	$ 800,000
Receivables	1,500,000	Bank loans	1,200,000
Inventories	700,000	Others	600,000
Total Current Assets	2,500,000	Total Current Liabilities	2,600,000
Land & building	1,000,000	Long-term debt	1,000,000
Fixed assets (net)	3,200,000	Common stock	3,000,000
Equipment (net)	1,300,000	Retained earnings	1,400,000
Total Fixed Assets	5,500,000		
Total Assets	$8,000,000	Total Claims	$8,000,000

Profit before tax for 1976: $800,000

(a) Assume that for the asset under consideration, the maximum rate for capital cost allowances is 20%, the marginal tax rate of the company is 40%, and the asset can be sold for a net amount of $1,000,000. Calculate the total net present value of the tax shield lost by selling the asset, given that the discount rate to be used is 8%.

(b) If the lease obligation is 10 years with annual payments of $135,000 each year, compute the present value of the tax shield received by the company as a consequence of the lease payments. What is the incremental tax shield? Lease payments are made at the end of each year.

(c) Compare the current ratio before and after the sale-and-leaseback arrangement.

(d) What would Alpex's profit before tax be if the lease arrangement had been in effect during 1976? (For simplicity, depreciation charges on the asset in 1976 can be estimated at $200,000.)

2. Halifax Company has decided to acquire a piece of equipment costing $100,000, and the maximum rate for capital cost allowances is 30%. The estimated life of the equipment is 10 years and the scrap value at the end of the 10th year is estimated to be $4,000. The asset can be purchased for cash using an 8% bank loan which will be repaid in equal amounts for 10 years, or leased at $15,600 a year. The firm's cost of capital is 12%. Assuming that the marginal tax rate of the company is 40%, use the present value method to make the decision to buy or to lease. (Payments under both the loan and the lease are made at the end of each year.)

3. The Lavish Carpet Manufacturing Co. has decided to acquire a new machine which has an economic life of 10 years. The machine can be purchased for \$80,000 and the supplier is willing to advance \$60,000 of the purchase price at 8%. The loan is to be repaid in equal instalments over 10 years. Lavish Carpets pays 40% corporate income tax, and plans to claim 20% capital cost allowance on the purchased asset. It expects to negotiate a further \$20,000 10-year loan with a financial institution at 10% interest, thereby financing any purchase entirely through debt. Meanwhile, Midland Leasing Ltd. has also offered to make the equipment available under a 10-year financial lease. Lease payments are to be \$12,000 annually. Assuming no residual value, lease payments starting at the end of the first year, and a cost of capital for Lavish Carpets of 13%, how should the asset be acquired?
4. An asset worth \$100,000 is leased by the XYZ Corporation for 5 years at \$28,000 per year. Lease payments are due at the end of the year. Assume that if purchased, capital cost allowances on the asset would amount to \$40,000, \$24,000, \$16,000, \$12,000, and \$8,000 over 5 years respectively. The XYZ Corporation faces a tax rate of 40%. What is XYZ's weighted average cost of capital if its capital structure is 80% common equity at an after-tax cost of 12%, and the remainder is lease financing?
5. A company considers acquiring a machine having a current market value of \$100,000 and an estimated useful life of 5 years. Capital cost allowance could be taken on the machine at a rate of 30% on a declining balance basis. A leasing firm has offered a 5-year lease involving lease payments of \$25,000 per annum, payable *at the beginning* of each year. Assume that the tax shield from the lease payments is available *at the end* of each year. Alternatively, a loan of \$100,000 could be obtained on which no periodic payments have to be made but, at the end of 5 years, a sum of \$161,000 has to be repaid (\$100,000 principal repayment and \$61,000 accumulated interest). The estimated salvage value at the end of year 5 is zero and the firm's corporate tax rate is 30%. The firm's weighted average cost of capital is 14%.
   (a) What is the effective annual interest rate which the firm would be paying on the loan?
   (b) Based on present value analysis, should the firm lease or purchase the asset?
   (c) How high would the estimated salvage value of the asset have to be for you to reverse your decision under item (b) above?
6. A government agency which does not pay any taxes is evaluating whether to lease an asset, or whether to purchase it, in which case 100% financing could be obtained in the form of a bank loan at an effective interest rate of 10%. Lease payments would be \$10,000 per year payable at the beginning of the year, and loan repayments would amount to \$12,000 per year payable at the end of the year, both to be incurred over the next 5 years. The anticipated salvage value of the asset is \$2,000. Given the uncertainty inherent in this estimate, the discount rate applicable to the residual value is 14%.
   (a) Which alternative would you prefer?
   (b) What would the salvage value have to be before you would reverse your decision under item (a) above?

7. A Crown corporation which does not pay any taxes is evaluating whether to lease an asset, or whether to purchase it, in which case 100% financing could be obtained in the form of a bank loan. Lease payments would be $4,000 per year and loan repayments would amount to $5,000 per year, both to be incurred for the next 7 years. Can you conclude from these figures alone that leasing is to be preferred? Give reasons.
8. You have decided to acquire a truck costing $10,000. You are offered a 4-year lease of $2,940 per year payable at the beginning of each year, or a term loan of $10,000 with payments at the end of each year in equal amounts of $3,223. The benefits of any tax shields are realized at the end of each year. The current loan rate is 11% per annum. The CCA rate is 20% and your cost of capital is 14%. Salvage value is zero and the corporate tax rate is 40%.
   (a) Which way would you finance the truck?
   (b) What other factors would influence your decision?
9. You are considering whether to purchase or lease a new machine costing $10,000. If you purchase, you can obtain a bank loan for the full $10,000 at an effective interest rate of 10%. The useful life of the machine is 2 years, and the bank loan would have to be repaid in 2 equal annual payments over the 2 years. The machine will be depreciated on a *straight-line* basis over the 2 years and has no salvage value. Lease payments would be $5,500 per year for the 2 years, payable at the end of the year. The marginal tax rate is 40%. The firm's average cost of capital is 14%.
   (a) Would you lease or purchase?
   (b) How would your analysis be altered if the machine had an estimated salvage value of $2,000 at the end of the 2 years?

Case

Dongara Industries

In 1972, Keith Best graduated from a business school in finance and was employed as an assistant to the financial executive of Dongara Industries. In 1974, he was assigned to assist the data processing manager in a study which would recommend a replacement for the company's computer. His main responsibility was to evaluate the various acquisition alternatives that were available and to recommend the best course of action.

In June of 1974, a joint planning session was held by data processing personnel and management of the company, and as a result a set of data processing objectives was formulated. These objectives were translated into required computer specifications by the data processing manager and sent to computer manufacturers and data centers as the basis for proposals. The specifications were detailed in a very thorough document explaining the company's data processing objectives, current volume of transactions, and anticipated growth over the next five years.

Three manufacturers and one data center responded with full proposals and after extensive meetings, studies, and demonstrations, the company decided on the particular computer to be chosen.

It was not proposed to introduce the whole new computer system at one time and a development schedule was drawn up calling for the introduction of the system in three phases. The manufacturer's proposal allowed Dongara to agree to the acquisition of the equipment for later phases at current prices, but to take delivery and make payments at a later date. A schedule of the planned implementation of the three phases is included in Exhibit 1.

The particular computer selected has only been recently announced and the first installation would not be operating until the first quarter of 1975. None are operating in the vicinity of Dongara's corporate office, although the computer manufacturer has one firm contract and several prospects for similar machines in the area. The manufacturer encourages their customers to cooperate in providing each other with back-up facilities in case of equipment failure.

A number of the peripherals and options were also new releases. As it is possible that the price of these may drop once the independent manufacturers of computer peripherals start producing this equipment, Dongara has already decided to acquire these on a one-year rental basis with a view to possibly purchasing them once the price is forced down by competition. The remainder of the equipment required and the expected dates of acquisition are listed in Exhibit 1, together with the anticipated expenditures to be classified as leasehold improvements.

Although the computer has been selected, the company still has to choose from a number of alternative acquisition methods. Another joint planning session is scheduled for the near future to make a final decision on the acquisition route to be followed.

Acquisition alternatives

The computer manufacturer is very flexible in providing alternative payment schedules. Basically, four plans are offered. Any or all of the equipment could be acquired under any of the plans, subject to the rules set out below. In addition to quoted prices, a sales tax of 5% is payable on purchase price or rentals at the time of payment. Maintenance is charged separately and charges are the same under all acquisition schemes with the exception that the 5% sales tax on maintenance only applies to rent or lease plans. Prices quoted by the manufacturer are listed in Exhibit 1.

1. *Purchase Plan*
   Payment of the full purchase price on delivery of the equipment. Equipment on rental schemes can be purchased at any time, and a credit of 75% of any rentals paid in the first year of rental may be applied to decrease the list purchase price.
2. *One-Year Rental*
   Rental payable at the full rental price which is in force at the commencement of each year, and which may change from year to year.
3. *Five-Year Level Lease*
   Rental payable at 80% of the one-year rental rate as quoted at the start of the

lease. Any additional equipment installed with 24 months of the initial agreement can be added to the lease. Additional equipment acquired after the first 24 months must be installed at the one-year rental rate then prevailing. No replacement of equipment is permissible.

4. *Five-Year Reducing Rate*
   Rentals are payable at reducing percentages of the one-year rental as quoted at the start of the lease.
   The percentages are:

Year	Percentage of One-Year Rate Payable
1	90%
2	85%
3	80%
4	75%
5	70%
all subsequent years	70%

Additional equipment can be added to the lease plan at any time. A similar condition applies to replacement of equipment (for example, more powerful equipment which may become necessary or desirable), provided the replacement has a higher rental. The equipment would start at the year 1 level and follow the same pattern of decreasing percentages except that after 48 months, additions and replacements are added to the lease at the full current one-year rental level.

After the original contract period, either party can cancel any lease by giving 90-days' notice.

Tax considerations clearly play a major role in evaluating these alternatives. Dongara's marginal tax rate is 48% of net income. The capital cost allowance on computer equipment is 20% on a declining balance and any equipment additions become part of an asset class with capital cost allowance being taken on the aggregate figures for the asset class. Leasehold improvements are amortized for tax purposes on a 20% per year, straight-line basis. Other expenditures—rental, lease payments, interest payments, maintenance—are all deductible for tax purposes. Dongara could borrow longer-term funds at a before-tax interest rate of 12 percent.

Keith Best was to prepare a written report for the upcoming meeting evaluating these four acquisition alternatives. He knew that the report would have to contain a quantitative analysis of the choices available. Given that several key variables—such as the useful life of the computer and its residual value—were subject to considerable uncertainty, he would have to conduct some sensitivity analysis to see how sensitive derived results would be to changes in such key variables. Also, any qualitative aspects which were not fully captured in the numerical analysis would have to be discussed; and an ultimate recommendation as to the most desirable course of action would have to be made and substantiated.

EXHIBIT 1

Computer Requirements and Quoted Prices
(All Subject to 5% Sales Tax)

Date	Equipment	Purchase Price $	Monthly Rental (based on 1-year rental)	Monthly Maintenance
Jan. 1975	Main Processor	91,640	1,940	339
	Card Reader	10,455	221	63
	Line Printer	27,120	579	185
	Disc Storage	26,130	550	158
	Disc Adaptor	10,890	230	53
	Other	35,540	753	112
	Total	201,775	4,273	910
Jan. 1976	Core Extension	38,765	818	105
	Disc Storage Extension	26,130	550	158
	Communications Adaptor	13,535	288	51
	Total	78,430	1,656	314
Jan. 1977	Core Extension	31,895	677	84
	Line Adaptor	3,840	80	18
	Total	35,735	757	102

Leasehold Improvements

Date	Improvement	Expected Cost
Jan. 1975	Physical Preparation	$50,950
Jan. 1976	Package Programs	5,500

Selected References

T. Beechy, "The Cost of Leasing: Comment and Correction", *Accounting Review*, October, 1970, pp. 769-773.

T. Beechy, "Quasi-Debt Analysis of Financial Leases", *Accounting Review*, April, 1969, pp. 375-381.

R. Bower, "Issues in Lease Financing", *Financial Management*, Winter, 1973, pp. 25-34.

R. Carlson and D. Wort, "A New Look at the Lease Versus Purchase Decision", *Journal of Economics and Business*, Spring, 1974, pp. 199-202.

F. Chapman, III, "Financial Lease Evaluation: Survey and Synthesis", paper presented at the Eastern Finance Association Meetings, April 12, 1973.

K. Cooper and R. Strawser, "Evaluation of Capital Investment Projects Involving Asset Leases", *Financial Management*, Spring, 1975, pp. 44-49.

C. Doenges, "The Cost of Leasing", *Engineering Economist*, Winter, 1971, pp. 31-44.

W. Ferrara and J. Wojdak, "Valuation of Long-Term Leases", *Financial Analysts Journal*, November-December, 1969, pp. 29-32.

M. Gordon, A General Solution to the Buy or Lease Decision: A Pedagogical Note", *Journal of Finance*, March, 1974, pp. 245-250.

R. Johnson and W. Lewellen, "Analysis of the Lease-or-Buy Decision", *Journal of Finance,* September, 1972, pp. 815-823.

W. Lewellen, M. Long and J. McConnell, "Asset Leasing in Competitive Capital Markets", *Journal of Finance*, June, 1976, pp. 787-798.

M. Miller and C. Upton, "Leasing, Buying, and the Cost of Capital Services", *Journal of Finance*, June, 1976, pp. 761-786.

G. Mitchell, "After-Tax Cost of Leasing", *Accounting Review*, April, 1970, pp. 308-314.

C. Moyer, "Lease Evaluation and the Investment Tax Credit: A Framework for Analysis", *Financial Management*, Summer, 1975, pp. 39-42.

S. Myers, D. Dill, and A. Bautista, "Valuation of Financial Lease Contracts", *Journal of Finance*, June, 1976, pp. 799-819.

T. Nelson, "Capitalized Leases—The Effect on Financial Ratios", *Journal of Accountancy*, July, 1963, pp. 49-58.

L. Schall, "The Lease-or-Buy and Asset Acquisition Decisions", *Journal of Finance*, September, 1974, pp. 1203-1214.

R. Vancil, "Lease or Borrow: New Method of Analysis", *Harvard Business Review*, September-October, 1961, pp. 122-136.

R. Vancil, *Leasing of Industrial Equipment*, New York: McGraw-Hill, 1963.

PART 5

The Canadian Monetary System

Chapter 19
The Canadian Monetary System

19-1. INTRODUCTION AND BACKGROUND

The purpose of this chapter is to examine and illustrate how the Canadian money supply is affected by a variety of financial transactions. We will also focus upon the critical role of our central bank, the Bank of Canada (commonly called *the Bank*). Before proceeding, however, we will briefly discuss: (a) the components of the money supply in Canada, (b) the role of monetary policy, its objectives, and how it is carried out, and (c) the manner in which the money supply may influence interest rates and the level of economic activity. Since interest rates are the prices at which financial managers must borrow and lend, knowledge of the effects of money supply changes and the ability to predict these changes should be an important part of the financial executive's work.

The second section of this chapter outlines very briefly the present structure of the Bank of Canada, and the third section stresses the basic principle upon which Canadian banking practice was founded. Finally, the effect of various types of financial transactions is discussed in section four.

The total money supply in Canada is, by the broader definition, equal to coin and Bank of Canada notes in circulation outside the banking system, plus the total Canadian dollar chartered bank deposits held by the public. Such chartered bank deposits are included since cheques, as well as notes, can be used directly for making payments. While notes held by the banks as vault cash are out of circulation and hence excluded from the money supply definition, it will be shown below that these balances, nevertheless, have an important role to play in our monetary system. As shown in Table 19-1, chartered bank deposits are by far the largest component of the money supply.

The level of money supply has an important effect on economic activity.

Monetary policy, which assists in the attainment of national economic objectives, is directly concerned with the provision of money to the economy and management of the money supply. Objectives generally include[1] high and stable levels of employment, adequate economic growth, reasonable price stability, and a viable balance of payments.[2] For Canada, a country heavily engaged in international trade, maintaining reasonable stability in the currency's external value is an important constraint.

[1] The Economic Council of Canada's *First Annual Review* was largely concerned with basic economic goals. See Economic Council of Canada, *First Annual Review: Economic Goals for Canada to 1970*, Ottawa: Queen's Printer, 1964.

[2] The economic environment and the level of output have very real effects on decision-making by financial executives, including the managers of financial institutions. In previous sections, for purposes of an introductory treatment, changes in prices, interest rates, government expenditures, and employment levels were often held constant in both the models and analytical frameworks used. Certain economic variables cannot, however, be assumed away, and more advanced and complex financial analysis will require an understanding of both their behaviour and consequent impact.

In continuous consultations with government, the Bank of Canada formulates monetary policy and carries it out on a day-to-day basis. The Bank has at its disposal a variety of tools by which it can affect changes in the money supply and in credit conditions. Most are directed at the banking system and will be detailed below. Traditional theory would suggest that the Bank decides on the amount of money it considers appropriate and supplies the chartered banks with the necessary reserve funds. The banking system then responds in a passive way, automatically increasing deposits. For ease of exposition, illustrations of the impact of financial transactions on the money supply will be based on just such a viewpoint. Recently, however, some economists have argued that since banks act in the best interests of their shareholders, the banking system's response to changes in the money supply will be influenced by expected changes in interest rates. Therefore, loans and investments may not be expanded to absorb excess reserves if interest rates are expected to rise.[3]

The precise ways in which the money supply influences the economy are hotly debated by economists, but nonetheless it is useful to review their thinking briefly.[4] One school, drawing on the quantity theory of money,[5] refined by Milton Friedman,[6] holds that the central bank's control of the money supply is the primary determinant of shifts in total spending or GNP and should, therefore, be the focus of stabilization policies. Where overall money holdings are increased, there is a tendency to increase spending. This is the *monetarist approach*. The other view called the *income-expenditure approach*, is linked to the work of Keynes[7] and neo-Keynesians[8] who believe that changes in the money supply have only an indirect effect on the economy via the rates of interest. In other words, an increase in the money supply is expected to reduce rates of interest thereby increasing the willingness of consumers to spend and of businesses to invest. While we need not be too concerned with subtleties of the debates being waged, we should recognize that regardless of whether money simply matters, or whether it matters most, it can affect the rate of interest as well as conditions in the money and capital markets. Consequently, it is imperative that the financial executive have an appreciation of the ways in which it is managed. Some comments of the senior deputy governor of the Bank of Canada are interesting in this respect.

> ...changes in credit conditions, that is changes in the availability and

[3] This theory of money supply determination might more precisely be interpreted as viewing the money supply as a function of the banking system's reserve base, interest rates, the Bank rate, the ratio of demand to time deposits and their respective reserve requirements, plus miscellaneous other factors.

[4] See, for example, S. Weintraub, "Keynes and the Monetarists", *Canadian Journal of Economics*, February 1971, pp. 37-49. Also, M. Friedman, *A Theoretical Framework for Monetary Analysis*, New York: National Bureau of Economic Research, 1971.

[5] For an example of the pre-Keynesian view, see I. Fisher, *The Purchasing Power of Money*, New York: Macmillan, 1911.

[6] M. Friedman, ed., *Studies in the Quantity Theory of Money and Other Essays*, Chicago: Aldine Press, 1969.

[7] J. Keynes, *The General Theory of Employment, Interest and Money*, New York: Harcourt Brace Javanovich, 1936.

[8] See, for example, W. Heller, *New Dimensions of Political Economy*, New York: Norton, 1966, and J. O'Brien, *Canadian Money and Banking*, Toronto: McGraw-Hill, 1964.

cost of money, have widespread effects on all financial markets as well as the economy generally.[9]

19-2. STRUCTURE OF THE BANK OF CANADA

The structure of the central bank is a simple one. It has a Board of Directors and a more viable Executive Council which acts for the Board. The latter includes the Governor, Senior Deputy Governor, Deputy Minister of Finance, and two Directors. Louis Raminsky, in taking over as Governor of the Bank, attempted to clarify both the responsibility of his office and the role of the Bank. The following excerpts are taken from his 1961 *Report* to the Minister of Finance:

> . . . it is essential that the responsibilities in relation to monetary policy should be clarified . . . I do not suggest a precise formula but have in mind two main principles to be established: (1) in the ordinary course of events, the Bank has the responsibility for monetary policy, and (2) if the Government disapproves of the monetary policy being carried out by the Bank it has the right and the responsibility to direct the Bank as to the policy which the Bank is to carry out.
>
> The first principle is designed to ensure that the Bank has the degree of independence and responsibility necessary if it is, in the language of the Bank of Canada Act, "to regulate credit and currency in the best interests of the economic life of the nation". To discharge this duty the Bank must be sufficiently independent and responsible in its operations to be able to withstand day-to-day pressures from any source. But in the longer run, if there should develop a serious and persistent conflict between the views of the Government and the views of the central bank with regard to monetary policy which, after prolonged and conscientious efforts on both sides, cannot be resolved, the Government should be able formally to instruct the Bank what monetary policy it wishes carried out and the Bank should have the duty to comply with these instructions. The exercise of this authority by Government would place on government direct responsibility for the monetary policy to be followed. If this policy, as communicated to the Bank, was one which the Governor felt he could not in good conscience carry out, his duty would be to resign and to make way for someone who took a different view.[10]

19-3. A BASIC PRINCIPLE OF CANADIAN BANKING PRACTICE

The money supply in Canada can be affected by a variety of financial transactions. These transactions may involve the Bank of Canada, the chartered

[9]Remarks by Gerald Bouey at the annual meeting of the Canadian Mutual Funds Association, Toronto, May 25, 1972. Mr. Bouey was subsequently appointed Governor of the Bank.

[10]Bank of Canada, *Annual Report of the Governor to the Minister of Finance, 1961*, Ottawa: Bank of Canada, February 1962, pp. 3-4.

banks, nonmonetary financial intermediaries (such as trust companies), deficit-spending units, as well as nonresidents. It is useful for students of finance to appreciate the impact of such transactions, and a review of a number of these will follow.[11]

To understand the transactions, we must bear in mind that Canadian banking practice is based upon the system of fractional reserve banking.[12] Chartered banks must maintain set fractions of their total deposits as reserves with the Bank of Canada. These reserve requirements exist only partially for the protection of depositors. The requirements, whose workings will be detailed below, are primarily there to facilitate control by the central bank of the banking system's ability to alter the money supply.

Under the *Bank Act*, two cash reserve requirements are set out. On demand deposits, the requirement is a cash ratio of twelve percent, while with notice deposits it is four percent. The weighted average of the two will vary and in mid-1975 it worked out to about 6.1 percent, with roughly 70 percent of the reserve kept on deposit at the Bank of Canada and the balance held by the chartered banks in notes and coin. If, for convenience, we were to assume an overall cash ratio of at least 6.25 percent, then, as shown below, the banking system and the public between them can create a maximum of about sixteen dollars of bank deposits for each new dollar of reserves created for the banks (this will be explained below).

To review how the banking system in a multibank economy can expand its deposits up to sixteen times, it is useful to first consider a single bank A's activities and the impact of a new $10,000 cash deposit. The balance sheet of the bank will initially show an increase in loanable cash of $9,375 and a reserve of $625 (which may not be loaned out) on the asset side and an increase in deposits or liabilities of $10,000. Note that this point emphasizes a basic rule in bank lending, namely that a bank may safely lend out an amount equal to its excess reserves; in the above case, this amount was $9,375, assuming a 6.25 percent legal reserve requirement. Once loans and investments are made to the allowable maximum, the increments to the balance sheet will appear as follows:

Chartered Bank A

Assets		Liabilities	
Cash & Reserves with Bank of Canada	+$ 625	Deposits	+ $10,000
Loans and Investments	+$9,375		
	$10,000		$10,000

[11] The illustrations which will follow are largely based on a more comprehensive set to be found in an excellent publication put out by the Economic Research Department of a chartered bank. See, Royal Bank of Canada, *How the Canadian Money Supply is Affected by Various Banking and Financial Transactions and Developments*, (4th ed.) Montreal: Royal Bank of Canada, 1970.

[12] For a review of the concept of fractional reserve banking, see P. Samuelson and A. Scott, *Economics, An Introductory Analysis*, (2nd Canadian ed.) Toronto: McGraw-Hill, 1968, Chapter 16.

The bank through its lending activites has increased the money supply by \$9,375 and, given the legal reserve requirements of 6.25 percent, it can do nothing more until it receives additional deposits.

The process does not, however, end here. Assume that the \$9,375 in loans from Bank A reappear as deposits in Bank B which, after reserving \$586 (.0625 × \$9,375), in turn makes loans of \$8,789 (0.9375 × \$9,375).

Such loans then reappear as deposits in Bank C, and so on. Algebraically, the sixteen-fold increase can be arrived at as follows:

new original deposit		= \$10,000
additional loans by Bank A	0.9375 × \$10,000	= \$9,375
additional loans by Bank B	0.9375 × \$9,375	= \$8,789
additional loans by Bank C	0.9375 × \$8,789	= \$8,240
⋮		⋮

When added together, this series yields[13]

$$\$10{,}000 + \$10{,}000(.9375) + \$10{,}000(.9375)^2 + \$10{,}000(.9375)^3 + \ldots$$

$$= \$10{,}000\,[1 + .9375 + (.9375)^2 + (.9375)^3 + \ldots]$$

$$= \$10{,}000\,[\tfrac{1}{1-.9375}] = \$10{,}000 \times \tfrac{1}{.0625}$$

$$= \$160{,}000.$$

More simply, the total possible *deposit* expansion that could occur in the banking system can be expressed as:

$$\frac{\text{Initial (Primary) Deposit}}{\text{Required Reserve Ratio}}$$

and in the above case, we have

$$\frac{\$10{,}000}{.0625} = \$160{,}000$$

Note that against these deposits, a required reserve of 6.25 percent must be maintained. Hence, \$10,000 must be kept on hand at the banks in the form of cash and/or reserves with the Bank of Canada. This permits a maximum possible expansion of \$150,000 in new loans and investments within the system.

In practice, however, the fullest possible expansion will not materialize since:

- in the course of deposit expansion, funds may leak outside the banking system, from banks into hand-to-hand circulation, for example;
- borrowers may not seek to take advantage of a bank's lending capacity; and

[13]We use the well known formula for an infinite geometric series which, for $x<1$, yields

$$1 + x + x^2 + \ldots + x^n + \ldots = \frac{1}{1-x}$$

- there is a tendency by banks toward maintaining excess reserves in anticipation, perhaps, of financial or political crises, seasonal factors, and the like.

The need for significant excess reserves is curtailed somewhat by the bank's extensions of day-to-day loans to money-market dealers. Such loans are callable daily before noon, thereby providing considerable flexibility.[14]

Thus, a basic principle upon which the Canadian banking system is founded is the system of fractional reserve banking and the related multiple deposit expansion as the initial increase in money supply works its way through the system.

19-4. FINANCIAL TRANSACTIONS AND THEIR EFFECT UPON THE MONEY SUPPLY

Given the preceding abstractive discussion of the Canadian banking system, attention can be shifted to various illustrations of the manner in which financial transactions may affect the money supply. For the sake of clarity, a number of simplifying assumptions need to be made. Specifically,

- excess reserves are precluded and bank response to any changed cash ratio is instantaneous, that is, there are no time lags,
- deposits rise or fall as bank portfolios of loans and investments increase or decrease, and
- currency holdings are only constant or, in other words, the money supply is held to vary only with bank deposits.

The following analyses are divided into a number of subsections involving the different ways in which the transactions of various groups may affect the Canadian money supply. The groups considered include the Bank of Canada, the Government in both an internal and an international context, and finally the public.

Transactions of the central bank

Open-Market Operations

Given the above assumptions, the first illustration is concerned with open-market operations by the Bank of Canada—the prime technique of monetary control. In the following example, the Bank purchases 10 million dollars of outstanding Government of Canada securities from the public who, in turn, deposit the drafts or cheques which were received in payment from the Bank of Canada with a chartered bank.

The chartered banks then simply exchange these cheques for increased balances with the Bank of Canada. This action thus adds to the cash position of the chartered banks (the cash ratio in the numerical example below becomes 6.367 percent) encouraging them to take on new loans and investments to eliminate their "excess" reserves. In actual fact, the public when buying or selling securities would deal through an investment dealer or bank and, as such, the transaction would not be directly consummated with the central bank. For the

[14]The dealer whose loan is called may turn to one of the other banks or, if necessary, to the Bank of Canada.

sake of simplicity, however, it is assumed that all transactions are carried out with the chartered banks. The resulting increase in bank deposits from the public selling the securities to the Bank, and hence the increase in money supply, is traced through the following balance sheets, while maintaining a 6.25 percent legal reserve ratio of bank cash to deposits.

Balance Sheets Prior to Open-Market Operations
(in millions of dollars)

Chartered Banks

Assets		Liabilities	
Notes	200	Can. $ Deps.	8000
Bal. at B of C	300		
Bank Cash	500		
Loans & Inv.	7500		
	8000		8000

Cash Ratio 500/8000 = 6.25%

Bank of Canada

Assets		Liabilities	
Securities	1500	Notes Outstanding	
		to banks	200
		to public	1000
		Deps. of Banks	300
	1500		1500

Balance Sheets After B of C Draft Cleared
and Balances with B of C Increased
(in millions of dollars); all changes are circled.

Chartered Banks

Assets		Liabilities	
Notes	200	Can. $ Deps.	(8010)
Bal. at B of C	(310)		
Bank Cash	(510)		
Loans & Inv.	7500		
	(8010)		(8010)

Cash Ratio 510/8010 = 6.367%

Bank of Canada

Assets		Liabilities	
Securities	1510	Notes Outstanding	
		to banks	200
		to public	1000
		Deps. of Banks	(310)
	(1510)		(1510)

Balance Sheets after Loans Increased to
Restore 6.25% Ratio of Bank Cash to Deposits
(in millions of dollars)

Chartered Banks

Assets		Liabilities	
Notes	200	Can. $ Deps.	8160
Bal. at B of C	310		
Bank Cash	510		
Loans & Inv.	7650		
	8160		8160

Cash Ratio 510/8160 = 6.25% restored.

Bank of Canada

Assets	Liabilities
No change	

The final result of the Bank of Canada's purchase of outstanding government securities is related in the third balance sheet. Through the 10 million dollar increase in the reserves of chartered banks, it was possible to increase loans and investments by 150 million dollars (7650-7500) and, in total, deposits by 160 million dollars (8160-8000).

Open-market operations by the Bank of Canada may just as readily be directed at reducing the money supply and this could be achieved by selling off holdings of government securities. In this case, the Bank would sell securities to the public who would pay with cheques drawn on their bank accounts, thereby reducing deposits and cash at chartered banks, which forces a corresponding reduction in loans and investment by the banks.

As we can see, through open-market operations the Bank of Canada may affect the supply of money in Canada. The magnitude of changes in the money supply is, of course, a critical issue to be faced by the Bank. The following remarks by Mr. Rasminsky are pertinent:

> Some economists, including some who have appeared before this Committee, advocate that the central bank should follow a money supply policy, that is, a policy which would produce over time a stable rate of growth in the money supply. The first thing that I would like to say about this proposition is that my life as Governor of the Bank of Canada would be a good deal easier if I could persuade myself that there was some such rule which was in fact valid for the conduct of monetary policy in Canada. It would be pleasant to be able to say that the money supply was being increased at exactly the right rate and that if the economy was not performing as well as it should then the trouble necessarily lay elsewhere than in monetary policy.
>
> To operate strictly according to a money supply rule, the central bank would have to be convinced that there is some specific and measurable definition of the money supply which was subject to its control and which exerted a reasonably predictable degree of control over the trend of economic activity. Although there has been a good deal of research on this matter, the evidence is far from being firm enough to justify an attempt to operate along these lines in Canada.[15]

While open-market operations remain the prime technique of monetary control utilized by the central bank, the proper magnitude of changes in the money supply required to balance complex and sometimes conflicting economic objectives (such as price stability and full employment) remains a challenge to which no conclusive answers have been found so far. Contributing to this difficulty are the time lags between actions taken and their effects, as well as the multiplicity of interacting factors in the economy which make it difficult to firmly establish cause and effect relationships. Thus, current activities by the Bank of Canada may not be fully felt for several months and the level of money

[15]Submission of Louis Rasminsky, then Governor of the Bank of Canada, to the Standing Senate Committee on National Finance, June 17, 1971, (mimeographed) pp. 15-16. It is interesting that in the autumn of 1975 the Bank of Canada for the first time announced publicly a target range for monetary expansion.

supply is but one of many factors influencing economic activity.

Table 19-1 shows how the major components of money have changed over time.

TABLE 19-1

Currency Outside Banks and Chartered Bank Deposits (in million of dollars)

	Coin	Currency	Deposits Less Float*	Total	% increase
Dec. 1966	288	2203	18,805	21,296	
Dec. 1968	390	2597	24,614	27,601	30%
Dec. 1970	457	3027	28,583	32,066	16%
Dec. 1972	509	3928	38,999	43,437	35%
Dec. 1974	646	5145	55,564	61,355	41%

Sources: Bank of Canada, *Statistical Summary, 1969 Supplement,* and *Bank of Canada Review,* Various Issues.

*Cheques which have been written against bank deposits but which have not yet been presented for payment—cheques in the mails for example—are defined as float. It is subtracted here to avoid double counting.

Variation in the Secondary Reserve Ratio

Another technique of central bank control involves the variation of the secondary reserve ratio. Under the *Bank of Canada Act*, the Bank has the right to impose and to vary a secondary reserve requirement quite distinct from the cash reserves discussed in the previous section.[16] When no requirement is in effect, one may be imposed up to six percent and this reserve may be increased by up to one percent a month, but is not to exceed twelve percent. Secondary reserves may include cash in excess of cash reserve requirements, treasury bills, which are the short-term debt issues of the Government of Canada, and day loans to money-market dealers. Clearly, these reserve requirements reduce the amount of funds which the banks have available for discretionary lending and investments.

TABLE 19-2

Minimum Secondary Reserve Ratios (Daily Averages for Period)

Period	%
1968	6.92
1969	7.58
1970	8.50
1971	9.00
1972	8.00
1973	8.00
1974	7.92

[16]The 1967 amendment to the *Bank of Canada Act* provided the legal authority for such impositions while revoking the power of the Bank of Canada to alter cash reserve requirements, a provision which, in any case, was never used because of its severity.

Table 19-2 shows some recent minimum average secondary reserve ratio requirements.

To illustrate how chartered bank liquidity can be immobilized or released by altering secondary reserve requirements without directly affecting the money supply, consider the impact of an increase from seven to nine percent.

Consequences of such increases in secondary reserves are an actual curtailment of lending and investments as indicated, with funds shifted from loans and general investments to investments in the narrow range of financial instruments which qualify as secondary reserves.

Balance Sheets of Chartered Banks with Secondary Reserves at 7%
(in millions of dollars)

Assets		Liabilities	
Bank Cash	500	Can. $ Deps.	8,000
Secondary Reserves	560		
Loans & Inv.	6,940		
	8,000		8,000

Secondary Reserve Ratio 7.0% Cash Ratio 6.25%

Balance Sheets with Secondary Reserves Raised to 9%
(in millions of dollars)

Assets		Liabilities	
Bank Cash	500	Can. $ Deps.	8,000
Secondary Reserves	720		
Loans & Inv.	6,780		
	8,000		8,000

Secondary Reserve Ratio 9% Cash Ratio 6.25%

Presented above were examples of actions which may be undertaken by the Bank of Canada, including the use of open-market operations and manipulation of the secondary reserve ratio. The Canadian Government through its operations may also have an effect upon the supply of money and credit conditions. Precisely how the Government of Canada may alter the situation is reviewed next.

Transactions of the Government of Canada

The following illustrations show the effect of transactions between the central bank and the Canadian Government upon the money supply via the operation of the money markets. Money-market transactions occur in maturities of under one year, and treasury bills occupy a central position in the market. Treasury bills are Government of Canada short-term debt issued weekly and generally possessing two maturities, 91 and 182 days, with one-year bills interjected periodically. The bills are usually sold at a discount, with the selling price below the face value to be paid at maturity. The difference between issue price and maturity value constitutes the yield on the bills. Since treasury bills are for our purposes the most relevant, attention will be focused only upon this basic money-market instrument.

A key position in the Canadian money market is occupied by a group of fifteen or so specialized investment dealers, "money-market dealers" or "jobbers" whose function it is to bring together borrowers and lenders of short-term funds. The main borrower in the money market is the Government of Canada, and those groups invited to bid at the weekly treasury bill auction include the Bank of Canada, the chartered banks, and the investment dealers. Those of the investment dealers who qualify as accredited money-market dealers have "purchase and resale privileges" with the central bank which they use only as a last resort. Purchase and resale agreements occur when "the Bank stands ready to buy treasury bills and government bonds of under three years' maturity from the dealers, subject to an agreement by the dealer to repurchase the securities within thirty days at a price to net the Bank a predetermined rate of interest."[17] In effect, it is just such agreements between the central bank and particular dealers which permit the latter to occupy a key position in the money market.

The government issues new treasury bills each week to replace maturing bills. The price and yield of the new issues are determined by an auction procedure, usually held on the Thursday of the week in which the new bills are to be issued. As was mentioned earlier, those eligible to bid are the banks, the central bank, and *all* the investment dealers. Though it is beyond the scope of this book to discuss the actual treasury bill auction procedures, the following illustration depicts the manner in which the weekly auctions enable the Bank of Canada to manage the money supply. Assume that the Canadian Government sells 50 million dollars' worth to replace an identical amount of maturing bills. Of bills maturing, 25 million are held by the Bank, 15 million by the chartered banks, and 10 million by money-market dealers. Assuming it is the Bank of Canada's intention to acquire only 15 million dollars of the new issue, with an extra 5 million dollars' worth left to each of the other bidders then, as set out below, a reduction in the money supply may follow.

It is readily apparent from the balance sheets that bank cash is *not* affected by transactions between the Government and the Bank of Canada. Furthermore, net purchases by the chartered banks and investment dealers restore the Government's balances with the Bank while reducing those of the chartered banks. The reduction in bank cash, however, decreases the overall cash ratio of the banks below 6.25 percent requiring, other things being equal, the sale of 155 million dollars of investments to the public. An offsetting decline in deposits by the public along with a 5 million dollar decline in the deposit of investment dealers results in a 160 million dollar decrease in the money supply. Thus, by a decision to absorb different proportions of a new issue, the Bank can affect the

[17]J. O'Brien, *Canadian Money and Banking*, Toronto: McGraw-Hill, 1968, Chapter 16, p. 116.

money supply, and can do so even when the net new issue of securities by the Government is zero.

Balance Sheets Prior to the Auctions
(in millions of dollars)

Chartered Banks

Assets		Liabilities	
Notes	200	Can. $ Deps.	
Bal. at B of C	300	of Inv. Dealers	200
Bank Cash	500	of Can. Govt.	800
Treasury Bills		of public	7000
maturing	15		
other	485		
Loans & Inv.	7000		
	8000		8000

Bank of Canada

Assets		Liabilities	
Treasury Bills		Notes Outstanding	
maturing	25	to banks	200
other	475	to public	960
Other Sec.	1000	Can. $ Deps.	
		of banks	300
		of Can. Govt.	40
	1500		1500

Balance Sheet Reflecting Bank of Canada Purchase
(in millions of dollars)

Chartered Banks

Assets	Liabilities
No change	

Bank of Canada

Assets		Liabilities	
Treasury Bills	490	Notes Outstanding	
Other Sec.	1,000	to banks	200
		to public	960
		Can. $ Deps.	
		of banks	300
		of Can. Govt.	30
	1,490		1,490

Balance Sheet Reflecting Purchases by Others
(in millions of dollars)

Chartered Banks

Assets		Liabilities	
Notes	200	Can. $ Deps.	
Bal. at B of C	290	of Inv. Dealers	195
Bank Cash	490	of Can. Govt.	800
Treasury Bills	505	of public	7,000
Loans & Inv.	7,000		
	7,995		7,995

Cash Ratio 6.13%

Bank of Canada

Assets		Liabilities	
Treasury Bills	490	Notes Outstanding	
Other Sec.	1,000	to banks	200
		to public	960
		Can. $ Deps.	
		of banks	290
		of Can. Govt.	40
	1,490		1,490

A net new offering of bonds by the Government of Canada to meet its expenditures will lead to an increase in the money supply to the extent that such bonds are bought by the Bank of Canada without further adjustments. Assume a net new 50 million dollar issue which does not just replace maturing bills, with the public picking up 30 million and the Bank of Canada the balance.

The public pays for the bonds by reducing its deposits with the chartered banks. Upon the Government depositing the cheques it receives into its account at the Bank of Canada, both deposits of the chartered banks at the Bank and their required cash ratio are reduced. If, however, the Government uses the entire proceeds of the bond sale to purchase goods and services from the Canadian public, which in turn deposits the payments received with the chartered banks, then bank reserves and deposits are restored leaving the money supply unaffected.

The 20 million dollars' worth of new debt purchased by the Bank of Canada works its way through the banking system as shown in the following balance sheets:

Balance Sheets Prior to New Gov't. Debt Issue
(in millions of dollars)

Chartered Banks				Bank of Canada			
Assets		Liabilities		Assets		Liabilities	
Notes	200	Can. $ Deps.		Securities	1500	Notes Outstanding	
Bal. at B of C	300	of Can. Govt.	800			to banks	200
Bank Cash	500	of public	7200			to public	960
Loans & Inv.	7500					Can. $ Deps.	
						of banks	300
						of Can. Govt.	40
	8000		8000		1500		1500

Cash Ratio 6.25%

Balance Sheets Reflecting New Gov't. Debt Issue and Government Purchase of Goods & Services from Public
(in millions of dollars)

Chartered Banks				Bank of Canada			
Assets		Liabilities		Assets		Liabilities	
Notes	200	Can. $ Deps.		Securities	1520	Notes Outstanding	
Bal. at B of C	320	of Can. Govt.	800			to banks	200
Bank Cash	520	of public	7220			to public	960
Loans & Inv.	7500					Can. $ Deps.	
						of banks	320
						of Can. Govt.	40
	8020		8020		1520		1520

The government's purchases increase the public's deposits. The government's cheques are returned to the Bank of Canada, and settlement results in the transfer of 20 million dollars from the Canadian government's deposits to those of the chartered banks. Unless the Bank of Canada then moves to offset the increase in bank cash, the money supply may increase by 320 million dollars as the chartered banks move to draw down their cash reserves from 6.48 percent by increasing deposits through the acquisition of additional loans and investment.

International financial transactions

Another set of financial transactions to be surveyed is the international one involving foreign exchange. The magnitude of such transactions is indicated by Table 19-3, with a minus sign indicating an outflow of capital from Canada.

The following illustration shows that, by themselves, neither inflows nor outflows of short- or long-term capital affect the internal money supply. Consider the case of a sale by a Canadian deficit-spending unit of 100 million dollars of long-term bonds in New York denominated in U.S. dollars.

Chartered Banks' Balance Sheet Prior to Borrowing in New York
(in millions of dollars)

Assets		Liabilities	
Notes	200	Can. $ Deps.	8000
Bal. at B of C	300	U.S. $ Deps.	500
Bank Cash	500		
Can. Loans & Inv.	7500		
U.S. $ Assets	500		
	8500		8500

Cash Ratio (Bank Cash to Can. $ Deps.) 6.25%

Chartered Banks' Balance Sheet Following Borrowing
(in millions of dollars)

Assets		Liabilities	
Notes	200	Can. $ Deps.	8000
Bal. at B of C	300	U.S. $ Deps.	
Bank Cash	500	of Can. Importers	100
Can. Loans & Inv.	7500	of others	500
U.S. $ Assets	600		
	8600		8600

Cash Ratio Unchanged

TABLE 19-3

Canadian Balance of International Payments
Capital Account
(in millions of dollars)

	1968	1971	1974
CAPITAL MOVEMENTS IN LONG-TERM FORMS			
Direct investment			
Direct investment in Canada	590	880	435
Direct investment abroad	—225	—220	—645
Canadian stocks			
Trade in outstanding stocks	114	—144	—111
New issues	67	22	15
Retirements	—5	—4	—6
Canadian bonds			
Trade in outstanding bonds	—70	—94	39
New issues			
Government of Canada	288	27	14
Provincial	852	725	1,726
Municipal	124	26	238
Corporate	586	389	444
Total	1,850	1,164	2,422
Retirements			
Government of Canada	—57	—31	—56
Provincial	—76	—318	—158
Municipal	—60	—99	—95
Corporate	—233	—374	—170
Total	—426	—822	—479
Columbia River Treaty: net	88	24	—
Foreign securities	—467	204	25
Government of Canada loans & subscriptions			
Advances	—73	—156	—311
Other long-term capital	226	—372	—440
Total capital movements in long-term forms	1,669	482	944
CAPITAL MOVEMENTS IN SHORT-TERM FORMS			
Resident holdings of foreign bank balances and other short-term funds	—449	843	211
Nonresident holdings of Canadian assets			
Canadian dollar deposits	72	92	592
Canadian government demand liabilities	21	50	45
Treasury bills	48	—3	79
Commercial paper		128	—63
Finance company paper	—132	—39	63
Other finance company obligations	24	—29	170
Other short-term capital movements	—807	—1,053	—140
Total capital movements in short-term forms	—1,223	—11	957
Net capital movements (excluding changes in reserves and I.M.F. positions)	446	471	1,901
Current account balance	—97	306	—1,877
Allocation of special drawing rights	—	119	—
Changes in official international reserves	350	896	24

Source: Bank of Canada, *Bank of Canada Review, April, 1975.*

The monies raised are deposited in the chartered banks and then sold for Canadian funds. If the Canadian dollars come from importers willing to buy the foreign currency to finance their imports, rather than the foreign exchange authority,[18] the transaction adds nothing to official holdings of foreign exchange. It is clear that the total of Canadian dollar deposits has remained constant and the money supply is unaffected.

Neither increases nor decreases in official foreign exchange reserves normally affect the money supply. Consider the case where the above U.S. dollar deposit cannot be matched with private demand for such monies. Sale of the foreign exchange by the chartered banks will, in the absence of private buyers, be to the Bank of Canada acting for the government. The foreign exchange will be held in the Exchange Fund Account. In settlement, balances of the banks with the Bank of Canada are increased while government balances with the Bank are reduced. As a consequence, cash reserves of the chartered banks increase above the required level. Following normal procedure, however, the Government will reduce its deposits with the chartered banks to restore its balances at the Bank of Canada. This move draws down bank cash and returns the cash reserves to the required levels. Failure to follow such normal procedure will clearly imply a potential increase in the money supply.

Shifts in bank deposits

A final illustration emphasizes the relevance of shifts in bank deposits or fluctuations in the public's propensity to hold currency and the Bank of Canada's adjustment of bank cash to compensate for this phenomenon.

Table 19-4 shows that the chartered banks have by far the largest proportion of their deposit liabilities in notice deposits. Any shifts from demand to notice

TABLE 19-4

Canadian Dollar Deposits of Chartered Banks
(millions of dollars, selected years)

End of	Gov't of Canada	Provincial Governments	Personal Savings	Other Notice	Other Banks	Public Demand	Total
1968	669	391	13,622	4,050	260	7,387	26,379
1971	2,239	587	17,783	6,215	351	8,436	35,611
1974	4,682	622	29,789	11,210	925	11,570	58,797

Source: Bank of Canada, *Bank of Canada Review*, April, 1975.

deposits, which carry a significantly lower four percent reserve requirement, will permit an increase in the money supply. Consequently, such shifting has important implications for the Bank of Canada, particularly as it is likely to occur in periods when the Bank pursues a policy of monetary constraint.

[18]Technically speaking, the foreign exchange authority involves the Exchange Fund Account, a special acount in the name of the Minister of Finance containing the bulk of Canada's official foreign exchange reserves.

During such periods, interest rates are likely to rise, providing added incentive for the public to increase their notice deposits in order to benefit from such increased rates. The resulting downward shift in chartered bank reserve requirements may, however, serve to increase the money supply and thus counteract the original policy of monetary constraint.

To illustrate, bank cash of 500 million dollars will meet the cash reserve requirements on 2,250 million dollars of demand deposits (12 percent requirement) and 5,750 million dollars of notice deposits (4 percent requirement). A shift of 500 million dollars from demand to notice deposits will drop legal cash requirements by $500(12% – 4%) = $40 million to a total of 460 million dollars and the overall reserve ratio to 5.75 percent. Therefore, unless the Bank of Canada reacts and reduces bank cash by 40 million dollars, the chartered banks will be free to loan or invest and thereby increase deposits by $40 million/.0575 or 696 million dollars, assuming that the public maintains the newly established balance between types of deposits (and thus, a new required cash ratio of 5.75%). Given varying reserve requirements for different types of deposits, shifts in the mix of deposits maintained by the public will affect the reserve position of the chartered banks. This, in turn, has a direct impact on the supply of money since the banks' lending and investment activities are determined by their reserve position.

As reflected in Table 19-1, the public's propensity to hold currency fluctuates. Changes are frequent and can be substantial with demand varying by seasons, months, and even days of the week. There are, for example, significant changes before Christmas, long weekends, and in agricultural regions before crops are harvested. In addition, increased business activity stimulates the need for currency.

Unless the Bank of Canada moves to offset the situation, an increase in the public's demand for pocket cash may reduce the money supply. Specifically, the public draws on its bank deposits to obtain cash—an action which will reduce bank reserves.

Though deposits have been reduced somewhat, the overall cash ratio also dips causing the banks to cut back on their loans and investments. The consequences of such action are a fall in deposits and a shrinking of the money supply.

19-5. SUMMARY

Money supply is a major factor influencing interest rates. The movement of interest rates is of critical importance not only for financing decisions but also in its effects on business investments and economic activity more generally. It is therefore essential for the student of finance to have at least a broad appreciation of the tools of monetary policy, and to understand both the role of the Bank of Canada and how a variety of financial transactions might have a bearing on the money supply. Money in this context is defined as coins and notes in circulation and chartered bank deposits held by the public, with the latter being by far the largest component.

The Bank of Canada, and the central banks in most countries, are semi-autonomous institutions established by governments to formulate and to implement monetary policy and to regulate the supply of money available in the economy. Canadian banking practice is based on the concept of fractional reserve banking, meaning that chartered banks have to maintain set percentages of their deposits as reserves or as "bank cash" with the Bank of Canada. Since the percentage of reserves to total deposits is small, this implies that any alteration in the chartered banks' reserve position is magnified in its effect on total bank deposits and on the chartered banks' lending and investment activities. By influencing the reserve positions of chartered banks, the Bank of Canada can affect the money supply.

The two principal ways in which the Bank of Canada intervenes to control the money supply are open-market operations and variations in the secondary reserve requirements. Open-market operations entail the purchasing or selling of financial securities (mainly Government debt instruments) by the Bank of Canada from or to the general public. When purchasing, the amounts paid to the public find their way to the chartered banks, thus adding to the banks deposits and reserves and increasing the lending and investment capacity of the banking system. The reverse takes place when the Bank of Canada sells securities: payment by the public is made by withdrawing deposits from banks, thus curtailing the money supply available in the economy. Secondary reserves which are in excess of bank cash are funds which have to be committed by chartered banks to a narrow range of financial assets, thereby freezing a part of bank assets by withdrawing them from lending and general investment activities. The Bank of Canada may vary the percentage of secondary reserve requirements.

Finally, the Bank can influence reserves of the banking system by the amounts of newly issued government debt (mainly treasury bills) it decides to purchase. The effects are identical to those of open-market operations. If the Bank finances additional government debt and if funds thus received by the government are used to purchase goods and services from the general public, these funds will result in new bank deposits and added reserves for the banking system.

International financial transactions generally have no effect on the internal money supply. If the supply and demand for foreign exchange is balanced, deposits due to foreign currency earnings are matched by withdrawals to pay for foreign currency liabilities, leaving total bank deposits unchanged. If the Bank of Canada has to absorb net differences, these will be posted to the government's account with the Bank. Following normal procedure the government will adjust its balances with chartered banks to restore its balances at the Bank of Canada, once again leaving the total reserves in the banking system unaltered.

Shifts between types of bank deposits with different reserve requirements (*e.g.*, notice and demand deposits) or fluctuations in the public's propensity to hold currency as against bank deposits, will alter the banking system's reserve position, thereby affecting the money supply, unless the central bank moves to offset the situation.

The appendix provides a brief discusion of the Weekly Financial Statistics published by the Bank of Canada.

Questions for Discussion

1. Chartered banks may fulfill their secondary reserve requirements by holding excess primary reserves, treasury bills, or day loans. Which of these investments constitute the largest percentage of the banks' portfolio which is used to fulfill secondary reserve requirements? Explain.

2. The banks are the major holders of treasury bills. When the secondary reserve requirement is reduced by the Bank of Canada, the banks which seek to maximize the return on their investment portfolio will sell treasury bills. For example, on November 3, 1971, with a 9% secondary reserve requirement, the banks held $2.877 billion in treasury bills. However, on March 1, 1972, with the secondary reserve requirement reduced to 8%, the banks held only $2.669 billion in treasury bills. Who purchased these excess treasury bills? Explain.

3. The lowering of the secondary reserve requirement is viewed by many as an indication that an easier monetary policy is to be effected. However, if the banks no longer have as great a need for treasury bills, they will tend to lower their bids at the weekly bill auction. Such action could increase yields and cause short-term interest rates to rise. The ultimate result would be exactly the reserve of the desired effect. How does one explain this apparent dichotomy?

4. Discuss some of the factors which prevent the Canadian banking system from expanding the money supply to the limits allowed by the Bank of Canada's reserve requirements.

5. The Bank of Canada is often referred to as a "lender of last resort". Explain the significance of this term.

Problems with Solutions

1. Assume an individual withdraws $25,000 from his account to use as a downpayment for a new house. If the overall reserve ratio is 8%, what is the effect of this transaction on deposits and the money supply?

Solution

The initial loss in reserves ($25,000) results in a multiple contraction of deposits and the money supply. Total deposit contraction may be given by the *initial* withdrawal of $25,000 divided by the overall reserve ratio of 8%. Thus, deposits fall by a total of $312,500. However, 8% of this amount must have been maintained as required reserves with the result that loans and investments worth $287,500 (23,000/.08) must be called in. Total money supply contraction then is $287,500 plus the initial withdrawal of $25,000.

2. In order to "dampen" an inflationary Canadian economy, the Bank of Canada decides to sell $80 million worth of Government of Canada securities to the

general public through the chartered banks. Show changes in both the Bank of Canada's and the chartered banks' balance sheets by using "T-accounts". Assume an overall reserve ratio of 8%.

Solution

Bank of Canada
(millions of dollars)

ASSETS		LIABILITIES	
Securities	–$80	Deposits of Banks	–$80

Chartered Banks (After Payment)
(millions of dollars)

ASSETS		LIABILITIES	
Bal. at B of C	–$80	Can. $ Deposits	–$80

Chartered Banks (Ultimate)
(millions of dollars)

ASSETS		LIABILITIES	
Bal. at B of C	–$80	Can. $ Deposits	–$1,000
Loans & Inv.	–$920		

Sale of $80 million in securities resulted in the chartered banks being short $80 million in reserves and this forces them to contract deposits by $1 billion—a "very painful process indeed"!

3. (a) Assume the following initial position of the chartered banking system:

ASSETS		LIABILITIES	
Bank Cash	$1,920	Can. $ Deps.	
Loans & Inv.	18,080	Demand	$14,000
	$20,000	Notice	6,000
			$20,000

Given a 12% required reserve ratio for demand and a 4% ratio for notice deposits, no excess reserves exist and the banking system is in a "fully loaned-up" position. What is the effect when the public shifts $3,000 from notice to demand deposits? Show the balance sheet changes.

(b) Assume now that only 50% of the deposit reduction in (a) comes from demand and 50% from notice balances.

Solution

(a) Balance Sheet Showing Deficiency Reserve Position

ASSETS		LIABILITIES	
Bank Cash:		Can. $ Deps.	
Required	$2,160*	Demand	$17,000
Actual	1,920	Notice	3,000
Deficiency	(240)		
Loans and Inv.	18,080		
	$20,000		$20,000

*[(.12 × $17,000) + (.04 × 3,000)]

To clear up this deficiency, some loans and investments must be called in unless the Bank of Canada moves in to clear up this deficiency. If we assume that the public in paying off the loans and investments called in, reduce only the balances in *their demand accounts*, then the contraction is simply (240/.12) or $2,000.

This is shown below:

ASSETS		LIABILITIES	
Bank Cash	$1,920	Can. $ Deposits	
Loans & Inv.	16,080	Demand	$15,000
	$18,000	Notice	3,000
			$18,000

(b) If this were the case (*i.e.*, 50% of the money coming from demand and 50% from notice deposits), loans and investments would be reduced by $\frac{240}{(.12 + .04)/2}$ = 3,000 or $1,500 each from the initial deficiency reserve position resulting in the following position:

ASSETS		LIABILITIES	
Bank Cash	$1,920	Can. $ Deps.	
Loans & Inv.	15,080	Demand	$15,500
	$17,000	Notice	1,500
			$17,000

Additional Problems

1. The Bank of Canada purchases a security for $500 from an individual who deals with bank *B*. Through the use of T-accounts, show the intermediate changes which take place in the balance sheets of (a) the individual, (b) bank *B*, and (c) the Bank of Canada.
2. Use the data given in problem 1 above. What is the change in the money supply? What is the level of actual reserves? Assume the funds were deposited in a demand deposit. The reserve requirement on demand deposits is 12%.

What volume of excess reserves does the banking system now have? To what maximum could the banking system expand the money supply?

3. For each of the following items, calculate the change in:
   (i) demand deposits—immediate
   (ii) demand deposits—final (*i.e.*, after the system has fully adjusted to the change)
   (iii) total chartered bank reserves
   (iv) total money supply—immediate

   In all cases, assume a 12% reserve requirement against demand deposits and a 4% reserve requirement against notice deposits.
   (a) The bank rate is lowered from 5% to 4%. Consider the immediate effects only.
   (b) Currency in circulation outside the banks increases by $1.2 million. Assume the funds are withdrawn from demand deposits.
   (c) The Department of Revenue collects taxes of $1.2 million and uses the funds to pay off government debt owned by nonbank holders. Assume the Bank of Canada takes offsetting action on the same day.
4. Assume the current Canadian reserve requirements. A large depositor of bank *X* decides to transfer $4.8 million from his current account to a new savings account.
   (a) How does such action affect the degree to which bank *X* can expand its loans?
   (b) What is the maximum amount by which bank *X* could expand its loan portfolio?
   (c) By how much could the entire banking system expand its loan portfolio?

   Assume new loans would only be made to demand deposit customers.
5. Assume bank *A* is fully loaned up. One day Customer *X* decides to transfer his $240,000 saving account to another bank. What is bank *A*'s reserve position after the transfer? If bank *A* is underreserved, what three methods can be used to overcome the deficiency? Explain showing what approximate volume of funds would have to be sought.
6. Assume that the reserve requirement for demand deposits is 10% while the requirement for notice deposits is 5%. Assume that a bank has a reserve deficiency of $100,000. One way to overcome this deficiency is by offering incentives to depositors to get them to transfer demand deposit balances to notice deposits. What volume of deposits would have to be transferred to make up the reserve deficiency?

Selected References

H. Binhammer, *Money, Banking and the Canadian Financial System*, (2nd ed.), Toronto: Methuen, 1972.

D. Bond and R. Shearer, *The Economics of the Canadian Financial System; Institutions, Theory and Policy*, Englewood Cliffs: Prentice-Hall, 1972.

Canadian Banker's Association, "The Role of the Chartered Banks in the Payment Mechanism", *CBA Bulletin*, January 1968.

Canadian Banker's Association, "The Growth of Banking—Some Highlights", *CBA Bulletin*, August 1968.

T. Comchene, and A. Kelly, "Money Supply and Money Demand: An Econometric Analysis for Canada", *Journal of Money, Credit and Banking*, May 1971, pp. 219-244.

D. Fand, and J. Tower, "An Analysis of the Money Supply Process in Canada", *Canadian Journal of Economics*, May 1968, pp. 380-400.

I. Fisher, *The Purchasing Power of Money*, New York; Macmillan, 1911.

M. Friedman, *A Theoretical Framework for Monetary Analysis*, New York: National Bureau of Economic Research, 1971.

M. Friedman, ed., *Studies in the Quantity Theory of Money and Other Essays*, Chicago: Aldine Press, 1969.

W. Heller, *New Dimensions of Political Economy,* New York: Norton, 1966.

J. Hugon, "Bank Impact on Corporate Liquidity", *Financial Executive*, June 1969, pp. 14-18.

J. Keynes, *The General Theory of Employment, Interest and Money*, New York: Harcourt, Brace, Jovanovich, 1936.

H. Leach, "Canadian Chartered Banks", *Financial Analysts Journal*, March-April 1969, pp. 133-140.

J. O'Brien, *Canadian Money and Banking*, Toronto: McGraw-Hill, 1964.

Royal Bank of Canada, *How the Canadian Money Supply is Affected by Various Banking and Financial Transactions and Developments,* (4th ed.), Montreal: Royal Bank of Canada, 1970.

P. Samuelson, and A. Scott, *Economics, An Introductory Analysis*, (2nd Canadian ed.), Toronto: McGraw-Hill, 1968 Chapter 16.

G. Watt, "The Origins and Background of Central Banking in Canada", *Bank of Canada Review*, May, 1972, pp. 15-26.

S. Weintraub, "Keynes and the Monetarists", *Canadian Journal of Economics*, February 1971, pp. 37-49.

CHAPTER 19: APPENDIX

The Bank of Canada weekly financial statistics[1]

1. Introduction

Each Thursday a most useful published set of financial data is issued by the Bank of Canada. The eleven-page *Weekly Financial Statistics* should be read and its contents appreciated by those active in the financial markets. It has been suggested that:

> Correct interpretation of the statistics contained in its weekly release can, if followed over a period of many weeks, help both borrowers and

[1]This appendix draws heavily on a paper in *The Canadian Banker*. Interested students are referred to C. Starrs, "A Guide to the Bank of Canada's Weekly Financial Statistics", *The Canadian Banker*, September-October, 1968, pp. 9-11, 34-36.

lenders answer the vital question of whether the Bank of Canada is content with the current level of interest rates or alternatively, whether it is actively promoting a change in the direction of interest rates, and if so, the methods used to achieve this change.[2]

The purpose of this appendix is to provide some introductory understanding of this important source of readily available information.

2. Yields on Financial Instruments

From the financial executive's standpoint, pages 5 and 11 of the *Weekly Financial Statistics* comprise some of the more important sets of tabulations and graphs contained in this publication. Data on money-market rates and Government of Canada bond yields covering a period of three consecutive weeks appear on page 5 while trends over about four years for selected Government of Canada issues, including treasury bills, are charted on page 11. Figures 1 and 2 provide examples of the format in which this vital material is presented.

The longer-term trend of security yields is particularly helpful in determining the overall direction of interest rates and, given the Bank of Canada's concern about and influence over the level of rates, in underlining the central bank's objectives. Furthermore, the Canadian series can usefully be contrasted with comparable foreign data for, in addition to international political developments, the size of interest-rate differentials between Canadian securities and those of comparable securities in other developed economies have an impact on the direction and size of capital flows and consequently on foreign exchange rates. Any unsought pattern of spreads may well precipitate Bank of Canada intervention to attempt to move the spreads.

In most instances, the reported yields on treasury bills can be viewed as reasonable indicators of both shifts in the trend of money-market borrowing costs and their levels. The cost of day-to-day loans and the bank rate are also set out on page 5 and can serve as supplementary indicators. It is, of course, the dominant role of chartered banks in providing a home for treasury bills (as part of their secondary reserves) that enhances the importance of treasury bills yields.

FIGURE 1

Illustrative Entry Taken From Page 5, of *Weekly Financial Statistics*

Average Treasury Bill Rate at Tender	July 17/75	July 10/75	Jully 3/75
91 day bills	7.25	7.15	7.11
182 day bills	7.45	7.39	7.40

[2] *Ibid.*, p. 9.

FIGURE 2

Graph of Government Security Yields Taken From Page 11, of *Weekly Financial Statements*

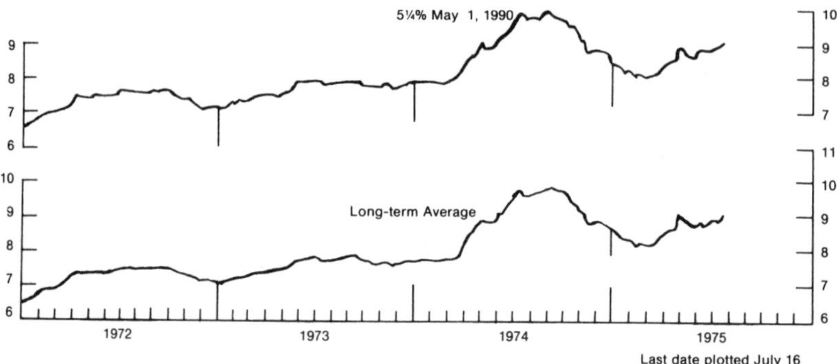

3. *Reserves and More Liquid Assets of the Chartered Banks*

The minimum cash and secondary reserve requirements of the chartered banks have already been reviewed. Given the opportunity cost of holding cash, the margin the banks have over and above their required cash ratio serves as a prominent indicator of credit conditions. On page 4 statistics are provided about the actual, required, and excess cash reserves. Specifically, average data is presented (i) covering the Wednesday before release of the publication (ii) for the current averaging period ended that Wednesday and (iii) for the previous semimonthly averaging period. A very approximate interpretation of excess cash reserves would be that 10 or more basis points above the quite frequently reported 6.15 percent required minimum[3] signals easier conditions, while an excess of less than .06 percent signals the reverse.

A related set of figures, also shown on page 4, is relevant to an evaluation of credit conditions as reflected in the cash reserves of chartered banks. Potential effects on the following week's cash reserves of both in-transit payments to or by the Bank of Canada and of its outstanding purchase and resale agreements[4] are estimated in millions of dollars.

Details on the more liquid Canadian assets of the chartered banks are set out on page 2 of the Bank's weekly release. As at July 9, 1975, these were reported (in millions of dollars) as follows:

[3]The actual requirement is, of course, a function of the balance between demand deposits with their minimum cash reserve requirement of 12 percent and notice deposits which require only 4 percent.

[4]With this arrangement, funds are advanced by the Bank to accredited money-market dealers who have sold the Bank money-market instruments with a promise of repurchase. Such agreements are generally indicative of tight credit conditions as the interest rate charged would exceed the yield on the instrument thus encouraging dealers to consider other alternatives first. It should be noted, however, that toward the end of the chartered banks' fiscal year in October, and also at the end of each semimonthly averaging period, the desire of such banks to show a strong cash position may force dealers to approach the Bank of Canada regardless of credit conditions.

Bank of Canada deposits	2,620
Bank of Canada notes	1,033
Day-to-day loans	233
Treasury bills	3,263
Other Government securities	
—3 years and under	2,381
—over 3 years	1,989
Special call loans	503
Other call and short loans	230
	12,252

A chart on page 6 of the release graphs the percentage of "free" liquid assets to total major assets over a 3- to 4-year period. This ratio is a useful indicator of the chartered banks' liquidity position.

Should a policy of restraint be introduced by the Bank, the chartered banks could be faced with inadequate primary reserves as cash is pulled out of the system. To rectify the situation, bonds and treasury bills might have to be sold and both call and day loans limited. Upward pressure on interest rates and reduction of more liquid assets would result, to be reversed as monetary restraints were relaxed. Consequently, a trend developing in either direction is a very significant indicator of the central bank's intentions.

Advances by the Bank of Canada to the chartered and savings banks are noted on the first page of the *Weekly Financial Statistics*. These advances are very seldom called for but may be resorted to by the banks in order to meet their cash reserve requirements. Granted at the Bank rate and for a minimum period of a day, such advances are used only as a last resort. When used, therefore, they may be viewed as supplementary evidence of tight credit conditions.

4. Attitude of the Central Bank

To this point, analysis of the Bank's weekly release will have afforded some indication of the extent of credit restraint or of its absence. By focusing on page 1 of the data, it is possible to infer something about the Bank of Canada's attitude toward existing conditions. Knowing the Bank's position would of course be critical to a financial officer contemplating long-term financing, for example, or to senior management attempting forecasts of business activity for the coming year.

Adjustments of the chartered banks' reserves by additions to or sale from the Bank of Canada's holdings of government securities or by shifting the maturities of such holdings are devices used by the Bank in implementing its policies. Changes in the central bank's holdings of government securities including their maturities are apparent from the scrutiny of balance sheet items subdivided into (i) treasury bills, (ii) other securities maturing in three years or less, and (iii) securities with maturities of over three years. Changes can be tied back to general credit conditions including the cash and secondary reserve position and liquid asset ratio of the banking system as well as the trend in interest rates.[5]

5. Loans by the Chartered Banks

On page 2 of the weekly release you will find a detailing of the several classifications of loans granted by the chartered banks. These can serve as important indicators of strength in the aggregate demand for funds. On page 8 of the publication, total Canadian loans, general loans, residential mortgages, loans to grain dealers, and other lesser loans by the chartered banks are graphed. Data for up to four years is shown on the charts and seasonal patterns, if any, can be observed.

6. The Money Supply

Currency outside the banks and chartered bank Canadian dollar deposits are reported on page 3 and graphed on page 9. Thus, changes in the money supply from both the previous week and from a year ago are indicated on page 3 while the pattern over the past three to four years is illustrated on page 9. From the *Weekly Financial Statistics* dated July 17, 1975 an analyst would note that the money supply (more broadly defined) stood at 65,662 billion dollars on July 9, 1975, up by a very significant 11.17 billion dollars from a year earlier.

7. Summary

The Bank of Canada's *Weekly Financial Statistics* provides a broad range of very valuable information to the discerning financial executive. If correctly interpreted, it can be used as an aid to forecasting credit conditions, economic activity, central bank policies, and consequently a particular firm's own opportunities.

[5]The reader is reminded that credit conditions may be altered without reference to the Bank's portfolio, for example, by transferring government cash balances between the banking system and the Bank of Canada. Data on government deposits with the chartered banks is found on page 3.

PART 6
Dividends and Valuation

Chapter 20
Dividend Policy and the Valuation of Common Shares

20-1. INTRODUCTION

Apart from its importance in practice, the area of dividend policy has received much attention in the academic literature. In this chapter, we will concentrate on the conceptual foundations developed for dividend policy, leaving the practical aspects of how dividend policies are actually formulated for the following chapter.

In presenting a conceptual framework for the analysis, our main concern is to explore how rational investors ought to value alternative dividend policies. Such valuations by investors should affect share prices accordingly. Given the objective of maximizing shareholder wealth, as set out in Chapter 1, we can then place a value on alternative dividend policies, and determine what ought to represent optimal dividend decisions by a firm.

We start by establishing the relevance of dividends for share valuation. In contrasting dividends per share with earnings per share and cash flows per share, we will demonstrate that investors should determine the value of a share by capitalizing its future stream of dividends.

The following section discusses the effects of alternative dividend policies on share prices. We explore various factors affecting dividend policy, and provide a framework within which optimal dividend policies can be developed. While the theory surrounding this topic draws heavily on mathematical formulation, we have avoided such formalism in this section. Rather, we present to the uninitiated reader who is not inclined towards abstract theory an intuitive grasp of the main arguments which have been advanced, and explain how such arguments relate to the real world.

The final sections in this chapter are somewhat more advanced and, hence, starred. A brief section introduces the potentials and difficulties of empirical testing in this area, reviewing the main results produced by statistical analysis to date. Finally, we present in simplified form the two main models which have been advanced to deal with the issue of share valuation and dividend policy: the Gordon model and the theory developed by Miller and Modigliani. Given the controversy which surrounds this significant topic both in practice and at an academic level, it is important that the serious reader obtains a clear understanding for the underlying issues being debated.

20-2. THE VALUATION OF COMMON SHARES BY INVESTORS: DIVIDENDS, EARNINGS AND CASH FLOWS

Given the stated financial objective of maximizing shareholder wealth it is of obvious importance to determine some of the key variables which influence a firm's share prices. Only if we have some understanding of what it is that investors value when acquiring shares can we establish the link between financial decisions and the enunciated objective of share price maximization. Because of the importance of the topic, researchers in finance have devoted considerable attention to the formulation and empirical testing of share valuation models, with the purpose of establishing relationships between the value which investors ascribe to shares and key financial variables characterizing the firm. Much of their work goes beyond the scope of this text. Therefore we shall limit ourselves to outlining in a simplified fashion some basic considerations, particularly as they affect the formulation of a firm's dividend policy.

Drawing on the concepts of basic economics, the market price of a firm's shares is ultimately determined by supply and demand, where demand equals supply at the equilibrium price. At the prevailing price, some investors will find the shares quite attractive and would hold them even if the price were to increase. Others would not purchase even if the price dropped sharply. In between these two extremes are what we call *investors at the margin*, for whom the decisions to buy or to sell are just marginal at the prevailing price. It is these latter investors who are the primary determinants of fluctuations in price, as they are the ones who are most likely to buy or to sell and, hence, to create incremental supply and demand.

Clearly, there are a multitude of factors which may determine the supply and demand for shares at given prices, some of which are related to the financial performance of the firm, while others may be quite unrelated. The latter may include such elusive concepts as general investor confidence or the general mood of the market. While recognizing the complexities of the stock markets, we are mainly interested in analyzing how rational investors ought to evaluate the financial performance of a firm.

Basically, three key variables have been proposed as determining the value of a firm's shares: per share dividends, earnings, and cash flows. The relations existing betwen these three variables are reviewed in Figure 20-1. In practice, dividends, earnings, and to a lesser extent, cash flows often appear to be used side-by-side without a clear appreciation as to their validity and relative importance in evaluating a firm's shares. For instance, dividend yields, price earnings ratios and measures of cash flow are used side-by-side by analysts and others, and you may wonder whether the market really ought to capitalize future dividends, earnings or cash flows.

While relatively comprehensive mathematical theories on this issue have been formulated, we will restrict ourselves to outlining the gist of the argument in an intuitive way through the use of simplified numerical examples.

FIGURE 20-1.

Relations between Cash Flows, Earnings and Dividends

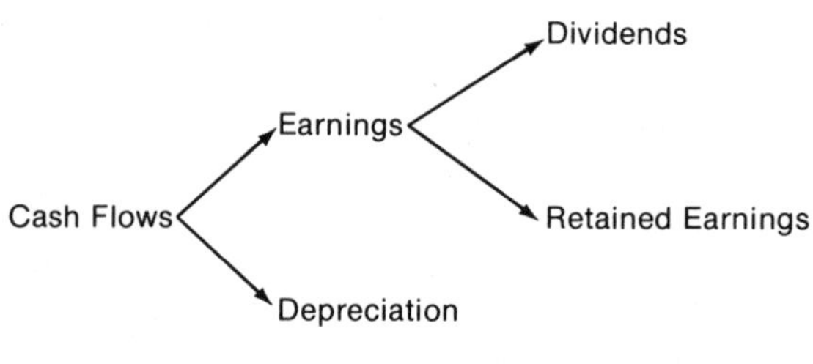

Retained Earnings + Dividends = Earnings
Earnings + Depreciation = Cash Flows

Dividends versus earnings per share

We start by focusing on the issue of dividends versus earnings.

Example

At the beginning of year 1 we form a corporation by investing \$100,000. We assume the assets do not depreciate, and no depreciation is charged. After-tax earnings per year are 20 percent of the amount invested, or \$20,000 for the first year. At the end of the first year, \$10,000 are paid in dividends, and \$10,000 are retained for reinvestment, implying a net asset value of \$110,000 second year. Earnings for the second year are 20% × \$110,000 = \$22,000 which are all paid out in dividends. At the end of the second year, the firm is liquidated and the assets sold for \$110,000, with a liquidating dividend of this amount being paid. Table 20-1 summarizes the example as outlined. Assume that you were the sole shareholder and were to place a value on this investment. It is clear that the only returns the shareholder actually receives from the investment are the dividends of \$10,000 and \$22,000 in years 1 and 2 and the liquidating dividend of \$110,000. The retained earnings of \$10,000 in year 1 only represent an indirect value to the shareholder in that they serve to increase dividends in year 2 to \$22,000, and in that they increase the firm's asset value by \$10,000 as reflected in the liquidating dividend. At the end of year 1, the shareholder has the choice of paying out all earnings in dividends, or of retaining some earnings to increase future dividends, with returns as follows

	Year 1	Year 2
No retentions, all earnings paid out in dividends	\$20,000	\$20,000 + \$100,000
Retentions of \$10,000 as outlined in example	\$10,000	\$22,000 + \$110,000

In order to increase future dividends, the shareholder foregoes earlier dividends which instead of being paid out, are reinvested. To count these retained earnings as representing a return to shareholders in addition to dividends as outlined, clearly would be double counting.

TABLE 20-1

Simplified Example to Outline Earnings versus Dividends as Alternative Bases for Evaluating a Firm's Shares.

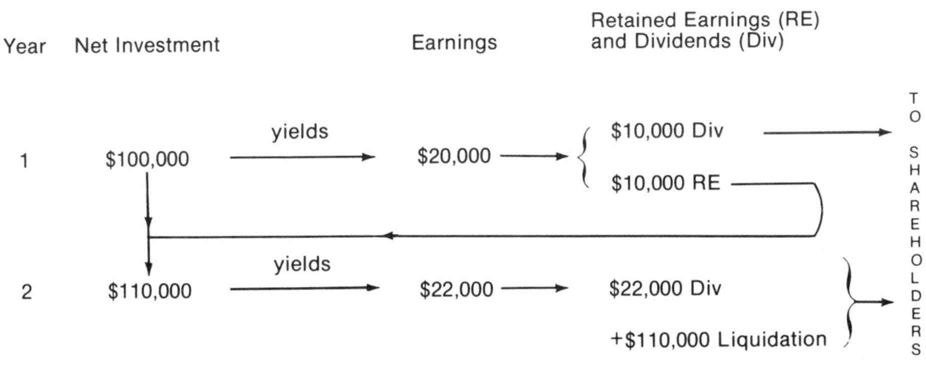

Generalizing from this example the only value of retained earnings to the shareholder lies in the fact that they are reinvested to increase dividend payments in the future. Ultimately, the only real return a shareholder receives are dividend payments. Retained earnings may provide an indication as to the likely growth rate of future dividend payments, and, hence, may be of indirect relevance in valuing a firm's shares. If, however, an investor capitalizes a projected earnings stream serious double counting will overstate the real expected returns.

Dividends versus cash flows

If cash flows were to form the basis of share valuation, we would not only need to include retained earnings alongside dividends, but we would also have to include depreciation. Having shown that retained earnings should not be considered explicitly, it is even easier to show that depreciation cannot rightly be considered a return to the shareholder. To demonstrate this, we again resort to a highly simplified numerical example. In this context, and to clarify our exposition, we will view depreciation as an economic concept defining the portion of an asset which wears out in a particular operating period. Funds set aside for depreciation are used to replace that portion of the asset which has been used up and to restore the asset to its original value. Again assume a firm which was established with an original investment of $100,000. Ten percent of the asset base wears out each year. Cash flow returns are 20 percent of the amount invested, or $20,000. Of these, $10,000 are set aside each year as depreciation to replace used up assets and to restore the asset base to the original $100,000. The remaining earnings of $10,000 are paid out in dividends. After 10 years, the firm is liquidated at a liquidation value of $100,000 which corresponds to the book value of the assets. It is probably obvious that the amounts set aside for depreciation can hardly be viewed as direct returns to shareholders. Their only benefit lies in the fact that in replacing worn out assets, the future earning power of the firm is protected, which again is reflected in future dividends. Thus, any components of cash flow (depreciation or retained earnings) which remain within the firm do so to protect and enhance future returns to shareholders in the form of dividends, and it is this stream of future dividends which we should look at to derive the value which the shareholder is willing to pay for a firm's shares.

Dividends and investor returns on common shares

In notation, we reintroduce the symbols and the formula derived in Chapter 13 for the return on equity or the equity capitalization rate, with

P_t = market price per share at the beginning of period t

D_t = dividends at the end of period t

$\hat{k}_e$ = the effective return required by equity investors[1]

With dividends assumed to be paid at year end, and dividends in the current period designated as D_0, the value of the shares was then given as

$$(1) \qquad P_0 = \frac{D_0}{(1+\hat{k}_e)} + \frac{D_1}{(1+\hat{k}_e)^2} + \ldots + \frac{D_n}{(1+\hat{k}_e)^{n+1}} + \ldots$$

In following the above discussion, one may argue that an investor is not primarily concerned about periodic returns to be realized during the period for which the shares are held, but rather that the investor hopes for capital gains when disposing of the shares at the prevailing market price at some time in the future. Therefore, if the investor plans on selling the shares at the end of period t for a price P_t, the share valuation model could be written as

$$(2) \qquad P_0 = \frac{D_0}{(1+\hat{k}_e)} + \frac{D_1}{(1+\hat{k}_e)^2} + \ldots + \frac{D_{t-1}}{(1+\hat{k}_e)^t} + \frac{P_t}{(1+\hat{k}_e)^t}$$

However, the issue of whether to value dividends, earnings or cash flows is not only important in assessing returns during the holding period, as illustrated by the above examples, but it is also critical in determining the potential for capital gains. If, for example, we can show that rational investors ought to use dividends as the basis for valuing shares, then the market price of the shares which can be realized at the time of disposition is again determined by dividend prospects subsequent to the date of disposition. Specifically, we would have

$$(3) \qquad P_t = \frac{D_t}{(1+\hat{k}_e)} + \frac{D_{t+1}}{(1+\hat{k}_e)^2} + \ldots.$$

which, if inserted into formula (2) above, brings us back to the original valuation formula (1).

[1]We recall that $\hat{k}_e$ was the market capitalization rate for equity *before investor taxes*. This rate is determined by the aggregate supply and demand for securities in the capital markets. The effecive after-tax yield of a security to a particular investor will also depend on the individual's specific marginal tax rates on dividends and capital gains.

Given the above discussion on finite holding periods and capital gains, another useful formulation emerges for the return which investors receive from holding a security. It focuses on expressing the return for holding a share for one period only. Assume an investor purchases the security at time t and intends to hold it for only one period, selling at time $t + 1$. We can then write

$$(4) \qquad P_t = \frac{D_t}{(1+\hat{k}_e)} + \frac{P_{t+1}}{(1+\hat{k}_e)}$$

That is, the price of the share at the beginning of the period is equal to the present value of the dividend during the period plus the present value of the share price at the start of the subsequent period. The above formulation has been called the *fundamental principle of share valuation,* and it will be encountered again later on in this chapter when we develop some of the theories which have been advanced on the issue of dividends. By rearranging equation (4), we can also write

$$(5a) \qquad \hat{k}_e = \frac{D_t + P_{t+1}}{P_t} - 1$$

or

$$(5b) \qquad 1 + \hat{k}_e = \frac{D_t + P_{t+1}}{P_t}$$

This is an intuitively appealing formulation for the one period return received from holding a security: if it were currently bought for P_t = \$100, pays a dividend of D_t = \$5 at yearend, and the investor expects to be able to sell it for P_{t+1} = \$110, we have $(1 + \hat{k}_e) = (110 + 5)/100 = 1.15$ and $\hat{k}_e = 0.15$ or 15 percent.

Having discarded the firm's cash flows as a basis for security valuation, the attentive reader may wonder how this can be reconciled with advocating cash flows as the basis for investment evaluations in capital budgeting. First, we note that basing the valuation of shares on the stream of future dividends is equivalent to advocating the evaluation of an investment (purchase of shares) on the basis of cash flows (future dividends). However, the relevant cash flows are those accruing *to the investor*, not those generated and also consumed by the firm. Where a firm evaluates a capital budgeting project based on its anticipated *net* cash flows, it is assumed that none of these cash flows need to be ploughed back into the project to protect or generate future cash flows as forecasted, but that the entire amount of such net cash flows is available to be used at the discretion of the owners—either to be paid out as current dividends, or to be reinvested to generate future dividends.

In summary, it should be recognized that the above discussion presents a simplified conceptual framework for the valuation of shares and the role of dividends in the valuation process. If, for example, current and future dividends were known with certainty, or if all investors were rational and had the same expectations about future dividends, the above model would probably come very close to explaining the actual behavior of securities markets. As it stands, price determinations in the stock market are obviously much more complex and cannot be characterized by one simple formula. It is useful, however, to at least clarify how a rational investor should approach the issue of security valuation, even in a simplified context, as it provides a framework which we can then alter and adjust in attempting to meet the complexities of real life.

20-3 THE EFFECT OF DIVIDEND POLICY ON THE VALUATION OF SHARES BY INVESTORS: SOME CONCEPTUAL CONSIDERATIONS

We have seen that, at least conceptually, the stream of current and future dividends ought to be viewed as the prime determinant of the value which investors attach to common shares. The question of how investors ought to value alternative dividend policies is therefore of obvious importance. Specifically, the issue of how a firm should decide on the proportion of earnings to be retained for reinvestment and, consequently, the proportion to be paid out in dividends deserves careful scrutiny. The main purpose of this section is again to clarify some basic issues at a conceptual level, and to provide a framework for analysis on how a rational investor ought to evaluate a firm's dividend policy. To this effect, we shall sometimes abstract from reality and present artificially simplified examples. After a point has been made at a conceptual level in such a simplified context, we will then explore how the conclusions derived may carry over into a more realistic world. At this stage, we are not concerned with describing how decisions on dividend policy are actually made in practice, as this will be the topic of the chapter to follow.

To clarify the issues having a bearing on dividend policy, and in following our subsequent arguments, it may sometimes be useful for the reader to assume the position of somebody who is the sole owner or who at least has a majority interest in a particular firm. That person not only determines what dividend policy is to be pursued, but also has relatively complete information about the operations of the firm, its investment opportunities and prospective returns. This may help to make our discussion more meaningful and to place the various arguments advanced in proper perspective.

Consider that the firm's earnings for the current period are given. Assuming that such earnings have not yet been committed and that the funds are available to be disbursed, a decision on the proportion to be paid out in dividends and the proportion to be ploughed back into the business for reinvestment is to be made. In assessing the situation to reach a decision, several factors may come to mind as having a potential bearing on the issue. Some of the more important considerations may be as follows:

- The firm's investment opportunities: how would earnings retained in the business be invested and what is the prospective rate of return on such new investments?
- The shareholders' own reinvestment opportunities: If monies were to be paid out in dividends, what use could the shareholders make of such funds and at what rate of return could they invest funds outside the firm?

- Tax considerations: What are the shareholders' taxes on dividends and on capital gains?
- The shareholders' current consumption needs: To what extent do shareholders rely on dividend income to finance their current consumption expenditures?
- Control considerations: These may restrict any selling of shares to outsiders by current shareholders who want to supplement their current income.

Investors' propensity for current income

The last two points as listed above, while potentially important in specific situations such as for closely held firms or family enterprises, will not form part of the main focus of our discussion. A few brief comments will clarify the reason for this. Where income from investments is important to supplement other revenue in financing a shareholder's consumption expenditures, this need not influence the firm's dividend policy. Except where considerations of corporate control are dominant, a shareholder could always sell a fraction of his shareholdings to realize such income.

Example

Consider, a shareholder who holds 1,000 shares of a firm at a market price of \$20 each. Current earnings are \$2 per share. These earnings could either be paid out in dividends or they could be reinvested. Assume that if dividends are paid, the share price remains at \$20. On the other hand, if these earnings were retained and reinvested, assume that the market price of the shares would move up to \$23 in anticipation of higher earnings and dividends to be realized in the future on the basis of the new investments. The shareholder requires investment income of \$2,000 to supplement other revenues. Rather than supplying him with these funds by paying out the firm's earnings in dividends (\$2 dividends per share x 1,000 shares = \$2,000), the shareholder would clearly be better off if these monies were reinvested and he simply sold 87 shares at the new price of \$23 per share (\$23 × 87 ≃ \$2,000), as illustrated below

(a) The firm pays \$2 per share dividend and the share price remains at \$20.
Shareholder's wealth position:

Receipts from dividends	
\$2 per share × 1,000 shares	\$ 2,000
Value of share holdings:	
1,000 shares at \$20	20,000
Total wealth	\$22,000

(b) The firm pays no dividends, reinvests earnings, and the share price moves up to \$23 per share.

Shareholder's wealth position:

913 shares at new price of $23 per share	$21,000
Cash realized from sale of 87 shares at $23 per share, to supplement income	$ 2,000
Total wealth	$23,000

Note that in making the above point we have ignored brokerage costs which may have to be paid in selling off shares. The difference in shareholder wealth for the two alternatives as set forth above would have to be sufficient to cover such brokerage and transaction costs. More importantly, we have also ignored taxes which the investor may have to pay on dividends received or on capital gains when disposing of shares. The conclusion reached certainly holds as long as tax considerations do not cause the investor to have a systematic preference for dividend income over capital gains. Only if dividends were generally taxed at a rate which is lower than taxes levied on capital gains, so that a dollar of dividend income was more valuable to investors than a dollar of capital gains, would our conclusions have to be modified accordingly. The issue of taxation is obviously very complex and may vary from one investor to another, making it difficult to draw simple and broad generalizations. Further discussions are therefore postponed until the matter can be considered in greater detail below.

We conclude that, where shareholders are mainly concerned about maximizing their wealth and where corporate control is not of concern, any propensity for current income by shareholders probably need not be of major concern in formulating corporate dividend policy. The firm should rather concentrate on finding the dividend policy which maximizes share prices. Shareholders who so desire can always sell off part of their shares. While brokerage costs and differential taxation of dividends and capital gains may have to be reckoned with in some instances, the gist of the argument remains valid and, for some investors at least, the reduced taxation of capital gains may even favor this approach to supplementing income.

Reinvestment versus dividends

We now turn to the more important issue of reinvestment opportunities, both at the level of the firm and at the level of the individual investor. To simplify the exposition and in order to concentrate on one issue at a time, we will again ignore taxes which the investor may have to pay on dividends or on capital gains. Subsequently, we will discuss the potential effects of such taxes on dividend policy.

Having dealt with the issue of using corporate funds to supplement investor income required for consumption purposes, the objectives of maximizing shareholders' financial wealth again becomes our guiding criterion. Given this framework, it should be clear that if a firm can reinvest retained earnings to yield an effective rate of return of say 20 percent, whereas the investor could only reinvest the dividends which he receives at a rate of return of 15 percent, it is in the best interest of the investor who wants to maximize wealth not to draw dividends, but rather to have the firm reinvest all earnings. If the investor owns 1,000 shares, and earnings for the current period are $2 per share, the $2,000 of earnings associated with his shares would grow at a rate of 20 percent if reinvested by the firm as compared to only 15 percent if they were taken out in dividends and reinvested privately. More generally, whenever the projects in which the firm can reinvest its earnings provide yields which exceed those which shareholders could achieve by reinvesting those same earnings elsewhere, the firm should retain the earnings for reinvestment. This obviously leads to the following important conclusion for dividend policy: in deciding how to use earnings, a firm should first look at its investment opportunities. As long as earnings can be reinvested at a rate which exceeds returns on opportunities available to shareholders such investments should be undertaken. Any amount left after the firm runs out of promising investments should then be paid out to shareholders in the form of dividends. Conceptually, therefore, what to pay in dividends is a residual decision which simply falls out once a firm has set its capital budget.

Assessing the reinvestment rate of shareholders warrants further comment for, as we have seen, it becomes the corporate hurdle rate in deciding whether or not to reinvest earnings. A firm's shareholders could clearly reinvest any proceeds from dividends to buy additional shares in the same company or in other firms with similar risk. Since they currently hold such shares, this use of funds for reinvestment would presumably be acceptable. The yield on such additional investments would simply be $\hat{k}_e$, the effective yield or current market capitalization rate on the firm's outstanding shares. If for simplicity we abstract from issuing and underwriting expenses, then, using the notation which we developed in the chapter dealing with the cost of capital, $\hat{k}_e = k_e$; or in other words, the yield on the firm's shares equals the cost of equity to the firm. Thus, the firm should use its cost of equity as a hurdle rate for determining whether earnings should be reinvested in the business or paid out in dividends. Where, in keeping with the firm's capital structure, new investments are financed from various sources, it follows that the weighted average cost of capital becomes the proper yardstick for evaluating new investments, as it includes k_e for that proportion financed from equity sources. Now we can confirm the conclusions reached in the chapters on capital budgeting and the cost of capital: a firm should undertake all investments which provide a yield exceeding the firm's cost of capital. Such investment will provide a yield exceeding k_e on the equity financed portion of the investment. Given that investors can only achieve a reinvestment rate of $\hat{k}_e$ on investments of a similar type if they themselves reinvest funds drawn out of the firm in the form of dividends, the firm should retain its earnings as long as it can generate new investments which promise positive net present values; or internal rates of return which exceed the firm's cost of capital.

Dividends versus capital gains

A simplified example will illustrate the important point we made in the preceding paragraphs.

Example

Consider a firm which has 100,000 shares outstanding. Earnings per share have been constant at \$2 per share for some time, with all earnings paid out in dividends. To invest in shares of this type, investors in the capital markets demand an effective return of $\hat{k}_e$ = 15 percent per year, from which we compute the current market price of the shares at \$2/0.15 = \$13.33. Assume that the firm could reinvest the current year's earnings of \$200,000 to earn a return of 20 percent, with the specific investment under consideration promising \$40,000 per year in additional net cash flows for the indefinite future. Hence, if the dividends are foregone in the current year, dividends of \$200,000 (current earnings) plus \$40,000 (returns from new investments) could be distributed in subsequent years, amounting to \$2.40 per share. At the old market price of \$13.33 per share, the effective return of the shares has now increased to \$2.40/\$13.33 = 18 percent. As this is higher than what would be dictated by supply and demand in a competitive capital market, investors will be attracted to buy these shares and, thereby, to bid up their price, until once again their yield is $\hat{k}_e$ = 15 percent. This implies a new market price of \$2.40/0.15 = \$16 per share. Therefore, by foregoing the current dividend of \$2 per share, investors can expect a capital gain of \$16 – \$13.33 = \$2.67 which is clearly to their advantage. This capital gain resulted from the firm reinvesting earnings to yield a rate of return (20%) which is higher than the competitive market rate for such investments ($\hat{k}_e$ = 15%). Discounting such future returns at the competitive market rate yields a present value which exceeds the amount of the current dividend foregone and, hence, serves to make the firm's shares more valuable, with the resulting capital gain exceeding the amount of the current dividend foregone.

Dividend policy and investors taxes

The above example can illustrate the important role of taxation in determining optimal dividend policy. Implied in our discussion up to this point was the assumption that investors are indifferent between receiving dividends or realizing capital gains. Insofar as differences in taxation cause a systematic preference of shareholders for one form of investment income versus another, our conclusions need to be modified accordingly. While this may be readily accomplished for a closely held firm where the shareholders and their tax brackets are known, it is quite difficult to reach clear conclusions for the widely held corporation with its constantly changing list of heterogeneous shareholders. Given the complexities of current tax legislation (for example, the initial tax free allowance on dividends and interest from Canadian corporations, the dividend tax credit, varying provincial tax rates and the likes) it is extremely difficult to ascertain whether a systematic general bias for dividends or capital gains does in fact exist in the capital markets and, if it does exist, to assess its direction and magnitude. If, as you might suspect, capital gains are preferred—firstly because for investors in higher tax brackets who have exhausted their allowance for tax-free investment income, the net tax to be paid will generally be lower, and second, because taxes on capital gains can be postponed until such gains are actually realized through sale of the shares—then this would further reinforce our conclusion that firms should view dividends as a residual which is to be paid after the financing of all profitable investments has been assured.

Example

Pursuing our earlier example, assume that an investor pays a net tax (after the dividend tax credit) of 30 percent on dividend income, and that his marginal tax rate is 50 percent, with tax to be paid on one-half of capital gains. Faced with the alternatives of a dividend before tax of $2 per share, or an incremental capital gain of $2.67 per share, the lower effective tax on capital gains further increases preference for the latter, since the investor now has to compare an after-tax dividend of $1.40 per share to an after-tax incremental capital gain of $2, with the additional possibility of being able to defer the tax on the capital gains.

In Canada, the recently introduced $1,000 exemption on taxable dividends or interest income has made dividend income for at least some investors relatively more appealing. It remains difficult, however, to ascertain the aggregate impact of this provision.

Dividend policy as a financing decision

If we accept the assertion that a firm should accept and find financing for all investment projects yielding a return in excess of its cost of capital, dividend policy may be viewed as a financing decision in the following sense: if a firm wants to pay dividends in excess of any portion of earnings left over after all new investment projects have been financed, it will have to supplement its earnings with external financing.

Example

If a firm with 100,000 shares outstanding wants to maintain its historical dividend of $2 per share, given current earnings of $300,000 and new investment opportunities requiring cash outlays of $200,000, external financing in the amount of $100,000 needs to be arranged. We have:

$$\underset{(\$100{,}000)}{\text{external financing}} = \underset{(\$200{,}000)}{\text{investments}} + \underset{(\$200{,}000)}{\text{dividends}} - \underset{(\$300{,}000)}{\text{earnings}}$$

With new investments and current earnings given, the amount of external financing becomes a direct function of dividend policy. To illustrate the implications of such a view of dividend policy let us assume that a firm finances itself solely through common equity. Then, any external financing will be through the issuance of additional common shares. If we assume away taxes and expenses associated with the issuing of new shares, it can be argued that the dividend policy which the firm pursues does not matter. If dividends to be paid exceed earnings minus retentions for new investments, the firm can simply issue new shares to cover the deficit. This is intuitively reasonable: if nothing is lost through taxes and transaction costs, the firm can always pay out money to shareholders in dividends and then ask them to reinvest these same funds by buying new shares. The money winds up where it started, namely in the firm. The proportionate ownership of shareholders is unchanged, and all that has been done has been to circulate money from the firm to shareholders and back to the firm. While the starred section at the end of this chapter will explore this point more fully, the following simple example may serve to make the point.

Example

> Again, a firm has 100,000 shares outstanding. It has no productive assets and no earnings, but just holds land with a market value of \$10,000,000. Its shares are valued accordingly at \$10,000,000/100,000 = \$100 per share. The firm decides to pay dividends of \$10 per share, and in order to finance such dividends, 12,500 new shares are sold through a rights offering to existing shareholders, with each 8 shares entitling the shareholder to subscribe for one new share at a price of \$80 per share. Consider a shareholder who holds 8 shares and who exercises his rights:[2] he will have received \$80 in dividends (\$10 × 8 shares) which he immediately reinvests to purchase one additional share. He now owns 9 shares, each of which should have a market value of \$10,000,000/112,500 = \$88.89, for a total of 9 × \$88.89 = \$800, and both his proportionate ownership of the firm and his total wealth remain unchanged. In essence, he has been financing his own dividend payments by providing the firm with the cash it required to pay dividends. Needless to say, this appears to be an unproductive exercise.

To pay dividends and to finance such payments by raising new funds externally becomes even less appealing if we recognize the reality of taxes and transaction costs.

Example

> In our above illustration, assume the shareholder paid a net tax (after the dividend tax credit) of 20 percent on dividends, and that the corporation paid issuing expenses of \$2 per share to implement the rights offering. We no longer have a senseless but harmless circulation of money from the firm to its shareholders and back to the firm, for such circulation actually results in the draining of cash to pay taxes and expenses. The investor no longer has \$80 in dividends to reinvest, but only \$80 (1 − 0.2) = \$64 net of taxes, and the corporation will have to sell the new shares for \$82 per share, implying that the investor pays \$82 − \$64 = \$18 out of his own pocket to close the circle, hardly a very attractive proposition.

Clearly, maintaining dividend payments at a time where external financing is called for to cover shortfalls in internally generated funds, for example in the

[2]We have seen in our discussion of rights offerings that the wealth position of a shareholder is unaffected by his decision to exercise or to sell the rights, so that this assumption is not critical for our argument.

face of growth and expansion, will generally not be in the best interest of a firm's shareholders.[3]

Informational effects of dividends

The main point which emerges from our disucssion is that the primary determinant of share prices ought to be a firm's investment policy, with dividends becoming a residual to be paid out of whatever funds are left after all profitable investments have been financed. To be able to assess the validity and potential limitations of our arguments in a real life setting, one additional implied assumption needs to be uncovered and discussed. Not only have we assumed rational investors who are guided by the sole objective of maximizing their financial wealth, but we have also assumed that such investors have reasonably complete information about the past operations and current financial position of the firm under consideration, and about the firm's prospective investment opportunities as well. To illustrate the importance of this assumption, the reader should assume the position of a shareholder who has just received a notice from a firm in which he holds shares saying that his anticipated dividend has been cut in half. The reason given is that the firm has enough profitable investment projects to make good use of retained earnings. While, according to our previous arguments, such a curtailing of dividends appears to be in the best interest of the owners, the shareholder may nevertheless have doubts about the sincerity of the announcement, in particular if such a step represents a drastic change from policies pursued in the past. In particular, the shareholder may not be able to dispel the suspicion that the real reason such action has been taken may be a deteriorating financial position which management may be attempting to hide. If the investor is not alone in this uncertainty, the firm's share price could suffer, at least in the short run, until the market has had an opportunity to fully appraise the situation. Also management may face a hostile shareholder group at the next annual meeting, in particular if, in light of the above, share prices have dropped following the cut in dividends. The practical importance of such considerations will become apparent in the next chapter when we look at actual dividend policies pursued by Canadian corporations. Given our earlier analysis, however, we can question whether such informational aspects of dividends really ought to dominate decisions on dividend policy, in particular in such well developed capital markets as we have in North America. The increasing importance of financial institutions as major equity investors casts a further doubt on the importance of incomplete information. The institutions' analysts certainly have available to them a wealth of information which goes beyond the financial statements and official reports issued by corporations.

[3]Note that this conclusion does not hinge on the assumption of the firm being financed solely through equity. If a firm maintains its long-term capital structure, any new financing will require some additional equity, and an argument paralleling the above can again be developed, leading to identical conclusions.

**ADDITIONAL SELECTED TOPICS

**20-4. THE EFFECT OF DIVIDEND POLICY ON THE VALUATION OF SHARES BY INVESTORS: EMPIRICAL TESTS

Given the importance of dividend policy and the controversies surrounding the topic it is obviously appealing to attempt to settle the issue by empirical observation, at least as far as actual behavior by investors in the capital markets is concerned. As we shall see, however, a major reason for the persistence of the controversy over the effect of dividend policy on share valuation is the difficulty of devising adequate empirical tests. A brief outline and discussion of the most common types of tests conducted, relating share prices to both dividends and retained earnings, follows. For a review of the basic approaches which may be relied on in empirical testing of this type and some of their limitations, the reader is referred to the earlier section on empirical testing of the effects of alternative capital structures in Chapter 14.

To test whether, in general, investors place a higher value on dividends than on retained earnings, several researchers[4] have run cross-sectional linear regressions, relating share price to dividends and retained earnings, of the basic form

$$(6) \qquad P_i = a + bD_i + cR_i$$

where P_i, D_i, and R_i are respectively the observed price, dividend, and retained earnings per share of company i, for the period under consideration. If the coefficients of D_i and R_i were to be approximately equal, we would conclude that investors have no systematic preference for dividends or for retained earnings. If, on the other hand, we found $b > c$, this would indicate that investors place a higher value on dividends than on retained earnings, as according to the above formula for each dollar per share which a corporation transfers from retained earnings to dividends it could raise its stock price by $(b - c)$ dollars. Estimates obtained in early studies suggested that $b > c$, implying that, on aggregate, dividend policy affects share valuation, with more generous dividend payments preferred. As was subsequently pointed out, however, these earlier tests may have suffered from various statistical biases[5], and a brief listing of these will illustrate at least in a cursory way the difficulties typically encountered in trying to resolve important issues in finance through such empirical testing.

[4]See, for example, D. Durand, *Bank Stock Prices and the Bank Capital Problem*, New York: NBER Occasional Paper No. 54, 1957: M. Gordon and E. Shapiro, "Capital Equipment Analysis; the Required Rate of Profit", *Management Science*, October, 1956, pp. 102-110: M. Gordon, (1962) *ibid.*, G. Fisher, "Some Factors Influencing Share Prices", *Economic Journal*, March, 1961.

[5]A full discussion of the various statistical biases inherent in such tests is given by I. Friend and M. Puckett, "Dividends and Stock Prices", *American Economic Review*, September, 1964, pp. 656-682.

- As brought out in our earlier arguments, the firm's investment policy ought to be a prime determinant of share prices. If the firms used in the samples pursue investment policies which vary according to the proportion of earnings they retain, and this appears likely, the above model may really measure the latter effect and not just a dividend preference by investors.
- The price of a share will depend on investors' expectations about future earnings and dividends. In view of the prevailing tendency by management to stabilize dividend payments, which will be discussed in more detail in the following chapter, such payments will provide investors with much better information about the corporation's future prospects than retained earnings which fluctuate year to year with variations in reported earnings. This information effect of dividends may be the primary cause for a strong relation between dividends and share prices and may bias the estimated coefficients.
- The risk of firms in the sample may vary in a way which is systematically related to the firms' dividend policies, resulting in bias in the estimated coefficients. For example, if "high payout" firms tended to be less risky than "low payout" firms, the sample may exhibit a supurious relationship between dividend policy and valuation which is really caused by investor attitudes regarding risk and the variations in risk within the observed sample of firms.
- Similar biases may result if there is any relationship between the rate of return a firm achieves on reinvested earnings and dividend policy, for example if "high payout" firms on aggregate have better investment opportunities available than "low payout" firms.

More recent studies[6] have attempted to overcome these statistical problems by introducing additional variables into the regression to hold constant the relative risk and other characteristics of the firms in the sample. Such refined studies have found either that b and c are approximately equal, or that $b > c$ for industries where the returns on marginal investments are low and $c > b$ for highly profitable growth industries.

These latter studies, while not conclusive, support the argument that investment policy is of primary importance in determining share prices, with dividend policy becoming a residual decision in the sense that funds to be paid out are determined by what is left after all profitable investments have been accepted.

A 1974 study by Black and Scholes, using different methodology, tested again the hypothesis that increasing dividends will increase the price of a company's shares.[7] Empirical results obtained failed to show that differences in dividend policy lead to differences in stock returns. Shares with high payout ratios did not have significantly different returns than those with low payout ratios, leading the researchers to conclude that a corporation which increases its dividends can expect no permanent effect on its share price.

[6]Friend and Puckett, *ibid.*, and J. Diamond, "Earnings Distribution and the Evaluation of Shares: Some Recent Evidence", *Journal of Financial and Quantitative Analysis*, March, 1967, pp. 14-29.

[7]F. Black and M. Scholes, "The Effects of Dividend Yield and Divided Policy on Common Stock Prices and Returns", *Journal of Financial Economics*, May, 1974, pp. 1-22.

**20-5. SOME THEORIES ON DIVIDENDS

For the reader who is interested in more formal expressions and derivations of financial theory, we present in this section simplified versions of the main arguments and models which have been advanced in the area of dividend policy and its effect on share valuation. This will not only provide a more precise formulation of some of the points which were made at a more intuitive level in previous sections, but it will also provide the reader with an introduction to the development of financial theories, and to an important controversy which has surrounded the topic of dividend policy in the academic literature. Models on dividend policy have generally been formulated under the assumption of perfect capital markets. Perfect capital markets in this context usually imply that all investors have equal and free access to the same information, the exclusion of transaction costs such as issuing and brokerage expenses, and no taxes on either dividends or capital gains[8]. Further, it is assumed that investors are rational, remaining indifferent between increments to wealth taking either the form of cash dividends or capital gains, and that they are strictly interested in maximizing their financial wealth. While the above assumptions may appear to be overly stringent to anyone familiar with real life capital markets, the reader is cautioned against rejecting out-of-hand theories developed in such a context because of the lack of realism in the underlying assumptions. What is important is not only how realistic the assumptions are on which the basic theoretical framework is developed, but the extent to which any conclusion derived can be carried over to a more realistic world by a subsequent relaxation of such assumptions, or at least the degree to which the theories developed contribute to a clearer understanding of the key issues involved.

The Gordon Model: An argument for the relevance of dividends

Two main schools of thought exist concerning the impact of dividend policy on valuation of the firm in perfect capital markets. The first and older view, originally argued by Myron Gordon[9] and still receiving widespread support among financial theorists and practitioners, can be paraphrased by the statement that the existence of both uncertainty about the future and investor risk aversion causes the price of a share and therefore, the value of a corporation to depend upon the dividend policy followed. More specifically, it is Gordon's view that investors prefer less risky current dividends over expected future ones. Hence, any decision to withhold current dividends, investing those dividends in marginal projects just yielding the firm's cost of capital, and paying consequently increased future dividends will drop share prices, even though funds retained and reinvested are expected to yield the firm's cost of capital.

[8]The point on taxes is a simplification. The more usual assumption is that when it comes to the taxing of dividends and capital gains, no differences exist.

[9]See M. Gordon, "Dividends, Earnings, and Stock Prices", *Review of Economics and Statistics*, May, 1959. pp. 99-105; M. Gordon, "The Savings, Investment and Valuation of a Corporation", *Review of Economics and Statistics*, February, 1962, pp. 37-51; M. Gordon, *The Investment, Financing and Valuation of a Corporation*, Homewood, Ill.: Richard D. Irwin, 1962; and M. Gordon, "Optimal Investment and Financing Policy", *Journal of Finance*, May, 1963, pp. 264-272.

To better understand the arguments, consider a no-growth firm with a 100 percent payout policy, no new outside financing, and earnings of X_O in all periods. Then,

$$(7) \qquad P_0 = \frac{X_0}{(1+k)} + \frac{X_0}{(1+k)^2} + \ldots + \frac{X_0}{(1+k)^t} + \ldots.$$

where k is the discount rate equating X_O in perpetuity with P_O, with this effective return on equity equal to the firm's cost of equity, or using the notation introduced earlier, $\hat{k}_e = k_e = k$. If the first year's earnings were retained for reinvestment to earn a return of k, with full payout subsequently, then,

$$(8) \qquad P_0 = \frac{0}{(1+k)} + \frac{X_0 + kX_0}{(1+k)^2} + \ldots + \frac{X_0 + kX_0}{(1+k)^t} + \ldots.$$

The investor, having given up X_O at the end of the current period, receives in exchange kX_O in perpetuity, which, discounted at k, is equal to X_O. The price per share will, therefore, be unchanged. This conclusion has intuitive appeal in that the marginal investment yields a return k on the equity financed portion which is just equal to the relevant discount rate (the cost of equity) so that its net present value, and hence its contribution to the value of the firm, is zero. What is being shown is that dividends should only be withheld and the funds reinvested in the business if the return on new investments exceeds the firm's cost of capital. If the returns to be realized just equal the firm's cost of capital, the investment becomes marginal, and it does not make any difference whether the firm reinvests or pays dividends. Assuming that the least attractive investments which a firm undertakes just fall in this category, a marginal shift of funds from such investments to dividends and *vice versa* would leave the value of the firm's shares unaffected, and, in that sense, dividend policy becomes irrelevant.

Example

To illustrate, reconsider the numerical example used earlier in this chapter. A firm has 100,000 shares outstanding. Earnings per share have been constant at \$2 per share, with all earnings paid out in dividends. To invest in shares of this type, investors in the capital markets require an effective return of $k = 15$ percent per year, from which we computed the current market price of the shares at \$2/0.15 = \$13.33. If the firm reinvested the current year's earnings of \$200,000 to earn the minimum required return of 15%, or \$30,000 per year, future dividends would increase to \$230,000/100,000 = \$2.30 per share, starting after the first year. The market price of the shares becomes

$$P_0 = \frac{0}{(1+0.15)} + \frac{\$2.30}{(1+0.15)^2} + \ldots + \frac{\$2.30}{(1+0.15)^t} + \ldots$$

which is easily shown to equal \$13.33.[10]

[10]The market price at the beginning of the first year becomes \$2.30/0.15 = \$15.33, which if discounted by one period to the present, becomes \$15.33/(1 + 0.15) = \$13.33.

Obviously however, if the dividend policy is changed by withholding the next dividend while raising more distant ones, and this causes a rise in the discount rate which investors apply in capitalizing future dividends while the yield of the marginal investment remains at k, then, by retaining earnings, the price of the shares will fall and dividend policy will be clearly relevant in establishing share prices. It is Gordon's position that because the uncertainty of dividends increases through time, the discount rate which investors apply becomes a function of time and should rise as we move out into the future. Therefore, equation (8) should be rewritten as:

$$(9) \qquad P'_0 = \frac{0}{(1+k_1)} + \frac{X_0 + kX_0}{(1+k_2)^2} + \ldots \frac{X_0 + kX_0}{(1+k_t)^t} + \ldots .$$

The present value of kX_O in perpetuity, discounted at rising rates k_t (where $k_t > k$), fails to make up X_O foregone during the current period, with the result that $P'_O < P_O$. Dividend policy has therefore influenced share price, which increases with more generous current dividends being paid.

Example

Pursuing the above illustration, assume investors discounted the dividend for the current period at 15 percent, but demanded a return of 16 percent on future dividends because future dividends were deemed to be more uncertain. Then, if all earnings were always paid out as a constant dividend of \$2 per share, the share price would be

$$P_0 = \frac{\$2}{(1+0.15)} + \frac{\$2}{(1+0.16)^2} + \ldots + \frac{\$2}{(1+0.16)^t} + \ldots$$

$$= \frac{\$2}{(1+0.15)} + \frac{1}{(1+0.16)} \times \left[\frac{\$2}{(1+0.16)} + \ldots + \frac{\$2}{(1+0.16)^t} + \ldots\right]$$

$$= \frac{\$2}{(1+0.15)} + \frac{1}{(1+0.16)} \times \frac{\$2}{0.16}$$

$$= \$12.50$$

If under these circumstances the firm retained current earnings and reinvested the funds to yield 15 percent per annum, the market price of the firm's shares would drop to

$$P_0 = \frac{0}{(1+0.15)} + \frac{\$2.30}{(1+0.16)^2} + \ldots + \frac{\$2.30}{(1+0.16)^t} + \ldots$$

$$= \frac{1}{(1+0.16)} \left[\frac{\$2.30}{(1+0.16)} + \ldots + \frac{\$2.30}{(1+0.16)^t} + \ldots\right]$$

$$= \frac{1}{(1+0.16)} \times \frac{\$2.30}{(0.16)}$$

$$= \$12.39$$

In critiquing Gordon's arguments[11], we first recognize an important and valid point: there is no compelling reason to assume that the rate at which investors discount or capitalize future dividends has to remain constant over time. While Gordon admits that it is not possible to determine conceptually what specific function of time the discount rate applied by investors to future dividends ought to be, he states: "The important point to note. however, is that there is nothing to guarantee that k_t is constant for all values of t."[12]

If this is the case, however, we can similarly argue that there is no reason why a firm has to use a discount rate which is constant over time in assessing the economic desirability of new investments. Gordon's result essentially stems from the inconsistency of applying a constant discount rate to assess the acceptability of new investments while assuming a discount rate which varies over time for returns required by investors. Clearly, if in the above example, in keeping with investor preferences, the firm had used a discount rate of 16 percent to assess investment returns after the current period, the reinvestment of current earnings would have yielded future earnings and dividends per share at \$2.32 to be acceptable, and we would again find

$$P_0 = \frac{0}{(1+0.15)} + \frac{\$2.32}{(1+0.16)^2} + \ldots + \frac{\$2.32}{(1+0.16)^t} + \ldots$$

$$= \$12.50$$

Discount rates which vary over time may be operationally less convenient as the firm no longer has a unique cost of capital.[13] Conceptually, however, there is no reason why an investment's net present value cannot and maybe should not be computed using varying discount rates which are a function of time.[14] Thus, Gordon's conclusion that a firm can affect its share price by paying out more generous current dividends at the expense of not financing marginal investments yielding an effective return of k derives from a conceptual inconsistency as outlined above. Once the discount rate a firm employs in its capital budgeting process fully reflects investor preferences as expressed in capital markets, so that the marginal investment's net present value makes a zero contribution to the firm's value, dividend policy once again becomes irrelevant, and the firm can shift dollars from such marginal investments to dividends and vice versa without affecting share prices. As one additional point, we note that although investors may perceive current cash dividends as more certain than future ones they may not necessarily pay more for shares offering high current dividends since they

[11]Our discussion on this point draws on M. Brennan, "A Note on Dividend Irrelevance and the Gordon Valuation Model", *Journal of Finance*, December, 1971, pp. 1115-1121.

[12]See M. Gordon, "The Savings, Investment, and Valuation of a Corporation", *Review of Economics and Statistics*, February, 1962, pp. 37-51.

[13]Where the firm attempts to use some generalized average of the individual k_t as an overall discount rate, it can be shown that inconsistencies as outlined are likely to prevail, as the weights to be applied in computing such an average would have to depend on the specific path over time of cash flows to be discounted. For a mathematical description of this, see the Appendix to Gordon, *ibid*.

[14]Use of the internal rate of return as an investment criterion becomes more problematic as it requires specification of a single hurdle rate.

can achieve "homemade dividends" through periodic sales of a fraction of their holdings of the firm's shares.[15]

A clear understanding of the Gordon model is of particular importance as its conclusions have strong appeal with many practitioners. Specifically, the widespread belief that dividend policy affects share prices, with more generous dividends being preferred by investors, is sometimes held to have solid conceptual foundations which are rooted in the arguments as presented in the Gordon model. It should have become clear, however, that such reasoning is not without problems, and that with a consistent application of discount rates, even the Gordon model need not lead to a conclusion of dividend policy affecting share valuation.

The Miller-Modigliani irrelevance argument

The contrary view, namely that given both perfect capital markets and the investment policy of a firm, the price of its shares is unaffected by dividend policy, has been advanced and clearly demonstrated by Miller and Modigliani (M-M).[16] In attempting to provide an overview of the theory surrounding dividend policy we cannot develop all aspects of the complex arguments presented, and in this section our discussion will be limited to a simplified presentation of the M-M position.

In focusing on the very comprehensive theoretical work by Miller and Modigliani on dividend policy some preliminary observations are useful.

The fundamental difficulty with any discussion of individual corporate financial decisions taken in isolation stems from the reality that, because of the corporation's budget constraint, all financial decisions are in fact interdependent. That is, payment of dividends represents a use of funds, and a change in the amount paid in dividends must be matched by a corresponding change in some other source or use of funds. Dividend policy may be regarded as more or less important for valuation depending on which other source or use is assumed to change. An increase in dividend payments, for example, matched by a reduction in the size of the investment budget may be expected to have quite different implications for valuation than if it were matched by an increase in the amount of new shares or bonds sold by the corporation.

A strong argument for taking the corporation's investment decision as given, and treating dividend policy as a financing decision, is that there has previously been developed a criterion for optimal investment policy—namely, the net present value rule (NPV)—and it follows from this rule that variations in the size of the investment budget will affect the valuation of the corporation, depending upon the NPV of the marginal investments. To focus properly on the effects of dividend policy, it is therefore necessary to hold the investment policy constant. This move reduces the dividend policy issue to a simple financing question, one of whether the value of the corporation is affected by the way in which a

[15]This critique is to be found in R. Higgins, "Dividend Policy and Increasing Discount Rates: A Clarification", *Journal of Financial and Quantitative Analysis*, June, 1972, pp. 1757-1762.

[16]M. Miller and F. Modigliani, "Dividend Policy, Growth, and the Valuation of Shares", *Journal of Business*, October, 1961, pp. 411-433.

particular level of investment is financed. The alternatives are to finance from retained earnings, or through debt and equity issues given a more generous dividend policy.

The Miller and Modigliani argument, apart from the assumption of perfect capital markets as outlined above is most easily introduced given the additional assumption of perfect certainty whereby investors have complete knowledge of any firm's future profits and investment activities. Given this assumption there is no point distinguishing between different forms of securities as all securities yield certain returns and, for convenience, M-M proceed to advance their argument using common equity as the available form of external financing. The assumption of certainty is relaxed later, and it is demonstrated that the conclusions carry over into a world with investor uncertainty about the firm's future earnings.

With their assumptions in place, M-M then note that the rate of return required by investors holding any security over any particular time period will be the same and reflects a combination of dividends and capital gains. As outlined earlier on in this chapter, this rate of return k can be expressed as:

$$(10) \quad k = \frac{d_t + P_{t+1} - P_t}{P_t}$$

where P_t = market price per share at the start of period t
d_t = dividend per share paid at the end of period t

which can be rewritten as

$$(11) \quad P_t = \frac{1}{1+k}(d_t + P_{t+1})$$

to provide the intuitively appealing statement that the price of a share at the start of a period is equal to the present value of the dividend paid during the period plus the present value of the share price at the start of the subsequent period.[17]

Example

Consider the case where the market requires a 20 percent return, the dividend to be received at year end is $1.00 and the price of a share a year hence is $11.00. The current market price, or what investors are prepared to pay for such a share, can be expressed as:

$$P_t = \frac{1}{1+.20}(1.00 + 11.00) = 0.833(12.00) = \$10.00$$

To be able to fully consider implications of the above principle of valuation for dividend policy, M-M go on to present equation (11) in terms of the total value of the firm. The transition is quite readily made. Letting n_t be the number of shares outstanding at time t, total dividend payments $D_t = d_t n_t$ and the firm's value $V_t = P_t n_t$, it follows that equation (11) may be rewritten as:

$$(12) \quad V_t = \frac{1}{1+k}(D_t + V_{t+1})$$

[17]Given the assumption of certainty as specified, the discount rate k would, naturally, be the pure or risk-free rate of interest.

Staying with our earlier numerical example, and assuming 10,000 shares to be outstanding,

$$V_t = 0.833\,(10{,}000 + 110{,}000) = \$100{,}000$$

We now look at the effects of any new financing which may be required to sustain current dividend policy. If, after dividends are paid and in order to raise additional funds, the firm issues m additional shares at the end of the year at a price of P_{t+1}, then mP_{t+1} represents contributions made by the new shareholders. It follows that the total value of the firm immediately after issue of the new shares would be inflated by funds received from such a sale, with only $V_{t+1} - mP_{t+1}$ of value perceived as being available to the "old" shareholders. To recognize this fact, M-M modify equation (12) and present it as:

$$(13)\quad V_t = \frac{1}{1+k}(D_t + V_{t+1} - mP_{t+1})$$

In terms of our earlier numerical illustration, if in order to finance both its new investments and its dividends, the firm had to sell 1,000 new shares at \$11 each, and because of the cash received from such sale, V_{t+1} is increased by \$11,000 to \$121,000, V_t would still remain at

$$0.833\,(\$10{,}000 + \$121{,}000 - \$11{,}000) = \$100{,}000$$

Through equation (13) M-M have more sharply identified ways in which the current value of the firm V_t can be affected, namely through current dividends, the firm's value in the next period, and through any new issue of shares, where all three of these variables are interrelated. This interrelation is demonstrated most clearly if we remind ourselves that for a given level of *net* investment I_t, any increase and, hence, potential positive influence of dividend payments is exactly offset by the issuing of additional shares required to finance them. To demonstrate this key point more formally, consider the volume of outside financing required, with X_t the firm's aggregate net profit and I_t its predetermined net investment for period t. We have

$$(14)\quad mP_{t+1} = I_t + D_t - X_t$$

In other words, if net profits are \$19,000, dividends \$10,000 and profitable net investments to be undertaken require \$20,000, then \$11,000 needs to be raised externally. If, however, dividends were to be increased to \$12,000, then \$13,000 would have to be raised. The issue faced is whether in the ideal world which we assumed it is better to finance the investments through retained earnings and to reduce dividends or whether one should increase dividend payments requiring additional outside financing. More specifically we have to resolve whether in fact the current value of the firm V_t (or equivalently the current market value of its shares P_t) is more favorably affected by reducing dividends and using retained earnings, or by increasing dividends and issuing new shares.

By simply substituting equation (14) into equation (13) Miller and Modigliani approach completion of the first phase of their argument showing that V_t is unaffected by the current dividend decision. Specifically,

$$V_t = \frac{1}{1+k}(D_t + V_{t+1} - [I_t + D_t - X_t])$$

or

$$(15) \quad V_t = \frac{1}{1+k}(X_t - I_t + V_{t+1})$$

Note that D_t neither appears directly nor does it influence the independent variables X_t, I_t and V_{t+1} in equation (15).

It is not difficult for M-M to go further and to show that V_t is unaffected by future dividend decisions which can only influence current value through some impact in the final term in equation (15), V_{t+1}. They point out that by reasoning along the lines above it can be shown that V_{t+1} and hence V_t is unaffected by D_{t+1}; that V_{t+2} and hence V_{t+1} and V_t are unaffected by D_{t+2} and so on into the future. Their conclusion is that

> . . . given a firm's investment policy, the dividend payout policy it chooses to follow will affect neither the current price of its shares nor the total return to its shareholders.[18]

Essentially, what is being shown is that in the perfect world being assumed, firms can pay dividends and finance them by simultaneously raising new funds from investors, with such transactions providing no benefit but doing no harm. As discussed earlier in this chapter, money simply circulates from the firm to investors in the form of dividends, and from investors back to the firm in the form of new share purchases. Nothing is lost in the process through either transaction costs or taxes. Hence, the wealth of the shareholders and the value of their shareholdings are left unaffected.

Dividend policy under uncertainty

The same arguments can be carried over into a setting where the assumption of certainty is relaxed. M-M, however, retain the assumptions of perfect markets, and extend their assumption of investor rationality by having each individual participant in the market viewing all other participants and the total market as rational.[19]

To prove that the irrelevance of dividend policy argument can be sustained even when allowing for uncertainty, M-M introduce a variation of their arbitrage approach which was outlined in Chapter 14.

[18]M. Miller and F. Modigliani, "Dividend Policy, Growth, and the Valuation of Shares", as reprinted in J. Van Horne, *Foundations for Financial Management*, Homewood: Irwin, 1966, p. 485.
[19]M-M offer the term "symmetric market rationality" for this extension.

Consider two firms A and B, with investors believing that total net profits and investments will be identical for both companies through time. Investors also believe that dividend payments *from the next period on* will be the same. Thus, the only possible way in which firms A and B might differ is with respect to their *current* dividends.[20] Expressed another way, the assumptions are that:

$$\tilde{X}_{At} = \tilde{X}_{Bt} \quad \text{for } t \text{ from 0 to } \infty$$

$$\tilde{I}_{At} = \tilde{I}_{Bt} \quad \text{for } t \text{ from 0 to } \infty$$

while $\tilde{D}_{At} = \tilde{D}_{Bt}$ for t from 1 to ∞

Tildes are added to reflect that the variables so characterized are subject to uncertainty.

Current period returns to the shareholders of firm A, $\tilde{R}_{A0}$, will be:

$$\tilde{R}_{A0} = \tilde{D}_{A0} + \tilde{V}_{A1} - \tilde{m}_A \tilde{P}_{A1} \tag{16}$$

Given equation (14), it is clear that

$$\tilde{m}_A \tilde{P}_{A1} = \tilde{I}_{A0} + \tilde{D}_{A0} - \tilde{X}_{A0}$$

and on substituting into equation (16) and simplifying, it is concluded that:

$$\tilde{R}_{A0} = \tilde{X}_{A0} - \tilde{I}_{A0} + \tilde{V}_{A1} \tag{17}$$

By an identical process an equivalent expression is derived for firm B, namely;

$$\tilde{R}_{B0} = \tilde{X}_{B0} - \tilde{I}_{B0} + \tilde{V}_{B1}. \tag{17a}$$

In comparing the returns available to current shareholders of the two firms, M-M note, first of all, that the net profit and net investment terms are identical by assumption. If, therefore, the returns are to differ, it must be because $\tilde{V}_{A1} \neq \tilde{V}_{B1}$.

The next point in their exposition stems from the "rationality" assumptions as a consequence of which values of the firm in period 1 can only depend on prospective future earnings, investment and dividends. Since these are assumed to be equal for both firms, $\tilde{V}_{A1}$ must equal $\tilde{V}_{B1}$. It follows that current period returns must therefore be equal and rationality requires that the current values of the firms be equal as well. The key conclusion is that $V_{A0} = V_{B0}$ regardless of any difference between current dividends which were not assumed equal.

In the final stage of their argument M-M allow dividends of the two firms to differ not just in the current period but in the subsequent one as well. We are then reminded that the only way in which the current returns and values of the two firms can be affected by differences between $\tilde{D}_{A1}$ and $\tilde{D}_{B1}$ is through $\tilde{V}_{A1}$ and $\tilde{V}_{B1}$ respectively. Having already shown that current values are unaffected by differences in current dividends, their logical conclusion is that

[20] M-M point out that the use of two identical firms is for ease of exposition only. We might just as readily view A and B as two alternative policy approaches which could be pursued by the same firm with investors "performing a series of mental experiments on the subject of dividend policy".

$\tilde{V}_{A1} = \tilde{V}_{B1}$ and hence $V_{A0} = V_{B0}$ regardless of possible differences in period 1 dividends. By extending their reasoning to all future values of the two firms they conclude that even under uncertainty

> . . . current valuation is unaffected by differences in dividend payments in *any* future period and thus that dividend policy is irrelevant for the determination of market prices, given investment policy.[21]

This statement carries some important conceptual implications. As we shall see in the following chapter, many firms behave as if dividend policy affected shareholders and their wealth and the price at which the firm's shares are traded. Given the arguments presented by Miller and Modigliani, we can understand more clearly what such beliefs will have to be based on if they are to withstand critical analysis, and to do so we will have to look at the assumptions underlying the M-M arguments. First, we can argue that dividend policy becomes relevant if we allow it to influence the firm's investment decisions. If, for example, dividends are paid at the expense of withdrawing funds from potentially profitable investments which then are not undertaken, share prices should be affected by dividend policy. However, to press this point, we would have to base the argument on suboptimal behavior by the firm's management. Even then, changes in the firm's value are ultimately caused not by changes in dividend policy, but by changes in the firm's investment policies. Second, and this appears more plausible, we can look at the effects of market imperfections such as incomplete and unequal information, transaction costs and taxes to cause dividend policy to become relevant.

Market imperfections and other qualifications

In assessing how their analysis of dividend policy carries over into a more real world, M-M acknowledge what they term to be the "informational content of dividends". In other words, they recognize that where a corporation has established a stable dividend policy investors are likely to interpret any change as reflecting management's informed estimate of the firm's future prospects. Such signals in the market may naturally trigger changes in share prices. M-M are careful to stress, however, that the cause of such adjustments to values do not stem *per se* from changes in dividends, but are in fact a reaction to messages being relayed about future growth and earnings expectations. Conceptually, no conflict with the irrelevance position is therefore involved as such information could potentially be relayed to investors in other ways.

When M-M go on to abandon their assumption of perfect capital markets they pursue only the more important implications of such a move. It is clear from their argument, however, that there exist imperfections in the capital market which may lead investors to systematically prefer dividends to capital gains or *vice versa*. We must therefore be prepared to modify the irrelevance conclusion

[21] M. Miller and F. Modigliani, "Dividend Policy, Growth, and the Valuation of Shares" as reprinted in J. Van Horne, *Foundations for Financial Management*, Homewood: Irwin, 1966, p. 508.

somewhat. Such modification helps align theory as we have pursued it with what on casual observation appears to be dividend policy and its rationale in practice.

The first set of major market imperfections which need to be recognized as biasing individual preferences—thereby causing dividend policy to effect values—can be considered under the general heading of transactions costs.

Allowing for underwriting and related issuing costs, it is apparent that with net investments set there are savings to the firm if dividends are limited and retained earnings relied upon. In other words, unlike what is set out in equation (14), once issuing expenses are introduced, each dollar paid in dividends could require more than a dollar of external financing. Hence dividend policy does matter, and it may no longer be reasonable to pay dividends and simultaneously raise new funds externally.

Unlike the impact of issuing expenses, the presence of brokerage costs may suggest that more dividends are to be preferred. When dividends are withheld and earnings reinvested by the firm, rational investors requiring income would simply sell some of their shares. Once brokerage costs are introduced the net amount realized will be reduced and proportionately more shares will have to be sold. As M-M correctly observe, however, firms tend to attract an investor "clientele" drawn by the particular payout being followed so that this effect may be negligible, since one clientele is as good as another in terms of the valuation implied for the corporation.

The difference in the tax treatment of dividends received and capital gains realized is another important real world imperfection which forces modification of the irrelevance conclusion discussed above. Clearly, if a dollar of pre-tax capital gains is felt to be more or less attractive than a dollar of pre-tax dividends, then the equal weighting given to dividends and capital appreciation which underlies the fundamental principle of valuation as set out in equation (11) above no longer holds. Introduction of this bias through personal taxation again suggests that dividend policy does matter.

We have to conclude that the major reasons for dividend relevance and its importance as a practical policy issue are attributable to the market imperfections outlined above. Unfortunately, it is not possible to readily assess how these and other market imperfections[22] and their interactions affect share prices as a function of dividend policy. Hence, while the arguments as set out in this section have allowed us to focus more clearly on what it is that makes dividend policy relevant and important, the question of dividend policy and share valuation remains a challenge to both the empirical researcher and the practitioner.[23]

[22]We might, for example, consider the restrictions placed on the investments of certain financial intermediaries and other institutions. The portfolio holdings of such investors are sometimes limited to the shares of firms which have paid reasonable and uninterrupted dividends.

[23]Because of conceptual difficulties and statistical biases, tests in this area have been inconclusive. See, for example, I. Friend and M. Puckett, "Dividends and Stock Prices", *American Economic Review*, September, 1964, pp. 656-682.

20-6. SUMMARY

We started this chapter by contrasting dividends, earnings and cash flows as alternative bases for the valuation of shares. It was demonstrated that earnings which are reinvested or funds set aside in the form of depreciation to replace worn out assets are only of indirect value to shareholders in that they protect and increase future dividends. Ultimately, dividends are the only valid basis for valuation, and shareholders ought to capitalize the stream of anticipated future dividends in arriving at the value of common shares.

In discussing how dividend policy should be formulated, we reviewed several factors which potentially may be relevant, including:

the firm's reinvestment opportunities,
the shareholders' reinvestment opportunities,
tax differentials between dividends and capital gains,
shareholders' propensity for current income,
consideration of corporate control.

We saw that if shareholders have a propensity for current income, this need not influence a firm's dividend policy, as such shareholders can always sell off part of their share holdings to realize additional income. This is particularly true where shareholders are only interested in maximizing their financial wealth, and other considerations such as corporate control need not be reckoned with. In a realistic setting, brokerage costs and, more importantly, differential taxes may have to be considered.

Tax considerations aside, where shareholders intend to maximize their wealth, a firm should retain all the earnings it requires to finance profitable investment projects which provide a return exceeding the firm's cost of capital. Such projects, by having a positive net present value, will enhance the total value of the firm, and hence, the price of its shares. Dividend policy becomes a residual decision in that any funds which are left over after all profitable investments have been financed should be paid out in dividends. Shareholders foregoing current dividends will be more than compensated by an appreciation in the value of their shares in anticipation of investment returns and, consequently, higher future dividends.

The above assumes that investors are indifferent between income in the form of either dividends or capital gains. Where different tax rates on dividends and on capital gains cause shareholders to have a systematic preference for one form of income versus another, the conclusions derived need to be modified accordingly. Given the complexities of tax legislation, it is not clear whether such a bias exists, and if it does, what its direction or magnitude may be. It appears plausible that firms pursuing different policies attract different clienteles of investors.

Where investors suffer from a lack of information and ascribe significant informational content to any change in dividend policy, such changes may have unsettling effects, even if in terms of what was established above the changes are in the best interest of shareholders.

Given the importance and complexity of the topic, it is appealing to attempt to settle the issue through empirical tests which measure how investors actually react to alternative dividend policies. Unfortunately, such statistical tests are fraught with difficulties, and results obtained to date are inconclusive.

The two major theoretical models presented in the area of dividend policy are those advanced by Gordon and by Miller and Modigliani. Gordon argues that, because of uncertainty and investor risk aversion, shareholders prefer current dividends. We have seen, however, that if the discount rate which the firm applies in evaluating investments truly reflects returns as required by investors in the capital markets, dividend policy once again becomes a residual decision in the above sense, even in the Gordon framework.

Miller and Modigliani analyze dividend policy as a financing decision and, under conditions of perfect capital markets, demonstrate the irrelevance of dividends on share prices, assuming the investment decisions of the firm are not altered. Under the conditions of perfect capital markets, a firm can pay dividends and at the same time raise funds externally without affecting its total value. The relevance of dividend policy for share prices stems from market imperfections such as transaction costs, taxes and perhaps limited information available to investors.

Questions for Discussion

1. The price/earnings ratio is widely used as an indicator in the evaluation of shares. Discuss its potentials and limitations.
2. In evaluating shares, earnings per share seems to be more widely used as an indicator than dividends per share. Discuss the reasons for which this might be so. What are the limitations of earnings per share as an indicator in assessing the value of shares?
3. How do you reconcile discounted cash flow criteria for investment evaluation with the argument that dividends ought to form the basis for valuing common shares?
4. What are some of the main considerations which may be relevant in determining a firm's dividend policy?
5. Why is there a direct tradeoff between dividend payments and capital gains? Illustrate using a numerical example.
6. Discuss some of the typical difficulties encountered when trying to test financial theories statistically.
7. Briefly summarize the arguments put forth by Gordon and by Miller and Modigliani. What is their relevance for a real-world setting, and what useful insights do they provide?

Problems with Solutions

1. Consider a firm with assets worth \$100,000. Assume the market value of the assets is always equal to their book value. Cash flows from operations after meeting all operating expenses amount to 25% of the firm's assets each year. Assets depreciate at a rate of 10% per year and the firm wants to maintain its asset base. \$10,000 of earnings are retained for reinvestment, with the

remainder paid out in dividends each year. At the end of the third year, the firm is liquidated, and a liquidating dividend is paid to shareholders. The firm has 1,000 shares outstanding, and shareholders require an effective return of 15% on their investments. How much should the shares sell for?

Solution

To determine how much the shares should trade for, it is necessary to determine all relevant cash flows and their ultimate use.

For year 1, given a beginning asset base of $100,000, cash flows are given as 25%, or $25,000. Of this, $10,000 must be set aside for depreciation (assets depreciate at a rate of 10%) and the remaining $15,000 are earnings. $10,000 of this are retained for reinvestment, leaving $5,000 to be distributed as dividends.

As the firm's market value is always equal to the book value of its assets, the value of the firm may be determined for the beginning of year 2. From year 1, the book value of the original assets is $100,000 – $10,000 (depreciation) = $90,000. In addition, assets are bought from $10,000 depreciation and $10,000 retained earnings, leaving the company with a net book value of $110,000 at the beginning of year 2.

This may be shown more clearly in a diagram. Years 2 and 3 are also included in the following diagram.

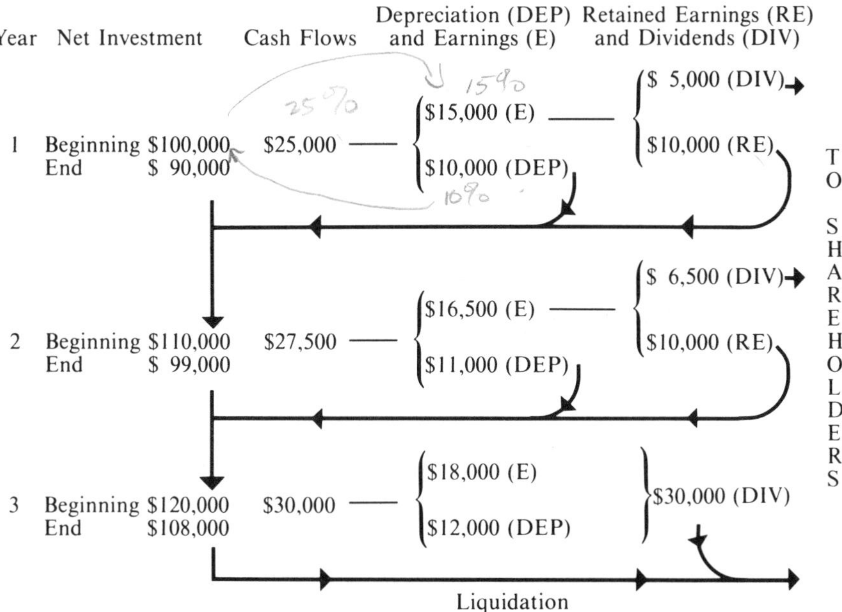

Given that there will be a dividend of $5,000 at the end of year 1, a dividend of $6,500 at the end of year 2, and a liquidating dividend of $138,000 at the end of year 3, it is possible to determine the current value of the firm, and thereby the value of a share, which is just 1/1,000 the value of the firm.

The value of the firm, given a 15% discount rate is:

$$V_t = \frac{D_1}{(1+\hat{k}_e)} + \frac{D_2}{(1+\hat{k}_e)^2} + \frac{D_3+L}{(1+\hat{k}_e)^3}$$

$$= \frac{\$5{,}000}{1.15} + \frac{\$6{,}500}{(1.15)^2} + \frac{\$138{,}000}{(1.15)^3}$$

$$= \$100{,}000$$

The value of the firm is \$100,000. Hence, the shares should sell for 1 / 1,000 this amount, or \$100.

This result occurs because earnings are always 25% of assets while depreciation is always 10% of assets, leaving net earnings as 15%—which just equals the shareholders' effective return requirements.

2. A firm has 100,000 shares outstanding. Earnings have been constant at \$3 per share, with all earnings paid out in dividends. The yield which shareholders require is 12%.
   (a) Compute the current market price of the shares.
   (b) The firm is considering to retain earnings, for the current year only, to finance new investments. In subsequent periods all earnings are again to be paid out in dividends. Compute the new market price per share for the following three cases: the investments being considered promise a return of 10%, 12%, and 15%. For simplicity, assume that the investments generate a constant annuity for the indefinite future. Do the results derived depend on this assumption?
   (c) Graphically portray the share price as a function of the yield provided by the investments.
   (d) Is it reasonable for the firm to claim that it will always have enough good investment opportunities yielding at least 15% and that, hence, it will never pay dividends?

Solution

(a) The market price of the shares should simply be the present value of an annuity of \$3 extending indefinitely into the future, discounted at the shareholder's required yield of 12%.

Thus,

$$\text{Share price} = \frac{A}{i} = \frac{\$3}{.12} = \$25.00$$

(b) If the new investments were financed with this year's dividend, then no dividend would be received by the investor until next year. However, this dividend would be larger than the dividend that otherwise would be received. A return of either 10%, 12%, or 15% on the \$3 foregone would be expected for years 2 to infinity, resulting in annual dividends of \$3.30, \$3.36, or \$3.45. Where the present value of the new annuity, discounted back one year, is equal to or greater than the \$25 computed in item (a) above, the new investments should be undertaken.

Present value of annuity, assuming 10% return from the new investments:

$$\frac{\$3.30}{.12} = \$27.50$$

This amount must be discounted one year at the shareholder's required yield, which is 12%.

$$\$27.50 \times .893 = \$24.56$$

Hence, the new investments should not be undertaken where the expected return is 10%.
Calculations for 12% and 15% returns are as follows:

$$12\% : \frac{\$3.36}{.12} = \$28.00 \qquad \$28.00 \times .893 = \$25.00$$

$$15\% : \frac{\$3.45}{.12} = \$28.75 \qquad \$28.75 \times .893 = \$25.67$$

Thus, given a 12% return on the new investments, the shareholder is indifferent to whether he receives a dividend this year or receives increased dividends from next year on. At 15%, he prefers the new investments.

The results derived do not depend on the assumption that the return from the new investments accrues as a perpetual annuity. For example, for the 12% return case, assume that the \$3 foregone and invested at the end of the year give a one-time return of \$3.36 at the end of the following year. The market price of the shares would be computed as:

$$\frac{\$3.36}{(1 + 0.12)^2} + \frac{\$25}{(1 + 0.12)} = \$25$$

where the second term of the above equation is the capitalized value of the regular \$3 annual dividend paid from the second period on.

We conclude that, quite generally, as long as investments yield a return which exceeds the return required by shareholders, such investments should be undertaken as this will increase the market price per share.

(c)

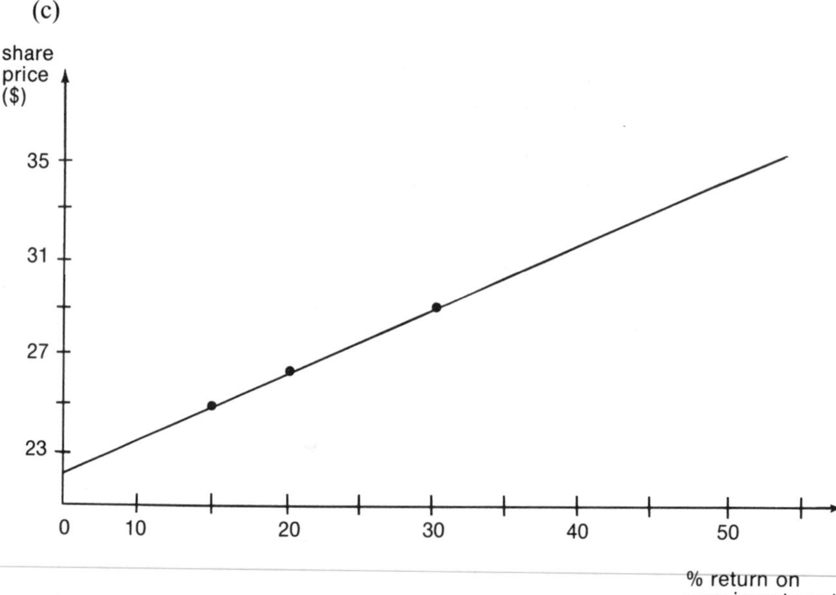

(d) No. If investments which are characteristic for the type of business the firm is in typically provide a return of 12% as indicated by the rate of return which shareholders require, it is not reasonable for a firm to believe that it can grow at a rate which is substantially higher forever. Sooner or later, the firm would have taken over the entire industry. No part of a system can constantly grow at a rate which is higher than the aggregate growth rate of the system. It follows that no part of the economy can grow at a rate which is higher than the overall economic growth rate forever. Abnormally high growth rates have to be viewed as strictly temporary phenomena.

3. Based on its current investment decisions and its anticipated future dividends, the value of a firm at the end of the year, excluding any additional financing which may be undertaken, and after payments of dividends for the current period, is expected to be $100,000,000. Earnings for the current year are expected to be $1.70 per share. $7,000,000 will be required to finance profitable new investments, with the remaining earnings to be paid out in dividends. Investors require an effective return on their shares of 10%. The firm currently has 10,000,000 shares outstanding.
   (a) What is the current value of the firm and the market price of its shares?
   (b) Given dividends of $1.50 per share are to be paid, and that new shares can be issued at $10 per share, how many new shares need to be issued? What is the current market value of the firm?
   (c) If dividends were increased to $2 per share, what effects would this have?

Solution

(a) The current value of the firm may be derived by taking the value expected at the end of the year and adding to that the value of the expected dividends. Referring to equation (15) in the chapter, this may be expressed as:

$$V_t = \frac{1}{1+k}(X_t - I_t + V_{t+1})$$
$$= \frac{1}{1.1}(\$17{,}000{,}000 - 7{,}000{,}000 + 100{,}000{,}000)$$
$$= \$100{,}000{,}000$$

Share price is simply:

$$\frac{\$100{,}000{,}000}{10{,}000{,}000 \text{ shares}} = \$10$$

(b) Expected earnings are to be \$1.70 per share, or a total of \$17,000,000. If the firm were to increase its dividends to \$1.50, this would leave only \$2,000,000 for new investments. Therefore, an additional \$5,000,000 needs to be raised and $\frac{\$5{,}000{,}000}{\$10} = 500{,}000$ new shares must be issued. Referring to equation (13) in the chapter, the value of the firm is now:

$$V_t = \frac{1}{1+k}(D_t + V_{t+1} - mP_{t+1})$$
$$= \frac{1}{1.1}(\$15{,}000{,}000 + \$100{,}000{,}000 - \$5{,}000{,}000)$$
$$= \$100{,}000{,}000$$

(c) Here dividends would require \$20,000,000 and investments \$7,000,000. This is \$10,000,000 more than expected earnings and thus, $\frac{\$10{,}000{,}000}{\$10}$ = 1,000,000 new shares must be issued. The value of the firm, V_t, would remain at \$100,000,000, or:

$$V_t = \frac{1}{1.1}(\$20{,}000{,}000 + \$100{,}000{,}000 - \$10{,}000{,}000)$$
$$= \$100{,}000{,}000$$

Additional Problems

1. Jhana Corporation is a business with \$1,500,000 in assets. Assume that the market value is always equal to the book value of the firm's assets. The assets depreciate at a rate of 15% per year and the firm wants to maintain its asset base. Earnings amount to 30% of assets each year. Investment plans call for \$100,000 of earnings to be invested next year and \$200,000 for each of the following three years, at which point Jhana will be liquidated and the proceeds distributed to shareholders. The firm has 250,000 shares out-

standing. If the shareholders require a 12% return, what is the current selling price for a share of Jhana?

2. (a) Given the same data as in question 1 above, what would be the current value of the firm's shares if Jhana were liquidated at the end of the 3rd year?

   (b) What would a share of Jhana sell for if all the money were reinvested in the firm for the 4 years?

3. A firm's 400,000 common shares have a market value of $50 per share. Dividends have been constant at $6.25, which represents 100% of earnings. The firm is considering retaining the next two years' dividends to finance an expansion which would yield a perpetual return of $700,000 per year, beginning in year 3. Find the expected share price, assuming all subsequent earnings are again paid out in dividends for the indefinite future. What is the minimum yield the investment would have to provide in order to maintain the present share price of $50?

4. Tomplex Ltd. is a small corporation with 200,000 shares outstanding. Given present policy, the firm's value is expected to be $3,000,000 at the end of the current year, after payment of dividends for the current period, with earnings for the current period predicted at $2.35 per share. Investors require an 8% return on the common shares. Assume perfect capital markets.
   Assuming that Tomplex plans to invest $320,000 in expansions and pay the rest of earnings out as dividends, find:
   (a) the market price of Tomplex shares.
   (b) the current value of the firm.
   (c) if Tomplex wished to pay dividends of $2 per share, and still maintain its investment program, how many new shares would have to be issued at $12.50 to supplement internally generated earnings?
   (d) if dividends paid were $2, how much less would the current market value of the firm be than in item (b) above? Explain.

Selected References

F. Black and M. Scholes, "The Effects of Dividend Yield and Dividend Policy on Common Stock Prices and Returns", *Journal of Financial Economics*, May, 1974, pp. 1-22.

W. Baumol, "On Dividend Policy and Market Imperfection", *Journal of Business*; January, 1963, pp. 112-115.

M. Brennan, "A Note on Dividend Irrelevance and the Gordon Valuation Model", *Journal of Finance*, December, 1971, pp. 1115-1121.

E. Brigham, and M. Gordon, "Leverage, Dividend Policy, and the Cost of Capital", *Journal of Finance*, March, 1968, pp. 85-104.

J. Brittain, *Corporate Dividend Policy*, Washington: Brookings Institute, 1966.

I. Diamond, "Earnings Distribution and the Valuation of Shares: Some Recent Evidence", *Journal of Financial and Quantitative Analysis*, March, 1967, pp. 14-29.

E. Elton and M. Gruber, "Marginal Stockholder Tax Rates and the Clientele Effect", *Review of Economics and Statistics*, February, 1970, pp. 68-74.

E. Fama, "The Empirical Relationships Between the Dividend and Investment Decisions of Firms", *American Economic Review*, June, 1974, pp. 304-318.

E. Fama and H. Babiak, "Dividend Policy: An Empirical Analysis", *Journal of the American Statistical Association*, December, 1968, pp. 1132-1161.

I. Friend, and M. Puckett, "Dividends and Stock Prices", *American Economic Review*, September, 1964, pp. 656-682.

M. Gordon, "Dividends, Earnings and Stock Prices", *Review of Economics and Statistics*, May, 1959, pp. 99-105.

M. Gordon, "The Savings, Investment and Valuation of a Corporation", *Review of Economics and Statistics*, February, 1962, pp. 37-51.

M. Gordon, *The Investment, Financing and Valuation of the Corporation*, Homewood: Irwin, 1962.

M. Gordon, "Optimal Investment and Financing Policy", *Journal of Finance*, May, 1963, pp. 264-272.

R. Higgins, "The Corporate Dividend-Saving Decisions", *Journal of Financial and Quantitative Analysis*, March, 1972, pp. 1527-1541.

R. Higgins, "Dividend Policy and Increasing Discount Rate: A Clarification", *Journal of Financial and Quantitative Analysis*, June, 1972, pp. 1757-1762.

J. Lintner, "Distribution of Incomes of Corporations Among Dividends, Retained Earnings and Taxes", *American Economic Review*, May, 1956, pp. 97-113.

J. Lintner, "Dividend, Earnings, Leverages, Stock Prices and the Supply of Capital to Corporations", *Review of Economics and Statistics*, August, 1962, pp. 243-269.

J. Lintner, "Optimal Dividend and Corporate Growth Under Uncertainty", *Quarterly Journal of Economics*, February, 1964, pp. 49-95.

M. Miller and F. Modigliani,"Dividend Policy, Growth, and the Valuation of Shares", *Journal of Business*, October, 1961, pp. 411-433.

R. Pettit, "Dividend Announcements, Security Performance, and Capital Market Efficiency", *Journal of Finance*, December, 1972, pp. 993-1007.

G. Pye, "Preferential Tax Treatment of Capital Gains, Optimal Dividend Policy, and Capital Budgeting", *Quarterly Journal of Economics*, May, 1972, pp. 226-242.

J. Van Horne and J. McDonald, "Dividend Policy and New Equity Financing", *Journal of Finance*, May, 1971, pp. 507-519.

B. Wallingford, "An Inter-Temporal Approach to the Optimization of Dividend Policy with Predetermined Investments", *Journal of Finance*, June, 1972, pp. 627-635.

J. Walter, *Dividend Policy and Enterprise Valuation*, Belmont: Wadsworth, 1967.

R. Watts, "The Information Content of Dividends", *Journal of Business*, April, 1973, pp. 191-211.

G. Whittington, "The Profitability of Retained Earnings", *Review of Economics and Statistics*, May 1972, pp. 152-160.

Chapter 21
Dividend Policy

21-1. INTRODUCTION

The focus of this chapter will be on the actual dividend policies of Canadian corporations and on the relevant institutional setting for dividend policies. We will look at considerations which seem to be prevalent in determining the dividends which firms pay, and we will discuss the aspects of dividend policy which appear to be of concern to investors. The emphasis will be on describing what seems to occur in practice. Procedures for declaring and paying dividends will be reviewed, and the chapter concludes with a discussion of stock dividends and stock splits.

21-2. SUMMARY OF DIVIDEND POLICIES OF CANADIAN FIRMS

The overall dividend policies pursued by management are reasonably depicted by data on past dividend payments. There is substantial U.S. evidence showing the prevalent policy to be one of favoring stable dollar dividend payments per share, with total dividends largely dependent upon the level of dividends in preceding periods and current after-tax corporate income.[1] Changes in corporate income tax rates were found to have no influence on the relationships. Dividends in Canada also appear to be mainly determined by after-tax corporate income and previous dividend levels. As in the United States, neither changes in corporate nor personal income tax rates appear to disturb the relationship.[2]

TABLE 21-1

Aggregated Data on Corporate Income After Taxes, Dividends, and Capital Cost Allowances

Year	Income After Taxes ($millions)	Dividends ($millions)	Payout Ratio*	Capital Cost Allowances ($millions)
1968	3,984	1,809	0.454	3,158
1969	4,126	1,803	0.436	3,261
1970	3,740	1,982	0.529	3,460
1971	4,438	1,946	0.438	3,867
1972	5,265	2,304	0.438	4,138
1973	7,540	2,599	0.345	4,871
1974	9,226	3,183	0.345	5,231

$$\text{*Payout Ratio} = \frac{\text{Dividends}}{\text{Income After Taxes}}$$

Source: Statistics Canada, *Industrial Corporations, Financial Statistics, Fourth Quarter*, 1974.

[1]See J. Lintner, "Distribution of Incomes of Corporations Among Dividends, Retained Earnings, and Taxes", *American Economic Review*, May, 1956, pp. 97-113; and J. Brittain, "The Tax Structure and Corporate Dividend Policy", *American Economic Review*, May, 1964, p. 272.

[2]Canada, *Report of the Royal Commission on Taxation*, Volume 2, Ottawa: Queen's Printer, 1966, p. 147.

FIGURE 21-1

Aggregated Data on Corporate Income After Taxes, Dividends and Capital Cost Allowances

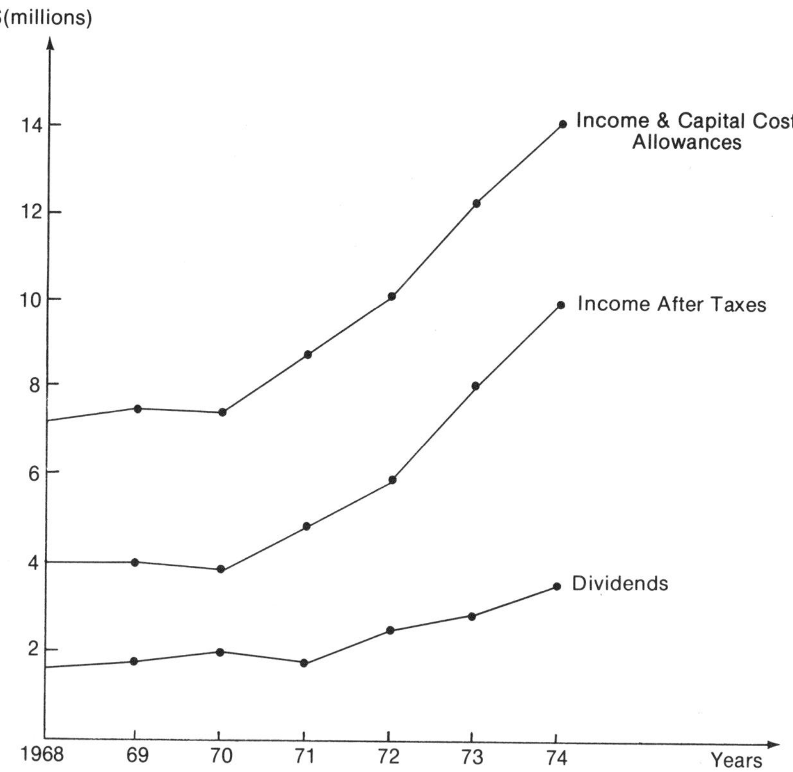

Table 21-1 and Figure 21-1 set out aggregated statistics on corporate income after taxes, dividend payments, dividend payout ratios and capital cost allowances of Canadian corporations. Capital cost allowances are included since the cash flows from which corporations can meet dividend payments are made up of after-tax earnings plus capital cost allowances. The stability of dividend payments relative to earnings is worth noting. While the period 1970-1974 is characterized by rapid growth in earnings, the comparable growth in dividend payments is quite modest. Two reasons for this can be found. For one, the growth in incomes in the early seventies is at least in part caused by inflation. With financial statements prepared on the basis of historical costs rather than replacement costs or current values, earnings figures appear artificially inflated. Corporations recognize that a portion of earnings will be required just to replace assets, and that failure to allow for this by paying generous dividends instead might amount to a gradual liquidation of the business. Secondly, we have seen that firms generally favor stable or gradually increasing dividends as any reduction in dividends may be interpreted as a sign of weakness by shareholders. Given the economic uncertainties of the early seventies, firms would have been reluctant to increase dividends proportionately with earnings since they could not be confident that such high earnings levels would prevail and, hence, that more generous dividend payments could be sustained. Finally, the stability of aggregate dividend payments for Canadian corporations probably reflects, in part, the significance of dividends paid to nonresidents, particularly the dividend transfers from Canadian subsidiaries to their parent corporations in line with long-standing instructions dictated from head office.[3]

This is not, however, to imply that all corporations maintain their dividends in face of declining incomes. The availability of cash and the maintenance of corporate liquidity are important considerations. While cash flows are related to earnings and, hence, to general economic activity, the two are not synonymous. For example, when there is a slowdown in business activity, some firms may in fact find that their cash positions improve because existing inventories and receivables revert to cash and only limited reinvestment in such assets is required. For other firms though, a business slowdown can result in a liquidity squeeze which, if severe enough, may rule out dividends altogether. Conversely, a successful and rapidly growing firm showing healthy profits may face cash shortages as additional investments in inventories, receivables and capital assets are required to sustain growth. Note that inflation has similar effects, since dollar sales increase even with constant physical volumes, and increasing dollar amounts are required as a consequence to sustain given levels of operation.

There is obviously considerable variance in the percentage of earnings being paid out as dividends by Canadian corporations. It is apparent from Table 21-2 that the differences are particularly striking across industry lines. Firms in the communications and transportation industries are generally utilities with moderate or low growth which attract investors seeking high dividend yields. In contrast, firms in non-metal mining and mineral fuels have reinvested substantial portions of their earnings, paying out only modest dividends and attracting shareholders mainly in anticipation of future growth. Even within the same industry, however, dividend policies and payments may vary from one firm to another, reflecting variations in operating performance, needs for funds, or simply differing attitudes towards dividend policy by senior management. This is shown in Table 21-3, which not only demonstrates quite different payout ratios for both firms, but the impact on dividend policy of severe reductions in 1975 earnings as well.

TABLE 21-2

Sample Industry Dividend Patterns

	Dividend Payout Ratios						
Industry	1968	1969	1970	1971	1972	1973	1974
Mineral Fuels	0.20	0.34	0.24	0.12	0.19	0.16	0.19
Non-metal Mining	0.29	0.22	0.19	0.20	0.18	0.09	0.27
Transportation	0.72	0.79	0.82	0.69	0.53	0.55	0.59
Communication	0.71	0.72	0.67	0.67	0.60	0.55	0.65

Source: Statistics Canada, *Industrial Corporations, Financial Statistics, Fourth Quarter,* 1974.

[3]In this respect, the authors differ with views expressed in the Carter Commission Report—on p. 146 of Volume 2, the statement is made that in contrast with the United States, our "less marked stability of aggregate dividend behavior reflects the much greater importance in this country of dividends paid to non-residents".

TABLE 21-3

Dividend Patterns
Forest Products Industry

	Abitibi Paper Co. Ltd.			MacMillian Bloedel Ltd.		
Year	Earnings per common share	Dividends per share	Payout ratio	Earnings per common share	Dividends per share	Payout ratio
1971	$0.23	$0	0	$1.08	$0.50	0.46
1972	0.43	0.07	0.16	1.80	1.00	0.56
1973	1.62	0.275	0.17	3.90	1.25	0.32
1974	2.50	0.65	0.26	3.41	1.75	0.51
1975	0.57	0.40	0.70	(0.89)*	0.65**	—

* (Loss)
** dividend payments were suspended during 1975.
Source: Financial Post Corporation Service

21-3. STABILITY OF DIVIDENDS

A corporation's earnings are apportioned into dividends and retained earnings. As mentioned above, most financial managers appear to treat retained earnings as a simple residual, concentrating instead first on the maintenance of stable or steadily rising dividends. This is best observed from patterns of payout and retention policies during business slowdowns. At such times, dividends tend to be maintained by increasing payout ratios and even drawing on retained earnings. On occasion, in fact, corporations have resorted to external financing in order to maintain the usual or perhaps reduced dividend payments.[4] Such maintenance of dividends is logical when the slump is expected to be short-lived, because a cutback in dividends may be interpreted by investors as signalling difficulties and the informational content of a maintained dividend reflecting management's optimism may cushion the drop in the shares' market price. Similarly, a firm may be reluctant to increase dividends immediately in a period of unusually high earnings. If the increase in earnings proves to be short-lived, the firm may not be able to maintain the increased dividends, and a subsequent reduction of dividends may project an image of instability to investors. Such variable dividends could impair the firm's standing in the eyes of those institutional and other investors particularly interested in stable returns. Beliefs about the value investors ascribe to and the premiums they are prepared to pay for dividend stability can be considered by reference to Figure 21-2. Specifically, proponents of stable dividends would hypothesize that the market price of the shares of Canadian Breweries would have been below what was actually the case if its management between, say, 1963 and 1971 had pursued a policy of paying out a constant percentage of earnings and therefore, of fluctuating its dividend payments.

Management may be prompted to follow a policy of dividend stability for a number of reasons. Given that firms pursuing quite different dividend policies do exist, investors with strong preferences in this regard have a choice of shares

[4]R. Plattner, "Fund Administration and Dividend Policy", *The Quarterly Review of Economics and Business*, Summer 1969, p. 25.

in which to invest. There is evidence to suggest that over time corporations attract a certain clientele of shareholders who value the particular dividend policy being pursued. It follows therefore, that sudden changes in dividend policy, while potentially beneficial in the long run, are likely to have an unsettling effect on at least a proportion of current shareholders. Because such disappointed and perhaps resentful shareholders are less likely to be tolerant toward management, a decision to cut dividends might well be construed as having a direct bearing on executive compensation including bonuses and pension benefits. In addition, the value of stock options could be reduced following a dividend cut because the market price of the shares will likely be depressed.[5]

The policy of maintaining stable dividends may periodically lead to difficult sets of decisions concerned with the length of time over which an existing level of dividends should be maintained in face of changed circumstances. If, for example, a business slowdown proves more severe and lasts longer than originally anticipated, or if the company encounters major difficulties unrelated to the business cycle, continuing to hold the dividends at historical levels could seriously impair the firm's liquidity and subsequent competitive position.

FIGURE 21-2

Earnings, Actual Dividends and Hypothetical Dividends per Share for Canadian Breweries Ltd., 1960-1971 (figures adjusted for changes in financial year end)

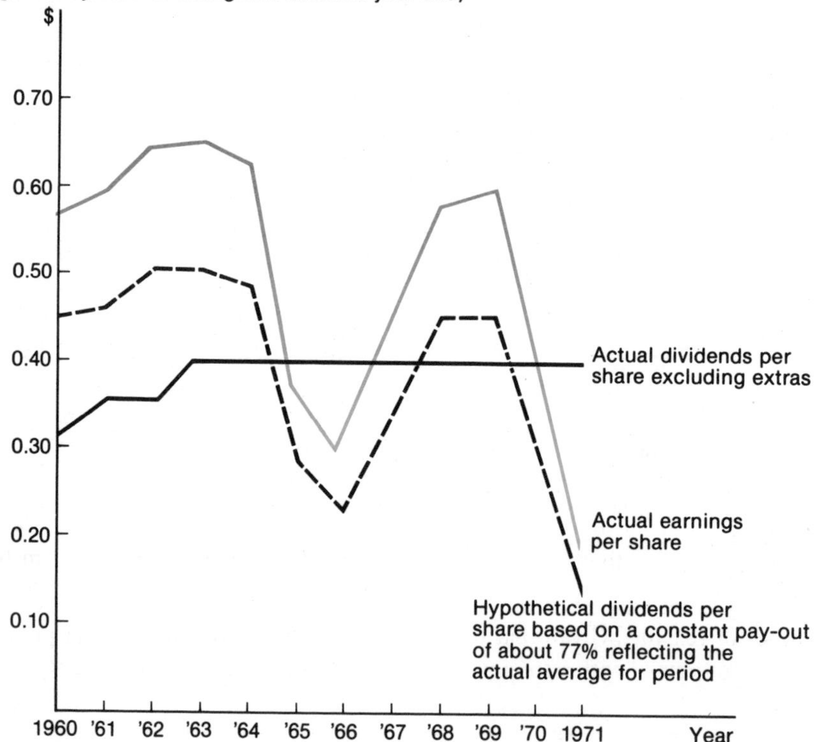

[5]J. Cohen and S. Robbins, *The Financial Manager*, New York: Harper & Row Publishers, 1966, p. 559.

Example

MacMillan Bloedel found that the combined impact of a worldwide recession which began in mid-1974, a costly three-month strike and a catastrophic loss of over $46 million in its shipping operations during 1975 forced a total suspension of dividend payments. A 1975 net loss of almost $19 million compared with net earnings of over $72 million the previous year made it impossible for the firm to sustain the 1974 dividend level of $37 million. After reluctantly distributing almost $14 million in 1975 no further dividends were declared. Interestingly enough it is noted in the *1975 Annual Report* that by the most onerous of the trust indentures under which MacMillan Bloedel has issued long-term debt, the firm's ability to pay dividends was limited (as of December 31, 1975) to future earnings plus about $10 million.

Investor valuation of stability

Investors apparently favor dividend stability for three main reasons. They recognize the informational content of stable or increasing dividends, in some instances they want predictable amounts of periodic dividend income, or they wish conformity with particular legal requirements. The arguments presented in support of these reasons are largely based on intuition and studies of prevalent practices. As yet, no satisfactory theoretical rationale has been developed on the value which rational and well informed investors should place on dividend stability, nor has much been done by way of statistically testing the effect of dividend stability on share prices.

It has been hypothesized that the payment of dividends reduces uncertainty in the minds of investors. For example, when earnings per share fall but dividends per share are maintained, it is argued that the market's evaluation of the corporation's future performance is revised to be relatively more optimistic. As a consequence, share prices hold up better than if dividends were cut to parallel earnings. The market will revise its expectations upward because stable dividends imply that insider evaluation of the firm's future prospects suggests better times than present depressed earnings might indicate.[6] In an extreme case, where management attempts to mislead the market by generating false impressions through its dividend policy, the deception will likely be short-lived. Furthermore, when the facts become known, investors may overreact causing share prices to fall below their warranted level. In any case, management will find it difficult to give the illusion of underlying stability for any length of time if the firm is intrinsically unstable or in difficulty.

A reduction of dividend payments may be contemplated where a firm has unusual growth prospects which make it appear desirable to retain larger proportions of earnings to finance such expansion. Such a reduction of

[6]It has been suggested that dividend policy may be affecting market value not because of informational content in the above sense but because the payments provide clear evidence of the firm's ability to generate cash. See E. Solomon, *The Theory of Financial Management*, New York, Columbia University Press, 1963, p. 142.

dividends could well be in the best interest of shareholders as any negative effects may be more than compensated by increased subsequent growth in earnings and consequently dividends. However, if shareholders are unclear as to whether such a cut in dividends signals hidden or unforeseen financial difficulties rather than exceptional growth prospects, an unsettling effect on the market price of the firm's shares could be experienced.

Propensity for Current Income
For shareholders largely dependent upon dividends received, stable payments are obviously important. Although funds could be obtained through the regular sale of some fraction of share holdings, many would prefer not to do so because of an aversion to what they perceive to be a reduction of capital. Increased brokerage costs and general difficulties to be faced in the sale of smaller lots of shares are also relevant. Moreover, share prices are typically depressed by the time a dividend cut is made and any sale of shares may have to be at quite unfavorable terms.

Institutional Constraints
Certain financial institutions, life insurance companies for example, are regulated with regard to securities in which they can invest while others voluntarily impose policy constraints on their investment managers. Under some circumstances, funds can be committed only for investment in shares of firms that appear on a so-called "approved list". In order to qualify and remain listed, a firm must generally have shown a particular pattern of dividend payments. Obviously it is to a corporation's advantage to build a record of stable dividends so that institutional investors, including trustees, remain free to purchase its shares.

Target payout ratios

Researchers have found that some firms follow the policy of a target dividend-payout ratio over the longer run and that dividends are adjusted to changes in a lagged fashion.[7] Dividends are increased only when management is satisfied that the increased level of earnings can be maintained, while dividends are reduced only when there is reasonably clear evidence that existing distributions can no longer be continued. This policy of hesitancy on management's part in initiating change produces the lagged relationships noted. A framework to represent such corporate policy would picture dividends as determined by a sustained ability to pay, tempered by shorter-run inertia. Empirically, the lag has been verified by several researchers using a target payout ratio model.[8]

Example

The hypothetical example set out in Table 21-4 illustrates how corporate management might be expected to react, given rising earnings

[7]See J. Lintner, "Distribution of Incomes of Corporations Among Dividends, Retained Earnings & Taxes", *American Economic Review*, May 1956, pp. 97-113.

[8]For example, J. Brittain, *Corporate Dividend Policy*, Washington Brookings Institute, 1966, Chapters 2-7, and E. Fama and H. Babiak, "Dividend Policy: An Empirical Analysis", *Journal of the American Statistical Association*, December, 1968, pp. 1132-1161.

per share and a target payout ratio of sixty percent. The lag is apparent in that after a sudden increase in earnings it takes years for actual payout ratios to again reach the target set. While it is possible to interpret the use of target payouts as evidence that stability of dividends is of primary importance, this is not the only reason for such behavior. The target ratio may have been set, but adjustments in payouts to reach it can be made only after management has estimated its long-term growth potential and the consequent total need for funds.[9]

TABLE 21-4

Lags and the Target Payout Ratio: Hypothetical Example

Year	Earnings per Share	Dividends per Share	Actual Payout Ratio
1970	$5.00	$3.00	60%
1971	5.10	3.00	59
1972	7.00	3.00	43
1973	8.10	3.50	43
1974	7.90	4.00	51
1975	8.05	4.80	60
1976	8.00	4.80	60

Extra dividends

When management has established a policy of paying fairly stable dividends, unexpected increases in earnings can pose something of a problem. On the one hand, management may wish to distribute some portion of increased profits to its shareholders. On the other hand, however, the rise in earnings may be viewed as a temporary phenomenon, casting doubts on the firm's ability to sustain the higher dividend payments for any length of time. It is in such situations that corporate management can usefully turn to the use of *extra dividends*. Resort to such extras signals the circumstances much more clearly, thus curtailing both false informational effects and loss of investor goodwill, if in the following periods such extras are not again forthcoming. The unsought and undesirable buildup of shareholder expectations about the permanence of the dividend increase is avoided, leaving the firm free to increase payments temporarily without jeopardizing its record of dividend stability. It must be appreciated, however, that when extras are declared regularly, investors will come to expect the payments and view them as part of the established dividend rate.

Example

Some recent instances of the use of extra dividends include the twenty-five cent distribution by Maple Leaf Gardens Ltd. during the first quarter of both 1970 and 1971 and the twenty-five cent extra dividend paid by the Canadian Salt Company in September 1971.[10] For Maple Leaf Gardens, operators of a sports arena and home ice for the Toronto

[9] R. Lindsay and A. Sametz, *Financial Management: An Analytical Approach*, Homewood, Ill., Richard D. Irwin, 1967, pp. 279-280.

[10] Dividend information is taken from the Financial Post Corporation Service, *Dividend Record*, November Edition, 1971.

Maple Leafs hockey team, the two years in question were very profitable ones. The unusually severe winter of 1970-71 was relevant in the case of the Canadian Salt Company. Sales of rock salt for road clearing purposes were the largest in the firm's history and produced earnings of $1.87 per share as opposed to $1.02 the previous year.

21-4. OTHER CONSIDERATIONS

A number of different factors have been identified as having direct bearing on the development of corporate dividend policy. The factors cited include the investment opportunities available to the firm since they influence the amount of earnings a firm may wish to retain for reinvestment, certain advantages of using retained earnings rather than further common share offerings as equity financing, the relative preferences of investors for dividends versus capital gains, and the apparent partiality investors have for dividend stability. However, there are a number of other considerations of a practical nature which constrain the firm in its setting of dividend policy and which, therefore, warrant attention.

The firm's cash position

Profitable firms are quite frequently illiquid and consequently unable to pay other than token cash dividends. This is most likely to be true in the case of growth companies which must commit a significant percentage of their earnings to investment in current and fixed assets. To sustain the growth while paying generous dividends would require more extensive use of debt or greater dilution of the common shareholder's position through issuance of additional common shares than company management could contemplate. As mentioned earlier, such growth could be either real (increasing physical volume) or inflationary (constant physical volume at increasing prices), with the effects on financing needs being identical. For low-growth firms, however, the cash position and general need for monies may not be as important a consideration. A study into factors which influence determination of the dividend payout policy of electric utilities concluded that managers seemed more concerned about potential shareholder dissatisfaction and market reaction than by the need for funds to finance expansion and replacement.[11]

An inadequate cash position might, of course, be offset by ready access to financial markets. Firms enjoying such flexibility and able to obtain funds on short notice can consider more generous dividends than their apparent liquidity would suggest. Since it is the better established corporations which generally have more liberal lines of credit and have their securities well received in both money and capital markets, such firms are able to go with higher dividend payouts than the typical new or smaller concern.

[11] R. Plattner, "How Electric Utility Managers Determine Dividend Policy", *Public Utilities Fortnightly*, April 24, 1969, p. 30.

Control

When retained earnings prove inadequate for the financing of available investment opportunities and management must turn to external sources, such as issuance of additional common shares, control of the corporation may emerge as an important consideration. In such circumstances, modest amounts of additional funds could probably be raised by selling new shares to existing shareholders through privileged subscription with the consequently increased equity base then permitting further debt to be issued. However, attention would also focus on the question of whether, in fact, lower payouts should be introduced to alleviate the problem—hence increasing the monies available from internal sources.

Actual situations are likely to be quite intricate and defy simple solutions. For example, those shareholders outside the group with working control may take umbrage at low payouts and through their actions encourage corporate raiders seeking to gain control of the firm, and proxy fights. This was just the circumstance faced by the management of Western Mines in late 1975, when Pat Sheridan of Toronto moved for control. He accumulated and subsequently sold a forty percent shareholding in Western Mines to Brascan Resources Ltd. and a restructuring of the Board of Directors followed. Management must therefore move very cautiously toward any lowering of dividend distributions. Researchers have recently looked at the question of whether degree of control influences corporate payout ratios, and one study focused on the conduct of the two-hundred largest U.S. firms over the 1959-64 period.[12] They found that firms which were effectively controlled by management (through obtaining proxy votes from dispersed shareholders) maintained significantly larger dividend payout ratios than firms which were under the effective control of one or a few large shareholders. This would suggest that management views payment of generous dividends as an important factor in maintaining good relations with shareholders.

Shareholders and their tax status

Where the corporation is closely held, management must naturally cater to the particular wishes and needs of the owners. Such individuals are likely to fall into the higher tax brackets and the differentiation for tax purposes between income and capital gains becomes significant. Clearly, funds which are retained within a business should contribute to increasing its value, so that a direct relationship can be postulated between the amount of retained earnings and the market price of a firm's share. It follows that there should be a tradeoff between dividends paid and potential capital gains to be realized by shareholders. This tradeoff is often recognized by resort to only modest cash dividends, leaving the bulk of shareholders' returns in the form of capital gains.

As a firm gets larger, its shares tend to be more widely held, making it difficult

[12]D. Komerschen and J. Pascucci, "Dividend Policy and Control Status", *Public Utilities Fortnightly*, May 21, 1970, pp. 43-44.

FIGURE 21-3

Exerpts from Letter to Shareholders Announcing Dividends

Hiram Walker-Gooderham & Worts Limited

Walkerville, Ontario
Canada

OFFICE OF
THE PRESIDENT

October 10, 1975

To our Shareholders:

Class A Convertible Common Shares Dividend

Directors of the Company have declared a dividend (No. 257) of 35 cents a share and an extra dividend (No. 258) of 10 cents a share, both payable October 15, 1975, in Canadian currency, on the outstanding Class A convertible common shares payable to shareholders of record September 22, 1975. Enclosed is a cheque in payment of the dividends on those Class A convertible common shares, if any, registered in your name.

Class B Convertible Common Shares Dividend

Directors of the Company have further declared, to be paid out of tax-paid undistributed surplus, a dividend (No. 11B) of 29 3/4 cents a share and an extra dividend (No. 12B) of 8 1/2 cents a share, both payable October 15, 1975, in Canadian currency, on the outstanding Class B convertible common shares payable to shareholders of record September 22, 1975, these dividends being the same as declared on Class A convertible common shares less 15% tax paid by the Company under the provisions of the Income Tax Act (Canada). Enclosed is a cheque in payment of the dividends on those Class B convertible common shares, if any, registered in your name.

for management to recognize the preferences of the owners and much less to cater to them. The dividend policy followed is consequently either a compromise in the form of a payout ratio in the middle range or a conscious attempt to attract and hold a particular type of investor with particular needs and expectations.

Increasingly, however, corporations are issuing two classes of interconvertible common shares and thereby recognizing different "clienteles" among their shareholders. As noted in the chapter on taxation, by paying a special fifteen percent tax on pre-1971 earnings, a firm can distribute such earnings to shareholders without shareholders being taxed on the receipts. For one class of common shares the corporation pays this special fifteen percent tax on pre-1971 earnings and effects distributions from these earnings which are then tax-deferred dividends.

Normal taxable dividends are issued on the other class of common shares and in this latter case the dividend tax credit is available to the recipients. Figure 21-3 illustrates this approach as used by Hiram Walker-Gooderham and Worts.

In evaluating the relative desirability of these two types of shares, the investor would compare the after-tax dividend yields which depend on his individual tax rates. For high marginal tax rates, shares offering the "tax-free" distribution would be preferred, and vice versa. The first problem with solution at the end of this chapter provides a numberical illustration of such an evaluation.

We note that if the March 1977 Federal Budget proposals are enacted, then from 1979 on tax-deferred dividends will have been eliminated.

Restrictions in debt contracts

Trust deeds and other longer-term debt contracts often limit the size of dividends payable by the debtor corporation. The restrictions aim at preserving the firm's ability to service its debt and typically relate dividend distributions to current earnings and cash flows, or to the maintenance of appropriate levels of working capital. As discussed in earlier chapters, the payment of cash dividends to common shareholders is also contingent on first meeting obligations on the outstanding preferred shares.

Small business

We saw in the chapter dealing with the tax environment that income of small businesses is taxed at a reduced rate. To confine the tax concession to smaller corporations, the lower rate is available only so long as the company's accumulated taxable income does not exceed the limit as stipulated by the Act. Small businesses are allowed to deduct from the accumulated total four dollars for every three dollars of taxable dividends distributed to the shareholders. While factors such as the net taxes which shareholders must pay on dividends will have to be considered in determining dividend policy, other things being equal this particular provision of the Act provides an incentive for small business to pay out at least a portion of earnings in dividends in order to retain the tax concession. Clearly, however, the current inflationary environment which combines expanding dollar sales with periods of restricted lending has placed many small businesses in a tight cash position, making generous dividends a luxury they no longer can really afford. Thus, management appears to face an unhappy choice between running short of cash on the one hand and losing the small business deduction with a subsequently increased tax bill on the other. If we add to this the fact that the ceiling on accumulated income is not automatically adjusted for inflation, leaving it to decrease in real terms, we can understand the deteriorating position in which small business has found itself in recent years.[13]

[13]The 1976 budget introduced some relief by providing for substantial increases in the ceilings applicable to the small business deduction.

Some general considerations

The opportunities available for the profitable use of retained earnings will certainly influence payouts. Where no attractive investment opportunities are available, all earnings should be paid out in dividends as shareholders themselves could reinvest such funds. It hardly seems to be rational, for example, for a firm to pursue a policy of large retentions in order to invest in money-market instruments or even government bonds.

Inflation may also influence dividend policy because, given major price level changes, the replacement cost of existing assets will exceed the funds generated through capital cost allowances. To preserve the firm's earning power by maintaining the level of its assets, an increasing fraction of earnings must be reinvested in the business to acknowledge the inadequacy of accounting depreciation, which is based on historical costs. Consider the following simplified example. A firm purchased assets at a cost of $10,000,000, 5 years ago. In order to maintain its productive capacity, about 10 percent of the assets need to be replaced each year. Assume for simplicity that the assets are depreciated on a straight-line basis over 10 years, *i.e.* 10 percent of the original cost or $1,000,000 each year. If, due to inflation, prices have doubled since original purchase of the assets, it will now take $2,000,000 to replace 10 percent of the assets, with depreciation based on historical costs clearly providing insufficient funds for such replacements. Consequently, the firm will have to draw on its earnings just to maintain its asset base, and failure to do so while paying generous dividends will be equivalent to a partial liquidation of the business. Though accelerated depreciation alleviates the problem to some degree, given double-digit inflation, the rates allowed on declining balance capital cost allowances will have to be high to compensate for the above effects.

21-5. PAYMENT PROCEDURES

Dividends are payable if and when declared by the corporation's board of directors. Distributions typically relate to a particular time span, therefore we tend to think in terms of quarterly or semiannual dividends being declared. The actual payment procedure would involve the formal dividend declaration at a meeting of directors specifying particulars including the type, amount, and form of the payment, the class of shares affected, and the dates of record and payment. The dividend may be labelled regular, extra, liquidating, or it may be left unlabelled.[14] Moreover, although dividends are usually paid out in cash, other available alternatives would include resort to stock, property, and scrip dividends, the latter a form of promissory note. Once the declaration is made, the shareholders are generally notified by publication of a notice in the financial pages of newspapers. Figure 21-4 illustrates one such announcement.

The corporation sets the date of record respecting the particular dividend, and payment will be made to those individuals or organizations appearing as

[14]See C. Prather and J. Wert, *Financing Business Firms*, (4th ed.), Homewood, Ill., Richard D. Irwin, 1971, pp. 335-337.

shareholders on the books of the company as at the date of record. A date of record usually precedes the payment date by two or three weeks, to allow for lags in cheque preparation and mailing. Given the lag between a sale of shares and registration of the new owner on the corporation's books, the stock exchanges will have shares trading ex-dividends a number of days prior to the date of record.[15] Shareholders lists are often updated and maintained by separate

FIGURE 21-4

Published Dividend Notice

The
Alberta Gas Trunk Line
Company Limited

NOTICE OF DIVIDENDS

Notice is hereby given that the following quarterly dividends have been declared payable on the 15th day of August, 1972, to shareholders of record at the close of business on the 1st day of August, 1972.

PREFERRED SHARES

Series C Dividend No. 28

Dividend of $1.1875 per share on the outstanding 4 3/4% Cumulative Redeemable Preferred Shares, Series C.

Series D Dividend No. 15

Dividend of $1.34375 per share on the outstanding 5 3/8% Cumulative Redeemable Convertible Preferred Shares, Series D.

COMMON SHARES

Class "A" and "B" Dividend No. 40

Dividend of $0.42 per share on the outstanding Class "A" and Class "B" common shares.

By order of the Board
W. J. Hopson
Vice-President and Secretary
Calgary, Alberta, June 9, 1972

Illustration Courtesy: The Alberta Gas Trunk Line Company Limited.

institutions, notably trust companies. In performing this service for a corporation, the trust company is said to act as the corporation's *transfer agent*. The treasurer or transfer agent will prepare cheques dated with the date of payment and the cheques are then mailed to arrive accordingly. Conceptually, we would

[15]Canadian stock exchanges usually establish the ex-dividend date on the second business day before the date of record.

expect the market price of a share to drop just after it goes ex-dividends. However, because many other factors also influence the market price of the shares, the theoretical drop in price is difficult to isolate and may not be observable.

When the board of directors meets to consider dividend payments, certain legal limitations beyond those spelled out in articles of association, by-laws, or trust deeds will have to be recognized. These statutory limitations exist largely for the protection of creditors but may not apply in the case of companies in extractive industries such as mining. The question of legality is quite complex and beyond the scope of this text. In general, however, restrictions are aimed at preventing (i) payments when the corporation is insolvent, (ii) payments which will impair the firm's capital, and (iii) payments which will render the company insolvent. Penalties for failure to comply are levied against the directors, with directors potentially being personally liable to creditors or shareholders where legal action is initiated.

In an international environment, laws restricting the payment of dividends to foreigners may also have to be recognized. Many countries with weak currencies exercise tight control over any outflow of funds which may influence their balance of payments unfavorably, and dividend payments abroad may be closely regulated. Such regulations, whether existing or anticipated, obviously become an important factor when evaluating foreign investments.

21-6. STOCK DIVIDENDS AND STOCK SPLITS

Though dividends are almost always paid out in cash, stock dividends are resorted to with some frequency. When such dividends are paid, the corporation merely distributes additional stock certificates to its shareholders on a pro-rata basis. There is, therefore, no change in the position of any individual owner as a consequence of the distribution. In an accounting sense, the disbursement simply involves transfering a portion of retained earnings to the capital account, leaving the net worth section of the balance sheet unchanged. The amount transferred generally reflects the fair market value of the additional shares issued.

Example

Consider the case of Consolidated Textile Mills Ltd. which had the following shareholders' equity position before declaring a 5 percent stock dividend on November 25, 1970:

Capital Stock:	
Authorized: 1,000,000 Common Shares without Nominal or Par Value	
Issued: 238,482 Common Shares	$ 416,712
Retained Earnings:	4,762,323
	$5,179,035

A five percent stock dividend meant that for each 20 shares held, the holder received one additional share, or that 238,482/20 = 11,924 new shares were issued. Payment altered the shareholders' equity position to:

Capital Stock:	
Authorized: 1,000,000 Common Shares without Nominal or Par Value	
Issued: 250,406 Common Shares	$ 559,260
Retained Earnings:	4,619,775
	$5,179,035

The amount transferred from retained earnings to the capital account reflects the fair market value of the common shares of Consolidated Textile Mills at that time—in this case, almost $12.

In theory, then, a shareholder receives nothing more than additional certificates when he or she receives stock dividends. Proportionate ownership of the firm is unchanged as is the total value of share holdings. The market price of each share should, however, drop. Thus, an investor holding 100 shares of Consolidated Textile Mills at a market price of $12 *cum*-dividends would expect the price of the stock to drop to $\$12 \times \frac{100}{105} = \$11.43$ after the stock dividend, while the total value of share holdings remain unchanged at $1,200 because of the additional shares received.

Problems with solutions at the end of this chapter provide additional illustrations of the above process.

Where, following payment of a stock dividend, the corporation returns to its usual per share distribution of cash dividends, the stock dividend would have had particular significance to those investors who value increased cash dividends. Quite obviously, their total receipts from cash dividends are increased after the stock dividend, as they now hold a greater number of shares. It should be noted that until the March 1977 Federal Budget there was no differentiation between stock and cash dividends for purposes of Canadian income taxation. It is proposed that effective April 1977, stock dividends will no longer be taxable when received from a public company by Canadian residents. Such dividends however, will be subject to capital gains tax on sale.

The possible informational content of the stock dividend may also be noted by investors. If, for example, such distributions are substituted for cash payments, it may signal that the expected future productivity of earnings presently retained in the business will more than offset dilution brought about by the increase in the number of shares outstanding. The Barber Oil Corporation might well provide an extreme example of such thinking. For fourteen years, since 1959, the corporation refrained from paying cash dividends. Stock dividends were introduced on October 1, 1959 and paid semiannually from 1960 until 1973.

In an economic sense, stock dividends are quite similar to stock splits. In either case, additional share certificates are issued. The motivation for issuing such new share certificates is different, however, and there are differences in the accounting treatment as well. Stock dividends are issued as a bonus (whether real or just perceived can be debated) to existing shareholders, and the number of new shares issued at one time as a stock dividend is generally small compared to the total number of shares already outstanding. In contrast, stock splits are introduced by corporate management to bring about a reduction in the price of the shares. The usual objective in dropping the price is to move the security into a more attractive price range. To achieve this, new share certificates are issued in a number which is a multiple of the shares currently outstanding. In a two-for-one split, for example, each shareholder would receive two new shares in return for every one share previously held. Conversely, a reverse split would reduce the number of shares outstanding, thereby increasing their market price. While it has been claimed that by dropping share prices to more popular trading ranges it is possible to broaden stock ownership,[16] the optimal price range for the trading of shares has yet to be identified. Thus, the five-for-one split by Canadian Pacific in October, 1971 moved the price to around $13.50 while the 2.5-for-1 split by International Nickel in June, 1968 only dropped the price to $42.00. Considering reverse splits, the September, 1971 one-for-four rollback of Comaplex Resource International Ltd. (formerly called Wollaston Lake Mines) lifted the price to around a dollar.

Distinctions from an accounting point of view also exist and require recognition. For example, a two-for-one split doubles the number of shares outstanding and, where the shares have a par value, this figure is accordingly halved. With a hundred percent stock dividend, twice the number of shares would also be outstanding, but the par value per share would remain unaltered. Additionally, unlike a stock dividend, the stock split requires no transfer between the balance sheet's retained earnings and capital accounts.

Example

Consider a two-for-one split, and assume the following entries for the equity section of the balance sheet before the split:

50,000 common shares, par value of $10 each	$500,000
Contributed surplus	$300,000
Retained earnings	$1,000,000
	$1,800,000

After the split, we would have:

100,000 common shares, par value of $5 each	$500,000
Contributed surplus	$300,000
Retained earnings	$1,000,000
	$1,800,000

With a hypothethical 100 percent stock dividend, we would have obtained:

100,000 common shares, par value of $10 each	$1,000,000
Contributed surplus	$ 300,000
Retained earnings	$ 500,000
	$1,800,000

[16]The point has specifically been made with respect to stock dividends, but is also applicable to splits. See C. Barker, "Evaluation of Stock Dividends", *Harvard Business Review*, July-August 1958, pp. 99-114.

Theoretically at least, a stock split like a stock dividend is of no value to the investor, for his proportional ownership of the corporation is unaffected and the total market value of his shares should remain unchanged. Like stock dividends, however, a split may have informational content. It may suggest that the previous growth and prosperity which moved share prices above the preferred range is expected to continue, thus prompting investors to bid the price higher. This view is supported by empirical research which found that where a split is anticipated or announced, the market price of the shares may increase and remain higher than would otherwise be expected.[17] Hence, reinforcement of growth expections and prospects of a more attractive trading price may combine to increase value.

Where a stock is split, the firm may reduce its dividends per share accordingly. In the case of the Canadian Pacific five-for-one split just cited, the dividend was dropped from $1.65 to $0.33 per share. International Nickel also reduced its dividend proportionately. Generally, however, shareholders have come to expect some increase in their aggregate dividends and may value the split stock accordingly.

21-7. OTHER TYPES OF DIVIDENDS

A survey of remaining forms of dividends requires brief mention of two possibilities. The first, a property dividend, calls for disbursement by the corporation of assets other than cash. Payments of this type are most usually made using various securities previously held for control or investment purposes, although inventories have been distributed on occasion.[18] Because the use of property dividends is quite limited, recent illustrations are difficult to come by. In January, 1962, Gatineau Power Co.,[19] in addition to paying the regular thirty cent dividend to its shareholders, distributed one share of Gelco Enterprises Ltd. This property dividend was held to have a taxable value of $1.20 per share.

Secondly, dividends may take the form of promissory notes or similar corporate liabilities. Such payments, depending on the maturities involved are referred to as scrip or bond dividends. Their use is so infrequent as to reduce them to academic interest only.

Stock repurchase and the dividend decision

An interesting alternative to the payment of cash dividends is the repurchase by the firm of its own common shares. Such repurchase, which may be effected either in the market or through a tender offer, is a well established practice in the United States and elsewhere. It is, however, a relatively new phenomenon in Canada, allowed for through appropriate amendments to provincial and federal

[17]R. Johnson, "Stock Splits and Price Change", *Journal of Finance*, December 1966, pp. 675-686.
[18]In the United States during World War II, some distillers took to distributing liquor as dividends.
[19]Purchased by Hydro-Quebec in 1963.

statutes, starting with those of Ontario in 1970.

With the legislation in place, those corporations lacking attractive investment opportunities but with spare cash on hand have an interesting choice. They may declare more generous dividends or alternatively buy back and retire their own shares.[20] Perhaps because of difficult economic conditions and associated cash shortages which prevailed during the early and mid-1970s, very few Canadian firms so far have resorted to share repurchases. Finding enough cash to maintain dividends appears to have been one major concern, while tax considerations are the other and perhaps more serious obstacle. If, however, the U.S. experience is any indication, we can expect to see some repurchase activity in Canada in the future.[21]

Example

To better appreciate the effects of share repurchases as an alternative to paying cash dividends, consider the simplified numerical example set out in Table 21-5. The illustration focuses on a company with 1,000,000 shares outstanding and total annual earnings of $1,000,000. A constant price-earnings ratio of 10 is assumed for deriving the market price of the shares, while special taxes which may have to be faced are ignored.

Our hypothetical corporation may on the one hand, distribute all of its earnings, in which case, a dividend of $1 per share can be sustained. If, on the other hand, earnings are used to repurchase shares, a number of interesting consequences are to be observed. For instance, with the number of outstanding shares reduced, reported earnings per share are increased. Furthermore, holding everything else constant, some appreciation in the market price of the remaining shares should follow. From the viewpoint of those shareholders who retain their holdings, the choice is simply between receiving cash dividends or of holding shares which increase in value.

TABLE 21-5

Basic Share Repurchase.

	Period 1	Period 2	Period 3
Earnings after taxes	$1,000,000	$1,000,000	$1,000,000
Shares outstanding	1,000,000	900,000	810,000
Earnings per share	$1.00	$1.11	$1.23
Price-earnings ratio (assumed constant)	10	10	10
Market price of shares	$10.00	$11.11	$12.30
Shares repurchased (total earnings/share price)	100,000	90,000	81,300

[20]Shares need not always be cancelled. They may be held for stock options, subsequent resale or use in a merger.

[21]For a useful review of U.S. activity, see P. Regan, "A Comment on the Recent Proliferation of Treasury Stock Purchase Programs," *Merrill Lynch, Pierce, Fenner, and Smith: Analysis*, April 2, 1973.

It has been suggested that, in the U.S. at least, managements have used share repurchases for cosmetic adjustment.[22] In this context there is the suggestion that repurchased shares are frequently those selling at depressed prices because of inferior operating results and prospects. The opportunities for cosmetic manipulation of, for example, earnings per share are more clearly identified if we reconsider "Period 3" in Table 21-5 and allow for a five percent decline in earnings after taxes to $950,000. Despite this slide in overall operating performance, earnings per share would still appear to rise from $1.11 in period 2 to $950,000/810,000 = $1.17 in period 3.

Any commentary on the advantages and disadvantages of share repurchases can only be set out in a fairly general way. Not only do specific circumstances differ in each case, but complex tax considerations are invariably involved in weighing the payment of cash dividends versus any repurchases of shares. Conceptually, share repurchase programs could offer tax advantages to some shareholders in that capital gains are substituted for cash dividends, and taxes on capital gains are only paid when such gains are realized, and then at a relatively low rate. While details on taxation go well beyond the scope of this text it should be appreciated, nevertheless, that Canadian taxation authorities have not left the corporation or its owners with much room for tax avoidance. Without going into exact details we might note, for example, that where a corporation purchases its shares *in the open market*, it faces a special 25 percent tax on the approximate spread between the purchase price and the paid-up capital account. The March 1977 Federal Budget proposes to drop this tax, however.

Corporate share repurchases may pose difficulties for management in quite another sense. Shares are purchased in the market from current owners offering them for sale. Such sellers have nowhere near as complete a grasp of the firm's current and future prospects as that enjoyed by corporate management engaged in buying on behalf of the remaining owners. For example, management may have good reasons to believe that, in the light of future prospects, share prices are currently undervalued, and it may use inside information to repurchase shares at bargain prices. Legislation governing the repurchase of shares does seek to limit abuses and conflicts of interest in such circumstances. Protection is also afforded creditors who may not want to see cash which could be used to service debt obligations channelled into share repurchase programs. The effectiveness of the statutory provisions has, however, been questioned. In the opinion of one authority who assisted in the drafting of repurchase legislation for both Ottawa and British Columbia,

> . . . restraints are not likely to prove significant and the opportunities for abuse are likely to prove significant in the hands of unscrupulous operators.[23]

[22]R. Norgaard and C. Norgaard, "A Critical Examination of Share Repurchase," *Financial Management*, Spring, 1974, pp. 44-50.

[23]See P. Brimelow, "Will Canadian Firms Follow U.S. Lead on Repurchase of Stock?" *Financial Post*, October 13, 1973, p. 8.

SUMMARY

Both the stability of aggregate dividends and, therefore, some evidence of a variability in corporate payout ratios are to be noted in Canada. The reasoning behind the maintenance of stable payments includes the informational content of such disbursements, the benefits in meeting the needs of institutional and other investors, and the propensity for current income on the part of some shareholders. Where additional distributions are contemplated but there is uncertainty about the firm's ability to maintain the new level of dividends, management frequently resorts to the use of extra dividends, thereby signalling the circumstances more clearly.

Furthermore, corporate dividend policy is often influenced by one or more of the following considerations:

- Reinvestment opportunities: where the firm can reinvest earnings retained in the business at high rates of return, it may prefer to do so in order to accumulate increased gains to shareholders in the future rather than paying out generous current dividends.
- Differential in investor taxes between dividends and capital gains: with capital gains often being taxed at lower effective rates than dividends (this is especially true for investors in the higher tax brackets), investors may prefer retention of earnings in the business and consequent capital appreciation in their shares rather than generous current dividends.
- Reluctance to issue new common shares: where additional funding is required and equity is the preferred choice (*e.g.* because the firm has reached its debt capacity) drawing on retained earnings is generally superior to issuance of new common shares since issuing expenses are avoided and dilution is minimized. It would not be very reasonable to pay out a generous dividend (taxed in the hands of investors) and then to ask investors to use their net proceeds to invest in new common shares which were just to be issued.
- The firm's cash position: cash needs to be available for the payment of dividends. Since availability of cash (liquidity) and profitability are not synonymous, high reported earnings are not sufficient to ensure that healthy dividends can be paid without compromising the firm.
- Trust deeds on outstanding debt issues: debt contracts may place restrictions on the payment of dividends in order to conserve cash for the servicing of outstanding debt.

Payment procedures are quite straightforward, with the board of directors declaring the amount of dividends to be paid. Certain critical dates associated with the declaration of dividends must be identified, specifically the date of record and the payment date. While we would expect the share price to drop by the amount of the dividend payment when the shares go ex-dividends, because of the many other factors influencing share prices such drops may often not be detectable.

The practice of paying other than cash dividends, while not very common, should be noted, and such forms as stock, property and scrip dividends may be encountered. Stock dividends involve issuance of additional share certificates to existing shareholders. While conceptually stock dividends do not affect the shareholders' wealth position their informational content and other market imperfections may serve as a positive factor influencing share prices.

Stock splits have strong similarities with stock dividends, but are resorted to for different purposes. The main objective in their use is to alter the price range in which the shares are currently trading. Again, conceptually, a stock split does not affect the wealth position of current shareholders and merely represents a rearrangement of outstanding share certificates which leaves the proportional ownership of each shareholder unchanged.

The repurchase by a firm of its own shares may be an alternative to paying cash dividends. With the number of outstanding shares reduced, reported earnings per share will increase and some appreciation in the market price of the remaining shares should follow. From the viewpoint of a shareholder, the choice is between receiving cash dividends or an appreciation in the value of their shares. While share repurchases are a well established practice in the United States, few Canadian firms have so far resorted to repurchase of their own shares.

Questions for Discussion

1. Is it reasonable for a firm which finds itself temporarily in a short cash position but which wants to maintain its dividend to resort to short-term borrowing in order to finance dividend payments? Discuss.
2. If management does believe that dividend policy has an effect upon share price, what would they do to keep dividends stable during business slowdowns?
3. (a) Why does a firm use extra dividends instead of increasing regular dividends?
   (b) What are the advantages to a company of using stock dividends?
4. "It is irrational to pay dividends and then issue common stocks to secure funds to finance growth."
   Do you think this statement is correct:
   (a) given perfect capital markets?
   (b) in the real world? Why?
5. If you were on the board of directors of a firm and had to vote on dividend policy, what would be some of the main considerations which would have a bearing on your decision? What information would you try to gather before arriving at a decision?
6. (a) A firm whose shares you have invested in just reduced its cash dividends. What information would you want to gather in order to evaluate such a reduction in cash dividends and its likely impact on the value of your shares?
   (b) At the same time as reducing its cash dividend, the above firm declared a stock dividend to supplement the reduced cash dividend. What factors would you consider in evaluating the stock dividend and its likely impact on the value of your shares?
7. Stock splits are used to alter the price range within which a firm's shares typically trade. How would you determine what is a "good" trading range for a firm's shares? What factors would you consider to be relevant?

8. If you were the majority shareholder of a firm and hence, through electing directors, could strongly influence a firm's dividend policy, would stability of dividends be something you would value and, hence, try to implement? What would be some of the main considerations in trying to answer this question?

Problems with Solutions

1. (a) As discussed in the chapter, Hiram Walker-Gooderham & Worts Ltd. offers two classes of shares (Class A and Class B) which are characterized by different types of dividend payments, with the details described in Figure 21-3. Assume you are an investor residing in a province where provincial tax is 30% of federal tax. If your total marginal tax rate (federal plus provincial tax) is 40%, which of the two types of shares would provide you with the higher current after-tax dividend yield? Assume that you have exhausted any tax-free amounts available on dividends, so that any dividends you receive are taxable.

Solution

Consider first the Class A shares. Each Class A share has a total dividend of 45¢ (35¢ + 10¢). Assuming the investor holds 1000 shares he will receive a total dividend of $450.

Dividend		$450.00
Add 33⅓% gross up		150.00
Taxable dividends		$600.00
Federal tax before credit (30.77%*)	$184.62	
Less 20% dividend tax credit on taxable dividends (20% × $600)	120.00	
Federal tax		$ 64.62
Provincial tax (30% of federal tax)		$ 19.39
Combined tax		$ 84.01
Net amount retained ($450 – $84.01)		$365.99

*30.77% federal tax + 9.23% provincial tax (30% of 30.77%) gives a total marginal tax rate of 40%. This is derived as follows:

$$\begin{aligned} \text{total tax} &= \text{federal tax} + \text{provincial tax} \\ &= \text{federal tax} + 0.30 \times \text{federal tax} \\ &= 1.3 \times \text{federal tax} \\ \text{federal tax} &= \text{total tax}/1.3 = 40\%/1.3 = 30.77\% \end{aligned}$$

Now consider the Class B shares. Each Class B share has a total dividend of 38.25¢ (29¾ + 8½¢). Assuming the investor holds 1000 shares he will receive a total dividend of $382.50. This dividend is non-taxable.

The investor would prefer the Class B shares given the 40% tax rate. He receives $382.50 from Class B shares, but only $365.99 from Class A shares.

An assumption in the above answer is that the shares are to be held indefinitely. Should the shares be sold in the near future the desirability of Class B shares may well change. As you will recall from Chapter 3, any dividends paid on Class B shares will reduce the purchase price for tax purposes. The result of this is that any capital gain realized on the sale of the shares will be increased through payment of dividends.

By way of example, assume the Class B shares are sold one year after this dividend. Any capital gain realized will be increased by the amount of the dividend, here \$382.50. One half of this is taxable at 40%, leading to an increase in taxes of $0.4 \times 0.5 \times \$382.50 = \$76.50$. Assuming a discount rate of 10%, the present value of this amount becomes $\$76.50/(1 + 0.1) = \$69.55$, leading to a net retention of $\$382.50 - \$69.55 = \$312.95$ for the investor. This is less than could be made from the Class A shares, making the Class A shares more favorable.

(b) At what marginal tax rate (combined federal and provincial) would you just be indifferent between the two classes of shares?

Solution

In providing a solution, we assume that the 1000 shares of Class B would be held indefinitely and, hence, that their effects on capital gains when the shares are disposed of can be ignored.

The net amount retained from Class A shares must match the \$382.50 retained from the Class B shares to make the investor indifferent between the two.

Actual dividends received (Class A)		\$450.00
Net amount retained (assumed)		382.50
Combined tax		\$ 67.50
Federal tax (combined tax/1.3)		\$ 51.92
Dividend	\$450.00	
Add 33⅓% gross up	150.00	
Taxable dividends	\$600.00	
20% dividend tax credit on taxable dividends	120.00	

Calling the federal tax rate F, we have

federal tax before credit − dividend tax credit = federal tax payable

$$F \times \$600 - \$120 = \$51.92$$

from which we compute

federal tax before credit = \$51.92 + \$120 = \$171.92

or

$$F = \frac{\$51.92 + \$120}{\$600} = 28.7\%$$

Federal tax as a percentage (\$171.92/\$600)	28.7%
Provincial tax as a percentage (30% of 28.7%)	8.6%
Combined tax rate for indifference (28.7% + 8.6%)	37.3%

2. In April 1969, Barber Ellis of Canada Ltd. implemented a ten-for-one stock split. The equity section of the balance sheet prior to the stock split is given below:

SHAREHOLDERS' EQUITY
Capital Stock:
Authorized: 1,200 7% cumulative redeemable first preference shares of a par value of $50 each
54,000 common shares with a par value of $10 each
Issued and fully paid:

	1,200 first preference shares (at $50 each)	$ 60,000	
	45,500 common shares (at $10 each)	455,000	
		$ 515,000	
Surplus:	Contributed	45,000	
	Retained Earnings	5,339,172	5,899,172

Determine the changes in the equity section of the balance sheet as affected by the stock split, given the following notes from the corporation's consolidated financial statements for the year ended December 31, 1969:

The company has obtained Supplementary Letters Patent dated April 22, 1969 authorizing the following changes in its capital stock:

(a) the 45,500 issued and the 8,500 unissued common shares with a par value of $10 each were subdivided and changed into 455,000 issued and 85,000 unissued common shares without par value
(b) the 1,200 authorized and issued preference shares with a par value of $50 each were redesignated as first preference shares with a par value of $50 each
(c) the authorized capital was increased (i) by creating 400,000 nonvoting second preference shares with a par value of $25 each issuable in series, and (ii) by creating in additional 960,000 common shares without par value.

Solution

SHAREHOLDERS' EQUITY
Capital Stock:
Authorized: 1,200 7% cumulative redeemable first preference shares of a par value of $50 each
400,000 nonvoting second preference shares of a par value of $25 each
1,500,000 common shares without par value
Issued and fully paid:

	1,200 first preference shares	$ 60,000	
	455,000 common shares	455,000	
		515,000	
Surplus:	Contributed	45,000	
	Retained Earnings	5,339,172	5,899,172

3. National Profit Company had the following shareholders' equity section before declaring a 5% stock dividend on July 30, 1972:

Capital stock:

Authorized: 500,000 common shares without nominal or par value.

Issued:	200,000 common shares	$2,000,000
	Retained earnings	600,000
		$2,600,000

(a) Show the change in the shareholders' section after the 5% stock dividend, given that the firm's shares are currently selling at $15 per share.
(b) If an investor is holding 100 shares of National Profits Company, show the total value of his holdings before and after the stock dividends.
(c) If the company intends to pay the same $2.00 per share as dividends after the stock dividends, what is the incremental dividend received by the above investor?

Solution

(a) Capital stock:

Authorized:	500,000 shares without nominal or par value	The split does not affect the number of shares authorized.
Issued:	210,000 common shares: $2,150,000	The number of shares issued increases by 5%. The value increases by number of new shares issued times the current market value, here $15 per share × 10,000 = $150,000.
Retained earnings:	$450,000	The $150,000 increase in the value of shares issued is transferred out of retained earnings.

(b) Total value of holdings before stock dividends:

100 × $15 = $1,500

After stock dividends the share price will drop to:

$\$15 - \$15\,(1 - \frac{100}{105}) = \$14.29.$

The value of his holdings = 105 × $14.29 or $1,500

(c) Incremental dividends:

The shareholder has 5% more dividends. Assuming the shareholder originally had 100 shares the increment is (105 – 100) × $2 dividend, or $10.

4. Using symbols to define the relevant variables, indicate the impact of an x % stock dividend on:
(a) the firm's book value per share
(b) the firm's market value per share
(c) the wealth position of an investor who initially holds k shares.

Solution

Assume:

C_0 = total stock (\$) before stock dividend, as per balance sheet
C_X = total stock (\$) after stock dividend, as per balance sheet
R_0 = retained earnings (\$) before stock dividend
R_X = retained earnings (\$) after stock dividend
N = number of shares outstanding before the dividend
P = market price of the shares before the dividend
n = number of new shares issued as a stock dividend
k = number of shares held by hypothetical investor before the dividend
V = original value of the shares held by hypothetical investor
x = stock dividend as a proportion of shares outstanding.

(a) Book Value per Share

(i) Book Value per share before dividend: $\dfrac{C_0 + R_0}{N}$

(ii) Book Value per share after dividend: $\dfrac{C_X + R_X}{N+n}$

However, $C_X = C_0 + (Pn)$, and $R_X = R_0 - (Pn)$

therefore $C_X + R_X = C_0 + (Pn) + R_0 - (Pn) = C_0 + R_0$

and Book Value per share after the dividend $= \dfrac{C_0 + R_0}{N+n}$

The value of the total stock as per balance sheet increases by the amount that retained earnings decrease. Thus the net worth of the firm does not change and the book value of a share is influenced only by the number of new shares issued.

(b) Market Value per Share

(i) Market Value before dividend: P

(ii) Market Value after dividend: $P - P\left(1 - \dfrac{100}{100(1+x)}\right)$

Because neither the net worth of the firm nor its operations have changed, the market value of the shares should adjust downward in proportion to the number of new shares issued.

(c) Wealth of Hypothetical Investor

(i) Wealth before dividend: $kP = V$

(ii) Wealth after dividend: $(k + kx)\left[P - P\left(1 - \dfrac{100}{100(1+x)}\right)\right]$

$$= k(1+x) \times P/(1+x) = V$$

The decrease in market value per share will be offset by the increased number of shares held so that the total value of shares held by any investor will not change.

A Numerical Example:
A company with \$1,000,000 common stock outstanding and \$300,000 retained earnings declares a 10% stock dividend. Current market value of the 100,000 outstanding shares is \$15 per share. Find the book value per share before and after the dividend, the market value before and after the dividend, and the wealth position of Jack Smith who owns 200 shares before the dividend.

Book Value before: $\frac{C+R}{N} = \frac{\$1{,}000{,}000 + \$300{,}000}{100{,}000} = \$13.00/\text{share}$

Book Value after: $\frac{C+R}{N+n} = \frac{\$1{,}000{,}000 + \$300{,}000}{100{,}000 + 10{,}000} = \$11.82/\text{share}$

Market Value before: $P = \$15$

Market Value after: $P - P\left(1 - \frac{100}{100(1+x)}\right) = \$15 - 15\left(1 - \frac{100}{100+10}\right) = \$13.64$

Jack Smith's wealth before: $k \times P = 200 \times 15 = \$3000$

Jack Smith's wealth after: $(k + kx)\left[P - P\left(1 - \frac{100}{100(1+x)}\right)\right]$

$$= (200 + 20)\left[15 - 15\left(1 - \frac{100}{100+10}\right)\right]$$

$$= (220)(\$13.64) = \$3000$$

Additional Problems

1. B.C. Resources had the following shareholders' equity section before a 2 for 1 stock split:

Capital stock:

Authorized: 600,000 common shares of a par value of \$5 each.

Issued and fully paid:	300,000 common shares	\$1,500,000
	Paid-in surplus	900,000
	Earned surplus	400,000
		\$2,800,000

(a) Show the change in the equity section after the 2 for 1 stock split.
(b) What should be the market value of B.C. shares after the split if they are currently selling at \$20 a share?

2. HPC Co. Ltd. has two classes of shares (Class A and Class B). On December 1, 1976 HPC declared a dividend of 60¢ per share on its Class A shares, and a dividend of 51¢ per share to be paid from tax-paid undistributed surplus on its Class B shares.

(a) For an investor holding 2000 shares, which class of share would provide the higher current after-tax dividend yield? Total marginal tax rate (provincial and federal tax) for the investor is 35%, and provincial tax is

40% of federal tax. Assume the investor plans to hold the shares indefinitely, and that he has exhausted any tax free amounts which may be available on dividend income, so that any dividends he receives are taxable.

(b) At what combined tax rate (provincial and federal tax) would this investor just be indifferent between the two classes of shares?

3. An investor currently holds 100 shares in Reliable Industries Inc. which are trading at $30 per share. The investor faces a federal marginal tax rate of 30%, plus a provincial tax rate which is 35% of the federal tax. Dividend payments for the current year are $3 per share. If this cash dividend were eliminated and the funds retained to finance business growth the investor would expect a capital appreciation in the share's market value of $3 per share.
   (a) Would it be advantageous for the shareholder if the dividend were eliminated with all earnings being reinvested in the business? Assume that the shareholder has exhausted any tax-free amounts which may be available on dividend income, so that any dividends she receives are taxable.
   (b) What would the marginal tax rate (combined federal and provincial) of the shareholder have to be to make her indifferent between the two alternatives?

4. Mr. B. Morris, head of Morris Sports Ltd., a small but rapidly growing public sporting goods company, has witnessed an escalating price of his company's shares. They have recently risen to $9 and he feels this to be too high a price for such a small company in this field. Morris has decided to meet this problem by either a 2 for 1 stock split or a 100% stock dividend.
   The present Owner's Equity section of Morris Sports Ltd. is as follows:

10,000 common shares without par value	$ 60,000
Retained earnings	$122,000
	$182,000

   Show what the effects of the 2 for 1 stock split, and of the stock dividend would be on the balance sheet of Morris Sports Ltd.

5. (a) In 1972 Burns Ltd. adopted a policy of buying back its own outstanding common stock instead of paying cash dividends. Earnings after taxes for the four years 1972-1975 stayed at a constant $7,000,000 and were used exclusively for the repurchase program. Assuming there were 28 million shares outstanding at the beginning of 1972, and that a fairly stable price/earnings ratio of 14 has existed since then, calculate the number of shares repurchased, the earnings per share and the market price per share obtained for the years 1972 through 1975.
   (b) Using the same data as above, determine the preference of a shareholder holding 3,000 shares of Burns Ltd. from 1972 to the end of 1974 for either cash dividends or share repurchases. Ignore the time value of money and assume earnings are either fully paid out in dividends or used for share repurchases, as described above. The shareholder's combined (provincial and federal) marginal tax rate is 38% with her federal tax being 30%. The shareholder has exhausted any tax-free amounts which may be available on dividend income, so that any dividends she receives are taxable.

Case

Prairie Land Holdings

Founded as a family business in 1946, Prairie Land grew very rapidly, first through land development activity and subsequently through oil and gas discoveries on its properties. In 1958, the corporation issued common shares to the public and by 1960 its shares were listed for trading on two major stock exchanges. Public offerings were made from time to time to finance exploration and development while long-term debt was issued with some regularity from 1960 onward. In late 1975 the Bailey family had working-control through its 25 percent holding of voting shares. The remaining shares were widely distributed with no other large blocks of holdings in existence. Further diversification of business activity was also taking place.

During 1975, the flow of letters from irate shareholders complaining about Prairie Lands' policy of paying only token cash dividends over the past five years increased significantly. The anger, no doubt, was precipitated by recent declines in share prices, as well as by prevailing rates of inflation. It became very apparent to Mr. Stewart Bailey, the firm's chief operating officer, that the issue of dividend policy would dominate discussion from the floor at the shareholders' annual general meeting now just three months away. Bailey was also concerned about some recent heavy trading activity in Prairie Land shares and wondered whether it was the prelude to a formal tender offer for Prairie Land stock. Members of the Bailey family had been approached in the past about selling their holdings, but only in a very casual way. Obviously, if shareholder unrest increased, it would become most difficult to resist a tender offer which aimed at control of the company.

Many of the letters from shareholders pointed to low dividends combined with significantly higher executive compensation including generous pension plans. Others noted the decline in share prices relative to book values and urged higher cash dividends, stock dividends, stock splits, and more recently, share repurchases. Declines in share prices were slightly more severe than those experienced by similar firms and the market generally. Bailey felt that despite the unattractiveness of several of these ideas to his family, whose members faced very high marginal tax rates, he would have to come up with a proposal regarding dividend policy in time for the annual general meeting. He was also aware of the firm's significant investment and expansion opportunities which would require additional security issues over the next several years.

EXHIBIT 1

Prairie Land Holdings
Financial Data, Selected Years

	EPS	Dividends/Share	Average MP/Share	Book Value/Share*
1974	$16.00	$0.30	$176.00	$198.00
1973	15.00	0.30	180.00	182.00
1972	14.50	0.30	290.00	167.00
1971	13.00	0.30	230.00	153.00
1970	12.00	0.30	180.00	136.00
1965	9.00	0.25	108.00	76.00
1960	4.00	0	41.00	39.00

*No reappraisals of land values or revenues had been undertaken since 1950.

EXHIBIT 2

Prairie Land Holdings,
Selected Balance Sheet
Data as at year ended December 31,
(in millions of dollars)

	1974	1973	1972	1971	1970
Cash and marketable securities	61	50	45	38	30
Accounts receivable	31	30	16	15	14
Inventories	44	40	19	18	16
Total current assets	136	120	80	71	60
Net fixed assets	662	655	527	505	443
Total assets	798	775	607	576	503
Current liabilities	217	220	123	115	105
Long-term liabilities	185	190	150	155	140
Common Shareholders' equity	396	365	334	306	258
Total liabilities and net worth	798	775	607	576	503

Selected References

C. Barker, "Evaluation of Stock Dividends", *Harvard Business Review*, July-August, 1958, pp. 99-114.

J. Brittain, *Corporate Dividend Policy*, Washington: Brookings Institute, 1966.

J. Brittain, "The Tax Structure and Corporate Dividend Policy", *American Economic Review*, May 1964, pp. 272-287.

Canada, *Report of the Royal Commission on Taxation*, Volume 2, Ottawa: Queen's Printer, 1966.

C. Ellis, "Repurchase Stock to Revitalize Equity", *Harvard Business Review*, July-August, 1965, pp. 119-128.

E. Elton and M. Gruber, "The Effect of Share Repurchases on the Value of the Firm", *The Journal of Finance*, March, 1968, pp. 135-149.

F. Finn, "Stock Splits: Prior and Subsequent Price Relationships", *Journal of Business Finance and Accounting*, Spring, 1974, pp. 93-108.

L. Guthart, "Why Companies are Buying Back Their Own Stock", *Financial Analysts Journal*, April-May, 1967, pp. 105-110.

W. Hausman, R. West, and J. Largay, "Stock Splits, Price Changes, and Trading Profits: A Synthesis", *Journal of Business*, January, 1971, pp. 69-77.

K. Johnson, "Stock Splits and Price Change", *Journal of Finance*, December, 1966, pp. 675-686.

D. Komerschen and J. Pascucci, "Dividend Policy and Control Status", *Public Utilities Fortnightly*, May 21, 1970, pp. 43-44.

L. Laporte, *Dividend Policy in the Smaller Company*, New York: The Conference Board, 1969.

J. Lintner, "Distribution of Incomes of Corporations Among Dividends, Retained Earnings, and Taxes", *American Economic Review*, May, 1956, pp. 97-113.

J. Miller and B. Fielitz, "Stock-Split and Stock Dividend Decisions," *Financial Management*, Winter, 1973, pp. 35-45.

R. Norgaard and C. Norgaard, "A Critical Examination of Share Repurchase", *Financial Management,* Spring, 1974, pp. 44-50.

R. Pettit, "Dividend Announcements, Security Performance, and Capital Market Efficiency," *Journal of Finance*, December, 1972, pp. 993-1007.

R. Plattner, "Fund Administration and Dividend Policy", *The Quarterly Review of Economics and Business,* Summer 1969, pp. 21-29.

R. Plattner, "How Electric Utility Managers Determine Dividend Policy", *Public Utilities Fortnightly,* April 24, 1969, pp. 27-30.

K. Smith, "Increasing Stream Hypothesis of Corporate Dividend Policy", *California Management Review,* Fall, 1971, pp. 56-64.

R. West and A. Brouilette, "Reverse Stock Splits", *Financial Executive,* January, 1970, pp. 12-17.

PART 7
Financial Analysis and Control

Chapter 22
Ratio Analysis

22-1. INTRODUCTION

At any given point in time a wide variety of interest groups may wish to analyze the financial condition of particular firms. Trade creditors will approach the task in a way that reflects their interest in establishing the firm's ability to meet its short-term obligations; bondholders, on the other hand, will wish to determine the firm's cash generating capacity over the longer run. The interest of financial analysts and shareholders may focus on the company's present and expected cash flows, earnings, and dividends, and how these will be reflected in the market price of the common stock. Corporate financial executives are also concerned about their firm's financial position. They must negotiate with outside suppliers of capital and must also be aware of general managerial effectiveness. This chapter will review and evaluate certain of the more basic or widely used concepts and tools of financial analysis. Given the range of possible approaches and techniques, greater detailing is not possible here.[1]

It should be appreciated right from the start that the effective use of the basic tools and techniques of financial analysis requires the exercising of a great deal of care. A number of points should be kept in mind. First, financial analysis cannot be viewed as a routine to be standardized. There exist many differences among industries and among firms within the same industry. The indiscriminate application of a standardized routine of analysis to all companies, regardless of size, industry, and peculiar characteristics, might well lead to grossly incorrect conclusions. Secondly, effective analysis requires identification of the tools most appropriate to particular lines of investigation. As will become evident later on, each of the techniques available to the analyst has been designed with a particular set of functions in mind. It is most important, therefore, that the goal or objective of the investigation be known in advance so that the most appropriate tools are used. Thirdly, in certain instances the outputs from the analyses provide nothing more than clues which may suggest a need for closer scrutiny. In-depth analysis should follow to explain a certain result and to establish its significance.

22-2. RATIO ANALYSIS

Though writers have related ratio analysis back to Euclid's work on ratios, dated around 300 B.C., as a tool of financial analysis it evolved quite recently.[2] Its initial and quite primitive usage was to provide benchmarks for credit analysis. Subsequently, ratios were recognized as having potential for more general

[1]Interested students are referred to Erich A. Helfert, *Techniques of Financial Analysis*, (3rd ed.), Homewood, Ill.: Richard D. Irwin, Inc., 1972, Chapter 2, and B. Lev, *Financial Statement Analysis: A New Approach*, Englewood Cliffs: Prentice-Hall, 1974, Chapters 2, 3 and 5.

[2]An interesting historical treatment is to be found in the work of J. Horrigan, "A Short History of Financial Ratio Analysis", *Accounting Review*, April, 1968, pp. 284-294.

managerial purposes and even held out as providing a scientific approach[3] which is clearly not the case.

It is fair to say that at present ratios are helpful devices for comparisons. In particular, contrasts may be made over time to discern trends in a firm's development or between similar firms in the same industry. Without comparisons, ratio analysis may provide nothing more than some rather meaningless numbers. Fortunately, however, various sources provide industry "standards" or averages which may be employed as norms. Among these sources are Dun & Bradstreet, the Canadian Imperial Bank of Commerce, trade associations, and various government agencies. A note of caution is again necessary, namely that industry comparisons must be made with care. The diversification phenomenon of recent years may make it very difficult to classify a company within a given industry. Even among firms within a given industry there likely exist wide differences in accounting methods employed, size, age, growth rate, and credit terms extended to customers and received from suppliers. Before drawing any positive conclusions, it is obviously important to confirm that reasonable and valid comparisons are being made.

In the future, ratios may hold greater promise despite an almost complete absence of underlying theory. For instance, statistical testing to establish the sufficiency of ratios as predictors illustrates one new direction. In particular, some modest success has been achieved in testing the ability of ratios to predict bankruptcy and to predict corporate bond ratings.[4] As additional progress is made in this area, ratio analysis should become more exact and comprehensive. Much additional work remains to be done, however, though the availability of computerized data files providing extensive collections of corporate financial statements should expedite matters significantly.

Type of ratios

When reviewing ratios it is useful to divide them into three basic classifications, namely: liquidity ratios, leverage ratios, and profitability and activity ratios. Clearly, only a limited set of examples will be used in focusing on each type or category of ratios. In the illustrations which follow, reference will be made to Tables 22-1 and 22-2, the Consolidated Balance Sheet and the Income Statement of Merchant Marts Limited respectively.

It is important to keep in mind that a ratio is merely a fraction—the comparison of one figure to another. The opportunity to "window dress" is

[3]See, for example, W. Justin, "Operating Control Through Scientific Analysis", *The Journal of Accountancy*, September, 1924, pp. 183-195.

[4]See W. Beaver, "Financial Ratios as Predictors of Failure", *Empirical Research in Accounting: Selected Studies, 1966*, University of Chicago, 1967, pp. 77-111; E. Altman, "Financial Ratios, Discriminant Analysis and the Prediction of Corporate Bankruptcy", *Journal of Finance*, September, 1968, pp. 589-609; J. Horrigan, "The Determination of Long-Term Credit Standing with Financial Ratios", *Empirical Research in Accounting: Selected Studies* in *Journal of Accounting Research*, 1966, pp. 44-62, R. Edmister, "An Empirical Test of Financial Ratio Analysis for Small Business Failure Predictions", *Journal of Financial and Quantitative Analysis*, March, 1972, pp. 1477-1493, and G. Pinches and K. Mingo, "A Multivariate Analysis of Industrial Bond Ratings", *Journal of Finance* March 1973, pp. 1-18.

always present in the preparation of financial statements and can influence ratios significantly. Take, for example, the *current ratio* which is defined as follows:

$$\frac{\text{Current Assets}}{\text{Current Liabilities}}$$

From Table 22-1, the 1970 fiscal year-end current ratio is

$$\frac{\$333{,}063{,}688}{\$130{,}263{,}991} = 2.56$$

The use of $20 million of cash just prior to the year-end to retire a current liability would have reduced both the numerator and the denominator by this amount, improving the current ratio as follows:[5]

$$\frac{\$313{,}063{,}688}{\$110{,}263{,}991} = 2.84$$

Other manipulations can also be employed to improve the current ratio. These might include the substitution of longer-term debt for current liabilities and the increase of current assets through the sale of fixed assets.

Liquidity ratios

Liquidity ratios are designed to reflect the short-term debt-paying ability of the firm. Simply stated, they spotlight the relationship between cash and "near cash" on the one hand and obligations which are currently maturing on the other.

The most widely used ratio in this category and perhaps the most widely used of all ratios is the current ratio which has already been introduced. From Table 22-1, the current ratios for Merchant Marts for the 1969 and 1970 fiscal year-ends are:

1969	1970
$\frac{\$321{,}876{,}638}{\$127{,}803{,}123} = 2.52$	$\frac{\$333{,}063{,}688}{\$130{,}263{,}991} = 2.56$

A very crude rule of thumb of 2.0 is cited from time to time as a suitable current ratio.[6] It must be stressed that such an overall standard is quite misleading and may be excessive for the service industry or utility field where cash flows are more predictable and current assets are comparably liquid; and inadequate in certain fields of manufacturing where the reverse may hold. Hence, a laundry must be viewed differently from a distillery where inventory requires aging. Table 22-3 provides information on a sample of key ratios across several industries in Canada. The wide variations among industries are worth noting and emphasize the importance of selection in industry groupings when comparisons are to be made.

[5]The use of cash to reduce liabilities will improve the current ratio only if the current ratio is 1.0 or greater before the manipulation is made. If the current ratio is less than 1.0, the situation will deteriorate rather than improve.

[6]See, for example, New York Stock Exchange, *Understanding Financial Statements*, 1967, p. 21.

TABLE 22-1

Merchant Marts Limited

Consolidated Balance Sheet

Assets	At Fiscal Year-end	
Current Assets:	January 6, 1971	January 7, 1970
Cash	$4,530,877	$2,452,646
Government of Canada bonds, at cost	112,669	112,669
Accounts receivable	203,100,502	188,804,533
Inventories valued at the lower of approximate cost or market	114,201,475	120,167,123
Prepaid advertising and other charges	11,118,165	10,339,667
	333,063,688	321,876,638
Investments and Other Assets:		
Investments and advances, at cost	9,337,408	13,143,119
Notes receivable on sales of Class A shares of Merchant Marts Limited under the Employees' Stock Purchase Plan	5,271,492	4,153,954
Refundable federal tax	——	194,621
	14,608,900	17,491,694
Fixed Assets, at cost:		
Land	15,648,113	14,042,835
Buildings and improvements	99,152,932	63,510,222
Equipment and fixtures	53,673,122	44,553,016
	168,474,167	122,106,073
Less accumulated depreciation	39,544,755	33,855,670
	128,929,412	88,250,403
Unamortized goodwill	2,512,307	2,346,820
	$479,114,307	$429,965,555
Liabilities		
Current Liabilities:		
Demand and short-term notes	$63,026,050	$71,934,000
Accounts payable	40,193,925	31,225,460
Accrued wages, rent, interest, etc.	15,779,770	15,381,540
Income and other taxes	8,065,996	5,329,497
Contribution payable to Merchant Marts Profit Sharing Retirement Fund	1,318,695	2,076,995
Dividend payable March 15, 1971	1,879,555	1,855,631
	130,263,991	127,803,123
Long-term debt	183,157,576	147,831,195
Deferred income taxes	9,228,000	7,352,000
	322,649,567	282,986,318
Shareholders' Equity Capital Stock:		
Authorized shares of no par value* 3,300,000 Class A shares 6,600,000 Class B shares 6,600,000 Class C shares		
Issued 2,458,208 Class A shares	$24,887,128	20,104,944
6,600,000 Class B shares	27,500,000	27,500,000
6,600,000 Class C shares	27,500,000	27,500,000
	79,887,128	75,104,944
Retained earnings	76,577,612	71,874,293
	156,464,740	146,979,237
	$479,114,307	$429,965,555

*Class A shares are participating preferred while Class B and C are common shares.

TABLE 22-2

Merchant Marts Limited

Consolidated Statements of Earnings

Consolidated Earnings	For Fiscal Year Ended January 6, 1971	January 7, 1970
Net sales	$646,887,585	$615,010,680
Dividends and other income	703,623	793,345
	647,591,208	615,804,025
Deduct		
Cost of merchandise sold and all expenses, except the items shown below	589,374,933	556,298,496
Provision for depreciation	7,705,309	6,337,696
Interest on long-term debt (including amortization of discount and expense)	12,378,056	8,917,121
Other interest	4,710,999	4,801,747
Municipal realty and business taxes	5,704,810	5,177,282
Contribution to Merchant Marts Profit Sharing Retirement Fund	1,318,695	2,076,995
Contribution to Canada and Quebec Pension Plans	1,458,615	1,350,373
	622,651,417	584,959,710
Earnings before provision for income taxes	24,939,791	30,844,315
Provision for income taxes	12,739,000	15,626,000
Net earnings for the fiscal year	$12,200,791	$15,218,315

The 2:1 ratio cited as a standard simply relays the expectation that at least one half of current assets are to be financed by long-term or permanent sources of funds. In addition, if the firm failed to realize 100 cents on the dollar through the liquidation of current assets, current liabilities could still be met with a wide margin of safety. In 1970, Merchant Marts would only have needed to realize approximately 39 cents on every dollar of current assets liquidated to meet its current obligations.

As already mentioned, inventories can create problems because they vary in liquidity and also because valuation methods may differ both over time and among different firms. This problem can be minimized by resort to the *acid test* or *quick ratio* which is expressed as:

$$\frac{\text{Current Assets minus Inventories}}{\text{Current Liabilities}}$$

From Table 22-1, the values for Merchant Marts are:

$$\underline{1969} \qquad\qquad \underline{1970}$$

$$\frac{\$201,709,515}{\$127,803,123} = 1.58 \qquad \frac{\$218,862,213}{\$130,263,991} = 1.68$$

TABLE 22-3

Selected Ratios in Canadian Industries

Industry	Current Ratio	Collection Period (days)	Total Debt to Tangible Net Worth (in %)
All Firms	1.13	62	194
Wholesale	1.37	51	175
Retail	1.59	16	111
Manufacturing	1.68	44	85
Services	0.98	55	155
Transportation, Storage, and Utilities	0.99	50	200
Mining	1.68	46	74

Source: Dun and Bradstreet of Canada, *Key Business Ratios,* 1974

While a rule of thumb of 1.0 is often suggested for the acid test ratio, again, blind adherence should be avoided. The acid test is, in fact, a useful example of a ratio which requires closer examination. Consider the case of a firm found to have identical ratios in two succeeding time periods. It is quite possible that currently 40 percent of its receivables are over 90 days past due while at the end of the previous year only 10 percent fell into this age category. The ratio itself is insensitive to this type of situation and the analyst must extend his scope to be concerned not only with the amount but also with the quality of accounts receivable.[7]

The *inventory turnover ratio* should be considered next. This ratio will provide not only a useful indication of the liquidity of inventories, and thereby a measure of short-term debt-paying ability, but also some insights into managerial efficiency. It could just as readily, therefore, be categorized under profitability and activity ratios. The ratio is found by:

$$\frac{\text{Cost of Goods Sold}}{\text{Average Inventory}}$$

Typically, the denominator is estimated by taking the average of beginning and ending inventories for the period, which for Merchant Marts for 1970 is given as $\frac{\$114{,}201{,}475 + 120{,}167{,}123}{2} = \$117{,}184{,}299$. From Tables 22-1 and 22-2, the ratio for Merchant Marts, with \$7,705,309 of depreciation included in cost of goods sold for 1970, works out to be:

$$\frac{\$597{,}080{,}242}{\$117{,}184{,}299} = 5.10$$

[7]The quality of accounts receivable refers to: (1) the time required for conversion to cash and (2) the probability of converting into cash. Clearly, this same reasoning can be applied to inventories.

An inventory turnover of 5.10 times annually is equivalent to inventory turning over every 365/5.10 = 72 days.

Obviously, if the year-end is either before or after a period of high business activity, some distortion is inevitable. A department store with its fiscal year-end in early January will have a far higher and impressive turnover than another with balance sheets drawn up sometime in late November with inventory levels built up to anticipate the Christmas rush. The inventory turnover ratio must, therefore, be used with extreme caution. The index is not, however, without merit. If, for example, we examine a firm over time, a slipping ratio might flag both overstocking and the buildup of obsolete inventories. On the other hand, a high inventory turnover is generally regarded as a signal of efficient management. Once again, closer scrutiny might be initiated with justification. It is quite possible, for example, to have an unusually high inventory turnover associated with too low a level of inventories and frequent costly stockouts.

To test the quality and liquidity of receivables, we can resort to the *average collection period.* This measure,

$$\frac{\text{Receivables times Days in Year}}{\text{Annual Credit Sales}}$$

indicates the number of days of credit sales outstanding and uncollected. The credit sales figure is often unavailable, however, and the total sales figure must be relied upon. When the majority of sales is, in fact, on credit terms, this does not pose much of a problem. From Tables 22-1 and 22-2, the average collection periods for Merchant Marts in 1969 and 1970 are:

1969	1970
$\frac{\$188{,}804{,}533 \times 365 \text{ days}}{\$615{,}010{,}680} = 112 \text{ days}$	$\frac{\$203{,}100{,}502 \times 365 \text{ days}}{\$646{,}887{,}585} = 115 \text{ days}$

The *receivables turnover ratio* is defined as:

$$\frac{\textbf{Annual Credit Sales}}{\textbf{Receivables}}$$

For Merchant Marts, the receivables turnover ratios are:

1969	1970
$\frac{\$615{,}010{,}680}{\$188{,}804{,}533} = 3.26 \text{ times.}$	$\frac{\$646{,}887{,}585}{\$203{,}100{,}502} = 3.19 \text{ times.}$

The average collection period and the receivables turnover ratio indicate the speed of collections. Obviously, if credit terms are n/30, and 90-days' sales are outstanding, a problem is indicated. If sales are not seasonal, thereby perhaps distorting the receivables figure, the problem may relate to either inefficient credit and collections or a reluctance on the part of management to write off bad debts. An average collection period which is low relative to industry standards may also require additional investigation. It may be the result of excessively restrictive credit policies which have the effect of decreasing sales. In this light, a firm's credit policy is really viewed as a part of its overall marketing strategy. Other things being equal, a potential customer will probably choose to purchase from the supplier granting the most favorable credit terms.

A more thorough analysis of the liquidity of receivables is accomplished by an *aging of accounts*. Although this is not a ratio technique, it is a most worthwhile auxiliary procedure. The process involves a categorization of receivables according to the length of time they have been outstanding. An example might be as follows:

Age of Accounts since Billing (days)	Percentage of Total Value of Receivables Outstanding
0-15	40
16-30	30
31-45	10
46-60	6
61-90	4
over 90	10
Total:	100

If credit terms are n/30, then the aging schedule shows 30 percent of the receivables' value to be past due, and there may be some real questions about the likelihood of collecting on accounts in the over 90 days category.

Leverage ratios

Leverage ratios provide measures of the firm's reliance on debt and other senior securities. There are basically two aspects of financial leverage which can be measured: the relationship of borrowed funds to funds contributed by the owners as shown on the balance sheet, and the ability of the firm to "service" its borrowings as reflected through the income statement. Obviously, a consideration of either aspect without an examination of the other would leave the analysis incomplete. It is one thing to establish the amount of debt a company has, but it is much more meaningful to determine whether or not that amount of debt is excessive.

The most frequently relied upon measure in this classification is the *debt-to-equity ratio* or *debt-to-net-worth ratio*, which is simply:

$$\frac{\text{Total Debt}}{\text{Tangible Net Worth}}$$

Depending on the direction the analysis is expected to take, preferred shares may be included under debt as they represent a senior or prior claim from the standpoint of the common shareholders. Where analysis is made from a bond or debenture holder's point of view, the preferred shares are excluded, however, because of their subordinate position *vis-à-vis* creditors.

It should be noted that the denominator of the ratio is tangible net worth. Where intangible assets make up a significant portion of total assets, they are to be subtracted from net worth. This is done because it is usually difficult to determine the true value of intangibles or what they contribute to the earnings potential of the firm. Furthermore, creditors are interested in the "cushion" or safety margin provided by the owners of the firm. In the event of liquidation, intangible assets such as "goodwill" may not contribute to this cushion.

Drawing on Table 22-1, with preferred or Class A shares included in the numerator as debt, and unamortized goodwill subtracted from net worth to obtain tangible net worth, the ratios for the two years under consideration are:

1969	1970
$\frac{\$303{,}091{,}262}{\$124{,}527{,}473} = 2.43$	$\frac{\$347{,}536{,}695}{\$129{,}065{,}305} = 2.69$

In other words, during 1969 and 1970, for every dollar contributed by the common shareholders, $2.43 and $2.69 respectively have been contributed by creditors and preferred shareholders. Where the firm has rather stable cash flows, the ability to service borrowings is enhanced and a higher ratio is generally tolerated. Therefore, a relatively high proportion of debt is to be found in the case of utilities where cash flows are less volatile and consequently creditors need be less concerned about the size of the cushion provided by the owners.

Efficient borrowing does contribute to the well-being of the owners of the business. Such borrowing requires, among other things, making certain the firm's ability to meet its interest payments is not jeopardized by excessive use of leverage. A widely used indicator of the "safety" of periodic interest payments is the *times-interest-earning ratio*, or the relationship:

$$\frac{\text{Earnings before Interest and Taxes}}{\text{Interest Charges}}$$

Table 22-2 gives the following times-interest-earning ratios for Merchant Marts:

1969	1970
$\frac{\$44{,}563{,}183}{\$13{,}718{,}868} = 3.25$	$\frac{\$42{,}028{,}846}{\$17{,}089{,}055} = 2.46$

Note that municipal and realty business taxes have been deducted as an operating cost prior to the determination of earnings before interest and taxes. The above ratio indicates that, for 1970, earnings before interest and taxes covered total interest charges 2.46 times, suggesting that there is a substantial, if declining, margin of safety. Earnings are taken before taxes because interest payments, being a tax deductible expense, are paid before taxes.

A serious shortcoming of this measure, however, is that it ignores sinking fund requirements and lease obligations which are also fixed charges and are likely to be more burdensome than interest payments in some situations. The *fixed coverage ratio*, which is:

$$\frac{\text{Earnings before Interest, Lease Charges and Taxes}}{\text{Fixed Charges}}$$

overcomes this objection. We work from Table 22-2 and note from the Annual Report that sinking fund payments of $1,772,000 and long-term lease payments of $3,735,000 are required during 1970. Assuming taxes at 50 percent, $3,544,000 are required before taxes to meet the sinking fund obligations which are not deductible for tax purposes. The coverage ratio for the fiscal year ending January 6, 1971 is derived as:

$$\frac{24{,}939{,}791 + 12{,}378{,}056 + 4{,}710{,}999 + 3{,}735{,}000}{12{,}378{,}056 + 4{,}710{,}999 + 3{,}735{,}000 + 3{,}544{,}000}$$

$$= \frac{45{,}763{,}846}{24{,}368{,}055} = 1.88$$

Variations of the above might be resorted to—for example, adding depreciation to the numerator as a further source of cash available, which in this instance would raise the coverage ratio to 2.19. While this particular extension may make sense for short-run analysis, over the longer term we should not, of course, look to the cash flow counterpart of depreciation provisions for the servicing of fixed charges.

Profitability and activity ratios

Through the use of profitability and activity ratios, the analyst hopes to gain insights into the managerial efficiency and operations of the firm in general. Profitability is usefully related to the dollar volume of sales, to the dollar value of assets employed to produce the sales, and to the method of financing total assets. Obviously, then, profitability and activity ratios make use of both the balance sheet and income statement. Comparisons of a firm's profitability and activity ratios over time and with the ratios of other firms in the same industry should provide relevant information to the analyst. Many of these ratios are also used by management to evaluate its own results and pinpoint areas where additional money and effort may be well spent.

Inventory turnover and the average collection period are measures already touched on which might just as readily have been reviewed here. Another important measure is the *asset turnover ratio*, defined as:

$$\frac{\text{Sales}}{\text{Total Tangible Assets}}$$

which indicates the dollar amount of sales created per dollar of investment in tangible assets. It is an indication of the efficiency achieved in employing assets to produce a given level of output. It is helpful to recognize that what may be an inadequate turnover for a food store chain would be unattainable by an electric utility. Furthermore, given inflation and depreciated assets, an older firm may look better in terms of the turnover than a newer company because its assets are depreciated and carried in the books at a low value relative to current replacement values. In this same light, a firm which is expanding rapidly may show a much lower turnover because of heavy investments in new assets than a firm which is undertaking no expansion. Where one company leases a substantial portion of its assets while another company owns its assets, comparisons are further complicated because leased assets are generally excluded from the balance sheet. Because of these problems, effective use of the turnover ratio may be somewhat curtailed.

The figures from Tables 22-1 and 22-2 produce the following results for Merchant Marts, where the unamortized goodwill has again been subtracted from total assets to obtain total tangible assets.

$$\underline{1969} \qquad\qquad \underline{1970}$$

$$\frac{\$615{,}010{,}680}{\$427{,}618{,}735} = 1.44 \qquad \frac{\$646{,}887{,}585}{\$476{,}602{,}000} = 1.36$$

In conjunction with the asset turnover ratio, it is useful to consider the *gross profit margin* or *net operating margin* which is defined as:

$$\frac{\text{Earnings before Interest and Taxes}}{\text{Sales}}$$

From Tables 22-1 and 22-2 the net operating margins for Merchant Marts for the two years under consideration are:

$$\underline{1969} \qquad\qquad \underline{1970}$$

$$\frac{\$\ 44{,}563{,}183}{\$615{,}010{,}680} = 7.25\% \qquad \frac{\$\ 42{,}028{,}846}{\$646{,}887{,}585} = 6.50\%$$

Neither of the above measures is complete in itself. The turnover ratio provides no indication of profitability on sales and the net operating margin fails to consider the assets which have been employed to produce these sales. A third ratio should therefore be looked at in conjunction, namely the *earnings power ratio*.[8] This measure is the product of the asset turnover ratio and the net operating margin, or:

$$\frac{\text{Sales}}{\text{Total Tangible Assets}} \times \frac{\text{Earnings before Interest and Taxes}}{\text{Sales}}$$

which reduces to:

$$\frac{\text{Earnings before Interest and Taxes}}{\text{Total Tangible Assets}}$$

Figure 22-1 illustrates this relationship between asset turnover, operating margin, and earning power.

[8]An early approach of this kind was made by E.I. du Pont de Nemours and Company. For additional detail, see C. Kline Jr. and H. Hessler, "The du Pont Chart System for Appraising Operating Performance," *N.A.C.A. Bulletin, 33,* August 1952, pp. 1595-1619.

FIGURE 22-1

The Components of Earning Power

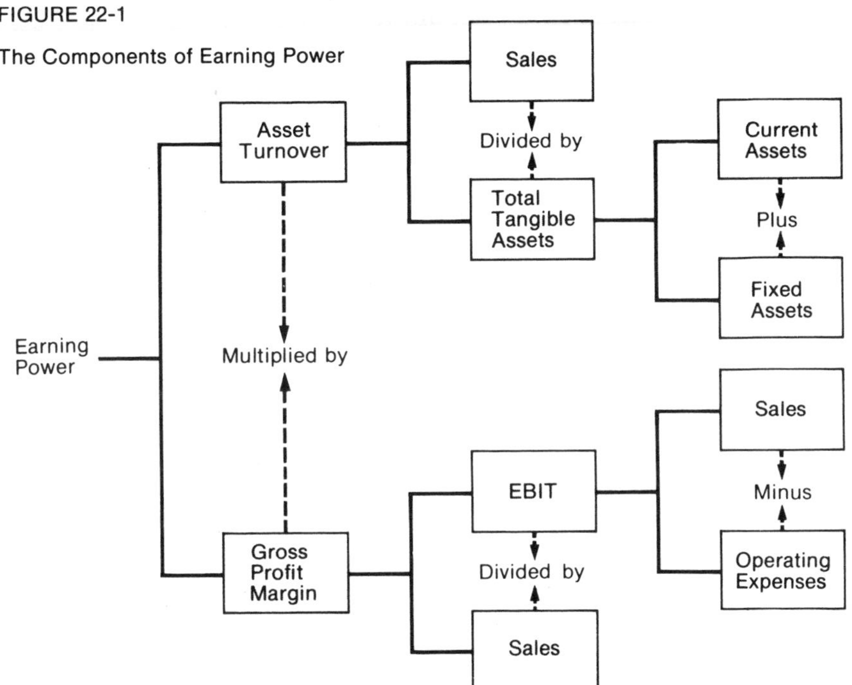

The 1969 and 1970 earnings power ratios for Merchant Marts are:

$$\underline{1969} \qquad\qquad\qquad \underline{1970}$$

$$\frac{\$\ 44{,}563{,}183}{\$427{,}618{,}735} = 10.42\% \qquad \frac{\$\ 42{,}028{,}846}{\$476{,}602{,}000} = 8.82\%$$

It is well to note that the earnings figures have been taken before interest and taxes in order to keep things independent of capital structure and the proportion of debt employed. This results in a more meaningful measure than that provided by the more traditional relating of net profits to total tangible assets. This particular group of ratios makes it obvious that the earning power of assets is not merely a function of the margin obtainable but of the turnover of the assets as well. For instance, a food store chain with a turnover of 5.0 times may have a net operating margin of only 2.0 percent, resulting in an earnings power ratio of 10.0 percent. However, an electric utility with a turnover of only 0.7 may have a net operating margin of 14 percent resulting in an almost identical earnings power ratio of 9.8 percent.

A final ratio to be considered measures the rate of return on common stockholders' equity. It is found by:

$$\frac{\text{Earnings after Taxes minus Preferred Dividends}}{\text{Net Worth minus Preferred Shares}}$$

This measure takes into account the leverage afforded by the use of debt and preferred shares and is an indication of the effectiveness with which management is serving the residual owners. Data from the Annual Report of Merchant Marts Limited but not reproduced here reveal a return of 8.37 percent for 1970.

A summary of the ratios discussed is provided in Table 22-6 at the end of this chapter.

22-3. COMMON-SIZE ANALYSIS

Significant difficulties can occur when, through the use of financial statements, attempts are made to contrast operating units or corporations which vary in size. Similar problems naturally arise when a corporation's balance sheets and earnings statements are analyzed over such an extended time period that the scale of operations has changed. Ratio analysis can certainly help in both instances, but common-size analysis, a somewhat related concept, provides a more complete overview and is, therefore, a useful point of departure for the analyst. The technique itself is fairly straightforward. It simply involves conversion of the dollar amounts indicated on the financial statements into percentage figures. In this way it is possible to pinpoint those changes which are not simply caused by a general increase or decrease in the overall size of the business, and which therefore warrant more careful scrutiny. More specifically, in the case of a balance sheet, total assets are held to equal 100 percent and all other values are arrived at accordingly. For the analysis of earnings statements, it is the net sales or net revenue figure that is set at 100 percent.

For illustrative purposes, Tables 22-4 and 22-5 set out the common-size analysis of Merchant Marts' consolidated balance sheets and earnings statements for fiscal 1969 and 1970. The increased cost of merchandise sold and its bearing on net earnings is, for example, clearly identified.

TABLE 22-4

Merchant Marts Limited

Common-size Consolidated Balance Sheet

	at Fiscal Year-end 1970	1969
Assets	%	%
Current Assets:		
Cash	0.94	0.57
Government of Canada bonds, at cost	0.02	0.02
Accounts receivable	42.39	43.92
Inventories valued at the lower of approximate cost or market	23.84	27.95
Prepaid advertising and other charges	2.32	2.40
	69.51	74.86
Investments and Other Assets:		
Investments and advances, at cost	1.94	3.05
Notes receivable on sales of Class A shares of Merchant Marts Limited under the Employees' Stock Purchase Plan	1.10	0.97
Refundable federal tax	—	0.04
	3.04	4.06
Fixed Assets, at cost:		
Land	3.27	3.27
Buildings, improvements, equipment, and fixtures, less depreciation	23.65	17.26
	26.92	20.53
Unamortized goodwill	0.53	0.55
	100.00	100.00
Liabilities		
Current Liabilities:		
Demand and short-term notes	13.16	16.73
Accounts payable	8.39	7.26
Accrued wages, rent, interest, etc.	3 29	3.57
Income and other taxes	1.69	1.23
Contributions payable to Merchant Marts Profit Sharing Retirement Fund	.28	.49
Dividend payable	.39	.44
	27.20	29.72
Long-term debt	38.22	34.39
Deferred income taxes	1.92	1.71
Stockholders' Equity		
Capital stock issued:		
2,458,208 Class A shares	5.19	4.68
6,600,000 Class B shares	5.74	6.39
6,600,000 Class C shares	5.74	6.39
	16.67	17.46
Retained earnings	15.99	16.72
	100.00	100.00

TABLE 22-5

Merchant Marts Limited

Common-Size Consolidated Statement of Earnings

	For Fiscal Year Ended 1970	1969
Consolidated Earnings	%	%
Net sales	100.00	100.00
Dividends and other income	.10	.12
	100.10	100.12
Deduct:		
Cost of merchandise sold and all expenses, except the items shown below	91.11	90.46
Provision for depreciation	1.20	1.04
Interest on long-term debt (including amortization of discount and expense)	1.92	1.45
Other interest	0.72	0.78
Municipal realty and business taxes	0.88	0.84
Contribution to Merchant Marts Profit Sharing Retirement Fund	0.20	0.33
Contributions to Canada and Quebec Pension Plans	0.22	0.21
	96.25	95.11
Earnings before provision for income taxes	3.85	5.01
Provision for income taxes	1.96	2.54
Net earnings for the fiscal year	1.89	2.47

22-4. SUMMARY

Ratio analysis, which relates items from financial statements to one another, represents one of the more basic approaches to financial analysis. It is relied upon not only by the firm's own management, but by creditors, potential investors, and existing shareholders as well.

The ratios most frequently resorted to can be classified as liquidity, leverage, and profitability and activity ratios. Liquidity ratios are aimed at highlighting the firm's short-term ability to meet financial obligations. Leverage ratios reflect the debt-equity structure of a firm, and its long-term ability to service outstanding debt. Profitability and activity ratios are derived with the purposes of portraying the earning power of an enterprise, and the efficiency with which its resources are used. All must be used with great care and, in most instances, additional in-depth analysis is required to confirm what the ratios appear to imply or point to. Analysis of corporate performance over time using ratios may prove quite useful to discern trends in performance; while comparisons with other companies in the same industry is also a possibility though the pitfalls are more numerous and may lead you to draw faulty conclusions.

Common-size analysis is offered as another important approach but one which is less well-known. Financial statement categories are expressed as percentages of total, thereby allowing comparisons of financial structure for firms of varying size of operations. It is in many ways akin to ratio analysis and provides another means of comparison over time as well as between firms within the same industry.

TABLE 22-6

Summary of Commonly Used Ratios and Financial Indices

Ratio	Definition
LIQUIDITY RATIOS	
Current	$\frac{\text{Current Assets}}{\text{Current Liabilities}}$
Quick (Acid test)	$\frac{\text{Current Assets — Inventories}}{\text{Current Liabilities}}$
Inventory Turnover	$\frac{\text{Cost of Goods Sold}}{\text{Average Inventory}}$
Average collection period	$\frac{\text{Receivables} \times \text{365 days}}{\text{Annual Credit Sales}}$
Receivables turnover	$\frac{\text{Annual Credit Sales}}{\text{Receivables}}$
LEVERAGE RATIOS	
Debt-to-net-worth (Debt-to-equity)	$\frac{\text{Total Debt}}{\text{Tangible Net Worth}}$
Times-interest-earning	$\frac{\text{Earnings before Interest and Taxes}}{\text{Interest Charges}}$
Fixed Coverage	$\frac{\text{Earnings before Interest, Lease Charges and Taxes}}{\text{Fixed Charges}}$
PROFITABILITY AND ACTIVITY RATIOS	
Asset turnover	$\frac{\text{Sales}}{\text{Total Tangible Assets}}$
Net operating margin (Gross profit margin)	$\frac{\text{Earnings before Interest and Taxes}}{\text{Sales}}$
Earnings power	$\frac{\text{Earnings before Interest and Taxes}}{\text{Total Tangible Assets}}$
Return on common equity	$\frac{\text{Earnings after Taxes − Preferred Dividends}}{\text{Net Worth − Preferred Shares}}$

Questions for Discussion

1. "The indiscriminate application of a standardized routine of analysis to all companies regardless of size, industry, and peculiar characteristics might well lead to grossly incorrect conclusions." "Yet a wide variety of groups make use of ratio analysis as one means of evaluating a company." Explain how these two statements can be reconciled.
2. Is it possible for a firm to have a high current ratio and still be unable to pay its current liabilities? Explain your answer.
3. Why may reviewing an aged list of accounts receivable be viewed as being necessary by a financial analyst even if the average collections period of accounts receivable is felt to be acceptable?
4. What is the major problem confronting the financial analyst when he attempts to calculate the inventory turnover ratio?
5. "The procedure whereby a firm sells certain of its assets to a financial intermediary and then leases back the same assets, induces a form of invisible debt." Do you agree with this statement? Comment on sales-leasebacks with regard to ratio analysis.
6. Certain ratios may be helpful in measuring the quality of a new debt issue from an investor's point of view. Discuss.

Problems with Solutions

1. SPRUCE-IT-UP LTD.

Wally Painter owns a small wall-washing and painting company. His current operations and commitments are such that at the start of 1975, his accountant has predicted a *pro-forma* financial statement for 1975 as follows:

ASSETS		
Current Assets:		
Cash		$10,000
Accounts receivable		25,000
		35,000
Fixed Assets:		
Trucks, scaffolding, garage, etc.	25,000	
Less: Accumulated depreciation	10,000	
		15,000
		$50,000
LIABILITIES AND SHAREHOLDERS' EQUITY		
Current Liabilities:		
Taxes payable		$1,000
Finance company loan		10,000
Accounts payable		9,000
		20,000
Long-term liabilities:		
Mortgage on storage garage		7,000
		27,000

Shareholder's Equity:		
Shares held by W. Painter	20,000	
Retained Earnings	3,000	
		23,000
		$50,000
EARNINGS		
Revenue		$100,000
Less:		
Cost of goods sold	50,000	
Salaries and wages (incl. Wally's salary)	40,000	
Provision for depreciation	4,000	
Interest on short-term debt	1,500	
Interest on mortgage	700	
		96,200
Net Income before Taxes		3,800
Income Taxes		1,000
Net Earnings		$2,800

Since the firm has strong possibilities for growth, Wally is trying to watch his financial ratios to keep the firm under control as it grows, to make it easy to borrow, and perhaps to sell his company to a larger firm. There are currently several decisions he must make about his operations and financing which could affect his ratios.

(a) He can use $8,000 of the firm's cash to pay off some accounts payable. What will this do to his current, and debt-to-net-worth ratios?

Solution

(a) Current ratio

$$\text{Original: } \frac{\$35{,}000}{\$20{,}000} = 1.75$$

$$\text{Modified: } \frac{\$35{,}000 - \$8{,}000}{\$20{,}000 - \$8{,}000} = 2.25$$

Debt-to-net-worth ratio

$$\text{Original: } \frac{\$27{,}000}{\$23{,}000} = 1.17$$

$$\text{Modified: } \frac{\$27{,}000 - \$8{,}000}{\$23{,}000} = 0.83$$

On paper, Spruce-It-Up's position seems more safe and conservative if Wally uses cash to reduce his current liabilities. But, Wally would be foolish to pay off any accounts payable a month before they were due unless he received a discount for doing so; otherwise he could at least earn bank interest on these funds. Also, it is clear that in the normal course of business Wally is using cash to pay accounts payable. If in the normal course of events he would have to pay the $8,000 on the day after the date of the statement, his ratios will change drastically. We should be wary of making judgments too quickly based on such potentially variable ratios, when cash forms such a large proportion of current assets.

(b) Wally normally carries no paint inventory, but a paint store in a nearby town is going out of business and is selling a $40,000 paint inventory for $25,000. Wally feels he can use this paint for special contracts in 1976 and 1977. Wally's wife is expecting an inheritance soon with which she can buy the inventory and gain a share of the firm herself. What would this do to the current ratio, quick ratio, debt-to-net-worth ratio and the times-interest-earning ratio? What would happen to these ratios if instead he borrowed the $25,000 at 15% for 3 years, where the principal is paid off only at the end of the term? What would happen if he borrowed $25,000 at 15% for 1 year? (We can safely ignore the negligible effect of interest payments on retained earnings via a change in after-tax income.) How would the purchase of the inventory (by any method) affect the earnings power ratio?

Solution

(b) Current ratio

Original: 1.75

After inventory financed by equity: $\dfrac{\$35{,}000 + \$25{,}000}{\$20{,}000} = 3.00$

After inventory financed by long-term debt: 3.00

After inventory financed by short-term debt: $\dfrac{\$35{,}000 + \$25{,}000}{\$20{,}000 + \$25{,}000} = 1.33$

Quick ratio

Original: $\dfrac{\$35{,}000}{\$20{,}000} = 1.75$

After inventory financed by equity: 1.75

After inventory financed by long-term debt: 1.75

After inventory financed by short-term debt: $\dfrac{\$35{,}000}{\$20{,}000 + \$25{,}000} = 0.78$

Debt-to-net-worth ratio

Original: 1.17

After inventory financed by equity: $\dfrac{\$27{,}000}{\$23{,}000 + \$25{,}000} = 0.56$

After inventory financed by short- or long-term debt: $\dfrac{\$27{,}000 + \$25{,}000}{\$23{,}000} = 2.26$

Times-Interest-Earning Ratio

Original or after inventory financed by equity: $\dfrac{\$3{,}800 + \$1{,}500 + \$700}{\$1{,}500 + \$700} = \$2.73$

After inventory financed by long or short-term debt: $\dfrac{\$3{,}800 + \$1{,}500 + \$700}{\$1{,}500 + \$700 + .15 \times \$25{,}000} = 1.01$

Earnings power ratio

$$\text{Original: } \frac{\$3{,}800 + \$1{,}500 + \$700}{\$50{,}000} = 12\%$$

$$\text{After inventory purchase: } \frac{\$3{,}800 + \$1{,}500 + \$700}{\$50{,}000 + \$25{,}000} = 8\%$$

COMMENTS:

This problem illustrates the need to use several ratios to analyze financial decisions. For example, equity or long-term debt financing of the inventory improves the current ratio, seemingly implying an improvement in liquidity. However, the inventory would be purchased essentially for speculative purposes and would not be needed for a year. Thus, the quick ratio, which did not rise, shows the liquidity position more fairly. Note how the current ratio falls after financing the inventory by short-term debt (the opposite analogue of using cash to pay off current liabilities).

The debt-to-net-worth ratio was shifted in the obvious ways, depending on the method of financing the inventory. The times-interest-earning ratio shows that the safety of coverage of interest charges is not hampered by equity financing, but is by debt financing, although, if the inventory added to the current year's income, this ratio might not have been impaired.

Finally, the fall in the earnings power ratio suggests the opportunity cost of purchasing an inventory now for later use.

2. FALLING TIMBER CO.

Following are exerpts from the Falling Timber Company's Annual Reports. Falling Timber is a vertically integrated forest resource conglomerate that concentrates on cutting timber and making lumber, but which also transports, wholesales and retails some of its products. Calculate all the relevant ratios defined in this chapter, and also prepare a common-size statement. Then comment on any significant changes in the firm's position from 1971 to 1974.

CONSOLIDATED BALANCE SHEETS (in thousands of dollars)

	1974	1971
ASSETS		
Current Assets:		
Cash	$ 6,049	$ 4,203
Short-term investments and deposits	15,383	14,927
Accounts receivable	149,206	111,984
Inventories	229,637	119,982
Prepaid expenses	5,406	3,033
	$405,681	$254,129

Investments:		
Partly owned companies	$ 85,347	$ 26,624
Investments, at cost	5,041	6,395
	$ 90,388	$ 33,019
Fixed Assets:		
Buildings and equipment	$983,627	$788,623
Less: Accumulated depreciation	486,323	375,267
	497,304	413,356
Timber less accumulated depletion	75,798	73,997
Logging roads and land	45,654	27,498
	$618,756	$514,851
Intangible Assets:		
Unallocated cost of shares in subsidiaries	26,583	28,503
	$1,141,408	$830,502

LIABILITIES		
Current Liabilities:		
Bank loans	$ 46,181	$ 43,867
Notes payable	40,962	—
Accounts payable and accrued liabilities	128,796	63,931
Income taxes payable	1,260	3,269
Current portion of long-term debt	11,537	7,929
	$228,736	$118,996
Bonds and Debentures	317,429	270,410
Income Tax Allocations in respect of future years	92,454	63,352
Minority Interests in Subsidiaries	44,383	14,390
	$683,002	$467,148
SHAREHOLDERS' EQUITY		
7% Cumulative Preferred Shares	21,947	22,326
Common Shares	147,396	141,440
Retained Earnings	289,063	199,588
	458,406	363,354
	$1,141,408	$830,502

CONSOLIDATED EARNINGS (thousands of dollars)	1974	1971
Sales and other income:		
Sales of products and services	$1,401,657	$790,775
Income from investments	3,256	1,787
Profit (loss) on disposal of assets	(602)	201
	$1,404,311	$792,763
Costs and expenses:		
Cost of sales and services	$1,053,134	$586,273
Depreciation	108,936	88,735
Depletion	12,610	10,695
Selling and administrative expense	93,275	46,835
Long-term debt interest	16,261	14,106
Bank and other interest	4,467	4,198
	1,288,683	750,842
Earnings before taxes	115,628	41,921
Income taxes:		
Current	44,781	21,672
Future years	16,893	(2,160)
	61,674	19,512
Earnings after tax, before items noted below	53,954	22,409
Dividends from partly owned companies	986	—
Equity in retained earnings of partly owned companies	17,936	438
Minority interest in subsidiaries	(1,685)	2,865
Net Earnings	$71,191	$25,712

Relevant notes to financial statements (thousands of dollars)

	1974	1973	1971	1970
1. Ending Inventories	221,984	159,367	119,382	98,928

2. Financial Commitments (at beginning of year)

	1974	1971
Leases	108,965	14,785
Payments for acquisition of cutting rights	2,410	2,273
Sinking fund requirements for debt	8,675	5,336

Solution

The data allow us to compute the following:

Current ratio

1974: $\frac{\$405,681}{\$228,736} = 1.77$ 1971: $\frac{\$254,129}{\$118,996} = 2.14$

Quick ratio

1974: $\frac{\$405,681 - \$229,637}{\$228,736} = 0.77$ 1971: $\frac{\$254,129 - \$119,982}{\$118,996} = 1.13$

Average Inventory

1974: $\frac{\$221,984 + \$159,367}{2} = \$190,676$ 1971: $\frac{\$119,382 + \$98,928}{2} = \$109,155$

Inventory turnover ratio

1974: $\frac{\$1,053,134}{\$190,676} = 5.52$ 1971: $\frac{\$586,273}{\$109,155} = 5.37$

Average collection period

Since most of Falling Timber's sales are to industrial consumers, we assume, in the absence of other information, that all sales are credit sales.

1974: $\frac{\$149,206 \times 365 \text{ days}}{\$1,401,657} = 38.9 \text{ days}$ 1971: $\frac{\$111,984 \times 365 \text{ days}}{\$790,775} = 51.7 \text{ days}$

Receivables turnover ratio

1974: $\frac{\$1,401,657}{\$149,206} = 9.39$ 1971: $\frac{\$790,775}{\$111,984} = 7.06$

Debt-to-net-worth ratio (from a creditor's viewpoint)

Preferred stock is counted in the denominator as equity or net worth. Intangible assets are deducted from the denominator to find tangible net worth. Since Falling Timber's accounts are consolidated to include debt of its subsidiaries, we leave "minority interests in subsidiaries" in the denominator as equity, even though it is not the equity of Falling Timber's shareholders. Alternatively, we might exclude the debt and equity of the subsidiaries altogether, but not enough information is provided to do this. Since the sums involved are relatively small, no significant change will result. Also, the accounts are not consolidated to include the accounts of partly owned companies (less than 50% owned), whose debt is somewhat more insulated from FT, so no adjustment for them is required.

1974: $\frac{\$228,736 + \$317,429 + \$92.454}{\$44,383 + \$458,406} = 1.27$

1971: $\frac{\$118,996 + \$270,410 + \$63,352}{\$14,390 + \$363,354} = 1.20$

Debt-to-net-worth ratio (from a common shareholder's viewpoint)

The same comments as above still apply except that preferred stock is shifted from the denominator to the numerator, since the preferred shareholders have a prior claim on assets and earnings before the common shareholders.

$$1974: \frac{\$228{,}736 + \$317{,}429 + \$92{,}454 + \$21{,}947}{\$44{,}383 + \$458{,}406 - \$21{,}947} = 1.37$$

$$1971: \frac{\$118{,}996 + \$270{,}410 + \$63{,}352 + \$22{,}326}{\$14{,}390 + \$363{,}354 - \$22{,}326} = 1.34$$

To compute the coverage ratios we note that Falling Timber may transfer money from its consolidated subsidiaries' accounts (*i.e.* declare dividends) to its own accounts to cover fixed charges, since it holds a majority of shares. Furthermore, the debt accounts of subsidiaries are consolidated so that consolidated income from subsidiaries is used to service consolidated debt charges of subsidiaries. Hence, we include subsidiary income as income available to service fixed charges. However, accounts of partly owned (less than 50%) companies are not consolidated, and Falling Timber is not at liberty to use their income to service its own debt, except insofar as these companies declare dividends. Therefore, we include only dividends from partly owned companies in earnings before interest and taxes.

Times-interest-earning ratio

$$1974: \frac{\$115{,}628 + \$16{,}261 + \$4{,}467 + \$986}{\$16{,}261 + \$4{,}467} = 6.63$$

$$1971: \frac{\$41{,}921 + \$14{,}106 + \$4{,}198}{\$14{,}106 + \$4{,}198} = 3.29$$

Fixed coverage ratio

The fixed charges include leases (which are deducted from income, and so must be added back to the numerator) and payments for cutting rights and sinking fund requirements (neither of which affected income, and thus aren't added back to the numerator).

$$1974: \frac{\$115{,}628 + \$16{,}261 + \$4{,}467 + \$986 + \$108{,}965}{\$16{,}261 + \$4{,}467 + \$108{,}965 + \$2{,}410 + \$8{,}675} = 1.75$$

$$1971: \frac{\$41{,}921 + \$14{,}106 + \$4{,}198 + \$14{,}785}{\$14{,}106 + \$4{,}198 + \$14{,}785 + \$2{,}273 + \$5{,}336} = 1.84$$

Cash flow coverage

To the numerator of the fixed coverage ratio, we add the depreciation and depletion reported on the income statement to get cash flows.

$$1974: \frac{\$115{,}628 + \$16{,}261 + \$4{,}467 + \$986 + \$108{,}965 + \$108{,}936 + 12{,}610}{\$16{,}261 + \$4{,}467 + \$108{,}965 + \$2{,}410 + \$8{,}675} = 2.61$$

$$1971: \frac{\$41{,}921 + \$14{,}106 + \$4{,}198 + \$14{,}785 + \$88{,}735 + \$10{,}695}{\$14{,}106 + \$4{,}198 + \$14{,}785 + \$2{,}273 + \$5{,}336} = 4.29$$

Asset turnover ratio

1974: $\frac{\$1,401,657}{\$1,141,408 - \$26,583} = 1.26$ 1971: $\frac{\$790,755}{\$830,502 - \$28,503} = 0.99$

Net operating margin

1974: $\frac{\$115,628 + \$16,261 + \$4,467}{\$1,401,657} = 9.73\%$

1971: $\frac{\$41,921 + \$14,106 + \$4,198}{\$790,775} = 7.62\%$

Earnings power ratio

1974: $1.26 \times 9.73\% = 12.3\%$

1971: $0.99 \times 7.62\% = 7.5\%$

Since the earnings power ratio represents a return on tangible assets, including investments in partly owned companies (whose income but not sales are reported on the income statements), it might be more meaningful to recompute the earnings power ratio to include earnings from partly owned companies. This would be essential in evaluating a holding company that owns few assets directly. However we have only a record of after-tax earnings of partly owned companies and cannot add this figure back to pre-tax earnings. Thus we can't perform this modification of the earnings power ratio.

Return on common equity

We assume the preferred dividends are paid at the end of the year on the preferred shares shown on the balance sheet.

1974: $\frac{\$71,191 - .07 \times \$21,947}{\$458,406 - \$21,947} = 16.0\%$

1971: $\frac{\$25,712 - .07 \times \$22,326}{\$363,354 - \$22,326} = 7.1\%$

COMMON-SIZE BALANCE SHEETS

	1974	1971
ASSETS		
Current Assets:		
Cash	0.53	0.51
Short-term investments and deposits	1.35	1.80
Accounts receivable	13.07	13.48
Inventories	20.12	14.45
Prepaid expenses	0.47	0.36
	35.54	30.60

Investments:		
Partly owned companies	7.48	3.21
Investments	0.44	0.77
	7.92	3.98
Fixed Assets:		
Buildings and equipment	86.18	94.96
Less: Accumulated depreciation	42.61	45.19
	43.57	49.77
Timber less accumulated depletion	6.64	8.91
Logging roads and land	4.00	3.31
	54.21	61.99
Unallocated cost of share in subsidiaries	2.33	3.43
	100.00	100.00
LIABILITIES		
Current Liabilities		
Bank loans	4.05	5.28
Notes payable	3.59	—
Accounts payable and accrued liabilities	11.28	7.70
Income taxes payable	0.11	0.39
Current portion of long-term debt	1.01	0.96
	20.04	14.33
Bonds and Debentures	27.81	32.56
Income Tax Allocations in respect of future years	8.10	7.63
Minority Interests in Subsidiaries	3.89	1.73
	59.84	56.25
SHAREHOLDERS' EQUITY		
7% Preferred Shares	1.92	2.69
Common Shares	12.91	17.03
Retained Earnings	25.33	24.03
	40.16	43.75
	100.00	100.00

COMMON SIZE EARNINGS	1974	1971
Sales and other income:		
Sales of products and services	100.00	100.00
Income from investments	0.23	0.23
Profit (loss) on disposal of assets	(0.04)	0.02
	100.19	100.25
Costs and expenses:		
Cost of sales and services	75.14	74.14
Depreciation	7.77	11.22
Depletion	0.90	1.35
Selling and administrative expense	6.65	5.92
Long-term debt interest	1.16	1.79
Bank and other interest	0.32	0.53
	91.94	94.95
Earnings before taxes	8.25	5.30
Income taxes:		
Current	3.19	2.74
Future years	1.21	(0.27)
	4.40	2.47
Earnings before items noted below	3.85	2.83
Dividends from partly owned companies	0.07	—
Equity in retained earnings of partly owned companies	1.28	0.06
Minority interests in subsidiaries	(0.12)	0.36
Net Earnings	5.08	3.25

COMMENTS:

From the viewpoint of performance, the firm's prospects seem to have brightened considerably from 1971 to 1974. First of all, the firm is more effective in using its assets to generate sales, for both the asset turnover ratio and the inventory turnover ratio improved, with a substantial improvement in the former. Also, the net operating margin increased by over 2% from 1971 to 1974. As a result of the compounding effect of the improved operating margin and asset turnover ratio, the earnings power ratio almost doubled. Another indication of improved performance is the return on common equity which more than doubled.

We must be aware that net income can change sharply from year to year, therefore any conclusive judgment of these performance indicators must include a comparison of several years in succession, not just two years, in order to distinguish trends from temporary changes.

To find the cause of the improved performance, we may examine the comparative common-size earnings statements. The cost of goods and services actually rose by 1% from 1971 to 1974, but depreciation and depletion charges (as a proportion of sales volume) had a combined drop of 3.9%. This was the major cause of the fall of 3% in costs and expenses. After taxes, the difference in earnings falls to 1%. The difference rises to almost 2% again as the income from partly owned companies is considered. Since such an important factor in the improved performance is the proportionately lower depreciation and depletion charges which are consistent with the higher asset turnover ratio, these improvements could have resulted from improved technology and management producing a higher volume with the same assets. Or, it could also result from a high level of inflation understating the value of assets and hence the required depreciation and depletion charges (recall that 1974 saw a surge in the rate of inflation). The firm could also be failing to upgrade its capital assets (avoiding new depreciation charges), which would harm its long-run position (although this is not likely the case here, since the balance sheet reports roughly the same proportion of accumulated depreciation of fixed assets for both years). Of course, inventory profits (from a period of inflation) could be a factor in improved performance, but that is not likely the case here, since the cost of sales as a proportion of sales actually increased from 1971 to 1974.

Now considering the firm from the viewpoint of its ability to continue operating, we may examine, for example, the current and quick ratios. From the common-size balance sheet, we see that the firm has increased both its current assets and current liabilities as a proportion of total assets, the net result being that the current ratio fell somewhat. Since the increase in current assets was almost solely due to the increase in inventories (again evident from the common-size analysis), the quick ratio fell even more sharply. Whether or not it is dangerously low requires comparison with other firms in the industry. However, in that the firm has reduced its average collection period by about 13 days, we might contend that it has improved its liquidity insofar as it is able to turn receivables into cash more readily. This may tend to offset the trend towards poorer liquidity resulting from a falling quick ratio.

Note one interesting anomaly regarding inventory figures. The sharply increased inventories on the common-size asset sheet suggest that inventories may be getting too large (slow sales, obsolete inventory, etc.), but the higher inventory turnover ratio suggests that, if anything, inventories may be getting too small. This could be explained if the firm changed its type of business to one with a lower margin and higher inventory turnover level. Another, and perhaps more viable, reason could be that a surge of inflation increased the cost of inventory (which was immediately passed on to the consumer, preserving the inventory turnover ratio), whereas the inflation made virtually no change in the historic costs of fixed assets, so that inventory increased as a proportion of total assets.

From a leverage viewpoint, the firm increased its use of debt slightly. Note that the proportionate reduction in use of preferred equity resulted in a smaller increase in leverage from a common shareholder's viewpoint than from a creditor's viewpoint. What is more interesting is the substitution of current liabilities for long-term liabilities as is evident from common-size analysis. In 1974, interest rates were high, and there was much resistance to long-term maturities by investors, due to the uncertainty created by the high rates of inflation. Consequently, many firms had to rely more on short-term debt than they normally would, and Falling Timber is no exception.

Falling Timber's coverage ratios have been increased and decreased. The times-interest-earning ratio increased mainly because of higher net earnings, with relatively fixed interest charges on long-term debt which was issued several years earlier. However, the fixed coverage ratio fell, mainly due to sharply increased lease commitments. If the firm is substituting lease financing for debt financing of long-term assets then the improved asset turnover ratios and increased proportion of current assets to total assets could be explained by the "off-balance sheet financing". So, along with the improved profit performance would go the risk inherent in meeting the fixed base charges as evidenced by the falling fixed coverage ratio. Alternatively, the increased lease commitments could represent a move into a new field of business, which must be analyzed on its own merits, considering the increased risk in the falling fixed coverage ratio.

The cash flow coverage fell more sharply, because of the proportionately smaller depreciation charges in 1974, and that change is discussed above. At any rate, fixed charges are all covered, usually several times over, by earnings and cash flow, providing some margin of safety to creditors and to the liquidity of the firm.

Additional Problems

1. The controller for the Prestige Department Store wanted to calculate the current ratio for the company. He had only been successful in obtaining the following information:

Acid Test Ratio	2.0
Current Liabilities	$2.5 million
Cost of Goods Sold	$2.6 million
Beginning Inventory	$0.5 million
Inventory Turnover Ratio	6.5

   Is it possible to determine the current ratio from this information? Calculate the required ratio, if possible, and explain the meaning and significance of the ratio.

2. The management of the Standout Pants Company was particularly pleased with its financial performance over the past year. Sales had increased to $360.5 million, net operating profit had increased, and nearly all other ratios had improved over the past year. However, their banker had noted that the average collection period had steadily deteriorated over the past few years to the point where at present it was 108 days. All the company's sales were made on credit, and their present policy was to offer terms of 1/30 n/60. Calculate the dollar volume of receivables outstanding and the receivables turnover ratio for the company. Before being able to properly assess this aspect of the

company's management, what additional information do you think the firm's banker should have?

3. Complete the following operating statement and the required ratios.

Cash Sales	$10.0	
Credit Sales	______	
Total Sales		______
Less: Cost of Goods Sold		
Beginning Inventory	$ 5	
Plus Purchases	$30	
Less Closing Inventory	______	
Cost of Goods Sold		$24.2
Gross Operating Margin		______
Expenses:		
Interest	______	
Leasing Expenses	0.5	
Other Expenses	______	
Total Expenses		______
Net Operating Profit		______
Less Income Taxes		______
Net Income		______

Calculate the following ratios:

(a) Times interest earning ratio	4.2
(b) Fixed coverage ratio	______
(c) Asset turnover ratio	______
(d) Earnings power ratio	______
(e) Average collection period	60 days
(f) Inventory turnover ratio	3 days

given that:

(i) Total debt outstanding—$5,000,000 @ 8% with a 10% annual sinking fund requirement

(ii) Total tangible assets—$50,000,000

(iii) Accounts receivable—$3,500,000

(iv) A 50% tax rate.

4. Choose two Canadian companies from the same industry and do a ratio analysis comparing the management policies of the two firms. This problem requires outside research as copies of the financial statements of the two firms will have to be obtained. Compare the ratios which you have calculated with the industry norms as calculated for at least two years. Can you make any statement about the management policies of the two firms as compared to the industry? Some examples of firms which could be chosen are:

Fields Stores Ltd. and Woodward Stores Limited
International Nickel Company Limited and Cominco
Royal Bank of Canada and Toronto Dominion Bank
Distillers Seagrams and Hiram Walker Gooderham and Worts.

5. The following data was taken from the financial statements of Imperial Oil Ltd.

Imperial Oil Limited and Subsidiary Companies
Consolidated Statements of Financial Position as at
December 31, 1968 and 1967
(thousands of dollars)

	1968	1967
Current Assets		
Cash including time deposits	44,289	46,808
Short-term commercial notes	100	3,095
Government securities	1,194	1,458
Accounts receivable	275,763	231,331
Prepaid taxes, insurance, and rentals	3,443	2,664
Inventories	170,625	163,579
	495,414	448,935
Fixed Assets		
Property, plant, equipment, less depreciation	811,365	713,034
Long-term accounts receivable	90,693	85,648
Total Assets	1,397,472	1,247,617
Current Liabilities		
Bank loans	36,600	—
Accounts payable and accrued liabilities	166,860	148,370
Income and other taxes payable	21,814	26,490
Long-term debt due within one year	20,000	—
	245,274	174,860
Long-Term Liabilities and Deferred Credit		
Long-term debt	128,500	102,350
Employee annuity contributions	12,724	12,724
Deferred income tax	105,340	87,645
Total Liabilities	491,838	377,579
Shareholders' Equity		
Capital stock	257,993	255,081
Retained earnings	647,641	614,957
Total Shareholders' Equity and Liabilities	1,397,472	1,247,617

(a) Prepare a common-size balance sheet for the two periods and note any variations which you consider significant.

(b) Calculate the acid test ratio for both years.

(c) Calculate the debt-to-net-worth ratio.

6. WESTERN FOREST RESOURCES LTD.

The following data are from Western's 1973 and 1974 financial statements (all figures in thousands of dollars):

CONSOLIDATED BALANCE SHEET	1974	1973
ASSETS		
Current Assets:		
Cash and short-term deposits	$ 100	$ 10,577
Accounts receivable	38,540	33,968
Inventories	66,789	44,635
	105,429	89,180
Investments in partly owned companies (less than 50% interest) at cost	9,695	8,700
Fixed Assets:		
Land, buildings and equipment	408,380	357,236
Less: accumulated depreciation	186,477	163,482
	221,903	193,754
Timber and cutting rights, less accumulated depletion	18,435	19,087
	240,338	212,841
Intangible Assets:		
Unamortized goodwill of subsidiaries	1,032	1,073
Patent rights of plywood process	620	705
	1,652	1,778
	$357,114	$312,499

LIABILITIES	1974	1973
Current Liabilities:		
Bank loan	$ 6,200	$ 1,085
Short-term notes payable	12,635	—
Accounts payable and accrued liabilities	33,649	23,172
Income taxes payable	4,650	14,742
Current portion of long-term debt	1,259	787
	58,393	39,786
Long-Term Debt	99,650	94,839
Deferred Income Taxes	62,563	56,675
	$220,606	$191,300

SHAREHOLDERS' EQUITY

5¾% Cumulative Preferred Shares	$ 9,775	$ 10,160
Common Shares (no par value)	62,132	61,872
Retained Earnings	64,621	49,167
	136,508	121,199
	$357,114	$312,499

CONSOLIDATED EARNINGS	1974	1973
Net sales	$285,163	$257,670
Costs and expenses:		
Cost of products sold	203,841	174,192
Depreciation	22,995	20,890
Depletion	1,902	1,838
Selling and administration expense	9,652	10,031
Interest on long-term debt	7,998	6,673
Other interest expense	1,067	1,320
	247,455	214,944
Net sales minus costs	37,708	42,726
Other income:		
Interest earned	1,838	1,271
Dividends from partly owned companies	50	100
Equity in retained earnings (loss) of partly owned companies	(408)	565
Earnings before income taxes	39,188	44,662
Income taxes		
Current	11,653	14,893
Deferred	6,271	5,051
	17,924	19,944
Net income	$ 21,264	$ 24,718

Other relevant data (in thousands of dollars):

	1974	1973	1972
1. Inventories	$66,789	$44,635	$38,290

	1974	1973
2. Sinking fund requirements for bonds and debentures	$3,010	$2,870
Lease payments (under prior commitments)	$2,850	$2,600

Required:

(a) Calculate the ratios and indices defined in this chapter, for both 1973 and 1974.

(b) Perform a common-size analysis for 1973 and 1974.

(c) Comment on any significant changes in the firm's position and performance. How would such changes affect your view of Western as
   (i) a common shareholder
   (ii) a preferred shareholder or bondholder
   (iii) Western's chairman of the board?

   Bear in mind that, in general, economic conditions for 1974 were:
   — start of a recession
   — record high rates of inflation and interest in most industrialized countries.

Case on Financial Statement Analysis

Given below are recent common-size balance sheets and selected financial ratios of 10 Canadian corporations in 10 different industries. These firms can be characterized as follows:

1. Railroad (with some diversification into other areas)
2. Farm machinery manufacturer
3. Forestry company
4. Heavy equipment dealer
5. Mining company
6. Motor hotel chain
7. Oil company
8. Pipeline company
9. Supermarket chain
10. Utility

After carefully analyzing the data given on the following page, match each company (A through J) to its appropriate industry classification. Give reasons to support your selections.

Balance Sheet Percentages	A	B	C	D	E	F	G	H	I	J
ASSETS										
Cash and marketable securities	5.0	11.4	0.0	0.0	0.9	3.9	3.3	8.6	1.3	5.8
Receivables	21.0	9.2	2.4	30.8	34.8	5.3	13.9	5.5	3.9	4.6
Inventories	10.3	37.1	0.5	39.2	34.3	1.8	13.6	10.9	1.3	1.2
Other current assets	0.4	0.3	2.7	—	3.2	—	0.6	—	0.1	0.9
Plant and equipment	58.3	37.4	86.6	12.8	17.1	58.3	61.2	48.8	84.7	63.9
Other assets	5.0	4.6	7.8	17.2	9.7	30.7	7.4	26.2	8.7	23.6
Total assets	100.0	100.0	100.0	100.0	100.0	100.0	100.0	100.0	100.0	100.0
LIABILITIES										
Notes payable	1.0	—	0.0	36.4	14.4	1.4	2.6	—	—	—
Accounts payable	13.6	15.6	2.7	14.3	19.9	4.0	8.6	3.4	3.1	7.8
Accrued taxes	0.4	3.4	0.0	2.6	3.3	0.6	1.3	0.6	0.0	0.6
Other current liabilities	—	0.8	3.8	0.9	0.4	6.9	1.1	6.6	1.3	1.8
Long-term debt	12.3	3.3	65.2	3.1	18.5	22.9	29.1	24.2	41.4	60.3
Other liabilities	10.2	3.7	—	6.9	1.5	6.8	12.6	5.2	8.3	10.8
Preferred stock	—	2.2	—	—	—	2.5	0.1	—	5.0	—
Common stock and capital surplus	15.4	1.8	19.5	11.0	16.7	22.7	17.7	8.5	32.3	10.6
Retained earnings and surplus reserves	47.1	69.2	8.8	24.8	25.3	32.2	26.9	51.5	8.6	8.1
Total liabilities and shareholders' equity	100.0	100.0	100.0	100.0	100.0	100.0	100.0	100.0	100.0	100.0
SELECTED RATIOS										
Current ratio	2.45	2.93	0.86	1.29	1.93	0.85	2.30	2.36	1.50	1.23
Quick ratio	1.73	1.04	0.37	0.57	0.94	0.71	1.26	1.33	1.18	1.02
Total debt/total assets	0.38	0.27	0.72	0.64	0.58	0.43	0.55	0.40	0.54	0.81
Long-term debt/capitalization	0.14	0.04	0.70	0.03	0.30	0.26	0.34	0.27	0.43	0.67
Net sales/total assets	1.14	4.77	0.26	1.62	1.13	0.29	1.07	0.30	0.28	0.64
Net profit/total assets	0.08	0.06	0.03	0.07	0.04	0.02	0.07	0.07	0.04	0.02
Net profit/total net worth	0.13	0.09	0.10	0.18	0.09	0.03	0.17	0.11	0.09	0.13
Net profit/net sales	0.07	0.01	0.12	0.04	0.03	0.06	0.07	0.22	0.15	0.04

Selected References

E. Altman, "Financial Ratios, Discriminant Analysis and the Prediction of Corporate Bankruptcy", *Journal of Finance*, September, 1968, pp. 589-609.

W. Beaver, "Financial Ratios as Predictors of Failure", *Empirical Research in Accounting: Selected Studies* in *Journal of Accounting Research* 1966, pp. 71-111.

W. Beranek, *Working Capital Management*, Belmont: Wadsworth, 1966

H. Bierman, "Measuring Financial Liquidity", *Accounting Review*, October, 1960, pp. 628-632.

O. Bowlin, "The Current Ratio in Current Position Analysis", *Financial Analysts Journal*, March-April, 1963, pp. 67-75.

Dun & Bradstreet of Canada, Ltd., *Key Business Ratios in Canada*, 1974, Toronto.

R. Edmister, "An Empirical Test of Financial Ratio Analysis for Small Business Failure Predictions", *Journal of Financial and Quantitative Analysis*, March, 1972, pp. 1477-1493.

E. Helfert, *Techniques of Financial Analysis,* (3rd ed.), Homewood: Richard D. Irwin, 1972, Chapter 2.

J. Horrigan, "A Short History of Financial Ratio Analysis", *Accounting Review*, April, 1968, pp. 284-294.

R. Jaedicke and R. Spouse, *Acounting Flows: Income, Funds, and Cash*, Englewood Cliffs: Prentice-Hall, 1965.

J. Jennings, "A Look at Corporate Liquidity", *Financial Executive*, February, 1971, pp. 123-135.

B. Lev, *Financial Statement Analysis: A New Approach*, Englewood Cliffs: Prentice-Hall, 1974, Chapters 2, 3, and 5.

G. Pinches and K. Mingo, "A Multivariate Analysis of Industrial Bond Ratings", *Journal of Finance*, March, 1973, pp. 1-18.

Chapter 23
Funds-Flow Analysis and Financial Forecasting

23-1. INTRODUCTION

In addition to the tools and approaches mentioned in the previous chapter, managers and analysts have a variety of other methods at their disposal for assessing business performance. This chapter deals with some such techniques which include the analysis of sources and uses of funds within the firm, and longer-term financial forecasting. Short-term financing and cash budgeting will be treated separately in the subsequent chapter dealing with cash management. It should be pointed out that the techniques examined in this chapter are widely used by both external analysts, including creditors, and by financial managers within the firm.

The *statement of sources and uses of funds* focuses on answers to two basic questions, namely: during a given period of time, where have the available funds been put to use within the firm, and how have these funds been obtained? As will be detailed below, such an analysis is carried out essentially by comparing the firm's balance sheets at the beginning and at the end of the period under consideration. These questions bring us to the heart of financial management: the procurement and allocation of funds.[1] Even though traditional funds-flow analysis deals with historical information, it can usefully be extended to encompass future periods, where such an analysis is then based on projected financial statements.

The remainder of this chapter deals with projected or *pro forma financial statements*. Through the use of such projected statements, the financial manager can forecast systematically where the firm will be some time in the future. Such forecasting is decidedly one of the more important tools of management and serves a variety of functions. Firstly, it will coordinate management thinking and action. The very process of forecasting requires future-oriented thinking on a concerted basis. It consequently has an impact not only on the financial side, but on every department or subsystem within the organization. Then, once the detailed plans have been set out, every phase of management will be concerned with the requirements for attaining prescribed goals. Hence, management thinking and action will continue to be coordinated. Secondly, effective forecasting will curtail the need for hurried decisions such as, for example, emergency financing. When forecasting, we are formally planning a course of action. This will encompass both the inputs needed to fulfil the plan satisfactorily, and the timing of these inputs. If, for example, we know in advance the timing and amount of funds needed, we may be able to select the most favorable

[1]For additional detail, see E. Solomon, *The Theory of Financial Management*, New York: Columbia University Press, 1963, pp. 1-25.

source of funds rather than be forced to settle on whatever happens to be available at the time. Hopefully, reducing the need for hurried decisions will produce better decisions. Thirdly, forecasting provides a means of control through the analysis of budget variances—the difference between the forecast and that which was achieved—whether favorable or unfavorable. Once a forecast has been made, management is capable of measuring actual performance at selected time intervals and comparing it against projections. If sufficient detail is available, the cause of variances may be determined and remedial action taken. In turn, forecasts may be revised or perhaps additional efforts expended to approach earlier expectations.

Definition of funds

For purposes of funds-flow analysis, the term *funds* may be defined in several ways, depending upon the approach or purpose of the analysis.[2] In the narrowest sense, the term is used to simply denote cash. Based on this narrow definition, funds-flow statements would simply reconcile cash balances from one time period to another. It follows that transactions which do not affect the cash account are excluded from the analysis.

In a somewhat broader context, funds are defined as working capital, or the excess of current assets over current liabilities. Changes in the noncurrent items of the balance sheet are analyzed only in terms of their combined effects on working capital. A funds-flow analysis based on this definition generally fails to consider changes in the firm's financial position which do not affect working capital.

In the broadest sense, funds are defined as all financial resources or all investments in assets and claims against these assets. Hence, changes are recognized in all balance sheet accounts, including the individual accounts which make up current assets and current liabilities. For purposes of this section, the broadest definition of funds-flow analysis will be used, covering all net sources and uses of funds.

23-2. PREPARATION OF THE STATEMENT OF SOURCES AND USES OF FUNDS

The process of preparing the statement of sources and uses of funds entails comparing the balance sheets of a company at two different points in time. Changes in the various entries on the balance sheet will indicate the net flows of funds which result from both management decisions and external influences during the period under scrutiny. The first step in such an analysis entails preparation of a *statement of balance sheet changes* (Table 23-1), which simply tabulates changes from one period to another, classifying them as either a source or a use of funds. The statement has also been termed the "Where-Got, Where-Gone Statement", to emphasize its function.

[2]For a detailed approach, see E. Helfert, *Techniques of Financial Analysis*, (3rd ed.), Homewood: Richard D. Irwin, 1972, pp. 3-30, also H. Simons and H. Karrenbrock, *Intermediate Accounting Comprehensive Volume*, (4th ed.), Cincinnati: South-Western Publishing Company, 1964, pp. 836-843.

TABLE 23-1

Merchant Marts Limited

Statement of Balance Sheet Changes Fiscal 1970 (millions of dollars)
(this table is prepared from the financial statements
as reproduced in Table 22-1 on p. 611)

Sources of Funds	
Increase in accounts payable	9.0
Increase in accruals	0.4
Increase in taxes payable	2.7
Increase in long-term debt	35.3
Increase in deferred income taxes	1.9
Increase in Class A shares	4.8
Increase in retained earnings	4.7
Decrease in inventories	6.0
Decrease in investments and advances	3.8
Decrease in refundable federal tax	0.2
Increase in accumulated depreciation	5.7
Total Sources	74.5

Uses of Funds	
Increase in cash	2.1
Increase in accounts receivable	14.3
Increase in prepayments	0.8
Increase in notes receivable	1.1
Increase in land	1.6
Increase in buildings, equipment	44.7
Increase in unamortized discount and expense	0.2
Decrease in notes payable	8.9
Decrease in contributions payable	0.8
Total Uses	74.5

Any increase in an asset account, or decrease in a liability account, represents a use of funds, whereas a decrease in an asset account or an increase in a liability account provides funds and is viewed as a source of funds. This is summarized in Table 23-2. For example, if assets such as plant and equipment or inventories are to be increased, or if liabilities such as a bank loan or accounts payable are to be reduced, funds are used up in the process. Similarly, funds can be provided either by liquidating assets such as inventories, or by incurring additional liabilities.

TABLE 23-2

Definitions of Sources and Uses of Funds

	Assets	Liabilities
Source of Funds	Decrease	Increase
Use of Funds	Increase	Decrease

It should be noted that such a statement of balance sheet changes depicts the shifts which occurred in accounts on a net basis. Thus, any fluctuations which may have taken place in an account during the time period under consideration are only recognized in terms of their net aggregate effect on the ending balance sheet. In the particular example provided, net changes which occurred from January 7, 1970 to January 6, 1971 are considered. Hence, a temporary building up of inventories prior to the traditional Christmas rush would not be detected because by January the bulk of those inventories would have been liquidated. Should the analyst wish to be more precise, he would have to draw up the funds-flow analysis over a shorter time-span, for example based on quarterly or even monthly data.

The statement of balance sheet changes does not in itself tell the full story. An additional refinement must be undertaken to arrive at a complete statement of sources and uses of funds, namely a breakdown of the noted change in retained earnings. If dividends have been paid by the firm, simply noting the net change in retained earnings will be incomplete. The retained earnings statement of Merchant Marts Limited indicates that in 1970 dividends of $7.5 million were declared. The income statement (Table 22-2) indicates that net earnings for 1970 were $12.2 million. Retained earnings are given as the difference between net earnings and dividends paid, and are computed as $12.2 million – $7.5 million = $4.7 million. It is this latter figure which appears on the statement of balance sheet changes (Table 23-1). If we substitute net earnings (as a source) and dividends paid (as a use) for the increase in retained earnings, not only is more detail shown, but for our example management's decision to pay out a sizable percentage of current earnings in the form of dividends is flagged. The following sources and uses of funds statement for Merchant Marts Limited, as shown in Table 23-3, includes the aforementioned alteration.

TABLE 23-3

Merchant Marts Limited

Statement of Sources and Uses of Funds
Fiscal 1970
(millions of dollars)

Sources of Funds	
Increase in accounts payable	9.0
Increase in accruals	0.4
Increase in taxes payable	2.7
Increase in long-term debt	35.3
Increase in deferred income taxes	1.9
Increase in Class A shares	4.8
Decrease in inventories	6.0
Decrease in investments and advances	3.8
Decrease in refundable federal tax	0.2
Income earned	12.2
Increase in accumulated depreciation	5.7
Total Sources	82.0
Uses of Funds	
Increase in cash	2.1
Increase in accounts receivable	14.3
Increase in prepayments	0.8
Increase in notes receivable	1.1
Increase in land	1.6
Increase in buildings, equipment	44.7
Increase in unamortized discount and expense	0.2
Decrease in notes payable	8.9
Decrease in contributions payable	0.8
Dividends paid	7.5
Total Uses	82.0

Table 23-3 provides a useful base from which we can analyze the firm's performance and certain decisions taken by company management. For example, we may question the sizable increase in cash balances, accounts receivable and buildings and equipment. Other items which may warrant additional detailed investigation include the large increase in accounts payable and in long-term debt. A comparison of the funds-flow statement of 1970 to those of preceding years may identify trends which could prompt further study. For example, have accounts payable also posted substantial increases in past years? If so, what are the underlying causes?

Other uses of the statement include analysis of the firm's method of financing. One obvious categorization of the financing methods employed is the division between internal and external sources. External sources may be refined further to determine the proportions of debt and equity financing, and the extent to which there is a reliance on short- as opposed to long-term debt. It then becomes possible to establish whether financing methods employed were appropriate given the types of assets financed, and the conditions of financial markets when the funds were obtained. For instance, if increases in plant and equipment were substantially financed through increases in accounts payable and notes payable and increases in short-term loans, we could become concerned about the future liquidity of the firm, as short-term funds have been committed to finance long-term investments. This type of analysis supplements the information which is available from a balance sheet. While the balance sheet represents the financial position of the firm at one point in time, a statement regarding sources and applications of funds provides insights into changes which have taken place over time.

23-3. PRO FORMA FINANCIAL STATEMENTS

In addition to an analysis of historical data, the financial officer or analyst may also be interested in the results of expected future operations. This is accomplished by means of projected financial statements, which are commonly called pro forma statements. The most important statements for forecasting purposes are the pro forma balance sheet and the pro forma income statement. Statements of projected sources and uses of funds can be derived by comparing a pro forma balance sheet with the current one, or by contrasting projected balance sheets for different points in time. In practice, approaches to developing such forecasted statements vary from strictly historical projections to the preparation of extremely detailed reports and schedules for each of the accounts dealt with.

In projecting financial statements, we normally start by preparing an income statement for the period under consideration. Figures from the projected income statement, such as retained earnings for the period, will be needed in preparing a pro forma balance sheet for the end of the period. As might be expected, preparation of pro forma financial statements invariably starts with a forecast of sales or revenues. Such forecasts can be based simply on projections of historical patterns, perhaps modified by subjective managerial judgment, or they can be based on detailed analyses of the economy, the industry, and the firm, drawing perhaps on sophisticated economic forecasting models and techniques. Whatever approach is used, forecasting the future is one of the most difficult and challenging tasks facing the manager or the analyst, particularly where longer time-spans are involved. Any results derived have to be viewed as tentative and subject to revisions through time as new information becomes available.

Based on the forecast of sales, we then relate other items making up the financial statements, such as cost of goods sold, inventories, and accounts receivable, to the projected sales figures, and possibly to each other. Some entries may be estimated fairly accurately by simply taking a constant proportion of sales, where the proportion to be applied could either be derived from the last financial statement, or could be taken as an average for several past periods. We may find, for example, that accounts receivable over time have amounted to a fairly constant proportion of sales. If credit terms and, hence, payment patterns have remained unaltered, it is easy to see why this may be so.

FIGURE 23-1

Various Types of Relationships Between Sales and Items From Financial Statements

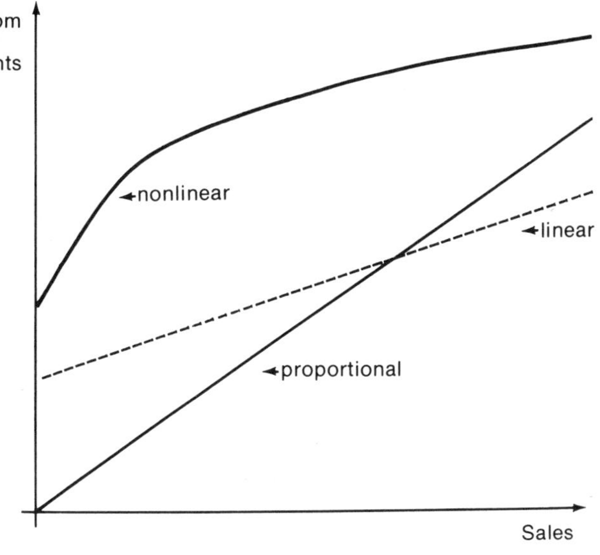

On the other hand, relationships between other items on the financial statements and sales may be more complex. In such cases, regression analysis may prove to be a useful tool in establishing the nature of the relationship.[3] For instance, we may find that inventory levels are not strictly proportional to sales in that even with reduced levels of sales, certain inventory levels need to be maintained in order to operate efficiently. Nevertheless, the relationship may be approximated as linear but, as illustrated in Figure 23-1, the function relating inventories to sales may not pass through the origin. By applying regression analysis to historical data points of inventories and sales, we can determine more exactly the

[3]For a description of such techniques, see any introductory statistics text. The risk of simply extrapolating using regression analysis, to the exclusion of judgment should be noted.

nature of the underlying relationship. In more complex cases where a straight-line relationship between variables may be inappropriate, we could even apply nonlinear regression models.

Table 23-4 provides an example of a pro forma income statement. Sales for the year just terminated were $8,000,000, and are expected to increase to $10,000,000 in the coming year. Once the basic sales forecast has been derived, several major categories of costs are then projected, specifically the cost of goods sold, selling and administrative expenses, and depreciation.

TABLE 23-4

Pro Forma Income Statement
for the Year Ended December 31, 197X

Sales		$10,000,000
Cost of goods sold	$6,900,000	
Selling and administrative expenses	800,000	
Depreciation	900,000	$ 8,600,000
Earnings before interest and taxes		$ 1,400,000
Interest		600,000
Earnings before taxes		$ 800,000
Tax (45%)		360,000
After-tax profit		$ 440,000
Dividends		140,000
Retained earnings		$ 300,000

In practice, there are several methods of estimating the cost of goods sold. A reasonably accurate estimate may be derived from past operating data, where the cost of goods sold is expressed as a percentage of sales (common-size analysis). We would rely on this proportion to remain relatively constant, and simply derive the cost of goods sold as a given percentage of projected sales. However, for firms with more complex cost structures, such as manufacturing firms as compared to merchandisers, a more detailed approach may be required, with each component of the cost of goods sold to be analyzed using cost-accounting techniques. Furthermore, the expected costs to be incurred during the period have to be allocated between the cost of goods sold and inventory. In other words, the costs charged to goods sold within the budget period will depend on whether a buildup or a reduction of inventories is planned. A detailed analysis of costs will thus require supporting data and schedules concerning materials and direct labor costs, as well as inventory analysis.

Once the costs of goods have been assessed, we need to estimate selling, administrative and other expenses in order to obtain earnings before interest and taxes. In practice, selling expenses are generally based upon a percentage of sales. This may also be true of general and administrative expenses, although both of these latter charges may not be strictly variable and, hence, proportional to sales, but rather fixed or semivariable. Therefore, such projections may have to be supported by more elaborate schedules. Other expenses include charges for depreciation which are easily established knowing the book value of the firm's assets and the rates of depreciation to be applied. Subtraction of all these costs and expenses from projected revenues yields anticipated earnings before interest and taxes.

Earnings before interest and taxes reflect the profitability of the firm's operations before any charges for the capital which is used in the enterprise have been deducted. It follows, therefore, that this measure of performance is independent of the actual capital structure employed by the corporation. Hence, as we have seen in the chapter on capital structure, it is used as the basis for evaluating the effects of alternative financing policies. Normally, interest expenses on outstanding debt and taxes to be paid can be predicted with a reasonable degree of accuracy, making the derivation of taxable income and after-tax earnings estimates relatively straightforward. The pro forma income statement will also include projected dividend payments based on the firm's established dividend policies. Clearly, for preparation of the pro forma balance sheet, it is necessary to arrive at the period's forecasted contribution to retained earnings.

Pursuing our numerical example, the current balance sheet and the pro forma balance sheet as at December 31, 197X are reproduced in Table 23-5.

TABLE 23-5

Current Balance Sheet and Pro Forma Balance Sheet as at December 31, 197X (millions of dollars)

	End of Current Year		Dec. 31, 197X (pro forma)	
Assets				
Cash and marketable securities		0.4		0.2
Inventories		2.6		3.2
Accounts receivable		2.0		2.5
Total current assets		5.0		5.9
Plant and equipment	7.0		9.0	
Minus accumulated depreciation	2.0		2.9	
Net plant and equipment		5.0		6.1
Total		10.0		12.0
Liabilities				
Accounts payable		1.5		2.0
Bank loan		2.0		3.2
Total current liabilities		3.5		5.2
Long-term debt		2.0		2.0
Capital stock		1.0		1.0
Retained earnings		3.5		3.8
Total		10.0		12.0

A few additional comments on the forecasts of individual balance sheet entries may be useful to illustrate the forecasting process.

Where longer-term forecasts are involved, forecasts of the cash account are typically derived from projected sales levels by the techniques described above. With relatively shorter-term projections of one year or less, a detailed month-by-month cash budget for the period under consideration would probably be available and form the basis for this particular projection. The preparation of cash budgets will be discussed in detail in a subsequent chapter.

Quite similar comments apply to the forecasting of inventory levels and accounts receivable. Short-term projections are most accurately derived by resorting to detailed monthly sales forecasts. This is particularly important where a firm's sales are subject to strong seasonal variations. In such situations, average annual sales figures may be meaningless and not usable for the computation of inventory or accounts receivable levels as at the particular date of the balance sheet. Longer-term forecasts may again be based on the techniques which were described above. Thus, the anticipated 25 percent increase in sales from $8,000,000 to $10,000,000 may be expected to increase accounts receivable by the same percentage or from $2,000,000 to $2,500,000. Inventories, on the other hand, may have been found to exhibit a linear relationship to sales, with the specific equation derived through regression analysis of past data, which yielded:

$$\text{inventories} = \$200{,}000 + 0.3 \times \text{sales}$$

Hence, with projected sales at $10,000,000, inventory levels would be forecast at $200,000 + 0.3 × $10,000,000 = $3,200,000.

Typically, the plant and equipment account is easily projected, as plans for expansion are generally laid out well in advance, and rates at which depreciation will be taken are known. Given the anticipated increase in sales, investments in new plant and equipment amounting to $2,000,000 are planned. With depreciation taken at a rate of 10 percent of book value, or $900,000 for the period, derivation of the ending balance at $6,100,000 becomes a matter of simple arithmetic.

On the liability side, assume that the firm does not contemplate raising any new long-term funds externally during the period under consideration, as current capital market conditions are not conducive to such financing. Then, the only change in this area of the balance sheet is given by the $300,000 in retained earnings for the period which were derived in the pro forma income statement and which serve to increase retained earnings from $3,500,000 to $3,800,000. The firm anticipates that the maximum increase in bank loans it can obtain will be another $1,200,000, which will bring total bank loans outstanding to $3,200,000. To balance its projected accounts, the firm plans to draw more heavily on trade credit, perhaps foregoing some cash discounts which are generally taken. Accordingly, accounts payable are anticipated to increase by 30 percent to $2,000,000.

Given the completed pro forma balance sheet, a comparison with the current balance sheet enables us to prepare a pro forma statement of sources and uses of funds. For our hypothetical example, such a statement is shown in Table 23-6. Together with the other pro forma statements, it provides a basis for analyzing the firm's projected operations. In this example, we could question the expectation that a significant portion of the investment in additional fixed assets will be financed from short-term sources. Should anticipated sales fail to materialize, it is entirely possible that with short-term borrowing pushed to the limit, the firm could find itself unable to meet obligations as they come due. Obviously, such planning statements are of vital importance, in that preventive or remedial action can be taken if something undesirable is noted.

It is also worth noting that since pro forma presentations are generally patterned after the regular statements, ratio analysis and other comparisons are also possible using the projections.

Before leaving our numerical example, it may be useful to note some general patterns which are typically a consequence of any substantial growth in sales. A growth in sales is likely to force increases in various asset accounts. Inventories and receivables will almost automatically follow trends in sales, and if the growth is substantial, new investments in fixed assets may also be required. It should not be surprising to find, therefore, that a firm with growing sales will find itself in a position of having to raise monies to finance such growth. Note that the projected growth need not be caused by increases in the physical volume of operations, but may merely be a reflection of inflation and price level changes, which push up dollar sales. Given widespread inflation in recent years, the increasing pressures by business on the capital markets becomes understandable. With stock markets often having performed poorly and long-term debt only available at historically high interest rates, many firms drew heavily on short-term financing including trade credit, with results quite similar to those portrayed in the above example.

TABLE 23-6

Pro Forma Statement of Sources and Uses of Funds
for the Year Ended December 31, 197X

Sources of Funds	
Decrease in cash and marketable securities	$ 200,000
Increase in accumulated depreciation	900,000
Increase in accounts payable	500,000
Increase in bank loans	1,200,000
Income earned	440,000
Total sources of funds	$3,240,000
Uses of Funds	
Increase in inventories	$ 600,000
Increase in accounts receivable	500,000
Increase in plant and equipment	2,000,000
Dividends paid	140,000
Total uses of funds	$3,240,000

It can readily be appreciated that the preparation of pro forma financial statements, which extend over several years, can become a tedious process. Even after forecasts of key variables have been made and typical relationships between different financial variables established, a fair amount of straightforward computation as well as bookkeeping must still be performed in order to derive complete and consistent financial statements. A variety of packaged computer programs and computer-based corporate financial models are readily available to assist in this task. Such aids greatly reduce the time and costs which financial planning entails and make feasible much more thorough analyses than were heretofore practical. Thus, with the aid of a computer, pro forma statements can be derived for alternate sets of forecasts. This enables management to ask a variety of "what if" type questions, and to explore the impact of alternative assumptions in projecting financial statements without facing a prohibitive clerical effort in preparing the reports. While it is not possible in this context to review the variety of financial models available,[4] they range from single programs performing accounting type calculations to sophisticated models of corporate activity encompassing forecasting modules and the likes. With the widespread availability and access to computer power and to packaged programs, the use of such models has expanded rapidly. Even many smaller firms have been placed in the position of being able to undertake systematic and comprehensive financial planning for the first time.

As a final word of caution, it should be noted that neither the computer nor quantitative models solve the problem of forecasting which underlies any planning. The pro forma statements derived from any model are as good or as unreliable as the forecasts on which they were based. While we have tools which can assist us with the task, there is no cookbook solution to forecasting the future, particularly where longer-term forecasts are called for.

23-4. SUMMARY

In this chapter, we reviewed several important tools of analysis which can assist either the manager or the external analyst in evaluating the operations of a firm. A statement of sources and uses of funds is derived by comparing the balance sheets of a firm at two different points in time. Any increase in an asset account, or any decrease in a liability, represents a use of funds. Similarly, any decrease in an asset, or increase in a liability, is viewed as a source of funds. Funds in this context are broadly defined as financial resources. A statement of sources and uses of funds provides useful information regarding a firm's investments over the time period under consideration, and the way in which such investments were financed.

Financial statements are not merely useful as historical records portraying the past operations of the firm, but they can also be used as planning tools to project the future. Projected financial statements are termed pro forma statements, and the most important pro forma statements are the income statement, the balance sheet, and the statement of sources and uses of funds. The basic forecast from which most other entries are derived is generally the forecast of sales or revenues for the period under consideration. Other entries in the financial statements are derived by relating the various items to anticipated sales, and possibly to each other. Regression analysis may be a useful tool in establishing such relationships. The preparation of pro forma financial statements has become much easier and, hence, more common with the widespread availability of computers and packaged computer programs to assist in this task.

The importance of systematic financial planning cannot be overstated. An early anticipation of financial needs will allow management to plan and to negotiate for new funding from a position of strength, affording flexibility in

[4]Interested readers are referred to A. Schrieber, ed., *Corporate Simulation Models*, Seattle: University of Washington, 1970.

searching for and finding those sources of funds which are optimal for the firm. Unpleasant surprises due to a lack of such planning will result in costlier financing at best. It should again be stressed that no recipes exist which will guarantee sound forecasting, and that subjective judgment will play an important role in any assessment of the future.

Questions for Discussion

1. In the context of funds-flow analysis, why does depreciation represent a source of funds?
2. Given inflationary growth in sales, what changes would you expect to note on a firm's balance sheet? How would such changes be reflected in a statement of sources and uses of funds?
3. Discuss the statement: "Carefully prepared pro forma statements reduce uncertainty".
4. Discuss the potentials and limitations of regression analysis in relating projected balance sheet entries to the sales forecast.

Problem with Solution

Prepare a sources and uses of funds statement using the actual 1974 and 1975 balance sheets for John Labatt Ltd., as provided in the case at the end of Chapter 13.

Solution

As a basis for the analysis, we use the consolidated balance sheets of John Labatt Ltd. as at April 30, 1974 and 1975, as provided in Exhibit 2 on pp. 388-89. Recalling Table 23-2, decreases in asset accounts and increases in liability accounts are sources of funds and increases in asset accounts and decreases in liability accounts are uses of funds. By taking the difference of all accounts on the balance sheets, we can draw up the following statement of balance sheet changes:

Sources of Funds:	
Increase in bank advances and short-term notes	$26,070,000
Increase in accounts payable	3,404,000
Increase in taxes payable	7,510,000
Increase in long-term debt due within one year	212,000
Increase in deferred income taxes	3,960,000
Increase in total minority interest in subsidiary companies	49,000
Increase in common shares issued and outstanding	2,493,000
Increase in retained earnings	10,155,000
Decrease in marketable securities	5,256,000
Decrease in investment in other companies	366,000
Decrease in the due from trustees and employees account	98,000
Decrease in unamortized debt financing expense	96,000
Total Sources	$59,669,000

Uses of Funds:	
Increase in cash	$ 320,000
Increase in accounts receivable	3,419,000
Increase in inventories	22,951,000
Increase in prepaid expenses	2,723,000
Increase in investment in corporate joint ventures	3,931,000
Increase in mortgages, loans, and advances	510,000
Increase in land and buildings and equipment, less accumulated depreciation	18,488,000
Increase in goodwill, store licences, and trademarks	2,939,000
Decrease in dividends payable	27,000
Decrease in long-term debt	2,447,000
Decrease in preferred shares	1,914,000
Total Uses	$59,669,000

This is as yet incomplete because John Labatt Limited paid dividends in 1975. Thus, the single "increase in retained earnings" figure of $10,155,000 should be replaced by an "income earned" figure of $22,176,000, found in Exhibit 1, and a corresponding "dividends paid" figure under uses of funds in the amount of $22,176,000 – $10,155,000 = $12,021,000.

In summary, we see that the main uses of funds were given by increases in inventories, investments in plant and equipment, and dividend payments. These uses of funds were primarily financed by an increase in short-term liabilities and by earnings.

Additional Problems

1. The current income statement and balance sheet for Antigua Ltd. are given as follows:

Antigua Ltd.
Income Statement

Sales	$7,200,000
Cost of goods sold	5,700,000
Depreciation expense	300,000
Selling and administration expenses	900,000
Interest and debt expense	160,000
Income before taxes	140,000
Tax	56,000
Net income	84,000

Antigua Ltd.
Balance Sheet

Cash		$ 90,000	Notes payable	$ 180,000
Marketable securities		40,000	Accounts payable	700,000
Accounts receivable		810,000	Other liabilities	360,000
Inventory		1,050,000	Long-term debt	2,100,000
Investments		185,000	Preferred shares	160,000
Other assets		1,140,000	Common shares	670,000
Plant and equipment	$4,500,000		Retained earnings	1,845,000
Less: accumulated depreciation	$1,800,000			
Net plant and equipment		$2,700,000		
		$6,015,000		$6,015,000

Prepare pro forma income statements and balance sheets for the next three years, given the following predictions:

(a) Inflation is expected to increase dollar sales by 8% annually while real sales growth will contribute 2%.
(b) Cost of goods sold, accounts receivable, inventories, and accounts payable are all expected to remain at a constant percentage of sales over the next three years.
(c) Selling and administrative expenses will grow at a rate which equals half the percentage increase of sales, plus an expected fixed increase of $30,000 per year.
(d) Cash, investments, and preferred share accounts are expected to remain at current levels.
(e) $100,000 of 10% long-term debt will be issued in year 2.
(f) Other assets will decrease $200,000 in year 1.
(g) Plant and equipment purchases will be $200,000 in year 1, $100,000 in year 2, and $300,000 in year 3.
(h) $40,000 in dividends are to be distributed each year.
(i) Assets are depreciated at the same current average rate over the 3 years.
(j) Any excess funds are used to reduce first other liabilities, then notes payable. If any funds are left after these two liability accounts are reduced to zero, such surplus funds will be invested in additional marketable securities. Otherwise, no additions to the marketable securities account are contemplated.

2. Assume that a financial institution in Western Canada releases the following comparative financial statements. The institution's fiscal year ends on October 31.

Assets

(in thousands of dollars)

	1970	1969
Cash on hand and due from banks	10,252	9,429
Cheques and other items in transit, net	4,855	465
Securities, at cost	35,103	23,382
Loans		
Day, call, and short loans	18,722	13,309
Other loans, less provision for losses	49,567	24,881
Bank premises, at cost less amounts written off	1,217	1,045
Securities of a corporation controlled by the Bank, at cost	662	143
Customers' liability under acceptances, guarantees, and letters of credit, as per contra account	722	1,185
Other assets	170	164
	121,270	74,003

Liabilities and Shareholders' Equity

	1970	1969
Deposits of the governments and banks	16,948	10,098
Personal savings deposits	19,963	10,706
Other deposits	70,223	38,834
Acceptances, guarantees, and letters of credit	722	1,185
Other liabilities	246	332
Accumulated appropriations for losses	474	311
Capital		
Issued and fully paid	5,106	5,106
Rest account and undivided profits	7,588	7,431
	121,270	74,003

Statement of Revenue, Expenses, and Undivided Profit

		1970		1969
Total revenue		7,444		3,384
Expenses				
Interest on deposits	4,067		1,618	
Salaries and staff benefits	1,407		836	
Property expenses including depreciation of $225,000 in 1970	453		268	
Other expenses	944		540	
Total expenses		6,871		3,262

Balance of revenue	573	122
Appropriation for losses	250	70
Balance of profit before tax	323	52
Provision for income taxes	116	–
Balance of profits for year	207	52

In addition, assume that:

(i) a dividend of $50,000 was declared and paid in the third quarter of 1970,

(ii) a temporary branch was sold for $150,000 on July 1, 1970.

Prepare a source and uses of funds statement for the institution for the fiscal year ended October 31, 1970.

Case

Verdun Manufacturing

In the Fall of 1976, Guy Richard, assistant to Maurice LaFleur, who was then the chief loan officer of the National Bank was reviewing the outstanding line of credit of the Verdun Manufacturing Company. Over the past five years credit had been extended each Spring to meet Verdun's seasonal requirements. This year, for the first time, the maximum credit line of $500,000 had proven inadequate and an additional $150,000 was advanced. Furthermore, although borrowings had always been retired by late July or early August, this time around no repayment had yet been made.

Mr. Richard had been asked by Mr. LaFleur to file a detailed analysis of the situation along with a recommendation on what should be done. In preparing to do so, Mr. Richard first reviewed the management team of Verdun Manufacturing, headed by Mr. Pierre LaLonde, and found them to be an impressive group combining engineering and marketing backgrounds. He also noted that sales and profits had grown fairly steadily over the past several years although in real terms (adjusting for inflation) the growth had not been dramatic.

Mr. Richard knew that his report had to be brief and to the point. He also recalled that his superior had a strong preference for presentations which included financial analysis.

Exhibits I and II below provide comparative income statements and balance sheets for Verdun Manufacturing.

EXHIBIT I

VERDUN MANUFACTURING
INCOME STATEMENTS FOR YEARS ENDED OCTOBER 31, 1974-1976
(Thousands of Dollars)

	1974	1975	1976
Net sales*	$6,000	$7,000	$9,000
Less cost of goods sold:			
Materials and labor	5,150	6,000	7,750
Overhead**	120	170	190
Earnings before interest and taxes	$ 730	$ 830	$1,060
Less interest expenses	30	30	60
Earnings before taxes	$ 700	$ 800	$1,000
Taxes at 50%	350	400	500
Earnings after taxes	$ 350	$ 400	$ 500
Dividends	260	300	300
Retained earnings	$ 90	$ 100	$ 200
*After quantity discounts	$ 60	$ 70	$ 105
**Includes capital cost allowances			
on plant of	$ 80	$ 90	$ 110
on equipment of	$ 35	$ 40	$ 50

EXHIBIT II

VERDUN MANUFACTURING
BALANCE SHEETS AS AT OCTOBER 31, 1974-1976
(Thousands of Dollars)

	1974	1975	1976
Cash	$ 181	$ 161	$ 81
Marketable securities	210	10	0
Accounts receivable	940	1,010	1,190
Inventories	1,010	1,150	1,310
Total current assets	$2,341	$2,331	$2,581
Loans to officers	100	100	150
Plant, net of depreciation	1,100	1,200	1,800
Equipment, net of depreciation	900	950	1,010
Total Fixed Assets	$2,100	$2,250	$2,960
TOTAL ASSETS	$4,441	$4,581	$5,541
Accounts payable	$ 870	$1,010	$1,120
Notes payable	100	0	0
Bank loan	0	0	650
Total Current Liabilities	$ 970	$1,010	$1,770
Common shares	801	801	801
Retained earnings	2,670	2,770	2,970
TOTAL LIABILITIES & SHAREHOLDERS' EQUITY	$4,441	$4,581	$5,541

Selected References

I. Ansoff, "Planning as a Practical Management Tool", *Financial Executive*, June, 1964, pp. 34-37.

H. Anton, *Accounting for the Flow of Funds*, Boston: Houghton Mifflin Co., 1962, Chapters 4 and 5.

J. Chambers, S. Mullick, and D. Smith, "How to Choose the Right Forecasting Technique", *Harvard Business Review*, July-August, 1971, pp. 45-74.

E. Helfert, *Techniques of Financial Analysis,* (3rd ed.) Homewood: Richard D. Irwin, Inc., 1972, Chapters 1 and 3.

R. Jaedicke, and R. Sprouse, *Accounting Flows: Income, Funds, and Cash.* Englewood Cliffs: Prentice-Hall, Inc., 1965, Chapters 5 and 6.

B. Lev, *Financial Statement Analysis: A New Approach*, Englewood Cliffs, Prentice-Hall, 1974.

A. Schrieber, ed., *Corporate Simulation Models*. Seattle: University of Washington, 1970.

F. Weston, "Financial Analysis: Planning and Control", *Financial Executive*, July, 1965, pp. 40-42 ff.

F. Weston, "Forecasting Financial Requirements", *Accounting Review*, July, 1958, pp. 427-440.

PART 8
Working Capital Management

Chapter 24
The Management of Cash and Marketable Securities

24-1. INTRODUCTION

The size of cash balances and the firm's holding of marketable securities are essentially determined by the corporate financial officer. Decisions taken in this area are critical for the firm in that insolvencies and bankruptcies frequently stem from inadequate cash management. In this context, the reader should appreciate that quite profitable firms can go bankrupt, for example, by allowing themselves to become illiquid through an overcommitment of funds to long-term projects. On the other hand, firms which have been unprofitable for some time may be perfectly solvent and may represent very little risk to short-term creditors.

Just as capital budgeting decisions are crucial in determining the long-term profitability of the firm, the liquidity of the firm hinges on cash management decisions which essentially revolve around tradeoffs between risk and profitability. Tight cash management increases the risk of insolvency, while excessive cash balances, being an unproductive investment, detract from the firm's profitability. The key issue is the striking of the right balance between the conflicting objectives of profitability and safety. Forecasting or cash budgeting is one important ingredient in this context, while the uncertainty inherent in the particular type of business is another. Given that cash management has to be an ongoing process, it is understandable that financial officers devote a relatively high proportion of their time to this particular responsibility.

In this chapter, we will briefly review the motives for holding cash balances. We will then discuss the process of forecasting such requirements through cash budgeting. Finally, we will look at the risk-return tradeoff in determining actual cash balances, and consider how surplus cash may be invested temporarily in a portfolio of marketable securities.

24-2. MOTIVES FOR HOLDING CASH

Economists have analyzed and categorized the various reasons behind people holding cash balances. A brief review of the motives will provide a conceptual framework for the analysis of cash management. In terms which are related to financial management, we can distinguish between the transactions motive, precautionary motive, speculative motive, and finance motive for holding cash. We will briefly discuss each of these in turn.

The *transactions motive* simply relates to the holding of cash to meet current transactions. The need for cash to transact company business arises because inflows do not always equal outflows and there are definite and often fixed costs involved in converting even highly liquid assets such as marketable securities into cash. Not surprisingly, it is both impractical and expensive to make such conversions too frequently and for small amounts each time. (Even as individuals we do not withdraw cash from our savings accounts several times a week in ten dollar amounts, simply because it would prove inconvenient as well as costly in terms of time and charges to do so.) Reasonable cash holdings are maintained, therefore, to meet daily transactions and to minimize the nuisance and costs of having to replenish one's holdings too frequently. The amount of cash to be maintained in this context clearly depends on the typical volume of transactions, and possibly on the interest which can be earned if excess cash is productively invested. We will discuss this point further when considering investments in marketable securities below.

The *precautionary motive* for holding cash relates to cash balances which are held to provide a cushion for unexpected events such as business declines. In economic downturns, not only may sales fall below expectations and anticipated inflows not materialize, but it also becomes more probable that additional accounts will have to be written off as bad debt. Similarly, outflows could quite unexpectely prove higher than was budgeted for. This seems to be a common pattern in environments characterized by sudden inflationary price level changes. For any of these reasons, some cash in excess of anticipated requirements may be maintained. In this context, however, it should be noted that the term cash may be used broadly to include near cash and even unused short-term borrowing capacity. Near cash comprises more liquid current assets such as treasury bills or other money market instruments which serve as revenue producing outlets for excess cash, but can be converted into cash on very short notice.

The *speculative motive* relates to holding cash in order to take advantage of special situations such as price declines or increases in interest rates. For instance, the manager of an investment account may temporarily hold large balances in cash in anticipation of a further rise in interest rates and declines in security prices. The manager may commit such cash once he feels that interest rates have peaked. Similarly, manufacturing or trading enterprises purchasing raw materials which are subject to cyclical price fluctuations, may build up cash in order to acquire inventories once prices have reached their lows.

Finally, the *finance motive* for holding cash balances ties in with the buildup of cash required to finance capital budget appropriations, dividend payments and similar large expenditures. Cash (again defined in a broad sense) may have to be built up over an extended period of time to finance such "lumpy" investments.

It should be clear from the above that determinants of cash management are reasonably complex, with the various motives superimposed on one another. Furthermore, circumstances vary and do depend on the particular business situation, making it impossible to derive clear rules which are universally applicable for the determination of optimal cash balances. Instead, we will have to consider general principles and techniques which can then be applied to a variety of specific situations to arrive at actual decisions.

24-3. THE TYPICAL FLOW OF FUNDS

Before discussing the process of cash budgeting, it may be useful to picture, in a simplified fashion, the typical flow of funds through a business. Such flow of funds can be depicted as a circular movement, originating from a pool or source which is the outgrowth of capital originally contributed by the owners. In most instances, the pool is augmented by credit received from lenders including suppliers. As depicted in Figure 24-1, available funds are then committed to the expenses of operations, to the purchase of fixed assets, and to various governmental agencies in the form of taxes or royalties. As sales are generated and accounts receivable collected, the funds flow back to replenish the pool. Hopefully, the inflow of funds resulting from sales will include a profit component. Miscellaneous inflows, through the sale of fixed assets, for example, also adds to the cash reservoir, while additional outflows of funds include interest on and repayment of borrowed funds as well as dividends paid to owners of the firm.

FIGURE 24-1

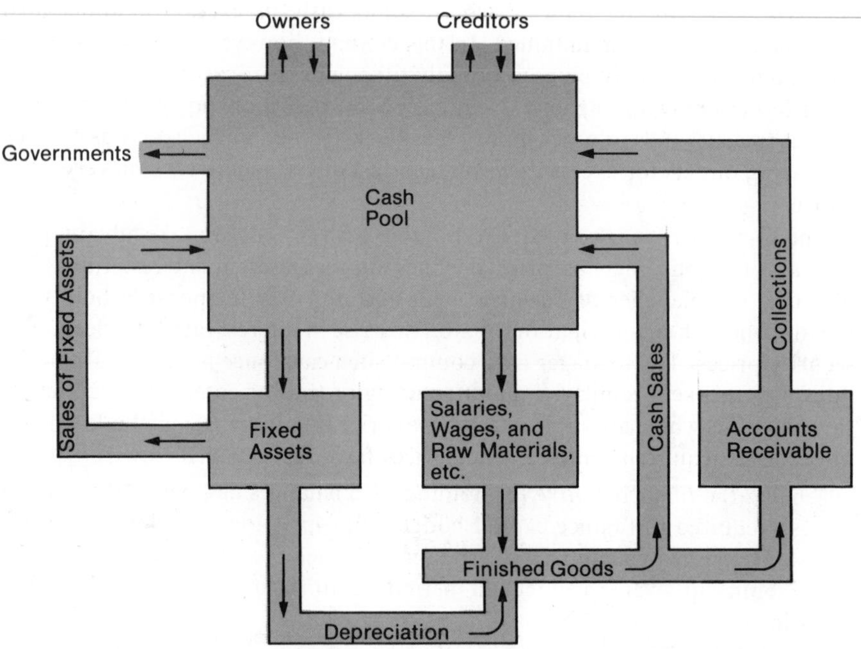

Of considerable importance to cash management and cash budgeting are the time lags which are typically involved in this circular flow of funds. Thus, operating costs are incurred to produce in-process and finished-goods inventories. Some time may elapse before sales are made from inventory, with further time delays until accounts receivable are collected and cash flows back into the business. Funds will be required to bridge these time lags and to finance investments in inventories and accounts receivable. The exact timing of outflows

TABLE 24-1

Time Lags in the Flow of Funds and their Impact on Financing

Example	:	wholesaler
Purchase terms	:	net 10
Selling terms	:	net 60
Inventory turnover	:	4 times per year

Time pattern of typical purchase and sale:

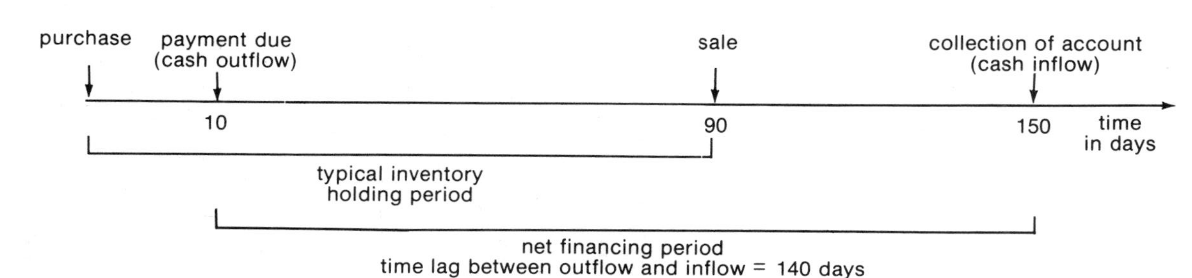

and inflows must be carefully considered in preparing a detailed cash budget. A numerical example of time lags in the flow of funds and of their impact on financing is provided in Table 24-1. Given a wholesaler purchasing goods on terms of net 10, selling on net 60, with an inventory turnover ratio of 4 times per year, the time lag between cash outflows required to procure the goods and the time to collections on sales is 140 days. Therefore, 140 days of average daily purchases will have to be financed. If, for example, annual purchases increase by $1,000,000, this implies an increase in daily purchases of $1,000,000/365 = $2,739, and increased investments in current assets (inventories and accounts receivable) of $2,739 × 140 = $383,562 for which funds will have to be found. This example illustrates why the combination of time lags which are inherent in the flow of funds and growth in the dollar volume of sales must be highlighted for management through cash budgeting, as it can pose significant problems in the procurement of funds. The point is important if we consider that dollar sales have increased significantly for most businesses in recent years, if for no other reason than a general upward movement of prices. It also illustrates that seasonal peaks in sales will have a major impact on a firm's cash flows and may necessitate temporary borrowing to finance buildups in inventories and receivables, with liquidation of the loan possible after the seasonal peak in sales. This particular topic will be expanded upon below.

24-4. CASH BUDGETING

The cash budget is simply an attempt to predict cash flows into and out of the company during some selected time span. Rather than merely being concerned with profits or account changes over a given period, this statement forecasts actual *cash* receipts and disbursements including their cumulative impact on cash balances. The budget may cover several years and may be broken down on a monthly, weekly, or daily basis depending upon the firm's operating characteristics and the intended use of the budget. Clearly, when cash flows are irregular and unevenly spread, smaller intervals may be required so as to pick up and more accurately predict extremes in the firm's cash balances. On the other hand, a cash budget prepared on a monthly basis may be adequate when both the inflows and outflows of cash are spread out in a relatively even way within the period.

Uses of the cash budget

Since the cash budget is a forecast of the effects of operations on the size of cash balances, it is an invaluable tool to financial officers concerned with corporate liquidity and planning for contingencies.[1] Through the lead time it provides, the cash budget permits planning for external financing in that the magnitude, timing, and duration of any expected cash shortage will be made apparent. In fact, a cash budget is often required by a bank's lending officer and may form part of a loan application, being one of the chief justifications for a line of credit.

[1] For an extended discussion, see G. Donaldson, "Strategy for Financial Emergencies," *Harvard Business Review*, November-December, 1969, pp. 67-79.

A cash budget also permits the planning of debt repayment schedules.

Not only does the budget indicate the characteristics of a cash shortage, but it also shows the size and timing of any subsequent cash buildup, hence detailing the firm's ability to reduce its obligations. Two questions which are important in loan applications are answered by the cash budget, namely: what are the borrowed funds to be used for, and how and when will the borrowed funds be repaid? In a short-term situation, the answers to these questions typically relate to increases in inventories and accounts receivable and to subsequent collections on the receivables. Obviously, if the forecast projects insufficient cash generation for repayment of the loan over an operating cycle, some form of longer-term or permanent capital requirement may be indicated.

The cash budget may also be important to the analysis of dividend policy: it will indicate the level of dividend payments which can readily be sustained. Dividend payments are often substantial, and their effects on the cash balance must be recognized.

Finally, the cash budget facilitates putting funds to work, thereby minimizing the opportunity cost occasioned by idle cash balances. The projections enable the financial executive to estimate the size and timing of cash shortages and surpluses, thereby facilitating decisions about the division of holdings between straight cash and marketable securities. Clearly, the amount or degree of help provided by the cash budget in this respect is a function of its precision and detail. An accurate budget prepared, for example, on a weekly basis may be much more valuable in managing cash than one which is prepared quarterly.

Preparation of the cash budget

The preparation of the cash budget requires inputs from many departments within the firm, with the accuracy of the budget a direct function of the reliability of these inputs. After deciding upon the time span to be covered and the breakdown of this time span into smaller segments, the financial manager must first obtain a forecast of future sales or revenues for the budget period. This is perhaps the most crucial estimate, as most other inputs are dependent upon the sales or revenue forecast.

There are various methods of forecasting sales, and typically senior personnel in the marketing area will be consulted. Basically, the sales forecast can be founded upon an internal approach, an external approach, or a combination of both. The internal approach consists of estimates made by various persons in the sales area concerning their particular product specialization. The individual estimates are reviewed by the marketing manager or marketing researcher who then prepares a forecast of sales by product lines and overall sales for the periods under consideration. The external approach to forecasting sales involves an analysis of both general economic expectations and of the particular industry in question. Once a forecast of industry sales has been made, factors such as market share, expected prices, and the likes are analyzed. The culmination of these studies will be a forecast of sales broken down by product lines, which is based upon external factors. In most instances, the internal and external approaches to forecasting sales will yield differing results, necessitating some sort of reconciliation. The method of achieving this compromise will depend upon such considerations as the size of the discrepancy, past experiences with both approaches, managerial judgment, and the possibility of substantial changes in economic conditions during the budget period.

Once sales forecasts have been made, the remaining estimates or schedules of purchases, production, inventory and payments can be determined. A simplified example will illustrate the cash budgeting process. Consider the preparation of a cash budget for a merchandising firm covering the 6-month period July to December, and to be broken down into monthly segments. The firm retails a single product which it expects to sell at $10 per unit. Forecasted sales are 1,000 units for each of July, August, and September, 1,200 units for October, 1,500 units for November, and 1,200 units for each of December and January. All sales are credit sales on terms of net 30 and experience indicates that 75 percent of accounts receivable are collected one month following the date of the sale with the balance collected after two months. No bad debts are expected. Table 24-2 indicates the firm's expected cash receipts from sales during the budget period.

Cash receipts from sources other than sales would obviously have to be included if they occur. Examples would include the sale of assets, issuance of common stock, and income from investments. It is well to note how seasonal patterns in sales affect the magnitude and timing of cash receipts for each of the months under consideration. Many companies, producers of winter sports equipment for example, could have even more severe seasonal fluctuations than those illustrated in Table 24-2.

TABLE 24-2

Schedule of Cash Receipts from Sales

	May	June	July	August	September	October	November	December
Total Sales	$8,000	$9,000	$10,000	$10,000	$10,000	$12,000	$15,000	$12,000
Collections:								
On previous month's sales		6,000	6,750	7,500	7,500	7,500	9,000	11,250
On sales two months previous			2,000	2,250	2,500	2,500	2,500	3,000
Totals			$8,750	$9,750	$10,000	$10,000	$11,500	$14,250

The forecast of cash outflows or disbursements is also based upon the sales forecast. Assume that the firm purchases enough units each month to cover sales expected during the following month. Purchase terms are net 30 and the company's policy is to avoid any stretching of its accounts payable. Costs of purchase are expected to total $7 per unit, wages paid are $1000 per month and miscellaneous operating expenses (excluding depreciation) are $1500 per month. Table 24-3 shows the expected cash outflows.

TABLE 24-3

Schedule of Cash Disbursements

	June	July	August	September	October	November	December
Purchases	$7,000	$7,000	$7,000	$8,400	$10,500	$8,400	$8,400*
Cash Outflow:							
Accounts payable		7,000	7,000	7,000	8,400	10,500	8,400
Wages		1,000	1,000	1,000	1,000	1,000	1,000
Miscellaneous		1,500	1,500	1,500	1,500	1,500	1,500
Totals		$9,500	$9,500	$9,500	$10,900	$13,000	$10,900

*Based on expected January sales of 1,200 units.

By combining Tables 24-2 and 24-3 and adding nonoperating cash receipts and disbursements, a typical, though simplified, cash budget emerges as in Table 24-4. Incorporated are assumptions about receipt of $750 from the sale of a fixed asset in September, dividend payments of $100 in August and November, income tax payments of $1,000 in September and December, and loan repayments (including interest) of $100 per month. The negative cash flow of $1,700 in November should be noted. This is caused by payments on larger October purchases to be made in anticipation of November sales. The income tax payments of $1,000 in September and December are also large cash drains which upset cash balances. As the budget demonstrates, a policy requiring minimum cash balances of $1,000 for precautionary reasons would entail borrowing beginning in July and building up to $3,350 by November. The large net cash inflow projected for December can be used to reduce the borrowings. It should also be noted that if the cash budget had been prepared on a quarterly basis, the large outflow in November would have been averaged with other months concealing true peaks in cash requirements. Where sales are seasonal care has to be taken to choose the basic time period small enough so that temporary peaks in the requirement for funds are fully detected. Finally, in our example the firm will not have idle cash balances available for investment during the 6 months under consideration.

As has previously been noted, the cash budget, like any other budget, is simply a forecast, and as such is in many instances no more than an educated guess. Hence, deviations from the budget are likely to occur and will have to be allowed for. This has several consequences. For one, it makes cash budgeting a continuous process, with budget revisions to be undertaken in the light of any new information becoming available as time moves on. For instance, if sales in a given month turn out below expectations, the executive should consider whether sales forecasts for subsequent months need to be adjusted accordingly. It is helpful to assess likely variations from forecasted expected values, and an analysis of past performance may be useful in this context. Finally, sensitivity analysis may be quite useful, implying the preparation of cash budgets for alternative forecasts of key variables. For example, if sales during the seasonal peak fall short by ten percent from the values forecasted, what will the impact be on the firm's cash position and its ability to meet payments on its short-term

TABLE 24-4

Cash Budget

	July	August	September	October	November	December
Receipts:						
Total sales receipts	$8,750	$9,750	$10,000	$10,000	$11,500	$14,250
Sale of fixed asset			750			
Total receipts	$8,750	$9,750	$10,750	$10,000	$11,500	$14,250
Disbursements:						
Operating expenses	$9,500	$9,500	$9,500	$10,900	$13,000	$10,900
Dividend payments		100			100	
Income taxes			1,000			1,000
Loan repayment	100	100	100	100	100	100
Total disbursements	$9,600	$9,700	$10,600	$11,000	$13,200	$12,000
Net cash flow	($850)	$50	$150	($1,000)	($1,700)	$2,250
Beginning cash balance	$1,000	$1,000	$1,000	$1,000	$1,000	$1,000
Ending cash balance	150	1,050	1,150	0	(700)	3,250
Minimum cash balance	1,000	1,000	1,000	1,000	1,000	1,000
New borrowing (repayment)	$850	($50)	($150)	$1,000	$1,700	($2,250)
Cumulative borrowings	$850	$800	$650	$1,650	$3,350	$1,100

debt? Based on such analysis, we can then determine the safety margin to be maintained in cash balances.

To illustrate once again the tradeoff between risk and profitability in this context, we return to the example in Table 24-4. Cumulative borrowings amounting to $3,350 are anticipated by November, with substantial repayments of $2,250 projected for December. Assume that a short-term loan with the bank has been arranged based on these figures. If actual sales in September then exceed forecasts, the firm may take this as an indication of a good season and commit itself to increased purchases in October, thus requiring additional funds. Should November sales then prove disappointing, the firm may sit on unsold inventory and find itself unable to meet previously contracted loan repayments, with a liquidity crisis the consequence. To protect itself against just such a contingency, the firm could have arranged for more liberal borrowings in the first place, but only at a higher cost. Although risk is thereby reduced, this is achieved at a price. If results actually deviate in the reverse direction, with cash requirements below those projected, the firm would incur unnecessary costs and reduce its profitability.

While models have been developed in an attempt to quantify such tradeoffs, they are largely of academic interest.[2] In practice, the optimal cash balances to be held are largely determined by resort to subjective judgment, essentially because information which would allow a meaningful quantification of risk in a statistical manner tends to be unavailable. Empirical evidence would suggest that cash balances which businesses hold, based on transactions and precautionary motives, appear to increase more than proportionally with sales.[3]

24-5. INVESTMENTS IN MARKETABLE SECURITIES

A firm's financial officer should consider putting excess cash balances to work by investing in securities which offer some returns. Cash balances may be built up to meet tax or dividend payments due on specific dates, or the balances may simply arise temporarily in the ordinary course of business. Firms should invest such periodic balances in short-term securities, a variety of which are available and were reviewed in the chapter covering short-term sources of funds. Shorter-term investments in money market instruments generally involve very limited risk and are quite liquid, allowing for rapid conversion into cash at a fair market price should the need arise. Factors to be aware of when investing temporary cash balances include the following

- The amounts to be invested and/or the period over which the funds are available to be invested should be sufficiently large to cover transaction costs and to justify the managerial time required to arrange and oversee such investments
- In the choice of securities you must deal with the typical risk *versus* expected return tradeoff
- The balance between holdings of cash and marketable securities needs to be determined.

We will briefly discuss each of these in turn.

Investment of temporary surplus cash is of limited interest to small businesses, simply because typical balances are of a size such that the opportunity costs of the management attention required, and the actual transaction costs of buying and selling securities would likely exceed the returns to be realized. Consequently, a small business may have a savings account or the likes, realizing some modest return on excess balances, but is unlikely to be involved in managing a portfolio of money market instruments. On the other hand, periodic cash buildups in large firms may warrant attention, even if they are only available for a few days. Thus, given an effective return of 8 percent per annum on short-term paper, and the availability of $1,000,000 for just 10 days, a gross return of approximately $2,192 could be realized. This may be more than enough to cover

[2]See, for example, W. Baumol, "The Transactions Demand for Cash: An Inventory Theoretic Approach", *The Quarterly Journal of Economics*, November, 1952, pp. 545-556; M. Miller and D. Orr, "A Model of the Demand for Money by Firms", *The Quarterly Journal of Economics*, August, 1966, pp. 413-435; and S. Archer, "A Model for the Determination of Firm Cash Balances", *Journal of Financial and Quantitative Analysis*, March, 1966, pp. 1-11.

[3]E. Whalen, "A Cross-Section Study of Business Demand for Cash", *Journal of Finance*, September, 1965, pp. 423-443.

transaction costs, and even the net return would justify a phone call to arrange the investment. With recent increases in the general level of interest rates, such investments have become comparatively more attractive, and an increasing number of firms have begun to take a more active approach towards the management of excess cash. Expressed another way, given higher rates of inflation, the opportunity cost of holding idle cash balances has increased, with such balances losing purchasing power over time. Investment in instruments which yield returns represents an attempt to protect against such erosion. Many larger firms have added staff specialists to the finance department to oversee the management of cash, with the productive investment of excess balances as their major function. Typically, we find in larger firms that these specialists have earned their salaries several times over.

Individuals charged with investing the firm's surplus cash face the typical risk and expected return tradeoff when selecting the particular securities. Risks to be reckoned with when investing in debt instruments include the risk of default, interest rate risk, and the risk of not being able to convert the security into cash at a fair market price should the need arise prior to maturity—which we may term the risk of liquidity. If investments in securities which are denominated in foreign currencies are contemplated, foreign exchange risk will also have to be reckoned with. For example, the effective yield on a certain type of commercial paper may exceed the yield available on treasury bills by 0.3 or 0.4 percent, which on an investment of $1,000,000 would amount to a difference of $3,000 to $4,000 per year. On the other hand, there is no risk of default on treasury bills, which are also more liquid, giving the firm a better chance to receive a fair market price if it has to liquidate the investment on short notice. The importance of the risk of liquidity will in part depend on the predictability of the firm's anticipated cash flows. Ideally, the maturity of the debt could be tailored exactly to the anticipated period of investment. Concerns about liquidity only become relevant where projected cash flows do not quite materialize, with the invested cash required sooner than was anticipated. If under such circumstances, securities have to be liquidated at depressed prices, this can more than offset any interest which was earned over the investment period. On the other hand, a larger portfolio committed entirely to treasury bills or demand paper is likely to be more liquid than necessary with income being sacrificed as a consequence. Referring back to the various purposes for which cash or near cash may be held, it is useful to divide portfolio holdings into

- Instruments convertible into cash on demand which are used for general liquidity purposes
- Securities maturing on or near specific payment dates, relating, for example, to taxes, dividend payments, or capital expenditures, and
- Longer-term notes for general reserve purposes.

In the absence of transaction costs, the financial manager's strategy should essentially be one of keeping the firm's cash flows close to zero by investing net cash flows which are positive, and selling off security holdings to cover negative net cash flows. Thus, the split between cash and marketable securities is basically determined by transaction costs which, as we have discussed, makes it impractical to make small adjustments to investment holdings on a continuous basis. It follows that investments must be limited to circumstances where it is expected that returns will exceed transactions and management costs.

24-6. SUMMARY

Cash management is of critical importance to most companies in that it determines the liquidity of the firm. In many cases, the immediate cause for insolvency can be attributable to inadequate cash planning.

Cash, which in the context of this chapter was often broadly defined as encompassing such "near cash" as marketable securities and even unused short-term borrowing capacity, may be held for various reasons. Economists have identified the transactions motive, the precautionary motive, the speculative motive, and the finance motive. Given that these motives may be superimposed on each other in a fairly complex way, it was impossible to determine universal rules on the proportion of assets which a firm should maintain in cash. Instead, this chapter reviewed some general principles and techniques which are useful in attempting to arrive at solutions for a variety of specific situations.

The flow of funds in a business can be depicted as a circular movement. Funds are committed to the expenses of operations, to the purchase of fixed assets, and to various governmental agencies. As sales are generated and accounts receivable collected, the funds flow back to replenish the pool. Of significance are the time lags involved in such flows, requiring the firm to undertake investments in inventories and accounts receivable.

A cash budget is a detailed plan laying out projected cash inflows and outflows for a number of periods. The cumulative net flow determines the cash balances which will be held, or if it is negative, the amount of borrowing which will have to take place. The basis for the forecast of cash flows is the forecast of sales or revenues, from which other expenses or incomes are then derived. The basic time period in the cash budget should be small enough to allow for the detection of cyclical or seasonal peaks which may exceed average requirements significantly. Even carefully prepared cash budgets represent nothing more than best estimates. Hence, contingency plans may have to be included in case anticipated developments do not fully materialize. Furthermore, cash budgets should be updated continuously.

Excess balances of cash may be invested temporarily in marketable securities in order to realize a return. Such anticipated returns will have to exceed transaction and management costs, making it impractical to invest lesser amounts for short periods of time. In the selection of marketable securities, the firm's financial officer has to be aware of the tradeoff between risk and return.

Questions for Discussion

1. What are the major motives for holding cash? Which of these do you think are most important for a manufacturing enterprise? In what types of business would you expect the speculative motive for holding cash to be significant?
2. Is the amount of capital cost allowances taken of relevance in preparing the cash budget? Discuss.

3. How can a firm shorten the time lags involved in the typical flows of funds as discussed in this chapter? What are the tradeoffs in contemplating such actions?
4. What are the main determinants influencing the decision of how far into the future a cash budget should be projected and the basic periods into which the cash budget is to be broken down? In this regard, if you were managing a firm, on what would you base your decisions?
5. Why do banks often require the submission of a cash budget as part of a loan application? Would the cash budget be more useful in evaluating the application for a short-term or longer-term loan? Discuss.
6. Define the term liquidity from the point of view of a firm investing in marketable securities. In this context, what are some of the factors which influence the liquidity of a particular type of security?
7. What are some of the risks which an investor faces when he invests in debt instruments? From the point of view of a firm investing temporary short-term cash, which of these risks are typically of greatest concern?

Problems with Solutions

1. (a) Given the following information for Christmas Cracker Corp., prepare a monthly cash budget for the coming fiscal year which starts July 1.

Christmas Cracker Corp. is the name given to a subsidiary of Party Stuff Inc., which for 9 months of each year manufactures novelties for the Christmas trade. The corporation owns no assets except for the $75,000 retained earnings from other years which are lent to the parent corporation for the idle 3 months of the year, interest free, but which are available as cash at the beginning of the season in July. Christmas Cracker has access to funds from Party Stuff, and for purposes of budget forecasting interest is charged at an annual rate of 7% on the average amount of loan outstanding for whatever time a loan is needed. Interest is paid at the end of the season.

Sales forecasts for the coming season are as follows:

July	$ 6,000
August	50,000
September	400,000
October	600,000
November	500,000
December	200,000
January	6,000

Accounts receivable are generally collected 10% cash, 40% after 30 days, and 50% after 60 days. Cost of goods sold, which is 80% of selling price, are incurred in the month in which the sale is made, and are paid 30% cash and 70% within 30 days. Selling and administrative expenses are $10,000 per month, plus 1% of monthly sales during the selling season, and are zero in months where there are no sales. The minimum cash which Christmas Cracker feels it is necessary to have on hand during the selling season is $25,000, and startup costs in July are $30,000. Taxes are paid in April and are 40% of net income.

(b) Calculate net income. Remember Christmas Cracker has no assets to depreciate.

(c) Prepare the cash budget on a quarterly basis. Comment on any inadequacies of such a quarterly budget as compared to the monthly budget.

Solution

(a) The first step in the preparation of the cash budget is to calculate the amount and timing of all receipts and expenditures. These are calculated on page 678.

Next we calculate sales and administrative expenses as $10,000 plus 1% of sales for the period July-January:

July	$10,060
August	$10,500
September	$14,000
October	$16,000
November	$15,000
December	$12,000
January	$10,060

We may now prepare the monthly cash budget using this information and information supplied in the question—see page 678.

(b)

Cash on hand at the end of March	$309,780
Cash on hand at beginning of July	75,000
Earnings before interest and taxes	$234,780
Interest*	3,184
Earnings before tax	$231,596
Tax	92,638
Net income for period	$138,958

*Interest is taken on the average amount over the total time a loan was outstanding. Thus,

$$\frac{9{,}360 + 84{,}360 + 223{,}360 + 204{,}360 + 24{,}360 \times 7\% \times 5/12}{5} = \$3{,}184$$

Due to taxes, there is a further cash outflow of $92,638 in April, plus payment of $3,184 in interest.

(c) The quarterly budget is prepared quite simply by combining the figures from the monthly budget prepared in item (a) of this question.

	Jul	Aug	Sep	Oct	Nov	Dec	Jan	Feb	Mar
Sales	$ 6,000	$ 50,000	$400,000	$600,000	$500,000	$200,000	$ 6,000	$ —	$ —
Receipts from sales: cash (10%)	600	5,000	40,000	60,000	50,000	20,000	600	—	—
net 30 (40%)	—	2,400	20,000	160,000	240,000	200,000	80,000	2,400	—
net 60 (50%)	—	—	3,000	25,000	200,000	300,000	250,000	100,000	3,000
Total collections	$ 600	$ 7,400	$ 63,000	$245,000	$490,000	$520,000	$330,600	$102,400	$ 3,000
Total cost of goods sold	$ 4,800	$ 40,000	$320,000	$480,000	$400,000	$160,000	$ 4,800	$ —	$ —
Cash payment (30%)	1,440	12,000	96,000	144,000	120,000	48,000	1,440	—	—
30 days payment (70%)	—	3,360	28,000	224,000	336,000	280,000	112,000	3,360	—
Total payment	$ 1,440	$ 15,360	$124,000	$368,000	$456,000	$328,000	$113,440	$ 3,360	$ —

Christmas Cracker Corp.
Monthly Cash Budgets

	Jul	Aug	Sep	Oct	Nov	Dec	Jan	Feb	Mar
Opening cash balance	$ 75,000	$ 34,100	$ 15,640	($ 59,360)	($198,360)	($179,360)	$ 640	$207,740	$306,780
Cash collections	600	7,400	63,000	245,000	490,000	520,000	330,600	102,400	3,000
Total	$ 75,600	$ 41,500	$ 78,640	$185,640	$291,640	$340,640	$331,240	$310,140	$309,780
Less: expenditures on cost of goods sold	$ 1,440	$ 15,360	$124,000	$368,000	$456,000	$328,000	$113,440	3,360	
sales and administrative expenses	10,060	10,500	14,000	16,000	15,000	12,000	10.060	—	
startup cost	30,000	—	—	—	—	—	—	—	
Total	$ 41,500	$ 25,860	$138,000	$384,000	$471,000	$340,000	$123,500	$ 3,360	
Balance at end of month	$ 34,100	$ 15,640	($ 59,360)	($198,360)	($179,360)	$ 640	$207,740	$306,780	
Less: desired level of cash	$ 25,000	$ 25,000	$ 25,000	$ 25,000	$ 25,000	$ 25,000	$ 25,000	—	
Loan outstanding	—	$ 9,360	$ 84,360	$223,360	$204,360	$ 24,360	—	—	

	Jul-Sep	Oct-Dec	Jan-Mar
Opening cash balance	$ 75,000	($ 59,360)	$ 640
Cash collections	71,000	1,255,000	436,000
Total	$146,000	$1,195,640	$436,640
Less: expenditures on cost of goods sold	$140,800	$1,152,000	$116,800
sales and administrative expenses	34,560	43,000	10,060
startup cost	30,000	—	—
Total	$205,360	$1,195,000	$126,860
Balance at end of quarter	($ 59,360)	$ 640	$309,780
Less: desired level of cash	25,000	25,000	
Loan outstanding	$ 84,360	$ 24,360	

Note that according to this quarterly budget, the maximum loan outstanding is shown as $84,360. From the monthly budget under item (a), we saw that at the end of October, the loan outstanding amounts to well over twice this amount, or $223,360. We see that temporary peaks may be concealed where budget information is aggregated into longer time periods.

Additional Problems

1. For 1976, the SL Company provides the following accounting information:

Net operating income	$50,000
Depreciation on equipment and building	12,000
Sale of land	20,000
Purchase of equipment	25,000
Retirement of long-term debt	15,000
Dividends declared	15,000

   (a) Which of the above are sources of funds?
   (b) Which of the above are uses of funds?
   (c) What is the increase (or decrease) in working capital?

2. Prepare a monthly cash budget for Student Services Incorporated, for the period January—April inclusive. The firm acts as a wholesaler to the various student retail shops which operate on campuses throughout Canada. They supply clothing, records, and confectionery items. They have a $75,000 line of operating credit with a local bank and they draw on their account in amounts of $5,000 at a time. In your budget, show if bank borrowing will be required and, if so, what amount. Also show the total loan outstanding at the

end of each month. As at December 31, the firm had a cash balance of $7,000.

Actual Sales		Forecasted Sales	
October	$100,000	January	$100,000
November	75,000	February	50,000
December	50,000	March	30,000
		April	100,000
		May	70,000
		June	70,000

Accounts Receivable: Terms are net 30 days. From past experience 60% of the accounts are collected the next month, 30% more within 60 days and 10% within 90 days. Bad debts are negligible.
Accounts Payable: Accounts are paid promptly with cash.
Cost of Goods Sold: 90% of sales. The goods have to be ordered 30 days before the month in which they are sold.
Administrative Expense: $3,000 per month plus a bonus of 4% of gross sales made the last quarter of the calendar year. The bonus is to be paid in February of each year.
Dividends: A $5,000 dividend will be paid in March.
Taxes: Calculated at 40% rate. $2,000 in deferred taxes for the past year must be paid by January 15, and no other taxes are payable in the period January to April.
No capital expenditures are planned.
Salaries: Paid to the labor force: 15% of the dollar sales of the month or $10,000 whichever is greater.
Round all figures to the nearest $1,000 and round any figures which are exactly in the middle of the range to the higher figure.

3. Using the data as outlined in problem 2, prepare a pro forma income statement for the first 4 months of the calendar year for Student Services Inc. The following additional information is also available. The plant from which the company operates is 5 years old and cost $600,000 to construct. The equipment was purchased at the same time at a cost of $120,000. The plant has a remaining life of 20 years while the equipment's remaining life is 5 years. The depreciation is calculated on a straight-line basis and there is no expected salvage value.
   The inventory which is produced is not shipped to the retailers until the month after it is purchased. All goods which are produced are shipped. There is no excess inventory.
4. Given the information developed in problems 2 and 3, prepare a pro forma balance sheet for Student Services Inc. as at April 30. Provide a detailed breakdown of the equity section of the balance sheet. The following information is also available to you.
   (i) There is a 5% mortgage on the building and the equipment. The amount outstanding as at December 31 was $425,000. Principal payments of $25,000 are due semi-annually on June 30 and December 31.

(ii) As at December 31, there were 20,000 shares of capital stock with a par value of $5 outstanding. The stock was only sold at par value and all of it has been fully paid for.

(iii) As at December 31, there was a balance of $137,000 in retained earnings.

5. Prepare a cash budget for Carly Corp. for August, September, and October, given the following information. As of July 31, the firm had a balance of $40,000 in cash, which is the amount which Carly considers the minimum balance to have on hand at all times.
Fifty percent of sales are for cash with the remaining sales collected equally in the following 2 months. Bad debts are negligible.

Actual Sales		Forecasted Sales	
April	$100,000	August	$140,000
May	$100,000	September	$160,000
June	$120,000	October	$200,000
July	$120,000	November	$200,000

Manufacturing costs are 70% of sales, with 90% of this cost paid during the first month after incurrence and the remaining 10% paid in the second month. Depreciation charges amount to $30,000, $32,000, and $36,000 for August, September, and October respectively. Sales and administration expense is $20,000 per month plus 10% of monthly sales. All of these expenses are paid in the month incurred. A semi-annual interest payment of $18,000 on bonds outstanding (6% coupon) is paid during October. A $100,000 sinking fund payment must also be made in October, along with a $20,000 dividend payment and a $2,000 income tax payment. Finally, the firm plans to invest $80,000 in plant and equipment in September.

(a) Based on the above information, what is the cumulative borrowing of the firm in August, September, and October?

(b) Suppose August receipts from sales come in uniformly during the month (assume a 30-day month); but payments for cost of goods manufactured and sales and administrative expenses are made on the 12th day of the month. Calculate the effect of this on the cash budget for August as you prepared it under part (a), and comment on the validity of the cash budget in (a) under these assumptions.

Selected References

S. Archer, "A Model for the Determination of Firm Cash Balances", *Journal of Financial and Quantitative Analysis*, March, 1966, pp. 1-11.

W. Baumol, "The Transactions Demand for Cash: An Inventory Theoretic Approach", *Quarterly Journal of Economics*, November, 1952, pp. 545-556.

H. Bierman and A. McAdams, *Management Decisions for Cash and Marketable Securities*, Ithaca: Cornell Graduate School of Business and Public Administration, 1962.

K. Brunner and A. Meltzer, "Economics of Scale in Cash Balances Reconsidered", *Quarterly Journal of Economics*, August, 1967, pp. 422-436.

P. Frost, "Banking Services, Minimum Cash Balances and the Firm's Demand for Money", *Journal of Finance*, December, 1970, pp. 1029-1039.

D. Jacobs, "The Marketable Security Portfolios of Nonfinancial Corporations: Investment Practices and Trends", *Journal of Finance*, September, 1960, pp. 341-352.

M. Miller and D. Orr, "A Model of the Demand for Money by Firms", *Quarterly Journal of Economics*, August 1966, pp. 413-435.

M. Miller and D. Orr, "The Demand for Money by Firms: Extension of Analytic Results",*Journal of Finance*, December, 1968, pp. 735-759.

E. Neave, "The Stochastic Cash-Balance Problem with Fixed Costs for Increases and Decreases", *Management Science*, March, 1970, pp. 472-490.

Y. Orgler, *Cash Management*, Belmont: Wadsworth Publishing, 1970.

W. Reed, Jr., "Cash: The Hidden Asset", *Financial Executive*, November, 1970, pp. 54-63.

P. Smith, *Economics of Financial Institutions and Markets*, Homewood: Richard Irwin, 1971, Chapter 4.

C. Sprenkle, "The Uselessness of Transactions Demand Models", *Journal of Finance*, December 1969, pp. 835-848.

E. Whalen, "A Cross-Section Study of Business Demand for Cash", *Journal of Finance*, September, 1965, pp. 423-443.

Chapter 25
The Management of Accounts Receivable

25-1. INTRODUCTION

Accounts receivable are amounts which customers owe. They result from the granting of trade credit by the firm for the purchase of its goods or services in the ordinary course of business. The management of such accounts receivable is a subject which is often not accorded the attention it deserves. For many firms, cash sales are the exception and receivables resulting from credit sales may comprise a significant fraction of total assets. This is the case, for example, in our wholesaling and construction industries where the size of the investment in receivables would warrant careful and continuing scrutiny by financial executives. Like most other assets, accounts receivable represent an investment which ties up scarce funds. For example, where goods are shipped with payment only required 60 days after delivery, the selling firm provides financing of such goods during the credit period. Such investments in receivables are made in order to stimulate sales and ultimately, to enhance the firm's profitability. Yet, beyond some particular level, the costs of granting additional credit may exceed any potential benefits and additional investments in accounts receivable will prove unproductive. The management of accounts receivable essentially is concerned with trading off the costs of granting credit against the benefits to be derived, and is an attempt to formulate an optimal credit policy in this context.

What represents an account receivable for the selling firm is the purchaser's account payable or trade credit. In this sense, study of the management of receivables and review of the management of trade credit are concerned with many of the same variables, albeit from opposite points of view. This particular chapter will deal with the credit analysis of individual accounts, the setting of overall credit policies, collection policies and procedures, the use of credit insurance, the evaluation of receivables management, and captive finance companies. As will be shown, these topics are closely interrelated and an arbitrary division of the topics has been made only for purposes of presentation.

25-2. CREDIT ANALYSIS OF INDIVIDUAL ACCOUNTS

The purpose of credit analysis is to assess the credit worthiness of a potential customer and the corresponding risk of default on his payments. Such credit analysis consists of three basic steps, namely (i) gathering of the necessary information concerning the potential customer, (ii) analysis of the information obtained to determine credit worthiness, and (iii) making the final credit decision which will establish the terms of payment and the maximum amount of trade credit to be granted.

Gathering credit information

There are several sources of information available for purposes of credit investigation and the subsequent classification of prospective customers. The particular ones to be used will depend, among other things, on the projected size of the new account, past experience with the customer and the amount of data available directly, the time required to secure information, and the costs involved. Obviously, a significant order from a new account with potential for further development will warrant assembling more comprehensive credit data despite the higher costs than a smaller routine order. Two important sources of information are the Dun and Bradstreet Ratings and the more comprehensive Dun and Bradstreet Reports, with similar data available from other mercantile agencies. Both the credit ratings and the comprehensive reports are prepared by reporters and correspondents working out of district offices. Such people are actually investigators who call on businesses or use questionnaires to gather financial data, analyze the firm's operations, its managerial efficiency, competitive position, and the likes. Outside information is also sought, especially from creditors including the firm's current suppliers. On the basis of these inputs the business is rated and conclusions are condensed into symbols as shown in Figure 25-1. In the ratings, *financial strength* refers to tangible net worth (tangible assets, excluding things such as goodwill, minus all liabilities), while *composite credit appraisal* encompasses the more subjective evaluation of managerial ability, business prospects, and past treatment of creditors.

A sample of the more comprehensive report is reproduced in the Appendix to this chapter. It typically includes a summary of the rating, details of maximum credit obtained from key suppliers, promptness of payments made, banking background, history of the company, and some insight into operations. A simplified balance sheet and earnings statement are also included. In the payments section which is reproduced in Figure 25-2, "HC" refers to the highest credit granted by that particular supplier during the past year; "Disc" indicates that the customer has been taking discounts; and "Ppt" means payments have been prompt. Also included are amounts still owed, past due, and the credit terms.

Although some financial statements are supplied with the Dun and Bradstreet reports, a current set of statements including projections may also be requested directly from the customer. Responses to such requests will, of course, vary, but suppliers are increasingly prepared to link unwillingness with financial inadequacy. Current statements and interim reports can provide more detailed and up-to-date information than would generally be available from Dun and Bradstreet reports.

Banks typically are capable and willing to assist their major clients with the gathering of credit information, occasionally on a confidential basis. Further, the company's own historical experience with the account must not be overlooked. This is an extremely useful source, as improved or deteriorating trends and seasonal patterns of payment can readily be spotted. Besides tapping its own records on a customer, the firm could seek information from other companies with whom the client has had dealings. Such exchanges of credit data are rather commonplace.

FIGURE 25-1

New Dun & Bradstreet Ratings

Dun & Bradstreet announces a new credit rating system.

Effective May 1, 1971, D&B®'s credit ratings on 3 million U.S. and Canadian businesses were converted to a new Rating Key.

New Key to Ratings (Effective May 1st)

Estimated Financial Strength			Composite Credit Appraisal			
			HIGH	GOOD	FAIR	LIMITED
5A	Over	$50,000,000	1	2	3	4
4A	$10,000,000 to	50,000,000	1	2	3	4
3A	1,000,000 to	10,000,000	1	2	3	4
2A	750,000 to	1,000,000	1	2	3	4
1A	500,000 to	750,000	1	2	3	4
BA	300,000 to	500,000	1	2	3	4
BB	200,000 to	300,000	1	2	3	4
CB	125,000 to	200,000	1	2	3	4
CC	75,000 to	125,000	1	2	3	4
DC	50,000 to	75,000	1	2	3	4
DD	35,000 to	50,000	1	2	3	4
EE	20,000 to	35,000	1	2	3	4
FF	10,000 to	20,000	1	2	3	4
GG	5,000 to	10,000	1	2	3	4
HH	Up to	5,000	1	2	3	4

Former Key to Ratings

Estimated Financial Strength			Composite Credit Appraisal			
			HIGH	GOOD	FAIR	LIMITED
AA	Over	$1,000,000	A1	1	1½	2
A+	$750,000 to	1,000,000	A1	1	1½	2
A	500,000 to	750,000	A1	1	1½	2
B+	300,000 to	500,000	1	1½	2	2½
B	200,000 to	300,000	1	1½	2	2½
C+	125,000 to	200,000	1	1½	2	2½
C	75,000 to	125,000	1½	2	2½	3
D+	50,000 to	75,000	1½	2	2½	3
D	35,000 to	50,000	1½	2	2½	3
E	20,000 to	35,000	2	2½	3	3½
F	10,000 to	20,000	2½	3	3½	4
G	5,000 to	10,000	3	3½	4	4½
H	3,000 to	5,000	3	3½	4	4½
J	Up to	3,000	3	3½	4	4½

Finally, mention must be made of such miscellaneous sources of credit material as the better business bureaus, trade associations, national credit associations, and specialized credit bureaus. In certain situations they can prove to be extremely helpful.

It should be clear that the gathering of comprehensive information will entail time delays and costs. Thus, the costs of such investigations have to be weighed against their potential benefits, which include some reduction in the risk of bad debt, and a proper balance must be found.

FIGURE 25-2
Business Information Report

Dun & Bradstreet BUSINESS INFORMATION REPORT RATING UNCHANGED

SIC	D-U-N-S	©DUN & BRADSTREET	STARTED	RATING
34 61	04-426-3226 ARNOLD METAL PRODUCTS CO	CD 34 APR 7 19-- METAL STAMPINGS	1957	DD 1 (D 1½)

53 S. MAIN ST.
TORONTO 2 ONT
TEL: 416 925-6218

SAMUEL B. ARNOLD)
GEORGE T. ARNOLD) PARTNERS

SUMMARY

PAYMENTS	DISC PPT
SALES	$177,250
WORTH	$42,961
EMPLOYS	8
RECORD	CLEAR
CONDITION	STRONG
TREND	UP

PAYMENTS

HC	OWE	P DUE	TERMS	APR 1 19--	SOLD
3000	1500		1 10 30	Disc	Over 3 yrs
2500	1000		1 10 30	Disc	Over 3 yrs
2000	500		2 20 30	Disc	Over 3 yrs
1000			30	Ppt	Over 3 yrs
500			30	Ppt	Over 3 yrs

FINANCE

On Apr 7 19-- S.B. Arnold, partner, submitted statement Dec 31 19--

Cash	$ 4,870	Accts Pay	$ 6,121
Accts Rec	15,472	Notes Pay (Curr)	2,400
Mdse	14,619	Accruals	3,583
Current	34,961	Current	12,104
Fixed Assets	22,840	Notes Pay (Def)	5,000
Other Assets	2,264	NET WORTH	42,961
Total Assets	60,065	Total	60,065

19-- sales $177,250; gross profit $47,821; net profit $4,204. Fire insurance mdse $15,000; fixed assets $20,000. Annual rent $3,000. Signed Apr 7 19-- ARNOLD METAL PRODUCTS CO by Samuel B. Arnold, partner Johnson & Singer, C.A.'s, Toronto.

-----0-----

Sales and profits increased last year due to increased sub-contract work and this trend is reported continuing. New equipment was purchased last Sept for $8,000 financed by a bank loan secured by a lien on the equipment payable $200 per month. With increased capacity, the business has been able to handle a larger volume. Arnold stated that for the first two months of this year volume was $32,075 and operations continue profitable.

BANKING

Medium to high four figure balances are maintained locally. An equipment loan is outstanding and being retired as agreed.

HISTORY

Style registered Feb 1 1965 by partners. SAMUEL, born 1918, married. 1939 graduated Queens University with B.S. degree in Mechanical Engineering. 1939-50 employed by Industrial Machine Limited, Toronto. 1950-56 production manager with Aerial Motors Ltd., Toronto. Started this business in 1957. GEORGE, born 1940, single, son of Samuel. Graduated in 1963 from Ryerson Polytechnical Institute. Served RCAF 1963-64. Admitted to partnership interest Feb 1965.

OPERATION

Manufactures light metal stampings for industrial concerns and also does some work on a sub-contract basis for aircraft manufacturers. Terms net 30. 12 accounts. Five production, two office employees, and one salesman. LOCATION: Rents one-storey cinder block building with 5,000 square feet located in industrial section in normal condition. Housekeeping is good.
4-8 (802 92)

Analyzing credit data

Once available data concerning a potential customer has been gathered, it must be analyzed so that a credit decision can be reached. Where a large number of accounts are involved, point systems have been devised wherein particular numerical values are assigned for specific characteristics and the applicant's total score can serve at least as a rough screen in determining the credit decision.[1] More commonly however, credit decisions are made on the basis of judgment. On occasion, the credit decision may be partially a function of factors other than the applicant's character, collateral, or capacity. For instance, a marginal customer's request for credit may be accepted when the firm is operating significantly below capacity, though the identical order would have been turned away during normal or peak times.

In general, the evaluation of credit data is geared toward establishing the applicant's liquidity and, in turn, his ability to pay bills over the shorter run. Ratio analysis, employing some of the techniques described in Chapter 22, such as the current and acid test ratios, is often performed by credit managers when financial statements are available. Data received from other sources, as discussed above, will also be included in the evaluation. Obviously, financial ability and responsible behavior towards creditors need not be synonymous.

The final outcome of the credit analysis would be the establishment of a particular credit classification for the account. If the analysis has been properly prepared, this should indicate the probabilities of slow payments or default associated with the account.

The credit decision

The actual decision to accept or reject an applicant and to establish limits on the maximum amount of trade credit to be granted is a matter of matching the analysis of the potential customer with the overall credit policies of the firm. The decision to reject an application for credit may not only entail the loss of the current order, but also of any future orders which might have been placed had the original one been accepted. Assessing the magnitude of this loss may be extremely difficult as various assumptions about the size and number of future orders and about the customer's future paying habits will have to be made. On the other hand, if the decision to accept an applicant proved incorrect the net loss would be the amount of bad debts, less the value of past profits which the firm realized on that customer's account to date.

25-3. CREDIT POLICIES

As we have seen, a firm's overall credit and collections policy is mainly determined by the tradeoff between higher profits from increased sales on the one hand and the costs of having large accounts receivable and additional bad debt losses on the other. This section will set out approaches for the evaluation of

[1] J. Myers and E. Forgy, "The Development of Numerical Credit Evaluation Systems", *Journal of the American Statistical Association*, September, 1963, pp. 799-806.

credit policies in light of the tradeoffs they pose for the financial officer. The particular policy variables to be considered include length of the credit period, quality of the credit standards, and size of the cash discount offered to customers.

Length of credit period

As noted in the chapter on trade credit, selling terms of "2/10, net 30" indicate that a customer is given a two percent discount if the bill is paid within ten days of the invoice date. Failure to pay by the tenth day requires the full amount to be paid within thirty days of the date of invoice. Hence, with terms of "2/10, net 30" the discount period is ten days and the total credit period thirty days. Although industry practice often determines the credit terms, there is little reason for the terms not to be considered a competitive tool.

To evaluate the suitability of lengthening the credit period, the financial officer must be in a position to judge the reaction of competitors and to estimate the profitability of added sales, the increase in volume of receivables, and the increase in bad debt losses as a consequence of such a move. The increased profits from added sales must be weighed against both the increased costs as outlined, and against the cash flow implications. A sudden increase in accounts receivable resulting from slower payments will represent a drain on the firm's cash position, and this effect needs to be reckoned with in the firm's cash budget.

Example

To illustrate the basic framework for an analysis of this type, consider a particular product characterized as follows:

current selling price	$5 per unit
current annual sales	360,000 units
current terms of sale	net 30
average cost per unit	$4.50

The firm considers an extention of its credit period to 60 days, with the proposed new terms of sale becoming net 60. Allowing for the reaction of competitors, such an alteration in credit terms is expected to produce the following results:

sales are expected to increase to 420,000 units
bad debt losses are expected to increase by $6,000 per year
the marginal cost per unit for the increased number of units to be produced would be $3 per unit

The firm's tax rate is 40 percent, and its required minimum rate of return on investments is 15 percent after tax. Given these data, how do we decide whether or not the credit period should be extended from the current 30 days to the proposed 60 days?

We first compute the increase in after-tax profits resulting from the increase in sales.

Increase in sales 60,000 units × $5		$300,000
Marginal cost of increased sales:		
60,000 units × $3	$180,000	
Increase in bad debts	$ 6,000	
	$186,000	$186,000
Before-tax profit from additional sales		$114,000
After-tax profit: $114,000 (1 – 0.4)		$68,400

This incremental profit must be weighed against the cost of having higher investments in accounts receivable. Assuming all customers pay at the end of the credit period granted, the amount of receivables outstanding will increase from 1 month's sales (30 days) to 2 months' sales (60 days), or in dollar amounts from

sales per month at old level = 360,000 × $5 × 1/12 = $150,000

to

sales for 2 months at new level = 420,000 × $5 × 2/12 = $350,000

Thus, the increased investment required by the firm to finance its growth in receivables would be computed as $350,000 – $150,000 = $200,000.

To achieve an annual return of 15 percent on this investment, annual profits would have to increase by 0.15 × $200,000 = $30,000. With annual after-tax profits expected to increase by $68,400 as calculated above, the firm should proceed and implement the proposed extension of the credit period to 60 days. Even if sales do not increase to 420,000 units per year as anticipated, the firm has a wide safety margin because the anticipated increase in profits ($68,400) far exceeds the minimum required ($30,000).

Speeding up collections through curtailment of the credit period can be evaluated in a similar fashion. The greatest practical difficulties in carrying out such evaluations do not lie in the basic approach, but in having to estimate the various consequences of altering the credit terms, such as effects on sales, bad debts, production costs, and competitive reaction. Many of these estimates will be nothing more than educated guesses. This makes it important to carry out some sort of sensitivity analysis in order to assess how vulnerable the ultimate conclusion is with regard to changes in the various forecasted values.

The Quality of credit standards

A change in the credit standards employed by the firm may also influence the level of sales, as a lowering of credit standards will result in the acceptance of additional accounts, but of a lesser quality. As already discussed, the increased sales potential has to be viewed against costs such as increased losses from bad debts and additional collection costs. Furthermore, since acceptance of lower quality accounts may imply slower collections on receivables, some increase in accounts receivable must also be anticipated.

The evaluation of alternative credit standards can be handled in a manner similar to that outlined above for evaluating alterations in the credit period. As long as anticipated net profits on the additional sales exceed losses from bad debts, increased collection costs, and the required returns on the incremental investment in receivables, consideration should be given to the lowering of standards.

The cash discount

The same basic framework of analysis can be applied to assess any cash discounts to be offered to customers. As we saw in the chapter dealing with trade credit, some discount on the selling price is commonly offered if payment is made at an early date. The purpose of granting such discounts is to provide an incentive for early payments, as this reduces the firm's investment in accounts receivable. On the other hand, such discounts clearly reduce the profit to be made on a sale. Again, policies regarding cash discounts should be evaluated by weighing reductions in revenues which result from discounts being taken, against the benefits of having lower investments in receivables.

Example

Consider a firm offering a 2 percent discount if payment is made within 10 days from the receipt of the invoice, with the full amount due within 30 days (terms of 2/10, net 30). Current sales are 600,000 units per year with a selling price of $5 per unit. Average per unit costs amount to 90 percent of the selling price, or $4.50 per unit. On 70 percent of the sales, cash discounts are currently taken with payments received on the 10th day after the sale. For the remaining 30 percent of sales, payment is received after 30 days. The firm's tax rate is 40 percent and its required rate of return on investments is 15 percent after tax. The firm is considering the elimination of cash discounts and wants to evaluate this alternative. We assume that the total volume of sales would not be affected by such a move, and compute annual after-tax profits with the current policy:

$$\begin{aligned}\text{Annual after-tax profit} &= (\text{annual sales} \times (\text{unit selling price} - \text{unit costs}) \\ &\quad - \text{discounts given})\ (1 - \text{tax rate}) \\ &= (600{,}000(\$5 - \$4.50) - 0.7 \times 0.02 \times 600{,}000 \times \$5)\ (1 - 0.4) \\ &= (300{,}000 - 42{,}000) \times 0.6 \\ &= \$154{,}800\end{aligned}$$

Under the new policy, discounts amounting to $42,000 (2 percent of 70 percent of annual sales) would be eliminated, increasing before-tax profits by that amount. After-tax profits become $300,000 × 0.6 = $180,000, resulting in an increase in after-tax profits of $180,000 – $154,800 = $25,200. Under the new policy, we assume that all payments are made 30 days after receipt of invoice. Thus, the 70 percent of sales on which discounts were previously taken will be outstanding for an additional (30 − 10) = 20 days. We have:

daily sales = (600,000 × \$5)/365 = \$8,220

daily sales on which discounts are currently taken = 70% × \$8,220
= \$5,754

increase in receivables if discounts are eliminated = 20 days of credit sales = 20 × \$5,754 = \$115,080

This increased investment in receivables of \$115,080 has to be viewed against an annual increase in after-tax profits of \$25,200, providing an annual return of \$25,200/\$115,080 = 21.90 percent. From these figures, discontinuation of the cash discount seems like an attractive proposition which merits active consideration. On the other hand, customers who up to now have availed themselves of the cash discount may view their elimination as an indirect price increase, and some of them may react by investigating alternative sources of supply. Before a final decision is made, the assumption that sales would remain unaffected by an elimination of discounts needs to be considered, and any potentially negative reactions by customers have to be assessed and included in the analysis.

25-4. COLLECTION POLICIES

The collection procedures where accounts become overdue comprise one of the more sensitive areas of supplier-customer relations. The objective in establishing collection procedures is to maintain a balance between being overly aggressive on the one hand and too relaxed on the other. Should a customer become irritated with the collection efforts used, he may well transfer his business elsewhere. This can be tolerated only if the lost customer is, in fact, a poor account. Where payment problems are of a temporary nature, the potential for future sales and profits should not be ignored.

In addition to interest being charged on overdue accounts, collection procedures typically followed by firms consist of a series of steps which gradually increase the pressure on a customer. The initial step may involve sending a standardized letter or reminder that the account is past due. This is usually done within a few days after the due date and may be followed by a telephone call from the credit department. Failure to produce results will prompt a final letter and the collection department may even send a representative to call on the client. The last step may involve either legal action or turning the account over to a collection agency. Both of these are costly alternatives, and fees to be paid to collection agencies can approach fifty percent of any amounts eventually collected.

The amount of time and money spent on collection efforts is a function of the size of the account and the likelihood of collecting. A company certainly should not spend $300 to collect a $250 account. It may not even be worthwhile to spend the identical amount in attempting to collect $1,000 if the customer is known to be close to bankruptcy and simply does not have the cash to pay. Organizations such as banks and sales finance companies, however, are sometimes willing to spend more on their collection efforts than the actual sum to be collected. Such institutions cannot afford to even hint at a willingness to write off bad accounts, as such a policy might result in increased abuses by other customers who would withhold payments in the hope of being written off.

25-5. CREDIT INSURANCE

Where receivables include a limited number of larger accounts, credit insurance can be extremely useful: default by any one of these more important customers could have serious financial consequences for the uninsured creditor. Credit insurance is designed to indemnify a business firm for *unexpected* losses caused by the insolvency of its customers. When purchasing such insurance, however, you should be careful not to overlook limitations and exclusions which may apply to the coverage afforded. For instance, under most insurance contracts the amount recoverable for losses from any single account is limited on the basis of ratings by agencies such as Dun and Bradstreet. This provision aims at curtailing careless credit extensions by the insured once the insurance protection is purchased. Furthermore, the normal loss experience which a particular firm has come to anticipate may be excluded from coverage. Another limit on recovery will be set out in a so-called *coinsurance clause* or participation stipulation which requires the insured to bear a percentage of any loss incurred. In practice, the magnitude of the participation ranges from 10 to 33⅓ percent of the loss. This provides a further incentive to suppliers to perform responsible credit screenings of potential customers.

We note that credit insurance will generally neither be suitable nor available to retailers since their business typically involves a very large number of relatively small accounts. By adequately screening its numerous credit customers and limiting each to relatively modest balances owing, the retailer can typically maintain low average credit losses and absorb them as a normal cost of doing business. Furthermore, the use of credit cards like Chargex may provide insurance against bad debt in that it shifts the risk of bad accounts to the bank which sponsors the credit card.

The decision on whether to purchase credit insurance depends upon several factors including the financial strength of the firm and, hence, its ability to absorb bad-debt losses. The coverage obviously comes at a cost and like most other insurance, it should only be purchased where unexpected losses can be of a magnitude which would severely affect the financial well-being of the firm.

25-6. THE USE OF CREDIT CARDS IN RETAILING

A retailer's management of his accounts receivable can be influenced significantly by his decision to accept a general credit card such as Chargex or

Mastercharge. These credit cards are sponsored and administered by the major Canadian banks. Their acceptance automatically provides the retailer with a variety of services, and in return he has to pay to the bank a percentage of his credit sales. This percentage is individually negotiated and typically ranges between 2 and 6 percent. By honoring credit cards and limiting all other sales to cash, a retailer may be able to avoid having to make credit investigations and decisions of his own, since, as mentioned earlier, the risk of losses from bad debts is generally shifted to the sponsoring bank. By depositing his credit card slips from sales with the bank, the retailer immediately receives cash and avoids having to finance receivables. Individual invoicing and collection procedures are also obviated. In reaching a decision on whether or not to honor a particular credit card, such benefits will have to be weighed against the costs with the outcome depending on the particular circumstances facing the retailer involved. For example, a business operating on a small margin and competing mainly on price may find the costs of an extra few percent of sales to be prohibitive, and may be forced to sell mainly on a cash basis. On the other hand, where some proportion of sales is caused by impulse-buying and markups are considerable, such as in the merchandising of fashion goods, the benefits provided by acceptance of a widely held credit card may well exceed its costs.

Some large retailers find it advantageous to retain the credit function within their own organization, administering credit through their own credit card. Some of the larger and better known department stores not only have their own credit cards, but refuse to accept any other more general ones. Not only does this give them more complete marketing information about their credit sales and credit customers, but the term-financing of receivables, which may be quite a profitable operation, is retained by the firm. For example, if interest on overdue balances is charged at a rate of 18 or 20 percent, handsome returns may be implied in the granting of credit.

25-7. RECEIVABLES AND EXPORT CREDITS INSURANCE

Receivables relating to exports are frequently denominated in foreign currencies thereby introducing additional risks through foreign exchange exposure. To illustrate the problems more clearly, a receivable denominated in pounds sterling, given its weak position in foreign exchange markets, is unlikely to have the same future value in Canadian dollar terms as one denominated in Swiss francs, even though they were equivalent at the time of the sale. In such situations, considerable care and attention must be expended in managing the receivables and techniques such as forward exchange or other hedging will be used. These approaches to the management of foreign exchange risks were explored in the chapter on short-term sources of funds, and will be reviewed in the chapter dealing with working capital management.

Foreign exchange exposure aside, in managing its accounts receivable an exporting firm cannot ignore the credit arrangements it will be expected to provide so as to meet foreign competition from large state-supported organizations or multinational firms. Quite obviously, however, only the largest

Canadian companies can cope with credit risks unique to marketing abroad and do so unassisted. This circumstance was well described in a recent address by the Chairman and President of the *Export Development Corporation* in which he stated that:

> . . . financial aspects of export marketing pose different business problems than those encountered domestically. The commercial credit risks vary with and are complicated by the remoteness of geography and the differences of culture, language, legal systems, and business practice; all too often compounded by a scarcity of reliable information. These differences are further overlaid with the imponderables of political risks which bear heavily on foreign exchange availability. Finally, the competitive environment is very different, and all too often more ruthless, thereby frequently establishing a buyer's market for the foreign customer to choose amongst competing offers.[2]

The Export Development Corporation, a Crown corporation, has done much to develop export trade and foreign investments, and to facilitate the work of financial officers attempting to manage accounts receivable. As part of its wide-ranging activities, the EDC will insure Canadian firms against nonpayment when Canadian goods and services are sold abroad. Included under such Export Credits Insurance are transactions involving consumer goods sold on short-term credit to a maximum of 180 days. Risks covered include insolvency of the buyer or failure to pay, war or revolution in the buyer's country, blockage of funds and other newly imposed restrictions. As at December 31, 1975, 726 million dollars of sales pertaining to consumer goods and services alone were insured through over 750 policies. The total volume of export credits insurance underwritten exceeded 910 million dollars.

In the case of capital goods, where sellers might ordinarily have to contemplate offering intermediate term credit in order to compete for the business, the EDC also plays a vital role. Not only does it grant loans (usually of at least five-years duration) to foreign buyers of Canadian capital equipment and technical services, but it guarantees any losses incurred by financial institutions making direct loans to such buyers. During 1975, 40 loan agreements totalling 1,135 million dollars were signed by EDC.[3]

25-8. EVALUATION OF ACCOUNTS RECEIVABLE MANAGEMENT

Evaluating the efficiency with which accounts receivable are managed is a difficult task at best. No simple measures or techniques are available which are universally applicable. The turnover of receivables or the average collection period are frequently used as aggregate indicators of credit-granting procedures, credit policies, and collection procedures. For instance, a decrease in the receivables turnover may be attributable to improper decisions in granting credit (stemming perhaps from a lack of valid data or incorrect analysis), overly lenient credit policies, and/or ineffective collection efforts. Pinpointing the exact cause

[2] J. MacDonald, "Financial Aspects of Selling to Export Markets", an address before the Marketing Conference of the Conference Board of Canada, Toronto, April 22, 1976.

[3] Export Development Corporation, *1975 Annual Report*, for all statistics reported.

for deteriorating performance indicators requires good managerial judgment.

25-9. CAPTIVE FINANCE COMPANIES

Manufacturing concerns producing such high-cost equipment as consumer durables and machinery have on occasion established financing subsidiaries known as captive finance companies. Their purpose is to provide customers with term-financing in the purchase of the firm's products. Examples of such parent firms include Simpson-Sears, The T. Eaton Co., Ltd., Canadian General Electric, Avco Delta Corp., and General Motors. In most cases, the parent company sells its products on a time contract, and then in turn this financing contract is sold to its subsidiary which collects the periodic payments.

The basic reasoning behind the use of captive finance companies appears to be the belief that it affords a lower cost of carrying the receivables. The assets of the finance subsidiary basically consist of financing contracts which provide for very predictable cash flows through the periodic payments made by customers. The subsidiary can borrow against these receivables and generally such finance subsidiaries rely on a much greater proportion of debt financing than could the parent company. As a consequence, the cost of capital to the organization may be reduced.[4] Whether or not this argument is borne out can be questioned. In selling its receivables to its subsidiary, the parent company loses some of its better current assets. Consequently, the parent corporation's debt capacity is probably reduced, and a mere transfer of debt capacity from parent to subsidiary takes place.

25-10. INFLATION AND INVESTMENTS IN ACCOUNTS RECEIVABLE

Discussions above showed how changes in a firm's credit decisions can affect the magnitude of outstanding accounts receivable. Such increased investments in receivables pose two problems:

- funds have to be made available to finance such expanded levels of current assets, and,
- these investments should yield an adequate return as reflected in growing sales and increased profitability.

Even with constant credit terms and policies, a firm's investment in receivables will change in proportion to its volume of credit sales. Given an inflationary environment characterized by price level increases, dollar sales expand considerably faster than indicated by any real growth which may characterize a business. Consider a firm with annual sales of $12,000,000 and an average collection period of one month. Investment in receivables is computed as $12,000,000/12 = $1,000,000. If, due to price level changes, sales increase by 50 percent to $18,000,000, receivables will grow to $1,500,000. This implies that the firm will have to find an additional $500,000 to finance the increase. If we remember that during past years policies of tight money were repeatedly pursued by governments to combat inflation while some industries faced eroding profit margins,

[4]The approach set out is essentially that of V. Andrews, "Captive Finance Companies", *Harvard Business Review*, July-August, 1964, pp. 80-92.

we can understand the challenges which such developments have presented to financial executives. We can also see that a firm's management of accounts receivable and determination of credit policies is not established once and for all, but has to be reviewed constantly in the light of changing economic conditions. Faced with a scarcity of funds and ever-expanding levels of accounts receivable, some firms have found in necessary to reappraise and to tighten their credit and collection policies.

25-11. SUMMARY

Accounts receivable represent a significant investment for most firms. Given our inflationary environment, investments in receivables have increased in proportion to growing dollar sales and such investments may represent a significant drain on the firm's scarce funds. Essentially, the management of accounts receivable is concerned with determining a level of investment which is commensurate with the returns which can be expected from such investment. Returns from investments in accounts receivable are realized through increased sales with consequently increased profitability. The level of investment in accounts receivable, apart from being a function of the level of sales, is determined by the credit decisions and policies of the firm, specifically by the length of the credit period, the rigor of credit standards, any cash discounts being offered, and collection policies.

In analyzing individual accounts, credit information is available from a variety of sources, including firms such as Dun and Bradstreet, credit bureaus, banks, a customer's other suppliers, and finally from the customers themselves. The information gathered needs to be analyzed to arrive at a decision. The ultimate decision will reflect the tradeoff between the benefits from anticipated sales and the costs of carrying the account, including risks of bad debt. This same tradeoff dominates the formulation of a firm's overall credit policy. Several numerical examples were provided illustrating how such tradeoffs can be quantified and how specific decisions can be reached. The most difficult aspect of such analysis is to assess the effects of altered credit policies on sales, and to estimate bad debts. Sensitivity analysis regarding these key forecasts is therefore indicated.

Credit insurance warrants consideration where acounts are large and where a customer's default can cause serious financial difficulties for the supplying firm. In retailing, acceptance of general credit cards sponsored by banks not only provides insurance against losses from bad debts, but a variety of other services as well. These are paid for through a percentage of credit sales which is charged by the bank. Where a firm is actively involved in exports, government agencies may provide assistance by assuming some of the risks occasioned by such receivables.

Captive finance companies are wholly owned subsidiaries which are typically set up by firms producing high-cost equipment in industries where sales involving extended credit are customary. Such captive finance companies are largely financed through debt which they issue against their receivables.

Questions for Discussion

1. What basic steps should be taken in a credit analysis of individual accounts? What are the major sources from which credit information can be gathered?
2. It has been said that credit terms should be extended until marginal revenues from increased sales equal the marginal costs of extended credit terms. What are some of the operational difficulties in implementing this rule?
3. What are the major factors which a firm should consider before making a decision to lengthen or shorten the credit period? Why do you think the particular factors are important?
4. (a) In what ways might a change in credit standards employed by the firm affect the profit level of the firm?
   (b) "In normal cases we would expect all firms to take advantage of the cash discounts offered." Do you agree? Why?
5. Why might an organization be willing to spend more on its collection costs than the actual amount to be collected?
6. How does a credit insurer make certain that the insured is prudent when extending credit?
7. What is the rationale behind setting up a captive finance company?

Problem with Solution

1. (a) A firm is currently selling on a cash basis only. The firm is contemplating offering credit terms of net 30 in order to stimulate sales. Current sales are $6,000,000 per year. If the proposal to offer credit terms of net 30 were implemented, a credit department would have to be established at a monthly operating cost of $2,000. It is expected that all customers will take full advantage of the credit period offered. Losses due to bad debt are estimated at 1½% of credit sales. Additional investments in accounts receivable would be financed by drawing more heavily on a line of credit with the bank. The bank currently charges 12% interest on outstanding balances. The firm's tax rate is 40%. Cost of goods sold amounts to 60% of the selling price, with variable operating expenses at 25% of sales. By how much would sales have to increase to make the proposed change in credit policy worthwhile?
   (b) In addition to offering credit terms, the firm considers offering a cash discount to customers who make payments within 10 days of receipt of the invoice. If a discount of 1% is offered, it is expected that the discount would be taken on 30% of all sales. If the amount of the discount is increased to 2%, it is expected that the discount would be taken on 80% of all sales. Should the firm offer a cash discount, and if it does, should the cash discount be 1% or 2%? Assume that the total sales are not affected by the offering of a cash discount.

Solution

(a) Current sales of $6,000,000 yield a profit margin of 15%, or $900,000, when cost of goods sold (60% of selling price) and variable operating expenses (25% of sales) are deducted. Therefore, for the credit policy to be worthwhile sales must increase to cover all credit expenses and still leave at least $900,000 before-tax profit.

Costs of implementing the credit policy may be determined as follows:

- Cost of operating credit department
  $2,000 per month × 12 months = $24,000 per year
- Losses from uncollectible accounts
  1½% of credit sales, or 0.015 × sales.
- Financing expense on accounts receivable. Given terms of net 30, and assuming all collections occur at the end of this period, 30 days of sales, or 30/365 of annual sales, will be outstanding as receivables. Given interest of 12%, the total financing expense is 12% × 30/365 of sales, or .00986 sales.

We know the 15% profit margin on the new sales level, less $24,000 operating costs, .015 sales loss from uncollectible accounts, and .00986 loss from financing expense must yield at least $900,000.

Putting this into numerical form, we solve for sales, where x = sales

$$.15x - .015x - .00986x - 24{,}000 = 900{,}000$$

$$0.12514x = 924{,}000$$

$$x = 7{,}383{,}730$$

Thus, sales must increase to $7,383,730 for the proposed change in credit policy to be worthwhile.

(b) Cost of implementing the 1% discount credit policy may be determined as follows:

- Cost of operating credit department
  $2,000 per month × 12 months = $24,000 per year
- Losses from uncollectible accounts
  Again, 1½% of credit sales are lost to bad debt, but in this case, credit sales are only 70% of total sales with only this amount subject to losses from bad debt
  1½% of credit sales × 70% sales = .0105 sales
- Financing expense on accounts receivable
  70% of sales will again be outstanding for 30/365 of the year, but the other 30% will be outstanding for only 10/365 of the year
  (70% sales × 30/365 year × 12% cost of debt) + (30% sales × 10/365 year × 12% cost of debt) = .0079 sales.

- Cost of credit discount
  1% of the sales price will be lost on 30% of sales, or .003 sales.
  In numerical form, where x = sales

$$.15x - .0105x - .0079x - .003x - 24{,}000 = 900{,}000$$
$$x = 7{,}185{,}070$$

Sales would have to increase to $7,185,070 for this policy to produce profits which are as high as those currently realized. Costs of implementing the 2% discount credit policy may be determined in a very similar way. In abbreviated fashion, costs would be:

- cost of operating credit department = $24,000
- losses from uncollectible accounts = 1½% of credit sales × 20% sales
  = .003 sales
- Financing expense on accounts receivable
  (20% sales × 30/365 year × 12% cost of debt) + (80% sales × 10/365 year × 12% cost of debt) = .0046 sales
- Cost of credit discount
  2% of the sales price is lost on 80% of the merchandise, or .016 sales.
  Hence,

$$.15x - .003x - .0046x - .016x - 24{,}000 = 900{,}000$$
$$x = 7{,}310{,}127$$

From the above figures, it is apparent the firm should offer the 1% discount if a credit policy is to be introduced, as the breakeven level for sales is lowest under this alternative.

Note that all calculations are based on before-tax figures. The results do not change if after-tax figures are used throughout, as all costs and benefits are multiplied by the same factor of 0.6 to derive after-tax figures.

Additional Problems

1. Taran Ltd. is reviewing its trade credit policy. Currently Taran offers terms of 1/10 net 60 on its selling price of $20 per unit. Production costs (including variable overhead) for a range of 600,000 to 900,000 units are $17/unit, with current sales at 800,000 units per year. Accounts receivable are financed through an account at the bank, which charges 13% interest. 40% of the units sold are paid for within ten days, and 1½% of the 60% of sales on which the cash discount is not taken have to be written off as bad debts.

   Taran is considering implementing a tighter credit policy with terms of net 30. If this policy were put into effect sales are expected to drop to 750,000 units, but it is felt that bad-debt expense would only amount to a flat $50,000 per year. If Taran's tax rate is 45%, should the proposed change in credit policy be implemented?

2. (a) The Imperial Socket Company has a subsidiary plant in Brazil. At present, the subsidiary offers its customers terms of 2/10, net 45. The Brazilian operation has been under considerable pressure to extend the terms granted to its customers in order to meet credit terms granted by competitors. After an appraisal of the situation, the company believes that the demand for its product is relatively price-inelastic. A proposal by the Brazilian executive states that prices could be increased by 10% if terms of 1/30, n/90 were offered with overall sales unaffected by these changes. At present, 75% of the customers take advantage of the full credit period offered. The balance takes advantage of any discounts offered. These proportions are expected to remain the same if the new credit terms were implemented. Credit sales average $200,000 per month. Local bank financing is available at 20% per annum (before-tax). All receivables are financed through the local bank. Assume all sales are made on the same day each month. The proposed price increase could not be imposed on cash sales. Past experience has shown that ½% of gross credit sales is written off each month as uncollectible. The corporate tax rate is 40%. Should the company introduce the proposal suggested by the Brazilian executive?

   (b) Are there other factors to be considered by the company before introducing such a change in policy?

3. At present, the Chocolate Cookie Company's products sell at $3 a unit with monthly sales of 50,000 units. Half of all sales are for cash, while the remainder are at net 30. The present average cost per unit is $2, while the marginal cost for the next 10,000 units per month is expected to be $1.50 per unit. If the credit terms are altered to 2/10, 1/30, net 60, sales are expected to increase by 3,000 units per month. It is assumed that 30% of future sales will be paid for within 10 days, 30% within 30 days, and the balance within the terms prescribed. Based on past experience, uncollectible accounts amount to 1% of gross credit sales. It is assumed that they will remain at 1% of any sales not paid after 10 days. The corporate tax rate is 50%. The company's required rate of return on investments is 7½% after tax. Should the firm alter its credit terms to purchasers of its products as indicated?

Selected References

V. Andrews, "Captive Finance Companies", *Harvard Business Review*, July-August, 1964, pp. 80-94.

W. Beranek, *Analysis for Financial Decisions*, Homewood: Richard D. Irwin, 1963, Chapter 10.

P. Davey, *Managing Trade Receivables*, New York: The Conference Board, 1972.

P. Davis, "Marginal Analysis of Credit Sales", *Accounting Review*, January, 1966, pp. 121-166.

Dun and Bradstreet, *Ten Keys to Basic Credits and Collections*, New York, 1973.

M. Greene, *Risk and Insurance*, (2nd ed.), Cincinnati: South-Western Publishing Co., 1968, Chapter 18.

C. Greer, "The Optimal Credit Acceptance Policy", *Journal of Financial and Quantitative Analysis*, December, 1967, pp. 399-415.

R. Kaplan, "Credit Risks and Opportunities", *Harvard Business Review*, March-April, 1967, pp. 83-88.

W. Lewellen, "Finance Subsidiaries and Corporate Borrowing Capacity", *Financial Management*, Spring, 1972, pp. 21-31.

W. Lewellen and J. Johnson, "Better Ways to Monitor Accounts Receivable", *Harvard Business Review*, May-June, 1972, pp. 101-109.

J. Mao and C. Sarndal, "Controlling Risk in Accounts Receivable Management", *Journal of Business Finance and Accounting*, Autumn, 1974, pp. 395-403.

F. Marrah, "Managing Receivables", *Financial Executive*, July, 1970, pp. 40-44.

D. Mehta, "The Formulation of Credit Policy Models", *Management Science*, October, 1968, pp. 30-50.

J. Myers and E. Forgy, "The Development of Numerical Credit Evaluation Systems", *Journal of the American Statistical Association*, September, 1963, pp. 799-806.

D. Smith, "Efficient Credit Management with Time Sharing", *Financial Executive*, March, 1971, pp. 26-30.

P. Smith, "Measuring Risk on Consumer Credit", *Management Science*, November, 1964, pp. 327-340.

R. Soldofsky, "A Model for Accounts Receivable Management", *N.A.A. Bulletin*, January, 1966, pp. 55-58.

D. Wrightsman, "Optimal Credit Terms for Accounts Receivable", *Quarterly Review of Economics and Business*, Summer, 1969, pp. 59-66.

CHAPTER 25: APPENDIX

DUN & BRADSTREET ANALYTICAL REPORT

PLEASE NOTE WHETHER NAME, BUSINESS AND STREET ADDRESS CORRESPOND WITH YOUR INQUIRY.

Dun & Bradstreet ANALYTICAL REPORT RATING UNCHANGED

SIC	D-U-N-S	© DUN & BRADSTREET	STARTED	RATING
36x51 36 32 36 34 36 79	10-001-1234 STAR RADIO & TELEVISION LTD (Subsidiary of Star Radio & Television Inc., New York City, N.Y.)	A-AD 34 SEP 18 19-- MFRS TV & RADIO RECEIVING SETS, REFRIDGERATORS, DE-HUMIDIFIERS & ELECTRONIC TUBE PARTS	1950	3A1 Also Branches

100 FIRST ST
TORONTO 128 ONT
TEL 416 999-1234

E.T. WRIGHT, PRES & CHIEF EXEC

SPECIMEN REPORT

SUMMARY

PAYMENTS	DISC PPT
SALES	$30,516,390
WORTH	$12,734,920
EMPLOYS	654 (920 here)
RECORD	CLEAR
CONDITION	STRONG
TREND	UP

PAYMENTS

HC	OWE	P DUE	TERMS	SEP 12 19--	SOLD
150000	75000		1 30	Disc	Over 3 yrs
70000	20000		1½ 30	Disc	Over 3 yrs
40000			1 10	Disc	Over 3 yrs
12000	6000		1 30	Disc	Over 3 yrs
104000	48000		30	Ppt	Over 3 yrs
66400	35600		30	Ppt	Over 3 yrs
41300			30	Ppt	Over 3 yrs
20500	1600		30	Ppt	Over 3 yrs
9300	9300		30	Ppt	Over 3 yrs
5000			30	Ppt	Over 3 yrs

HIGHLIGHTS

	DEC 19--	DEC 19--
Cash	$ 3,789,110	$ 3,994,176
Curr Liabs	3,550,575	3,807,614
Worth	10,854,847	11,306,492
Net Sales	26,774,115	30,516,390
Net Profit	792,876	927,047

19-- was the fourteenth consecutive year in which new records were achieved for both sales and earnings.

The financial structure of the company is very strong, with debt at all times at least well supported by cash balances alone. Trade dealings throughout the years have been most favourable, and activities conducted without outside assistance.

CURRENT September 15, 19--, E.T. Wright, President, submitted the following figures:

(CONTINUED)

SPECIMEN REPORT

STAR RADIO & TELEVISION LTD
TORONTO 2 ONT

A AD Page 2
9-18-7-

CURRENT

Statement of Consolidated Income for Six Months ended June 30:

	19--	19--
Sales	$ 14,350,884	$ 15,209,826
Cost of goods sold including selling general & administrative expenses	13,684,930	14,447,197
Operating Income	665,954	762,629
Income from investments	3,437	3,437
	669,391	766,066
Depreciation	96,565	82,000
Interest on indebtedness	2,625	2,625
	99,190	84,625
Net Income before taxes	570,201	681,441
Income taxes	105,000	110,000
Net Income for the period	465,201	571,441

Note: Subject to audit and year-end adjustments.

Statement of Consolidated Source and Application of Funds for Six Months ended June 30

	19--	19--
Source of Funds	$ 465,201	$ 571,441
Depreciation	96,656	82,000
Proceeds from sale of fixed assets	6,000	3,000
	567,857	656,441
Application of Funds	78,124	73,214
Expenditures on fixed assets	66,000	97,000
	144,124	170,214

Management is anticipating sales and profits will continue to move ahead of 19--.

Banking:
Account maintained at the same location since 1950 and dealings have all along been excellent. Balances range at times into moderate seven figure area and no support requested.
9-20-7- (75 7)

STAR RADIO & TELEVISION LTD
TORONTO 2 ONT

A CD Page 1

INDIVIDUAL FINANCIAL STATEMENTS

	DEC 31 19--	DEC 31 19--	DEC 31 19--
CASH	$ 3,175,415	$ 3,789,110	$ 3,994,176
MARKETABLE SECURITIES			
NOTES RECEIVABLE			
ACCOUNTS RECEIVABLE	4,715,662	4,998,712	5,194,216
INVENTORY	5,490,545	5,617,610	5,925,714
OTHER CURRENT ASSETS	-----------	-----------	-----------
TOTAL CURRENT ASSETS	13,381,622	14,405,422	15,114,106
FIXED ASSETS	1,114,780	1,214,694	1,316,214
INVESTMENTS			
PREPAID—DEFERRED	91,550	103,427	112,214
OTHER ASSETS	-----------	-----------	-----------
TOTAL	14,586,952	15,723,543	16,542,534
	===========	===========	===========
DUE BANKS			
NOTES PAYABLE			
ACCOUNTS PAYABLE	2,117,216	2,614,109	2,826,114
ACCRUALS	103,771	102,981	109,973
TAXES (Except Federal Income)	481,819	461,002	453,217
FEDERAL INCOME TAXES	315,010	372,483	418,310
LONG TERM LIABILITIES (Current)			
OTHER CURRENT LIABILITIES	-----------	-----------	-----------
TOTAL CURRENT LIABILITIES	3,017,816	3,550,575	3,807,614
LONG TERM LIABILITIES			
RESERVES			
PREFERRED STOCK	290,000	290,000	290,000
COMMON STOCK	1,000,000	1,000,000	1,000,000
CAPITAL SURPLUS			
EARNED SURPLUS	10,279,136	10,882,968	11,444,920
NET WORTH (Prop or Part)	-----------	-----------	-----------
TOTAL	14,586,952	15,723,543	16,542,534
	===========	===========	===========
NET WORKING CAPITAL	10,363,806	10,854,847	11,306,492
CURRENT RATIO	4.43	4.05	3.97
TANGIBLE NET WORTH	11,569,136	12,172,968	12,734,920
RESERVE FOR BAD DEBTS			
INVENTORY VALUED AT (BASIS)			
RESERVE FOR DEPRECIATION			

(CONTINUED)

STAR RADIO & TELEVISION LTD
TORONTO 2 ONT

A CD Page 2

INCOME STATEMENTS AND SURPLUS OR NET WORTH RECONCILIATIONS

FOR THE YEARS ENDED	DEC 31 19--	DEC 31 19--	DEC 31 19--
NET SALES	$ 23,518,711	$ 26,774,115	$ 30,516,390
COST OF GOODS SOLD			
GROSS PROFIT			
EXPENSES			
DEPRECIATION	127,104	138,104	184,595
NET INCOME ON SALES	1,218,230	1,392,541	2,029,924
OTHER INCOME	49,428	50,990	48,450
OTHER EXPENSES	101,041	105,655	175,827
FEDERAL INCOME TAXES	510,000	545,000	975,500
OTHER TAXES	------------	------------	------------
FINAL NET INCOME	656,617	792,876	927,047
	============	============	============
SURPLUS—NET WORTH—START	9,832,519	10,279,136	10,882,968
ADD: NET INCOME	656,617	792,876	927,047
ADJUSTMENTS			
DEDUCT: NET LOSS			
ADJUSTMENTS	210,000	189,044	365,095
DIVIDENDS-WITHDRAWALS	10,279,136	10,882,968	11,444,920
SURPLUS—NET WORTH—END	============	============	============
IF USED: D=DEFICIT, L=LOSS			

Figures prepared from statements contained in annual report to shareholders. Auditors: Price, Waterhouse & Co., C.A.'s, Toronto.

As at December 31, 19--, accounts receivable less allowance for doubtful accounts of $75,000. Inventory at lower of cost or market. Fixed assets less accumulated depreciation of $1,215,516. Fire insurance on merchandise $5,800,000, on building $1,500,000, on machinery and equipment $1,300,000.

As at December 31, 19--, other income of $48,450 represents amount charged to allowance for doubtful accounts and warranties. Other expenses of $175,827, represent executive remuneration $109,715; amortization of leasehold improvements $47,516; legal fees $18,596.

SUPPLEMENTAL DATA   Notes to Financial Statement as at December 31, 19--:

(1) Certain current assets and current liabilities in foreign currencies were converted at the rate of exchange prevailing at the close of the year.

(2) The minimum annual rentals (exclusive of taxes, insurance and other occupancy charges) under leases for office and warehouse facilities amounted to $151,474.

(3) The company is contingently liable under repurchase agreements, the effect of which, in the opinion of management, it will not materially affect the business of the company.

The following is summarized consolidated statement of the parent as at December 31, 19--:

	DEC 31 19--
Current Assets	$139,548,832
Current Liabilities	90,135,917
Working Capital	49,412,915
Total Assets	201,613,083
Net Worth	86,738,913
Net Sales	414,644,696
Net Profit	10,016,963

(CONTINUED)

STAR RADIO & TELEVISION LTD
TORONTO 2 ONT

A CD Page 4

HISTORY Started: 1924 as a proprietorship by S.R. Wright. Incorporated 1946, control acquired by Star Radio & Television Inc. in 1950.

Incorporated: Under Ontario laws January 7, 1946 as Wright Radio Limited, name amended by Supplementary Letters Patent February 3, 1951.
Authorized Capital Stock: 1,000,000 preference shares, par value $10 each and 1,000,000 common shares no par value.
Outstanding Capital Stock: 290,000 preference shares and 500,000 common shares, the latter at a declared valuation of $1,000,000 as at December 31, 1966.

Control: Held by Star Radio & Television Inc., New York City, N.Y. through ownership of all outstanding common stock with the exception of directors qualifying shares.

OPERATION The parent company Star Radio & Television Inc. has eleven direct and four indirect subsidiaries. This Canadian subsidiary is a direct and wholly owned subsidiary. The parent commenced in 1934 and was incorporated under Delaware laws 1940. It is engaged in producing radio sets, television sets, electric refrigerators, electric ranges and a wide variety of electronic equipment for the military forces. There are no inter-company relations between the various subsidiaries themselves. Merchandise transactions between subject and the parent take place on normal terms with settlement effected promptly.

Products: Star Radio & Television Ltd. manufactures television and radio receiving sets (45%) refrigerators (25%) dehumidifiers (15%) and electronic tube parts (15%). 90% of components manufactures locally with 10% imported.

Distribution: To franchised dealers and chain department stores and retailers.
Territory: Dominion wide. Sales branches maintained in most of the major cities throughout hte country. Exporting to the United Kingdom and western Europe accounts for 20% of volume.
Terms: 2% net 30 days.
Accounts: 2,500.
Seasons: Television and radio peak seasons August to December. The sale of refrigerators and dehumidifiers concentrated in warmer months.
Employees: 654.

Facilities: At 100 First Street, owns and occupies one-storey steel, frame, brick structure, which with recent additions provides 197,000 square feet of floor space. Buildings are in excellent repair and railway siding facilities available. The plant is capable of producing over 100,000 television sets, 75,000 radio sets and 35,000 appliances annually. At Hamilton, Ontario, company operates manufacturing plant in leased one-storey brick structure providing 31,000 square feet of floor space. At Fergus, Ontario and Montreal, Quebec, company leases major warehouses each providing 70,000 square feet of space.

(CONTINUED)

STAR RADIO & TELEVISION LTD
TORONTO 2 ONT

A CD Page 5

SAMUEL R. WRIGHT, CH OF THE BD
JOHN M. GODFREY, Q.C., SEC
DIRECTORS: The officers.

EDWARD T. WRIGHT, PRES
GERALD J. SAMPSON, TREAS

MANAGEMENT BACKGROUND:

SAMUEL R. WRIGHT born 1889, widower. 1924 began radio business on his own account. The business flourished and incorporation followed in 1946. He was President prior to becoming Chairman of the Board in 1963.

EDWARD T. WRIGHT born 1917, married. Is the son of the Chairman of the Board. He has been associated with this organization throughout his business career. Vice President prior to his appointment as President in 1963.

GODFREY, Q.C., is a local practicing solicitor and is legal advisor of the company. He was elected a director in 1952.

SAMPSON born 1906, married. He has been associated with Star Radio & Television Inc. throughout his business career and is President of that company.
9-18-7- (75 7) (40)

Chapter 26
Inventory Management

26-1. INTRODUCTION

For many individual firms, inventories represent a major fraction of current assets, and for the economy as a whole significant resources are committed to inventories. In April, 1975, the inventories held by manufacturers in Canada totalled about 15.2 billion dollars.[1] A more meaningful measure is perhaps provided through Table 26-1 which focuses on the sizable investments in inventories of a sample of better-known Canadian corporations.

TABLE 26-1

Inventories and Total Current Assets
of Selected Corporations, December 1971

Company	Inventory (in millions)	Current Assets (in millions)
Imperial Oil Ltd.	$189	$625
Crown Zellerbach	41	76
International Nickel	465	701

Source: 1971 Annual Reports.

Clearly, considerable importance must be attached to the management of inventories. Our concern in this chapter will be with the presentation of some of the more basic concepts and tradeoffs involved in the management of inventories. Most of the technical aspects of inventory control are, however, beyond the scope of this text and the interested reader is referred to the very extensive specialized literature available in this area.[2]

26-2. SOME FINANCIAL CONSIDERATIONS

While the management and control of inventory are not usually the direct responsibility of the financial officer, he is expected to consult and advise on the matter, as it is his responsibility to provide the necessary funds for the carrying of inventories.[3]

More obvious costs of carrying inventories include the expense of warehousing, handling, insurance, obsolescence, and spoilage. Equally important is the less apparent opportunity cost associated with funds being tied up in inventories. If one million dollars invested in inventories could be used elsewhere in the firm to earn an after-tax ten percent net return per annum, this would

[1]Statistics Canada, *Canadian Statistical Review*, September 1975, p. 66.

[2]For a practical introduction, see for example J. Magee, "Guides to Inventory Policy I, II and III, *Harvard Business Review*, Jan.-Feb. 1956, March-April 1956 and May-June 1956 respectively. A more thorough coverage is provided in J. Buchanan and E. Koenigsberg, *Scientific Inventory Management*, Englewood Cliffs, N.J.: Prentice-Hall, 1963, or A. Veinott, "The States of Mathematical Inventory Theory," *Management Science*, July 1966, pp. 745-777.

[3]See Chapter 1: Appendix.

FIGURE 26-1

Relationship Between Demand, Production, and Inventories

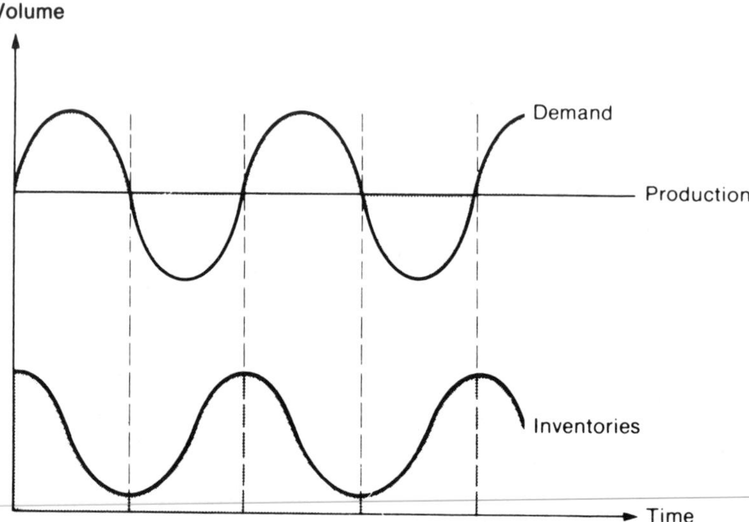

increase the effective annual costs of carrying the inventory by one hundred thousand dollars. Inventory holdings generally withdraw funds from other potentially profitable activities, and the opportunity cost has to be recognized.

The rationale for carrying inventories, despite the costs described, stems from the expectation that such investments will produce a net gain. The actual benefits to be derived are varied and depend on the particular circumstance. Goods-in-process, for example, are necessary in any production process and cannot be avoided. While the amount of such inventories may be reduced by scaling down the process, this may only be possible by incurring higher production expense. Because of fixed setup costs, unit production costs generally increase with any curtailment of the production run. On the other hand, should runs be increased beyond what is immediately required, the excess will represent inventories to be stored for future consumption.

Uncertainties in the demand, production, or order lead times induce business to carry safety-stocks. The benefit of such additional inventories is to reduce stockout costs which would otherwise have to be faced with greater frequency.[4] Finished goods inventories to absorb seasonal demands afford another example of the benefits to be derived from carrying inventories. Such holdings serve to level out production thereby reducing overall production costs. To illustrate, it would be expensive for a production process to have to match the pattern of seasonal demand reflected in Figure 26-1. Underutilized productive capacity

[4]Having a spare-tire for an automobile is analagous to the carrying of safety stocks. The tire serves to avoid stockout costs in case of an unpredictable demand resulting from damage to one of the tires in use. Airlines carrying spare parts for their aircraft represent another quite similar situation. Clearly, the stockout cost in having to wait for a part can be extremely large if a multimillion dollar piece of equipment must be grounded in the meantime.

would exist for much of the year and there would be constant fluctuations in the labor force employed. By making use of inventories, it is possible to satisfy the seasonal demand with a constant production schedule as shown in Figure 26-1; inventories are built up during periods where production exceeds demand and are then used to satisfy peak needs.

Inventory management is concerned with balancing the benefits and the costs of carrying inventories to achieve overall optimal economic results. In principle, this requires the measuring of relevant benefits and costs, and quantification of the tradeoffs. Much of the technical literature on inventory control is concerned with such quantification and we shall briefly discuss some basic models below. Operational difficulties are often encountered in the measurement of the relevant costs and benefits, and it is the rule rather than the exception that the necessary figures are not available from the firm's accounting records. It is, for example, a difficult task at best to quantify the costs of being unable to fill a customer's order because of a stockout (a loss of goodwill, perhaps, to be reflected by some diminution of future orders). The marginal benefits to be derived from increasing the inventory levels for a particular item may be no easier to ascertain. In practice, therefore, various approximations may have to take the place of more exact measurements, thus limiting the precision of inventory control schemes.

Another operational problem often encountered arises from the fact that when it comes to inventories, different operating departments within a firm generally have conflicting interests which can lead to misunderstandings and political frictions. For instance, production and marketing departments are generally interested in seeing higher inventory levels; production personnel because their prime concern is with production schedules and costs which can usually be improved by allowing inventories to expand, and marketing people because their major interest is customer service which implies minimizing the frequency of stockouts. The financial officer, on the other hand, is concerned with the best utilization of scarce funds and is likely to encourage the reduction of inventories so as to free resources for more profitable employment elsewhere. It is clear that good overall decisions can be reached only if each party involved has at least a basic understanding of the more general implications which inventory decisions will cause throughout the firm.

With the growth of interest in applying mathematics to business problems, exemplified by the development of operations research and management science in recent years, quantification of the tradeoffs entailed by inventory decisions has received increased attention to the point where inventory theory has emerged as a standard topic. Though the nature of this text lends itself only to a presentation of the most basic concepts, an understanding of them is useful not only because they provide the groundwork for more advanced techniques, but also because they illustrate an approach to quantifying inventory and similar types of decision.[5]

[5]Most practical inventory control systems tend to rely quite heavily on such basic concepts since many of the more sophisticated models have operational limitations due to measurement and data problems on the input side.

Probably the best known concept of inventory control is the economic order quantity or EOQ. It is directed at finding the order or production quantity which balances acquisition costs on the one hand with the costs of carrying inventories on the other. In particular, if fixed costs, perhaps production setup costs, are incurred with the placement of each order, the question becomes one of establishing the quantity to order, and how often an order should be placed.

In presenting the basic concept, the following notations and simplifying assumptions will be used:

- Q the order quantity in units
- C the variable costs per unit ordered; assumed to be independent of the quantity ordered
- K the fixed costs of placing an order; assumed to be independent of the quantity ordered
- H holding or inventory costs per unit, per period; assumed to be independent of the total number of items carried
- D the demand per period; assumed to be constant over the period and known with certainty.

If one orders Q items at the beginning of a period, the total costs of ordering are $K + QC$. With a constant demand of D, the inventory will be depleted at time $T = Q/D$. As shown in Figure 26-2, the average inventory carried during that period is $Q/2$, which would result in carrying costs of $THQ/2$. Additionally, whenever the inventory level reaches zero, a new order of Q would be placed.[6] The total costs per time-unit for such a policy are given by:

$$C_t = \frac{1}{T}\left(K + CQ + \frac{THQ}{2}\right)$$

and substituting $T = Q/D$

$$C_t = \frac{D}{Q}\left(K + CQ + \frac{HQ^2}{2D}\right)$$

(1) $$C_t = \frac{DK}{Q} + DC + \frac{HQ}{2}$$

Example

Suppose the demand for an item of inventory is constant at 10,000 units per month. Fixed ordering costs reflecting for example clerical and bookkeeping efforts and fixed delivery charges are \$200 per order. The item costs \$10 per unit, and variable storage costs amount to \$1 per unit each month. Assume that in the past the item had been ordered in shipments of Q = 10,000 items at a time.

Following the above notation, we have

D = 10,000 units/month
K = \$200

[6]If there is a known and constant lead time of x days required for filling orders, a new order would be placed x days before T.

$C = \$10$
$H = \$1$
$Q = 10{,}000$ units

We would have computed

time to depletion of inventory: $T = Q/D = 1$ month
average amount of inventory carried: $Q/2 = 5{,}000$ items
inventory carrying costs per month: $THQ/2 = \$5{,}000$
fixed ordering costs per month: $K = \$200$

This results in total costs per month of

$$C_t = \frac{DK}{Q} + DC + \frac{HQ}{2}$$

$$= \$200 + \$100{,}000 + \$5{,}000$$

$$= \$105{,}200$$

FIGURE 26-2

Inventory Levels, Average Inventory, and Order Points

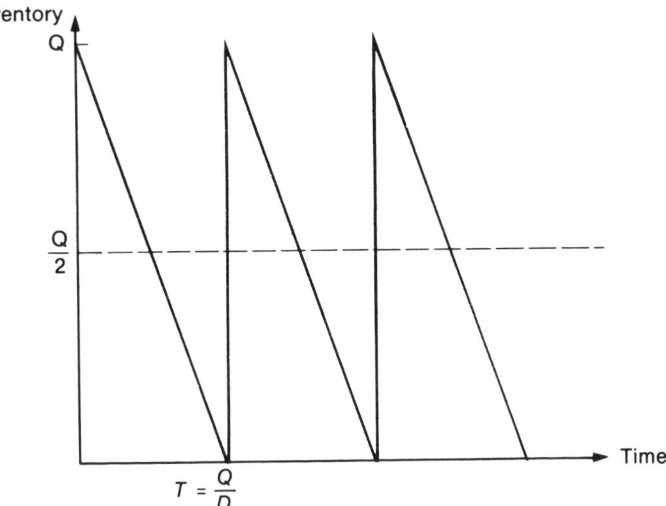

We want to choose an order quantity, Q, so as to minimize this total cost, but conflicts clearly arise. As we decrease Q, the costs of carrying inventory given by the last term in equation (1) are decreased, but this, in turn, increases the frequency with which orders are placed thus increasing the costs of ordering as given by the first term in equation (1). These points are set out graphically in Figure 26-3 along with the total cost curve. Note that the second term in equation (1) is independent of the order quantity, Q, and simply represents the variable costs in ordering goods. The total amount of goods ordered will always match demand, as the frequency of ordering is increased to compensate for decreasing order quantities and vice versa. Therefore, this term is constant, and since it will in no way influence the choice of Q, it can be disregarded in the decision.

FIGURE 26-3

The Economic Order Quantity

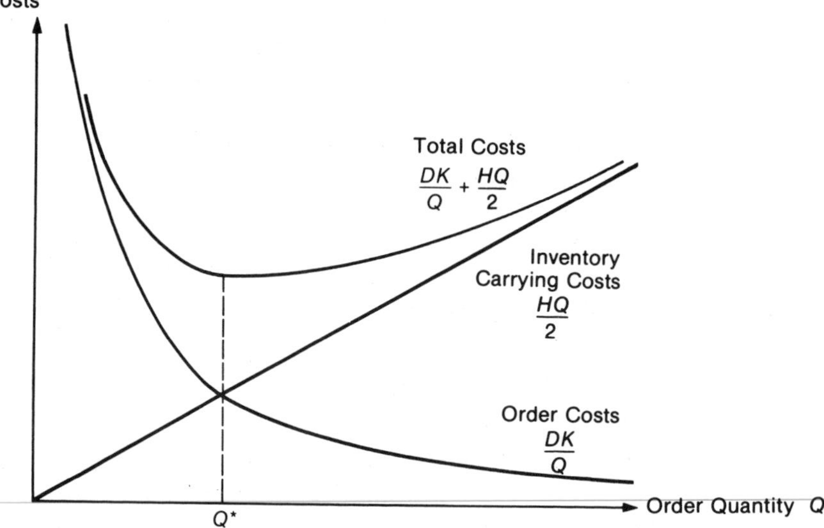

The minimum total cost, and hence the optimal order quantity, can be found by applying calculus, differentiating equation (1) with regard to Q and setting the first derivative equal to zero. We then have:

$$\frac{dC_t}{dQ} = \frac{-DK}{Q^2} + \frac{H}{2}$$

obtaining:

$$Q^2 = \frac{2DK}{H} \text{ by setting } \frac{-DK}{Q^2} + \frac{H}{2} = 0$$

or:

(2) $$Q^* = \sqrt{\frac{2DK}{H}}$$

where Q^* denotes the optimal or economic order quantity which minimizes total costs.[7]

Example

Pursuing the above example, the economic order quantity, using equation (2) becomes :

$$Q^* = \sqrt{\frac{2(10{,}000)\ (200)}{1}} = 2000 \text{ units}$$

[7]The sufficiency condition for a minimum clearly holds, as $\frac{d^2C_t}{dQ^2} = \frac{+2DK}{Q^3} > 0$

At this level, ordering costs have increased, but holding costs are reduced to more than offset this increase, and total costs per month are reduced to

$$C_t = \$1{,}000 + \$100{,}000 + \$1{,}000 = \$102{,}000$$

The assumptions made in developing the above solution may seem overly restrictive and suggest that the model is impractical. While inventory and order decisions made in feeding an assembly line which runs with a constant output rate may reasonably fit the above description, most operational situations are considerably more complex. Uncertainty, in particular, often plays an important role in inventory decisions, for demand is not generally known with certainty while unpredictable delivery dates merely compound the problem. Though modifications to the simple model presented are therefore often necessary, the concept of the economic order quantity is nevertheless fundamentally sound and is an important basic aspect of inventory control which has often been implemented in practice.[8]

When demand is not known with certainty and lead times exist, the above decision rule of placing an order only when inventories are depleted should be modified to consider safety-stocks. As the levels of such stocks are increased, the probability and hence the cost of stockouts are reduced, though at the expense of higher inventory levels and carrying costs. To derive the probabilities of stockouts, we need to know the probabilities for various levels of demand. In many situations we can obtain reasonable approximations by looking at historical demand, while in other circumstances (involving new products for instance) we may have to rely on subjective estimates. The decision rule which emerges from appropriate modifications to the basic economic order quantity model often takes this form: when inventory falls below a critical level termed the order point, *OP*, the economic order quantity should be requisitioned. The implementation of such a procedure is illustrated in Figure 26-4, which typifies many of the inventory control schemes actually used by industry.

It should be noted here that the computer may play a vital role in inventory control schemes. If we consider a fairly common situation where perhaps 25,000 different items are carried in inventory, it would be a formidable and perhaps prohibitively expensive task to routinely forecast demand for each item based on sales of the previous periods, to compute and adjust economic order quantities and order points, and to keep up-to-date records on actual inventory levels based on deliveries and shipments received. Many standard computer programs exist for inventory control applications, and some of these are available from the

[8]In finance, the economic order quantity has also been applied to assist in the management of cash and marketable securities. The inventory item in this context is cash, and there are obvious opportunity costs associated with the holding of cash. The firm's cash balance can be replenished through the sale of marketable securities or through borrowing, with each of these transactions entailing fixed and variable costs. Given a certain demand for cash per period, the frequency of such transactions and average cash balances become a function of magnitude (or "order quantity") of each sale or borrowing. The EOQ formula can be used to determine the optimum magnitude and frequency of transactions. See W. Baumol, "The Transactions Demand for Cash: An Inventory Theoretic Approach," *Quarterly Journal of Economics*, November 1952, pp. 545-556.

FIGURE 26-4

Inventory Control System

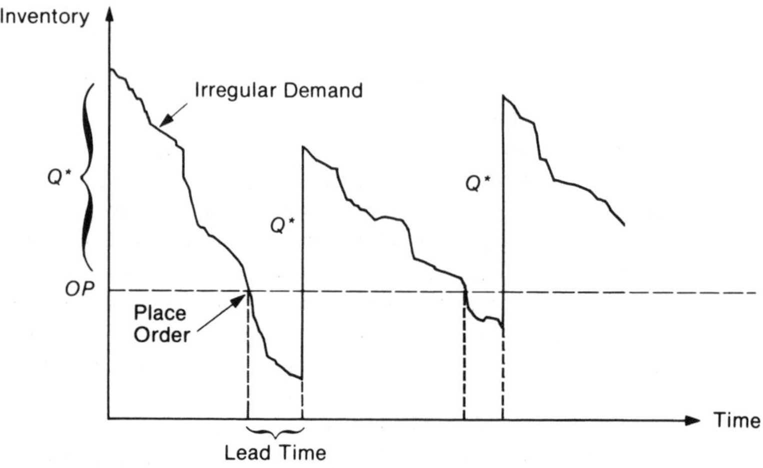

major computer manufacturers. Furthermore, by making use of computers, it may become operationally feasible to integrate inventory, production planning and scheduling, marketing and financial decision-making within the firm. Such integration would obviously improve the overall quality of decisions being taken. Some writers have gone so far as to suggest that one of the greatest potential payoffs from the introduction of computers into business organizations may be in this area of production and inventory control.[9] Through more efficient management, an overall reduction of just ten percent of an inventory amounting to $10,000,000 and an opportunity cost for funds of ten percent would suggest annual savings of $100,000 on the released monies alone, quite apart from the savings in inventory carrying costs.

26-3. THE IMPACT OF INFLATION OF INVENTORIES

With the costs of most items in inventory going up in periods of widespread inflation, a firm will find that it has to commit increasing amounts of cash toward inventories, even though the physical quantity of inventory on hand may remain unchanged. The effect is similar to the one experienced by firms facing rapid real growth in their sales. In either case, the financing of ever-increasing dollar amounts of inventories can represent a serious cash drain on the firm, and this aspect should be explicitly recognized, for example when projecting cash budgets. This phenomenon can also result in artificial changes in a firm's financial statements.[10] For example, where other items on a firm's balance sheet

[9]See, for example, J. Dearden and W. McFarlan, *Management Information Systems*, Homewood: Richard D. Irwin, 1966, p. 53.

[10]Because of such distortions caused by price level changes, accounting based on current values rather than on historical costs is finding an increasing number of advocates. See for example L.S. Rosen, *Current Value Accounting and Price-Level Restatements*, The Canadian Institute of Chartered Accountants, 1972.

(such as fixed assets which are carried at historical costs) are not influenced by inflation, distortions in the relative magnitudes of various asset accounts can occur, with inventories likely representing an increasing portion of the total balance sheet amounts.

Inventory profits which accrue because items held in inventory have gone up in price are a further consequence of inflation. In that case a firm's reported earnings may no longer accurately reflect the profitability of its regular operations but rather profits made from the holding of inventory. Where a sudden major price change occurs in an industry's key commodity, the effects could be dramatic, as illustrated by the earnings which major oil companies reported in periods following massive increases in the price of oil. Compounding the cash problem alluded to earlier is the fact that such inventory profits are subject to regular tax.

Example

> Consider the highly simplified example where an item in inventory was bought some time ago for $1,000 per unit, with the current price having jumped to $2,000 per unit, and the corporate tax rate being 50 percent. On current sales of each unit, the firm realizes a net cash inflow of $1,500 ($2,000 from the sale, minus $500 in taxes on the inventory profit). However, since the item needs to be replaced to stay in business, an outflow of $2,000 per unit for replacement must be incurred.[11]

Thus a sudden increase in price levels can simultaneously result in both inflated earnings figures and cash shortages with the consequent temptation to increase prices to bolster cash inflows from sales revenues. Needless to say, in periods where all sectors of the economy are called on to combat inflation and exercise restraint, situations of this type neither elicit general understanding nor sympathy. This was evidenced after the oil crisis. Nevertheless, inflation has become a general challenge to financial management, on occasion posing serious problems in financing and reporting, with inventories playing a prominent role because of their susceptability to price level changes.[12]

26-4. SUMMARY

Inventories play an important role in business and often amount to a significant portion of the current assets carried by a firm. Apart from the obvious costs of warehousing, insurance, obsolescence, and spoilage, the opportunity costs of tying up funds in inventories need to be recognized. The financial executive is

[11]This problem is aggravated in Canada by the fact that the last-in, first-out (LIFO) method of inventory valuation is currently unacceptable for tax purposes. See for example G.A. Welsch, C.T. Zlatkovich, D.A. Wilson and M. Zin, *Intermediate Accounting* (First Canadian Edition), Irwin Dorsey Ltd., 1974, pp. 328-329. For a general discussion and specific examples of distorted earnings figures caused by price level changes, see for instance C. Hutchins, "Why General Price Level Accounting," *CA Magazine*, September 1975, pp. 29-32, and M.O. Alexander and J.D. Barrington, "A Feasible Method of Current Value Accounting", *CA Magazine*, September, 1975, pp. 33-39.

[12]It is clear that Government has recently come to appreciate the problem. Thus, the March 1977 Federal Budget proposals would permit taxpayers to deduct from business income 3% of inventories on hand at the beginning of the year. Such allowances would be available from fiscal 1977 on.

concerned with the firm's inventory policy as he will have to arrange for funds to be available for the financing of inventories. Funds tied up in inventories are often withdrawn from other activities which the firm may pursue. Efficient inventory management is concerned with balancing the costs and benefits derived from inventories. Difficulties are often encountered in measuring or estimating these relevant variables. Models have been developed to quantify the tradeoffs in inventory decisions, resulting in the widely known concept of the economic order quantity. The basic formula for the economic order quantity was derived, and possible extensions dealing with uncertainty were indicated. In the implementing of inventory control schemes, computers are playing an increasingly important role. Price level changes caused by inflation can have a serious impact on inventories. Inflated earnings from inventory profits will result while at the same time cash shortages may arise due to increased replacement costs.

Questions for Discussion

1. What are some of the conflicts which could arise between the financial manager, the marketing manager, and the production manager regarding the proper inventory levels?
2. Why are inventory levels in many firms subject to strong seasonal fluctuations. Give an example of an industry where you would expect this to be the case. How could a firm in this industry avoid seasonal inventories? What are the tradeoffs?
3. Define the economic order quantity. How can the simple inventory control model be modified to incorporate uncertainties in demand and lead times?
4. What will be the effect on inventory holdings of the following developments:
   (a) greater use of air freight
   (b) greater standardization of parts
   (c) increases in the number of products produced
   (d) a manufacturer of winter sports equipment offers a sizable reduction in prices if orders are placed in June and July. How will the manufacturer be affected?
5. A retailer, handling a line of seasonal goods, finds that she is overstocked. Would she be justified in selling below cost to clean out her remaining stock? Discuss.
6. As the general level of interest rates in the economy goes up, and other things remaining equal, how would you expect general inventory levels to be affected? Discuss.
7. What are the assumptions on which the development of the formula for the economic order quantity is based? Describe a business situation where these assumptions appear reasonable, at least as an approximation.
8. How would the granting of quantity discounts affect the economic order quantity? How could the application of the formula for the economic order quantity be modified to take into account a quantity discount?
9. During a period of continued inflation, and other things remaining equal, would you expect it to be advantageous for firms to increase their physical level of inventories or to decrease their physical level of inventories? Discuss.

Problems with Solutions

1. A firm uses 1,000 items of a particular product each month in its assembly line. Fixed ordering costs are given at \$50 per order. The product costs \$3 per unit, and inventory holding costs are given as \$1.20 per unit per year.
   (a) Compute the economic order quantity and the total costs of procurement per year. How often are orders placed?
   (b) Assume the supplier of the product offers a quantity discount of 10% if the product is purchased in quantities of 2,000 units or more. What is the optimal ordering strategy now?
   (c) Assume that there is an ordering lead time of one week. Demand per week is not given with certainty, but has the following probability distribution:

Demand per week in units	Probability
175 - 200	0.05
200 - 225	0.15
225 - 250	0.3
250 - 275	0.3
275 - 300	0.15
300 - 325	0.05

   If the firm wants to make sure that the probability of a stockout does not exceed 5%, at what point should it reorder?

Solution

(a) Economic order quantity $Q^* = \sqrt{\frac{2DK}{H}}$

$$= \sqrt{\frac{2 \times 1{,}000 \times \$50}{\$1.20/12}}$$

$$= 1{,}000 \text{ units}$$

Note that inventory holding costs have to be converted to a monthly basis as all quantities in the above formula have to be based on the same time period.

Orders are placed every month, as the economic order quantity Q^* just covers one month's demand.

Total procurement costs per year = order costs + product costs + inventory holding costs

$$= 12 \times \$50 + 12{,}000 \times \$3 + \frac{\$1.20 \times 1{,}000}{2}$$

$$= \$600 + \$36{,}000 + \$600$$

$$= \$37{,}200$$

(b) Total annual cost of procurement by placing orders of 2,000 units every other month

$$= \$50 \times 6 + 12{,}000 \times \$2.70 + \frac{\$1.20 \times 2{,}000}{2}$$

$$= \$300 + \$32{,}400 + \$1{,}200$$

$$= \$33{,}900$$

The new ordering strategy of ordering 2,000 items every second month results in decreasing ordering costs (savings of $300), increased inventory costs (increase of $600), and decreased purchasing costs (savings of $3,600). Overall, the savings outweigh the increased inventory costs, indicating that the quantity discount should be taken.

(c) It should reorder whenever the inventory level falls below 300 units.

2. Assume that the inventory which a firm needs to maintain to ensure efficient operations was valued at $10,000,000 at the beginning of the year. A year later, the physical level of inventories has remained the same, but prices have increased by an average of 15% due to inflation. Thus, inventories are now valued at $11,500,000 in the firm's financial statements. The corporate tax rate is 40%. What effects do these price level changes have on the financial operations of the firm?

Solution

The firm's before-tax profits increase by the increase in the value of inventories, or $1,500,000.

The firm pays taxes on these inventory profits, amounting to 0.4 × $1,500,000 = $600,000.

The firm has to find $600,000 to finance the increased investment in inventories. Given the framework of a sources and uses of funds analysis, we have:

Uses of funds	:	increase in inventories	$1,500,000
Sources of funds	:	increase in retained earnings	$ 900,000
		to be found from other sources	$ 600,000

A major source of funds in this context is likely to be accounts payable, as this balance sheet account tends to increase automatically with increased dollar purchases.

Note that if dividends are paid out of inventory profits, the need for funds from other sources increases accordingly.

Should the March 1977 Federal Budget proposals become law, then 3% of inventories on hand at the beginning of the year may be deducted in arriving at business income.

Additional Problems

1. The Alpha Corporation has a steady demand for a particular raw material of 2,000 units in a 90-day period. Fixed ordering costs are $50 and holding costs per unit for 90 days are $5. The material costs $20 per unit.
   (a) What is the economic order quantity?
   (b) How often are orders placed?
   (c) Assume the supplier provides a quantity discount if orders of 500 units or more are placed. What would the minimum magnitude of the quantity discount (in percent of purchase price) have to be to make it attractive to order in batches of 500 units?
2. The Beta Corporation sells about 100,000 tillets per year. For each tillet it requires 4 wids. Ordering costs are $200 and carrying costs per wid per year are $10.
   (a) What is the economic order quantity of wids?
   (b) What are the total inventory costs (carrying costs plus ordering costs)?
3. (a) Suppose that in problem 1, management desires to maintain a safety stock of 50 units. Delivery lead times are 4 days. If the stock originally on hand is 250 units, at what level of inventory should a reorder be placed?
   (b) Suppose now that lead times are uncertain. Management has estimated the following probability distribution function of lead times:

lead time (days)	2	3	4	5	6
probability	.10	.20	.40	.20	.10

   If management is willing to risk a 10% chance of a stockout, how large a safety stock will it need?

Selected References

J. Dearden and W. McFarlan, *Management Information Systems: Text and Cases*, Homewood: Richard D. Irwin, 1966, ch. 1-3, pp. 298-307.

F. Hillier and G. Lieberman, *Introduction to Operations Research*, San Francisco: Holden Day, 1967, ch. 12.

J. Magee, "Guides to Inventory Policy I, II and III", *Harvard Business Review*, Jan.-Feb. 1956, March-April 1956, May-June 1956, respectively.

M. Schiff and Z. Lieber, "A Model for the Integration of Credit and Inventory Management", *Journal of Finance*, March, 1974, pp. 133-140.

A. Shapiro, "Optimal Inventory and Credit-Granting Strategies under Inflation and Devaluation," *Journal of Financial and Quantitative Analysis*, January 1973, pp. 37-46.

M. Starr and D. Miller, *Inventory Control—Theory and Practice*, Englewood Cliffs: Prentice-Hall, 1962.

A. Vienott, "The Status of Mathematical Inventory Theory", *Management Science*, July 1966, pp. 745-777.

H. Wagner, *Principles of Operations Research*, Englewood Cliffs: Prentice-Hall, 1969, ch. 9, 19, and Appendix II.

Chapter 27
Concepts of Working Capital Management

27-1. INTRODUCTION

Working capital has been defined in various ways.[1] It is sometimes defined quite narrowly as the firm's current assets, notably cash and marketable securities, accounts receivable, and inventories. A more useful definition of the term encompasses both current assets and current liabilities such as various payables and short-term borrowings. From this designation, it would follow that *working capital management* is concerned with management of interrelationships between these two balance sheet categories. *Net working capital* is typically defined as the difference between current assets and current liabilities, and as such is a single figure derived from the firm's balance sheet. For purposes of this chapter, we will use the broad definition of working capital which encompasses both current assets and current liabilities.

The preceding three chapters reviewed individual categories of current assets, including their efficient administration, while short-term sources of funds were surveyed in an earlier section of this text. Our concern here is with integrating some of the detail presented in earlier chapters, and with discussing some overall concepts which are useful in managing the firm's working capital. After reviewing some aggregate statistics, which establish the importance of working capital, we will discuss the framework for deciding on the level of current assets to be maintained and current liabilities to be incurred. We will also detail certain key considerations in working capital management set in an international context.

Tables 27-1 and 27-2 provide some aggregate working capital statistics for Canadian nonfinancial corporations and several aspects of the data are worth commenting on. It is evident from Table 27-1, that total levels of both current assets and current liabilities are sizable. As shown in Table 27-2, for many firms commitments in current assets represent a significant proportion of their total investments, while short-term liabilities provide a sizable proportion of the total funds raised by the firm. These facts are fully reflected in Table 27-2, making it easy to see why efficiency in the area of working capital management is vital to the overall financial success of a firm. For example, over-investment in unproductive current assets can reduce the overall profitability of the firm significantly; while management of current liabilities has a direct bearing on both the firm's cost of capital and, as will be detailed below, its risk.

It is also apparent from Table 27-1 that the magnitudes of both current assets and of current liabilities have increased steadily during the period from 1968 to 1971. The average growth rates for both balance sheet categories work out to approximately 10.5 percent and 12.7 percent respectively. This growth, which is a combination of real growth in the economy and inflationary price level changes, can also be looked at another way. It means that over the three-year

[1]See, for example, K. V. Smith (Ed.), *Management of Working Capital*, St. Paul, West Publishing Co., 1974, p. 4.

span, Canadian businesses in aggregate added just over 13 billion dollars to their investment in current assets. On the liability side, accounts payable and loans posted even larger annual growth rates, namely 15.7 percent and 13.5 percent respectively, with total current liabilities increasing by almost 11 billion dollars over the same period.

TABLE 27-1

Aggregate Figures of Current Assets and Current Liabilities for Canadian Nonfinancial Corporations, 1968-1971 (in millions of dollars)

	1971	1970	1969	1968
Cash	2,751.6	2,318.7	2,175.1	2,214.7
Marketable securities[1]	4,073.0	3,460.4	3,744.4	3,537.8
Accounts receivable	17,092.7	15,625.6	14,210.3	12,664.6
Inventories	21,607.5	20,322.0	17,852.3	16,098.1
Other current assets[2]	6,615.8	5,264.0	4,993.2	4,514.5
Total current assets	52,140.6	46,990.7	42,975.3	39,029.7
Bank Loans				
and other short-term loans[3]	11,686.2	11,155.0	9,280.7	8,070.4
Accounts payable	13,636.4	12,251.1	10,120.9	8,758.9
Long-term debt payable within 1 year	1,579.2	1,539.8	N/A	N/A
Other current liabilities[4]	9,242.1	8,005.1	8,605.8	8,372.1
Total current liabilities	36,143.9	32,951.0	28,007.4	25,201.4

[1]includes deposits and advances.
[2]includes prepaid expenses, due from affiliates, loans receivable, etc.
[3]includes advances and prepayments.
[4]includes taxes payable, valuation reserve, amounts due to affiliates, etc.

Source: Statistics Canada, *Corporate Financial Statistics*, 1969-1971.

It is one of the characteristics of current assets that the need for them tends to grow automatically with increasing sales. Assuming a constant credit policy, for example, investments in accounts receivable will be almost directly proportional to the dollar volume of sales. Similarly, increased inventories and perhaps larger cash balances are typically required to support expanded sales. While, over the longer term, the physical volume of sales will also affect a firm's investments in longer-term assets such as plant and equipment, the effects on working capital management tend to be much more direct and immediate. Furthermore, while new investments in plant and equipment may only be required if the physical volume of sales expands, an increased dollar volume of sales, which may have been caused solely by inflationary price level changes, will directly affect the dollar investment in current assets and the likely need for additional short-term as well as more permanent funds. As a consequence, the management of working capital has to be undertaken on a much more continuous basis than, for example, the formulation of capital budgeting decisions, and demands a proportionately greater amount of management's time on an ongoing basis. The impact on the firm's operations of such external environmental forces as the inflation rate and the availability of money, as reflected in short-term interest rates, also tends to be more direct in the area of working capital management than in other areas of financial decision-making.

TABLE 27-2

Current Assets and Current Liabilities for Selected Industries as a Percentage of Total Assets and Total Liabilities (Based on 1971 figures)

	Forestry	Mining	Manufacturing	Utilities	Wholesale Trade	Services
Cash	3.9	0.8	1.6	0.6	3.1	4.4
Marketable securities[1]	5.2	4.1	2.6	2.0	2.5	3.4
Accounts receivable	9.1	4.2	14.0	4.0	26.4	11.5
Inventories	7.6	4.8	20.2	1.2	31.5	2.8
Other current assets[2]	4.6	4.1	5.9	2.0	5.9	6.0
Total proportion current assets	30.4	18.0	44.3	9.8	69.4	28.1
Bank loans and other short term loans[3]	6.5	2.1	7.9	2.7	16.9	9.7
Accounts payable	8.4	4.5	9.5	3.5	20.5	8.7
Long-term debt payable within 1 year	6.9	0.9	0.8	1.0	0.9	2.3
Other current liabilities[4]	7.2	3.2	8.2	2.6	12.2	8.1
Total proportion current liabilities	29.0	10.7	26.4	9.8	50.5	28.8

[1]includes deposits and advances.
[2]includes prepaid expenses, due from affiliates, loans receivable, etc.
[3]includes advances and prepayments.
[4]includes taxes payable, valuation reserve, amounts due to affiliates, etc.

Source: Statistics Canada, *Corporate Financial Statistics 1971*, October, 1974.

Table 27-2 further illustrates the wide differences to be encountered in various industries as far as the relative importance of working capital is concerned. For instance, for utilities where several dollars of investment in fixed assets may be needed to generate one dollar of sales, current assets make up less than 10 percent of total assets, while in wholesaling they exceed 69 percent. Current assets approximately equal current liabilities for utilities and the service industry, while for mining current assets exceed current liabilities by a factor of almost two. It is evident from these statistics that it is impossible to derive general rules or guidelines regarding either absolute or proportionate amounts which a firm should carry in various working capital accounts. Rather, any conceptual framework to be developed for the management of working capital will have to be of sufficient generality to allow for specific solutions which may vary drastically depending on the characteristics of the industry and of the individual firm.

We note that working capital management may be of particular relevance to smaller firms. Such firms are often concentrated in retailing or the service industries, where large investments in plant and equipment are not called for. Furthermore, while buildings or machinery may be rented or leased, investments in current assets cannot be avoided and such assets are essential to most businesses. On the liabilities side, given that smaller firms find it very much more difficult to raise long-term funds, their relatively heavier reliance on short-term financing is quite understandable.

In spite of its importance in practical business management, at a theoretical level the area of working capital management has received little attention in the literature of finance. While relatively sophisticated theories are available to assist with such issues as capital budgeting decisions or choice of a firm's long-term capital structure, only a few fairly basic principles have been developed as guidelines in the area of working capital. As will become apparent from our subsequent discussion, the main difficulties in the area of working capital management are not of a conceptual nature, but stem from an inability to accurately quantify various inputs, including marginal costs and benefits, and risks. Thus, efficient working capital management continues to be very heavily dependent on subjective managerial judgment, guided by a few basic principles which will be reviewed below.

27-2. INVESTMENT IN CURRENT ASSETS

Conceptually, it is easy to formulate decision rules for determining the optimal level of investment in current assets. Expressed in economic terminology, a firm should invest until the marginal benefits to be derived from additional investments equal the marginal costs of financing such investments. In other words, just as with any other investments, funds should be provided to expand current assets as long as such committments yield a positive net present value. This is illustrated in Figure 27-1, using investments in inventories as an example. We assume that the total costs of carrying inventories increase proportionately with the level of inventories, which appears to be a reasonable approximation.

Thus, the marginal costs of carrying additional inventories would be constant. On the other hand, decreasing marginal benefits from additional investments in current assets are typically observed. For instance, initial investments in inventories are likely to have a major impact on the efficiency of production and on the quality of customer service. As additional inventories are accumulated, however, improvements in these areas of operations become less pronounced. While total benefits to be derived from inventory investments may still increase, they will do so at a decreasing rate. The optimal level of inventory investment is given at the point where marginal benefits equal marginal costs, since at this point the difference between total benefits and total costs is greatest, resulting in

FIGURE 27-1

Conceptually Optimal Investment in Current Assets:
Marginal Benefits Equal Marginal Costs

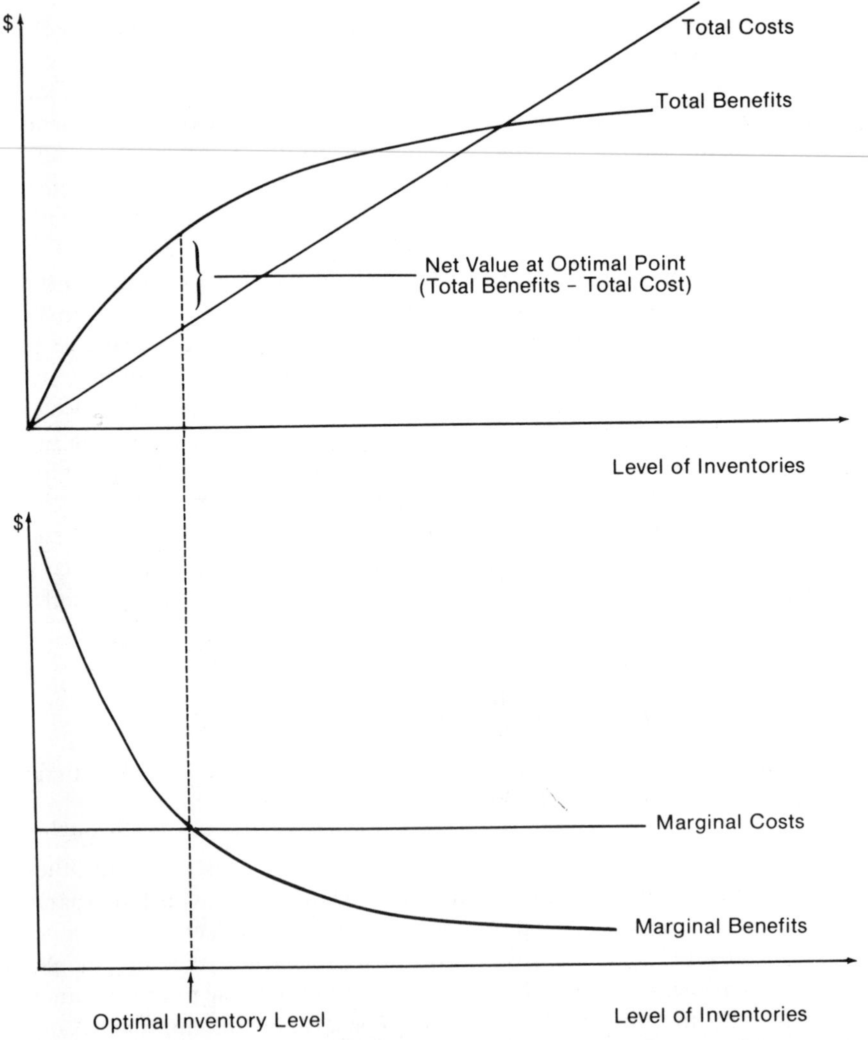

the highest net present value.[2] Quite similar arguments can be advanced for investments in accounts receivable or for the holding of cash.

While the setting out of a conceptual framework for determining optimal investments in current assets is relatively straightforward, the difficulties of translating such a general framework into specific decisions in a practical context can be formidable. Such difficulties essentially stem from our inability to readily quantify and measure relevant costs and benefits. Returning again to our example of inventories, cost accounting data as typically generated within firms are often inadequate for decision-making purposes, providing little information about marginal costs of incremental investments. However, while information on costs may be sparse, difficulties in any estimate of benefits are likely to be almost insurmountable. For example, in attempting to establish the benefits which are to be derived from increasing investments in inventories, we would not only have to estimate the probabilities of stockouts at various levels of inventory, but also the various costs associated with such stockouts. Loss of customer goodwill, which is often of major concern in this context, is a very elusive concept and hence, typically classified as an "intangible". Yet, if optimal decision-making is to be attempted in the context of the above framework, such intangibles need to be quantified, even if only through some subjective or "ball park" estimate. Thus, the art of good working capital management basically involves the exercise of informed judgment in quantifying various costs and benefits. More detailed models, some of which were discussed in previous chapters, can then be used to determine day-to-day operating decisions within such a general framework.

It should be emphasized that both the costs and benefits to be derived from various investments in current assets can be subject to significant fluctuations over relatively short periods of time. This means that decisions in this area need to be constantly monitored and adapted, serving to explain why working capital management typically occupies a fair proportion of a financial manager's time. To be more specific, the competitive situation will be crucial in the setting of credit policies and service levels; general business uncertainty and price levels will influence cash balances; and the availability and costs of monies, which have been subject to great fluctuations in recent years, will determine the opportunity costs of funds tied up in current assets. While liberal credit may have been granted in a highly competitive setting and where this has become common practice, such a policy may have to be reappraised by a firm which finds itself in a liquidity squeeze in periods of tight money. Competition on the basis of price and service with reduced credit terms may have to be considered as an alternative. Similarly, in an expanding and prospering industry, liberal credit policies may entail little risk, but if the same policies are maintained through a recession, losses from bad debts could become significant. Consequently,

[2]The reader who has taken an introductory economics course will be familiar with the fact that the marginal cost or benefit curve is just the first derivative of the total cost or benefit curve. At the point where marginal benefits equal marginal costs, the slope of the total cost curve and of the total benefit curve are identical, and this is a necessary condition for the distance between the two curves to be at a maximum.

the problem of measuring costs and benefits as discussed above is compounded by the dynamic nature of the process, and requires constant reappraisals.

27-3. THE USE OF SHORT-TERM LIABILITIES

There are three major reasons why firms may draw on short-term liabilities in financing their operations. First of all, there may be only a temporary need for funds, for example, to finance seasonal peaks. It would be wasteful to provide financing for such temporary peaks on a permanent basis, as the firm would then have excess cash balances in off-peak seasons and would incur higher financing costs than are necessary. Secondly, as we have seen in our discussion of the term structure of interest rates, debt with shorter maturities is often cheaper than long-term debt, thus providing an incentive for financing on a short-term basis. Finally, given that the raising of longer-term funds through an issue of securities in the capital markets is "lumpy", with significant amounts of money having to be raised at one time, a firm may temporarily draw on short-term sources until it has built up sufficient short-term liabilities to warrant turning to new long-term financing. The proceeds from such an issue are then used to pay off the short-term obligations. We will discuss each of these aspects which favor short-term financing.

The need for temporary financing is typical for, although not restricted to, seasonal businesses. Consider a manufacturer of winter sporting goods. The bulk of his sales may fall in the last third of each year, or in the period from September to December. Given more or less uniform levels of production throughout the year (which is necessary for maintaining a stable labor force and a good utilization of production facilities) inventories will build up throughout the first two-thirds of the year, reaching a peak just before the start of the heavy sales season. Concentrated sales lead to large investments in accounts receivable, with both inventories and receivables liquidated and reverting to cash sometime after the peak selling period, or early in the following year. This is illustrated in Figure 27-2. Inventories build up in periods where production exceeds sales, and *vice versa.* The aggregate investment in current assets is highly seasonal, having its peak sometime in the late fall and its low sometime at the end of the first third of the year. As shown in Figure 27-2, some investment in current assets is required at all times, which we may term the permanent component of current assets, and it is on this base that the seasonal component is superimposed. If the firm had secured adequate long-term financing to meet its peak needs, significant balances of excess cash would be available in the early half of the year. Even if such balances could be invested temporarily in marketable securities, the return earned on such investments is likely to fall short of the costs needed to service these funds. To minimize such net costs, the widely accepted *hedging approach* to financing is suggested by which the financial manager strives to match the maturities of corporate assets and liabilites. Temporarily increased assets which are not spontaneously financed through trade credit and accounts payable should be financed through short-term debt, while basic or permanent investments in current assets are provided for from long-term or permanent sources. Where such arrangements can be made, and the firm's financial needs have been accurately forecast, the firm need never have significant balances of excess cash, and should be in a position to liquidate all its current debt at least once a year.

FIGURE 27-2

A Seasonal Business' Sales, Production, Inventories and Accounts Receivable as a Function of Time

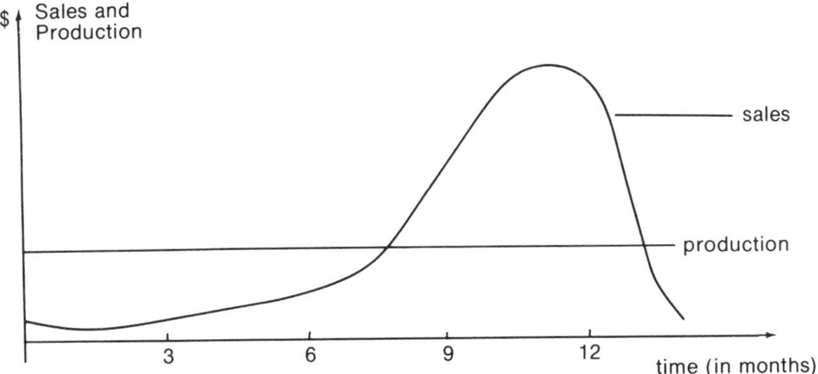

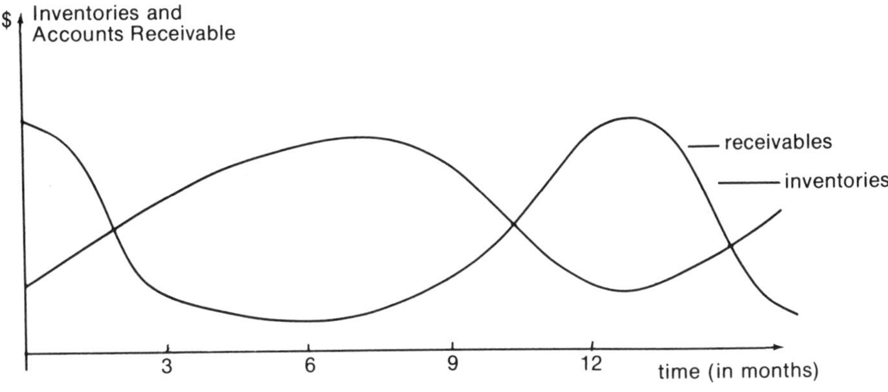

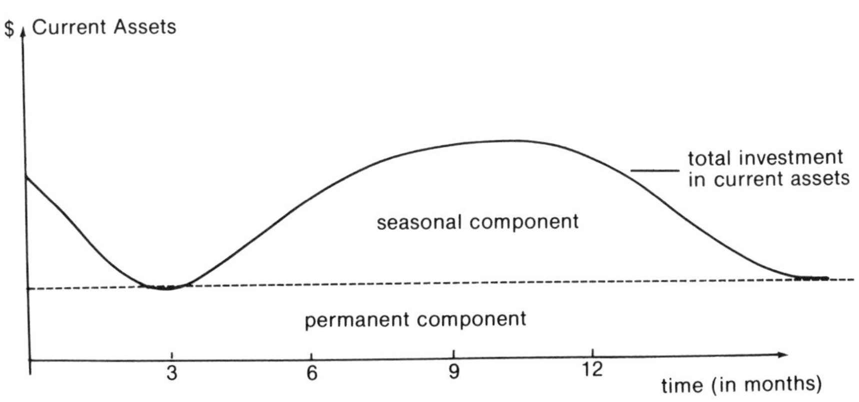

Given that short-term debt is often cheaper than debt with longer maturities, there is an incentive to carry short-term financing beyond what was just suggested, and to finance some permanent component of current assets and perhaps even long-term investments through current liabilities. While immediate savings may be realized, the risks of such financing policies must be quite obvious. In contrast to long-term debt which is usually provided for at fixed interest rates, short-term debt has to be rolled-over continually at whatever interest rates prevail. As evidenced by developments which we have witnessed in recent years, short-term interest rates change over time and may increase very significantly over relatively short time spans. Financing long-term requirements with short-term funds, therefore, introduces the risk of unpredictable future interest rates. More importantly, however, the actual availability of funds can change depending on economic conditions and on the monetary policies pursued by the Bank of Canada. During periods of monetary restraint, sources which were readily available earlier on have been known to dry up completely, and a notice from the bank regarding a significant reduction in its lending limits can prove embarassing for corporations which have invested those funds on a long-term basis.

It is evident from the above that we have once again encountered the now familiar tradeoff between risk and return in the management of working capital. An overly liquid firm, with current assets greatly exceeding current liabilities, incurs little risk, but may be sacrificing profit potential. On the other hand, a firm striving to minimize costs associated with its net working capital position by maintaining high current liabilities relative to current assets may be realizing its maximum profit potential, but at the expense of greatly increased risks. The optimal balance depends not only on the attitude of managers and shareholders towards this tradeoff, but also on the particular characteristics of the business. Where cash flows are very predictable, safety margins in net working capital need not be as large as they would have to be for businesses exposed to an unstable environment. Referring back to Table 27-2, we can see that for utilities, which are characterized by stable operating environments, current assets approximate current liabilities, implying little or no net working capital, while in less stable industries such as manufacturing or mining, current assets exceed liabilities by significant margins.

The use of short-term debt as a stopgap measure while preparing for a new long-term issue is quite common. For example, while long-term debt may be viewed as a permanent part of a firm's capital structure, a sinking fund feature requiring gradual retirement of the outstanding issue will likely be prescribed. Monies for payments could be provided through short-term borrowings, with another long-term issue placed once short-term liabilities reach a level which warrants the new offering. It may also be possible to temporarily delay new long-term financing in anticipation of falling interest-rate levels by relying on short-term borrowings. Again, the risks associated with such actions need to be borne in mind, for as noted earlier, a firm with a significant volume of short-term liabilities is vulnerable. Recently, however, despite long-term interest rates being at historical highs, and as a consequence of continued postponements of long-term financing, heavy reliance on short-term debt seems to have become almost traditional with many firms.

27-4. WORKING CAPITAL MANAGEMENT IN AN INTERNATIONAL CONTEXT

Procedures relating to the management of cash, accounts receivable, and short-term borrowings in an international context were introduced in earlier chapters of this text. Foreign exchange risks were acknowledged, and the potential role of forward exchange markets were identified. This section provides a brief overview of a few general principles which are important in controlling overall foreign exchange exposure in the context of working capital management.

The financial officer's response to risks of foreign exchange fluctuations may take the form of general defensive actions or, as we have already seen, involve specific contractual arrangements in the forward markets. General defensive postures include a variety of specific measures, most of which simply involve using basic common sense. For example, cash balances or assets denominated in weak or otherwise vulnerable foreign currencies should be minimized and funds transferred into strong or so-called "hard" currencies. Payments on outstanding hard currency debts should be made early, while liabilities denominated in vulnerable currencies could be incurred, perhaps through the purchase of useful raw materials or similar items. It must be apparent that if a currency is devalued, foreign borrowers who have outstanding liabilities in that currency stand to gain, while creditors suffer equivalent losses. Similarly, where a currency's value increases, foreign creditors having assets denominated in that currency gain, while borrowers lose.

Considering liabilities more fully and focusing, for example, on trade payables, it is possible that the discounts being offered on accounts payable denominated in a weak currency should be passed up and the debt actually "stretched out" to await devaluation.

Example

> We owe 900 million Italian lira billed at 2/10 net 60. If we expect the lira to drop in value, we may be better off not to take 18 million in discounts, but rather to wait for the lira to slip from the prevailing 680 to the dollar down to an expected 850 to the dollar. In other words, by foregoing discounts of about 18,000,000/680 = \$26,500, we could perhaps end up paying approximately 900,000,000/850 = \$1,059,000, instead of \$900,000,000/680 = \$1,323,500 to an Italian supplier.

In an earlier chapter, we discussed borrowings in international money markets as part of a hedging operation to eliminate foreign exchange exposure in accounts receivable. A more complete approach, feasible for larger multinational firms, would be to match the timing of future receipts in various currencies against obligations to be paid around those same dates and in the same currencies. Where a firm regularly has receipts and disbursements in various foreign currencies, it would not be optimal to hedge each individual transaction, but just the net balances which accumulate after various inflows and outflows are netted out. Considerable savings can result as the need for contractual hedging in the forward markets will be minimized by taking such an overall corporate viewpoint.

The mechanics of such foreign exchange hedging are not difficult to picture. A multinational corporation may find that after matching and netting all of its projected financial flows in pounds sterling, as of the first week in April, it expects to have £100,000 of surplus sterling on hand. It is also felt that although the future value of sterling in dollar terms is unpredictable, the pound is vulnerable. In such circumstances, £100,000 could be sold forward to the first week in April at a discount from today's spot rate, and the exposure is eliminated. While some costs are incurred, the expense is clearly less than would be incurred if a variety of individual transactions were entered into, with forward purchases and forward sales of pounds sterling arranged simultaneously perhaps by various divisions of the same firm. The opportunities afforded by netting foreign currency flows serve to illustrate why, even in decentralized firms, foreign exchange exposure is best managed by a centralized finance department which can take an overall corporate viewpoint.

27-5. SUMMARY

This chapter integrates earlier discussions dealing with the management of different categories of current assets and the use of various current liabilities as sources of funds. The chapter goes on to explain the importance of working capital and its efficient utilization for most types of businesses. Its rapid growth in recent years and its demands on management's time were also underscored.

Investments in current assets were analyzed. Conceptually, the optimal levels of investments occur where marginal costs equal marginal benefits. Because of difficulties in measuring the costs and benefits involved in such investments, little more than this broad conceptual framework for reaching decisions could be suggested. The resultant need for good judgment and constant monitoring by management was stressed.

The use of short-term liabilities was also considered with particular emphasis placed on the use of such financing when temporary and perhaps seasonal needs exist and when more permanent financing should be postponed. The temptation to use cheaper short-term funds for longer-term needs was also noted and evaluated in terms of the now familiar risk and return tradeoff.

Working capital management in the international context was looked at. It was observed that in addition to the use of specific contractual arrangements which involve forward exchange markets, the financial manager could use general defensive strategies to control foreign exchange exposure. Taking an overall corporate approach in the management of foreign exchange risk, a firm can reduce expenditures on hedging significantly.

Questions for Discussion

1. Under what circumstances might inventory levels increase by more than sales growth? By less?

2. Why should seasonality of sales have a bearing on corporate use of short-term debt?
3. Illustrate the risk-return tradeoff in the context of:
   (a) allowing net working capital to decline;
   (b) increasing the yield on the firm's holdings of marketable securities;
   (c) minimizing holdings of cash and near cash; and,
   (d) hedging foreign exchange exposure in accounts receivable.
4. Discuss two ways in which a firm may protect itself from foreign exchange risk when some of its receivables are denominated in a foreign currency. Assume the existence of forward exchange markets.
5. If suppliers extend credit, why might increases in inventories brought about by higher sales nevertheless cause cash shortages? Illustrate your answer.

Case

Robinson Laboratories (Abridged)

Jim Hodges, Vice-President of Finance for Robinson Laboratories (a medium sized firm located in Los Angeles, California) walked slowly back to his office from the weekly top management conference on January 17, 1974. The main topic of the session had been confirmation of the sale of a data communications system to a large British firm. The contract represented the largest non-military order yet received by Robinson Laboratories and was for the amount of 260,000 Pounds Sterling (£). A deposit of £25,000 was in transit to the United States, and the balance was to be paid upon successful installation and acceptance testing by the customer. Jack Reese, the manufacturing head, had promised completion by the end of April.

Mr. Hodges had shared the excitement of the sale, but after the meeting he began to think through the financial implications. The combination of a small percentage deposit followed by the balance due being receivable upon customer acceptance was quite usual. For the first time in his business career, however, the payments were in a foreign currency. He remembered that in early October, the management team had fixed a price in U.S. dollars (about $600,000) and then converted to quote in pounds at the exchange rate then prevailing—about $2.4150 = £1.00. Hodges had requested that the price be moved up to £260,000 to cover the uncertainty of foreign exchange. Since then, the pound had fluctuated in value relative to the dollar, moving up in mid-October, but declining since then to its current exchange rate of $2.1910. Robinson's management was reluctant to revise the quote upward in the middle of the contract negotiations, as would be indicated by the slump in the value of the pound. Even at current rates, the deal would show a profit.

Mr. Hodges was worried, however, about the time delay between January and April when the final payment would be received. If the pound should decline further relative to the dollar during this period, the contracted amount in pounds would be received, but there would be a significantly smaller number of dollars upon conversion. The sale might be thrown "into the red" by such a development. This would be certain to have a significant impact on Robinson's end-of-year financial statements. Mr. Hodges decided to call on his banker for help.

The bank manager, Ed Alston, explained that the foreign exchange market was similar to a commodities market, with national currencies as the products. In each market, there are "spot" transactions whereby the actual commodity changes hands immediately,[1] and "futures" transactions when a deal involved the delivery of the product at some specified time in the future. The dealers in the market are primarily the major offices of the European commercial and merchant banks, government central banks, and the European offices of American banks. Most trading is carried out in the cities of London, Frankfurt, and Zurich, though other active centers are developing in New York, Singapore, and Tokyo. Corporations and individuals generally conduct foreign exchange transactions through their primary banking connections.

In the futures, or forward foreign exchange sector of the market, it is possible to buy and sell currencies to be delivered and paid for at some future date. It is normal to fix rates for periods of up to one year in major world currencies. Hence it would be possible to buy or sell a 90-day forward contract for pounds sterling at a quoted "90-day forward rate". The rates quoted would reflect the interest yield differentials between the currencies based on interest yields domestically and internationally, and would also at times reflect the speculative pressures on the currencies in question.

The currently quoted "90-day forward rate" relating sterling to dollars was $2.1030 per pound, or equivalently, a discount of 8.80 cents from the current spot rate.

Mr. Hodges recalled a seminar he had recently attended where the speakers had discussed and shown applications of probability analysis. Their approach had been to examine possible "states-of-the-world" and the impact these would have on the problem at hand. Mr. Hodge decided to try to apply the techniques to his foreign exchange situation, in assessing the uncertainty about future values of the pound which would determine the proceeds of Robinson's sale. In this case, it seemed that the key factor amid the political and economic pressures that determine exchange rates was the effect of the energy crisis on the British economy. Developments in the Middle East had led to a substantial increase in the price of petroleum products worldwide, though supply restrictions were just beginning to be lifted.

More important to the British economy, however, was the labor unrest that threatened home energy supplies. For some months, United Kingdom coal miners had banned overtime work over a pay dispute with the government. Sporadic rail worker strikes impeded distribution of the available resources. The government, refusing to relax its prices and incomes policies, rejected the union pay demands. It had imposed a three-day per week power rationing scheme on British industry to conserve fuel consumption, but this reduced efficiency and

[1]Even in the spot market, there is a normal delay of two business days to permit both sides to execute the transfers and bookkeeping, but this may be waived.

seemed certain to aggravate Britain's deteriorating balance of trade and currency reserve position. Although negotiations between the miners' unions and government were still under way at several levels, talk of an all-out coal strike was increasingly reported. Such a strike, if sustained for any length of time, would certainly result in further substantial devaluation of the pound relative to the dollar.

If the negotiations could settle the dispute without a strike, Mr. Hodges believed that the pound would hold at its current level or increase slightly, as the market had already discounted the chances of reconciliation. However, he reckoned that there was only one chance in ten that the talks would be successful and the pound remain at about $2.20, as both government and union negotiators seemed firmly set in their positions. In the event of a breakdown in the talks, a strike was virtually sure to follow and an election would in all probability be called. Recent public opinion polls had given the incumbent Conservatives a narrow edge over the Labour opposition, and public support for a firm anti-inflationary stance might be forthcoming. However, the polls had proved inaccurate in the last election. Labour spokesmen had publicly called for meeting the union demands and could be expected to end the strike quickly if elected, but Mr. Hodges believed that this would trigger an inflationary spiral which would drop the pound to about $2.10. From his vantage point, he rated the election a toss-up, giving each side a 50-50 chance.

Even with a Conservative victory, the strike would be far from settled. It was quite possible that militant workers would remain on the picket lines, and it was just this possibility that Mr. Hodges feared would bring on the worst devaluation. Commentators were talking about spot rates of $1.80 per pound, which would be fully 25% below the prevailing rates just two months ago. Fortunately the chances of this were relatively slim—only about 20%. It would be much more likely if the government were re-elected, that a small concession would be made to the miners to save face, and coal production would be resumed. This would probably cause the pound to rebound upward. Mr. Hodges estimated that the spot rate would stabilize somewhere between $2.20 and $2.30 per pound, though he could not honestly foresee what value in that range it might assume.

He decided to lay out these possible outcomes and their probabilities to compute an average or expected value of the spot rate 90 days hence. He could then compare this with the certain forward foreign exchange quotation of $2.1030 he had now. This might provide at least some guidance in reaching a final decision.

EXHIBIT 1

Robinson Laboratories, Inc.—Operating Summary

Year Ended 30 June	Sales ($000)	Net Income ($000)	Reported EPS ($)
1973	11,747	338	.37
1972	11,234	265	.29
1971	10,212	(57)	(.06)
1970	9,249	(765)	(.84)
1969	9,796	236	.26
1968	9,450	302	.33
1967	6,848	267	.31
1966	6,033	253	.30

EXHIBIT 2

Robinson Laboratories, Inc.—Balance Sheet as of 30 June, 1973

Assets		
Cash	$195,131	
US Government securities	489,224	
Receivables, net	1,826,720	
Inventory	1,352,427	
Prepayments	67,128	
Total current assets		$3,930,630
Net property	$795,186	
Development costs, etc.	517,332	
Other assets	57,438	
Trademarks	56,333	
License agreement	19,984	
Deferred charges	121,584	
		$1,567,857
Total assets		$5,498,487
Liabilities and Equity		
Notes payable	$209,100	
Accounts payable	629,687	
Total current liabilities		$838,787
Debentures, 7½%, due 1990	$1,200,000	
Notes payable	244,425	
Deferred income tax	156,941	
		$1,601,366
Total liabilities		$2,440,153
Common stock	$910,245	
Paid-in surplus	817,946	
Retained earnings	1,330,143	
Total equity		$3,058,334
Total liabilities and equity		$5,498,487

Selected References

R. Cossaboom, "Let's Reassess the Profitability-Liquidity Trade-off", *Financial Executive*, May, 1971, pp. 46-51.

M. Glautier, "Towards a Reformulation of the Theory of Working Capital", *Journal of Business Finance*, Spring, 1971, pp. 37-42.

W. Knight, "Working Capital Management: Satisficing Versus Optimization", *Financial Management*, Spring, 1972, pp. 33-40.

L. Merville and L. Tavis, "Optimal Working Capital Policies: A Chance-Constrained Programming Approach", *Journal of Financial and Quantitative Analysis*, January, 1973, pp. 47-60.

K. Smith, "State of the Art of Working Capital Management", *Financial Management*, Autumn, 1973, pp. 50-55.

K. Smith, (ed.), *Management of Working Capital,* New York: West, 1974.

J. Van Horne, "A Risk-Return Analysis of a Firm's Working-Capital Position", *Engineering Economist*, Winter, 1969, pp. 71-89.

PART 9
Expansion

Chapter 28
Mergers and Consolidations

28-1. INTRODUCTION

In earlier sections on capital budgeting, attention was concentrated largely on internal growth achieved by a firm's acquisition of additional assets financed through retained earnings, depreciation and various external sources. During the postwar period, significant corporate growth, with its objectives of achieving both size and diversification, had also taken place by *external* means, specifically by the fusion of two or more going concerns. For instance, rather than gaining entry into a new line of business through appropriate internal investments, a firm would decide to combine with another which already had an established position in the area of interest. An illustration would be the 1972 takeover of Beaver Lumber by Molson Industries. Such business combinations have taken several forms including the *holding company, mergers,* and *consolidations.* Holding companies were considered in some detail in Chapter 2. A merger involves the fusion of two corporations only one of which survives, while with a consolidation both corporations would disappear and be replaced by an entirely new concern. As might be guessed, mergers usually involve firms of quite different size, with the smaller one usually being merged into the larger one, while consolidations, sometimes termed amalgamations, are more likely to take place between equals.

Business combinations through mergers and consolidations were an important Canadian phenomenon, particularly during the late sixties, with financial officers performing much of the evaluation which preceded negotiations leading to the final decision. It is essential, therefore, that our study of financial management provide some of the background required for an understanding of the complex issues involved.

28-2. DIRECTIONS FOR EXPANSION

Regardless of the form it takes, the thrust of external growth may be in several directions and be undertaken to achieve a range of objectives. The direction of a combination or acquisition might be *horizontal*, meaning that units engaged in the same stage of production and the distribution of identical products, perhaps over a wider market, are involved. The 1961 consolidation of the Canadian Bank of Commerce and the Imperial Bank of Canada into the Canadian Imperial Bank of Commerce affords an example of horizontal expansion. The objective of horizontal expansion is generally to strengthen a firm's market position within an established business field.

Vertical expansion is said to take place when successive stages of operation are integrated. In the case of manufacturing, for example, integration may be backward toward the source of raw materials or forward into the retailing end. Maple Leaf Mills Ltd. is an excellent illustration of vertical expansion. The focus of its business is the milling of flour but it has also moved into grain elevators, bakeries, poultry farming, animal foods, and seeds. Generally speaking, vertical growth would allow a company to exercise more control over both its distribution and purchasing.

Circular expansion brings together different products which can perhaps be handled by similar methods but, in any case, can be distributed through the same channels. The twenty-five percent interest of Simpsons-Sears Ltd. in each of the All State Insurance Company of Canada and the All State Life Insurance Company depict circular expansion to the extent that policies are sold in the department store and made available to the store's credit account customers.

Conglomerate expansion involves diversification in the sense that companies whose products or lines of business bear no relation to one another are combined. The activities of Neonex International Ltd. in branching out from the manufacture and leasing of neon advertising products into transportation, consumer goods, food services, and the leisure time industry is illustrative.

28-3. THE MOTIVES FOR COMBINATIONS

Many diverse reasons underly the fusion of business units and expansion in general. They may range all the way from the desire of an enterpreneur to be creative, or to increase power, through to improving efficiencies and straight profit considerations. A look at some of the more significant motivations follows.

Operating economies

Growth, either internally or externally, has been an important objective of many corporations because size allows a firm to take advantage of the economies inherent in large-scale operations. Often, an expansion through mergers and consolidations will confer such operating economies on a firm far more quickly than will internal growth, particularly if there are already many competitors in the market. It has, of course, been argued that external growth leading to large industrial complexes has in a variety of cases been pushed to the point where further economies are unattainable and where, in fact, the diseconomies of excessively large and cumbersome organizations are to be observed. In these instances, the motivating force underlying combinations may be market control rather than concern about economies of scale. Exactly what the facts are cannot be determined at this time because a great deal more empirical work is needed before conclusions can be drawn.[1]

Since the postwar period, many combinations appear to have aimed at attaining so-called *synergistic* effects, which imply operating economies such that outcomes are greater than the straight summation of individual parts

[1]For some recent research which does have some bearing, see Canada, *Concentration in the Manufacturing Industries of Canada*, Ottawa: Department of Consumer and Corporate Affairs, 1971.

would suggest.[2] Such effects are attainable for a variety of reasons. Two chemical companies may both, for example, be smaller than optimum economic size, yet, by combining into a single unit, they would be able to have more efficient production runs and lower their marketing, clerical, and general overhead costs through the elimination of redundancies. In other words, at constant prices, higher profits could be achieved than would be the case given two separate entities.

It may also be argued that the enlarged corporation which results will enjoy improved access to the financial markets and that its cost of funds would be favorably influenced because of an improved credit standing. Alternatively, complementary product lines may be involved which could be marketed through the same sales organization, or one firm may be strong in research and the other in production so that by joining together both strengths become available. The operating economies which could be achieved through the pooling of research facilities, sales efforts, and the development of a more integrated line of products was the reasoning cited behind the 1962 Benson and Hedges (Canada) Ltd. acquisition of Canadian Tabacofina Ltd. In addition, the Benson and Hedges management felt that horizontal expansion under the circumstances would help obtain at least five percent of the cigarette market which was viewed as economically comfortable for Canada's two smallest cigarette makers. Anticipated operating economies were also given as a major reason for the Acres Limited bid in 1970 to take over Traders Group Ltd., a large diversified financial concern.

Research effectiveness

The pace of scientific and business innovation has certainly quickened in recent years, thus placing a very considerable premium on productive research and development. In some situations it is even fair to equate corporate survival with competence in this particular endeavor. Since research is a time-consuming, extremely expensive and competitive undertaking, and since good individual researchers or teams of researchers are often scarce resources, it appears best conducted on an ongoing and centralized basis. This pattern, then, not only gives the edge to mature organizations but, in some cases, the time-consuming aspect of research including the very considerable startup time provides incentives for well-established businesses to seek out and acquire firms with either potential or developed exploitable scientific and business innovations which are not readily duplicated.

Senior management skills

A company needing to strengthen or replace its senior executives will generally

[2]One writer has termed this the 2 + 2 = 5 effect. See F. Weston, "Determination of Share Exchange Ratios in Mergers", in W. Alberts and J. Segall, eds., *The Corporate Merger*, Chicago: University of Chicago Press, 1966, p. 130.

look to its existing internal pool of talent in middle management or go outside the organization. It is entirely possible, however, that an external quest will prove unproductive even though some very attractive inducements are held out. Corporate management must then face the prospect of having the firm's competitive position erode over time unless a combination can be arranged with another concern endowed with the kind of superior managerial talent and technical skills that are required. Family controlled businesses frequently fall into this circumstance, with the founder-manager nearing retirement and his children lacking either the interest or the capacity to take over.

When different management groups are thrown together following corporate fusion, entrenched and conflicting philosophies may surface. Obviously, the behavioral problems of merging two existing organizations, each with its own traditions and patterns, should not be underestimated.

Diversification

An argument frequently advanced in favor of external growth, particularly for conglomerate mergers, is that through the acquisition of firms in unrelated industries, the cyclical instability of earnings can be moderated and corporate risk as perceived by investors can be reduced. This reduction of risk is alleged to result in the typical risk-averse investor valuing the expected earnings stream more highly and paying a premium for greater stability.[3]

Related to the diversification concept is the notion of spreading the exposure to risk when the opportunity for new ventures presents itself. A firm's size may rule out an undertaking because, given an unfavorable outcome, the losses would be too large to be absorbed. Following fusion with another corporation of sufficient size, the relative impact of any loss is reduced, for not only would such losses be smaller in terms of the "new" corporation's equity base and cash position, but they are more readily written off against available income for tax purposes.

While a more complete discussion of risk and diversification as well as the effect of risk on valuation will be provided in Chapter 29, some commentary on corporate diversification as an end in itself is useful here. Specifically, it has been argued that since investors are themselves able to diversify their holdings, they would not be willing to pay a premium for corporate diversification and it follows, therefore, that on theoretical grounds corporate diversification *per se* is irrelevant in maximizing shareholder wealth.[4]

Diversification, however, may yield an indirect benefit to shareholders. By being involved in several different industries and thereby stabilizing cash flows, a corporation may increase its debt capacity. Given the tax benefits associated

[3]While situations involving firms with negatively correlated earnings are very difficult to find, low correlations are a possibility and are often reflected in conglomerate expansion.

[4]A more rigourous argument for the irrelevance of corporate diversification for valuation is presented by S. Myers, "Procedures for Capital Budgeting Under Uncertainty", *Industrial Management Review*, Spring 1968, pp. 1-19; also H. Levy and M. Sarnat, "Diversification, Analysis and the Uneasy Case for Conglomerate Mergers", *Journal of Finance*, Sept. 1970, pp. 795-802.

with the use of corporate debt, this may lead to an increase in the value of the firm. Additionally, it must not be overlooked that while corporate diversification may not be regarded as risk-reducing by investors it certainly reduces the risks of management and this may be a significant motive in combinations. Diversification may reduce overall corporate vulnerability and risk as perceived by management since through operations in various areas which are more or less independent, the overall pattern of earnings and cash flows may become less erratic.

The recent rash of diversification programs entered into by tobacco companies provides some interesting illustrations of attempts to place eggs in different baskets. Such strategy is in sharp contrast to one of simply seeking out any undervalued situation with a view to acquisition. In 1969 and 1970, Rothmans of Pall Mall of Canada Ltd. acquired a fifty percent interest in Canadian Breweries Ltd., Benson and Hedges Canada Ltd. acquired Formosa Spring Brewereies Ltd., and MacDonald Tobacco Inc. took control of B.V.D. Ltd., a manufacturer of men's shirts and underwear. It is clear that resort to internal growth for diversification (or other reasons for that matter) would have been far slower, perhaps more costly, and certainly riskier than fusing with established businesses which command an identifiable and presumably satisfactory share of the market.

Improved financing

Even a quite profitable company may experience great difficulty in financing unusually rapid growth which, if not pursued, may impair the firm's competitive position. Fusion with a corporation that is quite liquid but lacking in reinvestment opportunities may be the solution and prove beneficial to both corporations. The business lacking cash would no longer have to postpone investments or limit its scope while the better endowed concern is regenerated. The Toronto-based company, Consolidated Computer Ltd., found that the more leases it put out on its successful Key Edit system the more pressed for funds it became. Despite assistance from governmental agencies, Consolidated found itself facing insolvency. Rather than forcing formal bankruptcy proceedings, however, creditors postponed any steps toward this end to allow the British giant, International Computers Ltd., to arrange the merging of its own Canadian subsidiary with Consolidated. Under the arrangements being considered, International Computers would supply Consolidated with the capital required to exploit its present and prospective business opportunities.[5]

It is generally appreciated that having a reasonably large number of shareholders is helpful when raising equity capital, particularly through rights offerings. One of the benefits derived from the acquisition of United Bata Resources by Pan Ocean Oil Corporation may thus have related to improved future financing since the move boosted the number of Pan Ocean shareholders from 500 to about 8,000.[6] Extending this point further, a company whose shares

[5]For greater detailing, see "How to Handle a Takeover Offer", *The Financial Post*, December 4, 1971, p. 19.
[6]"Stanley Rown and the Eight Oil Fimrs", *The Financial Post*, October 30, 1971, p. 19.

are not listed on a stock exchange and may not qualify for listing can get access to public markets by merging with a firm whose shares are traded on the exchange. Again, this may be important for a small successful concern experiencing rapid growth.

In the context of generally improving outside financing, it is interesting to note that one recent study of some seventy mergers prompted the observation that:

> . . . synergy is most easily accomplished where financial resources are pooled and . . . most difficult to achieve where production facilities are combined. Furthermore, the dollar payoff is actually lowest, on the average, where production and technological resources are put together, highest, where financial resources are combined.[7]

Competitive advantages

Greater product and market development may be achieved through carefully arranged combinations. More specifically, rigorous competition can be avoided and market control can be established more rapidly and with greater certainty through mergers or consolidations than would be possible by internal growth. Given the present state of legislation, coordinated price and output policies, which would be frowned upon if entered into by separate firms, are more readily attainable through fusion. In Canada, unlike the situation in the United States, even where a combination is expected to have an adverse effect on competition, prevailing attitudes and legislation ensure that government action need not be anticipated.

Miscellaneous considerations

Individuals holding controlling interests in publicly held corporations may find it extremely difficult to divest themselves of their holdings in a short span of time without depressing the market price of the shares. In many cases the only reasonable alternative involves sale of the controlling block of shares to another corporation for cash, or for the acquiring firm's shares if liquidity is improved through the switch of such securities. It may be more desirable to hold shares that are readily marketable for a variety of reasons including death duties.

Personal reasons are on occasion the basis for rejecting a takeover bid. For example, the rationale given by Mr. Jim Chapin for his past rejection of the numerous takeover bids for Canadian General Towers Ltd. were the family ties and the sentiment associated with the links. In his words, "the offers from a dollar standpoint are tremendous. I suppose my brother and I get a little emotional about the damned thing. . . ."[8]

Income tax considerations are frequently mentioned as a motive for combinations. A profitable corporation, for example, may seek to take over a company with losses not yet written off in order to reduce its own future taxes. It should be noted that in the absence of other motives for the fusion, the

[7]See J. Kitching, "Why Do Mergers Miscarry?" *Harvard Business Review*, November-December 1967, pp. 84-101.
[8]"Old Family Companies That Didn't Sell Out", *The Financial Post*, October 23, 1971, p. 18.

probability of any subsequent carry-forward of losses being allowed by the taxation authorities is likely to be low.

The recent economic environment of severe inflation and depressed equity prices has created opportunities for acquiring desirable assets at bargain prices. The opportunity is suggested when a company's shares are trading at twenty or thirty percent below their book value with attractive assets involved. Such circumstances were a definite consideration in Abitibi Paper's 1974 takeover of Price Company. In this instance, sought-after newsprint capacity was available very much more cheaply through Price's existing and efficient mills than through the construction of new facilities. Price Company with little debt and lots of liquid working capital offered other attractions as well.[9]

28-4. PROCEDURES

Mergers, consolidations, and more limited acquisitions of shares may be initiated through friendly negotiations between the managements of the corporations involved or may be the outcome of a tender offer. Where negotiations are entered into, the boards of directors of the respective companies are generally fully apprised and when a tentative understanding is reached about terms, ratification by the boards is sought. Upon ratification, and depending on the terms arranged, shareholder approval will have to be sought; supplementary letters patent or an alteration of the memorandum of association arranged; prospectus requirements, if any, accommodated; and a variety of statutes generally complied with. The legal considerations are clearly quite complex and fall outside of the financial officer's domain.

While shares are often acquired as an aftermath to extended negotiations, they may also be obtained by making tender offers. Under such an approach, the acquiring corporation makes a direct appeal to shareholders of the firm to be acquired and would do so along lines indicated in Figure 28-1. An offer need not be limited to an exchange of shares, however, but may involve the purchase of shares for cash. In either case, the bid extended would incorporate a premium over current market price in order to make it attractive to people holding the sought-after shares. While resort to a tender offer may follow the breakdown of negotiations, tenders are frequently used simply to avoid negotiating and thereby to speed up a takeover, merger, or consolidation. Thus, the offer by Molson Industries Ltd. for all of the common and class A shares of Beaver Lumber fell into the latter category. Molson's, by proffering a twenty-eight percent premium over the recent market price of Beaver Lumber shares, made its bid so attractive that Beaver Lumber's board of directors felt it had little choice but to recommend acceptance of the offer. Two months later, in January 1972, Molson Industries held 97 percent and 75 percent of the common and class A shares respectively.

Where a firm is subject to a takeover bid, its management may have good

[9]For greater detailing see "We Want to Go After Price", *The Financial Post*, April 3, 1976, p. 4.

personal or economic reasons for wanting to block the proposal. Though defense strategies can be quite complex and are therefore somewhat difficult to summarize, a few general comments on the subject are nevertheless useful.

On occasion, targets in a tender offer may look to the statute books to have the takeover blocked. For example, an undesirable reduction of competition might be argued where a horizontal combination is contemplated. In the event of a takeover bid from outside Canada, particularly careful government scrutiny may be called for under the Foreign Investment Review Act,[10] while pleading the point that the particular foreign takeover bid offers no significant benefit to Canada. Use of the media is naturally useful in either situation.

Support from employees, including their unions, as well as from the community may be solicited where it can be argued that a takeover would lead to a reduction in the number of jobs available in the locality. Private discussions with larger shareholders, including financial institutions, may also be held, perhaps as a prelude to getting a more acceptable party to step in with a counter-offer.

Obviously, any vigorous defense by the target firm's management virtually guarantees management's ouster if the defense tactics fail.

External growth may involve either the purchase of some or all of the assets of a business or the purchase of its shares.[11] Payment may be made in cash or in the securities of the acquiring corporation. Where only the assets are acquired, this then leaves the liabilities to be cleared away by the vendor. A business that sells off only part of its assets will probably continue to function but, if all operating assets are disposed of, it is then reduced to a corporate shell with assets comprised of the cash, or the securities in the purchasing corporation, or both. After redemption of existing liabilities a liquidating dividend may then be paid followed by surrender of the company charter. Where the vendor corporation decides not to distribute the proceeds of the sale to its shareholders, available cash is likely to be invested in other assets and a holding company of sorts may emerge. Should a minority group of stockholders decline to go along with the offer made for their shares, a merger or amalgamation can be delayed or even blocked. When, however, the minority controls less than ten percent of the shares outstanding, under the *Canada Corporations Act* and like statutes of several of the provinces, it can be required to accept the terms originally offered. Appeals to the courts are naturally provided for on grounds such as fraud or absence of full disclosure, but such actions are both difficult and costly.

An alternative to any complete combination is the purchase of a controlling block of the outstanding voting shares. Depending on the distribution of the remaining stock, effective control may be exerted by acquiring well under fifty

[10]Simply stated, the aim of this Act is to require the government to review foreign investment in Canada and to prevent such investment when it fails to offer significant benefit to Canada. The Act applies to the takeover of existing Canadian businesses as well as to the establishment of new ones and may have added significance as "oil money" moves around the globe in search of equity investment opportunities.

[11]Martin, in a study of business combinations found 80 percent to be through the purchase of shares. See S. Martin, "Business Combinations in Canada: 1960-1968", in D. Morin and W. Chippindale, eds., *Acquisitions and Mergers in Canada*, Toronto: Methuen, 1970, p. 295.

FIGURE 28-1

Advertisement Detailing A Tender Offer

ACRES

Offer by ACRES LIMITED

to acquire

Class A and Class B common shares

of

CANADIAN GENERAL SECURITIES LIMITED

and

TRADERS GROUP LIMITED

Acres Limited ("Acres") is offering to acquire Class B voting common shares in the capital of Canadian General Securities Limited ("CGS") on the following basis:

To Exchange: 1¾ common shares of Acres,

For: 1 Class B voting common share of CGS.

Acres is also offering to acquire (1) all the outstanding Class A common shares in the capital of CGS, (2) 2,065,000 Class A common shares in the capital of Traders Group Limited ("Traders"), and (3) 137,206 Class B common shares in the capital of Traders (being the balance of the shares of this class not held by CGS), in each case on the following basis:

To Exchange: (a) 1 7.20% Cumulative Redeemable Preferred Share Series B of the par value of $50 of Acres, plus

(b) 1 common share of Acres, plus

(c) 1 warrant to purchase 1 common share of Acres exercisable at $19.00 per share on or before April 1, 1973 and thereafter at $21.00 per share on or before April 1, 1975.

For: (i) 5 Class A common shares of CGS, or

(ii) 5 Class A common shares of Traders, or

(iii) 5 Class B common shares of Traders.

The foregoing offers are open for acceptance until the close of business on March 10, 1970. Shareholders of CGS and Traders may accept the offer pertaining to their respective shares by depositing their shares in the prescribed manner at any office of the Guaranty Trust Company of Canada, of which the principal ones are located as follows:

TORONTO, ONTARIO 88 University Avenue	OTTAWA, ONTARIO 109 Bank Street	MONTREAL, QUEBEC 427 St. James Street West
WINNIPEG, MANITOBA 430 Portage Avenue	REGINA, SASKATCHEWAN 2020-11th Avenue	CALGARY, ALBERTA 311-8th Avenue South West
EDMONTON, ALBERTA 10010 Jasper Avenue		VANCOUVER, BRITISH COLUMBIA 580 Hornby Street

In connection with these offers, the undersigned has formed a Soliciting Dealer Group in which all members of the Investment Dealers' Association of Canada and the Toronto, Montreal, Canadian, Winnipeg, Calgary and Vancouver Stock Exchanges have been invited to join for the purpose of soliciting and assisting the shareholders of CGS and Traders to accept the offer pertaining to the Class A common shares of CGS and the Class A and Class B common shares of Traders.

Copies of the offering letters, take-over bid circulars and letters of transmittal for depositing shares may be obtained by the shareholders of CGS and Traders from the offices of the Guaranty Trust Company of Canada, the undersigned or other members of the Soliciting Dealer Group.

McLEOD, YOUNG, WEIR & COMPANY
LIMITED

Reprinted Courtesy of McLeod, Young, Weir and Company Limited

percent of the voting shares. Because shareholders are generally quite passive when it comes to voting their shares, for most widely held companies ownership of around fifteen percent of the issued common stock provides working control. The corporation, after purchasing the necessary number of shares for control, assumes the position of a holding company and may thereby capture some of the benefits of complete fusion. Since the holding company device preserves separate legal entities (which would disappear with mergers or consolidations), such operational differences as disclosure, tax considerations, dividend policy, and general treatment of minority shareholders need to be recognized.

One of the important advantages associated with use of the holding company as a device for external expansion is that the dollar investment required for the acquisition of a controlling block of shares is smaller than that called for where the vehicle is to be a combination. Not only are far fewer shares required but, since share buying may take place gradually and informally, any inflating of share prices due to a sudden surge in demand for the shares is minimized. Argus Corporation Ltd. is one of the better-known holding companies in Canada and a useful illustration. It has substantial investments (in the range of thirteen to twenty-five percent of the shares outstanding) in B.C. Forest Products, Dominion Stores, DomTar, Hollinger Mines, and Massey-Ferguson, among others. Although the scope displayed may be atypical it does set out some measure of the opportunities afforded by holding companies as an alternative to combinations.

28-5. FINANCIAL ASPECTS

In order to simplify the discussion of the financial aspects of combinations, we shall abstract from synergistic effects or operating economies. This will help to clarify and underline the basic financial principles involved. Synergistic effects, if they are present, can then be incorporated into the basic analysis as an additional benefit of the merger or consolidation.[12]

Contrived growth in earnings per share

As mentioned earlier, mergers may be effected by an exchange of shares, or by one firm purchasing the other for cash or for a combination of cash and other securities.

The precise effects on earnings per share and share prices will depend on the financing employed. We should keep in mind, however, that a startling impact on earnings per share may relate not only to the mix of securities comprising the package being offered, but also to existing differentials between the price/earnings ratios of the acquiring and acquired corporation's shares. The

[12]For evidence that managers tend to overestimate the potential synergistic effects of mergers, see J. Kitching, "Why Do Mergers Miscarry?", *Harvard Business Review*, November-December 1967, pp. 84-101. And for evidence of the relative unprofitability of corporate growth through merger, see J. Segall, "Merging for Fun and Profit", *Industrial Management Review*, Winter 1968, pp. 17-29; M. Gort and T. Hogarty, "New Evidence on Mergers", *Journal of Law and Economics*, April, 1970, pp. 167-184: T. Hogarty, "The Profitability of Corporate Mergers", *Journal of Business*, July, 1970, pp. 317-327.

numerical illustrations given below serve to identify and clarify the issues involved.

Example

Assume the following financial information for two firms, only one of which will be merged with surviving Company A. The basis for the merger is to be a share-for-share exchange based on market prices, with Company A issuing new shares in return for the shares received from shareholders of Company 1 or Company 2.

	Company A	Company 1	Company 2
Total earnings	$16,000	$15,000	$12,000
Common shares outstanding	4,000	5,000	2,000
Earnings per share	$4.00	$3.00	$6.00
Price/earnings ratio	15	20	10
Market price of common	$60	$60	$60

The different price/earnings ratios shown in the above table may reflect different future prospects for the three firms. Company 1 may have exhibited a pattern of rapid growth, justifying its high price/earnings ratio relative to Company 2, with Company A being somewhere in between.

In the most straightforward case which would make no allowance for synergy, the expanded business entity should show earnings which are simply the sum of the earnings of the two firms being merged. Effects of the merger on earnings per share can be shown as follows:

	Total earnings after merger	Shares of Co. A outstanding	Earnings per share
Co. A fused with Co. 1	$16,000 + $15,000 = $31,000	4000 + 5000 = 9000	$31,000/9000 = $3.44
Co. A fused with Co. 2	$16,000 + $12,000 = $28,000	4000 + 2000 = 6000	$28,000/6000 = $4.67

The importance of the price/earnings ratio is obvious. If, as in the above setting, Firm A uses the market price of shares as the standard for the exchange of shares, and merges with another concern having higher earnings per share but a lower price/earnings ratio (Company 2) then expected earnings per share for Company A after the merger will be increased. New earnings per share are just a weighted average of such earnings for the two merging firms, that is

$\$4.67 = \$4 \times \frac{4000}{6000} + \$6 \times \frac{2000}{6000}$. Further, our assumed merger of A with Company 1 depicts that the reverse also holds, with earnings per share for Company A reduced to \$3.44 after the merger. By deliberately pursuing a policy of merging with other corporations having lower price/earnings ratios than itself, a firm will be able to show a growth in earnings per share.

It should be noted that owners of Company 2 need not object to receiving shares with projected earnings of \$4.67 in exchange for previous earnings per share of \$6.00, provided the lower earnings stream of the newly formed company was more highly valued by the market. If, for example, the price/earnings ratio of A, after the merger, settled at say 14, a share in A would be worth 14 × \$4.67 = \$65.38.

Growth in earnings per share which is achieved through mergers with firms having low price/earnings ratios has been termed *phantasmic growth.* The label stems from the fact that such contrived growth has no foundations in increased earning power stemming from more profitable operations, but is the side-effect of financial transactions which basically leave the earning power of the underlying business entities unchanged. Hence, in the above example, rational investors should simply react by adjusting the price-earnings ratio for shares of the acquiring firm downward to 12.85, leaving the market price of its shares (market price = increased new earnings per share × downward adjusted price/earnings ratio) unchanged. Clearly, in the absence of synergistic effects, the total market value of the combined firm should just equal the sum of the market values of the individual firms, which is given as \$60 × 4000 + \$60 × 2000 = \$360,000. In that the new firm will have 6000 shares outstanding (4000 original shares of Company A plus 2000 new shares issued to acquire Company 2), a price of \$60 per share is indicated after the merger, implying a price/earnings ratio of \$60/\$4.67 = 12.85. If, however, investors and analysts are gullible enough to perceive this increase in earnings per share as real increased profit potential, they may fail to scale down the price/earnings ratio and, in extreme cases, may even revise it upward to reflect their growing optimism.

In actual fact, during the past decade when the merger movement was at its peak, by seeking out and acquiring corporations which investors deemed relatively unattractive and which therefore had low price/earnings ratios, several conglomerates brought about fairly dramatic increases in their own earnings per share. Investors reacted by increasing price/earnings ratios, mistaking phantasmic growth for real growth. The higher ratio naturally tended to facilitate, if not accelerate, the acquisition program as it became even easier to find target firms meeting the lower price/earnings requisite. During this period, the game involving phantasmic growth was made possible largely because the reported earnings per share of firms completely dominated investor thinking and had a major impact on stock market prices. Understandably, the game itself has in retrospect been variously identified as "means by which ruthless capitalists practice the black arts of finance to their ends", as a "forward looking form of enterprise characterized by freedom from all that is hidebound in conventional corporate practice"; and as "a kind of business that services industry the way Bonnie and Clyde serviced banks."[13] Additional illustrations will complete our exposition of the game and give us a better understanding of what supposedly expert financial analysts apparently failed to grasp.[14]

We have shown that a systematic takeover of relatively unattractive firms (the shares of which sell at lower price/earnings multipliers) may cause earnings per share of the acquiring firm to rise. In this context we should also point out that the acquiring company's image as a dynamic growth firm may be sustained even when, in fact, its own real earnings potential may be deteriorating.

Example

In our earlier illustration, if the earnings of Company A were expected to dip by 20 percent, from \$16,000 to \$12,800, on merging with Company 2 it earnings per share would still show growth from \$4.00 to $\frac{\$12{,}800 + \$12{,}000}{6000} = \$4.13$.

To magnify the anticipated growth in earnings per share and perhaps sway investors into bidding up the price of its shares, Company A could have offered a mix of securities or even cash rather than just using common shares. The apparent monetary value of an offer could, in fact, have been increased and still have produced a higher earnings per share statistic. Consider an offer of one share plus \$70 of 10 percent debt by Company A for each two shares of Company 2. \$70,000 of new debt and 1000 additional common shares of A would potentially have to be issued for the latter firm's 2000 outstanding shares. With a 50 percent corporate tax rate, and in consideration of the interest on the new debt, earnings per share would have been

$$\frac{(\$16{,}000 + \$12{,}000) - (.5 \times .10 \times \$70{,}000)}{4000 + 1000} = \$4.90$$

A straight cash offer of \$80 per share, with monies raised from short-term sources at say 8 percent would have pushed earnings per share up even further to $\frac{\$28{,}000 - (.5 \times .08 \times \$160{,}000)}{4000}$ or an impressive \$5.40

The question of what might cause such contrived or phantasmic growth to end is an obvious one. To respond, a variety of possibilities need to be recognized

- debt financing at reasonable cost and with few restrictive provisions may no longer be available
- the servicing of debt may become too burdensome; with inadequate cash flows to meet fixed charges
- where short-term monies are used, on maturity refunding may be possible only at higher rates of interest
- the acquiring firm's high price/earnings ratio can no longer be sustained,

[13]For an interesting account of this period, see J. Brooks, *The Go-Go Years*, New York: Weybright and Talley, 1973, in particular Chapter 7, "The Conglomerateurs".

[14]See W. Rukeyser, "Why Rain Fell on 'Automatic' Sprinkler", *Fortune*, May 1969, pp. 88-91, 126-129.

perhaps because other firms of sufficient size with modest price/earnings ratios can no longer be located and taken over, thereby reducing the rate of growth in reported earnings per share.

It is not surprising, therefore, that during the early 1970s—a period characterized by tight money, high interest rates and declining stock market prices—the era of phantasmic growth and the earnings per share game came to an abrupt end.[15]

Example

Consider the well-known U.S. case of Litton Industries. During 1961, with earnings per share of $2.30, the common stock traded at price/earnings ratios of between 37 and 72, explainable in large measure by the growth illusions of investors. By 1970, with earnings down to $1.90 per share, the ratio was in the 8 to 20 range. In Canada, Neonex International Ltd. provides a useful, if less dramatic, example. After seven acquisitions in 1968, and with earnings per share of 60 cents, the price/earnings ratio ranged between 20 and 66. By 1971, earnings on the common were 43 cents while the ratio varied between 6 and 12.

Negotiations

A major area of emphasis in the bargaining process which attends any negotiated combination is the ratio to be used when shares are exchanged. Where publicly traded shares are involved, an obvious starting point for determining the exchange ratio is market price. However, in a merger situation, for example, there is little enticement for those controlling the firm to be acquired to recommend general acceptance of a one-to-one market value ratio of exchange. The acquiring corporation must consequently offer some premium for the sought-after shares. When a premium is offered the acquiring company's shareholders are better off only if the market value of the combined firm exceeds the total premium plus the pre-offer combined market values of the two firms.

In situations involving tendering, the offer of an inducement to shareholders of the sought-after corporation poses a problem in strategy for some owners. Because the market price of the sought after shares often adjusts upward immediately after a tender announcement to reflect the premium proffered, shareholders must decide whether to accept the terms or to hold off. If they do not turn in their shares it may be because they anticipate even better terms to be forthcoming.

A practical problem associated with any negotiated exchange or tender offer based on market values is that these values can fluctuate significantly over even relatively short time spans and the appropriate figures may be in doubt. As a consequence, some corporations vary the timing of their acquisitions in keeping with the price of their shares, becoming increasingly aggressive with any relative increase in the quotations on their stock.

[15]Where a company is legally permitted to buy back and retire its own common shares (see Chapter 21), declining stock prices facilitate a different earnings per share game, the so-called "split-off". Here, less profitable assets including whole operating units are sold off for cash which is then used to reduce the number of shares outstanding.

Generally speaking and for reasons outlined in Chapter 10, book values per share are rather unsatisfactory measures on which to base an exchange-of-shares ratio unless both the book and liquidation values for the given situation exceed the market price of the shares.[16] In such circumstances, it is possible that the major objective behind any proposed combination is a partial liquidation of the acquired firm making the working capital and book value per share quite significant in arriving at terms for the exchange.

A capital budgeting approach to evaluating combinations

The questionable preoccupation with earnings per share and phantasmic growth dominated appraoches to the evaluation of business combinations during the late 1960's. Thus, it is paradoxical that while most acquisitions of plant and equipment required a capital budgeting approach of one type or another, such systematic analysis was abandoned when the potential investment involved an entire business concern. Managerial and legal problems aside, the commitment of funds towards building a plant is not significantly different from investing to acquire an ongoing business. Though the latter will have a more immediate impact on reported earnings per share, both investments involve expectations about future cash flows and should be evaluated accordingly. Such consistency is both logical and over the longer run worthwhile.

Example

Using a very simple illustration to start with, consider a business planning to acquire a firm having the following characteristics: (a) no senior securities outstanding; (b) all its assets are useful to the acquiring firm and are to be retained; (c) physical assets match the firm's readily indentifiable lifespan of 10 years with no need of prior replacement; and (d) no prospects for synergy. After-tax net cash inflows anticipated from the acquisition are $10,000 per year for the first 5 years increasing to $12,000 per year for the remaining life of the firm. The acquiring firm imposes a required rate of return of 12 percent after taxes on all of its investments. Given these inputs, net present value analysis by the acquiring firm would dictate that the maximum cash or cash equivalent outlay for this particular acquisition should be limited to no more than the present value of expected cash inflows, in this case

$$\$10,000 \times 3.605 + \$12,000 \times (5.650 - 3.605) = \$60,590.$$

In altering the example to allow for more general circumstances, both the disposition of any redundant assets and the possible need to periodically invest further sums can readily be reflected in the cash flow projections. For instance, some assets may be sold at the time of acquisition to net $15,000 increasing the first year's cash inflow from $10,000 to $25,000. Further, replacement of a truck after 5 years at $6,000 would simply reduce the 6th year's inflow to $6,000.

[16]As at December 31, 1967, the J.H. Ashdown Hardware Co. Ltd. of Winnipeg had a book value of about $30 per share and working capital of $20 per share. The class A and B shares had market prices in the $8 to $10 range. By late 1968, Acklands Ltd. had acquired approximately 98% of all the outstanding shares.

In a net present value approach to the evaluation of business acquisitions, which is based on discounted cash flow analysis, the actual computation of future inflows resulting from the acquisition may not be straightforward and requires some interpretation.

An issue which frequently arises in merger analysis is how to account for the different capital structures of potential acquisitions. Consider two potential firms to be acquired, with identical levels of earnings before interest and taxes and the same business risk, one being all-equity financed and the other having debt outstanding. Adopting the Miller-Modigliani framework discussed in Chapter 14, it is apparent that, because of the tax deductibility of interest, the value of the levered firm may be higher than that of the unlevered concern. This then raises the question of whether the acquiring corporation is justified in paying more for the levered firm than the unlevered one. The answer is clearly that it would not, since by acquiring the *unlevered* firm and issuing new debt subsequently, it could leverage it up to the value of the levered company. Hence, what is important in determining the value of a potential acquisition is not its *current* capital structure but rather its optimal *potential* capital structure. In other words, we must ensure that inputs are not biased by the target company's particular capital structure since after the merger the acquiring firm can readily adjust the capital structure of the firm being acquired.

Example

> Assume the optimal capital structure in this instance to be 100 percent equity. If $10,000 of 10 percent debt forms part of the capital structure of the firm to be acquired, then to separate the investment from the financing decision, after-tax interest charges of $500 per year (.50 × .10 × $10,000, assuming a corporate tax rate of 50 per cent) must be added back when estimating the anticipated after-tax cash flows from the investment. This represents what cash flows would be if the debt were retired and the company financed entirely through common equity. In addition, from the present value of cash inflows we must subtract the present value of any of the acquired firm's liabilities which were not included in the computation of cash flows but which are being assumed as a consequence of the fusion, such as the $10,000 of principal to be repaid.

In determining value, the approach must also be amended to reflect those benefits of synergy with which the acquiring firm is prepared to credit the "to be acquired" entity. Assuming synergy to contribute an additional after-tax cash inflow of $4000 annually, the basis on which this amount is shared (between the parent firm and the newly acquired firm) is obviously critical.

A difficulty which frequently occurs in synergistic mergers is a difference of opinion between buyer and seller as to the value of the synergistic effects. If the difference is too great, then the merger will not be consummated. On the other hand, it is sometimes possible to devise contingent payment schedules which make the actual amount paid for the acquisition a function of success of the fusion. A common way in which this is done in mergers of publicly traded companies is by issuance of convertible securities. These will tend to be valued more highly by the optimistic sellers than by the pessimistic buyers of the company. Where estimates of future performance are dependent on managerial performance, consideration must also be given to providing incentives for the management of the acquired entity.

Lastly, selection of an appropriate time horizon is called for as a decision has to be made on how many years into the future cash flows are to be estimated and included in the analysis. With provision already made in the cash flows for the periodic replacement of physical assets, conceptually an infinite investment horizon may be argued, as this avoids any arbitrary choice of a time span. Problems associated with attempting to predict, over a long time horizon, growth in an acquired company's cash flows may be avoided by assuming zero growth after a finite number of years. In practice, however, some arbitrary finite horizon such as 10 or 20 years is likely to be set, beyond which cash flows will not be considered. Given the impact of discounting at currently prevailing rates, very little is lost by making this concession.

The influence of income taxes on business acquisitions is an important topic but one which is extremely technical, subject to periodic legislative change and, in general, outside the scope of an introductory course in finance. For our purposes it is sufficient to note that tax considerations must not be ignored when considering how the merger or acquisition transaction is to be effected, and that expert advice generally needs to be called for.[17]

28-6. SUMMARY

Business expansion can be achieved not only through internal investments, but also externally through combinations of separate business entities. Such combinations take several forms, such as holding companies, mergers and consolidations. Motivations leading to a combination may be varied, although ultimately the profit motive is the driving force behind most combinations. Synergy is said to exist if economies inherent in the fusion lead to improved efficiency for the combined entity as compared with individual and separate operations. A combination may be arranged through negotiations between management including boards of directors, with ratifications by shareholders, or through a tender offer whereby a direct appeal is made to the shareholders. A target company may be acquired through the purchase of its shares, or by a purchase of its assets. Tax considerations play an important role in determining exactly how a merger or acquisition is to be effected.

[17]It is interesting to note that in a project jointly sponsored by the Canadian Institute of Chartered Accountants and the University of Western Ontario, the authors reported that "In 71 of the 93 acquisitions (reviewed) we were told that income tax did not influence the transaction to any significant extent." See S. Martin, S. Laiken, D. Haslam *Business Combinations in the '60s: A Canadian Profile*, 1969, p. 34.

Financially, business combinations have an immediate effect on reported earnings per share for the shareholders of both business entities, and possibly on the shares' price earnings ratios and market prices as well. With no synergy present in a combination which is effected by an exchange of shares based on market values, the wealth position of shareholders should remain unaffected. Earnings per share, however, may grow if a firm whose shares trade at a high price-earnings ratio acquires another firm whose shares trade at lower price-earnings ratios, giving rise to the phenomenon of phantasmic growth. Rather than being primarily preoccupied with immediate effects on earnings per share, an acquisition ought to be viewed as an investment, and capital budgeting criteria based on discounted cash flow analysis are applicable. The framework for a net present value type of analysis was outlined.

Questions for Discussion

1. Critique the statement that "As a general rule, firms interested in contrived or phantasmic growth cannot afford to rely on capital budgeting approaches when evaluating potential acquisitions".
2. In a negotiated merger it is useful to consider a contingent payments schedule based on the success of the combination. Suggest ways in which this might be done.
3. (a) Why does the acquiring firm in a merger usually offer a premium for the sought-after shares?
   (b) Why would an all-common-equity offer probably involve a more modest premium than an offer package which included debt? Discuss.
4. Under what circumstances might the book value of a "potentially to be acquired" firm's common shares become important in determining the price to be paid?
5. For how long can a firm increase its earnings per share through mergers? Discuss.
6. "Economies of scale and diversification are the main factors leading to a combination of firms." Do you agree? Discuss.
7. "Both management and the shareholders should be willing to pay a premium for the acquisition of firms with earnings negatively correlated with ours." Discuss.
8. (a) What set of circumstances make a firm a more likely candidate for takeover?
   (b) Given an unfriendly takeover bid, suggest some defense tactics.

Problems with Solutions

1. A-2 Manufacturing Company is a welding and machine shop company that undertakes a balanced mix of custom and production-line type work. The quality of their product is well-regarded, partly because of the inventiveness of the firm's owner, Bob Aytu. However, business has been slow lately

because of an overall slowdown in capital spending in the firm's locality. Bob recently had a heart attack and would like to retire early, living on the proceeds from the sale of A-2. In his efforts to find a buyer, he first found a holding company, Liqui-Date, Inc., that continually negotiated as though it would simply liquidate A-2's assets. A-2 had net income of $60,000 last year (down from $70,000 the year before, on roughly the same capital base). Liqui-Date offered $500,000 cash for A-2. However, Bob felt A-2 had established a lot of goodwill in his community and this should enable the firm to continue operation, commanding a higher price. He also had close personal relationships with his employees and realized that, under the Liqui-Date offer, they would lose their jobs. So he searched harder and went to a major conglomerate, the South Seas Bubblegum Co. South Seas had a plant nearby which was expanding so rapidly that it needed a machine shop operation, and the conglomerate felt that the outright purchase of a functioning shop would generate savings of $15,000, $10,000 and $5,000, in each of the first three years, respectively, compared to the creation of a machine shop division from scratch. The A-2 shop could readily handle this new work in addition to its own previous work. Accordingly South Seas' management offered Bob 10,000 shares of its own common stock (recently trading at $70) in exchange for his firm. In addition to the synergistic effect already mentioned, South Seas' management analyzed the merger from an earnings per share viewpoint (before the offer, they had a net income of $1 million, or $2.50 per share). All three firms have a 50% corporate tax rate.

No other takeover possibilities are in sight.

(a) What P/E ratios seem applicable to the takeover bids?
(b) What will the takeover do for South Seas' eanings per share and P/E ratio?
(c) What would you recommend that Bob should do?

Solution

1\. (a) Applicable P/E ratios are those of the A-2 Manufacturing Company and South Seas Bubblegum Co. Since A-2 is a closely held firm with no public trading, it has no market price and we must use the prices offered by Liqui-Date and South Seas to arrive at its P/E ratio.

Using the Liqui-Date offer the P/E ratio is:

$$\frac{\text{Amount offered}}{\text{Last year's earnings}} = \frac{\$500{,}000}{\$60{,}000} = 8.33$$

Using South Seas' offer we determine the P/E ratio as:

$$\frac{10{,}000 \times \$70}{\$60{,}000} = \frac{\$700{,}000}{\$60{,}000} = 11.67$$

South Seas' P/E ratio is readily determinable from the question

$$\frac{\text{Market price}}{\text{Last year's earnings per share}} = \frac{\$70}{\$2.50} = 28$$

(b) We see that since South Seas has a higher P/E ratio than A-2 (based on the South Seas offering price) if A-2 continued at its current rate of earnings, a takeover would enhance South Seas' earnings per share, with no consideration of the synergistic effects.

This effect may be calculated as follows:

Before takeover, South Seas has earnings per share of \$2.50.

After a takeover South Seas would expect the following earnings:

Previous earnings	\$1,000,000
A-2 earnings	60,000
After-tax savings from the first year relating to the advantage of purchasing A-2 as opposed to building a machine shop: 15,000(1–.5)	7,500
Consolidated new earnings	\$1,067,500

Thus the earnings per share for South Seas rises to

$$\frac{\$1{,}067{,}500}{400{,}000 + 10{,}000^*} = \$2.60 \text{ per share.}$$

*The additional 10,000 shares issued to Bob Aytu.

It is not possible to say what South Seas' P/E will become. If phantasmic growth is perceived by investors then share prices may stay the same or fall, leading to a reduction in the P/E ratio of 28. Conversely it is possible that investors, in seeing the increasing earnings per share, will in fact bid up the price of the shares so that the P/E ratio will remain the same or even increase.

(c) Bob should take the South Seas offer if he can find a ready market for most or all of the South Seas shares he receives. Bob needs some diversification in his portfolio and South Seas may simply be exhibiting phatasmic growth—if stock prices fall, Bob could easily wind up with less than the Liqui-Date offer if he holds on to his South Seas shares.

2. If the management of South Seas Bubblegum was more thorough, it would have analyzed the takeover in Problem 1 from a capital budgeting standpoint. You are asked to undertake such an analysis. The following data, in addition to those supplied in Problem 1, are relevant:
   (i) South Seas requires at least a 12% return on its investments, after tax.
   (ii) A-2's earnings before depreciation and taxes are unlikely to change over the years (apart from the special synergistic savings in the first 3 years) since increased use of A-2's facilities by South Seas would complement a decline in business from the rest of the community.

A-2's current income statement can be abbreviated as:

Gross earnings before depreciation and interest	$235,000
Depreciation expense	85,000
Interest expense	30,000
Taxes	60,000
Net income	$ 60,000

(iii) A-2 currently has $300,000 of 10% debt outstanding.

(iv) A-2's facilities are quite new, and since no expansion of operations is forecast, no significant capital additions will be needed for 15 years. After 15 years, the land will probably be worth its original cost of $100,000 and the inventories worth $80,000. At that time the buildings and machinery will have a negligible salvage value.

(v) Currently A-2 has $50,000 in an asset class (its building) that has a declining balance capital cost allowance rate of 10%. Its machinery is in a $300,000 declining balance asset class, with a maximum rate of 30%.

(vi) South Seas would retire A-2's debt immediately.

Solution

A-2's basic cash flow before taxes and depreciation is now:

Gross revenue before depreciation and interest	$235,000
Taxes (before C.C.A. shield) @ 50%	117,500
Cash flow before C.C.A. tax shield	$117,500

(Interest is 0 as all debt is retired.)

We calculate the net present value of A-2, under the South Seas offer as:

Year		Cash Flow	P.V. Factor	P.V. of After Tax Cash Flows
0	10,000 shares @ $70 market value	–700,000	1.0	–700,000
	Debt incurred by A-2, paid off on acquisition	–300,000	1.0	–300,000
	P.V. of C.C.A. @ 30% (machinery) $\frac{300{,}000 \times .3 \times .5}{.3 + .12}$			107,143
	P. V. of C.C.A. @ 10% (building) $\frac{50{,}000 \times .1 \times .5}{.1 + .12}$			11,364
1	Synergistic effect (after tax) (0.5 × $15,000)	7,500	.893	6,698
2	Synergistic effect (after tax) (0.5 × $10,000)	5,000	.797	3,985
3	Synergistic effect (after tax) (0.5 × $5,000)	2,500	.712	1,780

Year	Cash Flow	P.V. Factor	P.V. of After Tax Cash Flows
1-15 Cash flow (excluding C.C.A tax shield)	117,500	6.811	800,293
15 Land	100,000	.183	18,300
Inventory	80,000	.183	14,640
Net present value of purchase A-2			–35,797

Thus, from a capital budgeting standpoint, South Sea should not acquire A-2 Manufacturing, but rather create its own smaller machinery division and invest its managerial talent and assets elsewhere. This shows how sole consideration of earnings per share can be misleading in decisions to acquire other firms.

Additional Problems

1. Consider the Alpha Company which plans to take over the Omega Company. Relevant data are as follows:

	Alpha	Omega
Earnings per share	$ 2.50	$ 3.50
Market share price	$35.00	$35.00
Number of shares outstanding	1,000	1,000

There would be no synergetic effects in a combination of Alpha and Omega.

(a) What are the P/E ratios of Alpha and Omega?

(b) If Alpha offered a one-for-one share exchange with Omega (based on their identical market prices) and the resulting market value per share was unchanged, what would the new P/E ratio and earnings per share be?

(c) If Alpha, noticing that its earnings per share rise with the offer in (b), decides to entice shareholders of Omega with a better offer of 5 shares of Alpha for 4 shares of Omega, what would the new earnings per share be after this takeover? What earnings in the new firm would now be available to a shareholder who originally held 10 shares of Alpha?

(d) Suppose the takeover bid failed, but a shareholder with 10 shares of Alpha sold 5 shares of Alpha and bought 5 shares of Omega (same price). What earnings would be available from his new diversified holdings? Compare this with the earnings available to him under schemes (b) and (c).

(e) Is the Alpha shareholder better off in (c) than (d)? Better off with (b) than (d)?

2. The Huge Co. is negotiating a takeover of the Tiny Co. and is using a capital budgeting approach. Huge currently has a cost of capital of 10% and because it is so much larger than Tiny, expects that there is no need to re-evaluate its

cost of capital after the takeover. Relevant performance estimates for Tiny are:

Annual operating cash flows after tax including tax shields:
Years 1 to 5: $20,000 in year 1, increasing by $5,000 annually,
Years 6 to 10: $40,000 annually

New equipment required in year 5 (capital cost allowance already included in the above): $50,000. Estimated market value of Tiny at the end of year 10, net of recaptured depreciation and capital gains: $100,000. Tiny has no long-term debt.

(a) What is the maximum cash offer Huge should make to the shareholders of Tiny?

(b) Huge is considering offering a mixture of its own securities for the 10,000 common shares of Tiny, on the basis of 100 shares of Tiny for:
   10 common shares of Huge (market value $50)
   10 preferred shares (8 percent) of Huge, with a negotiable par value (on which the 8 percent dividend will be paid).
   $1,000 secured note at 8% (market value is estimated to be par value).

   Huge has some other preferred stock outstanding that would rank equally with this preferred offering and is yielding 8% at current market prices.

   What is the maximum par value of the preferred securities that Huge can afford to offer?

3. Using data to be found in your library find an example of a combination of two firms. Briefly discuss the legal form of the combination. What do you think was the motivation behind it from each company's point of view. Pay particular attention to the financial implications of the arrangements made.

Case

SK Industries Ltd.

Mrs. Britt Bruzelius, senior planner in the corporate development department of SK Industries was preparing a final report to be considered by Bertil Ek, the firm's financial vice-president. Mrs. Bruzelius had been asked to report on whether $1,000,000 was a reasonable value to be placed on the outstanding common shares of Texon Plastics Ltd. The shares were owned by four descendants of Erik Andersson who founded the business.

It was specifically suggested to Mrs. Bruzelius that she use a capital budgeting approach in her analysis, making it the basis for her recommendation. Any assumptions made for purposes of the analysis were to be elaborated upon.

The following projected data based on Texxon's forecasts were accepted as reasonable and turned over to Mrs. Bruzelius for her consideration.

Financial Data (in millions of dollars)

	1976	1977	1978	1979	1980	1981	1982	1983	1984	1985
Earnings before interest, taxes and depreciation	1.26	1.31	1.30	1.41	1.40	1.50	1.70	1.80	1.90	1.90
Capital cost allowances	0.20	0.20	0.30	0.30	0.30	0.30	0.40	0.40	0.40	0.40
Bond interest	0.30	0.27	0.24	0.21	0.18	0.15	0.12	0.09	0.06	0.03
Capital expenditures	0.00	0.00	0.50	0.60	0.00	0.70	0.00	0.00	0.80	0.00
Increases in working capital	0.00	0.00	0.00	0.00	0.40	0.00	0.00	0.00	0.00	0.50

Sinking fund payments of $300,000 a year were called for in connection with the $3 million 10-year 10 percent mortgage bond issue only just placed privately by Texon. The issue incorporated a 5% call premium. Texon held marketable securities of $300,000 and a cash balance of $160,000 in excess of what would be required after the merger.

SK Industries paid corporate taxes of 50%, used a discount rate of 14% for all its investment decisions and followed a policy of avoiding the use of long-term debt. Mr. Ek was quite willing, however, to consider leaving the bonds outstanding until the end of 1980. It was also noted that he did not wish to consider any net inflows after 1985 in arriving at a valuation. Mr. Ek was, however, prepared to consider a liquidation value at the end of 1985, leaving the addressing of this point to Mrs. Bruzelius. He also recognized that for a variety of reasons, Texon had far greater debt capacity than SK Industries and wanted some consideration given to this fact.

Selected References

H. Ansoff and F. Weston, "Merger Objectives and Organization Structure", *Quarterly Review of Economics and Business*, August 1962, pp. 49-58.

A. Appleyard and G. Yarrow, "The Relationship Between Take-Over Activity and Share Valuation", *Journal of Finance*, December, 1975, pp. 1239-1249.

D. Austin, "The Financial Management of Tender Offer Takeovers", *Financial Management*, Spring, 1974, pp. 37-43.

A. Buckley, "A Review of Acquisition Valuation Models—a Comment", *Journal of Business Finance and Accounting*, Spring, 1975, pp. 147-151.

G. Burck, "The Merger Movement Rides High", *Fortune*, February 1969, pp. 79-83.

Canada, *Concentration in the Manufacturing Industries of Canada*, Ottawa: Department of Consumer and Corporate Affairs, 1971.

J. Franks, R. Miles and J. Bagwell, "A Review of Acquisition Valuation Models", *Journal of Business Finance and Accounting*, Spring, 1974, pp. 34-53.

J. Heath, "Valuation Factors and Techniques in Mergers and Acquisitions", *Financial Executive*, April, 1972, pp. 34-44.

T. Hogarty, "The Profitability of Corporate Mergers", *Journal of Business*, July 1970, pp. 317-327.

A. Kaplan, "The Current Merger Movement Analyzed", *Harvard Business Review*, May-June, 1955, pp. 91-98.

H. Kinard, "Financing Mergers and Acquisitions", *Financial Executive*, August 1963, pp. 13-16.

J. Kitching, *Acquisitions in Europe*, Geneva: Business International, 1973.

J. Kitching, "Why Do Mergers Miscarry?", *Harvard Business Review*, November-December 1967, pp. 84-101.

H. Levy and M. Sarnat, "Diversification, Portfolio Analysis and the Uneasy Case for Conglomerate Mergers", *Journal of Finance*, September 1970, pp. 795-802.

S. Martin, S. Laiken, and D. Haslam, *Business Combinations in the '60s: A Canadian Profile*, London: School of Business Administration, University of Western Ontario, 1969.

M. May, "The Chain Letter Revisited", *Financial Analysts' Journal*, May-June 1968, pp. 113-117.

R. Melicher, "Financing with Convertible Preferred Stock: Comment", *Journal of Finance*, March 1971, pp. 144-147.

R. Melicher and D. Rush, "Evidence on the Acquisition-Related Performance of Conglomerate Firms", *Journal of Finance*, March, 1974, pp. 141-149.

D. Morin and W. Chippindale, eds., *Acquisitions and Mergers in Canada*, Toronto: Methuen, 1970.

S. Myers, "Procedures for Capital Budgeting Under Uncertainty", *Industrial Management Review*, Spring 1968, pp. 1-19.

G. Pinches, "A Reply to Financing with Convertible Preferred Stock: Comment", *Journal of Finance*, March, 1971, pp. 150-151.

G. Pinches, "Financing With Convertible Preferred Stock, 1960-1967", *Journal of Finance*, March 1970, pp. 53-64.

F. Reilly, "What Determines the Ratio of Exchange in Corporate Mergers?", *Financial Analysts' Journal*, November-December 1962, pp. 47-50.

W. Reinhardt, *Mergers and Consolidations: A Corporate-Finance Approach*, Morristown: General Learning Press, 1972.

J. Segall, "Merging for Fun and Profit", *Industrial Management Review*, Winter 1968, pp. 17-29.

R. Schick, "The Analysis of Mergers and Acquisitions", *Journal of Finance*, May, 1972, pp. 495-502.

I. Silberman, "A Note on Merger Valuation", *Journal of Finance*, June 1968, pp. 528-534.

D. Smatter and R. Lancey, "P/E Analysis in Acquisition Strategy", *Harvard Business Review*, November-December 1966, pp. 85-95.

R. Sprecher, "A Note on Financing Mergers with Convertible Preferred Stock", *Journal of Finance*, June, 1971, pp. 683-686.

PART 10
Risk-Return Relationships in Finance

**Chapter 29
Some Conceptual Developments in Risk-Return Relationships

29-1. INTRODUCTION

In numerous places throughout this text, we found that the tradeoff between anticipated risk and expected return was an important component of financial decision-making. For example, in making capital budgeting decisions, the financial executive is typically faced with having to select from among competing project proposals which differ both in terms of their anticipated risks and rates of return. In financing a firm, debt may prove to be the cheapest source of funds, but increasing debt-equity ratios adds to the riskiness of the firm. We have discussed various techniques which the financial executive may use to guide decision-making in these areas. However, we have not yet systematically discussed the issue of risks *versus* returns, nor have we considered how the tradeoff between these two dimensions of financial decision-making might be handled.

Given the objective of maximizing long-run share prices which was developed in Chapter 1, we have to be guided by investor preference and behavior if we are to develop optimal rules for corporate decision-making. Clearly, a corporation will only be able to maximize its share prices if its behavior with regard to risk-return tradeoffs is consistent with the preferences expressed by investors in the capital markets. If, for example, a firm accepted undue risks for a given level of anticipated returns, investors would view the shares of such a firm to be relatively unattractive. It follows that share prices would decline until the shares once again promised a level of return which was in line with the risks to be borne. Consequently, in this chapter we will look largely at investor behavior, which will then help us to develop a conceptual framework for risk-return tradeoffs at the corporate level.

Two different approaches are possible in this context. We could simply attempt to find, through descriptive studies, how investors appear to behave. Alternatively, we could postulate certain hypotheses on how rational, well-informed investors ought to behave. Such hypotheses might lead us to expect certain tradeoffs between risk and return which ought to prevail in the capital markets. We could then set out to test empirically to what extent data observed in the capital markets confirm or disprove what we expected to find. Hence, the choice is between a purely descriptive approach, which simply attempts to state things as they are, and an approach which, relying on certain assumptions, derives things as they ought to be, and which then uses empirical testing to verify the model which was postulated. The latter approach is much more fruitful: if a given model appears to be borne out in practice, this not only provides us with information as to how the markets behave, but the model also enables us to better understand the markets and their underlying processes.

In recent years a great deal of effort in finance has been directed towards the development of models for capital markets, and the empirical testing of such models. Important new insights have resulted, both in terms of understanding key dimensions of rational investor behavior, and in terms of explaining capital markets as they were observed in practice. This body of knowledge has now matured to a point where it can no longer be ignored by the corporate financial officer. For example, institutional investors, in deciding on their portfolio holdings and in evaluating individual securities, rely increasingly on the modern concepts which have been developed in this area. With growing frequency these ideas also find their way into hearings before regulatory commissions which determine fair rates of return. It follows that even an introductory book such as this one should no longer side-step topics like portfolio theory and the capital asset pricing model (CAPM). It is the purpose of this chapter to provide the beginning student with a brief overview of the key concepts and models which are relevant in this context. The emphasis will be on providing an overview, stressing those aspects which may prove to have particular relevance for the practitioner. Nevertheless, presentation of the material in this chapter has to rely on basic concepts from probability and statistics. As it is not reasonable to attempt to inject a basic tutorial in statistics into a finance text, we assume the reader to have had at least an elementary exposure to statistics. The chapter is starred largely because it should be omitted by those who lack such a background.

A full development of all the theories which have emerged, and their empirical tests, is beyond the scope of this text, and properly belongs in a more advanced and specialized course.

We start by defining the concepts of risk and return, and how they may be conveniently measured. We proceed to introduce the concept of portfolio diversification, and to show how investors ought to select among alternative portfolios. Finally, drawing on portfolio theory, we derive and discuss the capital asset pricing model, which specifies how the market relates risk and expected return. A discussion of how these findings relate to financial decision-making completes this chapter.

29-2. MEASURES OF RISK AND RETURN

Returns from holding an asset or a security for a given period of time can be measured either in absolute or in percentage amounts. The absolute return is simply the value of the asset at the end of the period, including any cash flow realized from the asset during the holding period, minus the value of the asset at the beginning of the period. The percentage gain is best expressed by relating the absolute gain to the beginning value of the asset. Assume an investor holds a security for one period. We define the following notation:

V_0 = value of the security at the beginning of the period

V_1 = value of the security at the end of the period

D_1 = dividends paid on the security during the holding period. We assume for simplicity that such dividends are all paid just prior to the end of the period.

As discussed in Chapter 20, the one-period return from holding the security simply becomes:

$$(1) \quad \text{relative return} = R = \frac{D_1 + V_1 - V_0}{V_0}$$

$$(1a) \quad \text{absolute return} = R \times V_0 = D_1 + V_1 - V_0$$

The return thus measures the amount which can be withdrawn by the investor at the end of the period without affecting the amount of principal originally invested.[1]

In our subsequent discussion, returns are mostly expressed in relative terms, as more general results can be derived if returns are independent of the amounts actually invested. In any event, if relative returns are given, absolute returns are easily derived should it become necessary to evaluate individual decisions.

The concept of risk is somewhat more complex. At an intuitive level, the notion of risk appears to relate in some way to the variability of anticipated returns. If returns are known with certainty, and we can assume a particular value with a probability of one, then clearly no risk is present.

We saw in Chapter 6 that variables which are subject to uncertainty can conveniently be portrayed in terms of their probability distributions. We also discussed that, in the most general setting, the entire shape of the probability distribution may be of relevance in assessing and evaluating risk. On the other hand, working with probability distributions can be quite cumbersome, making any type of modelling unduly complex. Fortunately, there may be good reasons why certain types of simplifications yield perfectly acceptable results which are reasonable approximations for reality. Specifically, risk is often assumed to be associated with the standard deviation or variance of returns. Given that the variance measures the overall variability of a distribution around its expected value, resort to this measure of risk is not inconsistent with the intuitive notion as outlined above.[2]

Some writers have argued that risk-averse investors are only concerned about the lower half of the probability distribution, or about the possibility of returns which fall short of the expected value. If returns should exceed expectations, this

[1]Where returns over several periods are involved, computation of the average return per period becomes somewhat more complex, and several different averages can be relied on depending on the assumptions made. For example, reliance on the arithmetic average will only be meaningful if the amount invested at the beginning of each period is the same, which means that any intermediate gains are withdrawn and losses are made up through reinvestments. Where no intermediate withdrawals and reinvestments take place, the geometric average provides a better measure of average returns per period. See for example, F. Modigliani and G. Pogue, "An Introduction to Risk and Return; Concepts and Evidence", *Financial Analysts Journal*, March/April 1974, pp. 68-80.

[2]Strictly speaking, looking at only the variance as the proper measure of risk for a probability distribution is only permissable under either one of the following two assumptions: (1) either the probability distribution under consideration is normal, in which case it can be fully described by just its mean and variance, or, (2) the decision-maker's utility has a particular form which can be expressed by a quadratic function, in which case we can show that regardless of the mean of the probability distribution only its variance is of concern. In practice, returns are often more or less normally distributed, and a quadratic utility function provides a manageable way of portraying an investor's risk-aversion. Hence, resort to the variance as a measure of risk is not only mathematically convenient, but also defensible in terms of realism.

will be a pleasant surprise, but such possibilities should not be included in a measure of risk. This argument would lead us to postulate the semivariance of returns as a more appropriate measure of risk, as the semivariance just measures the variability of a distribution below its mean. Specifically, given:

$E(R)$ = expected value of R
$p(R)$ = probability distribution of R

the variance σ^2 of the probability distribution of R is defined as:[3]

$$(2)\quad \sigma_R^2 = \sum_{\text{all } R} (R - E(R))^2 p(R)$$

while the semivariance would be given as:

$$(3)\quad \sum_{\text{all } R < E(R)} (R - E(R))^2 p(R)$$

Thus, the variance measures the expected squared deviation of a variable from its means, while the semivariance just measures the expected squared deviation of values which are below the mean, with positive variations ignored and assigned a value of zero.

While the notion of semivariance may be intuitively appealing, in many practical situations the distinction between these two measures of risk (variance and semivariance) does not appear to be very important. Specifically, if the distribution of returns is symmetrical around its mean, it is easy to show that the semivariance will always be one-half the value of the variance.[4] Therefore, under such circumstances, the relative risk rankings of various investment alternatives will remain the same regardless of the measure which we use. We stress that in our search for a measure of risk, we are not concerned with finding an absolute measure; rather, we are concerned with being able to rank alternative investments according to their relative risk, and with being able to compare risks in terms of proportions—stating, for example, that one project is twice as risky as another. Given that empirical studies have shown the returns on many investments to be at least approximately symmetrical, and given that the variance is often computationally a more convenient measure than the semivariance, total variability of returns as measured by the variance is the most commonly used measure of risk in financial modelling.

[3] Where a continuous probability density function $f(R)$ is used, the formulas become:

$$\sigma_R^2 = \int_{-\infty}^{+\infty} (R - E(R))^2 f(R)\, dR$$

and

$$\text{semivariance} = \int_{-\infty}^{E(R)} (R - E(R))^2 f(R)\, dR$$

[4] For a distribution which is symmetrical around its mean, $E(R)$, we have:

$$\begin{aligned} \sigma_R^2 &= \int_{-\infty}^{+\infty} (R - E(R))^2 f(R)\, dR \\ &= \int_{-\infty}^{E(R)} 2(R - E(R))^2 f(R)\, dR \\ &= 2 \times \text{semivariance} \end{aligned}$$

Example

Consider that returns on holding a particular asset for a given period are distributed according to the following discrete symmetrical probability distribution:

Return R	Probability $p(R)$
8%	0.1
10%	0.2
12%	0.4
14%	0.2
16%	0.1

The expected return, $E(R)$, is given as:

$$
\begin{aligned}
E(R) &= \sum_{\text{all } R} R\,p(R) \\
&= 0.1 \times 0.08 + 0.2 \times 0.1 + 0.4 \times 0.12 + 0.2 \times 0.14 + 0.1 \times 0.16 \\
&= 0.12 \text{ or } 12\%
\end{aligned}
$$

For the variance (σ_R^2), standard deviation (σ_R), and semivariance, we obtain:

$$
\begin{aligned}
\sigma_R^2 &= \sum_{\text{all } R} (R - E(R))^2 p(R) \\
&= (0.08 - 0.12)^2 \times 0.1 + (0.10 - 0.12)^2 \times 0.2 + (0.12 - 0.12)^2 \times 0.4 \\
&\quad + (0.14 - 0.12)^2 \times 0.2 + (0.16 - 0.12)^2 \times 0.1 \\
&= 0.00048
\end{aligned}
$$

$$
\begin{aligned}
\sigma_R &= \sqrt{\sigma_R^2} \\
&= 0.0219
\end{aligned}
$$

$$
\begin{aligned}
\text{semivariance} &= \sum_{\text{all } R < E(R)} (R - E(R))^2 p(R) \\
&= (0.08 - 0.12)^2 \times 0.1 + (0.10 - 0.12)^2 \times 0.2 \\
&= 0.00024
\end{aligned}
$$

Given that the above probability distribution is symmetrical around $E(R) = 12\%$ we find that the semivariance just equals one-half the variance. The variance or standard deviation of absolute returns for a given amount invested is also readily computed. For an amount invested $I = \$1{,}000$, we have:

$$
\begin{aligned}
\text{expected absolute return} &= I\,E(R) \\
&= \$1{,}000 \times 12\% \\
&= \$120
\end{aligned}
$$

$$\sigma^2 = I^2\,\sigma_R^2 = 480$$

$$\sigma = I\,\sigma_R = 21.9$$

The variance is a computationally convenient measure for the dispersion or variability of a probability distribution. Unfortunately, values of variances are intuitively difficult to interpret. Given that distributions of returns are often reasonably symmetrical around the mean and roughly normal, the standard deviation, which is just the square root of the variance, has a more ready intuitive interpretation, as follows: there is a probability of roughly two-thirds that the value of the variable will not be further away from its expected value than one standard deviation, and chances are approximately 95 percent that the variable will remain within two standard deviations of the mean. For instance, if a distribution of returns is approximately normal and has an expected value of 12 percent and a standard deviation of 2 percent (*i.e.*, a variance of 4), chances are roughly 2 out of 3 that the eventual outcome will be within 2 points of 12 percent; and there is only a 5 percent probability that the return observed would be below 8 percent or above 16 percent.

Where several assets make up a portfolio, the above concepts are easily extended to compute the return and the risk for the overall portfolio.

We introduce the concepts of portfolio returns and risks by looking at an investor who holds two securities. These securities are characterized by returns R_1 and R_2, and x_1 and x_2 are the proportions of the portfolio invested in shares of corporation 1 and corporation 2 respectively, with $x_1 + x_2 = 1$. The expected return for such a portfolio is given simply by $E(R) = x_1\,E(R_1) + x_2\,E(R_2)$. That is, we just add the expected returns for each security, each multiplied by the proportional holdings. Thus, if shares of corporation 1 and corporation 2 are expected to return 8 percent and 12 percent respectively, and if the investor has invested 25 percent of his resources in corporation 1 and 75 percent of his resources in corporation 2, the expected return of his holdings would be $E(R) = 0.25 \times 8\% + 0.75 \times 12\% = 11$ percent. This result is readily extended to portfolios comprising more than two securities, and it is easy to show that the expected return for the overall portfolio is always just a weighted average of the individual security returns, with the weights being the proportions of the portfolio invested in the particular securities.

The expression for the portfolio variance is more complicated, as the portfolio variance not only depends on the variability of each individual security, but also on the statistical relationships between the two securities. As was briefly noted in Chapter 6, if high (or low) values in security 1 tend to go together with high (or low) values in security 2, the total variability of the portfolio will be much greater than if high values in one security tend to be cancelled out by simultaneous low values in the other security. In other words, the more the returns of the two securities tend to move together, the greater the portfolio risk, and *vice versa*.

Two alternative but equivalent statistics can be used to describe the relationship which exists between two variables R_1 and R_2: the covariance

($\text{cov}(R_1R_2)$) and the correlation coefficient (r_{12}). For discrete probability distributions, they are technically defined as follows:[5]

$$(4)\quad \text{cov}(R_1R_2) = \sum_{\text{all } R_1 R_2} (R_1 - E(R_1))(R_2 - E(R_2))p(R_1,R_2)$$
$$= E[(R_1 - E(R_1))(R_2 - E(R_2))]$$

$$(5)\quad r_{12} = \frac{\text{cov}(R_1R_2)}{\sigma_1\sigma_2}$$

where E again stands for expected value, and $p(R_1, R_2)$ is the joint probability distribution of the two variables R_1 and R_2. The correlation coefficient is simply the covariance divided by the product of the standard deviations for the two variables. Both the covariance and the correlation coefficient are positive if two variables move together, zero if the movements in the two variables are independent, and negative if high values in one variable are generally associated with low values in the other variable, and *vice versa*. However, while the covariance can assume any value, depending on the possible values of R_1 and R_2, the correlation coefficient is "scaled" in the sense that it can only take on values between +1 (perfect positive correlation, with both variables moving exactly together) and –1 (perfect negative correlation, with both variables moving in opposite directions). A problem with solution at the end of this chapter illustrates the numerical computations in deriving the covariance and the correlation coefficient.

The total portfolio risk for two securities is given by the formula:

$$(6)\quad \sigma_R^2 = x_1^2\sigma_{R_1}^2 + x_2^2\sigma_{R_2}^2 + 2x_1x_2\,\text{cov}(R_1R_2)$$

or, equivalently,

$$(6a)\quad \sigma_R^2 = x_1^2\sigma_{R_1}^2 + x_2^2\sigma_{R_2}^2 + 2x_1x_2r_{12}\sigma_1\sigma_2$$

If the covariance between 1 and 2 is positive, this adds to the portfolio risk, whereas a negative covariance diminishes overall risk. Only when the covariance is zero will the portfolio risk be solely determined by the variances of the individual securities. Hence, in computing portfolio risk, the statistical relationships between variables have to be considered. This is particularly crucial when we consider a diversified portfolio consisting of many different assets or securities. All the individual variances, and the covariances of each pair of securities enter into the more general formula for determining the portfolio risk.[6]

[5]The definitions for continuous probability distributions are equivalent, with integrals replacing the summation signs.

[6] The variance of a portfolio consisting of n different securities is given by:

$\text{Var}(R)$ = sum of (x^2 $\text{Var}(R)$ for all individual securities)
+ sum of ($2x_ix_j\,\text{Cov}(R_iR_j)$ for all possible pairs of securities)

or written more formally,

$$\text{Var}(R) = \sum_{i=1}^{n} x_i^2\,\text{Var}(R_i) + \sum_{i=1}^{n}\sum_{\substack{j=1\\ j\neq i}}^{n} x_ix_j\,\text{Cov}(R_iR_j) = \sum_{i=1}^{n}\sum_{j=1}^{n} x_ix_j\,\text{Cov}(R_iR_j)$$

where $\text{Cov}(R_iR_i) = \text{Var}(R_i)$

Thus, the addition of one new security to an existing portfolio consisting of n securities adds one new variance term and $2n$ new covariance terms to the above expression.

Consider the addition of one new type of security to an existing portfolio consisting of shares of 10 different corporations. The effect which this new security has on the overall risk of the portfolio will be determined by the variance of the new security, and by the covariances of the new securities with each one of the 10 different shares presently held in the portfolio. It is easy to see that the 10 new covariances are likely to have a more important effect on overall risk than the one variance term to be added. Generally, the risk which an asset adds to the existing asset portfolio of an investor is primarily determined by the statistical relationships of its returns with the returns of the other assets in the portfolio, as expressed by the covariances, and not by the variability of its own returns, as given by its variance.

This is an important point, which will be elaborated upon below, and which has implications both for investor behavior and for managerial decisions. It provides a new way of looking at risk where a multiplicity of assets or investments are involved. The implications are of very general applicability, since there are few firms or individuals holding only one asset. Risk is not something absolute which is inherent in a particular asset or investment, but it is something which has to be measured in a particular environment, with due reference to existing holdings and other available investments which a firm or an individual may pursue.

29-3. AN INTRODUCTION TO PORTFOLIO THEORY[7]

Risk aversion and the choice of investments

This section explores the application of the concepts just developed to the optimal selection of investments. We will go on to show how rational investors should approach the problem of portfolio selection. While our discussion will focus mainly on portfolios of shares, the reader should bear in mind that the ideas developed have broader applicability and can be carried over to analyze investments in other types of risky assets.

We assume throughout this section that investors are risk averse, and that risk is conveniently measured by the standard deviation or variance of anticipated returns. While, in particular circumstances, individuals may not be risk averse (otherwise the gambling casinos of Las Vegas or Monte Carlo would not survive), risk aversion on the part of most investors is well documented and reflected by the conditions prevailing in the capital markets. Consequently, as discussed in Chapter 7, riskier security issues typically have to offer a higher expected yield if they are to be sold in the capital markets.

Given this framework, a rational investor will choose those investments which maximize expected return for a given level of risk, or minimize risk for a particular level of return. The investor will tradeoff risks against returns according to personal preferences, always demanding an increase in the

[7]For a complete treatment see W. Sharpe, *Portfolio Theory and Capital Markets*, New York: McGraw-Hill, 1970. This section draws on many of the ideas developed in the first few chapters of Sharpe's work.

expected return for assuming higher risks. Such tradeoffs between risks and returns can be portrayed through *indifference curves*, as shown in Figure 29-1.

All points lying on one particular indifferences curve are equally desirable, while the slope of the indifference curve at each particular point specifies how the investor trades off risks against returns at that point. Given that expected returns are desirable and variations of returns are not, the investor's utility increases as we move towards the upper left portion of the diagram. For example, investments 2 and 3 in Figure 29-1 are equally desirable, while investment 1 lies on an indifference curve with a higher utility and, hence, is preferred to both 2 and 3. These specific curves show an investor whose risk aversion increases with increasing risk exposure: at low levels of risk, the curves are fairly flat, indicating a willingness to accept a higher risk for small additional compensations in expected returns. However, at points of higher risk (towards the right side of the diagram), the curves become increasingly steep, indicating more and more conservatism, with the compensation demanded for assuming greater risk growing rapidly.

FIGURE 29-1

Indifference Curves and the Risk-Return Tradeoff

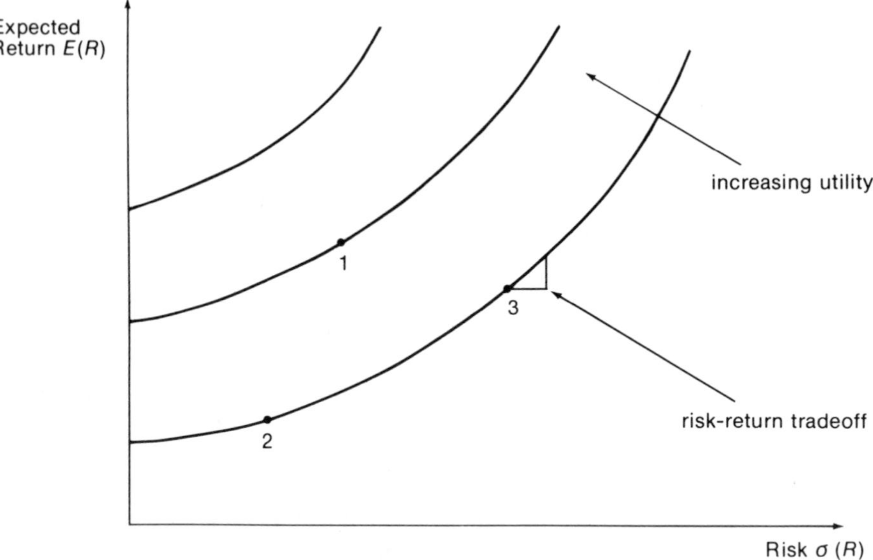

The particular choice of investments which is optimal for an investor not only depends on personal preferences or indifference curves, but also hinges on the set of available investments and their characteristics. An investor in the securities markets can invest either in individual securities, or in portfolios of securities. Given our discussion of diversification in the previous section, it is likely that a diversified portfolio will prove more attractive, as exposure to risk can be reduced through diversification. This point will be discussed in further detail below.

Alternative investment opportunities can be described in terms of their expected returns and standard deviations or variances, and portrayed diagrammatically, as the shaded area in Figure 29-2. The set of attainable investment portfolios will be centered in the lower right-hand part of the diagram, as will be shown below in Figure 29-4. The boundary curve *a-b* of the set of attainable portfolios is called the *efficiency frontier*, for it defines the points yielding the highest expected returns for a given level of risk.

Superimposing an investor's indifference curves on the set of attainable portfolios, we can determine the optimal investment. As shown in Figure 29-2, it is simply given by the point where the set of attainable portfolios just touches the indifference curve with the highest utility. Given risk averse investors, it is easy to show that the optimal portfolio will always lie on the efficiency frontier.

FIGURE 29-2

Risk-Return Characteristics of Attainable Portfolios

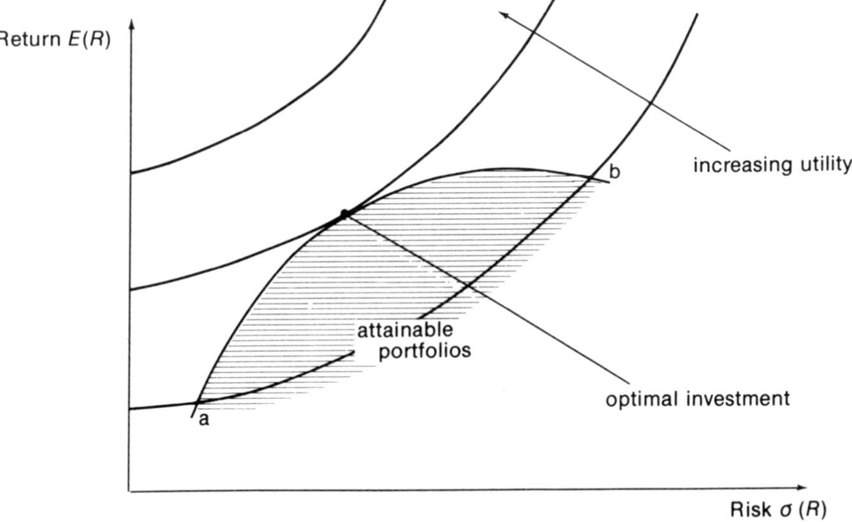

Combining investments into optimal portfolios

We saw that investors generally hold more than one risky asset. Under such circumstances, the investor's main concern ought to be with the expected return E_p and the standard deviation σ_p of the overall portfolio. In the previous section we discussed how the expected returns of individual securities combine to form the overall return for a portfolio, and how both the individual variances and, more importantly, the covariances or correlation coefficients determine the overall portfolio risk. Given several individual securities, we are now concerned with finding rules for combining such securities into optimal portfolios.

The subsequent points are most easily illustrated in the context of a portfolio consisting of only two securities. While this simplifies the exposition, we note that any results derived are readily generalized to portfolios consisting of

n securities. Given that some proportions x_1 and $x_2 = (1 - x_1)$ of the total portfolio are invested in securities 1 and 2 respectively, the total expected return and risk for the portfolio are simply given as:

$$E_P = x_1 E_1 + (1 - x_1) E_2 \quad (7)$$

$$\sigma_P = \sqrt{x_1^2 \sigma_1^2 + (1 - x_1)^2 \sigma_2^2 + 2x_1 (1 - x_1) r_{12} \sigma_1 \sigma_2} \quad (8)$$

If the returns of the two securities are perfectly correlated (they always move together), the correlation coefficient $r_{12} = 1$, and the portfolio standard deviation becomes:[8]

$$\sigma_P = x_1 \sigma_1 + x_2 \sigma_2$$

Similarly, if correlation is less than perfectly positive or even negative, with $r_{12} < 1$, overall risk as measured by σ_P is reduced through diversification. It is interesting to note that, through such diversification, the portfolio risk may be reduced below the risk of each individual security making up the portfolio.

Example

Assume the following values:

$x_1 = 0.6, E_1 = 10\%, \sigma_1^2 = 10.0$ or $\sigma_1 = 3.16$

$x_2 = 0.4, E_2 = 14\%, \sigma_2^2 = 16.0$ or $\sigma_2 = 4.00$

We compute σ_P for three different circumstances with r_{12} taken to be $+1.0, +0.6$, and -0.4. With $r_{12} = 1.0$,

$$\sigma_P = \sqrt{(0.6)^2(10.0) + (0.4)^2(16.0) + 2(0.6)(0.4)(1.0)(3.16)(4.0)}$$
$$= \sqrt{6.16 + 6.07} = \sqrt{12.23}$$
$$= 3.50$$

With $r_{12} = +0.6$,

$$\sigma_P = \sqrt{6.16 + 2(0.6)(0.4)(0.6)(3.16)(4.0)}$$
$$= \sqrt{6.16 + 3.64} = \sqrt{9.80}$$
$$= 3.13$$

With $r_{12} = -0.4$,

$$\sigma_P = \sqrt{6.16 + 2(0.6)(0.4)(-0.4)(3.16)(4.0)}$$
$$= \sqrt{6.16 - 2.43} = \sqrt{3.73}$$
$$= 1.93$$

[8] Given $r_{12} = 1$, by factoring, equation (8) may be rewritten as:
$\sigma_P = \sqrt{(x_1 \sigma_1 + x_2 \sigma_2)^2}$ and it follows that:
$\sigma_P = x_1 \sigma_1 + x_2 \sigma_2$

For all three cases, we have,

$$E_p = 0.6 \times 10\% + 0.4 \times 14\%$$
$$= 11.60\%$$

From the example, we see that the portfolio standard deviation decreases with decreasing correlation, and even with moderate positive correlation ($r_{12}=+0.6$), the standard deviation of the portfolio is lower than the standard deviation of either security taken by itself. It is this finding which makes portfolio diversification so important and which, no doubt, has contributed to the growth of investment funds and the likes, as they offer even the smallest investor a chance to hold a share of a diversified portfolio of securities. Similarly, this finding could explain the moves of many firms to diversify their operations.

Given two securities and their individual characteristics, we are next concerned with finding the optimal proportions in which the securities should be combined to form a portfolio, or more precisely, the optimal value of x_1. Using formulas (7) and (8), we can plot both the expected return and the risk of the portfolio as a function of x_1. Based on the figures given in the above numerical example, we would obtain the curves shown in Figure 29-3. As derived earlier, E_p is just a linear combination of the individual security returns, resulting in a straight line if plotted as a function of x_1. The standard deviation σ_p, on the other hand, is a linear function only if the securities in the portfolio are perfectly correlated, which represents the worst case from the point of view of minimizing risk. As r_{12} decreases, σ_p becomes smaller, and σ_p as a function of x_1 takes on a saucer shape, assuming a minimum at some middle value x_1^* which is easily computed through the use of calculus.[9] If the returns of the two securities showed a perfect negative correlation, risk could be completely eliminated through a proper combination of the two, with σ_p assuming a value of zero. Unfortunately, the returns on almost all investments and securities show some degree of positive correlation as all of them are dependent on the general state of the economy, moving up and down together in reaction to economic forecasts and conditions. Thus, for practical purposes, risk cannot be eliminated, but it can be reduced by combining securities which show only moderate degrees of correlation.

In assessing the desirability of a particular portfolio, and in determining whether it is efficient or not, we next need to plot the set of attainable portfolios for the two-security case in a diagram such as was introduced in Figure 29-2. The attainable curves, as a function of x_1, are readily found by inserting various

[9] x_1^*: is obtained by differentiating σ_p^2 as given through formula (8) above with respect to x and setting this derivative equal to zero, as follows:

$$\sigma_p^2 = x_1^2 \sigma_1^2 + (1 - 2x_1 + x_1^2)\sigma_2^2 + 2r_{12}\sigma_1\sigma_2(x_1 - x_1^2)$$
$$\frac{d\sigma_p^2}{dx} = 2\sigma_1^2 x_1 + 2\sigma_2^2 x_1 - 2\sigma_2^2 + 2r_{12}\sigma_1\sigma_2 - 4r_{12}\sigma_1\sigma_2 x_1$$
$$= 0$$

From which we obtain by rearranging:

$$x_1^* = \frac{\sigma_2(\sigma_2 - r_{12}\sigma_1)}{\sigma_1^2 + \sigma_2^2 - 2r_{12}\sigma_1\sigma_2}$$

FIGURE 29-3.

Portfolio Return and Risk as a Function of Portfolio Mix

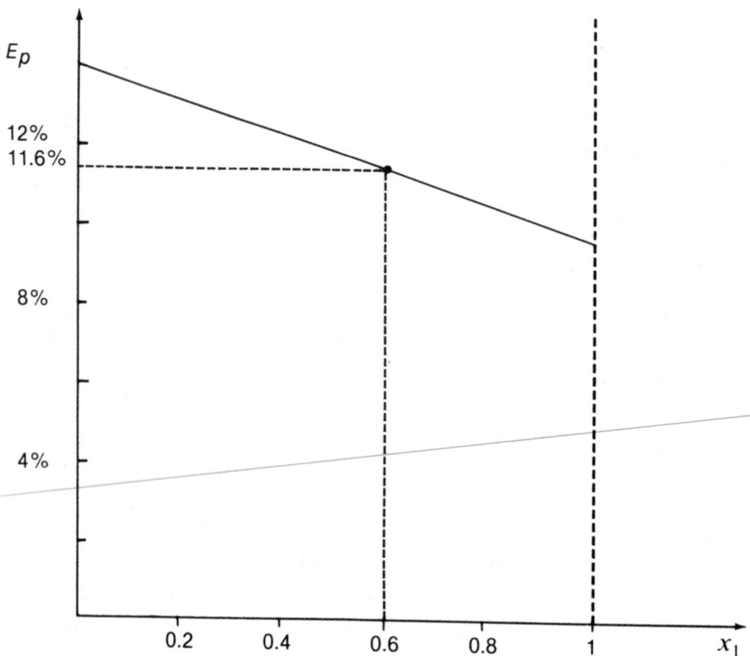

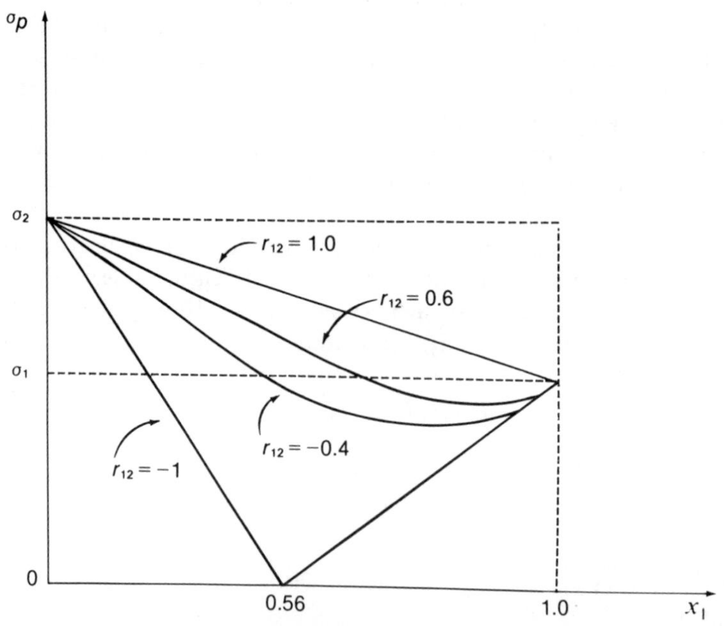

FIGURE 29-4

Two-Security Combinations and Risk-Return Relationships

(a) with $r_{12} = +1.0$

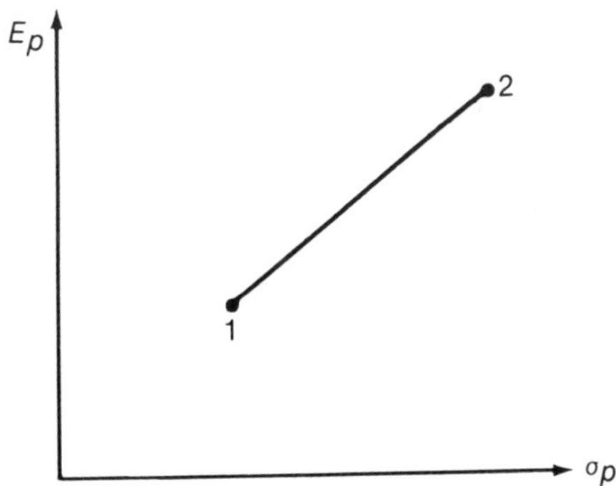

(b) with $r_{12} = +0.6$

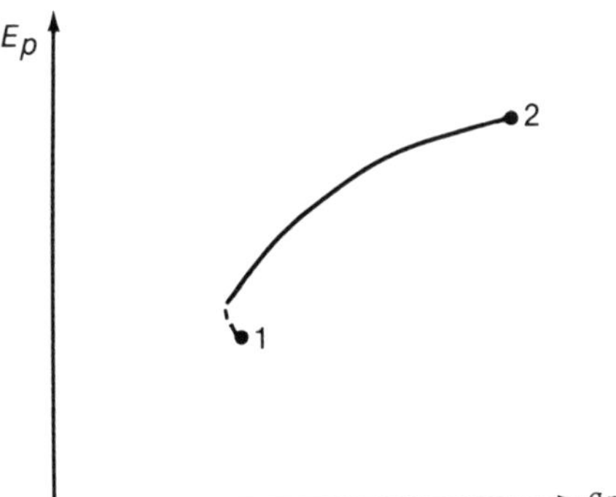

(c) with $r_{12} = -0.4$

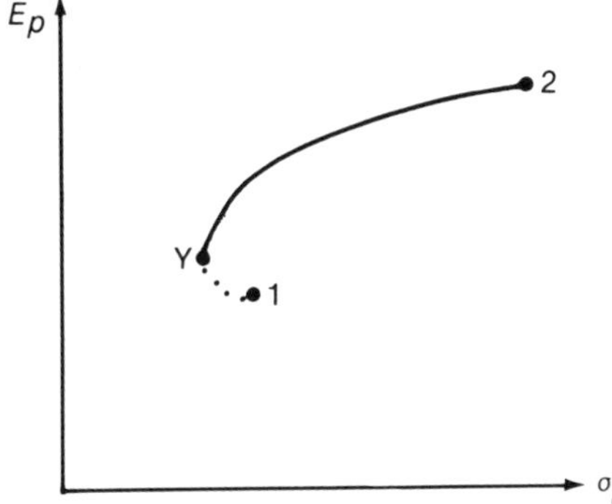

values of x_1 into equations (7) and (8) and simultaneously computing E_p and σ_p. The results for the numerical example which was introduced above are shown schematically in Figure 29-4. We see that the shape of the set of portfolios which are attainable depends on the correlation which exists between the individual securities making up the portfolio. The beginning and the end points 1 and 2 (for which $x_1 = 1$ and 0 respectively) are the same regardless of the value of r_{12} but, with decreasing correlation, the connecting curve exhibits an increasing bulge. In curve (c) with $r_{12} = -0.4$, combinations of the two securities in proportions x_1 and $(1 - x_1)$ which plot below Y are no longer efficient in that with different proportions, higher expected returns are possible at particular levels of risk. Given that $r_{12} = -0.4$, for example, it would never be optimal for a risk-averse investor to invest solely in security 1. As is easily computed, the same risk of $\sigma_p = \sigma_1 = 3.16$ can be maintained if securities 1 and 2 are combined with proportions 0.17 and 0.83 respectively, but the expected return has been increased from $E_1 =$ 10 percent to $E_p = 13.32$ percent.

It is possible to extend the approach to allow for combinations of many different securities, and even combinations of portfolios. Based on the concepts developed in Section 29-2, equations (7) and (8) can be rewritten for this more general case involving combinations of n securities. The set of attainable portfolios becomes an area of the form illustrated in Figure 29-2. While the computations can become formidable, we can again derive efficient portfolios and the efficiency frontier by computing the proportions of various securities which provide the highest expected return for given levels of risk, or conversely, which minimize risk for given levels of expected returns. It is worth noting in this context that individual securities will almost always fall in the interior of the feasible set and that efficient portfolios will involve a good deal of diversification.

Combinations of a riskless asset and risky portfolios

To complete our brief introduction to portfolio theory, we must next allow for the possibility of investing in riskless assets, such as short-term government treasury bills which provide a given return with certainty. Such an asset offers a risk-free return which we call E_f for which, by definition, $\sigma_f = 0$. It is represented by a point on the return axis, as shown in Figure 29-5. If an investor combined the riskless asset with a risky asset (such as a share) into a portfolio in proportions of $(1 - x_1)$ and x_1 respectively, the expected return and the standard deviation for such a portfolio become:

(9) $$E_p = (1 - x_1) E_f + x_1 E_1$$

and $$\sigma_p = \sqrt{(1 - x_1)^2 \sigma_f^2 + x_1^2 \sigma_1^2 + 2x_1(1 - x_1) r_{1f} \sigma_1 \sigma_f}$$

which for $\sigma_f = 0$ reduces to:

(10) $$\sigma_p = \sqrt{x_1^2 \sigma_1^2} = x_1 \sigma_1$$

The set of attainable portfolios is easily computed by substituting $x_1 = \sigma_p/\sigma_1$ from equation (10) into equation (9), which after rearranging yields:

$$(11) \quad E_p = E_f + \left(\frac{E_1 - E_f}{\sigma_1}\right)\sigma_p$$

Thus, the set of attainable portfolios is a straight line which joins the risk-free asset and the particular risky asset with which if was combined. If we allow for borrowing at the risk-free rate, using the proceeds to buy more of share 1, so that x_f becomes negative and x_1 exceeds 1, the line in Figure 29-5 is extended to include points which are to the upper right of share 1.

More generally, the combination of a riskless asset with the general set of attainable portfolios of risky securities, as introduced in Figure 29-2, yields a new efficiency frontier. Clearly, every attainable portfolio can be combined with the riskless asset in various proportions to form new portfolios which lie on the line joining the riskless asset with the particular portfolio. The optimal combinations arise if the riskless asset is combined with portfolio M, as shown in Figure 29-6, as the line connecting the riskless asset with portfolio M produces the highest expected returns for any given level of risk. This line $E_f - M$ (and its extension if borrowing takes place) becomes the new efficiency frontier. It is given by the equation:

$$(12) \quad E_p = E_f + \left(\frac{E_m - E_f}{\sigma_m}\right)\sigma_p$$

where E_m and σ_m are the expected return and standard deviation of portfolio M respectively. The optimal strategy for risk-averse investors under these circumstances is to combine various proportions of portfolio M and the riskless asset. For each individual investor, the optimal point on the line $E_f - M$ is determined by personal preferences regarding risks and returns. Those investors who are more risk-averse will pick up a larger proportion of the riskless asset and less of the risky portfolio M, thereby ending up closer to the riskless return E_f and *vice versa*.

Given rational and well-informed investors who have similar assessments about future returns and risks of securities, we shall see that portfolio M consists of all risky shares which are traded in the market, and is called the *market portfolio*. The efficiency frontier which results by combining the riskless asset with the market portfolio is called the *capital market line*. These results are important as they form the basis for the capital asset pricing model which we discuss in the next section.

Applications and limitations of portfolio theory

Some of the major contributions of portfolio theory are the insights which it provides regarding the effects of diversification. While at an intuitive level the benefits of diversification to reduce risk are widely recognized (not putting all your eggs into one basket) the findings of portfolio theory sharpen our understanding of the issues involved and allow us to structure decisions in a more systematic manner. Furthermore, portfolio theory provides some of the

FIGURE 29-5

Portfolio Combinations of the Riskless Asset and a Risky Share

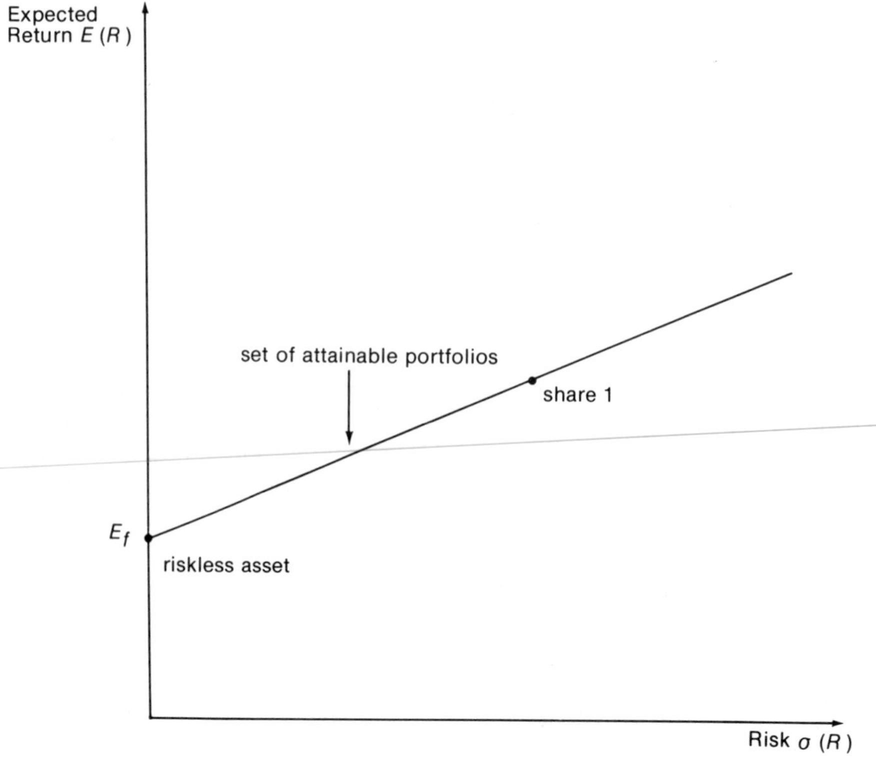

conceptual foundations for the capital asset pricing model to be discussed in the next section.

In terms of implementation, the general concepts of portfolio theory are widely recognized and provide a framework for decision-making, both for investment managers and corporate officers. For example, some firms in evaluating the risk of new investment projects make an explicit attempt to assess the correlations of the new project with existing operations.[10] Investment managers, in striving for "balanced portfolios", understand the concept of efficiency frontiers and attempt to select such portfolios.

In spite of such conceptual contributions, actual use of the formulas presented to compute efficient or optimal portfolios of investments is seldom found. Several difficulties have prevented more widespread operational applications.

For one, the problem of obtaining meaningful input information for use with the formulas is formidable. Not only do the expected returns and variances or standard deviations for all individual projects have to be assessed, but estimates of covariances or correlation coefficients have to be provided as well. Most of us

[10]See, for example, E. Carter, *Portfolio Aspects of Corporate Capital Budgeting*, Lexington: D. C. Heath & Co., 1974.

FIGURE 29-6

Combination of the Riskless Asset and the Set of Attainable Risky Portfolios

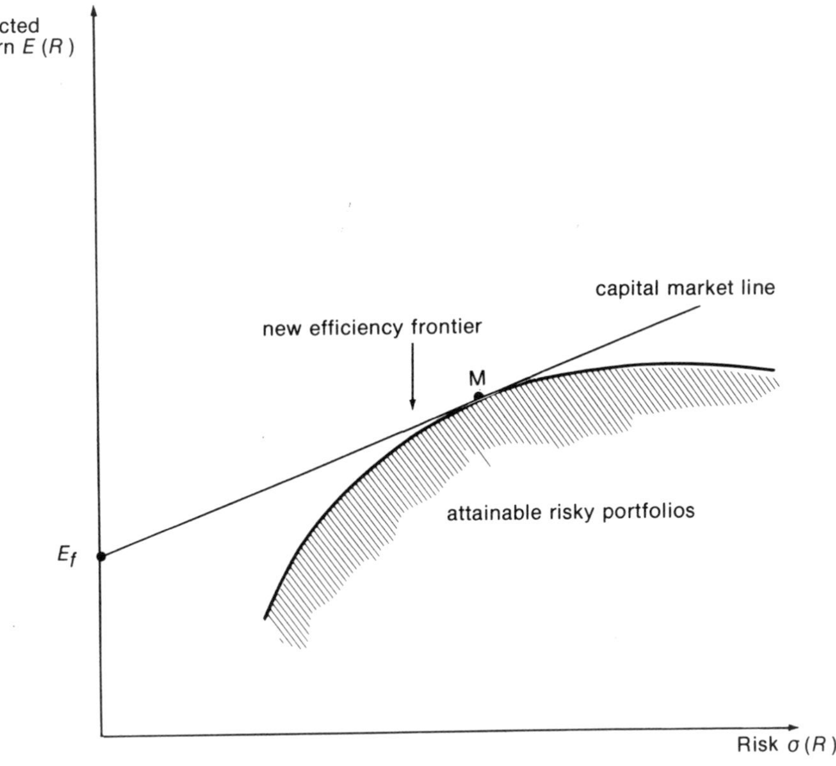

are not very well equipped to provide such estimates and in any event, the number of estimates required in any realistic problem tends to be enormous. For example, a portfolio of only 10 different securities would require 55 input estimates of variances and covariances, and this number increases with the square of the number of individual investments being considered. Secondly, the above formulations assume that assets are divisible. This is reasonably realistic where securities such as common shares make up the portfolio, but it is often inappropriate where a firm considers investments in capital assets. Finally, underlying the above formulations is the notion of a "one-period-model". All assets are assumed to be held for a given period, and this period is the same for all assets. Returns and risks are computed based on this common period, and the investor's objectives and indifference curves are stated in terms of one-period expected returns and risks. This is a convenient simplification as it makes for a relatively easy formulation of the problem as outlined. However, in an ongoing business operation, with assets characterized by different economic lives, the simplifications inherent in a one-period-model may not be justifiable.

The framework as outlined was originally proposed by Markowitz in the context of investments in common shares.[11] The securities environment has several advantages in this context. Not only are common shares in a portfolio divisible for all practical purposes, but a wealth of information is readily available on the past economic performance of individual common shares. Hence, we may rely on this past information to estimate expected future returns, variances, and covariances, thereby overcoming the input data problem which otherwise plagues portfolio formulations. Specifically, after deciding on the length of the period which forms the basis for the analysis, a month for example, we could statistically derive expected values, variances, and covariances of monthly returns by looking at the performance of individual shares for a sample of past months. The figures derived could then be used as an estimate of expected returns, variances, and covariances for the coming month. Technically speaking, *ex post* (backward looking) information is used to make *ex ante* (forward looking) predictions. In a relatively stable situation, extrapolation of past performance to predict the future may be a useful starting point which may yield workable approximations. As we shall see in the next section, it may be the only way to empirically test hypotheses about market behavior, as it is clearly not possible to obtain direct information as to the market's future expectations. When proceeding in this way, however, one should be mindful of the limitations of such an approach. Clearly, there is no inherent law which assures that the future has to be what the past was. In an economic environment such as ours which is subject to rapid and fundamental changes, stability of market behavior is subject to question, implying that any results which are derived in this fashion need to be interpreted with caution.

29-4. THE CAPITAL ASSET PRICING MODEL[12]

Given the risk-averse investors who require increasing expected returns as compensation for increasing variability of returns, it is quite reasonable to view the expected return on a particular security as a riskless rate of return to which are added one or more premiums for risk. As was mentioned in earlier chapters, the riskless rate of return is taken to be the interest rate paid on short-term borrowings by the federal government. A critical aspect of the valuation of shares is the determination of the relationship between risk and returns, specifically the risk premiums required by investors in the capital markets for different levels of risk. Determination of the risk-return relationships which prevail in the capital markets is a prerequisite for establishing rules of optimal behavior at the corporate level.

One formulation of risk-return tradeoffs in the capital markets which has held

[11]H. Markowitz, "Portfolio Selection", *Journal of Finance*, March, 1952, pp. 77-91.

[12]This section draws on some excellent summaries to be found in the literature, including M. Jensen, "Capital Markets: Theory and Evidence", *Bell Journal of Economics and Management Science*, Autumn, 1972, pp. 357-398; M. Rubinstein "A Mean-Variance Synthesis of Corporate Financial Policy", *Journal of Finance*, March, 1973, pp. 167-181; and F. Modigliani and G. Pogue, "An Introduction to Risk and Return: Concepts and Evidence", *Financial Analysts Journal*, March/April, 1974, pp. 68-80 and May/June, 1974, pp. 69-86.

the interest of researchers in finance for many years was developed by William Sharpe and others, and is termed the *Capital Asset Pricing Model* (CAPM).[13] Drawing on the concepts of portfolio diversification, and given certain assumptions about capital markets and the behavior of rational risk-averse investors, it is possible to establish risk-return relationships which should prevail. A variety of empirical tests have subsequently been carried out to verify how well the theory explains actual market behavior. This particular section provides an introduction to the basic CAPM, including a commentary on possible contributions of the model to some of the important issues introduced in earlier sections of this text, including the cost of capital and capital budgeting.

Components of risk

While some reduction of risk through portfolio diversification is possible, we saw that a total elimination of risk can only be achieved if securities with returns which exhibit a perfect negative correlation can be found. We also saw that in a real-life environment, all securities show some degree of positive correlation, because they are all correlated with the general market which in turn is tied to the general state of the economy. Consequently, while the percentage price changes of a particular share may be different from those of the general market (as expressed for example by the movement of some broadly based market index) the direction of the movements over the long run tend to coincide. Given such positive correlation, only a portion of risk can be diverisified away, with some risk remaining regardless of how well a portfolio is designed. It follows in this context that the total risk of each individual security can be broken down into two components: the security's *unsystematic risk*, or the riskiness which is unique to the particular security and which can be eliminated through diversification, and the *systematic risk* which is market related and therefore cannot be diversified away. Given that one component of risk can be diversified away through judicious choice of investment portfolios, we can argue that compensations for risk demanded by investors in the form of higher rates of return should relate only to undiversifiable or systematic risk rather than to the total risk of the asset, and that higher systematic risk should command higher expected returns.[14] Put another way, the volatility of returns, unique to a particular security and hence diversifiable, is not relevant. What matters in terms of a risk premium is the variability of returns relating to general movements in the market, as these cannot be eliminated.

At a conceptual level then, we can break down the return of any individual security into two components: one which is perfectly correlated with the returns from the market portfolio, and another which is a residual or unsystematic return. Using notation, we can express the expected return of a common share j as:

[13] W. Sharpe, "Capital Asset Pricing: A Theory of Market Equilibrium Under Conditions of Risk", *Journal of Finance*, September, 1964, pp. 425-447.
[14] W. Sharpe, *op. cit.*, pp. 425-426.

(13) $R_j = \beta_j R_m + \varepsilon_j$

with R_m the return on the market portfolio
ε_j the unsystematic return of the security
β_j a coefficient termed the *beta factor* of the security, which expresses the proportionality of the security's market related or systematic return with the return of the market portfolio.

Example

Assume a security is characterized by a beta factor of 2.0 (we shall see below how to measure beta factors). For a given period, the return of the market portfolio and of the individual security are measured as 7 percent and 15 percent respectively. The 15 percent return on the security can be thought of as a $\beta R_m = 2.0 \times 7 = 14\%$ return which is strictly related to overall market performance, plus a 1% unsystematic return which was caused by events which are unique to this security and not related in any way to the general market.

Equation (13) can be expressed in computationally more convenient form by setting $\varepsilon_j = \alpha_j + e_j$, such that e_j has an average value of zero over time and $\alpha_j = E(\varepsilon_j)$. Thus, α_j is the long-run expected unsystematic return of the security, and e_j becomes a residual "error term" which signals random fluctuations per period. It follows that:

(14) $R_j = \alpha_j + \beta_j R_m + e_j$

Equation (14) represents the standard model for simple regression analysis, and relates the dependent variable R_j to the independent variable R_m. Given the returns of the market and of an individual security over a number of sample periods, regression analysis can be used to estimate the parameters α_j and β_j in the above equation. Since data on past returns are readily available, estimates of α_j and β_j for individual securities are easy to obtain.

Example

Assume that actual returns for the general market and for an individual security were obtained for 11 past periods, as shown by the points in Figure 29-7. The resulting regression line which represents the line of "best fit" for these points is shown in the figure and is given by the equation:

$$R_j = 0.01 + 2.0\,R_m$$

with 0.01 and 2.0 being the estimates derived for α_j and β_j respectively. This line summarizing the relationship between R_j and R_m is called the security's *characteristic line*. It signifies that for every percentage increase or decrease in the market return, the return of the security is expected to increase or decrease by twice that amount. In addition, the security has a unique return which is not market-related with an average value of $\alpha_j = 1$ percent, and period-by-period random returns

e_j.[15] For instance, when the market return for 1975 was 7 percent, the market model indicated returns on our security of $0.01 + 2.0 \times 0.07 = 15$ percent, as shown by point A. Given that the security's actual return in 1975 was just 14 percent, e_j was in fact minus one percent. This downward "shock" would suggest that an unfavorable occurrence unique to the firm had taken place during that period.

FIGURE 29-7.

The Market Model for Security Returns

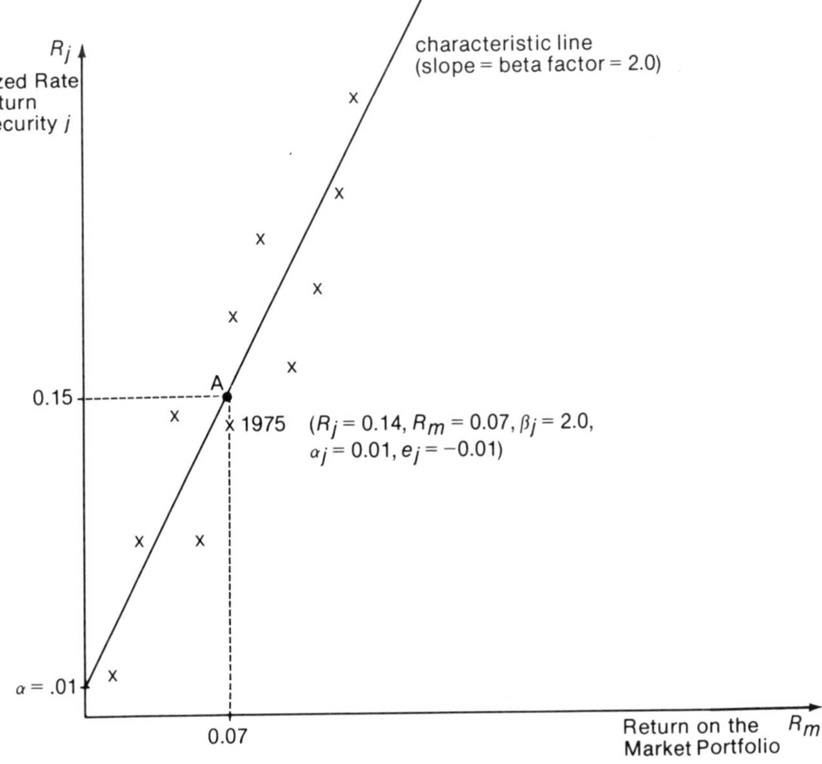

Having expressed an individual security's return in the form of equation (14), it becomes easy to derive the security's systematic and unsystematic risk. The total variance of a security, $\sigma^2(R_j)$, can be written as:

$$\sigma^2(R_j) = \sigma^2(\alpha_j + \beta_j R_m + e_j)$$

Given that α_j and β_j are constants, and e_j and R_m are independent, we have:

(15) $\quad \sigma^2(R_j) = \beta_j^2 \sigma^2(R_m) + \sigma^2(e_j)$

where $\sigma^2(R_m)$ is the risk of the market portfolio, which we abbreviate as σ_m^2 and $\sigma^2(e_j)$ is the risk of the residual or error terms, which we abbreviate as σ_e^2.

[15]For most shares, the intercept term for unsystematic returns is small and quite unstable, varying over time.

We see that the risk of an individual security can be thought of as having two components. One component, $\beta_j^2 \sigma_m^2$, is termed the security's systematic risk, and is strictly related to the volatility of the general market. The other component, σ_e^2, represents the security's unsystematic risk which is unique to the individual security and not market-related in any way.

The term for the systematic risk underscores the importance of the beta factor. β_j not only indicates how a security's returns are related to those of the market but it also specifies the security's systematic risk.[16] Thus, a beta coefficient of 1.0 would indicate a stock with returns which are as volatile as those of the market, whereas beta factors which are larger or smaller than one would indicate systematic risks which exceed or are more moderate than the risk of the market. For example, we typically find that shares of utilities are characterized by beta factors which are below one. While utilities are susceptible to general market conditions, they are more stable than the market in aggregate, implying reduced systematic risk. On the other hand, airline stocks typically have systematic risks which exceed those of the market (with beta factors larger than one) indicating that their returns are particularly sensitive to changes in general market conditions.

The unsystematic risk is caused by exceptional happenings which are unique to the particular firm. These occurrences are in no way related to general movements in the market, and are assumed to be independent of each other. Since both positive and negative happenings and e-values (error terms) are possible, chances are that the impacts of such occurrences across a variety of shares which make up a diversified portfolio cancel out, with the net aggregate effect being close to zero. It is in this sense that we can expect unsystematic risk to be eliminated through diversification.

Think of the portfolio return for two securities as $x_i R_i + x_j R_j = x_i \alpha_i + x_j \alpha_j + (x_i \beta_i + x_j \beta_j) R_m + x_i e_i + x_j e_j$, which can be rewritten as $\alpha_p + \beta_p R_m + e_p$, where the last term is very small. Then, with unsystematic risk eliminated, we can show that the total risk of a well-diversified portfolio is given as:

(16a) $$\sigma_p = \sigma_m \sum_{j=1}^{n} x_j \beta_j$$

where x_j is the proportion of the portfolio's market value represented by the jth security. Alternatively, we can define a beta coefficient for the portfolio β_p, such that:

(16b) $$\sigma_p = \beta_p \sigma_m$$

[16] β_j can be expressed more formally as the covariance between the return on share j and the return on the market portfolio, divided by the variance of the return on the market portfolio, or, in notation:

$$\beta_j = \frac{\text{cov}(R_j R_m)}{\sigma_m^2} = \frac{r_{jm} \sigma_j \sigma_m}{\sigma_m^2}$$

with r_{jm} the correlation coefficient.

where this beta coefficient is simply given as:

$$\beta_p = \sum_{j=1}^{n} x_j \beta_j$$

It follows that investors who are fully aware of the potential of diversification and who are free to form diversified portfolios need to focus their attention essentially on systematic risk.

The relationship between risks and returns

Throughout this text and in the opening section of this chapter we repeatedly indicated that risk-averse investors will demand a premium in the form of increased expected returns for bearing increased risks. From the discussion in the previous section, it should be clear that such risk premia or higher expected returns should relate not to the total risk of an investment, but only to its systematic risk since unsystematic risk can be eliminated by diversification. What remains to be determined is the exact relationship which ought to prevail in capital markets between a security's systematic risk and its expected return. The Capital Asset Pricing Model, based on a series of economic assumptions and straight reasoning, postulates the form which this relationship should take.

Given investors who are concerned only about the risks and returns of their investments, it must follow that securities which are subject to equal systematic risk should provide identical expected returns. If this did not hold, investors would sell the security with the lower expected return and buy the security with the higher expected return, thereby affecting their prices, until their expected returns are once again identical.

We saw in the previous section that combining the riskless asset with the set of attainable risky portfolios results in an efficient frontier which is given by the capital market line. We indicated that this efficient frontier is the line which joins the riskless asset with the market portfolio. In equilibrium, the market portfolio of risky securities must contain all securities, and it follows that the proportion of each security in the market portfolio equals its proportionate value in the market. Proceeding from this point, the capital asset pricing model is easily derived, as the risk-return preferences of the market are given by the capital market line which joins the riskless asset with the market portfolio. The market portfolio is characterized by expected returns $E(R_m) = E_m$ and risk σ_m respectively, and we saw that the return of the riskless asset is $E(R_f) = E_f$.

Consider an investor who can invest various proportions x of his investment budget in the market portfolio, with the remainder $(1 - x)$ invested in the riskless asset. Through varying x, he can alter the overall expected risk and return of his holdings, adapting them to his own preferences.

We saw that the beta coefficient of a portfolio, β_p, is simply a weighted average of the betas of the component securities which make up the portfolio. The beta for the riskless asset β_f is zero, while the beta of the market β_m is by definition 1.0. Thus, the beta of the investor's portfolio, β_p, is readily computed as:

$$(17) \qquad \beta_p = \sum x_j \beta_j = x\beta_m + (1-x)\beta_f = x$$

The expected return of his portfolio, $E(R_p)$, is similarly computed as:

$$(18) \qquad E(R_p) = xE_m + (1-x)E_f$$

Inserting $x = \beta_p$ into equation (18), we obtain the basic form of the capital asset pricing model:

$$E(R_p) = \beta_p E_m + (1-\beta_p)E_f$$

which can be rewritten as:

$$(19) \qquad E(R_p) = E_f + \beta_p (E_m - E_f)$$

Equation (19) represents a very important result which is easily generalized. For instance, equation (19) can be shown to be valid not only for portfolios consisting of a mix of the market portfolio and the riskless asset, but also for any other portfolio or individual risky asset. It states that the expected return of any security or portfolio should equal the risk-free return plus a risk premium. This risk premium equals the risk premium of the market portfolio, $E_m - E_f$, multiplied by the appropriate beta coefficient. Consequently, the risk premium demanded in the market is proportional to a security's beta coefficient and, hence, to its systematic risk. Furthermore, the relationship between expected returns and systematic risk is linear. This is illustrated diagramatically in Figure 29-8, with the line specifying the tradeoff between risks and returns as expressed in equation (19). No security can fall above this line, otherwise the market portfolio would no longer be efficient. Such a security would represent a bargain, and bargains do not exist in efficient capital markets. Similarly, a security which falls below this line is overpriced, not yielding adequate returns given its systematic risk. It follows that all securities traded in the capital markets should theoretically be represented by points on this line, which is called the *security market line.* Note the similarity to the capital market line as derived in Figure 29-6. However, while in the previous section we were still concerned with overall risk, the security market line as developed in this section and shown in Figure 29-8 is based solely on systematic risk, with β taking the place of σ on the horizontal axis.

Example

Consider the stock of an airline which is characterized by a beta factor of 2.0. The expected return on short-term treasury bills is 6 percent and the expected return of a broadly based market portfolio is 12 percent. Using equation (19), the expected return of the airline stock ought to be:

$$\begin{aligned} E(R) &= E_f + \beta(E_m - E_f) \\ &= 6\% + 2.0(12\% - 6\%) \\ &= 18\% \end{aligned}$$

FIGURE 29-8

Theoretical Relationship Between Security Risk and the Required Rate of Return

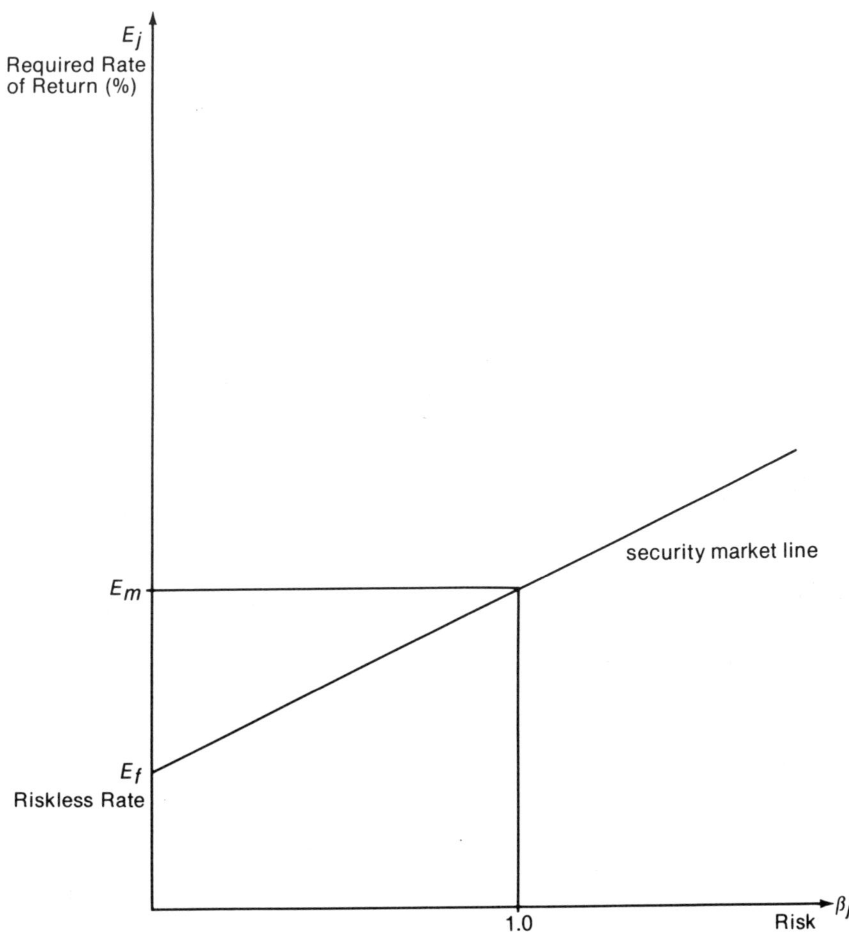

A number of fairly strong simplifying assumptions were made in the development of the capital asset pricing model. These include assumptions about risk-averse, rational, and well-informed investors who are solely concerned about risks and returns; who have a common time horizon for investment decisions as discussed earlier; and capital markets which are perfect, without transaction costs and the likes. Given these abstracting assumptions, the question which naturally arises is whether the results derived bear any resemblance to conditions encountered in real-life financial markets.

Financial researchers have directed significant effort towards answering this question empirically. Specifically, we attempt to measure *ex post* betas and expected returns by looking at the past behavior of securities, and we test statistically to determine the extent to which securities coincide with the security market line as presented in Figure 29-8. Unfortunately, as we have already noted in various sections of this text, statistical research in finance is fraught with difficulties, some of which are conceptual and some statistical. For example, the capital asset pricing model is formulated in terms of future expectations of returns and risks (*ex ante* information), while empirical research is by necessity based on historical data (*ex post* information). This and other limitations of empirical testing make any results suggestive rather than conclusive.

In this context, it is not possible to review the many and often highly sophisticated statistical tests which have been designed. Overall, in spite of the strong assumptions on which the CAPM is based and the difficulties of empirical research, the correspondence between the theoretical results and the practical findings are surprisingly good. It is for this reason that the CAPM is not just of conceptual interest, but is finding increasing application in practical decisions.

Some applications of the capital asset pricing model in financial management

The capital asset pricing model with its specification of risk-return tradeoffs has found applications in various areas of financial management. More important examples are the use of the model to estimate a firm's cost of equity capital and the evaluation of long-term investment projects.

When dealing with the assessment of a firm's cost of capital in Chapter 13, we saw that by far the most difficult aspect was the estimation of the cost of equity, k_e. It was clear that the return which investors required on a firm's shares was dependent on the risk perceived in the stream of future dividends, but we had no explicit way of quantifying this relationship. We can now use equation (19) as developed above to establish this relationship and quantify the expected return on common equity as a function of the β which characterizes the firm's shares. Then, given an estimate of β from past data, the cost of equity can be assessed. The capital asset pricing model is finding increasing applications at rate hearings of publicly regulated utilities, for example, where regulatory agencies attempt to establish rates which will allow the utility to earn a fair rate of return that is commensurate with its cost of capital.

It is interesting to note in this context that a firm's systematic risk or beta factor increases as the proportion of debt in its capital structure increases. While empirical research in this area is still somewhat tentative, it can provide useful additional insights regarding the issue of a firm's optimal capital structure as it was discussed in Chapter 14.

In the area of capital budgeting, given investment projects with different risks, the capital asset pricing model can again provide guidelines on how a firm might trade off risks against returns. While the equation of the capital asset pricing model was developed in the context of securities, it can clearly be applied to investments in other risky assets as well. If we can estimate a project's β, or its sensitivity to market fluctuations, the risk premium which is to be built into the discount rate for that project again becomes $\beta(E_m - E_f)$. Hence, the setting of risk-adjusted discount rates for capital expenditure decisions need no longer be a purely subjective exercise.

29-5. SUMMARY

The tradeoff between risks and returns is a key issue in financial decision-making. Given the financial manager's concern about the firm's share prices over the longer run, optimal decisions in this area can only be made by behaving in a way which is consistent with expressed market preferences. Thus, this chapter focused largely on how investors trade off risks against returns in the capital markets.

We started by introducing various measures for risks and returns. For our purposes, it was most convenient to use the expected value and the variance of relative returns. Using these measures, we computed the expected return and the risk of portfolios consisting of several individual investments. We saw that portfolio risk is largely determined by the covariances or correlations which exist between the individual assets making up the portfolio.

Risk can be reduced through portfolio diversification. We explored ways in which an investor can maximize expected returns for a given level of risk, or minimize risk for given expected returns, through a judicious combination of individual investments.

Given that the returns on most investments show some positive correlation with returns in the general market, only some of the risk can be diversified away. In this context, it is useful to think of the returns from a particular investment as having two components; one which is perfectly correlated with the market, and a residual which is unrelated to the market. Accordingly, we can distinguish two components of risk: one which is market determined and which is called systematic risk, and one which is unique to the particular investment, unrelated to the market, and labelled unsystematic risk. An investment's unsystematic risk can be diversified away through proper choice of investment portfolios, whereas the systematic, market-related risk has to be borne even by a well-diversified investor. Consequently, compensations for risk which investors demand should relate only to the systematic risk of an investment.

The capital asset pricing model specifies the nature of the relationship which should exist between an investment's systematic risk and its expected return. Specifically, the expected return can be viewed as a risk-free return plus a risk premium. The risk premium of an investment is given by the risk premium of the overall market multiplied by the investment's market sensitivity index or beta factor. Therefore, the relationship between expected return and systematic risk is linear.

Empirical tests have shown that the capital asset pricing model provides a reasonably accurate description of actual market behavior. It is of more than just conceptual interest, then, and can be used to guide financial managers in trading off risks against returns. Specifically, the capital asset pricing model has been used to estimate the cost of equity capital for firms and to provide guidance on how discount rates ought to be adjusted for risk in capital budgeting evaluations.

Questions for Discussion

1. Why is the variance or the standard deviation of returns often used as a convenient measure of risk? Can you think of individual situations where these measures would not be adequate?
2. A common saying advises, "Don't put all your eggs in one basket". Formulate the meaning of this statement in statistical terms—what exactly is the underlying reason for this saying?
3. To what extent are risk-return tradeoffs, as expressed by the market, relevant for managerial decision-making? Should the manager completely disregard the total risk of an investment and only be concerned with the component which is not diversifiable? Is the traditional concern which managers have about the stability of a firm's earnings and cash flows justified?
4. In developing models of capital markets in finance, the assumption is often made that all investors are rational and well-informed, and have the same expectations about the future performance of securities. Disregarding individual exceptions, do you think that broadly speaking this assumption provides a reasonable approximation of reality? Give reasons.
5. What do you think are some of the main difficulties in applying the capital asset pricing model to estimate a firm's cost of equity?
6. Give some examples of investors who may not be in a position to maintain a well-diversified portfolio of investments. To what extent are the findings of this chapter relevant to such situations?

Problems with Solutions

1. The current market price of a share is $10. The firm will pay dividends of $0.50 per share at the end of the period. The market price of the share at the end of the period is represented by the following probability distribution:

Probability	Market Price
0.05	$ 9.00
0.1	9.50
0.2	10.00
0.3	10.50
0.2	11.00
0.1	11.50
0.05	12.00

(a) Compute the expected value, the variance, standard deviation, and semivariance of the percentage return provided by investing in this share.
(b) Compute the quantities as under (a) for the absolute returns if an investor invests $1,000 at the beginning of the period.

Solution

(a) relative return $= R = \dfrac{D_1 + V_1 - V_0}{V_0} \times 100\%$

Probability	Market Price V_1	Return R
0.05	\$ 9.00	–5%
0.1	\$ 9.50	0%
0.2	\$10.00	5%
0.3	\$10.50	10%
0.2	\$11.00	15%
0.1	\$11.50	20%
0.05	\$12.00	25%

Expected percentage return

$= -5\%(0.05) + 0(0.1) + 5\%(0.2) + 10\%(0.3) +$

$15\%(0.2) + 20\%\ (0.1) + 25\%(0.05)$

$= 10\%$

Variance

$= (-0.05 - 0.1)^2\ (0.05) + (0 - 0.1)^2\ (0.1) + (0.05 - 0.1)^2\ (0.2) +$

$(0.1 - 0.1)^2\ (0.3) + (0.15 - 0.1)^2\ (0.2) + (0.2 - 0.1)^2\ (0.1) +$

$(0.25 - 0.1)^2\ (0.05)$

$= 0.00525$

Standard deviation

$= \sqrt{0.00525} \simeq 0.0725$

Semivariance

$= 0.00525/2$

$= 0.002625$

(b) Absolute expected value

$= \$1{,}000 \times 10\%$

$= \$100$

Absolute variance

$= (\$1{,}000)^2 \times .00525$

$= 5{,}250$

Absolute standard deviation

$= \$1{,}000 \times .0725$

$= \$72.50$

Absolute semivariance

= $(\$1{,}000)^2 \times .002625$

= 2,625

2. The returns of two shares 1 and 2 for the coming period are characterized by the following joint probability distribution:

returns security 2 \ returns security 1	8%	13%	18%
9%	0.15	0.1	0.05
11%	0.1	0.2	0.1
13%	0.05	0.1	0.15

Entries in the above table are probabilities.

(a) Compute $\sigma(R_1)$, $\sigma(R_2)$, $\text{cov}(R_1R_2)$, r_{12}.

(b) If an investor invests proportions x_1 and $x_2 = (1 - x_1)$ of his portfolio in shares 1 and 2 respectively, plot expected portfolio return and the portfolio variance as a function of x_1. Compute the value of x_1 which yields the lowest portfolio variance. What is the expected return at that point?

(c) Plot the set of attainable portfolios as a function of expected return and variance.

(d) Assume that what was called security 2 above is really the market portfolio. Compute β for security 1.

Note: use formula $\beta_1 = \dfrac{\text{cov}(R_mR_1)}{\sigma_m^2}$ as given in footnote 16.

Solution

(a) To compute the standard deviation of the individual security the information in the joint probability table must be condensed.
The returns to security 1, and the associated probabilities are as follows:

Return	Probability	
8%	.30	
13%	.40	$E(R_1) = 13\%$
18%	.30	

Similarly, for security 2:

Return	Probability	
9%	.30	
11%	.40	$E(R_2) = 11\%$
13%	.30	

For the standard deviations $\sigma(R_1)$ and $\sigma(R_2)$, we obtain:

$$\sigma(R_1) = \sqrt{0.3(0.08-0.13)^2 + 0.4(0.13-0.13)^2 + 0.3(0.18-0.13)^2}$$
$$= \sqrt{0.3(0.0025) + 0.3(0.0025)}$$
$$= \sqrt{0.0015}$$
$$= 0.03873$$
$$\sigma(R_2) = \sqrt{0.3(0.09-0.11)^2 + 0.4(0.11-0.11)^2 + 0.3(0.13-0.11)^2}$$
$$= 0.01549$$
$$\text{cov}(R_1 R_2) = \sum (R_1 - E(R_1))(R_2 - E(R_2))\, p(R_1 R_2)$$
$$= (.05)(.02)(.15) + (.05)(.02)(.05) + (.05)(.02)(.05) + (.05)(.02)(.15)$$
$$= 0.0004$$
$$r_{12} = \frac{\text{cov}(R_1 R_2)}{\sigma_1 \times \sigma_2}$$
$$= \frac{.0004}{.0006}$$
$$= .6667$$

(b) Expected portfolio return may be computed by using the formula:

$$E(R) = x_1(13\%) + (1 - x_1)(11\%)$$

Portfolio variance is computed using the formula given in section 29-2:

$$x_1^2 \sigma_{R_1}{}^2 + (1 - x_1)^2 \sigma_{R_2}{}^2 + 2x_1(1 - x_1)\,\text{cov}(R_1 R_2)$$

The following table was derived using the above formulas:

x_1	$E(R)$	Portfolio Variance
1	13.00%	0.00150
.75	12.50%	0.00101
.50	12.00%	0.00063
.25	11.50%	0.00038
0	11.00%	0.00024

These may be graphed as follows:

Expected Portfolio Return

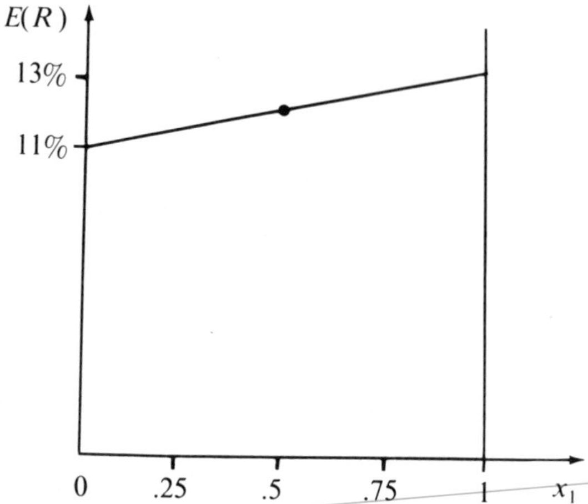

Expected Portfolio Variance

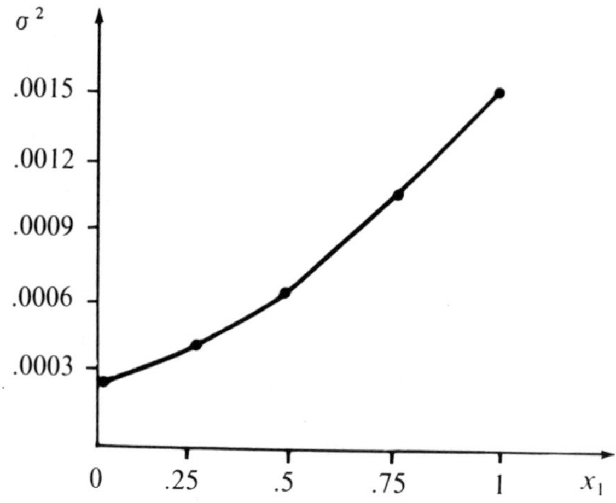

The lowest variance occurs where $x_1 = 0$. The expected return is 11%.

(c) This is done using the information found in part (b).

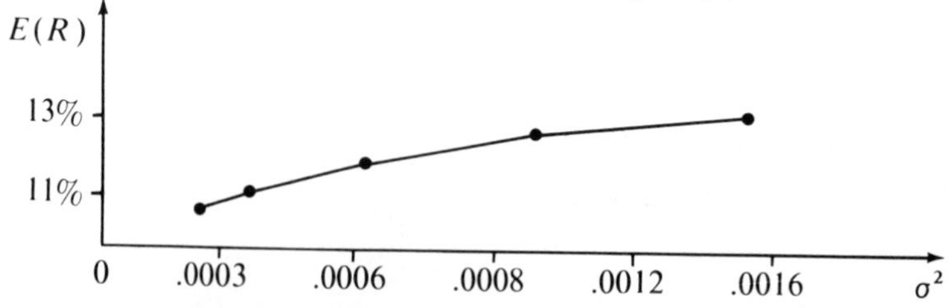

(d) $\beta_1 = \frac{\text{cov}(R_m R_1)}{\sigma_m^2}$

$= \frac{.00040}{.00024}$

$= 1.6667$

3. Two shares are characterized by the following expected values and variances of returns for the coming period:

$E(R_1) = 10\%$ $\qquad \sigma_1^2 = 4$

$E(R_2) = 14\%$ $\qquad \sigma_2^2 = 9$

An investor forms a portfolio, investing proportions x_1 of her money in share 1 and $x_2 = (1 - x_1)$ in share 2.

(a) Compute and graph the portfolio standard deviation as a function of x_1 for the cases $r_{12} = +1, +0.5, 0, -0.5, -1$. Compute the values of x_1 for which $\sigma(R_p)$ assumes its smallest value.

(b) Plot the set of attainable portfolios and the set of efficient portfolios as a function of $E(R_p)$ and $\sigma(R_p)$ for each of the cases given in (a) above.

Solution

(a) Equation (8) from the chapter is used here to compute the portfolio standard deviation. By varying the correlation coefficient and the value of x_1, the following table giving σ_R may be computed:

Correlation Coefficient	Proportions x_1 0	.25	.5	.75	1
+1	3.0000	2.7500	2.5000	2.2500	2.0000
+.5	3.0000	2.5372	2.1794	1.9843	2.0000
0	3.0000	2.3049	1.8028	1.6771	2.0000
−.5	3.0000	2.0463	1.3229	1.2990	2.0000
−1	3.0000	1.7500	.5000	.7500	2.0000

To properly graph these figures it is necessary to determine the value of x_1 for which the standard deviation is minimized.

We minimize:

$$\sigma_R^2 = x_1^2 \sigma_{R_1}^2 + (1 - x_1)^2 \sigma_{R_2}^2 + 2x_1(1 - x_1) r_{12}\sigma_1\sigma_2$$

as the square root will be minimized as well.

For a correlation coefficient of −1, we minimize:

$$\sigma_R^2 = x_1^2(4) + (1 - x_1)^2 9 + 2x_1(1 - x_1)(-1)(2)(3)$$

$$= 4x_1^2 + 9 - 18x_1 + 9x_1^2 + 12x_1^2 - 12x_1$$

$$= 25x_1^2 - 30x_1 + 9$$

We can approximate σ_R as a function of x_1 by computing various points and drawing a curve through them. We can use this to estimate the value of x_1^*, where σ_R assumes a minimum. More exactly, we take the derivative and set it equal to zero to find the minimum, as follows:

$$0 = 50x - 30$$

$$x_1^* = \frac{30}{50} = .6$$

For $x_1 = .6$, we obtain:

$$\sigma_R^2 = (.6)^2(4) + (.4)^2(9) + 2(.6)(.4)(-1)(2)(3)$$
$$= 0$$

Similarly, we find:

r_{12}	x_1^*	Minimum σ_p
.5	.8571	1.9640
0	.6923	1.6641
−.5	.6316	1.1921

The graphs appear as follows:

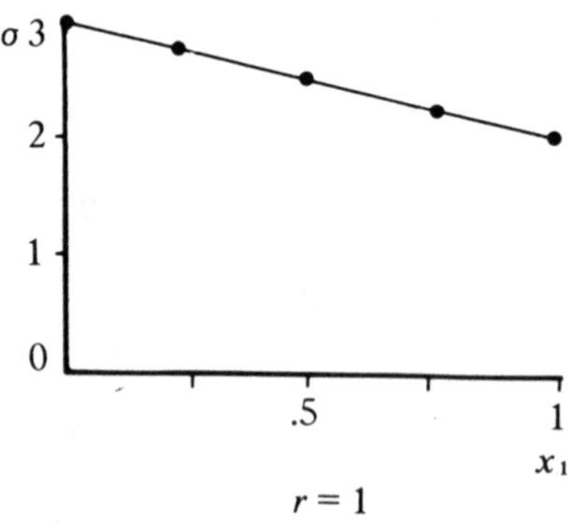

$r = 1$

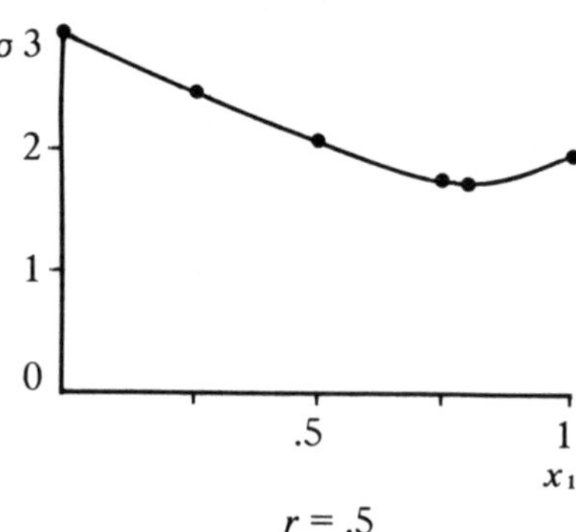

$r = .5$

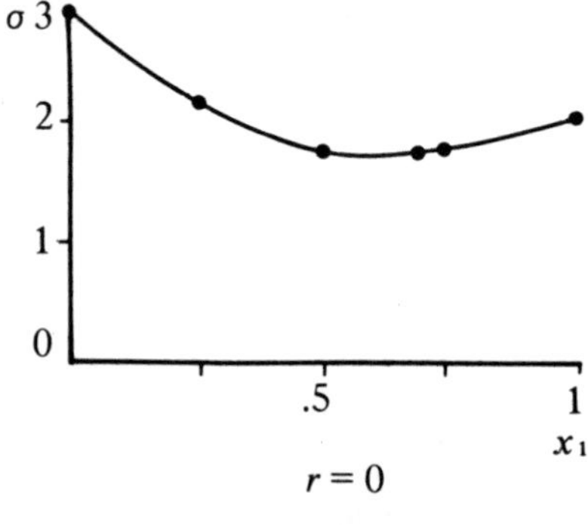

$r = 0$

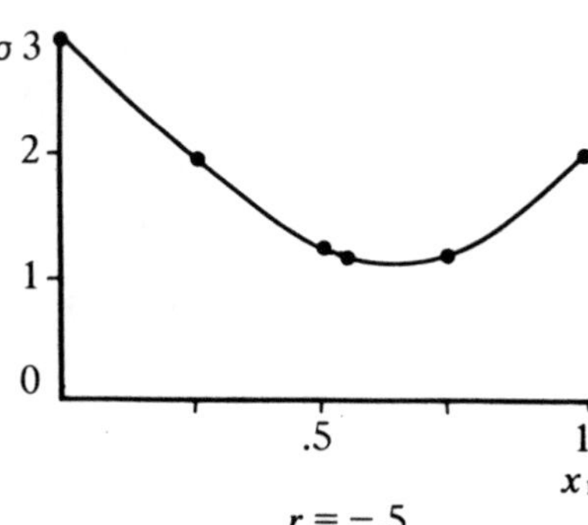

$r = -.5$

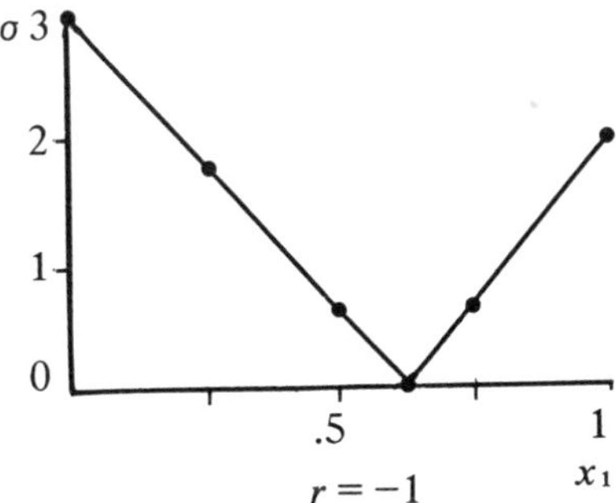

Note that footnote 9 of the chapter provides a more general approach to finding x_1^*. By use of calculus, we derived the general formula:

$$x_1^* = \frac{\sigma_2(\sigma_2 - r_{12}\sigma_1)}{\sigma_1^2 + \sigma_2^2 - 2r_{12}\sigma_1\sigma_2}$$

Which for our example becomes:

$$x_1^* = \frac{3(3 - 2r_{12})}{4 + 9 - 2r_{12}(2 \times 3)}$$

$$= \frac{9 - 6r_{12}}{13 - 12r_{12}}$$

The following values are easily verified:

r_{12}	x_1^*
0.5	0.8571
0	0.6923
−0.5	0.6316
−1	0.6000

where x_1^* is the value of x_1 where σ_R assumes the smallest value. Note that for $r_{12} = 1$, the value computed for x_1^* by the above formula would become $x_1^* = 3$. Since $0 < x_1 < 1$, this implies that there is no minimum value with a slope of zero within this range. The minimum value for σ_R occurs on the boundary of this range, with $x_1^* = 1$, as shown in the first figure above.

(b) We have the standard deviation from part (a) above, and expected return $= x_1E_1 + (1 - x_1)E_2$. We obtain:

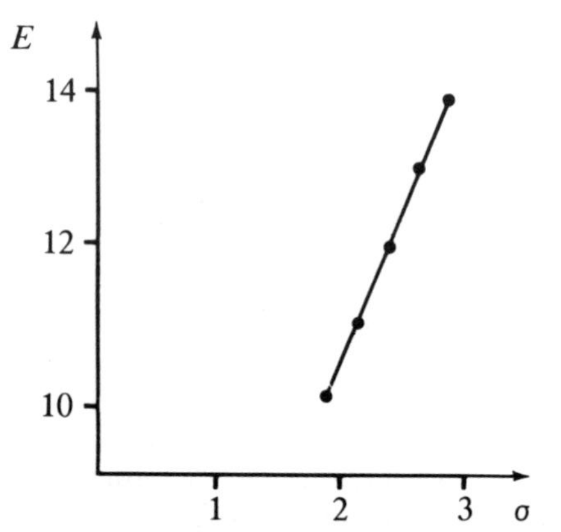
E
14
12
10
1
2
3
σ

$r = 1$

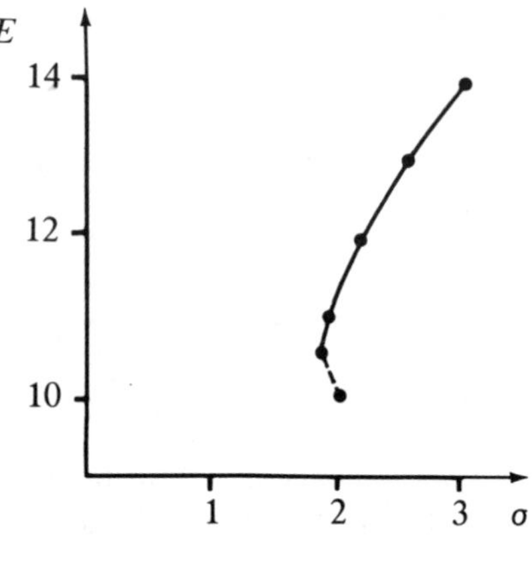
E
14
12
10
1
2
3
σ

$r = .5$

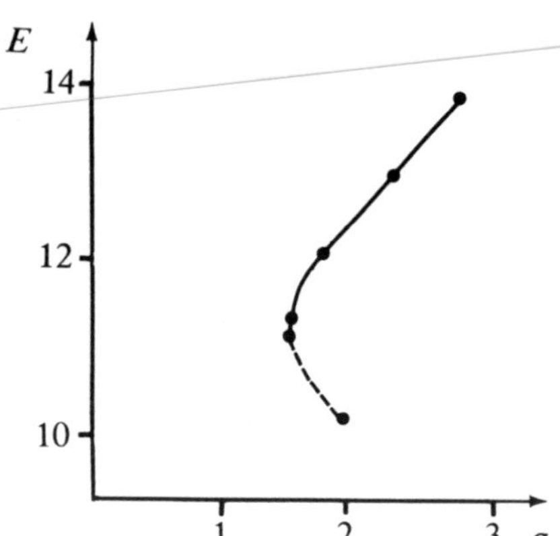
E
14
12
10
1
2
3
σ

$r = 0$

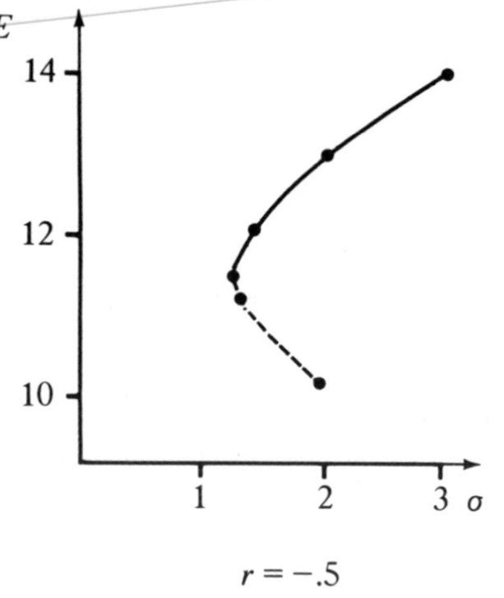
E
14
12
10
1
2
3
σ

$r = -.5$

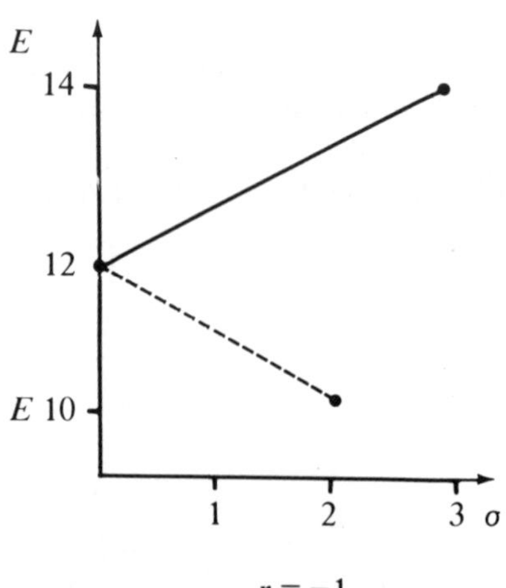
E
14
12
E 10
1
2
3
σ

$r = -1$

4. Over a sample of periods, the return on the market portfolio and on an individual share have been measured as follows:

Period	Market Return	Return on Share
1	8%	14%
2	5%	7%
3	10%	16%
4	13%	24%
5	6%	12%

(a) Compute the characteristic line for this share, estimating the values for α_j and β_j.

(b) For each period, show how the given return on this share can be split into the components $\alpha_j + \beta_j R_m$, and e.

Solution

(a) Using standard formulas of regression analysis, we can compute:

$$\alpha_j = \frac{\sum R_j \sum R_m^2 - \sum R_m \sum R_j R_m}{n \sum R_m^2 - (\sum R_m)^2}$$

$$\beta_j = \frac{n \sum R_j R_m - \sum R_j \sum R_m}{n \sum R_m^2 - (\sum R_m)^2}$$

where n is the number of observations, which is 5 in our example.

We compute the following:

R_m	R_j	R_m^2	$R_m R_j$	R_j^2
8	14	64	112	196
5	7	25	35	49
10	16	100	160	256
13	24	169	312	576
6	12	36	72	144
$\sum R_m = 42$	$\sum R_j = 73$	$\sum R_m^2 = 394$	$\sum R_m R_j = 691$	$\sum R_j^2 = 1221$

All the above entries are based on percentages.

We start by plotting the points in a diagram. The characteristic line can then be estimated by computing α_j and β_j using the techniques of regression analysis, as indicated above.

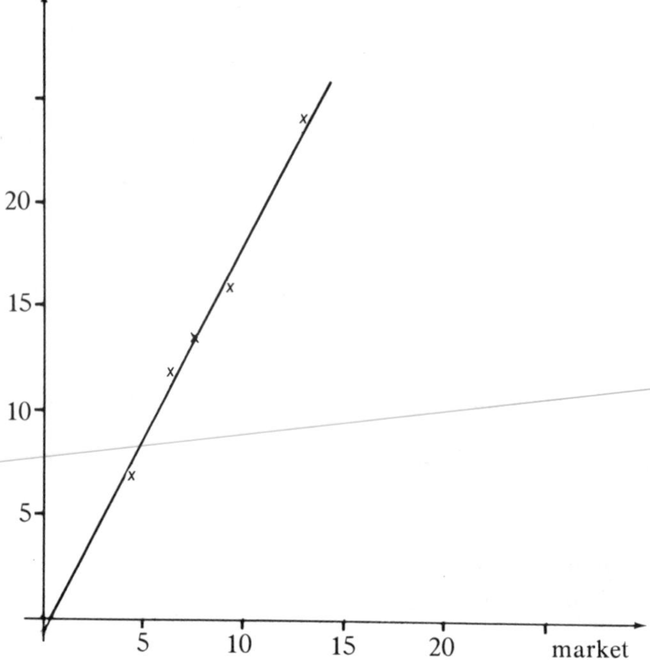

We can now compute:

$$\alpha_j = \frac{73 \times 394 - 42 \times 691}{5 \times 394 - 42 \times 42} = \frac{-260}{206} = -1.26$$

$$\beta_j = \frac{5 \times 691 - 73 \times 42}{5 \times 394 - 42 \times 42} = \frac{389}{206} = 1.89$$

(b)

R_m	$\alpha_j + \beta_j R_m$	$e = R_j - (\alpha_j + \beta_j R_m)$
8%	13.86%	0.14%
5%	8.19%	−1.19%
10%	17.64%	−1.64%
13%	23.31%	0.69%
6%	10.08%	1.92%
		$\sum e = -0.08\%$

We see that $\sum e \simeq 0$ (the small value of −0.08% computed is due to rounding).

5. The shares of a firm are characterized by a beta factor of $\beta = 1.5$. The expected market return is 12% and the risk-free rate of return is 8%. Using the capital asset pricing model, determine the expected return for the firm's shares. How is this expected return related to the firm's cost of equity capital?

Solution

We may determine the expected return for the firm's shares by using the equation:

$$E(R) = E_f + \beta_j(E_m - E_f)$$

Here,

$$E(R) = 8\% + 1.5(12\% - 8\%)$$
$$= 14\%$$

We may use this figure as an estimate of the market capitalization rate, or the effective yield which the firm's common shares have to provide. Because of issuing and underwriting expenses, the firm's cost of equity capital will be somewhat higher than this market capitalization rate, as was discussed in Chapter 13.

Additional Problems

1. The returns of shares A and B for the coming period are thought to be represented by the following joint probability distribution.

Returns Share B \ Returns Share A	7%	11%	15%
8%	.10	.20	.20
9%	.02	.04	.04
10%	.08	.16	.16

(a) Compute the expected value, the variance, and semivariance of the percentage return provided by investing in share B.
(b) Compute $\sigma(R_A)$, $\sigma(R_B)$, $\text{cov}(A, B)$, r_{AB}
(c) Plot the expected portfolio return and variance as a function of x, where x is the proportion of the portfolio invested in share A, and $(1 - x)$ is the proportion invested in portfolio B.
(d) Plot the set of attainable portfolios as a function of expected return and variance.

2. Assume the following information about two shares:

expected return of Q in next period = 10%

expected return of P in next period = 12%

$\sigma_Q = 6\%$

$\sigma_P = 10\%$

$r_{QP} = -1$

(a) What would the expected return and variance be of a portfolio consisting of 50% Q and 50% P?
(b) If the correlation coefficient r_{QP} were zero, would your answer to part (a) change? If so, recompute the standard deviation and expected return.
(c) Plot the set of attainable portfolios as a function of $E(R)$ and σ for part (b). Indicate any possible inefficient portfolios.

3. Over a 10-month period the return on the market portfolio and on a single share of Smythe Ltd. have been measured as follows:

Period	Market Return (%)	Smythe Return (%)
1	2	3
2	12	10
3	5	6
4	3	5
5	6	8
6	10	13
7	0	3
8	8	11
9	9	12
10	5	7

Compute and draw the characteristic line for Smythe Ltd., estimating the values for α and β. Break down each actual return measured for Smythe into the computed component $(\alpha_j + \beta_j R_m)$ and the error term e. Verify that $\Sigma e \simeq 0$.

4. Dr. Nowall, a rich lawyer, is interested in composing an investment portfolio from three securities that he has heard of. He has been informed by this son, a commerce student, that the beta factors of the three securities have been estimated at .25, .95, and 1.65. Dr. Nowall wishes to invest \$40,000, \$60,000, and \$25,000 in each of the securities respectively.
If the expected market return for the period under consideration is 8%, and the riskless asset carries a return of 2%, what is the expected return of this portfolio?

5. If the expected return of a firm's shares is 16%, the market return 11%, and the risk-free rate of return 7%, what should the beta factor of the firm be according to the Capital Asset Pricing Model?

Selected References

M. Blume, "Portfolio Theory: A Step Toward Its Practical Application", *Journal of Business,* April, 1970, pp. 152-173.

M. Brennan, "Capital Market Equilibrium with Divergent Borrowing and Lending Rates", *Journal of Financial and Quantitative Analysis*, December, 1971, pp. 1197-1205.

R. Hamada, "Portfolio Analysis, Market Equilibrium and Corporation Finance", *Journal of Finance*, March, 1969, pp. 13-32.

M. Jensen, "Capital Markets: Theory and Evidence", *Bell Journal of Economics and Management Science*, Autumn, 1972, pp. 357-398.

J. Lintner, "Security Prices, Risk, and Maximal Gain from Diversification", *Journal of Finance*, December, 1965, pp. 587-616.

H. Markowitz, "Portfolio Selection", *Journal of Finance*, March, 1952, pp. 77-91.

F. Modigliani and G. Pogue, "An Introduction to Risk and Return: Concepts and Evidence", *Financial Analysts Journal*, March/April, 1974, pp. 68-80 and May/June, 1974, pp. 69-86.

M. Rubinstein, "A Mean-Variance Synthesis of Corporate Financial Theory", *Journal of Finance*, March, 1973, pp. 167-181.

W. Sharpe, "Capital Asset Prices: A Theory of Market Equilibrium Under Conditions of Risk", *Journal of Finance*, September, 1964, pp. 425-442.

W. Sharpe, *Portfolio Theory and Capital Markets*, New York: McGraw-Hill, 1970.

APPENDIX A
Prospectus: Trans-Canada Pipe Lines Limited

This prospectus constitutes a public offering of these securities only in those jurisdictions where they may be lawfully offered for sale.
No Securities Commission or similar authority in Canada has in any way passed upon the merits of the securities offered hereunder and any representation to the contrary is an offence.

New Issue

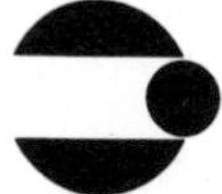

Trans-Canada Pipe Lines Limited

(Incorporated by Special Act of the Parliament of Canada)

$125,000,000
(2,500,000 shares)

$2.65 Cumulative Redeemable Convertible Second Preferred Shares Series A

(of the par value of $50 per share)

The $2.65 Cumulative Redeemable Convertible Second Preferred Shares Series A (the "Second Preferred Shares Series A"), when issued, will be preferred as to capital and dividends (subject to the Company's outstanding $2.80 Cumulative Redeemable Preferred Shares and $2.75 Cumulative Redeemable Convertible Preferred Shares Series A) and will be entitled to fixed cumulative preferred cash dividends, as and when declared by the Board of Directors, at a rate of $2.65 per share per annum, to accrue from March 21, 1972 and will be payable quarterly on the first days of May, August and November, 1972 and thereafter quarterly on the first days of February, May, August and November. The provisions to be attached to the Second Preferred Shares Series A including those with respect to priority, voting rights, redemption and purchase fund are set out under the heading "Details of the Offering" on page 16.

Conversion Privilege

Each Second Preferred Share Series A will be convertible at the option of the holder at any time on or prior to May 1, 1982, or the last business day prior to the date fixed for redemption of such shares, whichever is earlier, on the basis of 11 common shares for 10 Second Preferred Shares Series A so converted. This conversion basis will be subject to adjustment in certain events referred to under the heading "Conversion Privilege" on page 17.

In the opinion of counsel, these Second Preferred Shares Series A will be investments in which the Canadian and British Insurance Companies Act states that a company registered under Part III thereof may invest its funds without availing itself for that purpose of the provisions of subsection (4) of Section 63 of said Act.

Applications have been made to list the Second Preferred Shares Series A on the Montreal, Toronto, Winnipeg, Calgary and Vancouver stock exchanges. Acceptance of the listings will be subject to the filing of required documents and evidence of satisfactory distribution, both within ninety days.

Price: $50 per share

We, as principals, conditionally offer these Second Preferred Shares Series A, subject to prior sale, if, as and when issued by the Company and accepted by us in accordance with the conditions contained in the underwriting agreement referred to under the heading "Underwriting" on page 3 and subject to the approval of all legal matters on behalf of the Company by Messrs. McCarthy & McCarthy, Toronto, and on our behalf by Messrs. Borden, Elliot, Kelley & Palmer, Toronto.

	Price to public	Underwriting commission	Proceeds to Company (1)
Per Share..................	$50.00	$1.50	$48.50
Total......................	$125,000,000	$3,750,000	$121,250,000

(1) Before deducting expenses of issue, estimated at $200,000.

Subscriptions will be received subject to rejection or allotment in whole or in part and the right is reserved to close the subscription books at any time without notice. It is expected that Second Preferred Shares Series A will be available for delivery on or about March 21, 1972.

NESBITT THOMSON SECURITIES LIMITED

Offices in Principal Cities across Canada and in New York and London

THE COMPANY

Trans-Canada Pipe Lines Limited (the "Company") was incorporated by Special Act of the Parliament of Canada, 15 George VI, Chapter 92, which came into force on March 21, 1951. The said Special Act of Incorporation was subsequently amended by Special Act of the Parliament of Canada, 2-3 Elizabeth II, Chapter 80, which came into force on May 27, 1954 and by Special Act of the Parliament of Canada, 16-17 Elizabeth II, Chapter 46, which came into force on February 1, 1968.

At a meeting of the Board of Directors on March 1, 1972, the directors passed a resolution authorizing an application for letters patent continuing the Company as a company under Part I of the Canada Corporations Act, varying the name of the Company to TransCanada PipeLines Limited, increasing its authorized capital, and redesignating and varying in certain minor respects the terms of its presently outstanding preferred shares. Such resolution will be submitted for approval to a special general meeting of shareholders to be held in conjunction with the annual meeting of shareholders of the Company on April 18, 1972.

The Company's head office is located at 407 Eighth Avenue South West, Calgary, Alberta and its executive office is located at 150 Eglinton Avenue East, Toronto, Ontario.

APPLICATION OF PROCEEDS

The estimated net proceeds amounting to $121,050,000 to be derived by the Company from the sale of the Second Preferred Shares Series A will be applied:

(i) as to $10,000,000 to acquire additional shares in TransCanada GasProducts Ltd. ("GasProducts"), a wholly owned subsidiary of the Company, to enable GasProducts to retire outstanding bank loans of $4,000,000 incurred in connection with the acquisition from the Company of the Banner Companies referred to under the heading "TransCanada GasProducts Ltd." on page 15, the balance to be used by GasProducts as to $3,000,000 for investment in the GasProducts Extraction Plant and as to $2,000,000 for investment in the Pacific Extraction Plant both referred to on page 15 and as to $1,000,000 for working capital;

(ii) as to $5,000,000 to redeem the Preferred Shares Special Series, which were issued to provide funds to retire outstanding loans from United States banks in the total amount of U.S. $2,500,000 incurred to provide funds for the purchase by the Company of 25,000 common shares of Great Lakes Gas Transmission Company referred to under the heading "Great Lakes Pipe Line" on page 13 and as to the balance to purchase Subordinated Debentures due 1987 of the Company to be subsequently applied for sinking fund purposes in accordance with their terms; and

(iii) as to the balance, to reduce the Company's outstanding bank loans (which amounted to $65,600,000 on February 28, 1972) and short-term promissory notes (which amounted to $37,000,000 on February 28, 1972), which indebtedness was incurred primarily for the payment of construction expenditures related to the 1971 construction program and the 1972 construction program referred to on pages 5 and 6. The Company anticipates that its outstanding bank loans and short-term promissory notes will exceed $106,050,000 on March 21, 1972.

UNDERWRITING

Under an agreement dated March 1, 1972 between the Company and Nesbitt Thomson Securities Limited, Wood Gundy Limited, McLeod, Young, Weir & Company Limited and Midland-Osler Securities Limited, as underwriters, the Company has agreed to sell and the underwriters have agreed to purchase on March 21, 1972 the Second Preferred Shares Series A at a price of $50 per share, payable in cash to the Company against delivery of such Second Preferred Shares Series A. By the said agreement, the Company has agreed to pay the underwriters a commission of $1.50 per share in consideration of the obligations assumed thereunder by the underwriters. The obligation of the underwriters to take up the Second Preferred Shares Series A is several and not joint and may be terminated at their respective options on notice given as provided in the agreement on the basis of their assessment of the state of the financial markets and may also be terminated upon the occurrence of certain stated events. The underwriters are, however, obligated to take up and pay for all of the Second Preferred Shares Series A if any of the Second Preferred Shares Series A are purchased under such agreement.

The Banner Companies have been engaged in the business of exploring for and producing petroleum and natural gas, which activities will be continued by Gas Products.

As at December 31, 1971, Gas Products had natural gas reserves of approximately 79,365 billion cubic feet and oil reserves of approximately 3,177,500 barrels. As at the same date, Gas Products held oil and gas interests in 4,904,360 gross acres, representing 2,038,794 net acres after deduction of interests held by others. Of these interests, approximately 80% are located in Hudson Bay and the Gulf of St. Lawrence, with the remainder located in Western Canada. To date Gas Products has not expended any significant amounts of money for the development of its interests in Hudson Bay and the Gulf of St. Lawrence.

During 1971 Gas Products had production of 2,499 billion cubic feet of natural gas and 46,244 barrels of oil. This production was derived from acreages located in the Province of Alberta.

During 1972 Gas Products anticipates that it will expend approximately $2,700,000 on oil and gas exploration, development and land acquisitions. It is presently anticipated that expenditures at that approximate level will be continued during the next few years.

Regulation

Gas Products holds permits for the export of propane from Alberta under the provisions of The Energy Resources Conservation Act of Alberta and export licenses from the National Energy Board. As a result of the recent application by Gas Products and Dome the Alberta Board has authorized an increase in such export permits subject to the approval of the Lieutenant Governor in Council. Gas Products together with Dome and others have applied to the National Energy Board for increases in its licences to export propane.

Northwest Project

Discoveries of gas and oil on the north slope of Alaska and in the Mackenzie River Delta in Canada indicate that this area could be a significant source of gas supply in future years. Ecological and geological factors in the far northwest present problems in design and construction requiring extensive engineering research. The Company through the Northwest Project Study Group (consisting of the Company, Atlantic Richfield Company, Humble Oil & Refining Company, The Standard Oil Company (Ohio), Michigan Wisconsin Pipe Line Company and Natural Gas Pipeline Company of America) is participating in economic and engineering studies, including cost studies, of a natural gas pipe line from Prudhoe Bay, Alaska to Emerson, Manitoba.

As part of an initial $12,000,000 study program, the Northwest Project Study Group has constructed and is presently operating an extensive Arctic test facility at Sans Sault on the Mackenzie River. The Group also has under consideration the possibility of joint studies with others who have announced similar possibilities.

DETAILS OF THE OFFERING

The following is a brief summary of some of the preferences, privileges, rights, restrictions, conditions and limitations attaching to the Cumulative Second Preferred Shares as a class and to the 2,500,000 $2.65 Cumulative Redeemable Convertible Second Preferred Shares Series A (the "Second Preferred Shares Series A") offered by this prospectus and is subject in its entirety to the detailed provisions set out in Schedules I and II to this prospectus on pages 46 and 51, to which reference is expressly made. A summary of the share capital of the Company is set forth under the heading "Share Capital of the Company" on page 19.

Certain Provisions of the Second Preferred Shares as a Class

Subject to certain limitations, the directors may fix the provisions attaching to the Second Preferred Shares of each series. The Second Preferred Shares as a class have, amongst other provisions, provisions to the following effect attached thereto.

Priority

The Second Preferred Shares will rank junior to the $2.80 Cumulative Redeemable Preferred Shares and the Cumulative Preferred Shares (including the 5,000,000 additional Cumulative Preferred Shares provided for in the resolution of the directors referred to under the heading "Share Capital of the Company" on page 19) with respect to priority in payment of dividends and in the distribution of assets in the event of liquidation, dissolution or winding up of the Company, whether voluntary or involuntary, or any other distribution of the assets of the Company among its shareholders for the purpose of winding up its affairs and will be subject in all respects to the preferences, rights, conditions, restrictions, limitations and prohibitions attaching to the $2.80 Cumulative Redeemable Preferred Shares as a class and to the Cumulative Preferred Shares as a class and to each series of Cumulative Preferred Shares.

Voting Rights

The holders of the Second Preferred Shares of each series do not have any voting rights nor are they entitled to receive notice of or attend shareholders' meetings unless dividends on the Second Preferred Shares of any series are in arrears to the extent of six quarterly dividends. Until all arrears of dividends have been paid, such holders will be entitled to receive notice of and to attend all shareholders' meetings and to one vote in respect of each Second Preferred Share held. The holders of the Second Preferred Shares as a class and the holders of each series of Second Preferred Shares have the right to attend and vote at general meetings of the shareholders on any question directly affecting any of the rights or privileges attached to the Second Preferred Shares as a class, or to such series of Second Preferred Shares, as the case may be, including the right to attend and vote on any matter relating to the authorization of or to provide for the creation of additional preferred shares ranking prior to the Second Preferred Shares in any respect, save and except that the holders of the Second Preferred Shares shall not have the right to attend and vote at the special general meeting of the shareholders of the Company to be held on April 18, 1972 called for the purpose of approving the resolution authorizing an application for letters patent continuing the Company as a company under Part I of the Canada Corporations Act and, inter alia, increasing its authorized capital by the creation of a further 5,000,000 Cumulative Preferred Shares of the par value of $50 per share referred to under the heading "Share Capital of the Company" on page 19.

Changes in Terms

The provisions attaching to the Second Preferred Shares as a class and to each series of Second Preferred Shares which have been issued may be modified, amended or varied only with the sanction of the holders of the Second Preferred Shares as a class or of the holders of each such series, as the case may be. Any such sanction to be given by the holders of the Second Preferred Shares and any sanction of a change adversely affecting the rights or privileges of such shares or otherwise required by the terms thereof, may be given by the affirmative vote of the holders of not less than 66⅔% of the Second Preferred Shares or of each of such series, as the case may be, represented and voted at a meeting or adjourned meeting of such holders called and constituted in a specific manner.

Certain Provisions of the Second Preferred Shares Series A

Dividends

The holders of Second Preferred Shares Series A will be entitled to receive fixed cumulative preferential cash dividends, as and when declared by the board of directors, at the rate of $2.65 per share per annum, to accrue from March 21, 1972 and to be payable quarterly on the first days of May, August and November, 1972 and thereafter quarterly on the first days of February, May, August and November.

Redemption

The Second Preferred Shares Series A will not be redeemable prior to December 31, 1975. In addition, they will not be redeemable prior to May 1, 1977 unless the Company shall have filed with the Registrar and Transfer Agent for the Second Preferred Shares Series A on the day that notice of such redemption is first given a certificate certifying that the weighted average price at which the common shares of the Company have traded on The Toronto Stock Exchange during the 20 trading days ending on the fifth day preceding the date on which the notice of redemption is given, was not less than 125% of the conversion price in effect on the date of the filing of such certificate. Subject to the foregoing, the Second Preferred Shares Series A will be redeemable at the option of the Company, in whole at any time or in part from time to time, on not less than 30 days' notice at a redemption price of $52.50 per share if redeemed on or before April 30, 1982; $52.00 per share if redeemed thereafter and on or before April 30, 1984; $51.50 per share if redeemed thereafter and on or before April 30, 1986; $51.00 per share if redeemed thereafter and on or before April 30, 1988; and $50.50 per share if redeemed thereafter; together in each case with all accrued and unpaid preferential dividends calculated to the date fixed for redemption.

In addition, the Second Preferred Shares Series A will not be redeemable at any time if any part of the redemption price which constitutes a repayment of paid-up capital would for purposes of the Income Tax Act (Canada) be deemed to have been paid as a dividend by reason of the paid-up capital limit (as that term is defined in the said Act, as the same may be amended or re-enacted from time to time) of the Company being less than the paid-up capital in respect of those shares so to be redeemed.

Conversion Privilege

The Second Preferred Shares Series A will be convertible at any time up to but not after the close of business on May 1, 1982, or, in the case of shares called for redemption, up to the close of business on the last business day prior to the date fixed for redemption, whichever is earlier, into fully paid and non-assessable common shares of the Company, as presently constituted, on the basis of 1⅒ common shares for each Second Preferred Share Series A so converted.

The provisions attaching to the Second Preferred Shares Series A provide for an appropriate adjustment to be made in the conversion privilege in the event of any subdivision or consolidation of common shares or change of common shares into a different class or classes of shares, and also provide, in effect, that if the Company at any time after February 25, 1972 issues or sells (with certain exceptions) common shares at a price different from the then conversion price (initially $45.45 per share) the conversion basis referred to above shall be adjusted so as to protect the rights of the holders of the Second Preferred Shares Series A against dilution.

The Company will not pay any stock dividends upon its common shares or issue rights to the holders of such shares unless it shall so notify each registered holder of Second Preferred Shares Series A at least 14 days prior to the date for the determination of the holders of common shares entitled to receive the same.

The registered holder of any Second Preferred Share Series A on the record date for any dividend declared payable on such share will be entitled to such dividend notwithstanding that such share is converted after such record date and before the payment date of such dividend, and the registered holder of any common share resulting from any conversion shall be entitled to rank equally with the registered holders of all other common shares in respect of all dividends declared payable to holders of common shares of record on any date after the date of conversion. Subject as aforesaid, no payment or adjustment will be made on account of any dividend on the Second Preferred Shares Series A converted or the common shares resulting from any conversion. Fractional shares will not be issued on any conversion but in lieu thereof the Company shall adjust such fractional interest by the issue of non-voting and non-dividend bearing scrip certificates, which may become void after a period of not less than two years, entitling the bearers to receive fully paid common shares on surrender of scrip certificates aggregating a whole number of such shares.

Second Preferred Shares Series A may be converted at the offices of the Transfer Agent for the Company's common shares in Montreal, Toronto, Winnipeg, Calgary and Vancouver.

Purchase Fund

The Company shall on or before February 1 in each year commencing with the year 1975 credit to a purchase fund account for the Second Preferred Shares Series A an amount equal to 2% of the aggregate par value of the Second Preferred Shares Series A outstanding on the immediately preceding December 31 to be applied by the Company, subject as hereinafter provided, to the purchase for cancellation of Second Preferred Shares Series A to the extent such shares are available for purchase at a price not exceeding $50 per share plus costs of purchase, provided that the Company in each year subsequent to 1975 shall only be required to set aside that amount which shall be required to bring the balance in such purchase fund account on February 1 in such year up to an amount equal to 2% of the aggregate par value of the Second Preferred Shares Series A outstanding on the preceding December 31.

The Company shall only be obliged in any month to apply out of moneys standing to the credit of the purchase fund account to the purchase of Second Preferred Shares Series A an amount which if a like amount were used for such purpose in each of the remaining months, if any, up to the next succeeding January 31 would result in the aggregate of all such amounts not exceeding the balance standing to the credit of the purchase fund account at the commencement of such first mentioned month. The Company will not be required to purchase any Second Preferred Shares Series A if and so long as such purchase would constitute a breach by the Company of the provisions of any indenture securing bonds, debentures or other securities of the Company or if and so long as any such purchase would be contrary to any applicable law.

Rights on Liquidation

In the event of the liquidation, dissolution or winding-up of the Company or other distribution of assets of the Company among its shareholders for the purpose of winding-up its affairs, the holders of the Second Preferred Shares Series A shall be entitled to receive the amount paid up on such shares together with all accrued and unpaid cumulative preferential dividends thereon and, if such liquidation, dissolution, winding-up or distribution be voluntary, a premium of $2.50 per share if such event commences prior to May 1, 1977, and if such event commences thereafter, a premium equivalent to the premium payable on redemption if such shares were to be redeemed at the date of commencement of any such liquidation, dissolution, winding-up or distribution before any amount shall be paid or any property or assets of the Company shall be distributed to the holders of any shares ranking junior to the Second Preferred Shares Series A. After payment to the holders of the Second Preferred Shares Series A of the amounts so payable to them they shall not be entitled to share in any further distribution of the property or assets of the Company.

Right of Company to Purchase

Subject as hereinafter provided the Company may at any time or times purchase (if obtainable) for cancellation the whole or any part of the Second Preferred Shares Series A outstanding from time to time at a price per share not exceeding $52.50 if such purchase is made prior to May 1, 1977 and if such purchase is made thereafter, at a price per share not exceeding the then current redemption price plus in all cases costs of purchase.

Restrictions on Dividends and Retirement of Shares

So long as any of the Second Preferred Shares Series A are outstanding, the Company shall not

(a) pay any dividends on the common shares or any other shares of the Company ranking junior to the Second Preferred Shares Series A with respect to payment of dividends, or

(b) retire any shares of the Company ranking junior to the Second Preferred Shares Series A with respect to repayment of capital or with respect to payment of dividends, or

(c) retire less than all the Second Preferred Shares Series A and all Cumulative Preferred Shares and all the $2.80 Cumulative Redeemable Preferred Shares then outstanding

unless all dividends then payable on the Second Preferred Shares Series A, all Cumulative Preferred Shares and the $2.80 Cumulative Redeemable Preferred Shares then outstanding shall have been declared and paid.

SHARE CAPITAL OF THE COMPANY

The share capital of the Company, as authorized by the Special Act of Incorporation of the Company, as amended, consists of 5,000,000 preferred shares of the par value of $50.00 per share (less any shares which have been issued and subsequently purchased out of capital) and 25,000,000 common shares of the par value of $1.00 per share. 1,000,000 of the said preferred shares have been created as a class designated as $2.80 Cumulative Redeemable Preferred Shares (the "$2.80 Preferred Shares") and 4,000,000 of the said preferred shares have been created as a class of Cumulative Preferred Shares (the "Cumulative Preferred Shares") issuable in one or more series. By By-law No. 23 of the Company, enacted by the board of directors on January 25, 1972, pursuant to the provisions of the Company's Special Act of Incorporation, as amended, 2,500,000 of the said 4,000,000 Cumulative Preferred Shares have been reclassified as 2,500,000 Cumulative Second Preferred Shares (the "Second Preferred Shares") issuable in one or more series. By-law No. 23 of the Company was sanctioned, as amended, by a special general meeting of the common shareholders of the Company held on March 1, 1972. The amendment provided that the sanction of the holders of the Second Preferred Shares would not be required to the application for letters patent referred to below.

At a meeting of the Board of Directors held on March 1, 1972, the directors passed a resolution authorizing an application for letters patent continuing the Company as a company under the Canada Corporations Act and, inter alia, increasing its authorized capital by the creation of a further 5,000,000 Cumulative Preferred Shares of the par value of $50 per share ranking pari passu with the $2.80 Preferred Shares and the presently authorized Cumulative Preferred Shares, including the Preferred Shares Series A, and a further 5,000,000 Second Preferred Shares of the par value of $50 per share ranking pari passu with the Second Preferred Shares, including the Second Preferred Shares Series A. Such resolution will be submitted for approval to a special general meeting of shareholders to be held in conjunction with the annual meeting of shareholders of the Company on April 18, 1972.

Common Shares

As noted above, the authorized capital of the Company includes 25,000,000 common shares, of which as at December 31, 1971, 8,312,377 shares were issued and outstanding as fully paid and non-assessable. Each common share of the capital stock of the Company is equal to every other common share and all common shares participate equally on liquidation or distribution of assets. The holder of record of each common share is entitled to one vote.

The $2.80 Preferred Shares

The $2.80 Preferred Shares, of which 930,785 shares were outstanding on December 31, 1971, rank on a parity with the Cumulative Preferred Shares with respect to payment of dividends and repayment of capital and have attached thereto, among other provisions, provisions restricting the issuance of preferred shares ranking on a parity with the $2.80 Preferred Shares; provisions entitling the holders of the $2.80 Preferred

Shares on failure to pay six quarterly dividends on the $2.80 Preferred Shares and/or the Cumulative Preferred Shares to join with the holders of Cumulative Preferred Shares in electing one-third of the directors of the Company; and provisions restricting the payment of dividends on common shares or any other shares of the Company (including the Second Preferred Shares Series A) ranking junior to the $2.80 Preferred Shares and the reduction of junior capital (including the Second Preferred Shares Series A) as follows:

So long as any of the $2.80 Preferred Shares are outstanding the Company shall not:

(i) declare or pay or set apart for payment any dividends (other than stock dividends in shares of the Company ranking junior to the $2.80 Preferred Shares in all respects) on the common shares or any other shares of the Company ranking junior to the $2.80 Preferred Shares with respect to payment of dividends, or

(ii) call for redemption, purchase, reduce or otherwise pay off any shares of the Company ranking junior to the $2.80 Preferred Shares with respect to repayment of capital (except out of the proceeds of an issue of common shares or of an issue of other shares ranking junior to the $2.80 Preferred Shares in all respects made at any time after January 1, 1966 and prior to or contemporaneously with any such call for redemption, purchase, reduction or other payment) or

(iii) elect to pay or pay any tax under the provisions of former Section 105 of the Income Tax Act (Canada) or elect to pay or pay any tax under any similar provisions

at any time if immediately after giving effect to any such action the aggregate amount

(a) declared or paid or set apart for payment as dividends (other than stock dividends in shares of the Company ranking junior to the $2.80 Preferred Shares in all respects) on all shares of all classes of the Company, and

(b) distributed or paid on redemption, purchase, reduction or payment off in respect of all shares (other than shares purchased or redeemed out of capital) of all classes of the Company, and

(c) paid by way of tax as referred to in the foregoing subsection (iii),

in each case subsequent to January 1, 1966 would exceed such aggregate amount before giving effect to such action plus Consolidated Retained Earnings (as defined) as at such time determined in the manner applicable to the relevant action referred to in the foregoing subsections (i), (ii) and (iii).

The Cumulative Preferred Shares

The Cumulative Preferred Shares were created by By-law No. 20 of the Company as a single class of preferred shares issuable in one or more series, each series to consist of such numbers as may be determined by the directors of the Company. The following series of Cumulative Preferred Shares have been issued:

(i) 1,030,000 shares designated as $2.75 Cumulative Redeemable Convertible Preferred Shares Series A (the "Preferred Shares Series A"), of which 1,016,992 shares were outstanding on December 31, 1971; and

(ii) 100,000 shares designated as $3.50 Cumulative Redeemable Preferred Shares Special Series (the "Preferred Shares Special Series"), which are being redeemed out of the proceeds from the sale of the Second Preferred Shares Series A.

The Cumulative Preferred Shares rank on a parity with the $2.80 Preferred Shares with respect to payment of dividends and repayment of capital and have attached thereto, among other provisions, provisions restricting the issuance of preferred shares ranking on a parity with the Cumulative Preferred Shares, and provisions entitling the holders of the Cumulative Preferred Shares on failure to pay six quarterly dividends on the Cumulative Preferred Shares and/or the $2.80 Preferred Shares to join with the holders of $2.80 Preferred Shares in electing one-third of the directors of the Company.

Certain Provisions of the Preferred Shares Series A

The Preferred Shares Series A are convertible into common shares of the Company on the terms and conditions set out under the heading "1966 Warrants, Convertible Debentures and Preferred Shares Series A" on page 27.

The Preferred Shares Series A contain provisions restricting the payment of dividends on common shares or any other shares of the Company (including the Second Preferred Shares Series A) ranking junior to the Preferred Shares Series A and the reduction of junior capital (including the Second Preferred Shares Series A) as follows:

So long as any of the Preferred Shares Series A are outstanding, the Company shall not

(i) pay any dividends (other than stock dividends in shares of the Company ranking junior to the Preferred Shares Series A in all respects) on the common shares or any other shares of the Company ranking junior to the Preferred Shares Series A with respect to payment of dividends unless immediately thereafter Consolidated Retained Earnings (as defined) from incorporation available for the payment of such dividends under the provisions of each indenture securing bonds, debentures or other securities of the Company would be not less than an amount equal to two full years' dividend requirements on all Preferred Shares Series A and on all other series of Cumulative Preferred Shares and on the $2.80 Preferred Shares then outstanding, or

(ii) retire any shares of the Company ranking junior to the Preferred Shares Series A with respect to repayment of capital (except out of the proceeds of an issue of common shares or of an issue of other shares ranking junior to the Preferred Shares Series A in all respects made at any time after January 1, 1968 and prior to or contemporaneously with any such retirement) or pay any tax under former Section 105 of the Income Tax Act (Canada) unless immediately thereafter in each case the aggregate of Consolidated Retained Earnings (as defined) from incorporation and junior stock dividends and proceeds of junior issues (with certain exceptions) exceeds $29,440,091, or

(iii) pay any dividends or retire any shares as referred to in (i) and (ii) above out of premiums received on the issue, prior to January 1, 1968, of shares of the Company unless shareholders' equity, exclusive of amounts credited to the capital stock accounts, exceeds, in the case of a dividend, the sum of $87,866,567 and the two years' dividend requirements referred to in (i) or, in the case of a retirement of shares, $117,306,658.

Further Restrictions on Payment of Dividends and Purchases and Redemptions of Shares

In addition to the restrictions contained in the provisions attached to the $2.80 Preferred Shares, the Preferred Shares Series A and the Second Preferred Shares Series A, the right of the Company to pay dividends on and to purchase or redeem its shares is restricted as follows:

Mortgage Restrictions

The Mortgage referred to in Note (1) to the Consolidated Capitalization Table on page 4 provides in effect that so long as any of the Company's First Mortgage Pipe Line Bonds are outstanding the Company will not (with certain exceptions) declare or pay any dividend or make any other distribution on its common shares or purchase or redeem or otherwise acquire for a consideration any of its capital stock (excluding from such restriction and from all calculations required thereunder dividends paid in common shares and capital stock purchased, redeemed or otherwise acquired to the extent that it was so acquired in exchange for or from the proceeds of the substantially concurrent issue of other capital stock, with certain exceptions, and, to the extent permitted, preferred shares purchased or redeemed by the Company in compliance with any purchase or sinking fund provision), if after giving effect to such action,

(i) its outstanding funded debt (with certain exceptions) would then exceed 75% of its total capitalization, or

(ii) if thereafter the aggregate amount of

(a) dividends on, and amounts paid for repurchases or redemptions of, capital stock (other than preferred shares purchased or redeemed in accordance with permitted purchase or sinking fund provisions),

(b) interest not charged to construction,

(c) all payments (with certain exceptions) in respect of principal of its Convertible Debentures and Subordinated Debentures (both referred to in the Consolidated Capitalization Table on page 4),

(d) certain investments, and

(e) the excess of requirements for retirement of funded debt over the Company's property retirement appropriations,

would exceed net earnings of the Company available for interest after income taxes, computed for the period and in the manner provided in the Mortgage, after adding to such net earnings the amounts of interest deposits made by the Company with the trustee for its Subordinated Debentures. The Mortgage provides for certain additional deductions, but in determining the Company's right to declare or pay any cash dividend on any of its common shares, so long as the number of common shares outstanding does not exceed 10,000,000 the Company need not make such deductions if such dividend is at a quarterly rate not exceeding 25¢ per share. The issuance of common shares of the Company upon conversion of any security of the Company at the time outstanding pursuant to the conversion right granted therein to the holder of such security shall not require any adjustment of the 25¢ per share limit pursuant to the preceding sentence.

The Mortgage provides that, notwithstanding the foregoing provisions, the Company is not restricted from purchasing or redeeming any class or series of its preferred shares in accordance with purchase or sinking fund provisions attaching thereto at an annual rate not in excess of 3% of the aggregate par value of the largest number of preferred shares of such class or series theretofore outstanding.

Subordinated Debenture Restrictions

The indenture (the "Subordinated Debenture Indenture") securing the Company's Subordinated Debentures referred to in the Consolidated Capitalization Table on page 4 provides that so long as any of the Subordinated Debentures are outstanding the Company will not declare or pay any dividend or make any other distribution upon its common shares (excluding from such restriction and from the calculation in this paragraph dividends paid in common shares), (a) if after giving effect to such payment or distribution, the cumulative aggregate amount of all dividends and distributions declared or paid on the common shares subsequent to December 31, 1956 exceeds the aggregate amount of the Net Income (as defined in the Subordinated Debenture Indenture) of the Company subsequent to December 31, 1956, or (b) if any instalment of interest which is due and payable on the Subordinated Debentures has not been paid or if any sinking fund payment required to be made in accordance with the provisions of the Subordinated Debenture Indenture has not been so made.

Sinking Fund Debenture Restrictions

The indenture (the "Sinking Fund Debenture Indenture") securing the Company's Sinking Fund Debentures referred to in the Consolidated Capitalization Table on page 4 provides that so long as any of the Sinking Fund Debentures are outstanding, the Company will not declare or pay any dividends (other than stock dividends) or make any other distribution on its shares or redeem, reduce, purchase or otherwise retire or pay off any of its shares, if after giving effect thereto Consolidated Equity (as defined in the Sinking Fund Debenture Indenture) less Equity Fund Investments (as defined in the Sinking Fund Debenture Indenture) would be less than $175,000,000.

ASSET COVERAGE

The Consolidated Balance Sheet of the Company and subsidiary companies as at December 31, 1971 set out on page 34 shows the following consolidated net tangible assets available for $2.80 Preferred Shares, Preferred Shares Series A and Second Preferred Shares Series A (after taking into account the estimated net proceeds from the issue of the Second Preferred Shares Series A and the redemption of the Preferred Shares Special Series):

Current assets		$ 49,928,867
Investment in and advances to Great Lakes		28,243,393
Advance payments on future gas supply		22,238,683
Plant, property and equipment (less accumulated depreciation and depletion)		863,912,638
		964,323,581
Less: Current liabilities, including long-term debt due within one year	$ 89,057,158	
Advance payments received	21,955,050	
Long-term debt (Reference is made to Notes 7 and 14 to the Consolidated Financial Statements appearing on pages 41 and 43)	545,206,957	
Notes payable	78,800,000	735,019,165
		229,304,416
Add: Estimated net proceeds from this issue of Second Preferred Shares Series A (after giving effect to the redemption of the Preferred Shares Special Series)		116,050,000
		345,354,416
Less: Intangible assets included in plant, property and equipment above		8,788,400
Consolidated net tangible assets available for $2.80 Preferred Shares, Preferred Shares Series A and Second Preferred Shares Series A		336,566,016
Less: $2.80 Preferred Shares and Preferred Shares Series A		97,388,850
Consolidated net tangible assets available for Second Preferred Shares Series A		$239,177,166

The foregoing indicates that consolidated net tangible assets available for $2.80 Preferred Shares, Preferred Shares Series A and Second Preferred Shares Series A as at December 31, 1971 were equivalent to approximately $76 for each $50 par value preferred share to be outstanding and that consolidated net tangible assets available for Second Preferred Shares Series A at December 31, 1971 were equivalent to approximately $96 for each $50 par value Second Preferred Share Series A offered by this prospectus.

DIVIDEND COVERAGE

Maximum annual dividend requirements of the $2.80 Preferred Shares, Preferred Shares Series A and Second Preferred Shares Series A to be outstanding will amount to $12,027,926. The Consolidated Statement of Income on page 36 shows that consolidated net income averaged $19,067,895 for the three years ended December 31, 1971 and amounted to $22,249,258 for the year then ended. These amounts are respectively 1.59 times and 1.85 times the annual dividend requirements on the $2.80 Preferred Shares, Preferred Shares Series A and Second Preferred Shares Series A to be outstanding on completion of this financing.

Maximum annual dividend requirements of the Second Preferred Shares Series A to be outstanding will amount to $6,625,000. The consolidated net income of the Company (after providing for dividends on the $2.80 Preferred Shares and Preferred Shares Series A) averaged $13,552,432 for the three years ended December 31, 1971 and amounted to $16,813,697 for the year then ended. These amounts are respectively 2.05 times and 2.54 times the annual dividend requirements on the Second Preferred Shares Series A to be outstanding on completion of this financing.

Reference is made, however, to the restrictions on payment of dividends under the headings "Details of the Offering" and "Share Capital of the Company" on pages 16 and 19, respectively.

PRICE RANGE OF COMMON SHARES

The $2.80 Preferred Shares, the Preferred Shares Series A, the 1966 Warrants and the common shares of the Company are presently listed on the Montreal, Toronto, Winnipeg, Calgary and Vancouver stock exchanges.

The following table sets out the reported high and low prices and volume of trading of the common shares of the Company on The Toronto Stock Exchange for the years indicated:

Year	High	Low	Volume (shares)
1967	$33½	$24⅜	1,017,346
1968	39¾	23¾	1,021,144
1969	45	30⅛	896,732
1970	36	23¾	690,709
1971	37	30¾	833,900

The reported closing sale price on The Toronto Stock Exchange on February 29, 1972 was $40¾.

DIVIDEND RECORD

The following table sets out the dividends paid by the Company on each share of the capital stock of the Company outstanding during each of the last five completed financial years of the Company and the number of such shares outstanding on December 31 of each such year:

	Dividends Paid Per Share				Shares Outstanding as at December 31			
Year Ended December 31	$2.80 Cumulative Redeemable Preferred Shares	$2.75 Cumulative Redeemable Convertible Preferred Shares Series A	$3.50 Cumulative Redeemable Preferred Shares Special Series	Common Shares	$2.80 Cumulative Redeemable Preferred Shares	$2.75 Cumulative Redeemable Convertible Preferred Shares Series A	$3.50 Cumulative Redeemable Preferred Shares Special Series	Common Shares
1967	$2.80	—	—	$1.00	1,000,000	—	—	8,232,749
1968	2.80	$1.335	—	1.00	1,000,000	1,030,000	—	8,258,776
1969	2.80	2.75	—	1.00	978,275	1,024,788	—	8,285,717
1970	2.80	2.75	—	1.00	953,020	1,023,974	—	8,291,528
1971	2.80	2.75	$1.045	1.00	930,785	1,016,992	100,000	8,312,377

1966 Warrants, Convertible Debentures and Preferred Shares Series A

The 1966 Warrants, issued under an indenture (the "Warrant Indenture") made as of May 1, 1966 between the Company and Montreal Trust Company, confer on the holders thereof the right to purchase in the aggregate 499,951 common shares of the Company at $41.00 per share up to and including the close of business on April 30, 1976. The Warrant Indenture contains provisions to the effect, inter alia, that if the Company issues any common shares on the exercise of conversion rights at a price less than the purchase price (presently $41.00) then payable, the purchase price shall be adjusted downwards so as to protect the rights of the holders of the warrants against dilution.

The Convertible Debentures are convertible at any time up to the close of business on December 1, 1974, or, if called for redemption, on the last full business day next preceding the date specified for redemption, whichever is the earlier, into common shares of the Company at a conversion price of $41.00 per share being at the rate of $2^{18}/_{41}$ shares per $100 principal amount of Convertible Debentures. At December 31, 1971, 611,475 common shares were reserved against the exercise of such right of conversion. The indenture under which the Convertible Debentures have been issued contains anti-dilution provisions to the same effect as those described in the preceding paragraph with respect to the 1966 Warrants.

The Preferred Shares Series A are convertible at any time on or prior to May 1, 1978, or, if called for redemption, on the last business day prior to the date fixed for redemption, whichever is earlier, into common shares of the Company on the basis of $1^{6}/_{7}$ common shares for each Preferred Share Series A so converted. At December 31, 1971, 1,888,701 common shares were reserved against the exercise of such right of conversion. The provisions attaching to the Preferred Shares Series A provide for an appropriate adjustment to be made in the conversion privilege in the event of any subdivision or consolidation of common shares or change of common shares into a different class or classes of shares, and also provide, in effect, that if the Company at any time after April 15, 1968 issues or sells (with certain exceptions, including the exercise of employee stock options) common shares at a price different from the then conversion price (initially $26.92 per share) the conversion basis referred to above shall be adjusted so as to protect the rights of the holders of the Preferred Shares Series A against dilution.

The effect of the conversion privilege given to the holders of the Preferred Shares Series A will be to require an adjustment of the purchase price payable upon the exercise of the 1966 Warrants and the rate of conversion applicable to the Convertible Debentures. It is impossible to state the effect of the foregoing accurately since the adjustments are not required to be made until such time as Preferred Shares Series A have been converted from time to time. However, if all of the Preferred Shares Series A are converted prior to the expiration of the rights to purchase conferred by the 1966 Warrants and the rights of conversion conferred by the Convertible Debentures then the purchase price payable per share for common shares of the Company on the exercise of the 1966 Warrants may be reduced to approximately $38.17 per share and the Convertible Debentures may be convertible into common shares at a price of approximately $38.15 per share being at the rate of 2.621 shares per $100 principal amount of Convertible Debentures.

The privilege given to the holders of the Second Preferred Shares Series A to convert their Second Preferred Shares Series A into common shares of the Company at the rate of $1^{1}/_{10}$ common shares for each Second Preferred Share Series A held, which results in a conversion price of $45.45 per common share, will not require a further adjustment of the purchase price payable upon the exercise of the 1966 Warrants and the rate of conversion applicable to the Convertible Debentures, nor an adjustment of the rate of conversion applicable to the Preferred Shares Series A.

Copies of the Warrant Indenture and the indenture pursuant to which the Convertible Debentures were issued may be examined during normal business hours at the Company's executive office, 150 Eglinton Avenue East, Toronto during the period of distribution to the public of the Second Preferred Shares Series A and for a period of thirty days thereafter.

HOLDERS OF SECURITIES

The following table lists each shareholder who is known to have owned more than 10% of any class of the outstanding equity shares of the Company at December 31, 1971:

Name and Address	Designation of Class	Type of Ownership	Number of Shares Owned	Percentage of Class
Canadian Pacific Investments Limited, Windsor Station, Montreal, Quebec	Common	Of Record and Beneficial	1,383,840	16.65

At December 31, 1971 the directors and senior officers of the Company, as a group, beneficially owned, directly or indirectly, less than 1% of the common shares of the Company.

At February 25, 1972, counsel, partners and associates of Messrs. McCarthy & McCarthy, counsel for the Company, beneficially owned, directly or indirectly, 1,406 common shares, 300 Share Purchase Warrants, 600 $2.80 Cumulative Redeemable Preferred Shares, 450 $2.75 Cumulative Redeemable Convertible Preferred Shares Series A, $400 aggregate principal amount of Convertible Debentures and $23,700 aggregate principal amount of Subordinated Debentures. As of the same date, partners of Messrs. Borden, Elliot, Kelley & Palmer, counsel for the underwriters, beneficially owned, directly or indirectly, 33 common shares, 3 $2.75 Cumulative Redeemable Convertible Preferred Shares Series A, $200 aggregate principal amount of Convertible Debentures and $800 aggregate principal amount of Subordinated Debentures.

INTEREST OF DIRECTORS IN MATERIAL TRANSACTIONS

Nesbitt Thomson Securities Limited, of which Mr. A. D. Nesbitt, a director of the Company, is a director, has entered into the following agreements with the Company:

(a) Underwriting Agreement dated June 3, 1970 between the Company and Nesbitt Thomson Securities Limited, Wood Gundy Securities Limited, McLeod, Young, Weir & Company Limited and Midland-Osler Securities Limited as underwriters under which the Company agreed to sell and the underwriters agreed to purchase $50,000,000 principal amount of 10% Sinking Fund Debentures, Series A at a price of $97.60 per $100 principal amount thereof.

(b) Underwriting Agreement dated November 4, 1970 between the Company and Nesbitt Thomson Securities Limited, Wood Gundy Securities Limited, McLeod, Young, Weir & Company Limited and Midland-Osler Securities Limited as underwriters under which the Company agreed to sell and the underwriters agreed to purchase $60,000,000 principal amount of 9¾% Sinking Fund Debentures, Series B at $95.60 per $100 principal amount thereof.

(c) Underwriting Agreement dated February 18, 1971 between the Company and Nesbitt Thomson Securities Limited, Wood Gundy Securities Limited, McLeod, Young, Weir & Company Limited and Midland-Osler Securities Limited as underwriters under which the Company agreed to sell and the underwriters agreed to purchase $50,000,000 principal amount of 9% Sinking Fund Debentures, Series C at $97.75 per $100 principal amount thereof.

(d) Underwriting Agreement referred to on page 3.

Mr. W. P. Scott, a director of the Company, was a director of Wood Gundy Limited (formerly Wood Gundy Securities Limited) on the dates the agreements referred to in (a), (b) and (c) above were executed.

Copies of the above contracts may be examined during normal business hours at the Company's executive office, 150 Eglinton Avenue East, Toronto during the period of distribution to the public of the Second Preferred Shares Series A and for a period of thirty days thereafter.

In the ordinary course of its business the Company purchases natural gas at competitive prices from many producers in Western Canada, including Gulf Oil Canada Limited, CanDel Oil Ltd. and PanCanadian Petroleum Limited. Mr. Beverley Matthews, a director of the Company, is a director and shareholder of Gulf Oil Canada Limited. Mr. Smiley Raborn, Jr., a director of the Company, is a director and shareholder of CanDel Oil Ltd. Mr. I. D. Sinclair, a director of the Company, is a director and shareholder of Canadian Pacific Investments Limited, which is an affiliate of PanCanadian Petroleum Limited. Messrs. R. W. Campbell and J. M. Taylor, directors of the Company, are officers, directors and shareholders of PanCanadian Petroleum Limited.

Trans-Canada Pipe Lines Limited

and Subsidiary Companies

Consolidated Balance Sheet as at December 31, 1971

ASSETS

Plant, Property and Equipment		
Gas transmission plant—at cost (Note 1)	$995,050,969	
Less accumulated depreciation	162,678,093	
	832,372,876	
Interest in extraction plant project under construction—at cost	17,983,635	
Oil and gas properties—at cost (Note 2)	14,276,891	
Less accumulated depreciation and depletion	720,764	
	13,556,127	
	863,912,638	
Investment in and Advances to Great Lakes Gas Transmission Company—at cost (Note 3)	28,243,393	
Advance Payments on Future Gas Supply (Note 4)	22,238,683	
Current Assets		
Cash	3,478,334	
Deposits with Trustees	2,025,100	
Temporary cash investments	700,000	
Accounts receivable	35,082,802	
Materials and supplies—at cost	5,256,457	
Line pack gas—at cost	1,719,608	
Gas stored underground—at cost	626,710	
Prepayments and deposits	1,039,856	
	49,928,867	
Deferred Charges		
Unamortized debt discount and expense	12,525,807	
Great Lakes project (Note 3)		
Additional costs of gas	6,127,025	
Preliminary charges	159,039	
Other	2,307,723	
	21,119,594	
	$985,443,175	

On behalf of the Board:

(Signed) J. W. Kerr, Director

(Signed) Beverley Matthews, Director

(See accompanying notes to financial statements)

Trans-Canada Pipe Lines Limited

and Subsidiary Companies

Consolidated Balance Sheet as at December 31, 1971

SHAREHOLDERS' EQUITY AND LIABILITIES

SHAREHOLDERS' EQUITY	
Capital stock (Note 5)	
Preferred—Authorized—4,930,785 shares of a par value of $50.00 per share	
—Issued and outstanding	
—$2.80 cumulative redeemable shares	
— 930,785 shares	$ 46,539,250
—$2.75 cumulative redeemable convertible shares series A	
—1,016,992 shares	50,849,600
—$3.50 cumulative redeemable shares special series	
—100,000 shares	5,000,000
Common—Authorized—25,000,000 shares of a par value of $1.00 per share	
—Issued and outstanding	
—8,312,377 shares	8,312,377
	110,701,227
Contributed surplus—per Consolidated Statement	89,423,750
Retained earnings—per Consolidated Statement	49,204,211
Shareholders' equity	249,329,188
DEFERRED CREDIT (Note 6)	1,094,822
ADVANCE PAYMENTS RECEIVED (Note 4)	21,955,050
LONG-TERM DEBT (Note 7)	545,206,957
NOTES PAYABLE (Notes 8 and 17)	78,800,000
CURRENT LIABILITIES	
Long-term debt due within one year	26,848,025
Notes payable	1,881,826
Accounts payable	46,457,054
Interest accrued	10,353,927
Dividends payable	3,516,326
	89,057,158
	$985,443,175

(See accompanying notes to financial statements)

Trans-Canada Pipe Lines Limited

and Subsidiary Companies

Consolidated Statement of Income

	Year Ended December 31				
	1967	1968	1969	1970	1971
OPERATING REVENUES					
Gas sales	$167,258,898	194,712,753	231,403,387	279,880,913	315,972,770
Gas transportation	863,307	946,020	1,001,772	1,073,894	1,086,795
Other	116,283	131,529	215,243	530,626	942,019
	168,238,488	195,790,302	232,620,402	281,485,433	318,001,584
OPERATING EXPENSES					
Cost of gas sold (Note 3)	78,880,005	95,480,521	101,487,077	116,671,179	133,323,391
Gathering charges	15,801,627	17,243,110	20,264,050	30,101,982	38,324,244
Transmission by others (Note 3)	337,438	4,416,039	22,845,576	33,285,621	35,965,893
Operation and maintenance	19,418,962	22,341,055	24,893,078	27,692,772	28,952,846
Amortization of Deferred Credit (Note 6)	(1,094,817)	(1,094,817)	(1,094,817)	(1,094,817)	(1,094,817)
Depreciation (Note 1)	14,973,781	15,817,963	18,025,643	19,364,849	21,200,387
Taxes—provincial and municipal	2,745,498	3,238,539	3,986.885	4,387,166	4,330,826
	131,062,494	157,442,410	190,407,492	230,408,752	261,002,770
Operating profit	37,175,994	38,347,892	42,212,910	51,076,681	56,998,814
INTEREST AND OTHER DEDUCTIONS					
Interest on long-term debt	21,360,402	21,952,364	22,524,515	28,746,716	37,858,067
Amortization of debt discount and expense less gain on purchase of Subordinated Debentures	1,211,889	654,038	1,167,412	686,483	(326,942)
Other interest expense	605,447	1,512,012	6,070,936	4,758,269	1,683,556
Other income (credit) (Note 15)	(83,079)	(447,393)	(80,327)	(465,033)	(527,034)
Allowance for funds used during construction	(777,758)	(2,596,727)	(2,335,535)	(2,738,271)	(3,938,091)
	22,316,901	21,074,294	27,347,001	30,988,164	34,749,556
NET INCOME (Notes 9, 11 and 12)	$ 14,859,093	17,273,598	14,865,909	20,088,517	22,249,258

Consolidated Statement of Retained Earnings

	Year Ended December 31				
	1967	1968	1969	1970	1971
Balance at beginning of period (Note 9)	$ 25,610,447	29,440,091	33,588,260	34,587,138	40,878,316
Net income	14,859,093	17,273,598	14,865,909	20,088,517	22,249,258
	40,469,540	46,713,689	48,454,169	54,675,655	63,127,574
Dividends declared					
Preferred shares	2,800,000	4,883,703	5,588,815	5,509,670	5,620,548
Common shares	8,229,449	8,241,726	8,278,216	8,287,669	8,302,815
	11,029,449	13,125,429	13,867,031	13,797,339	13,923,363
Balance at end of period (Notes 10 and 11)	$ 29,440,091	33,588,260	34,587,138	40,878,316	49,204,211

(See accompanying notes to financial statements)

Auditors' Report

To the Directors of
TRANS-CANADA PIPE LINES LIMITED
Toronto, Ontario

We have examined the consolidated balance sheet of Trans-Canada Pipe Lines Limited and its subsidiary companies as of December 31, 1971 and the consolidated statements of income, retained earnings, contributed surplus and source and application of funds for the five years then ended. Our examination included a general review of the accounting procedures and such tests of accounting records and other supporting evidence as we considered necessary in the circumstances.

In our opinion, these consolidated financial statements present fairly the financial position of the company and its subsidiary companies at December 31, 1971 and the results of their operations and the source and application of their funds for the five years then ended, in accordance with generally accepted accounting principles applied on a consistent basis.

Toronto, Ontario
March 1, 1972

(Signed) PEAT, MARWICK, MITCHELL & CO.
Chartered Accountants

PURCHASER'S STATUTORY RIGHTS OF WITHDRAWAL AND RESCISSION

Sections 64 and 65 of The Securities Act (Alberta), sections 70 and 71 of The Securities Act, 1967 (Saskatchewan), sections 63 and 64 of The Securities Act (Manitoba) and sections 64 and 65 of The Securities Act (Ontario) provide, in effect, that where a security is offered to the public in the course of primary distribution:

(a) a purchaser will not be bound by a contract for the purchase of such security if written or telegraphic notice of his intention not to be bound is received by the vendor or his agent not later than midnight on the second business day after the prospectus or amended prospectus offering such security is received or is deemed to be received by him or his agent, and

(b) a purchaser has the right to rescind a contract for the purchase of such security, while still the owner thereof, if the prospectus or any amended prospectus offering such security contains an untrue statement of a material fact or omits to state a material fact necessary in order to make any statement therein not misleading in the light of the circumstances in which it was made, but no action to enforce this right can be commenced by a purchaser after the expiration of 90 days from the later of the date of such contract or the date on which such prospectus or amended prospectus is received or is deemed to be received by him or his agent.

Sections 61 and 62 of the Securities Act, 1967 (British Columbia) provide, in effect, that where a security is offered to the public in the course of primary distribution:

(a) a purchaser (other than a company) has a right to rescind a contract for the purchase of a security, while still the owner thereof, if a copy of the last prospectus, together with financial statements and reports and summaries of reports relating to the securities as filed with the British Columbia Securities Commission, was not delivered to him or his agent prior to delivery to either of them of the written confirmation of the sale of the securities. Written notice of intention to commence an action for rescission must be served on the person who contracted to sell within 60 days of the date of delivery of the written confirmation, but no action shall be commenced after the expiration of three months from the date of service of such notice, and

(b) a purchaser has the right to rescind a contract for the purchase of such security, while still the owner thereof, if the prospectus or any amended prospectus offering such security contains an untrue statement of a material fact or omits to state a material fact necessary in order to make any statement therein not misleading in the light of the circumstances in which it was made, but no action to enforce this right can be commenced by a purchaser after expiration of 90 days from the later of the date of such contract or the date on which such prospectus or amended prospectus is received or is deemed to be received by him or his agent.

Reference is made to the aforesaid Acts for the complete texts of the provisions under which the foregoing rights are conferred and the foregoing summary is subject to the express provisions thereof.

CERTIFICATES

Dated: March 1, 1972

The foregoing constitutes full, true and plain disclosure of all material facts relating to the securities offered by this prospectus as required by Part VII of the Securities Act, 1967 (British Columbia) and the regulations thereunder, by Part 7 of The Securities Act (Alberta) and the regulations thereunder, by Part VIII of The Securities Act, 1967 (Saskatchewan) and the regulations thereunder, by Part VII of The Securities Act (Manitoba) and the regulations thereunder, by Part VII of The Securities Act (Ontario) and the regulations thereunder, under the Quebec Securities Act and by Section 13 of the Securities Act (New Brunswick).

(Signed) J. W. Kerr
Chairman and Chief Executive Officer

(Signed) R. G. Wall
Vice-President and Treasurer

On behalf of the Board

(Signed) G. P. Osler
Director

(Signed) Beverley Matthews
Director

To the best of our knowledge, information and belief, the foregoing constitutes full, true and plain disclosure of all material facts relating to the securities offered by this prospectus as required by Part VII of the Securities Act, 1967 (British Columbia) and the regulations thereunder, by Part 7 of The Securities Act (Alberta) and the regulations thereunder, by Part VIII of The Securities Act, 1967 (Saskatchewan) and the regulations thereunder, by Part VII of The Securities Act (Manitoba) and the regulations thereunder, by Part VII of The Securities Act (Ontario) and the regulations thereunder, under the Quebec Securities Act and by Section 13 of the Securities Act (New Brunswick).

Nesbitt Thomson Securities Limited
By: (Signed) J. B. Aune

Wood Gundy Limited
By: (Signed) W. P. Wilder

McLeod, Young, Weir & Company Limited
By: (Signed) G. C. MacDonald

Midland-Osler Securities Limited
By: (Signed) R. G. McCulloch

The following includes the name of every person having an interest either directly or indirectly to the extent of not less than 5% in the capital of:

Nesbitt Thomson Securities Limited: A. D. Nesbitt, J. I. Crookston, J. R. Oborne, J. R. Learn, D. E. M. Schaefer, D. N. Stoker, T. E. Kierans, R. W. Crosbie and J. B. Aune;

Wood Gundy Limited: C. L. Gundy, W. P. Wilder, J. N. Cole, P. J. Chadsey, J. R. LeMesurier, C. E. Medland, J. N. Abell, D. C. H. Stanley and I. S. Steers;

McLeod, Young, Weir & Company Limited: J. S. Dinnick, G. C. MacDonald, C. P. Keeley, L. E. Barlow, J. L. McLaughlin, C. E. Godwin, A. T. L. Fraser, R. M. Grills, F. B. Farrill, A. S. Brooke and R. J. G. Reiner.

Midland-Osler Securities Limited: E. M. Kennedy, D. B. Weldon, R. G. McCulloch, E. H. Gunn and W. A. Stewart.

APPENDIX B
Compound Interest Tables

TABLE 1. COMPOUND SUM OF $1
TABLE 2. SUM OF AN ANNUITY OF $1 FOR *N* YEARS
TABLE 3. PRESENT VALUE OF $1
TABLE 4. PRESENT VALUE OF AN ANNUITY OF $1

TABLE 1

Compound sum of $1

Year	*1%*	*2%*	*3%*	*4%*	*5%*	*6%*	*7%*
1	1.010	1.020	1.030	1.040	1.050	1.060	1.070
2	1.020	1.040	1.061	1.082	1.102	1.124	1.145
3	1.030	1.061	1.093	1.125	1.158	1.191	1.225
4	1.041	1.082	1.126	1.170	1.216	1.262	1.311
5	1.051	1.104	1.159	1.217	1.276	1.338	1.403
6	1.062	1.126	1.194	1.265	1.340	1.419	1.501
7	1.072	1.149	1.230	1.316	1.407	1.504	1.606
8	1.083	1.172	1.267	1.369	1.477	1.594	1.718
9	1.094	1.195	1.305	1.423	1.551	1.689	1.838
10	1.105	1.219	1.344	1.480	1.629	1.791	1.967
11	1.116	1.243	1.384	1.539	1.710	1.898	2.105
12	1.127	1.268	1.426	1.601	1.796	2.012	2.252
13	1.138	1.294	1.469	1.665	1.886	2.133	2.410
14	1.149	1.319	1.513	1.732	1.980	2.261	2.579
15	1.161	1.346	1.558	1.801	2.079	2.397	2.759
16	1.173	1.373	1.605	1.873	2.183	2.540	2.952
17	1.184	1.400	1.653	1.948	2.292	2.693	3.159
18	1.196	1.428	1.702	2.026	2.407	2.854	3.380
19	1.208	1.457	1.754	2.107	2.527	3.026	3.617
20	1.220	1.486	1.806	2.191	2.653	3.207	3.870
25	1.282	1.641	2.094	2.666	3.386	4.292	5.427
30	1.348	1.811	2.427	3.243	4.322	5.743	7.612

Year	*8%*	*9%*	*10%*	*12%*	*14%*	*15%*	*16%*
1	1.080	1.090	1.100	1.120	1.140	1.150	1.160
2	1.166	1.188	1.210	1.254	1.300	1.322	1.346
3	1.260	1.295	1.331	1.405	1.482	1.521	1.561
4	1.360	1.412	1.464	1.574	1.689	1.749	1.811
5	1.469	1.539	1.611	1.762	1.925	2.011	2.100
6	1.587	1.677	1.772	1.974	2.195	2.313	2.436
7	1.714	1.828	1.949	2.211	2.502	2.660	2.826
8	1.851	1.993	2.144	2.476	2.853	3.059	3.278
9	1.999	2.172	2.358	2.773	3.252	3.518	3.803
10	2.159	2.367	2.594	3.106	3.707	4.046	4.411
11	2.332	2.580	2.853	3.479	4.226	4.652	5.117
12	2.518	2.813	3.138	3.896	4.818	5.350	5.936
13	2.720	3.066	3.452	4.363	5.492	6.153	6.886
14	2.937	3.342	3.797	4.887	6.261	7.076	7.988
15	3.172	3.642	4.177	5.474	7.138	8.137	9.266
16	3.426	3.970	4.595	6.130	8.137	9.358	10.748
17	3.700	4.328	5.054	6.866	9.276	10.761	12.468
18	3.996	4.717	5.560	7.690	10.575	12.375	14.463
19	4.316	5.142	6.116	8.613	12.056	14.232	16.777
20	4.661	5.604	6.728	9.646	13.743	16.367	19.461
25	6.848	8.623	10.835	17.000	26.462	32.919	40.874
30	10.063	13.268	17.449	29.960	50.950	66.212	85.850

Year	*18%*	*20%*	*24%*	*28%*	*32%*	*36%*
1	1.180	1.200	1.240	1.280	1.320	1.360
2	1.392	1.440	1.538	1.638	1.742	1.850
3	1.643	1.728	1.907	2.067	2.300	2.515
4	1.939	2.074	2.364	2.684	3.036	3.421
5	2.288	2.488	2.932	3.436	4.007	4.653
6	2.700	2.986	3.635	4.398	5.290	6.328
7	3.185	3.583	4.508	5.629	6.983	8.605
8	3.759	4.300	5.590	7.206	9.217	11.703
9	4.435	5.160	6.931	9.223	12.166	15.917
10	5.234	6.192	8.594	11.806	16.060	21.647
11	6.176	7.430	10.657	15.112	21.199	29.439
12	7.288	8.916	13.215	19.343	27.983	40.037
13	8.599	10.699	16.386	24.759	36.937	54.451
14	10.147	12.839	20.319	31.691	48.757	74.053
15	11.974	15.407	25.196	40.565	64.359	100.712
16	14.129	18.488	31.243	51.923	84.954	136.97
17	16.672	22.186	38.741	66.461	112.14	186.28
18	19.673	26.623	48.039	85.071	148.02	253.34
19	23.214	31.948	59.568	108.89	195.39	344.54
20	27.393	38.338	73.864	139.38	257.92	468.57
25	62.669	95.396	216.542	478.90	1033.6	2180.1
30	143.371	237.376	634.820	1645.5	4142.1	10143.

Year	*40%*	*50%*	*60%*	*70%*	*80%*	*90%*
1	1.400	1.500	1.600	1.700	1.800	1.900
2	1.960	2.250	2.560	2.890	3.240	3.610
3	2.744	3.375	4.096	4.913	5.832	6.859
4	3.842	5.062	6.544	8.352	10.498	13.032
5	5.378	7.594	10.486	14.199	18.896	24.761
6	7.530	11.391	16.777	24.138	34.012	47.046
7	10.541	17.086	26.844	41.034	61.222	89.387
8	14.758	25.629	42.950	69.758	110.200	169.836
9	20.661	38.443	68.720	118.588	198.359	322.688
10	28.925	57.665	109.951	201.599	357.047	613.017
11	40.496	86.498	175.922	342.719	642.684	1164.902
12	56.694	129.746	281.475	582.622	1156.831	2213.314
13	79.372	194.619	450.360	990.457	2082.295	4205.297
14	111.120	291.929	720.576	1683.777	3748.131	7990.065
15	155.568	437.894	1152.921	2862.421	6746.636	15181.122
16	217.795	656.84	1844.7	4866.1	12144.	28844.0
17	304.914	985.26	2951.5	8272.4	21859.	54804.0
18	426.879	1477.9	4722.4	14063.0	39346.	104130.0
19	597.630	2216.8	7555.8	23907.0	70824.	197840.0
20	836.683	3325.3	12089.0	40642.0	127480.	375900.0
25	4499.880	25251.	126760.0	577060.0	2408900.	9307600.0
30	24201.432	191750.	1329200.	8193500.0	45517000.	230470000.0

TABLE 2

Sum of an annuity of $1 for *N* years

Year	*1%*	*2%*	*3%*	*4%*	*5%*	*6%*
1	1.000	1.000	1.000	1.000	1.000	1.000
2	2.010	2.020	2.030	2.040	2.050	2.060
3	3.030	3.060	3.091	3.122	3.152	3.184
4	4.060	4.122	4.184	4.246	4.310	4.375
5	5.101	5.204	5.309	5.416	5.526	5.637
6	6.152	6.308	6.468	6.633	6.802	6.975
7	7.214	7.434	7.662	7.898	8.142	8.394
8	8.286	8.583	8.892	9.214	9.549	9.897
9	9.369	9.755	10.159	10.583	11.027	11.491
10	10.462	10.950	11.464	12.006	12.578	13.181
11	11.567	12.169	12.808	13.486	14.207	14.972
12	12.683	13.412	14.192	15.026	15.917	16.870
13	13.809	14.680	15.618	16.627	17.713	18.882
14	14.947	15.974	17.086	18.292	19.599	21.051
15	16.097	17.293	18.599	20.024	21.579	23.276
16	17.258	18.639	20.157	21.825	23.657	25.673
17	18.430	20.012	21.762	23.698	25.840	28.213
18	19.615	21.412	23.414	25.645	28.132	30.906
19	20.811	22.841	25.117	27.671	30.539	33.760
20	22.019	24.297	26.870	29.778	33.066	36.786
25	28.243	32.030	36.459	41.646	47.727	54.865
30	34.785	40.568	47.575	56.085	66.439	79.058

Year	*7%*	*8%*	*9%*	*10%*	*12%*	*14%*
1	1.000	1.000	1.000	1.000	1.000	1.000
2	2.070	2.080	2.090	2.100	2.120	2.140
3	3.215	3.246	3.278	3.310	3.374	3.440
4	4.440	4.506	4.573	4.641	4.770	4.921
5	5.751	5.867	5.985	6.105	6.353	6.610
6	7.153	7.336	7.523	7.716	8.115	8.536
7	8.654	8.923	9.200	9.487	10.089	10.730
8	10.260	10.637	11.028	11.436	12.300	13.233
9	11.978	12.488	13.021	13.579	14.776	16.085
10	13.816	14.487	15.193	15.937	17.549	19.337
11	15.784	16.645	17.560	18.531	20.655	23.044
12	17.888	18.977	20.141	21.384	24.133	27.271
13	20.141	21.495	22.953	24.523	28.029	32.089
14	22.550	24.215	26.019	27.975	32.393	37.581
15	25.129	27.152	29.361	31.772	37.280	43.842
16	27.888	30.324	33.003	35.950	42.753	50.980
17	30.840	33.750	36.974	40.545	48.884	59.118
18	33.999	37.450	41.301	45.599	55.750	68.394
19	37.379	41.446	46.018	51.159	63.440	78.969
20	40.995	45.762	51.160	57.275	72.052	91.025
25	63.249	73.106	84.701	98.347	133.334	181.871
30	94.461	113.283	136.308	164.494	241.333	356.787

Year	*16%*	*18%*	*20%*	*24%*	*28%*	*32%*
1	1.000	1.000	1.000	1.000	1.000	1.000
2	2.160	2.180	2.200	2.240	2.280	2.320
3	3.506	3.572	3.640	3.778	3.918	4.062
4	5.066	5.215	5.368	5.684	6.016	6.362
5	6.877	7.154	7.442	8.048	8.700	9.398
6	8.977	9.442	9.930	10.980	12.136	13.406
7	11.414	12.142	12.916	14.615	16.534	18.696
8	14.240	15.327	16.499	19.123	22.163	25.678
9	17.518	19.086	20.799	24.712	29.369	34.895
10	21.321	23.521	25.959	31.643	38.592	47.062
11	25.733	28.755	32.150	40.238	50.399	63.122
12	30.850	34.931	39.580	50.985	65.510	84.320
13	36.786	42.219	48.497	64.110	84.853	112.303
14	43.672	50.818	59.196	80.496	109.612	149.240
15	51.660	60.965	72.035	100.815	141.303	197.997
16	60.925	72.939	87.442	126.011	181.87	262.36
17	71.673	87.068	105.931	157.253	233.79	347.31
18	84.141	103.740	128.117	195.994	300.25	459.45
19	98.603	123.414	154.740	244.033	385.32	607.47
20	115.380	146.628	186.688	303.601	494.21	802.86
25	249.214	342.603	471.981	898.092	1706.8	3226.8
30	530.312	790.948	1181.882	2640.916	5873.2	12941.0

Year	*36%*	*40%*	*50%*	*60%*	*70%*	*80%*
1	1.000	1.000	1.000	1.000	1.000	1.000
2	2.360	2.400	2.500	2.600	2.700	2.800
3	4.210	4.360	4.750	5.160	5.590	6.040
4	6.725	7.104	8.125	9.256	10.503	11.872
5	10.146	10.846	13.188	15.810	18.855	22.370
6	14.799	16.324	20.781	26.295	33.054	41.265
7	21.126	23.853	32.172	43.073	57.191	75.278
8	29.732	34.395	49.258	69.916	98.225	136.500
9	41.435	49.153	74.887	112.866	167.983	246.699
10	57.352	69.814	113.330	181.585	286.570	445.058
11	78.998	98.739	170.995	291.536	488.170	802.105
12	108.437	139.235	257.493	467.458	830.888	1444.788
13	148.475	195.929	387.239	748.933	1413.510	2601.619
14	202.926	275.300	581.859	1199.293	2403.968	4683.914
15	276.979	386.420	873.788	1919.869	4087.745	8432.045
16	377.69	541.99	1311.7	3072.8	6950.2	15179.0
17	514.66	759.78	1968.5	4917.5	11816.0	27323.0
18	700.94	1064.7	2953.8	7868.9	20089.0	49182.0
19	954.28	1491.6	4431.7	12591.0	34152.0	88528.0
20	1298.8	2089.2	6648.5	20147.0	58059.0	159350.0
25	6053.0	11247.0	50500.0	211270.0	824370.0	3011100.0
30	28172.0	60501.0	383500.0	2215400.0	11705000.0	56896000.0

TABLE 3

Present value of $1

Year	*1%*	*2%*	*3%*	*4%*	*5%*	*6%*	*7%*	*8%*	*9%*	*10%*	*12%*	*14%*	*15%*
1	.990	.980	.971	.962	.952	.943	.935	.926	.917	.909	.893	.877	.870
2	.980	.961	.943	.925	.907	.890	.873	.857	.842	.826	.797	.769	.756
3	.971	.942	.915	.889	.864	.840	.816	.794	.772	.751	.712	.675	.658
4	.961	.924	.889	.855	.823	.792	.763	.735	.708	.683	.636	.592	.572
5	.951	.906	.863	.822	.784	.747	.713	.681	.650	.621	.567	.519	.497
6	.942	.888	.838	.790	.746	.705	.666	.630	.596	.564	.507	.456	.432
7	.933	.871	.813	.760	.711	.665	.623	.583	.547	.513	.452	.400	.376
8	.923	.853	.789	.731	.677	.627	.582	.540	.502	.467	.404	.351	.327
9	.914	.837	.766	.703	.645	.592	.544	.500	.460	.424	.361	.308	.284
10	.905	.820	.744	.676	.614	.558	.508	.463	.422	.386	.322	.270	.247
11	.896	.804	.722	.650	.585	.527	.475	.429	.388	.350	.287	.237	.215
12	.887	.788	.701	.625	.557	.497	.444	.397	.356	.319	.257	.208	.187
13	.879	.773	.681	.601	.530	.469	.415	.368	.326	.290	.229	.182	.163
14	.870	.758	.661	.577	.505	.442	.388	.340	.299	.263	.205	.160	.141
15	.861	.743	.642	.555	.481	.417	.362	.315	.275	.239	.183	.140	.123
16	.853	.728	.623	.534	.458	.394	.339	.292	.252	.218	.163	.123	.107
17	.844	.714	.605	.513	.436	.371	.317	.270	.231	.198	.146	.108	.093
18	.836	.700	.587	.494	.416	.350	.296	.250	.212	.180	.130	.095	.081
19	.828	.686	.570	.475	.396	.331	.276	.232	.194	.164	.116	.083	.070
20	.820	.673	.554	.456	.377	.312	.258	.215	.178	.149	.104	.073	.061
25	.780	.610	.478	.375	.295	.233	.184	.146	.116	.092	.059	.038	.030
30	.742	.552	.412	.308	.231	.174	.131	.099	.075	.057	.033	.020	.015

Year	*16%*	*18%*	*20%*	*24%*	*28%*	*32%*	*36%*	*40%*	*50%*	*60%*	*70%*	*80%*	*90%*
1	.862	.847	.833	.806	.781	.758	.735	.714	.667	.625	.588	.556	.526
2	.743	.718	.694	.650	.610	.574	.541	.510	.444	.391	.346	.309	.277
3	.641	.609	.579	.524	.477	.435	.398	.364	.296	.244	.204	.171	.146
4	.552	.516	.482	.423	.373	.329	.292	.260	.198	.153	.120	.095	.077
5	.476	.437	.402	.341	.291	.250	.215	.186	.132	.095	.070	.053	.040
6	.410	.370	.335	.275	.227	.189	.158	.133	.088	.060	.041	.029	.021
7	.354	.314	.279	.222	.178	.143	.116	.095	.059	.037	.024	.016	.011
8	.305	.266	.233	.179	.139	.108	.085	.068	.039	.023	.014	.009	.006
9	.263	.226	.194	.144	.108	.082	.063	.048	.026	.015	.008	.005	.003
10	.227	.191	.162	.116	.085	.062	.046	.035	.017	.009	.005	.003	.002
11	.195	.162	.135	.094	.066	.047	.034	.025	.012	.006	.003	.002	.001
12	.168	.137	.112	.076	.052	.036	.025	.018	.008	.004	.002	.001	.001
13	.145	.116	.093	.061	.040	.027	.018	.013	.005	.002	.001	.001	.000
14	.125	.099	.078	.049	.032	.021	.014	.009	.003	.001	.001	.000	.000
15	.108	.084	.065	.040	.025	.016	.010	.006	.002	.001	.000	.000	
16	.093	.071	.054	.032	.019	.012	.007	.005	.002	.001	.000		
17	.080	.060	.045	.026	.015	.009	.005	.003	.001	.000			
18	.069	.051	.038	.021	.012	.007	.004	.002	.001	.000			
19	.060	.043	.031	.017	.009	.005	.003	.002	.000				
20	.051	.037	.026	.014	.007	.004	.002	.001	.000				
25	.024	.016	.010	.005	.002	.001	.000	.000					
30	.012	.007	.004	.002	.001	.000	.000						

TABLE 4

Present value of an annuity of $1

Year	*1%*	*2%*	*3%*	*4%*	*5%*	*6%*	*7%*	*8%*	*9%*	*10%*
1	0.990	0.980	0.971	0.962	0.952	0.943	0.935	0.926	0.917	0.909
2	1.970	1.942	1.913	1.866	1.859	1.833	1.808	1.783	1.759	1.736
3	2.941	2.884	2.829	2.775	2.723	2.673	2.624	2.577	2.531	2.487
4	3.902	3.808	3.717	3.630	3.546	3.465	3.387	3.312	3.240	3.170
5	4.853	4.713	4.580	4.452	4.329	4.212	4.100	3.993	3.890	3.791
6	5.795	5.601	5.417	5.242	5.076	4.917	4.766	4.623	4.486	4.355
7	6.728	6.472	6.230	6.002	5.786	5.582	5.389	5.206	5.033	4.868
8	7.652	7.325	7.020	6.733	6.463	6.210	5.971	5.747	5.535	5.335
9	8.566	8.162	7.786	7.435	7.108	6.802	6.515	6.247	5.985	5.759
10	9.471	8.983	8.530	8.111	7.722	7.360	7.024	6.710	6.418	6.145
11	10.368	9.787	9.253	8.760	8.306	7.887	7.499	7.139	6.805	6.495
12	11.255	10.575	9.954	9.385	8.863	8.384	7.943	7.536	7.161	6.814
13	12.134	11.348	10.635	9.986	9.394	8.853	8.358	7.904	7.487	7.103
14	13.004	12.106	11.296	10.563	9.899	9.295	8.745	8.244	7.786	7.367
15	13.865	12.849	11.938	11.118	10.380	9.712	9.108	8.559	8.060	7.606
16	14.718	13.578	12.561	11.652	10.838	10.106	9.447	8.851	8.312	7.824
17	15.562	14.292	13.166	12.166	11.274	10.477	9.763	9.122	8.544	8.022
18	16.398	14.992	13.754	12.659	11.690	10.828	10.059	9.372	8.756	8.201
19	17.226	15.678	14.324	13.134	12.085	11.158	10.336	9.604	8.950	8.365
20	18.046	16.351	14.877	13.590	12.462	11.470	10.594	9.818	9.128	8.514
25	22.023	19.523	17.413	15.622	14.094	12.783	11.654	10.675	9.823	9.077
30	25.808	22.397	19.600	17.292	15.373	13.765	12.409	11.258	10.274	9.427

Year	*12%*	*14%*	*16%*	*18%*	*20%*	*24%*	*28%*	*32%*	*36%*
1	0.893	0.877	0.862	0.847	0.833	0.806	0.781	0.758	0.735
2	1.690	1.647	1.605	1.566	1.528	1.457	1.392	1.332	1.276
3	2.402	2.322	2.246	2.174	2.106	1.981	1.868	1.766	1.674
4	3.037	2.914	2.798	2.690	2.589	2.404	2.241	2.096	1.966
5	3.605	3.433	3.274	3.127	2.991	2.745	2.532	2.345	2.181
6	4.111	3.889	3.685	3.498	3.326	3.020	2.759	2.534	2.339
7	4.564	4.288	4.039	3.812	3.605	3.242	2.937	2.678	2.455
8	4.968	4.639	4.344	4.078	3.837	3.421	3.076	2.786	2.540
9	5.328	4.946	4.607	4.303	4.031	3.566	3.184	2.868	2.603
10	5.650	5.216	4.833	4.494	4.193	3.682	3.269	2.930	2.650
11	5.988	5.453	5.029	4.656	4.327	3.776	3.335	2.978	2.683
12	6.194	5.660	5.197	4.793	4.439	3.851	3.387	3.013	2.708
13	6.424	5.842	5.342	4.910	4.533	3.912	3.427	3.040	2.727
14	6.628	6.002	5.468	5.008	4.611	3.962	3.459	3.061	2.740
15	6.811	6.142	5.575	5.092	4.675	4.001	3.483	3.076	2.750
16	6.974	6.265	5.669	5.162	4.730	4.033	3.503	3.088	2.758
17	7.120	6.373	5.749	5.222	4.775	4.059	3.518	3.097	2.763
18	7.250	6.467	5.818	5.273	4.812	4.080	3.529	3.104	2.767
19	7.366	6.550	5.877	5.316	4.844	4.097	3.539	3.109	2.770
20	7.469	6.623	5.929	5.353	4.870	4.110	3.546	3.113	2.772
25	7.843	6.873	6.097	5.467	4.948	4.147	3.564	3.122	2.776
30	8.055	7.003	6.177	5.517	4.979	4.160	3.569	3.124	2.778

Glossary

ANNUITY. The flow of a given and constant amount of funds at uniform time intervals. One example is the periodic interest payments on a bond.

ARBITRAGE. The simultaneous buying and selling of the same asset or commodity, usually at a different place, for a profit; that is where the price differential is greater than the transaction cost. By regulating supply and demand, arbitrage will equalize prices in different markets.

BALLOON PAYMENT. Repayment of principal on outstanding debt, where the final payment at maturity exceeds amounts repaid periodically throughout the life of the debt. For example, a bond issue of $100 million could be repaid in installments of $10 million at the end of each of 5 years with a final balloon payment of $50 million due at the end of the 6th year.

BANKERS' ACCEPTANCES. A short-term debt instrument issued by a firm which is guaranteed by a bank. The bank levies a charge for making available such a guarantee.

BANKRUPTCY. The legal process through which an individual or corporation is deemed insolvent. Through procedures as specified in bankruptcy legislation, the assets of the insolvent firm are distributed among creditors. Further claims are then disregarded.

BENEFIT COST RATIO. See PROFITABILITY INDEX.

BETA FACTOR. A coefficient which expresses the proportionality of a security's return with the return on the market portfolio.

BOARD LOT. The smallest standard quantity of shares traded on an exchange. This quantity depends on the price range in which a share trades. For example, the board lot quantity could be 100 for a stock selling at $20, and 1000 for a stock trading at $0.25.

BOND. An interest-bearing debt instrument of longer maturity issued by corporations, institutions, and governments.

BOOK VALUE PER SHARE. The net worth of a firm as shown on the balance sheet less the par value of the outstanding preferred stock, divided by the number of outstanding common shares.

BUSINESS RISK. Risks inherent in the general operations of a business. Such risk is reflected in variations in operating revenue or earnings before interest and taxes, and may be caused by uncertainties in the economy, business cycles, or the paticular circumstances of the industry or the firm.

CALL PREMIUM. The amount to be paid over and above the face value of a security if the issuing corporation calls the security for redemption before maturity.

CAPITAL COST ALLOWANCE. The DEPRECIATION allowed on different asset classes for taxation purposes.

CAPITAL MARKETS. The places and institutions where longer-term instruments are traded, including bonds, debentures, mortgages, and preferred and common shares.

CASH DISCOUNT. The discount on the selling price which various suppliers offer to customers who make early payments on invoices rather than availing themselves of credit terms otherwise granted.

CASH FLOW. The total flow of funds in a given period. It differs from net profit, for example, in that non-cash accounting charges including depreciation and depletion are excluded when computing profits. They nevertheless represent a flow of funds and, hence, have to be added to profits to derive cash flows.

COMMON SHARES. Certificates representing proportional residual ownership of a corporation.

COMPENSATING BALANCES. A requirement of some banks or lenders stipulating that the borrower has to maintain a fixed percentage of a loan as an interest free deposit at the lending institution. This increases the effective interest rate of the loan.

CONGLOMERATE. A diversified firm whose subsidiary operations in various divisions or subsidiaries involve product lines or lines of business which bear no relation to one another.

CONVERTIBLE SECURITY. Financial instruments, usually debt or preferred shares, which at the option of the holder can be exchanged into another form of instrument, usually common shares.

CORPORATE PAPER. Negotiable, short-term, unsecured promissory notes issued by major corporations that are well known to investors and have excellent credit standing.

CORPORATION. A legal entity and form of business organization which offers owners limited liability and easy transfer of ownership. Shareholders are not automatically agents of the firm.

COST OF CAPITAL. The cost of funds to a firm. As the cost of capital varies with the type of instrument employed—debt, common shares, preferred shares, or retained earnings—the overall cost of capital of a firm which raises funds from various sources is a weighted average of these.

COUPON RATE. The fixed interest rate provided for on a long-term debt instrument.

CUMULATIVE FEATURE. A provision on preferred shares which provides for the accumulation of unpaid dividends from one time period to another. Previously unpaid dividends are referred to as 'arrears' and under the cumulative feature must be paid off before any distribution can be made to common shareholders.

DEBENTURE. A form of long-term corporate debt which is not secured by the pledge of specific assets. A debenture may be secured by a general or floating charge against any unpledged assets, or it is completely unsecured and backed only by the earning power of the firm.

DECISION TREE. A technique to aid in decision-making under uncertainty which structures potential outcomes and their probabilities across time.

DEPLETION ALLOWANCES. Such allowances (which are similar to DEPRECIATION) relate to non-renewable resources which will eventually be depleted (such as oil or minerals) and provide for deductions in computing net profits.

DEPRECIATION. An accounting allocation of expenses for the use of capital goods which approximates the amount of an asset 'used up' in a given time period.

DILUTION. This refers to a reduction in proportional ownership (encompassing voting power and rights to future earnings), as a consequence of a corporation issuing additional shares to the public.

DIRECT LEASE. A long-term lease through which the lessee obtains the use of an asset not previously owned. The direct lease contrasts with SALE AND LEASEBACK arrangements.

DIVIDEND. The amount periodically paid to shareholders of a firm as decided by the board of directors. Generally only a portion of a firm's earnings are distributed in this manner, with the remainder (RETAINED EARNINGS) being reinvested in the firm.

DIVIDEND TAX CREDIT. A credit against taxes payable on dividends received, allowed to non-corporate shareholders. It has the effect of reducing the effective tax paid on dividend income and provides some relief from double taxation (on corporate earnings, and again when dividends are paid).

EBIT. Earnings before interest and taxes (sometimes also called operating revenue). This quantity is independent of the particular capital structure of a firm and, hence, is used as a starting point for any analysis of the effects of alternate financing policies.

E.O.Q. The economic order quantity is the optimal quantity to be ordered when replenishing inventory. In balancing the cost of ordering and the costs of holding inventory, it provides the lowest overall cost for inventory management.

E.P.S. Earnings per share—the after-tax earnings of a corporation available to common shareholders divided by the number of outstanding common shares.

EQUIPMENT TRUST CERTIFICATES. Securities representing a particular form of long-term debt financing which is frequently resorted to by railroads and other transportation companies for the purchase of specific equipment. The financing is similar to a lease in that a trustee holds title to the assets, which serve as a collateral to holders of the equipment trust certificates.

EURO BOND MARKET. The market for longer term debt which is issued in countries other than the country of the currency in which the debt is denominated. An example may be debt denominated in U.S. dollars and issued in Europe.

EX-DIVIDEND DATE. The date after which purchase of a share no longer carries with it the right to the dividend declared for the current period, but not yet paid.

EXPECTED VALUE. The arithmetic average or mean value of a probability distribution.

EXTENDIBLES. Debt instruments which provide the holder of the debt with the option to extend the maturity date of the security beyond that originally specified.

FACE VALUE. The amount of principal owing on a debt instrument, which must be repaid at maturity.

FACTORING. The sale, at a discount, of a corporation's accounts receivable.

FINANCE COMPANY PAPER. The short-term debt (commercial paper) issued by finance companies, often secured by pledges of receivables in amounts providing a reasonable margin of safety.

FINANCIAL ASSETS. As opposed to REAL ASSETS, financial assets are pieces of paper which entitle the holder to some future payments. Because of this claim on future payments, financial assets have a value and command a market price. Examples are bonds, shares and the likes.

FINANCIAL INTERMEDIARY. Institutions which provide indirect financing channels by attracting funds from economic units with a surplus and making them available to deficit spending units. Examples are banks, insurance companies and the likes.

FINANCIAL LEASE. A long-term, non-cancellable lease whose maturity frequently matches the asset's economic life. A financial lease places an economic asset at the disposal of the lessee, but the lessor retains title to the asset. Financial leases are properly viewed as a form of debt financing.

FINANCIAL LEVERAGE. The partial use of debt to finance investments. The use of debt (with its fixed charges) in the capital structure has the effect of magnifying the potential variations of returns on the equity portion of the investment. The degree of financial leverage is sometimes defined as the percentage change in earnings per share caused by a given percentage change in earnings before interest and taxes. Financial leverage may also involve the use of senior securities other than debt.

FINANCIAL RISK. The risk caused by the firm's capital structure, as opposed to BUSINESS RISK which is caused by the underlying operations of the firm. Financial risk increases as the proportion of debt in a firm's capital structure increases.

FIXED EXCHANGE RATES. Exchange rates between currencies whose relative values are set, with central banks intervening to maintain established parities.

FLOATING EXCHANGE RATES. Exchange rates between currencies which are allowed to appreciate or depreciate on an ongoing basis *vis-à-vis* other currencies.

FORWARD EXCHANGE MARKET. A market where foreign currencies can be bought and sold for delivery at some future date. The prices for such transactions (forward prices) may differ from current exchange rates (SPOT RATES).

HOLDING COMPANY. A company which holds controlling interest through majority shareholdings in other companies. Often, the holding company itself does not carry on any active business.

HURDLE RATE. The minimum acceptable rate of return on an investment project. Sometimes also called the "cut-off rate".

INCOME BONDS. Bonds of a corporation which yield interest only in years in which the company reports earnings. The firm is not in default if it is unable to pay the interest; and unpaid interest does not accumulate. Thus, income bonds are a very weak form of debt in the hands of an investor.

INSOLVENCY. A firm is considered insolvent when it is no longer able to meet its financial obligations, that is, when it cannot make payments on its debts when they come due.

INTEREST-RATE RISK. The gains or losses incurred in fixed income securities (debt or preferred shares) through changes in prevailing interest-rate levels. For example, the prices of outstanding bonds depend on prevailing interest rates and increase/decrease as interest-rate levels move down/up. Thus, investors holding such securities are subject to interest rate risk. rate risk.

INTERNAL RATE OF RETURN. Often abbreviated IRR. The rate of discount which, when applied to the net cash flows of a contemplated investment, will yield a NET PRESENT VALUE of 0. The internal rate of return represents the effective yield which the project provides in each time period on the net funds which are invested.

LIMITED LIABILITY. The concept that a shareholder cannot lose any more money than the amount which he has invested in the shares of an incorporated business. Hence, if the business becomes insolvent, creditors cannot make claims against the personal property of shareholders. The claims can only be made against the corporation itself, which is a separate legal entity.

LIMITED PARTNERSHIP. A partnership where one or several partners enjoy limited liability. In any such partnership there must be at least one partner with unlimited liability.

LINE OF CREDIT. An arrangement with a financial institution (such as a bank) which enables one to overdraw one's account (or borrow money) up to a stipulated amount. Interest is only paid on the balances outstanding. This form of borrowing is often used to finance seasonal needs.

LISTED SECURITY. A financial instrument which is traded on a stock exchange, having met the requirements imposed by the exchange on which it is traded.

MARGIN REQUIREMENTS. When purchasing securities one may borrow money (usually from the brokerage house) to finance part of the purchase. The down payment required, or the proportion of funds which the investor has to put up, is called the margin requirement and is normally expressed as a percentage.

MARKET CAPITALIZATION RATE. The rate of return which investors find appropriate in establishing a market value for a security which is expected to produce a stream of future cash flows. In other words, the rate of discount which, if applied to future anticipated cash flows, equates the present value of such cash flows with the current market price of the security.

MATHEMATICAL PROGRAMMING. A mathematical model which takes the form of maximizing (or minimizing) an objective function subject to various constraints. Linear programming is the most widely used form of mathematical programming; in this case, both the objective function and the constraints are linear.

MERGERS. The fusion of two corporations, only one of which survives.

MONEY MARKET. The places and institutions where trading of short-term debt (with maturities of less than three years) takes place. Most of the trading is done in TREASURY BILLS and commercial paper, with maturities of less than one year.

MONTE CARLO SIMULATION. A computer based technique which relies on sampling and which allows one to assess how the uncertainties of a number of variables interact to determine the overall risk of a project.

MORTGAGE BOND. A bond which has real estate or physical assets pledged for security.

NET PRESENT VALUE. Often abbreviated NPV. The sum of all discounted cash flows generated by a project (all future cash flows are discounted back to the present). It represents the gain to be derived from a project, over and above returns on invested capital in the magnitude of the discount rate applied.

NET WORTH. The total assets of an individual or corporation minus the total liabilities. For a corporation, net worth is given by capital stock plus retained earnings.

ODD LOT. A quantity of shares traded which is not a BOARD LOT or multiple of a board lot.

OPEN ACCOUNT. A form of trade credit with no formal evidence of debt and where the account is open until payment is received.

OPERATING LEASE. A short-term lease which is similar to a rental agreement. The contractual commitment covers a time span which is relatively short in relation to the economic life of the asset, leaving the lessor to absorb any risks of obsolescence.

OVER-THE-COUNTER MARKET. A telephone market consisting of dealers who are in constant contact with each other and who arrange for the trading of securities which are not listed for trading on organized exchanges.

PARTICIPATING FEATURE. A feature to be found on some preferred shares providing extra dividend payments if corporate earnings or dividends per common share exceed some given amount. This is not a standard feature, with non-participating preferred shares being typical.

PARTNERSHIP. An unincorporated form of business organization in which two or more persons participate. The partners generally face unlimited liability.

PAYBACK. A criterion which is commonly used in practice to evaluate capital budgeting projects. It measures the time required for the expected after-tax cash inflows generated by the project to equal the original cash outlay.

PHANTASMIC GROWTH. Contrived growth in earnings per share which a firm may achieve through merging with firms whose shares trade at lower price-earnings ratios.

PRE-EMPTIVE RIGHT. The right of existing shareholders (by corporate charter or by statute) to purchase any new offerings of common stock, or of securities convertible into common stock. This right protects the current shareholder from dilution of ownership.

PREFERRED SHARES. These are shares which rank ahead of common shares in their claims on dividends. They may also have priority in their claim on assets in the event of liquidation. Typically, a fixed dividend is specified.

PRESENT VALUE. The current equivalent of a future dollar amount. It is derived by discounting the future amount at a rate which represents the TIME VALUE OF MONEY.

*PRIMARY DISTRIBUTION. The initial sale of newly issued securities to the investing public.

PRIME BUSINESS LOAN RATE. The loan rate at which banks will lend money to their most creditworthy customers.

PROFITABILITY INDEX. Also known as the benefit cost ratio of a capital expenditure project, it is given as the ratio of discounted after-tax cash inflows divided by discounted after-tax cash outflows. Projects for which this ratio exceeds 1 show a positive return and are deemed acceptable.

PROGRESSIVE TAX. A tax system characterized by the fact that successive increments of taxable income are subjected to increasingly higher tax rates. Personal income tax is a progressive tax.

PROMISSORY NOTE. A written commitment to pay a stated obligation by a specific date. It represents formal evidence of a credit arrangement.

PROSPECTUS. A legal document prepared by a corporation in the context of a public sale of securities which must contain full, true, and plain disclosure of all material facts related to the offering.

PROXY. A revokable power of attorney given by a shareholder to another person entitling that person to vote the shares at the shareholders' meeting. Proxies are generally solicited by the firm's current board of directors. A proxy fight is given where several competing parties actively solicit proxies from shareholders.

REAL ASSETS. Physical properties such as land, buildings, equipment and inventories. Note the distinction between REAL and FINANCIAL ASSETS.

RETAINED EARNINGS. Earnings of a corporation which are not distributed to the shareholders as dividends, but rather reinvested in the business.

RETRACTABLE DEBT. This is a bond or debenture which provides the holder with the option to cash in the security at full face value some time before its specified maturity.

RIGHTS. Negotiable securities with a relatively short life span (several weeks); rights represent options which are originally given to existing shareholders to buy additional shares at some specified subscription price. Rights may be exercised by the current shareholders, or they may be sold.

SALE AND LEASEBACK. Occurs when a corporation sells an asset to a financial institution (such as an insurance company), and the financial institution, as a lessor, leases the asset back to the corporation.

SECONDARY TRADING. The trading in previously issued securities. Securities merely change hands, but (as opposed to PRIMARY DISTRIBUTIONS) no flow of funds from investors to an issuing corporation takes place. The availability of secondary trading provides liquidity to investors.

SENIOR SECURITY. A security whose rights and claims on income or assets rank ahead of those of common shares; specifically debt and preferred shares.

SENSITIVITY ANALYSIS. An analytical approach which highlights how changes in a particular variable which may be subject to uncertainty affect a decision which is dependent on the value of that variable.

SHORT SELLING. The sale of shares or of a commodity which the seller does not currently own. The shares or commodity are borrowed (usually from a broker), and it is the seller's intent to replace what he has sold through later repurchase in the market at a lower price. Thus, short selling provides a vehicle for speculation in a market characterized by anticipated price declines.

SINKING FUND PAYMENTS. Periodic payments which the issuing corporation is to make in connection with the retirement of debt or preferred shares.

SOLE PROPRIETORSHIP. The simplest of all legal forms of business organization and the one most often used by small business. The owner faces unlimited liability, and effectively, his business and personal finances are not separated.

SPOT RATE. The current rate of exchange for immediate delivery of one currency against another.

STANDARD DEVIATION. A statistical measure which is commonly viewed as a reasonable measure of risk. It measures the variability of a probability distribution around its expected value or mean.

STOCK DIVIDEND. A dividend paid by the corporation in the form of additional shares rather than in cash.

STOCK SPLIT. As the term implies, existing shares are divided or split with several new shares issued for every original share outstanding. The market price per share adjusts accordingly. For example, if an investor owns 1 share of a firm which sells for $30, and management splits the stock 3 of 1, the investor will then own 3 new shares valued at approximately $10 per share.

SWAP DEPOSIT. A foreign currency short-term deposit purchased by an investor in his native currency. To eliminate foreign exchange risk, a "swap" or hedge is arranged whereby the purchase of foreign currency necessary for the deposit is combined with a forward sale of a like amount to coincide with the term of the deposit.

SYNERGISTIC EFFECT. Economies realized in the merger of two companies. The resulting unit is stronger and "adds up to more" than just the sum of its two individual components.

SYSTEMATIC RISK. Non-diversifiable risk which is market related and the only risk associated with an efficiently diversified portfolio.

TAX SHIELD. Tax saving or reduction in the amount of tax payable which results from being able to claim expenses or deductions (*e.g.* capital cost allowance or interest payments) against taxable income.

TERM STRUCTURE OF INTEREST RATES. Also called yield curve. The relationship between the effective yields on debt traded in the capital markets and their maturities.

TIME VALUE OF MONEY. Refers to the fact that $1.00 received now is worth more than $1.00 to be received at some time in the future, because money can earn a return over time. Hence, identical cash flows occuring at different points in time have different values. More specifically, the time value of money is the rate at which money is traded off over time.

TRADE CREDIT. Financing extended by a supplier to his customers allowing for payment for goods or services to be made some time after the delivery date of the goods or services.

TREASURY BILL. An interest-bearing promissory note issued by the Federal Government with a maturity of less than one year. The return on treasury bills is essentially risk free, as there is no risk of default and, because of the short maturities, INTEREST-RATE RISK is minimal.

TRUST DEED. Also called indenture. This is the contract drawn between a corporation which issues debt and a trust company acting as trustee for the creditors. The trust deed covers the various conditions and provisions under which the debt is issued.

UNDERWRITING. The purchase of a new offering of securities by an investment dealer from the issuing firm for future distribution to the public.

UNITS. A package of 2 or more financial securities (such as shares, bonds or warrants) which are issued together and have to be bought as a unit.

UNSYSTEMATIC RISK. Risk which is unique to a security and hence can be diversified away. It is not to be found in an efficiently diversified portfolio.

VARIANCE. The square of the STANDARD DEVIATION.

WARRANT. A transferable option to buy, within a given time period, a certain number of shares for a set price.

WORKING CAPITAL. In a narrow sense this is taken to be the difference between a firm's current assets and current liabilities, as taken from the financial statements. More broadly, working capital is defined as encompassing both a firm's current assets and liabilities, and working capital management is concerned with the management of current assets and liabilities.

YIELD CURVE. See TERM STRUCTURE OF INTEREST RATES.

Index